PORTRAIT OF HEALTH IN THE UNITED STATES

First Edition, 2001

PORTRAIT OF HEALTH IN THE UNITED STATES

First Edition, 2001

EDITORS
Daniel Melnick, Ph.D.
Beatrice Rouse, Ph.D.

BERNAN
Lanham, MD

© 2001 Bernan, a division of the Kraus Organization Limited.

No part of this publication may be reproduced, stored in a retrieval system, or transmitted, in any form or by any means, electronic, mechanical, photocopying, recording, or otherwise, without the prior written permission of the copyright holder. Bernan does not claim copyright in U.S. government information.

ISBN: 0-89059-189-X

ISSN: Pending

Printed by Automated Graphic Systems, Inc., White Plains, MD, on acid-free paper that meets the American National Standards Institute Z39-48 standard.

2002 2001   4 3 2 1

BERNAN
4611-F Assembly Drive
Lanham, MD 20706
800-274-4447
email: info@bernan.com
www.bernan.com

CONTENTS

LIST OF FIGURES AND TABLES

ACKNOWLEDGEMENTS

The snowstorm in early 2000 (that blanketed Washington and brought everything to a halt) was a great benefactor to this book. We found ourselves with all of our materials, an incomplete manuscript and cars that would not move. By the time the snow had cleared, we had completed our manuscript for Bernan.

Actually, a work such as this depends on the support of many people, including our colleagues in the statistical system, a patient publisher, and supportive families.

First and foremost, Dan Melnick would like to thank his wife, Vijaya L. Melnick, Ph.D. who taught him all of the biology and health science he knows and provided strong support for this effort. She was a consummate critic, ready source of information and close colleague. Her ideas and efforts are expressed throughout the work.

Beatrice Rouse takes this opportunity to gratefully acknowledge the contributions of her dedicated and outstanding professors at the University of North Carolina School of Public Health, especially H.A. (Al) Tyroler, M.D., for an international perspective and focus on rigorous methodology in epidemiology, Michel Ibrahim, M.D., M.P.H., Ph.D., for introducing her to the policy implications of health data, and Sherman A. James, Ph.D. (now at the University of Michigan School of Public Health) for emphasizing that health statistics are not merely data but represent human beings.

The authors of this book are grateful to their colleagues working in federal statistical and public health agencies who adhere to high standards of data collection and reporting. The federal policy of making the results of their work available in a timely and comprehensive manner has made this book possible. We salute their superb efforts.

This book was compiled from the results reported by federal public health agencies and other offices and departments in the federal government. It relies on the published material these agencies provide to the public and was greatly facilitated by the policy of releasing this information in readily accessible form on the World Wide Web. Chapter Six of this book reflects the authors' contribution to increasing the use of these resources.

We were greatly helped by the staffs of the Library of Congress, the National Library of Medicine, and the Library of the United States Bureau of the Census. In particular we would like to thank Bruce Martin for arranging research facilities at the Library of Congress where we conducted an early literature review that led to the approach used in this book. Betsy Humphreys, Marjorie Cahn, Mary E. Ryan, and Catherine Selden of the National Library of Medicine were extremely helpful.

We would also like to thank the staff of the National Center for Health Statistics, the Substance Abuse and Mental Health Services Administration, the Agency for Health Care Quality and Research, the Health Services and Resources Administration, the Indian Health Service, the Office of the Assistant Secretary for Planning and Evaluation in the Department of Health and Human Services, The Bureau of the Census, the Bureau of Labor Statistics, the Centers for Disease Control and Prevention, the Bureau of Transportation Statistics, and the United States Department of Agriculture. We received significant help from several Institutes at the National Institutes of Health including the National Cancer Institute, the National Heart Lung and Blood Institute, the National Institute of Child Health and Human Development, and the National Institute of Mental Health.

In the private sector, the Lexis-Nexis staff involved with LN Statistical Universe has been particularly helpful to us. We would particularly like to thank Mark Capaldini, Beth Bigman, Jeff Steinman, Kathleen Mufsud, Kim Steadman, and Leslie Sprigg.

Individuals who were extremely helpful included Joyce Abma, Chris Bachrach, Ross Arnett, Veronica Benson, Evelyn Christian, Christopher J. Conover, Anthony D'Angelo, Brenda Edwards, Anne Elixhauser, Meyer Glantz, Bridget Grant, Daniel J. Friedman, Lawrence Friedman, Joseph Gfroerer, Teresa Horan, Edward Hunter, Raynard Kington, Nancy Krieger, Linda F. McCaig, Paul S. Mead, Richard Mowery, Edna L. Paisano, Gibson Parish, Jim Scanlon, and the participants in a short course Dr. Melnick taught at the Medical Library Association meetings in May 2000.

The authors are particularly grateful to the staff of Bernan Associates who fully participated in creating this book. In particular, we would like to thank George Hall, who suggested the idea to us and provided helpful guidance throughout, and Katherine DeBrandt, who worked tirelessly to compile much of the material. We also are appreciative of the contributions of Courtney Slater, Vincent Eng, Steven Gstalder, Sean Long, Dan Parham, Sohair Abu-Aish, Kara Gottschlich, Lorrent Smith, Jacalyn Houston, and Tamera Wells-Lee.

Last but not least, our thanks go to Sara who provided warmth and support throughout this effort.

Dan Melnick, Ph.D. and Beatrice Rouse, Ph.D.
Editors

April 2001

PREFACE

The publics interested in improving the physical and mental health of the nation need current and reliable information to understand the health challenges of new and persistent infectious and chronic diseases, assess societal and environmental risks, implement cost effective interventions and prevention strategies, and develop appropriate health care financing and other health policies.

This book charts the health status of the nation presenting data on health correlates, conditions, care and consequences. In one place it provides information readers can use to monitor trends; identify emerging patterns or unusual changes in diseases, their correlates, treatment and consequences; identify high risk groups; and spot gaps in information. It also includes a guide to other resources keyed to locations on the World Wide Web.

The authors hope that layman interested in health policies as well as experts will find this volume of great help because it compiles and presents information from diverse sources that are often difficult to find. As well, health professionals, researchers, decision makers, and health planners, will find an organized and documented set of facts.

HEALTH INFORMATION AVAILABLE IN THIS BOOK

This source book covers both physical and mental health. Data are selected to provide insight into various facets of the nation's health from correlates and consequences of injury, disease, disability, and death to the health care system itself. Wherever possible, these data are presented by age group, sex, race, Hispanic status, income, poverty level, geographic area, employment status, and insurance status. Persons with special interests will find useful data throughout the book.

Persons interested in workplace health will find data on the correlates of work related injuries such as chemical exposure and physical stress (see Chapter 2), industries with tobacco smoke-free environments (see Chapter 2), the rate of occupational injuries and deaths (see Chapter 2), the nature of work related injuries and lost workdays (see Chapter 5), workplace drug testing (see Chapter 2), the effect of drinking and drug use on work (see Chapter 5), and employment and health insurance status (see Chapter 4).

Persons interested in mental health will find the estimated costs to society of specific conditions such as schizophrenia, depression and obsessive-compulsive disorder (see Chapter 5), the average length of stay, expenditures, and type of organization providing mental health care (see Chapter 4), the supply of clinically trained personnel (see Chapter 4), suicide and homicide rates (see Chapter 4), and the percent of persons with emotional problems unable to perform activities of daily living (see Chapter 5). Substance abuse issues are addressed in Chapter 2 and include current and former use of marijuana, cocaine,

alcohol, and tobacco, smoking during pregnancy, and alcohol, drug use, and driving.

Persons interested in health care will find a range of factors to describe the current state of the American health care system. Chapter 4 includes the percent of health plans complying with HEDIS quality measures, hospital acquired infection rates, principal hospitalization diagnosis and procedures as well as the supply of dentists, pharmacists, veterinarians, physicians, nurses and other health professionals. Data are presented not only for hospitalization and outpatient care but also for nursing home and hospice care. Persons interested in health care financing will find data not only on private health insurance, Medicare, and Medicaid but also on national health expenditures by type such as hospital care, physician services, dental services, home health care, and prescription drugs. Chapter 2 contains preventive care data that includes prenatal care, childhood immunizations, dental visits, and screening for cancer and heart disease.

Persons interested in disability will find a variety of measures in Chapter 5. These include the leading causes of disability, the number and percent distribution of persons by age with different levels of disability, activity limitations among diabetics, number of persons using wheel chairs and other assistive devices, difficulties experienced by persons with impaired vision and hearing, and the number of persons employed by severity of their disability.

In one handy document, this book contains data that are difficult to find or access elsewhere. This includes the estimated costs to society from premature death and lost productivity of almost 40 health conditions, including cardiovascular diseases, mental illness, cancer, AIDS, firearm injuries, foodborne illnesses, and diabetes (see Chapter 5). Transportation related injury and death rates are presented not only for passenger cars but also for motorcycles, boats, trains, airplanes and buses (see Chapter 3). Sport related injury rates are presented for 18 specific sports including basketball, swimming, skateboarding and bicycling (see Chapter 3). Information on nutrition includes dietary allowances and the percent of the population taking vitamin and mineral supplements (see Chapter 2).

Geographic areas vary in factors that influence health. These factors include climate, geologic characteristics, population and animal migration, population density, legislation, health services, socioeconomic characteristics, exposures to animal and other disease vectors, industrial exposures, and data collection and reporting systems. Regional data are presented for lost school days due to acute conditions (see Chapter 5) as well as source of regular health care, hospitalizations, hospice care, nursing care, unmet medical needs, and insurance coverage (see Chapter 4). State data presented include laws on child passenger safety, seatbelt use, and tobacco as well as data on air quality, child vaccination, heart disease risk factors, and traffic deaths (see Chapter 2). Variation in State level death rates, infant mortality, and notifiable diseases such as sexually transmitted diseases, hepatitis, and AIDS are shown (see Chapter 3).

DATA TYPES PRESENTED IN THIS BOOK

Graphics and tables interspersed in the text summarize major trends and relationships and the reference tables at the end of each chapter provide more detailed information. The usual types of data this book presents are averages, numbers, percentages, and rates. Averages are useful when there is a range of events that may vary widely, such as the charge for hospital stays for procedures as diverse as tonsil removal and organ transplant. Also, when the number of cases may not be sufficient for reliable estimates for smaller groups in the population, data may be combined and averaged over several years so that more reliable annual estimates can be obtained. For example, Table 3B presents data on deaths by States and racial and ethnic groups averaged over the years 1995, 1996 and 1997. Table 3.35 pools data from several years to show the frequency of various symptoms of gastrointestinal illness. Occasionally, ratios are presented as in Table 3.9 which presents the ratio of the age adjusted death rates for American Indians and Alaska Natives to that of whites in the United States.

The number of cases or other events helps indicate the magnitude of the problem in terms of the number of people that need care or intervention programs and may serve to determine the amount of resources needed, such as funding, hospital beds, physicians, therapists, and nurses. For example, Table 3.36 provides the number of cases reported to CDC for the various required notifiable diseases. The events may be new cases of a condition (incidence) or existing cases regardless of duration (prevalence).

Often policymakers, researchers, and others wish to compare the health of two or more groups. These groups may differ in important ways that are related to the condition of interest. For example, the groups may differ in age, health behavior, population size, or in physiological, socioeconomic, and other factors that need to be taken into consideration when making fair and useful comparisons. Rates are used to indicate the magnitude of a condition in a way that controls for group differences. Rates may be expressed as percentages, such as the percent of American households reporting hunger (see Table 2.9) or as number of events per specified size of population, such as cancer incidence and mortality rates that are expressed in number of cases per 100,000 population. (See Tables 3.16 and 3.18.)

Groups or conditions of interest often differ significantly by age. For example, the average age of African Americans is younger than that of whites and the average age of the residents of some States such as Florida and West Virginia is older than others such as Texas and California. These differences may be taken into account

by presenting either age adjusted rates such as the death rates in Table 3.1 or age-specific rates such as the cancer survival rates in Table 3.17. Both specific rates and adjusted rates may be presented for a variety of factors including race, gender, risk factors and disease.

Disease-specific rates are useful in controlling for differences in risk factors, in trying to determine different causes among the diseases, or in focusing on different prevention or intervention measures needed. For example, the infant mortality rate is an important measure of community health (see Tables 3.3 to 3.7). It can be used to indicate the adequacy of such public health issues as prenatal care, maternal nutrition, exposure to infectious disease, environmental exposures, and medical care. Measures for the different stages in infant development help focus on causes of death and the need for appropriate public health interventions. The components of the infant mortality rate are (1) neonatal mortality (deaths under 28 days of age) which shows the effect of prematurity, low birth weight, and congenital conditions, and (2) postneonatal mortality (deaths between 28 days and one year) which reflects exposure to factors such as infectious disease and malnutrition. These components are expressed as the rate per 1,000 live births.

Some indices of health or disease may indicate change in rates. A simple or crude change is a measure of the absolute change and is calculated by subtracting one rate from another to indicate the rate difference. In contrast, the percentage change takes into account the initial or base rate and provides a measure of the proportionate change compared with the base rate. For example, the infant mortality rate for the total United States changed from 10.4 percent in 1985–1987 to 7.4 percent in 1995–1997. The percent difference is 3.0 percent; that is, the infant mortality rate was 3.8 percentage points lower a decade later in 1995–1997. The percentage change, however, was 28.8 percent; that is, the rate in 1995–1997 was only 71.2 percent of its initial value a decade earlier. (See Table 3.7.)

It is important for readers to recognize that what follows is limited by the errors associated with data. Errors may be introduced into data by a variety of factors, including recall bias, incorrect measurement of the condition, or sampling variation (that is, if a different sample of people had been selected for the study, a different estimate of the rate might have resulted). In any case, errors may be systematic (that is, always higher or lower than the true value). This systematic error is also called bias. An example of bias might be the "healthy worker effect": that is, because many occupations require applicants to pass a health examination to get a job, studies of workers may be expected to find more healthy people than studies that included those both in and out of the workforce. In contrast, studies of hospital patients are more likely to find persons with several health conditions (i.e., comorbidity) than a random sample of persons in the community. Errors also may be random.

The standard error is a measure of how much the estimates vary around the true value. The smaller the standard error, the more confidence users can place in the estimate. Technically, standard deviations are presented for variation around the mean estimate, and standard errors are the average prediction errors around a regression line predicting the linear relationship between two variables. Another way of indicating the precision of the estimate presented is to provide a "confidence interval" that indicates the degree of confidence that the estimate is between the upper and lower boundaries presented. For example, among 18- to 25-year-olds in 1998, an estimated 2 percent used cocaine in the past month, with a 95 percent confidence interval of 1.5 percent to 2.6 percent. This information is interpreted as follows: on the basis of this sample, the observed estimate was 2 percent. On 95 percent of repeated samples when these statistics are calculated, the true mean will be between 1.5 percent and 2.6 percent. Another way of considering a confidence interval is to view it as the point estimate plus a margin of error. This book does not include indicators of uncertainty. Analysts and researchers are encouraged to consult the original sources. (See Chapter 6.)

GUIDELINES FOR READING THE GRAPHICS

Throughout the text are various maps, trend lines, bar charts, and other figures to illustrate some aspect of health in the United States. For example, maps are provided to show the geographic dispersion by state for various health conditions and risk factors. Some trend lines and bar charts are more complicated than others. Other figure types include Figure 2D, the food guide pyramid.

Some figures show simple comparisons for varying lengths of time. Figure 1A compares the trends in expenditures for total national health expenditures and the gross domestic product from 1960 to 1998. Figure 2F shows the change in three outcomes of teenage pregnancies (live births, abortions, and fetal loss) from 1976 to 1996. Figure 5F shows the years lost due to premature death from breast cancer by race from 1980 to 1997. Figure 4N shows the Medicaid population enrolled in fee-for-service and managed care from 1993 to 1998.

Other figures with trend lines are more complicated. One type shows the relationship between two conditions with different scales, such as Figure 5A which shows the change between 1967 and 1991 in the percent of the population drinking fluoridated water (shown on the left axis) and the average number of decayed, missing, and filled teeth among 12-year-olds (shown on the right hand axis). Another type shows the trend in terms of change from a base year, such as Figure 2J which shows the change in various air pollutants from the base year of 1988.

Some bar charts show bars side by side to demonstrate simple comparisons such as Figure 2B which compares the percent of current drug users and non drug users who would not like to work where various types of drug testing are conducted in the workplace. Others are stacked bars such as Figure 2M which shows the millions of pounds of toxic waste disposed by type of disposal for each year. Still others may show the relative proportion of the total, such as Figure 4B where all the stacked bars total 100% and are composed of the percentage for each place where each age or race group gets their regular care (emergency room, outpatient department, or physician office).

Other Figures are more complicated and show the relationship between conditions with different scales. For example, Figure 3K shows the death rates from specific diseases (diabetes, kidney disease, liver disease, and Alzheimer's disease) on the left axis that range by age up to 300 deaths per 100,000 population and the death rate from all causes on the right hand axis that ranges up to 16,000 per 100,000 population. Still other figures show the relationship between different concepts with different scales. For example, Figure 3AA shows the relationship between lung cancer incidence and mortality on the left axis (both measured in terms of cases per 100,000) and survival rate on the right axis (measured in terms of the percent who survive 5 years without dying from lung cancer).

In summary, this book provides a portrait of American health using a variety of measures from self perceived health status and reported acute and chronic health conditions to more objective measures such as life expectancy, medical diagnosis, hospitalization, and death rates. Data not easily found elsewhere are included to fill the needs of persons interested not only in describing the nation's health status but in promoting actions that increase the quality of life of all the nation's people.

CHAPTER 1: WHY WE NEED HEALTH STATISTICS

Good health is fundamental to a happy life, a strong economy, a vibrant society, and a strong nation. People can tell us how they perceive their health. Physicians can advise us about how to improve our health. However, promoting health is a public enterprise because societal decisions influence wellness. For example, government actions shape sanitation plans, personal behavior and practices, nutrition, the environment, and the availability of health care. The public allocation of resources—through the budget process, the licensing of care, and the regulation of insurance—influences the number of physicians, nurses, allied health workers, and hospitals as well as the conditions under which they deliver care. Wise health policies, whether personal or community based, flow from good information. Statistical indicators of health constitute the essential facts on which such information rests. To find, relate, understand, and use statistical information about trends in health, we must consult diverse materials, understand varied procedures, and comprehend many different concepts. In fact, analysts committed to the intelligent presentation of societal data on health trends face a truly challenging job of discovery and interpretation.[1]

Health statistics are becoming more plentiful but harder to find and use. The federal government's Centers for Disease Control and Prevention (CDC) and the National Center for Health Statistics (NCHS) provide sentinel health statistics indicators. Other agencies located within the Department of Health and Human Services (DHHS), the Department of Agriculture (USDA), the Department of Labor (DOL), the Department of Transportation (DOT), and the Environmental Protection Agency (EPA) provide health-related data as well. Some of these series are byproducts of administrative processes, such as the Medicare program. Others result from specialized surveys and data collections. State and local public health officials also play an important role in collecting and reporting information. In particular, their efforts and those of physicians and other health providers are key to the success of the reports that provide a rich source of information on health conditions and correlates or measures of factors associated with health. This book provides a road map to the many sources of health-related data and presents a guide to the signposts that point to them. Up to now there has been no single place to turn for help in finding these indicators.[2] In a book this size, we cannot hope to present all the important indicators. Rather, we have included a selection of some of the most relevant and a guide to finding the rest.

A SOCIAL DEFINITION OF HEALTH

The World Health Organization (WHO) defines health as "the state of complete physical, mental, and social well-being and not merely the absence of disease or infirmity."[3] Health status is an important element in societal progress. Analysts cannot understand how well a society is faring without considering the health of its members,

because vigorous and healthy living is a key to enjoying the fruits of the economy. But health status has been disconnected from standard economic indicators.[4] Health analysts focus on the factors contributing to disease and its absence among groups of individuals. They are less likely to examine its impact on how we live. Analysts studying the effect of health on the quality of life often stress what happens to an individual after recovering from disease rather than the effect of health status on our society and economy.

PUBLIC HEALTH

Public health practitioners employ art and science to maintain, protect, and improve health. They work to prevent disease, prolong life, and promote optimal mental and physical functioning. They focus their efforts on groups and intervene to serve the whole community. Public health agencies work to promote beneficial practices, reduce risks, and control diseases. They promote sanitation, insect and rodent control, food inspection, control of narcotics, health regulations for housing and industry, immunization programs, public health, nursing, and school health examinations. Governments adopt public health policies that require immunizations for school children and travelers, pasteurization of milk, chlorination of water, and waste disposal. They regulate housing, industrial pollution, and working conditions as well as food preparation and handling in restaurants, supermarkets, and food processing plants.

In contrast, the health care system is largely focused on responding to or preventing diseases. *Disease* is defined as the disruption of personal structure or function and is recognized by the signs and symptoms that indicate these pathologic changes. For example, rapid weight loss can be a symptom of a multitude of different conditions ranging from cancer to a parasitic disease.

The public health system collects and reports on health statistics as part of its function. These statistics include indicators of risk and protective factors present in the whole society as well as measures of characteristics and conditions of individuals. Health statisticians rely on procedures that frequently invoke governmental authority in the collection, analysis, and reporting of information. These procedures are designed to report on the health status of populations to facilitate public action. As such, public health advocates value statistics that facilitate action and thus they value timeliness more highly than precision. Knowing the direction of change or learning about emerging trends is frequently more important than knowing the exact number of persons afflicted.

Some of the procedures and activities involved in gathering health-related data, such as the system of disease notification, engage the regulatory powers of state governments, while others, such as the distribution of health surveys, rely on the legitimacy of the government to encourage compliance. The reporting of health-related statistics helps governments enhance their legitimacy by associating their activities with the well-being of the population. Surveillance, another activity used in collecting health statistics, focuses on spotting those events that call for immediate public and massive intervention. In view of the public nature of these activities, it is surprising to find that health statistics appear to focus on the diseases that affect individuals, rather than factors that shape the health of entire populations, such as environmental, societal, and educational trends.

HEALTH'S EFFECT ON THE ECONOMY

The way health affects our nation is a growing concern of decision makers who understand that health expenditures constitute an increasing share of economic activity. Health statistics help us understand how health conditions affect the economy. The economic impact of maintaining health is massive. The costs associated with pro-

viding care represent only a fraction of its effects, yet they constitute a substantial share of the nation's economy. The Office of the Actuary of the Health Care Financing Administration (HCFA) estimates that health expenditures grew from 5.1 percent of the gross domestic product (GDP) in 1960 to 13.5 percent in 1998. The GDP is the market value of goods and services produced within the United States.[5] Without taking inflation into account, HCFA estimates that from 1960 to 1998 health expenditures grew from $26.9 billion to $1,149.1 billion. At the same time, the public expenditures in health care increased from 25 percent of the total to more than 45 percent, and the per capita expenditure grew from $141 per year (in 1960 dollars) to $4,094 per year (in 1998 dollars). Health care expenditures grew at a faster pace than the economy. (See Figure 1A[6].) Policymakers concerned with providing adequate health care use these figures to estimate the various outcomes of proposed changes in health care coverage, insurance, and the societal cost of new procedures and interventions. (See Table 1A.)

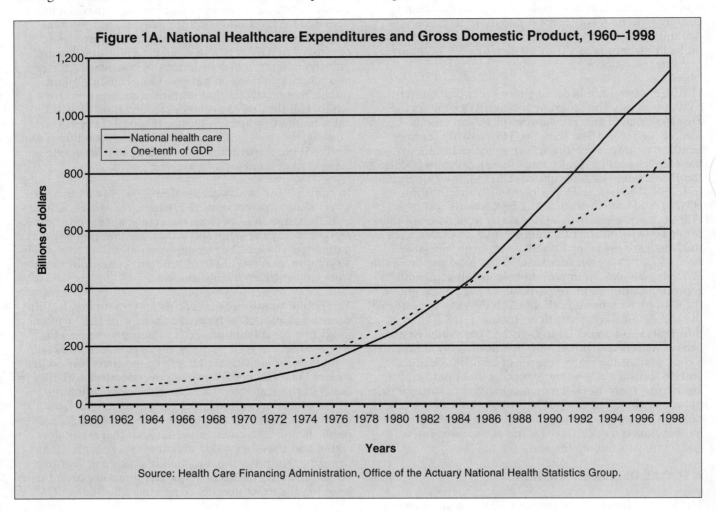

Figure 1A. National Healthcare Expenditures and Gross Domestic Product, 1960–1998

Source: Health Care Financing Administration, Office of the Actuary National Health Statistics Group.

Table 1A. National Healthcare Expenditures Aggregate and Gross Domestic Product (GDP)

Item	1960	1970	1980	1985	1990	1991	1992	1993	1994	1995	1996	1997	1998
AMOUNT IN BILLIONS OF CURRENT DOLLARS													
National healthcare expenditures	26.9	73.2	247.3	428.7	699.4	766.8	836.5	898.5	947.7	993.3	1 039.4	1 088.2	1149.1
Private	20.2	45.5	142.5	254.5	416.2	448.9	483.6	513.2	524.7	537.3	559.0	586.0	626.4
Public	6.6	27.7	104.8	174.2	283.2	317.9	353.0	385.3	423.0	456.0	480.4	502.2	522.7
Federal	2.9	17.8	72.0	123.2	195.2	222.5	251.8	275.4	301.2	326.1	347.3	363.0	376.9
State and local	3.7	9.9	32.8	51.0	88.0	95.4	101.2	110.0	121.8	129.8	133.1	139.2	145.8
PER CAPITA AMOUNT OF CURRENT DOLLARS													
National healthcare expenditures	141	341	1052	1734	2689	2918	3151	3351	3501	3637	3772	3912	4094
Private	106	212	606	1030	1600	1708	1821	1914	1938	1967	2028	2107	2232
Public	35	129	446	705	1089	1210	1329	1437	1563	1669	1743	1806	1862
Federal	15	83	306	498	750	847	948	1027	1113	1194	1260	1305	1343
State and local	20	46	140	206	338	363	381	410	450	475	483	500	520
PERCENT DISTRIBUTION													
National healthcare expenditures	100.0	100.0	100.0	100.0	100.0	100.0	100.0	100.0	100.0	100.0	100.0	100.0	100.0
Private	75.2	62.2	58.0	59.4	59.5	58.5	57.8	57.1	55.4	54.1	53.8	53.8	54.5
Public	25.0	38.0	42.0	40.6	40.5	41.5	42.2	42.9	44.6	45.9	46.2	46.2	45.5
Federal	11.0	24.0	29.0	28.7	27.9	29.0	30.1	30.6	31.8	32.8	33.4	33.4	32.8
State and local	14.0	14.0	13.0	11.9	12.6	12.4	12.1	12.2	12.9	13.1	12.8	12.8	12.7
ANNUAL PERCENT CHANGE													
National healthcare expenditures		10.6	12.9	11.6	11.0	9.6	9.1	7.4	5.5	4.8	4.6	4.7	5.6
Private		8.5	12.1	12.3	11.3	7.9	7.7	6.1	2.3	2.4	4.0	4.8	6.9
Public		15.3	14.2	10.7	10.5	12.3	11.0	9.2	9.8	7.8	5.4	4.5	4.1
Federal		19.8	15.0	11.3	10.5	14.0	13.1	9.4	9.4	8.3	6.5	4.5	3.8
State and local		10.2	12.7	9.2	10.4	8.4	6.1	8.6	10.8	6.6	2.5	4.6	4.7
U.S. population [1]		1.2	0.9	0.5	1.0	1.0	1.0	1.0	0.9	0.9	0.9	0.9	0.9
GDP		7.0	10.4	4.1	7.5	3.0	5.5	5.0	5.9	4.6	5.4	5.9	4.9
NUMBER IN MILLIONS													
U.S. population [1]	190	215	235	247	260	263	266	268	271	273	276	278	281
AMOUNT IN BILLIONS OF CURRENT DOLLARS													
GDP	527	1036	2784	4181	5744	5917	6244	6558	6947	7270	7662	8111	8511
PERCENT OF GDP													
National healthcare expenditures	5.1	7.1	8.9	10.3	12.2	13.0	13.4	13.7	13.6	13.7	13.6	13.4	13.5

SOURCE: Health Care Financing Administration, Office of the Actuary, National Health Statistics Group. 1998 National Health Expenditures: Table 1.

1. July 1 Social Security area population estimates for each year, 1960–1998.

NOTE: Numbers and percents may not add to totals because of rounding. The current and historical figures in this table are subject to periodic revision. For the latest exact figures, see <www.hcfa.gov/stats/nhe-oact/>.

Although difficult to quantify, the effect that health status has on productivity and personal freedom to enjoy life is most likely enormous. HCFA's National Health Accounts (NHA) track the direct costs of providing care, but they do not include data regarding the effect of health conditions on the economy, productivity, or quality of life.

HEALTH STATISTICS AS INDICATORS OF WELL-BEING

Health statistics aim to measure health status, the sense and reality of personal wellness resulting not merely from the absence of disease but also from the conditions that enable people to enjoy their lives. However, up to the 1960s, students of health who looked for nationally representative figures on conditions had to rely almost exclusively on measures that they derived from records of death. They analyzed the reported cause of death to track disease. However, since cause of death data only indirectly indicate health status, these records only approximately indicated health. Many conditions that cause long- or short-term disabilities do not cause death, although they might contribute to its early arrival. Consequently, diseases that affect the quality of life are not easily tracked by examining mortality statistics.[7]

Mortality is a term that refers to death, and *morbidity* is a term that refers to the diseases that affect life. While current, complete, and reliable mortality statistics date from the 1930s in the United States, national data on morbidity were only poorly or incompletely reported before the 1960s.[8] Nationally representative morbidity data based on modern sampling procedures date only from the enactment of the National Health Survey Act of 1956.[9]

Health statisticians use a variety of resources and tools to describe the forces that promote or impede the health of populations in society. These tools include sample surveys; compilations of birth and death records; surveillance of health events, including reports of outbreaks; and a large variety of incident data, such as accident statistics reported by the U.S. Department of Transportation. These resources draw heavily from the transactions between individuals and the institutions that respond to their needs. Students of health care recognize that overall wellness is a critical but largely unmeasured variable, and health outcomes are related to social status and the sense of personal control.

Health statistics fill an important void in measures of life quality obtained strictly from economic data. However, the field of health statistics generally lacks an overall theoretical framework that organizes its constituent elements coherently. This absence complicates the job of gaining access to these important statistics.

One approach to gathering and measuring health statistics is to ask individuals to rate their own health. Of course, this measure depends on the interaction between health conditions and each person's overall optimism or pessimism about his or her own life. However, this indicator does illustrate an important theme, the association of health conditions with social standing. People who are better off economically and socially and those who are less subject to the stress of discrimination tend to see their health in a more positive light and they are actually healthier.

It is important to consider people's perception of their own health as well as data on the conditions associated with injury, disability, disease, and death. When asked, most people in the general population are likely to consider their health as "very good" or "excellent," and only about 3 percent consider themselves to be in "poor" health. The distribution of perceptions, however, varies by such factors as age, gender, racial or ethnic group, and family income. Persons who are White, male, young and have a yearly family income of $35,000 or more are the most likely to consider themselves in "excellent" health. In fact, as Table 1B and Table 1.1 show, income is a key correlate of beliefs about one's own health. When age is held constant, those in lower-income families are less likely to rate their health positively.[10] (See Table 1.1.)

This is illustrated in Figure 1B, which shows how much each age and income group differs from the general population in their perception of their own health. Only persons in families with yearly incomes of at least $35,000 had better perceptions of their health at all age groups than the general population. Persons with low incomes, especially adults age 45 to 64, perceived their health more negatively than did the general population.

In fact, the data on subjectively reported health status show that income levels are a much more powerful predictor of health than race. For example, 32.6 percent of Blacks assessed their health as "excellent" compared to 38 percent of Whites. At the same time, 24.1 percent of persons with an annual income below $10,000 assessed their health as "excellent" compared with 47.2 percent of those with annual incomes of at least $35,000. Table 1.1 reports similar differences among occupational groups. One possible explanation for this difference is that perceived health status is related to the type of health insurance held by a person. Persons age 18 to 64 who had private health insurance had a consistently better perception of their health than those with public health insurance. For example, among Whites 36.9 percent of those who had private health insurance said that their health was "excellent" compared with 12.8 percent of those who had public health insurance; among Blacks 32.3 percent of those with private health insurance rated their health as "excellent" compared with 13.5 percent of those with public health insurance; and among Hispanics 32.4 percent of those with private insurance reported their health as "excellent" compared with 15.3 percent of those with public health insurance.[12]

Table 1B. How People Feel about Their Health by Income: 1996

(Respondent-assessed health status)

Income	Total [1] (thousands)	Percent					
		Total [2]	Excellent	Very good	Good	Fair	Poor
Under $10,000	19 879	100.0	24.1	23.9	28.3	16.5	7.2
$10,000–$19,999	36 871	100.0	27.7	25.7	29.3	12.8	4.6
$20,000–$34,999	54 093	100.0	34.6	31.2	24.8	7.1	2.4
$35,000 or more	109 609	100.0	47.2	30.6	17.8	3.5	0.9

1. Includes unknown health status.
2. Excludes unknown health status.

NOTE: P.F. Adams, G.E. Hendershot, and M.A. Marano. Current estimates from the National Health Interview Survey, 1996. National Center for Health Statistics. *Vital and Health Statistics* 10, no. 200. 1999: Table 70. Full table appears at the end of this chapter (table 1.1).

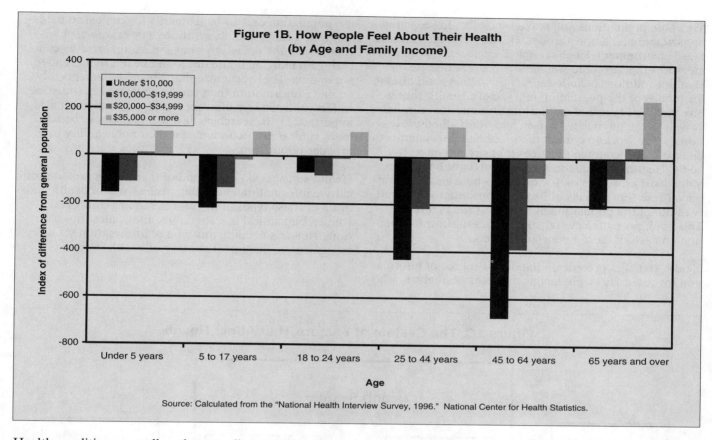

Figure 1B. How People Feel About Their Health
(by Age and Family Income)

Source: Calculated from the "National Health Interview Survey, 1996." National Center for Health Statistics.

Health conditions as well as the overall perception of health are best understood by examining the many variations of data across social and economic groups. The remainder of this volume presents those data and guides the reader to more detailed information. This volume shows health status and other related information for some of the major groups featured in various federal health statistics series.[13] It is important to recognize that these categories represent social facts; that is to say, they reflect the position of individuals, households, and families in society and do not represent innate biological differences between groups. While it is easy to see how this observation is correct for income, occupation, and geographical variables (such as region), the biological factors associated with health have been the subject of some controversy as they relate to age, sex, and race. Nancy Krieger and her colleagues argue that inferences related to the biological effects of race are largely spurious, except in the case of certain limited genetic diseases such as sickle cell anemia, which are more associated with the history of migrations than with any factor that is caused by racial differences.[14] However, there is more genetic variation within groups than between them. Indeed, viewed biologically, races do not really exist; they are merely social constructs. Yet, the effects of social disabilities associated with discrimination are manifest in poorer health conditions, reduced access to care, and more detrimental health consequences.

It is certain that health conditions can change with age because of the natural biological processes of maturation.

Some conditions are directly associated with gender, such as breast cancer or prostate cancer. However, the differences between the average health status of the groups presented in this volume represent social differences that are likely caused by different life circumstances, social and economic disabilities suffered, or privileges provided. As such, they are largely a product of societal impacts rather than a result of inherent biological differences. In general, it is best to observe the rule that biological differences are best established through the demonstration of genetic mechanisms while societal health indicators mostly reflect the effect of the social and physical environment. This is not to say that statistical data are not useful for providing clues to genetic patterns, but that those inferences are best established through controlled studies that demonstrate the mechanism of causal relationships.

Thus, the trends summarized in the tables throughout this book show the effect of health on groups rather than the effect of inherent group traits on health. They indicate groups in the population in need of medical help and the factors that are amenable to public health measures directed at improving equality of opportunity for health care and for the life circumstances that lead to a more healthy outcome.

WHAT HEALTH STATISTICS DESCRIBE

Health statistics describe four aspects of health—(1) correlates, (2) conditions, (3) care, and (4) consequences—

for whole populations and make it possible to see variations within and among groups. Health correlates include those environmental, behavioral, lifestyle, and preventive measures that promote wellness or prevent disease. Health conditions include aspects of wellness and disease for groups of the population in a society. Health care is provided by organized medical institutions and hospitals as well as the physicians, nurses, and other allied professionals who work to correct the problems associated with disease and encourage practices that strengthen well-being. Health consequences are the effect of health on individuals as well as on society as a whole and the economy. These four aspects of health contribute to the quality of life of the population as a whole. (See Figure 1C.) This book presents key statistical series to show information on each of those important aspects.

Health statistics provide an important source of information for researchers, physicians, and other caregivers who use population data as benchmarks for clinical studies, controlled trials, and observations. For example, physicians assess the deviation from expected norms by comparing an individual's health to the health of a broader population. They recognize that clinical judgments rely on more information than can be contained in statistics. In fact, statistical significance is not the same as clinical importance.[15] Researchers also use statistics to benchmark clinical protocols and test their applicability to a broader population.

Health statistics do not in and of themselves provide conclusive information about the mechanisms of health and disease. These types of inferences require controlled studies, biomedical investigations, and clinical observations. Readers needing this type of information should recognize the incomplete nature of health statistics.[16]

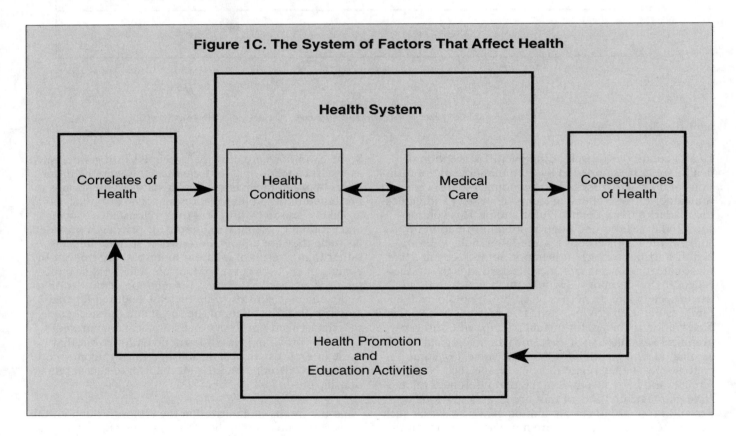

Figure 1C. The System of Factors That Affect Health

Health System

Correlates of Health

Health Conditions

Medical Care

Consequences of Health

Health Promotion and Education Activities

The findings of health statistics are most useful to describe the variation of health factors over time affecting social groups and to examine the correlates, conditions, care, and consequences of the broader population. Because health depends on factors and resources that go beyond the health care system, health statistics draw on data from a wide variety of sources. This volume presents some of the most important ones and provides a guide to finding the others.

FRAMEWORK OF THE PRESENTATION

This book organizes health statistics on the basis of a systematic analysis of the factors that influence public health. A population's health is only one of a number of aspects of its well-being. Clearly, health affects and is affected by the following:

1. Distribution of resources[17]
2. Personal security provided by community socialization, criminal justice agencies, the courts, and the procedures for equitably resolving disputes
3. Production and distribution of food, shelter, and clothing
4. Regulation of manufacturing, distribution, and exchange to reduce environmental risks
5. Availability of intellectual stimulation, literacy, and knowledge
6. Stability and welfare provided by families and other social support groups

Health statistics report on the factors that promote health and reduce disease, the health status of the population, the response of medical care providers, and the results of their activity. Figure 1C shows how the data presented in this book illustrate these factors and demonstrates how external factors (the correlates) affect health conditions, such as disease and wellness, and how medical care responds to these conditions, resulting in consequences that affect society as a whole, individuals, and the economy.

Table 1C relates the categories in the system of factors to the chapters in this book. You can use it to find the chapters that address the topics related in the diagram.

Public health activities aimed at improving health, such as immunization, food regulation, health screening, and efforts to promote healthy personal habits (which include educating individuals about the benefits of good nutrition and exercise, and the avoidance of harmful products like tobacco, drugs, and the excessive use of alcohol) attempt to modify the correlates of health and thereby improve the conditions presented to the health care system.

VARIATION IS KEY

Understanding variation puts public health efforts into focus. The tables presented throughout the book, which feature temporal, spatial, and social variation, are organized into four main chapters. They present statistics on the distribution of health correlates, conditions, care, and consequences in the population and make it possible for users to observe how major health trends affect groups of people at different times and in different places.

As analysts assess the effect of health on living conditions and the effect of living conditions on health, variation is a key consideration. It is the main tool for understanding health status, the care that is required to respond to disease, and the consequences for individuals as well as for our society and economy. The main chapters, which focus on correlates, conditions, care, and consequences, provide data on variation over time and between groups. Each one also includes information that shows how the factors of health vary across regions and states.

THE IMPORTANCE OF LOCATION

Health status in the United States varies within as well as between states. The variation across states could provide clues to causes of disease, but perhaps more importantly, it could allow public health planners to pinpoint those places where people need medical help or where education or prevention programs could affect the quality of life and health.

This book includes maps that illustrate the importance of state, regional, and local variation of health indicators and that show the dispersion of health conditions across

Table 1C. Topical Overview

Topic	Chapter
Care	Chapter 4
Conditions	Chapter 3
Consequences	Chapter 5
Correlates	Chapter 2
Health Accounts	Chapter 1
Health Promotion	Chapter 2
Sources of Health Data	Chapter 6

the nation. The maps provide data on deaths from breast cancer, lung cancer, homicide, suicide, and heart disease. There is also a map showing the rate of physicians per population.

As noted earlier in this chapter, health status constitutes a very large part of the U.S. economy and affects our society in substantial ways. Yet the public health and health care resources available to meet societal health needs are limited and, therefore, should be directed to the areas with the greatest need. The spatial dispersion of conditions provides a mechanism to channel resources to the places in greatest need or where interventions will do the most good. As a result, policymakers who allocate health resources are necessarily interested in the different patterns of dispersion. This book illustrates the dispersion and provides the kind of data policymakers might use to assess the match between the resources allocated and the dispersion of health problems.

RATIONALE FOR THE SELECTION OF DATA

A book of this size cannot present all of the findings related to health or even all of the most important ones. Rather, it includes some important health findings as examples of the information that readers can draw from federal statistical sources. The data were selected on the basis of availability, taking into consideration the influence of variables on personal health and the possibility that interventions could improve health.

The four main data chapters cover the following aspects:

1. Correlates that focus on the meaning and importance of risk and protective factors. The main ones featured in the book are listed.
2. Conditions, including disease and wellness.
3. Care, which examines trends in access to health insurance and the procedures and diagnoses that occasion hospital care.
4. Consequences showing how health status affects the economy, society, and the individual's well-being. This chapter also includes indicators that focus on the effect of consequences on external correlates.

REACHING BEYOND THIS BOOK

Chapter 6 of this book provides information about each of the major sources of health statistics included in this book and contains a detailed guide to finding more information on the Internet.

Table 1.1. How People Feel About Their Health: 1996

(Respondent-assessed health status)

Characteristic	Total [1] (thousands)	Percent					
		Total [2]	Excellent	Very good	Good	Fair	Poor
All persons [3]	264 259	100.0	37.4	29.5	23.1	7.4	2.6
AGE							
Under 5 years	20 087	100.0	54.1	27.8	15.6	2.2	*0.3
5–17 years	51 293	100.0	51.6	28.6	17.1	2.2	0.4
18–24 years	24 579	100.0	40.9	32.4	22.3	3.7	0.7
25–44 years	83 389	100.0	37.9	32.6	22.1	5.9	1.5
45–64 years	53 146	100.0	27.8	28.4	27.5	11.2	5.1
65 years and over	31 766	100.0	16.3	23.1	33.6	19.4	7.6
SEX AND AGE							
Men							
All ages	128 783	100.0	40.2	29.1	21.8	6.6	2.4
Under 5 years	10 279	100.0	53.9	27.5	16.0	2.1	*0.5
5–17 years	26 281	100.0	52.5	28.2	16.8	2.2	*0.3
18–24 years	12 191	100.0	46.3	30.3	19.9	3.0	*0.4
25–44 years	41 032	100.0	41.0	32.2	20.5	5.0	1.2
45–64 years	25 679	100.0	30.2	28.5	25.4	10.7	5.2
65 years and over	13 321	100.0	16.4	22.8	34.2	18.7	7.8
Women							
All ages	135 476	100.0	34.8	29.8	24.5	8.2	2.7
Under 5 years	9 808	100.0	54.2	28.2	15.1	2.2	*0.2
5–17 years	25 012	100.0	50.7	29.1	17.5	2.3	0.5
18–24 years	12 388	100.0	35.6	34.5	24.6	4.3	1.0
25–44 years	42 357	100.0	35.0	33.0	23.6	6.7	1.7
45–64 years	27 467	100.0	25.5	28.2	29.5	11.8	5.0
65 years and over	18 444	100.0	16.2	23.3	33.1	19.9	7.5
RACE AND AGE							
White							
All ages	220 058	100.0	38.1	29.9	22.5	7.0	2.4
Under 5 years	16 101	100.0	55.2	27.9	14.8	1.8	*0.3
5–17 years	40 688	100.0	53.6	28.6	15.4	1.9	0.4
18–24 years	19 682	100.0	41.7	32.8	21.5	3.2	0.7
25–44 years	69 296	100.0	38.9	33.3	21.1	5.3	1.3
45–64 years	45 730	100.0	29.1	29.0	27.1	10.3	4.5
65 years and over	28 560	100.0	16.8	23.6	33.8	18.6	7.2
Black							
All ages	33 183	100.0	32.6	26.9	26.7	10.3	3.4
Under 5 years	3 240	100.0	50.2	26.6	19.5	3.2	*0.6
5–17 years	8 126	100.0	43.0	28.2	24.6	3.9	*0.3
18–24 years	3 445	100.0	38.2	29.0	25.6	5.9	*1.4
25–44 years	10 341	100.0	31.3	28.9	27.7	9.7	2.3
45–64 years	5 419	100.0	16.0	24.5	30.7	20.0	8.9
65 years and over	2 612	100.0	10.8	18.3	31.1	27.5	12.4
FAMILY INCOME AND AGE							
Under $10,000							
All ages	19 879	100.0	24.1	23.9	28.3	16.5	7.2
Under 5 years	1 967	100.0	43.0	25.6	25.2	5.0	*1.1
5–17 years	3 820	100.0	33.5	26.7	33.1	6.0	*0.7
18–24 years	3 305	100.0	29.7	36.2	25.8	6.8	1.5
25–44 years	4 553	100.0	21.6	22.9	30.1	17.9	7.4
45–64 years	2 712	100.0	10.5	13.6	23.2	31.7	21.1
65 years and over	3 523	100.0	12.1	17.9	28.5	29.4	12.2
$10,000–$19,999							
All ages	36 871	100.0	27.7	25.7	29.3	12.8	4.6
Under 5 years	3 243	100.0	47.4	28.1	19.9	4.0	*0.5
5–17 years	6 853	100.0	40.0	28.7	26.8	3.7	*0.9
18–24 years	4 345	100.0	33.9	33.5	24.9	6.5	*1.3
25–44 years	9 772	100.0	27.3	28.3	30.1	11.3	2.9
45–64 years	5 556	100.0	13.6	18.6	34.0	21.7	12.2
65 years and over	7 102	100.0	14.9	18.8	33.6	24.3	8.4
$20,000–$34,999							
All ages	54 093	100.0	34.6	31.2	24.8	7.1	2.4
Under 5 years	4 224	100.0	53.7	29.3	14.9	1.9	*0.2
5–17 years	10 053	100.0	48.4	29.9	19.1	2.1	*0.4
18–24 years	4 907	100.0	43.9	32.1	20.6	2.7	*0.6
25–44 years	18 072	100.0	34.2	33.9	25.1	5.6	1.1
45–64 years	9 360	100.0	22.5	30.5	29.0	12.9	5.1
65 years and over	7 477	100.0	15.2	27.4	34.3	16.0	7.1
$35,000 or more							
All ages	109 609	100.0	47.2	30.6	17.8	3.5	0.9
Under 5 years	7 767	100.0	62.9	25.5	10.4	1.1	*0.1
5–17 years	23 222	100.0	61.8	27.0	10.1	1.0	*0.2
18–24 years	7 748	100.0	50.3	31.1	17.1	1.3	*0.3
25–44 years	38 481	100.0	46.0	34.0	16.6	2.9	0.5
45–64 years	26 253	100.0	35.9	31.0	25.4	5.8	1.8
65 years and over	6 139	100.0	24.5	27.1	32.3	12.1	4.0

See footnotes at end of table.

Table 1.1. How People Feel About Their Health: 1996—*Continued*

(Respondent-assessed health status)

Characteristic	Total [1] (thousands)	Percent					
		Total [2]	Excellent	Very good	Good	Fair	Poor
GEOGRAPHIC REGION							
Northeast	53 906	100.0	38.4	31.0	21.4	7.2	2.1
Midwest	63 413	100.0	37.3	31.6	22.3	6.7	2.0
South	90 561	100.0	36.2	27.6	24.6	8.3	3.4
West	56 380	100.0	38.7	28.5	23.5	6.9	2.4
PLACE OF RESIDENCE							
MSA [4]	208 354	100.0	38.6	29.8	22.6	6.8	2.2
Central city	78 116	100.0	35.4	29.8	24.0	8.1	2.6
Not central city	130 239	100.0	40.4	29.8	21.7	6.1	2.0
Not MSA [4]	55 905	100.0	33.2	28.2	25.2	9.5	3.8
MAJOR OCCUPATIONAL GROUPS (1993)							
Men							
White-collar	30 942	100.0	47.5	31.2	17.1	3.6	*0.6
Service	6 175	100.0	34.1	31.9	26.6	6.3	*0.8
Blue-collar	24 032	100.0	35.9	30.9	25.9	6.2	*0.9
Farm [5]	2 446	100.0	37.1	28.2	26.9	6.1	*1.5
Women							
White-collar	38 176	100.0	38.2	33.3	23.2	4.5	0.7
Service	9 336	100.0	29.6	30.0	29.1	9.7	1.4
Blue-collar	5 306	100.0	26.6	26.9	35.4	9.7	*1.4
Farm [5]	499	100.0	33.7	29.0	28.2	7.8	*0.5
HEALTH INSURANCE STATUS [6]							
Hispanic [7]							
Any private	7 866	100.0	32.4	30.3	26.1	**11.2	
Public only [8]	2 077	100.0	15.3	20.9	25.7	**38.0	
Uninsured	6 582	100.0	23.8	24.5	33.3	**18.4	
Black							
Any private	10 424	100.0	32.3	30.5	26.9	**10.4	
Public only [8]	3 042	100.0	13.5	16.9	36.3	**33.3	
Uninsured	5 547	100.0	32.2	25.8	24.4	**17.6	
White							
Any private	90 592	100.0	36.9	34.9	21.2	**7.1	
Public only [8]	7 211	100.0	12.8	19.8	28.6	**38.8	
Uninsured	19 138	100.0	32.3	29.0	26.4	**12.3	

SOURCE: P.F. Adams, G.E. Hendershot, and M.A. Marano. Current estimates from the National Health Interview Survey, 1996. National Center for Health Statistics. *Vital and Health Statistics* 10, no. 200. 1999: Table 70. Occupational groups from: D.K. Wagener, J. Walstedt, L. Jenkins, et al. Women: Work and Health. *Vital and Health Statistics* 3, no. 31. 1997: Table 32. Health insurance status from M.E. Weigers, S.K. Drilea. Health status and limitations: a comparison of Hispanics, Blacks, and Whites, 1996. Rockville, MD: Agency for Healthcare Research and Quality; 1999. MEPS Research Findings No. 10. AHCPR Pub. No. 00-0001: Table 3.

* Figure does not meet standard of reliability or precision.
** Fair and/or poor.
1. Includes unknown health status.
2. Excludes unknown health status.
3. Includes other races and unknown family income.
4. MSA is metropolitan statistical area.
5. Includes farming, forestry, and fishing occupations.
6. Adults age 18 to 64 were asked about their health insurance status during the first half of 1996.
7. Includes persons of all races.
8. Armed Forces related coverage, CHAMPUS/CHAMPVA, is classified as public insurance.

NOTE: This table is based on questions asked in the National Health Interview Survey that is conducted by CDC's National Center for Health Statistics (NCHS). In 1996, people in a nationally representative sample of more than 45,000 households were asked to rate their own health. The interviewers asked each adult who was present the following question "Would you say — health in general is excellent, very good, good, fair, or poor?" They also asked proxy respondents to provide this information on behalf of household members who were children or did not participate in the interview. The original source provides procedures for computing an estimate of the approximate standard errors and relative standard errors. As a rule of thumb, an estimate based on a population of 375,000 has a 10% Relative Standard Error (RSE); of 89,000, a 20% RSE; and of 40,000 a 30% RSE.

NOTES

1. The DHHS data council has issued a comprehensive catalog of DHHS databases that report data on health. This report cites more than 125 databases. See <http://ASPE.hhs.gov/datacncl/datadir/>.

2. For a review of these sources, see ed. Frieda Weise, et al., *Health Statistics: An Annotated Bibliographic Guide to Information Resources*, 2d ed. (Lanham, Md.: Medical Library Association and Scarecrow Press, 1997). Also see Frieda Weise, *Health Statistics: A Guide to Information Sources* (Detroit: Gale Research Co., 1980) and Frieda Weise, *A Bibliographic Guide to Statistics and Health Planning Information*, rev. ed. (Springfield: Illinois Cooperative Health Information System, State Center for Health Statistics, 1976).

3. See *Constitution of the World Health Organization, Basic Documents*, 15th ed. (Geneva: World Health Organization, 1948).

4. For an example of social and economic analysts who have called attention to this deficit in economics, see Martha C. Nussbaum and Amartya Sen, *The Quality of Life* (Oxford: Clarendon Press, 1993), and Amartya Sen, *Development as Freedom* (New York: Alfred A. Knopf, 1999). Also see Sen's discussion of the relationship between health and the distribution of economic power starting on page 44 of the latter work.

5. For a description of the methods they used, see Helen Lazenby, Katharine R. Levit, et al., "National Health Accounts: Lessons from the U.S. Experience," *Health Affairs* (Summer 1992). An updated version of this article can be obtained from the HCFA Web site at <http://www.hcfa.gov/stats/nhe-oact/lessons>.

6. HCFA compiles these figures from a variety of sources about health expenditures to determine the total societal costs of care.

7. For one project that attempts to combine mortality and morbidity indicators to show the overall impact on well-being, see Christopher J. L. Murray, et al., *The Global Burden of Disease: A Comprehensive Assessment of Mortality and Disability from Diseases, Injuries, and Risk Factors in 1990 and Projected to 2020* (Cambridge: Harvard School of Public Health on behalf of the World Health Organization and the World Bank, 1996). In that series, see also Christopher J. L. Murray, et al., *Global Burden of Disease and Injury Series*, Vol. 1 (Geneva: World Health Organization, 1994) and also Christopher J. L. Murray, et al., *Global Comparative Assessments in the Health Sector: Disease Burden, Expenditures, and Intervention Packages: Collected Reprints from the Bulletin of the World Health Organization* (Geneva: World Health Organization, 1994). Also see Christopher J. L. Murray and Alan D. Lopez, *Health Dimensions of Sex and Reproduction: The Global Burden of Sexually Transmitted Diseases, HIV, Maternal Conditions, Perinatal Disorders, and Congenital Anomalies* (Cambridge: Harvard School of Public Health, 1998) as well as Govindaraj Ramesh, *Health Expenditures in Latin America* (Washington, D.C.: World Bank, 1995). Also see Christopher J. L. Murray, *Global Health Statistics: A Compendium of Incidence, Prevalence, and Mortality Estimates for Over 200 Conditions* (Cambridge: Harvard University on behalf of the World Health Organization and the World Bank, 1996).

8. The paper by Daniel Melnick, *Building Robust Statistical Systems for Health* was prepared for the National Committee on Vital and Health Statistics, August 2000. See <http://www.melnickresearch.net> for a preprint of this paper.

9. The first attempt at fielding a national survey of morbidity occurred in the winter of 1935–36, but it did not use modern survey procedures such as probability sampling or a specified questionnaire. However, the Public Health Service used data from this survey from 1936 to 1956 as the basis for its estimates of the prevalence of disease conditions in the United States.

10. Table 1B is based on an index that combines the percentage difference between the group and all persons accounting for the number who say that their health is "excellent" or "very good" and those who say it is "fair" or "poor." The figure shows the sum of these differences, which is an overall indicator showing how the group stands compared to all persons regarding its sense of good health.

11. The index presented in Figure 1B is based on results from the National Health Interview Survey conducted in 1997. See Table 1.1 for the actual reported results.

12. These results were obtained from a question that was included on the Medical Expenditure Panel Survey by the Agency for Health Care Policy and Research. See Table 2 in *Health Status and Limitations: A Comparison of Hispanics, Blacks, and Whites* (Rockville, Md.: Agency for Health Care Policy and Research, 1996).

13. Reference tables, which are indicated with numbers (e.g., Table 1.1) are at the end of each chapter.

14. See N. Krieger, D. Williams, and S. Zierler, "Whiting Out: White Privilege Will Not Advance the Study of How Racism Harms Health," *American Journal of Public Health* 89, no. 5 (May 1999):782, and also J. W. Buehler, "Abandoning Race As a Variable in Public Health Research," *American Journal of Public Health* 89, no. 5 (May 1999):783, and R. Rabin, "The Use of Race As a Variable in Public Health Research," *American Journal of Public Health* 89, no. 5 (May 1999):783.

15. See James H. Ware, Frederick Mosteller, Fernando Delgao, Cristl Donnelly, and Joseph Ingelfinger, "P Values," in *Medical Uses of Statistics*, John C. Bailor III

and Frederick Mosteller, ed. (Boston: NEJM Books, 1992):196.

16. See Thomas Allen Lang and Michelle Secic, *How to Report Statistics in Medicine: Annotated Guidelines for Authors*, with a foreword by Edward J. Huth (Philadelphia: American College of Physicians, 1997).

17. See Martha Nussbaum and Amartya Sen, *The Quality of Life* (Oxford: Clarendon Press. New York: Oxford University Press, 1993). Also see Jean Dreze and Amartya Sen, *The Political Economy of Hunger* (Oxford: Clarendon Press. New York: Oxford University Press, 1990–91). And see Amartya Kumar Sen, *Development as Freedom* (New York: Knopf, 1999).

In the past decade, Americans greatly increased their chances of living longer and healthier lives by adopting better personal and social practices and improving the environment. However, the United States can still make substantial gains by continuing to address the health correlates that reduce risks and promote health and wellness. Health correlates include personal behaviors, environmental settings, social circumstances, and health care services. While individual action is important, concerted public action is also needed to promote health and prevent disease. Both individual and societal decisions to allocate money, time, personal commitment, and organizational attention to health education, awareness, and practices increase the possibility of success.

This chapter examines three types of factors associated with health and the quality of life. Each type of health correlate includes factors that protect against poor health and premature death as well as factors that increase the risk of disease, injury, and disability. Some of the factors are under the individual's control, but others are subject to social or organizational influences. This chapter presents examples of each type of health correlate together with the latest available data on its current prevalence and most recent trends. The reference tables for this chapter present more extensive and detailed statistics on health correlates and their trends by sociodemographic characteristics, such as gender, race, Hispanic origin, income, and place of residence.

The health correlates examined are grouped as follows:

1. Behavioral factors include personal characteristics and lifestyle behaviors of individuals, such as what they eat, how active they are, when they start having sexual relations, if they use seatbelts when riding in a car, and if they consume alcohol, tobacco, and other drugs.

2. Environmental factors often include variables that can be changed only by large-scale public health efforts and governmental regulations, such as those affecting air quality, workplace hazards, and toxic exposures.

3. Social, regulatory, health care factors are affected not only by individual health care choices but also by societal activities, including regulations regarding issues such as product, food, and drug safety; health insurance; and vehicle inspections. Finally, actions of the public health community are included as well as the medical establishment's decisions regarding treatment and preventive care, access to care, immunizations, screening for cancer, and prenatal care.

Federal statistics are available to determine the current level and trends in these types of health correlates. Such data permit an assessment of current needs and provide information to monitor progress in public and individual health efforts.

BEHAVIORAL CORRELATES

Some of the most important correlates of health depend on individual decisions about lifestyle or activity. A large body of epidemiological research documents the association of disease, disability, and premature death with behavioral correlates such as using tobacco, alcohol, and other drug use; poor nutrition; inactivity; and inappropriate sexual practices.

ALCOHOL, TOBACCO, AND OTHER DRUGS

Alcohol, tobacco, and other substances, such as cocaine, heroin, marijuana, and amphetamines, alter an individual's mental and physical functioning and can be addictive. When people use these substances they put their physical and emotional health at risk and create risks for others. For example, drug use increases the user's risk of HIV/AIDS and infectious diseases such as hepatitis C and tuberculosis.[1] A woman's alcohol or drug use during pregnancy can affect her baby's fetal and childhood development.[2] Finally, drinking increases not only the risk of liver disease, cancer, and hypertension but also the risk of injury to the drinker and others.[3] In 1998, drunk drivers were involved in highway crashes resulting in 15,935 deaths and 305,000 injured persons.[4]

From the mid-1980s to the beginning of the new millennium, Americans dramatically reduced their use of tobacco, cocaine, and marijuana. (See Figure 2A.) The official federal source of drug abuse statistics, the National Household Survey on Drug Abuse (NHSDA), reports on substance use in the general population age 12 and older. This scientific survey conducted by the Substance Abuse and Mental Health Services Administration (SAMHSA) found that the percentage of people who had smoked tobacco in the year before they were interviewed dropped from 40.5 percent in 1985 to 30.6 percent in 1998. At the same time, marijuana use dropped from 13.6 percent to 8.6 percent, and cocaine use dropped from 5.1 percent to 1.7 percent. Alcohol abuse also dropped. For example, the percentage of persons reporting that they consumed five or more drinks on a single occasion five or more times a month dropped from 8.3 percent in 1985 to 5.9 percent in 1998. (See Tables 2.1, 2.4, 2.5, and 2.6.)[5]

Smoking among pregnant women also decreased: 19.5 percent reported that they smoked cigarettes during pregnancy in 1989 compared to 13.2 percent in 1997. (See Table 2.3.)

By 1998, the rate of people who had stopped using marijuana or cocaine was higher than the rate of those who had stopped smoking tobacco. Because the NHSDA asks respondents about their use of tobacco, cocaine, and

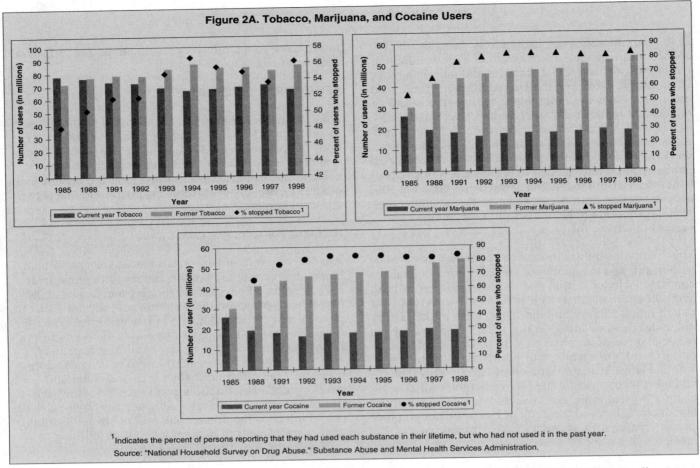

Figure 2A. Tobacco, Marijuana, and Cocaine Users

[1] Indicates the percent of persons reporting that they had used each substance in their lifetime, but who had not used it in the past year.

Source: "National Household Survey on Drug Abuse." Substance Abuse and Mental Health Services Administration.

marijuana over their entire lifetime, it is possible to estimate the percentage of users who have stopped using these substances. In 1985, these percentages were almost equal (tobacco, 48.1 percent; marijuana, 53.8 percent; and cocaine, 54.2 percent); by 1998 they diverged widely (tobacco, 56.2 percent; marijuana, 74.0 percent; and cocaine, 83.5 percent). (See Table 2A.) Experts disagree as to the reason for this trend. One view is that legal measures motivate users of illegal drugs to quit. Another is that the more severe behavioral effects of drug use discourage continued use. A third view is that drug treatment and social opprobrium motivate users to stop.

Table 2A. Persons Who Stopped Using Tobacco, Marijuana, or Cocaine

(Number in millions, except where noted)

	1985	1988	1991	1992	1993	1994	1995	1996	1997	1998
USERS WHO STOPPED (PERCENT) [1]										
Tobacco	48.1	50.2	51.7	51.8	54.7	56.7	55.5	54.9	53.6	56.2
Marijuana	53.8	67.9	70.8	73.7	72.7	72.7	72.9	73.2	72.7	74.0
Cocaine	54.2	66.0	77.3	80.7	83.1	83.2	83.1	81.8	81.6	83.5
LIFETIME USERS										
Tobacco	150.2	153.5	151.9	150.3	151.9	153.5	151.9	153.3	152.5	152.3
Marijuana	56.5	60.8	61.9	62.1	64.1	65.2	65.5	68.6	71.1	72.1
Cocaine	21.5	21.1	23.3	22.5	23.4	21.8	21.7	22.1	22.6	23.1
PAST YEAR USERS										
Tobacco	78.0	76.4	73.4	72.4	68.8	66.5	67.6	69.1	70.7	66.7
Marijuana	26.1	19.5	18.1	16.3	17.5	17.8	17.8	18.4	19.4	18.7
Cocaine	9.8	7.2	5.3	4.3	3.9	3.7	3.7	4.0	4.2	3.8
FORMER USERS [1]										
Tobacco	72.2	77.0	78.5	77.9	83.1	87.0	84.3	84.2	81.8	85.6
Marijuana	30.4	41.3	43.8	45.8	46.6	47.4	47.8	50.2	51.7	53.4
Cocaine	11.7	13.9	18.0	18.2	19.4	18.2	18.0	18.1	18.4	19.3

SOURCE: Substance Abuse and Mental Health Services Administration (SAMHSA), Office of Applied Studies, 1998. Data from the preliminary report of the National Household Survey on Drug Abuse. 1998 data provided by SAMHSA staff.

1. Persons reporting that they had used each substance in their lifetime, but who had not used it in the past year.

STATE RESTRICTIONS ON TOBACCO USE

Although tobacco smoking by adults is not illegal, many states have adopted measures to regulate its use. They restrict smoking in government buildings, private workplaces, restaurants, daycare centers, bars, shopping malls, grocery stores, buses and trains, hospitals, hotels, and other enclosed areas. States have also adopted laws requiring merchants to verify that tobacco purchasers are at least 18 or 19 years of age, and some impose license fees on automatic tobacco vending machines. (See Table 2.2 for detailed information about each state.)

Such smoking regulations encouraged private companies to restrict smoking in their workplaces. Women, however, are more likely than men to work in smoke-free environments. By 1993, 65.6 percent of employed women worked in smoke-free environments compared with 43.6 percent of men. One of the reasons for this difference is that a larger proportion of men work where it is more difficult to restrict smoking, such as outdoors or in vehicles. (See Table 2B.) A study of the workplace characteristics for working persons age 18 and older conducted in 1993 showed that these gender differences persisted even within different industries. For example, in an industry such as professional services where smoking restrictions can be applied to most workplaces, 74.8 percent of the women, compared with 59.2 percent of the men, worked in smoke-free environments.

Table 2B. Working in a Smoke-Free Environment: 1993

Sex and type of restriction	Total [1]	Farm [2]	Mining	Construction	Manufacturing	Transport utilities [2]	Wholesale	Retail trade
PERCENT DISTRIBUTION								
Total (age 18 years and older)	100.0	100.0	100.0	100.0	100.0	100.0	100.0	100.0
Female								
Not applicable [3]	20.9	59.8	(4)	36.2	10.4	27.8	24.6	20.0
Employer restricts smoking	65.6	20.6	(4)	28.6	74.4	58.9	62.5	59.5
Employer does not restrict	12.5	*15.2	(4)	*33.8	14.8	*12.0	*12.0	19.1
Unknown	1.1	*4.4	(4)	1.4	0.4	1.4	*0.9	*1.3
Male								
Not applicable [3]	45.2	91.4	60.0	84.8	24.4	61.5	55.4	33.5
Employer restricts smoking	43.6	*5.4	32.1	7.6	62.2	34.3	34.9	47.9
Employer does not restrict	10.4	*2.3	*4.2	*7.3	12.8	*3.7	*9.1	16.9
Unknown	0.9	*1.0	*3.6	*0.2	0.6	*0.5	*0.6	1.7
NUMBER OF PERSONS INTERVIEWED								
Female	6 517	85	16	76	804	281	122	1 060
Male	6 339	212	59	612	1 374	586	259	890

See footnotes at end of table.

Table 2B. Working in a Smoke-Free Environment: 1993—*Continued*

Sex and type of restriction	Finance, real estate [2]	Business, repair [2]	Personal services	Entertainment [2]	Professional [2]	Public administration	Unknown [2]
PERCENT DISTRIBUTION							
Total (age 18 years and older)	100.0	100.0	100.0	100.0	100.0	100.0	100.0
Female							
Not applicable [3]	16.3	35.3	32.8	31.8	17.8	18.2	*82.9
Employer restricts smoking	68.8	48.0	39.6	47.2	74.8	74.9	*14.8
Employer does not restrict	14.5	14.7	24.0	20.9	6.6	*6.6	*1.7
Unknown	*0.4	*2.0	*3.7	*—	0.9	*0.2	*0.7
Male							
Not applicable [3]	41.9	51.9	43.3	50.0	31.7	39.9	*83.8
Employer restricts smoking	47.4	30.1	*43.5	34.8	59.2	56.2	*10.1
Employer does not restrict	*9.6	16.5	*11.3	15.2	*7.7	3.9	*6.1
Unknown	*1.1	1.5	1.9	*—	*1.4	*—	*—
NUMBER OF PERSONS INTERVIEWED							
Female	553	279	327	94	2 439	304	77
Male	335	460	115	116	926	327	68

SOURCE: D.K. Wagener, J. Walstedt, L. Jenkins, et al. "Women: Work and Health." *Vital and Health Statistics* 3, no. 31. 1997: Table 43. Data from the National Health Interview Survey.

* Figure does not meet standards of reliability or precision.
*– Figure does not meet standards of reliability or precision and quantity zero.
1. Includes unknown industry and races other than Black and White.
2. "Farm" includes agriculture, forestry, and fisheries. "Transport, utilities" includes transport, communications, and other public utilities. "Finance, real estate" includes finance, insurance, and real estate. "Business, repair" includes business and repair services. "Entertainment" includes entertainment and recreational services. "Professional" includes professional and related services. "Unknown" includes unknown and Armed Forces.
3. Person works outside, in a motor vehicle, or at several locations.
4. Data not presented because based on 20 or fewer interviewed persons.

NOTE: The percents shown are weighted national estimates. Estimates for which the numerator has a relative standard error of more than 30 percent are indicated with an asterisk. Data are based on household interviews of civilian noninstitutionalized population.

Substance abuse has been associated with absenteeism, accidents and injuries, and increased medical costs in the workplace. Reduced worker productivity caused by drug use is estimated to cost $14 billion annually.[6] Therefore, many employers have adopted policies that restrict drug use in workplaces, such as pre-employment drug testing, random drug testing, and testing for probable cause after an accident. Drug testing is likely to discourage drug users from applying for a job in places known to test for illegal drug use. (See Figure 2B.) An evaluation of the costs and benefits of drug testing, therefore, needs to consider not only the percentage of individuals detected as drug users but also the preemptive effect of testing in discouraging high-risk workers from joining the workforce. Rather than change their drug using habits, such individuals may avoid employment with companies that test their employees for drug use. (See Table 2C.)

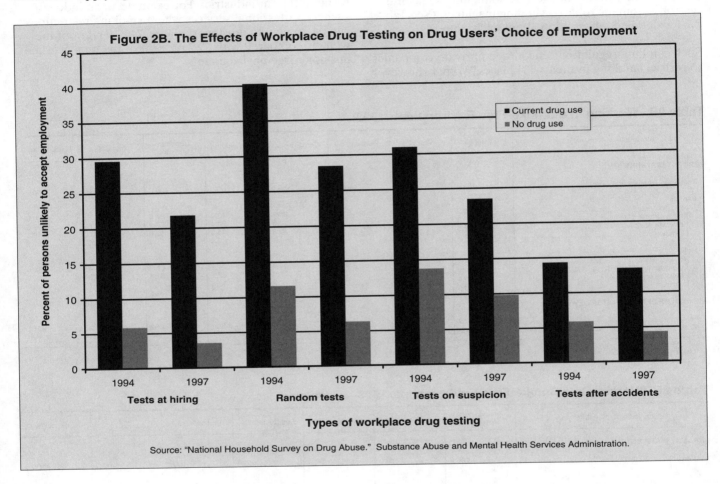

Figure 2B. The Effects of Workplace Drug Testing on Drug Users' Choice of Employment

Legend: ■ Current drug use ■ No drug use

Y-axis: Percent of persons unlikely to accept employment

X-axis categories: 1994 1997 Tests at hiring | 1994 1997 Random tests | 1994 1997 Tests on suspicion | 1994 1997 Tests after accidents

Types of workplace drug testing

Source: "National Household Survey on Drug Abuse." Substance Abuse and Mental Health Services Administration.

Table 2C. Workplace Drug Testing and Employment

(Percentage of full-time workers, age 18–49, reporting that they would be less likely to work for an employer who tests for drug use)

Establishment size	Tests for drugs at hiring				Tests for drugs randomly				Tests for drugs upon suspicion				Tests for drugs post-accident			
	Current illicit drug use		No current illicit drug use		Current illicit drug use		No current illicit drug use		Current illicit drug use		No current illicit drug use		Current illicit drug use		No current illicit drug use	
	1994	1997	1994	1997	1994	1997	1994	1997	1994	1997	1994	1997	1994	1997	1994	1997
Total	29.6	21.8	5.9	**3.5	40.3	**28.5	11.6	*6.4	31.0	23.5	13.7	**9.8	14.3	13.4	5.9	*4.3
1–24 employees	29.3	33.0	6.4	*3.7	38.0	37.0	10.3	*6.1	31.6	32.3	13.0	*9.5	15.2	13.6	5.8	4.7
25–499 employees	30.5	*15.1	5.5	*3.6	41.2	**24.6	11.7	*6.7	30.5	*18.1	13.3	*9.5	14.7	13.1	5.9	**4.7
Over 500 employees	28.8	**6.5	5.9	3.1	47.7	**13.2	14.1	*6.3	29.6	*12.1	15.9	11.1	9.7	14.1	6.0	**2.5

SOURCE: Office of Applied Studies, SAMHSA, National Household Survey on Drug Abuse, 1994-B, 1997. Worker Drug Use and Workplace Policies and Programs: Results from the 1994 and 1997 NHSDA: Table 5.4.

* Difference between 1994 and 1997 is statistically significant at the .05 level.
** Difference between 1994 and 1997 is statistically significant at the .01 level.

The impact of alcohol abuse and drug use is mediated by their effects on other behaviors that influence health and safety. For example, consider the relationship between drug use, alcohol abuse, and driving. Illicit drug users and heavy alcohol drinkers are four to five times more likely than the general population to drive an automobile under the influence of drugs or alcohol (40.7 percent of illicit drug users and 50.6 percent of heavy alcohol users drive under the influence compared to 10.7 percent of the general population). They are also about twice as likely to ride in an automobile without wearing seat belts (23.4 percent of illicit drug users and 26.8 percent of heavy alcohol drinkers ride without seat belts compared to 12.4 percent of the general population). Thus, drug and alcohol abuse work together with other risky behaviors, such as not wearing a seat belt when riding in an automobile, to increase the likelihood of serious injuries. (See Table 2.7.)

NUTRITION

Getting enough to eat and eating the right combination of foods are also critical to good health. Both the U.S. Department of Agriculture (USDA) and the National Center for Health Statistics (NCHS) report results from nutrition surveys that describe what people eat and how close their intake comes to what they should eat. In addition, the Economic Research Service of the USDA estimates the foods consumed by people on the basis of an analysis of commodity flows (that is, an analysis of the production and distribution of food). (See Table 2.10.) The USDA also uses data from the Census Bureau's Current Population Survey to identify the percentage of the population that does not have access to adequate amounts of food because they cannot afford to buy enough of the right foods. (See Tables 2.8 and 2.9.)

HUNGER

In 1998, the USDA identified households that did not have sufficient economic resources to obtain access to an "adequate quantity and/or quality of acceptable food." Its survey asked respondents to report on whether one or more members of the household were hungry at least sometime during the year before the interview. The results show that the overwhelming majority of households in the United States have enough money to buy sufficient amounts of healthy food. Only 10.2 percent of U.S. households reported difficulty buying adequate food, but this included about 3.7 million households that reported hunger. Persons in households with children under age 18 headed by women with no spouse were the most likely to report being hungry. (See Table 2.9.)

CALCULATING THE FOOD SECURITY INDEX

The USDA's Food Security Index was calculated on the basis of the following questions, which were asked of each household as a part of a supplement to the Census Bureau's Current Population Survey:

1. In the last 12 months, did you or other adults in your household ever cut the size of your meals or skip meals because there was not enough money for food? How often did this happen—almost every month, some months but not every month, or in only one or two months?

2. In the last 12 months, did you or other adults in your household ever not eat for a whole day because there was not enough money for food? How often did this happen—almost every month, some months but not every month, or in only one or two months?

3. In the last 12 months, did you ever eat less than you felt you should because there was not enough money to buy food?

4. In the last 12 months, were you ever hungry but did not eat because you could not afford enough food?

5. Sometimes people lose weight because they do not have enough to eat. In the last 12 months, did you lose weight because there was not enough food?

6. In the last 12 months, did you ever cut the size of any of the children's meals because there was not enough money for food?

7. In the last 12 months, did any of the children ever skip a meal because there was not enough money for food? How often did this happen—almost every month, some months but not every month, or in only one or two months?

8. In the last 12 months, were the children ever hungry but you just could not afford more food?

9. In the last 12 months, did any of the children ever not eat for a whole day because there was not enough money for food?

10. I worried whether our food would run out before we got money to buy more. Was that often, sometimes, or never true for you in the last 12 months?

11. The food that we bought just did not last, and we did not have money to get more. Was that often, sometimes, or never true for you in the last 12 months?

12. We could not afford to eat balanced meals. Was that often, sometimes, or never true for you in the last 12 months?

13. We could not feed the children a balanced meal because we could not afford that. Was that often, sometimes, or never true for you in the last 12 months?

14. The children were not eating enough because we

just could not afford enough food. Was that often, sometimes, or never true for you in the last 12 months?

15. We relied on only a few kinds of low-cost food to feed the children because we were running out of money to buy food. Was that often, sometimes, or never true for you in the last 12 months?

USDA analysts derived a scale based on the severity of the items in the questionnaire. This scale allows them to classify households into (1) those that do not have any problem buying food (food secure), (2) those that modify their buying behavior because of short funds but do not report any hunger (food insecure without hunger), (3) those that occasionally experience episodes of hunger (food insecure with moderate hunger), and (4) those that report severe hunger episodes such as denying food to

children because they do not have the resources to buy food (food insecure with severe hunger).

As shown in Table 2.9, households with incomes lower than the poverty level experience more hunger than other households. Furthermore, while the percentage of households reporting difficulty getting adequate food declined between 1995 and 1999, hunger rates among persons living at the poverty level increased during that period.[7] As expected, income is an important determinant of whether people experience hunger in the United States. However, other factors, such as education and food stamp program participation, also are important.[8] Households with children under age 18 headed by single women, as well as those in the southern and western regions of the United States continue to experience hunger. Figure 2C shows hunger rates by place of residence, and Table 2.8 shows the rates by each state.

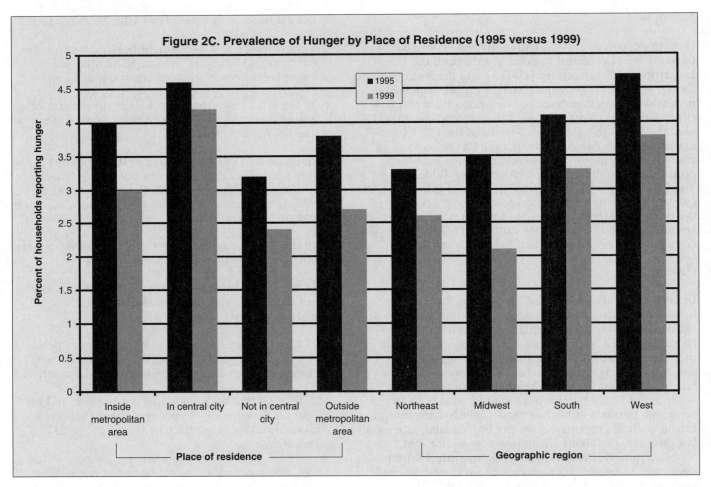

Figure 2C. Prevalence of Hunger by Place of Residence (1995 versus 1999)

EATING THE RIGHT FOODS

In the United States, more health problems are caused by the kinds of food people eat than by hunger.[9] On the basis of an analysis of the foods that are beneficial to good health, the USDA has identified the pattern of eating that promotes good health. Its advice is summarized in the Food Guide Pyramid. (See Figure 2D.) The USDA's detailed recommendations regarding the servings persons should eat vary with age, sex, and physiological status (i.e., activity and build).[10]

Compiling information from commodity flows (i.e., the production and distribution of food), the USDA concluded that people eat too much fat and sugar and not enough fruits, vegetables, dairy products, and lean meats. The USDA also found that the mix of grains may not be appropriate and suggested that American diets include more whole-grain products such as brown rice, barley, corn, whole-wheat breads, and whole-grain cereal. As a result, slow but steady progress has been made to educate the public about nutrition and to improve Americans' eating habits. Americans are increasing their

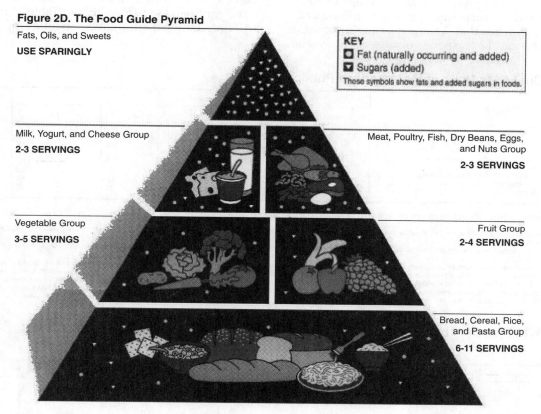

Figure 2D. The Food Guide Pyramid

Fats, Oils, and Sweets
USE SPARINGLY

KEY
◻ Fat (naturally occurring and added)
◥ Sugars (added)
These symbols show fats and added sugars in foods.

Milk, Yogurt, and Cheese Group
2-3 SERVINGS

Meat, Poultry, Fish, Dry Beans, Eggs, and Nuts Group
2-3 SERVINGS

Vegetable Group
3-5 SERVINGS

Fruit Group
2-4 SERVINGS

Bread, Cereal, Rice, and Pasta Group
6-11 SERVINGS

Source: Linda Scott Kantor, "A Dietary Assessment of the U.S. Food Supply: Comparing Per Capita Food Consumption with Food Guide Pyramid Serving Recommendations," December, 1998 *Agricultural Economic Report,* No. 772

consumption of vegetables and grains toward the recommended levels. (See Table 2D.) For example, from 1970 to 1975, Americans consumed an average of 6.8 servings of grains and 3.1 servings of vegetables a day. By 1996, consumption had increased to 9.7 servings of grains and 3.8 servings of vegetables. The latest figures come much closer to the Food Guide Pyramid's recommendations of 6 to 11 servings of grains and 3 to 5 servings of vegetables per day. However, Americans' consumption of fat and sugar not only exceeds the recommended levels but also continues to increase. The USDA estimates that, from 1970 to 1975, Americans consumed an average of 49 grams of fat and 27 teaspoons of sugar a day. By 1996, consumption had increased to a daily average of 60 grams of fat and 32 teaspoons of sugar. The Food Guide Pyramid recommends that Americans should consume 38 grams of fat and 12 teaspoons of sugar per day. The

composition of food consumed also has changed. For example, Americans reduced their consumption of whole milk from about 0.78 servings a day in 1970 to about 0.2 servings in 1996 and increased their consumption of non-fat and low-fat milk.[11]

USDA studies also show that large parts of the public are aware that they are not eating the best combination of foods. For example, 35.7 percent of men and 42.7 percent of women reported that they believe they consume too many calories, and 46.5 percent of men and 48.5 percent of women reported that they believe they eat too much fat. In addition, 29.5 percent of men and 34.1 percent of women reported that they believe they are not eating sufficient fiber. (See Table 2E and Tables 2.10 , 2.11, and 2.12 for additional information about nutrients.)[12]

Table 2D. Change in Diets of the American Public

Food group	Servings				Food Guide Pyramid serving recommendation [1]
	1970–1975	1980–1985	1990–1995	1996	
Grains	6.8	7.5	9.2	9.7	9
Vegetables	3.1	3.2	3.6	3.8	4
Fruits	1.1	1.2	1.3	1.3	3
Milk, yogurt, and cheese [2]	1.6	1.5	1.6	1.7	2.2
Meat, poultry, fish, dry beans, eggs, and nuts (ounces)	5.4	5.5	5.6	5.6	6.0
Added fats and oils (grams of fat) [3]	49	55	62	60	38
Added sugars (teaspoons) [4]	27	26	31	32	12

SOURCE: Economic Research Service/ U.S. Department of Agriculture, *A Dietary Assessment of the U.S. Food Supply*, AER-722: Table 2.

1. Recommendation based on a 2,200-calorie diet. A 2,200-calorie diet is close to the 2,247 calories recommended as an average caloric intake for the population in 1995. Recommended servings for other years may differ.
2. Three servings of milk, yogurt, and cheese are appropriate for teenagers and young adults to the age of 24 and for pregnant and breastfeeding women. Two servings are recommended for other adults.
3. *The 1995 Dietary Guidelines* recommend that consumers choose a diet that provides no more than 30 percent of total calories from fat. The upper limit on the grams of fat in a consumer's diet will depend on calorie intake. For example, a person consuming 2,200 calories per day, the upper limit on total daily fat intake is 660 calories. Seventy-three grams of fat contribute about 660 calories (73 grams x 9 calories per gram of fat = 660 calories). According to food supply data for 1994, added fats and oils account for 52 percent of the total fat provided by the food supply in that year. The recommendation shown here assumes that added fats and oils account for 52 percent of total fat intake for a daily upper limit of 38 grams of added fats and oils (73 x 0.52) = 38.
4. To avoid getting too many calories from sugar, dietary guidance suggests that consumers on a 2,200-calorie diet try to limit added sugars to the daily quantity listed.

Table 2E. What People Think They Eat: 1994–1995

(Percent)

Nutrient	Too low	Too high	About right	Don't know	Not ascertained
MEN (N = 1,889)					
Calories	6.8	35.7	53.7	3.6	0.2
Calcium	25.9	6.5	60.2	7.2	0.2
Iron	20.5	2.2	67.2	10.0	0.1
Vitamin C	25.4	3.7	66.7	4.1	0.1
Protein	8.8	11.7	75.7	3.8	0.1
Fat	7.7	46.5	42.8	2.9	0.1
Saturated fat	9.4	35.2	45.3	10.0	0.1
Cholesterol	7.6	30.6	53.8	7.7	0.3
Salt or sodium	11.9	25.3	60.2	1.8	0.8
Fiber	29.5	2.7	63.5	4.1	0.1
Sugar and sweets	11.7	28.9	57.6	1.4	0.3
WOMEN (N = 1,956)					
Calories	5.9	42.7	49.0	1.8	0.5
Calcium	43.6	2.8	50.6	2.7	0.4
Iron	34.7	1.5	59.1	4.6	0.1
Vitamin C	29.8	1.9	65.7	2.4	0.3
Protein	13.5	10.6	73.5	2.2	0.2
Fat	6.0	48.5	44.0	1.4	0.1
Saturated fat	7.3	35.9	48.5	8.0	0.4
Cholesterol	5.3	29.0	59.9	5.5	0.3
Salt or sodium	8.7	24.6	65.3	1.2	0.2
Fiber	34.1	2.9	59.6	3.2	0.1
Sugar and sweets	7.8	38.7	52.7	0.7	0.2

SOURCE: USDA Diet and Health Knowledge Survey, 1994–1995; Agricultural Research Service, U.S. Department of Agriculture, Beltsville Human Nutrition Research Center, Food Surveys Research Group: Table 13.

NOTE: Respondents were asked "Compared to what is healthy, do you think your diet is too low, too high, or about right in (nutrient/food component)?"

THE HEALTHY EATING INDEX

Although the commodity analysis and survey interviews provide information about the specific kinds of food people eat, they do not show the overall adequacy of the average U.S. diet. The USDA's Center for Nutrition Policy and Promotion developed a Healthy Eating Index to monitor people's eating patterns. The index compares Americans' eating habits with recommended standards for a varied and adequate diet for healthy living. It is constructed from information obtained during the USDA's Continuing Survey of Food Intakes by Individuals.[13] The ten components scored in the Healthy Eating Index include the five major food groups in the USDA's Food Guide Pyramid (illustrated in Figure 2D), total fat consumption as a percentage of total calorie intake, total cholesterol intake, total sodium intake, and variety in the diet.

Each component is given a score from 1 to 10 to indicate the degree of compliance with the recommended diet. Total scores lower than 51 imply poor diets, scores between 51 and 80 imply diets needing improvement, and scores of 80 to 100 imply good diets. (See Table 2F.) According to the index, most groups need to improve their eating habits. (See Table 2G.) People with higher incomes have better scores, as do the better educated and children under age three. The scores on this index might be elevated because of misreporting by the individuals tested. People often underreport caloric intake and fats consumed and overreport the consumption of fruits and vegetables.

PHYSICAL ACTIVITY

Health is improved by a combination of good eating habits and the appropriate level of exercise. In fact, the government's recommendations regarding eating patterns are based on the level of physical activity an individual achieves. In 1996, the surgeon general reviewed the state of physical activity in the United States and concluded that the rate of participation in physical activity was much lower than it should be.[14] In this report, the surgeon general linked physical activity to numerous health improvements and made the following statement:

Most significantly, regular physical activity greatly reduces the risk of dying from coronary heart disease, the leading cause of death in the United States. Physical activity also reduces the risk of developing diabetes, hypertension, and colon cancer; enhances mental health; fosters healthy muscles, bones, and joints; and helps maintain function and preserve independence in older adults.[15]

About one-quarter of all American adults age 18 and older participates in no physical activity at all other than the limited physical activity required by their jobs. Another quarter of the population participates in regular sustained physical activity on five or more occasions per week for at least 30 minutes. Younger adults are more likely to exercise on a regular basis than the very old. (See Tables 2.13, 2.14, 2.15, and 2.16.) Women who exercise regularly are more likely to prevent osteoporosis (a condition in which the bones break easily). Especially good for preventing osteoporosis are weight-bearing exercises, such as walking, climbing stairs, yoga, jogging, and lifting weights. Regular exercise is also helpful for weight control.

SEXUAL ACTIVITY

Teenage sexual activity is not only a risk factor for the birth of children into unstable environments, but it is also associated with sexually transmitted diseases. In one survey, a significant proportion of high school students as young as ninth graders reported that they had sexual relations. In 1997, 38 percent of 9th graders, 42.5 percent of 10th graders, 49.7 percent of 11th graders, and 60.9 percent of 12th graders reported that they had at least one episode of sexual relations. (See Table 2.19.) In another survey, 75.5 percent of young women age 19 reported that they have had sexual relations. (See Tables 2.17, 2.18, and 2.19.)

Although sexual activity among teenagers has increased over the years, both pregnancy rates and abortion rates among teenage women have decreased. At the beginning of the 1990s, there were 116.3 pregnancies per 1,000 teenage women age 15 to 19. By 1996, this rate dropped to 98.7 pregnancies per 1,000 teenage women.

Table 2F. Components of the Healthy Eating Index and Scoring System: 1994–1996

	Score ranges	Criteria for maximum score of 10	Criteria for minimum score of 0
Grain consumption	0 to 10	6–11 servings	0 servings
Vegetable consumption	0 to 10	3–5 servings	0 servings
Fruit consumption	0 to 10	2–4 servings	0 servings
Milk consumption	0 to 10	2–3 servings	0 servings
Meat consumption	0 to 10	2–3 servings	0 servings
Total fat intake	0 to 10	30% or less energy from fat	45% or more energy from fat
Saturated fat intake	0 to 10	Less than 10% energy from saturated fat	15% or more energy from saturated fat
Cholesterol intake	0 to 10	300 mg or less	450 mg or more
Sodium intake	0 to 10	2,400 mg or less	4,800 mg or more
Food variety	0 to 10	8 or more different items in a day	3 or fewer different items in a day

SOURCE: S.A. Bowman, M. Lino, S.A. Gerrior, P.P Basiotis. 1998. *The Healthy Eating Index: 1994–96.* U.S. Department of Agriculture, Center for Nutrition Policy and Promotion. CNPP-5.

1. People with consumption or intakes between the maximum and minimum ranges or amounts were assigned scores proportionately.
2. Number of servings depends on Recommended Energy Allowance. All amounts are on a per day basis.

Table 2G. Healthy Eating Index, Overall Mean Scores

Characteristic	Index score			
	1994	1995	1996	1994–1996
SEX				
Male	63.0	63.0	62.6	62.9
Female	64.2	64.0	65.0	64.4
AGE AND SEX				
Children 2–3 years	74.4	74.0	73.2	73.9
Children 4–6 years	66.4	68.8	68.0	67.7
Children 7–10 years	66.9	67.1	65.9	66.6
Females 11–14 years	63.1	63.5	64.0	63.5
Females 15–18 years	61.4	58.4	62.5	60.8
Females 19–50 years	61.8	61.2	62.7	61.9
Females 51 years and over	67.1	67.6	67.5	67.4
Males 11–14 years	62.4	63.2	61.2	62.3
Males 15–18 years	60.4	61.4	60.2	60.7
Males 19–50 years	61.2	60.6	60.6	60.8
Males 51 years and over	64.0	64.0	65.2	64.4
RACE				
White	64.2	63.9	64.4	64.2
Black	58.9	59.5	59.4	59.3
Asian or Pacific Islander	65.8	66.7	68.0	66.8
Other [1]	64.8	64.5	64.0	64.4
ETHNICITY				
Non-Hispanic	63.6	63.4	63.9	63.6
Hispanic	63.8	64.5	63.2	63.8
INCOME AS PERCENTAGE OF POVERTY				
0–50	58.8	61.2	60.7	60.2
51–100	60.5	61.4	60.5	60.8
101–130	61.5	61.6	61.6	61.6
131–200	62.8	61.4	63.7	62.6
201–299	63.8	63.6	63.6	63.7
300+	65.0	64.9	65.0	65.0
EDUCATION				
4 years of high school or less	60.8	60.6	61.0	60.8
Some college	63.5	63.0	63.2	63.2
4 years of college	66.6	65.4	67.1	66.4
More than 4 years of college	67.6	68.1	68.4	68.0
REGION				
Northeast	65.3	65.0	65.8	65.4
Midwest	64.1	64.0	65.2	64.4
South	61.7	61.7	61.3	61.6
West	64.5	64.6	64.7	64.6
URBANIZATION				
MSA [2], central city	64.0	63.2	64.3	63.8
MSA, outside central city	64.5	64.6	64.7	64.6
Non-MSA	61.0	61.6	61.6	61.4

SOURCE: S.A. Bowman, M. Lino, S.A. Gerrior, P.P. Basiotis. 1998. *The Healthy Eating Index: 1994–96*. U.S. Department of Agriculture, Center for Nutrition Policy and Promotion. CNPP-5: Table 5.

1. Includes American Indians and Alaskan Natives.
2. Metropolitan Statistical Area.

NOTE: The overall Healthy Eating Index (HEI) score ranges from 0–100. An HEI score over 80 implies a "good" diet, an HEI score between 51 and 80 implies a diet that "needs improvement," and an HEI score less than 51 implies a "poor" diet.

In contrast, pregnancies among older women have increased. Although fewer teenagers are becoming pregnant, more of the pregnant teenagers carry their babies to term: 40.7 percent of teenage pregnancies ended in abortion in 1990 compared to 33.8 percent in 1996.[16] (See Figures 2E and 2F.)

SOURCE OF DATA ON SEXUAL BEHAVIOR

The U.S. Department of Health and Human Services conducts four surveys that collect data on adolescent sexual behavior: the National Survey on Family Growth (NSFG) and the National Survey of Adolescent Males (NSAM); the National Survey of Adolescent Health (AddHealth); and the Youth Risk Behavior Survey (YRBS), which includes students from grades 9 through 12. The YRBS collects the data using questionnaires that students complete in school and does not survey school-age children who do not attend school.

When surveys do not yield the same results, the differences are likely caused by various factors, such as the way the instruments are administered, the selection of the questions asked, and the different sociodemographics of the populations surveyed. Each survey has specific strengths in measuring adolescent sexual behavior. For example, the school-based component of the YRBS provides national- and state-level trend data on young

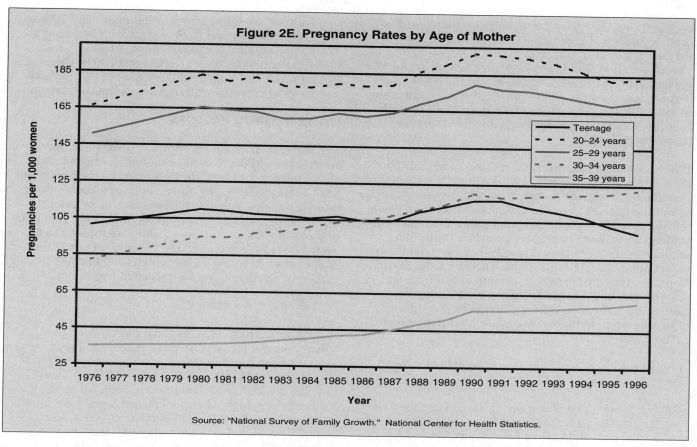

Figure 2E. Pregnancy Rates by Age of Mother

Source: "National Survey of Family Growth." National Center for Health Statistics.

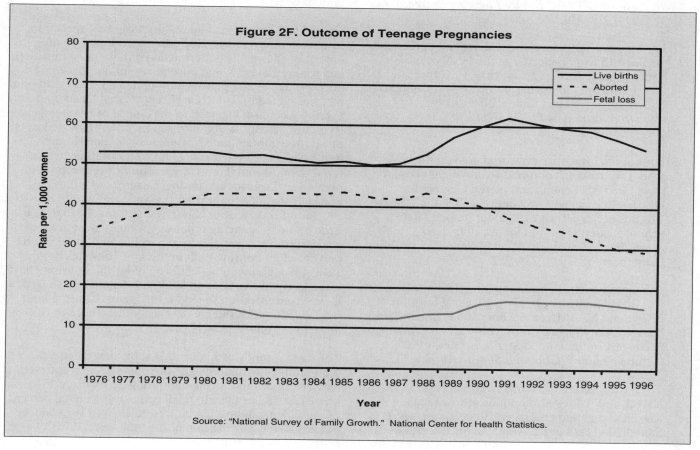

Figure 2F. Outcome of Teenage Pregnancies

Source: "National Survey of Family Growth." National Center for Health Statistics.

people who attend school. The NSFG includes adolescents regardless of their school status (that is, whether they are students, absentees, or school dropouts). Therefore, the NSFG is a good source of data about all young people. Because the NSAM and the NSFG samples are based on age, their data are directly comparable to vital statistics data, which provide the rates of adolescent pregnancy, unintended pregnancy, and sexually transmitted disease.

It is evident that the results from these surveys differ. (See Tables 2.17, 2.18, and 2.19.) When women are asked to recall their sexual behavior from the past, they provide somewhat different rates of sexual activities from when they are asked about their current sexual activities. When students are asked about their sexual behavior in a school-based survey, they report higher rates than they report in home-based interviews. Therefore, the results from these surveys should be examined carefully, and researchers should exercise care in interpreting the results and comparing different tables in this volume, especially when the tables are based on differing analytical approaches.

A list of resources that contain more detailed information on this subject follows:

1. For data on sexual activity of women collected in the NSFG, see S. Singh and J. Darroch, "Trends in Sexual Activity Among Adolescent American Women: 1982–1995," *Family Planning Perspectives* 31 (1999):212–219.

2. For national statistics on sexual activity of teenage men age 15 to 19 collected in the NSAM, see F. Sonenstein, L. Ku, L. D. Lindberg, C. Turner, and J. Pleck, "Changes in Sexual Behavior and Condom Use among Teenaged Males: 1988 to 1995," *American Journal of Public Health* 88 (1998):956–959.

3. For national statistics on sexual activity for high school students (as opposed to all young people) from the YRBS conducted by the Centers for Disease Control and Prevention (CDC) in 1998, see "Trends in Sexual Risk Behavior among High School Students: United States, 1991–1997," *Morbidity and Mortality Weekly Report* 47, no. 36 (September 18, 1998):749–752.

4. For more comprehensive statistics for both female and male teenagers age 15 to 19, using both the NSFG and NSAM, see J. Abma and F. Sonenstein, "Sexual Activity and Contraceptive Practices among Teenagers in the United States, 1988 and 1995," forthcoming in *Vital Health Statistics*, series 23.

5. For a comparison of results from the NSFG, NSAM, YRBS, and AddHealth on indicators of male and female sexual and contraceptive behavior, see J. Santelli, L. Lindberg, J. Abma, C. Sucoff, and M.

Resnick, "A Comparison of Estimates and Trends in Adolescent Sexual Behaviors in Four Nationally Representative Surveys," *Family Planning Perspectives* 32, no. 4 (July/August 2000). This analysis includes an in-depth discussion of the methodological and other differences among the surveys.

ENVIRONMENTAL FACTORS

The physical environment in which people live and work affects their exposure to hazards, pollutants, and other contaminants; the stress they endure; and their resulting health and safety. For example, some environments are more prone than other to hazards such as mudslides, floods, wildfires, and the mosquito-borne West Nile virus or diseases such as skin cancer and respiratory conditions. During the past decades, the environments in which Americans live and work have improved through the regulation of air, water, and work-related exposures.

LEAD EXPOSURE IN CHILDREN

According to the CDC's National Center for Environmental Health (NCEH), "Childhood lead poisoning is a major, preventable environmental health problem. Blood lead levels (BLLs) as low as 10 µg/dL are associated with harmful effects on children's learning and behavior. Very high BLLs (> 70 µg/dL) cause devastating health consequences, including seizures, coma, and death." The NCEH estimates that 890,000 American children have BLLs greater than 10 µg/dL.[17]

The NCEH points out that children can be exposed to lead from many sources, including lead-based paint; industrial sites and smelters; lead-contaminated dust, soil, and water; materials that parents use in occupations or hobbies; dishes and plates containing lead; and traditional medical remedies. The NCEH reports that "lead-contaminated house dust, ingested in the course of normal hand-to-mouth activity, is of major significance." House dust is most often contaminated by lead-based paint in the home when such paint is peeling, deteriorating, or scattered about during home renovation or preparation of painted surfaces for repainting. Lead-based paint in homes is the most important remaining source of lead exposure for American children. Substantial progress has been made in reducing other environmental sources of lead exposure, especially from gasoline and food. But 83 percent of all housing built in the United States before 1973 still contains some lead. The older the housing, the more likely it is to contain lead-based paint and to have a higher concentration of lead in the paint. Housing built before 1946 poses the greatest risk of exposure to children. (See Figures 2G, 2H, and 2I.)

The most recently available data show that when a random sample of children age one to five years was tested, 8.6 percent of those living in housing built before 1946 had BLLs higher than 10 µg/dl compared with 4.6 percent of those living in housing built from 1946 to 1973 and 1.6 percent of those living in housing built since 1973.

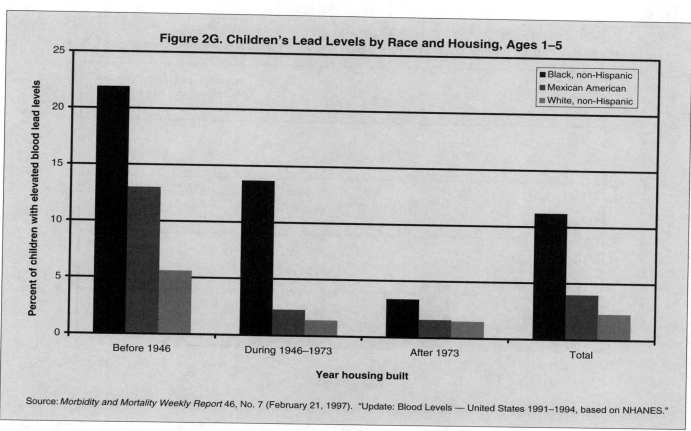

Figure 2G. Children's Lead Levels by Race and Housing, Ages 1–5

Percent of children with elevated blood lead levels (y-axis)

Legend:
- Black, non-Hispanic
- Mexican American
- White, non-Hispanic

Year housing built (x-axis): Before 1946, During 1946–1973, After 1973, Total

Source: *Morbidity and Mortality Weekly Report* 46, No. 7 (February 21, 1997). "Update: Blood Levels — United States 1991–1994, based on NHANES."

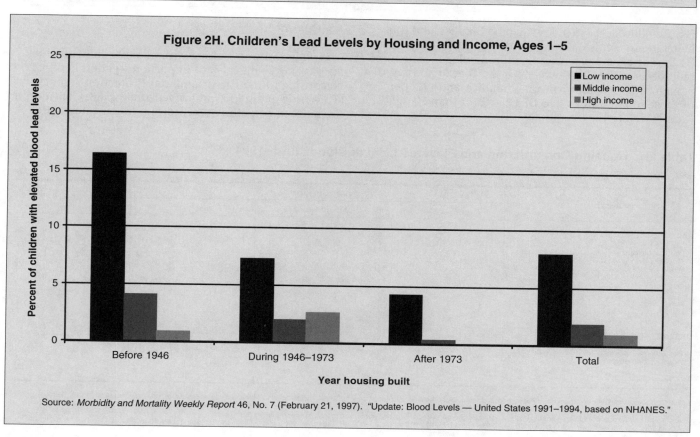

Figure 2H. Children's Lead Levels by Housing and Income, Ages 1–5

Percent of children with elevated blood lead levels (y-axis)

Legend:
- Low income
- Middle income
- High income

Year housing built (x-axis): Before 1946, During 1946–1973, After 1973, Total

Source: *Morbidity and Mortality Weekly Report* 46, No. 7 (February 21, 1997). "Update: Blood Levels — United States 1991–1994, based on NHANES."

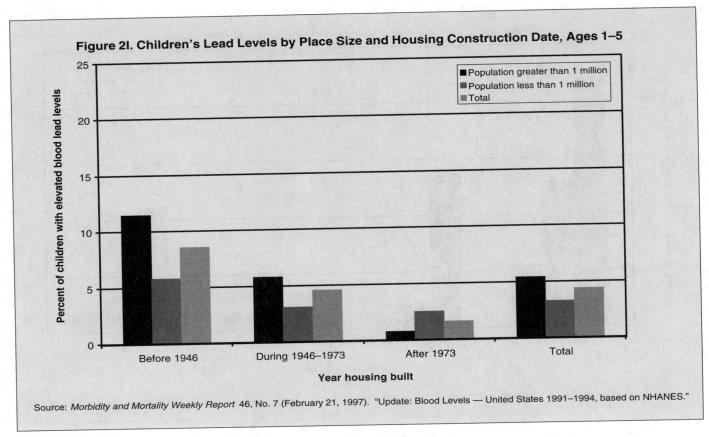

Figure 2I. Children's Lead Levels by Place Size and Housing Construction Date, Ages 1–5

Source: *Morbidity and Mortality Weekly Report* 46, No. 7 (February 21, 1997). "Update: Blood Levels — United States 1991–1994, based on NHANES."

Black children, those in low-income families, and those living in large cities were also more likely to have high BLLs. For example, of those children living in structures built before 1946, 21.9 percent of the Black children, 16.4 percent of those in low-income families, and 11.5 percent of those in large cities had BLLs greater than 10 µg/dL. (See Table 2H.)

AIR QUALITY

Clean air and water along with an environment with fewer toxic chemicals are important to good health. According to the Environmental Protection Agency (EPA), air quality has improved since 1988. Considering the amount of pollutants entering the air, substantial

Table 2H. Housing Construction and Elevated Lead in Blood: 1991–1994

(Percent with elevated blood lead levels [BLLs])

Characteristic	Year housing built [1]			Total
	Before 1946	During 1946–1973	After 1973	
RACE AND ETHNICITY [2]				
Black, non-Hispanic	21.9	13.7	3.4	11.2
Mexican American	13.0	2.3	1.6	4.0
White, non-Hispanic	5.6	1.4	1.5	2.3
INCOME [3]				
Low	16.4	7.3	4.3	8.0
Middle	4.1	2.0	0.4	1.9
High	0.9	2.7	*	1.0
URBAN STATUS [4]				
Population ≥ 1 million	11.5	5.8	0.8	5.4
Population < 1 million	5.8	3.1	2.5	3.3
TOTAL	8.6	4.6	1.6	4.4

SOURCE: Centers for Disease Control and Prevention. ""Update: Blood Levels – United States, 1991–94," *Morbidity and Mortality Weekly Report* 46, no. 7 (February 21, 1997): Table 2.

* No children in the sample had these characteristics; however, the true estimate for this population group is probably larger than zero.
1. Age of housing was unknown by the household respondent for 11.7% of children aged 1–5 years; approximately 5.6% of these children had BLLs ≥ 10 m g/dL.
2. Data for other racial/ ethnic groups were too small for reliable estimates.
3. Income categories were defined using the poverty-income ratio (PIR; the ratio of total family income to the poverty threshold for the year of the interview): low income was defined as PIR ≤ 1.300; middle, as PIR 1.301–3. 500; and high, as PIR ≥ 3. 501. Persons with data missing for income were not included in the analysis of income.
4. Urban status was based on U. S. Department of Agriculture codes that classify counties by total population and proximity to major metropolitan areas and divided into two categories: metropolitan areas with a population ≥ 1 million and metropolitan and nonmetropolitan areas with a population < 1 million.

improvements have occurred. However, the level of progress has varied depending on the type of pollutant.[18] For example, lead and particulate matter emissions have been reduced to about 55 percent of their 1988 levels, while nitrogen oxides have remained the same. (See Table 2I and Figure 2J.) Much of the improvement in lead levels has come from the introduction of regulations requiring cars to use unleaded fuel. In 1988, 48.9 percent of lead emitted into the air came from vehicles. By 1997, this source was reduced to 13.3 percent of the emissions, and the total emissions were reduced from 7,053 short tons to 3,915 short tons. (See Table 2J and Figure 2K; see also Table 2.20 for state emissions information.) As a result, during the 1990s

there was some improvement in population exposure to acceptable air quality. In 1990, 71 percent of the population lived in counties that met all of the air-quality standards, and by 1996 compliance had increased to 81.3 percent. In 1990 and 1996, more than 90 percent of the population lived in counties that met the air-quality standards for the levels of particulate exposure, carbon monoxide, sulfur dioxide, nitrogen dioxide, and airborne lead. A lower percentage lived in counties that met the air-quality standards for ozone levels set at the beginning of the decade (76.3 percent complied in 1990), but more lived in counties that complied by the mid-1990s (83.3 percent complied in 1996). (See Table 2K and Figure 2L.)

Table 2I. Change in Pollutants Released into the Air

(Percent of 1988 levels)

Type	1988	1989	1990	1991	1992	1993	1994	1995	1996	1997
Carbon monoxide	100.0	89.1	82.5	84.2	81.3	81.4	85.2	76.8	78.1	75.3
Lead	100.0	77.5	70.5	59.1	54.0	55.5	57.3	55.6	55.4	55.5
Nitrogen oxides	100.0	98.7	98.8	99.2	100.3	101.4	102.6	100.2	98.6	99.4
Organic compounds	100.0	92.7	87.1	87.7	85.9	86.7	89.3	85.6	80.4	80.0
Particulate matter	100.0	86.9	48.9	48.2	48.1	45.6	50.4	43.8	54.3	55.0
Sulfur dioxide	100.0	100.7	102.3	99.6	98.6	97.1	94.5	82.9	85.7	88.0

SOURCE: U.S. Environmental Protection Agency, Office of Air Quality Planning and Standards, *National Air Quality and Emissions Trends Report, 1997:* Table A-2–A-8.

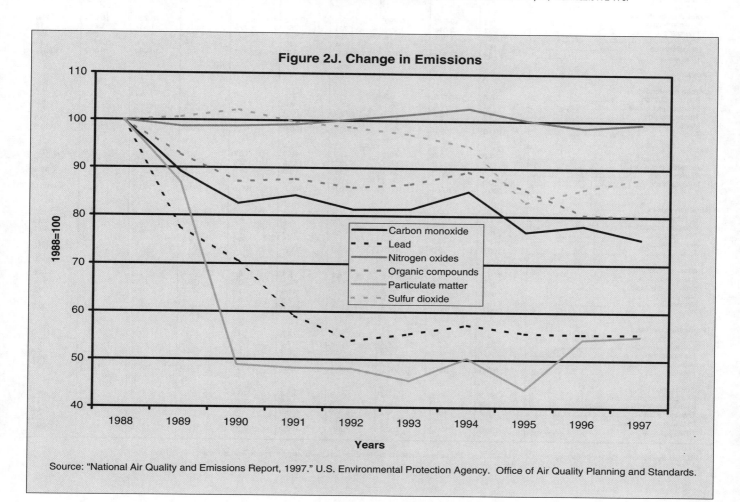

Figure 2J. Change in Emissions

Source: "National Air Quality and Emissions Report, 1997." U.S. Environmental Protection Agency. Office of Air Quality Planning and Standards.

Table 2J. Air Pollution Emission by Source

(Short tons)

Type and source	1988	1989	1990	1991	1992	1993	1994	1995	1996	1997
NUMBER										
Carbon monoxide (thousands)										
Fuel combustion	7 373	7 443	5 510	5 856	6 154	5 585	5 519	5 934	5 980	4 817
Industrial processes	7 034	7 013	5 852	5 740	5 683	5 898	5 839	5 791	5 816	6 052
Transportation	85 779	80 870	73 224	77 443	75 511	76 030	77 883	70 377	69 353	67 014
Miscellaneous	15 895	8 154	11 208	8 751	7 052	7 013	9 613	7 049	9 462	9 568
Total	116 081	103 480	95 794	97 790	94 400	94 526	98 854	89 151	90 611	87 451
Lead										
Fuel combustion	511	505	500	495	490	495	494	488	493	496
Industrial processes	3 090	3 161	3 278	3 081	2 734	2 869	3 005	2 873	2 892	2 897
Transportation	3 452	1 802	1 197	592	584	547	544	563	525	522
Miscellaneous	0	0	0	0	0	0	0	0	0	0
Total	7 053	5 468	4 975	4 168	3 808	3 911	4 043	3 924	3 910	3 915
Nitrogen oxides (thousands)										
Fuel combustion	10 472	10 538	10 895	10 779	10 928	11 111	11 015	10 828	10 519	10 724
Industrial processes	860	852	892	816	857	861	878	873	879	917
Transportation	11 659	11 731	11 278	11 639	11 750	11 849	12 069	11 830	11 650	11 595
Miscellaneous	727	293	371	286	254	225	383	237	343	346
Total	23 718	23 414	23 436	23 520	23 789	24 046	24 345	23 768	23 391	23 582
Organic compounds (thousands)										
Fuel combustion	1 360	1 372	1 005	1 075	1 114	993	989	1 073	1 079	861
Industrial processes	10 853	10 755	10 000	10 178	10 380	10 578	10 738	10 780	9 482	9 836
Transportation	10 583	9 506	8 765	8 965	8 569	8 619	8 940	8 106	7 899	7 660
Miscellaneous	1 231	642	1 164	845	579	641	798	599	846	858
Total	24 027	22 274	20 935	21 063	20 642	20 830	21 465	20 558	19 306	19 214
Particulate matter (thousands)										
Fuel combustion	1 381	1 382	1 196	1 147	1 184	1 124	1 113	1 179	1 192	1 101
Industrial processes	1 294	1 276	1 306	1 264	1 269	1 240	1 219	1 231	1 232	1 277
Transportation	852	849	831	841	835	806	802	751	733	734
Miscellaneous	57 555	49 562	26 512	26 199	26 093	24 706	27 622	23 599	30 031	30 468
Total	61 082	53 069	29 845	29 451	29 381	27 876	30 756	26 760	33 188	33 580
Sulfur dioxide (thousands)										
Fuel combustion	19 758	19 923	20 290	19 795	19 492	19 244	18 886	16 229	16 814	17 260
Industrial processes	2 052	2 010	1 900	1 721	1 758	1 723	1 676	1 637	1 644	1 718
Transportation	1 317	1 364	1 476	1 528	1 558	1 499	1 301	1 313	1 366	1 380
Miscellaneous	27	11	12	11	10	9	15	9	13	13
Total	23 154	23 308	23 678	23 057	22 819	22 478	21 880	19 189	19 836	20 371
PERCENT										
Carbon monoxide										
Fuel combustion	6.4	7.2	5.8	6.0	6.5	5.9	5.6	6.7	6.6	5.5
Industrial processes	6.1	6.8	6.1	5.9	6.0	6.2	5.9	6.5	6.4	6.9
Transportation	73.9	78.2	76.4	79.2	80.0	80.4	78.8	78.9	76.5	76.6
Miscellaneous	13.7	7.9	11.7	8.9	7.5	7.4	9.7	7.9	10.4	10.9
Total	100.0	100.0	100.0	100.0	100.0	100.0	100.0	100.0	100.0	100.0
Lead										
Fuel combustion	7.2	9.2	10.1	11.9	12.9	12.7	12.2	12.4	12.6	12.7
Industrial processes	43.8	57.8	65.9	73.9	71.8	73.4	74.3	73.2	74.0	74.0
Transportation	48.9	33.0	24.1	14.2	15.3	14.0	13.5	14.3	13.4	13.3
Miscellaneous	0.0	0.0	0.0	0.0	0.0	0.0	0.0	0.0	0.0	0.0
Total	100.0	100.0	100.0	100.0	100.0	100.0	100.0	100.0	100.0	100.0
Nitrogen oxides										
Fuel combustion	44.2	45.0	46.5	45.8	45.9	46.2	45.2	45.6	45.0	45.5
Industrial processes	3.6	3.6	3.8	3.5	3.6	3.6	3.6	3.7	3.8	3.9
Transportation	49.2	50.1	48.1	49.5	49.4	49.3	49.6	49.8	49.8	49.2
Miscellaneous	3.1	1.3	1.6	1.2	1.1	0.9	1.6	1.0	1.5	1.5
Total	100.0	100.0	100.0	100.0	100.0	100.0	100.0	100.0	100.0	100.0
Organic compounds										
Fuel combustion	5.7	6.2	4.8	5.1	5.4	4.8	4.6	5.2	5.6	4.5
Industrial processes	45.2	48.3	47.8	48.3	50.3	50.8	50.0	52.4	49.1	51.2
Transportation	44.0	42.7	41.9	42.6	41.5	41.4	41.6	39.4	40.9	39.9
Miscellaneous	5.1	2.9	5.6	4.0	2.8	3.1	3.7	2.9	4.4	4.5
Total	100.0	100.0	100.0	100.0	100.0	100.0	100.0	100.0	100.0	100.0
Particulate matter										
Fuel combustion	2.3	2.6	4.0	3.9	4.0	4.0	3.6	4.4	3.6	3.3
Industrial processes	2.1	2.4	4.4	4.3	4.3	4.4	4.0	4.6	3.7	3.8
Transportation	1.4	1.6	2.8	2.9	2.8	2.9	2.6	2.8	2.2	2.2
Miscellaneous	94.2	93.4	88.8	89.0	88.8	88.6	89.8	88.2	90.5	90.7
Total	100.0	100.0	100.0	100.0	100.0	100.0	100.0	100.0	100.0	100.0
Sulfur dioxide										
Fuel combustion	85.3	85.5	85.7	85.9	85.4	85.6	86.3	84.6	84.8	84.7
Industrial processes	8.9	8.6	8.0	7.5	7.7	7.7	7.7	8.5	8.3	8.4
Transportation	5.7	5.9	6.2	6.6	6.8	6.7	5.9	6.8	6.9	6.8
Miscellaneous	0.1	0.0	0.1	0.0	0.0	0.0	0.1	0.0	0.1	0.1
Total	100.0	100.0	100.0	100.0	100.0	100.0	100.0	100.0	100.0	100.0

SOURCE: U.S. Environmental Protection Agency, Office of Air Quality Planning and Standards, *National Air Quality and Emissions Trends Report, 1997*: Table A-2–A-8.

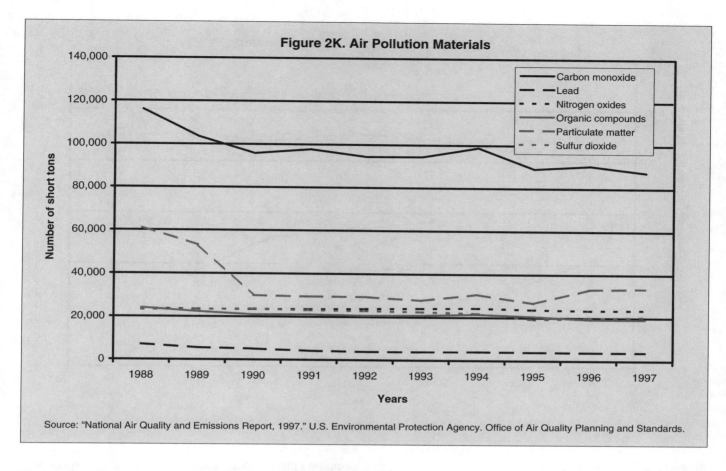

Figure 2K. Air Pollution Materials

Legend:
- Carbon monoxide
- Lead
- Nitrogen oxides
- Organic compounds
- Particulate matter
- Sulfur dioxide

Source: "National Air Quality and Emissions Report, 1997." U.S. Environmental Protection Agency. Office of Air Quality Planning and Standards.

Table 2K. Living in a County That Meets the Air-Quality Standards

(Percent)

Type of pollutant	1990	1991	1992	1993	1994	1995	1996
All pollutants	71.0	65.2	78.4	76.5	75.1	67.9	81.3
Ozone	76.3	71.9	81.9	79.5	79.9	71.6	83.3
Carbon monoxide	90.8	92.0	94.3	95.4	93.9	95.2	94.9
Particulates (PM-10) [1]	92.6	91.9	89.6	97.5	94.8	90.2	97.1
Sulfur dioxide	99.4	97.9	100.0	99.4	100.0	100.0	99.9
Nitrogen dioxide	96.4	96.4	100.0	100.0	100.0	100.0	100.0
Lead	94.1	94.1	98.1	97.8	98.3	98.1	98.3

SOURCE: E. Kramarow, H. Lentzner, R. Rooks, J. Weeks, S. Saydah. *Health and Aging Chartbook. Health, United States, 1999.* Hyattsville, Maryland : National Center for Health Statistics, 1999: Table 73.

1. Particulate matter smaller than 10 microns.

NOTE: Standard is met if the concentration of the pollutant does not exceed the criterion value more than once per calendar year. See Appendix II of *Health, United States, 1999*, National ambient air quality standards. 1990–96 data based on 1990 county population estimates.

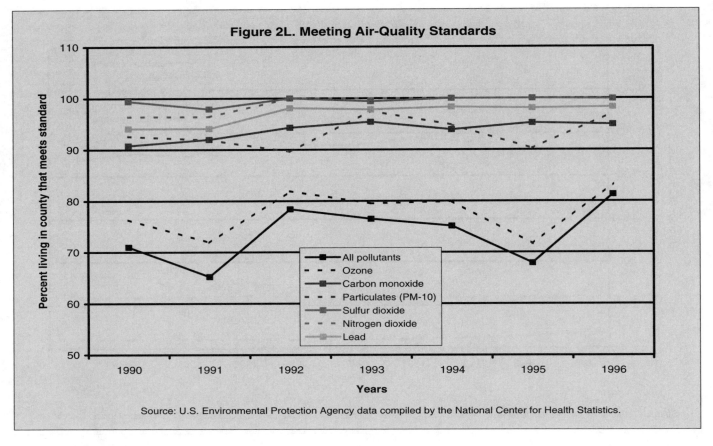

Figure 2L. Meeting Air-Quality Standards

Legend:
- All pollutants
- Ozone
- Carbon monoxide
- Particulates (PM-10)
- Sulfur dioxide
- Nitrogen dioxide
- Lead

Y-axis: Percent living in county that meets standard
X-axis: Years

Source: U.S. Environmental Protection Agency data compiled by the National Center for Health Statistics.

RELEASES OF TOXIC SUBSTANCES

Toxic substances used in manufacturing and for other purposes constitute a risk factor for chronic and acute illnesses. EPA monitors their release as part of a program established after the fatal chemical-release accident in Bhopal, India. Congress enacted the Emergency Planning and Community Right-to-Know Act (EPCRA) to "promote emergency planning, to minimize the effects of an accident such as occurred at Bhopal, and to provide the public with information on releases of toxic chemicals in their communities."[19]

As part of EPCRA, EPA established a national database to identify and monitor facilities, the chemicals that these facilities manufacture and use, and the annual amounts of those chemicals released. The database includes all chemical releases, whether in routine operations, in accidents, or from other one-time events. Between 1988 and 1997, industries reduced their on- and off-site releases of toxic chemicals by 42.8 percent, from 3.4 billion pounds to 1.9 billion pounds. These manufacturing industries disposed of their toxic wastes primarily to landfills and the air. (See Figure 2M and Table 2L.)

WORKPLACE HAZARDS

Throughout the last quarter of the 20th century a substantial reduction has occurred in the rate of occupationally related illnesses, injuries and deaths. For example,

nonfatal episodes decreased from 11.0 per 100 workers per year in 1973 to 7.1 in 1997, and most of the nonfatal injuries that did occur were not severe enough to lead to lost workdays. (See Table 2.21.) Workers who engage in operations requiring physical effort have a higher risk for work-related injuries than workers in less-physical occupations. (See Table 2M.) Still, most industries showed an improvement in the rate of work-related injuries.

Conway and Svenson examined the injury, illness, and lost workday rates by state, industry, regulatory, and related initiatives to determine the explanatory factors for this improvement.[20] Taking into account the fact that industries might underreport occupational injuries and deaths, the authors attribute the improvement in the workplace health and safety record to workers' compensation reforms, a growing worker and industry awareness of workplace hazards, and a shift in the Occupational Safety and Health Administration's (OSHA) inspection policy. In the mid-1990s, OSHA shifted its emphasis from records and field inspections to providing services to aid industry compliance.

Workers are injured or become ill for several reasons, including exposure to harmful substances and strenuous physical activity. For example, 23.0 percent of women and 39.1 percent of men reported that they were exposed to "substances believed to be harmful if breathed or on skin." (See Table 2.23.) Blue-collar workers and those not graduating from high school are more likely to

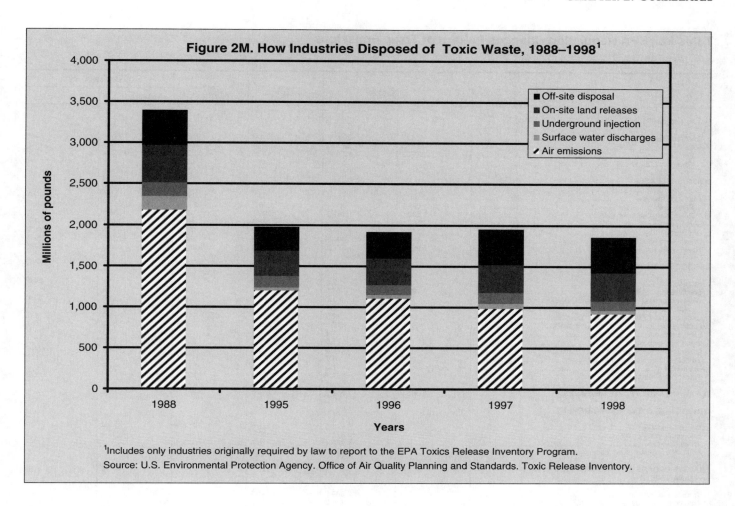

Figure 2M. How Industries Disposed of Toxic Waste, 1988–1998[1]

[1]Includes only industries originally required by law to report to the EPA Toxics Release Inventory Program.

Source: U.S. Environmental Protection Agency. Office of Air Quality Planning and Standards. Toxic Release Inventory.

Table 2L. EPA Regulation Changes Pattern of Toxic Emissions

(Pounds in millions, except where noted)

Type	1988	1995	1996	1997	Change 1988–1997 Number	Change 1988–1997 Percent
TOTAL (NUMBER)						
Total facilities	20 458	20 605	20 103	19 597	-861	-4.2
Total forms	62 763	62 586	60 844	60 095	-2 668	-4.3
Form Rs	62 763	57 305	54 835	51 534	-11 229	-17.9
Form As	—	5 281	6 009	8 561	—	—
ON-SITE RELEASES						
Total air emissions	2 182.2	1 196.6	1 094.2	982.3	-1 199.8	-55.0
Fugitive air emissions	681.2	305.1	268.7	240.2	-441.0	-64.7
Point source air emissions	1 500.9	891.5	825.5	742.1	-758.8	-50.6
Surface water discharges	164.6	36.6	44.3	61.4	-103.1	-62.7
Underground injection	162.0	139.9	118.2	126.5	-35.5	-21.9
On-site land releases	459.3	304.1	323.3	338.8	-120.5	-26.2
Total on-site releases	2 968.0	1 677.2	1 580.0	1 509.0	-1 458.9	-49.2
OFF-SITE RELEASES						
Storage only [1]	13.8	2.1	1.2	6.4	-7.5	-54.0
Solidification/stabilization [2]	29.5	26.4	57.7	144.3	114.8	388.7
Wastewater treatment (excluding POTWs) [3]	4.6	3.7	3.7	6.1	1.5	33.1
Transfers to POTWs [4]	9.6	2.5	2.4	2.4	-7.2	-74.9
Underground injection	9.0	12.5	9.1	10.9	1.9	21.3
Landfills/ Disposal surface impoundments	267.3	210.5	221.6	232.6	-34.7	-13.0
Land treatment	2.8	1.1	0.5	0.7	-2.1	-76.4
Other land disposal	9.6	11.6	6.1	8.0	-1.6	-17.1
Other off-site management	39.5	10.8	9.3	10.1	-29.4	-74.4
Transfers to waste broker for disposal	30.4	5.0	4.4	7.1	-23.3	-76.7
Unknown [5]	11.8	1.5	1.5	4.4	-7.5	-63.0
Total off-site releases	427.9	287.7	317.4	432.9	4.9	1.2
TOTAL ON- AND OFF-SITE RELEASES	3 395.9	1 964.9	1 897.4	1 941.9	-1 454.0	-42.8
OTHER ON-SITE WASTE MANAGEMENT						
Recycled on-site [6]	—	6 073.3	6 188.5	6 734.9	—	—
Energy recovery on-site [7]	—	2 674.2	2 587.5	3 551.9	—	—
Treated on-site	—	4 770.4	4 426.4	4 523.4	—	—
Total other on-site waste management [8]	—	13 517.9	13 202.3	14 810.2	—	—
TRANSFERS OFF-SITE FOR FURTHER WASTE MANAGEMENT						
Transfers to recycling	—	2 389.6	2 341.8	2 329.7	—	—
Transfers to energy recovery	—	489.2	447.5	470.0	—	—
Transfers to treatment	335.1	201.3	185.6	215.4	-119.8	-35.7
Transfers to POTWs	245.2	151.3	139.2	157.7	-87.5	-35.7
Other off-site transfers [9]	43.5	2.2	0.8	0.0	-43.5	-100.0
Total transfers off-site for further waste management	—	3 233.7	3 114.9	3 172.8	—	—

SOURCE: U.S. Environmental Protection Agency, Office of Air Quality Planning and Standards, *National Air Quality and Emissions Trends Report, 1997*: Table 3-3.

— Data not available.

1. "Storage only" (disposal code M10) indicates that the toxic chemical is sent off-site for storage because there is no known disposal method. Amounts reported as transferred to "storage only" are included as a form of disposal (off-site release).

2. Beginning in reporting year 1997, transfers to solidification/stabilization of metals and metal compounds (waste management code M41) are reported separately from transfers to solidification/stabilization of non-metal Toxic Release Inventory (TRI) chemicals (waste management code M40). Because this treatment method prepares a metal for disposal, but does not destroy it, such transfers are included as a form of disposal (off-site release). Reports under code M40 of metals and metal compounds have been included in solidification/stabilization of metals and metal compounds in this report.

3. Beginning in reporting year 1997, transfers to wastewater treatment (excluding publicly owned treatment works or POTWs) of metals and metal compounds (waste management code M62) are reported separately from transfers to wastewater treatment of non-metal TRI chemicals (waste management code M61). Because wastewater treatment does not destroy metals, such transfers are included as a form of disposal (off-site release). Transfers of metals and metal compounds reported under code M61 have been included in transfers of metals and metal compounds to wastewater treatment.

4. Reported as discharges to POTWs in Section 6.1 of Form R. EPA considers transfers of metals and metal compounds to POTWs as an off-site release because sewage treatment does not destroy the metal content of the waste material.

5. "Unknown" (disposal code M99) indicates that a facility is not aware of the type of waste management used for the toxic chemical that is sent off-site. Amounts reported as "unknown" transfers are treated as a form of disposal (off-site release).

6. One facility, Shintech Inc. in Freeport, Tex., reported on-site recycling of vinyl chloride of 200,000 pounds in 1995 and 244,000 pounds in 1996. The facility has since revised these quantities to 200,000,000 pounds in 1995 and 244,000,000 pounds in 1996. These revisions change on-site recycling to 6,273,065,292 pounds in 1995 and to 6,432,263,173 pounds in 1996.

7. One facility, TPI Petroleum in Ardmore, Okla., reported on-site energy recovery for ethylene of 82,500,000 pounds in 1995, 36,250,000 pounds in 1996, and 422,000,000 pounds in 1997. The facility also reported on-site energy recovery for propylene of 12,900,000 pounds in 1995, 16,300,000 pounds in 1996, and 272,000,000 pounds in 1997. The facility has since revised these quantities to zero. Another facility, Shell Chemical Co. in Geismar, La., reported on-site energy recovery for ethylene of 193,830,000 pounds in 1997. The facility has since revised this quantity to 13,000,000 pounds. These revisions change on-site energy recovery to 2,578,781,626 pounds in 1995, to 2,534,900,531 pounds in 1996, and to 2,677,099,018 pounds in 1997.

8. Revisions by three facilities change total other on-site waste management to 13,622,295,104 pounds in 1995, to 13,393,532,994 pounds in 1996, and to 13,935,393,752 pounds in 1997.

9. Other off-site transfers are transfers reported without a valid waste management code.

NOTE: Does not include delisted chemicals; chemicals added in 1990, 1991, 1994, and 1995; aluminum oxide; ammonia; hydrochloric acid and sulfuric acid. On-site releases from Section 5 of Form R. Off-site releases are from Section 6 (transfers off-site to disposal) of Form R. Off-site releases include metals and metal compounds transferred off-site for solidification/stabilization and for wastewater treatment, including to POTWs. Other On-site Waste Management from Section 8. Transfers off-site for further waste management from Section 6 (excluding transfers off-site to disposal) of Form R. Form A certification statement reporting began in 1995 reporting year. Breakdown of underground injection and on-site land releases (for the Resource Conservation and Recovery Act Subtitle C landfills) began in 1996 reporting year. Other on-site waste management began in 1991 reporting year.

Table 2M. Work-Related Injuries Leading to Fatalities: 1997

Occupational group [1]	Fatalities per 100,000 employed [2]
Managerial and professional specialty	4.7
Technical, sales, and administrative support	1.9
Service occupations	2.8
Farming, forestry and fishing	25.9
Precision production craft and repair	7.7
Operators, fabricators and laborers	11.7
Military [3]	7.5

SOURCE: U.S. Department of Labor, Bureau of Labor Statistics. *Report on the American Workforce, 1999*: Table 49.

1. Based on the 1990 Occupational Classification System developed by the Bureau of the Census.
2. The rate represents the number of fatal occupational injuries per 100,000 employed workers and was calculated as follows: (n/w) x 100,000, where n = the number of fatal work injuries, and w = the number of employed workers. There were 21 fatally injured workers under the age of 16 years that were not included in the rate calculations to maintain consistency with the Current Population Survey employment.
3. Resident armed forces.

experience physical stress at work. For example, 33.3 percent of men with fewer than 12 years of education work four or more hours a day at jobs requiring "repeated strenuous physical activity" compared with 4.6 percent of those with 15 years or more of education. (See Table 2.24.) Women are less exposed to work that requires repeated strenuous physical activity four or more hours a day (9.8 percent compared with 21.5 percent of men). However, women experience almost as much "bending or twisting of hands or wrists" as men; 35.9 percent of women compared with 40.4 percent of men work at tasks requiring this kind of activity at least four hours a day.

SOCIAL, REGULATORY, AND HEALTH CARE FACTORS

Some factors affecting health and safety are beyond the control of individuals and require societal or organizational actions to control them. For example, we have already identified the importance of regulations for improving water and air quality as well as in controlling the disposal of toxic wastes and the sale and use of tobacco products. Some regulations provide information to help consumers make healthy choices, such as nutritional information on food labels and potential adverse reactions on medication labels. Some reduce confusion and promote predictability and thereby safety, such as the "driving on the right side of the road" rule. Others establish standards to increase the likelihood of health and safety, such as licensing of physicians, building codes, immunization requirements for school children, and engineering specifications for public bridges. Still others establish procedures and standards for health care.

REGULATION OF TRANSPORTATION

Transportation-safety regulations help limit deaths and injuries not only from highway crashes but also from airplane, boating, and rail accidents. In 1996, of the more than 44,000 transportation fatalities, about 42,000 occurred on the highway, fewer than 600 on trains, and 380 on U.S. air carriers. (See Table 2N.) Traffic deaths were more likely to occur in states with more rural areas.[21] For example, in 1996, Mississippi, Wyoming, and New Mexico reported more than 28 traffic deaths per 100,000 persons compared to Connecticut, New York,

Rhode Island, and Massachusetts, which reported fewer than 10 deaths per 100,000 persons. (See Table 2.25.)[22]

States have enacted a variety of laws and regulations to promote highway safety. These include licensing drivers, regulating driving speed, mandating vehicle inspections, and requiring use of seat belts. By 1998, every state except New Hampshire had enacted a law requiring seat belt use. And every state had a law requiring younger children to use special child-safety seats. (See Tables 2.26 and 2.27.)

FOOD SAFETY

Science-based laws, regulations, and policies, as well as food inspection programs, have been established to protect America's food supply from harmful additives, drugs, pesticides, and toxic wastes and to ensure appropriate food processing and handling. In addition, food preparation guidelines and product labeling help inform the consumer about food choices and food handling. Governmental agencies at the federal, state, and local levels contribute to the nation's food safety. The Food and Drug Administration within the Department of Health and Human Services enforces food safety laws concerning domestic and imported food, except meat and poultry. The safety of domestic and imported meat and poultry products is the responsibility of the Department of Agriculture. The Department of Commerce's National Oceanic and Atmospheric Administration conducts a voluntary fish and seafood inspection program. The Environmental Protection Agency establishes safe drinking water standards and regulates toxic substances and waste to prevent contamination of food and drinking water.

The CDC monitors cases of disease that result from food-borne pathogens. The CDC estimates that food-borne diseases result in approximately 76 million episodes of illness, 325,000 hospitalizations, and 5,000 deaths each year.[23] Less than 20 percent of the cases can be attributed to specifically identified pathogens. Table 2.28 reports the CDC's best estimates of the annual number of cases of illness caused by known food-borne pathogens, some of which cause non-food-borne diseases.

Table 2N. Number of Transportation Deaths by Mode

Mode	1960	1965	1970	1975	1980	1985	1990
TOTAL FATALITIES	40 849	52 272	57 904	49 199	55 456	47 703	47 724
AIR							
U.S. air carrier [1]	499	261	146	124	1	526	39
Commuter carrier [2]	—	—	—	28	37	37	7
On-demand air taxi [3]	—	—	69	105	105	**76	**50
General aviation [4]	787	1 029	1 310	1 252	1 239	**956	**765
HIGHWAY							
Highway, total	36 399	47 089	52 627	44 525	51 091	43 825	44 599
Passenger car occupants	—	—	—	25 929	27 449	23 212	24 092
Motorcyclists	790	1 650	2 280	3 189	5 144	4 564	3 244
Truck occupants [5]	—	—	—	5 817	8 748	7 666	9 306
Bus occupants	—	—	—	53	46	57	32
Other [6]	35 609	45 439	50 347	9 537	9 704	8 326	7 925
RAIL							
Highway-rail grade crossing [7]	1 421	1 610	1 440	917	833	582	698
Railroad [7]	924	923	785	575	584	454	599
TRANSIT [8]	—	—	—	—	—	—	339
WATER							
Waterborne transport [9]	—	—	178	243	206	131	85
Recreational boating	819	1 360	1 418	1 466	1 360	1 116	865
PIPELINE							
Pipeline	—	—	30	15	19	33	9
Liquid pipeline	—	—	4	7	4	5	3
Gas pipeline	—	—	26	8	15	28	6

Mode	1991	1992	1993	1994	1995 **	1996 [10]
TOTAL FATALITIES	44 251	41 928	42 707	43 448	44 426	44 505
AIR						
U.S. air carrier [1]	*50	33	1	239	168	380
Commuter carrier [2]	*77	21	24	25	9	14
On-demand air taxi [3]	70	68	42	**63	52	63
General aviation [4]	**794	857	736	**730	734	631
HIGHWAY						
Highway, total	41 508	39 250	40 150	40 716	41 817	***41 907
Passenger car occupants	22 385	21 387	21 566	21 997	22 423	22 416
Motorcyclists	2 806	2 395	2 449	2 320	2 227	2 160
Truck occupants [5]	9 052	8 683	9 116	9 574	10 216	10 522
Bus occupants	31	28	18	18	33	21
Other [6]	7 234	6 757	7 001	6 807	6 918	6 786
RAIL						
Highway-rail grade crossing [7]	608	579	626	615	579	488
Railroad [7]	586	591	653	611	567	551
TRANSIT [8]	300	273	281	320	274	264
WATER						
Waterborne transport [9]	30	96	110	69	46	50
Recreational boating	924	816	800	784	829	709
PIPELINE						
Pipeline	14	15	17	22	21	20
Liquid pipeline	0	5	0	1	3	5
Gas pipeline	14	10	17	21	18	15

SOURCE: U.S. Department of Transportation, *National Transportation Statistics, 1998:* Table 3-1. Death data are derrived from accidents reported to the Department of Transportation.

* U.S. air carrier figure does not include 12 persons killed aboard a commuter aircraft when it and a USAir airliner collided; commuter air carrier figure does not include 22 persons killed aboard a USAir airliner when it and a commuter aircraft collided.
** Revised data.
*** Includes two fatalities that cannot be assigned to one of the four specified vehicle types.
— Data are nonexistent.
1. Carriers operating under 14 CFR 121, all scheduled and nonscheduled service.
2. All scheduled service operating under 14 CFR 135 (commuter air carriers).
3. Nonscheduled service operating under 14 CFR 135 (on-demand air taxis).
4. All operations other than those operated under 14 CFR 121 and 14 CFR 135.
5. Includes light and large trucks.
6. Includes occupants of other vehicle types and nonvehicle occupants (e.g., pedalcyclists and pedestrians) for all years shown. For 1960-1970, National Highway Traffic Safety Administration (NHTSA) did not break out fatality data to the same level of detail as in later years, so Fatalities for those years also include occupants of passenger cars, trucks, and buses.
7. Includes Amtrak. Highway-Rail Grade Crossing Fatalities data not comparable after 1970 due to change in reporting system. Fatalities include those resulting from train incidents, train incidents, and non-train incidents.
8. Fatalities include those resulting from all reportable incidents, not just from accidents.
9. Fatalities resulting from vessel casualties only.
10. Preliminary data.
NOTE: Total does not equal sum of rows because some fatalities are counted in more than one mode. To avoid double-counting, the following adjustments have been made: (i) most (not all) Highway-Rail Grade Crossing fatalities have not been added because most (not all) such fatalities involve motor vehicles, and thus they are already included in Highway fatalities; (ii) for Transit, all commuter rail fatalities and those motor bus, trolley bus, demand response and van pool fatalities arising from accidents have been subtracted, because they are counted either as Railroad, or Highway or Highway-Rail Grade Crossing fatalities. Note that the reader cannot reproduce the Total Fatalities row in this table by simply leaving out Highway-Rail Grade Crossing in the sum and subtracting the above Transit submodes, because in so doing, he or she has left out Grade Crossing Fatalities not involving Motor Vehicles. An example of such a fatality is a bicyclist hit by a train at a grade crossing. Caution must be exercised in comparing fatalities across modes, because significantly different definitions are used. In particular, rail and transit fatalities include incident-related (as distinct from accident-related) fatalities, such as fatalities from falls in transit stations, or railroad employee fatalities from a fire in a workshed. Equivalent fatalities for the air and highway modes (fatalities at airports not caused by moving aircraft, or fatalities from accidents in automobile repair shops) are not counted toward the totals for these modes. Thus, fatalities that are not necessarily directly related to transportation are counted for the transit and rail modes, potentially overstating the risk for these modes. For the waterborne mode, fatalities from vessel casualties are counted in the total, and other fatalities are not counted. (Vessel casualties are incidents involving damage to vessels, for example, from collisions or groundings.) Fatalities not from vessel casualties, include, for example, deaths from falling overboard or from accidents involving on-board equipment. Thus fatalities for the waterborne mode are potentially understated.

The table shows the number and percentage of illnesses, hospitalizations, and deaths. This table does not include illnesses that were not attributed to specific pathogens.[24] Of the 13.8 million food-borne cases that can be linked to identified pathogens, 60,854 resulted in hospitalizations and 1,809 resulted in death. About 79 percent of the deaths are caused by only three of the several dozen known agents. *Salmonella*[25] (nontyphoidal) accounted for 25.6 percent of the hospitalizations and 30.6 percent of the deaths. *Listeria monocytogenes*[26] and *Toxoplasma gondii*[27] each accounted for less than 5 percent of the hospitalizations but over 20 percent of the deaths. Whereas Norwalk-like viruses[28] accounted for 67 percent of the food-borne cases and 33 percent of the hospitalizations, this pathogen caused only 6.9 percent of the deaths. *Campylobacter spp*[29] also was a major cause of food-borne hospitalizations but caused only 5.5 percent of the deaths. CDC scientists estimated that of the 62 million cases that were not tied to specific pathogens, 265,000 resulted in hospitalizations and 3,200 in death.

HEALTH CARE FACTORS

Preventive care provided by physicians, dentists, nurses, and other health professionals can promote and maintain healthy behaviors, identify problems early, and help individuals improve their health and quality of life. More Americans are receiving prenatal care during the first trimester of pregnancy. In 1970, only 68 percent of the pregnant women received such early health care, but by 1997 the proportion had increased to 82.5 percent. (See Table 2.31.) Preventive care services include regular hearing, vision, and dental checkups as well as screening tests to detect cancer, diabetes, tuberculosis, and high levels of cholesterol and blood pressure early in the treatable stages of the diseases. (See Tables 2.29, 2.30, and 2.31.) Children, travelers, and adults at high risk for infectious diseases benefit from immunizations. Immunizations are available for conditions such as influenza, pneumonia, hepatitis, and tetanus. (See Table 2.32.) Access to this kind of care is a key indicator of the beneficial effect of the health care system. Data are available to report on several indicators of this kind of care. Together they provide a picture of the way access to care shapes our experience with illness and health. The most important aspect of these indicators is that they show the percentage of the population that receives attention when they are not reporting a specific complaint.

A PATTERN OF UNEVEN CARE

Several indicators, however, show a pattern of uneven preventive care associated with patient characteristics such as race, income, education, and area of residence. These significant differences were in important areas of preventive care such as prenatal care early in pregnancy, health checkups for children, and dental care. For example, in 1997, while 84.7 percent of White pregnant women reported that they received prenatal care during the first trimester of their pregnancy, only 72.3 percent of Black women received this needed care. Fortunately, only 3.9

percent of all pregnant women failed to meet with their doctor for prenatal care until the last trimester of their pregnancy. However, Black pregnant women were more than twice as likely as White pregnant women to receive their first prenatal visit in the last trimester of their pregnancy. (See Table 2.31.)

Another pattern in uneven preventive care can be seen in the health care statistics of children. One study showed that nearly 10 percent of children under the age of six years had not been examined by a physician within the year prior to the study. This finding was more common among children living in lower income households; 11.6 percent of children living in poor families, 10.7 percent of the near poor, and 6.2 percent of the others had not had a visit with a physician at all. These data mean that poor children under the age of six years were almost twice as likely as children who were not poor to have inadequate physician contact. (See Table 2.30.) However, this lack of physician contact does not appear to have affected immunization rates, which are almost equal for children living below the poverty level and the total population. (See Table 2.32.) Low-income children may have received their immunizations in settings without physician contact, such as public health clinics. Immunization rates did vary according to where the children lived. In 1997, only about 76 percent of children age 19 to 35 months received the standard 4:3:1:3 series of vaccinations. (See Table 2.33.)[30]

Dental visits also varied within the population. In 1993, 60.8 percent of the population visited a dentist at least once a year. However, only 35.9 percent of persons living in below poverty-level households reported that they had visited a dentist. These data also varied with years of schooling. Only 38 percent of those with less than 12 years of schooling visited a dentist compared with 73.8 percent of those with more than a high school education. (See Table 2.29.)

Cancer Screening

Clinical studies and population data show that several tests currently available to screen for cancer are effective in increasing the survival of cancer patients. The benefits of screening accrue from detection in early stages of the disease when treatment can be more effective. Such screening tests are available for cancer of the cervix, breast, and colon. Although the prostate-specific antigen (PSA) blood test was not approved for prostate-cancer detection by the U.S. Food and Drug Administration until 1994, preliminary analysis of available data indicates that the PSA test has been beneficial.[31] The widespread regular use of the Papanicolaou (Pap) test to screen for cervical cancer is credited for the substantial decrease in deaths from cervical cancer since the 1950s.[32] Furthermore, regular mammogram screening has been found to be more effective than self-examination or physician examinations to detect breast cancer in its earliest stage.[33] Early detection and timely treatment greatly affect the five-year survival rate for breast cancer, as with cancer in general. Women diagnosed in the early stage when the breast cancer is localized have a five-year relative survival rate of 94 percent. In contrast, women diagnosed after the disease spreads have a five-year relative survival rate of only 18 percent.[34]

Early and regular screening for cancer of the colon for both men and women is especially important because colorectal cancer is the second leading cause of cancer deaths in the United States. Screening includes a physical examination by a doctor, a fecal occult blood test (to detect hidden blood in feces), barium enema, and sigmoidoscopy or colonoscopy (that allows the doctor to examine on a video monitor either the lower part of the colon or the entire colon for growths or cancer). These tests are used to detect small growths inside the colon or rectum that may be precancerous or to detect colorectal cancer in its early stages when patients have over a 90 percent chance of survival. The Minnesota Colon Cancer Control Study, a large randomized clinical study, found that annual fecal occult blood tests reduced colorectal deaths by 33 percent. After following up on the participants for 18 years, the Minnesota study found that colorectal cancer deaths were reduced by 21 percent for those screened with a fecal occult blood test every two years.[35]

Although cancer screening has increased gradually over the past several years, many more men and women are still screened only once than are screened on a regular basis or as part of an annual physical examination. For example, even though the percentage of women age 50 to 59 who have ever been screened with a mammogram increased from 44 percent in 1987 to 75 percent in 1992, the proportion of those recently tested remained at 42 percent in 1992. By 1998, the percentage of women age 50 and over in each state who had been screened with a mammogram in the prior two years ranged from 64.9 percent in Minnesota to 84.2 percent in Massachusetts. Similarly, although the percentage of men age 50 to 59 who submitted a fecal occult blood test increased from 37 percent in 1987 to 42 percent in 1992, the rate for those who had a recent test in 1992 remained at 15 percent. (See Table 2O.) By 1997, the percentage of men and women age 55 to 64 in each state who had been screened with a fecal occult blood test for colorectal cancer in the prior two years ranged from 12.9 percent in Mississippi to 40 percent in North Carolina.[36]

Breast and Cervical Cancer Screening

Several screening procedures are readily available for the early detection of breast and cervical cancer. Effective screening campaigns need to understand the reasons that people do not get screened for these types of cancers on a regular basis. D. N. Pearlman and colleagues analyzed data from the Cancer Control Supplement of the 1992 National Health Interview Survey to determine the predictors of whether or not a woman will be screened for cervical and breast cancer. They found that women who knew the risk factors for cancer and perceived a good likelihood of surviving these diseases were the most like-

ly to have been screened recently.[37] Ashing-Giwa pointed out the importance of access to care and availability of health care resources as a factor, particularly for uninsured and low-income women. Women may be reluctant to get a baseline mammogram if they feel they do not have access to treatment or followup screening.[38] Women have three methods of screening for breast cancer: breast self-examination, mammography, and physical examination by a doctor or nurse. Random clinical trials and case studies have indicated the value of mammography in reducing deaths caused by breast cancer, especially in women over age 50 (most of whom were postmenopausal). In this age group, controlled studies indicate that mammography can eliminate about 25 percent of breast cancer deaths.[39] However, a single mammogram is not sufficient; regular monitoring is needed.

A computer simulation of various intervals between screening for breast cancer found that the optimal interval between mammograms to reduce the rate of tumor growth, spread to other parts of the body (metastasis), and death from breast cancer was six months to two years.[40] On the basis of controlled clinical trials, Fletcher and colleagues discussed the effectiveness of breast cancer screening for different age groups.[41] Sickles and Kopans focus their examination on the effectiveness of breast cancer screening for women age 40 to 49.[42]

At high risk for cervical cancer are women who have sexual intercourse at an early age and who have multiple sex partners. Women with HIV, human papillomavirus (HPV), or other sexually transmitted diseases are also at risk for cervical cancer. Early and frequent screening is recommended, especially for those at high risk for this condition. Cervical smear tests (Papanicolaou [Pap] smears) are used to detect changes in cells in the cervix that may indicate various conditions such as infection or inflammation and precancerous lesions as well as cancer.[43-47]

Between 1989 and 1997, the percentage of women over age 40 who had ever had a mammogram grew from 63.9 percent to 84.8 percent. However, in 1997 only 76.9 percent had the test as a part of a regular physical examination, and only 71.3 percent reported that they had a mammogram in the past two years. Similarly, although more than 90 percent of women had at least one Pap test, by 1997 only 79.7 percent reported having a Pap test within the past two years.[48] (See Tables 2.37, 2.38, 2.39, 2.40, and 2.41.) (See Figure 2N.)

As Figures 2O and 2P illustrate, having a regular mammogram or Pap test is closely related to income and health insurance coverage. Less than 50 percent of women with no health insurance had a recent mammogram, compared with more than 70 percent of those with insurance. By 1997, 79.9 percent of women with an annual family income of more than $50,000 had a recent mammogram compared with 58.4 percent of those with annual family incomes below $10,000. (See Figures 2O and 2P.)

Table 20. Persons Who Reported Ever or Recently [1] Having Had Screening Tests for Cancer

(Percent of persons)

Test and age group	Persons ever tested		Persons tested recently	
	1987	1992 [2]	1987	1992 [2]
PAPANICOLAOU TEST [3]				
18–29 years	84	85	70	73
30–39 years	95	95	77	76
40–49 years	94	97	71	71
50–59 years	91	94	67	64
60–69 years	88	92	57	59
70 years and over	76	82	41	43
CLINICAL BREAST EXAMINATION				
40–49 years	87	95	49	55
50–59 years	86	94	47	55
60–69 years	80	89	42	49
70 years and over	70	80	35	37
MAMMOGRAPHY				
40–49 years	41	70	17	35
50–59 years	44	75	20	42
60–69 years	38	68	17	39
70 years and over	28	58	12	28
DIGITAL RECTAL EXAMINATION				
Men				
40–49 years	46	53	12	14
50–59 years	48	55	17	22
60–69 years	54	55	21	29
70 years and over	51	53	23	31
Women				
40–49 years	51	57	26	29
50–59 years	53	60	25	34
60–69 years	55	57	26	27
70 years and over	46	43	18	18
FECAL OCCULT BLOOD TEST				
Men				
40–49 years	32	35	8	8
50–59 years	37	42	12	15
60–69 years	46	51	14	18
70 years and over	38	56	15	20
Women				
40–49 years	28	33	10	9
50–59 years	42	45	16	17
60–69 years	45	51	19	21
70 years and over	39	48	15	16
PROCTOSIGMOIDOSCOPY				
Men				
40–49 years	15	20	4	6
50–59 years	23	28	7	12
60–69 years	33	37	9	13
70 years and over	28	45	9	15
Women				
40–49 years	21	15	2	4
50–59 years	13	29	5	7
60–69 years	24	31	7	9
70 years and over	26	33	6	8

SOURCE: Centers for Disease Control and Prevention, *Morbidity and Mortality Weekly Report* 45, no. 3 (January 26, 1995): Table 1. Based on the National Health Interview Survey.

1. For papanicolaou and proctosigmoidoscopy, "recently" is defined as during the three years preceding the interview; for clinical breast examination, mammography, digital rectal examination, and fecal occult blood test, recently means during the year preceding the interview.
2. For 1987, the sample size was 122,859 (response rate: 95.3%), and for 1992 was 128,412 (response rate: 95.7%).
3. Excludes women who had a hysterectomy.

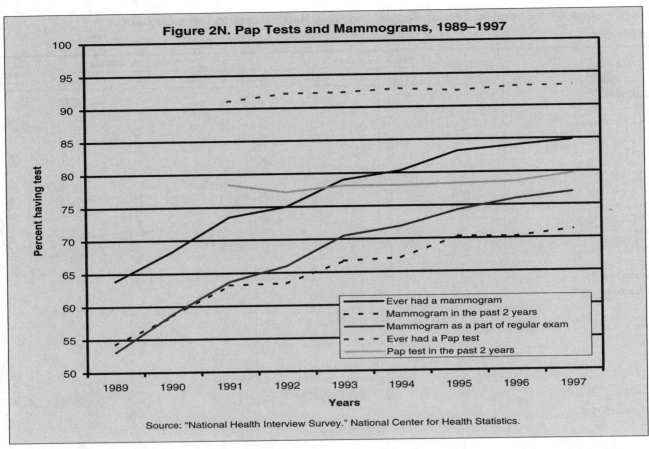

Figure 2N. Pap Tests and Mammograms, 1989–1997

Percent having test

Legend:
— Ever had a mammogram
■ ■ ■ Mammogram in the past 2 years
— Mammogram as a part of regular exam
- - - Ever had a Pap test
— Pap test in the past 2 years

Years

Source: "National Health Interview Survey." National Center for Health Statistics.

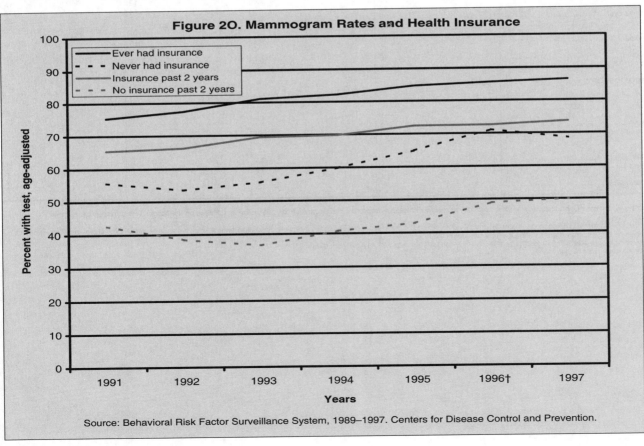

Figure 2O. Mammogram Rates and Health Insurance

Percent with test, age-adjusted

Legend:
— Ever had insurance
■ ■ ■ Never had insurance
— Insurance past 2 years
- - - No insurance past 2 years

Years

Source: Behavioral Risk Factor Surveillance System, 1989–1997. Centers for Disease Control and Prevention.

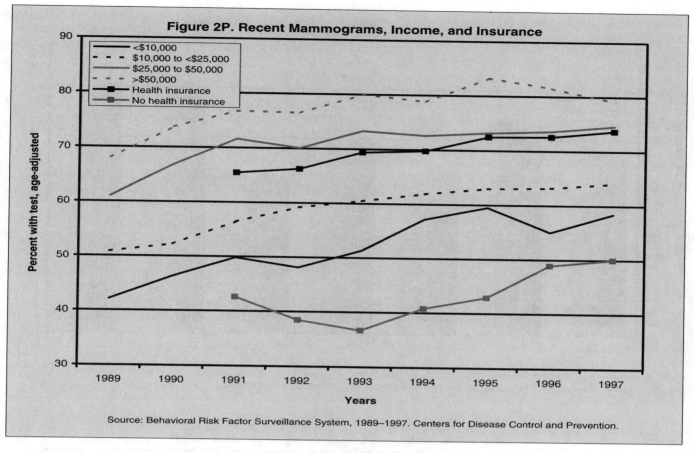

Figure 2P. Recent Mammograms, Income, and Insurance

Legend:
- <$10,000
- $10,000 to <$25,000
- $25,000 to $50,000
- >$50,000
- Health insurance
- No health insurance

Y-axis: Percent with test, age-adjusted (30 to 90)
X-axis: Years (1989 to 1997)

Source: Behavioral Risk Factor Surveillance System, 1989–1997. Centers for Disease Control and Prevention.

Differences in Cancer Screening Rates by State

States vary considerably in their rates of breast and cervical screening among women. (See Table 2.42.) In 1998, the jurisdictions with the lowest percentage of women age 50 and over with no mammogram in the past two years were the District of Columbia (10.6 percent), Massachusetts (15.8 percent), and Arizona (17.4 percent). The jurisdictions with the highest percentage of women with no mammogram in the past two years were Puerto Rico (43.2 percent) and Mississippi (35.1 percent). Between 1997 and 1998, the state with the greatest improvement was Arkansas.[49]

In 1998, the jurisdictions with the lowest percentage of women age 50 and over who did not have a breast examination by a doctor in the past two years were Delaware (16.5 percent), Arizona (17.3 percent), and North Carolina (18.4 percent). The jurisdictions with the highest percentage of women who did not have a breast examination by a doctor in the past two years were Arkansas (34.7 percent) and Wyoming (32.2 percent). The District of Columbia and Louisiana had the greatest improvement between 1997 and 1998. Some jurisdictions, however, did not show an improvement in breast screening

rates during that time. Puerto Rico, New York, and Georgia had the greatest increase in the percentage of women who lacked a breast examination between 1997 and 1998.

Blood Pressure and Cholesterol Screening

From 1960 to 1994 Americans greatly reduced their risk for heart disease and stroke by lowering their blood pressure and cholesterol levels. Although there was a steady decline during this period in the percentage of the population with high cholesterol, the decline for high blood pressure did not begin primarily until the late 1980s. These developments came as a result of the interaction between personal behavior and preventive health care, including screening for both conditions. As a result, the number of persons with high blood pressure levels was reduced by more than 35 percent and the number of persons with high cholesterol levels was reduced by approximately 40 percent. Overall, both men and women and both Blacks and Whites reduced their levels of those two heart disease risk factors (although Black men achieved only a 27 percent reduction in high blood pressure). (See Tables 2.34 and 2.35 and Figures 2Q and 2R.)

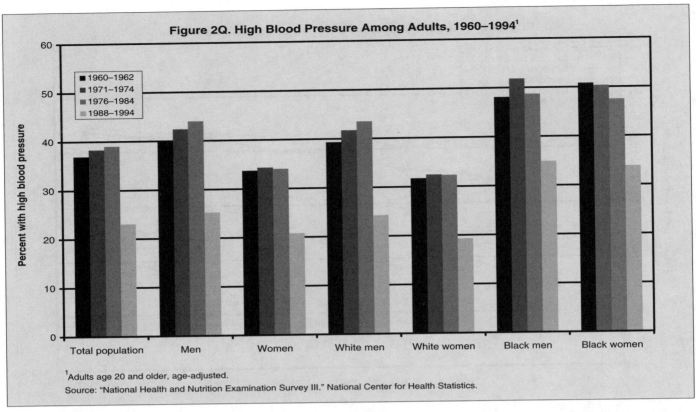

Figure 2Q. High Blood Pressure Among Adults, 1960–1994[1]

[1]Adults age 20 and older, age-adjusted.

Source: "National Health and Nutrition Examination Survey III." National Center for Health Statistics.

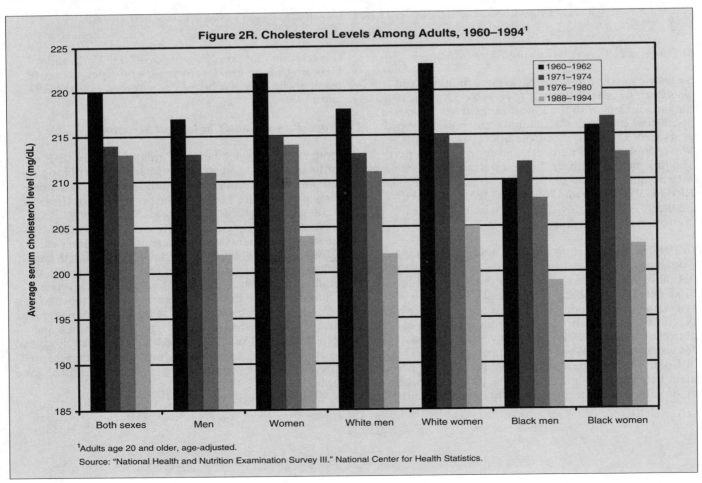

Figure 2R. Cholesterol Levels Among Adults, 1960–1994[1]

[1]Adults age 20 and older, age-adjusted.

Source: "National Health and Nutrition Examination Survey III." National Center for Health Statistics.

SUMMARY

This chapter presents information about the risk and protective factors that shape health conditions in society and for individuals. It shows how a combination of societal, personal, and economic factors accounts for most of the variation in health status. The provision of adequate preventive medical services also plays an important role in promoting health. Control of personal habits, nutrition, public safety, and environmental risks are very important. To be sure, public health authorities use their regulatory powers to control risks, but the data show how decisions made by other regulators can also have an important impact. The data show that these factors affect different parts of our population unevenly. In short, improving the health of our nation is a public enterprise that draws heavily on a variety of social resources.

Table 2.1. Smoking Tobacco

(Number in thousands)

Characteristic	1985	1988	1991	1992	1993	1994	1995	1996	1997	1998
LIFETIME										
Total	150 233	153 466	151 922	150 283	151 936	153 509	151 917	153 252	152 476	152 313
Age										
12–17 years	10 926	9 592	8 550	7 810	8 214	8 178	8 457	8 169	8 715	8 143
18–25 years	23 809	22 316	20 357	19 283	18 997	19 359	18 844	19 050	18 760	19 246
26–34 years	30 879	32 801	31 154	30 119	29 035	27 773	27 270	26 197	25 666	24 860
35 years or more	84 618	88 757	91 862	93 071	95 689	98 199	97 346	99 836	99 335	100 064
Race										
White	125 987	125 273	122 841	121 831	122 450	123 466	122 237	121 878	120 422	—
Black	13 884	14 884	14 780	14 242	13 463	14 473	14 595	14 932	15 119	—
Hispanic	8 013	10 306	10 845	10 650	11 731	11 617	11 083	11 748	12 129	—
Other	*	*	3 456	3 560	4 292	3 953	4 003	4 694	4 806	—
Sex										
Male	78 118	79 166	77 482	78 787	78 386	79 530	78 250	79 091	78 357	—
Female	72 115	74 299	74 440	71 496	73 550	73 979	73 667	74 161	74 119	—
PAST YEAR										
Total	78 026	76 446	73 419	72 409	68 831	66 475	67 639	69 098	70 709	66 735
Age										
12–17 years	6 447	5 436	4 775	4 427	4 783	5 345	5 901	5 453	5 957	5 404
18–25 years	15 780	15 108	13 371	13 099	12 391	11 519	11 825	12 433	12 697	13 175
26–34 years	17 786	18 212	16 247	16 341	14 399	13 176	13 824	13 917	13 277	12 651
35 years or more	38 013	37 690	39 027	38 542	37 258	36 435	36 089	37 295	38 777	35 506
Race										
White	63 391	60 884	58 110	57 560	54 006	51 841	52 469	53 403	54 255	—
Black	8 223	8 024	7 627	7 582	6 358	7 159	7 277	7 919	7 928	—
Hispanic	5 229	5 619	5 612	5 312	5 861	5 630	5 674	5 958	6 559	—
Other	*	*	2 070	1 955	2 606	1 845	2 218	1 818	1 967	—
Sex										
Male	41 595	40 867	38 050	37 608	36 431	34 882	35 143	36 066	36 042	—
Female	36 431	35 578	35 369	34 801	32 400	31 593	32 496	33 033	34 667	—
PAST MONTH										
Total	74 545	69 931	67 030	65 695	61 386	59 955	60 902	61 759	64 056	60 406
Age										
12–17 years	6 346	4 599	4 202	3 807	3 931	4 119	4 495	4 111	4 488	4 149
18–25 years	14 968	13 547	11 897	11 596	10 725	9 706	9 810	10 635	11 249	11 634
26–34 years	16 683	16 228	14 459	14 616	12 705	11 852	12 469	12 400	11 863	11 247
35 years or more	36 548	35 558	36 472	35 676	34 025	34 278	34 127	34 613	36 455	33 375
Race										
White	59 999	55 208	52 646	51 981	47 789	46 753	47 396	47 793	49 177	—
Black	8 109	7 621	7 192	7 059	6 027	6 641	6 667	7 311	7 265	—
Hispanic	5 296	5 317	5 430	4 925	5 360	4 938	4 868	5 138	5 915	—
Other	*	*	1 761	1 731	2 210	1 623	1 970	1 517	1 699	—
Sex										
Male	39 827	37 436	34 182	33 636	31 979	31 623	31 445	32 052	32 473	—
Female	34 718	32 495	32 848	32 058	29 407	28 332	29 457	29 707	31 583	—
FORMER SMOKERS [1]										
Number who stopped	72 207	77 020	78 503	77 874	83 105	87 034	84 278	84 154	81 767	85 578
Percent of total population who stopped	37.5	38.9	38.7	37.9	40.1	41.6	39.8	39.3	37.8	39.1
Percent of smokers who stopped	48.1	50.2	51.7	51.8	54.7	56.7	55.5	54.9	53.6	56.2

See footnotes at end of table.

Table 2.1. Smoking Tobacco—*Continued*

(Percent)

Characteristic	1985	1988	1991	1992	1993	1994	1995	1996	1997	1998
LIFETIME										
Total	78.0	77.4	74.9	73.1	73.3	73.3	71.8	71.6	70.5	69.7
Age										
12–17 years	50.7	47.4	42.4	37.8	38.7	37.6	38.1	36.3	38.7	35.8
18–25 years	75.3	75.2	71.4	69.0	67.1	69.1	67.7	68.5	67.7	38.8
26–34 years	84.7	85.0	80.4	78.8	78.1	75.9	75.8	73.8	72.8	71.8
35 years or more	82.2	80.8	79.5	78.3	79.4	79.8	77.5	77.8	76.0	75.2
Race										
White	81.7	79.9	78.1	76.9	77.7	77.6	76.5	76.0	74.7	—
Black	65.1	66.8	64.2	60.2	58.5	61.9	61.6	62.1	61.9	—
Hispanic	60.4	69.0	67.0	63.2	63.4	60.8	56.2	56.4	56.2	—
Other	*	*	55.0	52.2	53.6	50.0	47.7	53.2	53.1	—
Sex										
Male	85.1	83.4	79.7	79.8	78.9	79.2	77.1	76.8	75.3	—
Female	71.6	71.8	70.5	66.9	68.2	67.8	66.9	66.7	66.1	—
PAST YEAR										
Total	40.5	38.5	36.2	35.2	33.2	31.7	32.0	32.3	32.7	30.6
Age										
12–17 years	29.9	26.8	23.7	21.4	22.5	24.5	26.6	24.2	26.4	23.8
18–25 years	49.9	50.9	46.9	46.8	43.7	41.1	42.5	44.7	45.9	47.1
26–34 years	48.8	47.2	41.9	42.8	38.7	36.0	38.4	39.2	37.7	36.6
35 years or more	36.9	34.3	33.8	32.4	30.9	29.6	28.7	29.1	29.7	26.7
Race										
White	41.1	38.8	36.9	36.3	34.2	32.6	32.9	33.3	33.7	—
Black	38.5	36.0	33.1	32.1	27.6	30.6	30.7	32.9	32.5	—
Hispanic	39.4	37.6	34.7	31.5	31.7	29.5	28.7	28.6	30.4	—
Other	*	*	32.9	28.7	32.6	23.3	26.4	20.6	21.7	—
Sex										
Male	45.3	43.1	39.1	38.1	36.7	34.8	34.6	35.0	34.6	—
Female	36.2	34.4	33.5	32.5	30.0	29.0	29.5	29.7	30.9	—
PAST MONTH										
Total	38.7	35.3	33.0	31.9	29.6	28.6	28.8	28.9	29.6	27.7
Age										
12–17 years	29.4	22.7	20.9	18.4	18.5	18.9	20.2	18.3	19.9	18.2
18–25 years	47.4	45.6	41.7	41.5	37.9	34.6	35.3	38.3	40.6	41.6
26–34 years	45.7	42.1	37.3	38.2	34.2	32.4	34.7	35.0	33.7	32.5
35 years or more	35.5	32.4	31.6	30.0	28.2	27.9	27.2	27.0	27.9	25.1
Race										
White	38.9	35.2	33.5	32.8	30.3	29.4	29.7	29.8	30.5	27.9
Black	38.0	34.2	31.2	29.8	26.2	28.4	28.1	30.4	29.8	29.4
Hispanic	40.0	35.6	33.6	29.2	29.0	25.8	24.7	24.7	27.4	25.8
Other	*	*	28.0	25.4	27.6	20.5	23.5	17.2	18.8	23.8
Sex										
Male	43.4	39.5	35.2	34.1	32.2	31.5	31.0	31.1	31.2	29.7
Female	34.5	31.4	31.1	30.0	27.3	26.0	26.8	26.7	28.2	25.7

SOURCE: Substance Abuse and Mental Health Services Administration (SAMHSA), Office of Applied Studies, 1998. Data from the Summary of Findings from the National Household Survey on Drug Abuse (NHSDA). 1998 data provided by SAMHSA staff.

* Low precision; no estimate available.

— Data not available.

1. Persons reporting that they had smoked tobacco in their lifetime, but who had not smoked in the past year.

NOTE: The population distributions for the 1993–1997 NHSDA are poststratified to population projections of totals on the basis of the 1990 decennial census. NHSDAs for 1985–1992 used projections based on the 1980 census. The change from one census base to another has little effect on estimated percentages reporting drug use, but may have a significant effect on estimates of number of drug users in some subpopulation groups. Estimates from 1985–1993 may differ from estimates for these survey years that were published earlier by SAMHSA. The estimates shown here for 1985–1993 have been adjusted to improve their comparability with estimates based on the new version of the NHSDA instrument that was fielded in 1994 and subsequent NHSDAs. Because of the methodology used to adjust the 1985–1993 estimates, some logical inconsistency may exist between estimates for a given drug within the same survey year. For example, some adjusted estimates of past year use may appear to be greater than adjusted lifetime estimates. These inconsistencies tend to be small, rare, and not statistically significant.

Table 2.2. State Laws Regulating the Sale, Advertisement, and Use of Tobacco Products: 1998

Area	Cigarette tax		Places where smoking is restricted *							
	Per pack	Year enacted	Government building	Private work-places	Restaurants	Commercial day care	Home-based day care	Bars	Shopping malls	Grocery stores [1]
STATE										
Alabama	0.17	1984	No	No	No	No	No	No	No	No
Alaska	1.00	1997	Areas	No	Areas	Banned	Banned[2]	No	No	Areas
Arizona	0.58	1994	Areas	No	No	No	No	No	No	No
Arkansas	0.32	1993	No	No	No	Banned	No[3]	No	No	No
California [4]	0.37	1994	Areas	Areas	Areas	Banned	Areas	Areas	Areas	Areas
Colorado	0.20	1986	Banned	No	No	No	No	No	No	No
Connecticut	0.50	1994	Areas	Areas	Areas	No	No	No	No	Areas
Delaware	0.24	1991	Areas	Areas	Areas	Banned	No[3]	No	No	Areas
Florida	0.34	1990	Areas	Areas[5]	Areas	Banned	No[3]	No	No	No
Georgia	0.12	1971	No	No	No	Banned[2]	No	No	No	Areas
Hawaii	1.00	1998	Banned	No	Areas	Banned[2]	Banned[2]	No	No	Areas
Idaho	0.28	1994	Banned	No	Areas	No	No	No	No	Areas
Illinois	0.58	1997	Areas	Areas[5]	Areas	Banned[2]	Banned[2]	No	No	No
Indiana	0.16	1987	Areas	No	No	No	No	No	No	Areas
Iowa	0.36	1991	Areas	Areas	Areas	No	No	No	Areas	Areas
Kansas	0.24	1985	Banned	No	Areas	Banned[2]	No[3]	No	No	Areas
Kentucky	0.03	1970	No	No	No	No	No	No	No	No
Louisiana	0.20	1990	Areas	Areas	No	Banned	No[3]	No	No	Areas
Maine	0.74	1997	Areas	Areas	Areas	Areas	Areas[2]	No	Areas	Areas
Maryland	0.36	1992	Banned	No	Areas	No	No	No	No	Banned
Massachusetts	0.76	1996	Banned	No	Areas	Banned	Banned[2]	No	No	Areas
Michigan	0.75	1994	Banned	No	Areas	Banned[2]	Banned[2]	No	No	Areas
Minnesota	0.48	1992	Areas	Areas	Areas	Banned[2]	Banned[2]	No	No	No
Mississippi	0.18	1985	No	No	No	No	No	No	No	No
Missouri	0.17	1993	Areas	Areas	Areas	Banned[2]	No[3]	Areas	Areas	Areas
Montana	0.18	1993	Areas	Areas	Areas	No	No	No	No	Areas
Nebraska	0.34	1993	Areas	Areas	Areas	No	No	Areas	No	Areas
Nevada	0.35	1989	Areas	No	Areas	Areas	No	No	Areas	Areas
New Hampshire	0.37	1997	Areas	Areas	Areas	Banned[2]	No[3]	No	No	Areas
New Jersey	0.80	1998	Areas	Areas	No	Banned[6]	No	No	No	Banned
New Mexico	0.21	1993	Areas	No	No	No	No	No	No	No
New York	0.56	1993	Areas	Areas	Areas	Banned	No	No	No	Areas
North Carolina	0.05	1991	No	No	No	No	No	No	No	No
North Dakota	0.44	1993	Areas	No	Areas	Banned[2]	No[3]	No	No	No
Ohio	0.24	1993	Banned	No	No	Areas	Areas[3]	No	No	No
Oklahoma	0.23	1987	Areas	No	Areas	Banned	No[3]	No	No	Areas
Oregon	0.68	1997	Areas	No	Areas	No	No	No	No	No
Pennsylvania	0.31	1991	Areas	Areas	Areas	No	No	No	No	Areas
Rhode Island	0.71	1997	Areas	Areas	Areas	No	No	No	No	No
South Carolina	0.07	1977	Areas	No	No	Banned	No[3]	No	No	No
South Dakota	0.33	1995	Banned	No	No	Areas	Areas	No	No	No
Tennessee	0.13	1971	Banned	No	No	Areas[2]	Areas[2]	No	No	No
Texas	0.41	1990	No	No	No	No	No	No	No	No
Utah	0.52	1997	No	Areas	Banned	Banned[2]	Banned[2]	No	Banned	Banned
Vermont	0.44	1995	Areas	Areas	Banned	No	No	Areas	Areas	Areas
Virginia	0.03	1966	Areas	No	Areas	Areas	No	No	No	Areas
Washington	0.83	1996	Banned	No	No	No	No	No	Areas	Areas
West Virginia	0.17	1978	No	No	No	No	No	No	No	No
Wisconsin	0.59	1997	Areas	Areas	Areas	Banned[2]	No	No	No	Areas
Wyoming	0.12	1989	Areas	No	No	No	No	No	No	No
OTHER										
District of Columbia	0.65	1993	Areas	Areas	Areas	Areas	No[3]	No	No	Areas
NUMBER WITH PROVISION [7]	51	51	42	21	31	29	11	4	8	30

* No = no restrictions; Areas = smoking limited to certain areas; Banned = no smoking allowed.

See footnotes at end of table.

Table 2.2. State Laws Regulating the Sale, Advertisement, and Use of Tobacco Products: 1998—*Continued*

Area	Places Where Smoking is Restricted *—*Continued*					Minimum age for sale	Any retail license required	Vending machine license fee (machine operator fee/ fee per machine)	Does state preempt local law?
	Enclosed arenas	Public transportation	Hospitals	Prisons	Hotels and motels				
STATE									
Alabama	No	No	No	No	No	19	Yes	No	No
Alaska	No	Areas	Banned	Areas	No	19	Yes	$25/$0	No
Arizona	No	Areas	Areas	No	No	18	No	No	No
Arkansas	No	No	Areas	No	No	18	Yes	$100/$10	No
California [4]	Areas	Areas	Areas	No	Areas	18	No	No	Yes
Colorado	Areas	Areas	Areas	No	No	18	No	No	No
Connecticut	No	Areas	Areas	No	No	18	Yes	$25-$1,000 [8]/$0	Yes
Delaware	No	Banned	Banned	No	No	18	Yes	$0/$3	Yes
Florida	Areas	Banned	Areas	No	No	18	Yes	Up to $50 [9]	Yes
Georgia	No	Banned	No	No	No	18	Yes	$0/$1	No
Hawaii	No	Areas [10]	Areas	No	No	18	No	No	No
Idaho	Areas	Areas [11]	Areas	No	No	18	No	No	No
Illinois	Areas	Areas	Areas	No	No	18	No	No	Yes
Indiana	No	No	Areas	No	No	18	No	No	Yes
Iowa	Areas	Areas	Areas	No	Areas	18	Yes	$100/$0	Yes
Kansas	Areas	Banned	Areas	No	No	18	Yes	$0/$12	No
Kentucky	No	No	No	No	No	18	Yes	$25/$0	Yes
Louisiana	No	Banned	Areas	No	No	18	Yes	$75/$5	Yes
Maine	Areas	Areas	Areas	No	No	18	Yes	$0/$25	No
Maryland	No	Banned	Areas	No	Areas	18	Yes	$500/$0 [12]	No
Massachusetts	No	Areas [11]	Areas	No	No	18	Yes	$100/$5	Yes
Michigan	Areas	Areas	Areas	No	No	18	Yes	$5-$100/$0	Yes
Minnesota	Areas	Areas [11]	Banned	Banned [13]	Areas	18	Yes [14]	No	No
Mississippi	No	No	No	No	No	18	Yes	No	Yes
Missouri	Areas [15]	Areas	Areas	No	No	18	No	No	No
Montana	Areas	Areas [11]	Areas	No	No	18	Yes	$5-$50 [8]/$0	Yes
Nebraska	Areas	Areas	Areas	No	No	18	Yes	$10-$25 [9]/$0	No
Nevada	No	Areas	Areas	No	No	18	Yes	No	Yes
New Hampshire	Areas	Banned	Banned	Areas	Areas	18	Yes	$70/$10	No
New Jersey	No	Banned	Areas	No	No	18	Yes	$0/$50	Yes
New Mexico	No	No	No	No	No	18	No	No	Yes
New York	Areas	Banned	Areas	No	No	18	Yes	$0/$25	Yes
North Carolina	No	No	No	No	No	18	No [16]	No	Yes
North Dakota	No	Areas	Areas	No	No	18	Yes	$15/$0	No
Ohio	No	Areas [11]	Areas	No	No	18	Yes	$0/$25-$30	No
Oklahoma	Areas	Areas	Areas	No	No	18	Yes	$0/$50	Yes
Oregon	Areas	No	Areas	No	No	18	No	No	Yes
Pennsylvania	Areas	Areas	Areas	No	No	18	Yes	$25/$0	Yes
Rhode Island	No	Banned	Areas	No	No	18	Yes	$100 [17]/$25	No
South Carolina	Areas	Banned	Areas	No	No	18	Yes	No	Yes
South Dakota	No	Areas	Areas	No	No	18	No	No	Yes
Tennessee	No	No	Areas	No	No	18	No	No	Yes
Texas	No	Areas	Areas	No	No	18	Yes	No	No
Utah	Banned	Banned	Areas	No	Areas	19	Yes	$30/$0	Yes
Vermont	Areas	Areas	Areas	No	Areas	18	Yes	$10/$0	No
Virginia	Areas	Banned	Areas	No	No	18	No	No	Yes
Washington	Areas	Areas [11]	Areas	No	No	18	Yes	$93/$30	Yes
West Virginia	No	Banned	No	Banned [18]	No	18	No	No	Yes
Wisconsin	No	Areas [11]	Banned	No	No	18	Yes	$50/$0	Yes
Wyoming	No	No	No	No	No	18	No	No	Yes
OTHER									
District of Columbia	No	Banned	Areas	No	No	18	Yes	$0/$15	No
NUMBER WITH PROVISION [7]	23	41	43	4	7	51	35	29	30

* No = no restrictions; Areas = smoking limited to certain areas; Banned = no smoking allowed.

SOURCE: Centers for Disease Control and Prevention. CDC Surveillance Summaries, June 25, 1999. State Laws on Tobacco Contol—United States, 1998. *Morbidity and Mortality Weekly Report* 1999; 48 (No. SS-3) pp21–62: Tables 2–7, 9, 11, 12. This table is based on a study conducted by the Epidemiology Program Office of the CDC. They asked state governments to report on their enactment of laws or issuance of regulations governing the sale, use, and taxing of tobacco products.

1. Because law does not always explicitly refer to grocery stores, restrictions on retail stores are often included here.
2. Nonsmoking restrictions are in effect when children are on the premises.
3. Prohibits smoking in child-care facilities; however, language does not specify home-based child daycare.
4. Whereas most state law stipulate areas in which smoking is restricted, California's law designates places and circumstances under which smoking is allowed.
5. Restricts smoking in work sites but does not specify private-sector work sites.
6. Smoking restrictions are in effect only when children are on the premises. When children are not on the premises, smoking areas must be separately ventilated.
7. Total number of state laws that have restrictions, enforcement, penalties, or signage (i.e., sign is posted indicating where smoking is prohibited.)
8. Based on number of sites or vending machines operated.
9. Only one fee required if more than one vending machine is operated under the same roof.
10. Taxis only.
11. Prohibits smoking on certain forms of public transportation but allows designated smoking areas on others.
12. $200 application fee; $30 renewal fee.
13. State correctional facilities only.
14. Cities and towns are required to license and regulate retail tobacco sales. County boards are required to license and regulate retail tobacco sales in unorganized territories and in cities or towns that do not license or regulate retail tobacco sales.
15. Enclosed arenas with a capacity of >15,000 persons are exempt.
16. A retail license exists for those retailers who manufacture their own tobacco products or deal nontaxed tobacco products.
17. Only if vending machine operator has 25 machines.
18. Applies to inmates held by regional facility authority in regional jails operated solely by the authority.

Table 2.3. Mothers Who Smoked during Pregnancy

(Percent of mothers who smoked [1])

Characteristic of mother	1989	1990	1991	1992	1993	1994	1995	1996	1997
RACE OF MOTHER [2]									
All races	19.5	18.4	17.8	16.9	15.8	14.6	13.9	13.6	13.2
White	20.4	19.4	18.8	17.9	16.8	15.6	15.0	14.7	14.3
Black	17.1	15.9	14.6	13.8	12.7	11.4	10.6	10.2	9.7
American Indian or Alaska Native	23.0	22.4	22.6	22.5	21.6	21.0	20.9	21.3	20.8
Asian or Pacific Islander [3]	5.7	5.5	5.2	4.8	4.3	3.6	3.4	3.3	3.2
Chinese	2.7	2.0	1.9	1.7	1.1	0.9	0.8	0.7	1.0
Japanese	8.2	8.0	7.5	6.6	6.7	5.4	5.2	4.8	4.7
Filipino	5.1	5.3	5.3	4.8	4.3	3.7	3.4	3.5	3.4
Hawaiian and part Hawaiian	19.3	21.0	19.4	18.5	17.2	16.0	15.9	15.3	15.8
Other Asian or Pacific Islander	4.2	3.8	3.8	3.6	3.2	2.9	2.7	2.7	2.5
HISPANIC ORIGIN AND RACE OF MOTHER [4]									
Hispanic origin	8.0	6.7	6.3	5.8	5.0	4.6	4.3	4.3	4.1
Mexican	6.3	5.3	4.8	4.3	3.7	3.4	3.1	3.1	2.9
Puerto Rican	14.5	13.6	13.2	12.7	11.2	10.9	10.4	11.0	11.0
Cuban	6.9	6.4	6.2	5.9	5.0	4.8	4.1	4.7	4.2
Central and South American	3.6	3.0	2.8	2.6	2.3	1.8	1.8	1.8	1.8
Other and unknown Hispanic	12.1	10.8	10.7	10.1	9.3	8.1	8.2	9.1	8.5
White, non-Hispanic	21.7	21.0	20.5	19.7	18.6	17.7	17.1	16.9	16.5
Black, non-Hispanic	17.2	15.9	14.6	13.8	12.7	11.5	10.6	10.3	9.8
AGE OF MOTHER [2]									
Under 15 years	7.7	7.5	7.6	6.9	7.0	6.7	7.3	7.7	8.1
15–19 years	22.2	20.8	19.7	18.6	17.5	16.7	16.8	17.2	17.6
15–17 years	19.0	17.6	16.6	15.6	14.8	14.4	14.6	15.4	15.5
18–19 years	23.9	22.5	21.5	20.3	19.1	18.1	18.1	18.3	18.8
20–24 years	23.5	22.1	21.2	20.3	19.2	17.8	17.1	16.8	16.6
25–29 years	19.0	18.0	17.2	16.1	14.8	13.5	12.8	12.3	11.8
30–34 years	15.7	15.3	15.1	14.5	13.4	12.3	11.4	10.9	10.0
35–39 years	13.6	13.3	13.3	13.4	12.8	12.2	12.0	11.7	11.1
40–49 years	13.2	12.3	11.9	11.6	11.0	10.3	10.1	10.1	10.1
EDUCATION OF MOTHER [5]									
0–8 years	18.9	17.5	16.8	15.5	13.9	12.1	11.0	10.3	9.9
9–11 years	42.2	40.5	39.1	37.8	36.1	33.6	32.0	31.1	30.2
12 years	22.8	21.9	21.2	20.7	19.9	18.7	18.3	18.0	17.5
13–15 years	13.7	12.8	12.5	12.1	11.4	10.8	10.6	10.4	9.9
16 years or more	5.0	4.5	4.2	3.9	3.1	2.8	2.7	2.6	2.4

SOURCE: E. Kramarow, H. Lentzner, R. Rooks, J. Weeks, S. Saydah. *Health and Aging Chartbook. Health, United States, 1999*. Hyattsville, Maryland: National Center for Health Statistics. 1999: Table 10.

1. Excludes live births for whom smoking status of mother is unknown.
2. Includes data for 43 states and the District of Columbia (DC) in 1989, 45 states and DC in 1990, 46 states and DC in 1991–93, and 46 states, DC, and New York City (NYC) in 1994–97. Excludes data for California, Indiana, New York (but includes NYC in 1994–97), and South Dakota (1989–90), and Louisiana and Nebraska (1989), which did not require the reporting of mother's tobacco use during pregnancy on the birth certificate (see Appendix I of *Health, United States, 1999*).
3. Maternal tobacco use during pregnancy was not reported on the birth certificates of California and New York, which during 1989–91 together accounted for 43–66 percent of the births in each Asian subgroup (except Hawaiian).
4. Includes data for 42 states and DC in 1989, 44 states and DC in 1990, 45 states and DC in 1991–92, 46 states and DC in 1993, and 46 states, DC, and NYC in 1994–96. Excludes data for California, Indiana, New York (but includes NYC in 1994–96), New Hampshire (1989–92), Oklahoma (1989–90), and Louisiana and Nebraska (1989), which did not require the reporting of either Hispanic origin of mother or tobacco use during pregnancy on the birth certificate (see Appendix I in *Health, United States, 1999*).
5. Percentage of mothers 20 years of age and over who smoked. Includes data for 42 states and DC in 1989, 44 states and DC in 1990, 45 states and DC in 1991, 46 states and DC in 1992–93, and 46 states, DC, and NYC in 1994–96. Excludes data for California, Indiana, New York (but includes NYC in 1994–96), and South Dakota (1989–96), Washington (1989–91), Oklahoma (1989–90), and Louisiana and Nebraska (1989), which did not require the reporting of either mother's education or tobacco use during pregnancy on the birth certificate (see Appendix I of *Health, United States, 1999*).

NOTE: The race groups, White, Black, American Indian or Alaska Native, and Asian or Pacific Islander, include persons of Hispanic and non-Hispanic origin. Conversely, persons of Hispanic origin may be of any race.

Table 2.4. Past Month Heavy Alcohol Use

(Number in thousands)

Characteristic	1985	1988	1991	1992	1993	1994	1995	1996	1997	1998
NUMBER										
Total	15 757	11 468	13 540	12 689	13 681	12 650	11 319	11 215	11 249	12 427
Age										
12–17 years	2 017	805	1 193	703	717	536	600	646	685	648
18–25 years	4 327	3 547	4 277	4 181	3 921	3 565	3 220	3 463	2 971	3 760
26–34 years	4 154	2 743	3 018	3 216	3 119	2 801	2 756	2 413	2 557	2 399
35 years or more	5 260	4 374	5 052	4 588	5 924	5 748	4 743	4 692	5 037	5 620
Race										
White	13 977	9 900	11 271	10 680	11 689	9 892	8 891	8 587	8 846	9 443
Black	727	616	980	812	739	1 066	1 038	1 213	887	1 167
Hispanic	930	783	1 087	1 046	1 102	1 335	1 193	1 238	1 319	1 392
Other	*	170	203	151	150	356	197	177	197	425
Sex										
Male	12 543	9 598	10 325	9 845	11 620	9 990	9 238	9 141	8 942	9 801
Female	3 214	1 870	3 216	2 844	2 061	2 660	2 081	2 074	2 307	2 627
PERCENT										
Total	8.3	5.8	6.8	6.2	6.7	6.2	5.5	5.4	5.4	5.9
Age										
12–17 years	9.5	4.0	6.0	3.4	3.4	2.5	2.8	2.9	3.1	2.9
18–25 years	13.8	12.0	15.2	15.1	14.0	13.2	12.0	12.9	11.1	13.8
26–34 years	11.5	7.1	7.9	8.5	8.5	8.0	7.9	7.1	7.5	7.2
35 years or more	5.2	4.0	4.4	3.9	5.0	4.8	3.9	3.8	4.0	4.4
Race										
White	9.1	6.3	7.2	6.8	7.5	6.4	5.7	5.5	5.7	6.0
Black	3.5	2.8	4.3	3.5	3.3	4.8	4.6	5.3	3.8	4.9
Hispanic	7.1	5.3	6.8	6.3	6.0	7.3	6.3	6.2	6.3	6.5
Other	*	3.9	3.3	2.2	1.9	4.7	2.4	2.1	2.3	4.7
Sex										
Male	13.8	10.2	10.8	10.1	11.9	10.3	9.4	9.3	8.9	9.7
Female	3.2	1.8	3.1	2.7	1.9	2.5	2.0	1.9	2.1	2.4

SOURCE: Substance Abuse and Mental Health Services Administration (SAMHSA), Office of Applied Studies 1998. Data from the Summary of Findings from the National Household Survey on Drug Abuse (NHSDA). 1998 data provided by SAMHSA staff.

* Low precision; no estimate available.

NOTE: Numbers are estimates. Heavy Alcohol Use is defined as drinking five or more drinks on the same occasion on each of five or more days in the past 30 days. The population distributions for the 1993–1997 NHSDA are poststratified to population projections of totals based on the 1990 decennial census. NHSDAs from 1985–1992 used projections based on the 1980 census. The change from one census base to another has little effect on estimated percentages the basis of reporting drug use, but may have a significant effect on estimates of number of drug users in some subpopulation groups. Estimates for 1985–1993 may differ from estimates for these survey years that were published earlier by SAMHSA. The estimates shown here for 1985–1993 have been adjusted to improve their comparability with estimates based on the new version of the NHSDA instrument that was fielded in 1994 and subsequent NHSDAs. Because of the methodology used to adjust the 1985–1993 estimates, some logical inconsistency may exist between estimates for a given drug within the same survey year. For example, some adjusted estimates of past year use may appear to be greater than adjusted lifetime estimates. These inconsistencies tend to be small, rare, and not statistically significant.

Table 2.5. Marijuana Use

(Number in thousands)

Characteristic	1979	1982	1985	1988	1991	1992	1993	1994	1995	1996	1997	1998
LIFETIME												
Total	50 322	53 312	56 547	60 755	61 900	62 075	64 149	65 229	65 545	68 571	71 112	72 070
Age												
12–17 years	6 345	5 183	4 339	3 034	2 244	1 883	2 110	2 964	3 606	3 782	4 256	3 855
18–25 years	21 563	20 388	18 213	16 221	13 917	13 020	12 954	11 737	11 506	12 239	11 483	12 474
26–34 years	14 105	17 645	19 728	22 207	21 375	20 761	20 415	19 297	18 628	17 904	16 892	16 569
35 years or more	8 309	10 095	14 267	19 294	24 364	26 411	28 670	31 231	31 805	34 645	38 481	39 171
Race												
White	41 681	43 924	47 939	50 187	50 380	51 319	52 981	53 249	53 528	55 140	57 301	57 522
Black	5 480	5 684	5 677	5 974	6 609	5 910	5 666	6 430	6 673	7 111	6 962	7 494
Hispanic	2 191	2 799	2 444	3 236	3 403	3 375	4 024	4 129	3 990	4 579	4 818	5 175
Other	970	*	487	1 358	1 507	1 471	1 478	1 421	1 353	1 741	2 030	1 879
Sex												
Male	29 123	30 240	31 845	32 181	33 611	34 382	35 624	35 987	36 095	38 039	39 361	40 471
Female	21 199	23 073	24 701	28 574	28 289	27 692	28 525	29 242	29 450	30 532	31 751	31 598
PAST YEAR												
Total	29 869	29 685	26 145	19 492	18 067	16 322	17 510	17 813	17 755	18 398	19 446	18 710
Age												
12–17 years	5 054	3 949	3 598	2 177	1 718	1 427	1 797	2 491	3 145	2 925	3 556	3 197
18–25 years	14 414	12 417	10 755	7 741	6 536	5 928	6 049	6 105	6 076	6 628	6 184	6 739
26–34 years	6 416	7 327	7 353	5 466	4 484	4 407	4 134	4 208	4 234	4 021	3 946	3 362
35 years or more	3 985	5 993	4 439	4 108	5 328	4 560	5 529	5 009	4 300	4 825	5 759	5 412
Race												
White	24 701	24 805	21 677	15 519	14 265	13 349	13 727	13 672	13 671	13 749	14 655	13 686
Black	3 111	3 094	2 928	1 837	2 204	1 720	1 907	2 375	2 271	2 667	2 417	2 628
Hispanic	1 419	1 243	1 166	1 194	1 075	946	1 354	1 428	1 308	1 464	1 609	1 829
Other	639	*	375	*	522	307	522	338	505	517	765	566
Sex												
Male	18 291	18 826	15 839	11 725	10 780	10 052	10 984	11 327	10 641	11 716	12 103	11 332
Female	11 579	10 859	10 305	7 767	7 287	6 270	6 525	6 486	7 114	6 683	7 343	7 378
PAST MONTH												
Total	23 790	21 507	18 641	12 353	10 366	9 676	9 610	10 112	9 842	10 095	11 109	11 016
Age												
12–17 years	3 374	2 199	2 189	1 102	722	696	845	1 315	1 828	1 600	2 116	1 878
18–25 years	11 607	9 047	6 870	4 555	3 666	3 036	3 139	3 389	3 326	3 678	3 557	3 855
26–34 years	6 167	6 522	6 923	4 760	2 979	3 557	2 786	2 522	2 424	2 252	2 099	1 894
35 years or more	2 641	3 739	2 660	1 936	2 999	2 387	2 840	2 886	2 264	2 565	3 337	3 390
Race												
White	20 063	17 873	15 409	9 942	8 248	8 051	7 659	7 695	7 432	7 414	8 332	8 073
Black	2 123	2 308	2 103	1 045	1 269	932	974	1 386	1 409	1 576	1 488	1 627
Hispanic	1 202	1 012	842	731	587	513	722	791	768	776	872	1 000
Other	402	*	287	*	262	180	256	240	234	328	416	317
Sex												
Male	15 548	14 580	11 535	7 988	6 570	6 368	6 380	6 723	6 247	6 683	7 237	7 010
Female	8 242	6 927	7 106	4 365	3 797	3 308	3 230	3 389	3 596	3 412	3 871	4 006
FORMER USERS [1]												
Number who stopped	20 453	23 627	30 402	41 263	43 833	45 753	46 639	47 416	47 790	50 173	51 666	53 360
Percent of total population who stopped	11.3	12.7	15.8	20.8	21.6	22.3	22.5	22.6	22.6	23.4	23.9	24.4
Percent of users who stopped	40.6	44	54	68	71	74	73	73	73	73	73	74

See footnotes at end of table.

Table 2.5. Marijuana Use—*Continued*

(Percent)

Characteristic	1979	1982	1985	1988	1991	1992	1993	1994	1995	1996	1997	1998
LIFETIME												
Total	28.0	28.6	29.4	30.6	30.5	30.2	31.0	31.1	31.0	32.0	32.9	33.0
Age												
12–17 years	27.0	23.2	20.1	15.0	11.1	9.1	9.9	13.6	16.2	16.8	18.9	17.0
18–25 years	66.0	61.3	57.6	54.6	48.8	46.6	45.7	41.9	41.4	44.0	41.5	44.6
26–34 years	45.0	51.5	54.1	57.6	55.2	54.3	54.9	52.7	51.8	50.5	47.9	47.9
35 years or more	9.0	10.4	13.9	17.6	21.1	22.2	23.8	25.4	25.3	27.0	29.4	29.4
Race												
White	28.0	29.3	31.1	32.0	32.0	32.4	33.6	33.5	33.5	34.4	35.6	35.5
Black	28.0	28.2	26.6	26.8	28.7	25.0	24.6	27.5	28.2	29.6	28.5	30.2
Hispanic	21.0	23.7	18.4	21.7	21.0	20.0	21.8	21.6	20.2	22.0	22.3	23.2
Other	29.5	*	12.8	30.8	24.0	21.6	18.5	18.0	16.1	19.7	22.4	20.1
Sex												
Male	34.0	34.0	34.7	33.9	34.6	34.8	35.9	35.9	35.6	37.0	37.8	38.5
Female	22.0	23.6	24.5	27.6	26.8	25.9	26.4	26.8	26.8	27.5	28.3	27.9
PAST YEAR												
Total	16.6	15.9	13.6	9.8	8.9	7.9	8.5	8.5	8.4	8.6	9.0	8.6
Age												
12–17 years	21.3	17.7	16.7	10.7	8.5	6.9	8.5	11.4	14.2	13.0	15.8	14.1
18–25 years	44.2	37.4	34.0	26.1	22.9	21.2	21.4	21.8	21.8	23.8	22.3	24.1
26–34 years	20.5	21.4	20.2	14.2	11.6	11.5	11.1	11.5	11.8	11.3	11.2	9.7
35 years or more	4.3	6.2	4.3	3.7	4.6	3.8	4.6	4.1	3.4	3.8	4.4	4.1
Race												
White	16.8	16.5	14.1	9.9	9.1	8.4	8.7	8.6	8.6	8.6	9.1	8.4
Black	16.1	15.4	13.7	8.2	9.6	7.3	8.3	10.2	9.6	11.1	9.9	10.6
Hispanic	13.4	10.5	8.8	8.0	6.6	5.6	7.3	7.5	6.6	7.0	7.5	8.2
Other	19.5	*	9.9	*	8.3	4.5	6.5	4.3	6.0	5.9	8.4	6.1
Sex												
Male	21.3	21.2	17.2	12.4	11.1	10.2	11.1	11.3	10.5	11.4	11.6	10.8
Female	12.3	11.1	10.2	7.5	6.9	5.9	6.0	5.9	6.5	6.0	6.5	6.5
PAST MONTH												
Total	13.2	11.5	9.7	6.2	5.1	4.7	4.6	4.8	4.7	4.7	5.1	5.0
Age												
12–17 years	14.2	9.9	10.2	5.4	3.6	3.4	4.0	6.0	8.2	7.1	9.4	8.3
18–25 years	35.6	27.2	21.7	15.3	12.9	10.9	11.1	12.1	12.0	13.2	12.8	13.8
26–34 years	19.7	19.0	19.0	12.3	7.7	9.3	7.5	6.9	6.7	6.3	6.0	5.5
35 years or more	2.9	3.9	2.6	1.8	2.6	2.0	2.4	2.3	1.8	2.0	2.6	2.5
Race												
White	13.6	11.9	10.0	6.3	5.2	5.1	4.9	4.8	4.7	4.6	5.2	5.0
Black	11.0	11.5	9.9	4.7	5.5	3.9	4.2	5.9	5.9	6.6	6.1	6.6
Hispanic	11.4	8.6	6.4	4.9	3.6	3.0	3.9	4.1	3.9	3.7	4.0	4.5
Other	12.2	*	7.6	*	4.2	2.6	3.2	3.0	2.8	3.7	4.6	3.4
Sex												
Male	18.1	16.4	12.6	8.4	6.8	6.4	6.4	6.7	6.2	6.5	7.0	6.7
Female	8.7	7.1	7.1	4.2	3.6	3.1	3.0	3.1	3.3	3.1	3.5	3.5

SOURCE: Substance Abuse and Mental Health Services Administration (SAMHSA), Office of Applied Studies 1998. Data from the Summary of Findings from the National Household Survey on Drug Abuse (NHSDA). 1998 data provided by SAMHSA staff.

* Low precision; no estimate available.
1. Persons reporting that they had used marijuana in their lifetime, but not in the past year.

NOTE: The population distributions for the 1993–1997 NHSDA are poststratified to population projections of totals on the basis of the 1990 decennial census. NHSDAs for 1985–1992 used projections based on the 1980 census. The change from one census base to another has little effect on estimated percentages reporting drug use, but may have a significant effect on estimates of number of drug users in some subpopulation groups. Estimates for 1985–1993 may differ from estimates for these survey years that were published earlier by SAMHSA. The estimates shown here for 1985–1993 have been adjusted to improve their comparability with estimates based on the new version of the NHSDA instrument that was fielded in 1994 and subsequent NHSDAs. Because of the methodology used to adjust the 1985–1993 estimates, some logical inconsistency may exist between estimates for a given drug within the same survey year. For example, some adjusted estimates of past year use may appear to be greater than adjusted lifetime estimates. These inconsistencies tend to be small, rare, and not statistically significant.

Table 2.6. Cocaine Use

(Number in thousands)

Characteristic	1979	1982	1985	1988	1991	1992	1993	1994	1995	1996	1997	1998
LIFETIME												
Total	15 541	21 756	21 495	21 058	23 271	22 482	23 369	21 821	21 700	22 130	22 597	23 089
Age												
12–17 years	1 311	1 447	1 022	680	480	346	238	365	448	430	674	497
18–25 years	8 859	9 110	7 670	5 826	5 064	4 400	3 529	3 384	2 719	2 842	2 472	2 805
26–34 years	4 188	7 342	8 597	10 182	9 928	9 580	9 461	8 398	7 755	7 417	6 502	5 906
35 years or more	1 183	3 857	4 207	4 370	7 799	8 156	10 141	9 674	10 778	11 442	12 950	13 880
Race												
White	12 048	18 106	18 323	16 850	18 410	18 514	18 860	17 916	18 039	17 712	19 077	18 530
Black	1 860	2 394	2 013	2 062	2 569	2 023	2 145	1 831	1 915	1 989	1 583	2 094
Hispanic	1 243	912	1 025	1 625	1 793	1 626	1 755	1 543	1 489	1 771	1 582	1 980
Other	389	345	135	520	499	320	609	531	256	657	356	486
Sex												
Male	9 874	13 287	13 541	12 349	13 825	13 200	14 285	12 911	12 991	13 222	13 773	13 807
Female	5 666	8 468	7 955	8 709	9 446	9 282	9 083	8 910	8 709	8 908	8 825	9 282
PAST YEAR												
Total	8 608	10 458	9 839	7 151	5 284	4 332	3 947	3 664	3 664	4 033	4 169	3 811
Age												
12–17 years	861	816	735	515	263	199	141	240	367	311	491	379
18–25 years	5 551	5 276	4 285	3 122	1 905	1 537	1 246	1 008	1 208	1 308	1 078	1 306
26–34 years	1 796	3 189	3 841	2 691	1 706	1 628	1 419	1 273	1 108	1 251	1 102	942
35 years or more	399	1 178	977	823	1 409	968	1 141	1 142	981	1 163	1 498	1 185
Race												
White	6 676	8 962	8 036	5 421	3 806	3 262	2 721	2 369	2 727	2 760	3 054	3 811
Black	939	834	1 107	846	778	541	581	675	457	580	593	463
Hispanic	785	464	631	735	529	453	493	458	352	500	434	505
Other	208	*	*	149	171	76	152	162	127	194	88	94
Sex												
Male	5 495	6 831	6 244	4 596	3 437	2 769	2 743	2 447	2 325	2 564	2 625	2 399
Female	3 113	3 627	3 595	2 555	1 847	1 563	1 204	1 217	1 338	1 468	1 544	1 412
PAST MONTH												
Total	4 743	4 491	5 686	3 140	2 032	1 402	1 404	1 382	1 453	1 749	1 505	1 750
Age												
12–17 years	358	432	328	242	89	59	89	70	172	131	221	186
18–25 years	3 226	2 323	2 555	1 421	625	553	461	346	359	557	338	548
26–34 years	933	1 205	2 307	1 068	755	562	388	477	424	531	303	404
35 years or more	226	531	497	409	562	228	466	490	498	531	644	612
Race												
White	3 590	3 803	4 576	2 174	1 177	924	826	850	1 027	1 219	952	1 119
Black	531	489	721	480	444	247	320	305	254	252	332	313
Hispanic	508	181	332	412	277	223	220	217	147	232	178	293
Other	115	*	*	74	134	8	*	*	24	46	44	24
Sex												
Male	3 018	3 015	3 586	2 061	1 359	952	957	907	983	1 146	908	1 132
Female	1 725	1 476	2 100	1 079	672	450	447	475	470	603	597	618
FORMER USERS [1]												
Number who stopped	6 933	11 298	11 656	13 907	17 987	18 150	19 422	18 157	18 036	18 097	18 428	19 278
Percent of total population who stopped	3.8	6.1	6.1	7.0	8.9	8.8	9.4	8.7	8.6	8.4	8.6	8.9
Percent of users who stopped	44.6	51.9	54.2	66.0	77.3	80.7	83.1	83.2	83.1	81.8	81.6	83.5

See footnotes at end of table.

Table 2.6. Cocaine Use—*Continued*

(Percent)

Characteristic	1979	1982	1985	1988	1991	1992	1993	1994	1995	1996	1997	1998
LIFETIME												
Total	8.6	11.7	11.2	10.6	11.5	10.9	11.3	10.4	10.3	10.3	10.5	10.6
Age												
12–17 years	5.5	6.5	4.7	3.4	2.4	1.7	1.1	1.7	2.0	1.9	3.0	2.2
18–25 years	27.0	27.0	24.0	19.6	17.8	15.7	12.5	12.1	9.8	10.2	8.9	10.0
26–34 years	13.0	21.0	24.0	26.0	26.0	25.0	25.0	23.0	22.0	21.0	18.4	17.0
35 years or more	1.0	4.0	4.0	4.0	7.0	7.0	8.0	8.0	9.0	9.0	10.0	10.0
Race												
White	8.2	12.1	11.9	10.7	11.7	11.7	12.0	11.3	11.3	11.0	11.8	11.4
Black	10.0	12.0	9.0	9.0	11.0	9.0	9.0	8.0	8.0	8.0	7.0	9.0
Hispanic	12.0	8.0	8.0	11.0	11.0	10.0	10.0	8.0	8.0	9.0	7.0	9.0
Other	12.0	7.9	4.0	12.0	8.0	5.0	8.0	7.0	3.0	7.0	4.0	5.0
Sex												
Male	11.5	15.0	14.7	13.0	14.2	13.4	14.4	12.9	12.8	12.8	13.2	13.1
Female	6.0	9.0	8.0	8.0	9.0	9.0	8.0	8.0	8.0	8.0	8.0	8.0
PAST YEAR												
Total	4.8	5.6	5.1	3.6	2.6	2.1	1.9	1.7	1.7	1.9	1.9	1.7
Age												
12–17 years	3.6	3.7	3.4	2.5	1.3	1.0	0.7	1.1	1.7	1.4	2.2	1.7
18–25 years	17.0	15.9	13.6	10.5	6.7	5.5	4.4	3.6	4.3	4.7	3.9	4.7
26–34 years	5.7	9.3	10.5	7.0	4.4	4.3	3.8	3.5	3.1	3.5	3.1	2.7
35 years or more	0.4	1.2	0.9	0.7	1.2	0.8	0.9	0.9	0.8	0.9	1.1	0.9
Race												
White	4.5	6.0	5.2	3.5	2.4	2.1	1.7	1.5	1.7	1.7	1.9	1.7
Black	4.9	4.1	5.2	3.8	3.4	2.3	2.5	2.9	1.9	2.4	2.4	1.9
Hispanic	7.4	3.9	4.8	4.9	3.3	2.7	2.7	2.4	1.8	2.4	2.0	2.3
Other	6.3	*	*	3.4	2.7	1.1	1.9	2.1	1.5	2.2	1.0	1.0
Sex												
Male	6.4	7.7	6.8	4.8	3.5	2.8	2.8	2.4	2.3	2.5	2.5	2.3
Female	3.3	3.7	3.6	2.5	1.7	1.5	1.1	1.1	1.2	1.3	1.4	1.2
PAST MONTH												
Total	2.6	2.4	3.0	1.6	1.0	0.7	0.7	0.7	0.7	0.8	0.7	0.8
Age												
12–17 years	1.5	1.9	1.5	1.2	0.4	0.3	0.4	0.3	0.8	0.6	1.0	0.8
18–25 years	9.9	7.0	8.1	4.8	2.2	2.0	1.6	1.2	1.3	2.0	1.2	2.0
26–34 years	3.0	3.5	6.3	2.8	1.9	1.5	1.0	1.3	1.2	1.5	0.9	1.2
35 years or more	0.2	0.5	0.5	0.4	0.5	0.2	0.4	0.4	0.4	0.4	0.5	0.5
Race												
White	2.4	2.5	3.0	1.4	0.7	0.6	0.5	0.5	0.6	0.8	0.6	0.7
Black	2.8	2.4	3.4	2.2	1.9	1.0	1.4	1.3	1.1	1.0	1.4	1.3
Hispanic	4.8	1.5	2.5	2.8	1.7	1.3	1.2	1.1	0.7	1.1	0.8	1.3
Other	3.5	*	*	1.7	2.1	0.1	*	*	0.3	0.5	0.5	0.3
Sex												
Male	3.5	3.4	3.9	2.2	1.4	1.0	1.0	0.9	1.0	1.1	0.9	1.1
Female	1.8	1.5	2.1	1.0	0.6	0.4	0.4	0.4	0.4	0.5	0.5	0.3

SOURCE: Substance Abuse and Mental Health Services Administration (SAMHSA), Office of Applied Studies 1998. Data from the Summary of Findings from the National Household Survey on Drug Abuse (NHSDA). 1998 data provided by SAMHSA staff.

* Low precision; no estimate available.
1. Persons reporting that they had used cocaine in their lifetime, but not in the past year.

NOTE: The population distributions for the 1993–1997 NHSDA are poststratified to population projections of totals on the basis of the 1990 decennial census. NHSDAs for 1985–1992 used projections based on the 1980 census. The change from one census base to another has little effect on estimated percentages reporting drug use, but may have a significant effect on estimates of number of drug users in some subpopulation groups. Estimates for 1985–1993 may differ from estimates for these survey years that were published earlier by SAMHSA. The estimates shown here for 1985–1993 have been adjusted to improve their comparability with estimates based on the new version of the NHSDA instrument that was fielded in 1994 and subsequent NHSDAs. Because of the methodology used to adjust the 1985–1993 estimates, some logical inconsistency may exist between estimates for a given drug within the same survey year. For example, some adjusted estimates of past year use may appear to be greater than adjusted lifetime estimates. These inconsistencies tend to be small, rare, and not statistically significant.

Table 2.7. Alcohol, Drug Use, and Driving: 1997

(Percent of drivers over 16 years of age)

Characteristic	Illicit drug use in the past year		Heavy alcohol use in the past month		Total	
	Drove under the influence in the past year	Often drove or rode without wearing a seat belt	Drove under the influence in the past year	Often drove or rode without wearing a seat belt	Drove under the influence in the past year	Often drove or rode without wearing a seat belt
TOTAL	40.7	23.4	50.6	26.8	10.7	12.4
SEX						
Male	44.1	28.3	48.4	30.1	14.9	16.1
Female	35.2	15.7	59.4	13.7	6.9	9.0
AGE GROUP						
16–17 years	28.3	26.8	*	43.1	10.5	18.8
18–20 years	44.4	26.5	66.3	41.6	18.3	19.4
21–25 years	41.7	23.9	57.1	29.5	18.4	16.8
25–34 years	45.1	23.2	54.9	27.1	17.2	14.2
35 years and over	39.4	21.1	42.6	20.4	7.4	10.4
RACE/ ETHNICITY [1]						
White, non-Hispanic	45.9	23.0	55.4	27.0	12.3	12.0
Black, non-Hispanic	21.3	22.3	27.0	27.7	5.3	16.1
Hispanic	27.2	27.0	30.2	24.9	6.6	12.8
POPULATION DENSITY						
Large metro	38.1	19.8	42.8	24.1	9.8	11.7
Small metro	45.0	26.3	61.2	26.7	12.4	12.1
Nonmetro	38.2	26.2	49.6	32.2	9.9	14.3
REGION						
Northeast	27.2	20.1	*	*	5.9	15.4
North Central	49.1	34.0	54.5	36.0	15.1	14.6
South	44.0	25.6	53.6	23.1	10.4	12.6
West	36.4	13.5	56.1	13.0	10.8	7.3
ADULT EDUCATION [2]						
Less than 12 years	28.2	34.8	*	36.1	5.9	18.7
High school graduate	42.7	26.5	51.5	31.6	9.6	14.8
Some college	48.3	21.7	62.3	22.9	13.7	10.8
College graduate	48.0	4.4	*	*	13.2	4.8
CURRENT EMPLOYMENT [3]						
Full-time	48.1	24.8	55.7	26.2	14.9	12.2
Part-time	38.5	20.0	*	*	9.3	13.0
Unemployed	32.1	18.2	*	*	12.6	14.6
Other [4]	29.6	22.4	*	22.1	3.9	11.5

SOURCE: Substance Abuse and Mental Health Services Administration, Office of Applied Studies. National Household Survey on Drug Abuse (NHSDA), Main Findings 1997: Table 11.6.

* Low precision; no estimate report.
1. The category "other" for race/ethnicity is not included.
2. Data on adult education are not applicable to youth age 12 to 17. Total refers to adults aged 18 or older (unweighted n = 16,661).
3. Data on current employment are not applicable for youth aged 12 to 17. Total refers to adults aged 18 or older (unweighted n = 16,661).
4. Retired, disabled, homemaker, student, or "other."

NOTE: Because of improved procedures implemented in 1994, these estimates are not comparable with those presented in NHSDA Main Findings prior to 1994. Illicit drug use indicates use at least once in the past month of marijuana or hashish, cocaine (including crack), inhalants, hallucinogens (including PCP and LSD), or heroin, or nonmedical use of psychotherapeutics. Heavy alcohol use is defined as drinking five or more drinks on the same occasion on each of five or more days in the past 30 days. *Same occasion* means at the same time or within a couple hours of each other.

Table 2.8. Hunger

(Percent of households)

State	Food insecure (with or without hunger)			Food insecure with hunger		
	1996	1997	1998	1996	1997	1998
United States	10.4	8.7	10.1	4.1	3.1	3.5
STATE						
Alabama	12.7	10.5	10.7	4.4	3.3	2.0
Alaska	7.5	9.3	6.0	3.6	3.9	2.9
Arizona	13.1	11.0	14.4	4.9	3.9	3.8
Arkansas	13.8	12.3	11.7	6.3	4.9	2.7
California	12.6	9.5	12.2	5.1	3.0	4.1
Colorado	10.2	8.1	8.0	4.8	3.0	2.3
Connecticut	8.7	9.2	8.6	4.0	4.5	3.0
Delaware	6.1	6.2	8.1	3.1	1.1	3.7
Florida	13.4	9.6	11.4	5.2	3.5	3.9
Georgia	11.3	8.2	9.6	4.3	1.8	3.5
Hawaii	11.2	8.3	11.7	3.1	2.3	2.9
Idaho	11.5	8.6	10.3	4.4	2.0	3.5
Illinois	9.6	7.2	8.0	3.8	2.5	2.9
Indiana	6.6	9.2	7.5	2.8	2.6	3.0
Iowa	6.9	6.8	7.3	2.3	3.1	2.0
Kansas	10.4	10.4	9.0	3.9	4.2	4.0
Kentucky	9.2	6.8	9.1	3.3	2.6	3.6
Louisiana	13.3	10.4	14.8	3.8	3.6	5.7
Maine	8.2	8.7	9.3	3.9	3.8	3.3
Maryland	8.3	6.6	6.3	3.6	2.6	2.9
Massachusetts	4.8	6.4	7.6	1.5	1.6	2.9
Michigan	9.1	7.7	7.5	4.0	2.7	2.0
Minnesota	7.0	7.0	6.7	3.1	3.3	2.3
Mississippi	17.2	11.4	13.4	6.5	3.3	2.9
Missouri	9.6	7.8	8.3	3.3	2.9	2.6
Montana	9.1	10.1	11.5	2.4	3.2	3.5
Nebraska	8.0	7.0	7.5	2.2	2.3	2.6
Nevada	9.3	7.3	9.3	4.6	2.5	4.0
New Hampshire	7.6	6.1	8.4	3.6	2.0	3.3
New Jersey	6.4	6.5	9.0	3.0	2.1	3.3
New Mexico	17.0	12.3	16.0	5.2	3.7	5.3
New York	9.5	9.9	10.7	3.8	4.2	3.7
North Carolina	11.1	7.2	8.0	4.2	1.7	1.8
North Dakota	4.0	3.5	6.4	1.2	1.1	1.8
Ohio	9.5	7.9	8.0	3.9	3.1	3.1
Oklahoma	11.7	9.3	14.7	5.4	2.3	5.0
Oregon	11.4	10.8	15.6	6.2	4.4	6.8
Pennsylvania	7.1	6.6	7.5	2.5	2.1	2.4
Rhode Island	10.9	6.5	8.6	3.6	1.2	3.0
South Carolina	11.2	10.0	9.3	3.4	2.9	4.0
South Dakota	6.8	4.7	7.8	1.9	1.5	2.8
Tennessee	9.8	10.1	12.8	3.8	3.8	5.2
Texas	13.3	12.0	13.6	5.6	4.0	5.2
Utah	10.5	6.0	10.0	4.0	1.4	3.9
Vermont	8.1	5.5	9.5	3.0	1.2	3.7
Virginia	9.9	7.9	7.1	2.8	3.4	2.7
Washington	12.6	10.6	12.5	4.6	4.1	5.0
West Virginia	10.8	6.3	9.8	4.0	2.0	3.3
Wisconsin	7.8	6.2	7.8	2.2	3.1	1.7
Wyoming	8.9	9.1	9.1	3.4	4.1	2.5
OTHER						
District of Columbia	10.4	11.1	11.8	5.0	3.9	4.8
Median	9.6	8.2	9.1	3.8	3.0	3.3
Low	4.0	3.5	6.0	1.2	1.1	1.7
High	17.2	12.3	16.0	6.5	4.9	6.8

SOURCE: M. Nord, K. Jemison, and G. Bickel, *Measuring Food Security in the United States: Prevalence of Food Insecurity and Hunger, by State, 1996–1998*. Food and Rural Economics Division, Economic Research Service, U.S. Department of Agriculture. Food Assistance and Nutrition Research Report, No. 2. Based on Current Population Survey Food Security Supplement data, September 1996, April 1997, and August 1998.

NOTE: Care should be exercised in assessing trends over time for individual states. The margin of error for a single year's estimated prevalence is about 1.73 times that for the three-year average reported in Table 1. *Food security* has been defined as assured access to enough food for an active, healthy life. The household should have access to enough food, the food should be nutritionally adequate, it should be safe, and the household should be able to obtain it through normal channels. When food insecurity reaches severe levels, actual hunger for household members is the result.

Table 2.9. Hunger in the United States: 1998

(Number in thousands)

Characteristic	Total	Food secure	Food insecure		
			Total insecure	Without hunger	With hunger
ALL HOUSEHOLDS					
Total households	103 480	92 972	10 509	6 820	3 689
Adults in households	196 972	174 761	22 210	15 646	6 564
Children in households	71 296	57 252	14 044	10 653	3 391
HOUSEHOLD COMPOSITION					
With children under 6 years	17 176	14 381	2 796	2 132	664
With children under 18 years	38 178	32 365	5 812	4 216	1 596
Married couple families	26 415	23 873	2 542	2 019	523
Female head, no spouse	8 826	6 013	2 813	1 898	915
Male head, no spouse	2 167	1 832	336	225	111
Other household with child [1]	769	647	122	75	47
With no children under 18	65 302	60 607	4 695	2 603	2 092
More than one adult	38 691	36 634	2 057	1 219	838
Women living alone	15 525	14 091	1 434	807	627
Men living alone	11 086	9 882	1 203	577	626
Households with elderly	24 478	23 131	1 346	913	433
Elderly living alone	10 129	9 577	552	349	203
RACE/ ETHNICITY OF HOUSEHOLDS					
White, non-Hispanic	78 294	72 700	5 594	3 650	1 944
Black, non-Hispanic	12 529	9 941	2 588	1 560	1 028
Hispanic [2]	8 721	6 823	1 898	1 313	585
Other, non-Hispanic	3 937	3 508	429	298	131
HOUSEHOLD INCOME-TO-POVERTY RATIO					
Under 0.50	5 205	3 187	2 018	1 202	816
Under 1.00	12 358	7 980	4 378	2 712	1 666
Under 1.30	18 018	12 261	5 757	3 630	2 127
Under 1.85	29 540	21 985	7 555	4 870	17
1.85 and over	61 775	59 482	2 293	1 558	735
Income not known	12 165	11 505	660	391	269
AREA OF RESIDENCE [3]					
Inside metropolitan area	83 189	74 824	8 364	5 361	3 003
In central city	26 682	22 903	3 778	2 286	1 492
Not in central city	42 196	38 969	3 227	2 178	1 049
Outside metropolitan area	20 291	18 148	2 142	1 458	684
CENSUS GEOGRAPHIC REGION					
Northeast	19 635	17 852	1 784	1 161	623
Midwest	24 321	22 446	1 875	1 235	640
South	37 328	33 188	4 139	2 653	1 486
West	22 196	19 486	2 710	1 770	940

See footnotes at end of table.

Table 2.9. Hunger in the United States: 1998—*Continued*

(Percent)

Characteristic	Total	Food secure	Food insecure		
			Total insecure	Without hunger	With hunger
ALL HOUSEHOLDS					
Total households	100.0	89.8	10.2	6.6	
Adults in households	100.0	88.7	11.3	7.9	3.6
Children in households	100.0	80.3	19.7	14.9	3.3
					4.8
HOUSEHOLD COMPOSITION					
With children under 6 years	100.0	83.7	16.3	12.4	
With children under 18 years	100.0	84.8	15.2	11.0	3.9
Married couple families	100.0	90.4	9.6	7.6	4.2
Female head, no spouse	100.0	68.1	31.9	21.5	2.0
Male head, no spouse	100.0	84.5	15.5	10.4	10.4
Other household with child [1]	100.0	84.2	15.9	9.7	5.1
With no children under 18	100.0	92.8	7.2	4.0	6.1
More than one adult	100.0	94.7	5.3	3.2	3.2
Women living alone	100.0	90.8	9.2	5.2	2.2
Men living alone	100.0	89.1	10.9	5.2	4.0
Households with elderly	100.0	94.5	5.5	3.7	5.6
Elderly living alone	100.0	94.6	5.4	3.4	1.8
					2.0
RACE/ETHNICITY OF HOUSEHOLDS					
White, non-Hispanic	100.0	92.9	7.1	4.7	
Black, non-Hispanic	100.0	79.3	20.7	12.4	2.5
Hispanic [2]	100.0	78.2	21.8	15.1	8.2
Other, non-Hispanic	100.0	89.1	10.9	7.6	6.7
					3.3
HOUSEHOLD INCOME-TO-POVERTY RATIO					
Under 0.50	100.0	61.2	38.8	23.1	
Under 1.00	100.0	64.6	35.4	21.9	15.7
Under 1.30	100.0	68.0	32.0	20.1	13.5
Under 1.85	100.0	74.4	25.6	16.5	11.8
1.85 and over	100.0	96.3	3.7	2.5	9.1
Income not known	100.0	94.6	5.4	3.2	1.2
					2.2
AREA OF RESIDENCE [3]					
Inside metropolitan area	100.0	89.9	10.1	6.4	
In central city	100.0	85.8	14.2	8.6	3.6
Not in central city	100.0	92.4	7.6	5.2	5.6
Outside metropolitan area	100.0	89.4	10.6	7.2	2.5
					3.4
CENSUS GEOGRAPHIC REGION					
Northeast	100.0	90.9	9.1	5.9	
Midwest	100.0	92.3	7.7	5.1	3.2
South	100.0	88.9	11.1	7.1	2.6
West	100.0	87.8	12.2	8.0	4.0
					4.2

SOURCE: G. Bickel, S. Carlson, and M. Nord. "Measuring Food Security in the United States," *Household Food Security in the United States, 1995–1998* (Advance Report. Food and Nutrition Service U.S. Department of Agriculture, July 1999.): Table 2D.

1. Households with children in complex living arrangements (e.g., children of other relatives or unrelated roommate or border).
2. Hispanics may be of any race.
3. Subtotals do not add to metropolitan totals because central city residence is not identified for some areas. Households not identified as to area were 0.88 percent of all households.

NOTE: *Food security* is defined as assured access to enough food for an active, healthy life. *Food insecurity* is defined as inadequate access to enough food to meet basic needs. When food insecurity reaches severe levels, actual hunger results.

Table 2.10. What People Actually Eat: 1996

(Averages per day)

Characteristic	Food energy (kilocalories)	Protein (grams)	Total fat (grams)	Saturated fatty acids (grams)	Monusaturated fatty acids (grams)	Polyunsaturated fatty acids (grams)	Cholesterol (milligrams)	Total carbohydrate (grams)	Dietary fiber (grams)
MALES AND FEMALES									
Under 1 year	851	21.2	36.9	15.5	11.8	7.8	43	109.5	3.6
1–2 years	1 300	49.1	48.0	19.8	17.5	7.2	189	172.9	9.0
3–5 years	1 600	55.6	57.7	22.0	21.9	9.5	184	220.7	10.6
5 years and under	1 402	49.0	51.7	20.4	19.1	8.5	167	190.2	9.2
MALES									
6–11 years	1 960	68.1	72.1	26.4	27.8	12.5	207	266.8	13.5
12–19 years	2 807	99.6	106.1	38.0	41.8	18.3	325	365.3	17.0
20–29 years	2 781	100.3	102.3	34.6	39.7	19.9	348	344.1	18.3
30–39 years	2 596	100.4	99.5	34.2	38.3	19.3	331	314.0	19.5
40–49 years	2 508	94.8	94.5	31.2	37.0	18.9	322	309.3	18.8
50–59 years	2 292	91.0	87.3	29.1	33.6	17.6	336	279.5	19.5
60–69 years	2 018	80.3	74.1	24.4	27.8	16.0	289	252.9	18.8
70 years and over	1 785	69.7	66.4	21.6	25.7	13.7	254	227.7	17.8
20 years and over	2 435	92.8	91.5	30.7	35.4	18.2	322	299.8	18.9
FEMALES									
6–11 years	1 782	61.6	64.9	23.8	24.9	11.3	190	244.7	12.5
12–19 years	1 913	64.0	69.2	24.1	26.4	13.5	193	263.2	13.5
20–29 years	1 877	63.2	65.9	21.9	25.2	13.8	208	257.0	14.7
30–39 years	1 782	65.7	65.0	22.3	24.5	13.3	204	232.6	14.7
40–49 years	1 681	62.4	64.1	21.2	24.3	13.7	215	210.5	13.9
50–59 years	1 632	63.9	59.9	18.7	22.8	13.7	203	210.6	14.6
60–69 years	1 482	59.5	54.5	17.2	20.6	12.4	208	188.8	13.5
70 years and over	1 390	56.8	50.1	15.8	19.3	10.8	189	182.8	14.0
20 years and over	1 673	62.5	61.1	20.1	23.2	13.1	205	218.2	14.3
ALL INDIVIDUALS	2 005	74.0	74.3	25.4	28.5	14.6	247	257.9	15.4

Characteristic	Vitamin A (micrograms retinol equivalents)	Carotenes (micrograms retinol equivalents)	Vitamin E (micrograms alpha-tocopherol equivalents)	Vitamin C (milligrams)	Thiamin (milligrams)	Riboflavin (milligrams)	Niacin (milligrams)	Vitamin B-6 (milligrams)	Folate (micrograms)
MALES AND FEMALES									
Under 1 year	807	246	11	113	0.94	1.34	10.5	0.64	120
1–2 years	719	263	4	98	1.09	1.69	12.0	1.24	173
3–5 years	761	264	5	95	1.34	1.78	15.9	1.42	213
5 years and under	753	262	6	98	1.20	1.69	13.9	1.26	188
MALES									
6–11 years	878	241	6	91	1.68	2.19	21.1	1.77	263
12–19 years	1 057	412	9	114	2.18	2.57	28.0	2.15	292
20–29 years	948	444	10	113	1.94	2.25	28.4	2.19	302
30–39 years	1 041	518	10	102	1.97	2.28	29.2	2.20	311
40–49 years	1 085	561	10	103	1.89	2.18	27.8	2.13	302
50–59 years	1 218	587	10	108	1.79	2.14	25.9	2.03	299
60–69 years	1 231	679	10	103	1.79	2.11	24.0	2.13	318
70 years and over	1 163	595	8	105	1.61	1.87	21.3	1.86	281
20 years and over	1 087	545	10	106	1.87	2.17	26.9	2.12	303
FEMALES									
6–11 years	856	327	6	86	1.46	1.88	18.1	1.55	232
12–19 years	793	337	8	93	1.51	1.73	19.9	1.59	247
20–29 years	954	549	7	107	1.39	1.60	18.5	1.49	241
30–39 years	889	520	7	96	1.43	1.63	19.4	1.55	235
40–49 years	896	528	8	84	1.33	1.56	18.7	1.50	223
50–59 years	831	449	7	91	1.33	1.53	18.6	1.46	221
60–69 years	826	490	7	90	1.28	1.48	17.4	1.43	207
70 years and over	1 006	510	6	95	1.23	1.51	17.6	1.54	226
20 years and over	904	513	7	94	1.35	1.56	18.5	1.50	228
ALL INDIVIDUALS	952	(NA)	(NA)	(NA)	(NA)	1.89	21.7	1.75	256

See footnotes at end of table.

Table 2.10. What People Actually Eat: 1996—*Continued*

(Averages per day)

Characteristic	Vitamin B-12 (micrograms)	Calcium (milligrams)	Phophorus (milligrams)	Magnesium (milligrams)	Iron (milligrams)	Zinc (milligrams)	Copper (milligrams)	Sodium (milligrams)	Potassium (milligrams)
MALES AND FEMALES									
Under 1 year	2.04	670	529	103	16.0	6.6	0.7	449	1 119
1–2 years	3.20	869	972	189	10.4	7.3	0.7	1 888	1 977
3–5 years	3.35	824	1 029	200	12.6	8.7	0.8	2 485	2 004
5 years and under	3.13	819	945	183	12.3	8.0	0.7	2 020	1 881
MALES									
6–11 years	4.21	940	1 242	237	16.5	11.0	1.0	3 191	2 350
12–19 years	5.69	1 148	1 635	302	19.8	14.9	1.4	4 643	3 004
20–29 years	6.37	970	1 594	322	19.0	14.0	1.5	4 487	3 091
30–39 years	7.23	933	1 554	338	19.4	14.8	1.5	4 241	3 234
40–49 years	7.20	852	1 450	325	19.6	13.5	1.5	4 071	3 238
50–59 years	7.26	845	1 434	326	17.2	13.5	1.5	3 853	3 236
60–69 years	5.07	828	1 303	307	18.0	12.3	1.3	3 469	3 056
70 years and over	4.47	714	1 157	278	15.9	10.7	1.2	3 071	2 793
20 years and over	6.55	879	1 459	321	18.6	13.5	1.5	4 009	3 143
FEMALES									
6–11 years	3.88	836	1 106	215	14.1	9.6	0.9	2 795	2 156
12–19 years	3.57	739	1 081	225	13.9	9.8	1.1	3 010	2 212
20–29 years	3.91	678	1 067	231	13.8	9.2	1.1	3 068	2 299
30–39 years	3.64	679	1 074	240	13.5	9.9	1.1	2 977	2 392
40–49 years	4.34	623	998	230	13.2	9.2	1.0	2 729	2 291
50–59 years	3.83	617	1 019	244	12.2	8.5	1.1	2 690	2 445
60–69 years	3.36	600	954	225	11.7	8.3	1.0	2 480	2 310
70 years and over	4.34	568	925	227	12.9	8.3	1.0	2 363	2 335
20 years and over	3.92	635	1 017	234	13.1	9.0	1.0	2 768	2 346
ALL INDIVIDUALS	4.84	793	1 214	262	15.5	11.0	1.2	3 266	2 597

SOURCE: U.S. Department of Agriculture, Agricultural Research Service. 1997. Data tables: Results from USDA's 1996 Continuing Survey of Food Intakes by Individuals and 1996 Diet and Health Knowledge Survey. Table 1.

NOTE: Excludes breastfed children.

Table 2.11. Recommended Dietary Allowances: 1997

Compound	Units	Adult males	Adult females	Children 7–10 years	Infants	Pregnant and lactating women [*]
Protein	g	63	50	28	14	65
Vitamin A	RE	1 000	800	*700	*375	1,300
Vitamin D	IU	200	200	*200	*200	*200
Vitamin E	mg alphaTE	10	8	7	4	12
Vitamin K	ug	80	65	30	10	65
Vitamin C	mg	60	60	45	35	95
Folate	ug	200	180	100	35	400
Thiamin (B1)	mg	1.5	1.1	1.0	0.4	1.6
Riboflavin (B2)	mg	1.7	1.3	1.2	0.5	1.8
Niacin	mg	19	15	13	6	20
Pyridoxine (B6)	mg	2	1.6	1.4	0.6	2.2
Cyanocobalamine (B12)	ug	2	2	1.4	0.5	2.6
Biotin	mg	30–100	30–100	30	15	30–100
Pantothenic Acid	mg	4–7	4–7	4–5	3	4–7
Calcium (Ca)	mg	*1,000	*800	800	*270	*1,000
Phosphorus (P)	mg	**700	**700	**500	*275	**700
Iodine (I)	ug	150	150	120	50	200
Iron (Fe)	mg	**10	**15	**10	*10	30
Magnesium (Mg)	mg	**400	**310	**130	*75	**310–350
Copper (Cu)	mg	1.5–3	1.5–3	1–2	0.6–0.7	1.5–3
Zinc (Zn)	mg	15	12	10	5	19
Selenium (Se)	ug	70	55	30	15	75
Chromium (Cr)	ug	50–200	50–200	50–200	10–60	50–200
Molybdenum (Mo)	ug	75–250	75–250	50–150	15–40	75–250
Manganese (Mn)	mg	2–5	2–5	2–3	0.3–1.0	2–5
Fluoride (F)	mg	4.0	3.0	1.0	0.5	3.0
Sodium (Na)	mg	500	500	400	120–200	500
Chloride (Cl)	mg	750	750	600	180–300	750
Potassium (K)	mg	2 000	2 000	1 600	500–700	2 000

SOURCE: Nutrition Health Reports. U.S. Recommended Dietary Allowances (RDA).

* AI (Adequate Intake) from the new Dietary Reference Intakes, 1997: Calcium, Phosphorus, Magnesium, Vitamin D, and Fluoride. Values have changed from the previous RDA.
** RDA from the new Dietary Reference Intakes, 1997: Calcium, Phosphorus, Magnesium, Vitamin D, and Fluoride. Values have changed from the previous RDA.
1. Generally the higher number was reported.

NOTE: g = grams, mg = milligrams (0.001 g), ug = micrograms (0.000001g), IU = International Units, RE = Retinol Equivalent, alphaTE = alpha Tocopherol equivalent.

Table 2.12. Taking Vitamin and Mineral Supplements: 1994–1995

(Percent of individuals)

Characteristic	Individuals using supplements	Type of supplement			
		Multivitamin	Multivitamin with iron or other minerals	Combination of vitamin C and iron	Single vitamins/ minerals
MALES AND FEMALES					
Under 1 year	18.6	6.1	7.5	0.0	5.2
1–2 years	46.2	21.5	20.6	1.7	3.9
3–5 years	58.9	31.4	23.4	3.2	4.3
5 years and under	49.7	24.9	20.5	2.3	4.3
MALES					
6–11 years	46.9	24.7	17.7	3.6	4.1
12–19 years	31.3	16.2	6.4	4.7	9.3
20–29 years	36.6	20.4	8.7	3.5	9.9
30–39 years	41.1	21.5	13.9	3.9	10.4
40–49 years	42.0	21.2	11.4	1.7	14.3
50–59 years	45.0	22.4	11.3	3.0	19.0
60–69 years	45.5	20.9	13.7	2.0	19.0
70 years and over	44.8	20.0	12.9	2.4	20.6
20 years and over	41.6	21.1	11.8	2.9	14.1
FEMALES					
6–11 years	10.6	20.2	14.1	3.0	5.2
12–19 years	40.6	17.5	11.2	5.5	11.3
20–29 years	51.0	23.2	21.0	4.5	12.9
30–39 years	56.0	21.9	24.6	4.2	16.4
40–49 years	56.2	23.0	19.2	4.4	24.4
50–59 years	61.8	27.5	20.2	4.9	29.5
60–69 years	55.0	20.9	17.9	2.5	27.4
70 years and over	53.6	23.4	15.6	2.3	23.4
20 years and over	55.5	23.3	20.4	3.9	21.2
ALL INDIVIDUALS	47.0	21.9	15.8	3.5	14.6

SOURCE: U.S. Department of Agriculture, Agricultural Research Service. 1997. Data tables: Results from USDA's 1994–1996 Continuing Survey of Food Intakes by Individuals and 1994–1996 Diet and Health Knowledge Survey. On: 1994–1996 Continuing Survey of Food Intakes by Individuals and 1994–1996 Diet and Health Knowledge Survey. CD-ROM, NTIS Accession Number PB98-500457: Table 19.

NOTE: Excludes breastfed children. Respondents were asked, "How often, if at all, do you take any vitamin or mineral supplement in pill or liquid form? Would you say every day or almost every day, every so often, or not at all." Respondents who chose a category other than "not at all" were asked, "Looking at this card, which of these types of supplements do you usually take—a multivitamin; multivitamin with iron or other minerals; combination of vitamin C and iron; or single vitamins or minerals?" Responses are provided as a percent of all individuals, not just those who used supplements. Because multiple answers were possible and the categories "don't know" and "not ascertained" are not included in the table, percentages across a row may not add to the percentage in the column "Individuals using supplements."

Table 2.13. People Who Do Not Exercise[1]

(Percent of adults age 18 years and over)

Characteristic	1991 National Health Interview Survey (NHIS)[2]	1988–1991 Third National Health and Nutrition Examination Survey (NHANES III)[2]	1992 Behavioral Risk Factor Surveillance System (BRFSS)[2,3]
Total	24.3	21.7	28.7
SEX			
Males	21.4	15.8	26.5
Females	26.9	27.1	30.7
RACE AND ETHNICITY			
White, non-Hispanic	22.5	18.2	26.8
Males	20.3	12.9	25.3
Females	24.6	23.1	28.2
Black, non-Hispanic	28.4	30.4	38.5
Males	22.5	20.6	33.1
Females	33.2	38.1	42.7
Hispanic[4]	33.6	36.0	34.8
Males	29.6	29.1	30.2
Females	37.4	43.8	39.0
Other	26.7	*	31.4
Males	22.8	*	27.6
Females	30.8	*	35.8
AGE			
Males			
18–29 years	17.6	12.5	18.9
30–44 years	21.1	14.5	25.0
45–64 years	23.9	16.9	32.0
65–74 years	23.0	17.5	33.2
75 years and over	27.1	34.5	38.2
Females			
18–29 years	25.0	17.4	25.4
30–44 years	25.2	24.9	26.9
45–64 years	27.4	29.4	32.1
65–74 years	27.8	32.5	36.6
75 years and over	37.9	54.3	50.5
EDUCATION			
Less than 12 years	37.1	34.5	46.5
12 years	25.9	20.8	32.8
Some college (13–15 years)	19.0	15.7	22.6
College (16 years or more)	14.2	11.1	17.8
INCOME[5]			
Under $10,000	30.3	34.5	41.5
$10,000–19,999	30.2	28.5	34.6
$20,000–34,999	24.3	18.7	26.9
$35,000–49,999	19.5	15.9	23.0
Over $50,000	14.4	10.9	17.7
GEOGRAPHIC REGION			
Northeast	25.9	21.6	29.5
North Central	20.8	16.7	28.6
South	27.0	24.8	32.4
West	22.5	22.6	22.0

SOURCE: U.S. Department of Health and Human Services, *Physical Activity and Health: A Report of the Surgeon General.* (Atlanta, Ga.: U.S. Department of Health and Human Services, Centers for Disease Control and Prevention, National Center for Chronic Disease Prevention and Health Promotion, 1996.): Table 5-2.

* Estimates unreliable.
1. No participation in leisure-time physical activity.
2. NHIS asked about the prior two weeks; BRFSS asked about the prior month.
3. Based on data from 48 states and the District of Columbia.
4. Hispanic reflects Mexican-Americans in NHANES III.
5. Annual income per family (NHIS) or household (BRFSS).

Table 2.14. Physical Activity: 1994

(Percent of adults age 18 years and over)

Area	No activity	Regular, sustained activity	Regular, vigorous activity
United States	29.4	19.7	14.0
STATE			
Alabama	45.9	17.1	11.2
Alaska	22.8	28.3	15.1
Arizona	23.7	17.8	17.9
Arkansas	35.1	17.2	10.7
California	21.8	21.9	15.7
Colorado	17.2	26.5	15.9
Connecticut	22.1	26.9	16.9
Delaware	36.4	17.7	14.1
Florida	28.0	23.8	20.0
Georgia	33.0	18.0	13.5
Hawaii	20.8	25.5	18.3
Idaho	21.9	26.3	15.7
Illinois	33.5	15.7	14.6
Indiana	29.7	18.8	13.0
Iowa	33.2	15.9	13.3
Kansas	34.5	16.8	13.9
Kentucky	45.9	13.2	11.3
Louisiana	33.5	16.8	11.3
Maine	40.7	13.0	11.3
Maryland	30.5	17.6	14.5
Massachusetts	24.0	23.2	17.4
Michigan	23.1	21.8	14.5
Minnesota	21.8	20.1	15.4
Mississippi	38.5	14.0	9.8
Missouri	32.0	18.0	10.8
Montana	21.0	21.8	15.0
Nebraska	24.3	16.7	14.7
Nevada	21.7	25.3	14.1
New Hampshire	25.8	21.2	17.0
New Jersey	30.9	20.7	11.6
New Mexico	19.8	25.5	18.4
New York	37.1	14.8	10.6
North Carolina	42.8	12.7	9.3
North Dakota	32.0	20.2	13.9
Ohio	38.0	15.9	12.4
Oklahoma	30.4	23.0	11.1
Oregon	20.8	27.3	18.7
Pennsylvania	26.5	21.2	14.5
South Carolina	31.4	15.1	11.9
South Dakota	30.8	19.4	11.9
Tennessee	39.7	15.0	12.7
Texas	27.8	20.7	13.0
Utah	21.0	21.6	14.3
Vermont	23.3	25.7	18.4
Virginia	23.0	24.6	14.6
Washington	18.2	25.7	16.8
West Virginia	45.3	14.3	9.8
Wisconsin	25.9	22.7	12.7
Wyoming	20.9	27.9	16.3
OTHER			
District of Columbia	48.6	11.6	8.7

SOURCE: U.S. Department of Health and Human Services, *Physical Activity and Health: A Report of the Surgeon General*. (Atlanta, Ga.: U.S. Department of Health and Human Services, Centers for Disease Control and Prevention, National Center for Chronic Disease Prevention and Health Promotion, 1996.): Table 5-3. Based on data from the Behavioral Risk Factor Surveillance System, 1994.

NOTE: Data for Rhode Island were unavailabe.

Table 2.15. People Who Exercise Regularly [1]

(Percent of adults age 18 years and over)

Characteristic	1991 National Health Interview Survey (NHIS) [2]	1992 Behavioral Risk Factor Surveillance System (BRFSS) [2,3]
Total	23.5	20.1
SEX		
Males	26.6	21.5
Females	20.7	18.9
RACE AND ETHNICITY		
White, non-Hispanic	24.0	20.8
Males	26.7	21.9
Females	21.5	19.8
Black, non-Hispanic	22.9	15.2
Males	28.9	18.5
Females	18.0	12.6
Hispanic	20.0	20.1
Males	23.7	21.4
Females	16.5	18.9
Other	23.4	17.3
Males	25.5	19.7
Females	21.1	14.5
AGE		
Males		
18–29 years	32.0	26.8
30–44 years	24.1	17.4
45–64 years	24.2	18.9
65–74 years	29.2	26.8
75 years and over	24.6	23.2
Females		
18–29 years	23.2	19.9
30–44 years	20.4	18.5
45–64 years	20.6	19.4
65–74 years	21.3	19.0
75 years and over	13.8	15.0
EDUCATION		
Less than 12 years	18.1	15.6
12 years	21.9	17.8
Some college (13–15 years)	26.8	22.7
College (16 years or more)	28.5	23.5
INCOME [4]		
Under $10,000	23.6	17.6
$10,000–19,999	20.4	18.7
$20,000–34,999	23.2	20.3
$35,000–49,999	23.9	20.9
Over $50,000	28.0	23.5
GEOGRAPHIC REGION		
Northeast	23.9	20.2
North Central	24.2	18.2
South	21.1	19.0
West	26.1	24.0

SOURCE: U.S. Department of Health and Human Services, *Physical Activity and Health: A Report of the Surgeon General.* (Atlanta, Ga.: U.S. Department of Health and Human Services, Centers for Disease Control and Prevention, National Center for Chronic Disease Prevention and Health Promotion, 1996.): Table 5-4.

1. Participation in regular, sustained physical activity (5+ times per week for 30+ minutes per occasion).
2. NHIS asked about the prior two weeks; BRFSS asked about the prior month.
3. Based on data from 48 states and the District of Columbia.
4. Annual income per family (NHIS) or household (BRFSS).

Table 2.16. People Who Exercise Vigorously [1]

(Percent of adults age 18 years and over)

Characteristic	1991 National Health Interview Survey (NHIS) [2]	1992 Behavioral Risk Factor Surveillance System (BRFSS) [2,3]
Total	16.4	14.4
SEX		
Males	18.1	12.9
Females	14.9	15.8
RACE AND ETHNICITY		
White, non-Hispanic	17.2	15.3
Males	18.6	13.3
Females	15.9	17.1
Black, non-Hispanic	12.9	9.4
Males	16.0	9.5
Females	10.4	9.4
Hispanic	13.6	11.9
Males	15.6	12.4
Females	11.7	11.4
Other	16.8	11.8
Males	18.8	11.5
Females	14.8	12.2
AGE		
Males		
18–29 years	19.7	8.0
30–44 years	13.7	11.1
45–64 years	14.9	16.3
65–74 years	27.3	20.6
75 years and over	38.3	20.6
Females		
18–29 years	16.0	11.4
30–44 years	13.3	18.0
45–64 years	12.1	17.7
65–74 years	18.5	16.5
75 years and over	22.6	12.8
EDUCATION		
Less than 12 years	11.9	8.2
12 years	13.6	11.5
Some college (13–15 years)	18.9	14.9
College (16 years or more)	23.5	21.9
INCOME [4]		
Under $10,000	15.5	9.0
$10,000–19,999	14.4	10.8
$20,000–34,999	15.5	14.2
$35,000–49,999	16.0	16.3
Over $50,000	21.5	20.5
GEOGRAPHIC REGION		
Northeast	16.1	13.8
North Central	16.5	13.7
South	14.7	13.8
West	19.2	16.8

SOURCE: U.S. Department of Health and Human Services, *Physical Activity and Health: A Report of the Surgeon General.* (Atlanta, Ga.: U.S. Department of Health and Human Services, Centers for Disease Control and Prevention, National Center for Chronic Disease Prevention and Health Promotion, 1996.): Table 5-5.

1. Participation in regular, vigorous physical activity (3+ times per week for 20+ minutes per occasion at 50+ percent of estimate age- and sex-specific maximum cardiorespiratory capacity).
2. NHIS asked about the prior two weeks; BRFSS asked about the prior month.
3. Based on data from 48 states and the District of Columbia.
4. Annual income per family (NHIS) or household (BRFSS).

Table 2.17. Age Women Started Having Sexual Intercourse: 1995

(Women 20–44 years of age)

Characteristic	Number (thousands)	Percent reporting first intercourse before age			Mean age at first intercourse [1]
		15	18	20	
ALL WOMEN	51 240	9.2	52.3	75.0	17.8
AGE AT INTERVIEW					
20–24 years	9 041	13.6	62.2	80.2	16.6
25–29 years	9 693	10.9	54.9	75.0	17.5
30–34 years	11 065	10.1	53.1	75.8	17.8
35–39 years	11 211	7.6	52.2	75.2	18.0
40–44 years	10 230	4.6	40.6	69.2	18.6
FAMILY BACKGROUND					
Both parents from birth [2]	32 825	6.4	45.6	70.3	18.2
Single parent from birth	1 548	18.4	66.2	84.9	16.6
Both parents, then one parent	6 469	11.5	60.6	79.4	17.3
Stepparent [3]	6 655	15.2	70.4	88.1	16.6
Other	3 743	15.6	59.8	81.5	17.1
EDUCATION AT INTERVIEW [4]					
No high school diploma or GED [5]	5 424	20.4	73.0	87.1	16.5
High school diploma or GED [5]	18 169	11.2	59.8	83.1	17.3
Some college, no bachelor's degree ...	12 399	7.0	49.5	73.6	17.9
Bachelor's degree or higher	11 748	2.2	31.7	56.6	19.3
MOTHER'S EDUCATION					
0–11 years	15 798	11.5	55.3	77.1	17.6
12 years	21 813	9.1	54.0	77.5	17.6
13–15 years	6 866	7.2	47.8	70.1	18.1
16 years or more	6 456	5.1	43.0	65.7	18.3
No mother figure identified	307	31.8	81.5	90.9	15.9
RACE AND HISPANIC ORIGIN					
Hispanic	5 553	7.6	42.2	66.7	18.4
Non-Hispanic white	36 560	8.3	52.8	76.0	17.7
Non-Hispanic black	6 818	16.1	65.9	85.6	16.8
Non-Hispanic other	2 309	8.1	28.4	48.1	20.0

SOURCE: J. Abma, A. Chandra, W. Mosher, L. Peterson, L. Piccinino. National Center for Health Statistics. *Fertility, Family Planning, and Women's Health: New Data from the 1995 National Survey of Family Growth. Vital and Health Statistics* 23, no.19 (1997): Table 20. This table is based on recall regarding age when respondent started having sexual intercourse.

1. Mean ages are based only on women who ever had intercourse after menarche.
2. Includes women who lived with either both biological or both adoptive parents until they left home.
3. Parents separated or divorced, then custodial parent remarried.
4. Limited to women 22–44 years of age at time of interview.
5. GED is general equivalency diploma.

Table 2.18. Age of Women Who Have Had Sexual Intercourse: 1995

(Number in thousands)

Age and race and Hispanic origin	All women		Never-married women	
	Number	Percent	Number	Percent
All women [1]	60 201	89.3	22 679	71.5
AGE AT INTERVIEW				
15 years	1 690	22.1	1 674	21.4
16 years	1 874	38.0	1 874	38.0
17 years	1 889	51.1	1 831	49.6
18 years	1 771	65.4	1 641	62.7
19 years	1 737	75.5	1 542	72.4
15–19 years	8 961	50.4	8 562	48.1
15–17 years	5 452	37.6	5 379	36.8
18–19 years	3 508	70.4	3 183	67.4
20–24 years	9 041	88.6	5 939	82.6
25–29 years	9 693	95.9	3 456	88.6
30–44 years	32 506	98.2	4 722	87.4
AGE AT INTERVIEW AND RACE AND HISPANIC ORIGIN				
15–19 years				
Hispanic	1 150	55.0	1 078	52.0
White, non-Hispanic	5 962	49.5	5 693	47.1
Black, non-Hispanic	1 392	59.5	1 351	58.3
15–17 years				
Hispanic	688	50.0	673	48.8
White, non-Hispanic	3 534	34.9	3 485	33.9
Black, non-Hispanic	853	48.2	853	48.2
18–19 years				
Hispanic	462	62.5	405	57.2
White, non-Hispanic	2 428	70.7	2 208	67.8
Black, non-Hispanic	538	77.4	498	75.5

SOURCE: J. Abma, A. Chandra, W. Mosher, L. Peterson, L. Piccinino. National Center for Health Statistics: *Fertility, Family Planning, and Women's Health: New Data from the 1995 National Survey of Family Growth. Vital and Health Statistics* 23, no. 19 (1997): Table 19. Table based on information provided about the respondents' current status.

1. Includes women of other race and origin groups not shown separately.

Table 2.19. Sexual Behavior of High School Students

(Percent)

Year	Ever had sexual intercourse	Currently sexually active [1]	Condom use during last sexual intercourse [2]	Four or more sex partners during lifetime
SEX				
Male				
1991	57.4	23.4	36.8	54.5
1993	55.6	22.3	37.5	59.2
1995	54.0	20.9	35.5	60.5
1997	48.8	17.6	33.4	62.5
Female				
1991	50.8	13.8	38.2	38.0
1993	50.2	15.0	37.5	46.0
1995	52.1	14.4	40.4	48.6
1997	47.7	14.1	36.5	50.8
GRADE				
Nine				
1991	39.0	12.5	22.4	53.3
1993	37.7	10.9	24.8	61.6
1995	36.9	12.9	23.6	62.9
1997	38.0	12.2	24.2	58.8
Ten				
1991	48.2	15.1	33.2	46.3
1993	46.1	15.9	30.1	54.7
1995	48.0	15.6	33.7	59.7
1997	42.5	13.8	29.2	58.9
Eleven				
1991	62.4	22.1	43.3	48.7
1993	57.5	19.9	40.0	55.3
1995	58.6	19.0	42.4	52.3
1997	49.7	16.7	37.8	60.1
Twelve				
1991	66.7	25.0	50.6	41.4
1993	68.3	27.0	53.0	46.5
1995	66.4	22.9	49.7	49.5
1997	60.9	20.6	46.0	52.4
RACE/ETHNICITY [3]				
White, non-Hispanic				
1991	50.0	14.7	33.9	46.5
1993	48.4	14.3	34.0	52.3
1995	48.9	14.2	34.8	52.5
1997	43.6	11.6	32.0	55.8
Black, non-Hispanic				
1991	81.4	43.1	59.3	48.0
1993	79.7	42.7	59.1	56.5
1995	73.4	35.6	54.2	66.1
1997	72.6	38.5	53.6	64.0
Hispanic				
1991	53.1	16.8	37.0	37.4
1993	56.0	18.6	39.4	46.1
1995	57.6	17.6	39.3	44.4
1997	52.2	15.5	35.4	48.3
Total				
1991	54.1	18.7	37.4	46.2
1993	53.0	18.7	37.5	52.8
1995	53.1	17.8	37.9	54.4
1997	48.4	16.0	34.8	56.8

SOURCE: "Trends in Sexual Risk Behaviors Among High School Students — United States 1991–1997,"*Morbidity and Mortality Weekly Report* 47, no. 36 (September 18, 1998): Table 1. Data are based on questionnaire completed by high school students and does not include young people who were not attending school.

1. Sexual intercourse during three months preceding the survey.
2. Among currently sexually active students.
3. Numbers of students in other racial and ethnic groups were too small for meaningful analysis.

Table 2.20. Air Quality: 1997

(Percent of persons living in counties exceeding U.S. Environmental Protection Agency standards)

State	Carbon monoxide		Nitrogen oxides [1]		Volatile organic compounds [1]		Sulfur dioxide		Particulate matter (PM-10)	
	Rank	Emissions	Rank	Emissions	Rank	Emissions	Rank	Emissions	Rank	Emissions
United States		87 451		23 575		19 204		20 369		33 581
STATE										
Alabama	11	2 392	15	627	17	427	8	811	20	585
Alaska	42	486	49	42	46	64	51	5	41	183
Arizona	21	1 627	23	453	26	297	24	256	37	302
Arkansas	31	1 141	34	257	32	240	36	138	23	500
California	2	6 000	2	1 236	2	1 494	29	200	4	1 600
Colorado	28	1 259	25	414	28	293	35	141	26	476
Connecticut	39	747	40	153	35	165	40	90	45	101
Delaware	49	207	46	68	47	53	39	98	48	38
Florida	3	4 610	6	916	3	859	6	879	12	764
Georgia	4	3 917	11	691	11	595	13	639	7	1 017
Hawaii	48	212	47	49	50	30	47	34	49	33
Idaho	36	811	43	114	38	116	46	41	13	690
Illinois	8	3 046	4	1 129	4	851	4	1 190	8	1 007
Indiana	13	2 384	7	912	12	567	2	1 370	16	660
Iowa	33	997	29	329	30	257	22	273	21	580
Kansas	15	2 127	17	528	20	414	30	180	3	1 639
Kentucky	26	1 412	12	690	21	406	9	806	34	336
Louisiana	14	2 316	10	758	15	437	17	414	28	440
Maine	41	529	44	95	40	109	38	101	43	156
Maryland	30	1 160	28	331	31	243	19	387	40	208
Massachusetts	29	1 212	32	275	27	294	25	255	38	285
Michigan	9	2 996	8	839	7	705	12	653	22	530
Minnesota	25	1 476	22	463	22	398	32	168	10	962
Mississippi	23	1 565	27	351	25	339	27	235	25	479
Missouri	18	2 002	18	523	14	444	15	506	5	1 350
Montana	38	768	39	183	39	110	42	67	6	1 143
Nebraska	37	785	35	252	33	205	37	102	18	632
Nevada	40	545	41	135	42	98	43	65	44	150
New Hampshire	44	359	45	80	44	77	33	164	47	54
New Jersey	27	1 362	24	435	18	425	23	265	36	303
New Mexico	34	938	31	297	37	152	28	207	1	4 948
New York	7	3 116	13	667	5	767	11	663	11	818
North Carolina	10	2 759	14	643	8	685	14	610	24	480
North Dakota	46	317	36	239	41	99	20	308	29	412
Ohio	5	3 812	3	1 185	6	709	1	1 966	14	663
Oklahoma	20	1 733	20	470	23	350	26	239	9	999
Oregon	19	1 758	38	215	29	258	45	44	15	661
Pennsylvania	6	3 332	5	935	9	674	3	1 349	19	593
Rhode Island	50	203	50	31	48	50	49	13	50	27
South Carolina	22	1 606	26	364	24	340	21	299	30	410
South Dakota	45	317	42	120	43	78	44	57	35	311
Tennessee	12	2 391	9	797	10	610	7	840	32	384
Texas	1	6 479	1	1 843	1	1 615	5	1 151	2	3 307
Utah	32	1 029	37	233	34	170	41	83	39	248
Vermont	47	232	48	43	49	48	48	17	46	79
Virginia	16	2 082	16	564	13	492	16	486	27	445
Washington	17	2 062	30	325	16	431	34	150	31	392
West Virginia	35	843	19	516	36	157	10	759	42	158
Wisconsin	24	1 517	21	469	19	418	18	408	33	381
Wyoming	43	363	33	275	45	68	31	179	17	659
OTHER										
District of Columbia	51	111	51	19	51	21	50	9	51	4

SOURCE: Compiled from Environmental Protection Agency, and the Office of Air Quality Planning and Standards; Research Triangle Park, NC, December 1998. National Air Pollutant Emission Trends Update, 1970–1997: Table A-11. Based on actual measurements at 4,738 monitoring sites.

Table 2.20. Air Quality: 1997—*Continued*

(Percent of persons living in counties exceeding U.S. Environmental Protection Agency standards)

State	1992	1993	1994	1995	1996
United States	23.5	24.9	35.8	43.7	33.3
STATE					
Alabama	2.5	—	0.0	20.2	18.5
Alaska	60.1	55.3	55.9	55.9	55.1
Arizona	57.9	57.9	57.6	58.7	59.0
Arkansas	—		0.0	2.0	0.0
California	71.6	72.1	80.9	89.5	87.1
Colorado	14.0	0.0	13.6	26.6	0.9
Connecticut	96.9	79.9	100.0	100.0	37.6
Delaware	66.3	100.0	100.0	100.0	0.0
Florida	—		0.0	23.1	8.2
Georgia	20.4	10.0	10.9	23.6	19.5
Hawaii	—		11.5	11.6	11.7
Idaho	—	—	2.8	0.0	0.7
Illinois	2.4	2.5	58.3	48.0	50.4
Indiana	16.0	—	18.5	17.4	32.1
Iowa	—	—	8.6	8.6	13.4
Kansas	—		0.0	0.0	6.0
Kentucky	18.0	1.0	22.8	27.2	23.3
Louisiana	10.4	9.0	16.5	18.3	12.8
Maine	16.1	—	36.3	47.8	0.0
Maryland	44.3	42.4	60.9	79.9	25.3
Massachusetts	45.1	21.8	32.9	55.9	42.2
Michigan	0.3	32.0	50.6	58.2	43.2
Minnesota	—	11.1	10.6	10.5	0.0
Mississippi	—		0.0	0.0	3.2
Missouri	23.0	27.2	27.5	45.5	41.3
Montana	5.9	13.4	32.3	7.3	14.2
Nebraska	26.4	26.3	27.9	26.5	26.6
Nevada	61.7	82.9	64.4	65.0	65.4
New Hampshire	30.3	—	22.4	53.0	30.5
New Jersey	28.0	26.4	43.9	61.9	44.5
New Mexico	8.9	8.9	9.5	9.5	9.6
New York	8.8	26.5	47.6	54.0	24.7
North Carolina	8.3	—	0.0	13.8	18.9
North Dakota	—		0.0	0.0	0.0
Ohio	13.0	14.6	24.2	43.8	22.8
Oklahoma	—	16.0	35.3	35.2	16.1
Oregon	0.3	1.1	0.2	0.0	26.6
Pennsylvania	35.7	32.0	39.1	48.1	17.1
Rhode Island	—	—	75.1	74.9	0.0
South Carolina	12.0	—	0.0	0.9	1.4
South Dakota	—	—	0.0	0.0	11.9
Tennessee	22.0	16.9	18.7	21.0	41.8
Texas	35.0	29.8	35.3	46.9	47.1
Utah	24.5	—	57.9	52.4	57.4
Vermont	—	—	0.0	0.0	0.0
Virginia	16.9	16.0	14.5	29.8	13.5
Washington	7.4	32.0	46.9	36.8	7.3
West Virginia	2.0	2.0	12.1	7.2	1.9
Wisconsin	2.6	21.8	30.9	32.1	27.9
Wyoming	—	—	0.0	0.0	0.0
OTHER					
District of Columbia	—	66.3	65.4	82.1	0.0

SOURCE: Air quality data from *Healthy People 2000, Health Status Indicators, 1992–1996.*

— Data not available.
1. Excluding Biogenics.

Table 2.21. Occupational Injuries and Illnesses in Private Industry: 1997

Year	Injury incidence rate [2]				Number (in thousands)			
	Total cases	Lost workday cases		Cases without lost workdays	Total cases	Lost workday cases		Cases without lost workdays
		Total [3]	With days away from work [4]			Total [3]	With days away from work [4]	
1973	11.0	3.4	—	7.5	6 078.7	1 908.0	—	4 165.0
1974	10.4	3.5	—	6.9	5 915.8	2 001.8	—	3 908.1
1975	9.1	3.3	3.2	5.8	4 983.1	1 825.2	1 730.5	3 152.6
1976	9.2	3.5	3.3	5.7	5 163.7	1 978.8	1 875.4	3 180.4
1977	9.3	3.8	3.6	5.5	5 460.3	2 203.6	2 092.1	3 250.6
1978	9.4	4.1	3.8	5.3	5 799.4	2 492.0	2 327.5	3 302.0
1979	9.5	4.3	4.0	5.2	6 105.7	2 757.7	2 553.5	3 342.3
1980	8.7	4.0	3.7	4.7	5 605.8	2 539.9	2 353.8	3 060.4
1981	8.3	3.8	3.5	4.5	5 404.4	2 457.5	2 269.2	2 941.8
1982	7.7	3.5	3.2	4.2	4 856.4	2 182.4	2 016.2	2 668.6
1983	7.6	3.4	3.2	4.2	4 854.1	2 182.7	2 014.2	2 667.6
1984	8.0	3.7	3.4	4.3	5 419.7	2 501.5	2 303.7	2 913.4
1985	7.9	3.6	3.3	4.3	5 507.2	2 537.0	2 319.2	2 965.9
1986	7.9	3.6	3.3	4.3	5 629.0	2 590.3	2 356.9	3 034.6
1987	8.3	3.8	3.4	4.4	6 035.9	2 801.6	2 483.9	3 230.6
1988	8.6	4.0	3.5	4.6	6 440.4	2 977.8	2 585.8	3 458.7
1989	8.6	4.0	3.4	4.6	6 576.3	3 073.9	2 624.2	3 497.9
1990	8.8	4.1	3.4	4.7	6 753.0	3 123.8	2 613.5	3 625.6
1991	8.4	3.9	3.2	4.5	6 345.7	2 944.2	2 398.4	3 398.3
1992	8.9	3.9	3.0	5.0	6 799.4	2 953.4	2 331.1	3 846.0
1993	8.5	3.8	2.9	4.8	6 737.4	2 967.4	2 252.5	3 770.0
1994	8.4	3.8	2.8	4.6	6 766.9	3 061.0	2 236.6	3 705.9
1995	8.1	3.6	2.5	4.4	6 575.4	2 972.1	2 040.9	3 603.2
1996	7.4	3.4	2.2	4.1	6 238.9	2 832.5	1 880.6	3 406.4
1997	7.1	3.3	2.1	3.8	6 145.6	2 866.2	1 833.4	3 279.4

SOURCE: Bureau of Labor Statistics, U.S. Department of Labor. *Report on American Workforce* (1999): Table 54.

— Data not available.

1. Data for 1973–1975 are based on the *Standard Industrial Classification Manual*, 1967 Edition; data for 1976–1987 are based on the *Standard Industrial Classification Manual*, 1972 Edition; and data for 1988–1996 are based on the *Standard Industrial Classification Manual*, 1987 Edition.

2. The incidence rates represent the number of injuries and illnesses per 100 full-time workers and were calculated as
(n/eh) x 200,000, where
n = number of injuries and illnesses
eh = total hours worked by all employees during the calendar year
200,000 = base for 100 equivalent full-time workers (working 40 hours per week, 50 weeks per year).

3. Total includes cases involving restricted work activity only in addition to days-away-from-work cases with or without restricted work activity.

4. Days-away-from-work cases include those that result in days away from work with or without restricted work activity.

5. To maintain historical comparability with the rest of the series, data for small nonfarm employers in low-risk industries who were not surveyed were imputed and included in the survey estimates.

6. Data for 1992–1996 exclude fatal work-related injuries and illnesses.

NOTE: Because of rounding, components may not add to totals. Data for 1976–1997 exclude farms with fewer than 11 employees.

Table 2.22. Fatal Occupational Injuries: 1997

Occupation [1]	Fatalities		Employment [2] (in thousands)	Fatalities per 100,000 employed [3]
	Number	Percent		
Total	6 218	100.0	130 810	4.7
MANAGERIAL AND PROFESSIONAL SPECIALTY	667	10.7	37 686	1.8
Executive, administrative, and managerial	417	6.7	18 440	2.3
Professional specialty	250	4.0	19 245	1.3
TECHNICAL, SALES, AND ADMINISTRATIVE SUPPORT	733	11.8	38 309	1.9
Technicians and related support occupations	172	2.8	4 214	4.1
Airplane pilots and navigators	100	1.6	120	83.3
Sales occupations	458	7.4	15 734	2.9
Supervisors and proprietors, sales occupations	223	3.6	4 635	4.8
Salesworkers, retail and personal services	182	2.9	6 887	2.6
Cashiers	84	1.4	3 007	2.8
Administrative support occupations, including clerical	103	1.7	18 361	0.6
SERVICE OCCUPATIONS	492	7.9	17 537	2.8
Protective service occupations	283	4.6	2 300	12.3
Firefighting and fire prevention occupations, ...	49	0.8	268	18.3
Police and detectives, including supervisors	156	2.5	1 113	14.0
Guards, including supervisors	78	1.3	920	8.5
FARMING, FORESTRY, AND FISHING	923	14.8	3 503	25.9
Farm occupations	615	9.9	2 177	27.5
Forestry and logging occupations	128	2.1	108	118.5
Timber cutting and logging occupations	110	1.8	79	139.2
Fishers, hunters, and trappers	60	1.0	49	122.4
Fishers, including vessel captains and officers	58	0.9	47	123.4
PRECISION PRODUCTION, CRAFT, AND REPAIR	1 094	17.6	14 124	7.7
Mechanics and repairers	325	5.2	4 675	7.0
Construction trades	593	9.5	5 378	11.0
Carpenters	98	1.6	1 335	7.3
Electricians	94	1.5	774	12.1
Painters	39	0.6	545	7.2
Roofers	55	0.9	200	27.5
Structural metal workers	45	0.7	66	68.2
OPERATORS, FABRICATORS, AND LABORERS	2 161	34.8	18 399	11.7
Machine operators, assemblers, and inspectors	221	3.6	7 962	2.8
Transportation and material moving occupations	1 271	20.4	5 389	23.6
Motor vehicle operators	1 026	16.5	4 089	25.1
Truck drivers	857	13.8	3 075	27.9
Driver-sales workers	44	0.7	150	29.3
Taxicab drivers and chauffeurs	100	1.6	248	40.3
Material moving equipment operators	169	2.7	1 125	15.0
Handlers, equipment cleaners, helpers, and laborers	669	10.8	5 048	13.2
Construction laborers	333	5.4	811	41.1
Laborers, except construction	208	3.3	1 323	15.6
MILITARY [4]	94	1.5	1 252	7.5

SOURCE: Bureau of Labor Statistics, U.S. Department of Labor, in cooperation with state and federal agencies, Census of Fatal Occupational Injuries, 1997. *Report on American Workforce.* 1999: Table 49.

1. Based on the 1990 Occupational Classification System developed by the Bureau of the Census.
2. The employment figures, except for military, are annual average estimates of employed civilians, 16 years of age and older, from the Current Population Survey (CPS), 1997. The resident military figure, derived from resident and civilian population data from the Bureau of the Census, was added to the CPS employment total.
3. The rate represents the number of fatal occupational injuries per 100,000 employed workers and was calculated as follows: (n/w) x 100,000, where n = the number of fatal work injuries, and w = the number of employed workers. There were 21 fatally injured workers under the age of 16 years who were not included in the rate calculations to maintain consistency with the CPS employment.
4. Resident armed forces.

NOTE: Totals for major categories may include subcategories not shown separately. Percentages may not add to totals because of rounding. There were 64 fatalities for which there was insufficient information to determine an occupation classification.

Table 2.23. Exposure to Harmful Substances at Work: 1992

Sex, reported exposure to substance or radiation, and level of concern	Total [1]	Age				Race		Ethnicity	
		18–29 years	30–44 years	45–65 years	65 years and over	White	Black	Hispanic	Non-Hispanic
WOMEN									
Total (number in thousands)	53 189	13 868	22 405	5 222	1 694	44 792	6 415	3 460	49 729
Total (percent distribution)	100.0	100.0	100.0	100.0	100.0	100.0	100.0	100.0	100.0
Reported exposure to substances believed to be harmful if breathed or on skin:									
Yes	23.0	25.3	23.6	21.7	*7.8	23.0	25.1	24.2	22.9
No	73.7	71.9	73.0	75.7	79.9	73.9	71.7	70.7	73.9
Don't know	3.3	2.8	3.4	2.6	12.3	3.1	*3.2	5.0	3.2
Reported exposure to radiation [3]:									
Yes	4.8	5.5	5.7	3.2	*0.9	5.0	3.5	*4.2	4.8
No	92.0	91.7	91.1	93.9	88.8	91.9	93.8	89.8	92.2
Don't know	3.2	2.8	3.2	3.0	*10.3	3.1	*2.7	6.0	3.1
Reported exposure only (number in thousands)	12 813	3 677	5 549	3 439	148	10 850	1 637	852	11 962
Reported exposure only (percent distribution)	100.0	100.0	100.0	100.0	100.0	100.0	100.0	100.0	100.0
Concern level:									
Very concerned	25.6	21.5	27.6	26.6	(4)	23.4	39.2	*16.9	26.2
Somewhat concerned	27.3	30.1	27.7	24.3	(4)	27.5	27.0	*45.3	26.0
Slightly concerned	22.7	21.0	26.7	18.4	(4)	23.5	*15.5	*14.2	23.3
Not at all concerned	22.7	24.4	17.0	28.8	(4)	24.4	*13.4	*20.9	22.8
Unknown	1.8	2.9	1.0	*1.9	*99.9	*1.2	4.9	*2.7	*1.7
MEN									
Total (number in thousands)	63 813	17 284	26 630	17 673	2 226	54 909	6 335	4 459	59 354
Total (percent distribution)	100.0	100.0	100.0	100.0	100.0	100.0	100.0	100.0	100.0
Reported exposure to substances believed to be harmful if breathed or on skin:									
Yes	39.1	41.7	43.0	33.3	18.5	39.3	38.4	32.0	39.6
No	57.4	55.7	53.4	63.1	74.6	57.3	57.5	59.7	57.3
Don't know	3.5	2.7	3.6	3.6	*6.9	3.4	*4.1	8.3	3.1
Reported exposure to radiation [3]:									
Yes	6.3	4.7	8.0	5.7	*3.6	6.4	5.8	4.5	6.5
No	89.7	91.7	88.1	90.3	89.5	89.7	89.1	88.8	89.8
Don't know	4.0	3.7	3.8	4.1	*6.9	3.9	*5.1	6.8	3.8
Reported exposure only (number in thousands)	25 927	7 514	11 829	6 465	419	22 452	2 555	1 508	24 419
Reported exposure only (percent distribution)	100.0	100.0	100.0	100.0	100.0	100.0	100.0	100.0	100.0
Concern level:									
Very concerned	27.0	23.1	27.6	30.1	*36.0	23.1	57.0	29.3	26.9
Somewhat concerned	27.3	28.1	27.8	26.3	*14.6	28.4	21.3	29.8	27.1
Slightly concerned	26.0	30.5	25.5	22.4	*13.2	27.8	*10.5	25.2	26.1
Not at all concerned	18.5	*18.4	17.1	20.7	*32.6	19.6	*10.2	14.9	18.8
Unknown	1.1	*99.9	2.1	*0.6	3.6	*1.1	1.0	0.9	*1.2
NUMBER OF PERSONS INTERVIEWED									
Women	3 600	924	1 559	968	149	2 968	525	312	3 288
Reported exposure	846	239	385	210	12	709	118	66	780
Men	3 620	953	1 622	914	131	3 148	341	369	3 251
Reported exposure	1 443	406	708	301	28	1 259	132	125	1 318

See footnotes at end of table.

Table 2.23. Exposure to Harmful Substances at Work: 1992—*Continued*

Sex, reported exposure to substance or radiation, and level of concern	Educational level				Major occupational group			
	Less than 12 years	12 years	13–15 years	More than 15 years	White-collar	Service	Blue-collar	Farm [2]
WOMEN								
Total (number in thousands)	5 465	21 942	13 588	12 128	37 626	8 759	5 141	622
Total (percent distribution)	100.0	100.0	100.0	100.0	100.0	100.0	100.0	100.0
Reported exposure to substances believed to be harmful if breathed or on skin:								
Yes	28.8	23.2	22.6	20.7	17.6	36.1	*41.5	42.8
No	65.9	73.0	75.3	76.6	80.2	*61.8	*54.0	*44.1
Don't know	5.3	3.9	2.1	2.7	2.2	*2.1	4.5	*13.1
Reported exposure to radiation [3]:								
Yes	*1.9	2.3	7.1	8.0	4.9	5.7	*2.8	*6.5
No	93.3	94.2	90.1	89.5	92.5	92.5	95.1	79.8
Don't know	4.8	3.5	2.8	2.6	2.6	*1.9	*2.2	*13.8
Reported exposure only (number in thousands)	1 598	5 229	3 254	2 733	7 060	3 290	2 159	266
Reported exposure only (percent distribution)	100.0	100.0	100.0	100.0	100.0	100.0	100.0	100.0
Concern level:								
Very concerned	24.4	27.4	24.1	24.4	23.6	27.1	27.6	(4)
Somewhat concerned	26.9	26.4	27.7	28.8	27.0	22.0	39.4	(4)
Slightly concerned	*14.3	19.4	29.5	25.9	25.2	22.1	15.7	(4)
Not at all concerned	31.1	24.9	18.7	18.1	22.4	*26.2	16.6	(4)
Unknown	3.4	*1.9	*–	*2.8	1.8	*2.6	0.8	(4)
MEN								
Total (number in thousands)	8 031	23 510	13 969	18 220	31 574	6 207	22 780	2 631
Total (percent distribution)	100.0	100.0	100.0	100.0	100.0	100.0	100.0	100.0
Reported exposure to substances believed to be harmful if breathed or on skin:								
Yes	41.1	48.2	40.8	24.9	25.4	43.6	56.1	50.1
No	52.2	48.2	56.7	72.5	72.1	*52.9	40.2	43.5
Don't know	6.8	3.6	2.5	2.6	2.5	*3.5	3.8	6.4
Reported exposure to radiation [3]:								
Yes	4.8	5.4	8.1	6.8	6.8	8.4	5.9	*1.5
No	88.9	90.2	87.9	91.0	90.8	87.0	89.5	92.1
Don't know	6.3	4.4	4.1	2.2	2.5	*4.6	4.7	6.4
Reported exposure only (number in thousands)	3 405	11 635	5 959	4 864	8 688	2 862	12 923	1 332
Reported exposure only (percent distribution)	100.0	100.0	100.0	100.0	100.0	100.0	100.0	100.0
Concern level:								
Very concerned	30.7	27.2	28.3	22.0	24.5	30.7	27.4	29.6
Somewhat concerned	25.4	28.9	28.5	23.2	20.6	30.6	30.5	33.1
Slightly concerned	19.2	27.3	23.9	30.6	28.3	20.9	26.1	*21.6
Not at all concerned	24.6	15.5	17.2	23.3	25.0	17.8	15.0	14.2
Unknown	0.2	*1.0	*2.1	*1.0	*1.5	*–	1.0	1.5
NUMBER OF PERSONS INTERVIEWED								
Women	400	1 421	936	839	2 525	621	345	40
Reported exposure	103	344	217	182	476	219	132	17
Men	479	1 247	821	1 029	1 820	357	1 255	150
Reported exposure	195	623	343	279	487	161	708	79

SOURCE: D.K. Wagener, J. Walstedt, L. Jenkins, et al. "Women: Work and Health." *Vital and Health Statistics* 3, no. 31. (1997): Table 17.

* Figure does not meet standards of reliability or precision.
*– Figure does not meet standards of reliability or precision and quantity zero.
1. Includes races other than black and white and unknown occupations and unknown education.
2. Includes farming, forestry, and fishing occupations.
3. Excludes exposure to computer screens.
4. Data not presented because based on 20 or fewer interviewed persons.

NOTE: The percents shown are weighted national estimates. Estimates for which the numerator has a relative standard error of more than 30 percent are indicated with an asterisk.

Table 2.24. The Physical Stress of Work: 1988

(Percent, except where noted)

Work activity and hours spent [1]	Total [1]	Age				Race		Ethnicity	
		18–29 years	30–44 years	45–64 years	65 years and over	White	Black	Hispanic	Non-Hispanic
WOMEN									
Total (in thousands)	52 333	16 387	20 802	13 518	1 627	44 449	6 224	3 374	48 959
Total	100.0	100.0	100.0	100.0	100.0	100.0	100.0	100.0	100.0
Repeated strenuous physical activity									
None	76.7	74.2	77.0	78.0	85.8	76.7	75.5	76.7	76.7
Less than 2 hours	7.4	8.5	7.2	6.6	4.3	7.7	5.4	7.3	7.4
2–3 hours	4.7	5.2	4.5	4.3	4.1	4.8	4.0	4.0	4.7
4 hours or more	9.8	10.9	9.7	9.4	*3.8	9.5	12.3	4.0	9.8
Unknown	1.5	1.3	1.6	1.8	*2.0	1.4	2.8	*10.3 *1.6	1.5
Repeated bending, twisting, or reaching									
None	60.1	55.7	61.8	61.4	71.2	60.6	55.3	56.8	60.3
Less than 2 hours	6.2	6.5	5.9	6.6	5.0	6.4	5.1	7.8	6.1
2–3 hours	7.7	8.6	7.4	7.0	7.1	8.0	6.4	7.1	7.7
4 hours or more	23.5	27.1	22.7	21.8	12.3	22.9	28.3	26.9	23.3
Unknown	2.5	2.1	2.3	3.2	4.3	2.2	4.9	*1.5	2.6
Bending or twisting of hands or wrists									
None	52.6	50.7	53.5	52.1	63.3	52.7	51.8	50.0	52.8
Less than 2 hours	2.7	2.5	2.5	3.2	3.1	2.7	2.6	3.4	2.7
2–3 hours	5.9	6.2	5.7	5.7	7.1	5.9	5.0	4.5	6.0
4 hours or more	35.9	38.1	35.6	35.3	22.0	36.1	35.8	40.2	35.6
Unknown	2.9	2.5	2.6	3.8	4.6	2.7	4.9	1.9	3.0
Hand operation of vibrating machine									
None	91.4	89.6	91.8	92.5	94.5	91.9	88.0	88.1	91.6
Less than 2 hours	2.8	3.3	2.6	2.4	*2.0	2.8	2.4	*3.7	2.7
2–3 hours	1.4	1.5	1.5	1.2	*1.0	1.3	2.2	*1.6	1.4
4 hours or more	3.5	4.8	3.3	2.7	*0.8	3.3	5.9	*5.5	3.4
Unknown	0.9	0.7	0.8	1.2	*1.7	0.8	1.6	*1.1	0.9
MEN									
Total (in thousands)	63 852	18 945	25 590	17 288	2 029	55 702	6 150	4 551	59 301
Total	100.0	100.0	100.0	100.0	100.0	100.0	100.0	100.0	100.0
Repeated strenuous physical activity									
None	60.4	52.3	60.4	67.3	76.1	60.2	61.2	53.5	60.9
Less than 2 hours	7.9	9.0	8.2	6.6	5.9	8.2	4.8	8.7	7.9
2–3 hours	7.2	7.5	7.5	6.7	4.8	7.5	5.0	6.0	7.3
4 hours or more	21.5	28.4	21.0	16.2	10.0	21.2	25.3	27.9	21.1
Unknown	3.0	2.8	2.9	3.3	3.3	2.9	3.7	3.9	2.9
Repeated bending, twisting, or reaching									
None	48.8	39.5	50.7	54.5	63.7	49.2	42.9	39.5	49.6
Less than 2 hours	5.3	5.3	5.2	5.3	5.4	5.3	5.3	4.6	5.3
2–3 hours	7.6	8.8	7.6	6.4	7.2	7.8	6.8	7.0	7.7
4 hours or more	34.5	43.0	33.0	29.3	19.5	34.2	39.4	44.7	33.7
Unknown	3.8	3.4	3.6	4.5	4.1	3.5	5.6	4.3	3.7
Bending or twisting of hands or wrists									
None	46.8	39.5	48.5	50.6	62.8	46.8	45.5	38.1	47.5
Less than 2 hours	3.2	3.5	3.0	3.2	*2.7	3.3	3.2	2.5	3.3
2–3 hours	6.0	6.1	6.3	5.5	5.1	6.1	5.2	5.4	6.0
4 hours or more	40.4	47.7	38.6	36.7	24.9	40.5	40.9	49.1	39.7
Unknown	3.6	3.2	3.6	4.1	4.5	3.4	5.2	5.0	3.5
Hand operation of vibrating machine									
None	73.0	67.9	73.2	77.0	83.8	73.0	71.2	68.7	73.3
Less than 2 hours	7.1	8.1	7.2	6.2	*4.6	7.4	5.9	5.6	7.3
2–3 hours	5.6	6.4	5.9	4.8	*1.5	5.7	5.5	6.0	5.6
4 hours or more	11.6	15.1	11.5	8.7	6.7	11.5	13.3	17.8	11.2
Unknown	2.6	2.5	2.2	3.2	3.4	2.5	4.0	1.8	2.7
Number of persons interviewed									
Women	13 755	4 021	5 736	3 440	558	11 285	2 081	796	12 959
Men	13 653	3 689	5 741	3 714	509	11 875	1 415	878	12 775

See footnotes at end of table.

Table 2.24. The Physical Stress of Work: 1988—*Continued*

(Percent, except where noted)

Work activity and hours spent [1]	Educational level				Major occupational group			
	Less than 12 years	12 years	13–15 years	More than 15 years	White-collar	Service	Blue-collar	Farm [2]
WOMEN								
Total (in thousands)	6 188	22 257	12 824	10 964	37 043	8 669	5 859	598
Total	100.0	100.0	100.0	100.0	100.0	100.0	100.0	100.0
Repeated strenuous physical activity								
None	64.9	74.8	77.4	86.2	83.3	60.2	62.6	41.0
Less than 2 hours	8.5	7.0	8.4	6.2	6.8	10.3	6.5	11.5
2–3 hours	6.4	4.9	4.9	3.0	3.5	7.9	5.8	18.0
4 hours or more	17.1	11.7	8.2	3.7	5.5	19.1	22.4	23.2
Unknown	3.1	1.6	1.2	1.0	1.0	2.5	2.8	*6.3
Repeated bending, twisting, or reaching								
None	41.0	56.2	63.4	75.0	69.6	35.1	40.6	23.5
Less than 2 hours	6.2	5.8	7.2	6.1	6.3	7.2	4.4	9.2
2–3 hours	8.7	8.1	7.7	6.1	6.9	11.2	6.2	20.3
4 hours or more	40.0	27.1	20.1	10.7	15.6	42.4	44.8	34.5
Unknown	4.1	2.8	1.6	2.1	1.7	4.1	4.0	12.6
Bending or twisting of hands or wrists								
None	37.4	47.3	54.4	69.6	59.8	41.2	26.0	24.4
Less than 2 hours	3.3	2.2	3.0	3.0	2.7	3.0	1.5	*6.7
2–3 hours	6.2	5.4	6.8	5.8	5.4	7.9	4.8	19.0
4 hours or more	47.8	42.1	33.6	19.3	29.9	43.2	63.5	37.0
Unknown	5.5	3.0	2.1	2.3	2.2	4.7	4.2	13.0
Hand operation of vibrating machine								
None	85.1	90.3	92.9	95.4	95.4	83.6	78.5	79.5
Less than 2 hours	4.5	2.6	2.6	2.3	1.7	7.1	2.8	*9.6
2–3 hours	2.1	1.6	1.2	1.0	0.7	3.7	2.6	*2.5
4 hours or more	6.7	4.6	2.7	0.7	1.6	4.5	14.1	*5.7
Unknown	1.5	1.0	0.6	0.6	0.6	1.1	2.1	*2.8
MEN								
Total (in thousands)	10 080	23 954	13 683	15 945	29 926	5 615	25 363	2 732
Total	100.0	100.0	100.0	100.0	100.0	100.0	100.0	100.0
Repeated strenuous physical activity								
None	44.7	48.7	62.2	86.3	81.4	59.0	39.6	26.5
Less than 2 hours	8.4	9.0	9.7	4.5	6.3	12.6	8.7	9.7
2–3 hours	8.8	9.3	7.1	3.1	4.4	7.8	9.9	11.0
4 hours or more	33.3	29.3	18.8	4.6	6.5	16.6	38.0	44.3
Unknown	4.8	3.7	2.3	1.4	1.4	4.1	3.9	8.5
Repeated bending, twisting, or reaching								
None	28.3	35.0	51.6	80.3	73.3	42.2	25.1	16.1
Less than 2 hours	5.1	5.3	6.9	3.9	5.1	7.8	4.6	7.8
2–3 hours	7.2	9.0	8.8	4.9	5.5	8.7	9.5	11.9
4 hours or more	53.3	46.4	29.6	9.0	14.4	36.4	55.6	55.6
Unknown	6.1	4.4	3.1	1.9	1.7	5.0	5.3	8.5
Bending or twisting of hands or wrists								
None	28.0	35.2	50.4	73.1	66.5	46.4	26.0	26.7
Less than 2 hours	3.1	3.5	3.3	2.8	2.9	4.6	3.2	4.5
2–3 hours	5.5	6.4	7.3	4.4	5.5	7.0	6.1	7.3
4 hours or more	57.6	50.6	36.3	17.5	23.1	38.8	59.8	52.6
Unknown	5.7	4.3	2.7	2.2	2.1	3.1	4.9	9.0
Hand operation of vibrating machine								
None	60.8	65.4	74.3	91.1	90.2	76.3	54.2	51.6
Less than 2 hours	6.0	9.1	8.8	3.6	3.8	6.5	11.0	9.8
2–3 hours	8.3	7.3	5.2	1.7	2.0	6.9	9.3	8.4
4 hours or more	20.7	15.0	9.7	2.6	2.8	6.5	21.8	24.4
Unknown	4.3	3.3	2.1	1.0	1.2	3.7	3.7	5.8
Number of persons interviewed								
Women	1 680	5 617	3 385	3 049	9 635	2 397	1 526	147
Men	2 097	4 914	2 968	3 634	6 523	1 218	5 271	593

SOURCE: D.K. Wagener, J. Walstedt, L. Jenkins, et al. "Women: Work and Health." *Vital and Health Statistics* 3, no. 31. (1997): Table 19.

* Figure does not meet standards of reliability or precision.
1. Includes races other than black and white and persons with unknown occupations and unknown education.
2. Includes farming, forestry, and fishing occupations.

NOTE: The percents shown are weighted national estimates. Estimates for which the numerator has a relative standard of error of more than 30 percent are indicated with an asterisk. Data are based on household interviews of the civilian noninstitutionalized population.

Table 2.25. Traffic-Related Deaths by State: 1996

(Ranked by fatalities per 100,000 population)

Area	Licensed drivers (thousands)	Fatalities per 100,000 drivers	Registered vehicles (thousands)	Fatalities per 100,000 registered vehicles	Population (thousands)	Fatalities per 100,000 population	Total killed
United States	179 539	23.3	201 626	20.8	265 284	15.8	41 907
STATE							
Mississippi	1 700	47.7	2 182	37.2	2 716	29.9	811
Wyoming	343	41.7	562	25.4	481	29.7	143
New Mexico	1 179	40.8	1 545	31.1	1 713	28.1	481
Alabama	3 138	36.4	3 324	34.4	4 273	26.8	1 143
South Carolina	2 575	36.1	2 791	33.3	3 699	25.1	930
Arkansas	1 752	35.1	1 633	37.7	2 510	24.5	615
South Dakota	519	33.7	751	23.3	732	23.9	175
Oklahoma	2 396	32.2	3 082	25.0	3 301	23.4	772
Tennessee	3 806	32.6	4 830	25.6	5 320	23.3	1 239
Montana	574	34.8	973	20.6	879	22.8	200
Arizona	2 727	36.4	2 983	33.3	4 428	22.4	993
Nevada	1 117	31.2	1 096	31.8	1 603	21.7	348
Idaho	820	31.5	1 061	24.3	1 189	21.7	258
Kentucky	2 567	32.8	2 696	31.2	3 884	21.6	841
Missouri	3 749	30.6	4 350	26.4	5 359	21.4	1 149
Georgia	4 966	31.7	6 283	25.0	7 353	21.4	1 574
North Carolina	5 187	28.8	5 759	25.9	7 323	20.4	1 493
Texas	12 568	29.8	13 487	27.7	19 128	19.6	3 741
Florida	11 400	24.2	10 889	25.3	14 400	19.1	2 753
Kansas	1 788	27.5	2 110	23.3	2 572	19.1	491
West Virginia	1 274	27.1	1 406	24.5	1 826	18.9	345
Louisiana	2 624	29.8	3 318	23.5	4 351	18.0	781
Nebraska	1 160	25.3	1 479	19.8	1 652	17.7	293
Indiana	3 704	26.6	5 216	18.9	5 841	16.8	984
Oregon	2 613	20.0	2 851	18.4	3 204	16.4	524
Iowa	1 956	23.8	2 869	16.2	2 852	16.3	465
Colorado	2 757	22.4	3 433	18.0	3 823	16.1	617
Utah	1 319	24.3	1 455	22.2	2 000	16.0	321
Delaware	529	21.9	593	19.6	725	16.0	116
Michigan	6 717	22.4	8 010	18.8	9 594	15.7	1 505
Vermont	469	18.8	503	17.5	589	14.9	88
Wisconsin	3 724	20.4	3 972	19.2	5 160	14.8	761
Maine	874	19.3	959	17.6	1 243	13.6	169
North Dakota	449	18.9	679	12.5	644	13.2	85
Alaska	440	18.2	531	15.1	607	13.2	80
Virginia	4 692	18.6	5 576	15.7	6 675	13.1	875
Washington	3 908	18.2	4 603	15.5	5 533	12.9	712
California	20 249	19.7	25 214	15.8	31 878	12.5	3 989
Hawaii	733	20.2	786	18.8	1 184	12.5	148
Ohio	7 853	17.8	9 770	14.3	11 173	12.5	1 395
Illinois	7 610	19.4	8 817	16.8	11 847	12.5	1 477
Minnesota	2 830	20.4	3 861	14.9	4 658	12.4	576
Pennsylvania	8 221	17.9	8 640	17.0	12 056	12.2	1 469
Maryland	3 377	18.0	3 635	16.7	5 072	12.0	608
New Hampshire	915	14.6	1 112	12.0	1 162	11.5	134
New Jersey	5 486	14.9	5 822	14.0	7 988	10.2	818
Connecticut	2 344	13.2	2 609	11.9	3 274	9.5	310
New York	10 484	14.9	10 636	14.7	18 185	8.6	1 564
Rhode Island	669	10.3	696	9.9	990	7.0	69
Massachusetts	4 355	9.6	4 702	8.9	6 092	6.8	417
OTHER							
Puerto Rico	1 832	32.8	2 256	26.6	3 783	15.9	601
District of Columbia	333	18.6	237	26.2	543	11.4	62

SOURCE: Bureau of Transportation Statistics *Traffic Safety Facts 1996*, Table 103. Sources—Fatality Analysis Reporting System (FARS); Licensed drivers (estimated)—Federal Highway Administration; Registered vehicles by state (estimated)—Federal Highway Administration; Registered vehicles for USA—R. L. Polk and Co.; Population—Bureau of the Census.

NOTE: The number shown for registered vehicles for the United States is approximately 4 percent lower than the sum of the registered vehicles numbers shown for individual states, because of differing data sources.

Table 2.26. State Child Passenger Safety Laws: 1999

Area	Effective date	Restraint age	Safety seat age	May substitute safety belt	Penalty [1]	Children not covered
STATE						
Alabama	7/82	Under 6	Under 4	4–5 years of age	$10	Younger than 6 years; in out-of-state vehicle; 6+ years; in rear seat
Alaska	6/85	Under 16	Under 4	4–15 years of age	$50, 2 points	All children covered
Arizona	8/83	Under 16	Under 5	No	$50	5+ years; in rear seat
Arkansas	8/83	Under 14	Under 5[2]	4–14 years of age	$25–100	5+ years; in rear seat
California	1/83	Under 4[2]	Under 4[2]	4–15 years of age and 40+ pounds	$100	All children covered
Colorado	1/84	Under 15[2]	Under 4[2]	4–15 years of age or 40+ pounds	$50 and $6 service charge	All children covered
Connecticut	5/82	Under 16	Under 4[2]	4–15 years of age	$35–2 000	All children covered
Delaware	6/82	Under 16	Under 5	4–5 years of age	$28.75	All children covered
Florida	7/83	Under 16	Under 4	3 through 4 years of age	$60 plus $10	All children covered
Georgia	7/84	Under 4[2]	Under 3	No (7/1/99)	$50	4+ years; in rear seat
Hawaii	7/83	Under 4[2]	Under 3	No	$100 maximum	4+ years; or 40+ pounds; in rear seat
Idaho	1/85	Under 4	Under 4	No	$100 maximum	All children covered
Illinois	7/83	Under 6	Under 4	4–5 years of age	$25–50	6+ years; in rear seat; all children if driver is other than parent/guardian unless parent provides child restraint
Indiana	1/84	Under 5	Under 3	3–5 years of age	$500 maximum, 4 points	Younger than 4 years; in out-of-state vehicle; 12+ years; in rear seat
Iowa	1/85	Under 6	Under 3	3–5 years of age	$10	6+ years; in rear seat
Kansas	1/82	Under 14	Under 4	4–13 years of age	$20	14+ years; in rear seat
Kentucky	7/82	40 inches and under	40 inches and under	No	$50	All children covered
Louisiana	9/84	Under 13	Under 5	3–5 years of age, 3–12 in rear seat	$25–500	Younger than 13 years; if driver is nonresident of state; 13 years; in rear seat
Maine	9/83	Under 19	Under 4	No	$25	All children covered
Maryland	1/84	Under 16	Under 4[2]	40+ pounds through age 15	$25	All children covered
Massachusetts	1/82	Through 12	Under 5	5–11 years of age	$25	All children covered
Michigan	4/82	Through 16	Through 4	1–3 years of age in rear seat	$10	11+ years; in rear seat
Minnesota	8/83	Under 11	Under 4	No	$50	8+ years; in rear seat
Mississippi	7/83	Under 4	Under 4	No	$25	All children covered
Missouri	1/84	Under 4	Under 4	No	$25	All children covered
Montana[3]	1/84	Under 4[2]	Under 2	2–3 years of age or less than 40 pounds	$100 maximum	5+ years; in rear seat; younger than 5 years; if driver is nonresident of state
Nebraska	8/83	Under 5[2]	Under 4	40+ pounds or 4 years of age	$25	All children covered
Nevada	7/83	Under 5[2]	Under 5[2]	No	$35–100	All children covered
New Hampshire	7/83	Under 18	Under 4	4–17 years of age in all seats	$1 000	5+ years; in rear seat or pickup truck
New Jersey	4/83	Under 5	Under 5	1.5–4 years of age in rear seat; 5–10 in all seats	$10–25	11+ years; in rear seat
New Mexico	6/83	Under 11	Under 1	1–5 years of age in rear seat; 5–10 in all seats	$25	10+ years; in rear seat
New York	4/82	Under 10	Under 4	4–9 years of age in rear; 4–15 in front	$100 maximum, 3 points	All children covered
North Carolina	7/82	Under 12	Under 5	5–15 years of age (eff. 10/1/99)	$25	All children covered
North Dakota	1/84	Through 10	Under 3	4–17 years of age	$20	4+ years and 40 pounds; in rear seat; younger than 4 years; or less than 40 pounds; in out-of-state vehicle
Ohio	3/83	Under 4[2]	Under 4[2]	No	$100	All children covered
Oklahoma	11/83	Under 4[2]	Under 4[4]	Under 4 in rear; 4–5 in front or rear	$10 maximum	6+ years; in rear seat; younger than 6 years; if driver is nonresident of state
Oregon	1/84	Under 16	Under 4[2]	Over 4 years of age, over 40 pounds	$75	All children covered
Pennsylvania	1/84	Under 4	Under 4	No	$25	4+ years; in rear seat
Rhode Island	7/80	Through 12	Under 4	4–5 years of age; under 5 in rear	$150 maximum	All children covered
South Carolina	7/83	Under 6	Under 4	1–6 years of age in rear seat	$25	Younger than 6 years; in out-of-state vehicle; 6+ years; in rear seat without shoulder belt
South Dakota	7/84	Under 5	Under 5	40+ pounds and under 4 years of age	$20	5+ years; in rear seat
Tennessee	1/78	Under 12	Under 4	4–12 years of age	$50 maximum	13+ years; in rear seat
Texas	10/84	Under 4	Under 2	2–4 years of age	$25–50	15+ years; in rear seat
Utah	7/84	Under 10	Under 2	2–10 years of age	$75	10+ years; in rear seat
Vermont	7/84	Through 12	Under 5	5–12 years of age	$25	All children covered
Virginia	1/83	Over 4	Under 4	4–16 years of age	$50, 3 points	All children covered
Washington	1/84	Under 10	Under 3	3–10 years of age	$35	All children covered
West Virginia	7/81	Under 9	Under 3	3–8 years of age	$10–20	All children covered
Wisconsin	11/82	Under 8	Under 4	4–7 years of age	$75 maximum	8+ years; in rear seat without shoulder belt
Wyoming	4/85	Under 3[2]	Under 4[2]	No	$50	5+ years; in rear seat
OTHER						
District of Columbia	7/83	Under 16	Under 3	3–6 years of age	$55, 2 points	All children covered
Puerto Rico	1/89	Under 4	Under 4	Over 40 pounds	$10	—

SOURCE: *NCSL Transportation Series*, "State Traffic Safety Legislation, 1999," Appendix B. This table was compiled by the National Conference of State Legislatures from information provided by the National Highway Safety Administration and is used with permission.

— Data not available.
1. Most states waive fines upon proof of safety seat acquisition.
2. Or less than 40 pounds.
3. Law applies only to parents and legal guardians.
4. Or less than 60 pounds.

Table 2.27. State Seat Belt Use Laws: 1999

Area	Effective date	Enforcement	Fine	Seats	Vehicle and coverage by law [1]
STATE					
Alabama	6/9/99	Primary	$25	Front	Passenger car from model year 1965
Alaska	9/12/90	Secondary	$15	All	Motor vehicle; over age 16
Arizona	1/1/91	Secondary	$10	Front	Passenger car and van from model year 1972
Arkansas	7/15/91	Secondary	$25	Front	Passenger car, trucks and vans
California	1/1/86	Primary	$20	All	Passenger car, small trucks and vans
Colorado	7/1/87	Secondary	$15	Front	Passenger car, van, taxi, ambulance, RV and small truck
Connecticut	1/1/86	Primary	$37	Front	Passenger car, trucks and vans
Delaware	1/1/92	Secondary	$20	Front	Passenger car
Florida	7/1/86	Secondary	$20	Front	Motor vehicle and pickup truck
Georgia	9/1/88	Primary	$15	Front	Vehicle for under 8 people; pickup for under age 18
Hawaii	12/6/85	Primary	$20	Front	All vehicles made with seat belt or seat belt installed
Idaho	7/1/86	Secondary	$5	Front	Motor vehicle under 8,000 lbs.
Illinois	7/1/85	Secondary	$25	Front	Motor vehicle to carry under 10 people; RV
Indiana	7/1/87	Primary	$25	Front	Passenger car, bus and school bus
Iowa	7/1/86	Primary	$10	Front	Passenger car, van and truck 10,000 lbs. or less
Kansas	7/1/86	Secondary	$10	Front	Passenger car and van
Kentucky	7/13/94	Secondary	$25	All	Motor vehicles from model year 1965
Louisiana	7/1/86	Primary	$25	Front	Passenger car, van and truck under 6,000 lbs.
Maine	12/27/95	Secondary	$25	All	Passenger vehicle
Maryland	7/1/86	Primary	$25	Front	Passenger and multipurpose vehicle, truck, tractor and bus
Massachusetts	2/1/94	Secondary	$25	All	Passenger car, van and truck
Michigan	4/1/00	Primary	$25	Front	Motor vehicle
Minnesota	8/1/86	Secondary	$25	Front	Passenger car, pickup truck, van, and RV
Mississippi	3/20/90	Secondary	$25	Front	Passenger car and van
Missouri	9/28/85	Secondary	$10	Front	Passenger car to carry less than 10 people
Montana	10/1/87	Secondary	$20	All	Motor vehicle
Nebraska	1/1/93	Secondary	$25	Front	Motor vehicle
Nevada	7/1/87	Secondary	$25	All	Passenger car under 6,000 pounds
New Hampshire [1]	. . .	. . .	. . .	. . .	. . .
New Jersey	3/1/85	Secondary	$20	Front	Passenger car
New Mexico	1/1/86	Primary	$25	Front	Motor vehicle under 10,000 lbs.
New York	12/1/84	Primary	$50	Front	Passenger car
North Carolina	10/1/85	Primary	$25	Front	Passenger car to carry less than 10 people
North Dakota	7/14/95	Secondary	$20	Front	Motor vehicle
Ohio	5/6/86	Secondary	$25	Front	Passenger/ commercial car, van, tractor, and truck
Oklahoma	2/1/87	Primary	$10	Front	Passenger car, van, and pickup truck
Oregon	12/7/90	Primary	$75	All	Motor vehicle
Pennsylvania	11/23/87	Secondary	$10	Front	Passenger car, truck, and motor home
Rhode Island	6/18/91	Secondary	No	All	Passenger car; over age 12
South Carolina	7/1/89	Secondary	$10	Front	Passenger car, truck, van, RV, and taxi
South Dakota	1/1/95	Secondary	$20	Front	Passenger car, truck, van, RV, and taxi
Tennessee	4/21/86	Secondary	$10	Front	Vehicle under 8 500 lbs.
Texas	9/1/85	Primary	$25	Front	Passenger car, van, and certain trucks
Utah	4/29/86	Secondary	$10	Front	Motor vehicle
Vermont	1/1/94	Secondary	$10	All	Passenger car
Virginia	1/1/88	Secondary	$25	Front	Motor vehicle
Washington	6/11/86	Secondary	$35	All	Passenger/ multipurpose vehicle, bus, and truck
West Virginia	9/1/93	Secondary	$25	Front	Passenger car; age 18 and under in rear seat
Wisconsin	12/1/87	Secondary	$10	All	Motor vehicle
Wyoming	6/8/89	Secondary	No	All	Passenger car, van, and pickup truck
OTHER					
American Samoa	1/1/89	Primary	$25	All	Passenger car, truck, and van
District of Columbia	12/12/85	Primary	$50	All	Vehicle seating 8 or fewer, 2 points on license
Guam	11/20/86	Primary	$70	Front	Passenger car, truck, and van
Mariana Islands	4/20/90	Primary	$25	All	Passenger car, and truck
Virgin Islands	1/19/75	Primary	$10	Front	Passenger car; over age 4
Puerto Rico	1/1/98	Primary	$25	Front	Passenger car
TOTAL		20 Primary 35 Secondary		40 Front 15 All	

SOURCE: *NCSL Transportation Series*, "State Traffic Safety Legislation, 1999," Appendixes C and D. This table was compiled by the National Conference of State Legislatures from information provided by the National Highway Safety Administration and is used with permission.

1. No law.

Table 2.28. Food-borne Transmission of Illnesses

(Average annual number of cases reported to the CDC for 1983–1992)

Disease or agent	Illnesses			Hospitalizations			Deaths		
	Total	Food-borne	Percent of food-borne	Total	Food-borne	Percent of total food-borne	Total	Food-borne	Percent of total food-borne
BACTERIAL									
Bacillus cereus	27 360	27 360	0.2	8	8	0.0	0	0	0.0
Botulism, food-borne	58	58	0.0	46	46	0.1	4	4	0.2
Brucella spp.	1 554	777	0.0	122	61	0.1	11	6	0.3
Campylobacter spp	2 453 926	1 963 141	14.2	13 174	10 539	17.3	124	99	5.5
Clostridium perfringens	248 520	248 520	1.8	41	41	0.1	7	7	0.4
Escherichia coli O157:H7	73 480	62 458	0.5	2 168	1 843	3.0	61	52	2.9
E.coli, non-O157 STEC	36 740	31 229	0.2	1 084	921	1.5	30	26	1.4
E.coli, enterotoxigenic	79 420	55 594	0.4	21	15	0.0	0	0	0.0
E.coli, other diarrheogenic	79 420	23 826	0.2	21	6	0.0	0	0	0.0
Listeria monocytogenes	2 518	2 493	0.0	2 322	2 298	3.8	504	499	27.6
Salmonella Typhi [2]	824	659	0.0	618	494	0.8	3	3	0.1
Salmonella, nontyphoidal	1 412 498	1 341 873	9.7	16 430	15 608	25.6	582	553	30.6
Shigella spp.	448 240	89 648	0.6	6 231	1 246	2.0	70	14	0.8
Staphylococcus food poisoning	185 060	185 060	1.3	1 753	1 753	2.9	2	2	0.1
Streptococcus, food-borne	50 920	50 920	0.4	358	358	0.6	0	0	0.0
Vibrio cholerae, toxigenic	54	49	0.0	18	17	0.0	0	0	0.0
V.vulnificus	94	47	0.0	86	43	0.1	37	18	1.0
Vibrio, other	7 880	5 122	0.0	99	65	0.1	20	13	0.7
Yersinia enterocolitica	96 368	86 731	0.6	1 228	1 105	1.8	3	2	0.1
Subtotal	5 204 934	4 175 565	30.2	45 826	36 466	59.9	1 458	1 297	71.7
PARASITIC									
Cryptosporidium parvum	300 000	30 000	0.2	1 989	199	0.3	66	7	0.4
Cyclospora cayetanensis	16 264	14 638	0.1	17	15	0.0	0	0	0.0
Giardia lamblia	2 000 000	200 000	1.4	5 000	500	0.8	10	1	0.1
Toxoplasma gondii	225 000	112 500	0.8	5 000	2 500	4.1	750	375	20.7
Trichinella spiralis	52	52	0.0	4	4	0.0	0	0	0.0
Subtotal	2 541 316	357 190	2.6	12 010	3 219	5.3	827	383	21.2
VIRAL									
Norwalk-like viruses	23 000 000	9 200 000	66.6	50 000	20 000	32.9	310	124	6.9
Rotavirus	3 900 000	39 000	0.3	50 000	500	0.8	30	0	0.0
Astrovirus	3 900 000	39 000	0.3	12 500	125	0.2	10	0	0.0
Hepatitis A	83 391	4 170	0.0	10 841	90	0.9	83	4	0.2
Subtotal	30 833 391	9 282 170	67.2	123 341	21 167	34.8	433	129	7.1
TOTAL	38 629 641	13 814 920	100.0	181 177	60 854	100.0	2 718	1 809	100.0

SOURCE: P. Mead, L. Slutsker, V. Dietz, L. McCaig, J. Bresee, C. Shapiro, P. Griffin, and R. Tauxe. "Food-Related Illness and Death in the United States," *Emerging Infectious Diseases*, (Centers for Disease Control and Prevention) 5, no. 5 (September–October 1999): Table 3. Data sources include Foodborne Diseases Active Surveillance Network (Food Net), the National Notifiable Disease Surveillance System, the Public Health Laboratory Information System, the Gulf States Vibrio Surveillance System, the Foodborne Disease Outbreak Surveillance System, the National Ambulatory Medical Care Survey, the National Hospital Medical Care Survey, the National Hospital Discharge Survey, and the National Vital Statistics System.

Table 2.29. Visits to the Dentist

(Percent of population with a visit within the past year)

Characteristic	1983 [1]	1989 [1]	1990	1991	1993
Total [2,3]	53.9	58.9	62.3	58.2	60.8
AGE					
25–34 years	59.0	60.9	65.1	59.1	60.3
35–44 years	60.3	65.9	69.1	64.8	66.9
45–64 years	54.1	59.9	62.8	59.2	62.0
65 years and over	39.3	45.8	49.6	47.2	51.7
65–74 years	43.8	50.0	53.5	51.1	56.3
75 years and over	31.8	39.0	43.4	41.3	44.9
SEX [3]					
Male	51.7	56.2	58.8	55.5	58.2
Female	55.9	61.4	65.6	60.8	63.4
POVERTY STATUS [3,4]					
Below poverty	30.4	33.3	38.2	33.0	35.9
At or above poverty	55.8	62.1	65.4	61.9	64.3
RACE AND HISPANIC ORIGIN [3]					
White, non-Hispanic	56.6	61.8	64.9	61.5	64.0
Black, non-Hispanic	39.1	43.3	49.1	44.3	47.3
Hispanic	42.1	48.9	53.8	43.1	46.2
EDUCATION [3]					
Less than 12 years	35.1	36.9	41.2	35.2	38.0
12 years	54.8	58.2	61.3	56.7	58.7
13 years or more	70.9	73.9	75.7	72.2	73.8
EDUCATION, RACE, AND HISPANIC ORIGIN [3]					
Less than 12 years					
White, non-Hispanic	36.1	39.1	41.8	38.1	41.2
Black, non-Hispanic	31.7	32.0	37.9	33.0	33.1
Hispanic	33.8	36.5	42.7	28.9	33.0
12 years					
White, non-Hispanic	56.6	59.8	62.8	58.8	60.4
Black, non-Hispanic	40.5	44.8	51.1	43.1	48.2
Hispanic	48.7	56.5	59.9	49.5	54.6
13 years or more					
White, non-Hispanic	72.6	75.8	77.3	74.2	75.8
Black, non-Hispanic	54.4	57.2	64.4	61.7	61.3
Hispanic	58.4	66.2	67.9	61.2	61.8

SOURCE: E. Kramarow, H. Lentzner, R. Rooks, J. Weeks, S. Saydah. *Health and Aging Chartbook. Health, United States, 1999*. Hyattsville, Maryland: National Center for Health Statistics. 1999: Table 85. Based on data from the National Health Interview Survey.

1. Data for 1983 and 1989 are not strictly comparable with data for later years. Data for 1983 and 1989 are based on responses to the question "About how long has it been since you last went to a dentist?" Starting in 1990 data are based on the question "During the past 12 months, how many visits did you make to a dentist?"
2. Includes all other races not shown separately and unknown poverty status and education level.
3. Age adjusted.
4. Poverty status is based on family income and family size using Bureau of the Census poverty thresholds.

NOTE: Denominators exclude persons with unknown dental data. Estimates for 1983 and 1989 are based on data for all members of the sample household. Beginning in 1990 estimates are based on one adult member per sample household. Estimates for 1993 are based on responses during the last half of the year only.

Table 2.30. Children under Age Six Who Never Visit a Doctor

(Percent without physician contact within the past year)

Characteristic	1993–1994	1995–1996
ALL CHILDREN [1]	8.3	9.2
RACE [2]		
White	7.8	8.9
Black	10.1	9.9
American Indian or Alaska Native	12.7	16.4
Asian or Pacific Islander	8.9	11.5
RACE AND HISPANIC ORIGIN		
White, non-Hispanic	7.3	8.1
Black, non-Hispanic	10.3	10.0
Hispanic [2]	9.9	11.7
POVERTY STATUS [3]		
Poor	10.6	11.6
Near poor	9.9	10.7
Nonpoor	5.0	6.2
RACE AND HISPANIC ORIGIN AND POVERTY STATUS [3]		
White, non-Hispanic		
Poor	8.8	11.8
Near poor	10.0	9.3
Nonpoor	4.8	5.9
Black, non-Hispanic		
Poor	12.2	9.5
Near poor	8.7	11.8
Nonpoor	5.0	8.7
Hispanic [2]		
Poor	10.7	12.8
Near poor	10.3	12.3
Nonpoor	5.7	6.5
HEALTH INSURANCE STATUS [4]		
Insured	6.8	7.3
Private	6.6	6.9
Medicaid	7.2	7.9
Uninsured	15.6	18.5
POVERTY STATUS AND HEALTH INSURANCE STATUS [3, 4]		
Poor		
Insured	7.9	9.3
Uninsured	21.7	22.1
Near Poor		
Insured	8.6	8.9
Uninsured	13.7	18.4
Nonpoor		
Insured	4.8	5.5
Uninsured	8.7	15.2
GEOGRAPHIC REGION		
Northeast	4.4	5.5
Midwest	8.0	9.4
South	11.0	10.5
West	7.8	10.3
LOCATION OF RESIDENCE		
Within MSA [5]	7.6	8.9
Outside MSA [5]	10.8	10.9

SOURCE: E. Kramarow, H. Lentzner, R. Rooks, J. Weeks, S. Saydah. *Health and Aging Chartbook. Health, United States, 1999.* (Hyattsville, Maryland: National Center for Health Statistics, 1999.): Table 79. Data are based on the Health Insurance Supplement from the National Health Interview Survey.

1. Includes all other races not shown separately and unknown poverty status and unknown health insurance status.
2. The race groups White, Black, American Indian or Alaska Native, and Asian or Pacific Islander include persons of Hispanic and non-Hispanic origin; persons of Hispanic origin may be of any race.
3. Poverty status is based on family income and family size using Bureau of the Census poverty thresholds. Poor persons are defined as below the poverty threshold. Near poor persons have incomes of 100 percent to less than 200 percent of poverty threshold. Nonpoor persons have incomes of 200 percent or greater than the poverty threshold.
4. Health insurance categories are mutually exclusive. Persons who reported more than one type of health insurance coverage were classified to a single type of coverage according to the following hierarchy: Medicaid, private, other. Other health insurance includes Medicare or military coverage.
5. MSA is metropolitan statistical area.

NOTE: Physician contact is defined as a consultation with a physician in person or by telephone, for examination, diagnosis, treatment, or advice. The service may be provided by the physician or by another person working under the physician's supervision. In 1993–1994 and 1994–1995, between 8 and 9 percent of children had unknown health insurance status and about 13 percent of children had unknown poverty status.

Table 2.31. Prenatal Care

(Percent of live births [1])

Characteristic	1970	1975	1980	1981	1982	1983	1984	1985	1986	1987
PRENATAL CARE BEGAN DURING FIRST TRIMESTER										
All races	68.0	72.4	76.3	76.3	76.1	76.2	76.5	76.2	75.9	76.0
White	72.3	75.8	79.2	79.3	79.2	79.3	79.6	79.3	79.1	79.3
Black	44.2	55.5	62.4	62.1	61.1	61.2	61.9	61.5	61.2	60.8
American Indian or Alaska Native	38.2	45.4	55.8	56.6	57.7	56.6	57.4	57.5	58.2	57.6
Asian or Pacific Islander	—	—	73.7	73.2	73.3	73.9	74.7	74.1	74.9	75.0
Chinese	71.8	76.7	82.6	82.6	81.9	80.4	81.5	82.0	82.2	81.5
Japanese	78.1	82.7	86.1	85.2	85.6	86.6	87.0	84.7	85.7	86.6
Filipino	60.6	70.6	77.3	77.5	76.8	77.4	77.8	76.5	78.2	77.9
Hawaiian and part Hawaiian	—	—	68.8	—	—	—	—	67.7	—	—
Other Asian or Pacific Islander	—	—	67.4	—	—	—	—	69.9	—	—
Hispanic origin (selected states) 2, 3	—	—	60.2	60.6	61.0	61.0	61.5	61.2	60.3	61.0
Mexican	—	—	59.6	60.1	60.7	60.2	60.4	60.0	58.9	60.0
Puerto Rican	—	—	55.1	54.2	54.5	55.1	57.4	58.3	57.2	57.4
Cuban	—	—	82.7	80.1	79.3	81.2	82.2	82.5	81.8	83.1
Central and South American	—	—	58.8	58.3	58.5	59.3	61.1	60.6	58.8	59.1
Other and unknown Hispanic	—	—	66.4	66.9	66.0	66.6	66.7	65.8	66.6	65.5
White, non-Hispanic (selected states) 2	—	—	81.2	81.3	81.1	81.3	81.6	81.4	81.5	81.7
Black, non-Hispanic (selected states) 2	—	—	60.7	60.7	59.7	59.9	60.6	60.1	60.1	60.0
PRENATAL CARE BEGAN DURING THIRD TRIMESTER OR NO PRENATAL CARE										
All races	7.9	6.0	5.1	5.2	5.5	5.6	5.6	5.7	6.0	6.1
White	6.3	5.0	4.3	4.3	4.5	4.6	4.7	4.8	5.0	5.0
Black	16.6	10.5	8.9	9.2	9.7	9.8	9.7	10.2	10.7	11.2
American Indian or Alaska Native	28.9	22.4	15.2	14.7	14.0	14.4	13.8	12.9	12.9	13.1
Asian or Pacific Islander	—	—	6.5	6.6	6.6	6.5	6.4	6.5	6.2	6.3
Chinese	6.5	4.4	3.7	3.8	3.5	4.6	4.2	4.4	4.2	4.2
Japanese	4.1	2.7	2.1	2.5	2.5	2.4	2.6	3.1	3.1	2.8
Filipino	7.2	4.1	4.0	3.6	3.8	4.1	4.3	4.8	4.5	4.9
Hawaiian and part Hawaiian	—	—	6.7	—	—	—	—	7.4	—	—
Other Asian or Pacific Islander	—	—	9.3	—	—	—	—	8.2	—	—
Hispanic origin (selected states) 2, 3	—	—	12.0	11.6	12.1	12.5	12.6	12.4	13.0	12.7
Mexican	—	—	11.8	11.6	12.0	12.7	13.0	12.9	13.4	13.0
Puerto Rican	—	—	16.2	15.8	17.2	17.4	16.3	15.5	17.4	17.1
Cuban	—	—	3.9	4.2	4.9	4.0	4.0	3.7	4.2	3.9
Central and South American	—	—	13.1	12.4	13.4	13.3	12.6	12.5	13.8	13.5
Other and unknown Hispanic	—	—	9.2	8.3	9.3	9.0	9.1	9.4	9.0	9.3
White, non-Hispanic (selected states) 2	—	—	3.5	3.6	3.8	3.9	3.9	4.0	4.1	4.1
Black, non-Hispanic (selected states) 2	—	—	9.7	9.9	10.6	10.7	10.6	10.9	11.4	11.8

Characteristic	1988	1989	1990	1991	1992	1993	1994	1995	1996	1997
PRENATAL CARE BEGAN DURING FIRST TRIMESTER										
All races	75.9	75.5	75.8	76.2	77.7	78.9	80.2	81.3	81.9	82.5
White	79.3	78.9	79.2	79.5	80.8	81.8	82.8	83.6	84.0	84.7
Black	60.7	60.0	60.6	61.9	63.9	66.0	68.3	70.4	71.4	72.3
American Indian or Alaska Native	58.1	57.9	57.9	59.9	62.1	63.4	65.2	66.7	67.7	68.1
Asian or Pacific Islander	75.5	74.8	75.1	75.3	76.6	77.6	79.7	79.9	81.2	82.1
Chinese	82.3	81.5	81.3	82.3	83.8	84.6	86.2	85.7	86.8	87.4
Japanese	86.3	86.2	87.0	87.7	88.2	87.2	89.2	89.7	89.3	89.3
Filipino	78.4	77.6	77.1	77.1	78.7	79.3	81.3	80.9	82.5	83.3
Hawaiian and part Hawaiian	65.5	66.8	65.8	68.1	69.9	70.6	77.0	75.9	78.5	78.0
Other Asian or Pacific Islander	71.9	71.1	71.9	71.9	72.8	74.4	76.2	77.0	78.4	79.7
Hispanic origin (selected states) 2, 3	61.3	59.5	60.2	61.0	64.2	66.6	68.9	70.8	72.2	73.7
Mexican	58.3	56.7	57.8	58.7	62.1	64.8	67.3	69.1	70.7	72.1
Puerto Rican	63.2	62.7	63.5	65.0	67.8	70.0	71.7	74.0	75.0	76.5
Cuban	83.4	83.2	84.8	85.4	86.8	88.9	90.1	89.2	89.2	90.4
Central and South American	62.8	60.8	61.5	63.4	66.8	68.7	71.2	73.2	75.0	76.9
Other and unknown Hispanic	67.3	66.0	66.4	65.6	68.0	70.0	72.1	74.3	74.6	76.0
White, non-Hispanic (selected states) 2	81.8	82.7	83.3	83.7	84.9	85.6	86.5	87.1	87.4	87.9
Black, non-Hispanic (selected states) 2	60.4	59.9	60.7	61.9	64.0	66.1	68.3	70.4	71.5	72.3
PRENATAL CARE BEGAN DURING THIRD TRIMESTER OR NO PRENATAL CARE										
All races	6.1	6.4	6.1	5.8	5.2	4.8	4.4	4.2	4.0	3.9
White	5.0	5.2	4.9	4.7	4.2	3.9	3.6	3.5	3.3	3.2
Black	11.0	11.9	11.3	10.7	9.9	9.0	8.2	7.6	7.3	7.3
American Indian or Alaska Native	13.2	13.4	12.9	12.2	11.0	10.3	9.8	9.5	8.6	8.6
Asian or Pacific Islander	5.9	6.1	5.8	5.7	4.9	4.6	4.1	4.3	3.9	3.8
Chinese	3.4	3.6	3.4	3.4	2.9	2.9	2.7	3.0	2.5	2.4
Japanese	3.3	2.7	2.9	2.5	2.4	2.8	1.9	2.3	2.2	2.7
Filipino	4.8	4.7	4.5	5.0	4.3	4.0	3.6	4.1	3.3	3.3
Hawaiian and part Hawaiian	7.6	8.7	8.7	7.5	7.0	6.7	4.7	5.1	5.0	5.4
Other Asian or Pacific Islander	7.3	7.5	7.1	6.8	5.9	5.4	4.8	5.0	4.6	4.4
Hispanic origin (selected states) 2, 3	12.1	13.0	12.0	11.0	9.5	8.8	7.6	7.4	6.7	6.2
Mexican	13.9	14.6	13.2	12.2	10.5	9.7	8.3	8.1	7.2	6.7
Puerto Rican	10.2	11.3	10.6	9.1	8.0	7.1	6.5	5.5	5.7	5.4
Cuban	3.6	4.0	2.8	2.4	2.1	1.8	1.6	2.1	1.6	1.5
Central and South American	9.9	11.9	10.9	9.5	7.9	7.3	6.5	6.1	5.5	5.0
Other and unknown Hispanic	8.8	9.3	8.5	8.2	7.5	7.0	6.2	6.0	5.9	5.3
White, non-Hispanic (selected states) 2	4.1	3.7	3.4	3.2	2.8	2.7	2.5	2.5	2.4	2.4
Black, non-Hispanic (selected states) 2	11.0	12.0	11.2	10.7	9.8	9.0	8.2	7.6	7.3	7.3

SOURCE: E. Kramarow, H. Lentzner, R. Rooks, J. Weeks, S. Saydah. *Health and Aging Chartbook. Health, United States, 1999.* (Hyattsville, Maryland: National Center for Health Statistics. 1999.): Table 6. Based on birth certificate data compiled by the Division of Vital Statistics, National Center for Health Statistics.

— Data not available.
1. Excludes live births for whom trimester when prenatal care began is unknown.
2. Trend data for Hispanics and non-Hispanics are affected by expansion of the reporting area for an Hispanic-origin item on the birth certificate and by immigration. These two factors affect numbers of events, composition of the Hispanic population, and maternal and infant health characteristics. The number of states in the reporting area increased from 22 in 1980, to 23 and the District of Columbia (DC) in 1983–87, 30 and DC in 1988, 47 and DC in 1989, 48 and DC in 1990, 49 and DC in 1991–92, and 50 and DC in 1993 and later years.
3. Includes mothers of all races.

NOTE: Data for 1970 and 1975 exclude births that occurred in states not reporting prenatal care. The race groups, White, Black, American Indian or Alaska Native, and Asian or Pacific Islander, include persons of Hispanic and non-Hispanic origin. Conversely, persons of Hispanic origin may be of any race.

Table 2.32. Immunization of Children [1]: 1997

(Percent of children age 19–35 months)

Vaccine/Dose	White, non-Hispanic		Black, non-Hispanic		Hispanic		American Indian or Alaska Native		Asian or Pacific Islander	
	Living below the poverty level [2]	Total	Living below the poverty level [2]	Total	Living below the poverty level [2]	Total	Living below the poverty level [2]	Total	Living below the poverty level [2]	Total
DTP/DT [3]										
≥ 3 doses	93	97	95	95	92	93	92	92	96	95
≥ 4 doses	76	84	76	78	75	77	79	80	86	80
POLIOVIRUS ≥ 3 DOSES	90	92	90	90	89	90	93	91	89	88
HAEMOPHILUS INFLUENZAE **TYPE B (HIB) ≥ 3 DOSES**	90	94	92	92	89	90	93	87	85	89
MEASLES-CONTAINING VACCINE (MCV) [4] ≥ 1 DOSES	85	92	88	90	88	88	92	92	91	89
HEPATITIS B ≥ 3 DOSES	80	85	82	83	79	81	83	83	94	88
COMBINED SERIES										
≥ 4 DTP/ 3 Polio/ 1 MCV	73	80	72	74	72	74	78	78	82	75
≥ 4 DTP/ 3 Polio/ 1 MCV/ 3 Hib	72	79	71	73	70	72	78	72	73	70

SOURCE: Centers for Disease Control and Prevention; "Vaccination Coverage by Race/Ethnicity and Poverty Level Among Children Aged 19–35 Months — U.S., 1997," *Morbidity and Mortality Weekly Report* 47, no. 44 (November 13, 1998): Table 1. Data are based on the National Immunization Survey.

1. Children studied were born during February 1994–May 1996.
2. Poverty status is based on family income and household size using Bureau of the Census poverty thresholds for 1997. Children for whom poverty level was not determined were excluded from this analysis.
3. Diphtheria and tetanus toxoids and pertussis vaccine/diphtheria and tetanus toxoids.
4. Childhood Immunization Initiative goals are for measles-mumps-rubella vaccine; estimates are for MCV.

NOTE: The race groups White, non-Hispanic, Black, non-Hispanic, American Indian/ Alaskan Native, and Asian/Pacific Islander do not include children of Hispanic origin. Children of Hispanic origin may be of any race.

Table 2.33. Immunization of Children By State and Immunization Action Plan Areas

(Percent of children 19–35 months of age with 4:3:1:3 series 1)

Area	1994	1995	1996	1997	Difference from 1994–1997
United States	69	74	77	76	7
STATE					
Alabama	70	75	75	85	15
Alaska	65	72	69	75	10
Arizona	70	70	70	73	3
Arkansas	64	73	72	77	13
California	67	69	76	74	7
Colorado	66	77	76	72	6
Connecticut	81	83	87	85	4
Delaware	77	72	80	79	2
Florida	72	75	77	77	5
Georgia	75	77	80	79	4
Hawaii	78	78	77	79	1
Idaho	58	64	66	70	12
Illinois	60	79	75	74	14
Indiana	69	75	70	72	3
Iowa	75	82	80	76	1
Kansas	76	70	73	82	6
Kentucky	74	79	76	79	5
Louisiana	66	76	79	76	10
Maine	75	87	85	84	9
Maryland	75	78	78	80	5
Massachusetts	77	80	86	86	9
Michigan	55	67	74	75	20
Minnesota	74	76	83	78	4
Mississippi	79	81	79	80	1
Missouri	59	75	74	77	18
Montana	69	71	77	74	5
Nebraska	62	75	80	75	13
Nevada	63	65	70	71	8
New Hampshire	78	86	83	84	6
New Jersey	67	72	77	76	9
New Mexico	66	76	79	75	9
New York	72	77	79	76	4
North Carolina	75	80	77	80	5
North Dakota	73	81	81	82	9
Ohio	70	73	77	73	3
Oklahoma	70	73	73	71	1
Oregon	64	72	70	72	8
Pennsylvania	71	76	79	80	9
Rhode Island	78	82	85	81	3
South Carolina	78	80	84	79	1
South Dakota	67	79	80	76	9
Tennessee	68	73	77	77	9
Texas	65	73	72	74	9
Utah	62	66	63	69	7
Vermont	82	84	85	84	2
Virginia	76	71	77	72	-4
Washington	68	77	78	79	11
West Virginia	62	71	71	80	18
Wisconsin	70	74	76	79	9
Wyoming	71	71	77	72	1
SELECTED CITIES AND COUNTIES					
Baltimore, Maryland	74	75	81	83	9
Bexar County (San Antonio), Texas	60	74	74	79	19
Boston, Massachusetts	87	87	84	86	-1
Chicago, Illinois	55	69	74	68	13
Cuyahoga County (Cleveland), Ohio	82	71	80	73	-9
Dade County (Miami), Florida	73	77	76	75	2
Dallas County (Dallas), Texas	62	70	71	74	12
Davidson County (Nashville), Tennessee	65	73	77	77	12
Detroit, Michigan	45	57	63	65	20
Duval County (Jacksonville), Florida	69	71	76	70	1
El Paso County (El Paso), Texas	78	77	62	65	-13
Franklin County (Columbus), Ohio	71	74	78	74	3
Fulton/DeKalb Counties (Atlanta), Georgia	72	79	74	75	3
Houston, Texas	57	70	68	64	7
Jefferson County (Birmingham), Alabama	72	85	77	82	10
King County (Seattle), Washington	70	82	81	77	7
Los Angeles County (Los Angeles), California	65	70	79	71	6
Maricopa County (Phoenix), Arizona	71	69	71	72	1
Marion County (Indianapolis), Indiana	72	75	72	81	9
Milwaukee County (Milwaukee), Wisconsin	72	68	70	70	-2
New York City, New York	73	78	75	75	2
Newark, New Jersey	46	67	62	66	20
Orleans Parish (New Orleans), Louisiana	59	75	71	69	10
Philadelphia, Pennsylvania	67	67	75	78	11
San Diego County (San Diego), California	68	73	77	78	10
Santa Clara County (Santa Clara), California	78	74	79	73	-5
Shelby County (Memphis), Tennessee	67	68	70	70	3
District of Columbia	67	67	78	73	6
Median	70	74	77	76	
Low	45	57	62	64	
High	87	87	86	86	

SOURCE: E. Kramarow, H. Lentzner, R. Rooks, J. Weeks, S. Saydah. *Health and Aging Chartbook. Health, United States, 1999.* (Hyattsville, Maryland: National Center for Health Statistics, 1999.): Table 52. Centers for Disease Control and Prevention. "Vaccination Coverage by Race/Ethnicity and Poverty Level Among Children Aged 19–35 Months — U.S., 1997," *Morbidity and Mortality Weekly Report* 47, no. 28 (November 13, 1998): Table 1. Data are based on the National Immunization Survey. The selected cities and counties include all of the immunization action plan areas designated by the CDC.

1. The 4:3:1:3 combined series consists of 4 doses of diptheria-tetanus-pertussis (DTP) vaccine, 3 doses of polio vaccine, 1 dose of a measles-containing vaccine, and 3 doses of Haemophilus influnzae type b (Hib) vaccine.

NOTE: Urban areas were chosen because they were high risk for under-vaccination. Final estimates of data from the National Immunization Survey include an adjustment for children with missing immunization provider data. Data are based on telephone interviews of a sample of the civilian noninstitutionalized population supplemented by a survey of immunization providers for interview participants.

Table 2.34. Hypertension

(Percent)

Characteristic	1960–1962	1971–1974	1976–1980 [1]	1988–1994
20–74 YEARS, AGE ADJUSTED [2]				
Both sexes [3]	36.9	38.3	39.0	23.1
Male	40.0	42.4	44.0	25.3
Female [3]	33.7	34.3	34.0	20.8
White male	39.3	41.7	43.5	24.3
White female [3]	31.7	32.4	32.3	19.3
Black male	48.1	51.8	48.7	34.9
Black female [3]	50.8	50.3	47.5	33.8
White, non-Hispanic male	—	—	43.9	24.4
White, non-Hispanic female [3]	—	—	32.1	19.3
Black, non-Hispanic male	—	—	48.7	35.0
Black, non-Hispanic female [3]	—	—	47.6	34.2
Mexican male	—	—	25.0	25.2
Mexican female [3]	—	—	21.8	22.0
20–74 YEARS, CRUDE				
Both sexes [3]	39.0	39.7	39.7	23.1
Male	41.7	43.3	44.0	24.7
Female [3]	36.6	36.5	35.6	21.5
White male	41.0	42.8	43.8	24.3
White female [3]	34.9	34.9	34.2	20.4
Black male	50.5	52.1	47.4	31.5
Black female [3]	52.0	50.2	46.1	30.6
White, non-Hispanic male	—	—	44.3	25.0
White, non-Hispanic female [3]	—	—	34.4	20.9
Black, non-Hispanic male	—	—	47.5	31.6
Black, non-Hispanic female [3]	—	—	46.1	31.2
Mexican male	—	—	18.8	18.0
Mexican female [3]	—	—	16.7	15.8
MALE				
20–34 years	22.8	24.8	28.9	8.6
35–44 years	37.7	39.1	40.5	20.9
45–54 years	47.6	55.0	53.6	34.1
55–64 years	60.3	62.5	61.8	42.9
65–74 years	68.8	67.2	67.1	57.3
75 years and over	—	—	—	64.2
FEMALE [3]				
20–34 years	9.3	11.2	11.1	3.4
35–44 years	24.0	28.2	28.8	12.7
45–54 years	43.4	43.6	47.1	25.1
55–64 years	66.4	62.5	61.1	44.2
65–74 years	81.5	78.3	71.8	60.8
75 years and over	—	—	—	77.3

SOURCE: E. Kramarow, H. Lentzner, R. Rooks, J. Weeks, S. Saydah. *Health and Aging Chartbook. Health, United States, 1999.* (Hyattsville, Maryland: National Center for Health Statistics, 1999.): Table 68.

— Data not available.
1. Data for Mexicans are for 1982–1984. See Appendix I of *Health, United States, 1999*.
2. See Appendix II of *Health, United States, 1999* for age-adjustment procedure.
3. Excludes pregnant women.

NOTE: The race groups, White and Black, include persons of Hispanic and non-Hispanic origin. Conversely, persons of Hispanic origin may be of any race. A person with hypertension is defined by either having elevated blood pressure (systolic pressure of at least 140 mmHg or diastolic pressure of at least 90 mmHg) or taking antihypertensive medication. Percents are based on a single measurement of blood pressure to provide comparable data across the four time periods. In 1976–80, 31.3 percent of persons 20–74 years of age had hypertension, based on the average of three blood pressure measurements, in contrast to 39.7 percent when a single measurement is used.

Table 2.35. Cholesterol

(Percent)

Characteristic	High serum cholesterol				Mean serum cholesterol level, mg/dL			
	1960–1962	1971–1974	1976–1980 [1]	1988–1994	1960–1962	1971–1974	1976–1980 [1]	1988–1994
20–74 YEARS, AGE ADJUSTED [2]								
Both sexes	31.8	27.2	26.3	18.9	220.0	214.0	213.0	203.0
Male	28.7	25.8	24.6	17.5	217.0	213.0	211.0	202.0
Female	34.5	28.2	27.6	20.0	222.0	215.0	214.0	204.0
White male	29.4	25.9	24.6	17.8	218.0	213.0	211.0	202.0
White female	35.1	28.1	28.0	20.2	223.0	215.0	214.0	205.0
Black male	24.5	25.1	24.1	15.7	210.0	212.0	208.0	199.0
Black female	30.7	29.2	24.9	19.4	216.0	217.0	213.0	203.0
White, non-Hispanic male	—	—	24.7	17.3	—	—	211.0	202.0
White, non-Hispanic female	—	—	28.3	20.2	—	—	214.0	205.0
Black, non-Hispanic male	—	—	24.0	15.7	—	—	208.0	200.0
Black, non-Hispanic female	—	—	24.9	19.8	—	—	214.0	203.0
Mexican male	—	—	18.8	17.8	—	—	207.0	204.0
Mexican female	—	—	20.0	17.5	—	—	207.0	203.0
20–74 YEARS, CRUDE								
Both sexes	33.6	28.2	26.8	18.7	222.0	216.0	213.0	203.0
Male	30.7	26.8	24.9	17.6	220.0	214.0	211.0	202.0
Female	36.3	29.6	28.5	19.9	225.0	217.0	215.0	204.0
White male	31.4	26.9	25.0	18.1	221.0	215.0	211.0	203.0
White female	37.5	29.8	29.2	20.5	227.0	217.0	216.0	205.0
Black male	26.7	25.1	23.9	14.4	214.0	212.0	208.0	198.0
Black female	29.9	28.8	23.7	16.8	216.0	216.0	212.0	199.0
White, non-Hispanic male	—	—	25.1	17.9	—	—	211.0	203.0
White, non-Hispanic female	—	—	29.8	20.9	—	—	216.0	206.0
Black, non-Hispanic male	—	—	23.7	14.5	—	—	208.0	198.0
Black, non-Hispanic female	—	—	23.7	17.2	—	—	212.0	200.0
Mexican male	—	—	16.6	15.5	—	—	203.0	200.0
Mexican female	—	—	16.5	14.0	—	—	202.0	197.0
MALE								
20–34 years	15.1	12.4	11.9	8.2	198.0	194.0	192.0	186.0
35–44 years	33.9	31.8	27.9	19.4	227.0	221.0	217.0	206.0
45–54 years	39.2	37.5	36.9	26.6	231.0	229.0	227.0	216.0
55–64 years	41.6	36.2	36.8	28.0	233.0	229.0	229.0	216.0
65–74 years	38.0	34.7	31.7	21.9	230.0	226.0	221.0	212.0
75 years and over	—	—	—	20.4	—	—	—	205.0
FEMALE								
20–34 years	12.4	10.9	9.8	7.3	194.0	191.0	189.0	184.0
35–44 years	23.1	19.3	20.7	12.3	214.0	207.0	207.0	195.0
45–54 years	46.9	38.7	40.5	26.7	237.0	232.0	232.0	217.0
55–64 years	70.1	53.1	52.9	40.9	262.0	245.0	249.0	235.0
65–74 years	68.5	57.7	51.6	41.3	266.0	250.0	246.0	233.0
75 years and over	—	—	—	38.2	—	—	—	229.0

SOURCE: E. Kramarow, H. Lentzner, R. Rooks, J. Weeks, S. Saydah. *Health and Aging Chartbook. Health, United States, 1999*. Hyattsville, Maryland: National Center for Health Statistics. 1999: Table 69.

— Data not available.
1. Data for Mexicans are for 1982–1984. See Appendix I of *Health, United States, 1999*.
2. See Appendix II of *Health, United States, 1999* for age-adjustment procedure.

NOTE: The race groups, white and black, include persons of Hispanic and non-Hispanic origin. Conversely, persons of Hispanic origin may be of any race. High serum cholesterol is defined as greater than or equal to 240 mg/dL (6.20 mmol/L). Risk levels have been defined by the second report of the National Cholesterol Education Program Expert Panel on Detection, Evaluation and Treatment of High Blood Cholesterol in Adults. National Heart, Lung, and Blood Institute, National Institutes of Health. September 1993. (Summarized in the *Journal of the American Medical Association* 269, no. 23: 3015–23. June 16, 1993.)

Table 2.36. Cardiovascular Risk Factors: 1997

(Percent)

Area	Blood pressure			Cholesterol		
	Screened in the past two years	High blood pressure [1]		Screened in the past five years	High cholesterol [2]	
		Males	Females		Males	Females
STATE						
Alabama	95.4	24.8	32.5	71.0	28.7	28.9
Alaska	91.8	20.3	25.1	62.4	24.8	26.2
Arizona	93.5	15.3	17.3	68.5	30.1	33.5
Arkansas	93.3	24.7	27.8	58.6	32.7	28.1
California	90.7	20.5	22.0	65.8	30.2	30.5
Colorado	93.1	19.3	21.5	69.7	30.0	26.1
Connecticut	95.1	20.5	20.7	73.3	25.1	23.7
Delaware	94.3	24.3	26.6	69.3	27.9	29.7
Florida	94.3	25.2	26.8	75.3	30.3	33.3
Georgia	96.4	18.4	24.2	72.6	20.6	26.9
Hawaii	95.5	24.6	23.3	69.5	31.2	31.8
Idaho	91.3	24.5	23.7	65.0	30.3	29.3
Illinois	94.3	22.7	25.6	67.2	33.1	35.2
Indiana	93.1	23.8	26.4	66.4	26.8	30.9
Iowa	92.7	22.4	24.3	66.1	27.4	28.6
Kansas	94.7	19.0	22.6	54.9	27.2	28.8
Kentucky	93.8	26.5	27.7	65.6	28.5	31.5
Louisiana	94.4	23.1	26.9	66.3	24.1	28.5
Maine	94.5	22.3	23.3	71.8	32.7	31.7
Maryland	96.4	22.9	24.6	74.5	28.6	28.7
Massachusetts	96.0	20.1	19.5	74.7	24.7	25.2
Michigan	94.9	22.4	24.2	71.1	31.5	30.9
Minnesota	92.5	20.1	22.2	61.2	30.4	31.9
Mississippi	95.5	33.1	35.5	62.5	27.6	29.7
Missouri	94.7	25.0	29.4	70.4	30.1	30.8
Montana	92.3	22.2	23.5	63.2	29.9	32.0
Nebraska	93.2	21.5	23.1	65.5	32.5	28.0
Nevada	93.3	26.4	21.8	68.4	29.8	29.4
New Hampshire	94.0	23.4	21.9	73.0	30.8	31.1
New Jersey	94.4	24.0	23.3	75.3	26.4	29.2
New Mexico	90.8	22.7	20.0	62.8	28.7	27.3
New York	94.8	21.6	23.7	72.5	26.2	29.6
North Carolina	93.9	21.0	25.5	72.1	25.2	27.5
North Dakota	93.0	25.6	25.4	63.8	27.8	31.6
Ohio	95.5	21.2	22.7	66.5	28.4	27.0
Oklahoma	94.2	20.8	22.5	74.4	20.0	23.8
Oregon	92.2	22.3	23.3	68.2	31.2	32.6
Pennsylvania	95.6	20.7	22.5	68.5	25.5	26.2
Rhode Island	95.7	20.4	24.3	74.7	27.1	28.9
South Carolina	96.5	25.5	28.0	72.2	22.6	25.9
South Dakota	92.7	18.4	22.7	63.2	24.9	26.3
Tennessee	95.1	24.6	30.6	70.3	26.1	32.2
Texas	92.4	20.8	25.3	67.4	26.6	30.4
Utah	92.1	22.3	22.8	65.6	27.5	25.3
Vermont	93.6	21.6	20.3	68.9	26.1	25.7
Virginia	93.9	23.9	25.0	73.6	32.6	26.6
Washington	92.9	21.3	25.0	69.6	24.4	26.8
West Virginia	93.6	28.1	28.5	67.2	31.0	33.2
Wisconsin	92.6	24.3	22.1	70.2	26.6	27.2
Wyoming	90.7	21.1	23.1	70.2	32.2	27.8
OTHER						
District of Columbia	97.3	16.7	21.6	79.4	16.3	19.6
Puerto Rico	94.9	19.2	22.3	79.3	23.2	25.3

SOURCE: Centers for Disease Control and Prevention, 1997 Behavioral Risk Factor Surveillance System (BRFSS), *Summary Prevalence Report* (August 1998): Tables 9.3, 8.2, 11.3, and 12.2.

1. Ever told blood pressure is high by a health professional.
2. Ever told cholesterol is high by a health professional.

Table 2.37. Mammogram Testing

(Percent of women over 40 years of age who have ever had a mammogram [1])

Characteristic	1989	1990	1991	1992	1993	1994	1995	1996	1997
AGE									
40–49 years	63.3	68.6	74.0	75.6	77.4	78.2	80.4	80.6	80.4
50–59 years	71.1	72.2	78.5	79.4	83.2	84.0	87.6	87.7	89.2
60–69 years	65.2	70.7	74.3	75.7	81.4	83.1	86.2	86.6	88.5
70 years	56.2	61.3	67.2	69.2	74.4	76.2	79.1	81.8	82.3
RACE									
White	64.5	68.8	73.9	75.9	79.7	80.7	83.4	84.4	84.9
Black	63.8	66.4	72.0	70.1	75.4	78.8	81.7	83.7	85.1
Asian or Pacific Islander	48.2	60.8	65.3	70.9	75.3	79.2	81.8	83.9	86.3
American Indian or Alaska Native	62.5	59.7	78.0	75.7	79.7	66.6	85.2	75.3	78.7
Other	54.8	61.4	50.5	59.1	72.9	79.1	79.4	75.1	84.1
RACE AND AGE									
White									
40–49 years	65.0	69.5	74.1	76.8	78.5	79.0	80.5	81.4	80.0
50–59 years	70.9	72.7	79.1	80.7	84.1	84.2	87.9	88.1	89.9
60–69 years	66.2	71.5	75.3	76.2	81.6	83.8	86.2	86.9	88.8
70 years	55.6	61.1	67.1	69.7	74.7	76.0	79.6	81.8	82.3
Black									
40–49 years	58.7	66.2	72.9	69.3	75.9	74.4	79.8	78.0	82.4
50–59 years	73.5	68.5	75.9	73.0	78.1	81.0	86.9	88.7	87.2
60–69 years	64.2	67.2	71.1	75.1	77.7	80.7	84.8	86.4	86.9
70 years	60.3	63.8	68.1	63.0	69.3	80.2	75.9	83.2	84.7
ETHNICITY									
Hispanic	56.0	63.6	68.0	67.2	72.4	73.3	82.1	80.4	82.0
Non-Hispanic	64.5	68.6	74.0	75.6	79.5	80.7	83.3	84.3	85.1
ANNUAL HOUSEHOLD INCOME									
Under $10,000	51.6	57.2	62.4	62.2	66.6	71.3	73.3	73.1	76.7
$10,000–25,000	60.8	62.9	68.3	71.3	74.4	76.9	77.6	78.8	79.0
$25,000–50,000	70.0	75.7	80.1	80.5	83.7	84.0	85.4	86.6	87.5
Over $50,000	78.7	80.7	85.2	85.8	90.0	89.7	92.3	93.4	90.3
EDUCATION									
Less than 12 years	53.6	56.6	61.4	61.4	67.1	70.4	74.4	76.2	75.9
12 years	63.2	67.9	72.5	74.5	78.1	78.7	81.8	81.8	83.9
Over 12 years	70.6	74.6	79.9	81.6	84.4	85.8	87.7	88.4	88.6
HEALTH CARE INSURANCE									
Yes	—	—	75.4	77.4	81.1	82.2	84.7	85.7	86.5
No	—	—	55.7	53.5	55.8	59.9	64.9	71.1	68.5
TOTAL	63.9	68.3	73.5	75.0	79.0	80.3	83.2	84.0	84.8

SOURCE: D.K. Blackman, E.M. Bennett, and D.S. Miller. "Trends in Self-Reported Use of Mammograms (1989–1997) and Papanicolaou Tests (1991–1997)—Behavioral Risk Factor Surveillance System (BRFSS)," *Morbidity and Mortality Weekly Report* 48, no. SS06, October 8, 1999: Table 3. This table is based on the BRFSS of the 38 states that reported each year.

— Question not asked in 1989 or 1990.
1. Adjusted to the 1989 BRFSS age distribution for women.

Table 2.38. Papanicolaou Testing

(Percent of women who have ever had a Papanicolaou test [1])

Characteristic	1991	1992	1993	1994	1995	1996	1997
AGE							
Under 40 years	90.2	91.2	90.9	91.5	91.1	90.7	91.2
40–49 years	97.4	97.5	97.4	97.8	96.8	97.9	97.6
50–59 years	94.1	95.1	96.0	96.2	96.0	96.8	96.8
60–69 years	91.4	92.5	93.4	94.4	93.8	95.9	95.1
70 years	83.4	85.3	86.0	85.9	86.7	88.2	88.4
RACE							
White	92.0	92.7	93.2	93.6	93.0	93.8	93.7
Black	89.6	91.9	91.0	92.0	93.1	93.3	94.3
Asian or Pacific Islander	74.3	79.8	77.8	80.2	78.6	84.1	81.6
American Indian or Alaska Native	83.2	88.6	94.7	90.5	91.0	94.2	90.9
Other	88.4	84.0	79.5	81.0	85.6	78.5	83.1
RACE AND AGE							
White							
Under 40 years	91.3	91.8	92.0	92.5	91.6	91.8	91.8
40–49 years	97.6	97.9	98.3	98.3	97.4	98.7	98.4
50–59 years	95.2	96.1	96.6	97.0	96.5	97.3	97.2
60–69 years	92.1	92.7	94.2	95.3	94.4	96.0	95.8
70 years	84.0	85.9	86.6	86.5	87.5	88.8	89.2
Black							
Under 40 years	90.1	93.9	92.4	91.5	95.0	93.1	95.1
40–49 years	97.5	97.2	96.7	97.8	95.2	97.6	97.4
50–59 years	89.6	93.6	93.5	96.2	98.2	95.6	96.9
60–69 years	88.6	91.0	87.9	94.4	90.3	95.6	93.4
70 years	78.8	77.2	79.4	85.9	81.2	83.7	84.9
ETHNICITY							
Hispanic	84.0	84.3	84.0	84.0	86.1	84.4	86.7
Non-Hispanic	91.9	93.0	93.0	93.6	93.3	93.9	93.8
ANNUAL HOUSEHOLD INCOME							
Under $10,000	86.6	87.5	86.7	89.4	85.5	89.5	89.0
$10,000–25,000	91.3	92.5	92.1	94.2	92.2	91.9	92.9
$25,000–50,000	94.2	94.2	94.7	94.8	95.2	94.9	95.0
Over $50,000	93.4	94.1	95.6	94.2	94.6	94.5	93.8
EDUCATION							
Less than 12 years	84.2	86.4	86.3	89.0	86.8	88.2	88.6
12 years	91.4	92.3	92.6	92.6	92.6	92.9	93.5
Over 12 years	93.5	94.0	94.1	94.6	94.4	94.5	94.2
HEALTH CARE INSURANCE							
Yes	92.7	93.2	93.2	93.7	93.3	94.0	94.0
No	82.0	85.2	82.0	84.0	84.9	86.6	85.3
TOTAL	91.1	92.2	92.3	92.8	92.4	93.0	93.1

SOURCE: D.K. Blackman, E.M. Bennett, and D.S. Miller. "Trends in Self-Reported Use of Mammograms (1989–1997) and Papanicolaou Tests (1991–1997)—Behavioral Risk Factor Surveillance System," *Morbidity and Mortality Weekly Report* 48, no. SS06, October 8, 1999: Table 8. This table is based on the Behavioral Risk Factor Surveillance System (BRFSS) of the 38 states that reported each year.

1. Adjusted to the 1989 BRFSS age distribution for women.

Table 2.39. Recent Mammogram Testing

(Percent of women over 40 years of age who have had a mammogram in the past two years [1])

Characteristic	1989	1990	1991	1992	1993	1994	1995	1996	1997
AGE									
40–49 years	54.3	59.5	64.3	63.6	65.9	64.1	66.1	64.0	65.0
50–59 years	61.3	63.0	68.2	68.7	71.5	72.2	76.8	76.3	78.0
60–69 years	55.1	61.0	64.2	63.9	69.2	71.7	74.3	75.2	77.1
70 years	46.3	50.2	55.8	57.1	60.2	61.0	64.9	66.7	66.7
RACE									
White	54.7	59.2	63.4	64.2	67.0	67.3	70.2	70.5	71.4
Black	55.7	56.8	62.5	60.2	65.5	67.6	71.2	71.5	72.9
Asian or Pacific Islander	38.8	55.5	57.8	60.8	66.0	68.6	70.0	66.2	72.5
American Indian or Alaska Native	45.4	50.5	63.4	63.7	66.7	56.0	76.6	56.7	59.9
Other	43.3	45.9	49.1	46.7	60.2	66.0	67.1	62.7	59.7
RACE AND AGE									
White									
40–49 years	55.7	60.6	63.9	65.0	66.5	64.5	65.6	64.6	64.2
50–59 years	60.8	63.9	68.9	69.6	71.9	72.0	76.9	76.9	78.8
60–69 years	55.5	61.6	64.7	64.4	69.4	72.4	73.9	75.4	77.4
70 years	46.2	50.0	55.8	57.4	60.3	60.6	65.3	66.7	66.9
Black									
40–49 years	52.9	57.3	64.7	58.5	67.2	64.7	69.9	63.8	71.0
50–59 years	64.7	56.8	61.9	65.2	70.3	70.8	78.6	77.8	76.3
60–69 years	57.0	59.3	63.6	62.5	65.2	70.4	74.4	77.0	78.1
70 years	48.8	53.4	59.1	54.9	59.0	65.2	61.9	69.1	66.5
ETHNICITY									
Hispanic	45.2	53.3	57.4	54.2	61.4	61.3	71.8	67.3	67.0
Non-Hispanic	54.9	58.9	63.7	64.0	67.1	67.5	70.3	70.5	71.7
ANNUAL HOUSEHOLD INCOME									
Under $10,000	42.1	46.3	49.8	48.1	51.3	57.2	59.5	55.0	58.4
$10,000–25,000	50.8	52.2	56.4	59.2	60.5	61.9	63.0	63.2	64.1
$25,000–50,000	61.0	66.8	71.6	70.1	73.3	72.6	73.2	73.6	74.6
Over $50,000	68.0	73.7	76.7	76.5	80.0	78.8	83.3	81.5	79.1
EDUCATION									
Less than 12 years	44.1	46.6	51.7	48.2	53.3	56.5	61.0	60.0	58.8
12 years	53.0	58.0	61.2	62.8	65.7	65.1	68.6	68.7	71.0
Over 12 years	61.5	65.4	70.3	70.7	73.2	73.6	75.7	75.2	75.9
HEALTH CARE INSURANCE									
Yes	—	—	65.4	66.2	69.4	69.8	72.5	72.6	73.7
No	—	—	42.6	38.5	36.7	40.8	42.9	48.9	50.0
TOTAL	54.3	58.6	63.2	63.4	66.7	67.1	70.3	70.2	71.3

SOURCE: D.K. Blackman, E.M. Bennett, and D.S. Miller. "Trends in Self-Reported Use of Mammograms (1989–1997) and Papanicolaou Tests (1991–1997)—Behavioral Risk Factor Surveillance System," *Morbidity and Mortality Weekly Report* 48, no. SS06, October 8, 1999: Table 5. This table is based on the Behavioral Risk Factor Surveillance System (BRFSS) of the 38 states that reported each year.

— Question not asked in 1989 or 1990.
1. Adjusted to the 1989 BRFSS age distribution for women.

Table 2.40. Recent Papanicolaou Testing

(Percent of women who have had a Papanicolaou test in the past two years [1])

Characteristic	1991	1992	1993	1994	1995	1996	1997
AGE							
Under 40 years	84.4	83.9	83.8	84.2	83.5	83.0	84.2
40–49 years	84.0	81.2	82.4	81.9	82.0	82.6	83.0
50–59 years	78.5	76.7	78.8	76.2	80.1	80.1	82.8
60–69 years	68.7	68.2	71.9	72.5	71.3	74.2	76.5
70 years	58.5	56.6	56.9	57.4	59.6	58.9	58.7
RACE							
White	78.9	77.4	78.7	78.5	78.4	78.8	80.1
Black	80.4	79.9	79.5	80.6	82.5	81.6	83.9
Asian or Pacific Islander	59.7	67.2	66.5	67.0	68.9	72.6	72.9
American Indian or Alaska Native	67.6	76.4	77.6	77.8	75.1	74.2	69.2
Other	72.8	71.1	68.2	66.4	73.6	66.2	66.7
RACE AND AGE							
White							
Under 40 years	85.4	84.0	84.6	84.7	83.8	83.6	84.5
40–49 years	83.7	81.6	82.7	82.4	82.0	82.6	83.1
50–59 years	78.6	77.3	79.4	76.4	79.8	80.5	83.2
60–69 years	69.1	68.2	72.6	73.4	70.9	73.5	77.3
70 years	58.7	56.5	56.9	57.4	60.1	59.5	59.2
Black							
Under 40 years	85.5	89.8	88.8	89.6	89.3	88.6	91.0
40–49 years	86.9	83.2	84.4	82.7	84.5	85.9	89.0
50–59 years	80.5	78.3	73.3	76.7	85.9	78.8	84.6
60–69 years	71.8	66.4	66.2	70.1	72.2	81.7	75.4
70 years	61.8	54.4	58.0	58.9	60.9	52.5	58.6
ETHNICITY							
Hispanic	70.8	70.2	71.7	69.8	74.8	70.6	72.8
Non-Hispanic	79.1	78.0	78.8	78.9	78.9	79.5	80.5
ANNUAL HOUSEHOLD INCOME							
Under $10,000	70.3	68.3	67.9	72.0	66.0	68.1	68.7
$10,000–25,000	75.4	74.4	74.7	75.4	73.9	72.9	75.0
$25,000–50,000	83.6	81.9	82.2	81.7	81.4	81.5	81.7
Over $50,000	83.3	85.0	86.3	83.3	86.3	86.1	84.5
EDUCATION							
Less than 12 years	68.9	65.7	67.1	69.9	69.3	67.9	70.2
12 years	77.2	76.0	76.6	76.5	76.3	76.3	78.4
Over 12 years	82.5	81.5	82.6	81.8	82.7	82.7	83.1
HEALTH CARE INSURANCE							
Yes	80.7	79.4	80.4	80.4	80.5	81.1	82.2
No	63.2	61.7	58.1	60.1	62.0	59.3	64.5
TOTAL	78.4	77.2	78.1	78.1	78.3	78.5	79.7

SOURCE: D.K. Blackman, E.M. Bennett, and D.S. Miller. "Trends in Self-Reported Use of Mammograms (1989–1997) and Papanicolaou Tests (1991–1997)—Behavioral Risk Factor Surveillance System," *Morbidity and Mortality Weekly Report* 48, no. SS06, October 8, 1999: Table 9. This table is based on the Behavioral Risk Factor Surveillance System (BRFSS) of the 38 states that reported each year.

1. Adjusted to the 1989 BRFSS age distribution for women.

Table 2.41. Mammogram Testing as Part of a Regular Exam

(percent)

Characteristic	1989	1990	1991	1992	1993	1994	1995	1996	1997
AGE									
40–49 years	49.5	57.7	63.5	64.9	67.8	69.2	70.5	71.2	71.9
50–59 years	61.2	62.0	67.5	70.9	75.5	75.9	78.5	79.9	81.1
60–69 years	54.7	62.2	65.3	67.6	72.9	74.6	77.5	79.6	80.4
70 years	47.8	53.5	58.3	60.8	66.5	68.4	71.5	74.2	75.5
RACE									
White	53.1	59.1	63.7	66.6	70.8	72.0	74.0	76.0	76.8
Black	57.4	59.2	63.9	63.0	69.5	72.0	76.4	77.4	78.9
Asian or Pacific Islander	41.6	57.3	60.5	62.0	74.2	73.4	76.0	78.8	80.7
American Indian or Alaska Native	55.4	48.5	70.2	64.3	68.8	58.2	71.2	68.6	68.4
Other	49.4	54.0	44.7	54.3	66.6	69.4	71.3	67.0	76.6
RACE AND AGE									
White									
40–49 years	50.5	58.2	63.1	65.5	68.6	69.5	70.1	71.7	71.2
50–59 years	60.8	62.4	67.7	71.9	76.0	76.2	78.4	80.0	81.4
60–69 years	54.8	62.7	66.0	68.0	72.6	74.9	76.8	79.3	80.4
70 years	46.6	52.9	58.1	61.3	66.4	68.1	71.8	74.2	75.4
Black									
40–49 years	51.8	57.4	64.7	61.9	67.9	67.4	73.6	70.2	76.7
50–59 years	62.4	59.4	65.1	66.5	73.6	74.3	81.7	83.0	81.1
60–69 years	59.5	60.6	65.0	68.6	72.7	75.8	80.6	83.2	79.9
70 years	57.5	59.8	60.5	55.1	64.1	71.8	70.3	75.3	78.6
ETHNICITY									
Hispanic	45.2	56.3	60.3	59.4	66.0	66.3	73.2	71.7	77.2
Non-Hispanic	53.6	59.0	64.0	66.5	70.8	72.2	74.4	76.3	77.0
ANNUAL HOUSEHOLD INCOME									
Under $10,000	41.8	47.1	51.1	53.0	57.8	61.6	62.4	62.9	65.8
$10,000–25,000	48.8	53.7	58.2	61.7	65.1	69.0	69.6	70.1	70.7
$25,000–50,000	59.1	66.2	70.1	71.2	75.3	75.0	76.1	78.1	80.1
Over $50,000	68.9	71.7	75.5	75.6	81.1	80.9	82.7	86.2	82.4
EDUCATION									
Less than 12 years	43.2	48.1	51.7	53.1	58.2	61.9	66.4	65.7	67.7
12 years	52.0	58.6	62.0	65.9	69.7	70.2	72.8	74.3	76.1
Over 12 years	59.6	64.6	70.4	71.7	75.6	77.4	78.6	80.5	80.4
HEALTH CARE INSURANCE									
Yes	—	—	65.5	68.4	72.5	73.8	75.7	77.7	78.6
No	—	—	47.4	44.6	49.6	51.9	56.3	62.1	61.7
TOTAL	53.1	58.8	63.7	66.0	70.5	71.9	74.3	75.9	76.9

SOURCE: D.K. Blackman, E.M. Bennett, and D.S. Miller. "Trends in Self-Reported Use of Mammograms (1989–1997) and Papanicolaou Tests (1991–1997)—Behavioral Risk Factor Surveillance System," *Morbidity and Mortality Weekly Report* 48, no. SS06, October 8, 1999: Table 4. This table is based on the Behavioral Risk Factor Surveillance System (BRFSS) of the 38 states that reported each year.

— Question not asked in 1989 or 1990.

Table 2.42. Women Lacking Screening for Cancer

(Percent)

Area	Women age 50 years and over				Women age 18 years and over[1]	
	No mammogram in the past two years		No breast exam by doctor in past two years		No Pap smear in past three years	
	1997	1998	1997	1998	1997	1998
STATE						
Alabama	24.8	23.9	26.0	22.0	14.0	14.7
Alaska	21.8	20.9	20.3	20.2	9.7	10.5
Arizona	26.2	17.4	24.4	17.3	20.7	18.3
Arkansas	44.1	34.1	36.6	34.7	21.8	21.1
Colorado	23.9	22.6	21.5	22.0	12.4	13.0
Connecticut	22.3	22.0	23.7	22.2	17.0	13.8
Delaware	20.3	18.7	18.7	16.5	10.2	12.9
Florida	21.1	22.0	21.8	24.0	15.3	14.1
Georgia	24.6	27.5	17.2	27.1	7.7	13.9
Hawaii	17.6	22.9	19.1	20.4	13.2	13.7
Idaho	35.1	29.1	28.3	26.6	18.4	17.5
Illinois	27.0	28.6	27.6	27.6	17.3	15.5
Indiana	34.5	28.5	30.6	26.6	15.5	19.1
Iowa	32.1	28.6	26.3	27.7	19.5	15.5
Kansas	30.0	24.7	23.6	24.2	14.1	14.4
Kentucky	30.4	31.6	26.7	27.5	18.3	15.7
Louisiana	30.1	29.8	35.2	28.5	16.2	15.2
Maine	22.4	22.9	17.0	18.5	11.9	15.0
Maryland	19.5	19.2	15.6	22.5	11.3	10.8
Massachusetts	19.1	15.8	16.3	20.6	11.6	12.3
Michigan	20.1	21.1	22.4	24.6	13.7	11.9
Minnesota	26.3	35.1	21.3	27.8	16.6	15.0
Mississippi	35.3	32.1	26.7	29.9	14.1	15.6
Missouri	31.0	26.0	25.5	26.0	16.1	14.6
Montana	29.6	27.7	21.6	22.2	15.4	19.4
Nebraska	32.5	30.3	28.9	30.1	15.9	17.6
Nevada	32.3	28.4	30.3	29.5	14.4	14.9
New Hampshire	20.3	22.9	14.7	20.1	13.0	15.8
New Jersey	26.3	24.5	26.8	28.3	18.7	18.6
New Mexico	32.3	25.0	27.5	27.1	19.4	17.4
New York	21.9	22.9	13.6	23.5	13.0	16.2
North Carolina	25.6	21.0	17.6	18.4	12.7	12.3
North Dakota	27.4	25.1	24.4	23.3	17.6	14.5
Ohio	25.1	26.6	18.3	24.7	12.7	15.8
Oklahoma	34.8	29.1	18.3	25.5	15.6	15.2
Oregon	20.7	21.3	19.9	25.2	14.0	16.3
Pennsylvania	26.2	22.7	29.7	27.0	17.7	16.2
Rhode Island	16.9	18.8	20.4	22.2	12.6	14.8
South Carolina	24.5	22.8	17.0	24.8	10.3	15.0
South Dakota	29.2	25.0	24.1	19.2	15.0	13.7
Tennessee	26.0	24.8	20.2	20.5	12.3	13.9
Texas	31.9	27.3	28.1	29.3	19.1	18.5
Utah	29.8	28.8	22.8	30.1	21.5	21.6
Vermont	26.5	23.0	24.5	24.7	16.0	14.0
Virginia	23.7	22.2	21.5	24.4	12.1	15.1
Washington	26.6	21.6	22.3	22.3	13.0	14.6
West Virginia	30.7	25.0	27.3	22.8	21.1	19.0
Wisconsin	29.1	26.0	24.8	25.2	16.2	16.6
Wyoming	30.7	31.3	29.2	32.2	16.3	18.0
OTHER						
District of Columbia	16.4	10.6	16.7	9.8	7.9	6.1
Puerto Rico	38.1	43.2	23.2	41.0	28.2	32.4

SOURCE: Centers for Disease Control and Prevention, Behavioral Risk Factor Surveillance System. *1998 BRFSS Summary Prevalence Report (July 1999): Tables 29.2, 32.2, and 37.2.*

1. Among women with intact cervix.

NOTES

1. National Institutes of Health, National Institute on *Drug Abuse, Drug Abuse and Addiction Research: 25 Years of Discovery to Advance the Health of the Public. The Sixth Triennial Report to Congress from the Secretary of Health and Human Services* (Washington, D.C.: U.S. Government Printing Office, September 1999).

2. See S.I. Kelly, N. Day, and A.P. Streissguth, "Effects of Prenatal Alcohol Exposure on Social Behavior in Humans and Other Species," *Neurotoxicology and Teratology* 22, no. 2 (March–April 2000):143–149. See also M.H. Lifschitz, and G.S. Wilson, "Patterns of Growth and Development in Narcotic-Exposed Children, in *Methodological Issues in Controlled Studies on Effects of Prenatal Exposure to Drug Abuse*, NIDA Research Monograph Series #114, eds. M.M. Kilbey and K. Asghar (Washington, D.C.: U.S. Government Printing Office, 1991):323–339.

3. National Institutes of Health, National Institute on Alcohol Abuse and Alcoholism, *The Tenth Special Report to the U.S. Congress on Alcohol and Health from the Secretary of Health and Human Services* (Washington, D.C.: U.S. Government Printing Office, June 2000).

4. National Highway Traffic Safety Administration, *Traffic Safety Facts: Alcohol, 1998,* #DOT HS 808 950 (Washington, D.C.: U.S. Government Printing Office, October 1999).

5. For information on the effects of substance abuse, see National Institutes of Health, National Household Survey on Drug Abuse, which is conducted by the Substance Abuse and Mental Health Services Administration and is based on a national probability sample of the noninstitutionalized population of the United States. It provides national data on the use of illicit drugs, alcohol, and tobacco as well as the extent of drug dependence in the general population. Beginning with the 1999 HHSDA, the survey will provide estimates of substance in each state.

6. *Office of Drug Control Policy, The National Drug Control Strategy: 2000 Annual Report* (Washington, D.C.: U.S. Government Printing Office, July 2000).

7. M. Andrews, M. Nord, G. Bickel, and S. Carlson, *Household Food Security in the United States, 1999, Food Assistance and Nutrition Research Report No. 8* (Food and Rural Economic Division, Economic Research Service: U.S. Department of Agriculture, Fall 2000).

8. D. Rose, C. Gundersen, and V. Oliveira. *Socio-Economic Determinants of Food Insecurity in the United States: Evidence from the SIPP and CSFII Datasets, Technical Bulletin No. 1869* (Food and Rural Economic Division, Economic Research Service: U.S. Department of Agriculture, September 1998).

9. The following section draws on results from the USDA's Diet and Knowledge Survey, its Continuing Survey of Food Intakes, and the National Health and Nutrition Examination Survey conducted by NCHS. The NCHS and the USDA have announced the merger of their survey efforts, which are currently conducted as a single operation.

10. See Linda Scott Kantor, "A Dietary Assessment of the U.S. Food Supply: Comparing Per Capita Food Consumption with Food Guide Pyramid Serving Recommendations," *Agricultural Economic Report,* No. 772 (December 1998).

11. Ibid.

12. These tables are based on USDA surveys that ask people what they eat rather than based on measuring the consumption of commodities. While these tables do provide more information about the differences in eating habits among population groups, they also reflect misreporting by respondents. For example, the USDA has reported that the Continuing Survey of Food Intakes estimated an average person eats 1,969 calories per day, but commodity analysis shows the correct figure is 2,666 calories.

13. The Continuing Survey of Food Intakes is a nationally representative survey of American households that asks for information about their recent consumption of food.

14. See U.S. Department of Health and Human Services, *Physical Activity and Health: A Report of the Surgeon General* (Atlanta: U.S. Department of Health and Human Services, Centers for Disease Control and Prevention, National Center for Chronic Disease Prevention and Health Promotion, 1996). The tables presenting information on exercise participation that are contained in this book are drawn from this report. The original report contains technical material (including sampling errors) that was not included in this book because of space considerations.

15. Ibid; page v.

16. S. J. Ventura, W. D. Mosher, S. C. Curtin, J. C. Aabma, and S. Henshaw, "Highlights of Trends in Pregnancies and Pregnancy Rates by Outcome: Estimates for the United States, 1976–1996," *The Alan Guttmacher Institute 47,* no. 29 (December 15, 1999).

17. Centers for Disease Control and Prevention, *Screening Young Children for Lead Poisoning: Guidance for State and Local Public Health Officials* (Atlanta: CDC, November 1997).

18. These data come from the Environmental Protection Agency, Office of Air Quality Planning and Standards. Table 2J shows air pollution emission by source and type

of pollutant. For example, Table 2J shows the tonnage of carbon monoxide emissions from fuel combustion (fires, gas space heaters, etc.); industrial processes (use of carbon-based fuels by electric utilities and other industries); and transportation (automobile and other surface transportation). EPA based its calculations on direct measurements of pollutant concentrations at monitoring stations operated by state and local governments throughout the nation. The monitoring stations are generally located in larger urban areas. In 1997, 4,738 monitoring sites reported air-quality data to EPA. The panel used for these tables consisted of stations that had complete data for at least 8 of the 10 years between 1988 and 1997. See <http://www.epa.gov/airtrends/> for EPA air trends reports.

19. Congress passed the Emergency Planning and Community Right-to-Know Act (EPCRA) as part of the Superfund Amendments and Reauthorization Act (SARA) of 1986; therefore, EPCRA is also known as SARA Title III. This legislation also established the Toxics Release Inventory (TRI) program. In 1987, the TRI program began collective toxic release and waste management data from certain facilities, primarily those that manufactured or processed more than 25,000 pounds or otherwise used 10,000 pounds of designated chemicals during the reporting year. In 1998, seven new industries were required to report (mining, coal mining, electric utilities, chemicals distributors, petroleum bulk terminals, solvent recovery services, and RCRA Subtitle C hazardous waste treatment and disposal facilities).

20. H. Conway and J. Svenson, "Occupational Injury and Illness Rates, 1992–1996: Why They Fell," *Monthly Labor Review* 121, no. 11 (November 1998):36–58.

21. The transportation deaths by mode are compiled by various offices of the U.S. Department of Transportation (DOT) and combined in the DOT publication titled *National Transportation Statistics*. DOT offices get this information from the accident authorities (mostly the police). They cannot use the mortality data because typically the death certificates do not show the mode of transportation involved in accidents that cause deaths. See the Bureau of Transportation Web site for a detailed explanation of where each element comes from <http://www.bts.gov>. Deaths reported on Table 2N occurred within 30 days of the accident or incident. Most of the deaths come from highway accidents. These are reported in the Fatality Analysis Reporting System (FARS) and compiled by the National Transportation Safety Administration. The FARS is available on-line at the BTS Web site. Table 2N presents fatalities for transportation by air, highway, railroad, and water as well as those associated with the transport of liquid and gas energy through pipelines.

22. The data for Table 2.25 are not taken from death certificates, as is the case for most of the other mortality data reported in this book. Rather they are based on accident reports filed by traffic authorities and compiled

by DOT. DOT defines a traffic-related death as one related to a crash where the person dies within 30 days of the accident. States are rank ordered by their traffic fatality rate in 1996.

23. See Paul S. Mead, Laurence Slutsker, Vance Dietz, Linda F. McCaig, Joseph S. Bresse, Craig Shapiro, Patricia M. Griffin, and Robert V. Tauxe, "Food-Related Illness and Death in the United States," *Emerging Infectious Diseases* 5, no. 5 (September–October 1999). This study used multiple sources to estimate the total number and types of food-borne illnesses. (See page 78 for number of hospitalizations.)

24. The sources used for the study in Table 2.28 include the Food-Borne Diseases Active Surveillance Network (FoodNet), the National Notifiable Disease Surveillance System, the Public Health Laboratory Information System, the Gulf Coast States Vibrio Surveillance System, the Food-Borne Disease Outbreak Surveillance System, the National Ambulatory Medical Care Survey, the National Hospital Ambulatory Medical Care Survey, the National Hospital Discharge Survey, and the National Vital Statistics System.

25. This bacterium is found in raw meat and poultry and eggs. It multiplies at temperatures from 45 degrees Fahrenheit to 115 degrees Fahrenheit and causes headache, diarrhea, abdominal cramps, fever, nausea, and sometimes vomiting. Adequate cooking prevents illness.

26. This bacterium is associated with ingestion of unpasteurized milk and cheese and contaminated vegetables. It can cause meningoencephalitis and septicemia.

27. This protozoan can be transmitted in raw or inadequately cooked meat. It can cause symptoms similar to mononucleosis and may also lead to lesions involving the lungs, liver, heart, skin, muscle, brain, and meninges (membrane covering the brain and spinal cord). Treatment involves a 30-day course of drugs.

28. The Norwalk virus was identified in 1972 as the first virus known to cause diarrhea in humans. It is transmitted through contaminated water, food, or shellfish. See Roger Iglass and Paul E. Kilgore, "Etiology of Acute Viral Gastroenteritis," *Diarrheal Disease: Nestle Nutrition Workshop Series* 38 (Philadelphia: Lippincott-Raven, 1997):39–49.

29. *Campylobacter* is a microorganism that is found in infected poultry and other farm animals. Infected meat or poultry that is not properly cooked is the usual source of infection in humans, which results in chronic or persistent diarrhea.

30. Immunization rates are based on the National Immunization Survey conducted by the NCHS. This survey is one of the largest conducted by the federal government. It involves screening 1.2 million households to locate those with children age 19 to 35 months and to ask

their parents if the children have received immunizations. The text refers to rates for the so-called 4:3:1:3 series of inoculations. This series consists of four doses of Diphtheria-Tetanus-Pertussis, three doses of a polio vaccine, one dose of a measles-containing vaccine, and three doses of the *Haemophilus influenzae* type B (HIB) vaccine. The survey covered each of the 71 Immunization Action Plan areas designated by the CDC. These areas included the 50 states and 21 other selected cities and counties. More detailed information can be found in Tables 2.32 and 2.33.

31. B. F. Hankey, E. J. Feuer, L. X. Clegg, R. B. Hayes, J. M. Legler, P. C. Prorok, L. A. Ries, R. M. Merrill, and R. S. Kaplan, "Cancer Surveillance Series: Interpreting Trends in Prostate Cancer-Part I: Evidence of the Effects of Screening in Recent Prostate Cancer Incidence, Mortality, and Survival Rates," *Journal of the National Cancer Institute* 91, no. 12 (June 16, 1999):1017–1024.

32. D. K. Blackman, E. M. Bennett, and D. S. Miller, "Trends in Self-Reported Use of Mammograms (1989–1997) and Papanicolaou Tests (1991–1997)— Behavioral Risk Factor Surveillance System," *Morbidity and Mortality Weekly Report* 48 (SS06) (October 8, 1999):1–22.

33. U.S. Preventive Services Task Force, *Guide to Clinical Preventive Services: Report of the U.S. Preventive Services Task Force*, 2d ed. (Baltimore: Williams and Wilkins Publishing Co., 1996).

34. L. A. Ries, C. L. Kosary, B. E. Hankey, et al. (eds.) *SEER Cancer Statistics Review, 1973–1996* (Bethesda, Md.: National Cancer Institute, 1999).

35. J. S. Mandel, T. R. Church, F. Ederer, and J. H. Bond, "Colorectal Cancer Mortality: Effectiveness of Biennial Screening for Fecal Occult Blood," *Journal of the National Cancer Institute* 91, no. 5 (March 3, 1999):434–437.

36. G. R. Janes, D. K. Blackman, J. C. Bolen, L. A. Kamimoto, L. Rhodes, et al., "Surveillance for Use of Preventive Health-Care Services by Older Adults, 1995–1997," *Morbidity and Mortality Weekly Report* 48 (SS08) (December 17, 1999):51–88.

37. D. N. Pearlman, M. A. Clark, W. Rakowski, and B. Ehrick, "Screening for Breast and Cervical Cancers: The Importance of Knowledge and Perceived Cancer Survivability," *Women and Health* 28, no. 4 (1999):93–112.

38. K. Ashing-Giwa, "Health Behavior Change Models and Their Socio-cultural Relevance for Breast Cancer Screening in African American Women," *Women and Health* 28, no. 4 (1999):53–71.

39. I. Jatoi, "Breast Cancer Screening," *American Journal of Surgery* 177, no. 6 (June 1999):518–524.

40. J. S. Michaelson, E. Halpern, and D. B. Kopans, "Breast Cancer: Computer Simulation Method for Estimating Optimal Intervals for Screening," *Radiology* 212, no. 2 (August 1999):551–560.

41. S. W. Fletcher, W. Black, R. Harris, B. K. Rimer, and S. Shapiro, "Report of the International Workshop on Screening for Breast Cancer," *Journal of the National Cancer Institute* 85, no. 20 (October 20, 1993):1644–1656.

42. E. A. Sickles and D. B. Kopans, "Deficiencies in the Analysis of Breast Cancer Screening Data," *Journal of the National Cancer Institute* 85 no. 20 (October 20, 1993):1621–1624.

43. L. A. Brinton, "Epidemiology of Cervical Cancer-Overview," *International Agency for Research on Cancer Scientific Publications*, vol. 119 (1992):3–23.

44. N. S. Murthy and A. Mathew, "Risk Factors for Precancerous Lesions of the Cervix," *European Journal of Cancer Prevention* 9, no. 1 (February 2000):5–14.

45. J. S. Mandelblatt, M. Fahs, K. Garibaldi, R. T. Senie, and H. B. Peterson, "Association between HIV Infection and Cervical Neoplasia: Implications for Clinical Care of Women at Risk for Both Conditions," *AIDS* 6, no. 2 (February 1992):173–178.

46. E. J. Wilkinson and L. J. Smith, "Cervical Neoplasia. Its Association with Human Papillomavirus Infection," *Journal of the Florida Medical Association* 80, no. 2 (February 1993):106–11.

47. See note 36.

48. See note 32.

49. These results are based on the CDC's Behavioral Risk Factor Surveillance System. This program is conducted in cooperation with state health departments. Data are based on surveys conducted according to a common plan but carried out individually by each health department. CDC prepared a common analysis of the results. Table 2.42 shows the percentage of women who were not screened for breast cancer and cervical cancer in the past year. The data on women who were not screened for breast cancer are for the group age 50 and over.

Over the past six decades, Americans improved their health dramatically. Not only do Americans in general perceive that they have good health, but also the rates of diseases, injuries, and deaths have declined. The rate of infant mortality declined significantly from 47 per 1,000 live births in 1940 to 7.2 per 1,000 live births in 1997. (See Table 3.3.) The age-adjusted death rate for the total population also dropped from 1,076.1 per 100,000 persons in 1940 to 479.1 in 1997. (See Table 3.1.) However, not all Americans have shared equally in this health improvement. People living in low-income households, those without health insurance, and members of minority groups, particularly Black men, continue to have higher rates of disease, disability, and death than the general population.

The overall improvements in Americans' health were accompanied by a change in the kind of illnesses prevalent in the population. Before the 20th century, the primary sources of serious illnesses were infectious diseases such as typhoid fever, diphtheria, pneumonia, and tuberculosis. In 1900, pneumonia and influenza were the leading causes of death, with a mortality rate of 202 per 100,000 persons. Tuberculosis was the second leading cause of death, with a mortality rate of 194 per 100,000 persons; diarrhea and enteritis (a disease of the intestines) were third, with a mortality rate of 143 per 100,000 persons; and diphtheria was the ninth leading cause of death, with a mortality rate of 40 per 100,000 persons.[1] By the dawning of the new millennium, however, only pneumonia and influenza remained in the top 10 causes of death, and in most cases they occurred later in life.

As the life expectancy for the U.S. population increased in the 20th century, diseases that occur later in life became the leading causes of death. In 1998, the top four causes of death were diseases of the heart, malignant neoplasms (cancer), cerebrovascular diseases (stroke), and unintentional injuries (accidents).[2] Progress has been made in reducing heart diseases. Since 1950, the rate of deaths caused by heart disease has been cut in half, from 307.2 per 100,000 persons in 1950 to 130.5 per 100,000 persons in 1997. (See Table 3.8.) Unfortunately, despite all the technology that has evolved during the last part of the 20th century to control diseases and improve health, we have not witnessed a significant reduction in the rate of deaths from cancer. Furthermore, the second half of the 20th century has seen the identification of new health threats, such as Acquired Immunodeficiency Syndrome (AIDS). Not only have new diseases such as human immunodeficiency virus (HIV) disease and AIDS, Lyme disease, and Legionnaires' disease been identified, but also old diseases have reappeared in new forms, such as multidrug-resistant tuberculosis and Group A streptococcal bacteria.

This chapter reviews these trends and presents the results from several major federal data collection series on a variety of conditions that affect the length and quality of life. First, it presents some background information on ways of measuring diseases and other conditions that affect health status. This chapter categorizes diseases and other health conditions in terms of their duration—that is, whether they were chronic (long-term) or acute (short-term) conditions. Data are presented on the death rate from all causes as well as on the leading causes of death. Finally, this chapter includes information on health conditions by categories that have responded to various types of interventions and preventive approaches. These categories include malignancies and chronic diseases, such as cancers and heart diseases that are responsive to lifestyle interventions; notifiable, infectious, and communicable diseases, many of which have been eliminated or controlled with vaccines, animal control, and environmental regulations; transportation-related injuries and deaths that have been reduced by changed driving behaviors and safer vehicles, roads, and traffic practices; mental disorders, some of which have been effectively controlled with medications; and sexually transmitted diseases, which require education for informed decision making regarding individual behaviors.

MEASURES AND INDICES OF HEALTH

This book presents trends to show how diseases change when public health initiatives or improved health care practices intervene. It includes various measures to characterize and monitor the population's health. These measures include mortality (death) and morbidity rates. *Morbidity* refers to an illness, injury, or other serious impairment in function or structure. The numbers and rates of people affected are presented to show the total "burden" of each condition as well as to identify high-risk groups. Rates are sometimes based on the actual numbers, often referred to as *crude rates*. At other points, rates are age adjusted, meaning that statistical procedures are used to take into account age differences among groups.

MORBIDITY RATES

Health analysts examine the number of people with a disease from two perspectives: the current burden of a health condition (prevalence) and new cases (incidence). Prevalence and incidence are morbidity statistics. *Prevalence* is the total number or percent of people who have evidence of the condition at a given time and can include both active and inactive cases. *Incidence* refers to the newly reported cases of illness. Public health experts recognize that it is difficult to identify the inception of a disease or condition. Some conditions may be unnoticed by the health care system for a considerable time before they are identified and reported. This lag time means that reported incidence, the kind that can be captured in statistics, might be very different from actual incidence. In fact, some increases in incidence actually indicate better diagnosis—that is, identification of a disease at an earlier stage that results in potentially improved conditions, rather than an increase in the number of people who are sick.

Prevalence rates might be low if fewer people become ill, if more people recover quickly, or if more people die quickly. High prevalence rates may result when few cases develop but the condition lingers for a long time. Prevalence statistics are helpful to health service providers and others interested in the allocation and distribution of resources, training, and other health services because prevalence shows the number of people affected at a particular moment, although the data may be measured over a period of weeks or months. For example, data that represent an estimate of the number of people suffering from breast cancer at the beginning of 1999 may be based on a survey that covers reports collected throughout 1998. Incidence rates are important to researchers studying what leads to illness because they can compare the information that they collect with risk factors for various illnesses.

While public health attention often focuses on the most prevalent conditions, some conditions are important even when rare because of their perceived seriousness. Some rare conditions have such devastating impact that early trends can be useful to effectively institute initiatives to protect the public health or to identify conditions for scientific research into their causes, prevention, treatment, and elimination.

Changes in the definition of conditions can lead to dramatically higher reported incidence and prevalence rates in the period after new definitions are introduced. Because medical science continues to improve diagnosis and care, these increases are expected and do not actually mean that the disease has increased. Analysts face important choices in dealing with improved diagnoses and their impact on incidence and prevalence rates. Conservative statistical practice suggests that time series should not be presented where case definitions have changed; however, this practice would lead to a considerable loss of information. In this book, when longer time series are presented, tables show important changes in case definitions. It is important to understand when changes occur because of increases in disease and when they are an artifact of changed reporting procedures.

Misclassifying conditions or misreporting the size of groups also can lead to inaccurate incidence and prevalence rates. Trends may be distorted by such methodological changes as decennial revisions of the International Statistical Classification of Diseases, Injuries, and Causes of Death (ICD); the introduction of new disease categories; changes in the standard form used for death certificates; and coding changes for birth and death information, such as new rules for attributing the primary cause of death or for classifying pregnancies that result in a live birth.

MORTALITY RATES AS INDICATORS OF HEALTH

Ironically, statistics on death constitute the longest and most comprehensive record of the conditions that affect life. The National Center for Health Statistics (NCHS) compiles death statistics from certificates that have been filed by physicians, morticians, and family members with state health departments. Such death records are used, for example, by insurance companies to document claims and by governments to determine the manner of death and include the physician's certification of the immediate and underlying cause of death. Health statisticians and epidemiologists analyze the records to track changes in the cause of death. Death certificate information constitutes the longest running series of data on the diseases that afflict people. However, it suffers from an important limitation—it emphasizes diseases that result in death and does not cover other diseases that limit life activity. Therefore, mortality rates provide only a partial picture of the prevalence of health conditions.

VALIDITY

The validity and reliability of reported death rates depend on a number of factors. The death rate requires medical and demographic information from the death certificate and population information from the Bureau of the Census. Mortality rates are composed by combining information on the number of deaths drawn from death certificate data with population data drawn from the decennial census. Thus, these rates are dependent on the completeness of reporting from both sources and on the extent to which each data source includes the same person in the same group. Mortality rates may change because of changes to the definitions and procedures for determining who is included in the total population. For example, the calculation for death rates does not include fetal deaths, and since 1970 it has not included nonresidents of the United States.

Mortality rates for different racial and ethnic groups are affected by an undercount of racial and ethnic groups by the Census Bureau and by misclassification of an individual's race and ethnicity either by the Census Bureau or on the death certificate.

The death certificate provides information on demographic characteristics of the decedent, such as racial and ethnic group, provided by a funeral director, by an informant, or by observation. Before 1990, national data on Hispanic status were not collected routinely on death certificates. In fact, in 1985, only 17 states and the District of Columbia succeeded in obtaining information on Hispanic identity for at least 90 percent of reported deaths. By 1996, only Oklahoma had less than an 80 percent completion rate for this item on the death certificates.

Studies comparing the ethnic information on death certificates with the self-reported census data of American Indians, Asians, and Hispanics have shown that many death certificates have misreported American Indians as White and Hispanic persons as non-Hispanic. Sorlie and colleagues estimate that the death rates for American Indians are underestimated by 22 to 30 percent, for Asians by 12 percent, and for Hispanics by approximately 7 percent. (See source #4 below.)

Valid use of mortality data to describe health conditions also depends on the accurate reporting of the cause of death. The death certificate provides information on the conditions leading to death as determined by the certifying physician, medical examiner, or coroner. The ICD provides the classification system, defines the terms, and specifies the coding procedures used to identify or describe the medical conditions on the death certificate and in other data collections relating to mortality. In an effort to make this information consistent and comparable internationally, the World Health Organization (WHO) not only publishes the ICD but also coordinates systematic reviews and revisions to incorporate changes in health conditions and the medical field. The ICD is revised about every ten years, at which time diagnostic criteria for conditions may change and additional categories of diseases may be added. In the United States, the ICD is used to code and classify mortality. The ICD-Clinical Modification (ICD-CM) is used to code and classify health conditions from most surveys conducted by the National Center for Health Statistics (NCHS), diagnoses and procedures on inpatient and outpatient records from hospitals and physician offices, and other sources of data on morbidity.

Disease-specific mortality rates can be studied by the examination of the recorded underlying cause of death, which is defined by WHO as "the disease or injury that initiated the sequence of events leading directly to death or as the circumstances of the accident or violence that produced the fatal injury." The NCHS coded the underlying cause of death manually until 1968, when the coding was computerized. Computerization increased the reliability of the coding and increased confidence in the coding of multiple causes of death, which were coded manually until 1990. Since the coding has been computerized, the number of cases assigned to the "unspecified" category has decreased. In fact, since 1994, less than 2 percent of the cases reported have been assigned to this ICD category, allowing researchers to see more accurately the specific disease that actually caused the death.

Underreporting of a disease or condition as a cause of death can occur if the condition is not diagnosed, if it is not classified as a separate category, or if the certifying physician does not consider the condition a potential cause of death. Alzheimer's disease, for example, is considered to be underreported for this reason. Alzheimer's disease became a separate reportable category (ICD9–No. 331) in 1979. HIV/AIDS was introduced as a separate category in 1987. The definition for AIDS was modified several times. Before 1993, the diagnosis depended on a broad range of indicator diseases and conditions such as Kaposi's sarcoma, Pneumocystis carinii pneumonia, and wasting syndrome. After 1993, the definition added conditions that required laboratory confirmation of HIV infection (e.g., HIV infected persons with CD4+ T-lymphocyte counts of less than 200 cells/µL [microliter] or a CD4+ percentage of less than 14). The definition for pediatric cases of AIDS also changed during this period.

SOURCES

The following publications describe the procedures used to collect and classify information about deaths and discuss related validation issues:

1. Centers for Disease Control and Prevention (CDC), *Monthly Vital Statistics Report* 45 (11) S2 (1997).

2. CDC, *HIV/AIDS Surveillance Report—Year End Edition* 9(2) (1998).

3. National Center for Health Statistics, *Vital Statistics, Instructions for Classifying the Underlying Cause of Death: NCHS Instruction Manual Part 2A* (Hyattsville, Md.: Public Health Service, undated).

4. P. D. Sorlie, E. Rogot, and N. J. Johnson, "Validity of Demographic Characteristics on the Death Certificate," *Epidemiology* 3, no. 2 (1992):181–184.

5. World Health Organization, *Manual of the International Statistical Classification of Diseases, Injuries, and Causes of Death, Based on the Recommendations of the Ninth Revision Conference, 1975,* and adopted by the 29th World Health Assembly (Geneva: World Health Organization, 1977).

HOW MORBIDITY COMPARES WITH MORTALITY

Both morbidity and mortality rates are influenced by improved diagnostic procedures and changes in the definition of conditions. Both may be adjusted for age and other factors to provide more accurate rates. Because the fatal diseases before the 20th century were of relatively short duration, the mortality rate served as a realistic and acceptable measure for monitoring the nation's health status. However, during the 20th century, health statisticians recognized the need to collect information on diseases that disable or incapacitate people without necessarily leading to their death. The results showing acute and chronic conditions in the population present a different picture of conditions than is obtained by examining death rates. In contrast with mortality, or death rates, morbidity is the state of being affected with disease, disability, or injury. In the 20th century, chronic diseases, such as cardiovascular (i.e., heart) or renal (i.e., kidney) disease and cancer, had an important impact on health because they were among the leading causes of death. However, many conditions, including arthritis, rheumatism, and mental disease, are much more important causes of long-term morbidity than of mortality. Changing patterns in medical sciences, medical care, and public health programs led to fewer deaths, increasing the prevalence of chronic conditions as more people survived illnesses. Many people had an improved quality of life yet still required continuing medical care.

A variety of factors may affect morbidity rates besides the actual number of new cases and their survival rates. For example, health interviews could underestimate rates because many people do not know that they have a condition at the time of the interview. Some health surveys ask a member of a household to report on other people living in the household. The person providing information on others is called a *proxy respondent*. Data provided by proxy respondents may result in misreporting because such respondents may not know the full medical history of all of the members of the household.

The likelihood of a condition being detected or reported increases with the frequency of contact with the health system and surveillance programs, the duration of the condition, the explicitness of the associated symptoms, and the adequacy of the health screening technology. Insurance eligibility criteria and reimbursement procedures also affect how conditions are classified, which could lead to changes in the apparent prevalence or incidence of particular conditions—increasing some and decreasing others when no actual change has occurred.

TRENDS IN THE OVERALL DEATH RATE

Death rates differ by sociodemographic characteristics such as age, gender, race, and place of residence. Age-adjusted death rates are indicators of overall health because early death is the ultimate sign of poor health. While death rates declined for the entire population during the 20th century, there were very important differences among groups.[3] In 1940, the age-adjusted death rate for the whole population from all causes was 1,076.1 deaths for every 100,000 persons, but by 1997 it had been cut more than in half and dropped to 479.1 per 100,000 persons. (See Table 3.1.)

During the entire period, men had a higher total death rate from all causes than women, especially among young adults, and Blacks had a higher total death rate than Whites. (See Figure 3A.) By 1997, the age-adjusted death rate for men was 602.8 for every 100,000 persons, which was more than 1.6 times the rate for women, 375.7 per 100,000 persons. (See Table 3A.) Both Whites and Blacks improved, but Whites improved faster than Blacks and this difference increased the disparities in age-adjusted death rates between the groups. The rate for Black men was about 1.35 times the rate for White men in 1960 and about 1.59 times the rate for White men in 1997. The death rate among Black men declined from 1,246.1 per 100,000 persons to 911.9 between 1960 and 1997. The death rate was 917.7 per 100,000 persons for White men in 1960.

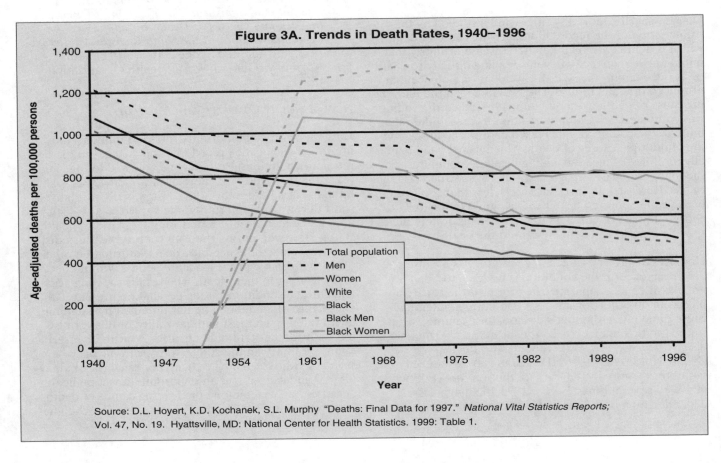

Figure 3A. Trends in Death Rates, 1940–1996

Source: D.L. Hoyert, K.D. Kochanek, S.L. Murphy "Deaths: Final Data for 1997." *National Vital Statistics Reports;* Vol. 47, No. 19. Hyattsville, MD: National Center for Health Statistics. 1999: Table 1.

Table 3A. Age-Adjusted Death Rates from All Causes

(Per 100,000 population)

Year	Both sexes	Male	Female
1940	1 076.1	1 213.0	938.9
1950	841.5	1 001.6	688.4
1960	760.9	949.3	590.6
1970	714.3	931.6	532.5
1975	630.4	837.2	462.5
1976	618.5	820.9	455.0
1977	602.1	801.3	441.8
1978	595.0	791.4	437.4
1979	577.0	768.6	423.1
1980	585.8	777.2	432.6
1981	568.6	753.8	420.8
1982	554.7	734.2	411.9
1983	552.5	729.4	412.5
1984	548.1	721.6	410.5
1985	548.9	723.0	410.3
1986	544.8	716.2	407.6
1987	539.2	706.8	404.6
1988	539.9	706.1	406.1
1989	528.0	689.3	397.3
1990	520.2	680.2	390.6
1991	513.7	669.9	386.5
1992	504.5	656.0	380.3
1993	513.3	664.9	388.3
1994	507.4	654.6	385.2
1995	503.9	646.3	385.2
1996	491.6	623.7	381.0
1997	479.1	602.8	375.7

SOURCE: D.L. Hoyert, K. D. Kochanek, S.L. Murphy ."Deaths: Final Data for 1997" National Center for Health Statistics. *National Vital Statistics Reports;* vol. 47, no. 19. June 30, 1999: Table 1.

NOTE: For method of computation see technical notes in "Deaths: Final Data for 1997." Rates are based on populations enumerated as of April 1 for census years and estimated as of July 1 for all other years. Beginning with 1970, deaths of nonresidents of the United States are excluded.

There are substantial differences in death rates among the states. (See Figure 3B.) In 1995-1997, the East South Central Census Division had the highest age-adjusted mortality rate (571.5 per 100,000 persons, compared with a national rate of 491.4 per 100,000 persons), with Mississippi exhibiting a rate of 611.7. Among the 12 states with the highest death rates, only three (West Virginia, Oklahoma, and Nevada) were not in the old Confederacy. (See Table 3.2 and Table 3B.)

INFANT MORTALITY

Deaths among American infants declined greatly from 1940 to 1997. (See Figure 3C.) The infant mortality rate was reduced from 47 deaths per 1,000 live births to 7.2 deaths per 1,000 live births, approximately 15 percent of the rate that it was in 1940. At the same time, racial disparities in infant mortality rates persisted. For example, the infant mortality rate of Blacks was 14.2 per 1,000 live births in 1997 which was two times the national rate for that year and greater than the national rate in 1977. (See Table 3.3.) According to the Indian Health Service, the infant mortality rate for American Indians and Alaska Natives was also about 1.3 times the U.S. national rate. (See Table 3.6.)

The infant mortality rate is also higher in the old Confederacy states. Mississippi reported 10.7 infant deaths per 1,000 live births compared with a national average of 7.4 per 1,000 live births. Other Southern states with high rates included Louisiana, Arkansas, Alabama, Georgia, North Carolina, South Carolina, and Tennessee. Illinois, Indiana, and Maryland also had high rates. (See Table 3.7.)

HOW INFANT MORTALITY IS MEASURED

Death rates for infants are among the most important indicators of the overall health status of a population. Epidemiologists use several standard measurements to show death rates among very young children. The *infant mortality rate* is the number of children who die before they reach their first birthday. It is defined as the number of deaths for every 1,000 live births and does not include fetal deaths. Neonatal deaths are those that occur to children less than 28 days old, and postneonatal deaths are those that occur to children between 28 and 364 days of age.

Reported infant mortality rates for groups, such as Blacks, Whites, and Hispanics, are affected by who reports the ethnic data for those who die (the numerators) and those who are born (the denominators). For example, in the case of infant deaths, the child's race is recorded on the death certificate. Since 1989, however, the race of the mother is used to indicate the race of the child at birth.

CAUSES OF INFANT DEATHS

In 1994, about a third of infant deaths were caused by sudden infant death syndrome. Other major causes included congenital anomalies or birth defects (19.5 percent of Whites and 10.9 percent of Blacks), infections (11.5 percent of Whites and 15.6 percent of Blacks), and injuries. (See Table 3C.) American Indian children had more than twice the deaths from congenital anomalies and four times the deaths from pneumonia and influenza as Whites. (See Table 3.6.) About half

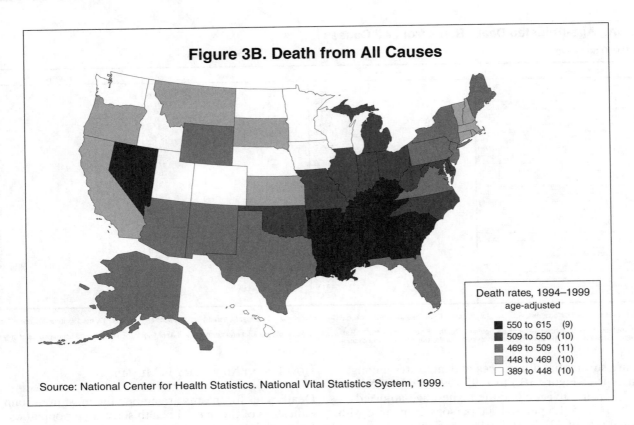

Figure 3B. Death from All Causes

Death rates, 1994–1999
age-adjusted

- 550 to 615 (9)
- 509 to 550 (10)
- 469 to 509 (11)
- 448 to 469 (10)
- 389 to 448 (10)

Source: National Center for Health Statistics. National Vital Statistics System, 1999.

Table 3B. Death Rate Differentials in States with the Highest Death Rates: 1995–1997

(Average annual deaths per 100,000 resident population; ranked by all persons' death rate)

Area	Rank	All persons	White	Black
United States		491.4	466.7	736.5
Mississippi	1	611.7	539.0	784.6
Louisiana	2	589.8	519.1	783.0
Alabama	3	576.3	526.7	764.7
South Carolina	4	573.8	504.8	785.6
Tennessee	5	564.6	527.2	821.7
Arkansas	6	561.1	531.1	788.3
Georgia	7	560.3	502.4	764.2
West Virginia	8	551.0	547.9	717.3
Kentucky	9	548.6	537.7	741.3
Nevada	10	543.8	543.8	653.5
Oklahoma	11	540.4	537.4	707.0
North Carolina	12	533.0	480.3	759.7
Missouri	13	521.5	496.1	778.5
Maryland	14	519.0	454.1	747.8
Delaware	15	518.9	481.2	748.5

SOURCE: E. Kramarow, H. Lentzner, R. Rooks, J. Weeks, S. Saydah. *Health and Aging Chartbook. Health, United States*, 1999. Hyattsville, Maryland: National Center for Health Statistics. 1999: Table 29, and unpublished data.

NOTE: The race groups, White and Black, include, persons of Hispanic and non-Hispanic origin.

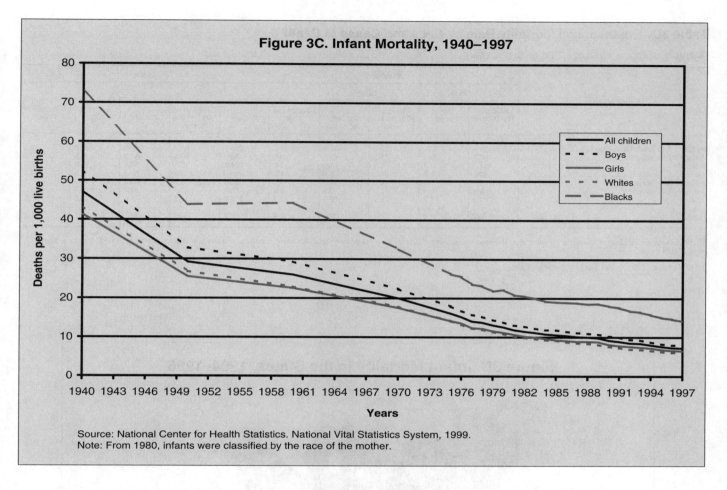

Figure 3C. Infant Mortality, 1940–1997

Source: National Center for Health Statistics. National Vital Statistics System, 1999.
Note: From 1980, infants were classified by the race of the mother.

of the birth defects involved cardiovascular defects, and nearly a quarter involved the central nervous system and genetic diseases. The primary illnesses that led to the deaths of these children age 28 to 364 days were infections involving the respiratory system and central nervous system, as well as gastrointestinal infections and septicemia. About half of the postneonatal deaths were caused by respiratory infections. The most frequent causes of injuries leading to death in these infants were suffocation, homicide, motor vehicle crashes, fires, and falls. Some deaths associated with prenatal conditions were caused by complications during birth. (See Table 3C.)

THE LEADING CAUSES OF DEATH

In the last half of the 20th century, as death rates declined, the leading causes of death changed for the total population and for different age and other demographic groups. Between 1950 and 1997, age-adjusted death rates for heart disease declined by more than half, while the death rates from cancer and injuries remained the same. (See Figure 3E and Table 3D.) By the end of the century, external causes, including injuries, homicide, and suicide, were the main causes of death among younger people, while heart disease and cancer were the top causes of death for older people. (See Table 3E and Figure 3F.)

Another change that can be seen throughout the 20th century is the decline in the number of tuberculosis (TB) cases. In 1953, the rate of TB cases was 53 per 100,000 persons, and the death rate was 12.4 per 100,000 persons. In 1997, the rate of TB cases had dropped to 7.4 per 100,000 persons, and the death rate had dropped to 0.5 per 100,000 persons. (See Figure 3G.) The number of TB cases has dropped even more dramatically in the last five years. In 1995, there were 84,000 cases of TB in the United States compared with 18,361 in 1998. In that same period the number of deaths dropped from almost 20,000 to 1,336.

These declines followed a resurgence of TB in the late 1980s. This increase was attributed to the AIDS epidemic; an increase in immigration from countries where TB is found; and increased poverty, injection drug use, and homelessness, as well as poor compliance with treatment regimens.

According to the National Institute of Allergy and Infectious Diseases (NIAID), TB is still "a serious public health problem." NIAID reports that there are 10 million to 15 million people in the United States with latent TB infections and estimates that about 10 percent of these "will develop active TB at some time in their lives." Blacks and Hispanics are particularly affected (with 54 percent of the cases) as are Asians (with 17.5 percent).

Table 3C. Postneonatal Mortality Rate by Race and Cause of Death

(Mortality rate for children age 28 days to one year)

Cause of death	White					Black				
	1980		1994		Percent Change Per Year	1980		1994		Percent Change Per Year
	Rate per 100,000 live births	Percent	Rate per 100,000 live births	Percent		Percent	Rate per 100,000 live births	Percent	Rate per 100,000 live births	
Sudden Infant Death Syndrome	117.4	33.8	79.8	37.0	-2.0	266.9	35.3	180.9	32.2	-1.8
Congenital Anomalies	67.1	19.3	46.2	19.5	-2.6	82.6	10.9	61.3	10.9	-1.2
Infections	41.9	12.1	27.3	11.5	-3.5	124.8	16.5	87.8	15.6	-2.2
Injuries	30.7	8.8	22.2	9.4	-1.6	69.0	9.1	58.7	10.5	-0.3
Perinatal Conditions	19.4	5.6	12.5	5.3	-3.3	50.3	6.7	53.9	9.6	0.5
Ill-defined Conditions	9.1	2.6	12.6	5.3	2.8	28.3	3.7	41.2	7.3	3.2
Others	61.6	17.7	36.7	15.5	-3.7	135.0	17.8	74.5	13.8	-3.8
Total	347	100	237	100	-2.4	757	100	561	100	-1.5

SOURCE: Centers for Disease Control and Prevention, "Postneonatal Mortality Surveillance — United States, 1980–1994" *Morbidity and Mortality Weekly Report* 47, no. SS-2 (July 3, 1998): 15-30, Table 2.

NOTE: Percent totals may not add to 100 due to rounding.

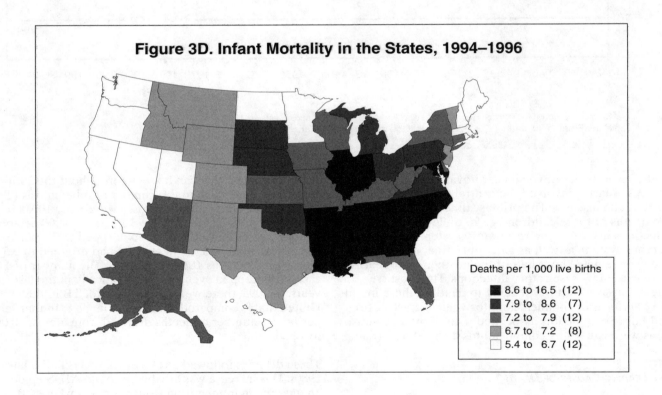

Figure 3D. Infant Mortality in the States, 1994–1996

Deaths per 1,000 live births

- 8.6 to 16.5 (12)
- 7.9 to 8.6 (7)
- 7.2 to 7.9 (12)
- 6.7 to 7.2 (8)
- 5.4 to 6.7 (12)

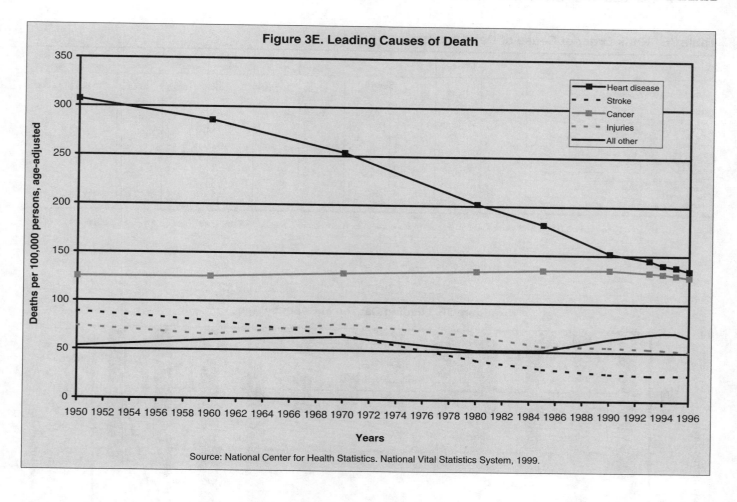

Figure 3E. Leading Causes of Death

Source: National Center for Health Statistics. National Vital Statistics System, 1999.

Table 3D. Leading Causes of Death for All Persons: 1997

(Number of deaths per 100,000 persons)

Diseases	Rank	Age-adjusted [1]	All ages [2]	1–4 years	5–14 years	15–24 years	25–34 years	35–44 years	45–54 years	55–64 years	65–74 years	75–84 years	85 years and over
All causes		479.1	864.7	35.8	20.8	86.2	115.0	203.2	430.8	1 063.6	2 509.8	5 728.2	15 345.2
Heart disease	1	130.5	271.6	1.4	0.8	3.0	8.3	30.1	104.9	302.4	753.7	1 943.6	6 198.9
Cancer	2	125.6	201.6	2.9	2.7	4.5	11.6	38.9	135.1	395.7	847.3	1 335.2	1 805.0
Accidents	3	30.1	35.7	13.1	8.7	36.5	31.8	33.0	31.0	32.6	46.4	103.4	276.5
Stroke	4	25.9	59.7	0.4	0.2	0.5	1.7	6.3	16.9	44.4	134.8	462.0	1 584.6
Chronic obstructive pulmonary diseases	5	21.1	40.7	0.3	0.3	0.5	0.9	2.0	8.4	46.3	165.3	359.6	561.9
Diabetes	6	13.5	23.4	0.0	0.1	0.4	1.6	4.2	12.9	38.4	88.2	294.1	
Pneumonia	7	12.9	32.3	1.2	0.4	0.6	1.3	3.2	6.6	17.2	57.0	233.7	1 024.7
Suicide	8	10.6	11.4	N/A	0.8	11.4	14.3	15.3	14.7	13.5	14.4	19.3	20.8
Homicide	9	8.0	7.4	2.4	1.2	16.8	12.8	8.4	5.6	3.9	2.9	2.9	3.8
Liver disease	10	7.4	9.4	0.0	0.0	0.1	1.3	8.0	16.7	24.1	31.4	30.2	22.8
AIDS	11	5.8	6.2	0.4	0.3	0.8	10.1	16.1	10.4	4.9	1.8	0.6	0.0
Nephritis	12	4.4	9.5	0.0	0.0	0.1	0.5	1.0	2.6	8.4	25.6	73.6	218.0
Septicemia	13	4.2	8.4	0.5	0.1	0.2	0.6	1.4	3.5	8.5	22.6	60.0	177.6
Alzheimer's disease	14	2.7	8.4	0.0	0.0	0.0	0.0	0.0	0.1	1.2	10.8	73.3	299.2
Atherosclerosis	15	2.1	6.0	0.0	0.0	0.0	0.0	0.1	0.6	2.4	9.8	40.5	225.5
Others		74.3	133.0	13.2	5.2	10.8	18.2	35.2	60.8	119.7	297.8	822.9	2 631.8

SOURCE: D.L. Hoyert, K.D. Kochanek, S.L. Murphy. "Deaths: Final Data for 1997" National Center for Health Statistics. *National Vital Statistics Reports;* vol. 47, no. 19. June 30, 1999: Table 7.

N/A Not applicable
1. For method of computation, see Technical Notes in "Deaths: Final Data for 1997."
2. Figures for age not stated included in "All ages" but not distributed among age groups.

Table 3E. Rank Order of Cause of Death by Age

Diseases	Age-adjusted	1–4 years	5–14 years	15–24 years	25–34 years	35–44 years	45–54 years	55–64 years	65–74 years	75–84 years	85 years and over
Deaths per 100,000 population	479.1	35.8	20.8	86.2	115.0	203.2	430.8	1 063.6	2 509.8	5 728.2	15 345.2
RANK											
Circulatory	1	3	3	3	4	3	2	2	1	1	1
Cancer	2	2	2	2	2	2	1	1	2	2	2
External causes	3	1	1	1	1	1	3	4	5	3	4
Respiratory	4	4	4	4	5	6	5	3	3	4	3
Diabetes	5	7	7	6	6	7	6	5	4	5	6
Liver disease	6	8	8	8	7	5	4	6	6	6	9
AIDS	7	6	5	5	3	4	7	9	10	7	10
Nephritis	8	9	9	9	9	9	9	8	7	8	7
Septicemia	9	5	6	7	8	8	8	7	8	9	8
Alzheimer's disease	10	10	10	10	10	10	10	10	9	10	5

SOURCE: D.L. Hoyert, K.D. Kochanek, S.L. Murphy. "Deaths: Final Data for 1997" National Center for Health Statistics. *National Vital Statistics Reports;* vol. 47, no. 19. June 30, 1999: Table 7.

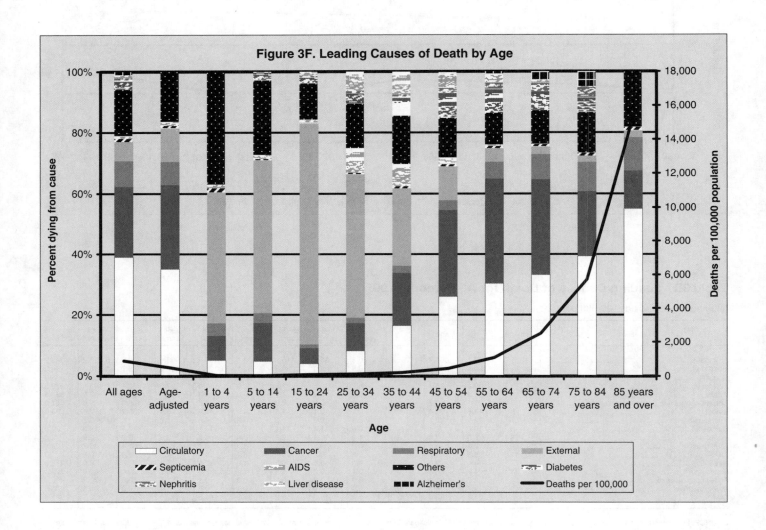

Figure 3F. Leading Causes of Death by Age

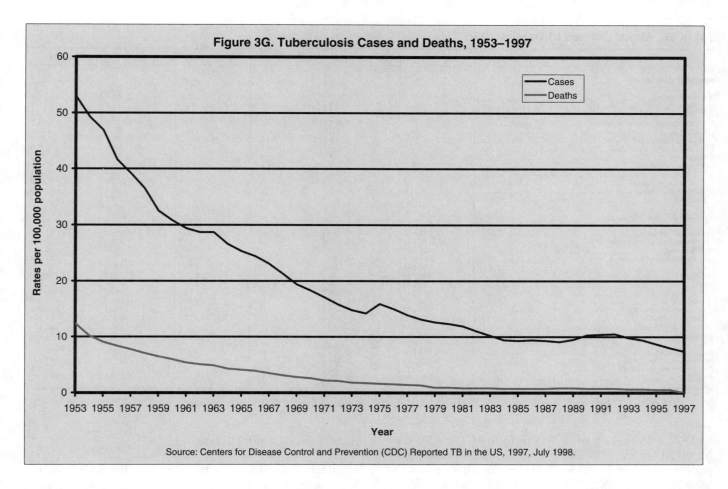

Figure 3G. Tuberculosis Cases and Deaths, 1953–1997

Source: Centers for Disease Control and Prevention (CDC) Reported TB in the US, 1997, July 1998.

NIAID reports that TB rates in some "sectors of U.S. society ... now surpass those in the world's poorest countries." For example, Black men age 35 to 44 living in New York City had a case rate of 318 per 100,000 in 1993 compared to a national rate of 9.8 per 100,000. NIAID also reports that in the 1990s drug-resistant TB cases were detected.[4]

AGE DIFFERENCES

As the life expectancy for the U.S. population has increased throughout the 20th century, diseases that occur later in life have become the most frequent causes of death for the population taken as a whole. Although diseases like cancer, heart disease, and stroke were once considered an inevitable consequence of aging, research in the last several decades has found risk factors such as genetics, diet, physical activity, and social and environmental exposures that now provide direction and methods for detecting, preventing, treating, and controlling these diseases.

According to data from 1997, causes external to biological health, such as accidents, homicides, and suicides, account for 61.4 percent of deaths for people between the ages of 5 and 34. (See Table 3F.) In that year, the death rate for people age 15 to 24 years was 86.2 per 100,000 persons. Of those who died, 36.5 per 100,000 died

from accidental injuries, 16.8 per 100,000 were victims of homicide, and 11.4 per 100,000 were suicides. For this age group, only 3 out of 100,000 persons died from heart disease and 4.5 out of 100,000 died from cancer. (See Table 3D.)

Starting at around age 35, heart disease and cancer account for more of the deaths. For example, among 45 to 54 year olds, 430.8 out of 100,000 persons died. Of these, 135.1 died as a result of cancer, 104.9 as a result of heart disease, and 16.9 were stroke victims. (See Table 3D.) Diabetes, liver disease, and nephritis also account for a substantial number of deaths for those over age 35. In this same age group (45 to 54), there were 31 deaths per 100,000 persons caused by accidental injury, 5.6 per 100,000 caused by homicide, and 14.7 per 100,000 caused by suicide. AIDS was the fourth leading cause of death for people between the ages of 35 and 44 (16.1 out of 203.2 deaths per 100,000 persons) and ranked third for individuals between the ages of 25 and 34 (10.1 out of 115 deaths per 100,000 persons). (See Tables 3E and 3D.) Alzheimer's disease starts to appear as a leading cause of death in people age 65 and older, but the rates are much higher in those age 85 and older. For those who survive beyond age 85, heart disease, stroke, and other circulatory disorders account for 46.3 percent of the deaths, cancer accounts for 11.8 percent, and respiratory diseases account for 10.3 percent. (See Figure 3F.)

Table 3F. Major Causes of Deaths: 1997

Major causes of death	All ages	Less than 1 year	1–4 years	5–34 years	35–64 years	65 years and over
PERCENT OF DEATHS						
External causes	6.5	4.1	44.0	61.4	11.8	2.2
Homicide and legal intervention	0.9	1.1	6.8	13.7	1.4	0.1
Suicide	1.3	0.0	0.0	11.9	3.1	0.3
Accidents and adverse effects	4.3	2.9	37.2	35.8	7.3	1.8
Cancer	23.3	0.3	8.0	8.6	31.9	22.1
Major cardiovascular diseases	40.8	3.2	5.0	7.1	29.9	46.1
AIDS	0.7	0.1	1.0	5.1	2.5	0.0
Respiratory	8.5	1.9	4.4	1.9	4.6	10.0
Infectious diseases	2.3	2.6	5.4	6.6	4.5	1.5
Childbirth, pregnancy, and congenital abnormalities	1.1	68.2	12.1	1.9	0.4	0.1
Diabetes mellitus	2.7	0.0	0.1	0.9	3.1	2.7
Alzheimer's disease	1.0	0.0	0.0	0.0	0.1	1.3
Nephritis	1.1	0.5	0.2	0.3	0.7	1.3
NUMBER OF DEATHS						
External causes	149 691	1 139	2 420	52 303	55 230	38 414
Homicide and legal intervention	19 846	317	375	11 678	6 399	1 029
Suicide	30 535	0	0	10 165	14 624	5 728
Accidents and adverse effects	95 644	765	2 005	29 336	32 052	31 386
Cancer	539 577	91	438	7 282	148 842	382 913
Major cardiovascular diseases	944 148	903	277	6 027	139 227	797 639
AIDS	16 516	19	54	4 371	11 651	415
Respiratory	195 943	538	241	1 593	21 267	172 291
Infectious diseases	53 202	722	295	5 640	20 769	25 769
Childbirth, pregnancy, and congenital abnormalities	25 331	19 113	664	1 631	1 663	2 256
Diabetes mellitus	62 636	2	3	777	14 563	47 289
Alzheimer's disease	22 475	0	1	2	317	22 154
Nephritis	25 331	136	11	250	3 147	21 787
Major causes	2 034 850	22 663	4 404	79 876	416 676	1 510 927
Not major causes	279 395	5 382	1 097	5 267	49 607	217 945
Percent not major causes	12.1	19.2	19.9	6.2	10.6	12.6
Total deaths	2 314 245	28 045	5 501	85 143	466 283	1 728 872

SOURCE: D.L. Hoyert, K.D. Kochanek, S.L. Murphy."Deaths: Final Data for 1997" National Center for Health Statistics, *National Vital Statistics Reports;* vol. 47, no. 19. June 30, 1999: Table 10.

In 1997, 54.6 percent of all deaths in the United States occurred after age 75. The primary causes of death in people age 75 and over were chronic conditions. For example, 41.9 percent of deaths caused by cancer, 65.9 percent caused by cardiovascular illnesses, and 66.9 percent caused by respiratory illnesses occurred in persons age 75 or older. Furthermore, 89.7 percent of Alzheimer's deaths occurred after age 75.[5]

GENDER DIFFERENCES

In 1997, age-adjusted death rates caused by heart disease were higher for men than for women (173.1 per 100,000 for men compared with 95.4 per 100,000 for women). (See Figure 3H.) On the other hand, more women in total died of heart disease—370,376 compared with 356,598 men—probably because women tended to die from heart disease later in life and more women than men were in the older population. Among individuals age 45 to 64 years, men had a heart disease death rate of 265 per 100,000 compared with 105 per 100,000 for women. Among those over age 65, men had a heart disease death rate of 1,944 per 100,000 compared with 1,781 for women. Even though the death rate for men was higher, more older women died of heart disease because more women are in the over 65 age group; 607,000 women over age 65 died of heart disease compared with 272,000 men. The sites for cancer deaths also differed by gender. (See Table 3.8.)

ETHNIC AND RACIAL DIFFERENCES

The impact of differential death rates on Blacks is evident from an examination of trends in death rates for men and women from heart disease. (See Figure 3H and Table 3.8.) From 1950 to 1998, age-adjusted death rates for heart disease dropped from 307.2 to 126.6 per 100,000 people for the whole population. Although death rates for heart diseases also declined among Blacks, their rates were still higher than those of Whites. In 1998, the age-adjusted death rate for heart disease for Black men was 231.8 per 100,000 people, 43 percent higher than the rate for White men. Furthermore, the age-adjusted death rate for heart disease for Black women was 146.8 per 100,000 people, 67 percent higher than the rate for White women.[6]

The leading causes of death also varied among racial and ethnic groups. Injuries took the place of cerebrovascular diseases in the top three causes of death for Hispanic men as well as American Indian/Alaska Native men and women. HIV infection took the place of cerebrovascular disease as one of the most frequent three causes of death for Black men. Homicide and legal intervention were among the top 10 causes of death for all men except Whites. Diseases of the kidneys (nephritis, nephritic syndrome, and nephrosis) were among the top 10 causes of death for all women except Hispanics. Alzheimer's disease was among the top 10 causes of death for White women only, and suicide was among the top 10 causes of death for American Indian/Alaska Native and Asian/Pacific Islander women only. (See Figures 3I, 3J, and 3K.)

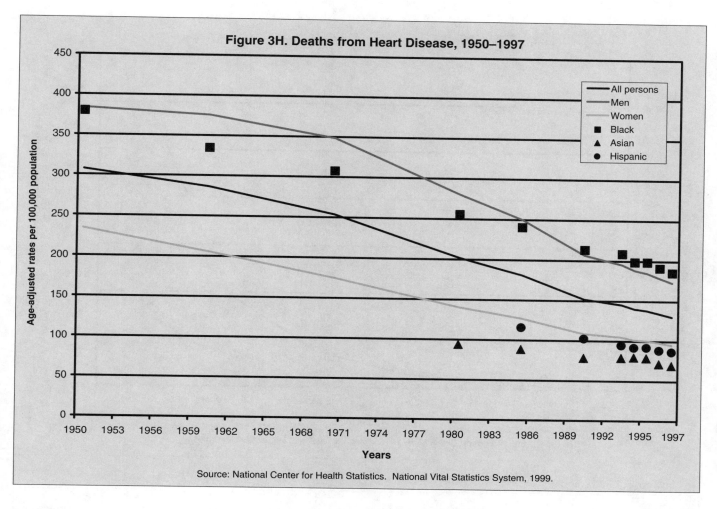

Figure 3H. Deaths from Heart Disease, 1950–1997

Source: National Center for Health Statistics. National Vital Statistics System, 1999.

INJURIES

Injury is a major public health problem. In 1998, unintentional injuries ranked as the fifth leading cause of death in the total population. In fact, an estimated 25 percent of the U.S. population is injured annually, and about 5 percent of those injured require hospitalization. Some injuries are so severe that they result in death. A variety of external causes contribute to deaths from injuries, including suicide, homicide, and accidental events such as traffic crashes, fires, and drownings. Most public health injury data do not include the adverse effects of such external causes as medical care, the therapeutic use of drugs, and war.

The earlier classification system of injury as a cause of death or disability grouped the injuries by cause, classifying them as either violent or accidental. The current classification system groups injuries by intent and mechanism. It includes intentional causes, such as homicide and suicide, and unintentional causes, also referred to as *accidents*. Intentional injuries can either be self-inflicted, such as suicide, or result from interpersonal violence, such as homicide, assault, child abuse, and rape. Unintentional injury may be the result of such mechanisms as traffic crashes, falls, fires, suffocation, drowning, and poisoning.

Injuries from firearms may be intentional or unintentional. Although most injury deaths are not intentional, many are preventable. Therefore, injury control professionals prefer the term *unintentional* to emphasize the possibility for prevention and control.

From 1979 to 1998, the age-adjusted injury rates declined from 66 per 100,000 to 48.3 per 100,000 persons. During that period, injury rates have declined in most age groups. (See Figure 3L.) Figure 3N, however, using 1979 as the base year for comparison, shows that injury deaths greatly increased beginning in the late 1980s for older adults.

In 1998, there were 146,941 total injury-related deaths, of which 35.4 percent were considered unintentional, 28.8 percent were motor vehicle related, 20.8 percent were caused by suicide, 12.2 percent were caused by homicide, and 2.8 percent resulted from other causes. (See Table 3G.) Children are more likely to die from unintentional injuries than any disease other than pneumonia and influenza, and most of their injuries are preventable. Elderly, especially the frail, are likely to die from such unintentional injuries as falls. In 1998, for example, the rate of deaths from falls among persons age 85 and older was 108.7 per 100,000 compared with 4.9 per 100,000 in

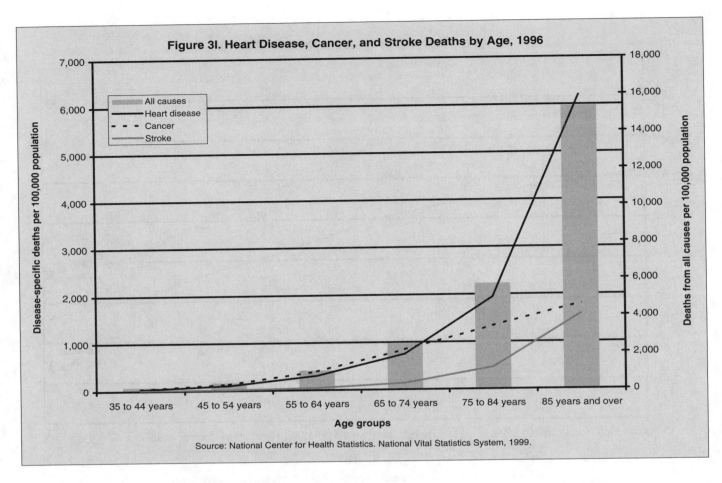

Figure 3I. Heart Disease, Cancer, and Stroke Deaths by Age, 1996

Source: National Center for Health Statistics. National Vital Statistics System, 1999.

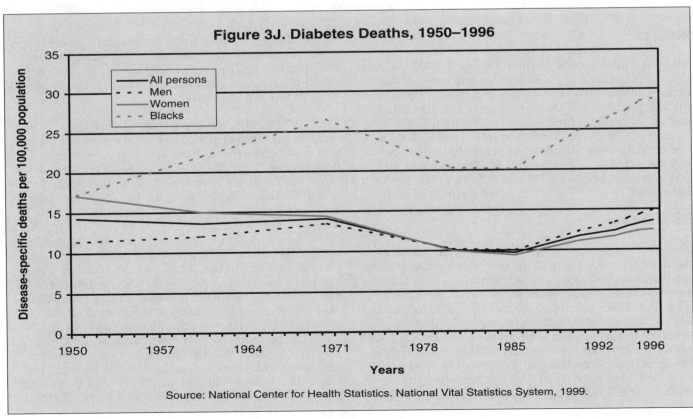

Figure 3J. Diabetes Deaths, 1950–1996

Source: National Center for Health Statistics. National Vital Statistics System, 1999.

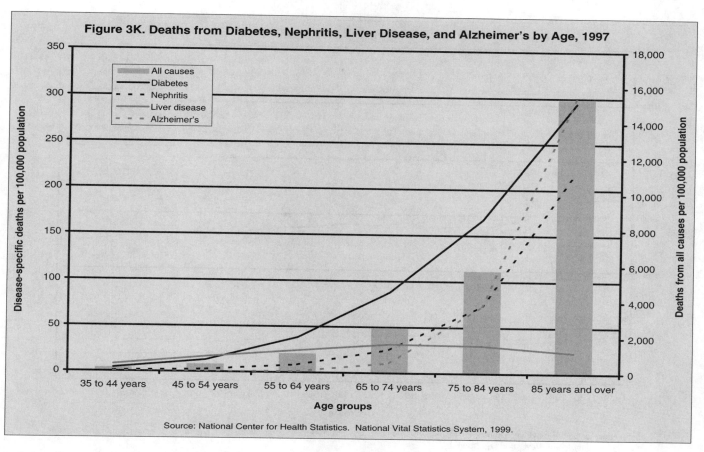

Figure 3K. Deaths from Diabetes, Nephritis, Liver Disease, and Alzheimer's by Age, 1997

Source: National Center for Health Statistics. National Vital Statistics System, 1999.

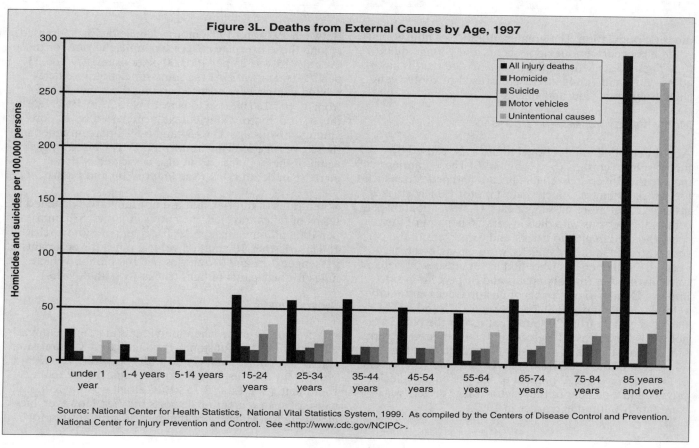

Figure 3L. Deaths from External Causes by Age, 1997

Source: National Center for Health Statistics, National Vital Statistics System, 1999. As compiled by the Centers of Disease Control and Prevention. National Center for Injury Prevention and Control. See <http://www.cdc.gov/NCIPC>.

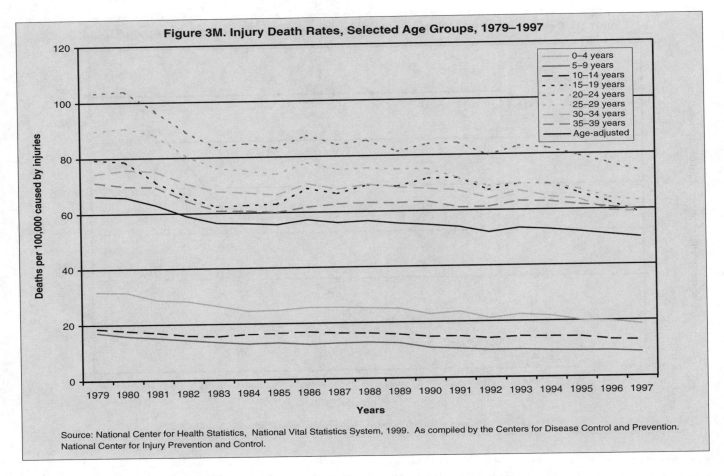

Figure 3M. Injury Death Rates, Selected Age Groups, 1979–1997

Source: National Center for Health Statistics, National Vital Statistics System, 1999. As compiled by the Centers for Disease Control and Prevention. National Center for Injury Prevention and Control.

the total population. The greatest number of injury-related deaths occurs among adolescents and young adults. (See Figure 3L.) Most of the injury-related deaths among adolescents and young adults are caused by motor vehicle crashes, homicide, and suicide.

MOTOR VEHICLE INJURIES AND DEATHS[7]

About half of all unintentional injuries are caused by motor vehicle crashes. (See Table 3.12.) These injuries include the drivers, passengers in cars, and pedestrians who are struck by motor vehicles. Most motor vehicle crashes involve one or more passenger cars. In 1997, about 39 percent of the persons who died in cars, 56 percent of the persons who died in pickup trucks, and 63 percent of the persons who died in utility vehicles were in single-vehicle crashes. Of the persons who died in car crashes, 51 percent were involved in frontal impacts and 31 percent in side impacts. Deaths to occupants of pickup trucks and utility vehicles have almost doubled between 1975 and 1997. On the basis of data from 20 states that report the blood alcohol levels for at least 80 percent of fatally injured drivers, blood alcohol levels of at least 0.10 percent were found in 34 percent of the pedestrians age 16 and older, 33 percent of the motorcyclists, 32 percent of the passenger-vehicle drivers, and 2 percent of the tractor-trailer drivers who were fatally injured in crashes in 1997.

Between 1979 and 1997, motor vehicle deaths increased among those over age 85. For example, the rate for those over age 85 was 25 per 100,000 persons in 1979 and 33 per 100,000 in 1997. At the same time, motor vehicle-related deaths were reduced among those age 20 to 24 from 47 per 100,000 persons in 1979 to 29 in 1997. During this period, motor vehicle deaths increased by 20 percent among persons age 35 to 54 and by 9.2 percent among those over age 55. This trend was partly caused by the aging of the population but also coincided with an increase in death rates. (See Figures 3O and Figure 3P.)

When rates of injuries that are not fatal are calculated in terms of miles traveled, they are as follows: 570 injuries per 100 million vehicle miles for riders of motorcycles, 166 injuries per 100 million vehicle miles for occupants of passenger cars, and 98 injuries per 100 million vehicle miles for occupants of light trucks. (See Table 3.13.)

SPORTS INJURIES

Other injuries occur when individuals are engaged in athletic activity. The Consumer Product Safety Commission reports on injuries associated with sports and recreation equipment that resulted in hospital emergency room treatment. (See Table 3.15.) Basketball was the leading cause of such recreational sports injuries. However, bicycles were associated with the most severe injuries; for

Table 3G. Deaths from Injuries: 1998

Cause of death	Number	Age-adjusted rate per 100,000 population
Total [1]	146 941	48.3
Firearm related	30 708	11.3
Motor vehicle	43 645	15.7
Pedestrian	6 319	2.1
Occupants of vehicles	24 783	9.0
Suicide	30 575	10.4
Firearm related	17 424	5.8
Homicide and legal intervention	17 893	7.2
Firearm related	11 798	4.9
Overall poisoning	18 392	6.3
Overall suffocation	11 095	3.5
Falls	13 301	2.5
Drownings/submersion	5 096	1.9
Fire/flames	3 691	1.2

SOURCE: Compiled from tables provided by the Centers for Disease Control and Prevention, National Center for Injury Prevention and Control.

1. Total injuries do not include adverse event–related injuries such as those associated with medical care and drugs.

NOTE: Each type of injury includes both intentional and unintentional injuries.

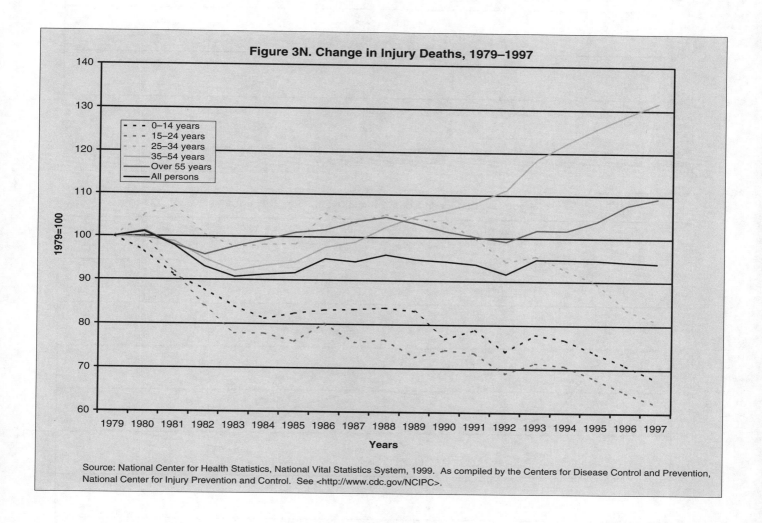

Figure 3N. Change in Injury Deaths, 1979–1997

Source: National Center for Health Statistics, National Vital Statistics System, 1999. As compiled by the Centers for Disease Control and Prevention, National Center for Injury Prevention and Control. See <http://www.cdc.gov/NCIPC>.

113

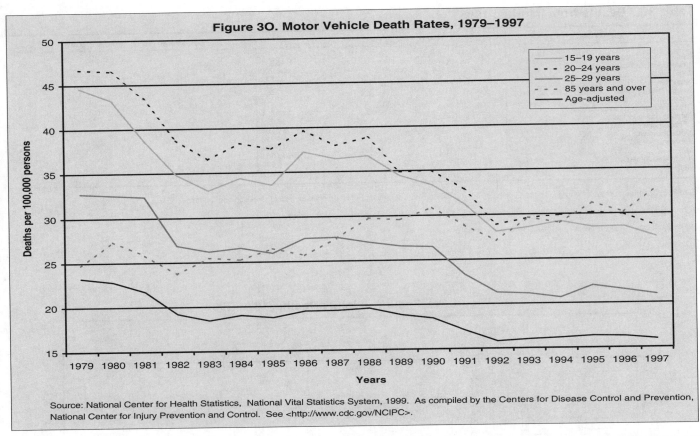

Figure 3O. Motor Vehicle Death Rates, 1979–1997

Source: National Center for Health Statistics, National Vital Statistics System, 1999. As compiled by the Centers for Disease Control and Prevention, National Center for Injury Prevention and Control. See <http://www.cdc.gov/NCIPC>.

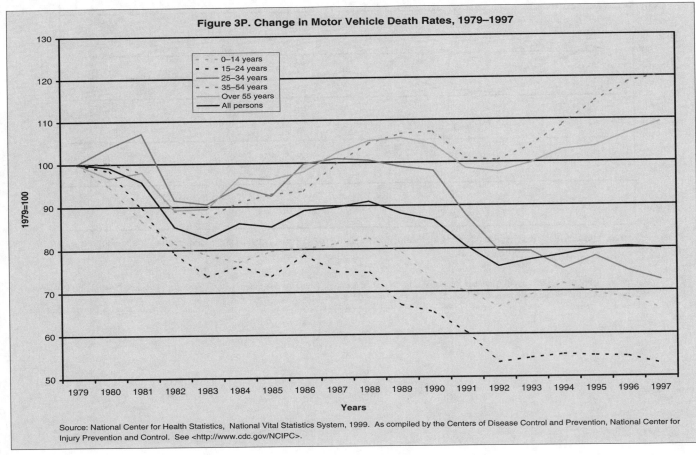

Figure 3P. Change in Motor Vehicle Death Rates, 1979–1997

Source: National Center for Health Statistics, National Vital Statistics System, 1999. As compiled by the Centers of Disease Control and Prevention, National Center for Injury Prevention and Control. See <http://www.cdc.gov/NCIPC>.

1998, the rate of hospitalizations or fatality (dead on arrival) was 9.8 per 100,000 population. Furthermore, bicycle-related injuries were twice as high as those associated with all-terrain vehicles, mopeds, and other related vehicles. This higher rate may be because of the greater number of people who use bicycles.

The data on bicycles are consistent with information collected by the Department of Transportation. Analysts there found that the number of bicyclists who were fatally injured in crashes increased between 1996 and 1997. Most deaths involved severe head injuries, occurred during the summer months, and occurred between 3:00 P.M. and 9:00 P.M. In 1997, 97 percent of the bicyclists who died were not wearing helmets.

Between 1994 and 1998, injuries associated with baseball and softball decreased, especially in children age 5 to 14 years. The rate in these children decreased from 410.7 per 100,000 to 297.3 per 100,000. Most of the baseball and softball game injuries are related to sliding into the stationary bases and resulted in injuries such as abrasions, sprains, ligament strains, and fractures. Use of break-away bases greatly reduced such injuries.

INJURIES IN THE WORKPLACE

The types of injuries that occur in the workplace have changed as the economy moves from heavy industry to more service-oriented businesses. This change is accompanied by a change in the nature and distribution of the people in the workforce, the hazards to which they are exposed, and the ability to regulate such hazards. The highest death rates occur in mining (30.5 per 100,000 workers); agriculture, forestry, and fishing (20.5 per 100,000 workers); and construction (15.5 per 100,000 workers). Between 1980 and 1994, the rate of occupational injury deaths declined from 7.5 to 4.4 per 100,000 workers.[8] By 1999, the number of workers had increased and the number of fatal work injuries had decreased. By 1999, 6,023 fatal occupational injuries occurred, compared with 6,588 in 1994.[9] Throughout this period, motor vehicles were the leading cause of death in the workplace. In 1999, 31 percent of all fatal injuries in the workplace involved motor vehicles. Machines, homicides, falls, and electrocution were the next top four causes.

In 1990, homicides moved to second place among the leading causes of death in the workplace and in 1994, the greatest number of workplace homicides occurred. Most of the homicides in the workplace occurred during a robbery or other crime. In 1994, 73 percent of the total homicides occurred during a robbery or other crime, and only 9 percent involved a co-worker or resulted from a business dispute. Homicides accounted for 16.3 percent of all workplace-related deaths among the total workforce, 11 percent among male workers and 42 percent among female workers. In 1999, homicides accounted for only 11 percent of all workplace deaths and dropped to third place among the leading causes of workplace deaths.

In a special study of violence in the workplace, the National Institute for Occupational Safety and Health examined its data from the National Traumatic Occupational Fatalities Surveillance System from 1980 through 1992 to obtain average annual rates.[10] The average rate over the 13-year period from 1980 through 1992 for workplace homicides for workers age 16 years and older was 0.70 per 100,000 workers. The highest rate by age was for workers age 65 and older (1.83 per 100,000 workers), and the highest rate by race was for Black workers (1.39 per 100,000 workers). The high-risk industries were retail trade (1.60 per 100,000 workers) and public administration (1.30 per 100,000 workers). The high-risk occupation was for taxi driver/chauffeur, which showed an increased rate from 15.1 per 100,000 workers in 1983–1989 to 22.7 per 100,000 workers in 1990–1992.

FIREARMS-RELATED INJURIES

About 26 percent of the total deaths from injuries in 1997 were associated with guns and other firearms. These weapons are involved in 57 percent of the suicides that occur and in 71 percent of the homicides. Deaths caused by firearms injuries increased from 12.7 per 100,000 persons in 1985 to 15.6 per 100,000 in 1993 and then fell back to 12.2 per 100,000 in 1997. Among 15- to 24-year-olds, the death rate caused by firearms injuries more than doubled between 1984 and 1993, increasing from 2,361 per 100,000 in 1984 to 4,961 per 100,000 in 1993. The rate in this young adult group then declined to 3,593 per 100,000 in 1997. The overall number declined from a high of 39,595 in 1993 to 32,436 in 1997. (See Figures 3Q and 3R and Table 3.14.)

DATA SOURCES FOR INJURIES

More detailed information on injuries is available from various sources. The following list provides sources of data for occupational injuries, traffic injuries, violence, and homicide in the workplace, as well as information from the Consumer Product Safety Commission.

1. Overall occupational injuries:

   Census of Fatal Occupational Injuries and Survey of Occupational Injuries and Illnesses, both from the Bureau of Labor Statistics.

   National Traumatic Occupational Fatality Surveillance System from the CDC.

2. Traffic injuries:

   Fatal Accident Reporting System from the National Highway Traffic Safety Administration.

3. Violence:

   National Crime Victimization Survey from the Bureau of Justice Statistics.

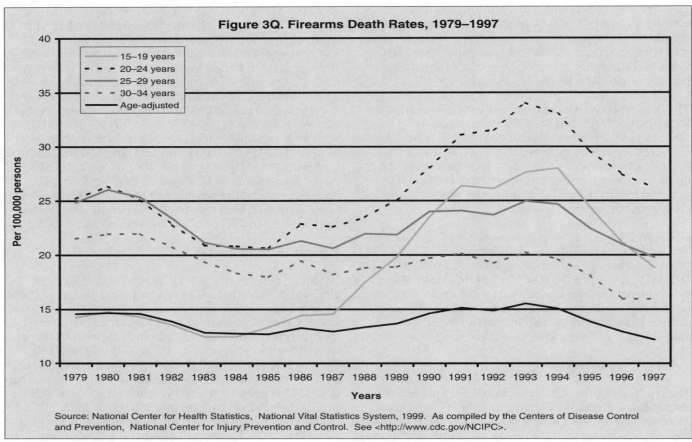

Figure 3Q. Firearms Death Rates, 1979–1997

Source: National Center for Health Statistics, National Vital Statistics System, 1999. As compiled by the Centers of Disease Control and Prevention, National Center for Injury Prevention and Control. See <http://www.cdc.gov/NCIPC>.

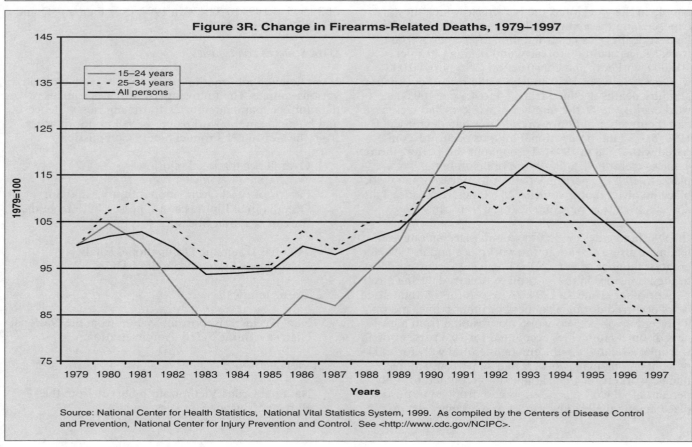

Figure 3R. Change in Firearms-Related Deaths, 1979–1997

Source: National Center for Health Statistics, National Vital Statistics System, 1999. As compiled by the Centers of Disease Control and Prevention, National Center for Injury Prevention and Control. See <http://www.cdc.gov/NCIPC>.

4. Consumer product safety:

National Electronic Injury Surveillance System from the Consumer Product Safety Commission.

5. Homicide in the workplace:

National Traumatic Occupational Fatalities Surveillance System from the CDC and the National Institute on Occupation Safety and Health (1980–1992), provides data on number, rate per 100,000 workers, causes, demographics, industry, state, and method (firearm, strangulation, cutting or piercing instrument, other).

Census of Fatal Occupational Injuries Program from the Bureau of Labor Statistics (1992–1994), includes data on the circumstances of workplace homicides.

MALIGNANCIES AND CHRONIC DISEASES

Heart disease is the leading cause of death, and malignant neoplasm (cancer) is the second leading cause of death, among men and women for all racial and ethnic groups. The trends in these conditions were discussed in this chapter in the section on the leading causes of death. As noted earlier, the death rates for heart disease have greatly declined while those for cancer have not.

Chronic conditions are defined as those that have lasted three months or longer. Important chronic conditions affect the skin, muscles, and skeletal system; hearing, vision, and speech; and the digestive, circulatory, respiratory, and other systems.

DISEASES OF THE CIRCULATORY SYSTEM (INCLUDING HEART DISEASE AND STROKE)

Diseases of the circulatory system, including heart disease and stroke, are believed to begin when people are young, to develop over time, and to get diagnosed in adulthood. Hypertension, otherwise known as high blood pressure, is the most prevalent circulatory condition reported by the general population (107.1 per 1,000 persons). A greater proportion of Blacks than Whites report that they suffer from hypertension, while Whites are more likely than Blacks to report having hardening of the arteries and heart disease. Most Americans living with heart disease report heart rhythm disorders (33 per 1,000 persons) and ischemic heart disease (29 per 1,000 persons). Reports of tachycardia or rapid heartbeats increase with age, while the rate of heart murmurs is similar across all age groups. (See Table 3.21.)

Hypertension (high blood pressure) and heart disease are often diagnosed in persons age 45 and older; while hardening of the arteries is most likely found in those age 65 and older. Contrary to popular belief, heart disease is the leading cause of death for women as well as for men. In fact, among persons under age 45, women are more likely than men to have heart disease and rheumatic fever with

or without heart disease. Among persons age 65 years and older, women are more likely than men to have hypertension. Men, however, are almost twice as likely to die of ischemic heart disease. (See Table 3.22.)

CANCER

Cancer is caused by malignant neoplasms, a group of diseases characterized by uncontrolled cell reproduction. Cancer is not infectious; however, evidence exists that some forms of cancer may be caused by a virus, environmental exposures, or certain diets. Several different treatment approaches are now available, depending on the type of cancer. Available treatments include destroying the cancerous growth by surgery, radiation, or chemotherapy; using hormones or steroids to stop the cancer cells from growing; or helping the body restore or increase its natural defenses against disease (immunotherapy). An increase in the recording of new kinds of cancer is the result of improved diagnosis and reporting systems as well as early access to screening and health care.

SOURCES OF DATA ON CANCER

The National Cancer Institute (NCI) and the American Cancer Society have cooperated to collect and report statistics on new cancer cases (incidence), survival of cancer patients after they have been diagnosed, and cancer deaths (mortality), through the Surveillance, Epidemiology, and End Results (SEER) program. The SEER program was established on January 1, 1973. The program collects information from 11 population-based registries of residents diagnosed with cancer during the year. According to the NCI, "Geographic areas were selected for inclusion in the SEER Program based on their ability to operate and maintain a high quality population-based cancer reporting system and for their epidemiologically significant population subgroups." The 11 SEER areas are San Francisco, Connecticut, Detroit, Iowa, New Mexico, Seattle, Utah, Atlanta, San Jose-Monterey, Los Angeles, and Hawaii. (See Table 3H.) The SEER data provide followup information on all previously diagnosed patients as well as information for cancer incidence and survival rates based on registries covering approximately 14 percent of the U.S. population. Information on more than 2.5 million cancer cases is included in the SEER database, and approximately 160,000 new cases are added each year. The mortality data are based on death certificate data compiled by state agencies and reported to the NCHS. The NCHS provides the NCI with a copy of these records for analysis.

The SEER program is conducted under contract with nonprofit, medically oriented organizations having statutory responsibility for registering diagnoses of cancer among residents of their respective geographic coverage areas. Each contractor maintains a cancer information reporting system; abstracts records for resident cancer patients seen in every hospital in and outside the cover-

Table 3H. Coverage of the SEER Program

Areas included	Dates participating
Connecticut, Iowa, New Mexico, Utah, Hawaii, and the metropolitan areas of Detroit and San Francisco–Oakland	1973–Present
The metropolitan area of Atlanta and the 13-county Seattle/Puget Sound area	1974/75–Present
Ten predominantly black rural counties in Georgia	1978–Present
American Indians residing in Arizona	1980–Present
New Orleans, Louisiana	1974–1977
Four counties in New Jersey	1979–1989
Puerto Rico	1973–1989
Increased coverage of minority populations, especially Hispanics, with the addition of Los Angeles County and four counties in the San Jose/Monterey area south of San Francisco	1992–Present
Alaskan Native Cancer Registry	1990–Present

SOURCE: L.A.G. Ries, C.L. Kosary, B.F. Hankey, B.A. Miller, L. Clegg , B.K. Edwards (eds). Surveillance, Epidemiology, and End Results (SEER) *Cancer Statistics Review*, 1973-1996, National Cancer Institute. Bethesda, MD, 1999.

age area; abstracts all death certificates on which cancer is listed as a cause of death for residents dying in and outside the coverage area; searches records of private laboratories, radiotherapy units, nursing homes, and other health services units that provide diagnostic service to ensure complete ascertainment of cases; registers all in situ and malignant neoplasms with the exception, since 1996, of certain histologies for cancer of the skin and in situ cancers of the cervix uteri; records data on all newly diagnosed cancers, including selected patient demographics, primary site, morphology, diagnostic confirmation, extent of disease, and first course of cancer-directed therapy; provides active followup on all living patients except those with in situ cancer of the cervix uteri; maintains confidentiality of patient records; and submits data electronically to the NCI twice each year covering all reportable diagnoses of cancer that were made for residents of the coverage area.

One problem with the SEER data is that it is based on a limited number of registries that have reported data to the NCI. In 1992, Congress passed the Cancer Registries Amendment Act (Public Law 102–515), which authorizes the Centers for Disease Control and Prevention to fund the development of cancer registries in all of the states. Under this program, CDC is authorized to extend the registry program to the entire country. CDC currently supports cancer registries in 45 states, three territories, and the District of Columbia: for 36 jurisdictions, CDC enhances established registries, and for 13 it develops and implements new registries. It is working closely with the NCI and the North American Association of Central Cancer Registries to improve existing cancer registries, to develop new ones, and to set standards for data completeness, timeliness, and quality. Once these registries are fully established and their results are compiled, they will provide more complete data that will greatly enhance the information currently reported in SEER.

CANCER INCIDENCE

The rate of new cases of all cancers combined has increased between 1973 and 1995 for both Whites and Blacks. (See Figure 3S.) During this period, however, the death rate for Whites diagnosed with cancer has been lower than Blacks and has remained relatively stable while it increased for Blacks. In 1996, the incidence

rate for invasive cancers for all sites was 388.6 per 100,000 persons. The rate of diagnosed new cases for those under age 65 is about the same for both men and women in both races. However, the rate of diagnosed new cases of cancers for all sites gradually increases with age for both sexes in both races. Furthermore, after age 65, the rates for new cases are much higher for both Black and White men than for Black and White women. (See Table 3.16.)

The incidence rates vary widely ranging from four new cases per 100,000 persons to over 100 per 100,000 for the different types of site-specific cancers. (See Table 3I.) Recent studies show that the incidence rates of kidney and renal cancer, liver and intrahepatic bile duct cancer, melanomas of the skin, non-Hodgkin's lymphomas, and thyroid cancer continue to increase. Although the rate of invasive cancers of the liver and the intrahepatic bile duct are on the rise, they are still among the rarest forms of cancer, along with cancer of the larynx and esophagus (fewer than four per 100,000). Invasive cancers of the prostate, breast, and lung and bronchus have the highest incidence rates.

Prostate Cancer

Prostate is the invasive cancer with the highest rate of new cases in the total population. Currently the incidence rate is 137.2 per 100,000 for the total population. The incidence rate for all races increased steadily from 64.2 per 100,000 in 1973 to its peak in 1992 of 190.8 and then decreased to 135.7 in 1996. During this time, the incidence rate for Black men rose from 106.3 per 100,000 in 1973 to 271.6 in 1993, and declined to 211.3 in 1996. Part of the increase may reflect a rise in the detection of this site-specific cancer from the recently available prostate-specific antigen (PSA) screening. (See Table 3.16.)

Breast Cancer

Although only men are at risk for prostate cancer, both sexes are at risk for breast cancer. The rates for men, however, are very low. In 1996, the incidence rate for breast cancer for White men was 1.1 per 100,000 and for Black men was 1.7. The incidence rate for White women was higher than for Black women, but has been increasing since 1973 for women of both races. In 1996, the inci-

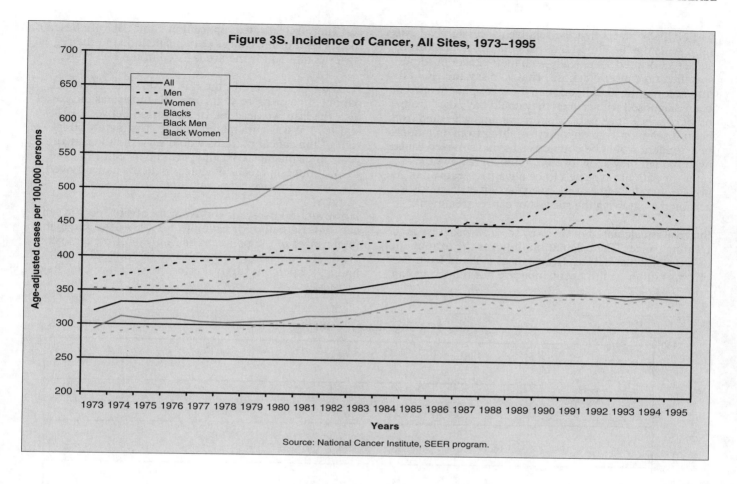

Figure 3S. Incidence of Cancer, All Sites, 1973–1995

Source: National Cancer Institute, SEER program.

Table 3I. Incidence of Cancer by Site: 1995

(Per 100,000 persons. Ranked by order of incidence.)

Site	New cases
All sites	388.6
Prostate cancer	135.7
Breast cancer (female)	110.7
Lung and bronchus cancer	54.2
Colon and rectum cancer	42.7
Corpus and uterus, NOS cancer	21.1
Urinary bladder cancer	16.2
Non-Hodgkin's lymphomas	15.5
Ovary cancer	14.1
Melanomas of skin	13.8
Oral Cavity and pharynx cancer	10.0
All leukemias	9.7
Kidney and renal pelvis cancer	9.4
Pancreas cancer	8.6
Cervix uteri cancer	7.7
Stomach cancer	6.6
Brain and other nervous system cancer	5.8
Thyroid cancer	5.5
Testis cancer	4.6
Liver and intrahepatic bile duct cancer	4.2
Multiple myeloma	4.2
Esophagus cancer	4.0
Larynx cancer	3.7
Hodgkin's disease	2.6

SOURCE: L.A.G. Ries, C.L. Kosary, B.F. Hankey, B.A. Miller, L. Clegg, B.K. Edwards (eds). Surveillance, Epidemiology, and End Results (SEER) *Cancer Statistics Review*, 1973-1996, National Cancer Institute. Bethesda, MD, 1999.

dence rate for breast cancer for White women was 110.7 per 100,000 and for Black women was 100.3.

Lung Cancer

Despite health campaigns about smoking and other behaviors that increase the risk of lung cancer, the rate of new cases in the total population has increased from 1973 to 1995. (See Figure 3T.) The rates of lung cancer increased especially for both White and Black women, greatly reducing the differences in incidence between men and women. In 1973, White men were four times more likely to develop lung cancer than White women. By 1995, the lung cancer incidence rate was only 1.5 times higher for White men than White women. The incidence rate for Black men was five times higher than for Black women in 1973 but only 2.2 times higher by 1995.

SURVIVAL OF PERSONS WITH CANCER

The NCI defines the *relative cancer survival rate* as "the observed survival rate ... adjusted for expected mortality."

The NCI also states that the relative cancer survival rate represents the likelihood that patients will not die from causes associated specifically with their cancer at some specified time after diagnosis. That is to say, the NCI takes into account the likelihood that, if cancer patients had not been diagnosed with cancer, they could have died from other causes. For example, cancer patients who died from heart disease or from an injury resulting from an automobile accident would be counted as having survived cancer even though they actually died. Table 3.17 shows these rates for patients expected to be alive five years after diagnosis; generally, survival for five years after diagnosis is accepted as showing the success of cancer treatment.

Survival is calculated in this way to show progress in treating cancer. The calculation requires the examination of mortality that derives from cancer isolated from the effect of other health events that are not related to can-

cer. The survival rates reported in Table 3.17 are based on the survival of the cancer patients included in the registries compiled for the areas listed in the text table.

As shown in Figure 3U, the rate of survival for cancer patients five or more years after diagnosis has increased over the last two decades. In the period between 1974 and 1976, it was anticipated that approximately 50 percent of the cancer patients would survive at least five years after diagnosis. By the period between 1989 and 1994, about 60 percent of cancer patients had survived the disease for five or more years.

However, the five-year survival rate of site-specific cancers differ greatly. For example, for 1989–1995 the highly fatal cancer of the pancreas had only a 4.1 percent survival rate compared with cancer of the thyroid, which had a 94.7 percent survival rate. The very rare cancers of

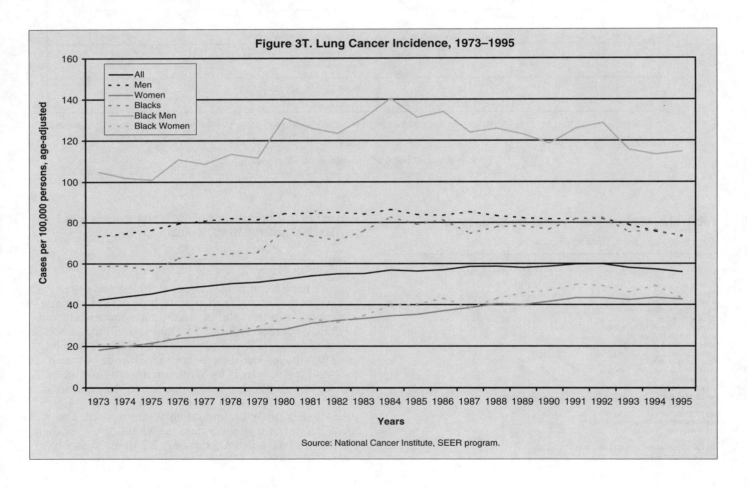

Figure 3T. Lung Cancer Incidence, 1973–1995

Source: National Cancer Institute, SEER program.

the esophagus and liver have low survival rates. In fact, only 5.3 percent of the people diagnosed with cancer of the liver and intrahepatic bile duct survive five or more years, and only 12.3 percent of those diagnosed with cancer of the esophagus survive five or more years. Not all rare cancers have low survival rates, and not all relatively common cancers have high survival rates. For example, cancer of the testes, also a relatively rare cancer, has a survival rate of 95.4 percent. The relatively common cancer of the breast has a survival rate of 82.7 percent, and prostate cancer has a survival rate of 91.9 percent. Conversely, lung cancer, another very common form of cancer, has a survival rate of only 13.9 percent.

CANCER MORTALITY (DEATHS)

The death rates for cancer vary according to patient characteristics, including sex, race, age, and place of residence, as well as the site of the cancer in the body. The mortality rate for all cancers combined increased slowly from 162 per 100,000 persons in 1973 to peak at 173.4 in 1991 and then declined to 166.9 in 1996. (See Figure 3V and Table 3.18.) Men have higher death rates from cancer than women (in 1996, 207.1 per 100,000 as compared to 139.1 per 100,000), and Blacks have higher rates than Whites. National mortality rates for American Indians and Alaska natives are generally lower than the rate for Whites.

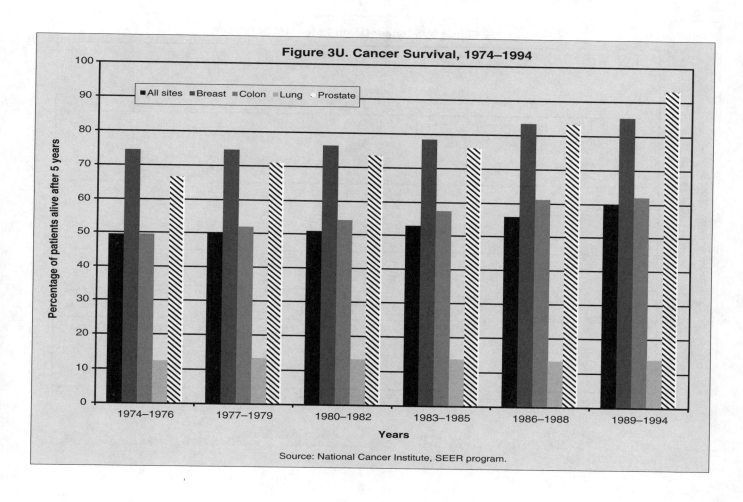

Figure 3U. Cancer Survival, 1974–1994

Source: National Cancer Institute, SEER program.

However, the mortality rates increased for almost all cancers when the data on the death certificates were adjusted for the misclassification of American Indians and Alaska Natives. (See Table 3.19.) Generally, the mortality rates are highest among people age 65 and over. For example, the rate for people under age 65 is 70.1 per 100,000, and for those age 65 and over the rate is 1,083.2 per 100,000. (See Table 3.18.)

The mortality rates for the various site-specific cancers range from less than one per 100,000 for thyroid cancer and Hodgkin's disease to 48.8 per 100,000 for lung can-cer. Lung cancer is the leading cause of cancer deaths for both men and women. In the 1990s, deaths from lung cancer among men decreased; however, among women, lung cancer deaths increased. Other cancers with high mortality rates include breast cancer (24.3 per 100,000 women) and prostate cancer (24.1 per 100,000 men). The cancer death rates for the total population are higher in Louisiana, Nevada, and the states east of the Mississippi. (See Table 3.20.) Lung, colon, and breast cancer death rates also have distinct geographic distributions. (See Figures 3W, 3X, 3Y, and 3Z.)

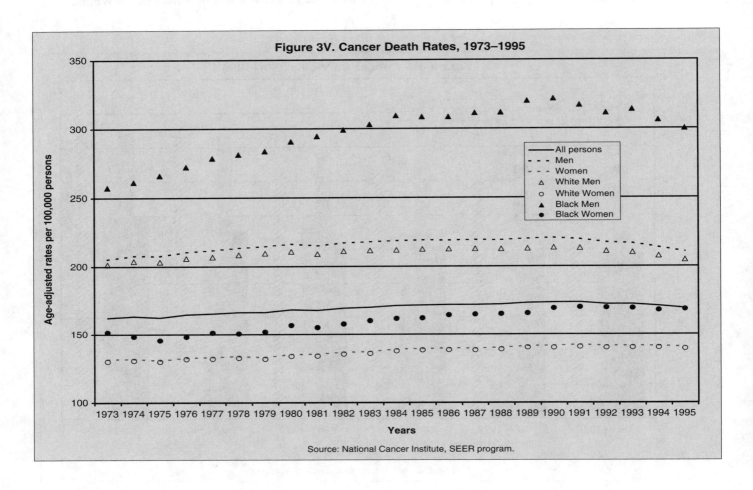

Figure 3V. Cancer Death Rates, 1973–1995

Source: National Cancer Institute, SEER program.

COMPARISON OF CANCER INCIDENCE, SURVIVAL, AND MORTALITY

Differential progress has been made in detecting and improving the survival rates of the various types of cancers. Overall, both the incidence and relative survival rates for cancers from all causes have increased more rapidly than the mortality rate. However, this relationship varies among the different site-specific forms of cancer. For

example, the rate of new cases of lung cancer continued to increase over the last two decades, and only recently has there been any evidence of some decrease. Lung cancer continues to be a highly fatal cancer with less than 20 percent surviving five years or more without dying from the cancer. (See Figure 3AA.) In contrast, colon cancer shows some improvement both in the development of new cases and in the relative survival rate and the data for prostate cancer show high and increasing relative survival rates and

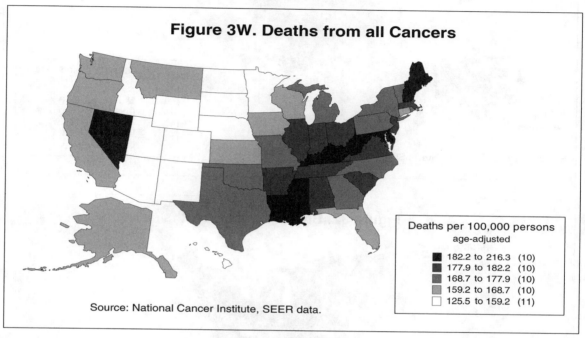

Figure 3W. Deaths from all Cancers

Deaths per 100,000 persons
age-adjusted

- 182.2 to 216.3 (10)
- 177.9 to 182.2 (10)
- 168.7 to 177.9 (10)
- 159.2 to 168.7 (10)
- 125.5 to 159.2 (11)

Source: National Cancer Institute, SEER data.

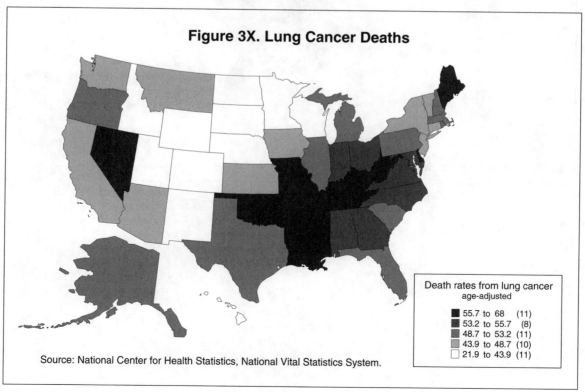

Figure 3X. Lung Cancer Deaths

Death rates from lung cancer
age-adjusted

- 55.7 to 68 (11)
- 53.2 to 55.7 (8)
- 48.7 to 53.2 (11)
- 43.9 to 48.7 (10)
- 21.9 to 43.9 (11)

Source: National Center for Health Statistics, National Vital Statistics System.

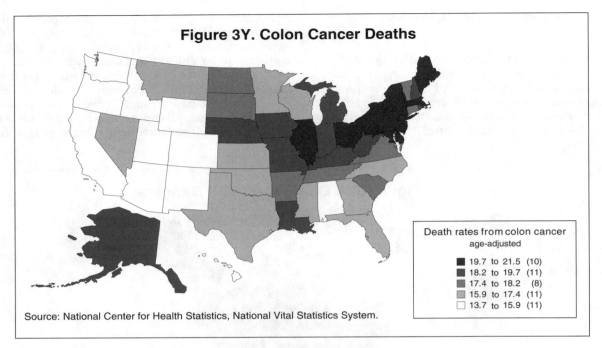

Figure 3Y. Colon Cancer Deaths

Death rates from colon cancer
age-adjusted

- 19.7 to 21.5 (10)
- 18.2 to 19.7 (11)
- 17.4 to 18.2 (8)
- 15.9 to 17.4 (11)
- 13.7 to 15.9 (11)

Source: National Center for Health Statistics, National Vital Statistics System.

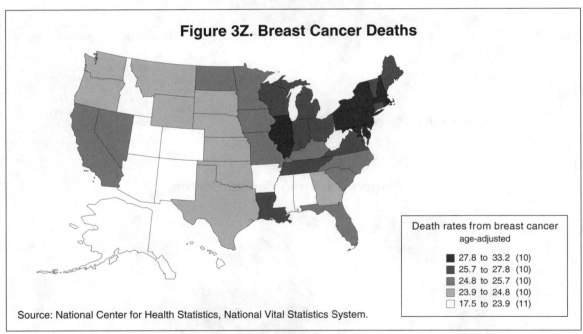

Figure 3Z. Breast Cancer Deaths

Death rates from breast cancer
age-adjusted

- 27.8 to 33.2 (10)
- 25.7 to 27.8 (10)
- 24.8 to 25.7 (10)
- 23.9 to 24.8 (10)
- 17.5 to 23.9 (11)

Source: National Center for Health Statistics, National Vital Statistics System.

very low mortality rates. (See Figures 3AB and 3AC.) However, this increase could reflect the development of the PSA test, which has enabled the identification of prostate cancer in its earlier stages. This early detection is desirable for cost-effective treatment, but the detection of asymptomatic cases may inflate the incidence rates temporarily. Breast cancer also has had high rates of new cases, but the survival rate also has been high and the mortality rate low. (See Figure 3AD.) So while new cases are diagnosed, over 80 percent of breast cancer patients survive five or more years after diagnosis.

Data on cancer incidence, survival, and mortality rates for specific racial groups such as American Indians and Asians are limited. Table 3.19 shows data for cancer deaths among American Indians and Alaska Natives based on analysis by the Indian Health Service. The SEER program conducted a special analysis providing data on American Indians and Asian groups such as Chinese, Korean, Japanese, and Hawaiians.[11] Special studies of cancer incidence, survival, and mortality among American Indians and Alaska Natives indicate unique patterns of site-specific cancers with recent increases in cancer incidence and mortality.[12–15]

CHRONIC CONDITIONS

A variety of long-term (chronic) conditions affects Americans' health and inhibits their ability to perform everyday activities. The National Center for Health

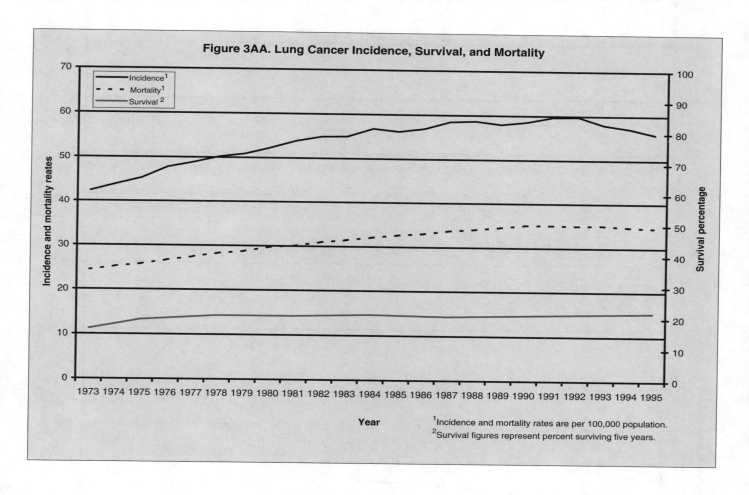

Figure 3AA. Lung Cancer Incidence, Survival, and Mortality

[1]Incidence and mortality rates are per 100,000 population.
[2]Survival figures represent percent surviving five years.

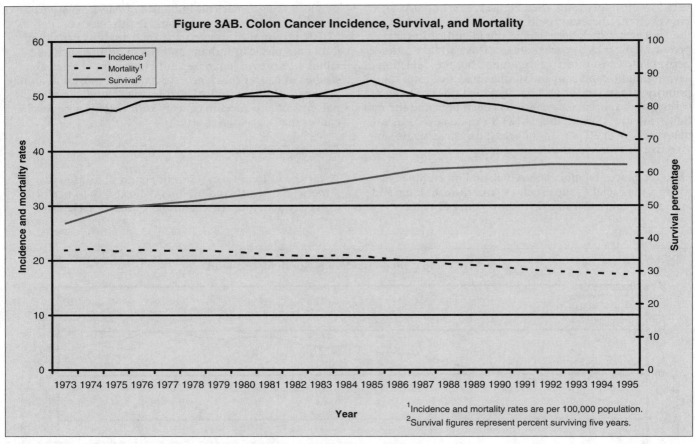

Figure 3AB. Colon Cancer Incidence, Survival, and Mortality

[1]Incidence and mortality rates are per 100,000 population.
[2]Survival figures represent percent surviving five years.

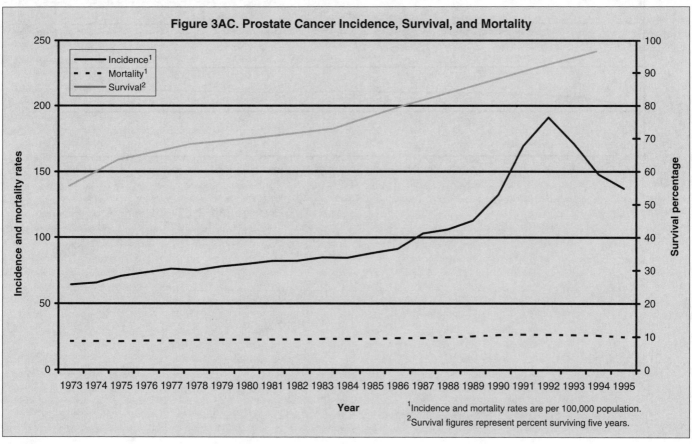

Figure 3AC. Prostate Cancer Incidence, Survival, and Mortality

[1]Incidence and mortality rates are per 100,000 population.
[2]Survival figures represent percent surviving five years.

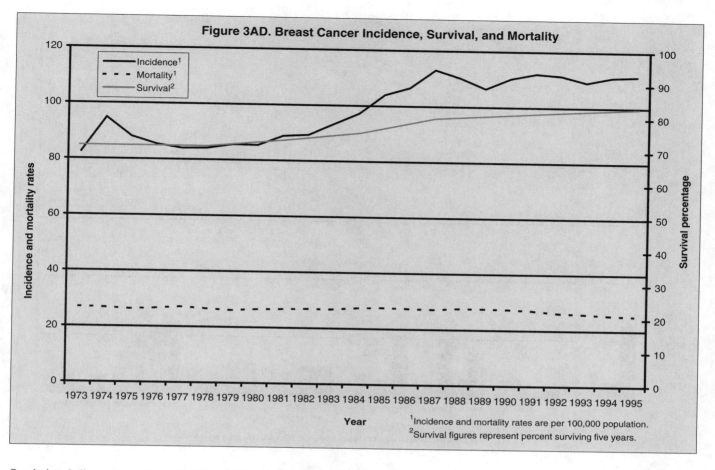

Figure 3AD. Breast Cancer Incidence, Survival, and Mortality

[Incidence¹]
[Mortality¹]
[Survival²]

¹Incidence and mortality rates are per 100,000 population.
²Survival figures represent percent surviving five years.

Statistics defines *chronic conditions* as those that were "first noticed more than three months before the reference date of the interview, or [are] a type of condition that ordinarily has a duration of more than three months." NCHS also states, "Examples of conditions that are considered chronic regardless of their time of onset are diabetes, heart conditions, emphysema, and arthritis." The primary source of annual information on chronic conditions in the general population is NCHS's National Health Interview Survey (NHIS).

The NHIS has collected information on self-reported health information from the household population since 1957. The NHIS reports chronic conditions using a period prevalence procedure. It shows the proportion of persons who had the condition at any time during the 12 months previous to the time when they were interviewed. Because the NHIS conducts interviews throughout the year, the estimates are best considered an average prevalence.[16]

Americans suffer from various chronic conditions that last three months or more, including arthritis, cataracts, ulcers, diabetes, anemia, heart conditions, emphysema, asthma, and chronic bronchitis. (See Figure 3AE.) Many people are not aware that they have any of these conditions until they see a doctor and receive medical attention. Therefore, surveys like the National Health Interview Survey that rely on self-reported medical conditions may present a very conservative estimate of the

actual extent of the problem in the nation. The chronic conditions most frequently self-reported are arthritis, chronic sinusitis, deformity or orthopedic impairment, and high blood pressure. (See Table 3J.) People age 45 and older are more likely than younger people to report having a chronic health condition, and most of the individuals in that age group suffer from arthritis, heart disease, and high blood pressure. Younger people are more likely to report conditions involving asthma and chronic bronchitis. (See Table 3.21.)

DIABETES MELLITUS

The Diabetes Program at CDC estimates that about 16 million people in the United States have diabetes, and approximately one-third are not aware that they have the disease. The rates of diabetes are higher among older adults than younger people and are also higher among Blacks than Whites. Since 1980, the prevalence of diabetes increased in all age groups, with the largest increases occurring among Blacks, especially among those age 65 and older. (See Table 3.28.) Deaths from diabetes in the general population decreased between 1950 and 1985. However, since 1985, the death rate from diabetes has risen. In fact, in 1996 the death rate for diabetes was as high as it was in 1960. The trends for men and women differ. Men had lower death rates from diabetes throughout the 1950s and 1960s than they did in 1996. Women had higher death rates from diabetes in the 1950s and

127

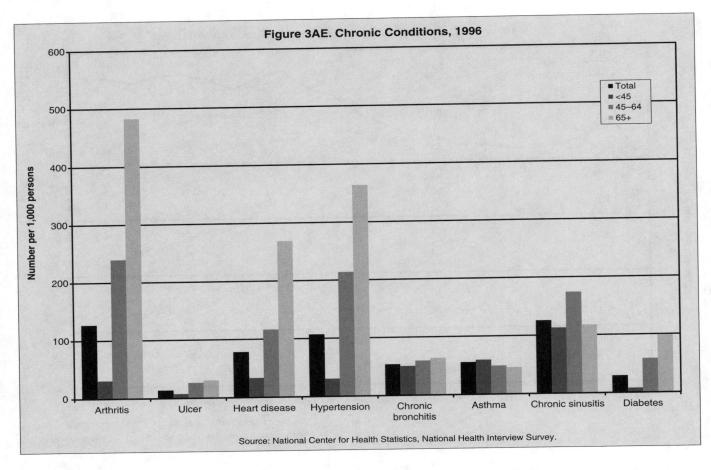

Figure 3AE. Chronic Conditions, 1996

Source: National Center for Health Statistics, National Health Interview Survey.

1960s than they did in 1996. During the 1950s through 1996, Asian/Pacific Islanders had the lowest death rates from diabetes. In the 1980s and 1990s, the death rates for Blacks and American Indian/Alaska Natives were twice as high as that for Whites. Furthermore, Whites were less likely than any other racial and ethnic group to have serious complications associated with diabetes. Blacks were more likely than Whites to suffer from eye disease, kidney failure, and amputations associated with their diabetes. Finally, more than half of the amputations that took place involving the lower extremities (legs and feet) that were not caused by events such as automobile crashes, lawn mower accidents, or other traumatic situations occurred among people with diabetes. (See Figure 3J and Table 3.28.)

MENTAL DISORDERS

The number of persons identified with a mental illness is highly dependent on the definition used for *mental illness*. According to one study, in 1994, more than 8 million Americans reported that they were suffering from a condition that would be classified as a mental illness. Women were more likely to report such conditions than men (3,830 men per 100,000 versus 5,914 women per 100,000). Poor people were more likely to report these conditions than those living in households with incomes over the poverty line (10,954 per 100,000 for those living in poverty households versus 4,050 per 100,000 for all others). And persons living alone were also more likely to report a mental or emotional problem (9,227 per 100,000 for those living alone versus 3,649 per 100,000 for those living with their spouse). Employed people also had a much lower rate of mental or emotional problems (2,955 per 100,000). (See Table 3.29.)

These data on mental or emotional problems are based on the 1994 Phase I National Health Interview Survey Disability Supplement. Face-to-face interviews were conducted in 45,705 households containing 116,179 persons. Information was obtained about each household member either by self-reporting or, if the person was unavailable or unable to respond, by proxy. Because respondents may have been unable or unwilling to report symptoms of mental illness for themselves or other household members, these data may be underestimates of the true prevalence of mental disorders in the general population. Adults were classified as having a mental or emotional disorder if they met one or more of the following three criteria within the past 12 months: (1) had one of six identified mental disorders, including schizophrenia, manic depression, Alzheimer's disease, or a severe personality disorder such as an antisocial personality or obsessive-compulsive personality; (2) had other mental

Table 3J. Rate of Chronic Conditions by Age: 1996

(Per 1,000 persons)

Type of chronic condition	Total	Under 18 years	18–44 years	45–64 years	65–74 years	75 years and over
SELECTED SKIN AND MUSCULOSKELETAL CONDITIONS						
Arthritis	127.3	*1.9	50.1	240.1	453.1	523.6
Intervertebral disc disorders	25.4	*1.0	21.1	62.7	38.2	24.0
Bursitis, unclassified	18.9	*0.8	13.1	43.9	43.0	31.1
Dermatitis	31.2	30.5	30.1	38.1	26.6	*23.1
SELECTED IMPAIRMENTS						
Visual impairment	31.3	*6.3	24.0	48.3	69.6	104.3
Hearing impairment	83.4	*12.6	41.9	131.5	255.2	369.8
Tinnitus	29.8	*2.6	16.0	59.6	96.0	76.2
Deformity or orthopedic impairment	111.6	*25.6	122.4	177.8	175.1	133.5
Back	64.0	*7.7	80.6	102.8	80.0	53.1
Upper extremities	15.8	*2.6	13.3	29.4	39.0	19.8
Lower extremities	48.0	*18.8	43.2	82.5	77.9	65.3
SELECTED DIGESTIVE CONDITIONS						
Ulcer	14.0	*1.3	11.8	26.1	36.9	20.7
Hernia of abdominal cavity	16.9	*1.7	10.8	30.9	38.3	62.4
Gastritis or duodenitis	14.1	*3.1	13.5	22.1	34.0	18.8
Diverticula of intestines	9.6	*—	2.4	17.6	36.0	50.0
SELECTED CONDITIONS OF THE GENITOURINARY, NERVOUS, ENDOCRINE, METABOLIC, AND BLOOD AND BLOOD-FORMING SYSTEMS						
Goiter or other disorders of the thyroid	17.4	*1.0	13.0	30.0	50.3	45.1
Diabetes	28.9	*1.2	11.8	58.2	98.4	102.3
Anemias	13.1	*5.0	16.7	10.7	13.7	35.9
Epilepsy	5.1	*4.9	4.4	5.8	5.4	7.4
Migraine headache	43.7	*15.2	60.0	57.9	28.6	28.4
Kidney trouble	9.7	*2.4	11.8	12.8	13.7	13.6
Bladder disorders	11.9	*3.3	11.3	15.7	19.9	36.4
Diseases of prostate	10.6	*—	2.2	14.7	48.8	66.0
Disease of female genital organs	16.7	*3.4	24.2	20.7	16.5	12.0
SELECTED CIRCULATORY CONDITIONS						
Heart disease	78.2	*23.6	39.3	116.4	238.2	310.7
Ischemic heart disease	29.0	*—	4.2	51.6	131.0	154.6
Heart rhythm disorders	33.0	*17.0	29.1	40.7	66.2	73.1
Tachycardia or rapid heart beat	8.7	*—	6.4	12.1	31.0	30.7
Heart murmurs	18.1	*16.6	18.8	17.6	21.4	17.3
Other selected diseases of heart, excluding hypertension	16.1	*6.6	6.0	24.0	41.0	83.1
High blood pressure (hypertension)	107.1	*0.5	49.6	214.1	356.0	373.8
Cerebrovascular disease	11.3	*0.4	2.0	12.8	40.2	99.4
Hardening of the arteries	5.9	*—	*—	6.7	28.4	50.9
Varicose veins of lower extremities	28.0	*—	22.2	46.8	74.0	86.2
Hemorrhoids	32.3	*0.3	34.4	53.6	72.8	45.4
SELECTED RESPIRATORY CONDITIONS						
Chronic bronchitis	*53.5	*57.3	*45.4	*59.1	*60.7	*67.3
Asthma	55.2	*62.0	56.9	48.6	43.7	48.0
Hay fever or allergic rhinitis without asthma	89.8	*58.7	*109.4	*104.8	61.9	75.7
Chronic sinusitis	125.5	*63.9	*144.7	*174.1	127.0	103.5
Emphysema	6.9	*—	0.8	13.2	32.3	32.6

SOURCE: P.F. Adams, G.E. Hendershot, and M.A. Marano. Current estimates from the National Health Interview Survey, 1996. National Center for Health Statistics. *Vital and Health Statistics* 10, no. 200 (1999): Table 57.

* Figure does not meet standard of reliability or precision.
*— Figure does not meet standard of reliability or precision and quantity zero.

NOTE: A condition is considered chronic if (a) the respondent indicates it was first noticed more than three months before the reference date of the interview, or (b) it is a type of condition that ordinarily has a duration of more than three months. Examples of conditions that are considered chronic regardless of their time of onset are diabetes, heart conditions, emphysema, and arthritis. A complete list of these conditions may be obtained by contacting the Division of Health Interview Statistics, National Center for Health Statistics.

or emotional disorders (were frequently confused, disoriented or forgetful, or had phobias or unreasonably strong fears) that seriously interfered with the ability to work, attend school, or manage day-to-day activities; and (3) used prescription medication for an ongoing mental or emotional condition.

ACUTE CONDITIONS

Morbidity data include information on short-term conditions that affect people's feelings of health and ability to perform their usual activities. *Acute conditions* are those that last fewer than three months but seriously restrict usual activities or require medical attention. Acute conditions include infections, influenza, injuries, and headaches. Older people are more likely to suffer from chronic conditions, but younger people are more likely to have acute conditions such as acute bronchitis, influenza, and other respiratory conditions. (See Figure 3AF.) Children under the age of five years were especially likely to get ear infections and the common cold. The rate of acute conditions in the total population in 1996 was 163.5

per 100 persons. For children under age five years, the rate of acute conditions was 317.9 per 100 compared with 117.3 per 100 for persons age 65 and over. (See Table 3.31.)

NOTIFIABLE, INFECTIOUS, AND COMMUNICABLE DISEASES

Whereas *contagious diseases* can be transmitted only through contact with other persons, *communicable diseases* are those capable of being transmitted from contact with an infected person, animal, or environmental reservoir (source of infection). *Infection* is the invasion of the host, which can be a person or an animal, by an organism that may be viral or bacterial or some other pathogen. An infected person may or may not show signs or symptoms of disease and may be considered an active or an inactive case. For example, with tuberculosis, being infected means that the tubercle bacilli have entered the body but not necessarily that they are reproducing and destroying tissue. A person is ill with tuberculosis when the infection has progressed to the point that there is evi-

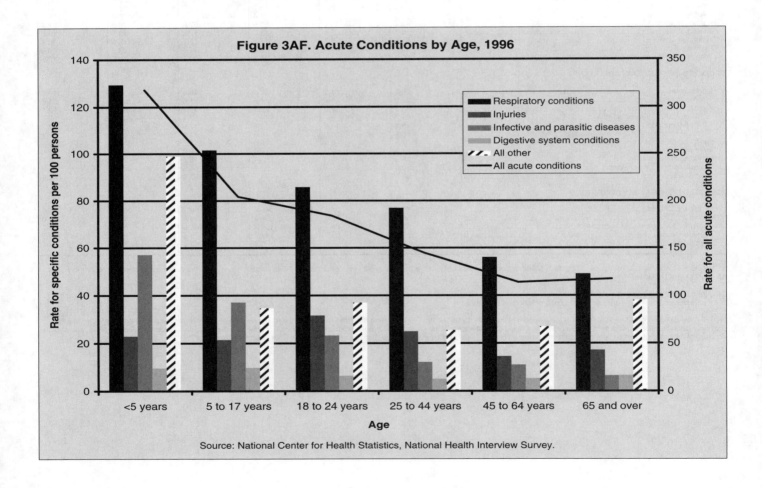

Figure 3AF. Acute Conditions by Age, 1996

Source: National Center for Health Statistics, National Health Interview Survey.

dence of destroyed tissue in the lungs or in other parts of the body.

Since 1900, the Public Health Service has encouraged states to adopt uniform laws that require physicians and hospitals to report cases of certain communicable diseases, or notifiable diseases, that come to their attention. All states currently transmit information about these cases to the Epidemiology Program Office of the Centers for Disease Control and Prevention as part of the National Notifiable Diseases Surveillance System (NNDSS). The CDC publishes weekly, semiannual, and annual summaries showing the number of new cases of notifiable diseases reported.

The completeness and accuracy of the CDC's summaries, however, depend on the cooperation of physicians, hospitals, and state health departments. Various factors, including reporting practices and the availability of screening and medical care, can artificially increase or decrease the number of cases reported. The CDC recognizes that physicians may more carefully report cases when they believe that they may be of special public concern, or when they consider the cases severe enough for the CDC to be notified, which can lead to differences in timeliness, accuracy, and completeness of the reported data.

ONGOING SURVEILLANCE

Because of the growing importance of some old infectious diseases and the emergence of new ones, surveillance for infectious diseases is still needed. Constant and improved surveillance can ensure timely and effective responses to emerging epidemics. Recent cases indicate how old diseases have become more important because they are changing and require new public health responses. In fact, some old diseases have become resistant to current drugs that have been designed to control them, and they require new drug designs for their treatment. Examples include pneumococci, which are becoming penicillin resistant, and tubercle bacilli, which have become multidrug resistant. Old diseases also have appeared in new forms. Streptococcal disease has reappeared as acute rheumatic fever and fatal toxic septicemias (often referred to as *flesh-eating bacteria* in the popular press when it first reappeared in this form). Hantavirus, considered a serious problem primarily in Asia, recently appeared in the rural southwest United States but was not immediately recognized because it emerged with a changed clinical picture—striking the lungs instead of the kidney. The Ebola virus, considered a problem primarily in Africa, also may be appearing in the United States. In addition, over the last three decades completely new diseases have been identified, including Legionnaires' disease, HIV, and Lyme disease.

The spread of infectious agents often occurs from persons traveling from regions of high incidence to places of low incidence or from contact with contaminated animals or goods that have been shipped into new regions. For example, cases of cholera have occurred because of inter-

national travel by U.S. residents. The major modes of transmission for infectious diseases are

1. Ingestion of causative agents such as pathogens from contaminated food and water (cholera)

2. Inhalation (respiratory) of causative agents (influenza, and fungal infections)

3. Direct skin contact with causative agents (schistosomiasis and hookworm)

4. Sexual transmission of causative agents (syphilis, gonorrhea, hepatitis B)

5. Vector-borne transmission of causative agents by mosquitoes, ticks, fleas, rodents, etc. (malaria, Lyme disease, and Rocky Mountain spotted fever)

Infectious diseases account for nearly 20 to 30 percent of physician's office visits, and most are diagnosed as acute respiratory diseases, such as bacterial pneumonia and influenza. In fact, bacterial pneumonia and influenza continue to rank as the most frequent cause for patients of all ages to seek medical attention, and they rank as the sixth leading cause of death for the total population. Acute otitis media, sinusitis, cervical adenitis, pharyngitis, and other less well-defined upper respiratory tract infections accounted for over half of the visits for children, while the common cold and sore throat (strep throat) were among the most popular symptoms for adults. Some respiratory tract infections can be life-threatening to both children and adults, including pneumonia and chronic obstructive pulmonary disease (bronchitis and emphysema). As a group, infectious and communicable diseases have declined in the United States.

WELL-KNOWN INFECTIOUS AND COMMUNICABLE DISEASES

TUBERCULOSIS

Tuberculosis is less of a public health problem at the end of the 20th century than it was in the 1950s. In general, TB is decreasing, but several groups are at high risk. These high-risk groups include alcoholics, injecting drug users, immigrants from high-prevalence areas, elderly people with a reactivation of disease acquired many years ago, and children exposed to these high-risk groups. The condition has been treatable, but recently multidrug-resistant cases of TB have emerged. Since 1987, about 1,000 to 2,000 deaths per year have been attributed to TB. (See Table 3.26.) More cases in the United States have been reported among U.S.-born persons than foreign-born persons. In the 1990s, however, the number of cases among U.S.-born persons has decreased, but the number of cases among foreign-born persons has increased.

The available data on TB cases have been verified using the laboratory or clinical definition and reported to the CDC from 1953 to 1998. Over time, the case definition has been refined, and additional information collected to monitor the trends, risk factors, and outcomes of the disease has been made available. Since 1993, items concerning drug-resistant TB, HIV test results, and TB therapy have been added to the standard case report form, Report of a Verified Case of Tuberculosis. Data reported in 1998 on persons with TB are available not only on sociodemographic characteristics but also on risk factors such as homelessness, injecting drug use, excess alcohol use, and HIV status.

HEPATITIS C

Hepatitis C is the most common blood-borne infection in the United States. It is an especially difficult condition because persons infected with the hepatitis C virus can infect others before they are even aware of their own status. For example, symptoms of hepatitis C liver-related chronic disease may not develop for 10 to 20 years after infection. Cirrhosis can develop in 10 to 20 percent of those diagnosed with hepatitis C liver-related chronic disease. In addition, an estimated 8,000 to 12,000 persons die from hepatitis C–related chronic liver disease yearly.

LYME DISEASE

Lyme disease is transmitted by tick-infested animals and was first recognized in 1976. Early treatment may decrease the prevalence and severity of associated arthritis. About 10 percent of those with Lyme disease show symptoms with neurological involvement. In 1997, cases were reported by 46 states and the District of Columbia, but most of the reported cases occurred in the northeastern states from Connecticut to Maryland, and in Wisconsin and Minnesota. (See Table 3.36.)

ROCKY MOUNTAIN FEVER

Rocky Mountain spotted fever (*Rickettsia rickettsii*) is another disease transmitted by ticks and is found in tick-infested terrain, in houses, and on dogs. It was originally detected in the Rocky Mountain area, but most cases now occur along the eastern seaboard. Rocky Mountain fever is a severe illness that may require hospitalization. It is difficult to diagnose in its early stages because it has such nonspecific symptoms as fever, severe headache, muscle pain, nausea, and vomiting. Furthermore, the level of antibodies needed to detect the disease with laboratory tests are not reached in the early stages of the disease. Therefore, the patient's being in a tick-infested area or having tick bites is important for the physician to know. Later symptoms include a rash, joint pain, abdominal pain, and diarrhea. If treatment is started early enough, all rickettsial diseases can be controlled by optimal doses of appropriate antimicrobial drugs. The largest number of cases was reported in the 1970s and early 1980s.

MALARIA

Malaria is a mosquito-borne infectious disease that has shown an increase since the 1990s. In the past, increases in the incidence of malaria were related to persons coming into the United States from malaria-endemic countries in Southeast Asia. In the early 1970s, an increase in the incidence of malaria in the United States resulted from the return of Vietnam veterans, and in the early 1980s, an increase was related to an influx of immigrants from Southeast Asia. In the 1990s, however, cases have been detected near urban areas that appear to have been locally acquired.

RABIES

Rabies appears to occur in three-year cycles, especially among wild animals. The number of cases among dogs and other domestic animals has remained relatively constant over the last decade because of pervasive antirabies immunization of domestic animals. However, cases associated with raccoons and other wild animals have increased lately.

SALMONELLOSIS

Salmonellosis is a preventable notifiable disease that can be transmitted by contaminated foods or by contact with the unwashed hands of an infected person. Thorough cooking of foods, treated municipal water, restaurant inspection, and proper hygiene by food handlers are just some of the effective ways of preventing salmonellosis and other food-borne diseases. Unfortunately, the number of cases has increased between 1966 and 1998. Furthermore, cases of the disease, especially the mild cases, are probably underreported because many people recover without treatment. The people most at risk for severe consequences are older persons, infants, and people with impaired immune systems.

ACQUIRED IMMUNODEFICIENCY SYNDROME AND OTHER SEXUALLY TRANSMITTED DISEASES

HIV/AIDS

When first recognized in the 1980s, AIDS was a serious problem because so many persons with the disease died and so little was known about how to prevent or treat the disease. In the 1990s, there were better and earlier diagnoses, more effective treatments, and widespread educational campaigns to prevent the disease. These efforts have been reflected in reduced new cases and deaths from AIDS in recent years. (See Table 3K and Figures 3AG and 3AH.) Yet AIDS is still a serious problem because of high fatality rates, the costs of treating the disease, and the difficulty of eliminating such HIV/AIDS risk factors as unprotected sex and injecting drug use.

Table 3.39 shows the number of AIDS cases reported to the CDC since 1995 and for the entire period of AIDS surveillance.[18] The table shows that most AIDS cases are concentrated in 10 states: New York, California, Florida, Texas, New Jersey, Illinois, Pennsylvania, Georgia, Maryland, and Massachusetts. Together, these states reported 69.8 percent of all AIDS cases ever reported in the United States, and when Puerto Rico and the District of Columbia are added to this list, the total increases to 74.7 percent. Since 1981, the CDC has changed the definition of AIDS on several occasions to incorporate improved laboratory and diagnostic methods and in response to increased knowledge of the natural history of the disease. The initial case definition was based on very specific clinical signs and symptoms. Later, most notably in 1993 for adults and 1994 for children under age 13

Table 3K. The AIDS Epidemic: Diagnosed Cases and Deaths Reported to CDC

Year	Incidence	Cumulative incidence	Deaths	Cumulative deaths
Before 1981	93	93	31	31
1981	332	425	128	159
1982	1 201	1 626	463	622
1983	3 145	4 771	1 508	2 130
1984	6 335	11 106	3 505	5 635
1985	11 990	23 096	6 972	12 607
1986	19 319	42 415	12 110	24 717
1987	28 999	71 414	16 412	41 129
1988	35 957	107 371	21 119	62 248
1989	43 168	150 539	27 791	90 039
1990	49 069	199 608	31 538	121 577
1991	60 124	259 732	36 616	158 193
Change in Case Definition	---------------	---------------	---------------	---------------
1992	79 054	338 786	41 094	199 287
1993	79 049	417 835	44 636	243 923
1994	71 209	489 044	48 663	292 586
1995	66 233	555 277	48 371	340 957
1996	54 656	609 933	36 194	377 151
1997	60 270	670 203	19 996	397 147

SOURCE: Centers for Disease Control and Prevention, compiled from CDC reports: *HIV/AIDS Surveillance Report* 8, no. 2 (1996): Table 13. *HIV/AIDS Surveillance Report* 10, no. 2 (1998): Table 2, Table 21.

NOTE: The criteria used to classify AIDS cases changed in 1992, which accounts for the increase in cases reported in subsequent years. The decline in cases in 1996 and 1997 may be a result of lags in reporting and the effect of the change in case definition.

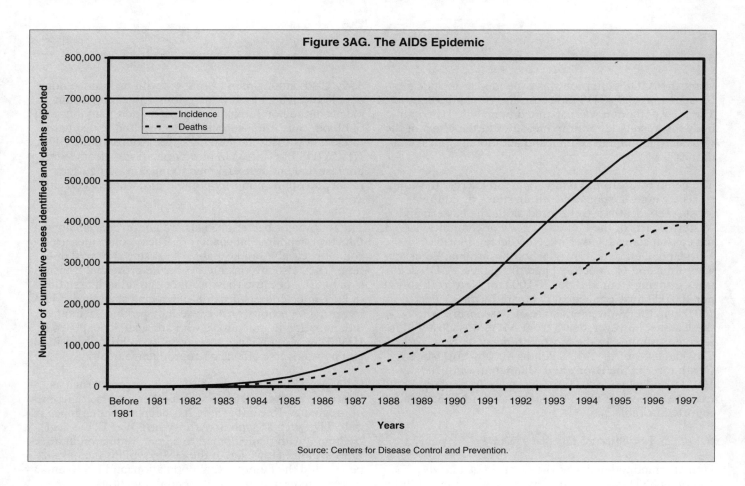

Figure 3AG. The AIDS Epidemic

Source: Centers for Disease Control and Prevention.

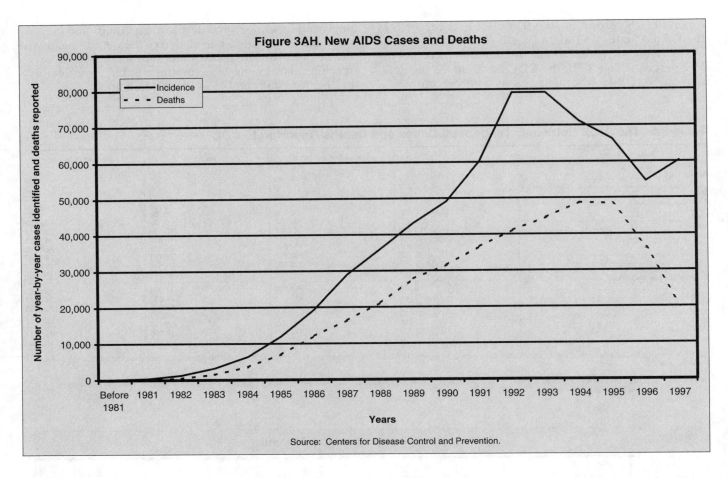

Figure 3AH. New AIDS Cases and Deaths

Source: Centers for Disease Control and Prevention.

years, the AIDS definition was expanded to include a broader range of AIDS indicator diseases and conditions. The later definition was expanded to include HIV antibody test results, laboratory measures of the effect of the virus on the immune system, and additional clinical conditions.

The death rates from AIDS vary greatly across the country as a whole, in states and within states by county.[19] Most AIDS deaths are clustered along the eastern and western coasts of the United States. For example, in 1998, ten coastal states [New York, New Jersey, Florida, Maryland, Delaware, Georgia, South Carolina, Louisiana, California and Connecticut] had the highest AIDS death rates [ranging from 31.3 per 100,000 for New York to 12.0 per 100,000 for Connecticut compared with 3.1 per 100,000 in the Midwestern state of Wisconsin]. Within these states, however, death from AIDS was clustered in selected counties. In the most extreme case, New York City had 84% of the AIDS deaths in New York state. Death rates in the Bronx and Manhattan were 100 per 100,000 and 94 per 100,000. Consequently, readers should exercise care when using the state AIDS incidence data reported in Table 3.39.

SEXUALLY TRANSMITTED DISEASES (STDs)

Human immunodeficiency virus disease is a newly emerging STD pathogen that was first identified in the early 1980s among men having sex with men and among people receiving blood transfusions. Educational campaigns in the homosexual population and the monitoring of blood transfusion supplies have resulted in decreased rates of new cases in these high-risk groups. In the 1990s, HIV/AIDS has shifted to new populations—from White homosexual and bisexual men to injecting drug users, racial and ethnic minority populations, women, and children.

The four major bacterial STDs are gonorrhea, chlamydial infection, syphilis, and chancroid. These conditions are common, curable, and capable of causing repeated infections. They also are risk factors for heterosexual transmission of HIV because they produce genital inflammation in HIV-infected persons, thus enhancing shedding of HIV in genital secretions, or because they produce genital inflammation in individuals who are sexually exposed to HIV. They also enhance susceptibility to HIV acquisition and have adverse effects on reproductive health.

STD organisms have caused diverse outcomes such as infertility, ectopic pregnancy, and other adverse outcomes of pregnancy. Recently, there has been a re-emergence of old STDs, such as syphilis. After World War II, medical treatment with penicillin led to a great reduction in infectious syphilis. However, in the 1990s, syphilis increased, penetrated the heterosexual population, and led to an increase in perinatal and congenital infections.

Rates of STDs over time can differ because of microbiologic, hormonal, and immunologic changes affecting both the STD agents and persons who are susceptible to STDs. In addition, high-risk lifestyles have affected the prevalence rates. Evidence exists of rates increasing when the following activities occur: sexual intercourse at younger ages, increased premarital sexual activity, sexual activity with multiple partners, commercial sex, and injecting drug use. Rates of STDs go down when there is increased condom use, STD screening, compliance with therapy, and early health care.

In 1998, the most frequently reported infectious disease in the United States was chlamydia. (See Table 3.40.) Once diagnosed, this sexually transmitted disease can be treated and cured. Untreated, however, chlamydia can cause severe and costly health problems. Because screening is not available in most states and more that half of those infected do not experience any symptoms, the number of cases is greatly underreported. Research shows that higher rates in some states reflect the availability of screening programs in those particular states.

VACCINE-PREVENTABLE DISEASES

Vaccines (immunizations) are one of the most cost-effective health interventions available to prevent disease in individuals and groups. Eventually, they may eliminate a disease entirely. Vaccines played an important role in the elimination of poliomyelitis from the United States and of smallpox from the world. Although cases of polio imported from other countries have been noted in the United States, no reported cases caused by the wild polio virus in this country have been acquired since 1979.[20] In 1988, WHO targeted polio for global eradication, and in 1994, an independent commission certified the American hemisphere to be free of polio.[21] In 1980, WHO declared that smallpox had been eradicated from the world.[21] The latest information on the several dozen vaccines licensed in the United States and their routes of administration, schedules, and other related information may be found in the *Red Book*,[22] for children, and in the *Guide to Clinical Preventive Services*,[23] for adults.

Immunizations are important when an effective and safe vaccine is available for a condition that imposes a large burden on the population or target group because of its prevalence or on the medical system because of its treatment difficulty or costs. Immunization programs are especially needed when the condition is not likely to respond to other prevention or interventions, such as improvements in sanitation and hygiene. The following are the most commonly recommended immunizations, especially among children: vaccines against hepatitis B, DTP (diphtheria, tetanus, and pertussis), H. influenza type B, MMR (measles, mumps, and rubella), and varicella (chicken pox).

Immunizations for influenza and pneumococcal disease are also recommended for people at high risk for major consequences from these conditions, including people older than age 65, people with certain underlying conditions (chronic diseases of the heart or lungs, HIV infection, liver disease, and sickle cell anemia), pregnant women, nursing home and other chronic-care facility residents, and health care workers who are needed for providing care during epidemics of these conditions. Influenza and pneumonia together are among the top 10 leading causes of death for the general population, and both can strike people of any age. In 1996, 83,727 people died of pneumonia and influenza. In fact, pneumococcal disease causes more deaths than any other vaccine-preventable bacterial disease. About 40,000 people die each year from this disease. The Advisory Committee on Immunization Practices estimates that pneumococcal disease accounts for 3,000 cases of meningitis, 50,000 cases of bacteremia, 500,000 cases of pneumonia, and 7 million cases of otitis media in the United States each year.[24]

Most of the infectious diseases that have effective vaccines, especially those targeted in childhood immunization programs, have declined in incidence over time. Some, however, persist and have been associated with death. These preventable infectious diseases for which childhood immunizations are provided include hepatitis B and chicken pox. Adults are especially likely to die from complications of influenza, pneumococcal infections, and hepatitis B. Hepatitis B was associated with 10,258 reported cases and 1,030 deaths in 1998. Although chicken pox was taken off the list of nationally notifiable diseases as of 1991, many states continue to report cases. In 1998, 82,455 cases of chicken pox were reported, and 99 deaths were associated with the disease.[25]

INFECTIOUS DISEASE DATA SOURCES

Trends in notifiable diseases are influenced by changes in reporting practices and case definitions, availability of diagnostic screening, awareness of the condition by the public or health professionals, discovery or emergence of new conditions or antimicrobial-resistant strains, and the effect of immunization, prevention, or other intervention programs. Official statistics on vaccine-preventable and other infectious diseases in the United States are available in reports from the National Notifiable Diseases Surveillance System (NNDSS). Currently, this system contains data on the number of cases and associated deaths for 52 infectious diseases, with a selected group of these infectious conditions reported to the CDC. The CDC operates the NNDSS in collaboration with the Council of State and Territorial Epidemiologists. Currently 57 jurisdictions (50 states, two cities, and five territorial health departments) submit data. Regulations regarding the types of infectious diseases that are required to be reported to the CDC may vary according to jurisdiction. Jurisdictions are not included in the calculation of rates for diseases that they were not required to report. The appropriate epidemiologist from each jurisdiction must approve the data before they are finalized in the *Morbidity and Mortality Weekly Report* Summary of Notifiable Diseases. Further information is available on the Internet at <http://www.cdc.gov/epo/phs.htm>.

SUMMARY

Changing patterns of disease and disability result from changes in personal lifestyles, in the physical environment, and in public health programs. The role of drug-resistant pathogens, as in multidrug-resistant tuberculosis, is also emerging. Medical advances and new screening technologies also have become available to detect and identify previously unknown or undetected diseases, such as AIDS and Legionnaires' Disease. Trends in new diseases are affected by methodological considerations such as revised standard forms of death certificates, coding changes of vital statistics and the decennial revisions of the ICD, which may include new diseases such as Alzheimer's disease.

In 19th century America, infectious diseases such as typhoid fever, diptheria, whooping cough, pneumonia, and tuberculosis predominated as the source of death and disability. Because these fatal diseases were of relatively short duration, the mortality rate was acceptable as a measure of ill health. In 20th century America, however, motor vehicle crashes and chronic diseases such as heart diseases and cancer became important sources of death and disability. Infectious diseases continue to be important to the health of Americans in this century because of international travel and the migration of various peoples from other parts of the world where infectious diseases still predominate. The changing demographics of the U.S. population, such as an increase in older residents, has led not only to increases in diseases in later life, but also to the need for morbidity statistics. Indeed, many conditions, such as injuries, arthritis, rheumatism, and mental disorders, are more likely to affect an individual's quality of life than to cause death.

The decline in communicable diseases demonstrates the importance of public health efforts as well as the importance of advances in scientific research. Medical microbiology, immunology, genetics, and virology contributed to the scientific discovery of causative infectious organisms and of the manner by which the diseases were spread. This knowledge was combined with intensive public health prevention campaigns such as water purification, milk pasteurization, sewage disposal systems to control typhoid fever, and programs to eliminate insect carriers such as the mosquito. Effective immunization programs have eliminated polio from the United States and smallpox from the world. Food-borne diseases have been controlled with regulations regarding cooking practices in fast-food chains, controls on the manufacture and distribution of imported products, and other food-handling standards. The transfusion transmission of hepatitis B and HIV has been controlled with mandatory screening of blood donors for serologic markers of hepatitis B infection and for HIV.

Although the health of Americans has improved in the last century, not all citizens have shared equally in this improvement. Both morbidity and mortality vary by age, gender, family income, health insurance status, racial and ethnic group, season, and geographic location. Injuries and chronic diseases such as cancers, however, remain important threats to the health of all Americans.

Table 3.1. Number of Deaths, Death Rates, and Age-Adjusted Death Rates, by Race and Sex: 1940, 1950, 1960, 1970, and 1975–1997

(Per 100,000 population)

Year	All races [1] Both sexes	Male	Female	White Both sexes	Male	Female	Black Both sexes	Male	Female
NUMBER									
1940	1 417 269	791 003	626 266	1 231 223	690 901	540 322	178 743	95 517	83 226
1950	1 452 454	827 749	624 705	1 276 085	731 366	544 719	169 606	92 004	77 602
1960	1 711 982	975 648	736 334	1 505 335	860 857	644 478	196 010	107 701	88 309
1970	1 921 031	1 078 478	842 553	1 682 096	942 437	739 659	225 647	127 540	98 107
1975	1 892 879	1 050 819	842 060	1 660 366	917 804	742 562	217 932	123 770	94 162
1976	1 909 440	1 051 983	857 457	1 674 989	918 589	756 400	219 442	123 977	95 465
1977	1 899 597	1 046 243	853 354	1 664 100	912 670	751 430	220 076	123 894	96 182
1978	1 927 788	1 055 290	872 498	1 689 722	920 123	769 599	221 340	124 663	96 677
1979	1 913 841	1 044 959	868 882	1 676 145	910 137	766 008	220 818	124 433	96 385
1980	1 989 841	1 075 078	914 763	1 738 607	933 878	804 729	233 135	130 138	102 997
1981	1 977 981	1 063 772	914 209	1 731 233	925 490	805 743	228 560	127 296	101 264
1982	1 974 797	1 056 440	918 357	1 729 085	919 239	809 846	226 513	125 610	100 903
1983	2 019 201	1 071 923	947 278	1 765 582	931 779	833 803	233 124	127 911	105 213
1984	2 039 369	1 076 514	962 855	1 781 897	934 529	847 368	235 884	129 147	106 737
1985	2 086 440	1 097 758	988 682	1 819 054	950 455	868 599	244 207	133 610	110 597
1986	2 105 361	1 104 005	1 001 356	1 831 083	952 554	878 529	250 326	137 214	113 112
1987	2 123 323	1 107 958	1 015 365	1 843 067	953 382	889 685	254 814	139 551	115 263
1988	2 167 999	1 125 540	1 042 459	1 876 906	965 419	911 487	264 019	144 228	119 791
1989	2 150 466	1 114 190	1 036 276	1 853 841	950 852	902 989	267 642	146 393	121 249
1990	2 148 463	1 113 417	1 035 046	1 853 254	950 812	902 442	265 498	145 359	120 139
1991	2 169 518	1 121 665	1 047 853	1 868 904	956 497	912 407	269 525	147 331	122 194
1992	2 175 613	1 122 336	1 053 277	1 873 781	956 957	916 824	269 219	146 630	122 589
1993	2 268 553	1 161 797	1 106 756	1 951 437	988 329	963 108	282 151	153 502	128 649
1994	2 278 994	1 162 747	1 116 247	1 959 875	988 823	971 052	282 379	153 019	129 360
1995	2 312 132	1 172 959	1 139 173	1 987 437	997 277	990 160	286 401	154 175	132 226
1996	2 314 690	1 163 569	1 151 121	1 992 966	991 984	1 000 982	282 089	149 472	132 617
1997	2 314 245	1 154 039	1 160 206	1 996 393	986 884	1 009 509	276 520	144 110	132 410
RATE									
1940	1 076.4	1 197.4	954.6	1 041.5	1 162.2	919.4	—	—	—
1950	963.8	1 106.1	823.5	945.7	1 089.5	803.3	—	—	—
1960	954.7	1 104.5	809.2	947.8	1 098.5	800.9	1 038.6	1 181.7	905.0
1970	945.3	1 090.3	807.8	946.3	1 086.7	812.6	999.3	1 186.6	829.2
1975	878.5	1 002.0	761.4	886.9	1 004.1	775.1	882.5	1 055.4	726.1
1976	877.6	993.8	767.6	887.7	997.3	783.1	875.0	1 041.6	724.5
1977	864.4	978.9	756.0	874.6	983.0	771.3	864.0	1 026.0	718.0
1978	868.0	977.5	764.5	880.2	982.7	782.7	855.1	1 016.8	709.5
1979	852.2	957.5	752.7	865.2	963.3	771.8	839.3	999.6	695.3
1980	878.3	976.9	785.3	892.5	983.3	806.1	875.4	1 034.1	733.3
1981	862.0	954.0	775.0	880.4	965.2	799.8	842.4	992.6	707.7
1982	852.4	938.4	771.2	873.1	951.8	798.2	823.4	966.2	695.5
1983	863.7	943.2	788.4	885.4	957.7	816.4	836.6	971.2	715.9
1984	864.8	938.8	794.7	887.8	954.1	824.6	836.1	968.5	717.4
1985	876.9	948.6	809.1	900.4	963.6	840.1	854.8	989.3	734.2
1986	876.7	944.7	812.3	900.1	958.6	844.3	864.9	1 002.6	741.5
1987	876.4	939.3	816.7	900.1	952.7	849.8	868.9	1 006.2	745.7
1988	886.7	945.1	831.2	910.5	957.9	865.3	888.3	1 026.1	764.6
1989	871.3	926.3	818.9	893.2	936.5	851.8	887.9	1 026.7	763.2
1990	863.8	918.4	812.0	888.0	930.9	846.9	871.0	1 008.0	747.9
1991	860.3	912.1	811.0	886.2	926.2	847.7	860.3	998.7	744.5
1992	852.9	901.6	806.5	880.0	917.2	844.3	850.5	977.5	736.2
1993	880.0	923.5	838.6	908.5	938.8	879.4	876.8	1 006.3	760.1
1994	875.4	915.0	837.6	905.4	931.6	880.1	864.3	987.8	752.9
1995	880.0	914.1	847.3	911.3	932.1	891.3	864.2	980.7	759.0
1996	872.5	896.4	849.7	906.9	918.1	896.2	842.0	939.9	753.5
1997	864.7	881.0	849.0	902.0	906.0	898.0	815.0	894.0	743.0
AGE-ADJUSTED RATE [4]									
1940	1 076.1	1 213.0	938.9	1 017.2	1 155.1	879.0	—	—	—
1950	841.5	1 001.6	688.4	800.4	963.1	645.0	—	—	—
1960	760.9	949.3	590.6	727.0	917.7	555.0	1 073.3	1 246.1	916.9
1970	714.3	931.6	532.5	679.6	893.4	501.7	1 044.0	1 318.6	814.4
1975	630.4	837.2	462.5	602.2	804.3	439.0	890.8	1 163.0	670.6
1976	618.5	820.9	455.0	591.3	789.3	432.5	870.5	1 138.5	654.5
1977	602.1	801.3	441.8	575.7	770.6	419.6	849.3	1 112.1	639.6
1978	595.0	791.4	437.4	569.5	761.1	416.4	831.8	1 093.9	622.7
1979	577.0	768.6	423.1	551.0	738.4	402.5	812.1	1 073.2	605.0
1980	585.8	777.2	432.6	559.4	745.3	411.1	842.5	1 112.8	631.1
1981	568.6	753.8	420.8	544.8	724.8	401.5	807.0	1 068.8	602.7
1982	554.7	734.2	411.9	532.3	706.8	393.6	782.1	1 035.4	585.9
1983	552.5	729.4	412.5	529.4	701.6	393.3	787.4	1 037.5	595.3
1984	548.1	721.6	410.5	525.2	693.6	391.7	783.3	1 035.9	590.1
1985	548.9	723.0	410.3	524.9	693.3	391.0	793.6	1 053.4	594.8
1986	544.8	716.2	407.6	520.1	684.9	388.1	796.8	1 061.9	594.1
1987	539.2	706.8	404.6	513.7	674.2	384.8	796.4	1 063.6	592.4
1988	539.9	706.1	406.1	512.8	671.3	385.3	809.7	1 083.0	601.0
1989	528.0	689.3	397.3	499.6	652.2	376.0	805.9	1 082.8	594.3
1990	520.2	680.2	390.6	492.8	644.3	369.9	789.2	1 061.3	581.6
1991	513.7	669.9	386.5	486.8	634.4	366.3	780.7	1 048.8	575.1
1992	504.5	656.0	380.3	477.5	620.9	359.9	767.5	1 026.9	568.4
1993	513.3	664.9	388.3	485.1	627.5	367.7	785.2	1 052.2	578.8
1994	507.4	654.6	385.2	479.8	617.9	364.9	772.1	1 029.9	572.0
1995	503.9	646.3	385.2	476.9	610.5	364.9	765.7	1 016.7	571.0
1996	491.6	623.7	381.0	466.8	591.4	361.9	738.3	967.0	561.0
1997	479.1	602.8	375.7	456.5	573.8	358.0	705.3	911.9	545.5

See footnotes at end of table.

Table 3.1. Number of Deaths, Death Rates, and Age-Adjusted Death Rates, by Race and Sex: 1940, 1950, 1960, 1970, and 1975–1997—*Continued*

(Per 100,000 population)

Year	American Indian [2]			Asian or Pacific Islander [3]		
	Both sexes	Male	Female	Both sexes	Male	Female
NUMBER						
1940	4 791	2 527	2 264	—	—	—
1950	4 440	2 497	1 943	—	—	—
1960	4 528	2 658	1 870	—	—	—
1970	5 675	3 391	2 284	—	—	—
1975	6 166	3 838	2 328	—	—	—
1976	6 300	3 883	2 417	—	—	—
1977	6 454	4 019	2 435	—	—	—
1978	6 959	4 343	2 616	—	—	—
1979	6 728	4 171	2 557	—	—	—
1980	6 923	4 193	2 730	11 071	6 809	4 262
1981	6 608	4 016	2 592	11 475	6 908	4 567
1982	6 679	3 974	2 705	12 430	7 564	4 866
1983	6 839	4 064	2 775	13 554	8 126	5 428
1984	6 949	4 117	2 832	14 483	8 627	5 856
1985	7 154	4 181	2 973	15 887	9 441	6 446
1986	7 301	4 365	2 936	16 514	9 795	6 719
1987	7 602	4 432	3 170	17 689	10 496	7 193
1988	7 917	4 617	3 300	18 963	11 155	7 808
1989	8 614	5 066	3 548	20 042	11 688	8 354
1990	8 316	4 877	3 439	21 127	12 211	8 916
1991	8 621	4 948	3 673	22 173	12 727	9 446
1992	8 953	5 181	3 772	23 660	13 568	10 092
1993	9 579	5 434	4 145	25 386	14 532	10 854
1994	9 637	5 497	4 140	27 103	15 408	11 695
1995	9 997	5 574	4 423	28 297	15 933	12 364
1996	10 127	5 563	4 564	29 508	16 550	12 958
1997	10 576	5 985	4 591	30 756	17 060	13 696
RATE						
1940	—	—	—	—	—	—
1950	—	—	—	—	—	—
1960	—	—	—	—	—	—
1970	—	—	—	—	—	—
1975	—	—	—	—	—	—
1976	—	—	—	—	—	—
1977	—	—	—	—	—	—
1978	—	—	—	—	—	—
1979	—	—	—	—	—	—
1980	487.4	597.1	380.1	296.9	375.3	222.5
1981	445.6	547.9	345.6	272.3	336.2	211.5
1982	434.5	522.9	348.1	271.3	338.3	207.4
1983	428.5	515.1	343.9	276.1	339.1	216.1
1984	419.6	502.7	338.4	275.9	336.5	218.1
1985	416.4	492.5	342.5	283.4	344.6	224.9
1986	409.5	494.9	325.9	276.2	335.1	219.9
1987	410.7	483.8	339.0	278.9	338.3	222.0
1988	411.7	485.0	339.9	282.0	339.0	227.4
1989	430.5	510.7	351.3	280.9	334.5	229.4
1990	402.8	476.4	330.4	283.3	334.3	234.3
1991	407.2	471.2	343.9	277.3	325.6	231.1
1992	417.7	487.7	348.9	283.1	332.7	235.8
1993	440.0	503.9	377.3	293.9	346.6	244.2
1994	436.1	502.6	371.0	301.5	354.0	252.2
1995	445.9	502.3	390.6	304.7	354.9	257.7
1996	442.6	489.8	396.0	302.8	350.7	257.9
1997	456.0	519.0	393.0	306.6	351.7	264.3
AGE-ADJUSTED RATE [4]						
1940	—	—	—	—	—	—
1950	—	—	—	—	—	—
1960	—	—	—	—	—	—
1970	—	—	—	—	—	—
1975	—	—	—	—	—	—
1976	—	—	—	—	—	—
1977	—	—	—	—	—	—
1978	—	—	—	—	—	—
1979	—	—	—	—	—	—
1980	564.1	732.5	414.1	315.6	416.6	224.6
1981	514.0	676.7	368.5	293.2	382.3	213.9
1982	494.3	634.6	371.6	293.6	389.2	212.8
1983	485.9	634.0	360.1	298.9	388.6	218.0
1984	476.9	614.2	347.3	299.4	386.0	223.0
1985	468.2	602.6	353.3	305.7	396.9	228.5
1986	451.4	591.6	328.4	296.7	385.3	220.3
1987	456.7	580.8	351.3	297.0	386.2	221.3
1988	456.3	585.7	343.2	300.2	385.4	226.5
1989	475.7	622.8	353.4	295.8	378.9	225.2
1990	445.1	573.1	335.1	297.6	377.8	228.9
1991	441.8	562.6	335.9	283.2	360.2	218.3
1992	453.1	579.6	343.1	285.8	364.1	220.5
1993	468.9	589.6	364.5	295.9	381.4	226.7
1994	460.7	585.9	350.8	299.2	386.5	229.3
1995	468.5	580.4	368.0	298.9	384.4	231.4
1996	456.7	555.9	367.7	277.4	355.8	214.4
1997	465.3	584.1	359.9	274.8	350.3	214.7

SOURCE: D.L. Hoyert, K.D. Kochanek, S.L. Murphy. Deaths: Final Data for 1997. *National Vital Statistics Reports;* vol. 47 no. 19. Hyattsville, Maryland: National Center for Health Statistics. 1999: Table 1.

— Data not available.
1. For 1940–1991 includes deaths among races not shown separately.
2. Includes deaths among Aleuts and Eskimos.
3. Includes deaths among Chinese, Filipino, Hawaiian, Japanese, and other Asian or Pacific Islander.
4. For method of computation see technical notes in "Deaths: Final Data for 1997"

NOTE: Rates are based on populations enumerated as of April 1 for census years and estimated as of July 1 for all other years. Beginning with 1970, excludes deaths of nonresidents of the United States.

Table 3.2. Age-Adjusted Death Rates from All Causes

(Average annual deaths per 100,000 resident population; ranked by all persons 1995–1997 rate)

Area	Total					
	1984–1986	1989–1991	1992–1994	1995–1997	Change 1996–1997	Difference from national rate 1995–1997
United States	547.7	522.0	508.3	491.4	-10.3	0.0
DIVISION						
East South Central	598.3	584.0	573.3	571.5	-4.5	80.1
West South Central	564.6	548.6	536.0	521.5	-7.6	30.1
South Atlantic	565.0	540.0	527.8	514.4	-9.0	23.0
East North Central	553.0	525.3	509.5	496.7	-10.2	5.3
Middle Atlantic	566.2	537.2	520.0	491.3	-13.2	-0.1
Mountain	502.4	479.1	472.9	459.2	-8.6	-32.2
West North Central	497.1	471.9	464.6	458.3	-7.8	-33.1
Pacific	516.6	491.9	473.4	446.7	-13.5	-44.7
New England	514.4	473.0	463.2	444.6	-13.6	-46.8
STATE						
Mississippi	625.3	621.3	616.5	611.7	-2.2	120.3
Louisiana	623.7	621.1	602.8	589.8	-5.4	98.4
Alabama	604.5	593.7	578.1	576.3	-4.7	84.9
South Carolina	618.6	596.4	578.5	573.8	-7.2	82.4
Tennessee	583.7	566.9	561.6	564.6	-3.3	73.2
Arkansas	575.7	564.7	562.6	561.1	-2.5	69.7
Georgia	614.9	592.6	572.7	560.3	-8.9	68.9
West Virginia	593.6	576.5	558.6	551.0	-7.2	59.6
Kentucky	592.6	571.0	555.0	548.6	-7.4	57.2
Nevada	586.6	569.3	560.4	543.8	-7.3	52.4
Oklahoma	550.4	534.1	538.3	540.4	-1.8	49.0
North Carolina	576.9	556.7	544.9	533.0	-7.6	41.6
Missouri	549.7	527.8	527.8	521.5	-5.1	30.1
Maryland	577.6	544.9	532.1	519.0	-10.1	27.6
Delaware	573.9	549.4	533.8	518.9	-9.6	27.5
Indiana	551.2	524.1	512.1	509.7	-7.5	18.3
Illinois	559.5	541.5	527.1	506.9	-9.4	15.5
Ohio	561.6	528.1	510.5	505.9	-9.9	14.5
Pennsylvania	562.5	525.8	511.6	500.5	-11.0	9.1
Virginia	564.2	528.6	512.8	499.1	-11.5	7.7
Texas	549.4	530.1	514.8	495.7	-9.8	4.3
Michigan	569.6	534.3	517.8	494.5	-13.2	3.1
New York	573.0	549.7	529.9	488.1	-14.8	-3.3
New Jersey	553.6	522.3	506.6	481.2	-13.1	-10.2
Florida	521.2	497.9	492.0	478.3	-8.2	-13.1
Arizona	511.9	488.4	497.3	476.5	-6.9	-14.9
Alaska	561.8	525.6	494.8	475.6	-15.3	-15.8
New Mexico	518.5	497.3	483.1	473.8	-8.6	-17.6
Maine	530.2	490.3	477.0	470.0	-11.4	-21.4
Wyoming	507.5	484.7	473.1	467.5	-7.9	-23.9
Oregon	510.9	479.9	470.5	461.6	-9.6	-29.8
Montana	513.7	484.1	470.7	460.8	-10.3	-30.6
Kansas	494.0	467.6	460.5	459.6	-7.0	-31.8
Vermont	528.5	480.5	472.5	456.5	-13.6	-34.9
California	523.4	500.7	479.9	449.0	-14.2	-42.4
New Hampshire	519.8	473.7	451.5	448.5	-13.7	-42.9
Rhode Island	517.3	478.8	464.3	448.0	-13.4	-43.4
South Dakota	497.2	459.4	460.1	444.9	-10.5	-46.5
Nebraska	484.1	464.1	449.7	442.9	-8.5	-48.5
Connecticut	497.3	461.4	455.0	441.8	-11.2	-49.6
Wisconsin	488.5	463.9	447.0	441.2	-9.7	-50.2
Massachusetts	518.7	475.0	467.0	439.7	-15.2	-51.7
Washington	496.9	463.7	454.6	436.8	-12.1	-54.6
Idaho	488.7	456.8	444.0	433.3	-11.3	-58.1
Iowa	472.7	448.9	435.6	430.7	-8.9	-60.7
Colorado	478.9	456.1	441.5	428.7	-10.5	-62.7
North Dakota	449.6	435.9	426.0	419.1	-6.8	-72.3
Minnesota	462.6	431.2	420.8	412.8	-10.8	-78.6
Utah	465.8	426.8	416.8	406.6	-12.7	-84.8
Hawaii	418.6	405.5	390.4	385.1	-8.0	-106.3
OTHER						
District of Columbia	765.8	824.5	826.2	774.4	1.1	283.0
Median	553.6	527.8	512.1	495.7	-8.6	495.7
Low	418.6	405.5	390.4	385.1	-15.3	385.1
High	765.8	824.5	826.2	774.4	1.1	774.4

See footnotes at end of table.

Table 3.2. Age-Adjusted Death Rates from All Causes—Continued

(Average annual deaths per 100,000 resident population; ranked by all persons 1995–1997 rate)

Area	White 1992–1994	White 1995–1997	Black 1992–1994	Black 1995–1997	Hispanic 1992–1994	Hispanic 1995–1997	Asian or Pacific Islander 1992–1994	Asian or Pacific Islander 1995–1997
United States	480.7	466.7	774.9	736.5	384.0	365.6	296.4	278.7
DIVISION								
East South Central	531.6	531.2	790.3	782.9	310.5	312.4	278.4	248.5
West South Central	507.4	496.4	770.1	735.7	431.3	411.6	247.6	227.8
South Atlantic	476.0	466.4	785.5	753.0	335.2	329.9	245.1	219.7
East North Central	477.6	466.9	796.8	769.7	308.8	305.2	234.9	229.6
Middle Atlantic	488.3	466.2	771.3	698.6	409.3	389.1	246.7	240.9
Mountain	464.8	452.4	650.7	596.6	456.6	428.7	303.1	286.2
West North Central	448.2	442.6	777.1	753.4	332.1	348.4	285.5	301.0
Pacific	473.8	448.2	729.5	681.8	308.1	316.2	252.9	237.1
New England	455.4	438.5	675.0	626.5	359.9	335.4	325.1	307.0
STATE								
Mississippi	539.7	539.0	798.7	784.6	165.5	186.5	241.6	288.6
Louisiana	528.1	519.1	810.6	783.0	207.1	248.0	262.2	254.1
Alabama	523.5	526.7	782.7	764.7	382.7	279.6	269.1	138.0
South Carolina	507.9	504.8	791.2	785.6	188.1	190.5	251.7	239.2
Tennessee	525.0	527.2	806.7	821.7	313.9	340.4	315.9	281.0
Arkansas	530.2	531.1	807.1	788.3	204.0	177.1	282.2	331.8
Georgia	510.5	502.4	789.6	764.2	231.2	216.1	279.8	263.3
West Virginia	556.8	543.8	723.0	653.5	278.5	260.0	310.7	335.5
Kentucky	544.0	537.7	751.2	741.3	350.8	433.7	254.9	274.6
Nevada	554.0	547.9	776.6	717.3	*	199.3	*	*
Oklahoma	535.4	537.4	723.7	707.0	*	*	376.6	279.4
North Carolina	487.8	480.3	784.8	759.7	204.0	168.8	267.7	247.3
Missouri	495.4	481.2	776.3	748.5	435.4	336.4	237.0	154.5
Maryland	467.6	454.1	764.6	747.8	138.0	93.7	286.5	223.6
Delaware	498.5	496.1	818.9	778.5	398.6	357.5	295.8	307.9
Indiana	480.3	463.2	859.9	828.3	323.0	294.7	222.5	222.0
Illinois	493.8	491.9	773.5	761.6	296.3	278.1	233.7	218.4
Ohio	475.2	456.4	800.8	753.0	340.8	342.4	281.9	260.8
Pennsylvania	488.5	484.5	726.7	718.8	222.1	364.7	208.0	198.8
Virginia	500.3	466.8	731.6	639.9	440.0	412.7	254.8	257.2
Texas	482.3	473.7	834.5	801.4	455.0	490.3	295.3	263.6
Michigan	471.0	459.2	743.4	720.2	243.6	186.7	250.3	227.0
New York	493.6	478.6	743.8	702.3	439.1	415.9	233.9	217.8
New Jersey	470.5	450.8	808.0	751.6	307.5	296.2	201.9	188.4
Florida	459.8	450.0	778.4	715.0	360.4	362.0	183.8	188.0
Arizona	453.5	440.1	541.0	468.7	285.3	282.9	240.7	335.4
Alaska	484.0	464.6	689.7	631.0	464.4	436.2	316.1	250.3
New Mexico	472.5	465.8	536.6	462.1	487.7	473.6	251.5	297.2
Maine	476.8	472.0	*	*	*	*	*	*
Wyoming	467.0	462.5	*	*	473.5	431.5	*	*
Oregon	469.4	460.1	725.2	668.6	299.1	280.3	310.5	306.1
Montana	447.8	447.2	713.7	722.7	333.2	316.3	249.0	254.8
Kansas	455.8	446.8	*	*	411.2	335.0	*	*
Vermont	480.3	451.0	737.9	691.5	362.6	337.4	306.8	285.7
California	473.5	457.2	*	*	*	*	*	*
New Hampshire	424.3	411.9	*	*	*	*	*	*
Rhode Island	434.2	425.6	737.0	659.5	330.3	347.9	175.7	173.2
South Dakota	452.6	449.7	*	*	*	179.7	*	225.4
Nebraska	462.0	434.9	624.6	599.8	312.2	317.2	269.8	264.4
Connecticut	456.9	441.4	732.3	682.9	238.0	256.7	310.8	255.5
Wisconsin	435.0	428.2	716.7	724.4	259.9	225.1	271.1	287.3
Massachusetts	440.0	431.7	730.9	776.5	288.5	315.4	214.6	237.8
Washington	451.6	435.1	664.5	618.6	287.8	289.8	337.1	290.7
Idaho	443.4	432.3	*	*	354.4	305.1	309.8	336.1
Iowa	432.6	427.2	684.3	704.6	346.5	335.0	327.3	301.2
Colorado	438.2	426.2	615.6	572.5	466.1	430.8	258.6	240.9
North Dakota	413.2	404.9	*	*	*	*	*	*
Minnesota	413.3	404.4	710.0	675.7	276.2	449.1	299.1	335.0
Utah	414.4	405.0	595.9	625.7	393.8	394.0	369.8	348.2
Hawaii	386.4	368.4	409.0	307.1	363.6	336.5	392.5	396.2
OTHER								
District of Columbia	455.4	401.5	1 036.0	1 003.0	148.1	88.6	217.0	210.0
Median	480.3	466.2	751.2	722.7	331.2	323.6	269.1	256.4
Low	386.4	368.4	409.0	307.1	138.0	88.6	175.7	138.0
High	556.8	547.9	1 036.0	1 003.0	487.7	490.3	392.5	396.2

SOURCE: E. Kramarow, H. Lentzner, R. Rooks, J. Weeks, S. Saydah. *Health and Aging Chartbook. Health, United States,* 1999. Hyattsville, Maryland: National Center for Health Statistics. 1999: Table 29, and unpublished data.

* Data for states with population under 10,000 in the middle year of a three-year period or fewer than 50 deaths for the three-year period are considered unreliable and are not shown.

NOTE: The race groups, White, Black, and Asian or Pacific Islander, include persons of Hispanic and non-Hispanic origin. Conversely, persons of Hispanic origin may be of any race. Consistency of race identification between the death certificate (source of data for numerator of death rates) and data from the Census Bureau (denominator) is high for individual white and black persons; however, persons identified as American Indian, Asian, or Hispanic origin in data from the Census Bureau are sometimes misreported as White or non-Hispanic on the death certificate, causing death rates to be underestimated by 22–30 percent for American Indians, about 12 percent for Asians, and about 7 percent for persons of Hispanic origin. (P.D. Sorlie, E. Rogot, and N.J. Johnson : Validity of Demographic Characteristics on the Death Certificate, *Epidemiology* 3, no. 2 (1992): 181–184. See Appendix II of Health, United States, 1999 for age-adjustment procedure.

Table 3.3. Infant[1] Mortality Rate

(Per 1,000 live births)

Year	Total			White			Black		
	Both sexes	Male	Female	Both sexes	Male	Female	Both sexes	Male	Female
RACE OF CHILD [2]									
1940	47.0	52.5	41.3	43.2	48.3	37.8	72.9	81.1	64.6
1950	29.2	32.8	25.5	26.8	30.2	23.1	43.9	48.3	39.4
1960	26.0	29.3	22.6	22.9	26.0	19.6	44.3	49.1	39.4
1970	20.0	22.4	17.5	17.8	20.0	15.4	32.6	36.2	29.0
1975	16.1	17.9	14.2	14.2	15.9	12.3	26.2	28.3	24.0
1976	15.2	16.8	13.6	13.3	14.8	11.7	25.5	27.8	23.2
1977	14.1	15.8	12.4	12.3	13.9	10.7	23.6	25.9	21.3
1978	13.8	15.3	12.2	12.0	13.4	10.6	23.1	25.4	20.8
1979	13.1	14.5	11.6	11.4	12.8	9.9	21.8	23.7	19.8
1980	12.6	13.9	11.2	11.0	12.3	9.6	21.4	23.3	19.4
RACE OF MOTHER [3]									
1980	12.6	13.9	11.2	10.9	12.1	9.5	22.2	24.2	20.2
1981	11.9	13.1	10.7	10.3	11.5	9.1	20.8	22.5	19.0
1982	11.5	12.8	10.2	9.9	11.1	8.7	20.5	22.5	18.4
1983	11.2	12.3	10.0	9.6	10.7	8.5	20.0	22.0	18.0
1984	10.8	11.9	9.6	9.3	10.4	8.2	19.2	20.7	17.6
1985	10.6	11.9	9.3	9.2	10.4	7.9	19.0	20.8	17.2
1986	10.4	11.5	9.1	8.8	9.9	7.7	18.9	20.9	16.8
1987	10.1	11.2	8.9	8.5	9.5	7.5	18.8	20.6	16.8
1988	10.0	11.0	8.9	8.4	9.4	7.3	18.5	20.0	17.0
1989	9.8	10.8	8.8	8.1	9.0	7.1	18.6	20.0	17.2
1990	9.2	10.3	8.1	7.6	8.5	6.6	18.0	19.6	16.2
1991	8.9	10.0	7.8	7.3	8.3	6.3	17.6	19.4	15.7
1992	8.5	9.4	7.6	6.9	7.7	6.1	16.8	18.4	15.3
1993	8.4	9.3	7.4	6.8	7.6	6.0	16.5	18.3	14.7
1994	8.0	8.8	7.2	6.6	7.2	5.9	15.8	17.5	14.1
1995	7.6	8.3	6.8	6.3	7.0	5.6	15.1	16.3	13.9
1996	7.3	8.0	6.6	6.1	6.7	5.4	14.7	16.0	13.3
1997	7.2	8.0	6.5	6.0	6.7	5.4	14.2	15.5	12.8

SOURCE: D.L. Hoyert, K.D. Kochanek, S.L. Murphy. Deaths: Final Data for 1997. *National Vital Statistics Reports;* vol. 47 no. 19. Hyattsville, Maryland: National Center for Health Statistics. 1999: Table 27.

1. Infant is defined as aged under one year.
2. Infant deaths based on race of child as stated on the death certificate; live births based on race of parents as stated on the birth certificate.
3. Infant deaths based on race of child as stated on the death certificate; live births based on race of mother as stated on the birth certificate.

Table 3.4. Postneonatal[1] Mortality Rate

(Per 1,000 live births)

Year	Total			White			Black		
	Both sexes	Male	Female	Both sexes	Male	Female	Both sexes	Male	Female
RACE OF CHILD [2]									
1940	18.3	19.9	16.6	16.0	17.5	14.5	33.0	36.4	29.7
1950	8.7	9.4	8.0	7.4	8.0	6.7	16.1	17.2	15.0
1960	7.3	8.1	6.5	5.7	6.3	4.9	16.5	18.0	14.9
1970	4.9	5.4	4.4	4.0	4.4	3.5	9.9	10.8	8.9
1975	4.5	4.9	4.0	3.8	4.2	3.3	7.9	8.5	7.2
1976	4.3	4.8	3.8	3.6	4.1	3.2	7.6	8.4	6.9
1977	4.2	4.8	3.7	3.6	4.1	3.1	7.6	8.3	6.8
1978	4.3	4.7	3.9	3.6	4.0	3.2	7.6	8.2	7.0
1979	4.2	4.7	3.7	3.5	4.0	3.0	7.5	8.2	6.7
1980	4.1	4.6	3.6	3.5	4.0	3.0	7.3	7.9	6.6
RACE OF MOTHER [3]									
1980	4.1	4.6	3.6	3.5	3.9	3.0	7.6	8.3	6.9
1981	3.9	4.3	3.5	3.4	3.8	2.9	6.8	7.4	6.3
1982	3.8	4.3	3.3	3.2	3.7	2.8	6.9	7.6	6.1
1983	3.9	4.3	3.4	3.3	3.7	2.9	7.0	7.8	6.3
1984	3.8	4.2	3.3	3.2	3.7	2.8	6.8	7.5	6.2
1985	3.7	4.2	3.2	3.2	3.6	2.7	6.4	7.0	5.8
1986	3.6	4.1	3.1	3.1	3.5	2.6	6.6	7.3	5.8
1987	3.6	4.1	3.2	3.1	3.5	2.6	6.4	7.1	5.8
1988	3.6	4.0	3.2	3.1	3.5	2.6	6.5	6.9	6.1
1989	3.6	4.0	3.1	2.9	3.4	2.5	6.7	7.2	6.2
1990	3.4	3.8	3.0	2.8	3.1	2.4	6.4	6.9	5.9
1991	3.4	3.8	2.9	2.8	3.2	2.3	6.3	6.8	5.8
1992	3.1	3.5	2.7	2.6	3.0	2.2	6.0	6.5	5.5
1993	3.1	3.5	2.6	2.5	2.9	2.1	5.8	6.6	5.1
1994	2.9	3.2	2.6	2.4	2.7	2.1	5.6	6.2	5.0
1995	2.7	3.0	2.4	2.2	2.5	1.9	5.3	5.7	4.8
1996	2.5	2.8	2.2	2.1	2.4	1.8	5.1	5.6	4.6
1997	2.5	2.8	2.1	2.0	2.3	1.8	4.8	5.3	4.2

SOURCE: D.L. Hoyert, K.D. Kochanek, S.L. Murphy. Deaths: Final Data for 1997. *National Vital Statistics Reports;* vol. 47 no. 19. Hyattsville, Maryland: National Center for Health Statistics. 1999: Table 27.

1. Postneonatal is defined as age 28 days–one year.
2. Infant deaths based on race of child as stated on the death certificate; live births based on race of parents as stated on the birth certificate.
3. Infant deaths based on race of child as stated on the death certificate; live births based on race of mother as stated on the birth certificate.

Table 3.5. Mortality of Children under Age One for Birth Cohorts

(Per 1,000 live births)

Race and Hispanic origin of mother	Single birth cohort							Multiple birth cohort		
	1983	1985	1988	1990	1991	1995[1]	1996[1]	1983–85	1986–88	1989–91
INFANT DEATHS (UNDER ONE YEAR OF AGE)										
All mothers	10.9	10.4	9.6	8.9	8.6	7.6	7.3	10.6	9.8	9.0
White	9.3	8.9	8.0	7.3	7.1	6.3	6.1	9.0	8.2	7.4
Black	19.2	18.6	17.8	16.9	16.6	14.6	14.1	18.7	17.9	17.1
American Indian or Alaska Native	15.2	13.1	12.7	13.1	11.3	9.0	10.0	13.9	13.2	12.6
Asian or Pacific Islander	8.3	7.8	6.8	6.6	5.8	5.3	5.2	8.3	7.3	6.6
Chinese	9.5	*5.8	*5.5	*4.3	*4.6	*3.8	*3.2	7.4	5.8	5.1
Japanese	*	*6.0	*7.0	*5.5	*4.2	*5.3	*4.2	6.0	6.9	5.3
Filipino	8.4	7.7	6.9	6.0	5.1	5.6	5.8	8.2	6.9	6.4
Hawaiian and part Hawaiian	*	*	*	*	*	*	*	11.3	11.1	9.0
Other Asian or Pacific Islander	8.1	8.5	7.0	7.4	6.3	5.5	5.7	8.6	7.6	7.0
Hispanic origin [2,3]	9.5	8.8	8.3	7.5	7.1	6.3	6.1	9.2	8.3	7.6
Mexican	9.1	8.5	7.9	7.2	6.9	6.0	5.8	8.8	7.9	7.2
Puerto Rican	12.9	11.1	11.6	9.9	9.7	8.9	8.6	12.3	11.1	10.4
Cuban	7.5	8.5	7.2	7.2	5.2	5.3	5.1	8.0	7.3	6.2
Central and South American	8.5	8.0	7.2	6.8	5.9	5.5	5.0	8.2	7.6	6.6
Other and unknown Hispanic	10.6	9.5	9.1	8.0	8.2	7.4	7.7	9.9	9.0	8.2
White, non-Hispanic [3]	9.2	8.7	8.0	7.2	7.0	6.3	6.0	8.9	8.1	7.3
Black, non-Hispanic [3]	19.1	18.3	18.1	16.9	16.6	14.7	14.2	18.5	17.9	17.2
NEONATAL DEATHS (UNDER 28 DAYS OF AGE)										
All mothers	7.1	6.8	6.1	5.7	5.4	4.9	4.8	6.9	6.3	5.7
White	6.1	5.8	5.0	4.6	4.4	4.1	4.0	5.9	5.2	4.7
Black	12.5	12.3	11.5	11.1	10.7	9.6	9.4	12.2	11.7	11.1
American Indian or Alaska Native	7.5	6.1	5.4	6.1	5.5	4.0	4.7	6.7	5.9	5.9
Asian or Pacific Islander	5.2	4.8	4.3	3.9	3.6	3.4	3.3	5.2	4.5	3.9
Chinese	5.5	*3.3	*3.1	*2.3	*2.3	*2.3	*1.9	4.3	3.3	2.7
Japanese	*	*3.1	*4.5	*3.5	*3.2	*3.3	*2.2	3.4	4.4	3.0
Filipino	5.6	5.1	4.4	3.5	3.4	3.4	4.1	5.3	4.5	4.0
Hawaiian and part Hawaiian	*	*	*	*	*	*	*	7.4	7.1	4.8
Other Asian or Pacific Islander	5.0	5.4	4.4	4.4	4.1	3.7	3.7	5.5	4.7	4.2
Hispanic origin [2,3]	6.2	5.7	5.2	4.8	4.5	4.1	4.0	6.0	5.3	4.8
Mexican	5.9	5.4	4.8	4.5	4.3	3.9	3.8	5.7	5.0	4.5
Puerto Rican	8.7	7.6	7.3	6.9	6.1	6.1	5.6	8.3	7.2	7.0
Cuban	5.0	6.2	5.5	5.3	4.0	3.6	3.6	5.9	5.3	4.6
Central and South American	5.8	5.6	4.8	4.4	4.0	3.7	3.4	5.7	5.0	4.4
Other and unknown Hispanic	6.4	5.6	5.9	5.0	5.1	4.8	5.3	6.2	5.8	5.2
White, non-Hispanic [3]	6.0	5.7	5.0	4.5	4.3	4.0	3.9	5.8	5.1	4.6
Black, non-Hispanic [3]	12.1	11.9	11.5	11.0	10.7	9.6	9.4	11.8	11.4	11.1
POSTNEONATAL DEATHS (BETWEEN 28 AND 365 DAYS OF AGE)										
All mothers	3.8	3.6	3.5	3.2	3.2	2.6	2.5	3.7	3.5	3.3
White	3.2	3.1	3.0	2.7	2.6	2.2	2.1	3.1	3.0	2.7
Black	6.7	6.3	6.3	5.9	5.9	5.0	4.8	6.4	6.2	6.0
American Indian or Alaska Native	7.7	7.0	7.4	7.0	5.8	5.1	5.3	7.2	7.3	6.7
Asian or Pacific Islander	3.1	*2.9	2.6	2.7	2.2	1.9	1.9	3.1	2.8	2.6
Chinese	*	*2.5	2.4	2.0	2.3	1.5	1.2	3.1	2.5	2.4
Japanese	*	*	*	*	*	*	*	2.6	2.5	2.2
Filipino	2.8	2.7	2.5	2.5	1.8	2.2	1.8	2.9	*2.4	2.3
Hawaiian and part Hawaiian	*	*	*	*	*	*	*	*	4.0	4.1
Other Asian or Pacific Islander	3.0	3.0	2.6	3.0	2.3	1.9	2.0	3.1	2.9	2.8
Hispanic origin [2,3]	3.3	3.2	3.1	2.7	2.6	2.1	2.1	3.2	3.0	2.7
Mexican	3.2	3.2	3.1	2.7	2.6	2.1	2.1	3.2	2.9	2.7
Puerto Rican	4.2	3.5	4.2	3.0	3.5	2.8	3.0	4.0	3.9	3.4
Cuban	*	*	*	*	*	*	*	2.2	2.0	1.6
Central and South American	2.6	2.4	2.4	2.4	1.9	1.9	1.6	2.5	2.6	2.2
Other and unknown Hispanic	4.1	3.9	3.2	3.0	3.1	2.6	2.5	3.7	3.2	3.0
White, non-Hispanic [3]	3.2	3.0	3.0	2.7	2.7	2.2	2.1	3.1	3.0	2.7
Black, non-Hispanic [3]	7.0	6.4	6.6	5.9	5.9	5.0	4.8	6.7	6.4	6.1

SOURCE: E. Kramarow, H. Lentzner, R. Rooks, J. Weeks, S. Saydah. Health and Aging Chartbook. *Health, United States, 1999.* Hyattsville, Maryland: National Center for Health Statistics. 1999: Table 19.

* Infant and neonatal mortality rates for groups with fewer than 10,000 births are considered unreliable. Postneonatal mortality rates for groups with fewer than 20,000 births are considered unreliable. Infant and neonatal mortality rates for groups with fewer than 7,500 births are considered highly unreliable and are not shown. Postneonatal mortality rates for groups with fewer than 15,000 births are considered highly unreliable and are not shown.
1. Rates based on a period file using weighted data to correct for the 2–3% of records that could not be linked. Data for 1995 not strictly comparable with unweighted birth cohort data for earlier years (see Appendix I of *Health, United States, 1999,* National Vital Statistics System). The 1995 weighted mortality rates shown in this table are less than 1 percent to 5 percent higher than unweighted rates for 1995.
2. Persons of Hispanic origin may be of any race.
3. Data shown only for states with a Hispanic-origin item on their birth certificates. The number of states reporting the item increased from 23 and the District of Columbia (DC) in 1983–1987, to 30 and DC in 1988, 47 and DC in 1989, 48 and DC in 1990, 49 and DC in 1991, and 50 and DC in 1995 (see Appendix I of *Health, United States, 1999*).

NOTE: The race groups, White, Black, American Indian or Alaska Native, and Asian or Pacific Islander, include persons of Hispanic and non-Hispanic origin. National linked files do not exist for 1992–1994 birth cohorts. Data are based on National Linked Birth/Infant Death Data Sets.

Table 3.6. Leading Causes of Infant Deaths by Age for American Indians and Alaska Natives: 1992–1994

(Rate per 1,000 live births)

Cause of death	American Indian and Alaskan Native				U.S. all races rate 1993	U.S. white rate 1993	Ratio [1] of American Indian and Alaska Native to:	
	Number		Rate				U.S. all races	U.S. white
	Actual	Adjusted	Actual	Adjusted				
INFANT DEATHS (UNDER ONE YEAR OF AGE)								
All causes	872	1 096	8.7	10.9	8.4	6.8	1.3	1.6
Sudden infant death syndrome	210	277	2.1	2.8	1.2	1.0	2.3	2.8
Congenital anomalies	193	229	1.9	2.3	1.8	1.7	1.3	1.4
Accidents	49	58	0.5	0.6	0.2	0.2	3.0	3.0
Pneumonia and influenza	37	44	0.4	0.4	0.1	0.1	4.0	4.0
Disorders relating to short gestation and low birthweight	31	38	0.3	0.4	1.1	0.7	0.4	0.6
Respiratory distress syndrome	27	36	0.3	0.4	0.5	0.3	0.8	1.3
Newborn affected by complications of placenta, cord, and membranes	26	33	0.3	0.3	0.2	0.2	1.5	1.5
Newborn affected by maternal complications of pregnancy	17	27	0.2	0.3	0.3	0.3	1.0	1.0
Intrauterine hypoxia and birth asphyxia	15	17	0.1	0.2	0.1	0.1	2.0	2.0
Homicide	15	16	0.1	0.2	0.1	0.1	2.0	2.0
All other causes	252	321						
NEONATAL DEATHS (UNDER 28 DAYS OF AGE)								
All causes	409	517	4.1	5.2	5.3	4.3	1.0	1.2
Congenital anomalies	138	163	1.4	1.6	1.3	1.3	1.2	1.2
Disorders relating to short gestation and low birthweight	30	37	0.3	0.4	1.1	0.7	0.4	0.6
Newborn affected by complications of placenta, cord, and membranes	26	33	0.3	0.3	0.2	0.2	1.5	1.5
Respiratory distress syndrome	23	30	0.2	0.3	0.4	0.3	0.8	1.0
Newborn affected by maternal complications of pregnancy	16	26	0.2	0.3	0.3	0.3	1.0	1.0
Sudden infant death syndrome	14	18	0.1	0.2	0.1	0.1	2.0	2.0
Intrauterine hypoxia and birth asphyxia	14	16	0.1	0.2	0.1	0.1	2.0	2.0
Infections specific to the perinatal period	14	15	0.1	0.2	0.2	0.1	1.0	2.0
Newborn affected by maternal conditions which may be unrelated to present pregnancy	7	8	0.1	0.1	0.0	0.0	*	*
Pneumonia and influenza	6	7	0.1	0.1	0.0	0.0	*	*
All other causes	121	164						
POSTNEONATAL DEATHS (BETWEEN 28 AND 365 DAYS OF AGE)								
All causes	463	579	4.6	5.8	3.1	2.5	1.9	2.3
Sudden infant death syndrome	196	259	2.0	2.6	1.1	0.9	2.4	2.9
Congenital anomalies	55	66	0.5	0.7	0.5	0.5	1.4	1.4
Accidents	26	54	0.3	0.5	0.1	0.1	5.0	5.0
Pneumonia and influenza	31	37	0.3	0.4	0.1	0.1	4.0	4.0
Homicide	14	15	0.1	0.2	0.1	0.1	2.0	2.0
Septicemia	5	6	0.0	0.1	0.1	0.0	1.0	1.0
Bronchitis and bronchiolitis	5	6	0.0	0.1	0.0	0.0	*	*
Respiratory distress syndrome	4	6	0.0	0.1	0.0	0.0	*	*
Viral diseases	4	5	0.0	0.1	0.0	0.0	*	*
Gastris and duodenitis	3	5	0.0	0.1	0.0	0.0	*	*
All other causes	120	120						

SOURCE: Indian Health Service, *Trends in Indian Health* (Rockville, Md.: 1997): Table 3.10.

* Not applicable.
1. Adjusted to compensate for miscoding of American Indian race on death certificate.

NOTE: 0.0 equals less than 0.1. Causes of death are ranked in the order of adjusted number of deaths.

Table 3.7. Infant [1] Mortality Rates

(Infant deaths per 1,000 live births; ranked by percent change for all races for 1987–1997)

Area	Total				
	1985–1987	1990–1992	1995–1997	Change 1987–1997	Percent change 1987–1997
United States	10.4	8.9	7.4	-3.0	-28.8
DIVISION					
Pacific	9.3	7.5	6.0	-3.3	-35.5
New England	8.6	6.9	5.7	-2.9	-33.7
Middle Atlantic	10.5	9.1	7.2	-3.3	-31.4
Mountain	9.5	8.1	6.7	-2.8	-29.5
South Atlantic	11.8	10.2	8.4	-3.4	-28.8
West South Central	10.1	8.5	7.2	-2.9	-28.7
West North Central	9.5	8.4	7.1	-2.4	-25.3
East North Central	10.8	9.8	8.3	-2.5	-23.1
East South Central	11.8	10.2	9.1	-2.7	-22.9
STATE					
New Hampshire	8.7	6.4	4.9	-3.8	-43.7
Washington	10.1	7.4	5.8	-4.3	-42.6
Oregon	9.9	7.5	5.8	-4.1	-41.4
Delaware	12.7	10.2	7.6	-5.1	-40.2
Maine	8.7	6.2	5.3	-3.4	-39.1
Wyoming	10.8	8.5	6.6	-4.2	-38.9
Massachusetts	8.3	6.7	5.1	-3.2	-38.6
Utah	9.0	6.5	5.7	-3.3	-36.7
Idaho	10.7	8.7	6.8	-3.9	-36.4
New Mexico	9.4	8.2	6.2	-3.2	-34.0
California	9.2	7.5	6.1	-3.1	-33.7
New York	10.7	9.3	7.1	-3.6	-33.6
New Jersey	9.9	8.7	6.6	-3.3	-33.3
Hawaii	9.0	6.8	6.0	-3.0	-33.3
Nevada	9.1	8.1	6.1	-3.0	-33.0
Texas	9.5	7.8	6.4	-3.1	-32.6
Florida	10.9	9.1	7.4	-3.5	-32.1
South Carolina	13.4	11.1	9.2	-4.2	-31.3
South Dakota	11.0	9.6	7.6	-3.4	-30.9
Minnesota	8.9	7.3	6.2	-2.7	-30.3
Montana	10.0	7.9	7.0	-3.0	-30.0
Alaska	10.7	9.3	7.5	-3.2	-29.9
Vermont	9.0	6.5	6.4	-2.6	-28.9
Virginia	10.9	9.9	7.8	-3.1	-28.4
Colorado	9.3	8.3	6.7	-2.6	-28.0
North Dakota	8.6	8.0	6.2	-2.4	-27.9
Missouri	10.4	9.4	7.5	-2.9	-27.9
Georgia	12.6	11.4	9.1	-3.5	-27.8
Kentucky	10.3	8.6	7.5	-2.8	-27.2
Michigan	11.2	10.4	8.2	-3.0	-26.8
Pennsylvania	10.5	9.2	7.7	-2.8	-26.7
Maryland	11.7	9.5	8.7	-3.0	-25.6
Illinois	11.8	10.5	8.8	-3.0	-25.4
Rhode Island	8.7	7.8	6.5	-2.2	-25.3
Connecticut	9.2	7.6	6.9	-2.3	-25.0
Tennessee	11.4	9.9	8.8	-2.6	-22.8
Indiana	10.8	9.4	8.4	-2.4	-22.2
Wisconsin	9.0	7.9	7.0	-2.0	-22.2
Arizona	9.5	8.6	7.4	-2.1	-22.1
Alabama	12.7	10.9	9.9	-2.8	-22.0
North Carolina	11.7	10.5	9.2	-2.5	-21.4
Oklahoma	10.3	9.2	8.1	-2.2	-21.4
Iowa	9.0	8.1	7.1	-1.9	-21.1
Louisiana	11.9	10.4	9.5	-2.4	-20.2
Ohio	10.1	9.6	8.1	-2.0	-19.8
Mississippi	13.3	11.8	10.7	-2.6	-19.5
West Virginia	10.3	9.1	8.3	-2.0	-19.4
Arkansas	10.8	9.9	8.9	-1.9	-17.6
Kansas	9.2	8.7	7.6	-1.6	-17.4
Nebraska	9.4	7.7	7.9	-1.5	-16.0
OTHER					
District of Columbia	20.4	20.4	14.8	-5.6	-27.5
Median	10.3	8.7	7.5	-3.0	-27.9
Low	8.3	6.2	4.9	-5.6	-43.7
High	20.4	20.4	14.8	-1.5	-16.0

See footnotes at end of table.

Table 3.7. Infant [1] Mortality Rates—Continued

(Infant deaths per 1,000 live births; ranked by percent change for all races for 1987–1997)

Area	White [2]					Black [2]					Difference in percent change between whites and blacks
	1985–1987	1990–1992	1995–1997	Change 1987–1997	Percent change	1985–1987	1990–1992	1995–1997	Change 1987–1997	Percent Change	
United States	8.8	7.3	6.1	-2.7	-30.7	18.9	17.5	14.7	-4.2	-22.2	-8.5
DIVISION											
Pacific	8.7	6.9	5.6	-3.1	-35.6	18.6	16.8	14.1	-4.5	-24.2	-11.4
New England	7.9	6.3	5.3	-2.6	-32.9	20.0	14.2	10.8	-9.2	-46.0	13.1
Middle Atlantic	8.7	7.1	5.8	-2.9	-33.3	18.9	18.1	13.8	-5.1	-27.0	-6.3
Mountain	9.1	7.6	6.4	-2.7	-29.7	18.5	18.3	15.1	-3.4	-18.4	-11.3
South Atlantic	9.1	7.4	6.2	-2.9	-31.9	19.0	17.2	14.5	-4.5	-23.7	-8.2
West South Central	8.7	7.2	6.2	-2.5	-28.7	16.6	14.7	12.8	-3.8	-22.9	-5.8
West North Central	8.7	7.3	6.3	-2.4	-27.6	18.6	19.0	16.2	-2.4	-12.9	-14.7
East North Central	8.9	7.7	6.6	-2.3	-25.8	21.0	20.2	17.4	-3.6	-17.1	-8.7
East South Central	9.4	7.8	7.1	-2.3	-24.5	18.5	16.5	15.0	-3.5	-18.9	-5.5
STATE											
New Hampshire	8.6	6.3	4.9	-3.7	-43.0						
Washington	9.8	7.0	5.5	-4.3	-43.9	17.6	16.9	15.8	-1.8	-10.2	-33.7
Oregon	9.7	7.2	5.7	-4.0	-41.2	*22.5	*21.5	*17.0	-5.5	-24.4	-16.8
Delaware	10.1	7.6	5.9	-4.2	-41.6	*21.4	*18.8	*13.4	-8.0	-37.4	-4.2
Maine	8.7	6.1	5.3	-3.4	-39.1	*	*	*	*	*	*
Wyoming	10.7	8.4	6.2	-4.5	-42.1	*	*	*	*	*	*
Massachusetts	7.4	6.2	4.8	-2.6	-35.1	19.6	12.5	8.9	-10.7	-54.6	19.5
Utah	9.0	6.4	5.7	-3.3	-36.7	*	*	*	*	*	*
Idaho	10.6	8.7	6.7	-3.9	-36.8	*	*	*	*	*	*
New Mexico	9.0	7.8	5.9	-3.1	-34.4	23.6	23.4	11.5	-12.1	-51.3	16.8
California	8.5	6.9	5.6	-2.9	-34.1	18.6	16.8	13.8	-4.8	-25.8	-8.3
New York	9.0	7.3	5.9	-3.1	-34.4	17.5	17.2	12.4	-5.1	-29.1	-5.3
New Jersey	7.9	6.3	5.2	-2.7	-34.2	19.3	18.5	13.9	-5.4	-28.0	-6.2
Hawaii	6.2	4.4	3.6	-2.6	-41.9	20.8	18.7	13.9	-6.9	-33.2	-8.8
Nevada	8.6	7.3	5.7	-2.9	-33.7	*17.0	*17.4	12.5	-4.5	-26.5	-7.3
Texas	8.6	6.9	5.8	-2.8	-32.6	16.1	14.5	*11.4	-4.7	-29.2	-3.4
Florida	8.6	7.1	5.8	-2.8	-32.6	18.8	16.1	12.9	-5.9	-31.4	-1.2
South Carolina	9.7	7.8	6.3	-3.4	-35.1	19.4	16.6	14.6	-4.8	-24.7	-10.3
South Dakota	8.9	8.0	5.9	-3.0	-33.7	*	*	*	*	*	*
Minnesota	8.5	6.5	5.4	-3.1	-36.5	20.8	21.0	16.2	-4.6	-22.1	-14.4
Montana	9.1	7.0	6.6	-2.5	-27.5	*	*	*	*	*	*
Alaska	8.9	7.7	6.2	-2.7	-30.3	17.4	13.2	16.6	-0.8	-4.6	-25.7
Vermont	8.9	6.5	6.4	-2.5	-28.1	*	*	*	*	*	*
Virginia	8.7	7.2	5.9	-2.8	-32.2	18.6	18.5	14.4	-4.2	-22.6	-9.6
Colorado	8.9	7.7	6.4	-2.5	-28.1	19.3	17.4	15.9	-3.4	-17.6	-10.5
North Dakota	8.2	7.5	5.9	-2.3	-28.0	*	*	*	*	*	*
Missouri	9.0	7.5	6.2	-2.8	-31.1	18.3	*18.6	*15.3	-3.0	-16.4	-14.7
Georgia	9.7	7.9	6.3	-3.4	-35.1	*18.5	*17.5	14.6	-3.9	-21.1	-14.0
Kentucky	9.7	8.0	7.1	-2.6	-26.8	16.1	14.2	11.8	-4.3	-26.7	-0.1
Michigan	8.8	7.4	6.1	-2.7	-30.7	22.9	21.8	17.5	-5.4	-23.6	-7.1
Pennsylvania	8.7	7.3	6.2	-2.5	-28.7	22.3	20.1	17.4	-4.9	-22.0	-6.8
Maryland	8.9	6.6	5.6	-3.3	-37.1	18.7	16.1	15.3	-3.4	-18.2	-18.9
Illinois	9.1	7.6	6.7	-2.4	-26.4	22.2	21.2	18.0	-4.2	-18.9	-7.5
Rhode Island	8.3	7.4	6.4	-1.9	-22.9	14.5	14.9	9.3	-5.2	-35.9	13.0
Connecticut	7.8	6.3	6.0	-1.8	-23.1	21.3	16.5	13.9	-7.4	-34.7	11.7
Tennessee	8.9	7.4	6.7	-2.2	-24.7	*19.8	*18.0	*16.6	-3.2	-16.2	-8.6
Indiana	9.6	8.2	7.4	-2.2	-22.9	*21.2	*19.0	17.2	-4.0	-18.9	-4.0
Wisconsin	8.2	7.1	6.1	-2.1	-25.6	17.9	15.5	17.1	-0.8	-4.5	-21.1
Arizona	8.9	7.9	7.0	-1.9	-21.3	18.1	19.2	17.2	-0.9	-5.0	-16.4
Alabama	9.6	8.0	7.6	-2.0	-20.8	18.8	16.5	14.8	-4.0	-21.3	0.4
North Carolina	9.2	7.8	6.9	-2.3	-25.0	18.2	*16.7	15.6	-2.6	-14.3	-10.7
Oklahoma	9.7	8.6	7.4	-2.3	-23.7	17.8	16.2	15.9	-1.9	-10.7	-13.0
Iowa	8.8	7.8	6.8	-2.0	-22.7	*18.0	*18.3	20.7	2.7	15.0	-37.7
Louisiana	8.4	7.4	6.4	-2.0	-23.8	17.4	14.6	*14.0	-3.4	-19.5	-4.3
Ohio	8.9	7.9	6.7	-2.2	-24.7	17.5	18.4	16.4	-1.1	-6.3	-18.4
Mississippi	9.3	7.9	7.4	-1.9	-20.4	17.9	15.9	14.7	-3.2	-17.9	-2.6
West Virginia	9.8	8.9	7.9	-1.9	-19.4	23.3	14.9	19.6	-3.7	-15.9	-3.5
Arkansas	9.4	8.3	7.6	-1.8	-19.1	15.3	15.5	14.1	-1.2	-7.8	-11.3
Kansas	8.5	7.7	6.7	-1.8	-21.2	18.4	19.8	19.3	0.9	4.9	-26.1
Nebraska	8.7	6.9	7.5	-1.2	-13.8	20.0	18.9	14.7	-5.3	-26.5	12.7
OTHER											
District of Columbia	11.0	10.9	5.8	-5.2	-47.3	23.7	24.0	18.1	-5.6	-23.6	-23.6
Median	8.9	7.5	6.2	-2.6	-30.3	18.6	17.4	15.0	-4.2	-21.7	-8.5
Low	6.2	4.4	3.6	-5.2	-13.8	23.7	24.0	20.7	-12.1	-54.6	-37.7
High	11.0	10.9	7.9	-1.2	-47.3	14.5	12.5	8.9	2.7	15.0	19.5

SOURCE: E. Kramarow, H. Lentzner, R. Rooks, J. Weeks, S. Saydah. *Health and Aging Chartbook. Health, United States,* 1999. Hyattsville, Maryland: National Center for Health Statistics. 1999: Table 23.

* Data for states with fewer than 5,000 live births for the three-year period are considered unreliable. Data for states with fewer then 1,000 live births are considered highly unreliable and are not shown.
1. Under one year of age.
2. Deaths are tabulated by race of decedent; live births are tabulated by race of mother.

NOTE: Infant mortality rates in this table are based on infant deaths from the mortality file (numerator) and live births from the natality file (denominator). Inconsistencies in reporting race for the same infant between the birth and death certificate can result in underestimated infant mortality rates for races other than White or Black. Infant mortality rates for minority population groups are available from the national linked files of live births and infant deaths.

Table 3.8. Selected Causes of Death by Race and Sex

(Age-adjusted rates; deaths per 100,000 resident population)

Sex, race, Hispanic origin, and cause of death	1950 [1]	1960 [1]	1970	1980	1985	1990	1995	1996	1997
ALL PERSONS									
All Causes	841.5	760.9	714.3	585.8	548.9	520.2	503.9	491.6	479.1
Natural Causes	766.6	695.2	636.9	519.7	493.0	465.1	451.7	440.6	429.2
Diseases of heart	307.2	286.2	253.6	202.0	181.4	152.0	138.3	134.5	130.5
Ischemic heart disease	—	—	—	149.8	126.1	102.6	89.5	86.7	82.9
Cerebrovascular diseases	88.8	79.7	66.3	40.8	32.5	27.7	26.7	26.4	25.9
Malignant neoplasms	125.4	125.8	129.8	132.8	134.4	135.0	129.9	127.9	125.6
Respiratory system	12.8	19.2	28.4	36.4	39.1	41.4	39.7	39.3	38.7
Colorectal	—	17.7	16.8	15.5	14.9	13.6	12.7	12.2	12.0
Prostate [2]	13.4	13.1	13.3	14.4	14.7	16.7	15.4	14.9	13.9
Breast [3]	22.2	22.3	23.1	22.7	23.3	23.1	21.0	20.2	19.4
Chronic obstructive pulmonary diseases	4.4	8.2	13.2	15.9	18.8	19.7	20.8	21.0	21.1
Pneumonia and influenza	26.2	28.0	22.1	12.9	13.5	14.0	12.9	12.8	12.9
Chronic liver disease and cirrhosis	8.5	10.5	14.7	12.2	9.7	8.6	7.6	7.5	7.4
Diabetes mellitus	14.3	13.6	14.1	10.1	9.7	11.7	13.3	13.6	13.5
Human immunodeficiency virus infection	—	—	—	—	—	9.8	15.6	11.1	5.8
External Causes	73.9	65.7	77.4	66.1	55.9	55.1	52.2	50.9	49.9
Unintentional injuries	57.5	49.9	53.7	42.3	34.8	32.5	30.5	30.4	30.1
Motor vehicle–related injuries	23.3	22.5	27.4	22.9	18.8	18.5	16.3	16.2	15.9
Suicide	11.0	10.6	11.8	11.4	11.5	11.5	11.2	11.0	10.6
Homicide and legal intervention	5.4	5.2	9.1	10.8	8.3	10.2	9.4	8.5	8.0
MALE									
All Causes	1 001.6	949.3	931.6	777.2	723.0	680.2	646.3	623.7	602.8
Natural Causes	—	—	—	675.5	637.9	595.8	567.0	547.2	528.0
Diseases of heart	383.8	375.5	348.5	280.4	250.1	206.7	184.9	178.8	173.1
Ischemic heart disease	—	—	—	214.8	179.6	144.0	123.9	119.3	114.2
Cerebrovascular diseases	91.9	85.4	73.2	44.9	35.5	30.2	28.9	28.5	27.9
Malignant neoplasms	130.8	143.0	157.4	165.5	166.1	166.3	156.8	153.8	150.4
Respiratory system	21.3	34.8	50.6	59.7	60.7	61.0	55.3	54.2	52.8
Colorectal	—	18.6	18.7	18.3	17.9	16.8	15.3	14.8	14.6
Prostate [2]	13.4	13.1	13.3	14.4	14.7	16.7	15.4	14.9	13.9
Chronic obstructive pulmonary diseases	6.0	13.7	23.4	26.1	28.1	27.2	26.3	25.9	26.1
Pneumonia and influenza	30.6	35.0	28.8	17.4	18.4	18.5	16.5	16.2	16.2
Chronic liver disease and cirrhosis	11.4	14.5	20.2	17.1	13.7	12.2	11.0	10.7	10.5
Diabetes mellitus	11.4	12.0	13.5	10.2	10.0	12.3	14.4	14.9	14.8
Human immunodeficiency virus infection	—	—	—	—	—	17.7	26.2	18.1	9.1
External Causes	—	—	—	101.7	85.2	84.4	79.3	76.5	74.8
Unintentional injuries	83.7	73.9	80.7	64.0	51.8	47.7	44.1	43.3	42.9
Motor vehicle–related injuries	36.4	34.5	41.1	34.3	27.3	26.3	22.7	22.3	21.7
Suicide	17.3	16.6	17.3	18.0	18.8	19.0	18.6	18.0	17.4
Homicide and legal intervention	8.4	7.9	14.9	17.4	12.8	16.3	14.7	13.3	12.5
FEMALE									
All Causes	688.4	590.6	532.5	432.6	410.3	390.6	385.2	381.0	375.7
Natural Causes	—	—	—	400.1	382.2	363.5	359.1	354.8	349.8
Diseases of heart	233.9	205.7	175.2	140.3	127.4	108.9	100.4	98.2	95.4
Ischemic heart disease	—	—	—	98.8	84.2	70.2	61.9	60.4	57.6
Cerebrovascular diseases	86.0	74.7	60.8	37.6	30.0	25.7	24.8	24.6	24.2
Malignant neoplasms	120.8	111.2	108.8	109.2	111.7	112.7	110.4	108.8	107.3
Respiratory system	4.6	5.2	10.1	18.3	22.5	26.2	27.5	27.5	27.5
Colorectal	—	16.9	15.4	13.4	12.6	11.3	10.6	10.2	10.0
Breast [3]	22.2	22.3	23.1	22.7	23.3	23.1	21.0	20.2	19.4
Chronic obstructive pulmonary diseases	2.9	3.5	5.4	8.9	12.5	14.7	17.1	17.6	17.7
Pneumonia and influenza	22.0	21.8	16.7	9.8	10.1	11.0	10.4	10.4	10.5
Chronic liver disease and cirrhosis	5.8	6.9	9.8	7.9	6.1	5.3	4.6	4.5	4.5
Diabetes mellitus	17.1	15.0	14.4	10.0	9.4	11.1	12.4	12.5	12.4
Human immunodeficiency virus infection	—	—	—	—	—	2.1	5.2	4.2	2.6
External Causes	—	—	—	32.5	28.1	27.0	26.1	26.2	25.9
Unintentional injuries	31.7	26.8	28.2	21.8	18.7	17.9	17.5	17.9	17.8
Motor vehicle–related injuries	10.7	11.0	14.4	11.8	10.5	10.7	10.0	10.2	10.2
Suicide	4.9	5.0	6.8	5.4	4.9	4.5	4.1	4.0	4.1
Homicide and legal intervention	2.5	2.6	3.7	4.5	3.9	4.2	4.0	3.6	3.3

See footnotes at end of table.

Table 3.8. Selected Causes of Death by Race and Sex—*Continued*

(Age-adjusted rates; deaths per 100,000 resident population)

Sex, race, Hispanic origin, and cause of death	1950 [1]	1960 [1]	1970	1980	1985	1990	1995	1996	1997
WHITE									
All Causes	800.4	727.0	679.6	559.4	524.9	492.8	476.9	466.8	456.5
Natural Causes	—	—	—	497.7	471.9	442.0	428.5	419.2	409.7
Diseases of heart	300.5	281.5	249.1	197.6	176.6	146.9	133.1	129.8	125.9
Ischemic heart disease	—	—	—	150.6	126.6	102.5	89.0	86.4	82.5
Cerebrovascular diseases	83.2	74.2	61.8	38.0	30.1	25.5	24.7	24.5	24.0
Malignant neoplasms	124.7	124.2	127.8	129.6	131.2	131.5	127.0	125.2	122.9
Respiratory system	13.0	19.1	28.0	35.6	38.4	40.6	39.3	38.9	38.4
Colorectal	—	17.9	16.9	15.4	14.7	13.3	12.3	11.8	11.6
Prostate [2]	13.1	12.4	12.3	13.2	13.4	15.3	14.0	13.5	12.6
Breast [3]	22.5	22.4	23.4	22.8	23.4	22.9	20.5	19.8	18.9
Chronic obstructive pulmonary diseases	4.3	8.2	13.4	16.3	19.2	20.1	21.3	21.5	21.7
Pneumonia and influenza	22.9	24.6	19.8	12.2	12.9	13.4	12.4	12.2	12.4
Chronic liver disease and cirrhosis	8.6	10.3	13.4	11.0	8.9	8.0	7.4	7.3	7.3
Diabetes mellitus	13.9	12.8	12.9	9.1	8.6	10.4	11.7	12.0	11.9
Human immunodeficiency virus infection	—	—	—	—	—	8.0	11.1	7.2	3.3
External Causes	—	—	—	61.9	53.0	50.8	48.4	47.5	46.8
Unintentional injuries	55.7	47.6	51.0	41.5	34.2	31.8	29.9	29.9	29.6
Motor vehicle–related injuries	23.1	22.3	26.9	23.4	19.1	18.6	16.4	16.3	15.9
Suicide	11.6	11.1	12.4	12.1	12.3	12.2	11.9	11.6	11.3
Homicide and legal intervention	2.6	2.7	4.7	6.9	5.4	5.9	5.5	4.9	4.7
BLACK									
All Causes	1 236.7	1 073.3	1 044.0	842.5	793.6	789.2	765.7	738.3	705.3
Natural Causes	—	—	—	740.2	713.5	701.3	685.8	662.3	632.7
Diseases of heart	379.6	334.5	307.6	255.7	240.6	213.5	198.8	191.5	185.7
Ischemic heart disease	—	—	—	150.5	130.9	113.2	103.4	99.4	96.3
Cerebrovascular diseases	150.9	140.3	114.5	68.5	55.8	48.4	45.0	44.2	42.5
Malignant neoplasms	129.1	142.3	156.7	172.1	176.6	182.0	171.6	167.8	165.2
Respiratory system	10.4	20.3	33.5	46.5	50.3	54.0	49.9	48.9	47.9
Colorectal	—	15.2	16.6	16.9	17.9	17.9	17.3	16.8	16.8
Prostate [2]	16.9	22.2	25.4	29.1	31.2	35.3	34.0	33.8	31.4
Breast [3]	19.3	21.3	21.5	23.3	25.5	27.5	27.5	26.5	26.7
Chronic obstructive pulmonary diseases	—	—	—	12.5	15.3	16.9	17.6	17.8	17.4
Pneumonia and influenza	57.0	56.4	40.4	19.2	18.8	19.8	17.8	17.8	17.2
Chronic liver disease and cirrhosis	7.2	11.7	24.8	21.6	16.3	13.7	9.9	9.2	8.7
Diabetes mellitus	17.2	22.0	26.5	20.3	20.1	24.8	28.5	28.8	28.9
Human immunodeficiency virus infection	—	—	—	—	—	25.7	51.8	41.4	24.9
External Causes	—	—	—	101.2	80.1	87.8	79.8	76.0	72.6
Unintentional injuries	70.9	66.4	74.4	51.2	42.3	39.7	37.4	36.7	36.1
Motor vehicle–related injuries	24.7	23.4	30.6	19.7	17.4	18.4	16.6	16.7	16.8
Suicide	4.2	4.7	6.1	6.4	6.4	7.0	6.9	6.6	6.3
Homicide and legal intervention	30.5	27.4	46.1	40.6	29.2	39.5	33.4	30.6	28.1
AMERICAN INDIAN OR ALASKA NATIVE									
All Causes	—	—	—	564.1	468.2	445.1	468.5	456.7	465.3
Natural Causes	—	—	—	436.5	375.1	360.3	385.4	374.5	381.1
Diseases of heart	—	—	—	131.2	119.6	107.1	104.5	100.8	102.6
Ischemic heart disease	—	—	—	87.4	77.3	66.6	65.4	63.8	64.2
Cerebrovascular diseases	—	—	—	26.6	22.5	19.3	21.6	21.1	19.9
Malignant neoplasms	—	—	—	70.6	72.0	75.0	80.8	84.9	86.6
Respiratory system	—	—	—	15.0	18.8	20.5	23.7	24.4	25.3
Colorectal	—	—	—	5.6	6.3	6.4	7.6	8.5	9.1
Prostate [2]	—	—	—	9.6	8.9	7.7	8.8	9.8	8.6
Breast [3]	—	—	—	8.1	8.0	10.0	10.4	12.7	9.4
Chronic obstructive pulmonary diseases	—	—	—	7.5	9.8	12.8	13.8	12.6	15.3
Pneumonia and influenza	—	—	—	19.4	14.9	15.2	14.2	14.0	13.4
Chronic liver disease and cirrhosis	—	—	—	38.6	23.6	19.8	24.3	20.7	20.6
Diabetes mellitus	—	—	—	20.0	18.7	20.8	27.3	27.8	30.4
Human immunodeficiency virus infection	—	—	—	—	—	1.8	7.0	4.2	2.4
External Causes	—	—	—	127.6	93.1	84.8	83.0	82.1	84.3
Unintentional injuries	—	—	—	95.1	66.2	59.0	56.7	57.6	58.5
Motor vehicle–related injuries	—	—	—	54.4	36.3	33.2	33.1	34.0	32.3
Suicide	—	—	—	12.8	12.1	12.4	12.2	13.0	12.9
Homicide and legal intervention	—	—	—	16.0	12.2	11.1	11.9	10.1	11.0

See footnotes at end of table.

Table 3.8. Selected Causes of Death by Race and Sex—*Continued*

(Age-adjusted rates; deaths per 100,000 resident population)

Sex, race, Hispanic origin, and cause of death	1950[1]	1960[1]	1970	1980	1985	1990	1995	1996	1997
ASIAN OR PACIFIC ISLANDER									
All Causes	—	—	—	315.6	305.7	297.6	298.9	277.4	274.8
Natural Causes	—	—	—	280.7	274.4	266.7	269.2	250.3	247.0
Diseases of heart	—	—	—	93.9	88.6	78.5	78.9	71.7	69.8
Ischemic heart disease	—	—	—	67.5	58.8	49.7	49.3	44.8	43.5
Cerebrovascular diseases	—	—	—	29.0	25.5	25.0	25.8	23.9	24.4
Malignant neoplasms	—	—	—	77.2	80.2	79.8	81.1	76.3	75.4
Respiratory system	—	—	—	18.1	17.2	18.3	18.5	17.4	17.4
Colorectal	—	—	—	9.3	9.6	8.3	8.2	7.7	7.6
Prostate[2]	—	—	—	4.0	5.9	6.9	7.4	5.8	5.3
Breast[3]	—	—	—	9.2	9.6	10.0	11.0	8.9	9.2
Chronic obstructive pulmonary diseases	—	—	—	5.9	8.4	8.7	9.0	8.6	8.6
Pneumonia and influenza	—	—	—	9.1	9.1	10.4	10.8	9.9	10.1
Chronic liver disease and cirrhosis	—	—	—	4.5	4.2	3.7	2.7	2.6	2.4
Diabetes mellitus	—	—	—	6.9	6.1	7.4	9.2	8.8	9.3
Human immunodeficiency virus infection	—	—	—	—	—	2.1	3.1	2.2	0.9
External Causes	—	—	—	34.9	31.4	30.9	29.7	27.1	27.7
Unintentional injuries	—	—	—	21.7	20.1	19.3	17.1	16.1	16.7
Motor vehicle–related injuries	—	—	—	12.6	12.0	12.5	10.8	9.5	9.7
Suicide	—	—	—	6.7	6.4	6.0	6.6	6.0	6.2
Homicide and legal intervention	—	—	—	5.6	4.2	5.2	5.4	4.6	4.3
HISPANIC[4]									
All Causes	—	—	—	—	397.4	400.2	386.8	365.9	350.3
Natural Causes	—	—	—	—	342.7	342.4	334.0	316.9	304.5
Diseases of heart	—	—	—	—	116.0	102.8	92.1	88.6	86.8
Ischemic heart disease	—	—	—	—	77.8	68.0	60.1	58.2	56.8
Cerebrovascular diseases	—	—	—	—	23.8	21.0	20.3	19.5	19.4
Malignant neoplasms	—	—	—	—	75.8	82.4	79.7	77.8	76.4
Respiratory system	—	—	—	—	14.3	16.9	15.6	15.4	15.2
Colorectal	—	—	—	—	7.5	8.2	7.6	7.3	7.5
Prostate[2]	—	—	—	—	8.5	9.5	10.9	9.9	8.6
Breast[3]	—	—	—	—	11.8	14.1	12.7	12.8	12.6
Chronic obstructive pulmonary diseases	—	—	—	—	8.2	8.7	9.4	8.9	8.7
Pneumonia and influenza	—	—	—	—	12.0	11.5	9.9	9.7	10.0
Chronic liver disease and cirrhosis	—	—	—	—	16.3	14.2	12.9	12.6	12.0
Diabetes mellitus	—	—	—	—	12.8	15.7	19.3	18.8	18.7
Human immunodeficiency virus infection	—	—	—	—	—	15.5	23.9	16.3	8.2
External Causes	—	—	—	—	54.7	57.8	52.9	49.0	45.8
Unintentional injuries	—	—	—	—	31.8	32.2	29.8	29.0	27.7
Motor vehicle–related injuries	—	—	—	—	16.9	19.3	16.6	16.1	15.2
Suicide	—	—	—	—	6.1	7.3	7.2	6.7	6.1
Homicide and legal intervention	—	—	—	—	15.7	17.7	15.0	12.4	11.1
WHITE, NON-HISPANIC[4]									
All Causes	—	—	—	—	510.7	493.1	475.2	466.7	458.5
Natural Causes	—	—	—	—	460.7	444.2	428.8	420.7	412.6
Diseases of heart	—	—	—	—	173.0	148.2	134.1	131.0	127.5
Ischemic heart disease	—	—	—	—	125.4	103.7	89.8	87.4	83.6
Cerebrovascular diseases	—	—	—	—	29.2	25.7	24.6	24.4	24.0
Malignant neoplasms	—	—	—	—	128.3	134.2	129.2	127.6	125.3
Respiratory system	—	—	—	—	38.0	41.9	40.5	40.2	39.8
Colorectal	—	—	—	—	14.4	13.6	12.5	12.1	11.8
Prostate[2]	—	—	—	—	13.0	15.6	14.1	13.6	12.7
Breast[3]	—	—	—	—	23.3	23.5	20.9	20.1	19.2
Chronic obstructive pulmonary diseases	—	—	—	—	19.7	20.7	21.8	22.1	22.4
Pneumonia and influenza	—	—	—	—	13.2	13.3	12.3	12.2	12.4
Chronic liver disease and cirrhosis	—	—	—	—	8.5	7.5	6.8	6.7	6.7
Diabetes mellitus	—	—	—	—	8.0	10.1	11.2	11.5	11.3
Human immunodeficiency virus infection	—	—	—	—	—	7.0	9.4	6.0	2.6
External Causes	—	—	—	—	50.0	48.9	46.4	46.0	45.9
Unintentional injuries	—	—	—	—	31.9	31.3	29.3	29.3	29.4
Motor vehicle–related injuries	—	—	—	—	17.8	18.4	16.0	16.0	15.8
Suicide	—	—	—	—	12.7	12.7	12.2	12.0	11.8
Homicide and legal intervention	—	—	—	—	4.5	4.2	3.8	3.5	3.5

SOURCE: E. Kramarow, H. Lentzner, R. Rooks, J. Weeks, S. Saydah. *Health and Aging Chartbook. Health, United States, 1999.* Hyattsville, Maryland: National Center for Health Statistics. 1999: Table 30.

— Data not available.

1. Includes deaths of persons who were not residents of the 50 states and the District of Columbia.
2. Male only.
3. Female only.
4. Excludes data from states lacking a Hispanic-origin item on their death certificates. See Appendix I, of *Health, United States, 1999,* National Vital Statistics System.

NOTE: For data years shown, categories for cause of death are based on the current revision of *International Classification of Diseases.* Categories for coding human immunodeficiency virus infection deaths were introduced in the United States in 1987. Consistency of race identification between the death certificate (source of data for numerator of death rates) and data from the Census Bureau (denominator) is high for individual White and Black persons; however, persons identified as American Indian, Asian, or Hispanic origin in data from the Census Bureau are sometimes misreported as White or non- Hispanic on the death certificate, causing death rates to be underestimated by 22–30 percent for American Indians, about 12 percent for Asians, and about 7 percent for persons of Hispanic origin. (P.D. Sorlie, E. Rogot, and N.J. Johnson : Validity of Demographic Characteristics on the Death Certificate, *Epidemiology* 3, no. 2 (1992): 181-184. See Appendix II of *Health, United States, 1999.* for age-adjustment procedure.

Table 3.9. Age-Adjusted Death Rates for American Indians and Alaska Natives: 1992–1994

(Rate per 100,000 population)

Cause of death	American Indian and Alaskan Native		U.S. all races rate 1993	U.S. white rate 1993	Ratio [1] of American Indian and Alaska Native to:	
	Actual	Adjusted			U.S. all races	U.S. white
All causes	601.3	690.4	513.3	485.1	1.3	1.4
Major cardiovascular diseases	167.0	194.6	181.8	173.9	1.1	1.1
Diseases of the heart	133.4	157.6	145.3	139.9	1.1	1.1
Cerebrovascular diseases	25.1	27.8	26.5	24.5	1.0	1.1
Atherosclerosis	2.2	2.3	2.4	2.4	1.0	1.0
Hypertension	1.8	1.8	2.2	1.7	0.8	1.1
Malignant neoplasms	97.5	112.2	132.6	129.4	0.8	0.9
Accidents	82.3	94.5	30.3	29.6	3.1	3.2
Motor vehicle	45.5	53.3	16.0	16.1	3.3	3.3
All other	36.9	41.2	14.4	13.5	2.9	3.1
Diabetes mellitus	35.1	41.1	12.4	11.0	3.3	3.7
Chronic liver disease and cirrhosis	30.7	35.0	7.9	7.6	4.4	4.6
Pneumonia and influenza	20.1	21.7	13.5	12.9	1.6	1.7
Suicide	17.3	19.2	11.3	12.0	1.7	1.6
Chronic obstructive pulmonary diseases and allied conditions	15.7	17.4	21.4	21.9	0.8	0.8
Homicide	13.4	15.1	10.7	6.0	1.4	2.5
Human immunodeficiency virus (HIV) infection	3.3	3.9	13.8	10.5	0.3	0.4
Tuberculosis, all forms	2.3	2.3	0.4	0.3	5.3	7.0

SOURCE: Indian Health Service, *Trends in Indian Health* (Rockville, Md.: 1997): Table 4.11.

1. Adjusted to compensate for miscoding of American Indian race on death certificate.

Table 3.10. All Injury and Adverse Event–Related Deaths and Rates: 1996

(Rate per 100,000)

Age Group	Total		Male		Female	
	Deaths	Rate	Deaths	Rate	Deaths	Rate
Under 5 years	3 815	19.8	2 175	22.0	1 640	17.4
5–9 years	1 794	9.2	1 077	10.8	717	7.6
10–14 years	2 503	13.2	1 679	17.3	824	8.9
15–19 years	11 663	62.5	8 903	92.6	2 760	30.5
20–24 years	13 419	76.4	11 057	122.9	2 362	27.6
25–29 years	12 180	64.1	9 633	101.0	2 547	26.9
30–34 years	12 697	59.4	9 772	91.7	2 925	27.3
35–39 years	13 699	60.7	10 346	91.9	3 353	29.6
40–44 years	12 366	59.4	9 353	90.7	3 013	28.7
45–49 years	9 989	54.2	7 437	82.1	2 552	27.2
50–54 years	7 092	50.9	5 171	76.3	1 921	26.8
55–59 years	5 663	49.8	4 129	75.7	1 534	26.0
60–64 years	5 188	51.9	3 624	76.9	1 564	29.6
65–69 years	5 741	58.0	3 894	86.4	1 847	34.3
70–74 years	6 545	74.6	4 196	109.9	2 349	47.4
75–79 years	7 030	102.3	4 191	148.6	2 839	70.1
80–84 years	7 360	161.5	3 956	237.5	3 404	117.7
85 years and over	11 324	301.0	4 616	431.5	6 708	249.2
Unknown	230		183		47	
Total	150 298	56.7	105 392	81.2	44 906	33.2
Age-adjusted rate		50.8		76.4		26.0

SOURCE: Centers for Disease Control and Prevention, National Center for Health Statistics, National Center for Injury Prevention and Control. National Injury Mortality Statistics (1997–1999).

Table 3.11. All Injury and Adverse Event–Related Deaths and Rates: 1997

(Rate per 100,000)

Age Group	Total		Male		Female	
	Deaths	Rate	Deaths	Rate	Deaths	Rate
Under 5 years	3 559	18.6	2 069	21.1	1 490	15.9
5–9 years	1 728	8.8	1 041	10.3	687	7.1
10–14 years	2 455	12.9	1 633	16.7	822	8.8
15–19 years	11 169	58.6	8 422	85.7	2 747	29.7
20–24 years	12 890	73.6	10 519	117.2	2 371	27.8
25–29 years	11 860	62.9	9 439	99.7	2 421	25.8
30–34 years	12 201	58.8	9 438	91.3	2 763	26.6
35–39 years	13 474	59.6	10 149	89.9	3 325	29.3
40–44 years	12 762	59.7	9 604	90.6	3 158	29.3
45–49 years	10 345	56.0	7 715	85.0	2 630	28.0
50–54 years	7 521	49.6	5 434	73.6	2 087	26.8
55–59 years	6 012	51.1	4 302	76.2	1 710	28.0
60–64 years	5 116	50.9	3 620	76.3	1 496	28.2
65–69 years	5 484	56.2	3 717	83.3	1 767	33.3
70–74 years	6 426	73.6	4 110	108.0	2 316	47.0
75–79 years	7 353	104.1	4 389	150.6	2 964	71.5
80–84 years	7 438	160.2	4 017	234.4	3 421	116.8
85 years and over	11 713	302.6	4 797	431.4	6 916	250.6
Unknown	185		154		31	
Total	149 691	55.9	104 569	79.8	45 122	33.0
Age-adjusted rate		49.8		74.7		25.8

SOURCE: Centers for Disease Control and Prevention, National Center for Health Statistics, National Center for Injury Prevention and Control. National Injury Mortality Statistics (1997–1999).

Table 3.12. Deaths from Injuries: 1998

(Rate per 100,000 population)

Cause of death	Total		Firearms related	
	Number	Age-adjusted rate	Number	Age-adjusted rate
Total [1]	146 941	48.3		
Motor vehicle	43 645	15.7	30 708	11.3
Pedestrian	6 319	2.1		
Occupants of vehicles	24 783	9.0		
Suicide	30 575	10.4	17 424	5.8
Homicide	17 893	7.2	11 798	4.9
Poisoning	18 392	6.3		
Suffocation	11 095	3.5		
Falls	13 301	2.5		
Drownings/submersion	5 096	1.9		
Fire/flames	3 691	1.2		

SOURCE: Compiled from tables provided by the Centers for Disease Control and Prevention, National Center for Injury Prevention and Control.

1. Total injuries do not include adverse event–related injuries such as those associated with medical care and drugs.

NOTE: Each type of injury includes both intentional and unintentional injuries.

Table 3.13. Transportation Injuries and Deaths by Vehicle Miles

	1975	1980	1985	1990	1991	1992	1993	1994	1995	1996
PASSENGER CAR OCCUPANT SAFETY DATA										
Fatalities	25 929	27 449	23 212	24 092	22 385	21 387	*21 566	*21 997	*22 423	22 416
Injuries	—	—	—	2 376 000	2 235 000	2 232 000	*2 265 000	*2 364 000	*2 469 000	2 478 000
Crashes	—	—	—	5 560 000	5 178 000	5 043 000	*5 045 000	*5 399 000	*5 523 000	5 659 000
Vehicle miles (billions)	1 030	—	—	1 425	1 411	1 436	*1 445	*1 459	*1 478	1 497
Rates per 100 million vehicle miles										
Fatality	2.5	2.5	1.9	1.7	1.6	1.5	*1.5	*1.5	*1.5	1.5
Injury	—	—	—	167	158	155	*157	*162	*167	166
Crash	—	—	—	390	367	351	*349	*370	*374	378
TRUCK OCCUPANT SAFETY DATA										
Total fatalities	5 817	8 748	7 666	9 306	9 052	8 683	9 116	9 574	*10 216	**10 522
Light	4 856	7 486	6 689	8 601	8 391	8 098	8 511	8 904	*9 568	**9 901
Large	961	1 262	977	705	661	585	605	670	*648	**621
Total injuries	—	—	—	547 000	591 000	579 000	*633 000	*661 000	752 000	**801 000
Light	—	—	—	505 000	563 000	545 000	601 000	631 000	*722 000	**768 000
Large	—	—	—	42 000	28 000	34 000	32 000	30 000	*30 000	**33 000
Total crashes	—	—	—	2 524 000	2 519 000	2 554 000	2 776 000	3 008 000	*3 071 000	**3293000
Light	—	—	—	2 152 000	2 200 000	2 191 000	2 395 000	2 564 000	*2 709 000	**2914000
Large	—	—	—	372 000	319 000	363 000	381 000	444 000	*362 000	**379 000
Vehicle miles (billions)										
Light	204	295	388	555	596	643	675	712	750	786
Large	81	108	127	150	151	153	160	170	*178	**183
Rates per 100 million vehicle miles										
Fatality										
Light	2.4	2.5	1.7	1.6	1.4	1.3	1.3	1.3	1.3	1.3
Large	1.2	1.2	0.8	0.5	0.4	0.4	0.4	0.4	*0.4	**0.3
Injury										
Light	—	—	—	91.0	95.0	85.0	89.0	89.0	*96.0	**98.0
Large	—	—	—	28	19	22	20	18	*17	16
Crash										
Light	—	—	—	388	369	341	355	360	*361	**371
Large	—	—	—	248	212	238	238	261	*203	**207
MOTORCYCLE RIDER SAFETY DATA										
Fatalities	3 189	5 144	4 564	3 244	2 806	2 395	*2 449	*2 320	*2 227	2 160
Injuries	—	—	—	84 000	80 000	65 000	*59 000	*57 000	*57 000	**56 000
Crashes	—	—	—	103 000	106 000	72 000	*72 000	*67 000	*63 000	**67 000
Vehicle miles (billions)	5.6	10.2	9.1	9.6	9.2	9.6	9.9	10.2	*9.8	9.9
Rates per 100 million vehicle miles										
Fatality	57	50	50	34	31	25	25	23	23	22
Injury [1]	—	—	—	880	870	680	*600	*560	*580	**570
Crash [1]	—	—	—	1 080	1 160	750	*730	*650	*640	680
RECREATIONAL BOATING SAFETY DATA, ALCOHOL INVOLVEMENT, AND PROPERTY DAMAGE										
Fatalities	1 466	1 360	1 116	865	924	816	800	784	*829	**709
Injuries	2 136	2 650	2 757	3 822	3 967	3 683	*3 559	4 084	*4 141	**4 442
Accidents	6 308	5 513	6 237	6 411	6 573	6 048	6 335	6 906	*8 019	8 026
Vessels involved	8 002	6 954	8 305	8 591	8 821	8 206	8 688	9 722	*11 534	11 306
Numbered boats [2] (millions)	7.3	8.6	9.6	11.0	11.1	11.1	11.3	11.4	11.7	11.9
Rates per 100,000 numbered boats										
Fatality	20.1	15.8	11.6	7.8	8.3	7.3	7.1	6.9	*7.1	6.0
Injury	29.3	30.8	28.7	34.7	35.7	33.2	31.5	35.8	*35.4	37.3
Accident	86.0	64.0	65.0	58.0	60.0	55.0	56.0	61.0	*69.0	67.0
Accident reports with alcohol involvement	—	—	279	568	513	504	381	389	*472	601
Property damage (millions of current dollars)	10.4	16.4	20.0	23.8	24.8	a34.8	20.2	25.2	*21.5	22.8
RAILROAD SYSTEM SAFETY DATA AND PROPERTY DAMAGE [3]										
Fatalities	575	584	454	599	586	591	653	611	567	551
Injuries	50 138	58 696	31 617	22 736	21 374	19 408	17 284	14 850	12 546	10 948
Accidents	8 041	8 205	3 275	2 679	2 658	2 359	2 611	2 504	2 459	2 443
Train miles (millions)	755	718	571	609	577	864	614	655	670	671
Rates per 100 million train miles										
Fatality	76	81	80	98	102	99	106	93	85	82
Injury	6 640	8 180	5 540	3 740	3 700	3 270	2 820	2 270	1 870	1 630
Accident	1 070	1 140	570	470	460	400	430	380	370	360
Property damage (millions of current dollars)	177.4	267.4	179.3	198.7	209.7	118.9	180.6	168.7	189.2	212.3

See footnotes at end of table.

Table 3.13. Transportation Injuries and Deaths by Vehicle Miles—*Continued*

	1975	1980	1985	1990	1991	1992	1993	1994	1995	1996
U.S. AIR CARRIER SAFETY DATA [4]										
Fatalities	124	1	526	*39	b*50	*33	*1	*239	*168	380
Serious injuries	81	19	30	*39	*26	*13	*16	*35	*25	*77
Accidents	37	19	21	*24	*26	*18	*23	*23	*36	38
Fatal	3	1	7	*6	*4	*4	*1	*4	*3	5
Aircraft miles (millions)	*2 478	2 924	3 631	*4 948	*4 825	*5 055	*5 249	*5 478	*5 651	5 843
Rates per 100 million aircraft miles										
Fatality	5	0.034	14	*0.79	*1.04	*0.65	*0.019	*4.4	*3.0	6.5
Serious injury	3.3	0.65	0.83	*0.79	*0.54	*0.26	*0.3	*0.64	*0.44	1.3
Accidents	1.5	0.65	0.58	*0.49	*0.54	*0.36	*0.44	*0.42	*0.64	0.65
Fatal	0.081	0.034	0.19	*0.12	*0.083	*0.079	*0.019	*0.073	*0.053	0.086
Aircraft departures (thousands) [5]	—	5 479	6 307	*8 092	*7 815	*7 881	*8 073	*8 242	*8 465	8 469
Rates per 100,000 aircraft departures										
Fatality	—	0.018	8.3	*0.48	*0.64	*0.42	*0.012	*2.9	*2	4.5
Serious injury	—	0.35	0.48	*0.48	*0.33	*0.16	*0.2	*0.42	*0.3	0.91
Accidents	—	0.35	0.33	*0.3	*0.33	*0.23	*0.28	*0.28	*0.43	0.45
Fatal	—	0.018	*0.11	*0.74	*0.051	*0.051	*0.012	*0.049	*0.035	0.059
Flight hours (thousands)	5 607	7 067	*8 710	*12 150	*11 781	*12 360	*12 706	*13 122	*13 124	13 510
Rates per 100,000 flight hours										
Fatality	2.2	0.014	6	*0.32	*0.42	*0.27	*0.008	*1.8	*1.3	2.80
Serious injury	1.4	0.27	0.34	*0.32	*0.22	*0.11	*0.13	*0.27	*0.19	0.57
Accidents	0.66	0.27	0.24	*0.2	*0.22	*0.15	*0.18	*0.18	*0.27	0.28
Fatal	0.054	0.014	0.08	*0.049	*0.034	*0.032	*0.008	*0.03	*0.023	0.037
BUS OCCUPANT SAFETY DATA [6]										
Fatalities	53	46	57	32	31	28	18	18	33	21
Injuries	—	—	—	33 000	21 000	20 000	17 000	* 16 000	*19 000	**20 000
Crashes	—	—	—	60 000	56 000	49 000	51 000	*56 000	*58 000	**57 000
Vehicle miles (billions)	6.1	6.1	4.5	5.7	5.8	5.8	6.1	*6.4	*6.4	**6.5
Rates per 100 million vehicle miles										
Fatality	0.9	0.8	1.3	0.3	0.5	0.5	0.3	*0.3	*0.5	**0.3
Injury	—	—	—	580	370	350	280	*300	*500	**310
Crash	—	—	—	1 050	980	860	840	*880	*910	**870

SOURCE: U.S. Department of Transportation, Bureau of Transportation Statistics Annual Report 1998 BTS98-S-01, Washington, D.C.: 1998: Tables 3-20, 3-22, 3-21, 3-40, 3-36, 3-9, 3-23.

* Revised
** Preliminary
— Data are nonexistent.
a. Includes $1.1 million damage due to a boat fire.
b. Does not include the 12 persons killed aboard the Skywest commuter aircraft when it and a US Air airliner collided.
1. U.S. Department of Transportation/ National Highway Traffic Safety Administration (DOT/NHTSA) rounds injury and crash data to the nearest thousand before publishing them, but calculates injury and crash rates using the unrounded data. U.S. DOT/NHTSA also calculates fatality, injury, and crash rates using vehicle miles expressed to a higher level of precision than shown here. Thus, the injury and crash rates shown in this table may differ slightly from the rates that would be calculated from the data in this table. U.S. DOT/ Bureau of Transportation Statistics (BTS) has rounded vehicle miles to the nearest 100 million. U.S. DOT/BTS has rounded fatality, injury, and crash rates to two significant digits (except for the crash rates for 1990 and 1991). The fatality rates, expressed to two significant digits, are not affected by rounding the vehicle-miles.
2. In 1994, the U.S. Coast Guard changed its methodology for calculating the number of recreational boats; from 1975 to present, the figures cited represent the number of numbered boats, not an estimate, as previously reported. Accident, fatality, and injury rates have been recalculated accordingly.
3. Fatalities and injuries from train accidents, train incidents, and nontrain incidents; excludes highway-rail grade crossing accidents. Train miles include Class I Rail, Group II Rail, and Other Rail. A train mile is the movement of a train (which can consist of many cars) the distance of one mile. Caution should be used when comparing train miles to vehicle miles.
4. Air carriers operating under 14 CFR 121, scheduled and nonscheduled service. Includes all scheduled and nonscheduled service accidents involving all deregulated cargo carriers and commercial operators of large aircraft when those accidents occurred during 14 CFR 121 operations. Since March 20, 1997, includes aircraft with 10 or more seats formerly operated under 14 CFR 135. This change makes it difficult to compare 14 CFR Part 121 and 14 CFR Part 135 accident statistics with previous years' data.
5. Prior to 1978, departure data is available for 14 CFR 121 scheduled service only.
6. Bus includes school, transit, and intercity buses.

Table 3.14. Deaths from Firearms

Year	All races			White			Black		
	Both sexes	Male	Female	Both sexes	Male	Female	Both sexes	Male	Female
NUMBER									
1979	33 019	27 476	5 543	24 234	20 039	4 195	8 304	7 031	1 273
1980	33 780	28 322	5 458	24 849	20 714	4 135	8 505	7 265	1 240
1981	34 050	28 343	5 707	25 237	20 846	4 391	8 324	7 109	1 215
1982	32 957	27 517	5 440	25 071	20 710	4 361	7 415	6 410	1 005
1983	31 099	25 945	5 154	24 038	19 911	4 127	6 589	5 647	942
1984	31 331	26 229	5 102	24 419	20 356	4 063	6 449	5 494	955
1985	31 566	26 382	5 184	24 507	20 389	4 118	6 565	5 584	981
1986	33 373	28 084	5 289	25 339	21 240	4 099	7 494	6 413	1 081
1987	32 895	27 569	5 326	24 789	20 687	4 102	7 586	6 452	1 134
1988	33 989	28 674	5 315	24 892	20 884	4 008	8 475	7 272	1 203
1989	34 776	29 596	5 180	25 023	21 149	3 874	9 077	7 904	1 173
1990	37 155	31 736	5 419	26 299	22 249	4 050	10 175	8 922	1 253
1991	38 317	32 882	5 435	26 455	22 448	4 007	11 025	9 733	1 292
1992	37 776	32 425	5 351	26 120	22 208	3 912	10 906	9 581	1 325
1993	39 595	33 711	5 884	26 948	22 680	4 268	11 763	10 310	1 453
1994	38 505	33 021	5 484	26 403	22 408	3 995	11 223	9 880	1 343
1995	35 957	30 724	5 233	25 438	21 510	3 928	9 643	8 494	1 149
1996	34 040	29 183	4 857	24 114	20 511	3 603	9 175	8 050	1 125
1997	32 436	27 756	4 680	23 270	19 673	3 597	8 389	7 430	959
RATE (PER 100,000 POPULATION)									
1979	14.7	25.2	4.8	12.5	21.2	4.2	31.6	56.5	9.2
1980	14.9	25.7	4.7	12.8	21.8	4.1	31.9	57.7	8.8
1981	14.8	25.4	4.8	12.8	21.7	4.4	30.7	55.4	8.5
1982	14.2	24.4	4.6	12.7	21.4	4.3	27.0	49.3	6.9
1983	13.3	22.8	4.3	12.1	20.5	4.0	23.6	42.9	6.4
1984	13.3	22.9	4.2	12.2	20.8	4.0	22.9	41.2	6.4
1985	13.3	22.8	4.2	12.1	20.7	4.0	23.0	41.3	6.5
1986	13.9	24.0	4.3	12.5	21.4	3.9	25.9	46.9	7.1
1987	13.6	23.4	4.3	12.1	20.7	3.9	25.9	46.5	7.3
1988	13.9	24.1	4.2	12.1	20.7	3.8	28.5	51.7	7.7
1989	14.1	24.6	4.1	12.1	20.8	3.7	30.1	55.4	7.4
1990	14.9	26.2	4.3	12.6	21.8	3.8	33.4	61.9	7.8
1991	15.2	26.7	4.2	12.5	21.7	3.7	35.4	66.0	7.9
1992	14.8	26.0	4.1	12.3	21.3	3.6	34.5	63.9	8.0
1993	15.4	26.8	4.5	12.5	21.5	3.9	36.6	67.6	8.6
1994	14.8	26.0	4.1	12.2	21.1	3.6	34.4	63.8	7.8
1995	13.7	23.9	3.9	11.7	20.1	3.5	29.1	54.0	6.6
1996	12.8	22.5	3.6	11.0	19.0	3.2	27.4	50.6	6.4
1997	12.1	21.2	3.4	10.5	18.1	3.2	24.7	46.1	5.4
AGE-ADJUSTED RATE (PER 100,000 POPULATION) [1]									
1979	14.6	24.9	4.9	12.2	20.6	4.3	33.6	61.5	9.5
1980	14.8	25.3	4.8	12.4	21.1	4.2	33.5	61.8	9.1
1981	14.6	24.9	4.9	12.5	21.0	4.4	31.9	58.6	8.7
1982	13.9	23.8	4.6	12.2	20.5	4.3	27.8	51.7	7.1
1983	12.9	22.1	4.3	11.5	19.4	4.0	24.2	44.6	6.5
1984	12.8	22.0	4.2	11.6	19.6	3.9	23.2	42.6	6.5
1985	12.7	21.8	4.2	11.4	19.4	3.9	23.2	42.2	6.5
1986	13.3	22.9	4.3	11.7	19.9	3.9	25.8	47.1	7.0
1987	13.0	22.3	4.2	11.3	19.2	3.8	25.7	46.4	7.3
1988	13.4	23.0	4.2	11.3	19.3	3.7	28.2	51.0	7.6
1989	13.7	23.7	4.1	11.4	19.5	3.6	30.0	54.9	7.4
1990	14.6	25.4	4.2	11.9	20.5	3.7	33.4	61.5	7.8
1991	15.2	26.4	4.2	12.0	20.7	3.7	35.9	66.4	8.0
1992	14.9	25.9	4.1	11.8	20.4	3.6	35.1	64.5	8.0
1993	15.6	26.9	4.6	12.2	20.7	3.9	37.6	68.8	8.8
1994	15.1	26.2	4.2	11.9	20.4	3.6	35.5	65.1	8.0
1995	13.9	24.1	4.0	11.3	19.3	3.5	30.3	55.6	6.8
1996	12.9	22.4	3.6	10.5	18.0	3.1	28.5	52.0	6.5
1997	12.2	21.1	3.4	10.0	17.1	3.1	25.7	47.4	5.6

SOURCE: D.L. Hoyert, K.D. Kochanek, S.L. Murphy. "Deaths: Final Data for 1997." *National Vital Statistics Reports;* vol. 47 no. 19. Hyattsville, Maryland: National Center for Health Statistics. 1999: Table 18.

1. For method of compuation, see Technical Notes of "Deaths: Final Data for 1997."

Table 3.15. Sports-Related Injuries: 1994 and 1998

(Injuries related to specified sport products treated in emergency rooms; sorted by total number of injuries; rate per 100,000 population)

Sport products	Estimated total number of injuries	Age						Sex		Disposition	
		Total	Under 4 years	5 to 14 years	15 to 24 years	26 to 64 years	65 years and over	Male	Female	Treated and released	Hospital and DOA
1994											
Basketball	716 114	275.1	13.4	584.0	955.3	111.6	3.2	468.3	90.8	272.9	1.8
Bicycles and accessories	604 455	232.2	247.8	908.2	243.2	87.5	28.2	333.7	135.3	223.3	8.6
Football	424 622	163.1	5.0	484.7	557.1	30.4	1.3	316.0	17.1	160.8	2.2
Baseball/ softball	404 364	155.3	45.0	410.7	294.4	100.1	3.3	219.0	94.5	153.4	1.7
Playground equipment	266 810	102.5	386.1	468.7	16.4	5.9	1.6	112.5	92.9	99.5	2.9
Soccer	162 115	62.3	2.7	190.6	180.7	18.5	0.6	86.4	39.1	61.4	0.8
Exercise equipment	155 231	59.6	45.2	68.8	134.6	49.6	16.6	76.1	43.9	58.5	1.0
Skating	146 082	56.1	15.6	226.8	57.3	27.1	2.6	44.4	67.3	54.8	1.3
ATV's, mopeds, minibikes	125 136	48.1	14.5	111.7	116.8	27.0	6.5	78.8	18.7	45.1	3.0
Swimming	115 139	44.2	62.4	128.8	63.3	21.1	10.1	52.4	36.4	42.5	1.7
Volleyball	97 523	37.5	2.0	52.4	111.4	27.7	0.6	35.5	39.3	37.2	0.2
Miscellaneous ball games	90 252	34.7	18.4	126.4	63.4	11.9	1.1	46.0	23.9	34.2	0.3
Hockey	81 885	31.5	5.4	85.1	81.9	14.4	0.3	53.6	10.3	30.9	0.5
In-line skating	75 994	29.2	2.3	115.6	40.4	12.9	0.7	35.1	23.6	28.3	0.8
Horseback riding	71 162	27.3	7.9	38.7	41.0	29.4	3.0	23.2	31.3	25.1	2.2
Trampolines	52 892	20.3	27.7	93.5	20.6	3.6	0.1	20.7	19.9	19.8	0.5
Skateboards	25 486	9.8	7.3	37.5	24.0	1.0	*	16.7	3.2	9.7	0.1
Track and field	18 774	7.2	*	24.3	24.2	0.5	1.0	8.2	6.3	7.1	0.1
1998											
Basketball	631 186	233.5	18.9	508.0	787.5	96.0	2.1	390.9	83.1	230.9	2.3
Bicycles	597 284	221.0	217.9	819.7	248.0	93.1	33.9	324.7	121.5	210.7	9.8
Football	355 247	131.4	5.0	407.8	411.8	29.0	1.2	254.0	14.1	128.4	2.9
Baseball/ softball	312 821	115.7	45.3	297.3	220.4	74.5	2.8	163.8	69.8	114.0	1.6
Playground equipment	248 372	91.9	346.8	426.0	16.4	6.3	2.3	101.0	83.1	88.2	3.5
Exercise equipment	215 831	79.8	51.9	84.1	151.5	74.2	36.1	95.2	65.1	76.7	2.9
Soccer	169 734	62.8	4.1	198.0	171.3	19.4	1.3	81.9	44.6	61.5	1.3
ATV's, mopeds, minibikes	145 258	53.7	13.2	114.3	133.1	33.5	4.0	88.4	20.6	49.1	4.5
Swimming	137 089	50.7	71.9	146.1	63.3	27.2	12.5	57.5	44.2	48.4	2.3
Skating	114 902	42.5	14.0	166.1	47.0	20.1	4.3	34.5	50.1	41.4	1.1
Trampolines	95 239	35.2	48.1	169.2	35.7	4.6	0.4	37.1	33.5	33.8	1.4
Miscellaneous ball games	79 333	29.3	15.1	103.4	57.0	10.0	2.2	40.7	18.5	28.6	0.6
Hockey	78 570	29.1	6.5	74.8	74.8	14.0	1.0	51.0	8.1	28.7	0.3
Volleyball	66 191	24.5	0.4	42.6	75.8	15.0	0.5	20.8	28.0	24.3	0.2
Horseback riding	64 692	23.9	5.1	33.4	26.6	28.1	3.7	18.1	29.5	21.1	2.7
Skateboards	54 532	20.2	7.9	70.6	57.9	2.7	0.1	36.4	4.6	19.5	0.6
Track and field	15 560	5.8	0.0	16.3	22.8	0.5	0.0	5.5	6.0	5.7	0.1

SOURCE: National Electronic Injury Surveillance System (NEISS), U.S. Consumer Product Safety Commission. Injuries associated with selected sports and recreation equipment treated in hospital emergency departments calendar year 1994. Consumer product safety review, Summer 1996 NEISS Data Highlights, 1998. Consumer Product Safety Review, Fall 1999.

* The sample size is too small for reliable estimates.

NOTE: Estimated injury rates are calculated using the July 1 census figures for the year. Product-related injuries: These data present national estimates of the number of persons treated in U.S. hospital emergency departments with consumer product related injuries during the given time period. The data system allows for up to two products for each person's injury. Therefore, a person's injury may be counted in two product groups. NEISS is a probability sample. ATV's (all terrain vehicles) category includes mopeds and other such motorized vehicles. Bicycle category includes bike accessories. Exercise is included in the exercise equipment category. Miscellaneous ball games include lacrosse and rugby. Skating category does not include in-line skating. Swimming category includes pools and other swimming equipment. Track and field category includes track and field activities and equipment.

Table 3.16. Cancer Incidence Rates

(Per 100,000 population; age-adjusted to the 1970 U.S. standard population, except where noted)

Site of cancer	All races			Whites			Blacks		
	Total	Males	Females	Total	Males	Females	Total	Males	Females
ALL SITES									
Year of Diagnosis									
1973	320.0	365.0	293.5	319.7	364.3	295.1	353.1	441.4	283.7
1974	332.9	372.6	311.8	334.1	373.7	314.7	349.8	427.0	289.4
1975	332.7	378.8	307.6	333.9	379.7	310.6	356.6	438.2	296.3
1976	338.0	389.9	308.4	339.7	389.7	313.3	355.6	456.4	282.3
1977	337.6	393.8	304.5	338.7	394.0	307.8	365.6	469.8	292.0
1978	337.7	395.8	303.3	339.6	396.2	308.1	363.3	471.8	284.9
1979	341.3	401.6	305.4	342.1	401.6	308.5	375.4	484.7	298.7
1980	345.8	409.2	307.1	346.4	407.5	311.3	390.7	510.4	305.0
1981	352.0	414.2	314.3	353.3	412.6	319.8	395.6	528.5	301.1
1982	351.7	413.7	314.6	353.8	413.3	320.4	389.7	516.4	300.3
1983	357.5	421.8	318.2	359.6	421.1	324.2	407.2	535.3	318.7
1984	364.6	425.9	328.0	366.6	425.7	333.5	410.2	537.9	322.4
1985	372.5	431.4	337.3	375.4	431.4	343.9	408.6	533.0	323.7
1986	374.5	436.9	336.7	377.4	438.5	341.9	412.9	533.0	331.4
1987	387.7	455.9	345.8	392.3	458.1	353.7	417.5	548.8	328.6
1988	385.2	452.3	343.9	389.7	455.4	351.0	421.3	544.2	338.6
1989	388.1	460.0	342.5	393.3	462.9	350.6	413.4	544.3	326.0
1990	399.7	479.6	348.7	405.1	483.0	356.9	427.1	561.4	337.5
1991	417.3	516.2	351.4	422.5	519.1	359.4	453.8	619.5	343.3
1992	425.6	536.3	349.3	428.7	535.6	356.3	470.9	657.2	343.5
1993	412.1	510.1	343.2	412.2	502.6	349.6	471.8	664.4	337.1
1994	403.8	483.5	347.8	404.2	476.7	354.5	465.4	636.5	344.8
1995	395.2	464.9	346.3	396.4	458.1	354.5	442.4	594.8	333.0
1996	388.6	454.6	342.0	387.3	445.8	347.1	430.9	563.1	336.1
Age at Diagnosis, 1992–1996									
All ages	404.8	489.1	345.8	405.6	483.0	352.5	455.8	621.9	338.7
Under 65 years	206.6	210.9	203.5	206.0	206.4	206.6	244.7	297.7	202.6
65 years and over	2 213.9	3 028.0	1 643.8	2 227.4	3 008.5	1 683.9	2 382.6	3 581.4	1 580.7
All ages (world standard) [1]	326.1	383.1	285.3	326.7	378.1	290.8	369.6	494.0	279.8
ALL SITES EXCLUDING LUNG AND BRONCHUS									
Year of Diagnosis									
1973	277.5	291.8	275.3	278.1	291.9	277.3	294.3	336.8	262.7
1974	289.0	298.1	292.0	290.7	299.6	294.9	290.9	324.9	267.6
1975	287.4	302.6	286.2	288.8	303.8	288.7	300.1	337.2	275.7
1976	290.2	310.6	284.6	292.5	311.3	289.4	293.0	345.5	257.1
1977	288.7	313.1	279.7	290.4	314.0	283.2	301.4	361.1	263.1
1978	287.5	313.8	277.2	289.8	315.1	281.6	298.2	358.3	257.8
1979	290.4	320.2	277.6	291.7	320.9	280.6	310.1	373.2	269.2
1980	293.4	324.8	279.0	295.2	325.3	283.0	314.7	379.4	271.2
1981	298.1	329.7	283.5	299.9	329.3	288.5	322.4	402.3	268.0
1982	296.8	328.6	282.2	299.2	329.5	287.1	318.5	392.9	268.9
1983	302.5	337.7	285.0	305.0	338.9	289.9	331.3	404.3	284.0
1984	307.8	339.4	293.4	310.9	341.5	298.6	327.6	397.5	282.7
1985	316.3	347.6	302.0	319.9	349.4	308.0	329.5	401.7	283.4
1986	317.6	353.3	299.7	321.0	356.6	304.3	331.6	399.0	288.3
1987	329.2	370.6	307.2	333.6	373.7	314.0	343.0	424.7	290.3
1988	326.5	369.0	303.6	330.8	373.1	309.3	343.5	418.2	295.7
1989	330.1	377.7	302.4	335.3	381.8	309.5	335.2	421.2	280.3
1990	341.1	398.0	307.1	346.3	402.1	314.4	351.8	445.5	291.1
1991	357.7	434.4	308.2	363.2	438.8	315.3	372.4	494.3	293.7
1992	366.0	454.7	306.1	369.6	456.3	312.0	389.0	529.6	294.7
1993	354.2	431.4	300.9	354.3	425.5	305.9	397.1	549.6	291.4
1994	346.6	407.9	304.5	347.0	402.2	310.1	389.5	523.7	295.8
1995	338.9	390.8	303.6	340.1	385.9	310.0	369.4	479.6	290.3
1996	334.4	384.6	299.8	333.0	377.4	303.4	361.1	461.7	288.9
Age at Diagnosis, 1992–1996									
All ages	347.8	413.2	303.0	348.7	408.8	308.3	380.8	507.7	292.1
Under 65 years	181.6	180.7	183.3	181.5	177.9	185.9	205.4	241.3	177.2
65 years and over	1 865.4	2 535.3	1 395.4	1 874.0	2 516.1	1 426.1	1 982.1	2 939.1	1 340.9
All ages (world standard) [1]	281.4	324.6	251.4	282.2	321.2	255.8	309.1	403.2	241.7
URINARY BLADDER CANCER									
Year of Diagnosis									
1973	14.6	25.6	6.3	15.4	27.3	6.5	7.0	10.6	4.0
1974	15.8	27.3	7.1	16.5	28.9	7.3	8.7	12.0	5.8
1975	15.5	27.1	7.1	16.3	28.8	7.3	8.7	13.5	5.0
1976	15.8	27.1	7.5	16.6	28.9	7.8	9.9	14.3	6.8
1977	15.3	26.5	7.0	16.1	28.2	7.3	10.6	17.8	5.3
1978	16.1	27.9	7.5	17.0	29.9	7.7	9.4	15.4	5.0
1979	16.1	27.9	7.5	17.1	30.1	7.8	8.7	13.0	5.4
1980	16.5	29.4	7.1	17.4	31.5	7.3	10.6	14.5	7.8
1981	16.7	29.0	7.7	17.7	30.9	8.1	9.6	16.3	4.9
1982	16.1	28.1	7.6	17.2	30.0	8.1	9.6	17.0	4.3
1983	16.3	28.7	7.2	17.3	30.8	7.5	10.1	15.4	6.3
1984	16.9	30.0	7.3	18.1	32.4	7.6	9.3	15.5	4.8
1985	16.8	28.9	8.0	17.9	31.2	8.3	10.6	16.3	6.6
1986	17.1	30.1	7.7	18.3	32.3	8.1	10.3	17.8	5.0
1987	17.5	31.4	7.3	18.7	33.9	7.6	10.7	17.3	6.2
1988	16.9	30.2	7.2	18.5	33.2	7.9	8.6	14.5	4.4
1989	17.0	29.7	7.7	18.4	32.4	8.1	9.1	13.9	5.7
1990	17.1	29.8	7.7	18.3	32.4	8.0	10.3	15.1	7.0
1991	16.9	29.6	7.5	18.4	32.4	8.0	10.0	15.1	6.5
1992	17.2	29.7	7.9	18.5	31.9	8.5	9.9	16.6	5.3
1993	17.3	29.9	7.9	18.5	32.0	8.4	10.9	18.1	6.2
1994	16.9	29.2	7.6	18.3	31.7	8.2	9.7	15.7	5.5
1995	16.6	28.4	7.7	18.0	30.8	8.2	9.4	14.3	5.6
1996	16.2	27.7	7.4	17.4	29.9	7.9	9.2	14.0	5.8
Age at Diagnosis, 1992–1996									
All ages	16.8	28.9	7.7	18.1	31.3	8.2	9.8	15.7	5.7
Under 65 years	6.4	10.1	3.0	7.0	10.8	3.3	3.7	5.9	1.9
65 years and over	111.6	201.3	50.4	119.8	217.8	53.2	65.5	105.1	39.9
All ages (world standard) [1]	12.8	21.7	5.9	13.8	23.4	6.3	7.3	11.7	4.2

See footnotes at end of table.

Table 3.16. Cancer Incidence Rates—*Continued*

(Per 100,000 population; age-adjusted to the 1970 U.S. standard population, except where noted)

Site of cancer	All races			Whites			Blacks		
	Total	Males	Females	Total	Males	Females	Total	Males	Females
BRAIN AND OTHER NERVOUS SYSTEM CANCER									
Year of Diagnosis									
1973	5.0	5.9	4.1	5.2	6.3	4.3	3.8	4.5	3.0
1974	5.1	6.0	4.3	5.4	6.5	4.5	2.5	2.5	2.5
1975	5.5	6.3	4.7	5.8	6.8	4.9	3.8	4.0	3.6
1976	5.4	6.6	4.3	5.7	6.9	4.7	3.0	4.9	1.4
1977	5.8	7.1	4.7	6.1	7.5	5.0	3.3	4.3	2.6
1978	5.4	6.3	4.6	5.7	6.7	4.9	3.7	4.0	3.4
1979	5.6	6.8	4.6	6.1	7.3	5.0	3.3	4.0	2.7
1980	5.8	6.9	4.8	6.2	7.4	5.2	3.2	3.5	2.8
1981	5.9	7.3	4.7	6.3	7.6	5.1	4.8	6.8	3.2
1982	5.8	7.1	4.8	6.3	7.6	5.2	3.5	4.2	2.9
1983	5.7	6.9	4.7	6.3	7.5	5.2	2.6	3.6	1.7
1984	5.6	6.5	4.8	5.9	7.0	5.0	4.1	4.7	3.7
1985	6.3	7.6	5.1	6.7	8.1	5.5	4.5	5.3	3.8
1986	6.2	7.4	5.3	6.7	7.8	5.7	3.9	4.5	3.3
1987	6.4	7.4	5.6	6.9	7.9	6.2	3.9	4.9	3.1
1988	6.2	7.2	5.3	6.7	7.8	5.8	4.0	4.1	3.8
1989	6.2	7.7	4.9	6.7	8.3	5.3	4.5	5.6	3.8
1990	6.5	7.4	5.7	6.9	8.0	6.1	4.1	4.8	3.5
1991	6.3	7.6	5.2	6.9	8.3	5.7	3.5	4.1	3.0
1992	6.3	7.7	5.2	6.9	8.3	5.7	3.4	3.8	3.1
1993	6.2	7.3	5.1	6.7	7.9	5.6	3.6	3.8	3.4
1994	6.0	7.1	5.0	6.4	7.6	5.3	4.0	4.1	4.0
1995	5.9	7.0	4.8	6.3	7.6	5.2	3.7	4.8	2.9
1996	5.8	7.2	4.5	6.2	7.7	4.9	3.5	4.2	3.1
Age at Diagnosis, 1992–1996									
All ages	6.0	7.3	4.9	6.5	7.8	5.3	3.7	4.2	3.3
Under 65 years	4.6	5.4	3.7	4.9	5.9	4.0	2.9	3.2	2.6
65 years and over	19.2	23.8	16.1	20.7	25.7	17.3	11.0	12.6	9.9
All ages (world standard) [1]	5.4	6.5	4.5	5.9	7.0	4.8	3.4	3.8	3.0
BREAST CANCER									
Year of Diagnosis									
1973	45.0	1.0	82.6	46.1	0.9	84.4	38.6	2.7	69.0
1974	51.7	1.0	94.9	52.9	1.0	96.7	43.5	1.5	79.3
1975	48.2	0.7	88.1	49.3	0.7	90.0	43.4	0.7	78.5
1976	46.8	0.8	85.5	48.1	0.8	87.8	39.3	1.0	70.5
1977	46.1	0.8	84.1	47.3	0.7	86.2	40.7	1.8	72.2
1978	46.1	0.7	84.1	47.5	0.7	86.5	39.9	0.3	71.8
1979	47.1	0.8	85.6	48.1	0.8	87.6	41.1	1.7	72.4
1980	47.0	0.7	85.4	48.3	0.8	87.8	41.8	0.7	74.5
1981	48.9	0.8	88.8	50.5	0.8	91.8	44.2	1.7	77.6
1982	49.1	0.8	89.3	50.6	0.8	92.3	44.3	1.6	77.5
1983	51.3	0.9	93.3	52.8	0.9	96.2	48.7	0.4	86.3
1984	53.4	0.8	97.2	55.1	0.8	100.5	48.2	1.2	85.0
1985	57.1	0.7	104.1	58.7	0.8	107.3	52.7	0.9	92.7
1986	58.5	0.8	106.7	60.0	0.8	109.6	54.6	1.1	95.6
1987	62.2	0.8	113.2	64.6	0.8	118.1	51.9	1.0	90.8
1988	60.6	1.0	110.3	62.7	0.9	114.5	57.2	2.2	99.4
1989	58.6	0.9	106.7	60.6	0.9	110.8	51.2	1.7	89.4
1990	60.5	0.9	110.4	62.5	1.0	114.5	55.1	1.0	96.5
1991	61.2	0.9	112.0	63.3	0.9	116.3	55.6	1.1	97.7
1992	60.7	0.8	111.1	62.0	0.8	114.2	58.4	1.1	102.2
1993	59.4	0.9	108.9	60.7	0.9	112.0	57.3	1.1	100.8
1994	60.3	1.0	110.8	61.9	1.0	114.6	58.3	1.6	102.1
1995	60.6	0.8	111.6	62.1	0.7	115.3	58.5	1.6	102.4
1996	60.1	1.2	110.7	61.1	1.1	113.3	57.3	1.7	100.3
Age at Diagnosis, 1992–1996									
All ages	60.2	0.9	110.6	61.6	0.9	113.9	58.0	1.4	101.5
Under 65 years	38.4	0.4	74.5	38.8	0.4	76.2	39.3	0.7	71.5
65 years and over	259.2	5.5	440.6	269.5	5.4	458.5	228.4	8.1	375.2
All ages (world standard) [1]	50.2	0.7	93.6	51.2	0.7	96.2	49.0	1.1	86.8
COLON AND RECTUM CANCER									
Year of Diagnosis									
1973	46.4	53.1	41.6	46.9	54.2	41.7	42.4	42.8	41.8
1974	47.7	56.2	41.6	48.4	57.4	41.9	41.3	46.8	37.5
1975	47.4	54.1	42.7	47.8	55.1	42.9	45.4	47.6	43.5
1976	49.1	57.3	43.2	49.6	57.8	43.8	44.4	48.9	40.3
1977	49.5	58.0	43.5	50.0	58.7	43.9	48.0	58.1	41.4
1978	49.4	57.2	43.9	49.9	58.4	44.1	49.4	51.3	48.5
1979	49.3	58.3	43.0	49.6	58.9	43.2	46.8	50.0	44.5
1980	50.4	58.7	44.5	50.4	58.7	44.7	55.7	63.7	49.6
1981	50.9	59.8	44.5	51.2	60.3	44.9	50.4	58.2	44.9
1982	49.7	59.2	42.9	50.1	60.0	43.3	48.9	55.1	44.5
1983	50.4	59.9	43.6	50.8	60.5	43.8	53.9	61.0	49.3
1984	51.5	61.6	44.2	52.2	62.9	44.6	49.9	54.8	47.1
1985	52.8	63.0	45.3	53.3	63.5	46.0	52.1	60.8	45.8
1986	51.2	61.9	43.3	51.2	62.4	43.1	52.9	59.8	47.8
1987	49.8	61.2	41.5	49.7	61.4	41.3	53.2	61.1	47.9
1988	48.6	59.5	40.6	48.6	59.8	40.3	50.9	58.1	45.9
1989	48.8	59.4	41.1	48.8	59.3	41.1	52.8	64.4	44.9
1990	48.3	58.9	40.5	48.2	59.1	40.2	52.4	58.1	48.6
1991	47.3	58.0	39.3	47.0	58.0	38.9	52.8	62.1	46.1
1992	46.4	56.3	38.9	46.2	56.4	38.4	52.1	61.8	45.8
1993	45.3	54.5	38.2	44.9	54.2	37.7	51.7	62.0	44.4
1994	44.3	53.1	37.6	44.0	52.9	36.9	51.7	59.6	46.5
1995	42.9	50.5	37.0	42.5	49.9	36.7	48.5	54.6	44.2
1996	42.7	51.1	36.2	42.2	50.7	35.5	45.7	50.9	41.8
Age at Diagnosis, 1992–1996									
All ages	44.3	53.0	37.6	43.9	52.8	37.1	49.9	57.6	44.5
Under 65 years	17.1	19.9	14.5	16.4	19.2	13.8	21.8	24.2	19.9
65 years and over	292.6	355.4	248.2	294.8	358.8	249.8	305.6	361.6	268.8
All ages (world standard) [1]	33.5	40.0	28.3	33.0	39.6	27.8	38.3	44.1	34.2

See footnotes at end of table.

Table 3.16. Cancer Incidence Rates—*Continued*

(Per 100,000 population; age-adjusted to the 1970 U.S. standard population, except where noted)

Site of cancer	All races			Whites			Blacks		
	Total	Males	Females	Total	Males	Females	Total	Males	Females
ESOPHAGUS CANCER									
Year of Diagnosis									
1973	3.4	5.5	1.8	3.0	4.8	1.6	9.0	13.3	5.2
1974	3.6	5.9	1.8	3.0	4.9	1.6	11.3	19.0	4.7
1975	3.5	5.8	1.8	3.0	4.8	1.7	9.6	17.6	3.2
1976	3.7	5.8	2.0	3.1	5.0	1.8	9.5	15.2	4.8
1977	3.5	5.5	1.9	2.9	4.5	1.6	10.5	17.7	4.9
1978	3.6	6.1	1.6	2.9	4.9	1.4	11.5	21.3	3.8
1979	3.7	6.2	1.9	3.1	5.1	1.7	11.4	20.1	4.5
1980	3.7	5.9	2.0	3.0	4.9	1.6	11.1	16.4	6.9
1981	3.5	5.5	2.0	2.8	4.3	1.6	12.3	19.4	6.8
1982	3.7	5.9	1.9	2.9	4.6	1.6	12.1	20.3	5.6
1983	3.7	6.3	1.7	3.0	5.0	1.5	11.2	20.3	3.9
1984	3.6	5.7	1.9	3.0	4.8	1.5	10.8	17.8	5.4
1985	3.8	6.3	1.9	3.2	5.3	1.6	11.3	19.4	5.2
1986	4.0	6.4	2.1	3.3	5.2	1.8	12.8	21.8	5.8
1987	3.9	6.4	1.9	3.3	5.4	1.6	10.3	17.9	4.4
1988	3.8	6.2	1.9	3.3	5.4	1.7	9.9	16.8	4.6
1989	3.7	6.1	1.8	3.1	5.1	1.6	9.4	15.7	4.7
1990	4.2	7.1	1.9	3.6	6.1	1.6	11.3	19.5	5.1
1991	3.9	6.3	2.0	3.5	5.7	1.8	9.0	15.2	4.5
1992	3.9	6.7	1.6	3.5	6.2	1.4	9.3	15.7	4.6
1993	4.0	6.6	1.9	3.6	5.9	1.7	8.9	15.2	4.3
1994	3.8	6.5	1.7	3.5	6.0	1.5	8.2	13.2	4.5
1995	3.7	6.0	1.8	3.4	5.5	1.6	7.5	12.4	3.8
1996	4.0	6.8	1.7	3.6	6.2	1.6	8.3	14.0	3.9
Age at Diagnosis, 1992–1996									
All ages	3.9	6.5	1.7	3.5	5.9	1.6	8.4	14.1	4.2
Under 65 years	1.9	3.2	0.7	1.6	2.7	0.6	5.2	8.6	2.5
65 years and over	21.7	36.9	10.9	20.8	35.1	10.6	37.9	64.2	19.8
All ages (world standard) [1]	3.1	5.1	1.3	2.8	4.6	1.2	7.0	11.7	3.4
HODGKIN'S DISEASE									
Year of Diagnosis									
1973	3.3	4.2	2.4	3.5	4.4	2.6	2.4	3.8	1.2
1974	3.1	3.7	2.6	3.2	3.8	2.7	2.5	2.9	2.1
1975	2.9	3.6	2.3	3.1	3.7	2.5	2.3	3.8	1.0
1976	2.6	3.1	2.2	2.7	3.2	2.4	2.4	3.6	1.3
1977	2.8	3.3	2.4	3.1	3.5	2.7	1.6	1.8	1.3
1978	2.7	3.2	2.3	3.0	3.5	2.5	1.4	1.8	1.1
1979	2.8	3.6	2.0	2.9	3.8	2.2	2.5	4.1	1.2
1980	2.6	3.1	2.2	2.8	3.3	2.4	1.7	2.0	1.4
1981	2.7	3.3	2.2	3.0	3.6	2.5	1.4	1.8	1.0
1982	2.8	3.2	2.4	3.0	3.4	2.7	2.3	2.9	1.7
1983	2.9	3.5	2.3	3.1	3.7	2.6	1.9	3.2	0.9
1984	2.9	3.5	2.4	3.3	3.8	2.8	2.0	3.1	1.1
1985	2.8	3.3	2.4	3.2	3.6	2.7	1.6	2.0	1.2
1986	2.6	3.1	2.2	2.8	3.2	2.5	2.0	2.4	1.6
1987	2.9	3.4	2.5	3.2	3.7	2.8	1.9	2.5	1.4
1988	2.9	3.3	2.6	3.3	3.7	2.9	1.8	1.9	1.8
1989	2.9	3.4	2.5	3.2	3.7	2.8	2.1	2.9	1.6
1990	2.9	3.3	2.5	3.1	3.6	2.6	2.7	2.8	2.6
1991	2.8	3.2	2.5	3.2	3.6	2.8	2.2	2.5	1.9
1992	2.8	2.9	2.6	2.9	3.1	2.9	2.6	2.6	2.5
1993	2.7	3.1	2.4	2.9	3.2	2.6	2.8	3.5	2.3
1994	2.7	2.9	2.5	3.0	3.3	2.7	2.0	2.2	2.0
1995	2.6	3.0	2.3	2.9	3.2	2.6	2.1	2.7	1.6
1996	2.6	3.1	2.2	2.8	3.2	2.4	2.4	3.0	1.8
Age at Diagnosis, 1992–1996									
All ages	2.7	3.0	2.4	2.9	3.2	2.6	2.4	2.8	2.0
Under 65 years	2.6	2.8	2.4	2.8	3.0	2.6	2.4	2.8	2.1
65 years and over	3.6	4.5	3.0	4.0	4.9	3.3	1.8	2.6	1.3
All ages (world standard) [1]	2.6	2.9	2.4	2.8	3.1	2.6	2.4	2.7	2.0
KIDNEY AND RENAL PELVIS CANCER									
Year of Diagnosis									
1973	6.7	9.6	4.4	6.7	9.6	4.5	6.6	9.1	4.4
1974	6.3	8.9	4.2	6.3	9.1	4.1	6.8	8.7	5.3
1975	6.1	8.8	3.9	6.3	9.2	4.0	5.4	7.5	3.5
1976	6.9	9.6	4.7	7.0	9.8	4.8	6.9	10.1	4.3
1977	6.8	9.5	4.6	6.8	9.7	4.6	7.1	9.5	5.2
1978	6.7	10.0	4.1	6.8	10.2	4.2	7.1	9.7	5.1
1979	6.5	9.3	4.3	6.7	9.7	4.4	5.9	7.1	4.8
1980	6.8	9.8	4.6	7.1	10.2	4.7	5.3	7.3	3.7
1981	7.2	10.7	4.5	7.3	10.8	4.5	8.7	13.6	5.0
1982	7.1	10.0	4.9	7.2	10.1	4.9	6.8	9.9	4.4
1983	7.7	11.3	4.9	8.0	11.7	5.0	7.6	11.3	5.0
1984	7.8	11.1	5.3	8.1	11.5	5.4	7.6	10.1	5.8
1985	7.7	11.1	4.9	7.9	11.5	5.1	7.5	10.6	5.1
1986	8.2	11.7	5.6	8.4	11.8	5.7	8.8	13.0	5.6
1987	8.5	11.9	5.8	8.6	12.2	5.9	9.6	13.5	6.5
1988	8.5	11.7	6.0	8.6	11.9	6.0	9.9	13.2	7.4
1989	8.8	12.3	6.1	9.1	12.7	6.2	9.3	12.9	6.7
1990	8.9	12.5	6.0	9.1	12.7	6.3	8.9	13.3	5.7
1991	9.1	12.7	6.1	9.2	12.9	6.3	10.3	15.3	6.5
1992	9.2	12.9	6.3	9.5	13.1	6.6	9.6	14.2	6.3
1993	9.2	12.5	6.5	9.2	12.5	6.6	11.2	15.1	8.3
1994	9.7	13.3	6.7	9.9	13.5	6.9	10.9	15.4	7.3
1995	9.3	12.9	6.4	9.3	12.8	6.4	11.8	17.8	7.5
1996	9.4	12.9	6.5	9.4	13.1	6.3	11.3	14.4	8.9
Age at Diagnosis, 1992–1996									
All ages	9.3	12.9	6.5	9.4	13.0	6.5	11.0	15.4	7.7
Under 65 years	5.3	7.1	3.6	5.2	7.0	3.6	6.9	9.7	4.6
65 years and over	46.5	66.1	32.6	47.8	68.0	33.5	48.5	68.0	35.6
All ages (world standard) [1]	7.7	10.5	5.3	7.8	10.6	5.4	9.2	12.8	6.5

See footnotes at end of table.

Table 3.16. Cancer Incidence Rates—*Continued*

(Per 100,000 population; age-adjusted to the 1970 U.S. standard population, except where noted)

Site of cancer	All races			Whites			Blacks		
	Total	Males	Females	Total	Males	Females	Total	Males	Females
LARYNX CANCER									
Year of Diagnosis									
1973	4.5	8.4	1.3	4.4	8.4	1.2	6.3	11.9	1.8
1974	4.5	8.2	1.4	4.5	8.3	1.4	6.0	10.1	2.4
1975	4.5	8.3	1.3	4.4	8.3	1.3	6.4	11.9	1.8
1976	4.7	8.9	1.2	4.7	8.9	1.3	6.6	13.0	1.3
1977	4.5	8.5	1.2	4.4	8.5	1.2	6.4	11.9	2.0
1978	4.7	8.6	1.6	4.7	8.6	1.7	6.3	11.7	2.0
1979	4.8	8.9	1.5	4.8	9.0	1.5	6.7	11.8	2.7
1980	4.7	8.8	1.4	4.6	8.7	1.4	6.6	12.6	1.8
1981	4.8	8.6	1.7	4.7	8.4	1.8	7.2	14.5	1.6
1982	4.7	8.6	1.6	4.7	8.6	1.6	7.2	13.0	2.6
1983	4.8	8.8	1.6	4.9	8.9	1.6	6.1	11.0	2.3
1984	4.6	8.5	1.4	4.4	8.4	1.3	7.9	14.1	3.1
1985	4.9	8.7	1.8	4.8	8.7	1.8	7.5	13.4	3.0
1986	4.5	8.2	1.5	4.4	8.0	1.5	7.0	13.8	1.9
1987	4.7	8.3	1.8	4.6	8.2	1.7	7.3	13.3	2.8
1988	4.6	8.3	1.7	4.6	8.3	1.7	7.3	13.2	3.0
1989	4.5	7.8	1.8	4.5	7.8	1.8	7.0	12.6	2.9
1990	4.5	8.1	1.7	4.5	7.9	1.7	8.2	15.0	3.2
1991	4.2	7.5	1.6	4.2	7.4	1.7	5.9	11.2	1.9
1992	4.4	7.9	1.6	4.3	7.7	1.6	7.7	14.1	2.9
1993	3.9	7.0	1.3	3.8	6.8	1.4	6.2	12.5	1.4
1994	4.1	7.2	1.6	4.0	7.1	1.5	7.9	13.9	3.4
1995	3.8	6.8	1.4	3.8	6.8	1.4	5.8	10.9	2.0
1996	3.7	6.5	1.4	3.7	6.4	1.4	5.6	9.8	2.3
Age at Diagnosis, 1992–1996									
All ages	4.0	7.1	1.5	3.9	6.9	1.5	6.6	12.2	2.4
Under 65 years	2.3	3.7	0.9	2.2	3.5	0.9	4.4	7.7	1.6
65 years and over	19.7	37.6	6.6	20.0	38.1	6.7	27.1	53.2	9.3
All ages (world standard) [1]	3.3	5.7	1.2	3.2	5.6	1.2	5.6	10.1	2.0
ALL LEUKEMIAS									
Year of Diagnosis									
1973	10.6	13.8	8.1	10.8	14.3	8.1	9.6	12.0	8.0
1974	10.8	14.2	8.3	11.0	14.6	8.4	10.4	13.1	8.1
1975	10.6	13.7	8.3	10.9	14.3	8.4	9.3	12.5	7.1
1976	11.2	14.9	8.6	11.4	15.4	8.6	9.4	11.6	7.9
1977	10.6	13.3	8.5	11.0	13.9	8.8	8.1	10.7	6.3
1978	10.6	13.9	8.1	11.1	14.7	8.5	7.8	9.7	6.3
1979	10.3	13.5	7.9	10.7	14.1	8.2	8.9	11.0	7.4
1980	10.7	14.2	8.2	11.0	14.6	8.3	10.0	13.1	7.7
1981	10.4	13.5	8.2	10.6	13.8	8.3	10.6	12.7	9.0
1982	10.9	14.7	8.1	11.1	15.2	8.2	9.2	12.3	7.1
1983	10.8	14.5	8.1	11.1	15.0	8.2	10.1	13.0	8.0
1984	10.9	14.0	8.5	11.1	14.5	8.7	9.6	10.8	8.5
1985	11.1	14.4	8.7	11.4	14.8	8.9	9.7	13.0	7.5
1986	10.7	14.4	7.9	11.1	15.0	8.2	8.3	10.6	6.7
1987	10.9	14.3	8.5	11.2	14.7	8.6	10.3	14.3	7.6
1988	10.6	14.1	7.9	10.9	14.6	8.1	9.5	11.8	7.5
1989	11.1	14.4	8.6	11.5	14.8	9.0	9.4	13.0	6.7
1990	10.5	13.9	7.9	10.9	14.5	8.2	8.9	11.7	6.8
1991	10.8	13.6	8.5	11.2	14.3	8.7	9.2	9.9	8.7
1992	10.6	14.0	8.0	10.9	14.7	8.0	8.9	11.4	7.1
1993	10.4	13.3	8.1	10.6	13.8	8.1	9.2	12.2	7.1
1994	10.2	13.0	8.1	10.6	13.5	8.3	7.7	9.8	6.2
1995	10.5	13.5	8.2	11.0	14.1	8.5	7.9	10.2	6.2
1996	9.7	12.3	7.7	9.8	12.4	7.7	8.1	10.1	6.6
Age at Diagnosis, 1992–1996									
All ages	10.3	13.2	8.0	10.6	13.7	8.1	8.3	10.7	6.6
Under 65 years	5.8	6.9	4.7	5.9	7.0	4.7	4.7	5.8	3.8
65 years and over	51.4	70.6	38.4	53.5	74.2	39.5	41.8	55.6	32.7
All ages (world standard) [1]	8.6	10.9	6.8	8.9	11.2	6.9	7.1	8.9	5.6
LIVER AND INTRAHEPATIC BILE DUCT CANCER									
Year of Diagnosis									
1973	2.3	3.3	1.5	1.9	2.7	1.4	3.9	6.7	1.7
1974	2.2	3.2	1.5	2.0	2.8	1.4	3.2	4.9	1.7
1975	2.2	3.3	1.3	1.8	2.7	1.1	4.2	6.0	2.6
1976	2.2	3.2	1.4	1.9	2.6	1.3	3.4	5.4	1.8
1977	2.2	3.5	1.3	1.9	2.9	1.1	3.1	4.6	1.9
1978	2.3	3.5	1.3	1.8	2.7	1.2	3.7	6.0	1.9
1979	2.2	3.4	1.3	1.8	2.7	1.2	3.6	6.2	1.6
1980	2.2	3.2	1.4	1.8	2.6	1.2	3.2	4.6	2.1
1981	2.4	3.8	1.3	2.0	3.1	1.2	3.8	6.3	1.9
1982	2.4	3.6	1.5	1.9	2.8	1.3	3.4	4.9	2.3
1983	2.4	3.9	1.3	2.0	3.1	1.1	3.7	5.8	2.0
1984	2.4	3.5	1.6	1.9	2.8	1.4	2.8	4.6	1.5
1985	2.6	4.2	1.4	2.1	3.4	1.2	3.5	6.6	1.2
1986	2.7	4.0	1.6	2.2	3.2	1.3	4.2	6.6	2.5
1987	2.8	4.1	1.8	2.2	3.0	1.5	4.5	6.8	2.8
1988	2.8	4.6	1.5	2.2	3.5	1.3	4.1	7.7	1.3
1989	3.0	4.6	1.8	2.4	3.5	1.6	4.7	7.9	2.4
1990	3.3	5.0	1.9	2.5	3.8	1.5	5.4	8.8	2.8
1991	3.6	5.5	2.1	2.9	4.5	1.8	5.1	8.0	2.8
1992	3.3	4.9	1.9	2.6	3.9	1.6	4.6	6.9	2.8
1993	3.7	5.9	2.0	3.0	4.7	1.6	5.4	8.9	2.6
1994	3.7	5.7	2.0	2.9	4.5	1.7	4.2	7.9	1.4
1995	3.8	5.6	2.3	2.9	4.3	1.9	5.3	7.6	3.4
1996	4.2	6.4	2.4	3.4	5.1	2.0	5.6	9.0	3.0
Age at Diagnosis, 1992–1996									
All ages	3.7	5.7	2.1	3.0	4.5	1.7	5.0	8.1	2.6
Under 65 years	1.9	2.8	1.0	1.3	1.9	0.8	3.0	5.2	1.2
65 years and over	21.1	32.7	12.8	18.2	28.6	10.8	23.6	34.7	15.9
All ages (world standard) [1]	3.0	4.6	1.7	2.3	3.5	1.4	4.1	6.7	2.0

See footnotes at end of table.

Table 3.16. Cancer Incidence Rates—*Continued*

(Per 100,000 population; age-adjusted to the 1970 U.S. standard population, except where noted)

Site of cancer	All races			Whites			Blacks		
	Total	Males	Females	Total	Males	Females	Total	Males	Females
LUNG AND BRONCHUS CANCER									
Year of Diagnosis									
1973	42.4	73.2	18.2	41.6	72.4	17.8	58.7	104.6	20.9
1974	43.9	74.5	19.9	43.4	74.2	19.8	58.9	102.0	21.7
1975	45.3	76.2	21.5	45.1	75.9	21.8	56.5	101.0	20.6
1976	47.8	79.3	23.8	47.2	78.4	23.8	62.6	110.9	25.2
1977	48.9	80.7	24.7	48.3	80.0	24.6	64.2	108.7	28.9
1978	50.2	82.0	26.2	49.7	81.1	26.5	65.0	113.5	27.1
1979	50.9	81.4	27.8	50.4	80.7	27.9	65.4	111.6	29.4
1980	52.3	84.4	28.1	51.2	82.2	28.2	76.0	131.0	33.8
1981	53.9	84.5	30.9	53.4	83.3	31.3	73.3	126.1	33.1
1982	54.9	85.1	32.3	54.6	83.8	33.3	71.1	123.5	31.4
1983	55.0	84.1	33.3	54.5	82.2	34.4	75.9	130.9	34.7
1984	56.8	86.5	34.6	55.7	84.2	34.8	82.7	140.3	39.7
1985	56.1	83.8	35.3	55.5	82.0	35.9	79.0	131.3	40.2
1986	56.9	83.6	37.0	56.4	81.9	37.7	81.3	134.0	43.0
1987	58.5	85.3	38.6	58.6	84.3	39.8	74.4	124.1	38.3
1988	58.7	83.4	40.4	58.9	82.3	41.6	77.8	125.9	42.8
1989	58.0	82.2	40.1	58.0	81.1	41.1	78.1	123.1	45.7
1990	58.6	81.7	41.5	58.8	80.9	42.6	75.3	115.9	46.3
1991	59.6	81.8	43.2	59.3	80.3	44.1	81.4	125.2	49.6
1992	59.6	81.7	43.2	59.1	79.3	44.3	81.9	127.6	48.7
1993	57.9	78.7	42.3	57.9	77.1	43.8	74.7	114.8	45.7
1994	57.1	75.6	43.4	57.2	74.5	44.4	75.9	112.8	49.0
1995	56.2	74.1	42.7	56.4	72.3	44.5	73.1	115.2	42.7
1996	54.2	70.0	42.3	54.2	68.4	43.7	69.9	101.4	47.2
Age at Diagnosis, 1992–1996									
All ages	57.0	75.9	42.8	56.9	74.3	44.1	75.0	114.2	46.6
Under 65 years	25.0	30.3	20.2	24.5	28.4	20.7	39.3	56.3	25.4
65 years and over	348.6	492.8	248.4	353.4	492.5	257.8	400.5	642.3	239.8
All ages (world standard)[1]	44.7	58.5	33.9	44.5	56.9	34.9	60.5	90.7	38.1
MELANOMAS OF SKIN									
Year of Diagnosis									
1973	5.7	6.1	5.4	6.2	6.7	5.9	0.7	0.6	0.7
1974	5.9	6.2	5.7	6.5	6.9	6.3	0.5	0.2	0.7
1975	6.7	7.1	6.3	7.3	7.8	6.9	0.9	1.1	0.8
1976	6.9	7.4	6.5	7.6	8.1	7.1	1.4	1.7	1.2
1977	7.6	8.3	7.0	8.4	9.1	7.8	0.7	0.5	0.8
1978	7.6	8.0	7.3	8.5	9.0	8.3	0.6	0.3	0.8
1979	8.1	8.9	7.5	9.1	9.9	8.5	0.8	0.7	1.0
1980	8.9	9.9	8.2	10.1	11.2	9.4	0.7	0.7	0.7
1981	9.4	10.2	8.8	10.5	11.3	10.0	1.1	1.7	0.7
1982	9.4	10.5	8.6	10.6	11.8	9.8	0.8	1.0	0.6
1983	9.3	10.6	8.4	10.4	11.8	9.4	0.7	0.4	1.0
1984	9.6	10.9	8.7	10.8	12.3	9.8	0.6	0.1	0.9
1985	10.8	12.7	9.4	12.0	14.1	10.5	0.8	0.2	1.2
1986	11.2	13.2	9.8	12.5	14.6	11.0	0.4	0.2	0.5
1987	11.4	13.2	10.2	12.7	14.6	11.4	1.0	1.1	0.9
1988	10.8	12.5	9.6	12.4	14.4	11.0	0.9	0.9	0.9
1989	11.6	13.8	9.9	13.2	15.6	11.4	1.0	1.3	0.9
1990	11.6	13.9	9.9	13.3	15.8	11.4	0.9	1.2	0.7
1991	12.3	14.6	10.5	14.2	16.8	12.2	1.0	1.4	0.7
1992	12.5	15.2	10.4	14.2	17.3	11.9	0.3	0.1	0.4
1993	12.4	15.2	10.3	14.1	17.1	11.8	0.7	0.5	0.8
1994	13.0	16.3	10.5	14.9	18.5	12.1	0.9	0.9	0.8
1995	13.5	16.5	11.3	15.5	18.6	13.2	1.4	2.6	0.6
1996	13.8	17.0	11.4	15.9	19.3	13.2	0.9	1.3	0.6
Age at Diagnosis, 1992–1996									
All ages	13.0	16.0	10.8	14.9	18.2	12.4	0.8	1.1	0.6
Under 65 years	9.8	10.8	8.8	11.2	12.3	10.3	0.5	0.7	0.3
65 years and over	43.2	64.1	28.6	48.4	72.3	31.8	3.8	4.6	3.3
All ages (world standard)[1]	11.5	13.7	9.9	13.2	15.5	11.4	0.7	0.9	0.5
MULTIPLE MYELOMA									
Year of Diagnosis									
1973	3.8	4.5	3.3	3.4	4.0	3.1	9.7	12.8	7.2
1974	3.8	4.5	3.3	3.5	4.2	3.0	8.5	10.0	7.4
1975	4.0	5.2	3.2	3.8	5.0	2.9	8.2	9.4	7.1
1976	4.2	4.9	3.7	3.9	4.6	3.5	7.8	9.2	6.9
1977	4.1	5.1	3.4	3.9	4.9	3.2	7.6	8.9	6.6
1978	3.9	4.7	3.2	3.6	4.4	3.0	7.8	9.0	6.8
1979	3.9	4.8	3.3	3.6	4.3	3.0	8.8	11.8	6.8
1980	4.0	4.7	3.4	3.6	4.4	3.1	8.4	9.3	7.6
1981	4.0	4.8	3.5	3.7	4.4	3.2	8.8	11.7	6.8
1982	4.3	5.1	3.9	4.0	4.7	3.5	9.7	11.9	8.0
1983	4.3	5.5	3.4	3.8	4.9	3.0	11.0	12.9	9.5
1984	4.4	5.6	3.5	4.1	5.1	3.3	9.0	12.9	6.3
1985	4.2	5.1	3.5	3.9	4.8	3.3	7.7	10.3	5.7
1986	4.3	5.1	3.8	4.0	4.8	3.3	9.0	9.7	8.5
1987	4.8	5.8	4.1	4.6	5.6	3.9	9.0	10.7	7.9
1988	4.4	5.3	3.8	4.1	5.1	3.5	9.1	10.5	8.0
1989	4.3	5.4	3.5	4.0	5.0	3.3	8.6	10.7	7.1
1990	4.5	5.8	3.6	4.2	5.5	3.3	9.3	11.3	7.9
1991	4.8	6.1	3.8	4.4	5.7	3.5	10.4	12.7	8.7
1992	4.8	5.7	4.1	4.5	5.5	3.8	9.1	10.1	8.3
1993	4.5	5.9	3.4	4.1	5.4	3.2	10.0	13.2	7.6
1994	4.5	5.3	4.0	4.0	4.8	3.5	10.2	11.3	9.9
1995	4.4	5.4	3.6	4.0	5.1	3.2	8.9	11.0	7.5
1996	4.2	5.3	3.4	3.9	5.0	3.0	9.3	10.1	8.6
Age at Diagnosis, 1992–1996									
All ages	4.5	5.5	3.7	4.1	5.1	3.3	9.5	11.2	8.4
Under 65 years	1.9	2.2	1.5	1.6	2.0	1.3	4.4	5.0	3.9
65 years and over	28.2	35.4	23.4	26.6	33.9	21.9	56.0	66.9	49.1
All ages (world standard)[1]	3.4	4.2	2.8	3.1	3.9	2.5	7.4	8.6	6.5

See footnotes at end of table.

Table 3.16. Cancer Incidence Rates—*Continued*

(Per 100,000 population; age-adjusted to the 1970 U.S. standard population, except where noted)

Site of cancer	All races			Whites			Blacks		
	Total	Males	Females	Total	Males	Females	Total	Males	Females
NON-HODGKIN'S LYMPHOMAS									
Year of Diagnosis									
1973	8.6	10.0	7.4	8.8	10.4	7.6	7.0	8.8	5.5
1974	8.9	10.4	7.7	9.2	10.7	8.0	5.9	7.5	4.6
1975	9.4	11.0	8.0	9.8	11.5	8.5	5.6	7.0	4.2
1976	9.5	10.7	8.5	9.8	11.1	8.9	5.3	6.5	4.3
1977	9.3	10.8	8.2	9.7	11.3	8.5	5.6	6.2	5.1
1978	10.0	11.9	8.4	10.4	12.3	8.9	6.2	8.3	4.3
1979	10.4	11.8	9.3	10.8	12.1	9.8	7.4	10.1	5.3
1980	10.5	12.4	8.9	10.8	12.6	9.2	7.4	9.3	6.0
1981	11.3	13.2	9.7	11.6	13.5	10.1	6.4	9.1	4.3
1982	11.2	13.0	9.6	11.7	13.7	10.0	8.5	8.7	8.1
1983	11.6	13.8	9.8	12.1	14.5	10.2	8.8	9.7	8.1
1984	12.6	15.1	10.6	13.2	15.6	11.2	8.2	11.2	5.8
1985	12.9	15.2	10.9	13.5	15.9	11.4	8.3	10.0	7.0
1986	13.1	15.9	10.7	13.8	16.9	11.3	8.8	10.8	7.1
1987	13.9	17.3	11.1	14.7	18.4	11.6	8.8	9.3	8.2
1988	14.2	17.5	11.6	15.0	18.3	12.3	9.9	13.5	7.1
1989	14.3	17.7	11.5	15.1	18.8	12.0	9.7	11.9	7.9
1990	15.3	18.9	12.3	16.0	19.7	12.9	11.3	14.0	9.2
1991	15.6	19.6	12.0	16.3	20.5	12.6	11.8	15.8	8.6
1992	15.3	18.9	12.2	16.0	19.6	12.9	11.4	15.3	8.2
1993	15.6	19.3	12.4	16.2	20.0	12.8	11.6	15.7	8.1
1994	16.3	20.3	13.0	16.9	20.7	13.5	12.0	17.7	7.2
1995	16.2	20.5	12.4	16.6	20.9	12.8	13.6	19.1	9.1
1996	15.5	19.2	12.2	15.9	19.7	12.7	12.0	15.0	9.5
Age at Diagnosis, 1992–1996									
All ages	15.8	19.7	12.5	16.3	20.2	12.9	12.1	16.6	8.5
Under 65 years	9.2	11.9	6.7	9.4	12.0	6.8	9.2	13.3	5.7
65 years and over	75.5	90.6	65.2	79.3	94.5	68.9	38.9	46.8	33.8
All ages (world standard) [1]	13.1	16.4	10.1	13.4	16.8	10.4	10.7	14.9	7.2
ORAL CAVITY AND PHARYNX CANCER									
Year of Diagnosis									
1973	11.3	17.5	6.2	11.2	17.6	6.1	10.9	16.6	6.0
1974	11.1	17.4	6.1	11.2	17.6	6.1	10.8	16.1	6.3
1975	11.4	18.0	6.2	11.4	18.3	6.0	11.7	17.2	7.3
1976	11.5	17.8	6.5	11.4	17.8	6.4	13.2	20.4	7.4
1977	11.1	17.4	6.1	11.0	17.1	6.1	12.8	21.1	6.0
1978	11.6	17.7	6.7	11.5	17.6	6.7	13.2	21.5	6.7
1979	12.1	18.7	6.9	11.8	18.4	6.6	16.5	24.9	9.9
1980	11.6	17.4	6.8	11.2	17.0	6.6	15.3	23.1	8.6
1981	11.8	18.0	6.9	11.6	17.5	6.9	14.9	25.1	6.7
1982	11.5	17.4	6.8	11.3	17.0	6.7	15.4	24.7	7.9
1983	11.6	18.2	6.3	11.5	18.1	6.3	14.3	23.3	7.1
1984	11.8	17.9	6.9	11.3	17.2	6.7	16.9	26.9	8.9
1985	11.5	17.1	7.0	11.4	16.8	7.1	14.1	22.6	7.5
1986	11.0	16.8	6.2	10.8	16.4	6.2	14.3	24.8	6.0
1987	11.6	17.8	6.5	11.5	17.5	6.6	14.8	26.2	6.1
1988	10.8	16.2	6.3	10.4	15.7	6.1	14.8	23.3	8.0
1989	10.7	16.2	6.3	10.5	15.6	6.3	14.2	24.2	6.4
1990	11.2	17.0	6.3	10.9	16.4	6.4	14.2	24.5	6.1
1991	10.8	16.3	6.2	10.7	16.1	6.2	12.9	21.2	6.5
1992	10.5	16.1	6.0	10.4	15.7	5.9	13.3	22.6	6.2
1993	10.9	16.5	6.1	10.6	16.0	6.1	14.2	22.9	7.2
1994	10.4	15.7	5.8	10.0	14.8	5.8	14.6	25.0	6.4
1995	10.0	14.7	6.0	9.8	14.3	6.1	12.2	20.3	5.9
1996	10.0	14.8	5.9	9.5	14.0	5.7	13.5	21.9	6.8
Age at Diagnosis, 1992–1996									
All ages	10.3	15.5	6.0	10.0	14.9	5.9	13.5	22.5	6.5
Under 65 years	6.5	9.7	3.6	6.1	8.9	3.4	10.7	17.6	4.9
65 years and over	45.0	69.2	27.6	46.0	70.3	28.7	39.8	67.0	20.8
All ages (world standard) [1]	8.6	12.9	4.9	8.3	12.3	4.9	11.8	19.5	5.6
PANCREAS CANCER									
Year of Diagnosis									
1973	10.0	12.9	7.7	9.8	12.8	7.5	13.6	15.9	11.6
1974	9.6	11.6	8.2	9.2	11.1	7.8	14.9	18.7	12.0
1975	9.5	12.5	7.3	9.4	12.5	7.1	13.5	15.6	11.6
1976	9.6	11.9	7.9	9.4	11.7	7.7	14.3	18.0	11.4
1977	9.5	11.8	7.8	9.3	11.6	7.6	14.0	16.2	12.1
1978	9.0	11.5	7.1	8.8	11.3	6.9	12.7	16.8	9.6
1979	9.2	11.3	7.7	9.0	11.0	7.4	13.2	15.9	11.2
1980	9.3	11.4	7.7	8.9	11.1	7.3	14.8	17.6	13.0
1981	9.3	11.0	8.0	9.1	10.7	7.8	13.9	17.6	11.0
1982	9.4	11.0	8.1	9.1	10.7	7.9	13.6	16.7	11.4
1983	9.8	11.7	8.4	9.4	11.2	8.1	14.9	18.6	12.2
1984	9.7	11.1	8.6	9.5	11.0	8.4	14.1	15.2	13.2
1985	9.6	11.3	8.2	9.2	10.7	8.1	14.7	19.7	11.3
1986	9.4	11.0	8.2	9.1	10.8	7.8	14.2	16.3	12.9
1987	9.3	11.0	8.1	8.8	10.6	7.5	15.5	16.1	15.0
1988	9.3	10.9	8.2	8.8	10.6	7.6	15.6	16.9	14.4
1989	9.0	10.4	7.9	8.7	10.2	7.5	11.9	13.1	11.0
1990	9.0	10.4	8.0	8.8	10.1	7.8	12.1	15.0	10.0
1991	9.0	10.3	8.0	8.7	10.0	7.6	13.5	14.6	12.7
1992	9.3	10.7	8.2	9.1	10.4	8.0	14.1	15.9	12.8
1993	8.7	10.0	7.6	8.3	9.6	7.3	13.6	15.4	12.0
1994	9.0	10.6	7.8	8.6	9.8	7.6	14.2	17.3	11.9
1995	8.7	9.9	7.7	8.3	9.5	7.5	14.2	16.4	12.4
1996	8.6	10.0	7.4	8.2	9.5	7.1	13.1	15.9	10.8
Age at Diagnosis, 1992–1996									
All ages	8.9	10.2	7.8	8.5	9.8	7.5	13.8	16.2	12.0
Under 65 years	3.3	4.0	2.7	3.1	3.7	2.5	5.9	7.4	4.6
65 years and over	59.6	67.2	54.0	57.7	64.7	52.7	86.5	96.6	79.0
All ages (world standard) [1]	6.7	7.8	5.8	6.4	7.4	5.5	10.6	12.6	9.1

See footnotes at end of table.

Table 3.16. Cancer Incidence Rates—*Continued*

(Per 100,000 population; age-adjusted to the 1970 U.S. standard population, except where noted)

Site of cancer	All races			Whites			Blacks		
	Total	Males	Females	Total	Males	Females	Total	Males	Females
STOMACH CANCER									
Year of Diagnosis									
1973	10.2	15.1	6.6	9.5	14.0	6.2	16.7	25.9	9.5
1974	10.0	14.5	6.5	9.1	13.3	5.9	15.1	21.4	10.0
1975	9.2	13.5	6.1	8.4	12.5	5.4	13.8	19.9	9.2
1976	9.5	13.9	6.2	8.7	12.6	5.7	12.9	19.3	8.0
1977	9.1	13.1	6.0	8.1	11.9	5.3	13.9	20.0	9.1
1978	9.1	13.0	6.2	8.1	11.8	5.4	14.3	19.1	10.5
1979	9.4	13.6	6.3	8.3	12.0	5.7	14.8	22.6	9.2
1980	8.9	13.5	5.4	8.1	12.3	4.9	12.4	21.4	5.9
1981	8.8	13.0	5.6	7.9	11.7	5.1	14.3	22.6	8.1
1982	8.7	13.0	5.5	7.6	11.5	4.8	15.6	25.8	8.1
1983	8.6	12.5	5.7	7.5	10.8	5.0	14.1	22.0	8.5
1984	8.3	12.0	5.6	7.3	10.8	4.8	13.0	17.6	9.4
1985	8.1	11.9	5.4	7.1	10.5	4.7	12.9	18.8	8.5
1986	8.1	11.9	5.3	7.2	10.8	4.5	12.9	18.4	9.0
1987	8.1	11.9	5.3	7.1	10.5	4.6	13.4	20.8	8.4
1988	8.1	12.3	5.0	7.0	10.7	4.2	13.2	20.2	7.9
1989	8.0	12.1	4.9	7.0	10.8	4.1	12.4	18.3	8.3
1990	7.4	10.9	4.8	6.3	9.4	4.0	11.7	17.8	7.3
1991	7.7	11.2	5.2	6.6	9.7	4.3	13.0	20.0	8.1
1992	7.4	10.7	4.8	6.4	9.4	4.0	11.0	15.9	7.3
1993	7.2	10.7	4.5	6.1	9.1	3.8	11.3	18.5	6.2
1994	7.2	10.9	4.4	6.1	9.4	3.6	12.1	19.4	6.9
1995	6.6	9.9	4.1	5.8	8.9	3.4	10.5	14.6	7.5
1996	6.6	9.8	4.2	5.6	8.4	3.5	11.5	17.6	6.9
Age at Diagnosis, 1992–1996									
All ages	7.0	10.4	4.4	6.0	9.0	3.7	11.3	17.2	7.0
Under 65 years	2.8	4.0	1.7	2.4	3.5	1.3	4.7	7.1	2.7
65 years and over	45.1	68.5	29.0	39.0	59.8	24.9	71.4	109.7	46.0
All ages (world standard)[1]	5.3	7.9	3.3	4.5	6.8	2.7	8.6	13.3	5.2
THYROID CANCER									
Year of Diagnosis									
1973	3.6	2.0	5.1	3.5	1.9	4.9	2.6	1.3	3.7
1974	4.0	2.5	5.4	3.8	2.4	5.2	2.8	1.4	4.0
1975	4.1	2.7	5.5	4.0	2.4	5.4	2.6	1.4	3.7
1976	4.2	2.5	5.7	4.0	2.5	5.6	2.9	1.2	4.3
1977	4.6	2.9	6.3	4.6	2.9	6.2	3.3	1.5	4.7
1978	4.3	2.6	6.0	4.2	2.5	5.9	2.5	1.4	3.4
1979	3.8	2.3	5.3	3.8	2.2	5.3	2.7	1.6	3.7
1980	3.7	2.0	5.3	3.7	1.9	5.3	2.0	1.0	2.9
1981	3.8	2.2	5.4	3.8	2.2	5.4	2.1	1.0	2.9
1982	4.0	2.5	5.3	3.9	2.4	5.3	2.8	1.7	3.7
1983	4.1	2.4	5.7	4.2	2.3	6.0	2.5	1.7	3.1
1984	4.2	2.3	6.0	4.1	2.2	5.9	2.6	1.6	3.5
1985	4.5	2.6	6.2	4.4	2.7	6.2	2.4	1.6	3.1
1986	4.6	2.6	6.5	4.5	2.7	6.4	2.8	1.1	4.3
1987	4.3	2.4	6.1	4.3	2.5	6.1	2.3	0.9	3.5
1988	4.3	2.5	6.0	4.2	2.6	5.9	2.2	1.5	2.8
1989	4.6	2.5	6.6	4.7	2.7	6.7	2.1	0.6	3.3
1990	4.7	2.5	6.9	4.8	2.5	7.1	3.0	1.8	4.0
1991	4.7	2.7	6.6	4.8	2.8	6.8	2.7	1.5	3.6
1992	5.1	3.1	7.0	5.1	3.0	7.2	3.7	2.9	4.4
1993	4.8	3.0	6.6	4.9	3.2	6.7	2.8	1.8	3.8
1994	5.3	2.8	7.6	5.4	2.9	7.8	3.2	1.6	4.5
1995	5.4	2.9	7.8	5.5	3.1	7.9	2.5	1.1	3.6
1996	5.5	2.9	8.0	5.6	3.0	8.2	3.2	1.2	4.9
Age at Diagnosis, 1992–1996									
All ages	5.2	2.9	7.4	5.3	3.0	7.6	3.1	1.7	4.2
Under 65 years	4.8	2.4	7.1	4.9	2.6	7.3	2.6	1.3	3.7
65 years and over	9.3	7.6	10.6	8.9	7.3	10.0	7.4	5.2	8.9
All ages (world standard)[1]	5.0	2.7	7.2	5.1	2.8	7.4	2.8	1.5	3.9

See footnotes at end of table.

Table 3.16. Cancer Incidence Rates—*Continued*

(Per 100,000 population; age-adjusted to the 1970 U.S. standard population, except where noted)

Site of cancer	Females								
	All races			Whites			Blacks		
	All	Under 50 years	50 years and over	All	Under 50 years	50 years and over	All	Under 50 years	50 years and over
BREAST CANCER									
Year of Diagnosis									
1973	82.6	29.0	247.7	84.4	29.4	254.0	69.0	25.9	201.9
1974	94.9	33.0	285.8	96.7	32.9	293.4	79.3	30.4	230.0
1975	88.1	30.0	267.4	90.0	30.1	274.8	78.5	30.9	225.5
1976	85.5	29.7	257.5	87.8	30.3	265.1	70.5	27.5	203.2
1977	84.1	28.8	254.4	86.2	29.1	262.2	72.2	27.2	211.0
1978	84.1	28.5	255.5	86.5	28.8	264.4	71.8	29.6	202.0
1979	85.6	28.0	263.0	87.6	28.4	270.2	72.4	27.6	210.5
1980	85.4	27.7	263.4	87.8	28.0	272.1	74.5	27.8	218.6
1981	88.8	28.8	274.2	91.8	29.3	284.5	77.6	28.6	228.8
1982	89.3	29.9	272.7	92.3	30.3	283.4	77.5	28.0	229.9
1983	93.3	29.6	289.9	96.2	30.0	300.2	86.3	30.3	259.1
1984	97.2	31.1	301.3	100.5	31.6	313.1	85.0	32.1	248.1
1985	104.1	32.6	324.6	107.3	32.7	337.3	92.7	33.5	275.1
1986	106.7	32.6	335.0	109.6	33.1	345.4	95.6	32.6	290.1
1987	113.2	33.5	359.1	118.1	34.2	376.7	90.8	31.5	274.0
1988	110.3	32.3	350.8	114.5	33.0	366.0	99.4	31.4	308.8
1989	106.7	32.0	337.0	110.8	32.8	351.6	89.4	31.4	268.4
1990	110.4	33.4	347.6	114.5	33.5	364.4	96.5	35.4	285.0
1991	112.0	34.6	350.5	116.3	34.7	368.2	97.7	37.3	284.1
1992	111.1	31.9	355.3	114.2	32.0	367.7	102.2	34.0	312.4
1993	108.9	31.5	347.4	112.0	31.6	360.0	100.8	33.2	309.3
1994	110.8	31.2	356.3	114.6	31.3	371.7	102.1	34.9	309.6
1995	111.6	31.7	357.9	115.3	31.8	372.8	102.4	33.4	315.3
1996	110.7	31.3	355.8	113.3	31.1	366.9	100.3	30.9	314.1
1992–1996	110.6	31.5	354.7	113.9	31.5	368.0	101.5	33.2	312.3
CERVIX UTERI CANCER									
Year of Diagnosis									
1973	14.2	8.7	31.2	12.8	7.6	28.8	29.9	17.9	66.8
1974	12.7	7.6	28.7	11.6	7.0	25.9	25.2	12.0	65.7
1975	12.4	7.3	28.2	11.1	6.8	24.6	27.9	13.2	73.2
1976	11.9	7.2	26.6	10.8	6.7	23.6	24.6	12.0	63.6
1977	10.9	6.4	24.7	9.8	5.7	22.2	23.1	12.4	55.9
1978	10.5	6.3	23.5	9.5	5.8	20.8	19.8	9.3	52.3
1979	10.6	6.6	23.1	9.2	5.8	19.7	23.5	12.0	59.3
1980	10.2	6.1	22.7	9.1	5.5	20.3	19.0	10.0	46.8
1981	9.0	5.5	19.7	8.0	5.0	17.3	19.1	10.1	47.0
1982	8.9	5.4	19.7	7.9	5.1	16.5	17.8	7.6	49.0
1983	8.8	5.6	18.6	8.1	5.2	16.9	15.2	8.9	34.5
1984	9.2	6.1	18.7	8.3	5.7	16.4	17.4	9.7	41.0
1985	8.5	5.3	18.4	7.6	5.1	15.3	15.9	6.8	43.8
1986	9.0	5.9	18.5	8.0	5.4	16.0	15.3	8.0	37.7
1987	8.3	5.4	17.4	7.5	5.2	14.5	15.3	6.7	41.7
1988	8.8	6.0	17.6	8.0	5.6	15.1	15.4	8.0	38.2
1989	8.9	5.9	18.0	8.3	5.9	15.6	13.3	5.9	36.1
1990	8.9	6.1	17.7	8.3	5.9	15.9	13.8	7.2	34.0
1991	8.4	5.3	17.9	7.7	5.1	15.6	13.4	6.7	34.0
1992	8.3	5.6	16.6	7.9	5.5	15.3	11.1	7.3	22.8
1993	8.1	5.5	16.4	7.6	5.4	14.6	11.3	6.6	25.6
1994	7.9	5.2	16.3	7.3	5.1	13.9	11.6	5.3	31.1
1995	7.4	5.0	14.8	6.6	4.7	12.3	11.3	6.0	27.9
1996	7.7	5.4	14.8	7.0	5.1	12.7	10.6	5.8	25.3
1992–1996	7.9	5.3	15.8	7.3	5.2	13.8	11.2	6.2	26.6
CORPUS AND UTERUS, NOS CANCER									
Year of Diagnosis									
1973	28.4	5.3	99.5	29.5	5.4	103.8	15.0	2.2	54.3
1974	30.8	4.9	110.6	32.4	5.0	116.6	13.0	2.3	46.1
1975	32.1	4.9	116.1	33.7	5.1	122.1	17.0	2.7	61.3
1976	31.0	4.7	112.0	32.6	4.7	118.8	14.4	2.4	51.2
1977	28.5	4.3	103.2	29.8	4.4	108.3	17.1	2.6	61.9
1978	26.5	4.5	94.3	28.0	4.7	99.8	15.9	2.8	56.1
1979	24.9	4.0	89.4	26.1	4.0	94.2	14.4	2.9	49.9
1980	24.2	3.7	87.5	25.3	3.7	92.0	14.1	1.8	52.0
1981	24.1	4.1	85.6	25.1	4.0	90.1	14.3	2.0	52.4
1982	23.6	3.8	85.0	24.8	3.8	89.6	14.7	1.9	54.0
1983	23.4	3.6	84.4	24.6	3.7	89.1	16.0	2.5	57.6
1984	22.6	3.4	81.9	23.9	3.6	86.6	14.7	1.2	56.3
1985	22.1	3.4	79.5	23.2	3.6	83.6	15.4	1.6	57.7
1986	21.3	3.6	75.8	22.4	3.7	80.1	14.2	1.9	52.0
1987	21.5	3.7	76.6	22.8	3.9	80.9	13.4	1.3	50.7
1988	20.5	3.4	73.3	21.4	3.3	77.4	14.1	2.1	50.9
1989	21.3	3.4	76.4	22.2	3.6	79.7	16.3	1.4	62.5
1990	21.8	3.3	78.6	23.1	3.5	83.6	14.4	1.6	54.0
1991	21.3	3.2	77.0	22.5	3.3	81.8	14.7	2.3	53.2
1992	21.5	3.6	76.8	22.7	3.6	81.6	14.6	2.0	53.5
1993	21.0	3.9	73.7	22.1	3.8	78.8	14.7	2.8	51.5
1994	21.8	3.8	77.5	22.7	3.7	81.3	15.7	2.1	57.7
1995	21.9	3.5	78.5	22.8	3.4	82.5	15.8	1.8	59.0
1996	21.1	3.3	75.9	21.8	3.1	79.5	15.7	2.3	56.7
1992–1996	21.5	3.6	76.5	22.4	3.5	80.8	15.3	2.2	55.8

See footnotes at end of table.

Table 3.16. Cancer Incidence Rates—*Continued*

(Per 100,000 population; age-adjusted to the 1970 U.S. standard population, except where noted)

Site of cancer	Females								
	All races			Whites			Blacks		
	All	Under 50 years	50 years and over	All	Under 50 years	50 years and over	All	Under 50 years	50 years and over
OVARY CANCER									
Year of Diagnosis									
1973	14.1	4.7	43.1	14.6	4.9	44.6	10.5	2.3	36.0
1974	14.7	4.9	44.9	15.3	5.1	46.8	10.2	2.1	35.1
1975	14.1	4.9	42.3	14.4	4.9	43.9	10.1	3.7	29.8
1976	13.7	4.3	42.4	14.3	4.5	44.6	9.4	2.9	29.8
1977	13.6	4.6	41.2	14.1	4.7	43.0	9.6	3.8	27.5
1978	13.2	4.2	41.1	13.9	4.3	43.3	8.5	2.8	26.0
1979	13.2	4.5	40.0	13.5	4.6	41.0	10.5	3.3	32.5
1980	13.3	4.1	41.8	14.0	4.2	44.0	10.1	2.6	33.4
1981	13.2	4.1	41.3	13.7	4.2	43.1	9.8	2.6	32.0
1982	13.4	3.9	42.5	13.8	4.1	43.9	10.8	3.3	33.9
1983	13.8	4.3	42.9	14.1	4.3	44.3	11.5	2.9	38.1
1984	14.1	4.4	43.7	14.8	4.6	46.1	9.4	2.5	30.6
1985	14.3	4.3	45.2	15.1	4.5	47.5	10.1	3.1	31.7
1986	12.9	3.8	41.1	13.5	4.1	42.4	9.3	1.1	34.7
1987	13.9	3.8	45.0	14.7	4.0	47.6	10.2	2.9	32.6
1988	14.9	5.0	45.7	15.6	5.2	47.8	10.9	4.0	31.9
1989	15.3	5.3	46.1	16.2	5.6	48.9	10.8	3.0	35.0
1990	15.2	5.1	46.4	16.1	5.4	49.1	10.1	2.4	33.7
1991	15.4	5.1	47.1	16.3	5.4	50.0	10.1	3.0	31.8
1992	15.0	5.3	44.8	15.8	5.7	47.0	10.6	3.7	31.9
1993	15.0	4.9	46.1	15.7	5.2	48.0	11.1	3.1	35.9
1994	14.5	5.4	42.6	15.0	5.3	44.7	12.4	4.3	37.1
1995	14.5	5.3	43.0	15.4	5.7	45.3	9.9	2.8	31.7
1996	14.1	4.9	42.6	15.3	5.2	46.4	8.5	2.9	25.7
1992–1996	14.6	5.2	43.8	15.4	5.4	46.3	10.5	3.4	32.4

See footnotes at end of table.

Table 3.16. Cancer Incidence Rates—*Continued*

(Per 100,000 population; age-adjusted to the 1970 U.S. standard population, except where noted)

Site of cancer	Males		
	All races	Whites	Blacks
PROSTATE CANCER			
Year of Diagnosis			
1973	64.2	62.6	106.3
1974	65.6	64.8	100.7
1975	70.6	69.0	111.5
1976	73.5	72.7	110.4
1977	76.1	74.5	122.2
1978	75.1	73.6	116.6
1979	78.0	77.1	123.1
1980	79.8	78.8	126.6
1981	82.1	81.0	127.0
1982	82.2	81.3	130.7
1983	84.8	83.9	134.6
1984	84.6	83.0	139.6
1985	88.3	87.2	133.8
1986	91.4	91.1	132.6
1987	103.0	103.1	148.2
1988	106.2	106.5	148.7
1989	113.0	113.1	150.2
1990	132.5	133.4	168.4
1991	169.2	169.3	222.9
1992	190.8	188.7	258.0
1993	171.1	163.9	271.6
1994	148.4	141.0	246.9
1995	139.3	132.3	218.3
1996	135.7	127.8	211.3
Age at Diagnosis, 1992–1996			
All ages	156.5	150.2	240.4
Under 65 years	49.6	47.5	89.1
65 years and over	1 131.9	1 087.2	1 622.1
All ages (world standard) [1]	118.2	113.5	184.7
TESTIS CANCER			
Year of Diagnosis			
1973	3.0	3.2	0.4
1974	3.3	3.5	1.5
1975	3.3	3.7	0.6
1976	3.2	3.5	1.1
1977	3.8	4.3	0.4
1978	3.2	3.6	1.3
1979	3.5	3.9	0.8
1980	4.0	4.5	0.8
1981	3.8	4.3	0.6
1982	4.0	4.6	0.7
1983	4.2	4.8	1.0
1984	4.0	4.5	0.6
1985	4.1	4.7	1.1
1986	4.3	5.0	0.5
1987	4.4	5.0	0.8
1988	4.1	4.8	0.6
1989	4.9	5.6	1.0
1990	4.5	5.3	0.6
1991	4.6	5.1	0.7
1992	4.6	5.4	0.4
1993	4.5	5.3	0.7
1994	4.9	5.6	1.2
1995	4.2	4.7	1.3
1996	4.6	5.4	0.9
Age at Diagnosis, 1992–1996			
All ages	4.5	5.3	0.9
Under 65 years	4.9	5.7	1.0
65 years and over	1.2	1.2	0.2
All ages (world standard) [1]	4.8	5.5	1.0

SOURCE: L.A.G. Ries, C.L. Kosary, B.F. Hankey, B.A. Miller, L. Clegg, B.K. Edwards (eds). SEER *Cancer Statistics Review*, 1973–1996, National Cancer Institute. Bethesda, MD, 1999.

1. Rates are per 100,000 and are age-adjusted to the world standard population.

Table 3.17. Cancer Survival Rates

(Percent of patients expected to be alive five years after diagnosis)

Site of cancer	All Races			Whites			Blacks		
	Total	Males	Females	Total	Males	Females	Total	Males	Females
ALL SITES									
Year of Diagnosis									
1960–1963 [1]	—	—	—	39.0	—	—	27.0	—	—
1970–1973 [1]	—	—	—	43.0	—	—	31.0	—	—
1974–1976 [2]	49.5	41.0	56.9	50.5	42.1	57.7	39.1	31.6	47.0
1977–1979 [2]	50.0	43.3	56.2	51.1	44.6	57.0	39.2	32.4	46.7
1980–1982 [2]	50.9	45.2	56.2	52.0	46.6	57.0	39.7	34.2	45.9
1983–1985 [2]	52.4	46.8	57.7	53.8	48.4	58.8	39.8	34.7	45.4
1986–1988 [2]	*55.2	*49.9	*60.2	*56.6	*51.6	*61.3	*42.5	*37.6	*47.6
1989–1995 [2]	*59.4	*57.5	*61.4	*60.9	*59.2	*62.6	*47.7	*46.5	*49.1
Age at Diagnosis, 1992–1996									
Under 45 years	67.8	55.3	77.8	70.1	57.9	80.2	51.6	36.9	62.6
45–54 years	62.4	50.8	71.1	64.8	53.5	73.0	46.5	36.5	56.1
55–64 years	59.2	56.8	61.8	60.8	58.8	63.3	47.5	47.3	47.7
65–74 years	59.7	62.0	56.4	60.9	63.3	57.7	49.8	54.6	42.2
75 years and over	52.4	56.7	48.4	53.5	57.8	49.7	42.4	48.3	36.2
Under 65 years	62.5	55.0	69.5	64.5	57.3	71.2	48.4	41.8	55.3
65 years and over	56.7	60.0	52.9	57.9	61.2	54.1	47.2	52.6	39.9
ALL SITES EXCLUDING LUNG AND BRONCHUS									
Year of Diagnosis									
1960–1963 [1]	—	—	—	—	—	—	—	—	—
1970–1973 [1]	—	—	—	—	—	—	—	—	—
1974–1976 [2]	55.3	49.0	60.0	56.4	50.3	60.8	44.7	38.8	49.7
1977–1979 [2]	56.2	51.8	59.8	57.3	53.2	60.6	45.4	40.4	49.7
1980–1982 [2]	57.6	54.1	60.4	58.8	55.6	61.3	46.1	42.4	49.6
1983–1985 [2]	59.2	55.6	62.3	60.7	57.3	63.5	46.4	43.2	49.3
1986–1988 [2]	*62.3	*58.5	*65.6	*63.8	*60.4	*66.9	*49.1	*45.6	*52.4
1989–1995 [2]	*66.5	*65.8	*67.3	*68.1	*67.5	*68.7	*54.7	*55.2	*54.2
Age at Diagnosis, 1992–1996									
Under 45 years	69.5	57.1	79.1	71.6	59.4	81.4	54.3	39.8	64.5
45–54 years	68.9	58.3	76.2	71.2	60.8	78.1	54.0	44.6	61.7
55–64 years	68.1	67.0	69.3	69.9	68.9	71.1	56.5	58.4	53.9
65–74 years	68.8	72.2	64.2	70.1	73.5	65.6	58.8	65.3	48.9
75 years and over	59.0	65.1	53.5	60.3	66.4	54.9	47.7	55.9	39.5
Under 65 years	68.7	62.1	74.6	70.7	64.2	76.5	55.1	49.7	60.1
65 years and over	64.7	69.4	59.4	66.0	70.7	60.7	54.7	62.1	45.0
URINARY BLADDER CANCER									
Year of Diagnosis									
1960–1963 [1]	—	—	—	53.0	53.0	53.0	24.0	24.0	24.0
1970–1973 [1]	—	—	—	61.0	61.0	60.0	36.0	38.0	**27.0
1974–1976 [2]	72.6	73.8	69.4	73.8	74.7	71.6	47.7	54.2	**36.5
1977–1979 [2]	75.0	76.7	70.5	75.9	77.1	72.6	55.1	62.9	**40.3
1980–1982 [2]	77.9	79.1	74.7	78.8	79.8	76.0	58.3	62.6	**49.8
1983–1985 [2]	77.6	79.2	73.0	78.2	79.5	74.5	59.0	64.2	**49.5
1986–1988 [2]	*79.7	*81.4	*74.8	*80.6	*82.2	*76.0	*62.0	*67.5	*49.7
1989–1995 [2]	*80.7	*83.1	*74.1	*81.8	*83.9	*75.7	*62.2	*66.6	*54.6
Age at Diagnosis, 1992–1996									
Under 45 years	92.1	93.0	89.4	93.4	93.9	92.0	**78.5	**81.7	—
45–54 years	87.4	88.1	85.0	88.0	88.4	86.5	**73.1	**78.5	**57.8
55–64 years	85.3	86.6	81.1	86.4	87.6	82.6	64.0	**67.4	**55.4
65–74 years	81.7	84.3	74.0	82.5	85.0	74.8	63.0	**65.6	**58.6
75 years and over	70.9	74.0	64.8	72.3	75.0	67.0	50.1	**52.3	**46.2
Under 65 years	86.7	87.8	83.3	87.7	88.5	85.0	68.7	72.7	**58.6
65 years and over	77.2	80.4	69.4	78.3	81.2	70.8	57.7	60.8	52.8

See footnotes at end of table.

Table 3.17. Cancer Survival Rates—*Continued*

(Percent of patients expected to be alive five years after diagnosis)

Site of cancer	All Races			Whites			Blacks		
	Total	Males	Females	Total	Males	Females	Total	Males	Females
BRAIN AND OTHER NERVOUS SYSTEM CANCER									
Year of Diagnosis									
1960–1963 [1]	—	—	—	18.0	16.0	21.0	19.0	17.0	21.0
1970–1973 [1]	—	—	—	20.0	18.0	22.0	19.0	19.0	19.0
1974–1976 [2]	22.4	20.6	24.7	22.2	20.6	24.2	26.7	17.3	**39.5
1977–1979 [2]	24.4	23.0	26.2	23.8	22.6	25.4	27.3	25.0	**29.9
1980–1982 [2]	25.2	24.5	26.2	24.6	23.9	25.5	31.1	33.9	**27.3
1983–1985 [2]	26.5	25.1	28.3	25.8	24.7	27.2	32.4	31.6	33.5
1986–1988 [2]	30.3	28.9	32.2	29.6	27.7	31.9	32.3	35.9	28.1
1989–1995 [2]	*30.4	*31.2	*29.5	*29.6	*30.0	*29.0	*38.6	*42.3	34.8
Age at Diagnosis, 1992–1996									
Under 45 years	57.9	57.7	58.1	58.4	57.6	59.8	55.5	59.1	51.4
45–54 years	22.0	19.2	26.2	21.6	18.4	26.4	**22.0	**24.2	**18.9
55–64 years	10.6	9.2	12.5	10.1	8.5	12.2	8.9	**10.9	**7.3
65–74 years	6.2	6.3	6.2	5.9	6.1	5.7	**13.2	**11.8	**15.9
75 years and over	3.7	2.9	4.2	3.5	2.9	3.9	*9.1	—	**11.0
Under 65 years	40.3	39.2	41.8	39.8	38.2	42.1	43.8	47.5	39.9
65 years and over	5.3	5.2	5.4	5.1	5.1	5.0	12.0	*9.7	**14.2
COLON AND RECTUM CANCER									
Year of Diagnosis									
1960–1963 [1]	—	—	—	—	—	—	—	—	—
1970–1973 [1]	—	—	—	—	—	—	—	—	—
1974–1976 [2]	49.8	48.9	50.7	50.1	49.2	50.9	44.9	41.5	47.7
1977–1979 [2]	51.9	50.7	53.0	52.2	51.2	53.2	45.7	43.7	47.3
1980–1982 [2]	54.3	53.8	54.8	54.8	54.4	55.1	46.5	43.5	49.2
1983–1985 [2]	56.9	56.8	56.9	57.6	57.7	57.6	47.9	46.9	48.8
1986–1988 [2]	60.1	60.3	59.9	60.7	61.2	60.3	52.1	50.6	53.5
1989–1995 [2]	*61.0	*61.2	*60.8	*61.8	*62.0	*61.5	*51.7	*51.7	*51.7
Age at Diagnosis, 1992–1996									
Under 45 years	58.2	56.4	60.2	59.5	57.9	61.3	51.4	48.5	54.4
45–54 years	62.6	61.5	64.1	63.6	62.2	65.6	54.9	54.2	55.7
55–64 years	62.9	62.9	62.8	63.4	63.6	63.1	55.7	56.5	55.0
65–74 years	63.1	63.6	62.6	64.1	64.6	63.7	52.0	51.7	52.3
75 years and over	57.2	56.9	57.5	58.1	57.7	58.3	44.5	44.3	44.6
Under 65 years	62.1	61.6	62.7	62.9	62.5	63.5	54.7	54.2	55.1
65 years and over	60.4	61.0	59.9	61.3	61.9	60.8	49.1	49.2	49.0
ESOPHAGUS CANCER									
Year of Diagnosis									
1960–1963 [1]	—	—	—	4.0	4.0	6.0	1.0	0.0	2.0
1970–1973 [1]	—	—	—	4.0	4.0	4.0	4.0	4.0	3.0
1974–1976 [2]	4.6	3.7	6.8	5.1	4.4	6.6	4.0	2.1	9.0
1977–1979 [2]	5.0	4.7	5.8	5.6	5.6	5.6	2.8	2.4	4.3
1980–1982 [2]	6.8	6.1	8.5	7.4	6.6	9.2	5.4	4.6	7.2
1983–1985 [2]	8.3	7.0	11.8	9.3	7.8	13.1	6.3	5.2	9.5
1986–1988 [2]	9.9	*10.0	9.7	10.8	11.4	13.1	7.3	7.1	8.0
1989–1995 [2]	*12.3	*12.1	*13.1	*13.3	*13.2	*13.6	*8.9	*8.0	10.7
Age at Diagnosis, 1992–1996									
Under 45 years	17.3	16.6	**21.5	21.4	21.9	—	9.1	0.0	—
45–54 years	15.1	14.5	17.1	16.9	16.2	**20.5	10.0	8.9	**13.1
55–64 years	13.5	12.5	17.2	15.0	13.7	20.0	9.1	8.4	10.9
65–74 years	11.2	11.6	10.3	11.6	12.1	9.9	9.2	8.6	10.6
75 years and over	9.8	9.1	10.7	10.8	10.1	11.5	4.6	3.9	**5.5
Under 65 years	14.3	13.4	17.6	16.0	15.0	20.3	9.4	8.3	12.0
65 years and over	10.7	10.8	10.5	11.3	11.5	10.7	8.0	7.6	9.1

See footnotes at end of table.

Table 3.17. Cancer Survival Rates—*Continued*

(Percent of patients expected to be alive five years after diagnosis)

Site of cancer	All Races			Whites			Blacks		
	Total	Males	Females	Total	Males	Females	Total	Males	Females
HODGKIN'S DISEASE									
Year of Diagnosis									
1960–1963 [1]	—	—	—	40.0	34.0	48.0	—	—	—
1970–1973 [1]	—	—	—	67.0	66.0	69.0	—	—	—
1974–1976 [2]	71.1	69.5	73.0	71.5	69.6	73.8	68.8	**72.1	**61.2
1977–1979 [2]	73.1	70.8	76.2	73.2	70.8	76.3	72.8	**72.0	**73.5
1980–1982 [2]	74.5	73.9	75.2	75.0	74.6	75.5	71.8	**73.2	**69.5
1983–1985 [2]	78.8	77.6	80.4	79.0	77.9	80.4	77.8	**74.0	**85.6
1986–1988 [2]	79.3	77.0	82.3	80.1	77.6	83.3	71.5	**74.3	*67.9
1989–1995 [2]	*82.1	*79.2	*85.5	*82.9	*80.4	*85.9	76.2	68.6	84.3
Age at Diagnosis, 1992–1996									
Under 45 years	89.3	85.9	93.1	90.7	87.5	94.3	**78.3	**71.5	86.0
45–54 years	74.1	72.0	78.5	74.1	72.6	77.4	**71.4	63.3	—
55–64 years	73.4	71.4	75.4	74.2	**72.0	**77.1	***66.2	—	—
65–74 years	54.5	*54.8	**53.3	53.4	**54.4	**50.2	—	—	—
75 years and over	30.8	**18.3	**38.4	29.3	**15.5	**37.6	—	—	—
Under 65 years	86.6	83.0	91.0	87.8	84.4	92.0	**76.7	69.6	84.7
65 years and over	45.3	44.3	46.3	44.3	44.1	44.3	***54.9	—	—
KIDNEY AND RENAL PELVIS CANCER									
Year of Diagnosis									
1960–1963 [1]	—	—	—	37.0	36.0	39.0	38.0	38.0	37.0
1970–1973 [1]	—	—	—	46.0	44.0	50.0	44.0	40.0	**49.0
1974–1976 [2]	51.6	51.0	52.5	51.8	51.1	52.9	48.7	49.4	**47.4
1977–1979 [2]	50.9	50.9	50.9	50.9	51.2	50.3	51.8	44.7	**60.9
1980–1982 [2]	51.5	51.9	51.0	51.0	51.8	49.8	55.4	52.6	**59.8
1983–1985 [2]	55.6	56.3	54.4	55.7	56.6	54.2	54.8	53.6	56.4
1986–1988 [2]	56.9	57.3	56.2	57.5	*58.1	*56.7	53.0	51.7	54.8
1989–1995 [2]	*60.3	*60.5	*60.1	*61.1	*61.7	*60.1	57.7	54.7	62.0
Age at Diagnosis, 1992–1996									
Under 45 years	78.1	76.8	79.8	79.3	77.9	81.3	69.2	68.4	**69.7
45–54 years	64.2	61.2	70.8	65.5	62.8	71.1	56.0	51.7	**69.5
55–64 years	60.9	59.7	63.0	61.4	60.5	63.2	60.6	**55.9	**67.7
65–74 years	57.5	59.2	55.0	58.6	60.9	55.1	**50.7	**47.4	**55.3
75 years and over	48.2	50.9	45.9	49.0	52.0	46.5	**47.9	49.0	44.5
Under 65 years	65.7	63.6	69.6	66.5	64.6	69.9	61.8	57.5	**68.8
65 years and over	54.0	56.5	51.0	55.0	58.0	51.3	49.8	**48.9	**51.1
LARYNX CANCER									
Year of Diagnosis									
1960–1963 [1]	—	—	—	53.0	54.0	46.0	—	—	—
1970–1973 [1]	—	—	—	62.0	63.0	56.0	59.7	58.8	**64.0
1974–1976 [2]	65.6	65.3	67.2	66.4	66.1	67.9	56.0	54.3	**63.0
1977–1979 [2]	67.0	67.9	63.0	68.3	69.4	62.9	58.4	59.9	**50.4
1980–1982 [2]	68.1	68.0	68.5	69.2	69.0	70.4	55.3	56.5	**51.3
1983–1985 [2]	67.0	68.1	61.7	68.5	69.5	63.6	54.2	52.4	**61.5
1986–1988 [2]	66.7	67.3	*64.2	68.6	69.6	64.4	53.3	54.2	**50.5
1989–1995 [2]	64.6	66.2	*58.6	66.1	67.7	59.9			
Age at Diagnosis, 1992–1996									
Under 45 years	63.1	63.7	**60.5	68.4	68.2	**68.8	**43.6	**47.4	—
45–54 years	66.8	67.8	63.0	71.1	71.7	68.5	49.8	**51.6	**44.5
55–64 years	65.8	66.4	63.4	67.6	68.4	64.3	52.0	**50.5	**58.3
65–74 years	64.4	66.3	*57.2	64.2	65.9	*57.6	61.0	**62.9	***53.3
75 years and over	59.8	64.4	**44.6	60.4	65.4	**44.5	***57.1	***58.9	—
Under 65 years	65.7	66.4	63.0	68.6	69.3	65.9	50.0	**50.2	**49.2
65 years and over	63.2	65.9	53.7	63.3	65.9	53.8	60.5	**63.1	**52.4

See footnotes at end of table.

Table 3.17. Cancer Survival Rates—Continued

(Percent of patients expected to be alive five years after diagnosis)

Site of cancer	All Races Total	All Races Males	All Races Females	Whites Total	Whites Males	Whites Females	Blacks Total	Blacks Males	Blacks Females
ALL LEUKEMIAS									
Year of Diagnosis									
1960–1963 [1]	—	—	—	14.0	—	—	—	—	—
1970–1973 [1]	—	—	—	22.0	—	—	—	—	—
1974–1976 [2]	34.4	33.2	35.8	35.1	33.9	36.7	31.2	32.6	29.7
1977–1979 [2]	37.1	36.4	37.9	37.9	37.2	38.8	30.1	29.2	31.2
1980–1982 [2]	38.6	38.3	39.0	39.3	39.4	39.3	33.2	30.2	36.7
1983–1985 [2]	40.2	39.7	40.9	41.6	41.2	42.0	33.4	32.3	34.6
1986–1988 [2]	*42.4	*43.4	*40.9	*43.4	44.8	*41.6	36.8	35.8	38.0
1989–1995 [2]	*43.1	*43.7	*42.3	*44.4	45.5	*43.0	33.5	29.7	37.5
Age at Diagnosis, 1992–1996									
Under 45 years	55.9	55.4	56.6	58.2	58.3	58.1	**43.5	**38.3	**49.9
45–54 years	47.3	48.1	46.0	49.9	51.0	47.9	**33.5	**31.3	**35.4
55–64 years	45.7	45.9	45.5	48.0	48.4	47.5	32.0	24.9	39.9
65–74 years	39.1	38.6	39.8	40.7	40.4	41.1	27.9	25.7	**31.6
75 years and over	27.8	27.7	27.9	28.8	29.0	28.7	20.0	**13.7	23.2
Under 65 years	51.2	50.9	51.6	53.3	53.5	53.1	38.9	33.8	45.0
65 years and over	33.9	34.2	33.5	35.2	35.8	34.5	24.5	22.1	26.8
LIVER AND INTRAHEPATIC BILE DUCT CANCER									
Year of Diagnosis									
1960–1963 [1]	—	—	—	—	—	—	—	—	—
1970–1973 [1]	—	—	—	—	—	—	—	—	—
1974–1976 [2]	3.8	2.5	6.1	4.3	2.5	7.0	2.0	1.4	*3.3
1977–1979 [2]	3.7	2.1	6.6	3.5	2.2	5.5	4.9	3.4	*8.6
1980–1982 [2]	3.5	2.6	5.1	3.9	2.8	5.5	1.6	2.2	0.0
1983–1985 [2]	5.5	3.8	8.7	6.0	4.4	8.8	4.0	1.1	**10.8
1986–1988 [2]	*6.1	*4.1	10.0	*6.9	*4.4	10.9	5.3	4.6	6.6
1989–1995 [2]	*5.3	*4.3	*7.2	*6.0	*4.9	8.0	2.8	1.4	7.3
Age at Diagnosis, 1992–1996									
Under 45 years	16.8	12.6	27.9	23.0	18.3	**31.8	11.9	5.7	—
45–54 years	6.1	5.1	8.9	7.9	6.6	11.4	0.0	0.0	—
55–64 years	4.4	3.6	6.5	4.9	4.1	6.5	1.7	0.0	5.3
65–74 years	3.1	2.2	4.9	3.3	2.6	4.9	0.0	0.0	0.0
75 years and over	3.0	2.6	3.4	3.2	2.3	4.2	2.1	2.3	0.0
Under 65 years	7.7	6.1	11.9	9.7	7.8	13.7	3.5	1.4	12.8
65 years and over	3.1	2.4	4.1	3.3	2.5	4.6	1.3	1.5	0.0
LUNG AND BRONCHUS CANCER									
Year of Diagnosis									
1960–1963 [1]	—	—	—	8.0	7.0	11.0	5.0	5.0	6.0
1970–1973 [1]	—	—	—	10.0	9.0	14.0	7.0	6.0	10.0
1974–1976 [2]	12.5	11.2	15.8	12.5	11.1	16.0	11.5	11.0	13.1
1977–1979 [2]	13.4	11.8	17.2	13.7	12.1	17.3	11.1	9.1	17.0
1980–1982 [2]	13.4	12.1	16.1	13.5	12.2	16.2	12.2	11.0	15.4
1983–1985 [2]	13.6	11.9	16.8	13.9	12.1	17.0	11.5	10.4	14.1
1986–1988 [2]	*13.3	*12.0	*15.3	*13.5	*12.1	*15.8	11.8	11.9	11.7
1989–1995 [2]	*13.9	*12.4	*16.1	*14.2	*12.7	*16.4	11.3	9.9	14.0
Age at Diagnosis, 1992–1996									
Under 45 years	21.2	17.2	26.8	23.0	18.5	28.8	15.7	11.8	22.7
45–54 years	16.7	14.5	20.0	17.5	15.2	20.6	12.5	10.8	15.7
55–64 years	15.4	13.7	18.1	15.8	14.3	18.1	12.2	10.1	16.3
65–74 years	13.8	12.6	15.5	14.0	12.7	15.9	10.5	10.1	16.3
75 years and over	9.3	7.8	11.1	9.5	8.0	11.4	6.9	10.4	10.7
								4.8	10.7
Under 65 years	16.2	14.2	19.3	16.8	14.8	19.6	12.7	10.5	17.0
65 years and over	12.2	11.0	13.9	12.5	11.1	14.2	9.6	9.0	10.6

See footnotes at end of table.

Table 3.17. Cancer Survival Rates—*Continued*

(Percent of patients expected to be alive five years after diagnosis)

Site of cancer	All Races			Whites			Blacks		
	Total	Males	Females	Total	Males	Females	Total	Males	Females
MELANOMAS OF SKIN									
Year of Diagnosis									
1960–1963[1]	—	—	—	60.0	51.0	68.0	—	—	—
1970–1973[1]	—	—	—	68.0	62.0	75.0	**66.6	—	—
1974–1976[2]	79.9	74.9	84.8	80.2	75.4	84.9	***50.5	—	—
1977–1979[2]	81.9	77.5	86.1	82.2	77.8	86.4	***60.9	—	***70.1
1980–1982[2]	82.8	77.3	88.2	83.0	77.6	88.2	***74.4	—	
1983–1985[2]	84.5	80.2	89.0	84.6	80.3	89.2	***65.9	—	
1986–1988[2]	87.4	84.1	90.8	87.6	84.4	91.0	67.6	**58.9	**75.2
1989–1995[2]	*87.7	*85.1	*90.8	*87.9	*85.3	*91.0	*67.6		
Age at Diagnosis, 1992–1996									
Under 45 years	90.2	86.1	93.5	90.2	86.2	93.6	**71.4	—	—
45–54 years	87.8	84.5	91.9	88.0	84.9	91.9	—	—	—
55–64 years	88.2	85.6	92.5	88.3	85.9	92.5	***69.6	—	—
65–74 years	86.8	85.9	88.4	87.3	86.5	88.7	—	—	—
75 years and over	80.7	80.1	80.7	81.0	80.2	81.2	***67.7	—	—
Under 65 years	89.0	85.5	92.9	89.1	85.7	93.0	**70.4	**60.9	**83.7
65 years and over	84.8	84.3	85.1	85.2	84.7	85.5	***62.8	—	—
MULTIPLE MYELOMA									
Year of Diagnosis									
1960–1963[1]	—	—	—	12.0	13.0	10.0	—	—	—
1970–1973[1]	—	—	—	19.0	20.0	17.0	—	—	—
1974–1976[2]	24.3	23.7	24.9	23.9	23.2	24.7	27.8	27.6	28.1
1977–1979[2]	26.2	25.6	26.8	24.6	24.7	24.5	34.0	30.0	38.0
1980–1982[2]	27.9	25.6	30.2	27.7	26.3	29.1	29.3	25.8	32.9
1983–1985[2]	28.0	28.1	27.8	27.5	27.3	27.6	30.3	33.1	27.1
1986–1988[2]	29.3	30.6	28.0	29.3	*31.1	27.6	30.5	*28.7	32.1
1989–1995[2]	*28.4	*29.2	*27.6	*28.0	*28.7	*27.2	30.6	32.9	28.4
Age at Diagnosis, 1992–1996									
Under 45 years	44.6	41.9	**48.9	41.8	**39.4	**45.9	**49.9	**50.9	***48.5
45–54 years	40.7	40.1	41.5	40.2	39.5	41.3	**42.4	**42.6	**41.9
55–64 years	32.3	34.2	29.8	33.1	34.4	31.1	30.4	**35.8	**25.0
65–74 years	26.2	25.6	27.1	26.2	25.2	27.6	26.5	**27.4	25.8
75 years and over	20.0	20.4	19.8	19.6	20.8	18.8	20.4	**17.0	21.8
Under 65 years	36.2	36.8	35.4	36.0	36.3	35.7	37.6	41.2	33.5
65 years and over	23.6	23.7	23.5	23.3	23.5	23.2	24.3	24.7	24.2
NON-HODGKIN'S LYMPHOMAS									
Year of Diagnosis									
1960–1963[1]	—	—	—	31.0	31.0	31.0	—	—	—
1970–1973[1]	—	—	—	41.0	39.0	43.0	—	—	—
1974–1976[2]	47.1	47.1	47.2	47.7	48.0	47.4	48.3	**43.7	**54.1
1977–1979[2]	48.4	45.8	50.9	48.6	46.4	50.7	51.2	44.5	59.8
1980–1982[2]	51.2	50.1	52.4	51.7	50.8	52.7	50.0	47.3	53.3
1983–1985[2]	53.8	52.6	55.0	54.3	53.3	55.4	44.8	43.6	46.3
1986–1988[2]	52.2	49.4	*55.6	52.8	*50.1	*55.9	49.8	46.6	53.9
1989–1995[2]	*51.0	46.8	*56.5	51.9	*47.7	57.3	*41.3	*37.6	47.6
Age at Diagnosis, 1992–1996									
Under 45 years	48.9	40.9	69.2	50.6	41.9	72.9	34.8	31.2	44.6
45–54 years	58.7	53.1	68.7	60.1	54.7	69.8	45.6	**36.5	**62.4
55–64 years	58.3	54.7	62.8	58.9	55.2	63.6	55.8	**57.2	**53.8
65–74 years	52.5	50.6	54.4	53.4	50.9	55.9	39.6	**39.5	**38.6
75 years and over	38.7	36.0	40.5	38.9	36.5	40.5	**45.1	**37.1	**47.7
Under 65 years	54.4	47.8	66.3	55.8	49.1	68.1	41.5	**37.0	51.4
65 years and over	46.7	45.2	48.0	47.2	45.5	48.6	41.6	**39.6	41.8

See footnotes at end of table.

Table 3.17. Cancer Survival Rates—Continued

(Percent of patients expected to be alive five years after diagnosis)

Site of cancer	All Races			Whites			Blacks		
	Total	Males	Females	Total	Males	Females	Total	Males	Females
ORAL CAVITY AND PHARYNX CANCER									
Year of Diagnosis									
1960–1963[1]	—	—	—	45.0	—	—	—	—	—
1970–1973[1]	—	—	—	43.0	—	—	—	—	—
1974–1976[2]	53.3	52.3	55.7	55.0	54.5	56.2	36.3	31.3	45.9
1977–1979[2]	52.7	51.5	55.4	54.6	53.9	56.1	36.8	31.2	49.1
1980–1982[2]	52.7	51.1	56.1	55.4	54.3	57.6	30.8	26.2	42.3
1983–1985[2]	53.0	51.5	56.2	55.1	54.3	56.8	35.1	29.9	47.3
1986–1988[2]	52.8	49.2	*60.6	55.1	52.0	*61.9	34.8	29.6	49.0
1989–1995[2]	53.3	50.0	*60.2	55.5	52.7	*61.3	33.8	28.4	48.4
Age at Diagnosis, 1992–1996									
Under 45 years	58.5	50.9	77.9	60.5	52.7	81.6	40.3	32.4	**58.4
45–54 years	54.5	50.1	67.6	59.4	54.5	73.0	31.9	27.0	**49.1
55–64 years	51.4	48.6	58.5	54.1	51.6	60.3	32.9	28.8	**44.7
65–74 years	52.2	49.8	56.4	53.4	51.8	56.4	**32.9	**27.6	**43.9
75 years and over	52.6	54.7	50.1	53.9	56.8	50.6	**26.2	**22.6	***33.6
Under 65 years	54.1	49.6	66.0	57.2	52.7	68.8	34.4	28.9	**50.3
65 years and over	52.3	51.3	54.1	53.6	53.3	54.2	31.3	26.4	**42.1
PANCREAS CANCER									
Year of Diagnosis									
1960–1963[1]	—	—	—	1.0	1.0	2.0	1.0	0.0	3.0
1970–1973[1]	—	—	—	2.0	2.0	2.0	2.0	0.0	3.0
1974–1976[2]	2.5	2.9	2.1	2.6	3.1	2.0	2.5	1.9	3.1
1977–1979[2]	2.4	2.3	2.6	2.3	2.3	2.3	3.8	2.8	4.8
1980–1982[2]	3.1	2.7	3.5	2.9	2.6	3.1	4.7	3.6	5.7
1983–1985[2]	3.2	2.7	3.7	2.9	2.5	3.3	5.4	4.8	5.8
1986–1988[2]	*3.6	*3.4	*3.7	3.0	2.9	3.2	*6.2	6.6	5.9
1989–1995[2]	*4.1	*3.7	*4.4	*4.1	*3.8	*4.4	*3.6	3.3	3.9
Age at Diagnosis, 1992–1996									
Under 45 years	13.1	5.5	24.3	13.0	5.6	26.2	14.3	10.6	**21.0
45–54 years	7.2	7.0	7.6	8.3	8.9	7.5	3.0	0.0	9.9
55–64 years	5.0	5.0	5.0	5.2	5.0	5.4	4.0	5.1	2.2
65–74 years	2.9	2.2	3.5	2.9	2.2	3.6	1.9	1.5	2.3
75 years and over	2.5	2.5	2.5	2.5	2.3	2.7	2.6	5.3	1.6
Under 65 years	6.6	5.6	7.8	6.9	6.1	8.0	5.2	3.7	7.2
65 years and over	2.7	2.4	3.0	2.7	2.2	3.1	2.3	2.6	1.9
STOMACH CANCER									
Year of Diagnosis									
1960–1963[1]	—	—	—	11.0	10.0	13.0	8.0	5.0	14.0
1970–1973[1]	—	—	—	13.0	12.0	14.0	13.0	15.0	10.0
1974–1976[2]	15.4	14.2	17.3	14.7	13.5	16.6	16.5	15.9	17.6
1977–1979[2]	16.6	15.1	18.8	15.9	14.3	18.3	15.1	14.6	16.1
1980–1982[2]	17.7	16.6	19.6	16.5	15.5	18.0	19.4	18.5	21.3
1983–1985[2]	17.3	15.8	19.7	16.3	14.6	18.9	18.6	17.8	19.6
1986–1988[2]	*20.1	*17.0	25.2	*19.1	*16.1	24.2	18.9	14.5	25.7
1989–1995[2]	*21.1	*18.6	*25.2	*19.3	*16.7	*23.6	21.6	20.6	23.2
Age at Diagnosis, 1992–1996									
Under 45 years	22.9	18.9	29.4	20.8	15.6	31.9	19.6	**18.4	**22.0
45–54 years	20.2	16.5	27.8	20.7	15.4	33.1	18.1	18.9	**17.8
55–64 years	20.9	18.6	26.4	18.6	16.4	24.4	20.9	22.7	17.2
65–74 years	22.9	20.4	27.8	19.6	17.8	23.0	26.9	21.4	**37.9
75 years and over	19.3	17.2	21.3	18.7	16.4	20.7	17.7	17.5	17.1
Under 65 years	21.1	18.1	27.5	19.6	16.0	28.4	19.9	20.5	18.8
65 years and over	21.2	19.1	24.1	19.2	17.3	21.7	23.2	20.6	26.7

See footnotes at end of table.

Table 3.17. Cancer Survival Rates—*Continued*

(Percent of patients expected to be alive five years after diagnosis)

Site of cancer	All Races			Whites			Blacks		
	Total	Males	Females	Total	Males	Females	Total	Males	Females
THYROID CANCER									
Year of Diagnosis									
1960–1963[1]	—	—	—	83.0	75.0	87.0	—	—	—
1970–1973[1]	—	—	—	86.0	82.0	87.0	—	***76.8	90.7
1974–1976[2]	92.2	90.4	92.7	92.1	90.6	92.6	87.8	—	96.6
1977–1979[2]	92.5	89.7	93.4	92.2	90.4	92.9	91.5	**93.3	93.9
1980–1982[2]	94.3	91.7	95.2	93.9	91.1	94.8	94.3	**92.8	90.6
1983–1985[2]	93.4	89.8	94.6	93.3	89.0	94.5	91.6	**89.3	92.7
1986–1988[2]	95.2	93.6	95.6	95.1	93.5	95.6	92.5	**86.0	89.6
1989–1995[2]	*94.7	90.5	*96.1	*95.1	91.0	*96.6	88.7		
Age at Diagnosis, 1992–1996									
Under 45 years	99.4	98.2	99.7	99.4	98.2	99.7	98.0	**92.2	98.8
45–54 years	96.3	90.6	98.1	96.8	91.2	98.7	91.9	—	92.9
55–64 years	90.9	86.7	93.0	91.4	87.4	93.4	**77.8	—	***77.9
65–74 years	84.7	**76.1	89.0	85.6	**77.4	89.9	**85.8	—	***85.0
75 years and over	66.1	**66.5	63.1	68.5	**64.5	67.9	***34.9	—	***29.7
Under 65 years	97.5	94.0	98.6	97.7	94.3	98.8	93.7	87.8	**95.4
65 years and over	78.9	75.7	80.3	80.4	76.1	82.4	**66.4	—	**63.3

See footnotes at end of table.

Table 3.17. Cancer Survival Rates—*Continued*

(Percent of patients expected to be alive five years after diagnosis)

Site of cancer	Females								
	All Races			Whites			Blacks		
	All	Under 50 years	50 years and over	All	Under 50 years	50 years and over	All	Under 50 years	50 years and over
BREAST CANCER									
Year of Diagnosis									
1960–1963 [1]	—	—	—	63.0	—	—	46.0	—	—
1970–1973 [1]	—	—	—	68.0	—	—	51.0	—	—
1974–1976 [2]	74.6	76.3	74.0	75.3	77.4	74.6	63.1	64.2	62.5
1977–1979 [2]	74.7	75.8	74.3	75.4	76.7	75.0	63.2	65.3	62.0
1980–1982 [2]	76.3	77.2	76.1	77.1	78.0	76.9	65.9	69.1	64.0
1983–1985 [2]	78.1	77.4	78.3	79.2	79.1	79.3	63.5	63.4	63.6
1986–1988 [2]	*82.7	*80.0	*83.7	*83.8	*81.4	*84.7	*69.2	*67.4	*70.3
Age at Diagnosis, 1992–1996									
Under 45 years	80.8	—	—	82.9	—	—	67.2	—	—
45–54 years	85.2	—	—	86.5	—	—	74.1	—	—
55–64 years	85.3	—	—	86.3	—	—	73.5	—	—
65–74 years	87.4	—	—	88.4	—	—	73.2	—	—
75 years and over	84.3	—	—	85.4	—	—	66.4	—	—
Under 65 years	84.0	—	—	85.4	—	—	71.3	—	—
65 years and over	86.2	—	—	87.2	—	—	70.7	—	—
CERVIX UTERI CANCER									
Year of Diagnosis									
1960–1963 [1]	—	—	—	58.0	—	—	47.0	—	—
1970–1973 [1]	—	—	—	64.0	—	—	61.0	—	—
1974–1976 [2]	69.0	81.3	58.0	69.7	82.2	58.5	63.7	75.2	53.8
1977–1979 [2]	68.3	78.0	59.5	69.5	79.8	60.3	62.1	71.4	52.9
1980–1982 [2]	67.3	79.0	56.0	67.9	80.3	55.8	61.0	72.0	50.9
1983–1985 [2]	68.5	78.1	57.6	70.3	80.3	58.5	59.9	69.2	50.0
1986–1988 [2]	68.8	78.5	56.6	71.6	81.4	58.5	55.4	64.1	47.3
1989–1995 [2]	69.7	*77.9	58.6	71.4	80.5	58.4	58.8	*63.5	53.1
Age at Diagnosis, 1992–1996									
Under 45 years	79.9	—	—	82.8	—	—	64.7	—	—
45–54 years	68.3	—	—	69.4	—	—	55.0	—	—
55–64 years	62.9	—	—	62.2	—	—	**57.4	—	—
65–74 years	55.4	—	—	54.6	—	—	**56.3	—	—
75 years and over	45.3	—	—	45.8	—	—	**40.2	—	—
Under 65 years	73.9	—	—	76.0	—	—	61.0	—	—
65 years and over	51.5	—	—	51.2	—	—	49.2	—	—
CORPUS AND UTERUS, NOS CANCER									
Year of Diagnosis									
1960–1963 [1]	—	—	—	73.0	—	—	31.0	—	—
1970–1973 [1]	—	—	—	81.0	—	—	44.0	—	—
1974–1976 [2]	87.9	92.1	87.3	88.8	92.9	88.3	60.9	84.2	56.1
1977–1979 [2]	84.9	92.0	84.0	86.3	92.9	85.4	57.6	80.8	52.3
1980–1982 [2]	81.6	91.0	80.4	82.8	92.3	81.7	54.1	85.1	49.3
1983–1985 [2]	82.8	92.6	81.6	84.5	93.4	83.4	54.0	81.0	50.1
1986–1988 [2]	*82.7	92.2	*81.3	84.3	93.4	83.4	56.5	86.4	51.1
1989–1995 [2]	*83.5	*88.9	*82.7	*85.5	90.9	*84.7	56.1	74.2	52.6
Age at Diagnosis, 1992–1996									
Under 45 years	88.7	—	—	89.7	—	—	**83.6	—	—
45–54 years	89.5	—	—	91.5	—	—	**60.2	—	—
55–64 years	86.1	—	—	88.8	—	—	53.5	—	—
65–74 years	82.9	—	—	85.1	—	—	**52.9	—	—
75 years and over	73.5	—	—	74.9	—	—	**46.6	—	—
Under 65 years	87.5	—	—	89.7	—	—	61.1	—	—
65 years and over	79.7	—	—	81.7	—	—	50.6	—	—

See footnotes at end of table.

Table 3.17. Cancer Survival Rates—*Continued*

(Percent of patients expected to be alive five years after diagnosis)

Site of cancer	Females								
	All Races			Whites			Blacks		
	All	Under 50 years	50 years and over	All	Under 50 years	50 years and over	All	Under 50 years	50 years and over
OVARY CANCER									
Year of Diagnosis									
1960–1963 [1]	—	—	—	32.0	—	—	32.0	—	—
1970–1973 [1]	—	—	—	36.0	—	—	32.0	—	—
1974–1976 [2]	36.8	56.3	30.0	36.5	56.1	30.0	40.9	**61.1	30.4
1977–1979 [2]	38.4	63.0	29.8	37.8	62.1	29.8	40.0	**67.2	24.3
1980–1982 [2]	39.0	64.9	31.1	38.6	63.9	31.3	38.6	**70.2	25.8
1983–1985 [2]	40.9	65.2	33.0	40.2	63.3	33.1	41.7	79.7	26.4
1986–1988 [2]	42.1	71.2	32.4	41.9	71.1	32.6	38.6	**72.6	24.0
1989–1995 [2]	*50.0	*75.8	*38.9	*49.9	*76.2	*39.1	*47.2	*74.8	33.2
Age at Diagnosis, 1992–1996									
Under 45 years	80.7	—	—	81.3	—	—	76.8	—	—
45–54 years	61.5	—	—	62.1	—	—	**57.2	—	—
55–64 years	47.2	—	—	48.4	—	—	**35.5	—	—
65–74 years	34.4	—	—	34.6	—	—	27.4	—	—
75 years and over	24.4	—	—	24.2	—	—	**23.8	—	—
Under 65 years	63.5	—	—	63.9	—	—	59.4	—	—
65 years and over	30.2	—	—	30.2	—	—	26.7	—	—

See footnotes at end of table.

Table 3.17. Cancer Survival Rates—*Continued*

(Percent of patients expected to be alive five years after diagnosis)

Site of cancer	Males		
	All races	White	Black
PROSTATE CANCER			
Year of Diagnosis			
1960–1963 [1]	—	50.0	35.0
1970–1973 [1]	—	63.0	55.0
1974–1976 [2]	67.1	68.1	58.3
1977–1979 [2]	71.1	72.2	62.5
1980–1982 [2]	73.4	74.5	64.7
1983–1985 [2]	74.7	76.2	64.1
1986–1988 [2]	81.0	82.6	69.0
1989–1995 [2]	*91.9	*93.1	*83.6
Age at Diagnosis, 1992–1996			
Under 45 years	81.6	80.6	**81.9
45–54 years	89.8	90.3	88.7
55–64 years	93.4	94.6	85.9
65–74 years	95.0	95.9	88.3
75 years and over	88.7	90.2	74.2
Under 65 years	92.7	93.8	86.1
65 years and over	92.3	93.5	83.4
TESTIS CANCER			
Year of Diagnosis			
1960–1963 [1]	—	63.0	—
1970–1973 [1]	—	72.0	—
1974–1976 [2]	78.5	78.6	**75.9
1977–1979 [2]	87.4	87.8	***66.2
1980–1982 [2]	91.7	92.0	**89.7
1983–1985 [2]	91.1	91.4	**87.9
1986–1988 [2]	95.1	95.6	—
1989–1995 [2]	*95.4	*95.7	88.1
Age at Diagnosis, 1992–1996			
Under 45 years	95.6	95.8	89.8
45–54 years	97.1	96.9	—
55–64 years	**87.1	**88.3	—
65–74 years	**80.9	**83.3	—
75 years and over	***95.9	—	—
Under 65 years	*95.5	*95.7	88.1
65 years and over	**85.9	**88.2	—

SOURCE: L.A.G. Ries, C.L. Kosary, B.F. Hankey, B.A. Miller, L. Clegg, B.K. Edwards (eds). SEER *Cancer Statistics Review,* 1973–1996, National Cancer Institute. Bethesda, MD, 1999.

* The difference in rates between 1974–1976 and 1989–1995 is statistically significant (p< .05).
** The standard error of the survival rate is between 5 and 10 percentage points.
*** The standard error of the survival rate is greater than 10 percentage points.
— Data not available.
1. Rates are based on end results data from a series of hospital registries and one population-based registry.
2. Rates are from the Surveillance, Epidemiology, and End Results (SEER) Program. They are based on data from population-based registries in Connecticut, New Mexico, Utah, Iowa, Hawaii, Atlanta, Detroit, Seattle-Puget Sound, and San Francisco–Oakland. Rates are based on follow-up of patients through 1996.

Table 3.18. Cancer Mortality Rates [1]

(Per 100,000 population; age-adjusted to the 1970 U.S. standard population, except where noted)

Site of cancer	All races			Whites			Blacks		
	Total	Males	Females	Total	Males	Females	Total	Males	Females
ALL SITES									
Year of Death									
1973	162.0	205.3	131.4	159.3	201.5	129.7	197.0	257.2	151.4
1974	163.1	207.8	131.7	160.5	203.9	130.4	196.6	261.1	148.3
1975	162.3	207.7	130.6	159.6	203.4	129.6	196.8	266.0	145.4
1976	164.5	210.5	132.5	161.8	205.9	131.5	201.0	272.2	148.1
1977	165.1	211.8	132.9	162.0	206.8	131.6	204.8	278.6	151.1
1978	166.1	213.6	133.5	163.0	208.5	132.3	205.4	281.3	150.5
1979	166.1	214.6	132.8	163.0	209.6	131.5	206.7	283.6	151.8
1980	168.0	216.4	135.0	164.6	210.8	133.5	212.2	290.7	156.6
1981	167.4	215.1	135.1	164.0	209.1	133.8	212.5	294.4	155.0
1982	169.0	217.2	136.5	165.5	211.2	135.2	215.5	299.0	157.5
1983	169.6	218.0	137.1	166.0	211.7	135.7	218.3	303.0	159.8
1984	170.9	218.8	138.9	167.1	212.0	137.5	221.7	309.4	161.5
1985	171.3	219.2	139.3	167.7	212.5	138.1	221.1	308.5	161.8
1986	171.5	219.1	139.7	168.0	212.8	138.3	221.9	308.5	164.0
1987	171.6	219.4	139.6	168.0	212.9	138.1	223.0	311.3	164.5
1988	171.9	219.2	140.2	168.2	212.7	138.8	223.2	311.7	164.8
1989	173.0	220.2	141.4	169.2	213.0	140.2	226.6	320.0	165.2
1990	173.3	220.8	141.6	169.4	213.7	140.1	228.9	321.5	168.8
1991	173.4	219.9	142.2	169.6	213.3	140.7	227.5	316.8	169.6
1992	172.1	217.5	141.6	168.5	211.1	140.0	224.9	311.1	169.3
1993	172.0	216.8	141.7	168.4	210.2	140.2	225.8	313.7	169.0
1994	170.7	213.9	141.5	167.4	207.7	140.2	221.9	305.9	167.5
1995	169.0	210.5	140.8	165.8	204.7	139.3	219.9	299.8	168.2
1996	166.9	207.1	139.1	163.8	201.4	138.0	216.2	295.2	165.0
Age at Death, 1992–1996									
All ages	170.1	213.1	140.9	166.7	207.0	139.5	221.6	304.9	167.7
Under 65	70.1	77.3	63.5	67.6	73.5	62.1	100.9	124.7	82.4
65 and over	1 083.2	1 452.3	846.9	1 072.0	1 425.2	845.9	1 323.6	1 950.0	946.3
All ages (world standard) [2]	130.3	159.7	109.5	127.4	154.7	108.3	172.5	232.2	132.6
ALL SITES EXCLUDING LUNG AND BRONCHUS									
Year of Death									
1973	127.3	142.9	118.1	124.9	139.9	116.5	156.1	182.0	137.8
1974	127.1	143.7	117.4	125.0	140.7	116.1	154.1	182.6	134.0
1975	125.5	142.6	115.5	123.2	139.3	114.3	153.6	186.3	130.5
1976	126.4	143.8	116.2	124.1	140.2	115.0	156.3	190.2	132.2
1977	125.9	143.6	115.6	123.5	140.0	114.2	157.0	190.8	133.7
1978	125.7	144.1	115.0	123.2	140.3	113.6	156.9	192.4	132.6
1979	125.0	144.5	113.5	122.5	140.8	112.0	157.3	193.9	132.5
1980	125.5	144.9	114.1	122.8	140.8	112.6	160.4	198.0	135.1
1981	124.4	143.4	113.4	121.7	139.1	112.0	159.4	198.9	133.0
1982	124.8	144.3	113.5	122.0	139.9	112.0	160.9	201.1	134.5
1983	124.7	145.0	112.7	121.7	140.4	111.1	162.6	205.0	134.8
1984	125.2	144.8	113.7	122.1	140.0	112.1	164.7	207.3	137.1
1985	124.8	145.0	112.9	121.7	140.2	111.3	163.6	206.9	135.8
1986	124.5	144.9	112.5	121.5	140.4	110.8	163.6	205.9	136.9
1987	123.5	144.3	111.3	120.5	139.7	109.5	163.3	206.7	136.2
1988	123.3	144.4	110.8	120.2	139.7	109.0	163.3	207.6	135.5
1989	123.7	145.5	110.6	120.5	140.4	109.0	165.0	213.4	134.9
1990	123.2	145.5	110.0	120.0	140.5	108.1	166.3	214.5	137.0
1991	123.3	145.4	110.0	120.1	140.7	108.0	165.9	212.2	137.6
1992	122.1	144.6	108.5	119.0	140.1	106.5	163.4	208.7	135.9
1993	121.9	144.3	108.2	118.7	139.5	106.1	164.9	211.4	136.6
1994	121.2	143.0	107.7	118.2	138.5	105.8	161.9	206.8	134.3
1995	119.8	141.0	106.6	116.8	136.7	104.5	160.5	202.8	134.7
1996	118.0	138.9	104.8	115.2	134.7	102.9	157.9	200.7	131.6
Age at Death, 1992–1996									
All ages	120.6	142.3	107.1	117.6	137.9	105.2	161.7	206.0	134.6
Under 65	49.2	50.0	48.6	47.2	47.5	47.0	71.7	79.3	66.0
65 and over	772.0	985.1	641.6	759.9	962.7	636.2	982.3	1 361.8	760.6
All ages (world standard) [2]	91.9	105.7	83.1	89.3	102.1	81.4	124.9	154.7	106.1
URINARY BLADDER CANCER									
Year of Death									
1973	4.2	7.2	2.1	4.2	7.4	2.1	4.1	5.6	3.0
1974	4.2	7.2	2.1	4.2	7.4	2.0	4.1	5.7	3.0
1975	4.1	7.2	2.0	4.1	7.4	1.9	3.9	5.4	2.8
1976	4.1	7.2	2.1	4.2	7.4	2.0	4.1	6.1	2.7
1977	4.1	7.1	2.1	4.1	7.3	2.0	4.0	5.8	2.8
1978	4.0	6.9	2.0	4.0	7.1	2.0	3.9	5.6	2.7
1979	3.8	6.7	1.9	3.9	6.9	1.9	3.8	5.8	2.5
1980	3.8	6.6	2.0	3.8	6.8	1.9	3.6	4.8	2.8
1981	3.7	6.5	1.9	3.7	6.6	1.8	3.8	5.5	2.6
1982	3.7	6.4	1.8	3.7	6.6	1.8	3.8	5.3	2.7
1983	3.6	6.3	1.8	3.6	6.4	1.8	3.6	5.4	2.4
1984	3.4	6.1	1.8	3.5	6.2	1.7	3.6	5.2	2.5
1985	3.4	6.0	1.7	3.4	6.2	1.7	3.4	5.1	2.3
1986	3.3	5.8	1.7	3.3	6.0	1.7	3.2	4.3	2.5
1987	3.2	5.6	1.6	3.2	5.8	1.6	3.3	4.8	2.3
1988	3.2	5.6	1.7	3.3	5.7	1.6	3.2	4.4	2.4
1989	3.3	5.7	1.7	3.3	5.9	1.6	3.4	5.1	2.4
1990	3.3	5.7	1.7	3.3	5.8	1.7	3.3	4.8	2.4
1991	3.2	5.6	1.7	3.3	5.8	1.6	3.3	4.8	2.3
1992	3.2	5.6	1.7	3.3	5.8	1.7	3.2	4.7	2.3
1993	3.3	5.7	1.7	3.3	5.9	1.6	3.1	4.6	2.2
1994	3.3	5.6	1.7	3.3	5.8	1.7	3.2	4.6	2.3
1995	3.2	5.5	1.6	3.2	5.7	1.6	3.0	4.1	2.3
1996	3.2	5.5	1.7	3.3	5.7	1.7	3.1	4.3	2.3
Age at Death, 1992–1996									
All ages	3.2	5.6	1.7	3.3	5.8	1.7	3.1	4.4	2.3
Under 65	0.7	1.1	0.4	0.7	1.1	0.4	0.8	1.1	0.5
65 and over	26.2	46.4	13.8	26.7	48.2	13.6	24.3	35.1	18.1
All ages (world standard) [2]	2.3	3.8	1.2	2.3	4.0	1.1	2.2	3.1	1.6

See footnotes at end of table.

Table 3.18. Cancer Mortality Rates [1]—Continued

(Per 100,000 population; age-adjusted to the 1970 U.S. standard population, except where noted)

Site of cancer	All races			Whites			Blacks		
	Total	Males	Females	Total	Males	Females	Total	Males	Females
BRAIN AND OTHER NERVOUS SYSTEM CANCER									
Year of Death									
1973	3.7	4.5	3.1	3.9	4.7	3.2	2.4	3.0	1.9
1974	3.7	4.5	3.0	3.9	4.8	3.2	2.1	2.5	1.8
1975	3.8	4.5	3.1	4.0	4.7	3.3	2.3	3.0	1.7
1976	3.9	4.8	3.2	4.1	5.0	3.4	2.5	3.2	1.9
1977	4.0	4.9	3.2	4.2	5.1	3.4	2.4	2.8	2.0
1978	4.1	4.9	3.4	4.3	5.2	3.5	2.5	3.1	2.0
1979	3.8	4.7	3.1	4.0	4.9	3.3	2.4	2.9	2.0
1980	3.9	4.9	3.1	4.1	5.1	3.3	2.3	2.8	1.9
1981	3.9	4.7	3.2	4.1	4.9	3.4	2.3	3.0	1.9
1982	3.9	4.7	3.3	4.2	5.0	3.5	2.4	3.1	1.9
1983	3.9	4.7	3.2	4.1	5.0	3.4	2.3	2.7	2.0
1984	4.0	4.9	3.3	4.3	5.1	3.5	2.3	3.1	1.8
1985	4.0	4.9	3.3	4.3	5.2	3.5	2.3	2.9	1.8
1986	4.0	4.9	3.2	4.2	5.2	3.4	2.3	2.9	1.8
1987	4.1	5.0	3.5	4.4	5.2	3.4	2.5	3.1	2.1
1988	4.1	5.1	3.3	4.4	5.2	3.7	2.6	3.2	2.1
1989	4.1	5.0	3.4	4.4	5.4	3.5	2.6	3.2	2.2
1990	4.3	5.2	3.5	4.5	5.3	3.6	2.5	3.0	2.1
1991	4.3	5.2	3.6	4.6	5.5	3.7	2.6	3.3	2.1
1992	4.2	5.1	3.5	4.5	5.4	3.8	2.5	3.0	2.2
1993	4.2	5.1	3.4	4.5	5.4	3.8	2.5	3.0	2.1
1994	4.2	5.1	3.5	4.5	5.5	3.7	2.5	3.2	2.0
1995	4.1	4.9	3.4	4.3	5.2	3.6	2.4	2.9	2.0
1996	4.2	5.0	3.4	4.5	5.4	3.7	2.5	3.0	2.1
Age at Death, 1992–1996									
All ages	4.2	5.1	3.4	4.5	5.4	3.7	2.4	3.0	2.0
Under 65	2.7	3.2	2.1	2.9	3.4	2.3	1.6	2.0	1.3
65 and over	18.0	21.8	15.3	19.0	23.0	16.2	9.8	11.8	8.5
All ages (world standard) [2]	3.5	4.3	2.9	3.8	4.6	3.1	2.1	2.6	1.8
BREAST CANCER									
Year of Death									
1973	15.0	0.3	26.9	15.1	0.3	27.1	14.8	0.5	26.3
1974	14.9	0.3	26.7	14.9	0.3	26.8	15.1	0.5	26.7
1975	14.6	0.3	26.2	14.8	0.3	26.5	14.1	0.3	24.8
1976	14.8	0.3	26.5	15.0	0.3	26.8	14.4	0.5	25.2
1977	15.2	0.3	27.1	15.2	0.3	27.2	15.7	0.4	27.4
1978	14.8	0.3	26.5	14.9	0.3	26.7	15.3	0.5	26.7
1979	14.6	0.2	26.0	14.7	0.2	26.2	14.8	0.4	25.7
1980	14.8	0.2	26.4	14.9	0.2	26.6	15.2	0.3	26.4
1981	14.9	0.2	26.6	15.0	0.2	26.8	15.6	0.4	27.1
1982	15.0	0.3	26.8	15.1	0.2	26.9	16.3	0.4	28.2
1983	15.0	0.2	26.7	15.0	0.2	26.8	16.2	0.4	28.0
1984	15.4	0.2	27.3	15.3	0.2	27.3	17.4	0.4	30.0
1985	15.4	0.3	27.5	15.4	0.3	27.6	16.9	0.3	29.1
1986	15.3	0.2	27.3	15.3	0.2	27.4	17.1	0.3	29.6
1987	15.2	0.3	27.1	15.2	0.3	27.1	17.8	0.4	30.6
1988	15.5	0.2	27.5	15.3	0.2	27.4	18.3	0.6	31.4
1989	15.4	0.3	27.5	15.4	0.2	27.5	17.7	0.4	30.4
1990	15.4	0.2	27.4	15.2	0.2	27.3	18.5	0.4	31.6
1991	15.1	0.2	27.0	15.0	0.2	26.8	18.6	0.3	31.8
1992	14.7	0.2	26.2	14.5	0.2	26.0	18.0	0.4	31.0
1993	14.5	0.3	25.9	14.3	0.3	25.6	18.5	0.5	31.5
1994	14.3	0.3	25.5	14.1	0.3	25.2	18.4	0.5	31.3
1995	14.1	0.3	25.2	13.8	0.3	24.8	18.7	0.6	31.9
1996	13.6	0.3	24.3	13.3	0.2	24.0	18.1	0.6	30.8
Age at Death, 1992–1996									
All ages	14.2	0.3	25.4	14.0	0.2	25.1	18.3	0.5	31.3
Under 65	7.7	0.1	14.7	7.4	0.1	14.3	11.3	0.2	20.4
65 and over	74.1	1.7	122.9	74.5	1.6	124.0	82.1	3.4	130.9
All ages (world standard) [2]	11.4	0.2	20.7	11.1	0.2	20.4	15.1	0.4	26.2
COLON AND RECTUM CANCER									
Year of Death									
1973	21.9	24.9	19.8	22.0	25.3	19.8	21.0	22.0	20.4
1974	22.2	25.8	19.7	22.3	26.0	19.8	21.2	23.6	19.5
1975	21.7	25.3	19.3	21.9	25.6	19.3	21.5	23.9	19.7
1976	22.0	25.6	19.5	22.1	25.9	19.5	22.3	24.4	20.8
1977	21.8	25.6	19.1	21.8	25.7	19.1	22.0	25.0	19.9
1978	21.9	25.9	19.2	22.0	26.1	19.2	21.9	24.4	20.2
1979	21.7	25.7	18.9	21.7	25.9	18.8	22.4	24.8	20.8
1980	21.5	25.8	18.6	21.5	25.9	18.5	22.7	26.1	20.3
1981	21.1	25.2	18.2	21.1	25.3	18.1	22.7	25.7	20.7
1982	20.9	25.2	18.0	20.8	25.2	17.8	23.0	26.4	20.6
1983	20.8	25.3	17.7	20.8	25.4	17.6	22.7	26.1	20.3
1984	21.0	25.3	18.0	20.9	25.3	17.8	23.3	27.3	20.6
1985	20.6	25.1	17.5	20.5	25.1	17.2	24.0	27.0	21.8
1986	20.1	24.5	17.0	19.9	24.5	16.7	23.3	27.5	20.6
1987	19.9	24.4	16.7	19.6	24.3	16.4	23.7	27.8	20.9
1988	19.3	23.7	16.3	19.1	23.6	16.0	22.9	27.0	20.2
1989	19.1	23.5	15.9	18.8	23.2	15.6	23.5	28.3	20.3
1990	18.8	23.4	15.6	18.4	23.1	15.2	24.0	29.2	20.7
1991	18.3	22.6	15.4	18.0	22.3	15.0	23.3	27.6	20.5
1992	18.0	22.3	15.0	17.7	22.0	14.6	23.0	27.9	19.8
1993	17.8	21.8	15.0	17.5	21.5	14.5	23.3	27.8	20.3
1994	17.6	21.6	14.6	17.2	21.3	14.3	22.8	27.8	19.4
1995	17.3	21.2	14.5	16.9	20.8	14.1	23.2	28.0	20.0
1996	16.8	20.5	14.0	16.4	20.1	13.6	22.5	26.9	19.5
Age at Death, 1992–1996									
All ages	17.5	21.5	14.6	17.1	21.1	14.2	22.9	27.6	19.8
Under 65	5.8	6.9	4.8	5.6	6.7	4.5	8.6	10.3	7.4
65 and over	124.1	154.0	104.2	122.7	152.9	102.4	153.4	186.2	133.3
All ages (world standard) [2]	12.9	15.7	10.7	12.6	15.4	10.4	17.2	20.7	14.8

See footnotes at end of table.

Table 3.18. Cancer Mortality Rates [1]—Continued

(Per 100,000 population; age-adjusted to the 1970 U.S. standard population, except where noted)

Site of cancer	All races			Whites			Blacks		
	Total	Males	Females	Total	Males	Females	Total	Males	Females
ESOPHAGUS CANCER									
Year of Death									
1973	3.0	5.0	1.4	2.5	4.2	1.2	8.3	13.9	3.7
1974	3.0	5.1	1.4	2.5	4.3	1.2	8.3	14.0	3.7
1975	3.1	5.4	1.4	2.6	4.5	1.2	8.6	15.0	3.6
1976	3.2	5.4	1.5	2.6	4.4	1.2	9.1	15.8	3.8
1977	3.2	5.3	1.5	2.6	4.3	1.2	8.9	15.5	3.8
1978	3.2	5.4	1.5	2.7	4.5	1.3	8.9	15.6	3.8
1979	3.2	5.4	1.5	2.6	4.4	1.2	9.2	16.4	3.7
1980	3.3	5.5	1.5	2.7	4.6	1.2	9.4	16.1	4.3
1981	3.3	5.6	1.5	2.7	4.5	1.2	9.3	16.5	3.9
1982	3.3	5.5	1.5	2.7	4.5	1.3	9.3	16.4	4.0
1983	3.3	5.6	1.5	2.7	4.7	1.2	9.1	15.9	4.0
1984	3.3	5.7	1.5	2.7	4.7	1.3	9.4	16.6	4.2
1985	3.3	5.7	1.4	2.7	4.8	1.2	8.9	15.8	3.8
1986	3.4	5.7	1.5	2.8	4.8	1.3	9.1	16.0	4.0
1987	3.4	5.8	1.5	2.9	5.0	1.2	8.6	15.0	3.9
1988	3.4	5.9	1.5	2.9	5.0	1.3	8.8	16.2	3.4
1989	3.5	6.0	1.5	3.0	5.2	1.2	8.7	15.4	3.7
1990	3.5	6.0	1.5	3.0	5.2	1.2	8.3	14.3	3.8
1991	3.5	6.1	1.5	3.1	5.4	1.3	8.2	14.5	3.7
1992	3.5	6.1	1.5	3.1	5.5	1.3	7.7	13.3	3.6
1993	3.6	6.2	1.5	3.1	5.5	1.3	8.0	14.0	3.6
1994	3.6	6.4	1.4	3.2	5.8	1.2	7.6	13.3	3.4
1995	3.6	6.4	1.4	3.3	5.8	1.3	7.1	12.7	3.0
1996	3.6	6.3	1.5	3.4	5.9	1.3	6.9	11.9	3.2
Age at Death, 1992–1996									
All ages	3.6	6.3	1.5	3.2	5.7	1.3	7.4	13.0	3.4
Under 65	1.7	2.9	0.6	1.4	2.5	0.4	4.4	7.6	1.9
65 and over	20.8	36.8	9.5	19.7	35.0	8.9	34.7	62.3	16.8
All ages (world standard) [2]	2.8	4.9	1.1	2.5	4.4	0.9	6.1	10.6	2.7
HODGKIN'S DISEASE									
Year of Death									
1973	1.3	1.7	1.0	1.4	1.8	1.1	0.9	1.4	0.5
1974	1.2	1.6	0.9	1.3	1.6	1.0	0.8	1.2	0.6
1975	1.1	1.5	0.9	1.2	1.5	0.9	0.9	1.3	0.6
1976	1.0	1.3	0.8	1.0	1.3	0.8	0.9	1.2	0.5
1977	1.0	1.2	0.7	1.0	1.3	0.8	0.8	1.0	0.6
1978	0.9	1.1	0.7	0.9	1.2	0.7	0.7	1.0	0.4
1979	0.8	1.1	0.6	0.9	1.1	0.6	0.7	0.9	0.4
1980	0.8	1.0	0.7	0.9	1.1	0.7	0.7	1.0	0.4
1981	0.8	1.0	0.6	0.8	1.0	0.6	0.7	0.8	0.6
1982	0.7	0.9	0.6	0.8	1.0	0.6	0.6	0.7	0.5
1983	0.7	0.9	0.6	0.8	1.0	0.6	0.6	0.8	0.4
1984	0.7	1.0	0.5	0.8	1.0	0.5	0.7	1.0	0.4
1985	0.7	0.8	0.5	0.7	0.8	0.5	0.6	0.8	0.5
1986	0.7	0.9	0.5	0.7	0.9	0.5	0.6	0.7	0.4
1987	0.6	0.8	0.5	0.7	0.8	0.5	0.6	0.8	0.4
1988	0.6	0.7	0.4	0.6	0.8	0.4	0.5	0.6	0.4
1989	0.6	0.8	0.5	0.6	0.8	0.5	0.6	0.8	0.4
1990	0.6	0.7	0.4	0.6	0.7	0.4	0.5	0.7	0.3
1991	0.6	0.7	0.4	0.6	0.7	0.4	0.6	0.8	0.4
1992	0.6	0.7	0.4	0.6	0.7	0.4	0.5	0.6	0.4
1993	0.5	0.7	0.4	0.5	0.7	0.4	0.5	0.7	0.3
1994	0.5	0.6	0.4	0.5	0.6	0.4	0.5	0.6	0.4
1995	0.5	0.6	0.4	0.5	0.6	0.4	0.5	0.7	0.3
1996	0.5	0.5	0.4	0.5	0.5	0.4	0.4	0.6	0.3
Age at Death, 1992–1996									
All ages	0.5	0.6	0.4	0.5	0.6	0.4	0.5	0.6	0.4
Under 65	0.4	0.4	0.3	0.4	0.4	0.3	0.4	0.5	0.3
65 and over	1.8	2.2	1.5	1.8	2.2	1.6	1.1	1.7	0.8
All ages (world standard) [2]	0.4	0.5	0.3	0.4	0.5	0.4	0.4	0.6	0.3
KIDNEY AND RENAL PELVIS CANCER									
Year of Death									
1973	2.9	4.2	1.9	3.0	4.4	2.0	2.2	3.1	1.5
1974	3.0	4.4	2.0	3.1	4.5	2.0	2.3	3.2	1.5
1975	3.0	4.3	2.0	3.1	4.4	2.1	2.4	3.5	1.6
1976	3.0	4.4	2.0	3.1	4.5	2.0	2.5	3.6	1.6
1977	3.1	4.4	2.0	3.1	4.6	2.1	2.4	3.5	1.7
1978	3.1	4.5	2.0	3.1	4.6	2.0	2.7	4.1	1.7
1979	3.0	4.4	2.0	3.1	4.5	2.0	2.5	3.6	1.7
1980	3.1	4.5	2.0	3.1	4.6	2.0	2.6	3.7	1.7
1981	3.1	4.4	2.1	3.1	4.5	2.1	2.7	4.0	1.8
1982	3.2	4.7	2.1	3.2	4.7	2.1	2.9	4.1	2.0
1983	3.2	4.6	2.1	3.3	4.7	2.2	2.8	4.1	1.8
1984	3.2	4.7	2.1	3.3	4.8	2.1	2.9	4.1	2.0
1985	3.3	4.7	2.2	3.3	4.7	2.2	3.2	5.0	2.0
1986	3.3	4.8	2.3	3.4	4.8	2.3	3.1	4.4	2.1
1987	3.4	4.9	2.3	3.5	5.0	2.3	3.1	4.6	2.0
1988	3.3	4.8	2.2	3.4	4.8	2.2	3.2	4.8	2.0
1989	3.4	4.9	2.3	3.5	5.0	2.3	3.3	5.0	2.2
1990	3.4	5.0	2.3	3.5	5.1	2.3	3.5	5.3	2.3
1991	3.5	5.0	2.4	3.6	5.1	2.4	3.6	5.2	2.4
1992	3.5	5.1	2.3	3.6	5.2	2.4	3.3	4.9	2.1
1993	3.4	5.0	2.2	3.5	5.1	2.3	3.4	5.0	2.3
1994	3.5	5.0	2.3	3.6	5.1	2.4	3.5	5.2	2.3
1995	3.6	5.0	2.4	3.6	5.1	2.5	3.6	5.1	2.6
1996	3.5	5.1	2.3	3.6	5.1	2.3	3.5	4.9	2.4
Age at Death, 1992–1996									
All ages	3.5	5.0	2.3	3.6	5.1	2.4	3.5	5.0	2.3
Under 65	1.6	2.3	1.0	1.6	2.3	1.0	1.7	2.6	1.1
65 and over	20.8	30.1	14.4	21.1	30.7	14.7	19.1	27.7	13.8
All ages (world standard) [2]	2.7	3.9	1.8	2.8	4.0	1.8	2.7	4.0	1.8

See footnotes at end of table.

Table 3.18. Cancer Mortality Rates [1]—Continued

(Per 100,000 population; age-adjusted to the 1970 U.S. standard population, except where noted)

Site of cancer	All races			Whites			Blacks		
	Total	Males	Females	Total	Males	Females	Total	Males	Females
LARYNX CANCER									
Year of Death									
1973	1.4	2.8	0.3	1.3	2.7	0.3	2.2	4.3	0.5
1974	1.5	2.9	0.4	1.4	2.8	0.3	2.3	4.6	0.6
1975	1.5	2.8	0.4	1.4	2.7	0.4	2.3	4.4	0.7
1976	1.5	2.9	0.4	1.4	2.7	0.4	2.3	4.4	0.7
1977	1.5	2.9	0.4	1.4	2.7	0.4	2.4	4.7	0.6
1978	1.5	2.9	0.4	1.4	2.7	0.4	2.6	5.1	0.6
1979	1.4	2.8	0.4	1.4	2.7	0.4	2.3	4.6	0.6
1980	1.4	2.7	0.4	1.3	2.5	0.4	2.6	5.0	0.8
1981	1.4	2.7	0.5	1.3	2.6	0.4	2.6	4.8	1.0
1982	1.4	2.7	0.5	1.4	2.6	0.5	2.5	4.8	0.7
1983	1.4	2.7	0.5	1.3	2.5	0.4	2.4	4.6	0.8
1984	1.4	2.7	0.5	1.3	2.4	0.5	2.8	5.5	0.7
1985	1.3	2.5	0.5	1.2	2.3	0.4	2.6	5.0	0.8
1986	1.4	2.6	0.5	1.3	2.3	0.4	2.7	5.2	0.9
1987	1.4	2.6	0.5	1.3	2.4	0.4	2.6	5.1	0.8
1988	1.4	2.5	0.5	1.2	2.3	0.4	2.8	5.9	0.7
1989	1.4	2.5	0.5	1.2	2.2	0.5	2.8	5.7	0.8
1990	1.3	2.5	0.5	1.2	2.3	0.4	2.6	5.0	1.0
1991	1.4	2.6	0.6	1.3	2.3	0.5	2.9	5.5	1.1
1992	1.4	2.5	0.5	1.3	2.3	0.5	2.9	5.6	1.0
1993	1.4	2.5	0.5	1.2	2.3	0.4	2.9	5.5	0.9
1994	1.3	2.4	0.5	1.2	2.2	0.5	2.8	5.5	0.9
1995	1.3	2.4	0.5	1.2	2.1	0.4	2.7	5.1	0.9
1996	1.3	2.3	0.5	1.2	2.1	0.5	2.8	5.6	0.9
Age at Death, 1992–1996									
All ages	1.3	2.4	0.5	1.2	2.2	0.5	2.8	5.5	0.9
Under 65	0.7	1.1	0.2	0.6	0.9	0.2	1.7	3.2	0.6
65 and over	7.5	14.3	2.8	7.1	13.6	2.7	12.6	25.9	4.1
All ages (world standard) [2]	1.1	1.9	0.4	1.0	1.7	0.4	2.3	4.4	0.8
ALL LEUKEMIAS									
Year of Death									
1973	6.7	8.8	5.2	6.9	9.0	5.3	5.8	7.7	4.4
1974	6.7	8.7	5.2	6.8	8.9	5.3	5.5	7.0	4.3
1975	6.6	8.8	5.1	6.8	9.0	5.2	5.5	7.1	4.4
1976	6.6	8.8	5.1	6.8	9.0	5.1	5.7	7.2	4.6
1977	6.6	8.7	5.1	6.7	8.9	5.2	5.7	7.1	4.7
1978	6.5	8.6	5.0	6.6	8.8	5.1	5.6	7.6	4.2
1979	6.7	8.8	5.2	6.8	9.0	5.3	5.8	7.3	4.7
1980	6.8	8.9	5.2	6.9	9.2	5.3	5.9	7.5	4.7
1981	6.5	8.7	5.0	6.7	8.9	5.1	5.9	7.3	4.8
1982	6.6	8.7	5.1	6.7	8.9	5.1	6.0	7.7	4.8
1983	6.5	8.6	5.0	6.6	8.8	5.1	5.9	7.5	4.8
1984	6.5	8.5	5.1	6.6	8.6	5.2	5.9	7.5	4.8
1985	6.5	8.5	5.1	6.6	8.6	5.2	5.9	7.8	4.7
1986	6.4	8.5	4.9	6.5	8.6	5.0	5.8	7.6	4.5
1987	6.2	8.1	4.9	6.3	8.3	4.9	5.9	7.6	4.8
1988	6.2	8.3	4.8	6.3	8.5	4.8	5.8	7.8	4.5
1989	6.4	8.4	4.9	6.5	8.5	5.0	6.0	8.3	4.5
1990	6.4	8.4	4.9	6.5	8.6	5.0	6.1	8.1	4.8
1991	6.4	8.3	5.0	6.5	8.4	5.1	6.0	8.0	4.7
1992	6.4	8.4	4.9	6.5	8.6	5.0	5.8	7.6	4.6
1993	6.3	8.4	4.9	6.4	8.5	4.9	6.0	8.0	4.7
1994	6.3	8.3	4.8	6.4	8.5	4.9	5.8	7.8	4.5
1995	6.3	8.4	4.8	6.4	8.6	4.8	5.9	7.9	4.6
1996	6.3	8.2	4.8	6.4	8.4	4.9	6.1	7.9	4.8
Age at Death, 1992–1996									
All ages	6.3	8.4	4.8	6.4	8.5	4.9	5.9	7.8	4.6
Under 65	2.8	3.4	2.2	2.8	3.4	2.2	3.0	3.7	2.4
65 and over	38.6	54.0	28.6	39.6	55.4	29.3	32.8	45.2	25.2
All ages (world standard) [2]	4.9	6.4	3.8	5.0	6.5	3.8	4.7	6.2	3.7
LIVER AND INTRAHEPATIC BILE DUCT CANCER									
Year of Death									
1973	2.4	3.2	1.7	2.2	2.9	1.6	3.9	5.8	2.3
1974	2.4	3.3	1.7	2.2	3.0	1.6	3.8	5.5	2.5
1975	2.3	3.2	1.6	2.1	2.9	1.6	3.6	5.5	2.1
1976	2.2	3.1	1.6	2.0	2.8	1.5	3.8	5.8	2.2
1977	2.3	3.2	1.6	2.1	2.8	1.5	3.8	6.1	2.0
1978	2.2	3.2	1.5	2.0	2.8	1.4	3.9	6.0	2.3
1979	2.3	3.2	1.6	2.1	2.9	1.5	3.7	5.6	2.2
1980	2.3	3.1	1.6	2.1	2.8	1.5	3.8	5.8	2.3
1981	2.3	3.3	1.6	2.1	3.0	1.5	3.8	5.8	2.3
1982	2.4	3.4	1.6	2.2	3.0	1.5	3.9	5.9	2.4
1983	2.4	3.4	1.6	2.1	3.0	1.5	4.0	6.1	2.4
1984	2.4	3.5	1.6	2.2	3.1	1.6	4.0	6.6	2.2
1985	2.5	3.6	1.7	2.3	3.2	1.6	3.8	6.0	2.3
1986	2.5	3.7	1.7	2.3	3.3	1.6	3.9	6.1	2.3
1987	2.6	3.7	1.7	2.4	3.3	1.6	3.9	5.7	2.6
1988	2.7	3.9	1.7	2.4	3.5	1.6	3.9	6.1	2.4
1989	2.8	4.1	1.8	2.5	3.6	1.7	4.2	6.7	2.5
1990	2.9	4.2	1.9	2.6	3.8	1.8	4.3	6.4	2.9
1991	3.0	4.3	2.0	2.7	3.9	1.8	4.3	6.5	2.8
1992	3.2	4.6	2.0	2.9	4.2	1.9	4.5	7.1	2.7
1993	3.3	4.7	2.2	3.0	4.3	2.0	4.5	6.8	2.8
1994	3.4	4.9	2.2	3.1	4.4	2.0	4.7	7.3	2.8
1995	3.6	5.1	2.3	3.2	4.6	2.1	5.1	7.6	3.4
1996	3.6	5.3	2.3	3.3	4.8	2.2	4.9	7.5	2.9
Age at Death, 1992–1996									
All ages	3.4	4.9	2.2	3.1	4.4	2.1	4.8	7.3	2.9
Under 65	1.5	2.1	0.8	1.2	1.8	0.8	2.4	3.8	1.2
65 and over	21.1	30.5	14.7	20.0	28.9	13.9	26.6	38.5	18.9
All ages (world standard) [2]	2.6	3.8	1.7	2.4	3.4	1.5	3.8	5.8	2.2

See footnotes at end of table.

Table 3.18. Cancer Mortality Rates [1]—*Continued*

(Per 100,000 population; age-adjusted to the 1970 U.S. standard population, except where noted)

Site of cancer	All races Total	All races Males	All races Females	Whites Total	Whites Males	Whites Females	Blacks Total	Blacks Males	Blacks Females
LUNG AND BRONCHUS CANCER									
Year of Death									
1973	34.8	62.4	13.3	34.3	61.6	13.3	40.8	75.1	13.6
1974	36.0	64.1	14.3	35.5	63.2	14.3	42.5	78.5	14.2
1975	36.8	65.1	15.2	36.4	64.2	15.3	43.3	79.7	14.9
1976	38.1	66.7	16.4	37.7	65.7	16.5	44.7	82.0	15.9
1977	39.2	68.2	17.3	38.6	66.8	17.4	47.8	87.8	17.3
1978	40.4	69.5	18.6	39.9	68.2	18.7	48.5	88.8	17.9
1979	41.1	70.1	19.4	40.5	68.8	19.5	49.4	89.7	19.2
1980	42.5	71.5	20.9	41.9	70.0	21.0	51.8	92.7	21.4
1981	43.0	71.7	21.7	42.3	70.0	21.8	53.1	95.5	21.9
1982	44.2	72.9	23.0	43.6	71.3	23.2	54.6	97.9	23.0
1983	44.9	72.9	24.4	44.3	71.3	24.6	55.7	98.0	25.0
1984	45.8	73.9	25.1	45.1	72.0	25.4	56.9	102.1	24.5
1985	46.6	74.1	26.4	46.0	72.3	26.8	57.5	101.6	26.0
1986	47.1	74.3	27.2	46.4	72.4	27.5	58.3	102.6	27.0
1987	48.1	75.1	28.3	47.4	73.3	28.5	59.8	104.6	28.4
1988	48.6	74.8	29.4	48.0	73.0	29.8	59.9	104.1	29.3
1989	49.3	74.7	30.8	48.7	72.6	31.2	61.6	106.7	30.3
1990	50.1	75.2	31.6	49.4	73.2	32.0	62.5	107.0	31.8
1991	50.0	74.4	32.2	49.5	72.5	32.6	61.6	104.6	32.0
1992	50.0	72.9	33.1	49.4	71.0	33.5	61.5	102.4	33.4
1993	50.1	72.5	33.5	49.7	70.7	34.1	60.9	102.4	32.4
1994	49.6	70.8	33.8	49.2	69.2	34.4	60.0	99.1	33.2
1995	49.3	69.5	34.2	49.0	67.9	34.8	59.4	97.0	33.5
1996	48.8	68.2	34.3	48.6	66.8	35.0	58.3	94.4	33.5
Age at Death, 1992–1996									
All ages	49.5	70.8	33.8	49.2	69.1	34.4	60.0	99.0	33.2
Under 65	20.9	27.3	15.0	20.4	26.0	15.2	29.2	45.4	16.4
65 and over	311.2	467.2	205.3	312.1	462.5	209.7	341.3	588.3	185.7
All ages (world standard) [2]	38.4	54.0	26.4	38.1	52.5	26.9	47.6	77.4	26.5
MELANOMAS OF SKIN									
Year of Death									
1973	1.6	2.0	1.3	1.7	2.2	1.4	0.4	0.6	0.4
1974	1.7	2.2	1.3	1.9	2.5	1.4	0.3	0.4	0.3
1975	1.7	2.2	1.3	1.9	2.4	1.4	0.4	0.5	0.4
1976	1.9	2.4	1.4	2.0	2.6	1.6	0.4	0.6	0.3
1977	1.9	2.4	1.4	2.1	2.6	1.6	0.4	0.5	0.3
1978	1.9	2.5	1.4	2.1	2.7	1.6	0.4	0.5	0.4
1979	2.0	2.6	1.5	2.2	2.9	1.7	0.4	0.5	0.4
1980	1.9	2.5	1.4	2.1	2.8	1.5	0.5	0.4	0.5
1981	2.0	2.6	1.5	2.2	2.8	1.7	0.4	0.5	0.4
1982	2.0	2.7	1.5	2.2	3.0	1.6	0.4	0.5	0.4
1983	2.0	2.7	1.5	2.3	3.0	1.7	0.4	0.5	0.3
1984	2.1	2.8	1.5	2.3	3.1	1.6	0.4	0.4	0.4
1985	2.1	2.8	1.5	2.3	3.1	1.7	0.4	0.5	0.4
1986	2.1	2.9	1.5	2.4	3.2	1.7	0.4	0.6	0.2
1987	2.2	3.1	1.5	2.4	3.4	1.7	0.4	0.5	0.4
1988	2.2	3.0	1.5	2.4	3.3	1.7	0.4	0.4	0.3
1989	2.2	3.1	1.5	2.5	3.4	1.7	0.4	0.4	0.4
1990	2.3	3.1	1.6	2.5	3.4	1.8	0.4	0.5	0.4
1991	2.2	3.2	1.5	2.5	3.5	1.6	0.5	0.5	0.4
1992	2.2	3.1	1.5	2.5	3.5	1.7	0.4	0.5	0.3
1993	2.2	3.1	1.5	2.5	3.5	1.7	0.4	0.3	0.5
1994	2.2	3.1	1.5	2.5	3.5	1.7	0.3	0.4	0.3
1995	2.2	3.2	1.5	2.5	3.6	1.7	0.4	0.4	0.3
1996	2.3	3.2	1.5	2.6	3.6	1.7	0.3	0.4	0.3
Age at Death, 1992–1996									
All ages	2.2	3.2	1.5	2.5	3.5	1.7	0.4	0.4	0.3
Under 65	1.3	1.8	0.9	1.5	2.0	1.1	0.1	0.2	0.1
65 and over	10.5	15.9	6.9	11.4	17.4	7.5	2.4	2.3	2.4
All ages (world standard) [2]	1.8	2.6	1.2	2.1	2.9	1.4	0.3	0.3	0.3
MULTIPLE MYELOMA									
Year of Death									
1973	2.3	2.8	1.9	2.1	2.6	1.8	4.2	5.0	3.6
1974	2.3	2.9	1.9	2.1	2.6	1.8	4.2	5.4	3.3
1975	2.4	3.0	2.0	2.2	2.8	1.8	4.4	5.3	3.7
1976	2.5	3.1	2.1	2.3	2.9	1.9	4.7	5.8	3.9
1977	2.5	3.1	2.1	2.3	2.9	1.9	4.6	5.8	3.7
1978	2.5	3.1	2.1	2.3	2.9	2.0	4.7	5.7	4.1
1979	2.6	3.3	2.1	2.4	3.0	2.0	4.9	6.0	4.0
1980	2.6	3.3	2.2	2.4	3.0	2.0	5.0	6.0	4.3
1981	2.6	3.2	2.2	2.4	2.9	2.0	5.3	6.5	4.5
1982	2.7	3.3	2.3	2.5	3.0	2.1	5.4	6.7	4.4
1983	2.7	3.4	2.3	2.5	3.1	2.1	5.5	7.0	4.5
1984	2.8	3.4	2.4	2.5	3.1	2.2	5.4	6.7	4.4
1985	2.8	3.5	2.4	2.6	3.2	2.2	5.6	6.9	4.7
1986	2.8	3.5	2.4	2.6	3.2	2.2	5.8	7.3	4.8
1987	2.9	3.6	2.3	2.6	3.3	2.1	5.7	7.3	4.6
1988	2.9	3.6	2.4	2.6	3.4	2.1	5.6	6.5	5.0
1989	2.9	3.6	2.4	2.7	3.3	2.2	5.6	7.0	4.7
1990	3.0	3.7	2.5	2.7	3.4	2.2	5.8	7.6	4.7
1991	3.1	3.8	2.6	2.8	3.4	2.3	6.2	7.6	5.3
1992	3.0	3.7	2.5	2.7	3.4	2.3	6.0	7.4	5.1
1993	3.1	3.8	2.7	2.9	3.5	2.4	6.2	7.3	5.5
1994	3.1	3.9	2.6	2.9	3.6	2.4	6.1	7.6	5.2
1995	3.2	3.8	2.7	2.9	3.6	2.4	6.3	7.3	5.7
1996	3.1	3.8	2.6	2.8	3.5	2.3	6.2	7.5	5.4
Age at Death, 1992–1996									
All ages	3.1	3.8	2.6	2.8	3.5	2.4	6.2	7.4	5.3
Under 65	1.0	1.2	0.9	0.9	1.1	0.7	2.4	2.8	2.1
65 and over	21.9	27.4	18.4	20.5	25.8	17.0	40.6	49.9	35.1
All ages (world standard) [2]	2.3	2.8	1.9	2.1	2.6	1.7	4.6	5.6	4.0

See footnotes at end of table.

Table 3.18. Cancer Mortality Rates [1]—*Continued*

(Per 100,000 population; age-adjusted to the 1970 U.S. standard population, except where noted)

Site of cancer	All races			Whites			Blacks		
	Total	Males	Females	Total	Males	Females	Total	Males	Females
NON-HODGKIN'S LYMPHOMAS									
Year of Death									
1973	4.7	5.8	3.9	4.9	6.0	4.1	3.2	4.3	2.3
1974	4.8	5.9	4.0	5.0	6.1	4.1	3.3	4.4	2.4
1975	4.7	5.7	3.8	4.8	5.9	3.9	3.2	4.2	2.5
1976	4.7	5.7	3.9	4.9	5.9	4.1	3.0	3.9	2.3
1977	4.8	5.7	4.0	4.9	5.9	4.1	3.3	4.2	2.6
1978	4.9	6.0	4.0	5.0	6.2	4.2	3.3	4.5	2.4
1979	4.9	6.0	4.0	5.1	6.3	4.1	3.1	3.9	2.5
1980	5.1	6.1	4.2	5.3	6.3	4.4	3.3	4.3	2.5
1981	5.0	6.0	4.2	5.2	6.2	4.4	3.3	4.1	2.7
1982	5.3	6.4	4.4	5.5	6.7	4.6	3.4	4.4	2.7
1983	5.4	6.6	4.5	5.6	6.8	4.7	3.6	4.8	2.7
1984	5.4	6.5	4.6	5.7	6.8	4.8	3.5	4.4	2.8
1985	5.7	7.0	4.6	5.9	7.3	4.8	3.8	4.7	3.1
1986	5.9	7.2	4.8	6.1	7.4	5.0	4.1	5.5	3.0
1987	5.8	7.0	4.8	6.0	7.3	5.0	3.9	5.1	3.0
1988	6.0	7.4	4.9	6.2	7.6	5.1	4.1	5.5	3.0
1989	6.2	7.7	5.1	6.4	7.9	5.3	4.4	5.8	3.3
1990	6.2	7.9	5.0	6.5	8.2	5.2	4.4	5.9	3.4
1991	6.5	8.0	5.3	6.7	8.3	5.5	4.7	5.9	3.7
1992	6.5	8.1	5.3	6.8	8.4	5.5	4.6	5.9	3.6
1993	6.5	8.0	5.4	6.8	8.2	5.6	4.7	6.1	3.6
1994	6.9	8.5	5.6	7.2	8.8	5.9	4.6	5.7	3.7
1995	6.9	8.5	5.6	7.2	8.8	5.9	4.7	6.2	3.6
1996	6.9	8.6	5.6	7.2	8.9	5.9	5.1	6.8	3.9
Age at Death, 1992–1996									
All ages	6.8	8.4	5.5	7.0	8.6	5.8	4.7	6.1	3.7
Under 65	2.8	3.6	2.1	2.9	3.7	2.1	2.7	3.7	1.9
65 and over	42.8	51.7	37.0	44.9	54.1	38.9	23.4	28.5	20.2
All ages (world standard) [2]	5.2	6.4	4.1	5.4	6.6	4.3	3.9	5.1	2.9
ORAL CAVITY AND PHARYNX CANCER									
Year of Death									
1973	3.6	5.9	1.9	3.5	5.7	1.8	5.0	8.3	2.3
1974	3.6	5.9	1.9	3.5	5.8	1.8	4.7	7.8	2.2
1975	3.7	5.8	1.9	3.5	5.6	1.9	5.1	8.7	2.1
1976	3.6	5.8	1.9	3.4	5.5	1.8	5.3	9.2	2.3
1977	3.7	5.9	1.9	3.5	5.6	1.9	5.4	9.4	2.3
1978	3.6	5.7	1.9	3.4	5.4	1.8	5.4	9.3	2.3
1979	3.6	5.7	2.0	3.4	5.3	1.9	5.8	9.9	2.6
1980	3.5	5.6	1.9	3.3	5.1	1.8	6.1	10.9	2.3
1981	3.4	5.5	1.9	3.2	5.0	1.8	5.7	9.9	2.4
1982	3.4	5.4	1.8	3.1	5.0	1.8	5.8	10.0	2.5
1983	3.3	5.3	1.8	3.1	4.8	1.7	5.8	10.3	2.4
1984	3.3	5.2	1.8	3.0	4.7	1.8	5.6	10.3	2.1
1985	3.2	5.0	1.8	2.9	4.6	1.7	5.5	9.7	2.3
1986	3.1	4.9	1.8	2.9	4.4	1.7	5.6	9.8	2.5
1987	3.0	4.6	1.7	2.8	4.2	1.6	5.0	8.7	2.2
1988	3.0	4.7	1.7	2.8	4.3	1.6	5.3	9.4	2.2
1989	3.0	4.5	1.7	2.7	4.1	1.6	5.3	9.3	2.3
1990	3.0	4.7	1.6	2.7	4.2	1.6	5.4	9.7	2.2
1991	2.9	4.5	1.7	2.7	4.1	1.6	5.2	8.9	2.4
1992	2.8	4.3	1.6	2.6	3.9	1.5	5.0	8.9	2.0
1993	2.8	4.4	1.6	2.6	3.9	1.5	5.0	8.9	2.1
1994	2.7	4.1	1.5	2.4	3.7	1.4	4.7	8.2	2.0
1995	2.7	4.1	1.5	2.4	3.7	1.4	4.7	8.2	2.2
1996	2.6	3.9	1.4	2.4	3.6	1.4	4.3	7.7	1.8
Age at Death, 1992–1996									
All ages	2.7	4.2	1.5	2.5	3.7	1.4	4.7	8.4	2.0
Under 65	1.4	2.3	0.7	1.2	1.9	0.6	3.3	5.9	1.3
65 and over	14.1	21.4	9.0	13.9	20.7	9.1	17.5	30.9	8.8
All ages (world standard) [2]	2.2	3.3	1.2	2.0	3.0	1.1	4.0	7.1	1.7
PANCREAS CANCER									
Year of Death									
1973	8.6	11.2	6.7	8.5	11.1	6.5	10.4	13.3	8.2
1974	8.6	10.8	6.8	8.4	10.7	6.7	10.2	12.6	8.4
1975	8.6	11.1	6.7	8.4	10.9	6.6	10.8	13.9	8.5
1976	8.6	11.0	6.8	8.4	10.8	6.7	10.7	13.5	8.6
1977	8.7	11.1	7.0	8.5	10.8	6.8	11.0	14.2	8.6
1978	8.7	10.9	7.0	8.5	10.8	6.8	10.8	13.3	8.9
1979	8.6	10.8	7.0	8.4	10.6	6.7	11.0	13.2	9.4
1980	8.5	10.5	7.0	8.3	10.3	6.8	11.4	13.8	9.7
1981	8.5	10.6	7.0	8.4	10.3	6.9	11.0	14.1	8.8
1982	8.5	10.4	7.0	8.2	10.2	6.8	11.5	14.1	9.5
1983	8.5	10.3	7.2	8.2	9.9	6.9	12.1	14.8	10.1
1984	8.6	10.4	7.3	8.3	10.1	7.0	12.3	14.5	10.6
1985	8.5	10.3	7.1	8.2	10.0	6.9	11.7	14.2	9.9
1986	8.4	10.0	7.2	8.2	9.7	7.0	11.8	13.7	10.3
1987	8.4	10.0	7.2	8.1	9.7	7.0	11.7	14.2	10.0
1988	8.3	10.0	7.0	8.0	9.7	6.7	11.8	14.0	10.1
1989	8.4	10.0	7.2	8.1	9.7	6.9	12.1	14.4	10.5
1990	8.5	10.0	7.2	8.2	9.7	6.9	12.2	14.6	10.5
1991	8.4	10.0	7.2	8.2	9.8	7.0	11.6	13.7	10.0
1992	8.5	10.1	7.2	8.2	9.7	7.0	12.4	14.7	10.7
1993	8.5	9.9	7.4	8.2	9.6	7.1	12.1	14.1	10.7
1994	8.4	9.9	7.3	8.1	9.6	7.0	12.2	14.2	10.7
1995	8.3	9.6	7.2	8.1	9.5	7.0	11.1	12.6	9.9
1996	8.3	9.6	7.2	8.0	9.4	7.0	11.6	13.2	10.4
Age at Death, 1992–1996									
All ages	8.4	9.8	7.3	8.1	9.5	7.0	11.8	13.8	10.5
Under 65	3.0	3.7	2.4	2.9	3.5	2.3	4.6	5.7	3.7
65 and over	57.6	65.8	51.8	56.1	64.5	50.2	78.4	87.6	72.4
All ages (world standard) [2]	6.3	7.4	5.3	6.1	7.2	5.1	8.9	10.5	7.8

See footnotes at end of table.

Table 3.18. Cancer Mortality Rates [1]—*Continued*

(Per 100,000 population; age-adjusted to the 1970 U.S. standard population, except where noted)

Site of cancer	All races			Whites			Blacks		
	Total	Males	Females	Total	Males	Females	Total	Males	Females
STOMACH CANCER									
Year of Death									
1973	7.0	10.1	4.8	6.5	9.4	4.5	11.8	17.2	7.7
1974	6.8	9.9	4.7	6.3	9.1	4.3	12.0	17.7	7.7
1975	6.6	9.5	4.5	6.1	8.7	4.3	11.2	17.1	6.8
1976	6.4	9.3	4.3	5.9	8.5	4.0	10.8	16.4	6.7
1977	6.1	8.9	4.1	5.6	8.2	3.8	10.7	15.6	7.0
1978	6.0	8.6	4.1	5.5	7.9	3.8	10.2	15.1	6.6
1979	5.9	8.5	4.0	5.4	7.8	3.7	10.3	15.2	6.8
1980	5.7	8.2	3.9	5.2	7.6	3.6	9.7	14.6	6.3
1981	5.6	8.2	3.8	5.1	7.6	3.4	9.9	14.5	6.6
1982	5.5	7.9	3.7	5.0	7.2	3.4	9.7	15.2	5.9
1983	5.3	7.7	3.6	4.8	7.0	3.3	9.8	14.7	6.3
1984	5.3	7.7	3.5	4.8	7.0	3.2	9.4	14.2	6.1
1985	5.1	7.4	3.4	4.6	6.8	3.1	9.1	13.5	5.9
1986	5.0	7.4	3.2	4.5	6.7	2.9	9.0	13.8	5.7
1987	4.8	7.1	3.2	4.4	6.4	2.8	8.9	13.5	5.8
1988	4.7	6.9	3.1	4.3	6.2	2.9	8.7	13.6	5.3
1989	4.8	7.1	3.1	4.3	6.4	2.8	9.1	14.2	5.6
1990	4.7	6.9	3.1	4.2	6.1	2.8	8.9	13.5	5.8
1991	4.7	6.9	3.0	4.2	6.2	2.7	9.1	14.0	5.7
1992	4.4	6.3	3.0	3.9	5.6	2.6	8.4	12.3	5.7
1993	4.4	6.4	2.9	3.9	5.7	2.6	8.3	12.7	5.3
1994	4.2	6.1	2.8	3.7	5.4	2.5	8.1	12.1	5.3
1995	4.2	6.0	2.8	3.7	5.3	2.4	8.1	11.7	5.6
1996	4.0	5.7	2.7	3.5	5.1	2.4	7.7	11.6	5.1
Age at Death, 1992–1996									
All ages	4.2	6.1	2.8	3.7	5.4	2.5	8.1	12.1	5.4
Under 65	1.6	2.2	1.0	1.4	1.9	0.8	3.2	4.8	1.9
65 and over	28.1	41.2	19.5	25.4	37.3	17.4	53.4	78.4	37.8
All ages (world standard) [2]	3.2	4.6	2.1	2.8	4.0	1.8	6.1	9.1	4.0
THYROID CANCER									
Year of Death									
1973	0.4	0.3	0.5	0.4	0.3	0.5	0.5	0.4	0.6
1974	0.4	0.3	0.5	0.4	0.3	0.5	0.5	0.3	0.5
1975	0.4	0.3	0.5	0.4	0.3	0.5	0.4	0.3	0.5
1976	0.4	0.4	0.5	0.4	0.4	0.5	0.4	0.3	0.5
1977	0.4	0.4	0.5	0.4	0.4	0.5	0.5	0.5	0.6
1978	0.4	0.3	0.5	0.4	0.4	0.5	0.4	0.3	0.5
1979	0.4	0.3	0.4	0.4	0.4	0.4	0.4	0.3	0.5
1980	0.4	0.3	0.4	0.4	0.3	0.4	0.3	0.2	0.4
1981	0.4	0.3	0.4	0.4	0.4	0.4	0.4	0.2	0.5
1982	0.4	0.3	0.4	0.4	0.3	0.4	0.4	0.3	0.4
1983	0.3	0.3	0.4	0.3	0.3	0.4	0.3	0.2	0.4
1984	0.4	0.3	0.4	0.4	0.3	0.4	0.4	0.2	0.5
1985	0.3	0.3	0.4	0.3	0.3	0.4	0.4	0.3	0.5
1986	0.4	0.3	0.4	0.3	0.3	0.4	0.4	0.3	0.5
1987	0.4	0.3	0.4	0.3	0.3	0.4	0.4	0.3	0.5
1988	0.3	0.3	0.3	0.3	0.3	0.3	0.3	0.3	0.4
1989	0.3	0.3	0.3	0.3	0.3	0.3	0.4	0.3	0.4
1990	0.3	0.3	0.4	0.3	0.3	0.4	0.4	0.2	0.4
1991	0.3	0.3	0.4	0.3	0.3	0.3	0.4	0.3	0.4
1992	0.4	0.3	0.4	0.4	0.3	0.4	0.3	0.3	0.4
1993	0.4	0.3	0.4	0.4	0.3	0.4	0.4	0.2	0.5
1994	0.3	0.3	0.3	0.3	0.3	0.3	0.3	0.3	0.3
1995	0.3	0.3	0.3	0.3	0.4	0.3	0.3	0.2	0.4
1996	0.4	0.3	0.4	0.4	0.3	0.4	0.3	0.3	0.4
Age at Death, 1992–1996									
All ages	0.3	0.3	0.4	0.3	0.3	0.4	0.3	0.2	0.4
Under 65	0.1	0.1	0.1	0.1	0.1	0.1	0.1	0.1	0.1
65 and over	2.3	2.0	2.5	2.3	2.0	2.4	2.2	1.6	2.6
All ages (world standard) [2]	0.3	0.2	0.3	0.3	0.3	0.3	0.2	0.2	0.3

See footnotes at end of table.

Table 3.18. Cancer Mortality Rates—*Continued*

(Per 100,000 population; age-adjusted to the 1970 U.S. standard population, except where noted)

Site of cancer	Females								
	All races			Whites			Blacks		
	All	<50	50+	All	<50	50+	All	<50	50+
BREAST CANCER									
Year of Death									
1973	26.9	7.0	88.4	27.1	6.8	89.7	26.3	8.9	79.8
1974	26.7	6.9	87.6	26.8	6.7	88.6	26.7	8.7	82.0
1975	26.2	6.8	86.1	26.5	6.7	87.5	24.8	7.9	77.1
1976	26.5	6.5	88.3	26.8	6.4	89.9	25.2	7.5	79.7
1977	27.1	6.6	90.2	27.2	6.5	91.1	27.4	7.8	88.0
1978	26.5	6.4	88.3	26.7	6.3	89.5	26.7	8.4	83.1
1979	26.0	6.3	86.6	26.2	6.2	88.2	25.7	8.4	79.0
1980	26.4	6.3	88.4	26.6	6.2	89.7	26.4	8.0	83.2
1981	26.6	6.2	89.3	26.8	6.0	90.7	27.1	8.5	84.3
1982	26.8	6.2	90.2	26.9	6.0	91.1	28.2	8.3	89.7
1983	26.7	6.0	90.6	26.8	5.8	91.6	28.0	8.2	89.2
1984	27.3	6.3	92.2	27.3	6.0	93.0	30.0	9.2	94.3
1985	27.5	6.3	92.7	27.6	6.1	93.7	29.1	8.8	91.8
1986	27.3	6.4	91.9	27.4	6.1	93.0	29.6	9.4	91.7
1987	27.1	6.2	91.7	27.1	5.9	92.4	30.6	9.5	95.7
1988	27.5	6.2	93.4	27.4	5.9	93.9	31.4	9.3	99.5
1989	27.5	6.2	93.1	27.5	5.9	93.9	30.4	9.2	96.0
1990	27.4	6.1	92.9	27.3	5.9	93.3	31.6	8.8	101.7
1991	27.0	6.0	91.8	26.8	5.7	92.0	31.8	9.1	102.0
1992	26.2	5.8	89.1	26.0	5.5	89.3	31.0	8.9	99.0
1993	25.9	5.5	88.7	25.6	5.2	88.7	31.5	8.6	102.0
1994	25.5	5.5	87.3	25.2	5.1	87.1	31.3	8.7	101.2
1995	25.2	5.4	86.3	24.8	5.0	85.8	31.9	8.8	103.2
1996	24.3	5.2	83.4	24.0	4.8	83.2	30.8	8.8	98.9
1992–1996	25.4	5.5	86.9	25.1	5.1	86.8	31.3	8.7	100.9
CERVIX UTERI CANCER									
Year of Death									
1973	5.2	2.0	15.0	4.4	1.6	12.9	13.1	5.0	37.9
1974	5.0	1.9	14.6	4.3	1.6	12.9	11.7	4.6	33.6
1975	4.6	1.8	13.4	3.9	1.4	11.6	11.1	4.2	32.1
1976	4.5	1.6	13.4	3.9	1.4	11.5	10.7	3.6	32.4
1977	4.1	1.5	12.3	3.5	1.2	10.6	10.1	3.7	30.0
1978	4.0	1.6	11.6	3.4	1.3	10.0	9.6	3.5	28.3
1979	3.8	1.4	11.2	3.3	1.2	9.8	8.8	3.3	25.8
1980	3.7	1.5	10.6	3.1	1.2	9.1	8.9	3.4	25.8
1981	3.6	1.4	10.5	3.1	1.2	9.0	8.2	2.7	24.9
1982	3.4	1.3	9.8	2.9	1.1	8.3	8.1	2.7	24.6
1983	3.3	1.3	9.6	2.8	1.1	8.1	8.1	2.9	24.3
1984	3.3	1.3	9.2	2.8	1.1	7.8	7.6	2.9	22.1
1985	3.1	1.3	8.9	2.7	1.1	7.6	7.3	2.5	22.3
1986	3.2	1.3	8.9	2.7	1.1	7.5	7.7	3.0	22.2
1987	3.0	1.3	8.3	2.6	1.1	7.1	6.8	2.7	19.6
1988	3.0	1.3	8.3	2.6	1.1	7.0	6.7	2.2	20.6
1989	3.0	1.3	8.2	2.5	1.1	6.8	7.1	2.4	21.5
1990	3.0	1.3	8.3	2.6	1.2	7.1	6.4	2.5	18.5
1991	2.9	1.3	8.0	2.5	1.1	6.7	6.4	2.3	18.8
1992	2.9	1.3	7.9	2.5	1.1	6.6	6.7	2.5	19.6
1993	2.8	1.2	7.7	2.4	1.1	6.6	6.3	2.3	18.7
1994	2.8	1.2	7.7	2.5	1.1	6.8	5.6	2.1	16.2
1995	2.7	1.2	7.2	2.3	1.1	6.2	5.7	2.2	16.5
1996	2.7	1.2	7.4	2.4	1.1	6.4	5.2	1.9	15.4
1992–1996	2.8	1.2	7.6	2.4	1.1	6.5	5.9	2.2	17.3
CORPUS AND UTERUS, NOS CANCER									
Year of Death									
1973	4.6	0.5	17.4	4.3	0.4	16.4	8.0	1.1	29.5
1974	4.5	0.5	16.8	4.2	0.4	15.9	7.0	0.7	26.6
1975	4.3	0.4	16.4	4.1	0.4	15.7	6.6	0.7	24.8
1976	4.3	0.4	16.6	4.1	0.4	15.8	6.8	0.6	25.6
1977	4.3	0.4	16.2	4.0	0.4	15.4	7.0	0.6	26.5
1978	4.2	0.4	15.8	3.9	0.4	15.0	6.8	0.6	25.8
1979	4.1	0.3	15.7	3.8	0.3	14.9	6.6	0.6	25.4
1980	4.2	0.3	16.0	3.9	0.3	15.1	6.9	0.6	26.3
1981	4.0	0.3	15.3	3.8	0.3	14.6	6.1	0.4	23.8
1982	3.9	0.3	15.2	3.7	0.3	14.3	6.3	0.3	24.7
1983	3.9	0.3	15.1	3.7	0.2	14.4	6.0	0.5	23.1
1984	3.8	0.3	14.7	3.6	0.2	13.9	6.3	0.5	23.9
1985	3.7	0.3	14.5	3.6	0.3	13.7	6.1	0.4	23.6
1986	3.6	0.3	13.9	3.4	0.2	13.1	6.0	0.4	23.3
1987	3.6	0.3	13.7	3.4	0.2	13.0	5.9	0.4	22.9
1988	3.5	0.2	13.6	3.3	0.2	12.7	6.1	0.3	23.8
1989	3.4	0.3	13.2	3.2	0.3	12.3	5.9	0.4	23.0
1990	3.5	0.2	13.5	3.3	0.2	12.6	6.0	0.3	23.4
1991	3.4	0.2	12.9	3.1	0.2	12.0	6.0	0.4	23.3
1992	3.4	0.2	13.1	3.2	0.2	12.3	5.7	0.3	22.4
1993	3.4	0.2	12.9	3.1	0.2	12.0	6.0	0.3	23.4
1994	3.3	0.2	13.0	3.1	0.2	12.1	5.9	0.2	23.2
1995	3.3	0.3	12.8	3.2	0.3	12.1	5.3	0.3	20.9
1996	3.3	0.2	12.9	3.1	0.2	11.9	5.9	0.3	23.2
1992–1996	3.3	0.2	12.9	3.1	0.2	12.1	5.8	0.3	22.6

See footnotes at end of table.

Table 3.18. Cancer Mortality Rates—*Continued*

(Per 100,000 population; age-adjusted to the 1970 U.S. standard population, except where noted)

Site of cancer	Females								
	All races			Whites			Blacks		
	All	<50	50+	All	<50	50+	All	<50	50+
OVARY CANCER									
Year of Death									
1973	8.4	1.9	28.4	8.5	1.9	29.0	7.1	1.6	24.0
1974	8.5	1.9	28.8	8.7	2.0	29.5	6.8	1.6	23.1
1975	8.4	1.8	28.9	8.7	1.8	29.7	6.3	1.3	21.4
1976	8.5	1.7	29.6	8.7	1.7	30.4	6.9	1.3	24.1
1977	8.2	1.5	28.9	8.4	1.5	29.8	6.3	1.3	21.9
1978	8.2	1.5	28.8	8.4	1.5	29.6	6.3	1.1	22.6
1979	7.9	1.4	27.9	8.1	1.4	28.6	6.5	1.4	22.4
1980	7.8	1.3	27.9	8.0	1.4	28.6	6.7	1.2	23.7
1981	7.8	1.3	27.9	8.0	1.3	28.7	6.2	1.0	22.3
1982	7.8	1.3	27.9	8.0	1.3	28.7	6.3	0.9	22.8
1983	7.8	1.2	28.1	8.0	1.2	28.9	6.5	1.1	22.8
1984	7.7	1.2	27.4	7.9	1.3	28.2	6.3	1.0	22.8
1985	7.7	1.2	27.6	7.9	1.2	28.4	6.3	0.9	22.8
1986	7.8	1.2	27.9	8.0	1.3	28.7	6.3	0.9	22.9
1987	7.7	1.1	28.1	8.0	1.1	29.0	6.3	1.0	22.7
1988	7.8	1.1	28.5	8.0	1.1	29.3	6.6	1.0	24.0
1989	7.7	1.1	28.2	8.0	1.1	29.2	6.1	0.9	22.4
1990	7.8	1.1	28.3	8.0	1.2	29.2	6.5	0.9	23.9
1991	7.9	1.1	29.1	8.1	1.1	30.0	6.9	1.0	24.8
1992	7.9	1.0	28.9	8.1	1.1	29.7	6.8	0.9	25.0
1993	7.5	1.0	27.6	7.8	1.1	28.4	6.3	0.7	23.6
1994	7.8	1.0	28.8	8.1	1.0	29.7	6.5	0.8	24.0
1995	7.6	1.0	27.9	7.9	1.0	29.0	6.1	0.7	22.5
1996	7.4	1.0	27.1	7.6	1.0	28.0	6.1	0.8	22.3
1992–1996	7.6	1.0	28.1	7.9	1.0	29.0	6.3	0.8	23.5

See footnotes at end of table.

Table 3.18. Cancer Mortality Rates [1]—Continued

(Per 100,000 population; age-adjusted to the 1970 U.S. standard population, except where noted)

Site of cancer	Males		
	All races	Whites	Blacks
PROSTATE CANCER			
Year of Death			
1973	21.7	20.3	39.5
1974	21.7	20.2	39.7
1975	21.6	20.1	40.6
1976	22.1	20.6	40.8
1977	22.1	20.6	41.2
1978	22.6	21.0	42.5
1979	22.7	21.1	43.0
1980	22.8	21.1	44.6
1981	22.9	21.0	45.8
1982	23.0	21.3	44.7
1983	23.4	21.6	46.6
1984	23.4	21.5	47.1
1985	23.4	21.5	48.1
1986	24.1	22.2	48.3
1987	24.1	22.2	49.1
1988	24.7	22.8	49.5
1989	25.4	23.5	51.1
1990	26.4	24.3	54.8
1991	26.7	24.7	54.9
1992	26.6	24.5	55.6
1993	26.4	24.3	56.2
1994	25.9	23.8	55.1
1995	24.9	22.9	53.5
1996	24.1	22.0	53.7
Age at Death, 1992–1996			
All ages	25.6	23.4	54.8
Under 65	2.7	2.3	7.1
65 and over	234.3	216.3	490.4
All ages (world standard) [2]	16.7	15.2	36.4
TESTIS CANCER			
Year of Death			
1973	0.8	0.8	0.3
1974	0.7	0.8	0.2
1975	0.7	0.7	0.2
1976	0.6	0.7	0.3
1977	0.6	0.7	0.2
1978	0.5	0.5	0.2
1979	0.5	0.5	0.3
1980	0.4	0.4	0.2
1981	0.3	0.4	0.2
1982	0.4	0.4	0.2
1983	0.3	0.4	0.2
1984	0.3	0.3	0.2
1985	0.3	0.3	0.2
1986	0.3	0.3	0.1
1987	0.3	0.3	0.2
1988	0.3	0.3	0.1
1989	0.2	0.3	0.1
1990	0.2	0.3	0.2
1991	0.2	0.3	0.1
1992	0.3	0.3	0.1
1993	0.2	0.3	0.1
1994	0.2	0.3	0.1
1995	0.2	0.2	0.1
1996	0.2	0.3	0.1
Age at Death, 1992–1996			
All ages	0.2	0.3	0.1
Under 65	0.2	0.3	0.1
65 and over	0.3	0.3	0.2
All ages (world standard) [2]	0.2	0.3	0.1

Source: L.A.G. Ries, C.L. Kosary, B.F. Hankey, B.A. Miller, L. Clegg, B.K. Edwards (eds). SEER *Cancer Statistics Review,* 1973-1996, National Cancer Institute. Bethesda, MD, 1999.

1. NCHS public use tape. Rates are per 100,000 and are age-adjusted to the 1970 U.S. standard population, except where noted.
2. NCHS public use tape. Rates are per 100,000 and are age-adjusted to the world standard population.

Table 3.19. Cancer Deaths Among American Indians and Alaska Natives: 1992–1994

(Per 100,000 population)

Site of fatal cancer	Number		Rate	
	Actual	Adjusted [1]	Actual	Adjusted [1]
MALE				
All sites	1 578	1 792	82.0	93.2
Trachea, bronchus, and lung	436	531	22.7	27.6
Prostate	188	204	9.8	10.6
Colon	103	127	5.4	6.6
Stomach	94	109	4.9	5.7
Liver	81	87	4.2	4.5
Kidney	80	87	4.2	4.5
Leukemia	64	65	3.3	3.4
Pancreas	58	65	3.0	3.4
Esophagus	51	61	2.7	3.2
Pharynx	34	34	1.8	1.8
Multiple myeloma	33	34	1.7	1.8
Brain	28	31	1.5	1.6
Gallbladder	30	30	1.6	1.6
Rectum, rectosigmoid junction, and anus	24	29	1.2	1.5
Connective and other soft tissue	12	15	0.6	0.8
Larynx	14	14	0.7	0.7
Bladder	13	14	0.7	0.7
Melanoma of skin	7	8	0.4	0.4
Tongue	6	7	3.0	0.4
Bone and articular cartilage	6	7	0.3	0.4
Penis	3	3	0.2	0.2
Thyroid gland	2	3	0.1	0.2
Testis	2	2	0.1	0.1
All other sites	209	225		
FEMALE				
All sites	1 519	752	76.6	88.4
Trachea, bronchus, and lung	321	384	16.2	19.4
Female breast	204	243	10.3	12.3
Colon	116	136	0.9	6.9
Ovary	78	90	3.9	4.5
Pancreas	67	80	3.4	4.0
Cervix uteri	60	71	3.0	3.6
Stomach	52	62	2.6	3.1
Liver	51	55	2.6	2.8
Gallbladder	50	51	2.5	2.6
Kidney	48	50	2.4	2.5
Leukemia	46	50	2.3	2.5
Rectum, rectosigmoid junction, and anus	25	31	1.3	1.6
Multiple myeloma	25	25	1.3	1.3
Connective and other soft tissue	16	23	0.8	1.2
Brain	21	22	1.1	1.1
Bladder	14	18	0.7	0.9
Melanoma of skin	10	13	0.5	0.7
Pharynx	10	11	0.5	0.6
Esophagus	7	8	0.4	0.4
Tongue	6	6	0.3	0.3
Thyroid gland	6	6	0.3	0.3
Bone and articular cartilage	5	6	0.3	0.3
Larynx	5	5	0.3	0.3
All other sites	276	306		

SOURCE: Indian Health Service, *Trends in Indian Health* (Rockville, Md.: 1997): P. 110. This table is based on data covering the period from 1992 to 1994 and is based on a special analysis of mortality data from the National Vital Statistics System, which corrects for the underreporting of American Indian deaths.

1. Adjusted to compensate for miscoding of American Indian race on death certificates.

Table 3.20. Cancer Deaths Distributed by State: 1996

(Per 100,000 population; age-adjusted to the 1970 U.S. standard population)

Area	All sites	Urinary bladder cancer	Brain and other nervous system cancer	Female breast cancer	Cervix uteri cancer	Colon and rectum cancer	Corpus and uterus, NOS cancer	Esophagus cancer
United States	170.1	3.2	4.2	25.4	2.8	17.5	3.3	3.6
STATE								
Alabama	179.3	2.5	4.1	23.2	3.3	15.1	2.7	3.4
Alaska	167.1	3.0	3.2	23.2	1.8	18.8	1.6	3.9
Arizona	155.3	3.1	3.8	22.3	2.4	15.0	2.6	3.4
Arkansas	180.9	3.1	5.0	23.1	3.0	17.3	3.0	2.8
California	156.4	3.0	4.1	24.4	2.6	15.3	3.2	3.2
Colorado	142.3	2.9	4.2	21.6	2.1	14.7	2.7	2.9
Connecticut	162.8	3.6	3.9	25.7	1.9	17.1	3.1	3.8
Delaware	194.5	4.3	4.1	27.8	3.8	19.2	4.1	5.0
Florida	165.9	3.4	4.4	24.5	3.1	16.4	2.9	3.5
Georgia	175.2	2.8	4.0	24.0	2.9	15.8	3.1	3.8
Hawaii	132.9	2.0	2.3	17.6	1.9	14.3	2.5	2.7
Idaho	147.9	3.0	4.3	22.3	2.0	14.1	2.6	3.0
Illinois	177.9	3.3	3.9	27.5	2.9	19.3	3.5	4.1
Indiana	177.6	3.4	4.3	25.9	3.0	18.9	3.5	3.6
Iowa	159.2	3.1	4.9	24.6	2.3	18.3	4.0	3.3
Kansas	158.9	2.8	5.1	23.4	2.5	16.3	3.3	2.8
Kentucky	191.9	3.2	4.9	24.8	3.7	19.4	3.2	3.5
Louisiana	193.1	3.0	3.9	26.4	3.5	18.7	3.2	3.9
Maine	185.4	4.1	4.4	25.3	3.1	19.8	3.4	4.0
Maryland	184.2	3.7	3.8	27.3	2.7	20.1	3.4	4.5
Massachusetts	177.5	3.7	4.1	27.9	2.1	19.7	3.3	4.1
Michigan	172.5	3.6	4.4	26.0	2.6	17.6	3.6	3.9
Minnesota	155.6	3.0	4.6	24.5	1.7	15.8	3.1	3.1
Mississippi	182.2	2.6	4.8	23.8	3.7	16.5	2.7	3.3
Missouri	175.5	2.9	4.3	24.6	3.0	18.0	3.5	3.4
Montana	159.4	3.2	4.5	24.6	2.3	16.0	3.2	3.2
Nebraska	155.2	2.6	4.8	24.8	2.2	18.2	2.8	3.4
Nevada	183.5	4.1	3.7	24.9	3.0	17.3	2.7	3.5
New Hampshire	181.0	3.9	5.3	27.5	3.0	19.6	3.4	4.6
New Jersey	179.0	3.9	3.5	28.4	2.9	20.6	4.0	3.8
New Mexico	146.2	2.5	3.2	23.1	2.4	14.2	3.1	2.9
New York	169.3	3.6	3.6	28.2	3.0	19.2	4.0	3.9
North Carolina	174.8	2.9	4.5	24.9	3.0	17.1	3.3	3.7
North Dakota	154.5	2.8	4.8	24.4	2.6	17.3	2.4	2.5
Ohio	179.8	3.6	4.1	27.2	2.8	19.2	3.9	3.8
Oklahoma	169.6	2.8	4.4	24.2	3.0	16.2	2.7	2.8
Oregon	165.5	3.2	4.8	24.0	2.1	15.4	3.3	3.7
Pennsylvania	176.5	3.5	4.0	27.7	2.7	20.0	3.7	3.8
Rhode Island	177.6	3.8	4.7	28.0	2.8	19.6	3.6	3.8
South Carolina	177.9	3.3	4.5	24.4	3.6	17.7	3.4	4.3
South Dakota	155.0	2.9	5.1	24.2	1.7	17.4	3.3	3.2
Tennessee	181.3	3.2	5.0	25.3	3.5	17.5	3.2	3.3
Texas	168.1	2.8	4.5	23.5	3.3	16.3	3.0	3.2
Utah	122.0	2.3	4.1	20.8	2.3	12.9	3.3	1.9
Vermont	171.9	3.7	4.0	24.8	3.5	18.3	4.1	3.9
Virginia	176.6	3.2	3.9	25.8	2.7	17.7	3.5	4.1
Washington	162.3	3.2	4.3	24.1	2.0	15.5	2.9	3.4
West Virginia	184.3	3.4	4.4	23.4	3.7	18.5	3.1	3.2
Wisconsin	162.5	3.4	4.4	24.8	2.3	16.9	3.4	3.8
Wyoming	156.5	2.7	4.3	24.0	1.6	15.7	3.6	3.4
OTHER								
District of Columbia	212.3	3.4	2.5	32.8	4.6	20.6	5.3	8.9
Median	172.5	3.2	4.3	24.6	2.8	17.4	3.3	3.5
Low	122.0	2.0	2.3	17.6	1.6	12.9	1.6	1.9
High	212.3	4.3	5.3	32.8	4.6	20.6	5.3	8.9

See footnotes at end of table.

Table 3.20. Cancer Deaths Distributed by State: 1996—*Continued*

(Per 100,000 population; age-adjusted to the 1970 U.S. standard population)

Area	Hodgkin's disease	Kidney and renal pelvis cancer	Larynx cancer	All leukemias	Liver and intrahepatic bile duct cancer	Lung and bronchus cancer	Melanomas of skin	Multiple Myeloma
United States	0.5	3.5	1.3	6.3	3.4	49.5	2.2	3.1
STATE								
Alabama	0.5	3.0	1.2	6.5	3.7	54.0	2.3	3.3
Alaska	0.6	4.5	0.4	6.0	3.1	52.3	2.1	2.8
Arizona	0.5	3.1	1.1	6.0	3.0	44.8	2.5	2.7
Arkansas	0.6	3.7	1.2	6.6	4.6	62.1	2.0	3.2
California	0.5	3.1	1.0	6.1	3.9	43.1	2.3	2.8
Colorado	0.4	3.2	1.0	6.2	2.7	35.8	2.5	2.9
Connecticut	0.6	3.3	1.3	6.3	3.0	43.8	2.3	2.6
Delaware	0.5	3.6	1.7	6.4	3.0	59.9	2.6	3.4
Florida	0.5	3.2	1.5	6.0	3.2	51.1	2.4	2.7
Georgia	0.4	3.3	1.3	6.3	3.2	54.4	2.2	3.3
Hawaii	0.2	2.3	0.8	4.6	5.7	33.4	1.2	1.7
Idaho	0.5	3.3	0.9	6.5	2.2	38.4	2.6	3.2
Illinois	0.5	3.8	1.6	6.6	3.7	50.9	2.0	3.2
Indiana	0.5	4.0	1.2	6.5	3.1	55.4	2.2	3.1
Iowa	0.4	3.9	1.2	6.7	2.3	45.6	2.1	3.2
Kansas	0.5	3.8	1.0	6.4	2.4	45.9	2.4	3.6
Kentucky	0.5	4.1	1.6	6.1	3.4	67.9	2.3	3.3
Louisiana	0.6	3.9	1.9	6.6	4.6	59.9	1.9	3.7
Maine	0.6	4.4	1.4	6.1	2.4	56.3	2.3	2.8
Maryland	0.5	3.5	1.6	5.9	3.6	53.9	2.2	3.5
Massachusetts	0.6	3.6	1.5	6.2	3.4	48.8	2.6	3.0
Michigan	0.6	3.7	1.4	6.4	3.2	51.0	1.8	3.5
Minnesota	0.5	3.9	0.8	7.0	2.6	40.0	1.9	3.3
Mississippi	0.5	3.5	1.2	5.9	4.6	56.2	1.6	3.2
Missouri	0.4	3.9	1.2	6.4	3.1	55.8	2.4	3.0
Montana	0.5	2.9	1.0	6.5	2.9	43.4	2.1	2.8
Nebraska	0.6	3.8	1.1	5.8	2.7	43.0	2.1	2.9
Nevada	0.4	3.7	1.7	6.6	3.4	57.6	2.7	3.0
New Hampshire	0.8	3.6	1.5	6.1	3.2	51.8	2.3	2.9
New Jersey	0.5	3.4	1.4	6.6	3.5	47.5	2.5	3.0
New Mexico	0.7	3.6	1.0	6.0	4.2	34.2	2.2	3.2
New York	0.6	3.1	1.7	6.0	3.5	44.8	2.0	3.0
North Carolina	0.4	3.6	1.3	6.1	2.8	54.0	2.4	3.7
North Dakota	0.6	4.4	1.1	6.4	2.8	38.7	1.9	3.7
Ohio	0.5	3.8	1.5	6.5	2.8	54.3	2.1	3.2
Oklahoma	0.4	4.0	1.1	6.5	2.9	55.8	2.5	3.0
Oregon	0.4	3.5	1.0	6.5	2.5	50.5	2.6	3.0
Pennsylvania	0.5	3.6	1.4	6.6	3.1	48.6	2.3	3.0
Rhode Island	0.7	3.3	1.8	5.5	3.4	52.1	2.0	2.3
South Carolina	0.4	3.6	1.6	6.1	3.0	52.6	2.1	3.8
South Dakota	0.7	4.2	0.9	6.3	2.4	42.0	2.3	2.7
Tennessee	0.4	3.8	1.4	6.4	3.3	60.0	2.5	3.4
Texas	0.5	3.8	1.4	6.4	4.7	50.9	2.2	3.1
Utah	0.4	2.6	0.4	5.6	2.4	21.6	2.7	3.0
Vermont	0.4	4.0	1.2	6.3	2.7	49.1	3.2	2.8
Virginia	0.4	3.4	1.4	6.2	3.3	52.9	2.3	3.6
Washington	0.5	3.1	0.9	6.5	3.2	48.4	2.3	3.2
West Virginia	0.7	3.8	1.7	6.9	2.9	60.7	2.5	3.2
Wisconsin	0.5	3.8	1.0	6.8	3.1	41.7	2.0	3.1
Wyoming	0.4	3.8	1.3	6.7	2.6	42.4	2.8	3.0
OTHER								
District of Columbia	0.6	3.0	3.5	6.4	5.1	52.6	0.8	4.5
Median	0.5	3.6	1.3	6.4	3.1	50.9	2.3	3.1
Low	0.2	2.3	0.4	4.6	2.2	21.6	0.8	1.7
High	0.8	4.5	3.5	7.0	5.7	67.9	3.2	4.5

See footnotes at end of table.

Table 3.20. Cancer Deaths Distributed by State: 1996—*Continued*

(Per 100,000 population; age-adjusted to the 1970 U.S. standard population)

Area	Non-Hodgkin's lymphoma	Oral cavity and pharynx cancer	Ovary cancer	Pancreas cancer	Prostate cancer	Stomach cancer	Testis cancer	Thyroid cancer
United States	6.8	2.7	7.6	8.4	25.6	4.2	0.2	0.3
STATE								
Alabama	6.3	2.8	7.2	8.6	28.7	4.0	0.2	0.3
Alaska	5.2	2.9	7.1	7.9	20.8	4.8	0.2	0.4
Arizona	6.6	2.2	7.4	7.8	23.2	3.6	0.2	0.4
Arkansas	6.7	2.6	7.6	8.6	27.1	4.0	0.3	0.3
California	6.3	2.8	7.6	8.1	23.0	4.7	0.3	0.4
Colorado	6.3	2.0	6.5	7.8	23.9	3.5	0.3	0.3
Connecticut	6.9	2.7	7.2	8.8	23.1	4.7	0.2	0.4
Delaware	6.9	4.0	8.1	8.7	30.0	4.6	0.1	0.5
Florida	6.5	3.3	7.5	8.2	23.1	4.0	0.3	0.3
Georgia	5.7	3.1	7.4	8.2	31.7	4.1	0.1	0.3
Hawaii	5.9	3.1	5.9	7.8	16.8	8.6	0.2	0.7
Idaho	6.9	2.3	8.6	6.9	26.7	3.0	0.3	0.3
Illinois	7.1	2.8	7.9	8.6	25.8	4.5	0.2	0.4
Indiana	7.0	2.1	8.0	8.5	25.4	3.1	0.2	0.3
Iowa	7.3	2.1	7.4	7.6	24.2	3.0	0.3	0.3
Kansas	6.8	2.3	8.1	8.3	24.1	3.4	0.3	0.3
Kentucky	6.8	2.8	7.4	8.4	25.2	3.6	0.2	0.3
Louisiana	6.9	3.5	6.4	10.0	30.8	5.1	0.2	0.3
Maine	7.3	2.9	8.9	8.9	26.4	3.7	0.3	0.3
Maryland	6.2	3.3	7.2	8.8	29.3	4.7	0.2	0.3
Massachusetts	7.1	2.7	8.0	8.6	24.8	4.6	0.3	0.3
Michigan	7.0	2.5	7.6	8.4	26.2	3.9	0.3	0.3
Minnesota	7.8	2.0	7.9	8.3	25.9	3.6	0.2	0.4
Mississippi	5.9	3.2	6.1	9.1	32.6	4.3	0.2	0.3
Missouri	6.9	2.4	7.3	8.0	24.5	3.4	0.2	0.3
Montana	6.7	2.9	8.2	8.5	26.9	0.3	0.3	0.3
Nebraska	6.5	2.1	7.2	7.9	21.5	0.2	0.2	0.3
Nevada	6.7	2.3	7.5	8.8	24.9	0.2	0.3	0.3
New Hampshire	7.4	3.3	9.2	8.8	24.6	0.2	0.3	0.3
New Jersey	7.2	2.8	8.8	9.0	26.3	0.1	0.2	0.4
New Mexico	5.9	2.2	7.0	7.8	24.8	0.2	0.2	0.4
New York	7.2	2.7	8.1	8.9	24.6	0.1	0.3	0.4
North Carolina	6.1	3.0	6.9	8.6	30.4	0.1	0.2	0.3
North Dakota	7.2	1.8	8.3	7.7	28.8	0.3	0.4	0.6
Ohio	7.4	2.5	7.8	8.3	26.1	0.1	0.2	0.3
Oklahoma	7.1	2.2	7.1	7.9	23.5	0.1	0.2	0.3
Oregon	6.9	2.2	7.9	8.4	24.8	0.1	0.3	0.3
Pennsylvania	7.1	2.3	8.2	8.3	25.8	0.1	0.2	0.4
Rhode Island	7.6	2.6	7.0	8.5	23.7	0.3	0.5	0.3
South Carolina	5.9	3.9	7.8	9.1	32.8	0.2	0.2	0.3
South Dakota	6.3	2.2	6.8	7.3	27.0	0.3	0.3	0.5
Tennessee	6.8	2.9	7.3	8.5	26.4	0.1	0.2	0.3
Texas	6.7	2.9	7.0	8.3	25.8	0.1	0.2	0.4
Utah	6.7	1.4	7.9	6.1	26.2	0.2	0.3	0.3
Vermont	7.6	2.6	9.0	7.4	27.9	0.3	0.2	0.2
Virginia	6.5	2.7	7.4	8.5	29.1	0.1	0.2	0.3
Washington	6.7	2.3	8.8	8.2	23.9	0.1	0.2	0.3
West Virginia	6.6	2.5	7.1	7.8	24.4	0.2	0.2	0.4
Wisconsin	7.0	2.5	8.5	8.4	27.3	0.1	0.2	0.3
Wyoming	6.3	2.0	7.0	7.7	27.7	0.4	0.2	0.3
OTHER								
District of Columbia	6.2	6.7	7.4	10.3	45.4	7.9	0.2	0.4
Median	6.8	2.6	7.5	8.4	25.8	3.0	0.2	0.3
Low	5.2	1.4	5.9	6.1	16.8	0.1	0.1	0.2
High	7.8	6.7	9.2	10.3	45.4	8.6	0.5	0.7

SOURCE: L.A.G. Ries, C.L. Kosary, B.F. Hankey, B.A. Miller, L. Clegg, B.K. Edwards (eds). Surveillance, Epidemiology, and End Results (SEER) *Cancer Statistics Review*, 1973-1996, National Cancer Institute. Bethesda, MD, 1999.

Table 3.21. Rate of Chronic Conditions by Age: 1996

(Per 1,000 persons)

Type of chronic condition	Total	Under 18 years	18–44 years	Under 45 years	45–64 years	65 years and over	65–74 years	75 years and over
SELECTED SKIN AND MUSCULOSKELETAL CONDITIONS								
Arthritis	127.3	*1.9	50.1	30.9	240.1	482.7	453.1	523.6
Gout, including gouty arthritis	9.4	*—	3.0	1.8	22.4	30.8	31.7	29.4
Intervertebral disc disorders	25.4	*1.0	21.1	13.1	62.7	32.2	*38.2	24.0
Bone spur or tendinitis, unspecified	11.1	*—	10.9	6.6	23.2	16.4	*14.6	18.8
Disorders of bone or cartilage	6.5	*0.5	3.1	2.1	10.0	26.2	*15.6	40.6
Trouble with bunions	8.9	*1.3	6.5	4.5	16.2	22.0	*21.2	23.0
Bursitis, unclassified	18.9	*0.8	13.1	8.2	43.9	38.0	43.0	31.1
Sebaceous skin cyst	4.5	0.4	5.7	3.6	*9.1	2.0	3.4	*—
Trouble with acne	18.7	24.4	27.5	26.3	*4.5	*—	*16.3	*13.2
Psoriasis	11.1	3.2	10.5	7.6	20.7	15.0	26.6	23.1
Dermatitis	31.2	30.5	30.1	30.3	38.1	25.2	37.5	64.4
Trouble with dry (itching) skin, unclassified	25.1	12.7	24.4	19.7	28.9	48.9	34.0	42.7
Trouble with ingrown nails	22.0	*5.2	26.0	17.8	26.8	37.7	27.1	33.2
Trouble with corns and calluses	14.3	*1.1	13.0	8.3	25.4	29.7		
IMPAIRMENTS								
Visual impairment	31.3	*6.3	24.0	17.0	48.3	84.2	69.6	104.3
Color blindness	10.6	4.0	10.0	*7.6	16.1	18.8	*20.6	16.4
Cataracts	26.6	*0.5	*2.8	*1.9	23.3	171.5	151.9	198.6
Glaucoma	9.8	*—	2.0	1.2	10.3	57.8	46.7	73.1
Hearing impairment	83.4	12.6	41.9	30.2	131.5	303.4	255.2	369.8
Tinnitus	29.8	2.6	16.0	10.7	59.6	87.7	96.0	*76.2
Speech impairment	10.3	16.3	7.8	11.1	6.6	*11.7	10.0	14.1
Absence of extremities (excludes tips of fingers or toes only)	4.9	*1.0	*2.7	*2.0	*5.7	19.4	*21.5	*16.7
Paralysis of extremities, complete or partial	8.1	3.8	5.1	4.6	13.5	18.9	12.4	27.8
Deformity or orthopedic impairment	111.6	25.6	122.4	83.9	177.8	157.6	175.1	133.5
Back	64.0	*7.7	80.6	51.6	102.8	68.7	80.0	*53.1
Upper extremities	15.8	*2.6	13.3	9.1	29.4	30.9	39.0	19.8
Lower extremities	48.0	18.8	43.2	33.5	82.5	72.6	77.9	65.3
SELECTED DIGESTIVE CONDITIONS								
Ulcer	14.0	*1.3	11.8	7.6	26.1	30.1	36.9	*20.7
Hernia of abdominal cavity	16.9	*1.7	10.8	7.2	30.9	48.4	38.3	*62.4
Gastritis or duodenitis	14.1	*3.1	13.5	9.4	22.1	27.6	34.0	*18.8
Frequent indigestion	24.3	*3.3	26.7	17.4	42.1	33.5	38.6	*26.4
Enteritis or colitis	6.4	*1.7	6.9	4.8	10.0	9.2	*8.4	*10.5
Spastic colon	7.9	*0.7	*7.9	*5.0	13.7	14.3	16.9	10.9
Diverticula of intestines	9.6	*—	2.4	*1.5	17.6	41.9	36.0	50.0
Frequent constipation	11.9	*5.3	8.5	7.2	14.7	33.8	23.9	47.5
SELECTED CONDITIONS OF THE GENITOURINARY, NERVOUS, ENDOCRINE, METABOLIC, AND BLOOD AND BLOOD-FORMING SYSTEMS								
Goiter or other disorders of the thyroid	17.4	*1.0	13.0	8.2	30.0	48.1	50.3	45.1
Diabetes	28.9	*1.2	11.8	7.6	58.2	100.0	*98.4	102.3
Anemias	13.1	*5.0	16.7	12.0	10.7	23.0	*13.7	35.9
Epilepsy	5.1	*4.9	4.4	4.6	5.8	6.2	5.4	*7.4
Migraine headache	43.7	15.2	60.0	42.2	57.9	28.5	28.6	*28.4
Neuralgia or neuritis, unspecified	1.3	*0.2	0.3	0.3	2.4	5.6	*2.6	9.8
Kidney trouble	9.7	*2.4	11.8	8.0	12.8	13.7	*13.7	*13.6
Bladder disorders	11.9	3.3	11.3	*8.1	15.7	26.9	*19.9	36.4
Diseases of prostate	10.6	*—	2.2	*1.3	14.7	56.1	*48.8	*66.0
Disease of female genital organs	16.7	*3.4	24.2	15.9	20.7	14.6	*16.5	12.0
SELECTED CIRCULATORY CONDITIONS								
Rheumatic fever with or without heart disease	6.7	*1.2	6.9	4.6	10.4	*11.9	*7.8	*17.5
Heart disease	78.2	23.6	39.3	33.1	116.4	268.7	238.2	310.7
Ischemic heart disease	29.0	*—	4.2	2.5	51.6	140.9	131.0	154.6
Heart rhythm disorders	33.0	17.0	29.1	24.3	40.7	69.1	66.2	73.1
Tachycardia or rapid heart	8.7	*—	6.4	3.8	12.1	30.9	*31.0	30.7
Heart murmurs	18.1	16.6	18.8	18.0	17.6	19.6	*21.4	*17.3
Other and unspecified heart rhythm disorders	6.1	0.4	3.9	2.5	11.0	18.6	*13.9	25.1
Other selected diseases of heart, excluding hypertension	16.1	*6.6	6.0	6.3	24.0	58.7	41.0	83.1
High blood pressure (hypertension)	107.1	*0.5	49.6	30.1	214.1	363.5	356.0	373.8
Cerebrovascular disease	11.3	*0.4	2.0	1.4	12.8	65.1	40.2	99.4
Hardening of the arteries	5.9	*—	*—	*—	6.7	37.8	28.4	50.9
Varicose veins of lower extremities	28.0	*—	22.2	13.4	46.8	79.1	74.0	86.2
Hemorrhoids	32.3	*0.3	34.4	20.8	53.6	61.2	72.8	45.4
SELECTED RESPIRATORY CONDITIONS								
Chronic bronchitis	53.5	57.3	45.4	50.1	59.1	63.5	60.7	67.3
Asthma	55.2	62.0	56.9	58.9	48.6	45.5	43.7	48.0
Hay fever or allergic rhinitis without asthma	89.8	58.7	109.4	89.2	104.8	67.7	61.9	75.7
Chronic sinusitis	125.5	63.9	144.7	112.6	174.1	117.1	127.0	103.5
Deviated nasal septum	7.5	1.7	8.0	5.5	15.0	*6.2	*3.2	10.4
Chronic disease of tonsils or adenoids	9.5	20.2	*8.2	13.0	3.0	0.8	1.4	*—
Emphysema	6.9	*—	*0.8	0.5	13.2	32.4	32.3	32.6

SOURCE: P.F. Adams, G.E. Hendershot, and M.A. Marano. Current Estimates from the National Health Interview Survey, 1996. National Center for Health Statistics. *Vital and Health Statistics* 10, no. 200 (1999): Table 57.

* Figure does not meet standard of reliability or precision.
*— Figure does not meet standard of reliability or precision and quantity zero.

NOTE: A condition is considered chronic if (a) the respondent indicates it was first noticed more than three months before the reference date of the interview, or (b) it is a type of condition that ordinarily has a duration of more than three months. Examples of conditions that are considered chronic regardless of their time of onset are diabetes, heart conditions, emphysema, and arthritis. A complete list of these conditions may be obtained by contacting the Division of Health Interview Statistics, National Center for Health Statistics.

Table 3.22. Rate of Chronic Conditions by Sex and Age: 1996

(Per 1,000 persons)

Type of chronic condition	Male					Female				
	Under 45 years	45–64 years	65–74 years	65 years and over	75 years and over	Under 45 years	45–64 years	65–74 years	65 years and over	75 years and over
SELECTED SKIN AND MUSCULOSKELETAL CONDITIONS										
Arthritis	26.1	193.0	394.6	411.2	437.9	35.8	284.0	500.3	534.5	576.4
Gout, including gouty arthritis	3.4	33.5	42.6	46.4	52.6	0.2	12.0	22.9	19.5	15.2
Intervertebral disc disorders	15.2	62.8	41.7	37.4	30.4	10.9	62.7	35.4	28.4	20.0
Bone spur or tendinitis, unspecified	6.2	19.7	16.5	12.0	4.7	7.0	26.4	13.1	19.5	27.5
Disorders of bone or cartilage	1.2	6.9	7.1	8.9	12.0	2.9	13.0	22.6	38.6	58.5
Trouble with bunions	1.6	6.2	23.5	17.0	6.5	7.3	25.6	19.4	25.6	33.2
Bursitis, unclassified	7.5	39.6	24.8	25.7	27.5	8.8	47.9	57.7	46.8	33.4
Sebaceous skin cyst	4.7	10.6	5.0	3.1	—	2.6	7.6	2.1	1.1	—
Trouble with acne	24.9	3.6	—	—	—	27.6	5.4	—	—	—
Psoriasis	7.3	22.4	24.2	28.2	34.5	7.9	19.2	9.8	5.4	—
Dermatitis	24.1	28.6	31.1	32.6	34.9	36.4	47.0	23.0	19.8	16.0
Trouble with dry (itching) skin, unclassified	15.0	23.1	37.3	50.9	73.0	24.4	34.3	37.7	47.4	59.3
Trouble with ingrown nails	21.1	24.4	40.1	40.7	41.6	14.4	29.1	29.0	35.5	43.4
Trouble with corns and calluses	6.9	19.6	25.4	26.7	28.8	9.6	30.9	28.5	31.8	35.8
IMPAIRMENTS										
Visual impairment	21.7	61.0	90.6	103.8	125.1	12.2	36.4	52.6	70.0	91.4
Color blindness	13.8	29.6	38.6	40.2	42.9	1.3	3.5	6.2	3.4	—
Cataracts	1.6	17.3	109.3	140.1	189.6	2.1	29.0	186.4	194.3	203.9
Glaucoma	1.6	11.0	34.9	54.1	85.3	0.8	9.6	56.2	60.4	65.6
Hearing impairment	34.0	183.4	342.6	386.8	457.9	26.4	82.9	184.5	243.2	315.5
Tinnitus	11.0	76.9	119.5	117.4	114.1	10.4	43.4	77.1	66.1	52.8
Speech impairment	15.3	7.9	17.5	15.2	11.4	7.0	5.4	3.9	9.2	15.6
Absence of extremities (excludes tips of fingers or toes only)	3.2	9.8	34.8	26.6	13.5	0.8	1.9	10.7	14.3	18.6
Paralysis of extremities, complete or partial	5.8	16.8	19.5	20.8	22.9	3.3	10.3	6.7	17.5	30.7
Deformity or orthopedic impairment	84.8	187.5	165.5	156.5	142.0	82.9	168.6	182.8	158.4	128.4
Back	46.7	102.8	59.7	50.1	34.7	56.6	102.9	96.4	82.1	64.5
Upper extremities	10.7	37.6	50.1	43.4	32.6	7.4	21.7	30.0	21.8	11.9
Lower extremities	36.3	90.0	63.6	69.9	80.0	30.7	75.4	89.4	74.5	56.2
SELECTED DIGESTIVE CONDITIONS										
Ulcer	6.6	26.7	28.0	30.0	32.9	8.6	25.5	44.2	30.3	13.2
Hernia of abdominal cavity	7.8	35.0	49.3	53.3	59.8	6.6	27.1	29.6	44.9	64.0
Gastritis or duodenitis	7.1	19.4	20.1	17.9	14.3	11.6	24.6	45.3	34.6	21.5
Frequent indigestion	20.8	44.7	28.1	20.3	7.6	14.0	39.7	46.9	43.0	38.1
Enteritis or colitis	3.6	3.7	9.0	7.1	4.1	6.1	15.8	7.9	10.7	14.3
Spastic colon	3.2	5.3	12.3	10.7	8.0	6.8	21.6	20.6	17.0	12.6
Diverticula of intestines	1.2	17.4	30.0	22.8	11.4	1.8	17.7	41.0	55.6	73.8
Frequent constipation	4.7	6.5	12.8	21.3	35.1	9.8	22.4	32.8	42.8	55.1
SELECTED CONDITIONS OF THE GENITOURINARY, NERVOUS, ENDOCRINE, METABOLIC, AND BLOOD AND BLOOD-FORMING SYSTEMS										
Goiter or other disorders of the thyroid	3.5	15.5	25.8	22.2	16.5	13.0	43.6	70.0	66.9	62.9
Diabetes	6.1	56.9	117.4	121.8	129.0	9.0	59.4	83.1	84.3	85.8
Anemias	1.9	3.4	8.4	22.2	44.5	22.2	17.5	18.1	23.6	30.4
Epilepsy	4.0	3.6	8.6	8.6	8.4	5.2	7.8	2.7	4.6	6.9
Migraine headache	20.2	20.2	1.5	8.3	19.4	64.1	93.3	50.6	43.1	33.9
Neuralgia or neuritis, unspecified	0.2	1.1	1.5	7.2	16.7	0.3	3.6	3.4	4.4	5.7
Kidney trouble	5.3	13.2	20.1	23.9	30.2	10.7	12.4	8.6	6.3	3.4
Bladder disorders	2.4	7.2	1.8	6.0	12.7	13.8	23.5	34.6	41.9	51.0
Diseases of prostate	2.7	30.4	109.3	133.7	173.0	N/A	N/A	N/A	N/A	N/A
Disease of female genital organs	N/A	N/A	N/A	N/A	N/A	31.9	40.0	29.9	25.2	19.5
SELECTED CIRCULATORY CONDITIONS										
Rheumatic fever with or without heart disease	4.1	3.7	4.4	17.7	39.2	5.1	16.7	10.6	7.7	4.1
Heart disease	30.7	133.5	259.5	311.3	394.8	35.5	100.3	221.0	238.0	258.7
Ischemic heart disease	3.2	76.7	171.1	184.8	207.1	1.8	28.2	98.6	109.1	122.1
Heart rhythm disorders	20.8	31.1	54.2	69.7	94.5	27.8	49.7	75.9	68.7	59.9
Tachycardia or rapid heart	4.5	6.2	21.3	28.2	39.4	3.1	17.7	38.9	32.7	25.2
Heart murmurs	14.1	14.3	23.1	23.9	25.3	21.8	20.8	19.9	16.5	12.3
Other and unspecified heart rhythm disorders	2.1	10.7	9.9	17.4	29.6	2.9	11.2	17.1	19.5	22.4
Other selected diseases of heart, excluding hypertension	6.7	25.7	34.2	56.8	93.4	5.9	22.5	46.6	60.1	76.7
High blood pressure (hypertension)	30.0	214.8	314.6	298.0	271.0	30.1	213.3	389.5	410.8	437.0
Cerebrovascular disease	1.3	16.3	59.0	93.8	149.8	1.5	9.6	24.9	44.4	68.3
Hardening of the arteries	—	10.5	39.5	45.8	55.9	—	3.1	19.2	32.1	47.8
Varicose veins of lower extremities	3.8	17.6	38.2	46.2	59.2	22.9	74.1	102.9	102.9	102.9
Hemorrhoids	16.7	47.8	46.1	40.4	31.2	25.0	59.1	94.3	76.3	54.2
SELECTED RESPIRATORY CONDITIONS										
Chronic bronchitis	48.4	41.0	57.9	48.8	34.1	51.9	76.1	63.2	74.1	87.7
Asthma	49.8	30.4	39.8	37.5	33.7	68.1	65.5	46.8	51.3	56.8
Hay fever or allergic rhinitis without asthma	86.3	85.6	57.9	45.7	26.1	92.1	122.8	65.1	83.6	106.3
Chronic sinusitis	93.5	140.5	119.4	109.6	93.7	131.7	205.5	133.1	122.5	109.6
Deviated nasal septum	6.4	7.0	7.2	10.7	16.5	4.6	22.5	—	3.0	6.7
Chronic disease of tonsils or adenoids	9.9	0.6	—	—	—	16.0	5.2	2.6	1.4	—
Emphysema	1.0	16.5	39.6	33.2	22.7	—	10.1	26.4	31.9	38.6

SOURCE: P.F. Adams, G.E. Hendershot, and M.A. Marano. Current Estimates from the National Health Interview Survey, 1996. National Center for Health Statistics. *Vital and Health Statistics* 10, no. 200 (1999): Table 58.

* Figure does not meet standard of reliability or precision.
*— Figure does not meet standard of reliability or precision and quantity zero.
N/A Not applicable.

NOTE: A condition is considered chronic if (a) the respondent indicates it was first noticed more than three months before the reference date of the interview, or (b) it is a type of condition that ordinarily has a duration of more than three months. Examples of conditions that are considered chronic regardless of their time of onset are diabetes, heart conditions, emphysema, and arthritis. A complete list of these conditions may be obtained by contacting the Division of Health Interview Statistics, National Center for Health Statistics.

Table 3.23. Rate of Chronic Conditions by Race and Age: 1996

(Per 1,000 persons)

Type of chronic condition	White					Black				
	Under 45 years	45–64 years	65–74 years	65 years and over	75 years and over	Under 45 years	45–64 years	65–74 years	65 years and over	75 years and over
SELECTED SKIN AND MUSCULOSKELETAL CONDITIONS										
Arthritis	30.7	244.6	447.4	477.6	517.8	37.5	256.5	511.8	536.4	583.3
Gout, including gouty arthritis	1.9	21.0	31.2	31.0	30.8	0.7	35.6	44.1	35.2	18.6
Intervertebral disc disorders	15.6	63.3	37.8	32.3	24.9	2.0	72.9	50.0	38.3	16.4
Bone spur or tendinitis, unspecified	7.4	25.4	15.1	17.4	20.5	4.1	4.1	13.5	8.8	—
Disorders of bone or cartilage	2.0	10.7	17.6	28.4	42.6	1.6	7.6	—	8.0	23.0
Trouble with bunions	4.9	17.1	22.5	23.2	24.0	3.7	10.0	13.5	13.8	14.3
Bursitis, unclassified	9.1	48.3	37.9	34.5	29.9	4.1	17.7	72.9	66.2	53.7
Sebaceous skin cyst	4.0	9.6	3.8	2.2	—	2.5	3.1	—	—	—
Trouble with acne	28.1	5.3	—	—	—	18.8	—	—	—	—
Psoriasis	8.6	23.7	18.4	16.6	14.4	2.3	3.0	—	—	—
Dermatitis	29.1	42.6	27.7	26.1	24.1	34.7	14.0	10.6	12.3	15.4
Trouble with dry (itching) skin, unclassified	19.2	28.5	41.5	52.3	66.8	19.4	13.3	8.8	22.2	47.1
Trouble with ingrown nails	19.5	27.0	32.5	35.9	40.3	10.7	31.4	55.9	65.8	84.4
Trouble with corns and calluses	7.6	21.1	24.4	29.0	35.0	11.9	62.4	59.4	44.4	15.4
IMPAIRMENTS										
Visual impairment	17.0	47.8	70.6	86.1	106.7	20.1	63.1	75.9	81.9	93.2
Color blindness	8.7	17.9	22.0	20.2	17.9	2.1	3.0	11.8	7.7	—
Cataracts	1.8	23.7	153.7	174.8	202.9	2.7	20.9	144.7	157.7	182.0
Glaucoma	0.9	10.1	43.4	55.7	72.0	3.3	15.1	88.8	93.8	103.1
Hearing impairment	33.1	139.0	270.6	320.3	386.5	19.0	77.0	137.1	155.4	189.7
Tinnitus	11.8	63.4	102.4	90.7	75.2	7.4	31.2	46.5	55.1	71.3
Speech impairment	9.5	4.7	11.3	13.0	15.3	20.4	20.7	—	—	—
Absence of extremities (excludes tips of fingers or toes only)	2.4	6.2	22.2	19.5	16.0	0.7	3.9	19.4	22.6	29.6
Paralysis of extremities, complete or partial	3.7	11.9	13.6	18.4	24.8	11.4	31.9	4.1	18.0	43.9
Deformity or orthopedic impairment	88.5	176.0	180.4	161.9	137.4	69.5	205.6	147.6	134.4	109.6
Back	55.5	104.8	82.5	70.8	55.3	38.9	97.3	74.7	60.9	36.2
Upper extremities	9.5	29.2	42.4	32.4	18.9	9.9	29.2	14.7	21.8	35.1
Lower extremities	34.0	78.4	77.4	73.3	67.8	33.8	112.8	82.4	69.3	45.0
SELECTED DIGESTIVE CONDITIONS										
Ulcer	8.3	20.3	33.2	27.9	20.9	5.2	74.2	40.6	34.5	23.0
Hernia of abdominal cavity	8.2	33.9	41.7	53.0	68.1	2.3	17.2	14.7	9.6	—
Gastritis or duodenitis	9.5	22.7	32.6	26.7	18.9	10.5	25.3	55.9	43.6	20.8
Frequent indigestion	19.3	44.0	34.5	29.9	23.6	8.1	37.6	85.9	80.4	70.2
Enteritis or colitis	5.3	11.0	8.8	9.9	11.4	0.9	4.8	5.9	3.8	—
Spastic colon	5.9	15.8	17.7	15.1	11.8	1.4	1.7	13.5	8.8	—
Diverticula of intestines	1.8	20.4	40.7	44.3	49.0	—	—	—	25.7	73.5
Frequent constipation	7.4	12.8	24.3	34.9	48.8	8.5	23.6	24.7	29.9	39.5
SELECTED CONDITIONS OF THE GENITOURNARY, NERVOUS, ENDOCRINE, METABOLIC, AND BLOOD AND BLOOD-FORMING SYSTEMS										
Goiter or other disorders of the thyroid	8.3	32.8	53.4	50.2	45.9	8.8	17.2	31.8	36.4	45.0
Diabetes	7.5	44.7	89.5	87.5	85.0	8.4	149.5	154.7	199.1	281.8
Anemias	10.4	9.5	12.5	22.7	36.2	21.7	19.2	28.8	32.2	38.4
Epilepsy	4.3	5.8	6.1	6.9	8.1	6.1	8.3	—	—	—
Migraine headache	43.8	58.4	28.5	26.9	24.9	38.5	61.1	23.5	44.0	81.1
Neuralgia or neuritis, unspecified	0.3	2.8	0.7	5.0	10.7	—	—	20.6	13.4	—
Kidney trouble	9.1	13.7	14.1	14.5	14.9	4.3	9.4	12.9	8.4	—
Bladder disorders	8.8	16.7	21.6	28.7	38.2	6.2	12.9	8.8	12.6	19.7
Diseases of prostate	1.5	15.2	53.2	58.6	65.8	—	10.3	18.2	41.3	83.3
Disease of female genital organs	14.5	20.4	18.6	16.2	13.1	22.7	14.8	—	—	—
SELECTED CIRCULATORY CONDITIONS										
Rheumatic fever with or without heart disease	4.9	11.9	8.8	13.2	19.1	4.7	1.5	—	—	—
Heart disease	34.4	117.4	247.1	278.2	319.6	35.0	129.4	108.8	150.5	228.1
Ischemic heart disease	2.7	54.8	140.7	148.5	158.7	2.6	34.5	29.4	64.7	130.5
Heart rhythm disorders	25.3	41.1	69.2	72.9	77.8	25.2	52.2	21.8	23.4	26.3
Tachycardia or rapid heart	4.3	12.1	33.8	33.1	32.1	2.1	16.6	11.8	13.8	17.5
Heart murmurs	18.2	18.6	20.8	20.0	18.9	21.6	16.2	—	—	—
Other and unspecified heart rhythm disorders	2.8	10.5	14.6	19.9	26.9	1.4	19.4	10.0	9.2	7.7
Other selected diseases of heart, excluding hypertension	6.5	21.5	37.3	56.9	83.0	7.2	42.4	58.2	62.8	71.3
High blood pressure (hypertension)	27.6	200.4	336.9	348.1	362.9	47.5	375.7	499.4	487.0	463.8
Cerebrovascular disease	1.4	11.6	40.1	65.1	98.3	1.9	24.9	36.5	70.8	134.9
Hardening of the arteries	—	7.0	32.0	40.2	51.0	—	6.3	—	21.1	60.3
Varicose veins of lower extremities	14.2	47.8	74.8	78.5	83.5	11.7	44.7	51.8	45.9	35.1
Hemorrhoids	23.3	57.5	71.4	62.0	49.5	13.4	33.8	64.7	42.1	—
SELECTED RESPIRATORY CONDITIONS										
Chronic bronchitis	50.4	61.4	58.3	63.4	70.4	51.3	51.7	54.7	39.1	9.9
Asthma	56.9	47.4	43.0	45.3	48.3	76.6	50.7	35.9	41.7	53.7
Hay fever or allergic rhinitis without asthma	92.0	111.0	62.5	68.2	75.7	66.2	64.6	37.1	46.7	64.7
Chronic sinusitis	112.8	174.9	127.6	118.3	105.9	121.5	180.5	150.6	121.7	69.1
Deviated nasal septum	6.8	17.0	3.6	6.9	11.3	—	3.7	—	—	—
Chronic disease of tonsils or adenoids	13.8	2.4	1.6	0.9	—	8.2	2.6	—	—	—
Emphysema	0.4	13.6	35.6	35.2	34.5	—	14.6	8.2	10.0	13.2

SOURCE: P.F. Adams, G.E. Hendershot, and M.A. Marano. Current Estimates from the National Health Interview Survey, 1996. National Center for Health Statistics. *Vital and Health Statistics* 10, no. 200 (1999): Table 59.

* Figure does not meet standard of reliability or precision.
*— Figure does not meet standard of reliability or precision and quantity zero.

NOTE: A condition is considered chronic if (a) the respondent indicates it was first noticed more than three months before the reference date of the interview, or (b) it is a type of condition that ordinarily has a duration of more than three months. Examples of conditions that are considered chronic regardless of their time of onset are diabetes, heart conditions, emphysema, and arthritis. A complete list of these conditions may be obtained by contacting the Division of Health Interview Statistics, National Center for Health Statistics.

Table 3.24. Rate of Chronic Conditions by Family Income and Age: 1996

(Per 1,000 persons)

Type of chronic condition	Less than $10,000					$10,000–$19,999				
	Under 45 years	45–64 years	65–74 years	65 years and over	75 years and over	Under 45 years	45–64 years	65–74 years	65 years and over	75 years and over
SELECTED SKIN AND MUSCULOSKELETAL CONDITIONS										
Arthritis	82.6	395.3	453.0	520.6	580.0	39.4	378.3	445.7	469.6	496.8
Gout, including gouty arthritis	*—	54.9	57.6	36.6	18.1	*—	23.9	25.1	34.9	46.2
Intervertebral disc disorders	*28.1	66.0	48.5	25.3	4.8	18.8	98.3	25.9	27.7	29.9
Bone spur or tendinitis, unspecified	11.1	48.7	12.7	6.0	*—	3.2	38.3	11.9	9.3	6.3
Disorders of bone or cartilage	4.0	8.5	29.7	33.5	36.8	*—	26.8	15.1	29.3	45.6
Trouble with bunions	7.0	12.9	13.9	6.5	*—	1.6	26.3	7.9	21.3	36.5
Bursitis, unclassified	10.3	65.6	74.0	34.6	*—	9.1	51.1	35.9	46.6	59.1
Sebaceous skin cyst	2.5	*—	*—	*—	*—	4.5	8.5	*—	*—	*—
Trouble with acne	43.2	*—	*—	*—	*—	13.6	10.6	*—	*—	*—
Psoriasis	13.7	*—	39.4	35.5	32.0	3.9	30.1	13.2	7.0	*—
Dermatitis	38.7	29.1	5.5	7.9	10.1	25.8	23.2	25.6	25.8	25.9
Trouble with dry (itching) skin, unclassified	20.2	30.2	68.5	46.0	25.6	20.2	34.9	34.9	56.2	80.2
Trouble with ingrown nails	29.5	80.8	69.1	56.8	45.9	18.3	20.0	67.3	53.2	37.1
Trouble with corns and calluses	7.8	48.3	14.6	17.6	20.3	8.2	42.3	26.9	42.4	59.7
IMPAIRMENTS										
Visual impairment	38.2	*131.3	66.7	122.3	*171.3	23.9	82.3	123.1	113.8	*103.2
Color blindness	7.6	16.2	23.7	11.1	*—	7.3	5.4	27.2	23.7	19.6
Cataracts	5.6	52.7	151.6	219.4	279.6	3.6	29.9	220.2	215.9	210.9
Glaucoma	1.6	22.9	55.2	44.6	35.2	*—	6.1	41.7	51.1	61.8
Hearing impairment	48.3	220.1	307.5	360.2	406.6	34.9	179.6	294.2	328.2	367.4
Tinnitus	15.5	106.6	141.3	128.0	*116.3	21.2	115.2	129.1	99.5	65.8
Speech impairment	21.3	35.8	42.4	19.9	*—	22.7	11.0	5.5	3.0	*—
Absence of extremities (excludes tips of fingers or toes only)	5.7	*—	26.1	26.7	27.2	2.4	9.7	15.3	17.9	20.8
Paralysis of extremities, complete or partial	5.5	42.0	*—	17.6	33.1	8.2	20.0	21.1	21.3	21.4
Deformity or orthopedic impairment	119.5	399.7	246.8	209.5	176.1	102.7	256.3	216.0	204.0	190.3
Back	66.8	237.8	94.6	85.7	77.9	58.3	135.0	86.1	93.8	102.6
Upper extremities	20.6	88.9	28.5	59.9	87.5	19.4	57.2	30.1	21.8	12.4
Lower extremities	49.0	220.9	*130.4	*112.4	96.6	39.1	143.4	127.3	106.7	83.6
SELECTED DIGESTIVE CONDITIONS										
Ulcer	*20.6	*59.7	*43.7	*45.4	*47.0	*10.4	*48.2	*69.2	51.7	*32.0
Hernia of abdominal cavity	12.1	*51.3	*19.4	65.6	106.2	9.8	65.7	40.4	46.6	53.7
Gastritis or duodenitis	*19.7	42.8	42.4	42.6	42.2	6.4	16.9	17.2	23.7	31.1
Frequent indigestion	19.9	73.4	37.6	52.2	65.1	14.2	50.0	8.7	11.7	15.1
Enteritis or colitis	4.1	33.9	6.1	11.4	15.5	10.9	4.7	6.1	3.2	*—
Spastic colon	7.1	8.5	*—	11.6	21.9	5.0	8.5	6.9	6.3	6.0
Diverticula of intestines	*—	31.3	24.3	31.8	38.4	1.1	15.1	29.6	39.8	51.6
Frequent constipation	14.2	49.8	38.8	72.9	103.0	6.1	34.7	32.7	31.0	28.7
SELECTED CONDITIONS OF THE GENITOURINARY, NERVOUS, ENDOCRINE, METABOLIC, AND BLOOD AND BLOOD-FORMING SYSTEMS										
Goiter or other disorders of the thyroid	*4.9	*26.9	*33.4	66.7	*96.1	*3.9	*9.5	*41.2	*42.9	*44.9
Diabetes	0.9	80.0	152.8	116.1	83.8	12.9	93.1	103.2	110.5	118.6
Anemias	21.8	10.0	47.9	42.0	36.8	14.1	16.0	*—	24.1	51.6
Epilepsy	13.2	24.7	16.4	7.7	*—	5.9	4.0	7.1	5.2	2.7
Migraine headache	47.7	87.4	46.7	49.7	52.3	41.6	60.5	16.9	18.0	19.3
Neuralgia or neuritis, unspecified	*—	11.1	12.7	14.8	16.5	1.2	4.3	3.2	4.9	6.9
Kidney trouble	9.9	49.8	16.4	13.3	10.7	20.0	27.2	5.8	10.0	14.8
Bladder disorders	5.1	19.9	43.7	37.5	32.0	13.5	21.4	20.9	28.2	36.5
Diseases of prostate	*—	10.7	75.2	44.0	16.5	1.1	9.5	72.4	65.2	57.0
Disease of female genital organs	16.3	12.2	21.2	16.5	12.3	13.3	21.8	*—	3.2	6.9
SELECTED CIRCULATORY CONDITIONS										
Rheumatic fever with or without heart disease	*10.9	*11.4	*—	10.5	19.7	*5.5	*21.8	*10.6	22.0	*35.0
Heart disease	51.2	*128.7	292.9	310.5	326.0	50.2	205.0	284.4	301.9	321.9
Ischemic heart disease	8.5	46.1	144.9	143.6	142.5	3.2	102.4	190.9	168.0	141.8
Heart rhythm disorders	40.2	52.7	40.0	50.0	58.7	43.0	46.3	56.2	59.8	64.0
Tachycardia or rapid heart	10.6	19.2	23.7	29.8	35.2	9.5	31.0	8.7	14.2	20.5
Heart murmurs	26.3	21.8	16.4	20.2	23.5	32.7	11.0	31.7	33.2	35.0
Other and unspecified heart rhythm disorders	3.3	11.8	*—	*—	*—	0.9	4.3	15.8	12.4	8.4
Other selected diseases of heart, excluding hypertension	2.4	29.9	107.9	116.9	124.9	4.0	56.3	37.2	74.1	116.1
High blood pressure (hypertension)	38.5	387.2	527.0	461.3	403.4	39.7	291.6	384.5	386.4	388.5
Cerebrovascular disease	1.4	26.5	78.8	56.8	37.4	0.6	33.1	39.6	64.2	92.0
Hardening of the arteries	*—	22.1	17.0	24.7	31.5	*—	14.0	62.3	42.9	20.8
Varicose veins of lower extremities	20.2	73.7	195.9	145.9	101.9	10.7	68.0	84.5	121.4	163.5
Hemorrhoids	13.0	35.8	131.6	116.1	102.5	20.4	85.3	58.6	45.1	29.9
SELECTED RESPIRATORY CONDITIONS										
Chronic bronchitis	37.5	*67.8	*75.8	*100.2	*121.7	51.7	78.8	*75.3	71.8	*67.9
Asthma	39.6	60.8	36.4	64.4	89.1	80.5	75.2	97.2	73.8	46.8
Hay fever or allergic rhinitis without asthma	82.7	106.9	29.1	80.9	125.9	69.1	111.8	36.4	50.1	65.8
Chronic sinusitis	105.3	135.0	132.2	134.5	136.6	110.0	154.4	165.3	149.3	130.9
Deviated nasal septum	3.5	*—	*—	*—	*—	5.8	25.6	*—	4.1	8.7
Chronic disease of tonsils or adenoids	23.2	4.4	*—	*—	*—	24.2	10.4	*—	*—	*—
Emphysema	2.3	45.0	47.9	42.0	36.8	1.0	29.5	31.4	36.6	42.5

See footnotes at end of table.

Table 3.24. Rate of Chronic Conditions by Family Income and Age: 1996—*Continued*

(Per 1,000 persons)

Type of chronic condition	$20,000–$34,999					$35,000 or more				
	Under 45 years	45–64 years	65–74 years	65 years and over	75 years and over	Under 45 years	45–64 years	65–74 years	65 years and over	75 years and over
SELECTED SKIN AND MUSCULOSKELETAL CONDITIONS										
Arthritis	38.7	284.1	493.6	485.0	469.1	16.7	193.0	395.3	430.2	495.8
Gout, including gouty arthritis	1.4	29.8	33.3	21.5	*—	2.8	18.3	17.2	28.5	49.7
Intervertebral disc disorders	10.2	64.4	34.3	34.9	36.0	11.3	58.8	67.6	49.8	16.4
Bone spur or tendinitis, unspecified	8.6	21.3	*—	6.8	19.3	6.5	21.2	48.2	31.4	*—
Disorders of bone or cartilage	2.4	13.8	13.0	26.5	50.8	2.0	3.1	15.2	24.6	42.2
Trouble with bunions	6.3	12.4	25.0	16.2	*—	4.8	15.8	13.2	8.6	*—
Bursitis, unclassified	12.9	46.4	48.8	34.0	6.8	7.1	44.3	57.1	51.5	40.8
Sebaceous skin cyst	3.1	22.6	4.3	2.8	*—	4.8	7.4	10.2	6.7	*—
Trouble with acne	28.2	2.2	*—	*—	*—	28.8	5.3	*—	*—	*—
Psoriasis	8.0	27.9	16.7	10.8	*—	7.4	22.1	*—	15.1	43.6
Dermatitis	34.0	54.4	38.4	27.8	8.3	31.2	39.3	28.0	36.7	52.5
Trouble with dry (itching) skin, unclassified	22.5	42.6	60.6	69.4	86.0	20.8	27.8	16.7	42.0	89.6
Trouble with ingrown nails	23.8	41.7	18.6	31.7	55.3	16.0	20.2	19.0	16.6	12.2
Trouble with corns and calluses	11.3	37.5	30.0	23.9	12.5	8.4	15.9	18.2	20.0	23.5
IMPAIRMENTS										
Visual impairment	20.6	60.0	50.2	61.7	82.2	14.4	38.1	72.6	75.4	81.1
Color blindness	7.2	23.9	26.3	20.1	9.1	10.3	18.0	*—	9.9	28.6
Cataracts	2.6	43.1	113.7	124.2	143.6	0.7	11.9	117.8	157.0	230.8
Glaucoma	0.9	18.4	29.4	54.8	101.6	1.6	6.2	59.6	70.2	89.6
Hearing impairment	29.0	175.1	271.0	325.8	426.3	29.2	117.0	206.4	268.3	384.6
Tinnitus	6.1	63.4	96.7	98.8	102.7	10.0	51.2	67.4	76.1	92.4
Speech impairment	14.8	5.3	*—	8.7	24.6	5.3	3.2	15.7	14.7	13.1
Absence of extremities (excludes tips of fingers or toes only)	3.3	13.1	28.5	22.2	10.6	0.9	2.6	31.2	25.4	14.5
Paralysis of extremities, complete or partial	3.2	4.9	9.1	12.6	18.9	4.1	6.4	15.0	23.1	38.5
Deformity or orthopedic impairment	88.9	219.7	161.0	137.6	94.7	81.0	143.9	112.1	133.6	174.0
Back	54.3	139.5	77.7	66.1	44.3	52.5	83.4	78.9	68.9	50.2
Upper extremities	9.2	19.7	41.5	30.9	11.7	6.2	26.3	13.2	13.2	13.1
Lower extremities	35.8	87.7	62.0	53.0	36.4	32.9	57.8	19.0	42.4	86.3
SELECTED DIGESTIVE CONDITIONS										
Ulcer	8.0	35.5	28.3	18.3	*—	4.5	12.5	28.7	22.0	9.4
Hernia of abdominal cavity	5.0	18.2	31.0	39.2	54.2	8.0	29.4	43.2	42.0	39.9
Gastritis or duodenitis	10.8	17.7	35.6	28.8	15.9	8.9	24.1	55.4	36.2	*—
Frequent indigestion	15.0	29.3	49.6	39.6	21.6	20.4	46.0	55.9	49.5	37.5
Enteritis or colitis	4.4	0.9	14.5	12.4	9.1	4.9	11.9	*—	10.4	30.0
Spastic colon	1.9	18.8	15.1	9.8	*—	6.9	17.2	31.7	29.0	23.9
Diverticula of intestines	1.5	16.2	49.2	45.3	38.3	1.6	17.9	30.2	43.7	68.9
Frequent constipation	4.5	3.6	24.8	19.1	8.7	9.1	8.6	8.7	27.0	61.4
SELECTED CONDITIONS OF THE GENITOURINARY, NERVOUS, ENDOCRINE, METABOLIC, AND BLOOD AND BLOOD-FORMING SYSTEMS										
Goiter or other disorders of the thyroid	9.3	40.8	91.2	73.7	41.7	11.1	34.2	47.7	37.6	18.8
Diabetes	9.2	80.4	111.2	113.4	117.5	7.5	36.5	82.6	92.2	109.8
Anemias	10.0	11.5	*—	7.6	21.6	11.9	10.8	20.5	23.9	30.5
Epilepsy	5.8	2.6	6.2	16.0	34.1	3.0	2.7	*—	*—	*—
Migraine headache	45.1	76.4	26.0	24.5	21.2	44.8	56.0	27.5	24.6	19.2
Neuralgia or neuritis, unspecified	*—	5.6	3.1	4.7	8.0	0.2	0.9	6.7	9.3	26.7
Kidney trouble	9.3	17.7	29.6	28.4	26.1	4.6	6.7	6.7	5.9	3.8
Bladder disorders	9.2	23.5	25.2	22.3	17.1	7.8	11.0	23.5	24.9	27.7
Diseases of prostate	*—	5.8	35.3	57.9	99.3	2.1	22.2	72.9	88.1	116.8
Disease of female genital organs	14.3	23.5	39.5	31.6	17.1	18.3	21.9	9.2	13.8	22.5
SELECTED CIRCULATORY CONDITIONS										
Rheumatic fever with or without heart disease	5.7	9.5	*—	*—	*—	4.3	10.9	16.7	24.3	38.5
Heart disease	30.6	107.6	231.3	277.5	362.3	31.7	106.9	230.8	244.8	271.1
Ischemic heart disease	1.3	43.2	95.7	129.2	190.6	2.1	46.4	157.7	156.9	155.3
Heart rhythm disorders	19.7	39.0	86.0	94.8	111.0	23.5	40.6	36.9	48.4	69.9
Tachycardia or rapid heart	1.3	6.4	58.7	57.9	56.5	3.0	8.4	5.5	13.8	29.1
Heart murmurs	15.9	12.4	15.7	10.2	*—	17.2	24.5	20.7	19.9	18.8
Other and unspecified heart rhythm disorders	2.5	20.3	11.6	26.7	54.6	3.3	7.7	10.5	14.5	22.0
Other selected diseases of heart, excluding hypertension	9.5	25.3	49.4	53.5	60.6	6.1	19.8	36.2	39.6	46.0
High blood pressure (hypertension)	31.3	242.1	324.3	315.0	297.8	27.0	182.2	309.2	333.0	377.6
Cerebrovascular disease	0.8	10.3	36.4	58.2	98.1	1.4	7.4	44.7	67.6	110.7
Hardening of the arteries	*—	2.5	31.0	65.3	128.1	*—	5.3	21.7	27.4	38.0
Varicose veins of lower extremities	13.0	35.3	61.0	39.5	*—	13.9	46.6	56.7	60.6	68.0
Hemorrhoids	17.8	55.2	71.5	59.9	38.7	28.2	56.7	83.4	79.2	71.8
SELECTED RESPIRATORY CONDITIONS										
Chronic bronchitis	58.8	64.0	59.5	66.9	80.7	50.2	50.0	60.1	68.3	83.5
Asthma	69.5	58.8	18.8	39.1	76.2	56.8	41.8	19.0	27.5	43.6
Hay fever or allergic rhinitis without asthma	75.1	105.0	58.5	78.5	115.2	108.9	109.2	110.1	85.4	38.9
Chronic sinusitis	140.9	200.6	131.0	119.2	97.4	109.6	187.5	123.3	114.2	96.6
Deviated nasal septum	5.7	10.1	*—	10.0	28.4	6.7	18.1	7.2	10.6	16.9
Chronic disease of tonsils or adenoids	13.8	5.6	*—	*—	*—	9.2	*—	*—	*—	*—
Emphysema	0.9	15.0	31.6	32.9	35.2	*—	5.2	11.0	15.8	24.9

SOURCE: P.F. Adams, G.E. Hendershot, and M.A. Marano. Current Estimates from the National Health Interview Survey, 1996. National Center for Health Statistics. *Vital and Health Statistics* 10, no. 200 (1999): Table 60.

* Figure does not meet standard of reliability or precision.
*— Figure does not meet standard of reliability or precision and quantity zero.

NOTE: A condition is considered chronic if (a) the respondent indicates it was first noticed more than three months before the reference date of the interview, or (b) it is a type of condition that ordinarily has a duration of more than three months. Examples of conditions that are considered chronic regardless of their time of onset are diabetes, heart conditions, emphysema, and arthritis. A complete list of these conditions may be obtained by contacting the Division of Health Interview Statistics, National Center for Health Statistics.

Table 3.25. Rate of Chronic Conditions by Geographic Region and Place of Residence: 1996

(Per 1,000 persons)

Type of chronic condition	Geographic region				Place of residence			
					MSA [1]			Not MSA [1]
	Northeast	Midwest	South	West	All MSA [1]	Central city	Not central city	
SELECTED SKIN AND MUSCULOSKELETAL CONDITIONS								
Arthritis	126.1	118.8	138.9	119.4	121.0	117.9	122.9	150.6
Gout, including gouty arthritis	9.3	9.8	9.2	9.4	8.5	5.6	10.3	12.8
Intervertebral disc disorders	23.3	23.3	28.0	25.4	25.8	23.1	27.4	23.7
Bone spur or tendinitis, unspecified	7.1	*9.6	10.0	18.2	9.8	10.7	9.3	16.0
Disorders of bone or cartilage	9.2	3.0	7.0	*7.3	6.6	5.3	7.4	*6.2
Trouble with bunions	9.9	7.9	10.3	*6.9	9.4	7.8	10.4	*7.0
Bursitis, unclassified	17.5	17.7	20.1	19.8	18.3	11.2	22.6	21.2
Sebaceous skin cyst	3.0	4.3	4.9	5.6	4.7	3.4	5.5	3.7
Trouble with acne	12.9	23.8	15.1	24.4	18.4	14.9	20.4	20.1
Psoriasis	7.9	12.9	9.0	15.6	10.1	9.2	10.7	14.9
Dermatitis	31.5	32.5	28.8	33.4	31.5	30.5	32.0	30.3
Trouble with dry (itching) skin, unclassified	29.3	27.1	21.1	25.2	24.7	23.6	25.4	26.3
Trouble with ingrown nails	16.2	20.2	24.4	25.6	21.9	22.8	21.3	22.3
Trouble with corns and calluses	15.0	12.2	14.4	15.9	15.5	19.9	12.8	9.8
IMPAIRMENTS								
Visual impairment	30.8	28.9	37.1	25.3	27.2	29.1	26.1	46.8
Color blindness	10.0	10.4	13.7	6.6	8.9	8.9	8.9	17.2
Cataracts	21.4	29.1	26.7	28.5	25.4	27.9	23.9	30.9
Glaucoma	11.2	11.1	8.3	9.5	9.5	12.3	7.8	11.1
Hearing impairment	72.6	86.1	84.3	89.2	74.7	71.8	76.4	116.1
Tinnitus	19.4	29.9	34.6	31.7	27.2	28.5	26.4	39.5
Speech impairment	10.6	*9.5	11.8	*8.6	11.0	11.8	10.5	*7.7
Absence of extremities (excludes tips of fingers or toes only)	*4.1	5.8	4.3	*5.5	4.6	4.7	4.5	*5.9
Paralysis of extremities, complete or partial	6.2	9.8	10.5	*4.2	8.4	9.2	8.0	*6.9
Deformity or orthopedic impairment	99.5	125.8	100.8	124.7	106.4	106.4	106.4	131.0
Back	59.1	72.1	52.2	78.3	62.1	60.8	62.8	71.1
Upper extremities	13.4	18.7	12.8	19.5	14.7	13.9	15.1	20.0
Lower extremities	37.3	57.1	49.2	46.1	44.9	45.5	44.6	59.7
SELECTED DIGESTIVE CONDITIONS								
Ulcer	10.1	10.9	16.4	17.5	13.1	14.5	12.2	17.5
Hernia of abdominal cavity	19.2	17.5	17.2	13.7	16.4	9.9	20.3	18.8
Gastritis or duodenitis	16.7	13.8	12.3	14.9	14.6	15.7	14.0	12.2
Frequent indigestion	14.4	28.6	28.9	21.6	24.0	26.6	22.4	25.5
Enteritis or colitis	9.0	*5.0	6.9	4.6	6.8	8.2	5.9	*4.8
Spastic colon	8.2	*4.3	9.8	8.4	8.8	7.7	9.4	*4.6
Diverticula of intestines	9.5	10.3	10.2	7.9	9.3	7.1	10.6	10.7
Frequent constipation	12.9	10.3	12.7	11.7	12.2	14.2	11.0	11.0
SELECTED CONDITIONS OF THE GENITOURINARY, NERVOUS, ENDOCRINE, METABOLIC, AND BLOOD AND BLOOD-FORMING SYSTEMS								
Goiter or other disorders of the thyroid	11.0	12.5	21.8	21.9	18.3	22.1	16.0	14.1
Diabetes	24.9	25.2	35.3	26.5	28.9	29.4	28.6	28.7
Anemias	16.1	7.9	15.2	12.7	13.3	16.0	11.7	12.2
Epilepsy	4.4	7.9	3.7	4.6	4.8	5.7	4.2	6.1
Migraine headache	45.8	40.1	46.3	41.5	41.9	39.9	43.1	50.4
Neuralgia or neuritis, unspecified	1.6	0.9	1.1	*2.1	1.1	1.8	0.6	*2.4
Kidney trouble	8.5	9.1	12.8	*6.4	8.4	11.5	6.5	14.3
Bladder disorders	9.5	9.8	12.0	16.3	11.2	12.0	10.7	14.5
Diseases of prostate	10.0	7.4	14.0	9.3	10.5	9.4	11.2	10.9
Disease of female genital organs	15.7	16.8	17.3	16.8	17.5	14.9	19.1	13.8
SELECTED CIRCULATORY CONDITIONS								
Rheumatic fever with or without heart disease	*7.1	6.9	6.7	*5.9	6.2	5.2	6.8	8.4
Heart disease	88.5	78.0	77.0	70.4	72.6	70.4	73.9	98.8
Ischemic heart disease	28.9	30.0	30.7	25.5	26.4	24.9	27.3	38.8
Heart rhythm disorders	40.2	34.0	28.1	32.9	32.0	32.2	31.8	36.8
Tachycardia or rapid heart	6.5	11.3	9.0	7.5	7.9	8.9	7.3	11.8
Heart murmurs	26.5	16.1	13.4	19.9	18.4	18.8	18.1	17.1
Other and unspecified heart rhythm disorders	7.2	6.5	5.7	*5.4	5.7	4.5	6.4	7.9
Other selected diseases of heart, excluding hypertension	19.5	14.0	18.2	12.0	14.2	13.4	14.8	23.2
High blood pressure (hypertension)	109.3	108.2	113.5	93.7	101.3	107.9	97.4	128.8
Cerebrovascular disease	10.3	9.0	13.0	12.4	10.4	12.0	9.4	15.1
Hardening of the arteries	2.5	8.5	5.2	7.3	4.8	5.5	4.3	10.1
Varicose veins of lower extremities	33.8	29.6	20.1	33.5	27.1	25.4	28.1	31.3
Hemorrhoids	32.4	34.3	27.9	37.0	32.1	28.6	34.3	32.8
SELECTED RESPIRATORY CONDITIONS								
Chronic bronchitis	51.0	59.0	53.0	50.7	53.3	49.0	55.8	54.6
Asthma	61.8	56.6	51.8	52.9	57.5	61.7	54.9	46.9
Hay fever or allergic rhinitis without asthma	78.3	85.5	94.9	97.3	90.6	86.3	93.3	86.5
Chronic sinusitis	85.3	143.1	162.9	83.9	120.7	121.3	120.4	143.3
Deviated nasal septum	10.3	5.8	6.7	8.1	7.7	5.9	8.8	6.8
Chronic disease of tonsils or adenoids	*8.1	8.6	10.6	10.1	9.0	10.6	8.0	11.5
Emphysema	*6.8	8.6	6.4	5.9	6.1	7.0	5.6	9.7

SOURCE: P.F. Adams, G.E. Hendershot, and M.A. Marano. Current Estimates from the National Health Interview Survey, 1996. National Center for Health Statistics. *Vital and Health Statistics* 10, no. 200 (1999): Table 61.

* Figure does not meet standard of reliability or precision.
1. MSA is metropolitan statistical area.

NOTE: A condition is considered chronic if (a) the respondent indicates it was first noticed more than three months before the reference date of the interview, or (b) it is a type of condition that ordinarily has a duration of more than three months. Examples of conditions that are considered chronic regardless of their time of onset are diabetes, heart conditions, emphysema, and arthritis. A complete list of these conditions may be obtained by contacting the Division of Health Interview Statistics, National Center for Health Statistics.

Table 3.26. Number of Cases and Deaths from Tuberculosis

Year	Tuberculosis cases		Tuberculosis deaths	
	Number	Index change 1953=100	Number	Index change 1953=100
1953	84 304	100.0	19 707	100.0
1954	79 775	94.6	16 527	83.9
1955	77 368	91.8	15 016	76.2
1956	69 895	82.9	14 137	71.7
1957	67 149	79.7	13 390	67.9
1958	63 534	75.4	12 417	63.0
1959	57 535	68.2	11 474	58.2
1960	55 494	65.8	10 866	55.1
1961	53 726	63.7	9 938	50.4
1962	53 315	63.2	9 506	48.2
1963	54 042	64.1	9 311	47.2
1964	50 874	60.3	8 303	42.1
1965	49 016	58.1	7 934	40.3
1966	47 767	56.7	7 625	38.7
1967	45 647	54.1	6 901	35.0
1968	42 623	50.6	6 292	31.9
1969	39 120	46.4	5 567	28.2
1970	37 137	44.1	5 217	26.5
1971	35 217	41.8	4 501	22.8
1972	32 882	39.0	4 376	22.2
1973	30 998	36.8	3 875	19.7
1974	30 122	35.7	3 513	17.8
1975	33 989	40.3	3 333	16.9
1976	32 105	38.1	3 130	15.9
1977	30 145	35.8	2 968	15.1
1978	28 521	33.8	2 914	14.8
1979	27 669	32.8	2 007	*10
1980	27 749	32.9	1 978	10.0
1981	27 373	32.5	1 937	9.8
1982	25 520	30.3	1 807	9.2
1983	23 846	28.3	1 779	9.0
1984	22 255	26.4	1 729	8.8
1985	22 201	26.3	1 752	8.9
1986	22 768	27.0	1 782	9.0
1987	22 517	26.7	1 755	8.9
1988	22 436	26.6	1 921	9.7
1989	23 495	27.9	1 970	10.0
1990	25 701	30.5	1 810	9.2
1991	26 283	31.2	1 713	8.7
1992	26 673	31.6	1 705	8.7
1993	25 287	30.0	1 631	8.3
1994	24 361	28.9	1 478	7.5
1995	22 860	27.1	1 336	6.8
1996	21 337	25.3	1 202	6.1
1997	19 851	23.5	1 166	5.9
1998	18 361	21.8	—	—

SOURCE: Centers for Disease Control and Prevention, Reported Tuberculosis in the United States, 1998 (Atlanta, Ga.: U.S. Department of Health and Human Services, August 1999): Table 1.

* The large decrease in 1979 occurred because late effects of tuberculosis (e.g., bronchiectasis or fibrosis) and pleurisy with effusion (without mention of cause) are no longer included in tuberculosis deaths.
— Data not available.

NOTE: Case data after 1974 are not comparable to prior years because of changes in surveillance case definitions that became effective in 1975.

Table 3.27. Rate of Cases and Deaths from Tuberculosis

(Per 100,000 population)

Year	Tuberculosis cases		Tuberculosis deaths	
	Rate	Index change 1953=100	Rate	Index change 1953=100
1953	53.0	100.0	12.4	100.0
1954	49.3	93.0	10.2	82.3
1955	46.9	88.5	9.1	73.4
1956	41.6	78.5	8.4	67.7
1957	39.2	74.0	7.8	62.9
1958	36.5	68.9	7.1	57.3
1959	32.5	61.3	6.5	52.4
1960	30.8	58.1	6.0	48.4
1961	29.4	55.5	5.4	43.5
1962	28.7	54.2	5.1	41.1
1963	28.7	54.2	4.9	39.5
1964	26.6	50.2	4.3	34.7
1965	25.3	47.7	4.1	33.1
1966	24.4	46.0	3.9	31.5
1967	23.1	43.6	3.5	28.2
1968	21.3	40.2	3.1	25.0
1969	19.4	36.6	2.8	22.6
1970	18.3	34.5	2.6	21.0
1971	17.1	32.3	2.2	17.7
1972	15.8	29.8	2.1	16.9
1973	14.8	27.9	1.8	14.5
1974	14.2	26.8	1.7	13.7
1975	15.9	30.0	1.6	12.9
1976	15.0	28.3	1.5	12.1
1977	13.9	26.2	1.4	11.3
1978	13.1	24.7	1.3	10.5
1979	12.6	23.8	*0.9	7.3
1980	12.3	23.2	0.9	7.3
1981	11.9	22.5	0.8	6.5
1982	11.0	20.8	0.8	6.5
1983	10.2	19.2	0.8	6.5
1984	9.4	17.7	0.7	5.6
1985	9.3	17.5	0.7	5.6
1986	9.4	17.7	0.7	5.6
1987	9.3	17.5	0.7	5.6
1988	9.1	17.2	0.8	6.5
1989	9.5	17.9	0.8	6.5
1990	10.3	19.4	0.7	5.6
1991	10.4	19.6	0.7	5.6
1992	10.5	19.8	0.7	5.6
1993	9.8	18.5	0.6	4.8
1994	9.4	17.7	0.6	4.8
1995	8.7	16.4	0.5	4.0
1996	8.0	15.1	0.5	4.0
1997	7.4	14.0	0.4	3.2
1998	6.8	12.8	—	—

SOURCE: Based on data from the Centers for Disease Control and Prevention, Reported Tuberculosis in the United States, 1998 (Atlanta, Ga.: U.S. Department of Health and Human Services, August 1999): Table 1.

* The large decrease in 1979 occurred because late effects of tuberculosis (e.g., bronchiectasis or fibrosis) and pleurisy with effusion (without mention of cause) are no longer included in tuberculosis deaths.
— Data not available.

NOTE: Case data after 1974 are not comparable to prior years because of changes in surveillance case definitions that became effective in 1975. The case definition changed between 1974 and 1975. Readers should use caution in interpreting the data. The index is presented to facilitate long-term comparisons.

Table 3.28. Persons Living with Diabetes: 1980–1994

(Per 1,000 population)

Year	All people					
	0–44 years	45–64 years	65–74 years	75 years and over	Total	Age-adjusted total
1980	6.2	55.4	91.4	88.9	25.4	25.4
1981	6.2	56.0	92.2	84.3	25.3	25.3
1982	6.1	57.6	86.5	82.3	25.1	25.1
1983	6.1	53.2	92.9	84.1	25.4	25.3
1984	6.2	54.3	97.8	90.9	25.7	25.6
1985	6.2	55.9	101.7	100.6	26.8	26.7
1986	6.9	57.1	99.1	100.2	27.4	27.2
1987	6.9	57.6	94.5	97.1	27.1	26.9
1988	7.2	56.0	93.7	89.9	26.7	26.4
1989	6.7	53.8	95.7	83.8	25.9	25.4
1990	7.5	54.9	98.4	85.8	27.0	26.5
1991	7.5	54.2	106.1	92.6	27.9	27.2
1992	8.3	58.0	105.8	101.3	29.8	28.8
1993	8.0	60.0	105.4	103.4	30.3	29.1
1994	8.3	62.2	101.5	103.3	30.8	29.5

Year	White Male						White Female					
	0–44 years	45–64 years	65–74 years	75 years and over	Total	Age-adjusted total	0–44 years	45–64 years	65–74 years	75 years and over	Total	Age-adjusted total
1980	5.1	51.2	92.8	73.7	22.2	23.2	6.8	48.1	84.9	92.5	26.6	24.1
1981	5.3	51.3	84.3	78.8	22.0	23.0	6.9	48.1	88.5	83.8	26.5	24.0
1982	5.7	51.4	73.3	84.0	21.8	22.8	6.5	49.9	82.5	78.3	25.9	23.4
1983	5.6	47.8	73.9	91.0	21.3	22.3	6.5	50.7	88.8	76.0	26.5	23.9
1984	5.6	46.0	85.1	93.4	21.8	22.8	6.6	49.6	91.6	82.5	27.0	24.3
1985	5.0	51.5	93.8	98.1	23.3	24.3	7.5	49.5	92.3	91.3	28.3	25.3
1986	6.0	55.6	97.4	104.0	25.3	26.4	7.8	48.1	88.8	86.3	27.7	24.7
1987	6.4	56.3	89.8	104.3	25.3	26.3	7.1	48.0	85.5	80.5	26.6	23.7
1988	6.9	53.0	84.0	89.1	24.5	24.9	6.8	47.2	89.1	76.9	26.5	23.5
1989	6.1	48.6	85.6	78.9	22.6	23.1	6.7	47.2	90.9	75.4	26.6	23.5
1990	6.5	50.2	88.8	77.2	23.4	23.8	8.2	50.2	90.9	81.9	28.7	25.4
1991	6.6	50.3	100.1	89.6	24.9	25.2	8.3	50.7	95.0	86.7	29.6	26.0
1992	7.5	56.1	95.9	100.3	27.1	27.2	8.6	52.5	98.2	95.1	31.3	27.2
1993	7.3	56.9	100.1	104.8	27.9	27.7	8.0	51.9	98.6	92.7	30.8	26.6
1994	7.8	57.7	96.0	106.8	28.4	28.0	7.9	51.9	97.2	89.2	30.5	26.2

Year	Black Male						Black Female					
	0–44 years	45–64 years	65–74 years	75 years and over	Total	Age-adjusted total	0–44 years	45–64 years	65–74 years	75 years and over	Total	Age-adjusted total
1980	7.4	98.7	108.1	103.6	27.6	36.4	10.6	108.2	132.5	151.2	38.1	44.3
1981	6.4	97.2	116.8	79.3	24.4	35.0	9.0	120.8	172.3	144.9	41.0	48.2
1982	6.0	93.2	120.1	83.7	25.6	34.4	7.9	135.6	197.9	134.4	41.5	51.6
1983	3.5	104.2	142.7	79.8	26.1	36.2	10.5	124.9	243.6	160.1	47.3	55.6
1984	5.2	108.3	145.0	111.6	28.8	39.7	9.7	115.4	224.0	170.6	44.5	52.3
1985	5.9	110.1	159.2	107.3	30.0	41.3	8.1	104.8	216.6	211.6	42.7	50.4
1986	7.6	99.8	143.3	119.5	29.3	40.0	7.6	112.0	167.8	219.7	41.2	48.4
1987	8.2	100.9	160.5	104.4	30.3	41.1	9.4	110.2	163.5	247.1	43.2	50.2
1988	7.2	116.8	128.6	150.9	31.5	43.3	11.4	94.2	174.6	230.1	42.3	48.6
1989	6.7	117.3	116.7	159.4	30.8	42.7	11.2	89.8	199.4	190.6	41.2	47.5
1990	5.0	115.1	109.4	172.9	29.1	41.2	11.8	84.1	226.1	140.7	40.3	46.4
1991	5.2	80.5	173.1	127.6	26.0	36.9	12.1	100.9	222.2	148.1	43.3	49.9
1992	7.5	89.5	211.6	83.0	29.9	41.0	12.4	104.0	201.0	167.5	43.9	50.2
1993	8.5	95.6	190.5	109.3	31.4	42.5	12.6	127.3	181.2	181.8	47.5	54.2
1994	10.6	120.8	157.3	120.6	35.9	47.1	12.1	134.5	171.8	173.5	47.9	54.2

SOURCE: Centers for Disease Control and Prevention, Diabetes Surveillance, 1997 (Atlanta, Ga.: U.S. Department of Health and Human Services, 1997): Tables 2.8, 2.11–2.14.

NOTE: Three-year moving average.

Table 3.29. Mental Illness in the Adult Household Population: 1994

Characteristic	Persons with mental or emotional problem		
	Number (in thousands)	Percent	Rate (per 100,000 population)
SEX			
Male	3 144	38.2	3 830
Female	5 095	61.8	5 914
RACE			
White	6 974	84.7	4 974
Black	969	11.8	4 835
Other	296	3.6	3 716
AGE			
18–24 years	781	9.5	3 089
25–44 years	4 089	49.6	4 933
45–64 years	2 901	35.2	5 756
65–69 years	468	5.7	4 844
MARITAL STATUS			
Married	4 050	49.2	3 666
Widowed, divorced, or single	2 326	28.2	10 573
Never married	1 847	22.4	5 209
EMPLOYMENT STATUS			
Employed	3 516	42.7	2 955
Unemployed	637	7.7	7 918
Not in labor force	4 086	49.6	9 920
POVERTY STATUS			
At or above threshold	5 650	68.6	4 050
Below threshold	1 895	23.0	10 954
LIVING ARRANGEMENT			
Lives alone	1 766	21.4	9 227
With nonrelative	266	3.2	5 918
With spouse	3 974	48.2	3 649
With relative, other	2 233	27.1	6 255

SOURCE: 1994 National Health Interview Survey, A.G. Willis, G.B. Willis, A. Male, M.J. Henderson, and R.W. Manderscheid. "Mental Illness and Disability in the U.S. Adult Household Population," in *Mental Health, United States, 1998,* ed. R.W. Manderscheid and M.J. Henderson, DHHS Pub. No. (SMA) 99-3285. SAMHSA Center for Mental Health Services. (Washington D.C.: Supt. of Docs., U.S. Govt. Printing Office, 1998): Table 1 and pp. 113-123.

NOTE: Some percentages total less than 100 because values for "Don't know" and "Refusal" are not listed.

Table 3.30. Rate of Acute Conditions by Age: 1996

(Per 100 persons)

Type of acute condition	All ages	Under 5 years	5–17 years	18–24 years	25–44 years	45 years and over	45–64 years	65 years and over
ALL ACUTE CONDITIONS	163.5	317.9	204.4	184.2	144.3	115.0	113.7	117.3
INFECTIVE AND PARASITIC DISEASES	20.5	57.0	37.1	23.2	12.2	9.3	11.0	6.5
Common childhood diseases	1.2	*6.8	*2.3	*0.9	*0.4	*—	*—	*—
Intestinal virus, unspecified	6.0	14.2	10.4	*6.2	4.7	2.8	*2.8	*2.7
Viral infections, unspecified	5.7	22.6	9.6	*2.8	2.6	3.2	4.5	*1.1
Other	7.6	13.4	14.8	13.2	4.4	3.3	3.7	*2.7
RESPIRATORY CONDITIONS	78.9	129.4	101.5	86.0	76.9	53.3	55.9	49.0
Common cold	23.6	48.6	33.8	23.8	18.7	16.1	16.4	15.7
Other acute upper respiratory infections	11.3	13.1	15.0	16.1	11.6	7.0	7.5	6.1
Influenza	36.0	53.7	44.3	40.5	38.1	23.3	26.1	18.6
Acute bronchitis	4.6	*7.2	4.3	*3.9	5.1	3.8	3.5	*4.4
Pneumonia	1.8	*3.9	*1.7	*1.4	*1.3	*2.0	*0.9	*3.8
Other respiratory conditions	1.7	*2.9	*2.4	*0.4	2.0	1.1	1.5	0.5
DIGESTIVE SYSTEM CONDITIONS	6.7	9.6	9.8	*6.4	5.1	5.8	5.3	6.6
Dental conditions	1.1	*3.6	*1.0	*1.1	*0.9	*0.9	*0.9	*0.8
Indigestion, nausea, and vomiting	3.0	*2.3	7.4	*2.5	*2.2	1.5	*1.7	1.2
Other digestive conditions	2.5	*3.8	*1.4	2.8	*2.0	3.4	*2.7	4.5
INJURIES	21.7	22.9	21.4	31.5	24.9	15.6	14.6	17.2
Fractures and dislocations	3.2	*1.2	5.9	*3.0	*1.8	3.5	3.5	*3.5
Sprains and strains	4.9	0.5	*3.5	*7.3	8.3	2.8	3.8	*1.2
Open wounds and lacerations	3.4	6.8	2.0	6.6	4.4	1.6	1.7	1.5
Contusions and superficial injuries	3.8	*3.6	3.9	*5.8	4.4	2.5	*2.7	2.2
Other current injuries	6.4	10.8	6.1	8.7	6.0	5.2	3.0	8.8
SELECTED OTHER ACUTE CONDITIONS	23.9	79.9	24.4	25.4	16.8	16.8	15.4	19.2
Eye conditions	1.3	*3.8	*0.7	*1.6	*0.4	*2.0	*1.7	*2.3
Acute ear infections	8.2	55.0	12.4	*3.8	2.9	*1.2	*1.1	*1.3
Other ear conditions	1.5	*3.0	*2.2	*0.8	1.2	1.1	*1.3	0.7
Acute urinary conditions	3.2	*2.4	*2.0	*2.9	*3.0	4.3	3.3	6.1
Disorders of menstruation	*0.3	N/A	*0.3	*0.7	*0.6	*—	*—	*—
Other disorders of female genital tract	*0.6	*—	*0.1	*1.8	*0.7	*0.6	*0.7	*0.5
Delivery and other conditions of pregnancy and puerperium	1.2	N/A	*0.6	*4.5	2.2	*—	*—	N/A
Skin conditions	1.9	*2.8	*1.4	*2.0	1.4	2.4	*2.3	*2.5
Acute musculoskeletal conditions	3.2	*3.0	*0.8	*5.4	3.0	4.2	3.5	*5.5
Headache, excluding migraine	*0.7	*—	*0.8	*1.1	0.7	0.6	0.7	0.3
Fever, unspecified	1.8	10.0	*3.1	*0.9	*0.5	0.5	*0.8	*—
ALL OTHER ACUTE CONDITIONS	11.8	19.1	10.2	11.6	8.6	14.2	11.5	18.8

SOURCE: P.F. Adams, G.E. Hendershot, and M.A. Marano. Current Estimates from the National Health Interview Survey, 1996. National Center for Health Statistics. *Vital and Health Statistics* 10, no. 200 (1999): Table 1.

* Figure does not meet standard of reliability or precision.
*— Figure does not meet standard of reliability or precision and quantity zero.
N/A Not applicable.

NOTE: A condition is considered acute if (a) it was first noticed no longer than three months before the reference date of the interview, and (b) it is not one of the conditions considered chronic regardless of the time of onset. However, any acute condition not associated with either at least one doctor visit or at least one day of restricted activity during the reference period is considered to be of minor consequence and is excluded from the final data produced by the survey.

Table 3.31. Rate of Acute Conditions by Sex and Age: 1996

(Per 100 persons)

Type of acute condition	Male — All ages	Male — Under 5 years	Male — 5–17 years	Male — 18–44 years	Male — 45 years and over	Female — All ages	Female — Under 5 years	Female — 5–17 years	Female — 18–44 years	Female — 45 years and over
ALL ACUTE CONDITIONS	150.1	339.4	187.1	128.3	105.0	176.2	295.4	222.5	177.7	123.6
Infective and parasitic diseases	17.9	62.0	32.9	10.4	6.5	23.0	51.7	41.5	18.8	11.7
Common childhood diseases	*1.3	*8.1	*1.8	*0.6	*-	*1.1	*5.5	*2.9	*0.4	*—
Intestinal virus, unspecified	5.0	*14.5	7.8	4.0	*1.9	7.1	*14.0	13.1	6.1	*3.5
Viral infections, unspecified	6.0	28.5	10.3	*2.60	*1.9	5.4	*16.4	8.9	*2.7	4.3
Other	5.7	*11.0	13.0	*3.20	*2.7	9.4	*15.9	16.6	9.6	*3.8
RESPIRATORY CONDITIONS	70.3	136.9	85.7	66.8	47.3	87.1	121.6	118.3	90.8	58.4
Common cold	21.9	52.8	31.1	16.0	15.7	25.1	44.1	36.6	23.7	16.5
Other acute upper respiratory infections	7.8	*10.7	10.2	7.7	5.7	14.6	*15.6	20.1	17.4	8.1
Influenza	34.1	59.4	38.1	36.2	21.8	37.8	47.6	50.9	41.1	24.6
Acute bronchitis	3.2	*5.9	*4.1	*3.4	*1.8	5.9	*8.5	*4.5	6.2	5.6
Pneumonia	1.8	*6.2	*1.0	*1.2	*2.1	1.8	*1.5	*2.5	*1.5	*1.9
Other respiratory conditions	1.4	*1.8	*1.2	*2.3	*0.3	2.0	*4.1	*3.7	*1.0	*1.8
DIGESTIVE SYSTEM CONDITIONS	5.9	*8.1	7.9	3.5	7.3	7.4	*11.2	11.8	7.2	4.4
Dental conditions	*1.2	*3.9	*1.7	*0.6	*1.1	*1.0	*3.3	*0.3	*1.3	*0.6
Indigestion, nausea, and vomiting	2.0	*1.4	*4.5	*1.0	*1.8	4.0	*3.1	*10.4	3.5	*1.3
Other digestive conditions	2.7	*2.8	*1.7	*2.0	*4.4	2.4	*4.8	*1.1	*2.4	*2.5
INJURIES	24.6	27.6	27.6	28.8	16.2	18.9	*17.9	14.8	24.1	15.1
Fractures and dislocations	3.3	*1.0	8.3	*1.3	*3.2	3.1	*1.5	*3.3	*2.8	*3.7
Sprains and strains	5.4	*1.0	*3.1	8.8	*3.4	4.4	*-	*4.0	7.3	*2.3
Open wounds and lacerations	4.9	*10.5	*3.2	6.7	*2.1	2.0	*3.0	*0.7	*3.1	*1.2
Contusions and superficial injuries	4.6	*5.7	*5.2	6.1	*2.1	2.9	*1.3	*2.6	3.5	*2.9
Other current injuries	6.4	*9.5	7.9	5.9	5.4	6.3	*12.1	*4.2	7.4	5.0
SELECTED OTHER ACUTE CONDITIONS	20.6	77.9	23.6	12.0	15.3	27.0	82.0	25.3	25.3	18.1
Eye conditions	*1.3	*3.8	*1.2	*0.6	*1.7	*1.3	*3.7	*0.1	*0.8	*2.2
Acute ear infections	8.7	53.8	14.9	*2.2	*1.4	7.8	56.1	9.9	3.9	*2.2
Other ear conditions	*1.1	*2.4	*1.5	*0.7	*1.0	1.8	*3.6	*3.0	*1.4	*1.2
Acute urinary conditions	1.7	*—	*0.6	*1.0	*3.7	4.6	*4.9	*3.4	4.9	4.9
Disorders of menstruation	N/A	N/A	N/A	N/A	N/A	*0.6	N/A	*0.5	*1.3	*—
Other disorders of female genital tract	N/A	N/A	N/A	N/A	N/A	*1.2	*—	*0.2	*1.9	*1.1
Delivery and other conditions of pregnancy and puerperium	N/A	N/A	N/A	N/A	N/A	2.4	N/A	*1.2	5.4	*—
Skin conditions	1.9	*2.9	*1.5	*1.4	*2.6	1.8	*2.8	*1.4	*1.7	*2.1
Acute musculoskeletal conditions	3.4	*0.8	*0.4	4.9	*4.0	3.0	*5.3	*1.3	*2.2	4.5
Headache, excluding migraine	*0.6	*—	*0.9	*0.8	*0.3	0.7	*—	*0.6	*0.8	*0.8
Fever, unspecified	2.0	*14.2	*2.6	*0.4	*0.5	1.6	*5.6	*3.7	*0.9	*0.5
ALL OTHER ACUTE CONDITIONS	10.7	26.9	9.5	6.8	12.4	12.9	*11.0	10.9	11.6	15.8

SOURCE: P.F. Adams, G.E. Hendershot, and M.A. Marano. Current Estimates from the National Health Interview Survey, 1996. National Center for Health Statistics. *Vital and Health Statistics* 10, no. 200 (1999): Table 2.

* Figure does not meet standard of reliability or precision.
*— Figure does not meet standard of reliability or precision and quantity zero.
N/A Not applicable.

NOTE: A condition is considered acute if (a) it was first noticed no longer than three months before the reference date of the interview, and (b) it is not one of the conditions considered chronic regardless of the time of onset. However, any acute condition not associated with either at least one doctor visit or at least one day of restricted activity during the reference period is considered to be of minor consequence and is excluded from the final data produced by the survey.

Table 3.32. Rate of Acute Conditions by Race and Age: 1996

(Per 100 persons)

Type of acute condition	White				Black			
	All ages	Under 18 years	18–44 years	45 years and over	All ages	Under 18 years	18–44 years	45 years and over
ALL ACUTE CONDITIONS	168.7	253.1	158.3	116.8	143.1	174.5	143.9	97.5
Infective and parasitic diseases	21.0	45.0	15.3	9.6	19.0	34.7	*12.8	*7.4
Common childhood diseases	1.1	3.9	*0.2	*—	*1.7	*3.1	*1.7	*—
Intestinal virus, unspecified	6.3	12.0	5.6	2.7	5.5	*8.7	*3.5	*4.2
Viral infections, unspecified	5.5	13.0	2.5	3.5	7.2	16.2	*2.9	*1.7
Other	8.1	16.0	7.0	3.4	*4.6	*6.8	*4.6	*1.5
RESPIRATORY CONDITIONS	81.4	116.1	81.7	54.5	66.6	81.8	67.6	43.3
Common cold	23.3	38.1	19.8	16.2	26.0	40.3	21.0	*14.4
Other acute upper respiratory infections	11.9	16.2	12.9	7.5	8.3	*8.9	*12.3	*0.9
Influenza	37.3	50.1	40.7	23.4	28.1	29.3	28.9	24.9
Acute bronchitis	5.2	6.1	5.4	4.4	*1.9	*1.7	*3.2	*—
Pneumonia	2.0	*2.9	*1.4	*1.9	*0.8	*—	*—	*3.1
Other respiratory conditions	1.7	*2.7	*1.5	*1.1	*1.5	*1.6	*2.2	*—
DIGESTIVE SYSTEM CONDITIONS	6.8	10.0	5.4	6.0	6.9	*8.6	*7.0	*4.2
Dental conditions	0.9	*1.4	*0.7	*0.9	*2.1	*2.9	*2.8	*—
Indigestion, nausea, and vomiting	3.1	6.1	2.3	*1.7	*3.2	*5.8	*2.6	*0.5
Other digestive conditions	2.8	*2.6	2.5	3.4	*1.5	*—	*1.6	*3.7
INJURIES	22.1	22.3	27.0	16.1	20.8	20.3	26.5	*11.6
Fractures and dislocations	3.6	5.4	2.1	4.0	*1.8	*1.8	*2.9	*—
Sprains and strains	4.7	*2.9	7.7	2.6	6.4	*1.3	*12.5	*2.9
Open wounds and lacerations	3.5	3.5	5.1	*1.6	*3.2	*2.4	*4.4	*2.3
Contusions and superficial injuries	3.7	3.6	4.7	2.7	*4.3	*6.0	*4.7	*1.4
Other current injuries	6.6	7.0	7.5	5.2	*5.0	*8.8	*2.0	*5.0
SELECTED OTHER ACUTE CONDITIONS	25.0	45.5	18.9	16.8	19.8	19.8	23.3	*13.6
Eye conditions	1.3	*1.9	*0.5	*1.8	*1.3	*—	*1.8	*2.5
Acute ear infections	9.0	28.2	3.2	*1.3	*5.0	*10.5	*2.9	*0.7
Other ear conditions	1.6	*2.8	*1.2	*1.2	*0.9	*1.6	*0.8	*—
Acute urinary conditions	3.3	*2.4	2.8	4.6	*2.8	*1.1	*5.2	*1.1
Disorders of menstruation	*0.4	*0.2	*0.8	*—	*—	*—	*—	*—
Other disorders of female genital tract	*0.7	*0.1	*1.1	*0.6	*0.4	*—	*0.6	*0.5
Delivery and other conditions of pregnancy and puerperium	1.2	*0.5	*2.7	*—	*1.2	*—	*2.9	*—
Skin conditions	1.9	*1.8	*1.7	*2.3	*2.2	*2.3	*1.2	*3.6
Acute musculoskeletal conditions	3.2	*1.5	3.4	4.3	*3.0	*—	*5.8	*2.3
Headache, excluding migraine	*0.5	*0.4	*0.7	*0.3	*1.5	*1.7	*1.5	*1.3
Fever, unspecified	1.9	5.7	*0.7	*0.4	*1.6	*2.6	*0.7	*1.6
ALL OTHER ACUTE CONDITIONS	12.4	14.1	10.0	13.9	10.2	*9.2	*6.7	*17.3

SOURCE: P.F. Adams, G.E. Hendershot, and M.A. Marano. Current Estimates from the National Health Interview Survey, 1996. National Center for Health Statistics. *Vital and Health Statistics* 10, no. 200 (1999): Table 3.

* Figure does not meet standard of reliability or precision.
*— Figure does not meet standard of reliability or precision and quantity zero.

NOTE: A condition is considered acute if (a) it was first noticed no longer than three months before the reference date of the interview, and (b) it is not one of the conditions considered chronic regardless of the time of onset. However, any acute condition not associated with either at least one doctor visit or at least one day of restricted activity during the reference period is considered to be of minor consequence and is excluded from the final data produced by the survey.

Table 3.33. Rate of Acute Conditions by Income and Age: 1996

(Per 100 persons)

Type of acute condition	Family income							
	Less than $10,000				$10,000–$19,999			
	All ages	Under 18 years	18–44 years	45 years and over	All ages	Under 18 years	18–44 years	45 years and over
ALL ACUTE CONDITIONS	215.2	273.4	228.5	144.3	153.1	200.0	159.0	109.2
INFECTIVE AND PARASITIC DISEASES	25.7	49.0	24.3	*5.6	16.5	34.0	14.7	*4.4
Common childhood diseases	*1.2	*4.1	*—	*—	*1.2	*2.5	*1.4	*—
Intestinal virus, unspecified	*8.7	*11.2	*11.8	*2.3	*4.7	*8.7	*6.1	*—
Viral infections, unspecified	6.6	*15.3	*4.0	*1.8	4.4	*8.0	*2.8	*3.5
Other	9.2	*18.4	*8.5	*1.6	6.1	*14.9	*4.4	*1.0
RESPIRATORY CONDITIONS	94.3	126.3	90.9	69.1	68.4	80.8	80.8	44.5
Common cold	30.9	45.6	*30.2	*18.2	18.9	*23.4	24.9	*8.7
Other acute upper respiratory infections	12.6	6.9	19.5	9.2	7.5	12.7	7.6	3.2
Influenza	41.8	66.6	31.1	32.5	33.7	36.6	41.9	22.3
Acute bronchitis	*3.5	3.6	*3.7	*3.1	3.6	4.2	2.6	*4.3
Pneumonia	*1.9	*—	*3.6	*1.6	*2.3	0.3	*1.9	*4.4
Other respiratory conditions	3.5	*3.6	*2.8	*4.5	*2.3	*3.6	*2.0	*1.6
DIGESTIVE SYSTEM CONDITIONS	*7.0	*9.5	*4.0	*8.6	8.0	*11.9	*5.4	*7.8
Dental conditions	*0.9	*—	*2.2	*—	*1.8	*3.2	*1.8	*0.9
Indigestion, nausea, and vomiting	*4.0	9.5	*0.4	*3.6	4.1	*7.1	*2.7	*3.3
Other digestive conditions	*2.1	*—	*1.4	5.0	2.1	1.7	1.0	3.7
INJURIES	28.0	*22.6	42.3	*14.8	25.8	23.9	32.6	19.9
Fractures and dislocations	*4.6	*8.0	*5.9	*—	*3.3	*3.0	*2.3	*4.8
Sprains and strains	*3.3	*—	*8.4	*—	*5.1	*2.8	*9.6	*1.9
Open wounds and lacerations	*6.9	*4.8	*10.0	*4.9	*4.8	*3.1	*7.7	*2.9
Contusions and superficial injuries	*5.3	*3.9	*7.3	*4.3	*4.5	*3.6	*6.3	*3.2
Other current injuries	7.8	6.0	10.8	5.6	8.1	11.5	6.7	7.1
SELECTED OTHER ACUTE CONDITIONS	39.0	41.2	48.7	*24.6	20.0	38.3	15.1	*10.9
Eye conditions	*3.4	*3.0	*3.3	*4.0	*0.8	*—	*2.2	*—
Acute ear infections	8.4	*17.6	*6.8	*1.8	7.6	25.4	*1.1	*0.7
Other ear conditions	*3.4	4.7	*5.2	*—	*1.3	*3.0	*0.6	*0.7
Acute urinary conditions	3.2	*—	*6.1	*2.4	2.1	1.0	2.1	2.9
Disorders of menstruation	*—	*—	*—	*—	0.5	*—	*1.2	*—
Other disorders of female genital tract	*2.5	*—	*4.4	*2.3	0.2	*0.4	*0.2	*—
Delivery and other conditions of pregnancy and puerperium	*2.6	*—	*6.5	*—	*0.8	*—	*2.2	*—
Skin conditions	*1.4	*4.9	*—	*—	2.8	*2.7	*3.2	*2.5
Acute musculoskeletal conditions	8.7	*1.8	*11.3	*11.9	2.0	*0.8	*1.8	*3.2
Headache, excluding migraine	*2.3	*2.7	*2.3	*2.1	0.7	*0.6	*0.7	*0.8
Fever, unspecified	3.1	6.6	*2.9	*—	1.2	*4.4	*—	*—
ALL OTHER ACUTE CONDITIONS	21.2	*24.8	*18.4	*21.6	14.4	*11.0	*10.4	21.6

See footnotes at end of table.

Table 3.33. Rate of Acute Conditions by Income and Age: 1996—*Continued*

(Per 100 persons)

Type of acute condition	Family income							
	$20,000–$34,999				$35,000 or more			
	All ages	Under 18 Years	18–44 years	45 years and over	All ages	Under 18 Years	18–44 years	45 years and over
ALL ACUTE CONDITIONS	166.6	236.6	154.7	123.5	166.2	258.5	145.2	107.9
INFECTIVE AND PARASITIC DISEASES	18.7	34.7	14.7	*10.6	23.5	52.3	12.6	11.5
Common childhood diseases	*0.9	*3.3	*—	*—	*1.5	*4.7	*0.5	*—
Intestinal virus, unspecified	6.1	9.7	*6.3	*2.8	6.5	14.5	*3.3	*3.3
Viral infections, unspecified	4.7	12.7	*1.4	*2.4	7.3	16.6	3.0	*4.6
Other	7.0	9.0	*7.0	*5.4	8.2	16.5	5.8	*3.6
RESPIRATORY CONDITIONS	79.2	102.3	84.2	52.9	84.1	118.9	80.5	56.0
Common cold	23.0	39.9	18.0	15.3	24.4	35.4	20.5	19.3
Other acute upper respiratory infections	10.8	15.7	9.1	8.8	14.1	18.3	15.5	8.1
Influenza	39.7	40.9	50.9	23.5	37.1	53.8	36.2	22.5
Acute bronchitis	*3.6	*3.1	*5.0	*2.0	*5.6	*6.5	*5.8	*4.6
Pneumonia	*1.1	*—	*0.7	*2.6	*1.3	*2.9	*0.9	*0.5
Other respiratory conditions	*1.1	*2.7	*0.5	*0.5	*1.5	*2.0	*1.6	1.0
DIGESTIVE SYSTEM CONDITIONS	7.5	14.0	*6.0	*3.9	6.0	9.4	5.4	*3.7
Dental conditions	*1.9	*4.5	*1.2	*0.8	*0.5	*0.7	*0.3	*0.4
Indigestion, nausea, and vomiting	*3.3	*6.8	*2.5	*1.3	2.8	*5.8	*2.3	*0.7
Other digestive conditions	*2.3	*2.7	*2.3	*1.8	2.8	*2.9	*2.8	*2.6
INJURIES	21.7	24.2	22.8	18.1	20.6	22.4	22.9	15.5
Fractures and dislocations	*1.7	*2.8	*0.3	*2.7	3.5	*5.8	*2.1	*3.4
Sprains and strains	5.0	*2.0	*7.0	*4.8	5.3	*3.8	7.5	*3.7
Open wounds and lacerations	3.3	*3.8	*5.4	*—	2.9	*4.0	3.3	*1.4
Contusions and superficial injuries	4.2	*5.9	*4.1	*2.9	3.6	*3.7	4.0	*3.0
Other current injuries	7.5	*9.8	6.0	*7.7	5.1	*5.1	6.0	*4.0
SELECTED OTHER ACUTE CONDITIONS	27.3	45.5	19.1	22.9	23.6	43.9	17.1	13.6
Eye conditions	*0.7	*0.9	*0.3	*1.2	*1.3	*2.6	*0.2	*1.8
Acute ear infections	9.0	27.5	*2.8	*1.7	*9.9	28.2	*3.7	*1.2
Other ear conditions	*1.6	*1.9	*1.0	*2.3	*1.3	*2.5	*1.0	*0.5
Acute urinary conditions	4.5	*3.5	*2.7	7.9	2.6	*1.9	*2.8	*3.2
Disorders of menstruation	*0.5	*—	*1.3	*—	*0.3	*0.4	*0.5	*—
Other disorders of female genital tract	*0.9	*—	*1.2	*1.2	*0.4	*—	*0.9	*0.1
Delivery and other conditions of pregnancy and puerperium	*2.0	*2.2	*3.3	*—	*0.8	*—	*1.9	*—
Skin conditions	2.0	*1.0	*1.5	*3.5	1.7	*1.5	*1.7	*2.0
Acute musculoskeletal conditions	3.6	*2.4	*4.0	*4.1	2.8	*1.3	*3.0	*3.8
Headache, excluding migraine	*0.4	*—	*0.5	*0.6	0.6	*0.4	*0.8	*0.5
Fever, unspecified	*2.1	*6.3	*0.7	*0.6	1.8	*5.0	*0.6	*0.4
ALL OTHER ACUTE CONDITIONS	12.2	15.9	7.9	15.1	8.4	11.7	6.7	7.6

SOURCE: P.F. Adams, G.E. Hendershot, and M.A. Marano. Current Estimates from the National Health Interview Survey, 1996. National Center for Health Statistics. *Vital and Health Statistics* 10, no. 200 (1999): Table 4.

* Figure does not meet standard of reliability or precision.
*— Figure does not meet standard of reliability or precision and quantity zero.
0.0 Quantity more than zero but less than 0.05.

NOTE: A condition is considered acute if (a) it was first noticed no longer than three months before the reference date of the interview, and (b) it is not one of the conditions considered chronic regardless of the time of onset. However, any acute condition not associated with either at least one doctor visit or at least one day of restricted activity during the reference period is considered to be of minor consequence and is excluded from the final data produced by the survey.

Table 3.34. Rate of Acute Conditions by Geographic Region and Place of Residence: 1996

(Per 100 persons)

Type of acute condition	Geographic region				Place of residence			
					MSA			
	Northeast	Midwest	South	West	All MSA [1]	Central city	Not central city	Not MSA [1]
ALL ACUTE CONDITIONS	150.5	170.8	160.6	172.3	162.1	164.9	160.4	168.5
Infective and parasitic diseases	21.3	17.9	25.5	14.7	19.2	14.6	21.9	25.4
Common childhood diseases	*0.6	*0.8	*1.5	*1.5	1.0	*0.8	*1.1	*1.8
Intestinal virus, unspecified	6.2	1.6	10.7	3.4	5.1	4.1	5.7	9.5
Viral infections, unspecified	7.0	5.3	7.1	2.7	6.0	4.7	6.8	4.5
Other	7.5	10.1	6.2	7.1	7.0	5.0	8.3	9.6
RESPIRATORY CONDITIONS	69.1	87.2	69.9	93.7	80.5	89.7	74.9	73.3
Common cold	21.7	26.0	19.2	29.6	24.8	30.4	21.4	18.9
Other acute upper respiratory infections	9.3	11.9	13.7	8.6	11.0	10.8	11.0	12.6
Influenza	28.3	41.5	28.8	48.7	37.3	41.4	34.9	30.8
Acute bronchitis	5.2	4.9	4.3	4.1	4.2	3.9	4.4	6.0
Pneumonia	*2.8	*1.6	*1.6	*1.5	*1.5	*1.5	1.4	*3.1
Other respiratory conditions	*1.9	*1.4	2.2	1.2	1.7	*1.7	1.7	*1.8
DIGESTIVE SYSTEM CONDITIONS	4.8	7.7	7.4	6.1	6.7	6.1	7.1	6.6
Dental conditions	*0.7	*0.6	*1.2	*1.9	1.1	*1.1	*1.1	*1.3
Indigestion, nausea, and vomiting	*2.9	3.3	3.1	2.8	3.4	3.0	3.7	*1.5
Other digestive conditions	*1.2	3.8	3.2	1.4	2.2	*2.0	2.3	3.7
INJURIES	21.9	24.3	20.4	20.5	21.2	21.1	21.3	23.4
Fractures and dislocations	3.4	3.0	3.6	2.7	2.9	3.6	2.5	4.3
Sprains and strains	6.4	4.9	3.6	5.6	4.8	4.6	5.0	5.2
Open wounds and lacerations	3.4	4.6	3.8	1.6	3.1	*2.3	3.5	4.7
Contusions and superficial injuries	4.1	5.5	2.9	2.8	4.1	4.1	4.0	*2.7
Other current injuries	4.7	6.3	6.5	7.9	6.3	6.5	6.3	6.5
SELECTED OTHER ACUTE CONDITIONS	22.3	23.4	24.1	25.5	23.1	21.4	24.2	26.6
Eye conditions	*1.0	*1.6	*1.4	*1.2	1.3	*1.5	*1.2	*1.3
Acute ear infections	8.2	8.4	8.6	7.5	8.2	6.1	9.5	8.4
Other ear conditions	*1.7	*1.8	*1.1	*1.4	1.5	*1.6	1.4	*1.3
Acute urinary conditions	*2.1	3.5	4.0	2.6	3.1	3.6	2.9	3.3
Disorders of menstruation	*—	*0.4	*0.4	*0.4	*0.3	*0.3	*0.3	*0.3
Other disorders of female genital tract	*0.5	*0.9	*0.2	*1.0	*0.6	*0.8	*0.4	*0.7
Delivery and other conditions of pregnancy and puerperium	*1.0	*0.5	*1.6	*1.6	*1.1	*1.0	*1.2	*1.6
Skin conditions	*1.8	*1.8	*1.6	*2.6	1.7	*2.1	1.5	*2.6
Acute musculoskeletal conditions	4.1	*2.7	2.8	3.5	2.9	*1.8	3.6	4.3
Headache, excluding migraine	*0.2	*0.7	*0.5	*1.3	*0.6	*0.9	*0.4	*1.0
Fever, unspecified	*1.7	*1.3	*1.9	*2.2	1.8	*1.8	1.7	*1.9
ALL OTHER ACUTE CONDITIONS	11.1	10.2	13.4	11.8	11.4	12.0	11.1	13.2

SOURCE: P.F. Adams, G.E. Hendershot, and M.A. Marano. Current Estimates from the National Health Interview Survey, 1996. National Center for Health Statistics. *Vital and Health Statistics* 10, no. 200 (1999): Table 5.

* Figure does not meet standard of reliability or precision.
*— Figure does not meet standard of reliability or precision and quantity zero.
1. MSA is metropolitan statistical area.

NOTE: A condition is considered acute if (a) it was first noticed no longer than three months before the reference date of the interview, and (b) it is not one of the conditions considered chronic regardless of the time of onset. However, any acute condition not associated with either at least one doctor visit or at least one day of restricted activity during the reference period is considered to be of minor consequence and is excluded from the final data produced by the survey.

Table 3.35. Frequency of Gastrointestinal Illness in the General Population

(Episodes per person per year, as determined by three studies)

Symptom	FoodNet Population Survey 1996–1997 Age-adjusted	Tecumseh Study 1965–1971 Crude	Tecumseh Study 1965–1971 Age-adjusted	Cleveland Study 1948–1957 Crude	Cleveland Study 1948–1957 Age-adjusted
Diarrhea or vomiting	—	0.98	0.81	1.28	0.87
Diarrhea, any	0.75	0.63	0.52	0.83	0.56
Without vomiting	0.61	0.40	0.33	0.48	0.33
With vomiting	0.14	0.23	0.19	0.35	0.23
Vomiting without diarrhea	—	0.35	0.29	0.45	0.31

SOURCE: P. Mead, L. Slutsker, V. Dietz, L. McCaig, J. Bresse, C. Shapiro, P. Griffin, and R. Tauxe, "Food-Related Illness and Death in the United States," Emerging Infectious Diseases, (Centers for Disease Control and Prevention) 5, no. 5 (September–October 1999): Table 4.

— Data not available.

Table 3.36. Notifiable Diseases with More Than 10,000 Cases Reported to CDC in 1997

(Cases per 100,000 resident population; ranked by total)

Area	Chlamydia Trachomatis infection [1]	Gonorrhea [1]	AIDS [2]	Syphilis, all stages [1]	Hepatitis A, B, and C	Salmonellosis	Shigellosis	Tuberculosis [3]	Lyme disease	Total
United States	196.8	121.4	21.9	17.4	16.5	15.7	8.6	7.4	4.8	410.5
DIVISION										
East South Central	217.1	216.9	12.6	34.8	11.2	10.8	6.9	8.1	0.6	519.0
West South Central	243.5	157.0	21.4	27.5	29.5	14.3	14.3	9.5	0.5	517.6
South Atlantic	220.8	192.8	28.7	27.5	8.9	17.6	9.3	7.8	1.6	515.2
Middle Atlantic	153.5	104.5	48.0	20.8	10.2	17.0	8.3	9.2	19.8	391.3
East North Central	196.9	135.8	9.9	9.9	11.7	14.1	5.8	4.4	1.4	389.8
Pacific	202.6	50.3	18.9	9.5	25.6	17.4	9.6	11.1	0.4	345.4
Mountain	177.2	49.0	11.2	6.3	33.6	15.7	11.6	3.9	0.1	308.8
West North Central	177.5	80.0	6.3	4.7	15.6	12.3	4.9	3.3	1.6	306.3
New England	137.8	44.0	17.7	8.8	6.7	17.5	4.4	3.6	23.3	263.8
STATE										
South Carolina	332.7	305.5	20.7	30.2	6.6	16.0	2.3	8.7	0.1	722.9
Mississippi	289.2	304.9	12.7	52.7	14.2	17.8	4.2	9.0	1.0	705.7
Maryland	270.2	227.1	36.8	48.2	7.3	24.2	8.3	6.7	9.7	638.4
Louisiana	265.3	247.7	25.1	41.5	17.2	14.2	4.2	9.3	0.3	624.9
Delaware	357.0	173.9	31.6	15.4	5.2	13.8	4.8	5.3	14.9	621.9
Georgia	212.5	246.7	23.0	37.8	13.2	18.1	15.1	9.3	0.1	576.0
Alabama	201.5	278.6	13.2	34.3	4.2	10.9	6.3	9.4	0.3	558.6
Tennessee	232.9	205.3	14.6	44.1	20.7	8.3	5.4	8.7	0.8	540.5
North Carolina	230.4	227.4	11.4	29.7	7.1	16.5	5.2	6.2	0.5	534.5
Texas	260.7	136.9	24.3	27.7	31.6	14.4	18.0	10.2	0.5	524.1
Oklahoma	223.6	143.4	8.5	12.2	45.9	11.8	8.8	6.4	1.4	462.0
Arizona	236.7	83.5	9.8	13.2	56.2	18.7	23.6	6.5	0.1	462.0
Missouri	227.8	147.0	10.7	9.1	28.2	10.5	4.1	4.6	0.1	448.3
Michigan	218.9	161.0	9.0	8.0	22.7	9.3	3.5	3.8	0.5	442.6
Connecticut	185.4	92.6	37.4	9.8	6.3	16.7	3.1	3.9	70.2	436.6
Florida	182.8	130.2	41.6	18.7	11.0	17.7	13.3	9.6	0.4	425.4
Illinois	193.5	154.9	15.5	16.4	10.4	16.3	9.8	8.2	0.1	425.3
Ohio	204.1	133.7	7.6	6.8	4.0	13.8	7.5	2.6	0.4	425.1
New Mexico	232.4	49.5	7.6	6.0	38.7	18.0	19.1	4.1	0.1	380.4
California	212.7	55.6	21.8	11.8	27.7	18.6	10.9	12.6	0.5	377.6
Virginia	172.5	129.7	17.4	16.4	6.1	16.6	6.2	5.2	0.5	372.2
Alaska	265.2	64.4	8.5	2.0	8.0	8.2	1.0	12.8	1.0	371.1
Rhode Island	209.6	42.8	15.4	8.5	16.3	16.9	1.0	3.9	44.8	370.4
Arkansas	99.2	173.7	9.6	22.3	13.7	17.6	10.8	7.9	1.1	367.9
New Jersey	128.5	94.2	40.1	14.0	7.0	18.6	7.8	8.9	25.3	355.9
Wisconsin	184.8	83.5	4.9	6.1	15.1	23.8	2.3	2.5	9.3	344.5
Pennsylvania	165.0	82.9	15.9	9.8	7.8	13.0	2.5	4.4	22.3	332.3
Kentucky	162.0	103.0	9.2	10.3	3.6	9.5	6.5	4.4	6.3	323.6
Indiana	163.7	105.0	8.9	8.9	7.5	10.1	1.5	2.9	0.5	314.8
New York State	—	123.5	72.7	31.1	13.3	19.0	9.7	12.5	0.6	309.0
Colorado	184.8	59.6	9.8	4.0	15.1	15.6	6.6	2.4	—	300.0
Hawaii	154.1	43.0	7.9	4.0	28.7	32.4	5.5	14.1	—	297.9
Nebraska	167.0	73.0	5.5	1.9	8.6	5.5	14.1	1.3	—	289.6
Kansas	154.3	67.1	6.1	5.6	11.8	17.2	5.1	3.0	0.1	285.8
Washington	170.7	35.1	11.4	2.4	20.9	12.1	5.7	5.4	0.2	270.3
Iowa	172.1	46.0	3.5	2.5	19.7	10.4	3.2	2.6	0.2	263.8
Nevada	116.4	32.7	35.3	6.1	32.0	17.4	3.1	6.7	0.3	260.3
West Virginia	171.1	52.7	7.2	1.0	2.5	7.3	1.5	3.0	0.1	249.7
South Dakota	196.5	23.4	1.5	0.9	3.8	12.2	4.2	2.6	0.6	246.9
Oregon	162.5	23.8	9.4	1.5	15.4	11.3	5.8	5.0	0.1	245.3
Massachusetts	130.5	36.4	14.1	11.9	6.2	20.6	5.2	4.4	4.8	235.4
Minnesota	141.5	51.6	4.6	2.6	6.7	13.5	2.9	3.4	5.5	234.0
Idaho	141.2	13.1	4.3	2.0	24.0	11.7	6.5	1.2	5.5	232.3
Wyoming	132.3	11.3	3.3	0.2	29.8	10.2	1.0	0.4	0.6	204.3
North Dakota	140.7	10.6	2.0	—	3.9	10.8	1.6	1.9	0.6	189.2
Montana	130.4	7.5	4.7	0.6	12.2	7.2	1.3	2.0	—	171.5
Utah	86.2	13.5	7.4	2.7	31.5	13.2	4.9	1.7	—	165.8
Maine	85.8	5.3	4.1	1.0	5.8	11.0	1.2	1.7	2.7	161.1
Vermont	73.7	9.0	4.9	0.2	5.1	14.9	1.9	1.0	1.4	118.8
New Hampshire	69.6	8.2	4.7	2.0	4.5	12.9	4.6	1.4	3.3	112.1
OTHER										
District of Columbia	580.2	861.4	188.7	121.9	12.5	21.7	8.9	20.8	1.9	1 818.0
New York City	389.5	213.3	127.7	67.8	18.7	24.6	13.1	23.7	2.4	880.7
Guam	253.8	32.4	1.4	0.7	2.1	16.6	24.1	—	—	331.0
Puerto Rico	55.5	13.7	53.3	41.2	29.2	21.9	1.8	6.7	—	223.3
Virgin Islands	12.3	35.1	86.8	8.8	29.8	8.8	1.8	0.9	—	184.2
Upstate New York	—	62.8	35.6	6.3	9.6	15.2	7.4	4.9	29.1	171.0

SOURCE: Centers for Disease Control and Prevention, National Center for Health Statistics, Division of Health Examination Statistics. Unpublished data.

— Data not available.
1. Cases were updated through the Division of Sexually Transmitted Diseases Prevention, National Center for HIV, STD, and TB Prevention (NCHSTP), as of July 13, 1998.
2. Totals reported to Division of HIV/ AIDS Prevention—Surveillance and Epidemiology, NCHSTP, as of December 31, 1997. Total includes 49 cases in persons with unknown state of residence.
3. Cases were updated through the Division of Tuberculosis Elimination, NCHSTP, as of April 15, 1998.

Table 3.37. Reported Cases of Notifiable Diseases: National Trends

Disease	1966	1967	1968	1969	1970	1971	1972	1973	1974	1975	1976
AIDS [1]	(2)	(2)	(2)	(2)	(2)	(2)	(2)	(2)	(2)	(2)	(2)
Amebiasis	2 921	3 157	3 005	2 915	2 888	2 752	2 199	2 235	2 743	2 775	2 906
Anthrax	5	2	3	4	2	5	2	2	2	2	9
Aseptic meningitis	3 058	3 082	4 494	3 672	6 480	5 176	4 634	4 846	3 197	4 475	3 510
Botulism	9	5	7	16	12	25	22	34	28	20	55
Food-borne	(3)	(3)	(3)	(3)	(3)	(3)	(3)	(3)	(3)	(3)	(3)
Infant	(3)	(3)	(3)	(3)	(3)	(3)	(3)	(3)	(3)	(3)	(3)
Brucellosis	262	265	218	235	213	183	196	202	240	310	296
Chancroid [4]	838	784	845	1 104	1 416	1 320	1 414	1 165	945	700	628
Chlamydia [5]	(2)	(2)	(2)	—	(2)	1	(2)	1	(2)	(2)	(2)
Cholera	—	—	—	—	—	—	—	—	—	—	—
Cryptosporidiosis	(3)	(3)	(3)	(3)	(3)	(3)	(3)	(3)	(3)	(3)	(3)
Diphtheria	209	219	260	241	435	215	152	228	272	307	128
Encephalitis, primary [6]	2 121	1 478	1 781	1 613	1 580	1 524	1 059	1 613	1 164	4 064	1 651
Post-infectious [6]	964	1 060	502	304	370	439	243	354	218	237	175
California	(2)	(2)	(2)	(2)	(2)	(2)	(2)	(2)	(2)	(2)	(2)
Eastern Equine	(2)	(2)	(2)	(2)	(2)	(2)	(2)	(2)	(2)	(2)	(2)
St. Louis	(2)	(2)	(2)	(2)	(2)	(2)	(2)	(2)	(2)	(2)	(2)
Escherichia coli O157: H7	(2)	(2)	(2)	(2)	(2)	(2)	(2)	(2)	(2)	(2)	(2)
NETSS [7]	—	—	—	—	—	—	—	—	—	—	—
PHLIS [8]	—	—	—	—	—	—	—	—	—	—	—
Gonorrhea [4]	351 738	404 836	464 543	534 872	600 072	670 268	767 215	842 621	906 121	999 937	100 199
Granuloma inguinale	148	154	156	154	124	89	81	62	47	60	71
Haemophilus influenzae, invasive	(2)	(2)	(2)	(2)	(2)	(2)	(2)	(2)	(2)	(2)	(2)
Hansen disease (leprosy)	109	81	123	98	129	131	130	146	118	162	145
Hepatitis A (infectious)	32 859	38 909	45 893	48 416	56 797	59 606	54 074	50 749	40 358	35 855	33 288
Hepatitis B (serum)	1 497	2 458	4 829	5 909	8 310	9 556	9 402	8 451	10 631	13 121	14 973
Hepatitis, C/ non-A, non-B [9]	(2)	(2)	(2)	(2)	(2)	(2)	(2)	(2)	(2)	(2)	(2)
Hepatitis, unspecified	(2)	(2)	(2)	(2)	(2)	(2)	(2)	(2)	(2)	7 158	7 488
Legionellosis [10]	(2)	(2)	(2)	(2)	(2)	(2)	(2)	(2)	(2)	(2)	235
Leptospirosis	72	67	69	89	47	62	41	57	68	93	73
Lyme disease	(2)	(2)	(2)	(2)	(2)	(2)	(2)	(2)	(2)	(2)	(2)
Lymphogranuloma venereum	308	371	485	520	612	692	756	408	394	353	365
Malaria	565	2 022	2 317	3 102	3 051	2 375	742	237	293	373	471
Measles (rubeola)	204 136	62 705	22 231	25 826	47 351	75 290	32 275	26 690	22 094	24 374	41 126
Indigenous	—	—	—	—	—	—	—	—	—	—	—
Imported [11]	—	—	—	—	—	—	—	—	—	—	—
Meningococcal disease	3 381	2 161	2 623	2 951	2 505	2 262	1 323	1 378	1 346	1 478	1 605
Mumps	(2)	(2)	152 209	90 918	104 953	124 939	74 215	69 612	59 128	59 647	38 492
Murine typhus fever	33	52	36	36	27	23	18	32	26	41	69
Pertussis (whooping cough)	7 717	9 718	4 810	3 285	4 249	3 036	3 287	1 759	2 402	1 738	1 010
Plague	5	3	3	5	13	2	1	2	8	20	16
Poliomyelitis, total	113	41	53	20	33	21	31	8	7	13	10
Paralytic [12]	106	40	53	18	31	17	29	7	7	13	10
Psittacosis	50	41	43	57	35	32	52	33	164	49	78
Rabies, animal	4 178	4 481	3 591	3 490	3 224	4 310	4 369	3 640	3 151	2 627	3 073
Rabies, human	1	2	1	1	3	(13)	(13)	(13)	(13)	(13)	(13)
Rheumatic fever, acute	4 472	3 985	3 470	3 229	3 227	2 793	2 614	2 560	2 431	2 854	1 865
Rocky Mountain spotted fever	268	305	298	498	380	432	523	668	754	844	937
Rubella (German measles)	46 975	46 888	49 371	57 686	56 552	45 086	25 507	27 804	11 917	16 652	12 491
Rubella, congenital syndrome	11	10	14	31	77	68	42	35	45	30	30
Salmonellosis, excluding typhoid fever	16 841	18 120	16 514	18 419	22 096	21 928	22 151	23 818	21 980	22 612	22 937
Shigellosis	11 888	13 474	12 180	11 946	13 845	16 143	20 207	22 642	22 600	16 584	13 140
Streptococcal sore throat and scarlet fever	427 752	453 351	435 013	450 008	433 405	(13)	(13)	(13)	(13)	(13)	(13)
Syphilis, all stages	105 159	102 581	96 271	92 162	91 382	95 997	91 149	87 469	83 771	80 356	71 761
Primary and secondary [4]	21 414	21 053	19 019	19 130	21 982	23 783	24 429	24 825	25 385	25 561	23 731
Congenital (< 1 year)	(2)	(2)	(2)	(2)	(2)	(2)	(2)	(2)	(2)	(2)	(2)
Tetanus	235	263	178	192	148	116	128	101	101	102	75
Toxic-shock syndrome	(2)	(2)	(2)	(2)	(2)	(2)	(2)	(2)	(2)	(2)	(2)
Trichinosis	115	66	77	215	109	103	89	102	120	252	115
Tuberculosis [14]	47 767	45 647	42 623	39 120	37 137	35 217	32 882	30 998	30 122	33 989	32 105
Tularemia	208	184	186	149	172	187	152	171	144	129	157
Typhoid fever	378	396	395	364	346	407	398	680	437	375	419
Varicella (chicken pox)	(2)	(2)	(2)	(2)	(2)	(2)	164 114	182 927	141 495	154 248	183 990
Yellow fever	(15)	(15)	(15)	(15)	(15)	(15)	(15)	(15)	(15)	(15)	(15)

See footnotes at end of table.

Table 3.37. Reported Cases of Notifiable Diseases: National Trends—*Continued*

Disease	1977	1978	1979	1980	1981	1982	1983	1984	1985	1986	1987
AIDS[1]	(2)	(2)	(2)	(2)	(2)	(2)	—	4 445	8 249	12 932	21 070
Amebiasis	3 044	3 937	4 107	5 271	6 632	7 304	6 658	5 252	4 433	3 532	3 123
Anthrax	6	2	9	1	9	9	9	1	9	9	1
Aseptic meningitis	4 789	6 573	8 754	8 028	9 547	9 680	12 696	8 326	10 619	11 374	11 487
Botulism	129	105	45	89	103	—	133	123	122	109	82
Food-borne	(3)	(3)	(3)	(3)	(3)	(3)	(3)	(3)	70	79	59
Infant	(3)	(3)	(3)	(3)	(3)	(3)	(3)	(3)	49	23	17
Brucellosis	232	179	215	183	185	173	200	131	153	106	129
Chancroid[4]	455	521	840	788	850	1 392	847	665	2 067	3 756	4 998
Chlamydia[5]	(2)	(2)	(2)	(2)	(2)	(2)	(2)	(2)	(2)	(2)	(2)
Cholera	3	12	1	9	19	5	1	1	4	23	6
Cryptosporidiosis	(3)	(3)	(3)	(3)	(3)	(3)	(3)	(3)	(3)	(3)	(3)
Diphtheria	84	76	59	3	5	2	5	1	3	—	3
Encephalitis, primary[6]	1 414	1 351	1 504	1 362	1 492	1 464	1 761	1 257	1 376	1 302	1 418
Post-infectious[6]	119	78	84	40	43	36	34	108	161	124	121
California	(2)	(2)	(2)	(2)	(2)	(2)	(2)	(2)	(2)	(2)	(2)
Eastern Equine	(2)	(2)	(2)	(2)	(2)	(2)	(2)	(2)	(2)	(2)	(2)
St. Louis	(2)	(2)	(2)	(2)	(2)	(2)	(2)	(2)	(2)	(2)	(2)
Escherichia coli O157: H7	(2)	(2)	(2)	(2)	(2)	(2)	(2)	(2)	(2)	(2)	(2)
NETSS[7]	(2)	(2)	(2)	(2)	(2)	(2)	(2)	(2)	(2)	(2)	(2)
PHLIS[8]	—	—	—	—	—	—	—	—	—	—	—
Gonorrhea[4]	1 002 219	1 013 436	1 004 058	1 004 029	990 864	960 633	900 435	878 556	911 419	900 868	780 905
Granuloma inguinale	75	72	76	51	66	17	24	30	44	61	22
Haemophilus influenzae, invasive	(2)	(2)	(2)	(2)	(2)	(2)	(2)	(2)	(2)	(2)	(2)
Hansen disease (leprosy)	151	166	185	223	256	250	259	290	361	270	238
Hepatitis A (infectious)	31 153	29 500	30 407	29 087	25 802	23 403	21 532	22 040	23 210	23 430	25 280
Hepatitis B (serum)	16 831	15 016	15 452	19 015	21 152	22 177	24 318	26 115	26 611	26 107	25 916
Hepatitis, C/ non-A, non-B[9]	(2)	(2)	(2)	(2)	(2)	(2)	3 470	3 871	4 184	3 634	2 999
Hepatitis, unspecified	8 639	8 776	10 534	11 894	10 975	8 564	7 149	5 531	5 517	3 940	3 102
Legionellosis[10]	359	761	593	475	408	654	852	750	830	980	1 038
Leptospirosis	71	110	94	85	82	100	61	40	57	41	43
Lyme disease	(2)	(2)	(2)	(2)	(2)	(2)	(2)	(2)	(2)	(2)	(2)
Lymphogranuloma venereum	348	284	250	199	263	235	335	170	226	396	303
Malaria	547	731	894	2 062	1 388	1 056	813	1 007	1 049	1 123	944
Measles (rubeola)	57 345	26 871	13 597	13 506	3 124	1 714	1 497	2 587	2 822	6 282	3 655
Indigenous	—	—	—	—	—	—	—	—	—	—	—
Imported[11]	—	—	—	—	—	—	—	—	—	—	—
Meningococcal disease	1 828	2 505	2 724	2 840	3 525	3 056	2 736	2 746	2 479	2 594	2 930
Mumps	21 436	16 817	14 225	8 576	4 941	5 270	3 355	3 021	2 982	7 790	12 848
Murine typhus fever	75	46	69	81	61	58	62	53	37	67	49
Pertussis (whooping cough)	2 177	2 063	1 623	1 730	1 248	1 895	2 463	2 276	3 589	4 195	2 823
Plague	18	12	13	18	13	19	40	31	17	10	12
Poliomyelitis, total	19	8	22	9	10	12	13	9	8	10	9
Paralytic[12]	19	8	22	9	10	12	13	9	8	10	9
Psittacosis	94	140	137	124	136	152	142	172	119	224	98
Rabies, animal	3 130	3 254	5 119	6 421	7 118	6 212	5 878	5 567	5 565	5 504	4 658
Rabies, human	(13)	(13)	(13)	(13)	(13)	(13)	(13)	(13)	(13)	(13)	(13)
Rheumatic fever, acute	1 738	851	629	432	264	137	88	117	90	147	141
Rocky Mountain spotted fever	1 153	1 063	1 070	1 163	1 192	976	1 126	838	714	760	604
Rubella (German measles)	20 395	18 269	11 795	3 904	2 077	2 325	970	752	630	551	306
Rubella, congenital syndrome	23	30	62	50	19	7	22	5	—	14	5
Salmonellosis, excluding typhoid fever	27 850	29 410	33 138	33 715	39 990	40 936	44 250	40 861	65 347	49 984	50 916
Shigellosis	16 052	19 511	20 135	19 041	19 859	18 129	19 719	17 371	17 057	17 138	23 860
Streptococcal sore throat and scarlet fever	(13)	(13)	(13)	(13)	(13)	(13)	(13)	(13)	(13)	(13)	(13)
Syphilis, all stages	64 621	64 875	67 049	68 832	72 799	75 579	74 637	69 888	67 563	68 215	86 545
Primary and secondary[4]	20 399	21 656	24 874	27 204	31 266	33 613	32 698	28 607	27 131	27 883	35 147
Congenital (< 1 year)	(2)	(2)	(2)	(2)	(2)	(2)	(2)	(2)	(2)	(2)	(2)
Tetanus	87	86	81	95	72	88	91	74	83	64	48
Toxic-shock syndrome	(2)	(2)	(2)	(2)	(2)	(2)	502	482	384	412	372
Trichinosis	143	67	157	131	206	115	45	68	61	39	40
Tuberculosis[14]	30 145	28 521	27 669	27 749	27 373	25 520	23 846	22 255	22 201	22 768	22 517
Tularemia	165	141	196	234	288	275	310	291	177	170	214
Typhoid fever	398	505	528	510	584	425	507	390	402	362	400
Varicella (chicken pox)	188 396	154 089	199 081	190 894	200 766	167 423	177 462	221 983	178 162	183 243	213 196
Yellow fever	(15)	(15)	(15)	(15)	(15)	(15)	(15)	(15)	(15)	(15)	(15)

See footnotes at end of table.

Table 3.37. Reported Cases of Notifiable Diseases: National Trends—*Continued*

Disease	1988	1989	1990	1991	1992	1993	1994	1995	1996	1997	1998
AIDS [1]	31 001	33 722	41 595	43 672	45 472	103 691	78 279	71 547	66 885	58 492	46 521
Amebiasis	2 860	3 217	3 328	2 989	2 942	2 970	2 983	(13)	(13)	(13)	(13)
Anthrax	2	—	—	—	1	—	—	—	—	—	—
Aseptic meningitis	7 234	10 274	11 852	14 526	12 223	12 848	8 932	(13)	(13)	(13)	(13)
Botulism	84	89	92	114	91	97	143	97	119	132	—
Food-borne	28	23	23	27	21	27	50	24	25	31	22
Infant	50	60	65	81	66	65	85	54	80	79	66
Brucellosis	96	95	85	104	105	120	119	98	112	98	79
Chancroid [4]	5 001	4 692	4 212	3 476	1 886	1 399	773	606	386	243	189
Chlamydia [5]	(2)	(2)	(2)	(2)	(2)	(2)	(2)	477 638	498 884	526 671	607 602
Cholera	8	—	6	26	103	18	39	23	4	6	17
Cryptosporidiosis	(2)	(2)	(2)	(2)	(2)	(2)	(2)	(2)	(2)	2 566	3 793
Diphtheria	2	3	4	5	4	—	2	—	2	4	1
Encephalitis, primary [6]	882	981	1 341	1 021	774	919	717	(13)	(13)	(13)	(13)
Post-infectious [6]	121	88	105	82	129	170	143	(13)	(13)	(13)	(13)
California	(2)	(2)	(2)	(2)	(2)	(2)	(2)	(2)	(2)	(2)	109
Eastern Equine	(2)	(2)	(2)	(2)	(2)	(2)	(2)	(2)	(2)	(2)	4
St. Louis	(2)	(2)	(2)	(2)	(2)	(2)	(2)	(2)	(2)	(2)	26
Escherichia coli O157: H7	(2)	(2)	(2)	(2)	(2)	(2)	1 420	2 139	2 741	2 555	3 161
NETSS [7]	—	—	—	—	—	—	—	—	—	—	2 172
PHLIS [8]	—	—	—	—	—	—	—	—	—	—	—
Gonorrhea [4]	719 536	733 151	690 169	620 478	501 409	439 673	418 068	392 848	325 883	324 907	355 642
Granuloma inguinale	11	7	97	29	6	19	3	(13)	(13)	(13)	(13)
Haemophilus influenzae, invasive	(2)	(2)	(2)	2 764	1 412	1 419	1 174	1 180	1 170	1 162	1 194
Hansen disease (leprosy)	184	163	198	154	172	187	136	144	112	122	108
Hepatitis A (infectious)	28 507	35 821	31 441	24 378	23 112	24 238	26 796	31 582	31 032	30 021	23 229
Hepatitis B (serum)	23 177	23 419	21 102	18 003	16 126	13 361	12 517	10 805	10 637	10 416	10 258
Hepatitis, C/ non-A, non-B [9]	2 619	2 529	2 553	3 582	6 010	4 786	4 470	4 576	3 716	3 816	3 518
Hepatitis, unspecified	2 470	2 306	1 671	1 260	884	627	444	(13)	(13)	(13)	(13)
Legionellosis [10]	1 085	1 190	1 370	1 317	1 339	1 280	1 615	1 241	1 198	1 163	1 355
Leptospirosis	54	93	77	58	54	51	38	(13)	(13)	(13)	(13)
Lyme disease	(2)	(2)	(2)	9 465	9 895	8 257	13 043	11 700	16 455	12 801	16 801
Lymphogranuloma venereum	185	189	277	471	302	285	235	(13)	(13)	(13)	(13)
Malaria	1 099	1 277	1 292	1 278	1 087	1 411	1 229	1 419	1 800	2 001	1 611
Measles (rubeola)	3 396	18 193	27 786	9 643	2 237	312	963	309	508	138	—
Indigenous	(2)	(2)	(2)	(2)	(2)	(2)	(2)	(2)	(2)	(2)	74
Imported [11]	(2)	(2)	(2)	(2)	(2)	(2)	(2)	(2)	(2)	(2)	26
Meningococcal disease	2 964	2 727	2 451	2 130	2 134	2 637	2 886	3 243	3 437	3 308	2 725
Mumps	4 866	5 712	5 292	4 264	2 572	1 692	1 537	906	751	683	666
Murine typhus fever	54	41	50	43	28	25	(13)	(13)	(13)	(13)	(13)
Pertussis (whooping cough)	3 450	4 157	4 570	2 719	4 083	6 586	4 617	5 137	7 796	6 564	7 405
Plague	15	4	2	11	13	10	17	9	5	4	9
Poliomyelitis, total	(13)	(13)	(13)	(13)	(13)	(13)	(13)	(13)	(13)	(13)	(13)
Paralytic [12]	9	(13)	(13)	(13)	(13)	(13)	(13)	(13)	(13)	(13)	(13)
Psittacosis	114	116	113	94	92	60	38	64	42	33	47
Rabies, animal	4 651	4 724	4 826	6 910	8 589	9 377	8 147	7 811	6 982	8 105	7 243
Rabies, human	—	1	—	3	1	3	6	5	3	2	1
Rheumatic fever, acute	158	144	108	127	75	112	112	(13)	(13)	(13)	(13)
Rocky Mountain spotted fever	609	623	651	628	502	456	465	590	831	409	365
Rubella (German measles)	225	396	1 125	1 401	160	192	227	128	238	181	364
Rubella, congenital syndrome	6	3	11	47	11	5	7	6	4	5	7
Salmonellosis, excluding typhoid fever	48 948	47 812	48 603	48 154	40 912	41 641	43 323	45 970	45 471	41 901	43 694
Shigellosis	30 617	25 010	27 077	23 548	23 931	32 198	29 769	32 080	25 978	23 117	23 626
Syphilis, all stages	103 437	110 797	134 255	128 569	112 581	101 259	81 696	68 953	52 976	46 540	37 977
Primary and secondary [4]	40 117	44 540	50 223	42 935	33 973	26 498	20 627	16 500	11 387	8 550	6 993
Congenital (< 1 year)	(2)	(2)	(2)	(2)	(2)	(2)	(2)	(2)	(2)	(2)	801
Tetanus	53	53	64	57	45	48	51	41	36	50	41
Toxic-shock syndrome	390	400	322	280	244	212	192	191	145	157	138
Trichinosis	45	30	129	62	41	16	32	29	11	13	19
Tuberculosis [14]	22 436	23 495	25 701	26 283	26 673	25 313	24 361	22 860	21 337	19 851	18 361
Tularemia	201	152	152	193	159	132	96	(13)	(13)	(13)	(13)
Typhoid fever	436	460	552	501	414	440	441	369	396	365	375
Varicella (chicken pox)	192 857	185 441	173 099	147 076	158 364	134 722	151 219	120 624	83 511	98 727	—
Yellow fever	(15)	(15)	(15)	(15)	(15)	(15)	(15)	(15)	1	—	—

SOURCE: Centers for Disease Control and Prevention, "Summary of Notifiable Diseases United States, 1997," *Morbidity Mortality Weekly Report* 46, no. 54 (November 20, 1998): pp. 1–87, Table 2–5. 1998 data from "Final 1998 Reports of Notifiable Diseases," *Morbidity Mortality Weekly Report* 48, no. 36 (September 17, 1999): pp. 804–805, 815–822.

* Cutaneous diptheria is no longer nationally notifiable.
— Data not available or quantity zero.
1. Acquired immunodeficiency syndrome. Totals for 1998 reported to the Division of HIV/AIDS Prevention–Surveillance and Epidemiology, National Center for HIV, STD, and TB Prevention (NCHSTP), through December 31, 1998.
2. Not previously nationally notifiable.
3. Not reported as distinct categories during this period.
4. Totals for 1998 reported to the Division of Sexually Transmitted Diseases Prevention, NCHSTP, as of July 19, 1999.
5. Chlamydia refers to genital infections caused by *C. trachomatis*. Totals for 1998 reported to the Division of Sexually Transmitted Diseases Prevention, NCHSTP, as of July 19, 1999.
6. Beginning in 1984, data reflect change in categories for tabulating encephalitis reports that were recorded by date of record to state health departments. Data for previous years are from surveillance records reported by onset date.
7. National Electronic Telecommunications System for Surveillance.
8. Public Health Laboratory Information System. Totals for 1998 reported to the National Center for Infectious Diseases as of August 26, 1999.
9. Anti-HCV antibody test was available as of May 1990.
10. Beginning in 1982, data were recorded by date of report to the state health department. Data for 1976–1981 are from surveillance records reported by onset date.
11. Imported cases include only those resulting from importation from other countries.
12. No cases of paralytic poliomyelitis caused by wild virus have been reported in the United States since 1979. Since 1989, categories other than paralytic are no longer reported. Numbers might not reflect changes because of retrospective case evaluations or late reports (see *MMWR* 1986; 35: 180–2).
13. No longer nationally notifiable.
14. Case data subsequent to 1974 are not comparable with earlier years because of changes in reporting criteria that became effective in 1975. Totals for 1998 reported to the Division of Tuberculosis Elimination, NCHSTP, as of June 3, 1999.
15. Last indigenous case of yellow fever was reported in 1911; before 1996, the last imported case was reported in 1924.

Table 3.38. AIDS Cases by Sex, Age at Diagnosis, and Race or Ethnicity: Cumulative to June 1999

Age at Diagnosis	White, Non-Hispanic		Black, Non-Hispanic		Hispanic		Asian/Pacific Islander		American Indian/ Alaska Native		Total [1]	
	Number	Percent	Number	Percent	Number	Percent	Number	Percent	Number	Percent	Number	Percent
MALE												
Under 5 years	513	0.0	2 064	1.0	755	1.0	16	0.0	12	1.0	3 364	1.0
5–12 years	334	0.0	438	0.0	277	0.0	9	0.0	4	0.0	1 064	0.0
13–19 years	829	0.0	792	0.0	469	0.0	23	1.0	19	1.0	2 134	0.0
20–24 years	7 452	3.0	6 586	3.0	3 973	4.0	156	3.0	73	4.0	18 266	3.0
25–29 years	37 007	13.0	23 902	12.0	15 511	15.0	562	12.0	307	18.0	77 384	13.0
30–34 years	66 541	23.0	40 769	21.0	25 274	24.0	985	22.0	447	27.0	134 150	23.0
35–39 years	64 874	23.0	44 016	23.0	23 520	22.0	983	22.0	374	22.0	133 954	23.0
40–44 years	47 251	17.0	34 527	18.0	16 466	16.0	780	17.0	254	15.0	99 416	17.0
45–49 years	28 426	10.0	19 971	10.0	9 203	9.0	477	11.0	103	6.0	58 257	10.0
50–54 years	15 336	5.0	10 242	5.0	4 865	5.0	251	6.0	41	2.0	30 779	5.0
55–59 years	8 320	3.0	5 630	3.0	2 700	3.0	156	3.0	26	2.0	16 860	3.0
60–64 years	4 622	2.0	3 084	2.0	1 468	1.0	65	1.0	16	1.0	9 267	2.0
65 years or older	3 826	1.0	2 573	1.0	1 179	1.0	61	1.0	9	1.0	7 657	1.0
Male subtotal	285 331	100.0	194 594	100.0	105 660	100.0	4 524	100.0	1 685	100.0	592 552	100.0
FEMALE												
Under 5 years	476	2.0	2 052	3.0	748	3.0	14	2.0	13	4.0	3 308	3.0
5–12 years	176	1.0	463	1.0	211	1.0	7	1.0	—	—	860	1.0
13–19 years	236	1.0	943	1.0	241	1.0	7	1.0	2	1.0	1 430	1.0
20–24 years	1 543	6.0	3 922	6.0	1 406	6.0	35	6.0	29	8.0	6 944	6.0
25–29 years	4 332	17.0	9 878	15.0	3 824	16.0	79	13.0	51	15.0	18 179	15.0
30–34 years	5 908	23.0	14 948	22.0	5 579	23.0	113	19.0	82	24.0	26 679	22.0
35–39 years	5 185	20.0	14 865	22.0	4 900	21.0	110	18.0	68	20.0	25 164	21.0
40–44 years	3 374	13.0	10 221	15.0	3 167	13.0	90	15.0	43	12.0	16 916	14.0
45–49 years	1 800	7.0	4 982	7.0	1 713	7.0	61	10.0	29	8.0	8 606	7.0
50–54 years	1 007	4.0	2 454	4.0	953	4.0	26	4.0	15	4.0	4 460	4.0
55–59 years	662	3.0	1 371	2.0	584	2.0	21	3.0	9	3.0	2 648	2.0
60–64 years	442	2.0	821	1.0	302	1.0	24	4.0	4	1.0	1 595	1.0
65 years or older	903	3.0	803	1.0	267	1.0	22	4.0	3	1.0	2 000	2.0
Female subtotal	26 044	100.0	67 723	100.0	23 895	100.0	609	100.0	348	100.0	118 789	100.0
TOTAL [2]	311 377		262 317		129 555		5 133		2 034		711 344	

SOURCE: Centers for Disease Control and Prevention, *HIV/AIDS Surveillance Report*, June 1999; 11, no. 1: Table 7. Cases reported through June 1999.

— Data not available.
1. Includes 758 males and 170 females whose race or ethnicity is unknown.
2. Includes three persons whose sex is unknown.

Table 3.39. AIDS Cases Reported to CDC

(Per 100,000 population; ranked by number of AIDS cases ever reported)

Area	1995 Number	1995 Rate	1996 Number	1996 Rate	1997 Number	1997 Rate	1998 Number	1998 Rate	Number ever reported Adults/ adolescents	Number ever reported Children <13 years old	Number ever reported Total
United States [1]	73 767	28.0	69 151	26.0	60 270	22.0	48 269	18.0	679 739	8 461	688 200
STATE											
New York	12 369	68.0	12 379	68.1	13 117	72.3	8 714	47.9	126 495	2 180	128 675
California	11 054	35.0	9 610	30.1	6 958	21.6	5 654	17.3	109 481	575	110 056
Florida	7 979	56.3	7 330	50.9	6 051	41.2	5 448	36.5	68 939	1 337	70 276
Texas	4 456	23.7	4 830	25.3	4 672	24.1	3 967	20.1	47 994	356	48 350
New Jersey	4 400	55.3	3 613	45.2	3 235	40.1	2 134	26.3	37 517	713	38 230
Illinois	2 215	18.8	2 199	18.6	1 833	15.3	1 304	10.8	21 442	242	21 684
Pennsylvania	2 370	19.7	2 348	19.5	1 910	15.9	1 740	14.5	20 755	285	21 040
Georgia	2 310	32.0	2 411	32.8	1 719	23.0	1 295	16.9	19 816	191	20 007
Maryland	2 567	50.9	2 253	44.4	1 851	36.3	1 639	31.9	18 430	286	18 716
Massachusetts	1 438	23.7	1 307	21.5	850	13.9	924	15.0	13 610	199	13 809
Virginia	1 605	24.3	1 195	17.9	1 175	17.4	998	14.7	11 110	159	11 269
Louisiana	1 079	24.9	1 470	33.8	1 090	25.0	951	21.8	11 018	118	11 136
Connecticut	1 645	50.3	1 112	34.0	1 221	37.4	666	20.3	10 231	173	10 404
Ohio	1 101	9.9	1 161	10.4	851	7.6	685	6.1	10 138	117	10 255
Michigan	1 193	12.5	965	10.1	880	9.0	714	7.3	9 865	104	9 969
North Carolina	1 000	13.9	895	12.2	850	11.4	788	10.4	8 838	110	8 948
Washington	882	16.2	804	14.5	634	11.3	441	7.8	8 618	33	8 651
Missouri	786	14.8	858	16.0	569	10.5	443	8.1	8 190	55	8 245
South Carolina	976	26.6	869	23.5	770	20.3	777	20.3	7 692	75	7 767
Tennessee	892	17.0	826	15.5	775	14.4	695	12.8	6 940	48	6 988
Colorado	672	17.9	522	13.7	380	9.8	314	7.9	6 416	28	6 444
Arizona	675	15.7	594	13.4	446	9.8	645	13.8	6 090	21	6 111
Indiana	523	9.0	596	10.2	519	8.8	484	8.2	5 382	37	5 419
Alabama	637	15.0	607	14.2	568	13.1	484	11.1	5 251	67	5 318
Oregon	458	14.5	463	14.5	303	9.3	204	6.2	4 349	16	4 365
Nevada	494	32.2	427	26.6	588	35.0	258	14.8	3 875	26	3 901
Mississippi	440	16.3	450	16.6	345	12.6	415	15.1	3 562	53	3 615
Minnesota	365	7.9	304	6.5	211	4.5	190	4.0	3 372	22	3 394
Oklahoma	295	9.0	272	8.2	282	8.5	285	8.5	3 274	26	3 300
Wisconsin	349	6.8	270	5.2	254	4.9	203	3.9	3 204	26	3 230
Kentucky	296	7.7	401	10.3	362	9.3	280	7.1	2 839	22	2 861
Arkansas	277	11.1	269	10.7	242	9.6	203	8.0	2 553	38	2 591
Hawaii	258	21.9	198	16.7	95	8.0	161	13.5	2 234	15	2 249
Delaware	316	44.1	285	39.3	230	31.3	174	23.4	2 163	18	2 181
Kansas	304	11.9	239	9.3	159	6.1	126	4.8	2 082	11	2 093
Rhode Island	221	22.3	178	18.0	152	15.4	128	12.9	1 839	20	1 859
New Mexico	164	9.7	205	12.0	168	9.7	209	12.0	1 812	8	1 820
Utah	164	8.4	196	9.8	152	7.4	139	6.6	1 651	21	1 672
Iowa	116	4.1	112	3.9	100	3.5	75	2.6	1 138	9	1 147
West Virginia	125	6.8	121	6.6	126	6.9	86	4.7	945	8	953
Nebraska	115	7.0	100	6.1	91	5.5	72	4.3	942	9	951
Maine	129	10.4	50	4.0	51	4.1	31	2.5	827	9	836
New Hampshire	110	9.6	93	8.0	55	4.7	42	3.5	801	8	809
Idaho	48	4.1	39	3.3	52	4.3	32	2.6	447	2	449
Alaska	69	11.5	36	5.9	51	8.4	29	4.7	435	5	440
Vermont	43	7.4	25	4.2	29	4.9	20	3.4	344	4	348
Montana	25	2.9	34	3.9	41	4.7	29	3.3	294	3	297
Wyoming	18	3.8	7	1.5	16	3.3	6	1.2	157	2	159
South Dakota	18	2.5	14	1.9	11	1.5	15	2.0	140	4	144
North Dakota	5	0.8	12	1.9	12	1.9	6	0.9	96	—	96
OTHER											
Puerto Rico	2 578	68.7	2 243	59.0	2 037	53.2	1 711	44.3	21 915	382	22 297
District of Columbia	1 027	185.2	1 262	232.3	997	188.2	989	189.1	11 228	166	11 394
Virgin Islands, U.S.	39	37.4	18	17.2	98	83.8	35	29.6	396	15	411
Guam	—	—	4	2.8	2	1.4	2	1.3	21	—	21
Pacific Islands, U.S.	—	—	1	0.4	1	0.3	—	—	4	—	4

SOURCE: Centers for Disease Control and Prevention, *HIV/AIDS Surveillance Report, 1996*; 8, no. 2 (1997): Table 1; *HIV/AIDS Surveillance Report, 1998*; 10, no. 2 (1999): Table 2.

— Data not available.
1. Includes data from the United States (50 states and the District of Columbia) and from U.S. dependencies, possessions, and independent nations in free association with the United States. Includes persons whose state of residence is unknown.

Table 3.40. Rates of Sexually Transmitted Diseases Other Than AIDS

(Per 100,000 population)

Year [1]	Syphilis all stages	Chlamydia	Gonorrhea	Chancroid	Other
1941	368.2	—	146.7	2.5	1.4
1942	363.4	—	160.9	4.1	2.3
1943	447.0	—	213.6	6.4	3.3
1944	367.9	—	236.5	6.1	3.5
1945	282.3	—	225.8	4.3	3.4
1946	271.7	—	275.0	5.2	3.5
1947	252.3	—	270.0	6.7	3.5
1948	218.2	—	239.8	5.3	3.4
1949	175.3	—	217.3	4.6	2.9
1950	146.0	—	192.5	3.3	2.2
1951	116.1	—	168.9	2.8	1.8
1952	110.2	—	160.8	2.5	1.4
1953	95.9	—	153.9	2.2	1.0
1954	82.9	—	153.5	1.9	1.0
1955	76.2	—	147.0	1.7	0.8
1956	78.7	—	135.7	1.3	0.5
1957	73.5	—	127.4	1.0	0.5
1958	66.4	—	135.6	0.9	0.5
1959	69.2	—	137.6	0.9	0.5
1960	68.8	—	145.4	0.9	0.5
1961	68.8	—	145.8	0.8	0.7
1962	68.7	—	143.6	0.7	0.5
1963	66.6	—	149.2	0.7	0.4
1964	60.4	—	159.0	0.7	0.4
1965	58.9	—	169.6	0.5	0.5
1966	54.4	—	181.9	0.4	0.6
1967	52.5	—	207.3	0.4	0.3
1968	48.8	—	235.7	0.4	0.3
1969	46.3	—	268.6	0.6	0.3
1970	45.3	—	297.2	0.7	0.4
1971	46.9	—	327.2	0.6	0.4
1972	43.9	—	369.7	0.7	0.3
1973	41.7	—	402.0	0.6	0.4
1974	39.6	—	428.2	0.4	0.2
1975	37.6	—	467.7	0.3	0.2
1976	33.2	—	464.0	0.3	0.2
1977	29.6	—	459.0	0.2	0.2
1978	29.4	—	459.0	0.2	0.1
1979	30.1	—	450.0	0.4	0.1
1980	30.5	—	445.0	0.3	0.1
1981	32.0	—	435.2	0.4	0.1
1982	32.9	—	417.9	0.6	0.1
1983	32.1	—	387.6	0.4	0.1
1984	29.8	3.2	374.8	0.3	0.1
1985	28.5	10.8	384.3	0.9	0.1
1986	28.3	24.1	372.8	1.3	0.1
1987	35.9	47.8	323.6	2.0	0.1
1988	42.5	81.8	300.3	2.0	0.1
1989	46.6	96.6	297.1	1.9	0.1
1990	54.3	161.0	277.4	1.7	0.1
1991	51.0	180.0	246.7	1.4	0.2
1992	44.3	183.4	197.1	0.7	0.1
1993	39.3	180.0	172.5	0.5	0.1
1994	31.4	194.5	165.6	0.3	0.1
1995	26.4	190.4	149.4	0.2	0.1
1996	20.1	192.9	123.2	0.1	0.0
1997	17.4	206.9	122.0	0.1	0.0
1998	14.2	236.6	132.9	0.1	0.0

SOURCE: Division of STD Prevention, U.S. Department of Health and Human Services, Public Health Service. *Sexually Transmitted Disease Surveillance, 1998.* (Atlanta, Ga.: Centers for Disease Control and Prevention (CDC), September 1999.): Table 1.

— Data not available.

1. For 1941–1946, data were reported for the federal fiscal year ending June 30 of the year indicated. From 1947 to the present, data were reported for the calendar year ending December 31. For 1941–1958, data for Alaska and Hawaii were not included.

NOTE: Adjustments to the number of cases reported from state health departments were accepted through June 15, 1999 (see Appendix of *Sexually Transmitted Disease Surveillance, 1998*). The number of cases and the rates shown here supersede those published in previous reports. Military cases are no longer categorized separately and are included with civilian cases. Georgia did not report gonorrhea statistics for 1994 (see Appendix of *Sexually Transmitted Disease Surveillance, 1998*). Cases and rates shown in this table exclude the outlying areas of Guam, Puerto Rico, and Virgin Islands.

NOTES

1. See Louis I. Dublin, *Factbook on Man: From Birth to Death*, 2d ed. (New York: Macmillan Co., 1965):103.

2. Heart disease and cancer accounted for both the largest number of deaths and the highest age-adjusted death rates. Cerebrovascular disease (stroke) accounted for the third largest number of deaths, but accidents had a higher age-adjusted death rate because most strokes occur late in life and accident rates are highest among young people.

3. Adjusting the rates for age discounts differences in age between places or groups. Older people are more likely to die because of the biological process of maturation. But this is a natural process that should apply equally to all groups. The age-adjusted death rates facilitate comparison between other factors holding age constant.

4. National Institute of Allergy and Infectious Diseases, National Institutes of Health. Fact Sheet on Tuberculosis. See <http://www.niaid.nih.gov/factsheets/tb.htm>. For the most recent CDC report on tuberculosis, see Centers for Disease Control and Prevention, *Tuberculosis in the United States, 1998.* August 1999.

5. Calculations are based on data in Table 10 of D. L. Hoyert, K. D. Kochanek, and S. L. Murphy, "Deaths: Final Data for 1997," National Vital Statistics Reports 47, no. 19 (June 30, 1999).

6. See Table 37 in A. P. MacKay, L. A. Fingerhut, and C. R. Duran, *Health, United States, 2000* (Hyattsville, Md.: National Center for Health Statistics, 2000).

7. All data in this section is from U.S. Department of Transportation, National Highway Traffic Safety Administration, *Traffic Safety Facts, 1997: A Compilation of Motor Vehicle Crash Data from the Fatality Analysis Reporting System and the General Estimates System* (Washington, D.C., 1998).

8. National Institute for Occupational Safety and Health. "Fatal Occupational Injuries—United States, 1980–1994," *Morbidity and Mortality Weekly Report* 47, no. 15 (April 24, 1998):297–302.

9. U.S. Department of Labor, Bureau of Labor Statistics, National Census of Fatal Occupational Injuries. Washington, D.C. Annual reports from 1994 to 1999.

10. L. Jenkins, "Violence in the Workplace: Risk Factors and Prevention Strategies." National Institute for Occupational Safety and Health Current Intelligence Bulletin #57, DHHS (NIOSH) Publication No. 96-100, July 1996.

11. B. A. Miller, L. N. Kolonel, and L. Bernstein et al. (eds.), *Racial/Ethnic Patterns of Cancer in the United States 1988–1992,* NIH Pub. No. 96–4104 (Bethesda, Md.: National Cancer Institute, 1996).

12. M. C. Mahoney and A. M. Michalek, "The Health Status of American Indians and Alaska Natives: 2. Lessons for Cancer Educators," *Journal of Cancer Education* 14, no. 1 (1999):23–27.

13. N. Cobb and R. W. Paisano, "Patterns of cancer mortality among Native Americans," *Cancer* 83, no. 11 (1998):2377–2383.

14. S. L. Parker, K. J. Davis, P. A. Wing, L. A. Ries, and C. W. Heath Jr., "Cancer Statistics by Race and Ethnicity," *CA: A Cancer Journal for Clinicians* 48, no. 1 (1998):31–48.

15. J. S. Kaur, "Native women and cancer." *Health Care for Women International* 20, no. 5 (1999):445–453.

16. See J. G. Collins, "Prevalence of Selected Chronic Conditions: United States, 1990–1992," *Vital and Health Statistics* 10, no. 194 (1997):4–5 for a description of the procedures used to collect data on chronic conditions in the National Health Interview Survey.

17. L. S. Geiss, M. Engelgau, E. Frazier, and E. Tierney, *Diabetes Surveillance*, 1997 (Atlanta, Ga.: DHHS, 1997). Also see Centers for Disease Control and Prevention, *Diabetes Surveillance Updates*, 1999 (Atlanta, Ga.: DHHS, 2000).

18. The CDC began collecting information on AIDS cases in the 1980s. During the epidemic, the CDC has changed the definition of an AIDS case on several occasions.

19. For the actual data, see R.K. Thomas, *Health and Health Care in the U.S.* (Lanham, Md.: Bernan, 1999).

20. Centers for Disease Control and Prevention. "Epidemiologic Notes and Follow-Up on Poliomyelitis—United States, Canada, Netherlands," *Morbidity and Mortality Weekly Report* 46, no. 50 (December 19, 1997):1195-1199. Reprinted in *Morbidity and Mortality Weekly Report* 48 (LMRK) (March 3, 1999):61–66.

21. Centers for Disease Control and Prevention. "Recommendations of the International Task Force for Disease Eradication," *Morbidity and Mortality Weekly Report* 42, no. RR-16 (December 31, 1993). Anthony S. Fauci et al. (eds.), *Harrison's Principles of Internal Medicine*, 14th ed. (New York: McGraw-Hill, 1998):1095, 1120.

22. G. Peter (ed.) See also, *1997 Red Book: Report of the Committee on Infectious Diseases*, 24th ed. (Elk Grove Village, Ill.: American Academy of Pediatrics, 1997).

23. Immunization Practices Advisory Committee (ACIP), "Update on Adult Immunization Recommendations of the ACIP," *Morbidity and Mortality Weekly Report* 40, no. RR-12 (November 15, 1991):1–52.

24. Advisory Committee on Immunization Practices (ACIP), "Recommendations of the ACIP," *Morbidity and Mortality Weekly Report* 46, no. RR-08 (April 4, 1997):1–24.

25. Centers for Disease Control and Prevention, Epidemiology Program Office, "Summary of Notifiable Diseases, United States 1998." (Tables 2 and 6.) *Morbidity and Mortality Weekly Report* 47, no. 53 (December 31, 1999):1–93.

Appropriate and timely diagnoses and treatments can reduce the development and severity of disabilities as well as prevent premature death. The care that patients receive depends on various characteristics of the patient, the particular illness or disability, and the patient's access to the health care delivery system. National health monitoring systems provide data on patient characteristics and the types of care received.

In the second half of the 20th century, access to health care improved for the very young and the very old, but a substantial proportion of adults failed to receive needed high-quality care. Although health care has improved, it is unevenly available. For example, people who do not have insurance, those with low incomes, and young adults are less likely to have a regular provider of care. Furthermore, people with no health insurance or only public insurance are more likely than others to use the emergency room as their regular source of care. (See Figure 4A.) Recently, more people are receiving health care from managed care organizations and through preferred provider networks. In fact, private health care insurance pays for physician and hospital services but covers only limited dental, home health, and nursing home care. These developments have occurred in the context of increasing expenditures, although in recent years the rate of increase has slowed.

Both low and high use of health care resources are undesirable. Low use marks inadequate access, while high use increases costs, which can lead to future restrictions. For example, high costs of care, discrimination, and inaccessibility of services could result in less use of preventive services and regular medical checkups to detect diseases in their earlier, more readily treated stages. This delay in needed treatment could result in more emergency room and hospital admissions, longer stays, and higher fatality rates because the patient shows up for treatment with a more serious medical problem. Higher use of care by a particular population group could mean that they are sicker, are more likely to seek medical care, receive poorer care, or have more care available to them. Therefore, statistical series alone may not provide a complete picture. An accurate picture requires controlled studies that account for various factors.

The volume and intensity of health care services are influenced by the severity of the patient's condition, whether medical specialists or primary care providers deliver care, and whether they practice defensive medicine to avoid threats of malpractice suits.[1] As the population increases, both the use of and expenditures for health care can be expected to increase over time. On the one hand, because rates are adjusted for population growth, they are preferred to actual numbers when comparing trends for health care services. On the other hand, health care planners need to know the demand for services in terms of the actual number of probable cases to determine the resources that will be required. Health care expenditures can be influenced by variables other than the actual number and kinds of prevention and treatment services delivered. These factors include the general inflation rate for the costs of goods and services and the medical care price inflation above general inflation.

This chapter presents data on health care use, expenditures for health care, insurance coverage, and other sources of payment for medical services. It also discusses the availability of health practitioners and other aspects of the health care system.

USE OF HEALTH CARE SERVICES

ACCESS TO CARE

The Institute of Medicine defines access to care as "the timely use of personal health services to achieve the best possible health outcomes."[2] The use of health care services is determined by a variety of factors, including access to a regular source of care for timely prevention, for screening, and for continuity of care. The source of care needs to be affordable, convenient, and responsive to the person's needs.

Most Americans have a regular source of medical care. In 1996, the predominant source of regular health care was office based, usually with a private doctor, group practice, or clinic. (See Figures 4A and 4B and Table 4A.) About half of the persons whose regular source of care was a physician's office, a hospital outpatient facility, or a free-standing urgent care clinic had access to their provider at night or on weekends; only 23.2 percent found their usual health care provider difficult to contact by telephone. (See Table 4B.) Hispanics and Blacks, however, were more likely than Whites to use hospital clinics and emergency departments for their regular source of health care. (See Table 4.1.)

In 1996, over 46 million Americans did not have a regular source of medical care. (See Table 4.1.) The reasons such people usually gave for having no regular source of care were that they could not pay for the care or that they did not need a doctor. Some said that they did not know where to go or that no source of care was available or convenient. A small percentage reported that they did not like, trust, or believe in doctors. (See Table 4D.)

Studies show that both the youngest and oldest individuals in our society have more access to health care than adults in the middle age groups. Surprisingly, the age group most likely to be in the workforce is that most likely to report no regular source of medical care. In this working-age group, people of higher income are more likely to report no regular source of medical care because they believe that they do not need one.

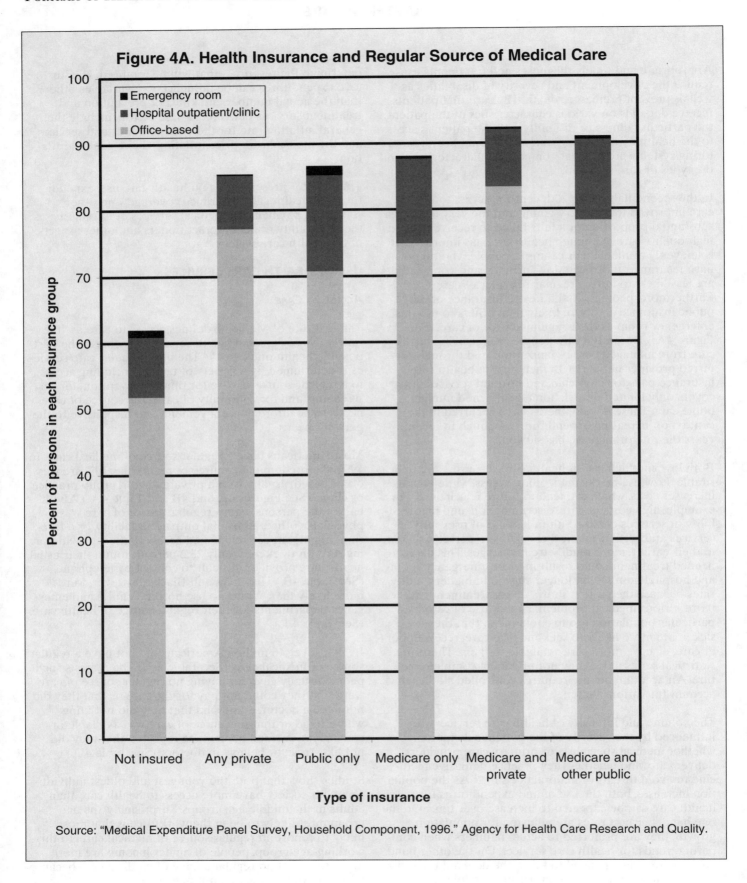

Figure 4A. Health Insurance and Regular Source of Medical Care

■ Emergency room
■ Hospital outpatient/clinic
■ Office-based

Percent of persons in each insurance group (y-axis)

Type of insurance (x-axis)

Not insured · Any private · Public only · Medicare only · Medicare and private · Medicare and other public

Source: "Medical Expenditure Panel Survey, Household Component, 1996." Agency for Health Care Research and Quality.

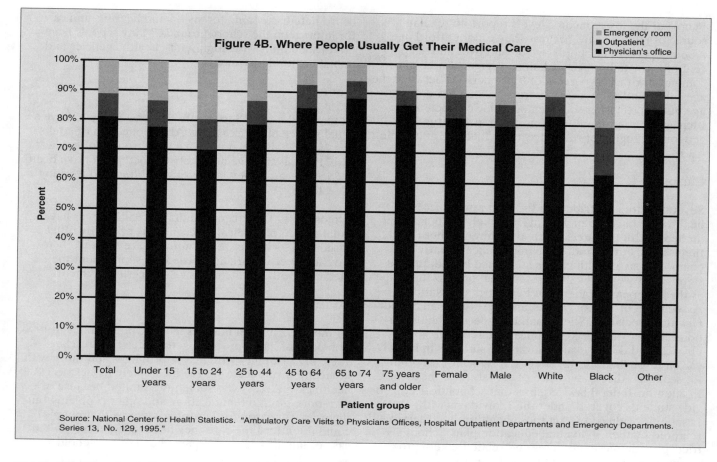

Figure 4B. Where People Usually Get Their Medical Care

Source: National Center for Health Statistics. "Ambulatory Care Visits to Physicians Offices, Hospital Outpatient Departments and Emergency Departments. Series 13, No. 129, 1995."

Table 4A. Regular Source of Care by Age: 1996

(Percent, except where noted)

Age	Number		Place of regular source of care			
	Population	No usual source of care	No usual source of care	Office based	Hospital outpatient or clinic	Emergency room
All ages	262 654 000	46 227 104	17.6	72.7	9.2	0.5
0–5 years	24 164 000	1 329 020	5.5	83.8	10.1	*0.5
6–17 years	47 253 000	4 914 312	10.4	80.2	9.0	*0.4
18–24 years	24 854 000	8 450 360	34.0	57.4	7.6	*1.0
25–54 years	114 359 000	25 959 493	22.7	68.1	8.8	0.4
55–64 years	22 899 000	3 022 668	13.2	75.2	10.9	*0.7
65 years and over	31 125 000	2 863 500	9.2	80.3	10.1	*0.4

SOURCE: R.M. Weinick, S.H. Zuvekas, and S. Drilea, *Access to Health Care—Sources and Barriers, 1996,* (Rockville, Md.: Agency for Health Care Policy and Research, Center for Cost and Financing Studies—Medical Expenditure Panel Survey, Household Component, 1996): Table 1.

*Figure does not meet standard of reliability or precision; relative standard error is greater than or equal to 30%.

NOTE: The survey was restricted to the civilian, noninstitutionalized population of the United States. Percents may not add to 100 because of rounding. The total includes persons with unknown health status and those few individuals age 65 and over who did not have Medicare. Total excludes a small number of persons who were eligible for data collection in the first half of 1996 but died or were institutionalized in the second half of the year. Office-based includes all types of physicians and nonphysician providers seen in an office setting as well as office-based group practices or clinics. Hospital outpatient department or clinic includes outpatient departments and clinics owned and operated by hospitals. The agency named in the source became the Agency for Healthcare Research and Quality in December 1999. It is part of the U.S. Department of Health and Human Services.

Table 4B. When Regular Care is Available: 1996

Characteristics of usual source of care	Percent	Population
Has office hours at night or on weekends	48.6	104 676 000
Usually sees patients by appointment	76.3	164 137 000
Somewhat difficult or very difficult to contact by telephone	23.2	49 904 000

SOURCE: R.M. Weinick, S.H. Zuvekas, and S. Drilea, *Access to Health Care—Sources and Barriers,* 1996 (Rockville, Md.: Agency for Health Care Policy and Research, Center for Cost and Financing Studies—Medical Expenditure Panel Survey, Household Component, Rounds 1 and 2, 1996).

NOTE: The survey was restricted to the civilian, noninstitutionalized population of the United States. This table does not include persons whose usual source of care is an emergency room.

221

People at the lower income levels report no regular source of medical care because they cannot afford one. About 9 percent of people age 65 and over and 5.5 percent of those under age six had no regular source of care compared with 17.3 percent of those persons between the ages of 18 and 64. Access to care is related not only to age but also to other sociodemographic characteristics, such as sex, race, family income, insurance status, and geographic region of residence. (See Table 4C and Table 4.3.)

CHILDREN

Several factors contribute to the high rate of access to health care in children. Parents are likely to spend their limited health resources on their children rather than themselves. Furthermore, the importance of early and comprehensive health care is addressed by federal and state law as well as health professional organizations such as the American Academy of Pediatrics, the National Association of School Nurses, and the American School Health Association. States mandate specific immunizations against various communicable diseases as well as physical and dental examinations for students in kindergarten through grade 12. Some states include screening for scoliosis (that is, evidence of curvature of the spine). In addition, federal law requires that school districts provide students covered under the Individuals with Disabilities Education Act those health-related services required by their individual education plan. School districts provide these measures and related school programs in the interest of public health as well as to remove or deal with health-related barriers to learning.

School-age children can take advantage of school health services provided by the school nurse or health technicians. Some school districts routinely provide services such as emergency first aid, health education programs, coordinated screening for vision and hearing, and care for injuries on the school grounds. Many schools have established links with community health agencies and public health departments.

ADULTS

Young adults, age 18 to 24, are the least likely to have a usual source of medical care. About one-fifth of adults age 25 to 54 also do not have a usual source of medical care. Persons this age are likely to need preventive health services because they are raising children and working. (See Table 4A.)

Almost all (90.8 percent) adults age 65 and over have a usual source of medical care, and it is primarily office based. Adults in this age group who are most likely to have a source of care are those who supplement their Medicare with private or other sources of payment.

FAMILIES

Of the 110.2 million families in the United States in 1996, 11.6 percent had a problem getting health care. (See Table 4D.) Families with health problems and those with no health insurance were the most likely to lack access to health care. Access was sometimes limited because of transportation, communication, and other problems, but the primary reason for lack of access was that people could not afford the care they needed, especially in the case of families with a Hispanic head of household.

The source of regular care differs for Americans, depending on their racial and ethnic group. A special study of access to care in 1993 found that Whites were more likely than Blacks and Hispanics to receive their regular care from a private doctor. Blacks and Hispanics were more likely than Whites to receive their care at clinics and

Table 4C. Regular Source of Care by Insurance Status: 1996

(Percent)

Health insurance status	No usual source	Office based	Outpatient	Emergency room
UNDER AGE 65				
Any private	14.5	77.2	8.1	0.2
Public only	13.3	70.8	14.5	1.4
Not insured	38.0	51.8	9.1	1.1
AGE 65 AND OVER				
Medicare only	11.9	74.9	12.8	0.4
Medicare and private	7.5	83.4	8.7	0.3
Medicare and other public	8.9	78.3	10.4	0.5

SOURCE: R.M. Weinick, S.H. Zuvekas, and S. Drilea, *Access to Health Care—Sources and Barriers*, 1996 (Rockville, Md.: Agency for Health Care Policy and Research, Center for Cost and Financing Studies—Medical Expenditure Panel Survey, Household Component, 1996, Rounds 1 and 2, 1996).

Table 4D. Difficulty Finding Health Care: 1996

(Percent of families, except where noted)

Family characteristics	Total number of families	Percent with any problem	Percent distribution of main problems		
			Cannot afford care	Insurance related	Other problems
Total	110 207 000	11.6	59.9	19.5	20.7
RACE / ETHNICITY OF HEAD OF FAMILY					
White	88 029 000	11.4	58.5	20.9	20.6
Black	12 770 000	9.9	60.4	12.3	27.3
Hispanic	9 408 000	15.1	69.1	15.8	15.0
PERCEIVED HEALTH STATUS					
All family members in good to excellent health	86 938 000	9.9	59.3	20.3	20.4
Any family member in fair or poor health	23 227 000	17.9	60.9	17.9	21.3
HEALTH INSURANCE STATUS OF FAMILY					
All members, private insurance	68 539 000	7.0	36.7	32.2	31.1
All members, public insurance	12 495 000	12.2	46.2	21.8	32.0
All members, not insured	12 125 000	27.1	87.0	6.0	7.0
Some private, some not insured	8 006 000	18.1	77.4	14.2	*8.5
Some public, some not insured	4 250 000	21.8	80.8	*2.5	16.7
Some private, some public	3 830 000	12.6	—	—	—
Some private, some public, some not insured	962 000	27.5	—	—	—
METROPOLITAN STATISTICAL AREA (MSA)					
MSA	87 972 000	11.5	59.4	19.9	20.7
Not MSA	22 235 000	12.0	61.6	17.9	20.6

SOURCE: R.M. Weinick, S.H. Zuvekas, and S. Drilea, *Access to Health Care—Sources and Barriers,* 1996 (Rockville, Md.: Agency for Health Care Policy and Research 1997. Medical Expenditure Panel Survey, Household Component, 1996, MEPS Research Findings No. 3 AHCPR Pub. No. 98-0001): Table 4.

* Figure does not meet standard of reliability or precision, relative standard error is greater than or equal to 30%.
— Sample size is too small for a reliable estimate.

NOTE: Insurance-related reasons include insurance company would not approve, cover, or pay for care; preexisting condition; insurance required a referral but could not get one; and doctor refused to accept family's insurance plan. Other problems include transportation problems, physical problems, communication problems and other problems. Transportation problems included medical care was too far away, cannot drive or do not have car, no public transportation available, and too expensive to get there. Physical problems included hard to get into building, hard to get around inside building, and no appropriate equipment in office. Communication problems included hearing impairment or loss and different language. Other problems included could not get time off work, did not know where to go to get care, was refused service, could not get child care and did not have time or took too long. Health insurance status refers to status during the first half of 1996. Not insured refers to person uninsured during the entire period. Public and private insurance categores refer to persons with public or private insurance at any time during the period. Persons with both public and private insurance are considered privately insured. CHAMPUS and CHAMPVA (Armed Forces–related coverage) are considered private health insurance for this table.

emergency rooms. Among children, for example, 25.3 percent of the Blacks and 25 percent of the Hispanics received their regular medical care in a clinic compared with 5 percent of the Whites. In general, the children most likely to receive their regular medical care in a clinic were those living in central cities (about 20 percent), those not living with both parents (about 22 percent), and those with family incomes under $10,000 (about 32 percent) or $10,000–$19,999 (about 20 percent). (See Table 4.2.) In addition, non-Hispanic Black children were more likely than any other group to receive their regular medical care in an emergency room.[3]

The average American has about 5.9 contacts (in person or by telephone) with a doctor in a year as an outpatient for examination, diagnosis, treatment, or advice. (See Table 4.4.) The doctor or another person working under the doctor's supervision may provide the service. More than three of those contacts were visits to the doctor's office, 0.8 were on the telephone, 0.7 were in the hospital, and 1.1 were in other settings. These contacts included primarily physicians in general and family practice, internists, and pediatricians. The primary reasons for doctor visits were general medical examinations, respiratory problems, routine prenatal examinations, and followup care after surgery.[4]

About 68 percent of the people with an acute condition receive some kind of health care. Conditions most likely to receive medical care include injuries, eye problems, acute ear infections, acute urinary conditions, pregnancy, acute respiratory disorders, and acute skin conditions. (See Table 4.5.) Almost all persons with injuries and these conditions were likely to receive care, regardless of income or other sociodemographic characteristics. Conditions less likely to receive medical care include intestinal virus, influenza, and digestive upset characterized by indigestion, nausea, and vomiting.[5] Such digestive symptoms, however, may indicate a serious gastrointestinal illness that could result in hospitalization and even death. (See Table 4.6.) Children under 5 years and people age 65 and older were more likely to be treated for their acute conditions than younger adults.

Chronic conditions, like asthma, are treated both in the doctor's office and in the emergency room and hospital. (See Tables 4.7 and 4.8.)

OUTPATIENT CARE

More procedures, including surgery that used to be conducted in hospitals, are now performed on an outpatient basis. For example, about half of the surgical procedures performed in 1996 were on an outpatient basis. (See Table 4.9.) Office visits now include more than the usual medical examinations, blood pressure readings, psychotherapy, and specimen gathering for urinalysis, strep test, or pregnancy test. Now, patients can go to the doctor's office for tests using new technology, such as electrocardiogram, mammography, magnetic resonance imaging, and computerized axial tomography scan.

Blacks are more likely than Whites to receive their outpatient care in an emergency department. Older persons are more likely than younger persons to receive their care in a doctor's office. (See Table 4.10.)

INPATIENT HOSPITAL CARE

Only about 7 percent of the population receives treatment in a short-stay hospital, as reported in the 1996 National Health Interview Survey. (See Table 4.11.) About 19.4 million persons were reported to have had at least one hospitalization in the past year. When hospitalizations based on the delivery of children were excluded, hospitalization was associated with older age groups (age 65 and older) but not gender, region, or population density. In the general population age 45 to 64, 7.8 percent had been hospitalized at least once in the past year. Among Blacks age 45 to 64, 10.1 percent had been hospitalized. Among persons age 45 to 64 with a family income under $10,000, 14.6 percent had been hospitalized; 12.5 percent had been hospitalized among those with a family income of $10,000 to $19,999. Persons age 45 to 64 with higher family incomes were less likely to have been hospitalized: 8.7 percent of those with family incomes of $20,000 to $34,999, and 6 percent of those with family incomes of $35,000 or more.

Based on data collected by the American Hospital Association (AHA) for the federal government, the rate of admissions to community hospitals and average length of stay has tended to decrease between 1994 and 1997. Furthermore, on the basis of these data, the Health Care Financing Administration (HCFA) estimates that in 1997 the average hospital expenses were $1,202 per inpatient day and $224 per outpatient visit. The AHA collected these data from its National Hospital Panel Survey, a sample of about one-third of all U.S. community hospitals. (See Table 4.12.)

In 1996, there were about 34.9 million discharges from short-stay community hospitals. The average age for hospital discharges was 47.1 years. The leading conditions for hospital discharges were circulatory system diseases (18.7 percent), complications of pregnancy (12.5 percent), perinatal conditions (11.3 percent), and respiratory diseases (9.3 percent). The most fatal principal diagnosis was an infectious or parasitic disease. More than 10 percent of those hospitalized with this diagnosis died compared with 6 percent of those diagnosed with neoplasms (cancer) and 5.8 percent of those diagnosed with a respiratory disease. (See Table 4E.) Neoplasms and infectious and parasitic diseases also were among the most costly. (See Figure 4C.) Only congenital anomalies, with an average hospital charge of $23,193, had a higher charge than neoplasms ($16,034). Infectious and parasitic diseases ranked a close third place at $15,760. Infectious or parasitic diseases also had relatively longer average lengths of stay (7.7 days), exceeded only by mental disorders (8.4 days) and a catchall category of symptoms, signs, and ill-defined conditions and factors influencing health status (8.2 days). (See Figure 4D.) The principal diagnosis at discharge is based on evaluation of the patient while hospitalized and indicates the best medical judgment for the primary reason the patient was hospitalized. (See Table 4.14.)

Table 4E. Principal Diagnosis for Hospital Discharges: 1996

Diagnosis	Discharges		Mean charges	Mean length of stay (days)	Percent died	Patient's mean age
	Number	Percent				
All discharges	34 872 474	100.0	10 647	5.0	2.5	47.1
Infectious and parasitic diseases	738 424	2.1	15 760	7.7	10.3	53.4
Neoplasms	2 027 921	5.8	16 034	6.3	6.0	60.0
Respiratory system diseases	3 235 193	9.3	11 787	5.9	5.8	54.6
Circulatory system diseases	6 522 102	18.7	14 826	5.3	4.2	67.8
Endocrine, nutritional, and metabolic diseases and immunity disorders	1 059 659	3.0	8 845	5.2	2.3	54.0
Unclassified conditions	43 572	0.1	7 704	4.2	2.3	54.7
Digestive system diseases	3 001 774	8.6	11 569	5.1	2.2	55.5
Circulatory system diseases	281 881	0.8	10 075	5.1	1.9	48.9
Injury and poisoning	2 718 444	7.8	14 646	5.4	1.9	53.1
Congenital anomalies	108 510	0.3	23 193	5.9	1.6	16.2
Ill-defined conditions	979 806	2.8	11 132	8.2	1.6	61.1
Nervous system diseases	681 769	2.0	9 598	5.0	1.4	48.7
Genitourinary system diseases	1 592 254	4.6	8 382	3.9	1.4	53.7
Skin diseases	423 323	1.2	9 516	6.3	1.1	54.7
Musculoskeletal diseases	1 391 458	4.0	14 032	4.7	0.4	59.2
Perinatal conditions	3 948 024	11.3	3 786	3.0	0.4	0.0
Mental disorders	1 759 206	5.0	7 517	8.4	0.2	43.0
Pregnancy and childbirth	4 346 935	12.5	4 528	2.2	0.0	27.1

SOURCE: Agency for Healthcare Research and Quality (AHRQ), Healthcare Cost and Utilization Project (HCUP), Hospital Inpatient Statistics, 1996: Table 1.

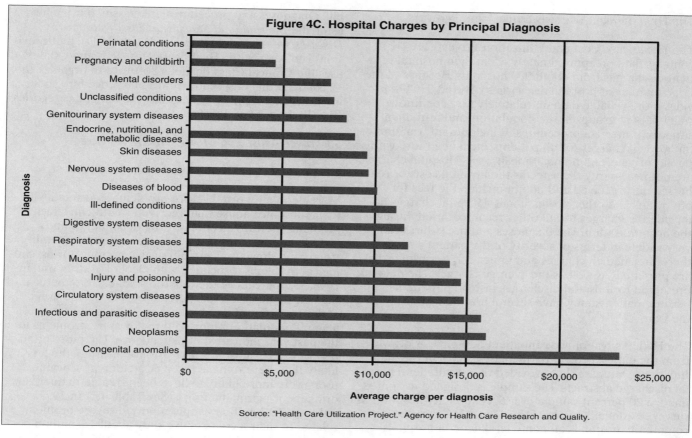

Figure 4C. Hospital Charges by Principal Diagnosis

Source: "Health Care Utilization Project." Agency for Health Care Research and Quality.

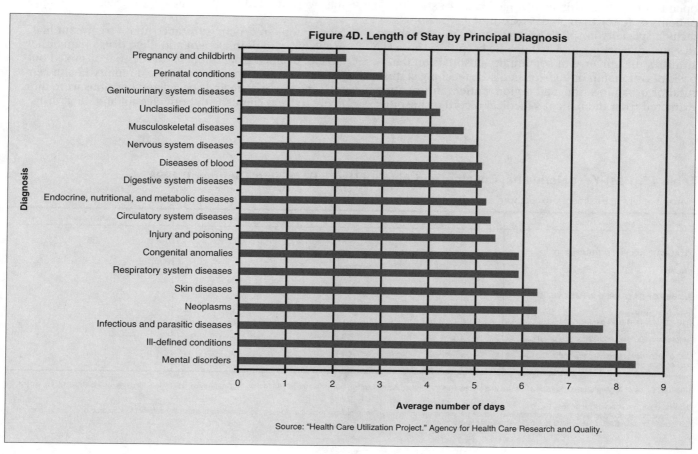

Figure 4D. Length of Stay by Principal Diagnosis

Source: "Health Care Utilization Project." Agency for Health Care Research and Quality.

THE HEALTHCARE COST AND UTILIZATION PROJECT

The Healthcare Cost and Utilization Project (HCUP) contains data on approximately 6.5 million hospital inpatient discharges from about 900 hospitals. Because of the large number of hospital discharges covered, HCUP provides more reliable data on relatively rare conditions, small patient groups in the population, and infrequent surgical or medical procedures. It includes information on hospital charges for all patients, including those with public, private, and no health insurance. Hospital charges are not necessarily the same as the hospital costs or reimbursements received and do not include the fees for physicians and other professionals. Hospital charges do include the charges for all other resources used during the hospitalization. The diagnoses and procedures can vary widely in terms of severity of the patient's condition; therefore, median charges and upper and lower quartiles are presented as well as the average charges. The data are presented for hospital discharges instead of patients because patients may have several hospitalizations during the year.

The HCUP's Nationwide Inpatient Sample was drawn from the data sets of 19 participating states in the State Inpatient Database that provided their nonfederal hospital discharge abstracts. The sample is designed to approximate a 20 percent sample of U.S. community hospitals as surveyed annually by the AHA. The AHA classifies as community hospitals all nonfederal general hospitals open to the public with an average length of stay for patients of fewer than 30 days. Community hospitals include specialty hospitals such as rehabilitation, obstetrics and gynecology, and orthopedic hospitals. The AHA stratifies the universe of community hospitals on the basis of ownership or control, bed size, teaching status, rural or urban location, and region. Patient information is extracted from the patient's medical record or hospital

bill. Diagnoses and procedures are classified originally using the *International Statistical Classification of Diseases, Injuries, and Causes of Death* (ICD), ninth revision. The Agency for Healthcare Research and Quality uses the Clinical Classifications Software to organize the 12,000 *ICD* diagnosis codes and 3,500 procedure codes into a smaller number of clinically meaningful categories. (See Tables 4.14 and 4.15.)

SUBSTANCE ABUSE AND MENTAL HEALTH SERVICES

TREATMENT FOR ALCOHOL AND ILLICIT DRUG ABUSE

More people reported severe problems associated with their substance abuse than received treatment.[6] Such problems indicate alcohol or drug dependence and include tolerance for the substance's effect; an inability to stop or cut down use; and physical, emotional, or psychological problems associated with alcohol or drug use. In 1998, 33.7 percent of the tobacco smokers, 17.4 percent of the marijuana users, 18.0 percent of the cocaine users, and 7.7 percent of the drinkers age 12 and over in the general population reported three or more problems in the past year indicative of dependence. The more often people used a substance like alcohol or drugs, the less likely they were to have received treatment. Cocaine users were more likely to have been treated than either drinkers or marijuana users. (See Table 4F.) In 1999, although 10.3 million people reported severe problems related to their alcohol abuse, only about 1.7 million persons were treated for their alcohol or drug dependence.

More people receiving substance abuse treatment had problems with both alcohol and illicit drugs than either alcohol or illicit drugs alone.[7] Residential or mixed outpatient and residential facilities, community health centers, and psychiatric and specialized hospitals were more likely to treat clients with both alcohol and illicit drug

Table 4F. Past-Year Marijuana, Cocaine, and Alcohol Users Receiving Treatment: 1998

(Percent receiving treatment 1, except where noted)

Frequency of drug use	Marijuana users	Cocaine users	Alcohol users
TOTAL WHO RECEIVED TREATMENT			
Number	701 000	375 000	1 664 000
Percent	3.7	9.9	1.2
NUMBER OF DAYS USED IN PAST YEAR			
Fewer than 12 days	3.0	8.5	0.6
12–50 days (1–4 days per month)	2.8	10.3	0.9
51–300 days (1–6 days per week)	4.6	*	2.1
More than 300 days (daily or almost daily)	6.3	*	2.0
12 or more days (1+ days per month)	4.3	12.0	1.5
51 or more days (1+ days per week)	5.1	*	2.0

SOURCE: Office of Applied Studies, Substance Abuse and Mental Health Services Administration, National Household Survey on Drug Abuse, 1998 Main Findings, 1999: Table 12.3 and 12.4.

* Low precision, no estimate reported.
1. The percentage receiving drug abuse treatment may include people receiving treatment for problems related to drug abuse, as well as to those in treatment to stop drug use. This category may also include some individuals who have also received alcohol abuse treatment.

problems. Clients in private for-profit facilities and outpatient specialty substance abuse treatment facilities were more likely to abuse only illicit drugs. Facilities operated by the Department of Defense or the Indian Health Service or tribal governments were more likely to have a high proportion of clients receiving treatment for only alcohol. (See Table 4.16.)

TREATMENT FOR MENTAL ILLNESS

Most persons with psychological or emotional difficulties do not receive treatment; those who do are more likely to receive treatment on an outpatient basis. Among adolescents age 12 to 17 in the general population, 4.8 percent (about 1 million adolescents) received treatment for psychological problems or emotional difficulties on an outpatient basis in the past year in the specialty mental health sector (that is, by a mental health professional or at a mental health clinic or facility). Among adults age 18 and older, 4.7 percent (about 8.7 million adults) received such treatment for their psychological problems or emotional difficulties. Adults with agoraphobia were less likely to have received treatment. In fact, studies show that only 15 percent of those with agoraphobia reported receiving outpatient mental health treatment in the past year as compared to 23 percent of those with a major depressive episode, 27 percent with a generalized anxiety disorder, and 27 percent of those with a panic attack.

Overall only about 19 percent of the adults reporting one or more of those four mental syndromes received treatment.[8]

Some individuals have a mental disorder that is serious enough to be treated on a hospital inpatient basis or in a mental health residential treatment organization. The rate of persons receiving residential mental health care decreased markedly, from 236.8 per 100,000 population in 1969 to 91.1 per 100,000 population in 1994. (See Table 4.17.) As shown in Figures 4E and 4F, there has been a major move away from institutionalization of persons with serious mental disorders. In 1969, 78.5 percent of the hospitalized patients were receiving their care in state and county mental hospitals. By 1994, only 30.6 percent of the patients were in state and county mental hospitals. More persons are now receiving residential mental health care in private psychiatric hospitals and other mental health settings, such as free-standing psychiatric partial-care organizations, free-standing outpatient clinics, and multiservice mental health organizations.

Between 1969 and 1994, the percentage of persons receiving inpatient care in private psychiatric hospitals increased from 2.3 percent to 11.2 percent. The percentage of persons in residential treatment centers for emotionally disturbed children also increased from 2.9 percent in 1969 to 12.5 percent in 1994. The greatest change,

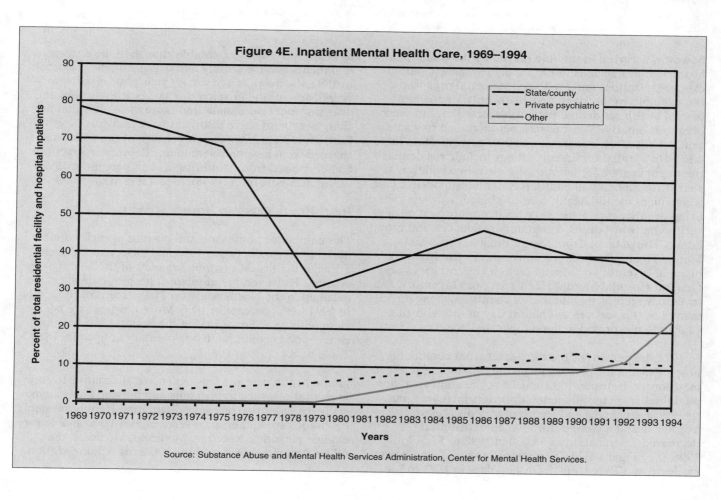

Figure 4E. Inpatient Mental Health Care, 1969–1994

Source: Substance Abuse and Mental Health Services Administration, Center for Mental Health Services.

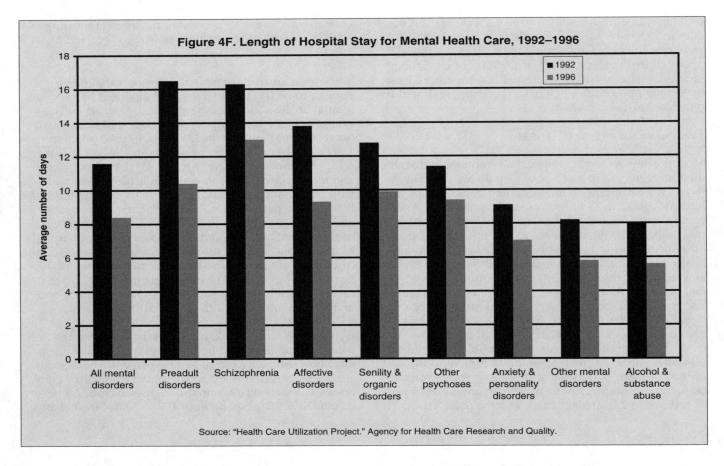

Figure 4F. Length of Hospital Stay for Mental Health Care, 1992–1996

Source: "Health Care Utilization Project." Agency for Health Care Research and Quality.

however, occurred in the role played by the other mental health settings, such as free-standing psychiatric partial-care organizations and multiservice mental organizations. For example, in the 1960s and 1970s, only 1 percent of mental health residential patients received care in such organizations. By 1986, this number increased to 8.5 percent, and by 1994, it increased to 20.9 percent. (See Table 4.17.) Residential treatment settings include residential treatment centers for emotionally disturbed children as well as for mentally ill adults. Residential supportive care is overnight mental health care combined with supervised living or other supportive services in nonhospital settings, such as halfway houses, community residences, and group homes. The data are from the Substance Abuse and Mental Health Services Administration's (SAMHSA) biennial Inventory of Mental Health Organizations and General Hospital Mental Health Services Inventory. The inventory records the number of clients receiving direct mental health services on the last day of the reporting year so that it provides an unduplicated count of clients.

In 1992, 4.3 percent of the discharges from community hospitals were for persons receiving treatment for a mental disorder. Between 1992 and 1996, the number of hospital discharges for all mental disorders increased, but the average charges and length of stay decreased. The average hospital charges for all mental disorders decreased 7 percent, from $8,050 in 1992 to $7,517 in 1996. (See Figure 4G.) The average length of stay, however, decreased 28 percent, from 11.6 days in 1992 to 8.4

days in 1996. The most notable change in the average age of patients was for senility and organic mental disorders. In 1992, the average age was 69 years; by 1996, it was 74 years. More of the hospital discharges with alcohol and drug disorders were male, and more of the hospital discharges with affective disorders were female. Furthermore, in 1996, the percentage of the males discharged from hospitals with manic depressive psychosis had decreased from that in 1992 (42.8 percent in 1992 versus 36.5 percent in 1996). (See Table 4G.)

HOME HEALTH CARE AND HOSPICE SERVICES

The number of home care and hospice agencies doubled in the five years between 1991 and 1996, making such agencies the fastest-growing segment of the health care system.[9] However, the number of hospice care agencies declined in the Northeast from 24.8 percent of the total in 1994 to 9.7 percent in 1996. More hospice care agencies continue to be located in the South. Most hospice care agencies continue to be voluntary nonprofits. (See Table 4.18.)

Home health care is a less-expensive alternative to care in institutions such as hospitals and nursing homes, especially for older persons with disabilities. Reimbursement for home care and hospice services may be available for eligible persons covered by Medicaid, Medicare, the Older Americans Act, and the Veterans Administration.

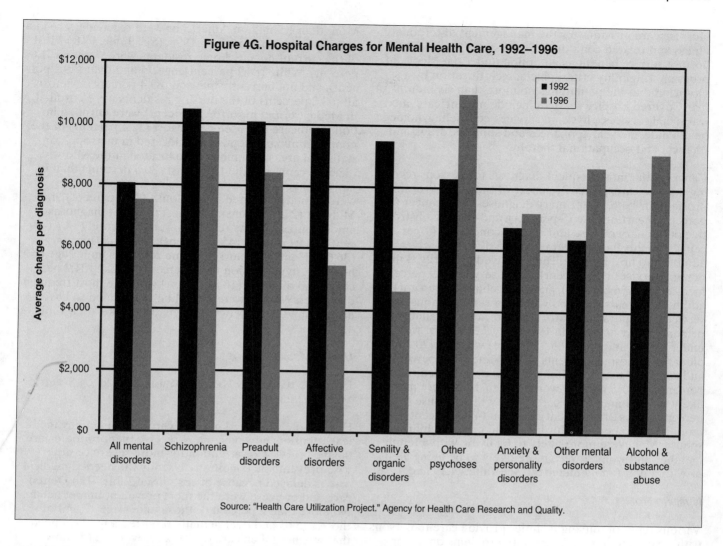

Figure 4G. Hospital Charges for Mental Health Care, 1992–1996

Source: "Health Care Utilization Project." Agency for Health Care Research and Quality.

Table 4G. Hospitalization for Mental Disorders

Principal Diagnosis	Number of discharges		Percent of discharges		Mean charges ($)		Mean length of stay (days)		Percent male		Mean age	
	1992	1996	1992	1996	1992	1996	1992	1996	1992	1996	1992	1996
All mental disorders	1 510 162	1 759 206	4.31	5.04	8 050	7 517	11.6	8.4	50.2	50.8	43.0	43.0
Mental retardation	461	636	*	*		9 584	*	10.6	*	63.2	*	36.0
Alcohol and substance-related mental disorders	429 911	513 099	1.23	1.47	5 071	4 631	8.0	5.6	70.0	68.2	39.0	40.0
Alcohol-related mental disorder	290 550	277 610	0.83	0.80	5 052	5 048	7.9	6.0	72.6	73.4	41.0	42.0
Substance-related mental disorder	139 361	235 490	0.40	0.68	5 110	4 142	8.3	5.1	64.7	62.1	35.0	36.0
Opioid dependence	24 828	49 373	0.07	0.14	4 433	3 588	6.8	4.6	65.9	63.7	35.0	36.0
Cocaine dependence	45 940	58 519	0.13	0.17	5 186	3 946	9.4	5.4	67.8	63.7	32.0	34.0
Senility and organic mental disorders	106 695	134 427	0.30	0.39	9 500	9 733	12.8	9.9	46.2	43.1	69.0	74.0
Affective disorders	467 113	574 133	1.33	1.65	9 900	8 435	13.8	9.3	36.2	37.6	44.0	43.0
Major depressive disorder, single episode ...	159 640	167 354	0.46	1.65	9 601	7 386	13.2	8.0	37.6	39.5	42.0	41.0
Major depressive disorder, recurrent	154 517	219 637	0.44	0.63	10 692	8 743	14.7	9.6	31.8	34.4	48.0	45.0
Neurotic depression	29 981	24 043	0.09	0.07	6 597	5 451	9.5	6.5	36.4	36.4	34.0	34.0
Bipolar affective disorder	107 331	145 908	0.31	0.42	10 279	9 665	14.6	10.8	39.3	40.2	44.0	35.0
Manic-depressive psychosis	8 469	8 754	0.02	0.03	9 336	8 531	13.3	9.8	42.8	36.5	41.0	42.0
Other affective disorders	7 176	8 436	0.02	0.02	8 103	8 339	11.4	9.0	41.6	41.7	45.0	43.0
Schizophrenia and related disorders	221 902	248 833	0.63	0.71	10 465	11 048	16.3	13.0	53.4	55.2	40.0	41.0
Paranoid schizophrenia	88 837	86 805	0.25	0.25	9 925	11 664	16.1	13.9	60.1	61.6	40.0	42.0
Schizo-affective type	75 853	100 449	0.22	0.29	10 856	10 804	16.1	12.5	44.4	47.0	40.0	41.0
Other schizophrenia	59 212	61 579	0.17	0.18	10 768	10 577	16.8	12.7	54.9	59.7	40.0	41.0
Other psychoses	55 577	59 908	0.16	0.17	8 300	8 693	11.4	9.4	44.2	47.2	55.0	49.0
Anxiety, somatoform, dissociative, and personality disorders	66 590	64 904	0.19	0.19	6 746	7 209	9.1	7.0	34.5	37.5	38.0	40.0
Pre-adult disorders	16 833	17 593	0.05	0.05	10 076	9 138	16.5	10.4	71.1	76.8	13.0	13.0
Other mental conditions	144 774	145 183	0.41	0.42	6 368	5 441	8.2	5.8	42.0	45.0	33.0	33.0

SOURCE: Agency for Healthcare Research and Quality (AHRQ). Healthcare Cost and Utilization Project (HCUP).

* Low precision, no estimate reported.

Hospice care provides for the management of terminal illness and related conditions. Some states provide the hospice service benefit as an option under the Medicaid program. Eligibility criteria include certification by a physician that the patient has no more than six months to live. Covered hospice services include nursing care, medical social services, physician services, counseling, home health aide, medical appliances and supplies, drugs, and physical and occupational therapy.

Cancer is the most frequent diagnosis for persons receiving hospice care, primarily cancer of the lungs, breast, and prostate. In 1996, the primary diagnoses were cancer (58 percent), heart disease (8 percent), and chronic obstructive pulmonary disease and related conditions (7 percent). Patients had an average of 2.5 diagnoses when admitted to hospice care. They received primarily skilled nursing services (93 percent), social services (79 percent), medications (56 percent), and counseling (53 percent). In addition, patients received volunteer services, household services, and physician care. Hospice care is available for persons of any age, but, in 1996, only 7.3 percent were under age 45 and most (69.3 percent) were age 70 and older. Most hospice patients were White (83.7 percent) and currently married (43.7 percent) or widowed (32.2 percent), and 55 percent were women. Men were more likely than women to be cared for by their spouse (62.5 percent versus 21.5 percent). Women (48.7 percent) were more likely to be cared for by a child or their child's spouse. Men were more likely to be living with a family member and women were more likely to be living alone or with a non-family member. (See Tables 4.19 and 4.20.)

NURSING HOMES

Various types of nursing facilities provide care to persons with severe medical and disability problems on a long-term basis. Nursing homes may be hospital based, consist of only nursing home beds, contain personal care units, or be part of continuing-care retirement communities and retirement centers. While most nursing facilities consist only of nursing home beds, the trend is toward nursing homes that include assisted living or other independent living beds. In addition, nursing homes are increasingly being certified by both Medicare and Medicaid.[10] The percentage certified by both increased from 27.8 percent in 1987 to 73.2 percent in 1996. Apparently, the need for nursing homes has decreased because both the availability and the occupancy rate of nursing home beds decreased during that period. The rate of nursing home beds decreased from 141 per 1,000 persons age 75 and over in 1987 to 117 per 1,000 in 1996. During that time, the overall occupancy rate decreased from 92.3 percent in 1987 to 88.8 percent in 1996. However, the residents of nursing homes were older and more functionally disabled in 1996 than in the decade earlier. This increased need for skilled nursing care has resulted in an increase in special care units, such as units for Alzheimer's disease and other dementias, AIDS/HIV, hospice, and brain injury.

More than 1.5 million Americans were receiving care in a nursing home on January 1, 1996. (See Table 4.21.) Most of the current nursing home residents were women (71.6 percent), White (88.7 percent), age 75 and over (79.2 percent), and not currently married (83.4 percent). Almost all (93.2 percent) of the nursing residents were enrolled in Medicare, and most (63.5 percent) were enrolled in both Medicare and Medicaid. Most (72.4 percent) of the nonprofit nursing homes were located in metropolitan statistical areas, and more were located in the Midwest (38.6 percent) and the Northeast (30.5 percent) than in any other region. For-profit nursing homes, however, were primarily located in the South (36.6 percent) and Midwest (27.6 percent). The most frequent diagnoses among nursing home residents were dementia (47.7 percent), heart disease (45.5 percent), and hypertension (36.6 percent). For nursing home residents under age 65, however, hypertension (41.1 percent), stroke (21.2 percent), and diabetes (18.8 percent) were the most frequent diagnoses. Women were more likely than men to have arthritis and less likely to have had a stroke. (See Table 4.22.)

UNMET MEDICAL NEEDS

INABILITY TO OBTAIN NEEDED MEDICAL CARE OR SPECIFIC MEDICAL SERVICES

Few people who need medical care do not get any medical attention; however, many receive inappropriate care, delayed service, or attention for more severe or otherwise preventable conditions. Usually the needed medical care is delayed because of costs. (See Table 4H.) Dental care and eye care were the most prevalent unmet need. No more than 2 percent of those under age 17 and of those age 65 and over actually reported a medical need that was not taken care of. Persons over age 65 show racial differences only in need for drug prescriptions, eyeglasses, and dental care. Unmet needs are generally higher in the working-age group (age 18 to 64) and in the lower-income groups. About 4 percent of people age 18 to 64 reported an unmet medical need, and an additional 12.5 percent reported delays in needed medical care because of costs. Dental care was the most prevalent service needed that was either delayed or not received. (See Table 4.23.)

MEASURING UNMET NEEDS

The estimate of unmet medical needs can vary by population group, type of survey data collection method, and definition of unmet medical need.[11] The estimate can range from 4.5 million people when the definition is the number of people with fair or poor health status who did not see a doctor during the year to 41.5 million people when the definition is the inability to obtain a specific medical service. Other definitions used for unmet medical need include lack of health insurance, inability to obtain medical care, and use of the emergency room as the usual source of care. Use of the emergency room for

Table 4H. Unmet Medical Needs: 1993

(Percent)

Age	Any unmet need	Needed but not able to get care	Delayed medical care because of cost
0–17 years	10.8	1.9	4.1
0–4 years	6.2	1.7	2.5
5–17 years	12.6	2.0	4.8
18–64 years	20.9	3.7	12.5
18–44 years	22.5	3.9	13.2
45–64 years	17.5	3.2	11.1
65 years and over	10.6	1.6	4.7
65–74 years	11.4	1.6	5.3
75 years and over	9.3	1.7	3.8

SOURCE: G. Simpson, B. Bloom, R.A. Cohen, and P.E. Parsons, "Access to Health Care—Part 1: Children," *Vital and Health Statistics* (National Center for Health Statistics—NCHS) 10, no. 196 (1997): Table 9. B. Bloom, G. Simpson, R.A. Cohen, and P.E. Parsons, "Access to Health Care—Part 2: Working-Age Adults," *Vital and Health Statistics* (NCHS) 10, no. 197 (1997): Table 10. R.A. Cohen, B. Bloom, G. Simpson, and P.E. Parsons, "Access to Health Care—Part 3: Older Adults," *Vital and Health Statistics* (NCHS) 10, no. 198 (1997): Table 3. Based on data from the National Health Interview Survey.

health care that is not urgent is considered medically inappropriate and more costly than other outpatient settings. Unmet medical need as defined by recency of last contact with a doctor would vary from a high of 11.4 percent of the population (if defined as last visit two or more years ago) to a low of 3.4 percent (if defined as five years or more ago). (See Table 4.4.) Among adults age 18 to 64, men are more likely than women not to have seen a doctor in the past two years. (See Figure 4H.)

Data are available that use various approaches to indicate unmet medical needs. *Unmet medical need* is defined in Table 4.23 as the inability to obtain a specific medical service; in Table 4.24, by recency of last contact with a doctor; and in Tables 4.26 and 4.27, as lack of health insurance.

Table 4.23 is based on the Access to Care and Health Insurance Components of the 1993 National Health Interview Survey (NHIS). People with no regular source of medical care were asked to indicate why they had no regular source from a list that included responses related to lack of need, insurance, access, and trust. Unmet need was defined as the inability to obtain needed medical services at least once in the last 12 months. Needed medical services included surgery, dental care, prescription medicine, eyeglasses, or mental health care.

ANNUAL DOCTOR VISITS

About 90 percent of Americans see their doctors each year, suggesting increased attention to preventive care. About 80 percent of the population had at least one contact with a doctor less than a year prior to the survey interview, either as an outpatient or while hospitalized. Almost all children under age five (94.9 percent) and people age 75 and over (92.1 percent) saw a doctor less than a year ago. Males of all ages and people age 18 to 44, however, are the least likely to participate in annual doctor visits. (See Tables 4.4 and 4.24.) Annual dental and physical examinations, including screening for cancer, visual, and hearing disorders, are considered good preventive health care. For some groups of people, contact with a doctor is still restricted to dealing with perceived health problems and conditions rather than

including annual preventive screening and care. People whose last contact with a doctor is two years ago or more are losing the opportunity to detect serious diseases in their earlier, preventable, and treatable stages.

HEALTH INSURANCE COVERAGE IN THE POPULATION

Generally, persons are considered uninsured if they do not have private health insurance, Medicare, Medicaid, public assistance, a state-sponsored health plan, military insurance, or another government-sponsored health program. However, people with only Indian Health Service coverage are not considered insured. Private health insurance includes health maintenance organizations (HMOs) and other managed care. HMOs are prepaid health plans that provide preventive and treatment services to their members through designated providers. In contrast, *fee-for-service health insurance* reimburses the providers for services rendered to the insured person. Single-service plans other than those covering hospital and physician services, such as dental health plans, are generally not included. (See Tables 4.25, 4.26, and 4.27.)

Public insurance plans include Medicare and Medicaid. Medicare (Title XVIII, Health Insurance for the Aged of the Social Security Act) became effective in 1966. It covers primarily people age 65 and older. People with disabilities and people with end-stage renal disease are also eligible. Medicare is a federal insurance program supported by a trust fund of monies contributed by workers. Medicare consists of Part A (hospital insurance) and Part B (supplementary medical insurance that covers doctors' services such as surgery and other procedures for the diagnosis or treatment of illness and injury). Medicare does not cover all health care costs, such as payments for routine screening and dental services not related to an underlying medical condition. Therefore, Medigap coverage is available as private health insurance that people can purchase to supplement Medicare's benefits. Medicaid serves low-income people regardless of age. It is a joint federal and state program funded by federal, state, and local tax funds. Medicaid is developed and administered by state and local governments within federal guidelines; therefore, Medicaid programs, eligibility criteria, and benefits can differ by state.

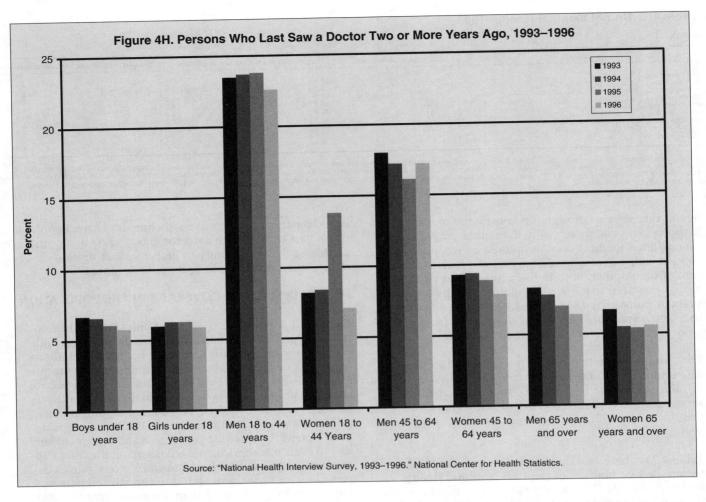

Figure 4H. Persons Who Last Saw a Doctor Two or More Years Ago, 1993–1996

Source: "National Health Interview Survey, 1993–1996." National Center for Health Statistics.

CONTINUOUS HEALTH INSURANCE COVERAGE[12]

For the first time in over a decade, the number and percent of Americans with health insurance increased in 1999. About 16 percent are covered by Medicare, 12 percent by Medicaid, and 71 percent by private insurance, which is mostly employment based. Hispanics are more likely than Blacks or Whites not to have any health insurance coverage. (See Table 4.25.) Lapses in insurance coverage last five months or more for about half of those who lose their insurance. Whites are twice as likely as Blacks to have continuous private health insurance for a three-year period. Blacks, Hispanics, and Asians and Pacific Islanders are more likely than Whites to have continuous health coverage because of Medicaid. Although most people have some kind of health insurance at some time, certain groups are uninsured for extended periods of time. Only 71 percent of the total population had either public or private health insurance for the total 36 months between 1993 and 1996. (See Table 4.25.) Men and Hispanics are the most likely to be without health insurance of any kind for extended periods of time. Almost 10 percent of Hispanics had no health insurance in any month between 1993 and 1996 compared with 2.9 percent of Whites, 3.9 percent of Blacks, and 4 percent of Asians or Pacific Islanders.

While the majority of Americans have health insurance, many are underinsured; that is, they do not have adequate insurance to cover their health and medical needs. (See Figures 4I, 4J, 4K, and 4L for the geographic dispersion of the population with adequate and inadequate health insurance.)

INSURANCE DATA SOURCES

Four major nationally representative surveys provide information on the insurance status of the civilian population of the United States. These federal surveys are (1) the National Health Interview Survey, (2) the Medical Expenditure Panel Survey (MEPS), (3) the Current Population Survey (CPS) March Supplement, and (4) the Survey of Income and Program Participation (SIPP). Since 1960, The National Health Interview Survey has collected data on whether people are covered by insurance. It is the only one of the four surveys that asks directly whether the respondent was not insured. Because the NHIS is conducted continuously throughout the year, it provides estimates of health insurance status for the population during an average month. The NHIS also collects data to correlate insurance status with both health conditions and care received.

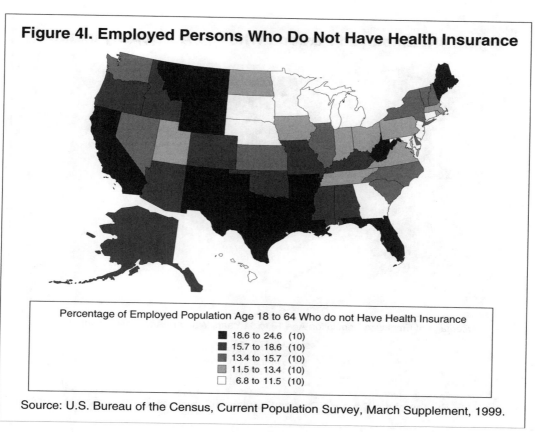

Figure 4I. Employed Persons Who Do Not Have Health Insurance

Percentage of Employed Population Age 18 to 64 Who do not Have Health Insurance

- 18.6 to 24.6 (10)
- 15.7 to 18.6 (10)
- 13.4 to 15.7 (10)
- 11.5 to 13.4 (10)
- 6.8 to 11.5 (10)

Source: U.S. Bureau of the Census, Current Population Survey, March Supplement, 1999.

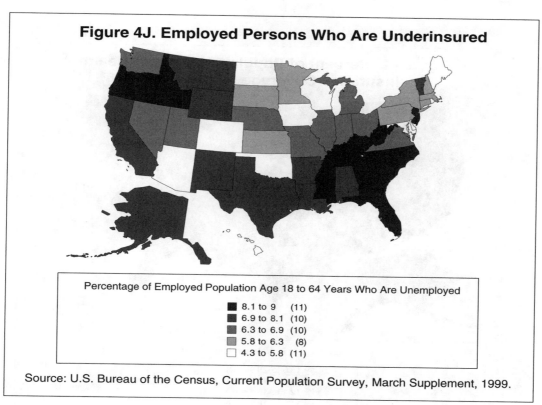

Figure 4J. Employed Persons Who Are Underinsured

Percentage of Employed Population Age 18 to 64 Years Who Are Unemployed

- 8.1 to 9 (11)
- 6.9 to 8.1 (10)
- 6.3 to 6.9 (10)
- 5.8 to 6.3 (8)
- 4.3 to 5.8 (11)

Source: U.S. Bureau of the Census, Current Population Survey, March Supplement, 1999.

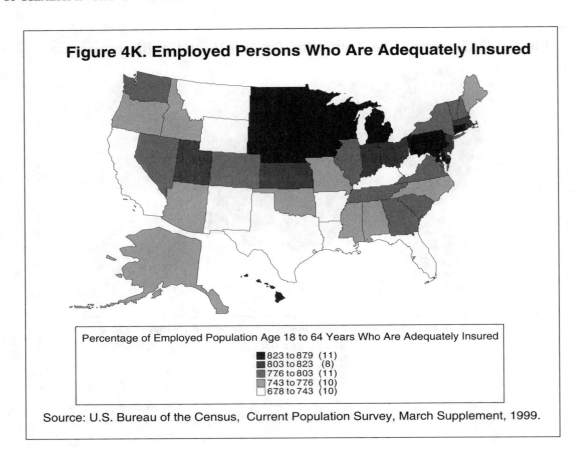

Figure 4K. Employed Persons Who Are Adequately Insured

Percentage of Employed Population Age 18 to 64 Years Who Are Adequately Insured

- ■ 823 to 879 (11)
- ■ 803 to 823 (8)
- ■ 776 to 803 (11)
- ■ 743 to 776 (10)
- □ 678 to 743 (10)

Source: U.S. Bureau of the Census, Current Population Survey, March Supplement, 1999.

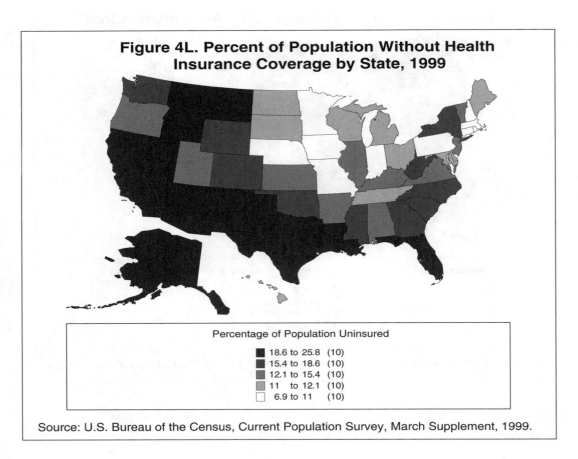

Figure 4L. Percent of Population Without Health Insurance Coverage by State, 1999

Percentage of Population Uninsured

- ■ 18.6 to 25.8 (10)
- ■ 15.4 to 18.6 (10)
- ■ 12.1 to 15.4 (10)
- ■ 11 to 12.1 (10)
- □ 6.9 to 11 (10)

Source: U.S. Bureau of the Census, Current Population Survey, March Supplement, 1999.

Since 1977, the Medical Expenditure Panel Survey has collected information on insurance coverage of households in its sample from householders, employers, unions, and other private health insurance companies.

The March Supplement of the Census Bureau's Current Population Survey collects data on income and work experience and details sources of income including non-cash sources such as health insurance. Because of its large sample of households, state-level estimates are reported. (See Table 4.27.) Because Medicaid coverage is underreported in the CPS, the Census Bureau imputes Medicaid coverage to persons who receive other benefits that make them Medicaid eligible. Data show health insurance status for the entire prior calendar year. Estimates of the uninsured from the CPS, therefore, are based on persons without health insurance during the entire prior calendar year. (See Tables 4.26 and 4.27, and Figures 4I, 4J, 4K and 4L.)

The Survey of Income and Program Participation supplements the CPS estimates by providing information on monthly changes in insurance status over about a three-year period. The SIPP is a longitudinal survey of a continuous series of overlapping national panels. SIPP provides data on the characteristics of the population without health insurance for varying periods of time between 1 and 36 months. (See Table 4.25.)

HEALTH INSURANCE—RELATED LEGISLATIVE PROVISIONS

Legislation has been passed to address insurance issues that interfered with appropriate, timely, effective, and affordable health care. These laws include the Health Insurance Portability and Accountability Act of 1996 (Public Law 104–191), the State Children's Health Insurance Program (Title XXI of the Social Security Act of 1997), and the Mental Health Parity Act of 1996 (Public Law 104–204).

When insurance disallowed reimbursement for preexisting conditions, persons who lost or changed their insurance because of job changes were especially affected. This exclusion resulted in persons with preexisting conditions either not getting needed treatment or receiving treatment at later, more severe, and costly stages of their diseases. The Health Insurance Portability and Accountability Act of 1996, however, allowed eligible persons to maintain health insurance coverage without their preexisting conditions being excluded from coverage when they changed jobs or insurance companies or lost their job. The *preexisting condition* is conceived of in broad terms as a health condition that is present before the person enrolls in the health insurance plan. An eligible person may not be excluded from coverage for a condition regardless of whether any prior medical advice, diagnosis, care, or treatment may have been recommended or received. Eligible individuals are allowed a defined period of creditable health insurance coverage, which may be carried forward so that they may avoid the impo-

sition of the preexisting condition exclusion when enrolling in a new health plan. States may implement alternative mechanisms to ensure access to insurance coverage for eligible persons without the preexisting condition exclusion. These alternative mechanisms, however, must provide eligible persons with a choice of health insurance coverage.

The State Children's Health Insurance Program helps make health insurance coverage available to low-income children who are presently uninsured but not eligible for Medicaid. Examples of free or low-cost health services include regular checkups and immunizations, physical examinations for school and sports, dental care, vision and hearing testing, hospital visits, and medications. Income eligibility levels are established by each state and are based on a percentage of the federal poverty level. States provide annual reports that include their progress in reducing the number of uninsured children. These state reports are available at the following Web site: <http://www.hcfa.gov/INIT/children.htm>.

The Mental Health Parity Act of 1996 applies to group health plans and to health insurance coverage offered in connection with group health plans. This act does not require that insurance cover mental health benefits, nor does it apply to benefits for substance abuse or chemical dependency treatment. Rather, it applies only to the group health plans that provide mental health benefits and requires that such plans do not apply lifetime or annual dollar limits for mental health medical and surgical coverage unless they also impose such limits for all medical and surgical benefits. Group health plans covered by the Mental Health Parity Act may not have lower lifetime and annual dollar limits for mental illness than for physical illness. The act applies to Medicaid managed care organizations but not Medicaid fee-for-service arrangements. In states with more favorable mental health insurance requirements, state law takes precedence over the Mental Health Parity Act provisions.

QUALITY OF CARE

SETTING STANDARDS AND ASSESSING QUALITY OF HEALTH CARE

Consumers want health care that is accessible, timely, effective, safe, and affordable. They want to be informed concerning their health status and options in a clear, understandable, and respectful way. Clinicians want access to the latest available information on effective treatments and the resources and ability to provide the best patient care they can. Employers, labor unions, and other private group purchasers and their health plans want to provide cost-effective treatment and maintain healthy enrollees. Quality-improvement programs, "report cards," and other indicators are being developed to help both individuals and organizations decide on health plans on the basis of quality of care as well as cost and the nature of benefits received.

Researchers have identified various health care interventions that improve health, including screening and treatment that have been found effective in reducing disabling complications, more costly treatment needed later, and death. Such measures of quality care include immunizations, mammograms, cervical cancer screening, yearly foot and eye examinations for persons with diabetes, and followup care for persons hospitalized for mental illness. Markers for poor health care quality include medication errors, unnecessary hysterectomies, routinely prescribed antibiotics for acute bronchitis and colds, and incorrectly reported Pap smears and other laboratory tests.

Health care providers are being urged to increase their emphasis on preventive measures, improve their treatment outcomes, ensure accountability, and increase availability and access to underserved populations. Information systems are needed to monitor such progress. Such systems require that the information be collected in a standard manner and that the security and confidentiality of records be ensured.

In the public sector, the Department of Veterans Affairs (DVA) and the Department of Health and Human Services (DHHS) are among the governmental organizations that monitor health care services for compliance with federal health, safety, and program standards. The DVA established the National Performance and Data Resource Center (earlier called the Quality Management Institute) to promote research and training to enhance the quality of patient care. The DVA measures of health care quality include monitoring surgical complications, infection control, adverse drug events, suicide, and other violence. Quality is also assessed with indices for chronic disease, prevention, practice guidelines, and palliative care. In addition, the DVA uses standardized assessment instruments such as the Addiction Severity Index to determine the functional status of persons with alcohol or other drug problems. The DHHS's Agency for Healthcare Research and Quality, formerly known as the Agency for Healthcare Policy and Research, has sponsored or developed several mechanisms to help consumers assess health plans and to help providers evaluate and improve the quality of their care. The HCUP Quality Indicators, for example, consist of 33 clinical performance measures to help hospitals assess their own potentially avoidable adverse hospital outcomes, inappropriate use of hospital procedures, and hospital admissions that could be prevented with appropriate primary care. The Health Care Financing Administration has several programs to monitor and improve the health care services provided to Medicaid and Medicare beneficiaries, including the Outcome and Assessment Information Set for home health care.

The need for careful monitoring to ensure quality of care in nursing homes was emphasized when, in 1995, strong protective regulations were instituted to protect the estimated 1.6 million elderly and disabled persons receiving care in nearly 17,000 nursing homes.[13] HCFA has promoted new approaches to improve the quality of life and care for nursing home residents. Constant vigilance is needed. Quality-of-care measures include prevention of bed sores, dehydration, malnutrition, physical and verbal abuse, neglect, and misappropriation of resident property; the implementation of criminal background checks of nursing home workers; and an ombudsman program for nursing home residents.[14]

A number of organizations in the private sector are also working to develop quality-of-care standards and to assess and report on the quality of care. These organizations include the Joint Commission on Accreditation of Healthcare Organizations (JCAHO), the Foundation for Accountability, the American Accreditation HealthCare Commission, the Commission on Accreditation of Rehabilitation Facilities, and the National Committee for Quality Assurance (NCQA). Several of these organizations have developed uniform data collection systems. For example, JCAHO accredits both hospital and non-hospital providers and routinely collects and analyzes data on outcome and other performance measures. In addition, JCAHO has a catalogue of health care indicators for use in JCAHO accreditation programs. In May 1999, JCAHO chose five core performance measures for hospitals: acute myocardial infarction (including coronary artery disease), congestive heart failure, pneumonia, surgical procedures and complications, and pregnancy and related conditions (including newborn and maternal care). NCQA established the Health Plan Employer Data and Information Set (HEDIS) with guidelines to help measure the performance of health care plans.

HEALTH PLAN EMPLOYER DATA AND INFORMATION SET

The National Committee for Quality Assurance established guidelines to help measure the performance of health care plans as well as to assess the quality of care received by groups in the population. The Health Plan Employer Data and Information Set was developed to help employers make choices about HEDIS available health plans for their employees. HEDIS has been adapted to assess the quality of care for Medicare and Medicaid enrollees. The performance measures assess the effectiveness, availability, use, and cost of health care as well as the health plan membership's satisfaction with their experiences in the plan.

NCQA assesses and reports on managed health care organizations that voluntarily provide information on the various HEDIS measures of quality of care. In NCQA 1999 report, data were collected from 247 managed care organizations in the United States for a public report of their plan-specific performance. These organizations represent 410 health plans, including HMOs and point-of-service plans, and cover over 52 million people. An additional 112 managed care organizations provided their data on the performance measures for analysis and to be used in national averages but not for public reporting. Managed care health plans that publicly reported their performance provided higher quality of care on the indicators than the non-publicly reporting plans. (See Table 4I.) Furthermore, the publicly reporting plans continued to maintain their quality or to improve over time. Several hundred health plans, however, do not participate in this monitoring system and provide no data at all.[15]

Two indicators, beta-blocker treatments and eye exams for diabetics, are especially noteworthy for their value and the variability in their application. Researchers have found that beta-blocker medications taken after a heart attack can reduce death in heart patients by 43 percent.[16] Yet NCQA found that the plans vary from 40 to 100 percent in their provision of beta-blockers to eligible heart patients. Yearly eye examinations for persons with diabetes can prevent blindness. Yet, overall less than half of the health plans conduct such yearly exams, and the rates range from less than 10 percent to over 80 percent. Notably, plans sharing the same physicians and market differ in their quality report card based on whether they are accountable—that is, either publicly report or are accredited. Therefore, NCQA concludes that health plans, not just the physicians or other health care providers, are important factors in improving the quality of health care.

HOSPITAL-ACQUIRED DISEASES (NOSOCOMIAL INFECTIONS)

Another measure of the quality of care is the rate of hospital-acquired diseases (nosocomial infections). These infections are usually associated with high-risk surgery or other medical procedures. Because of the concentration of people with lowered immune conditions who are otherwise at risk for illness, and the variety of infectious diseases that are found in hospitals, people can acquire diseases in the hospital other than the conditions for which they were hospitalized. Nosocomial infections have occurred since care of patients in hospitals began, but the properties and species of the infecting microorganisms have changed over time. An estimated 2 million patients

annually develop nosocomial infections. In 1992, the additional patient care costs for these infections were more than $4.5 billion.[17]

A variety of factors cause these hospital-acquired infections. There has always been increased risk for certain groups of inpatients to acquire additional infections while hospitalized because of their individual susceptibility and the nature of their underlying illness. In the last several decades, the number of older patients has increased because of the longer life expectancy in the population as a whole. This increase, along with the complex nature of the underlying disease or associated illness, has contributed to the rise in nosocomial infections.

The most notable change contributing to recent hospital-acquired infections has been the type of surgical and systemic therapies now available for treating diseases that were formerly untreatable. These therapies include organ transplants, intensive chemotherapy, and innovations in cardiac and orthopedic surgery. Such innovative procedures may involve prolonged anesthesia, insertion of foreign objects into the body during the operation, invasive manipulations during the postoperative period, and several surgical operations. For example, in reconstructive orthopedic surgical procedures such as a hip replacement, a foreign object is inserted into the hip that increases the risks for developing postoperative infections. Some nosocomial conditions include operative wound infections, lower respiratory tract infections (secondary to prolonged anesthesia, intubation, etc.), urinary tract infections (secondary to indwelling urinary catheters), and blood stream infections (from intravenous catheters used while the patient is recovering from extensive surgery). In addition, the National Nosocomial Infections Surveillance (NNIS) system has reported that the number of drug-resistant pathogens associated with nosocomial infections in the intensive care unit has continued to increase in the last five years.[18]

Table 4I. Health Plans Complying with HEDIS[1] Quality Measures: 1996–1998

(Percent)

Measure	National averages			3–Year public reporters[2]	Public reporting all three years[2]		
	1996	1997	1998		1996	1997	1998
Adolescent immunization status	51.5	52.2	52.3	67.9	60.6	65.4	67.9
Antidepressant medication management	—	—	54.4	55.0	—	—	55.0
Advice to quit smoking[3]	61.0	64.0	62.5	66.1	63.2	67.1	66.1
Beta-blocker treatment	62.5	74.0	79.9	85.0	70.5	82.4	85.0
Breast cancer screening	70.3	71.3	72.2	76.1	73.8	74.6	76.1
Cervical cancer screening	70.4	71.3	69.9	75.4	74.2	76.6	75.4
Cholesterol screening	—	—	59.1	63.6	—	—	—
Childhood immunization status–combo 1	65.1	65.4	64.8	—	—	—	—
Chicken pox vaccination	—	40.1	51.9	52.6	—	—	—
Eye exams for people with diabetes	38.0	39.0	40.9	49.4	45.2	47.6	49.4
Followup after hospitalization for mental illness[4]	72.3	67.3	67.4	76.1	75.8	76.0	76.1
Prenatal care in the 1st trimester	83.4	83.1	83.6	87.7	86.8	87.7	87.7
Overall rating of health plan[3]	56.2	55.7	57.0				

SOURCE: National Committee for Quality Assurance, State of Managed Care Quality Report, 1999. As reported to HEDIS.

— Data not available.
1. HEDIS is the Health Plan Employer Data and Information Set (HEDIS) performance measures.
2. Health plans that have publicly reported HEDIS data consistently for the past three years.
3. The survey instrument related to this measure changed between the 1997 and 1998 reporting years.
4. Specifications for this measure changed between the 1996 and 1997 reporting years.

The most common nosocomial infections in intensive care units (ICUs) are pneumonia, urinary tract infections, catheter sepsis, and wound infection. The more risk factors an individual has, the more likely the person is to have a surgical site infection, regardless of the specific surgical procedure. The rates for infections at surgical sites, however, are generally low. The surgical site infection rate among patients with no risk factor for 21 of the 44 reported surgical procedures in the NNIS was 1 percent or less. Only 7 of the 44 surgical procedures with any risk factors had infection rates of 10 per 100 operations or higher. The highest rates were 17.9 per 100 operations for persons with three risk factors and a coronary artery bypass graft with incisions in both the chest and leg (or other donor site), and 21.3 per 100 operations for persons with three risk factors and an organ transplant. (See Table 4.29.)

HOSPITAL CONTROL OF INFECTIONS FOLLOWING SURGERY FOR SPECIFIC PROCEDURES

An estimated 5 to 10 percent of all hospitalized patients, compared to about 28 percent of ICU patients, have developed a nosocomial infection.[19] Appropriate and meaningful comparisons of nosocomial rates among hospitals or units within hospital, however, require careful attention to comparability. For example, it is important to have uniform definitions and case-finding techniques. It is also necessary to have sufficiently large samples and to adjust for infection risk factors such as disease severity and specific surgical or medical procedures. Comparisons are best made for specific procedures controlling for the general condition of the patients as well as for the site of the surgery and the procedures performed.

The National Nosocomial Infections Surveillance System uses standardized methods of surveillance. Data on the rate of nosocomial infections for hospitals participating in the Surgical Patient Component of the NNIS with 30 or more operations in a given risk factor are shown in Table 4.30. Their average hospital-acquired infection rate for most reported procedures was less than 5 per 100 procedures. Rates of nosocomial infections over 5 per 100 procedures generally were for digestive tract operations on high-risk patients. Abdominal hysterectomies on high-risk patients also had a high rate of nosocomial infections.

To be accredited by JCAHO, ICUs must have written policies and procedures on infection control. The low rate of nosocomial infections in the general hospital population reflects a variety of control measures that hospital personnel have instituted. Routine measures to control infectious diseases include the following: separating patients with highly infectious diseases from other patients; using barriers such as masks, gloves, and gowns to avoid direct exposure to transmissible organisms; sterilizing instruments; controlling the disposal of syringes, gloves, and other possibly contaminated items; careful hand washing after direct contact with patients; and constant monitoring of patients, especially those who have

catheters or other devices. Because devices contribute to so many nosocomial infections, however, new designs or materials are needed that resist contamination or spread of infectious diseases.

AVAILABILITY OF HEALTH PRACTITIONERS

Policymakers are interested in the number and rate of health practitioners as a means of monitoring the adequacy of the availability and provision of health care services. They are concerned about the balance between sufficient numbers of health practitioners to provide ready access to quality care and an excess of care that results in unnecessary medical procedures and increased health costs. These health practitioners come from several disciplines and provide a variety of health care services.

In particular, health services researchers have examined the role of the size, composition, and distribution of physicians in the nation.[20] Because an increase in medical specialists has been associated with decreased continuity of care and higher costs, there is concern about the increased number of medical specialists compared with primary care providers.[21] Between 1965 and 1992, the rate of medical specialists increased from 56 per 100,000 to 123 per 100,000 population. In contrast, the rate of primary physicians only increased during that period from 59 per 100,000 population to 67 per 100,000.[22]

The rate of all physicians, regardless of specialty, increased from 155.6 per 100,000 population in 1970 to 260 per 100,000 population in 1996. (See Table 4.32.) The Bureau of Health Professions in the federal Health Resources and Services Administration produced these data from a variety of sources, including the American Medical Association (AMA), the American Osteopathic Association, and the American Board of Medical Specialties. The ratio of physicians to the population increased about 67 percent between 1970 and 1996. The ratio of veterinarians increased about 70 percent. The supply of optometrists, pharmacists, and dentists, however, has not shown such great increases. Between 1970 and 1996, the rate of each of these three types of health practitioners increased only about 25 percent.

The increase in physicians during that time is overshadowed by the increase in the supply of registered nurses. This increase in registered nurses remains when measured as the ratio of full-time equivalents of hospital registered nurses to patients, but not when adjustments are made for the severity of the patient case mix in the hospitals.[23] In addition, when the number of all types of nurses is examined, a different picture emerges. Aiken, Sochalski, and Anderson found that when nursing personnel were considered in terms of patient days, the rate decreased. Between 1981 and 1993 the national rate of all nursing personnel decreased 7.3 percent per 1,000 patient days when adjusted for case mix. In contrast, during that same period, non-nursing hospital administrative personnel per 1,000 patient days increased by 46.5 percent when adjusted for case mix. Nurses as a group used to be a major component of the hospital workforce. In 1981, nursing personnel constituted 45 percent of the hospital workforce, but by 1993 nurses accounted for only 37 percent of the hospital workforce.

The rate of clinically trained psychiatric nurses is lower than that of other mental health professionals per 100,000 population. (See Table 4.33.) The source for most of the information on clinically trained and clinically active mental health professionals by discipline comes from the discipline's professional association membership surveys. These surveys were conducted at varying times, and the data are presented for the latest available year of the association study. Because not all health professionals are members of their discipline's association, the data presented underestimate the number actually working in the mental health field. Among the mental health professionals who are actively working in the field, the largest category is psychosocial rehabilitation workers. These mental health professionals usually work in psychosocial rehabilitation programs for individuals with severe mental illness in the community. Psychosocial rehabilitation workers provide training in areas such as community living skills and vocational rehabilitation. The services they provide include socialization, crisis management, and case management. Psychosocial rehabilitation workers also have worked with persons with substance abuse, mental retardation, and physical disabilities such as deafness. The rate of psychosocial rehabilitation workers was 37.7 per 100,000 population in 1996 compared with the rates of marriage and family therapists (16.7 per 100,000 population in 1998), psychiatrists (11.3 per 100,000 population in 1996), and school psychologists (8.4 per 100,000 population in 1995). (See Table 4.33.)

The availability of physicians, such as psychiatrists and family practice physicians, to provide mental health care is greater in urban than in rural areas and for nonmetropolitan counties near a metropolitan area. (See Table 4.31.) Most counties, regardless of population density, have a family practice physician, and almost all metropolitan counties have at least one psychiatrist. However, the percentage of nonmetropolitan counties with a psychiatrist ranges from 5.2 percent in rural areas with fewer than 2,500 residents located away from a metropolitan area to 88.2 percent for urban areas with more than 20,000 residents near a metropolitan area. SAMHSA based Table 4.31 on data it took from the AMA's master file of data on all physicians practicing in the United States. The AMA master file includes both AMA members and nonmembers and specialty as designated by the physicians. Medical residents, students, and inactive physicians are not included in the table.

Although the number and rate of health practitioners are useful in monitoring the availability of various needed health services, other indicators provide a better measure of health care availability, need, and quality. For example, Grumbach, Vranizan, and Bindman evaluated the impact of the number of available physicians on access to care in urban areas in California and found that income, insurance status, and racial and ethnic group were more important determinants of access to care even in high physician supply areas.[24] Also, the need for certain disciplines can take into account the demands of necessary medical care. Such a needs-based estimate of the adequate numbers and rates of health practitioners could take into account the prevalence of various health conditions and the best practices guidelines for needed prevention and treatment services. Such an approach, however, needs to provide flexibility for unexpected public health emergencies, such as the AIDS epidemic.

Consumers want to be able to choose health practitioners who are readily available and responsive to their needs. They seek medical services from those who can communicate effectively with them concerning their health condition and the required compliance with treatment regimens and prescriptions. For example, the practice setting and the racial and ethnic diversity of physicians were found to be as important as the number of physicians to respond to the health care needs of minority and other underserved populations. Hispanic and other minority physicians were found to be more likely to practice in health care shortage areas and to care for minority patients than their non-Hispanic White physician counterparts.[25] Therefore, medical training for interested persons of all racial and ethnic groups would contribute to providing health care for persons of minority and other underserved populations.

Market forces have been used to encourage people to choose careers in the health care professions. Simon, Dranove, and White found that incomes for primary care physicians increased by 4.78 percent annually in states in the highest quartile of managed care growth compared with increased incomes of 1.20 percent in states in the lowest quartile of managed care growth. (See Table 4.34.)[26] The information was collected by the Bureau of Labor Statistics (BLS) in its monthly survey of employment for all workers in nonagricultural industries. The BLS survey collects industry-specific information on wage and salary jobs in a sample of approximately 305,000 establishments. Self-employed persons and the military are not included. Unlike the Current Population Survey, which counts each person's employment status once regardless of the number of jobs held, the BLS defines *employment* as the number of jobs. The BLS estimates that about 5 percent of the population has more than one job at any one time.

NATIONAL HEALTH CARE EXPENDITURES

The United States spends more for health care services than any other industrialized country whether measured by percentage of its gross domestic product or amount per capita (adjusted for purchasing power).[27] Health expenditures in the United States have increased over time; the rate of growth in spending was especially high between 1970 and 1990. Only 28 percent of the increase in expenditures for personal health care in the past 20 years is attributed to an increase in the number and type of services. General inflation is estimated to account for 30 percent of the increase, medical care price inflation for 17 percent, and population growth for 9 percent.[28] Total national health care expenditures reached 1 trillion dollars for the first time in 1996. The annual growth rate of health spending, however, actually slowed between 1993 and 1996 from 7.4 percent to 4.9 percent but by 1998 had increased to 5.6 percent. (See Table 1A.)

WHAT THE U.S. HEALTH DOLLARS BUY

The major categories of national health expenditures are personal health care (i.e., health care spent on individuals as opposed to public health campaigns or hospital construction), program administration and net cost of private health insurance, government public health activities, health research, and health-related construction. (See Table 4.35.) In 1997, approximately $969 billion was spent for personal health care, $50 billion for program administration, $38.5 billion for government public health activities, $18 billion for research, and $16.9 billion for construction.

The largest factors of spending within the category of personal health care are for hospital care, physician services, drugs and other medical nondurables, and nursing home care. In 1997, the expenditures were $371.1 billion for hospital care, $217.6 billion for physician services, $108.9 billion for drugs and other medical nondurables, and $82.8 billion for nursing home care. *Nursing home care expenditures* refers to spending for free-standing facilities only. Expenditures for nursing care in hospitals are included in the hospital spending categories.

From 1965 until 1997, the amounts spent increased for each category of health expenditures in terms of current dollars for the year. (See Table 4.35.) However, the average annual growth in spending from the prior year has decreased in recent years. The rate of spending growth for hospital care, physician services, and nursing home care has slowed down in the later part of the 1990s.[29] Spending for hospital care increased at an annual rate of over 10 percent from 1970 to 1991, but has decreased steadily since then to 3.4 percent in 1998. Physician service expenditures increased annually from 1970 to a high of 13.1 percent in 1985. From that time, the annual growth in spending for physician services decreased to 5.4 percent in 1998. Spending growth for nursing home care expenditures peaked in 1970 with an annual growth of 17.4 percent and have decreased steadily to 3.7 percent in 1998. These decreases could be caused by a variety of factors, including fewer people using the services, lower costs, or shorter lengths of stays or treatment.[30]

The rate of growth for expenditures for prescription drugs, however, has fluctuated from 1970 to 1997. In 1970, the annual rate of growth was 7.4 percent and increased to a high of 12.2 percent in 1990. In the earlier 1990s, expenditures for prescription drugs decreased to 8.7 percent in 1993. In the later 1990s, the annual growth rate for prescription drug expenditures increased until it

reached 14.1 percent in 1997. This increase could be caused by higher cost drugs, more prescriptions being filled, or both.

THE NATIONAL HEALTH ACCOUNTS

The expenditures are in terms of current dollars for the year. The data are based on the National Health Accounts (NHA) system, a statistical system to monitor health care expenditures. The NHA uses data reported from both private and public data collection surveys. The trends in actual national health expenditures are presented for 1960 to 1997. The amounts for 1998 through 2007 are projected expenditures. The projected expenditures are based on assumptions about the consequences of current spending trends and the demographic and economic status of the nation in the coming years. The broad types of health care expenditures covered are health care to prevent or treat various conditions, government public health activity to organize and deliver health and preventive services, program administration, and research and new construction for hospitals and nursing homes. Most expenditures are for health services and supplies. This category does not include nutrition programs such as the Women, Infants, and Children program. Programs to improve environmental and sanitation conditions also are not included.

The Standard Industrial Classification (SIC) for health services (SIC categories 801 to 809) is used to determine which services are included. The category in which costs are assigned depends on the location of the delivered services. Hospital care costs include all services provided by the hospital to patients, such as room and board charges, operating room fees, inpatient pharmacy charges, resident physician service fees, and any other charges billed by the hospital. Physician costs include services provided in the offices and clinics of doctors of medicine and doctors of osteopathy, and independently billing medical laboratories. Dental costs include services in offices and clinics of doctors of dental surgery and doctors of dental medicine. Other professional care costs include services in offices and clinics of other health practitioners and miscellaneous health and allied services (except staff model HMOs).

Home health care costs are for services delivered in the home, such as Meals on Wheels or nursing services provided by temporary help agencies, and exclude the costs of services provided by facility-based home health agencies. Personal care costs are Medicaid-covered services that are delivered in the home by qualified professionals. Drugs and other nondurable medical product costs are limited to products purchased from retail outlets. Vision products and other medical durables include eyeglasses, hearing aids, surgical appliances and supplies, and bulk and cylinder oxygen and equipment rental. Nursing home care costs are for inpatient nursing care. Other personal health care costs include unspecified care paid for by the government and industrial services that are facilities or supplies provided by employers either onsite or offsite for the health care needs of their workers.

MENTAL HEALTH EXPENDITURES

Although expenditures for inpatient care are usually higher than those for outpatient care, this does not appear to be the case for residential mental health care. (See Table 4.36.) In 1969, for example, 78.5 percent of the inpatient or residential clients received their mental health care in state or county mental hospitals; yet only 55.1 percent of the mental health care expenditures were for these facilities. By 1994, when 30.6 percent of the mental health residential clients were in state or county mental hospitals, 23.6 percent of the expenditures were for these facilities.

In 1994, Veterans Administration medical centers cared for 7.6 percent of the mental health residential clients but received only 4.2 percent of the mental health care expenditures. Residential treatment centers for emotionally disturbed children cared for 12.5 percent of the residential clients but received only 7.1 percent of the mental health care expenditures. Private psychiatric hospitals, free-standing psychiatric partial care organizations, and multiservice mental health organizations tended to receive a greater percentage of the mental health care expenditures than their percentage of the residential clients.

The data are from SAMHSA's biennial Inventory of Mental Health Organizations and General Hospital Mental Health Services Inventory. The inventory collects data from the organizational administrators or designated staff on all expenses associated with providing patients with psychiatric or other mental health services.

The expense categories included salary and contract personnel expenses, but not value in kind by volunteers, operating expenses, and costs for construction and purchasing durable equipment. The number of dollars spent to provide mental health care is presented in current dollars from 1969 to 1994 and as expenditures per capita of the civilian population.

WHO PAYS FOR HEALTH CARE IN THE U.S.

In 1960, private funds paid for 75.2 percent of the national health expenditures. Private funds include the consumer's payment for private insurance premiums as well as out-of-pocket health care expenses not paid by private insurance or other private funds. Private funds also include the employer's share of premiums for workplace-based health insurance. Since 1960, public programs such as Medicaid and Medicare have assumed an increasingly larger share of the expenditures. By 1997, private funds paid for 53.6 percent, federal funds paid for 33.6 percent, and state and local funds paid for 12.8 percent. Medicare is the largest federal public insurance program, and Medicaid is funded jointly by federal and state and local governments. In 1997, Medicare spent $214.6 billion and Medicaid spent $95.4 billion on health care for the programs' participants. (See Table 4.35.)

In 1998, more government funds than private funds were spent for hospital care, home health care, nursing home care, and health-related research. (See Table 4J and Figure 4M.) Consumers paid much more out of pocket ($55.4 billion) for their drugs and other medical nondurables than for physician services ($35.7 billion) or

Table 4J. Payment for Each Type of Health Expenditure: 1998

(Billions of dollars)

| Type of expenditure | Total | Private | | | | | Government | | |
| | | All private funds | Consumer | | | Other | Total | Federal | State and local |
			Total	Out of pocket payments	Private health insurance				
National health expenditures	1 149.1	626.4	574.6	199.5	375.0	51.8	522.7	376.9	145.8
Health services and supplies	1 113.7	613.4	574.6	199.5	375.0	38.8	500.4	360.4	140.0
Personal health care	1 019.3	574.5	536.5	199.5	337.0	37.9	444.9	343.6	101.3
Hospital care	382.8	149.9	130.9	12.8	118.0	19.1	232.9	187.4	45.5
Physician services	229.5	156.2	151.7	35.7	116.0	4.5	73.3	60.8	12.4
Dental services	53.8	51.5	51.3	25.8	25.5	0.2	2.3	1.3	1.0
Other professional services	66.6	52.4	47.4	27.2	20.2	5.0	14.2	11.2	3.0
Home health care	29.3	13.7	10.0	6.0	4.0	3.7	15.5	13.1	2.4
Drugs and other medical nondurables	121.9	103.1	103.1	55.4	47.8	*	18.8	10.7	8.1
Vision products and other medical durables	15.5	9.0	9.0	8.2	0.8	*	6.5	6.4	0.1
Nursing home care	87.8	34.8	33.2	28.5	4.7	1.6	53.0	35.4	17.7
Other personal health care	32.1	3.8	*	*		3.8	28.3	17.1	11.2
Cost of private health insurance	57.7	38.9	38.0	*	38.0	0.9	18.8	12.6	6.2
Government public health activities	36.6	*	*	*	*	*	36.6	4.2	32.4
Research and construction	35.3	13.0	*	*	*	13.0	22.3	16.5	5.8
Research [1]	19.9	1.6	*	*	*	1.6	18.3	15.5	2.8
Construction	15.5	11.5	*	*	*	11.5	4.0	1.0	3.0

SOURCE: Health Care Financing Administration, Office of the Actuary, National Health Statistics Group. 1998 National Health Expenditures: Table 3.

* Low precision, no estimate reported.
1. Research and development expenditures of drug companies and other manufacturers and providers of medical equipment and supplies are excluded from research expenditures, but are included in the expenditure class in which the product falls.

NOTE: Numbers may not add to totals because of rounding.

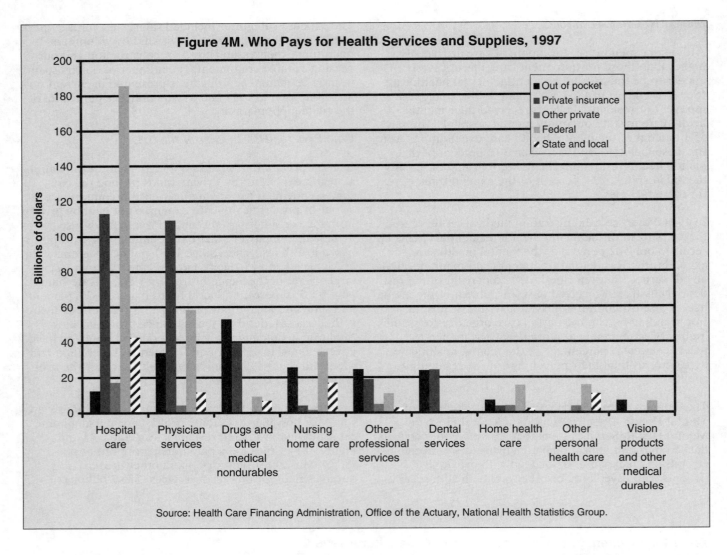

Figure 4M. Who Pays for Health Services and Supplies, 1997

Billions of dollars

Legend:
- Out of pocket
- Private insurance
- Other private
- Federal
- State and local

Categories: Hospital care; Physician services; Drugs and other medical nondurables; Nursing home care; Other professional services; Dental services; Home health care; Other personal health care; Vision products and other medical durables

Source: Health Care Financing Administration, Office of the Actuary, National Health Statistics Group.

dental services ($25.8 billion). Out-of-pocket expenses include copayments, deductibles, and any services not covered by the insurer. More private insurance funds ($116.1 billion) than public funds ($73.3 billion) were spent for physician services. Private funds ($11.5 billion), other than consumer out of pocket or insurance premiums, were more likely than public funds ($4 billion) to be spent on construction of health care and institutional facilities. These construction costs exclude housing or offices for health care providers, as reported by the Bureau of Census Survey of New Construction.

THE HEALTH CARE SYSTEM

Health care services depend not only on the patient's health conditions but also on the organization and financing of the health care system. However, as pointed out by the National Academy of Science, a national monitoring system is not available to track the effect of changes in the entire health care system on the appropriateness, quality, cost, and outcomes of prevention and treatment.[31]

The financing and organization of the health care system is in flux.[32] Gabel discussed changes within HMOs in the past decade that also apply to other parts of the health care system.[33] These changes included the rapid growth of for-profit health care organizations. Needleman, Chollet, and Lamphere found that hospital ownership changed the most in California, Florida, Georgia, and Texas.[34] One question is the effect this change had on access to care. Because communities benefit from non-profit hospitals, health services researchers are examining whether the ownership status (private or public) affects access and quality of care.[35] The conversion of nonprofit hospitals to for-profit organizations does not always result in less care for those unable to pay.[36]

Mergers, acquisitions, and other forms of consolidation of health organizations have also increased. Consumers have been most directly affected by the changed arrangements and organization of physicians and other provider personnel. The model of a physician practicing alone or in a group setting has been augmented by different arrangements. For example, the physician may be part of a network of preferred providers or part of an independent practice association. People enrolled in health plans may choose from independent practice associations, preferred providers organizations, or point of service plans where the enrollee is encouraged to use the providers in the plan but can choose outside the plan at extra cost when the service is used.

The major change in the health care system most felt by the consumer involved the move away from reimbursement for costs and toward fixed payments per patient or enrollee (capitation). This change resulted in a shift of the financial risk for health costs from the health plan to the health care provider, giving physicians incentives to reduce costs, reduce services, and select less costly patients. This change also resulted in increased cost sharing by the patient. In 1987, the average out-of-pocket cost for an HMO member for a doctor's visit was $1.18; by 1993 it was $4.51. For mental health treatment, the out-of-pocket cost for outpatient care was $4.74 in 1987; by 1993 it was $12.24. In 1987, the prescription drug copayment was $3.90 per prescription; by 1993 it was $4.60 per prescription. The shift from fee-for-service programs to capitation was joined by the public health insurers and resulted in the changing use of hospitals.[37]

In prior decades, the infrastructure and services provided by the health care system were driven by the fee-for-service insurance plan. Indeed, most persons with either private or public health insurance had a regular source of medical care. (See earlier discussion of Access to Care and Tables 4C and 4.3.) In 1993, over 90 percent of persons under age 18 and of persons age 45 to 64 with either private or public insurance had a regular source of medical care. Among those with no health insurance, 78.9 percent of those age under age 18, 58.9 percent of those age 18 to 44, and 66.1 percent of those age 45 to 64 had a regular source of medical care. Characteristics of the uninsured are shown in Table 4.26. Surprisingly, persons of working age (18 to 64 years old) were less likely than younger persons to have a regular source of medical care, regardless of insurance status.

At present, HMOs and other managed care organizations play an increasingly important role in the availability, delivery, and structure of health care services. In 1996, 60 percent of the population was enrolled in managed care organizations compared with 36 percent in 1992.[38] This figure included enrollment in public insurance programs as well as private employer-sponsored programs. In Medicare alone, more than 4.8 million persons were enrolled in managed care plans, and by 1996, HCFA estimated that 80,000 Medicare beneficiaries were voluntarily enrolling in risk plan HMOs each month. Risk plans are paid a set amount per beneficiary based on 95 percent of the projected average expenses for fee-for-service beneficiaries. Under risk plan contracts, the health plan must provide all Medicare-covered services and assumes full financial risk for all care provided to Medicare beneficiaries. In 1999, only about 15 percent of Medicare beneficiaries were enrolled in managed care plans compared with over half of Medicaid beneficiaries. The increase in managed care enrollees in the Medicaid program has been recent. (See Table 4K.)

MEDICAID

The Medicaid program was established in 1965. It provides medical assistance for lower-income children and their adult caretakers, and elderly, blind, and disabled persons who meet the eligibility criteria. The federal government contributes to each state Medicaid program on the basis of the average per capita income in each state. The federal government establishes broad guidelines for the program, some mandatory Medicaid eligibility groups, and minimum services that must be covered. Within those guidelines, the states administer their own programs, establish their own eligibility standards, and determine the services to be covered and the rate of payment. Therefore, the Medicaid program varies from state to state. HCFA estimates that 20 percent of the nation's children are covered by Medicaid. Fewer elderly, blind, and disabled persons are covered by Medicaid; yet 72 percent of the health care expenditures in the Medicaid program are for these groups.

Table 4K. Medicaid and Managed Care: 1993–1998

Year	Total Medicaid population	Fee for service population	Managed care population	Percent managed care enrollment
1993	33 430 051	28 621 100	4 808 951	14.4
1994	33 634 000	25 839 750	7 794 250	23.2
1995 [1]	33 373 000	23 573 000	9 800 000	29.4
1996	33 241 147	19 911 028	13 330 119	40.1
1997	32 092 380	16 746 878	15 345 502	47.8
1998	30 896 635	14 322 639	16 573 996	53.6

SOURCE: Health Care Financing Administration, Center for Medicaid and State Operations, Data and Systems Group, data from the Medicaid Managed Care: Enrollment Report. See <http://www.hcfa.gov/medicaid/trends98.htm>. Total Medicaid population data for 1993 and 1994 are based on data submitted by the states using HCFA form 2082 that is derived from their administrative records for the program. For these years, the table shows the recipient count, which includes anyone who ever had a service paid for during the fiscal year. For 1995, HCFA estimated the June 30, 1995, total Medicaid enrollment by interpolating full-year-equivalent enrollment figures, which HCFA calculated from state-submitted HCFA form 2082 data. From 1996 on, all data come from the Managed Care Survey that collects Medicaid and managed care enrollment as of June 30 each year.

1. Data for 1995 are approximate.

NOTE: The total Medicaid population for 1996 was collected by states at the same time the managed care enrollment numbers were collected. In prior years, HCFA form 2082 data were used to develop estimates of the total Medicaid population.

In 1993, only 14.4 percent of the Medicaid population was enrolled in managed care health plans; by 1998, managed care enrollment had increased to 53.6 percent. (See Figure 4N.) The impact of this shift to managed care enrollment is reflected in changes in the utilization rates of various health care services, the size and composition of the health care workforce, and national health expenditures. Medicaid covers about 31 million persons and is jointly funded by federal and state governments. Medicaid pays for skilled nursing facility care, intermediate care facilities for the mentally retarded and developmentally disabled, and other long-term institutional care. HCFA estimates that Medicaid covers 68 percent of the residents in nursing homes and is the largest insurer of long-term care in the United States.

SUMMARY

The current U.S. health care system is undergoing changes, including the trend toward more medical care delivered in ambulatory settings. Many nations are joining the United States in examining the health care factors that might provide cost-effective measures to prevent disease, injury, and illness and to promote public health.[39] The initial approach was to increase health resources. This approach resulted in providing more training for health care providers, increasing the number of physicians for the population, constructing additional health care facilities, and so forth. These changes resulted in some improvement, but the focus shifted to improve access to health care. In the United States, the adoption of Medicare and Medicaid provided increased access and improved care for the elderly and those most in need but unable to pay for their medical care. Finally, the focus has shifted to health outcomes, with emphasis on cost-effective procedures to prevent and treat health conditions.

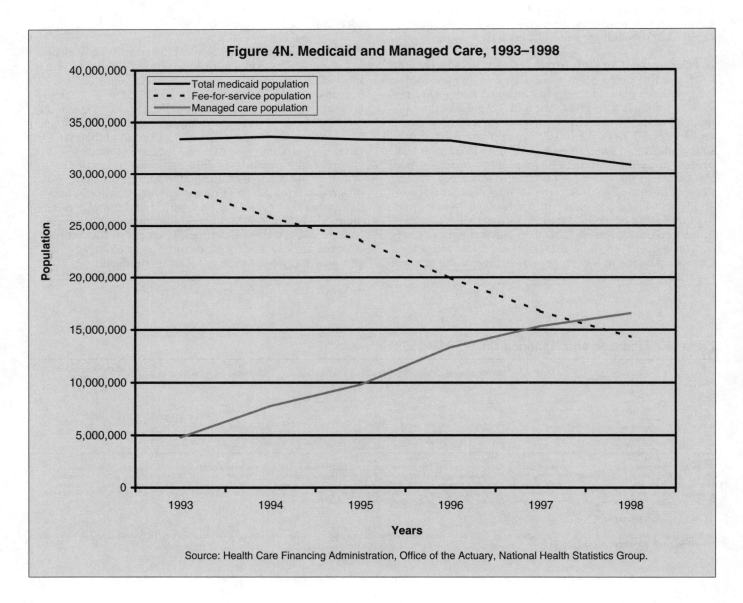

Figure 4N. Medicaid and Managed Care, 1993–1998

Source: Health Care Financing Administration, Office of the Actuary, National Health Statistics Group.

Table 4.1. Regular Source of Medical Care: 1996

(Percent, except where noted)

Characteristic	Number		Place of regular source of care			
	Total population	No usual source of care	No usual source of care	Office based [1]	Hospital outpatient or clinic [2]	Emergency room
Total [3]	262 654 000	46 227 104	17.6	72.7	9.2	0.5
AGE						
0–5 years	24 164 000	1 329 020	5.5	83.8	10.1	*0.5
6–17 years	47 253 000	4 914 312	10.4	80.2	9.0	0.4
18–24 years	24 854 000	8 450 360	34.0	57.4	7.6	1.0
25–54 years	114 359 000	25 959 493	22.7	68.1	8.8	0.4
55–64 years	22 899 000	3 022 668	13.2	75.2	10.9	*0.7
65 years and over	31 125 000	2 863 500	9.2	80.3	10.1	*0.4
RACE AND/OR ETHNICITY						
White	201 466 000	31 227 230	15.5	76.3	7.8	0.3
Black	32 838 000	6 633 276	20.2	63.6	14.9	*1.3
Hispanic	28 350 000	8 391 600	29.6	57.9	11.9	0.6
SEX						
Male	127 922 000	27 247 386	21.3	69.3	8.9	0.4
Female	134 732 000	18 997 212	14.1	76.0	9.4	0.5
PERCEIVED HEALTH STATUS						
Excellent	95 817 000	17 630 328	18.4	73.0	8.2	0.3
Very good	79 193 000	14 492 319	18.3	72.4	8.8	0.5
Good	58 405 000	10 512 900	18.0	71.9	9.5	*0.5
Fair	21 115 000	2 808 295	13.3	73.1	12.8	*0.8
Poor	7 868 000	794 668	10.1	77.8	10.9	*1.2
HEALTH INSURANCE STATUS [4] UNDER AGE 65						
Any private	161 356 000	23 396 620	14.5	77.2	8.1	0.2
Public only	26 278 000	3 494 974	13.3	70.8	14.5	1.4
Not insured	43 896 000	16 680 480	38.0	51.8	9.1	1.1
Medicare only	8 123 000	966 637	11.9	74.9	12.8	*0.4
Medicare and private	19 344 000	1 450 800	7.5	83.4	8.7	*0.3
Medicare and other public	3 056 000	271 984	8.9	78.3	12.2	*0.5
METROPOLITAN STATISTICAL AREA (MSA)						
MSA	208 887 000	37 808 547	18.1	72.3	9.1	0.4
Not MSA	53 767 000	8 495 186	15.8	74.3	9.3	*0.6

SOURCE: R.M. Weinick, S.H. Zuvekas, and S. Drilea, *Access to Health Care—Sources and Barriers,* 1996 (Rockville, Md.: Agency for Health Care Policy and Research, Center for Cost and Financing Studies—Medical Expenditure Panel Survey, Household Component, 1996, Rounds 1 and 2, 1996).

*Figure does not meet standard of reliability or precision, relative standard error is greater than or equal to 30%.
1. Office based includes all types of physicians and nonphysician providers seen in an office setting as well as office-based group practices or clinics.
2. Hospital outpatient department or clinic includes outpatient departments and clinics owned and operated by hospitals.
3. The total includes persons with unknown health status and those few individuals age 65 and over who did not have Medicare. The total excludes a small number of persons who were eligible for data collection in the first half of 1996 but died or were institutionalized in the second half of the year.
4. Health insurance status refers to status during the first half of 1996. Not insured refers to person uninsured during the entire period. Public and private insurance categories refer to persons with public or private insurance at any time during the period. Persons with both public and private insurance are considered privately insured. CHAMPUS and CHAMPVA (Armed Forces–related coverage) are considered private health insurance in this report.

NOTE: The survey was restricted to the civilian, noninstitutionalized population of the United States. Percents may not add to 100 because of rounding.

Table 4.2. How Many People Have a Regular Source of Medical Care: 1993

(Percent)

Characteristic	Children 0–17 years			Adults 18–64			Persons 65 years and over		
	Private doctor [1]	Clinic	Emergency room	Private doctor [1]	Clinic	Emergency room	Private doctor [1]	Clinic	Emergency room
Total [2]	84.4	11.1	1.4	85.9	8.8	1.6	91.3	4.3	0.6
SEX									
Male	84.1	11.1	1.5	85.6	8.3	1.9	89.1	4.4	0.6
Female	84.6	11.0	1.3	86.2	9.2	1.3	93.0	4.3	0.5
AGE									
0–4 years	82.0	13.3	1.3	—	—	—	—	—	—
5–17 years	85.4	10.1	1.4	—	—	—	—	—	—
18–44 years	—	—	—	84.2	10.2	1.9	—	—	—
45–64 years	—	—	—	89.3	6.0	1.0	—	—	—
65–74 years	—	—	—	—	—	—	90.9	4.2	0.5
75 years and over	—	—	—	—	—	—	92.0	4.5	0.6
RACE AND/OR ETHNICITY									
White, non-Hispanic	91.5	5.0	0.6	89.7	5.8	1.2	**92.8	**3.3	**0.4
Black, non-Hispanic	66.9	25.3	*4.7	71.2	19.9	*4.3	**77.9	**14.4	**1.7
Hispanic	70.0	25.0	*1.8	76.5	18.4	*1.6	—	—	—
Mexican-American	69.9	25.3	*1.8	75.1	19.0	*1.5	—	—	—
Other Hispanic	70.1	24.6	*1.7	78.3	17.6	*1.6	—	—	—
REGION									
Northeast	86.3	11.3	*0.9	87.0	8.5	1.7	91.4	4.9	*0.6
Midwest	87.5	10.2	1.0	87.0	9.2	1.3	92.2	5.1	0.2
South	83.0	11.1	*2.3	85.8	7.6	2.0	92.3	3.2	*0.8
West	81.3	11.7	*1.0	83.9	10.2	1.2	88.5	4.7	*0.6
PLACE OF RESIDENCE									
MSA [3]	82.9	12.4	1.4	85.2	9.7	1.4	90.6	4.8	0.6
Central city	73.3	20.2	*2.6	78.0	15.2	2.2	86.7	7.2	0.9
Noncentral city	89.1	7.5	*0.6	89.5	6.4	0.9	93.2	3.2	*0.3
Not MSA [3]	89.3	6.3	1.5	88.6	5.6	2.2	93.5	2.9	0.6
FAMILY STRUCTURE									
Both parents	87.7	8.0	1.1	—	—	—	—	—	—
Mother only	73.2	21.5	*2.0	—	—	—	—	—	—
Mother and other adult	72.4	21.7	*2.7	—	—	—	—	—	—
Other	74.2	19.6	*2.9	—	—	—	—	—	—
EMPLOYMENT STATUS									
Currently in labor force	—	—	—	87.8	7.6	1.4	—	—	—
Currently employed	—	—	—	88.3	7.2	1.4	—	—	—
Currently unemployed	—	—	—	77.2	16.2	2.4	—	—	—
Not in labor force	—	—	—	79.3	13.1	2.1	—	—	—
FAMILY INCOME									
Less than $10,000	62.5	32.2	3.2	61.1	29.9	3.7	87.9	6.7	*1.4
$10,000–$19,999	72.8	20.2	*2.9	75.6	15.5	3.7	90.7	4.7	*0.6
$20,000–$ 34,999	86.2	8.6	*1.1	87.7	6.9	1.5	93.0	3.6	*0.3
$35,000–$49,000	93.8	3.3	*0.6	91.3	4.8	0.8	92.2	3.5	*0.2
$50,000 or more	94.0	3.2	*0.2	92.5	4.3	0.6	92.1	3.4	*0.3

SOURCE: G. Simpson, B. Bloom, R.A. Cohen, and P.E. Parsons, "Access to Health Care—Part 1: Children," *Vital and Health Statistics* (National Center for Health Statistics—NCHS) 10, no. 196 (1997): Table 5. B. Bloom, G. Simpson, R.A. Cohen, and P.E. Parsons, "Access to Health Care—Part 2: Working-Age Adults," *Vital and Health Statistics* (NCHS) 10, no. 197 (1997): Table 5. R.A. Cohen, B. Bloom, G. Simpson, and P.E. Parsons, "Access to Health Care—Part 3: Older Adults," *Vital and Health Statistics* (NCHS) 10, no. 198 (1997): Table 2. Based on data from the National Health Interview Survey.

* Figure does not meet standard of reliability or precision.
** Includes persons of Hispanic origin.
— Data not available.
1. Includes health maintenance organizations (HMOs).
2. Persons of races other than white or black, persons with unknown income, poverty status, health insurance coverage, and health status are included in the total but not shown separately.
3. MSA is metropolitan statistical area.

Table 4.3. Regular Source of Medical Care and Type of Health Insurance: 1993

(Percent)

Characteristic	0–4 years	0–17 years	5–17 years	18–44 years	18–64 years	45–64 years	65 years and over	65–74 years	75 years and over
REGULAR SOURCE OF MEDICAL CARE									
Total[1]	96.3	93.7	92.6	80.1	82.7	88.3	93.9	93.6	94.2
Sex									
Male	96.3	93.5	92.3	73.9	77.7	85.7	93.3	92.7	94.4
Female	96.3	93.9	93.0	86.0	87.6	90.7	94.3	94.3	94.2
Race and/or ethnicity									
White, non-Hispanic	97.1	95.3	94.6	81.7	84.2	88.9	93.9	93.8	94.1
Black, non-Hispanic	95.5	92.5	91.2	80.5	83.1	89.7	93.4	92.2	95.3
Hispanic	92.7	87.1	84.0	69.7	71.9	79.2	—	—	—
Mexican-American	92.5	86.0	82.2	67.0	69.5	79.5	—	—	—
Other Hispanic	93.1	88.9	86.8	74.0	75.3	78.9	—	—	—
Region									
Northeast	97.9	97.3	97.0	86.0	87.3	90.0	94.3	94.2	94.4
Midwest	96.9	95.7	95.2	82.5	85.2	91.1	93.9	93.9	94.0
South	94.2	90.9	89.5	76.6	79.9	86.5	93.9	93.4	94.7
West	97.1	92.8	90.9	77.7	80.3	86.4	93.3	93.0	93.7
Place of residence									
MSA[2]	96.3	93.6	92.4	79.2	82.0	87.9	93.7	93.7	93.8
Central city	95.3	92.3	90.9	76.0	78.9	86.1	93.0	92.9	93.1
Noncentral city	97.1	94.4	93.3	81.4	83.9	88.8	94.2	94.2	94.2
Not MSA[2]	96.1	94.1	93.4	83.4	85.6	89.6	94.2	93.3	95.6
Family structure									
Both parents	96.7	94.6	93.8	79.7	82.1	87.9	—	—	—
Mother only	95.5	92.1	91.1	80.1	82.5	88.0	—	—	—
Mother and other adult	95.5	92.1	89.8	72.0	74.8	84.8	—	—	—
Other	88.6	83.2	82.1	81.7	84.9	89.4	—	—	—
Family income									
Less than $10,000	—	—	—	71.9	74.4	82.9	92.1	88.4	95.2
$10,000–$19,999	—	—	—	71.2	74.6	83.3	93.0	92.6	93.6
Less than $20,000	94.0	89.4	87.0	—	—	—	—	—	—
$20,000–$34,999	96.3	93.7	92.6	78.3	81.0	87.6	95.4	95.5	95.3
$35,000 or more	99.0	97.5	97.0	—	—	—	—	—	—
$35,000–$49,000	—	—	—	86.3	87.5	90.3	94.2	95.1	91.7
$50,000 or more	—	—	—	88.7	90.2	92.5	95.7	95.3	96.8
PRIVATE HEALTH INSURANCE									
Total[1]	98.6	96.8	96.2	86.2	87.9	91.2	—	—	—
Sex									
Male	98.6	96.6	95.9	81.4	84.0	88.7	—	—	—
Female	98.7	97.1	96.5	90.8	91.8	93.6	—	—	—
Race and/or ethnicity									
White, non-Hispanic	98.6	97.1	96.5	86.2	88.0	91.0	—	—	—
Black, non-Hispanic	98.4	95.5	94.7	85.9	88.4	94.0	—	—	—
Hispanic	98.2	96.0	95.0	87.4	88.6	92.0	—	—	—
Mexican-American	98.5	95.4	94.1	84.7	86.0	90.5	—	—	—
Other Hispanic	97.9	96.7	96.1	90.8	91.5	93.2	—	—	—
Region									
Northeast	99.9	99.0	98.7	89.5	90.3	91.8	—	—	—
Midwest	98.5	97.4	97.0	86.4	88.7	92.8	—	—	—
South	97.5	94.8	93.9	82.8	85.3	89.7	—	—	—
West	98.9	96.9	96.1	87.4	88.6	90.9	—	—	—
Place of residence									
MSA[2]	98.8	97.1	96.4	85.8	87.6	91.0	—	—	—
Central city	98.7	96.9	96.2	84.6	86.4	90.4	—	—	—
Noncentral city	98.8	97.1	96.5	86.5	88.2	91.3	—	—	—
Not MSA[2]	98.1	96.0	95.3	87.6	89.2	91.8	—	—	—
Family structure									
Both parents	98.7	97.1	96.5	85.7	87.4	90.9	—	—	—
Mother only	97.8	95.4	94.9	85.7	87.4	90.9	—	—	—
Mother and other adult	98.2	96.0	95.1	86.0	87.9	91.7	—	—	—
Other	100.0	91.8	90.6	89.6	90.9	92.2	—	—	—
Family income									
Less than $10,000	—	—	—	81.6	82.8	87.4	—	—	—
$10,000–$19,999	—	—	—	80.0	83.1	89.1	—	—	—
Less than $20,000	97.9	94.1	92.6	—	—	—	—	—	—
$20,000–$34,999	97.9	95.8	95.0	82.9	85.0	89.6	—	—	—
$35,000 or more	99.2	97.9	97.5	—	—	—	—	—	—
$35,000–$49,000	—	—	—	88.1	89.2	91.5	—	—	—
$50,000 or more	—	—	—	90.1	91.2	92.8	—	—	—

See footnotes at end of table.

Table 4.3. Regular Source of Medical Care and Type of Health Insurance: 1993—*Continued*

(Percent)

Characteristic	0–4 years	0–17 years	5–17 years	18–44 years	18–64 years	45–64 years	65 years and over	65–74 years	75 years and over
PUBLIC HEALTH INSURANCE									
Total [1]	95.9	94.1	92.8	84.9	86.9	94.1	—	—	—
Sex									
Male	96.2	93.7	91.8	78.6	82.0	90.8	—	—	—
Female	95.6	94.5	93.7	87.0	88.8	96.0	—	—	—
Race and/or ethnicity									
White, non-Hispanic	96.6	94.9	93.7	81.8	84.7	95.1	—	—	—
Black, non-Hispanic	94.3	93.8	93.4	88.6	89.8	93.9	—	—	—
Hispanic	95.9	92.8	89.8	85.0	86.4	*92.6	—	—	—
Mexican-American	96.4	94.5	92.0	82.1	83.6	94.5	—	—	—
Other Hispanic	95.0	90.5	87.4	88.2	89.1	91.7	—	—	—
Region									
Northeast	94.5	95.6	96.1	92.1	93.2	96.6	—	—	—
Midwest	96.2	94.9	93.8	82.6	83.6	90.0	—	—	—
South	96.1	93.8	91.9	85.1	87.7	94.4	—	—	—
West	96.0	92.7	90.2	81.3	84.1	93.8	—	—	—
Place of residence									
MSA [2]	95.7	93.7	92.2	84.0	86.1	93.7	—	—	—
Central city	95.4	94.4	93.6	85.1	86.9	93.5	—	—	—
Noncentral city	96.2	92.5	89.6	81.9	84.3	94.0	—	—	—
Not MSA [2]	96.6	95.6	94.9	89.3	90.8	96.0	—	—	—
Family structure									
Both parents	96.6	94.7	93.1	78.5	79.9	91.3	—	—	—
Mother only	95.1	93.7	93.0	79.8	81.4	*92.3	—	—	—
Mother and other adult	96.4	96.6	96.9	75.3	75.3	*76.6	—	—	—
Other	91.2	89.8	89.4	88.1	89.9	94.6	—	—	—
Family income									
Less than $10,000	96.1	94.2	92.9	84.1	86.5	94.3	—	—	—
$10,000–$19,999	—	—	—	87.0	88.3	94.1	—	—	—
$20,000–$34,999	90.8	90.3	89.8	82.4	84.3	95.1	—	—	—
$35,000 or more	100.0	100.0	100.0	—	—	—	—	—	—
$35,000–$49,000	—	—	—	*84.1	85.6	*100.0	—	—	—
$50,000 or more	—	—	—	*100.0	100.0	*100.0	—	—	—
NO HEALTH INSURANCE									
Total [1]	86.3	78.9	76.3	58.9	60.5	66.1	—	—	—
Sex									
Male	86.3	78.9	76.3	52.2	53.4	59.3	—	—	—
Female	86.2	78.9	76.4	67.5	68.5	71.5	—	—	—
Race and/or ethnicity									
White, non-Hispanic	87.5	83.8	82.5	62.6	63.7	67.7	—	—	—
Black, non-Hispanic	93.4	81.9	78.2	66.4	67.5	71.4	—	—	—
Hispanic	78.1	67.0	62.6	44.3	46.0	53.3	—	—	—
Mexican-American	78.9	67.8	63.5	46.6	49.1	62.0	—	—	—
Other Hispanic	75.7	64.5	59.9	39.2	39.5	40.6	—	—	—
Region									
Northeast	93.3	89.4	87.7	69.2	69.7	71.6	—	—	—
Midwest	86.8	85.4	84.9	64.3	65.1	69.0	—	—	—
South	81.3	75.4	73.4	59.4	61.4	67.8	—	—	—
West	89.8	75.3	70.6	48.3	50.1	57.5	—	—	—
Place of residence									
MSA [2]	85.9	76.8	73.4	56.1	57.7	63.7	—	—	—
Central city	84.9	73.3	68.3	51.5	53.5	61.4	—	—	—
Noncentral city	87.0	79.8	77.4	60.5	61.6	65.8	—	—	—
Not MSA [2]	87.4	85.3	84.6	69.4	70.4	73.3	—	—	—
Employment status									
Currently in labor force	—	—	—	58.1	59.2	63.9	—	—	—
Currently employed	—	—	—	58.3	59.4	63.8	—	—	—
Currently unemployed	—	—	—	56.6	57.7	64.0	—	—	—
Not in labor force	—	—	—	61.7	64.3	70.4	—	—	—
Family structure									
Both parents	85.9	80.8	78.7	—	—	—	—	—	—
Mother only	91.8	78.6	75.5	—	—	—	—	—	—
Mother and other adult	87.4	77.5	73.3	—	—	—	—	—	—
Other	71.0	62.8	61.5	—	—	—	—	—	—
Family income									
Less than $10,000	—	—	—	53.1	56.3	67.5	—	—	—
$10,000–$19,999	—	—	—	57.0	58.6	64.7	—	—	—
Less than $20,000	84.1	75.8	72.8	—	—	—	—	—	—
$20,000–$34,999	91.0	83.7	81.0	60.3	62.1	70.6	—	—	—
$35,000 or more	93.5	88.6	87.0	—	—	—	—	—	—
$35,000–$49,000	—	—	—	70.9	70.1	66.6	—	—	—
$50,000 or more	—	—	—	69.2	71.8	81.1	—	—	—

SOURCE: G. Simpson, B. Bloom, R.A. Cohen, and P.E. Parsons, "Access to Health Care—Part 1: Children," *Vital and Health Statistics* (National Center for Health Statistics—NCHS) 10, no. 196 (1997): Tables 1–4. B. Bloom, G. Simpson, R.A. Cohen, and P.E. Parsons, "Access to Health Care—Part 2: Working-Age Adults," *Vital and Health Statistics* (NCHS) 10, no. 197 (1997): Tables 1–4. R.A. Cohen, B. Bloom, G. Simpson, and P.E. Parsons, "Access to Health Care—Part 3: Older Adults," *Vital and Health Statistics* (NCHS) 10, no. 198 (1997): Table 1. Based on data from the National Health Interview Survey.

* Figure does not meet standard of reliability or precision.
— Data not available.
1. Includes persons with all types of health insurance coverage including those for which health insurance coverage is unknown. Non-Hispanic persons of races other than white or black, persons with unknown income, unknown family structure, unknown poverty status, and unknown health status are included in the total but not shown separately.
2. MSA is metropolitan statistical area.

NOTE: Children with unknown regular source of medical care were excluded from the analysis. Percent distribution includes other and unknown places of regular source of care but are not shown separately.

Table 4.4. Physician Care: 1995

Characteristic	Place of contact number per person per year					Interval since last contact percent [1]				
	All places [2]	Telephone	Office	Hospital	Other	All intervals [3]	Less than 1 year	1 year to less than 2 years	2 years to less than 5 years	5 years or more
All persons [4]	5.9	0.8	3.3	0.7	1.1	100.0	79.1	9.4	8.0	3.4
AGE										
Under 5 years	6.5	1.0	3.8	0.8	0.9	100.0	94.9	4.1	0.7	0.2
5–17 years	3.4	0.4	2.0	0.4	0.5	100.0	79.1	12.5	6.9	1.5
18–24 years	3.9	0.4	2.0	0.6	0.8	100.0	71.8	13.1	11.1	4.1
25–44 years	5.2	0.8	2.9	0.6	0.8	100.0	72.9	10.9	11.4	4.8
45–64 years	7.1	0.9	3.9	0.9	1.3	100.0	79.9	7.8	8.0	4.4
65–74 years	9.8	1.1	5.6	1.2	1.9	100.0	88.5	4.4	4.1	3.1
75 years and over	12.9	1.2	6.5	1.0	4.0	100.0	92.1	3.5	2.5	1.8
SEX AND AGE										
Male										
All ages	4.9	0.6	2.7	0.7	0.9	100.0	73.6	10.9	10.7	4.8
Under 18 years	4.4	0.6	2.6	0.6	0.6	100.0	83.5	10.4	4.9	1.2
18–44 years	3.3	0.4	1.7	0.5	0.7	100.0	62.3	13.9	16.5	7.3
45–64 years	6.0	0.7	3.2	0.8	1.2	100.0	75.1	8.8	10.5	5.6
65 years and over	10.4	1.0	5.9	1.1	2.3	100.0	88.9	4.2	4.0	3.0
Female										
All ages	6.9	0.9	3.8	0.8	1.3	100.0	84.4	8.1	5.5	2.0
Under 18 years	4.2	0.6	2.4	0.5	0.6	100.0	83.8	9.9	5.3	1.0
18–44 years	6.4	1.0	3.6	0.7	1.0	100.0	82.6	9.0	6.3	2.0
45–64 years	8.1	1.0	4.5	1.0	1.4	100.0	84.3	6.8	5.7	3.2
65 years and over	11.6	1.2	6.0	1.2	3.1	100.0	90.7	4.0	3.1	2.3
RACE AND AGE										
White										
All ages	6.1	0.8	3.4	0.7	1.1	100.0	79.3	9.3	8.0	3.4
Under 18 years	4.5	0.6	2.8	0.5	0.6	100.0	83.9	9.9	5.1	1.1
18–44 years	5.0	0.7	2.8	0.6	0.8	100.0	72.8	11.4	11.3	4.5
45–64 years	7.0	0.9	3.9	0.9	1.3	100.0	79.6	7.8	8.1	4.4
65 years and over	11.2	1.2	6.1	1.1	2.7	100.0	90.1	4.1	3.3	2.6
Black										
All ages	5.2	0.5	2.5	1.0	1.2	100.0	80.0	10.0	7.4	2.5
Under 18 years	3.5	0.5	1.6	0.7	0.7	100.0	83.2	11.2	4.9	0.7
18–44 years	4.5	0.4	2.3	1.0	0.9	100.0	74.3	11.4	10.4	3.8
45–64 years	8.0	*0.6	4.0	1.4	1.9	100.0	83.0	7.3	6.5	3.2
65 years and over	10.4	*0.7	4.9	1.5	3.2	100.0	89.9	3.5	4.4	2.2
FAMILY INCOME AND AGE										
Under $10,000										
All ages	8.2	0.9	3.6	1.3	2.5	100.0	81.2	8.5	7.2	3.1
Under 18 years	5.0	0.6	2.4	0.7	1.2	100.0	83.2	10.2	5.7	1.0
18–44 years	6.1	0.7	2.7	1.0	1.7	100.0	75.4	10.6	9.7	4.3
45–64 years	13.8	1.4	5.4	2.8	4.0	100.0	82.8	5.5	9.7	4.3
65 years and over	13.9	1.2	5.9	1.6	5.1	100.0	88.9	4.1	3.7	3.2
$10,000–$19,999										
All ages	7.0	0.8	3.6	1.0	1.6	100.0	76.9	9.8	9.0	4.3
Under 18 years	4.4	0.6	2.2	0.7	0.8	100.0	80.1	11.0	7.2	1.7
18–44 years	5.7	0.5	2.9	0.9	1.2	100.0	68.2	12.8	13.3	5.8
45–64 years	9.2	1.0	4.4	1.1	2.5	100.0	77.0	7.2	8.7	7.1
65 years and over	11.7	1.3	6.3	1.2	2.8	100.0	89.8	4.0	3.3	2.9
$20,000–$34,999										
All ages	5.7	0.7	3.1	0.7	1.1	100.0	77.0	10.3	8.9	3.8
Under 18 years	3.9	0.5	2.2	0.5	0.6	100.0	81.4	11.2	5.8	1.6
18–44 years	4.5	0.6	2.4	0.6	0.8	100.0	70.2	12.3	12.6	4.9
45–64 years	7.3	0.7	4.3	1.0	1.2	100.0	76.8	8.9	8.8	5.4
65 years and over	10.9	1.4	6.0	1.0	2.4	100.0	90.3	4.2	3.1	2.3
$35,000 or more										
All ages	5.4	0.9	3.3	0.6	0.7	100.0	81.2	9.0	7.2	2.7
Under 18 years	4.6	0.7	2.9	0.5	0.5	100.0	86.8	8.7	3.9	0.6
18–44 years	5.1	0.9	3.0	0.5	0.6	100.0	75.8	10.6	9.8	3.7
45–64 years	6.0	0.9	3.5	0.6	0.9	100.0	81.9	7.6	7.2	3.3
65 years and over	10.3	1.3	5.8	1.0	2.2	100.0	91.1	3.4	3.7	1.9
GEOGRAPHIC REGION										
Northeast	5.8	0.8	3.5	0.7	0.8	100.0	82.9	7.9	6.2	3.0
Midwest	6.0	0.9	3.1	0.8	1.1	100.0	79.9	9.4	7.8	2.9
South	5.9	0.7	3.3	0.7	1.2	100.0	77.5	10.4	8.6	3.5
West	5.8	0.6	3.2	0.7	1.2	100.0	77.5	9.4	9.1	4.0
PLACE OF RESIDENCE										
MSA [5]	6.0	0.8	3.3	0.7	1.1	100.0	79.7	9.3	7.8	3.3
Central city	5.9	0.7	3.0	0.9	1.2	100.0	78.9	9.6	8.2	3.4
Not central city	6.0	0.8	3.5	0.7	1.0	100.0	80.2	9.1	7.5	3.3
Not MSA [5]	5.6	0.6	3.0	0.6	1.3	100.0	77.0	10.2	9.1	3.7

SOURCE: V. Benson and M.A. Marano, *Current Estimates from the National Health Interview Survey, 1995.* National Center for Health Statistics. *Vital and Health Statistics* 10, no. 199 (1998): Tables 71, 72.

* Figure does not meet standard of reliability or precision.
1. Includes physician contacts while an overnight patient is in a hospital.
2. Includes unknown place of contact.
3. Excludes unknown interval.
4. Includes other races and unknown family income.
5. MSA is metropolitan statistical area.

NOTE: Data are based on household interviews of the civilian noninstitutionalized population. The standard errors (SEs) and relative standard errors (RSEs) for age, sex and age, and race and age for columns 1–5 can be computed by using parameter set VI of table II, the frequencies of table 71 and the formula presented in rule 2 of appendix I. The SE's and RSE's for family income and age, geographic region, and place of residence for columns 1–5 can be computed by using parameter sets VI and X of table II, the frequencies of tables 71 and 78 and the formula presented in rule 4 of appendix I. The SE's and RSE's for columns 6–10 can be computed by using parameter set VI of table II and the formula presented in rule 1 of appendix I. An estimate of 21.0 million has a 10-percent RSE; of 5.2 million, a 20-percent RSE; and of 2.3 million, a 30-percent RSE.

Table 4.5. Who Gets Care for Acute Conditions: 1996

(Percent medically attended)

Type of acute condition	All ages	Under 5 years	5–17 years	18–24 years	25–44 years	45 years and over	45–64 years	65 years and over
ALL ACUTE CONDITIONS	67.9	81.2	61.6	65.0	63.8	72.4	68.7	78.5
INFECTIVE AND PARASITIC DISEASES	67.6	79.0	70.8	68.1	54.3	60.1	57.2	*68.5
Common childhood diseases	60.5	*73.5	*53.9	*38.9	*44.9	*—	*—	*—
Intestinal virus, unspecified	36.3	*52.9	37.8	*18.1	*32.9	*30.3	*26.6	*37.0
Viral infections, unspecified	67.1	84.7	70.6	*37.8	*53.2	*50.1	*47.7	*67.4
Other	94.1	100.0	96.9	100.0	78.4	94.7	92.3	*100.0
RESPIRATORY CONDITIONS	51.1	67.9	47.6	40.8	47.9	55.1	52.1	60.8
Common cold	43.0	73.8	36.3	*22.0	41.1	40.6	37.4	46.2
Other acute upper respiratory infections	87.0	100.0	83.1	82.1	82.5	97.1	97.5	96.2
Influenza	36.3	47.9	35.5	28.5	32.1	41.4	38.6	47.8
Acute bronchitis	90.7	*100.0	92.1	*86.2	87.2	91.7	100.0	*80.8
Pneumonia	89.8	*78.2	*84.0	*100.0	*88.0	*97.3	*90.6	*100.0
Other respiratory conditions	91.8	*100.0	*100.0	*100.0	*84.7	*87.5	*85.1	*100.0
DIGESTIVE SYSTEM CONDITIONS	63.5	*74.5	*33.5	*74.1	70.1	80.9	72.1	92.7
Dental conditions	*59.6	*62.2	*31.8	*100.0	*31.5	*89.9	*83.9	*100.0
Indigestion, nausea, and vomiting	40.5	*51.9	*22.6	*74.9	*57.0	*49.3	*39.9	*72.1
Other digestive conditions	92.5	*100.0	*92.8	*63.2	*100.0	93.1	*89.1	*96.9
INJURIES	91.4	100.0	92.1	93.1	89.8	89.3	89.4	89.0
Fractures and dislocations	97.8	*100.0	97.1	*100.0	*93.4	100.0	100.0	*100.0
Sprains and strains	84.1	*100.0	*90.3	*96.1	82.4	*74.7	*70.0	*100.0
Open wounds and lacerations	97.9	*100.0	*100.0	*100.0	94.7	*100.0	*100.0	*100.0
Contusions and superficial injuries	90.6	*100.0	94.8	*89.0	91.5	*83.0	*94.1	*60.3
Other current injuries	90.7	100.0	83.9	85.5	94.0	89.6	*91.9	88.4
SELECTED OTHER ACUTE CONDITIONS	92.8	95.7	82.0	98.5	91.5	98.0	98.4	97.4
Eye conditions	100.0	*100.0	*100.0	*100.0	*100.0	*100.0	*100.0	*100.0
Acute ear infections	98.6	99.2	96.4	*100.0	100.0	*100.0	*100.0	*100.0
Other ear conditions	97.5	*100.0	*100.0	*100.0	*90.4	*100.0	*100.0	*100.0
Acute urinary conditions	99.4	*100.0	*100.0	*100.0	98.1	100.0	*100.0	100.0
Disorders of menstruation	*74.3	. . .	*24.1	*100.0	*78.6	*—	*—	*—
Other disorders of female genital tract	*97.2	*—	*100.0	*100.0	*100.0	*91.2	*87.4	100.0
Delivery and other conditions of pregnancy and puerperium	97.5	. . .	*100.0	*100.0	*95.6	*—	*—	0.0
Skin conditions	88.8	*100.0	*65.5	*100.0	*74.5	100.0	*100.0	*100.0
Acute musculoskeletal conditions	91.5	*100.0	*78.8	*100.0	84.8	93.2	*95.5	*90.8
Headache, excluding migraine	*75.3	*—	*18.5	*100.0	*81.9	*100.0	*100.0	*100.0
Fever, unspecified	57.2	*69.6	*21.5	*58.0	*86.9	*100.0	*100.0	*—
ALL OTHER ACUTE CONDITIONS	89.8	98.8	81.4	83.5	87.4	93.5	92.9	94.2

See footnotes at end of table.

Table 4.5. Who Gets Care for Acute Conditions: 1996—*Continued*

(Percent medically attended)

Type of acute condition	Male					Female				
	All ages	Under 5 years	5–17 years	18–44 years	45 years and over	All ages	Under 5 years	5–17 years	18–44 years	45 years and over
ALL ACUTE CONDITIONS	68.8	80.2	65.2	62.6	73.8	67.2	82.5	58.4	65.2	71.5
INFECTIVE AND PARASITIC DISEASES	70.1	84.0	74.6	47.4	69.9	65.7	72.8	67.7	65.6	55.5
Common childhood diseases	*73.2	*94.6	*55.1	*44.9	*—	*46.7	*41.2	*53.1	*38.9	*—
Intestinal virus, unspecified	49.2	*69.7	*56.5	*30.1	*41.8	27.7	*34.6	*26.1	*27.9	*25.0
Viral infections, unspecified	65.6	82.1	*64.7	*38.3	*55.0	68.7	*89.5	*77.7	*60.2	*48.3
Other	92.8	*100.0	96.0	*76.9	*100.0	94.8	*100.0	97.6	92.3	*91.5
RESPIRATORY CONDITIONS	49.7	63.8	46.8	43.4	54.5	52.3	72.6	48.1	48.1	55.5
Common cold	43.0	72.0	37.6	31.6	40.4	43.0	76.0	35.2	38.7	40.7
Other acute upper respiratory infections	89.1	*100.0	90.3	79.5	100.0	86.0	*100.0	79.3	83.6	95.3
Influenza	37.4	44.4	35.4	33.0	44.6	35.3	52.4	35.7	29.7	38.9
Acute bronchitis	92.9	*100.0	*100.0	*83.4	*100.0	89.6	*100.0	*84.5	88.9	89.5
Pneumonia	84.7	*73.1	*45.3	*100.0	*94.4	94.7	*100.0	*100.0	*83.5	*100.0
Other respiratory conditions	*86.0	*100.0	*100.0	*79.0	*100.0	95.8	*100.0	*100.0	*100.0	*86.0
DIGESTIVE SYSTEM CONDITIONS	64.3	*67.6	*43.8	*60.5	80.9	62.8	*79.7	*26.1	*76.3	*81.0
Dental conditions	*49.2	*59.2	*28.5	*15.9	*83.4	*71.6	*65.7	*51.3	*65.4	*100.0
Indigestion, nausea, and vomiting	*31.6	*27.5	*28.7	*28.8	*39.3	44.7	*63.6	*19.8	*70.3	*61.0
Other digestive conditions	95.0	*100.0	*100.0	*87.7	*97.4	89.8	*100.0	*80.8	*90.6	*86.7
INJURIES	93.2	*100.0	94.3	93.8	87.5	89.0	*100.0	87.6	87.0	90.9
Fractures and dislocations	100.0	*100.0	100.0	*100.0	*100.0	95.6	*100.0	*89.4	*93.5	*100.0
Sprains and strains	85.8	*100.0	*93.8	87.2	*74.9	82.1	*—	*87.5	82.8	*74.4
Open wounds and lacerations	100.0	*100.0	*100.0	100.0	*100.0	93.0	*100.0	*100.0	*88.8	*100.0
Contusions and superficial injuries	90.0	*100.0	*92.3	93.8	*64.0	91.4	*100.0	*100.0	*85.6	*94.7
Other current injuries	93.1	*100.0	87.6	95.1	92.4	88.4	*100.0	*76.7	88.7	87.1
SELECTED OTHER ACUTE CONDITIONS	91.3	93.2	82.1	89.6	100.0	94.0	98.1	81.9	95.5	96.5
Eye conditions	* 100.0	* 100.0	* 100.0	* 100.0	* 100.0	* 100.0	* 100.0	* 100.0	* 100.0	* 100.0
Acute ear infections	98.3	*98.5	97.3	*100.0	*100.0	98.8	100.0	95.0	100.0	*100.0
Other ear conditions	*93.3	*100.0	*100.0	*75.5	*100.0	100.0	*100.0	*100.0	*100.0	*100.0
Acute urinary conditions	100.0	*—	*100.0	*100.0	*100.0	99.2	*100.0	*100.0	98.2	100.0
Disorders of menstruation	. . .	. . .	. . .	. . .	. . .	*74.3	. . .	*24.1	*83.7	*—
Other disorders of female genital tract	. . .	. . .	. . .	. . .	. . .	*97.2	*—	*100.0	*100.0	*91.2
Delivery and other conditions of pregnancy and puerperium	. . .	. . .	. . .	. . .	. . .	97.5	. . .	*100.0	97.2	*—
Skin conditions	81.7	*100.0	*61.1	*60.7	*100.0	95.9	*100.0	*70.5	*100.0	*100.0
Acute musculoskeletal conditions	95.2	*100.0	*100.0	92.0	*100.0	87.6	*100.0	*71.8	*85.5	88.1
Headache, excluding migraine	*68.0	*—	*—	*100.0	*100.0	*81.0	*—	*47.7	*76.6	*100.0
Fever, unspecified	*55.5	*68.4	*10.3	*68.8	*100.0	*59.2	*72.8	*29.9	*80.7	*100.0
ALL OTHER ACUTE CONDITIONS	95.1	100.0	88.8	95.5	95.3	85.6	*95.8	74.6	81.0	92.3

See footnotes at end of table.

Table 4.5. Who Gets Care for Acute Conditions: 1996—*Continued*

(Percent medically attended)

Type of acute condition	White				Black			
	All ages	Under 18 years	18–44 years	45 years and over	All ages	Under 18 years	18–44 years	45 years and over
ALL ACUTE CONDITIONS	68.1	69.5	63.7	72.8	68.7	68.7	69.3	67.4
INFECTIVE AND PARASITIC DISEASES	67.5	74.3	59.6	58.0	68.9	68.9	*67.2	*73.9
Common childhood diseases	*55.7	*60.8	*—	*—	*92.2	*87.0	*100.0	*—
Intestinal virus, unspecified	35.0	41.1	*31.6	*22.7	*41.5	*50.4	*—	*75.4
Viral infections, unspecified	68.6	80.4	*50.4	*50.3	*64.1	*62.4	*78.1	*47.1
Other	93.4	97.4	87.2	94.1	*100.0	*100.0	*100.0	*100.0
RESPIRATORY CONDITIONS	50.7	54.0	45.0	55.3	54.3	59.6	52.7	*44.9
Common cold	42.1	49.3	34.9	39.9	43.0	52.5	*33.7	*28.4
Other acute upper respiratory infections	87.0	85.9	82.4	98.2	83.4	*100.0	*77.1	*—
Influenza	34.9	38.3	29.5	40.4	51.1	*52.5	49.6	*51.5
Acute bronchitis	90.2	94.9	85.8	91.7	*100.0	*100.0	*100.0	*—
Pneumonia	89.9	*81.2	*89.6	*100.0	*81.5	*—	*—	*81.5
Other respiratory conditions	92.6	*100.0	*88.1	*86.1	80.8	*100.0	*69.5	*—
DIGESTIVE SYSTEM CONDITIONS	67.3	48.9	75.7	81.8	*49.4	*34.5	*51.5	*86.9
Dental conditions	*70.0	*52.5	*60.0	*100.0	*49.4	*66.0	*35.5	*—
Indigestion, nausea, and vomiting	41.3	*28.0	*60.2	*47.9	*41.2	*18.9	*76.0	*100.0
Other digestive conditions	94.7	96.5	94.3	94.0	*65.8	*—	*38.6	*85.3
INJURIES	91.8	94.3	90.7	91.6	92.5	97.8	91.4	*83.6
Fractures and dislocations	98.9	97.1	100.0	100.0	*83.7	*100.0	*75.4	*—
Sprains and strains	85.0	*92.5	85.9	*75.6	87.5	*66.7	*87.7	*100.0
Open wounds and lacerations	97.5	100.0	95.7	*100.0	*100.0	*100.0	*100.0	*100.0
Contusions and superficial injuries	89.6	95.0	88.6	*86.3	*94.0	*100.0	*100.0	*24.8
Other current injuries	91.2	89.8	90.8	93.3	*95.9	*100.0	*100.0	*83.3
SELECTED OTHER ACUTE CONDITIONS	93.1	90.3	93.3	98.7	91.9	85.4	95.2	*96.0
Eye conditions	100.0	*100.0	*100.0	*100.0	*100.0	*—	*100.0	*100.0
Acute ear infections	98.4	98.1	100.0	*100.0	*100.0	*100.0	*100.0	*100.0
Other ear conditions	97.3	*100.0	*91.1	*100.0	*100.0	*100.0	*100.0	*—
Acute urinary conditions	99.3	*100.0	98.1	100.0	*100.0	*100.0	*100.0	*100.0
Disorders of menstruation	*74.3	*24.1	*83.7	*—	*—	*—	*—	*—
Other disorders of female genital tract	*100.0	100.0	100.0	100.0	64.2	*—	100.0	*—
Delivery and other conditions of pregnancy and puerperium	97.0	*100.0	96.6	*—	*100.0	*—	*100.0	*—
Skin conditions	86.9	*75.6	*80.0	*100.0	*100.0	*100.0	*100.0	*100.0
Acute musculoskeletal conditions	91.9	89.7	89.3	95.0	*93.7	*—	*92.4	*100.0
Headache, excluding migraine	*71.7	*—	*83.9	*100.0	*76.3	*38.0	*100.0	*100.0
Fever, unspecified	60.7	*51.7	*89.8	*100.0	*41.0	*28.5	*—	*100.0
ALL OTHER ACUTE CONDITIONS	91.1	89.8	88.2	94.7	82.1	*80.6	*82.5	*83.0

See footnotes at end of table.

Table 4.5. Who Gets Care for Acute Conditions: 1996—*Continued*

(Percent medically attended)

Type of acute condition	Family income							
	Less than $10,000				$10,000–$19,999			
	All ages	Under 18 years	18–44 years	45 years and over	All ages	Under 18 years	18–44 years	45 years and over
ALL ACUTE CONDITIONS	71.6	72.0	68.9	76.2	65.6	69.7	57.1	73.5
INFECTIVE AND PARASITIC DISEASES	49.0	*59.2	*37.6	*27.6	*74.2	*76.1	*63.9	*100.0
Common childhood diseases	*78.8	*78.8	*—	*—	*30.2	*54.8	*—	*—
Intestinal virus, unspecified	*3.3	*8.6	*—	*—	*51.6	*42.5	*60.8	*—
Viral infections, unspecified	*32.3	*42.0	*16.7	*—	*74.7	*74.5	*46.5	*100.0
Other	100.0	*100.0	*100.0	*100.0	100.0	*100.0	*100.0	*100.0
RESPIRATORY CONDITIONS	57.3	65.5	46.4	61.5	43.3	49.3	33.2	54.9
Common cold	56.5	73.4	*34.3	*63.7	37.1	*42.3	*31.3	*44.7
Other acute upper respiratory infections	88.5	*100.0	*81.1	*100.0	79.3	*87.3	*62.0	*100.0
Influenza	39.5	52.9	*19.1	*38.5	27.0	*29.3	*22.7	*33.0
Acute bronchitis	*100.0	*100.0	*100.0	*100.0	*100.0	*100.0	*100.0	*100.0
Pneumonia	*100.0	*—	*100.0	*100.0	*79.4	*100.0	*50.0	*92.0
Other respiratory conditions	*100.0	*100.0	*100.0	*100.0	*88.6	*100.0	*66.2	*100.0
DIGESTIVE SYSTEM CONDITIONS	*66.5	*34.6	*100.0	*79.9	61.4	*59.8	*54.3	*68.9
Dental conditions	*100.0	*—	*100.0	*—	*41.3	*53.4	*—	*100.0
Indigestion, nausea, and vomiting	*42.0	*34.6	*100.0	*52.7	*53.5	*52.9	*73.1	*37.2
Other digestive conditions	*100.0	*—	*100.0	*100.0	*94.3	*100.0	*100.0	*90.5
INJURIES	93.2	*100.0	92.2	*87.2	91.3	91.1	90.9	90.8
Fractures and dislocations	*89.2	*100.0	*78.4	*—	*100.0	*100.0	*100.0	*100.0
Sprains and strains	*83.9	*—	*83.9	*—	97.5	*100.0	*96.6	*100.0
Open wounds and lacerations	*96.1	*100.0	*93.1	*100.0	*100.0	*100.0	*100.0	*100.0
Contusions and superficial injuries	*89.0	*100.0	*100.0	*56.0	*78.3	*100.0	*77.5	*61.0
Other current injuries	*100.0	*100.0	*100.0	*100.0	77.9	*90.5	*58.2	*82.3
SELECTED OTHER ACUTE CONDITIONS	95.4	88.9	97.5	*100.0	95.4	95.3	100.0	88.3
Eye conditions	*100.0	*100.0	*100.0	*100.0	*100.0	*—	*100.0	*—
Acute ear infections	*100.0	*100.0	*100.0	*100.0	97.0	96.8	*100.0	*100.0
Other ear conditions	*100.0	*100.0	*100.0	*—	*100.0	*100.0	*100.0	*100.0
Acute urinary conditions	*100.0	*—	*100.0	*100.0	*100.0	*100.0	*100.0	*100.0
Disorders of menstruation	*—	*—	*—	*—	*100.0	*—	*100.0	*—
Other disorders of female genital tract	*100.0	*—	*100.0	*100.0	*100.0	*100.0	*100.0	*—
Delivery and other conditions of pregnancy and puerperium	*100.0	*—	*100.0	*—	*100.0	*—	*100.0	*—
Skin conditions	*100.0	*100.0	*—	*—	*100.0	*100.0	*100.0	*100.0
Acute musculoskeletal conditions	*100.0	*100.0	*100.0	*100.0	*78.5	*100.0	*100.0	*60.5
Headache, excluding migraine	*67.0	*—	*100.0	*100.0	*77.3	*—	*100.0	*100.0
Fever, unspecified	*66.1	*70.8	*58.0	*—	*90.7	*90.7	*—	*—
ALL OTHER ACUTE CONDITIONS	92.0	*90.9	*85.7	*100.0	81.2	*65.2	*81.1	87.8

See footnotes at end of table.

Table 4.5. Who Gets Care for Acute Conditions: 1996—*Continued*

(Percent medically attended)

Type of acute condition	Family income							
	$20,000–$34,999				$35,000 or more			
	All ages	Under 18 years	18–44 years	45 years and over	All ages	Under 18 years	18–44 years	45 years and over
ALL ACUTE CONDITIONS	65.5	66.3	58.4	76.5	67.6	70.1	65.1	66.5
INFECTIVE AND PARASITIC DISEASES	66.2	77.0	53.4	*60.4	69.4	74.3	66.2	53.1
Common childhood diseases	*24.3	*24.3	*—	*—	*76.6	*72.9	*100.0	*—
Intestinal virus, unspecified	*51.8	*73.6	*30.0	*55.2	33.7	41.6	*19.0	*21.0
Viral infections, unspecified	*63.0	*84.8	*—	*15.8	72.2	79.6	*80.2	*39.3
Other	86.2	*89.3	*85.3	*83.4	93.8	98.0	*82.9	*100.0
RESPIRATORY CONDITIONS	46.6	46.0	41.2	59.1	52.9	56.8	49.5	51.9
Common cold	35.1	35.9	*32.2	*38.1	44.5	55.7	36.5	37.0
Other acute upper respiratory infections	87.7	86.1	*84.3	*95.1	85.7	85.5	82.1	96.2
Influenza	35.6	32.9	31.9	50.3	36.8	38.6	34.2	38.9
Acute bronchitis	*85.7	*100.0	*75.9	*100.0	91.7	100.0	85.0	*92.5
Pneumonia	*100.0	*—	*100.0	*100.0	*100.0	*100.0	*100.0	*100.0
Other respiratory conditions	*100.0	*100.0	*100.0	*100.0	*89.0	*91.0	*91.0	*62.9
DIGESTIVE SYSTEM CONDITIONS	57.4	*37.5	*75.3	*80.0	58.0	*45.1	*64.0	*76.9
Dental conditions	*40.9	*23.7	*51.5	*100.0	*78.1	*100.0	*29.6	*100.0
Indigestion, nausea, and vomiting	*44.7	*21.5	*84.7	*41.5	*—	*14.0	*37.7	*44.5
Other digestive conditions	*89.8	*100.0	*77.0	*100.0	*88.8	*94.3	*89.7	*81.5
INJURIES	90.6	90.4	88.0	86.6	91.7	94.0	89.7	92.5
Fractures and dislocations	*100.0	*100.0	*100.0	*100.0	97.7	*95.1	*100.0	*100.0
Sprains and strains	72.6	*82.3	*71.4	*71.6	79.9	*89.5	80.6	*68.2
Open wounds and lacerations	*100.0	*100.0	*100.0	*—	95.7	*100.0	*90.8	*100.0
Contusions and superficial injuries	96.3	*100.0	*100.0	*82.7	90.6	*91.1	*85.4	*100.0
Other current injuries	89.8	*89.5	*87.5	*92.6	98.3	*93.7	100.0	*100.0
SELECTED OTHER ACUTE CONDITIONS	90.6	89.7	83.7	100.0	91.6	88.4	94.0	97.1
Eye conditions	*100.0	*100.0	*100.0	*100.0	*100.0	*100.0	*100.0	*100.0
Acute ear infections	97.8	97.3	*100.0	*100.0	98.9	98.6	*100.0	*100.0
Other ear conditions	*100.0	*100.0	*100.0	*100.0	*93.3	*100.0	*79.3	*100.0
Acute urinary conditions	100.0	*100.0	*100.0	*100.0	98.3	*100.0	*96.2	*100.0
Disorders of menstruation	*100.0	*—	*100.0	*—	*42.7	*24.1	*52.9	*—
Other disorders of female genital tract	*100.0	*—	*100.0	*100.0	*89.9	*—	*100.0	*—
Delivery and other conditions of pregnancy and puerperium	*92.3	*100.0	*89.1	*—	*100.0	*—	*100.0	*—
Skin conditions	*86.2	*100.0	*56.1	*100.0	*86.6	*78.1	*80.7	*100.0
Acute musculoskeletal conditions	*80.2	*100.0	*57.8	*100.0	97.2	*100.0	*100.0	*93.2
Headache, excluding migraine	*46.7	*—	*—	*100.0	*81.8	*—	*100.0	*100.0
Fever, unspecified	*51.2	*37.3	*100.0	*100.0	*38.7	*26.5	*78.0	*100.0
ALL OTHER ACUTE CONDITIONS	93.9	88.7	*92.1	100.0	89.8	93.2	92.1	81.7

See footnotes at end of table.

Table 4.5. Who Gets Care for Acute Conditions: 1996—*Continued*

(Percent medically attended)

Type of acute condition	Geographic region				MSA			Not MSA [1]
	Northeast	Midwest	South	West	All MSA [1]	Central City	Not Central City	
ALL ACUTE CONDITIONS	69.7	68.1	71.8	60.5	67.2	65.7	68.1	70.6
INFECTIVE AND PARASITIC DISEASES	69.0	81.8	59.5	69.0	69.9	71.7	69.2	61.1
Common childhood diseases	*100.0	*35.1	*74.6	*39.1	*65.7	*57.5	*69.4	*49.9
Intestinal virus, unspecified	*32.0	*34.5	41.3	*19.6	40.1	*45.8	37.7	*28.7
Viral infections, unspecified	67.5	83.8	54.9	*81.1	67.1	79.6	61.9	*67.4
Other	98.7	*—	92.8	94.1	94.6	88.1	97.0	92.6
RESPIRATORY CONDITIONS	53.6	49.5	59.0	41.6	50.0	47.7	51.7	55.7
Common cold	45.5	46.0	51.7	29.1	42.3	41.0	43.4	46.3
Other acute upper respiratory infections	88.2	82.0	88.6	89.4	86.9	85.4	87.8	87.4
Influenza	36.0	33.4	40.1	35.5	36.3	34.5	37.7	35.8
Acute bronchitis	84.6	95.0	94.1	86.8	87.2	100.0	80.4	100.0
Pneumonia	*91.2	*100.0	*100.0	*56.7	98.5	*96.3	100.0	*74.1
Other respiratory conditions	*100.0	*100.0	*87.0	*82.7	92.2	*84.0	97.0	*90.5
DIGESTIVE SYSTEM CONDITIONS	*48.2	73.7	67.6	52.3	60.3	76.6	51.9	75.3
Dental conditions	*100.0	*100.0	*53.9	*35.6	*65.4	*70.8	*62.0	*42.2
Indigestion, nausea, and vomiting	*13.6	*44.2	*53.0	*40.0	*39.5	*68.7	*25.2	*48.7
Other digestive conditions	*100.0	94.6	87.0	*100.0	90.0	*91.6	89.2	97.9
INJURIES	91.2	88.6	96.0	87.8	91.7	89.9	92.8	90.2
Fractures and dislocations	*89.7	100.0	100.0	*100.0	96.9	96.5	97.2	100.0
Sprains and strains	82.4	85.7	91.8	76.2	84.4	76.3	88.9	83.0
Open wounds and lacerations	100.0	95.2	100.0	*93.9	97.0	*97.0	97.0	100.0
Contusions and superficial injuries	93.9	86.1	92.3	*93.0	92.0	92.4	91.8	*82.6
Other current injuries	95.7	82.6	95.4	88.9	92.1	91.6	92.4	85.6
SELECTED OTHER ACUTE CONDITIONS	93.3	93.5	92.9	91.6	93.0	94.3	92.3	92.4
Eye conditions	*100.0	*100.0	*100.0	*100.0	100.0	*100.0	*100.0	*100.0
Acute ear infections	98.1	95.7	100.0	100.0	98.8	98.2	99.0	97.7
Other ear conditions	*100.0	*91.5	*100.0	*100.0	96.9	*100.0	*94.9	*100.0
Acute urinary conditions	*100.0	100.0	100.0	*96.7	99.3	100.0	98.7	100.0
Disorders of menstruation	*—	*57.0	*100.0	*52.9	*67.8	*53.8	*76.0	*100.0
Other disorders of female genital tract	*100.0	*100.0	*100.0	*92.4	*96.3	*100.0	*92.4	*100.0
Delivery and other conditions of pregnancy and puerperium	*100.0	*75.1	*100.0	*100.0	96.5	*100.0	*94.9	*100.0
Skin conditions	*73.7	*100.0	*89.2	*89.9	88.6	*90.7	*86.8	*89.3
Acute musculoskeletal conditions	92.8	*94.6	93.3	*85.1	93.7	*95.4	93.2	86.0
Headache, excluding migraine	*—	*100.0	*75.9	*72.5	*73.3	*68.0	*79.8	*79.9
Fever, unspecified	*78.8	*56.8	*36.0	*71.4	56.8	*76.7	*44.2	*58.6
ALL OTHER ACUTE CONDITIONS	90.0	90.8	89.3	89.6	89.4	93.8	86.5	91.2

SOURCE: P.F. Adams, G.E. Hendershot, and M.A. Marano, *Current Estimates from the National Health Interview Survey, 1996.* National Center for Health Statistics. *Vital and Health Statistics* 10, no. 200 (1999): Tables 11–15.

* Figure does not meet standards of reliability or precision.
*— Figure does not meet standards of reliability or precision, and quantity zero.
... Category not applicable.
1. MSA is metropolitan statistical area.

NOTE: A condition is considered acute if (a) it was first noticed no longer than 3 months before the reference date of the interview, and (b) it is not one of the conditions considered chronic regardless of the time of onset. This table refers only to acute conditions that involved at least one doctor visit or resulted in at least one day of restricted activity.

Table 4.6. Average Annual Hospitalizations and Deaths for Gastrointestinal Illness by Diagnostic Category: 1992–1996

Cause of enteritis [1]	First diagnosis		All diagnoses	
	Hospitalizations	Deaths	Hospitalizations	Deaths
Bacterial (001-005,008-008.5)	27 987	*148	54 953	1 139
Viral (008.6-008.8)	82 149	*0	132 332	*194
Parasitic (006-007)	2 806	*82	5 799	*127
Unknown etiology (009,558.9)	186 537	*868	423 293	5 148
Total	299 479	1 898	616 377	6 608

SOURCE: P. Mead, L. Slutsker, V. Dietz, L. McCaig, J. Bresse, C. Shapiro, P. Griffin, and R. Tauxe, "Food-Related Illness and Death in the United States," *Emerging Infectious Diseases* (Centers for Disease Control and Prevention) 5, no. 5 (September–October 1999): Table 5.

* Estimate unreliable because of small sample size.
1. ICD-9-CM code.

Table 4.7. Estimated Average Rates of Hospitalizations for Asthma as the First-Listed Diagnosis

(Per 10,000 population)

Characteristic	1979–1980	1981–1983	1984–1986	1987–1989	1990–1992	1993–1994
RACE [1]						
White	14.2	16.2	15.9	14.1	11.9	10.9
Black	26.0	34.8	33.2	38.1	40.1	35.5
Other	28.2	30.6	32.7	33.6	24.4	23.0
SEX [1]						
Male	16.3	18.4	18.7	18.3	18.0	15.9
Female	18.7	21.4	21.8	21.0	20.8	20.0
AGE GROUP						
0–4 years	34.3	42.8	48.5	52.2	58.3	49.7
5–14 years	15.9	19.2	18.9	18.7	20.6	18.0
15–34 years	8.7	9.5	9.5	9.5	9.3	10.0
35–64 years	18.2	20.3	19.0	16.7	15.4	15.2
65 years and over	31.5	33.6	37.5	35.2	29.7	25.6
Total	17.6	20.0	20.5	19.8	19.7	18.1

SOURCE: D.M. Mannino, D.M. Homa, C.A. Pertowski, A. Ashizawa, L.L. Nixon, C.A. Johnson, L.B. Ball, E. Jack and D.S. Kang. "Surveillance for Asthma—United States," 1960–1995. In: CDC Surveillance Summaries, *Morbidity and Mortality Weekly Report* 47 (No. SS-1), April 24, 1998, pages 1–28: Table 8.

1. Age-adjusted to the 1970 U.S. population.

NOTE: All relative standard errors are <30% (i.e. relative confidence interval <59%) unless otherwise indicated. These estimates are based on hospitalization data from the National Hospitalization Discharge Survey, 1979–1994.

Table 4.8. Treatment for Asthma

Characteristic	Number					Per 100,000 office visits		
	Cases 1993–1994	Office visits 1993–1995	Emergency room 1995	Hospitalizations 1993–1994	Deaths 1993–1995	Emergency room 1995	Hospitalizations 1993–1994	Deaths 1993–1995
RACE								
White	1 070 000	8 316 000	1 018 000	240 000	4 084	12 241.5	2 886.0	49.1
Black	1 880 000	1 373 000	775 000	115 000	1 182	56 445.7	8 375.8	86.1
Other	5 400 000	6 860 000	*73 000	26 000	165	10 641.4	3 790.1	24.1
Missing	(NA)	(NA)		85 000				
SEX								
Male	6 150 000	4 252 000	725 000	191 000	2 036	17 050.8	4 492.0	47.9
Female	7 400 000	6 122 000	1 140 000	275 000	3 394	18 621.4	4 492.0	55.4
AGE GROUP								
0–4 years	1 280 000	1 024 000	248 000	97 000	34	24 218.8	9 472.7	3.3
5–14 years	2 790 000	2 004 000	322 000	67 000	136	16 067.9	3 343.3	6.8
15–34 years	4 050 000	1 876 000	566 000	78 000	489	30 170.6	4 157.8	26.1
35–64 years	4 090 000	3 982 000	630 000	139 000	1 798	15 821.2	3 490.7	45.2
65 years and over	1 480 000	1 488 000	101 000	85 000	2 972	6 787.6	5 712.4	199.7
Total	13 690 000	10 374 000	1 867 000	466 000	542 900	1 799 690	449 200	5 230

SOURCE: D.M. Mannino, D.M. Homa, C.A. Pertowski, A. Ashizawa, L.L. Nixon, C.A. Johnson, L.B. Ball, E. Jack and D.S. Kang. "Surveillance for Asthma—United States," 1960–1995. In: CDC Surveillance Summaries, *Morbidity and Mortality Weekly Report* 47 (No. SS-1), April 24, 1998, pages 1–28: Tables 1, 3, 5, 7, 9.

* Relative standard error of the estimate is 30%–50%; the estimate is unreliable.
1. Numbers for each variable may not add up to total because of rounding error.

NOTE: All relative standard errors are <30% (i.e., relative confidence interval <59%) unless otherwise indicated.

Table 4.9. Ambulatory and Inpatient Surgery: 1996

(Per 1,000 population)

Sex and age	Total	Ambulatory [1]	Inpatient [2]
BOTH SEXES			
All ages	272.4	119.3	153.0
Under 15 years	75.1	41.3	33.8
Under 1 year	242.1	57.8	184.3
1–4 years	93.4	63.1	30.3
5–14 years	51.2	30.8	20.4
15–44 years	203.5	80.5	123.0
15–24 years	154.9	46.6	108.4
25–34 years	235.0	82.7	152.3
35–44 years	214.7	106.7	108.0
45–64 years	337.6	164.3	173.2
45–54 years	282.2	143.7	138.6
55–64 years	421.4	195.7	225.7
65 years and over	746.7	317.2	429.5
65–74 years	668.2	300.0	368.2
75–84 years	863.9	368.7	495.2
85 years and over	779.6	245.7	533.9
MALE			
All ages	232.2	107.9	124.3
Under 15 years	86.3	48.0	38.3
Under 1 year	292.8	74.9	217.9
1–4 years	109.5	75.6	33.9
5–14 years	56.8	34.3	22.5
15–44 years	119.4	62.4	57.0
15–24 years	75.0	37.4	37.6
25–34 years	111.1	60.7	50.3
35–44 years	165.0	85.4	79.6
45–64 years	341.8	155.9	185.9
45–54 years	267.9	129.4	138.5
55–64 years	456.6	197.1	259.5
65 years and over	819.4	339.6	479.8
65–74 years	729.6	314.5	415.1
75–84 years	961.3	395.7	565.5
85 years and over	922.9	299.5	623.4
FEMALE			
All ages	310.6	130.3	180.3
Under 15 years	63.2	34.2	29.0
Under 1 year	189.0	39.8	149.2
1–4 years	76.6	50.1	26.5
5–14 years	45.4	27.2	18.3
15–44 years	287.4	98.6	188.9
15–24 years	237.9	56.0	181.9
25–34 years	356.7	104.2	252.4
35–44 years	263.3	127.5	135.8
45–64 years	333.7	172.3	161.4
45–54 years	295.9	157.3	138.6
55–64 years	389.4	194.4	195.0
65 years and over	696.1	301.6	394.5
65–74 years	618.8	288.4	330.4
75–84 years	801.0	351.2	449.7
85 years and over	722.7	224.3	498.4

SOURCE: M.F. Owings and L.J. Kozak, "Ambulatory and Inpatient Procedures in the United States, 1996." National Center for Health Statistics. *Vital and Health Statistics* 13, no. 139 (1998): Table 2.

1. Data from the National Survey of Ambulatory Surgery. Excludes ambulatory patients who become inpatients.
2. Data from the National Hospital Discharge Survey. Excludes newborn infants.

NOTE: Procedures estimated from the National Survey of Ambulatory Surgery and the National Hospital Discharge Survey. Not all procedures are covered by these surveys.

Table 4.10. Ambulatory Care Visits: 1995

Ambulatory care setting	Total	Age						Sex		Race		
		Under 15 years	15–24 years	25–44 years	45–64 years	65–74 years	75 years and over	Male	Female	White	Black	Other
NUMBER OF VISITS (PER 100,000 PERSONS) [1]												
Combined settings	328 700	284 600	222 100	277 200	364 200	560 300	683 200	277 100	377 700	338 200	280 800	288 700
Physician offices	266 200	221 100	155 700	218 600	308 500	494 400	588 300	220 100	309 900	280 700	178 300	248 000
Outpatient departments	25 700	25 300	23 000	22 400	28 600	32 800	34 000	20 600	30 500	23 100	44 900	17 900
Emergency departments	36 900	38 200	43 400	36 200	27 000	33 100	60 900	36 500	37 300	34 400	57 600	22 800
NUMBER OF VISITS (THOUSANDS)												
Combined settings	860 859	169 297	80 266	230 265	188 320	102 605	90 106	353 484	507 375	733 087	93 984	33 788
Physician offices	697 082	131 548	56 278	181 590	159 531	90 544	77 591	280 762	416 320	608 384	59 678	29 020
Outpatient departments	67 232	15 039	8 307	18 588	14 811	6 004	4 482	26 221	41 011	50 110	15 022	2 100
Emergency departments	96 545	22 709	15 681	30 086	13 978	6 057	8 033	46 501	50 044	74 593	19 284	2 668
PERCENT DISTRIBUTION												
Combined settings	100.0	100.0	100.0	100.0	100.0	100.0	100.0	100.0	100.0	100.0	100.0	100.0
Physician offices	81.0	77.7	70.1	78.9	84.7	88.2	86.1	79.4	82.1	83.0	63.5	85.9
Outpatient departments	7.8	8.9	10.3	8.1	7.9	5.9	5.0	7.4	8.1	6.8	16.0	6.2
Emergency departments	11.2	13.4	19.5	13.1	7.4	5.9	8.9	13.2	9.9	10.2	20.5	7.9

SOURCE: S.M. Schappert, "Ambulatory Care Visits to Physician Offices, Hospital Outpatient Departments, and Emergency Departments: United States, 1995." National Center for Health Statistics. *Vital and Health Statistics* 13, no. 129 (1997): Table 1.

1. Based on U.S. Bureau of the Census estimates of the civilian noninstitutionalized population as of July 1, 1995. Figures used are monthly postcensal estimates and are consistent with Census reports PE-10/PPL-41, Addendum 1, and have been adjusted for net underenumeration using the 1990 National Population Adjustment Matrix.

NOTE: Numbers may not add to totals because of rounding.

Table 4.11. Short-Stay Hospital Care: 1996

(Percent distribution)

Characteristic	Total	All causes Number of episodes				Total	All causes excluding deliveries [1] Number of episodes			
		None	One	Two	Three or more		None	One	Two	Three or more
All persons [2]	100.0	92.7	5.9	1.0	0.4	100.0	93.9	4.8	0.9	0.4
AGE										
Under 5 years	100.0	94.5	4.6	0.6	*0.3	100.0	94.5	4.6	0.6	*0.3
5–17 years	100.0	97.8	2.0	0.2	*0.1	100.0	98.0	1.8	*0.2	*0.0
18–24 years	100.0	92.7	6.6	0.5	*0.2	100.0	96.4	3.2	*0.3	0.1
25–44 years	100.0	93.0	6.1	0.6	0.3	100.0	95.5	3.8	0.5	0.3
45–64 years	100.0	92.2	5.9	1.4	0.6	100.0	92.2	5.9	1.4	0.6
65–74 years	100.0	85.8	10.5	2.6	1.2	100.0	85.8	10.5	2.6	1.2
75 years and over	100.0	79.6	14.2	4.3	1.9	100.0	79.6	14.2	4.3	1.9
SEX AND AGE										
Male										
All ages	100.0	94.1	4.6	0.9	*0.4	100.0	94.1	4.6	0.9	*0.4
Under 18 years	100.0	96.8	2.8	0.3	*0.1	100.0	96.8	2.8	0.3	*0.1
18–44 years	100.0	96.2	3.2	0.4	0.2	100.0	96.2	3.2	0.4	0.2
45–64 years	100.0	92.5	5.5	1.3	0.7	100.0	92.5	5.5	1.3	0.7
65 years and over	100.0	81.5	13.1	3.9	1.5	100.0	81.5	13.1	3.9	1.5
Female										
All ages	100.0	91.3	7.2	1.1	*0.5	100.0	93.6	5.0	0.9	*0.4
Under 18 years	100.0	97.0	2.6	0.3	*0.1	100.0	97.3	2.3	0.3	*0.1
18–44 years	100.0	89.7	9.2	0.8	0.4	100.0	95.2	4.1	0.5	0.3
45–64 years	100.0	91.9	6.3	1.4	0.5	100.0	91.9	6.2	1.4	0.5
65 years and over	100.0	84.4	11.3	2.9	1.4	100.0	84.4	11.3	2.9	1.4
RACE AND AGE										
White										
All ages	100.0	92.7	5.9	1.0	*0.4	100.0	93.9	4.8	0.9	*0.4
Under 18 years	100.0	97.0	2.6	0.3	*0.1	100.0	97.1	2.5	0.3	0.1
18–44 years	100.0	93.1	6.1	0.5	0.3	100.0	95.9	3.5	0.4	0.2
45–64 years	100.0	92.5	5.7	1.3	0.5	100.0	92.5	5.7	1.3	0.5
65 years and over	100.0	83.2	12.1	3.3	1.4	100.0	83.2	12.1	3.3	1.4
Black										
All ages	100.0	92.0	6.4	*1.0	0.6	100.0	93.3	5.3	*0.9	0.6
Under 18 years	100.0	95.9	3.4	*0.5	*0.2	100.0	96.3	3.0	*0.5	*0.2
18–44 years	100.0	91.5	7.3	0.8	*0.4	100.0	94.3	4.8	*0.5	*0.3
45–64 years	100.0	89.9	7.5	1.4	*1.1	100.0	89.9	7.5	1.4	*1.1
65 years and over	100.0	82.1	12.4	3.4	*2.1	100.0	82.1	12.4	3.4	*2.1
FAMILY INCOME AND AGE										
Under $10,000										
All ages	100.0	89.0	8.1	*1.8	*1.1	100.0	90.6	6.6	*1.7	*1.1
Under 18 years	100.0	94.5	4.4	*0.7	*0.4	100.0	94.8	4.1	*0.7	0.4
18–44 years	100.0	89.5	8.3	1.1	*1.1	100.0	93.4	4.7	*0.8	*1.1
45–64 years	100.0	85.4	9.7	3.1	*1.8	100.0	85.4	9.7	3.1	*1.8
65 years and over	100.0	81.5	12.4	4.1	*1.9	100.0	81.5	12.4	4.1	*1.9
$10,000–$19,999										
All ages	100.0	89.7	7.8	*1.7	*0.9	100.0	91.0	6.6	*1.6	*0.8
Under 18 years	100.0	95.7	3.4	*0.5	*0.4	100.0	96.0	3.1	*0.6	*0.3
18–44 years	100.0	90.7	8.1	0.7	0.5	100.0	93.9	5.1	0.6	0.4
45–64 years	100.0	87.5	8.8	2.1	1.5	100.0	87.5	8.8	2.1	1.5
65 years and over	100.0	80.8	12.8	4.7	1.8	100.0	80.8	12.8	4.7	1.8
$20,000–$34,999										
All ages	100.0	92.2	6.3	*1.0	*0.5	100.0	93.5	5.1	0.9	*0.4
Under 18 years	100.0	97.1	2.5	*0.3	*0.1	100.0	97.3	2.3	0.3	*0.1
18–44 years	100.0	92.4	6.7	0.7	*0.2	100.0	95.4	4.0	0.5	*0.1
45–64 years	100.0	91.3	6.5	1.4	0.8	100.0	91.3	6.5	1.4	0.8
65 years and over	100.0	83.2	12.3	2.8	1.7	100.0	83.2	12.3	2.8	1.7
$35,000 or more										
All ages	100.0	94.7	4.6	*0.6	*0.2	100.0	95.7	3.6	*0.5	*0.1
Under 18 years	100.0	97.4	2.3	*0.2	*0.0	100.0	97.5	2.3	*0.2	*0.0
18–44 years	100.0	94.2	5.2	0.5	*0.1	100.0	96.6	3.0	0.4	*0.0
45–64 years	100.0	94.0	4.8	1.0	*0.3	100.0	94.0	4.7	1.0	*0.3
65 years and over	100.0	87.3	10.4	1.2	*1.0	100.0	87.3	10.4	1.2	*1.0
GEOGRAPHIC REGION										
Northeast	100.0	93.5	5.4	0.8	0.3	100.0	94.6	4.3	0.8	0.3
Midwest	100.0	92.6	6.0	1.0	0.5	100.0	93.7	4.9	0.9	0.5
South	100.0	91.7	6.6	1.2	0.5	100.0	92.9	5.5	1.1	0.5
West	100.0	93.6	5.2	0.8	0.3	100.0	94.9	4.0	0.8	0.3
PLACE OF RESIDENCE										
MSA [3]	100.0	93.1	5.6	0.9	0.4	100.0	94.3	4.5	0.9	0.4
Central city	100.0	92.6	6.0	1.0	0.4	100.0	93.9	4.8	0.9	0.4
Not central city	100.0	93.4	5.4	0.9	0.4	100.0	94.5	4.3	0.8	0.4
Not MSA [3]	100.0	91.1	7.1	1.3	0.6	100.0	92.1	6.1	1.2	0.6

SOURCE: P.F. Adams, G.E. Hendershot, and M.A. Marano, "Current Estimates from the National Health Interview Survey, 1996." National Center for Health Statistics. *Vital and Health Statistics* 10, no. 200 (1999): Table 73.

* Figure does not meet standard of reliability or precision.
0.0 Quantity more than zero but less than 0.05.
1. Based on reason for admission or other indication of delivery.
2. Includes other races and unknown family income.
3. MSA is metropolitan statistical area.

NOTE: Data are based on household interviews of the civilian noninstitutionalized population. The survey design, general qualifications, and information on the reliability of the estimates are given in Appendix I of Current Estimates from the National Health Interview Survey. Definitions of terms are given in Appendix II of Current Estimates from the National Health Interview Survey.

Table 4.12. Community Hospitals Care, Revenue, and Expenditures

Item	1994	1995	1996	1997
ALL AGES				
Admissions (thousands)	32 938	33 389	33 268	33 388
Admissions (per 1,000 population) [1]	122	122	121	120
Inpatient days (thousands)	196 117	190 377	183 495	181 313
Adult length of stay (days)	6.0	5.7	5.5	5.4
65 YEARS AND OVER				
Admissions (thousands)	12 456	12 820	12 870	13 050
Admissions (per 1,000 population) [1]	368	375	373	375
Inpatient days (thousands)	94 877	91 164	86 431	85 315
Adult length of stay (days)	8	7	7	6
UNDER 65 YEARS				
Admissions (thousands)	20 483	20 569	20 398	20 339
Admissions (per 1,000 population) [1]	87	86	85	84
Inpatient days (thousands)	101 240	99 213	97 064	95 999
Adult length of stay (days)	5	5	5	5
SURGICAL OPERATIONS (THOUSANDS)	23 286	23 739	24 165	24 601
OUTPATIENT VISITS (THOUSANDS)	417 684	452 558	481 298	507 523
CAPACITY				
Adjusted patient days (thousands) [2]	276 209	273 638	270 023	275 864
Beds (thousands)	891	874	854	833
Adult occupancy rate [3]	60	60	59	60
REVENUE (MILLIONS OF DOLLARS)				
Total hospital revenues [4]	309 354	324 961	338 118	349 329
Total patient revenues	293 285	307 228	318 183	327 938
Inpatient revenues	208 262	213 771	216 242	215 558
Outpatient revenues	85 023	93 457	101 941	112 380
EXPENSES (DOLLARS)				
Total hospital expenses (millions)	292 801	308 411	320 789	331 482
Labor (millions)	156 826	163 842	168 796	173 047
Nonlabor (millions)	135 975	144 569	151 993	158 435
Inpatient expense (millions) [5]	207 897	214 570	217 994	217 869
Amount per patient day	1 060	1 127	1 188	1 202
Amount per admission	6 312	6 426	6 553	6 525
Outpatient expense (millions) [5]	84 903	93 841	102 796	113 614
Amount per outpatient visit	203	207	214	224

SOURCE: Compiled by the Health Care Finance Administration, National Health Statistics Group from data provided by the Social Security Administration and the American Hospital Association. Some of the data can be found in American Hospital Association (AHA); Trend Analysis Group: *National Hospital Panel Survey Reports*. Chicago. Monthly Reports for January 1995—September 1998, See <http://www.hcfa.gov/stats/indicatr>, Health Care Indicators: Table 1.

1. Admissions per 1,000 population is calculated using population estimates prepared by the Social Security Administration.
2. Adjusted patient days is an aggregate figure reflecting the number of days of inpatient care, plus an estimate of the volume of outpatient services, expressed in units equivalent to an inpatient day in terms of level of effort. It is derived by multiplying the number of outpatient visits by the ratio of outpatient revenue per outpatient visit to inpatient revenue per inpatient day and adding the product to the number of inpatient days.
3. The adult occupancy rate is calculated by the National Health Statistics Group. The AHA does not publish this statistic. Adult occupancy rate is the ratio of average daily census to average number of beds maintained during the reporting period.
4. Total hospital revenue is the sum of total patient revenue and all other operating revenue. Total patient revenue is the sum of inpatient revenue and outpatient revenue.
5. Inpatient expense and outpatient expense are calculated by the National Health Statistics Group. These statistics are calculated by applying the ratio of inpatient or outpatient revenue to total patient revenue multiplied by total hospital expenses.

Table 4.13. Hospital Discharges by Sex, Age, and Region: 1996

Sex, age, and region	Discharges		Days of care		Average length of stay (days)
	Number (thousands)	Rate (per 1,000 population)	Number (thousands)	Rate (per 1,000 population)	
BOTH SEXES					
All ages					
United States	30 545	115.7	159 883	605.6	5.2
Northeast	6 665	129.4	41 343	802.5	6.2
Midwest	7 107	114.7	35 574	573.9	5.0
South	11 085	120.0	57 392	621.3	5.2
West	5 688	97.9	25 574	440.0	4.5
Under 15 years					
United States	2 207	38.2	10 064	174.4	4.6
Northeast	575	54.3	2 836	267.4	4.9
Midwest	509	37.9	2 221	165.2	4.4
South	642	32.0	2 866	142.6	4.5
West	480	35.4	2 142	157.9	4.5
15–44 years					
United States	10 325	87.0	39 645	333.9	3.8
Northeast	2 134	93.4	10 274	449.9	4.8
Midwest	2 241	80.6	8 060	290.0	3.6
South	3 823	92.3	14 427	348.3	3.8
West	2 127	79.7	6 884	258.0	3.2
45–64 years					
United States	6 294	117.2	33 521	624.3	5.3
Northeast	1 390	129.1	8 353	776.1	6.0
Midwest	1 372	108.8	6 790	538.3	4.9
South	2 469	129.7	13 287	698.0	5.4
West	1 064	94.3	5 092	451.3	4.8
65 years and over					
United States	11 718	346.1	76 652	2 263.7	6.5
Northeast	2 566	350.8	19 880	2 717.3	7.7
Midwest	2 985	367.2	18 503	2 276.5	6.2
South	4 151	351.1	26 811	2 267.5	6.5
West	2 016	305.7	11 457	1 737.5	5.7
MALE					
All ages					
United States	12 110	94.1	69 928	543.4	5.8
Northeast	2 807	112.9	18 552	746.0	6.6
Midwest	2 880	95.3	15 676	518.9	5.4
South	4 289	95.9	24 787	554.3	5.8
West	2 134	73.9	10 913	377.7	5.1
Under 15 years					
United States	1 240	42.0	5 710	193.2	4.6
Northeast	327	60.3	1 717	316.0	5.2
Midwest	298	43.3	1 328	192.7	4.5
South	344	33.5	1 561	151.8	4.5
West	271	39.0	1 105	159.0	4.1
15–44 years					
United States	2 831	47.7	15 604	263.2	5.5
Northeast	700	61.6	4 528	398.5	6.5
Midwest	657	47.2	3 224	231.9	4.9
South	998	48.8	5 362	262.1	5.4
West	476	35.1	2 491	183.5	5.2
45–64 years					
United States	3 138	120.8	17 107	658.8	5.5
Northeast	690	133.9	4 198	815.2	6.1
Midwest	679	110.9	3 401	555.3	5.0
South	1 233	134.9	6 811	745.2	5.5
West	536	96.5	2 697	485.5	5.0
65 years and over					
United States	4 901	353.1	31 507	2 269.8	6.4
Northeast	1 090	373.0	8 109	2 775.1	7.4
Midwest	1 246	377.6	7 723	2 341.1	6.2
South	1 714	354.3	11 053	2 284.7	6.4
West	851	301.6	4 621	1 637.6	5.4

See footnotes at end of table.

Table 4.13. Hospital Discharges by Sex, Age, and Region: 1996—*Continued*

Sex, age, and region	Discharges		Days of care		Average length of stay (days)
	Number (thousands)	Rate (per 1,000 population)	Number (thousands)	Rate (per 1,000 population)	
FEMALE					
All ages					
United States	18 435	136.2	89 955	664.8	4.9
Northeast	3 859	144.8	22 791	855.1	5.9
Midwest	4 226	133.0	19 898	626.3	4.7
South	6 796	142.6	32 605	684.2	4.8
West	3 553	121.6	14 661	501.6	4.1
Under 15 years					
United States	967	34.3	4 355	154.6	4.5
Northeast	248	48.0	1 119	216.3	4.5
Midwest	211	32.2	893	136.2	4.2
South	298	30.4	1 306	133.0	4.4
West	210	31.7	1 037	156.8	4.9
15–44 years					
United States	7 495	126.1	24 041	404.4	3.2
Northeast	1 434	125.0	5 747	500.9	4.0
Midwest	1 585	114.0	4 836	348.0	3.1
South	2 825	134.8	9 065	432.6	3.2
West	1 651	125.9	4 393	335.0	2.7
45–64 years					
United States	3 156	113.8	16 414	592.0	5.2
Northeast	700	124.7	4 155	740.2	5.9
Midwest	692	106.7	3 389	522.3	4.9
South	1 236	124.9	6 476	654.4	5.2
West	528	92.1	2 395	418.0	4.5
65 years and over					
United States	6 817	341.2	45 145	2 259.5	6.6
Northeast	1 476	336.0	11 771	2 678.9	8.0
Midwest	1 739	360.1	10 780	2 232.4	6.2
South	2 437	348.9	15 758	2 256.0	6.5
West	1 165	308.8	6 836	1 812.3	5.9

SOURCE: E.J. Graves and L.J. Kozak, "National Hospital Discharge Survey: Annual Summary, 1996." National Center for Health Statistics. *Vital and Health Statistics* 13, no. 140 (1998): Table 3.

NOTE: Discharges of inpatients from nonfederal hospitals. Excludes newborn infants.

Table 4.14. Reasons Why People Are in the Hospital: 1996

(Principal diagnosis only)

Multilevel Clinical Classifications Software (CCS) category [1]	Number of discharges	Percent of discharges [2]	Mean charges (dollars)	25 percentile charges (dollars)	Median charges (dollars)	75 percentile charges (dollars)	Mean length of stay (days)	Percent died	Percent male	Mean age
ALL DISCHARGES	34 872 474	100.00	10 647	2 911	5 737	11 414	5.0	2.5	41.3	47.1
1 INFECTIOUS AND PARASITIC DISEASES	738 424	2.12	15 760	4 692	8 786	17 167	7.7	10.3	50.1	53.4
1.1 **Bacterial infection**	452 392	1.30	17 096	5 708	10 100	18 772	8.4	13.0	44.8	64.2
1.1.1 Tuberculosis [1.]	13 495	0.04	24 845	7 323	13 930	26 346	14.2	5.9	66.0	51.7
1.1.2 Septicemia (except in labor) [2.]	419 175	1.20	17 022	5 775	10 156	18 754	8.2	13.7	44.2	65.9
1.1.2.1 Streptococcal septicemia	31 368	0.09	19 177	6 691	11 735	21 257	9.4	10.7	49.0	61.1
1.1.2.2 Staphylococcal septicemia	66 395	0.19	22 787	7 724	13 546	24 878	10.8	14.5	47.9	65.3
1.1.2.3 E. Coli septicemia	69 830	0.20	14 586	5 965	9 565	16 385	7.5	5.9	31.6	69.9
1.1.2.4 Other gram negative septicemia	48 427	0.14	20 486	7 070	12 064	22 173	9.3	12.4	49.3	67.8
1.1.2.5 Other specified septicemia 6	18 037	0.05	18 652	6 065	10 697	19 504	8.5	10.4	49.1	54.8
1.1.2.6 Unspecified septicemia	185 118	0.53	14 446	4 879	8 606	16 149	7.1	17.6	45.1	65.9
1.1.3 Sexually transmitted infections (not HIV or hepatitis) [9.]	5 788	0.02	9 094	3 580	5 796	10 320	5.5	0.4	31.0	32.7
1.1.4 Other bacterial infections [3.]	13 934	0.04	15 097	4 206	8 259	15 793	7.2	3.3	45.1	39.4
1.2 **Mycoses** [4.]	16 294	0.05	24 986	5 940	11 422	24 518	10.2	9.0	50.2	55.1
1.2.1 Candidiasis of the mouth (thrush)	1 080	0.00	7 724	3 138	5 078	10 235	4.9	0.9	49.0	41.4
1.2.2 Other mycoses	15 214	0.04	26 223	6 391	12 115	26 450	10.6	9.6	50.3	56.0
1.3 **Viral infection**	251 871	0.72	13 072	3 382	6 501	13 760	6.6	6.1	59.9	34.4
1.3.1 HIV infection [5.]	128 760	0.37	18 875	6 010	11 108	21 590	9.3	11.0	71.7	37.6
1.3.2 Hepatitis [6.]	21 958	0.06	12 719	3 559	5 906	10 799	5.5	4.0	49.4	45.6
1.3.3 Other viral infections [7.]	101 153	0.29	5 756	2 343	3 669	6 111	3.4	0.3	47.2	28.0
1.3.3.1 Herpes zoster infection	12 779	0.04	9 264	3 727	6 269	10 831	5.5	1.0	35.2	65.7
1.3.3.2 Herpes simplex infection	4 039	0.01	8 320	2 627	4 841	9 234	4.8	0.5	38.0	23.8
1.3.3.3 Other and unspecified viral infection	84 335	0.24	5 100	2 236	3 428	5 439	3.0	0.2	49.5	22.5
1.4 **Other infections, including parasitic** [8.]	16 998	0.05	11 650	3 800	6 591	12 197	5.8	2.0	47.8	45.1
1.5 **Immunizations and screening for infectious disease** [10.]	869	0.00	5 105	2 022	3 792	6 875	4.6	1.3	61.8	40.6
2 NEOPLASMS	2 027 921	5.82	16 034	5 768	9 691	17 355	6.3	6.0	40.1	60.0
2.1 **Colorectal cancer**	165 393	0.47	22 546	11 125	17 159	26 611	9.7	5.0	48.8	70.8
2.1.1 Cancer of colon [14.]	118 494	0.34	22 753	11 228	17 100	26 668	9.8	5.5	47.1	71.5
2.1.2 Cancer of rectum and anus [15.]	46 899	0.13	22 023	10 761	17 330	26 505	9.3	3.9	53.1	68.8
2.2 **Other gastrointestinal cancer**	97 588	0.28	25 494	7 493	15 459	29 478	10.3	13.3	55.4	68.1
2.2.1 Cancer of esophagus [12.]	13 492	0.04	28 124	5 966	13 419	29 490	10.9	12.6	74.8	66.7
2.2.2 Cancer of stomach [13.]	24 502	0.07	30 249	9 836	19 489	35 493	11.6	11.1	63.2	68.8
2.2.3 Cancer of liver and intrahepatic bile duct [16.]	10 531	0.03	17 751	5 586	11 434	20 851	7.8	19.3	60.7	65.1
2.2.4 Cancer of pancreas [17.]	31 040	0.09	21 905	6 159	13 180	26 412	9.6	15.7	46.5	69.5
2.2.5 Cancer of other GI organs, peritoneum [18.]	18 024	0.05	27 760	10 243	17 816	32 152	10.8	9.4	42.6	67.6
2.3 **Cancer of bronchus, lung** [19.]	158 150	0.45	19 392	7 134	14 012	23 748	8.1	15.8	57.0	67.5
2.4 **Cancer of skin**	11 860	0.03	11 929	4 752	7 777	12 781	4.5	3.3	53.2	66.0
2.4.1 Melanomas of skin [22.]	4 887	0.01	10 449	4 719	7 650	11 411	4.1	5.9	51.5	60.3
2.4.2 Other non-epithelial cancer of skin [23.]	6 973	0.02	12 968	4 793	7 903	13 739	4.8	1.4	54.3	70.0
2.5 **Cancer of breast** [24.]	125 663	0.36	9 229	4 789	6 855	9 900	2.9	1.5	0.6	61.6
2.6 **Cancer of uterus and cervix**	77 015	0.22	11 534	6 093	9 015	13 472	4.3	1.2	0.0	56.2
2.6.1 Cancer of uterus [25.]	40 820	0.12	12 173	6 621	9 643	14 128	4.8	1.2	0.0	64.5
2.6.2 Cancer of cervix [26.]	36 195	0.10	10 822	5 588	8 285	12 434	3.8	1.1	0.0	47.0
2.7 **Cancer of ovary and other female genital organs**	31 992	0.09	20 360	8 106	13 553	23 055	7.5	4.9	0.0	61.8
2.7.1 Cancer of ovary [27.]	24 724	0.07	21 639	8 779	14 687	24 563	7.9	5.7	0.0	60.9
2.7.2 Cancer of other female genital organs [28.]	7 268	0.02	16 022	6 263	10 296	16 374	6.0	2.1	0.0	65.1
2.8 **Cancer of male genital organs**	109 794	0.31	11 724	6 553	9 940	14 456	4.3	1.6	100.0	67.0
2.8.1 Cancer of prostate [29.]	107 106	0.31	11 646	6 576	9 929	14 400	4.3	1.6	100.0	67.7
2.8.2 Cancer of testis [30.]	1 890	0.01	16 111	5 723	11 747	18 576	5.2	3.6	100.0	32.3
2.8.3 Cancer of other male genital organs [31.]	798	0.00	11 694	4 853	7 877	14 816	4.7	1.3	100.0	66.9
2.9 **Cancer of urinary organs**	83 528	0.24	15 790	5 335	10 178	18 722	6.1	3.0	68.4	69.8
2.9.1 Cancer of bladder [32.]	51 035	0.15	13 842	4 193	7 334	15 617	5.4	2.6	73.9	73.2
2.9.2 Cancer of kidney and renal pelvis [33.]	29 163	0.08	18 920	9 294	14 031	21 325	7.3	3.7	59.9	63.5
2.9.3 Cancer of other urinary organs [34.]	3 330	0.01	18 410	8 629	14 303	22 131	6.9	3.7	59.0	71.4
2.10 **Cancer of lymphatic and hematopoietic tissue**	113 492	0.33	32 952	7 181	14 518	31 928	11.4	15.4	52.8	60.0
2.10.1 Hodgkin's disease [37.]	5 676	0.02	28 716	7 570	13 662	28 396	9.2	6.4	51.6	42.7
2.10.2 Non-Hodgkin's lymphoma [38.]	50 476	0.14	26 516	7 540	14 213	27 662	10.0	13.2	52.8	62.9
2.10.3 Leukemias [39.]	39 487	0.11	46 726	6 876	16 211	53 271	14.1	19.7	54.6	55.2
2.10.4 Multiple myeloma [40.]	17 854	0.05	21 971	6 670	13 364	24 547	10.4	15.4	49.4	68.3
2.11 **Cancer, other primary**	104 590	0.30	20 409	6 307	12 289	23 782	7.1	4.8	55.1	55.1
2.11.1 Cancer of head and neck [11.]	32 944	0.09	25 077	7 717	15 457	28 743	8.6	4.8	69.7	62.5
2.11.2 Cancer, other respiratory and intrathoracic [20.]	2 903	0.01	18 363	7 848	14 250	22 842	8.4	7.9	76.2	67.9
2.11.3 Cancer of bone and connective tissue [21.]	11 368	0.03	22 457	7 706	13 337	25 022	7.3	5.0	52.2	50.0
2.11.4 Cancer of brain and nervous system [35.]	31 389	0.09	22 129	7 434	15 246	27 155	7.8	5.9	56.1	52.4
2.11.5 Cancer of thyroid [36.]	17 565	0.05	8 112	4 025	6 274	9 654	2.5	0.9	26.1	48.6
2.11.6 Cancer, other and unspecified primary [41.]	8 421	0.02	19 298	6 477	11 726	21 246	7.2	7.4	51.4	51.8
2.12 **Secondary malignancies** [42.]	264 057	0.76	16 789	5 792	10 810	19 875	7.9	13.8	43.6	64.9
2.12.1 Secondary malignancy of lymph nodes	17 812	0.05	17 011	6 271	10 498	18 416	6.1	8.1	46.4	60.7
2.12.2 Secondary malignancy of lung	23 602	0.07	15 455	5 220	10 302	18 756	6.8	21.4	43.2	63.7
2.12.3 Secondary malignancy of liver	31 428	0.09	15 783	5 106	9 796	18 373	7.2	20.4	47.9	66.1
2.12.4 Secondary malignancy of brain/spine	39 605	0.11	14 430	5 150	9 520	17 900	7.0	10.8	48.3	63.1
2.12.5 Secondary malignancy of bone	47 493	0.14	15 713	5 531	10 169	18 611	8.6	11.4	50.8	66.1
2.12.6 Other secondary malignancy	104 116	0.30	18 747	6 525	12 165	22 263	8.7	13.2	36.9	65.6
2.13 **Malignant neoplasm without specification of site** [43.]	9 560	0.03	14 429	4 266	9 117	16 929	7.9	29.6	44.5	68.1
2.14 **Neoplasms of unspecified nature or uncertain behavior** [44.]	42 094	0.12	14 631	5 095	9 116	16 217	6.0	3.3	43.2	62.7
2.15 **Maintenance chemotherapy, radiotherapy** [45.]	258 600	0.74	10 460	4 197	6 724	10 786	3.8	0.8	44.2	52.3
2.15.1 Radiotherapy	15 994	0.05	8 866	3 664	6 200	10 502	4.5	2.1	42.3	57.3
2.15.2 Chemotherapy	242 606	0.70	10 565	4 233	6 748	10 809	3.8	0.7	44.4	51.9
2.16 **Benign neoplasms**	374 544	1.07	10 697	5 700	8 105	11 640	3.7	0.3	11.8	48.1
2.16.1 Benign neoplasm of uterus [46.]	222 765	0.64	8 551	5 702	7 746	10 317	3.0	0.0	0.0	43.8
2.16.2 Other and unspecified benign neoplasm [47.]	151 779	0.44	13 848	5 700	9 017	15 389	4.6	0.6	29.2	54.4
2.16.2.1 Benign neoplasm of ovary	37 784	0.11	9 528	5 755	7 920	10 999	3.4	0.1	0.0	46.8
2.16.2.2 Benign neoplasm of colon	26 537	0.08	13 071	5 756	9 785	15 546	5.9	0.7	48.5	69.4
2.16.2.3 Benign neoplasm of the thyroid	12 419	0.04	6 806	4 265	5 936	8 074	1.7	0.0	18.6	49.3
2.16.2.4 Benign neoplasm of cerebral meninges	12 413	0.04	28 726	10 717	20 925	34 866	8.1	2.8	32.1	61.9
2.16.2.5 Other and unspecified benign neoplasms	62 625	0.18	15 345	5 834	10 107	17 999	4.7	0.5	40.3	52.2

See footnotes at end of table.

Table 4.14. Reasons Why People Are in the Hospital: 1996—*Continued*

(Principal diagnosis only)

Multilevel Clinical Classifications Software (CCS) category [1]	Number of discharges	Percent of discharges [2]	Mean charges (dollars)	25 percentile charges (dollars)	Median charges (dollars)	75 percentile charges (dollars)	Mean length of stay (days)	Percent died	Percent male	Mean age
3 ENDOCRINE, NUTRITIONAL, AND METABOLIC DISEASES AND IMMUNITY DISORDERS	1 059 659	3.04	8 845	2 925	5 157	9 529	5.2	2.3	42.3	54.0
3.1 Thyroid disorders [48.]	35 665	0.10	8 124	4 206	6 323	9 286	3.1	0.5	16.4	52.7
3.1.1 Thyrotoxicosis with or without goiter	9 529	0.03	8 697	4 117	6 567	10 215	4.1	0.7	18.1	49.3
3.1.2 Other thyroid disorders	26 136	0.07	7 914	4 249	6 252	9 007	2.8	0.5	15.8	53.9
3.2 Diabetes mellitus without complication [49.]	9 854	0.03	4 666	1 902	3 058	5 104	4.4	0.3	52.9	41.8
3.3 Diabetes mellitus with complications [50.]	403 460	1.16	11 030	3 420	6 095	11 730	6.2	1.6	49.1	54.6
3.3.1 Diabetes with ketoacidosis or uncontrolled diabetes	160 292	0.46	6 765	2 825	4 596	7 671	4.2	0.6	47.2	44.5
3.3.2 Diabetes with renal manifestations	28 234	0.08	20 034	4 910	9 461	20 408	7.4	3.2	46.8	57.5
3.3.3 Diabetes with ophthalmic manifestations	4 006	0.01	7 847	2 959	4 942	8 395	4.0	0.0	45.1	54.5
3.3.4 Diabetes with neurological manifestations	43 492	0.12	10 585	3 914	6 743	11 851	6.7	0.6	45.1	57.8
3.3.5 Diabetes with circulatory manifestations	57 115	0.16	20 641	7 440	13 463	24 725	10.7	3.3	58.0	66.3
3.3.6 Diabetes with unspecified complications	2 479	0.01	5 195	2 287	3 492	5 664	4.6	0.0	41.5	51.0
3.3.7 Diabetes with other manifestations	107 841	0.31	10 398	3 379	6 104	11 540	6.4	2.1	49.6	61.5
3.4 Other endocrine disorders [51.]	36 662	0.11	9 617	3 663	6 362	11 124	5.2	1.8	33.4	58.6
3.5 Nutritional deficiencies [52.]	16 199	0.05	12 095	4 546	7 798	13 369	8.2	5.6	38.2	68.9
3.5.1 Unspecified protein-calorie malnutrition	9 469	0.03	11 441	4 550	7 457	12 659	7.8	5.4	36.2	70.8
3.5.2 Other malnutrition	6 729	0.02	13 019	4 538	8 316	14 634	8.7	5.8	40.9	66.2
3.6 Disorders of lipid metabolism [53.]	636	0.00	11 334	3 230	4 762	6 992	4.0	2.7	46.6	49.3
3.7 Gout and other crystal arthropathies [54.]	8 990	0.03	6 807	2 844	4 654	7 685	4.7	0.3	64.4	66.9
3.8 Fluid and electrolyte disorders [55.]	492 750	1.41	6 596	2 481	4 229	7 458	4.5	3.0	39.4	54.3
3.8.1 Hyposmolality	49 981	0.14	7 654	3 233	5 191	8 568	4.9	2.0	29.4	69.1
3.8.2 Hypovolemia	383 036	1.10	6 223	2 313	3 937	6 995	4.4	3.1	41.1	51.0
3.8.3 Hyperpotassemia	13 300	0.04	8 151	3 194	5 335	9 342	4.1	2.7	47.4	65.8
3.8.4 Hypopotassemia	21 352	0.06	6 822	3 024	4 643	7 795	4.3	1.3	27.9	64.2
3.8.5 Other fluid and electrolyte disorders	25 080	0.07	9 161	3 610	6 015	10 317	5.5	5.0	39.6	59.9
3.9 Cystic fibrosis [56.]	5 441	0.02	26 088	9 080	15 802	27 705	9.9	1.6	49.8	18.3
3.10 Immunity disorders [57.]	1 462	0.00	17 080	4 053	6 589	13 316	6.8	2.0	34.4	37.1
3.11 Other nutritional, endocrine, and metabolic disorders [58.]	48 540	0.14	11 454	3 687	7 325	14 200	5.4	2.4	36.3	43.1
3.11.1 Disorders of mineral metabolism	13 323	0.04	9 166	3 707	6 364	10 707	5.4	4.5	40.2	61.4
3.11.2 Obesity	10 288	0.03	17 614	11 624	15 402	19 620	5.1	0.4	16.7	39.7
3.11.3 Other and unspecified metabolic, nutritional, and endocrine disorders	24 929	0.07	10 103	2 859	5 419	10 153	5.6	2.2	42.4	34.7
4 DISEASES OF THE BLOOD AND BLOOD-FORMING ORGANS	281 881	0.81	10 075	3 550	6 136	10 925	5.1	1.9	43.7	48.9
4.1 Anemia	186 272	0.53	8 703	3 269	5 490	9 532	5.0	1.3	43.1	47.1
4.1.1 Acute posthemorrhagic anemia [60.]	9 845	0.03	7 626	2 977	4 920	8 452	4.0	1.6	31.4	64.3
4.1.2 Sickle cell anemia [61.]	76 386	0.22	8 045	3 392	5 578	9 334	5.5	0.3	49.8	25.5
4.1.3 Deficiency and other anemia [59.]	100 040	0.29	9 312	3 200	5 468	9 807	4.7	2.0	39.1	62.0
4.1.3.1 Iron deficiency anemia	15 667	0.04	7 250	3 495	5 464	8 919	4.2	0.4	29.4	64.1
4.1.3.2 Other deficiency anemia	5 523	0.02	8 765	3 732	6 042	9 945	5.5	1.0	37.8	67.0
4.1.3.3 Aplastic anemia	22 529	0.06	14 835	4 027	7 704	14 855	5.9	3.5	47.5	55.6
4.1.3.4 Chronic blood loss anemia	17 125	0.05	6 699	2 930	4 691	7 954	3.9	1.8	32.5	66.3
4.1.3.5 Acquired hemolytic anemia	6 142	0.02	15 743	5 059	9 109	17 510	6.8	2.8	41.4	56.9
4.1.3.6 Other specified anemia	5 934	0.02	8 369	2 960	4 754	9 230	4.2	1.4	41.3	45.0
4.1.3.7 Anemia, unspecified	27 119	0.08	6 443	2 629	4 328	7 416	3.8	1.8	41.2	67.3
4.2 Coagulation and hemorrhagic disorders [62.]	45 530	0.13	12 478	3 800	7 229	13 518	5.1	4.1	46.7	51.9
4.2.1 Coagulation defects	14 424	0.04	13 153	3 606	6 980	13 573	5.5	5.4	50.2	63.0
4.2.2 Thrombocytopenia	27 451	0.08	12 836	4 236	7 806	14 338	5.0	3.6	44.0	48.8
4.2.3 Other coagulation and hemorrhagic disorders	3 655	0.01	7 119	2 376	4 145	8 202	4.1	1.9	53.5	30.7
4.3 Diseases of white blood cells [63.]	42 558	0.12	12 302	4 824	7 986	13 545	5.7	2.1	42.2	51.8
4.4 Other hematologic conditions [64.]	7 521	0.02	16 996	5 485	10 357	18 728	7.1	4.9	46.5	58.9
5 MENTAL DISORDERS	1 759 206	5.04	7 517	2 718	4 782	8 782	8.4	0.2	50.8	43.0
5.1 Mental retardation [65.]	636	0.00	9 584	4 037	5 958	9 831	10.6	0.0	63.2	36.4
5.2 Alcohol and substance-related mental disorders	513 099	1.47	4 631	2 100	3 187	5 267	5.6	0.1	68.2	39.6
5.2.1 Alcohol-related mental disorders [66.]	277 610	0.80	5 048	2 087	3 428	5 778	6.0	0.1	73.4	42.6
5.2.1.1 Acute alcoholic intoxication	49 356	0.14	3 714	1 807	2 859	4 346	3.5	0.1	72.4	43.7
5.2.1.2 Other and unspecified alcohol dependence	127 172	0.36	5 241	2 247	3 658	6 250	8.1	0.0	72.7	40.7
5.2.1.3 Nondependent alcohol abuse	14 519	0.04	3 794	1 709	2 791	4 609	3.0	0.0	66.5	37.2
5.2.1.4 Other alcohol-related mental disorders	86 563	0.25	5 728	2 163	3 707	6 377	4.8	0.2	76.1	45.7
5.2.2 Substance-related mental disorders [67.]	235 490	0.68	4 142	2 113	3 011	4 586	5.1	0.0	62.1	36.1
5.2.2.1 Opioid dependence	49 373	0.14	3 588	2 142	2 970	4 209	4.6	0.0	63.7	36.0
5.2.2.2 Cocaine dependence	58 519	0.17	3 946	2 169	2 996	4 224	5.4	0.0	63.7	34.5
5.2.2.3 Other, combined, and unspecified drug dependence	59 241	0.17	4 059	2 223	2 943	4 205	5.4	0.0	64.5	33.4
5.2.2.4 Cocaine abuse	3 712	0.01	4 372	2 077	3 319	5 154	3.5	0.0	64.6	33.2
5.2.2.5 Other, mixed, or unspecified drug abuse	6 170	0.02	4 613	2 006	3 394	5 691	5.4	0.1	61.8	30.1
5.2.2.6 Other substance-related mental disorders	58 475	0.17	4 832	1 863	3 299	5 861	5.0	0.2	56.5	41.4
5.3 Senility and organic mental disorders [68.]	134 427	0.39	9 733	4 054	6 859	11 474	9.9	1.2	43.1	74.4
5.3.1 Senile dementia, uncomplicated	16 894	0.05	9 268	3 823	6 347	10 988	10.3	1.2	39.2	80.7
5.3.2 Arteriosclerotic dementia	16 769	0.05	10 886	4 753	7 794	12 608	11.1	1.6	45.1	78.3
5.3.3 Transient organic psychotic conditions	27 198	0.08	8 839	3 589	6 197	10 372	7.8	0.9	45.7	65.1
5.3.4 Specific nonpsychotic mental disorders caused by organic brain damage	9 157	0.03	7 933	3 214	5 414	9 216	8.2	1.7	48.7	57.3
5.3.5 Presenile dementia, uncomplicated	1 093	0.00	9 309	3 857	6 436	9 909	10.3	2.9	47.6	72.4
5.3.6 Senile dementia with delirium	13 549	0.04	9 141	4 143	6 657	10 854	9.1	1.2	40.9	81.4
5.3.7 Other senility and organic mental disorders	49 767	0.14	10 491	4 392	7 392	12 614	11.1	1.1	41.9	77.2
5.4 Affective disorders [69.]	574 133	1.65	8 435	3 293	5 693	10 095	9.3	0.1	37.6	42.6
5.4.1 Major depressive disorder, single episode	167 354	0.48	7 386	2 972	5 037	8 709	8.0	0.1	39.5	41.4
5.4.2 Major depressive disorder, recurrent episode	219 637	0.63	8 743	3 419	5 867	10 393	9.6	0.1	34.4	44.7
5.4.3 Neurotic depression	24 043	0.07	5 451	2 226	3 784	6 341	6.5	0.0	36.4	35.3
5.4.4 Bipolar affective disorder	145 908	0.42	9 665	3 912	6 719	11 806	10.8	0.1	40.2	42.1
5.4.5 Manic-depressive psychosis	8 754	0.03	8 531	3 195	5 479	10 212	9.8	0.1	36.5	39.5
5.4.6 Other affective disorders	8 436	0.02	8 339	3 074	5 523	9 613	9.0	0.2	41.7	43.2
5.5 Schizophrenia and related disorders [70.]	248 833	0.71	11 048	4 378	7 528	12 950	13.0	0.1	55.2	41.0
5.5.1 Paranoid schizophrenia	86 805	0.25	11 664	4 508	7 744	13 494	13.9	0.1	61.6	41.6
5.5.2 Schizo-affective type	100 449	0.29	10 804	4 408	7 523	12 738	12.5	0.0	47.0	40.7
5.5.3 Other schizophrenia	61 579	0.18	10 577	4 137	7 211	12 475	12.7	0.1	59.7	40.6

See footnotes at end of table.

Table 4.14. Reasons Why People Are in the Hospital: 1996—*Continued*

(Principal diagnosis only)

Multilevel Clinical Classifications Software (CCS) category [1]	Number of discharges	Percent of discharges [2]	Mean charges (dollars)	25 percentile charges (dollars)	Median charges (dollars)	75 percentile charges (dollars)	Mean length of stay (days)	Percent died	Percent male	Mean age
5.6 Other psychoses [71.]	59 908	0.17	8 693	3 469	6 041	10 289	9.4	0.2	47.2	48.6
5.7 Anxiety, somatoform, dissociative, and personality disorders [72.]	64 904	0.19	7 209	2 443	4 236	7 396	7.0	0.0	37.5	39.9
5.7.1 Anxiety states	17 301	0.05	4 986	2 248	3 713	5 988	4.1	0.0	34.1	52.6
5.7.2 Personality disorders	8 076	0.02	12 952	2 246	4 546	9 450	13.4	0.0	39.1	34.6
5.7.3 Other anxiety, somatoform, dissociative, and personality disorders	39 527	0.11	7 003	2 586	4 463	7 850	7.0	0.1	38.6	35.5
5.8 Pre-adult disorders [73.]	17 593	0.05	9 138	3 584	6 073	10 863	10.4	0.0	76.8	13.0
5.9 Other mental conditions [74.]	145 183	0.42	5 441	1 960	3 381	5 914	5.8	0.1	45.0	33.1
5.9.1 Adjustment reaction	69 614	0.20	3 861	1 670	2 741	4 491	4.3	0.0	45.5	32.3
5.9.1.1 Brief depressive reaction	33 945	0.10	3 643	1 700	2 724	4 357	4.0	0.0	45.5	32.8
5.9.1.2 Other adjustment reaction	35 669	0.10	4 070	1 637	2 760	4 618	4.5	0.0	45.5	31.8
5.9.2 Depressive disorder, not elsewhere classified	48 873	0.14	5 380	2 169	3 725	6 360	5.9	0.1	46.8	35.8
5.9.3 Other and unspecified mental conditions	26 695	0.08	9 656	3 077	5 400	10 025	9.6	0.1	40.1	30.2
5.10 Personal history of mental disorder, screening for mental condition [75.]	489	0.00	2 614	1 389	2 151	2 786	2.6	0.0	45.6	35.5
6 DISEASES OF THE NERVOUS SYSTEM AND SENSE ORGANS	681 769	1.96	9 598	3 151	5 338	9 664	5.0	1.4	46.0	48.7
6.1 Central nervous system infection	54 004	0.15	16 865	4 195	7 880	17 394	7.3	3.2	50.4	32.0
6.1.1 Meningitis (except that caused by TB or STD) [76.]	40 308	0.12	12 014	3 741	6 380	12 327	5.7	2.5	49.2	27.6
6.1.2 Encephalitis (except that caused by TB or STD) [77.]	8 170	0.02	25 825	7 210	14 034	28 162	10.5	4.6	49.4	42.1
6.1.3 Other CNS infection and poliomyelitis [78.]	5 526	0.02	39 367	12 178	24 043	46 015	14.7	5.7	60.5	49.4
6.2 Hereditary and degenerative nervous system conditions	71 604	0.21	11 871	4 210	7 133	12 907	7.0	1.6	44.9	58.7
6.2.1 Parkinson's disease [79.]	17 008	0.05	9 352	4 039	6 439	10 864	7.7	1.5	56.2	74.4
6.2.2 Multiple sclerosis [80.]	18 970	0.05	8 982	3 501	5 871	9 409	6.8	0.3	25.6	44.5
6.2.3 Other hereditary and degenerative nervous system conditions [81.]	35 626	0.10	14 647	4 880	8 795	16 198	6.8	2.4	49.8	58.8
6.2.3.1 Disorders of the autonomic nervous system	2 742	0.01	13 590	5 084	10 575	19 857	4.7	0.4	61.5	66.7
6.2.3.2 Other and unspecified hereditary and degenerative nervous conditions	32 884	0.09	14 735	4 875	8 720	15 791	7.0	2.6	48.8	58.1
6.3 Paralysis [82.]	20 141	0.06	23 772	5 965	13 782	29 977	16.4	2.0	50.7	56.1
6.3.1 Hemiplegia	11 834	0.03	27 047	7 030	17 488	35 205	20.5	2.8	46.6	66.6
6.3.2 Other paralysis	8 307	0.02	19 064	5 078	10 237	21 322	10.7	0.9	56.5	41.1
6.4 Epilepsy, convulsions [83.]	217 431	0.62	7 709	2 966	4 932	8 380	4.0	1.1	52.3	43.2
6.4.1 Epilepsy	47 167	0.14	10 242	3 159	5 570	10 427	4.8	1.8	52.3	38.4
6.4.2 Convulsions	170 264	0.49	7 010	2 919	4 804	7 992	3.8	0.9	52.3	44.5
6.5 Headache, including migraine [84.]	51 180	0.15	5 437	2 516	4 183	6 967	3.3	0.0	26.0	43.0
6.5.1 Migraine	33 744	0.10	5 549	2 477	4 270	7 234	3.5	0.0	21.9	40.8
6.5.2 Other headache	17 436	0.05	5 219	2 602	4 057	6 394	2.8	0.1	34.0	47.3
6.6 Coma, stupor, and brain damage [85.]	15 226	0.04	16 268	3 591	6 758	14 757	7.4	16.8	48.7	60.8
6.7 Eye disorders	62 208	0.18	5 777	2 916	4 424	6 786	2.7	0.2	46.7	52.3
6.7.1 Cataract [86.]	5 389	0.02	4 282	2 645	3 536	5 418	1.5	0.1	37.9	72.0
6.7.2 Retinal detachments, defects, vascular occlusion, and retinopathy [87.]	15 806	0.05	6 176	3 564	4 999	7 335	1.9	0.1	54.8	58.5
6.7.2.1 Retinal detachment with defect	4 671	0.01	6 038	3 657	5 216	7 728	1.5	0.0	59.1	57.4
6.7.2.2 Other retinal detachment or defect	5 455	0.02	5 484	3 557	4 668	6 718	1.4	0.0	57.6	56.6
6.7.2.3 Other retinal disorders	5 680	0.02	6 956	3 480	5 115	7 787	2.7	0.2	48.4	61.3
6.7.3 Glaucoma [88.]	6 092	0.02	4 020	2 472	3 293	4 605	1.9	0.0	37.9	67.7
6.7.4 Blindness and vision defects [89.]	2 168	0.01	5 729	2 724	4 219	6 583	3.4	0.0	46.0	58.3
6.7.5 Inflammation, infection of eye (except that caused by TB or STD) [90.]	19 501	0.06	6 188	2 606	4 322	7 368	3.9	0.4	48.7	32.2
6.7.6 Other eye disorders [91.]	13 252	0.04	6 119	3 300	4 914	7 160	2.6	0.1	41.8	58.2
6.8 Ear conditions	83 245	0.24	5 081	2 398	3 823	6 076	2.9	0.1	41.7	52.2
6.8.1 Otitis media and related conditions [92.]	19 804	0.06	5 350	2 277	3 721	6 061	2.8	0.1	53.7	17.1
6.8.1.1 Suppurative and unspecified otitis media	10 585	0.03	4 055	1 907	3 024	4 873	2.6	0.0	56.7	10.1
6.8.1.2 Other otitis media and related conditions	9 220	0.03	6 838	2 981	4 623	7 740	3.1	0.1	50.3	25.2
6.8.2 Conditions associated with dizziness or vertigo [93.]	54 379	0.16	4 723	2 374	3 752	5 860	2.9	0.1	36.7	67.2
6.8.3 Other ear and sense organ disorders [94.]	9 062	0.03	6 675	2 930	4 697	7 673	3.2	0.1	45.2	39.0
6.9 Other nervous system disorders [95.]	106 730	0.31	12 427	3 960	7 022	13 144	5.9	1.3	42.6	56.4
6.9.1 Disorders of the peripheral nervous system	46 236	0.13	14 538	4 077	7 359	14 554	5.9	1.1	44.8	55.8
6.9.2 Other central nervous system disorders	33 441	0.10	13 360	4 925	8 575	14 915	6.0	2.3	41.9	51.6
6.9.3 Other nervous system symptoms and disorders	27 052	0.08	7 711	3 130	5 186	8 970	5.5	0.4	39.8	63.3
7 DISEASES OF THE CIRCULATORY SYSTEM	6 522 105	18.70	14 826	4 565	8 240	16 341	5.3	4.2	51.3	67.8
7.1 Hypertension	282 621	0.81	11 963	4 128	7 114	12 818	5.5	3.0	42.1	65.2
7.1.1 Essential hypertension [98.]	40 877	0.12	5 449	2 482	4 047	6 480	3.2	0.2	36.4	60.2
7.1.2 Hypertension with complications and secondary hypertension [99.]	241 745	0.69	13 064	4 625	7 838	14 020	5.9	3.5	43.0	66.1
7.1.2.1 Hypertensive heart and/ or renal disease	210 342	0.60	13 937	5 013	8 406	14 966	6.2	3.9	44.2	67.0
7.1.2.2 Other hypertensive complications	31 402	0.09	7 224	2 975	4 859	8 129	3.8	0.4	35.2	59.8
7.2 Diseases of the heart	4 584 160	13.15	15 219	4 460	8 292	17 175	4.9	3.6	53.3	67.2
7.2.1 Heart valve disorders [96.]	88 783	0.25	45 305	11 400	37 923	59 657	9.2	4.6	49.4	67.5
7.2.1.1 Chronic rheumatic disease of the heart valves	23 326	0.07	50 209	13 564	41 191	66 069	10.6	5.6	37.5	66.6
7.2.1.2 Nonrheumatic mitral valve disorders	20 264	0.06	43 781	8 657	34 445	58 361	9.0	4.3	45.3	63.3
7.2.1.3 Nonrheumatic aortic valve disorders	43 883	0.13	44 081	12 796	38 663	57 847	8.7	4.3	57.6	70.5
7.2.1.4 Other heart valve disorders	1 309	0.00	22 370	3 896	8 805	22 694	8.7	3.5	51.5	49.1
7.2.2 Peri-, endo-, and myocarditis, cardiomyopathy (except that caused by TB or STD) [97.]	83 553	0.24	19 301	5 273	9 409	18 454	7.4	5.8	58.0	57.5
7.2.2.1 Cardiomyopathy	34 324	0.10	16 617	5 044	8 307	13 918	6.2	6.7	59.8	60.6
7.2.2.2 Other peri-, endo-, and myocarditis	49 229	0.14	21 172	5 497	10 621	22 149	8.3	5.2	56.8	55.4
7.2.3 Acute myocardial infarction [100.]	743 677	2.13	21 367	7 902	13 987	25 629	6.0	8.9	61.2	67.3
7.2.4 Coronary atherosclerosis and other heart disease [101.]	1 417 670	4.07	18 210	4 952	10 174	23 706	4.3	0.9	59.0	65.9
7.2.4.1 Angina pectoris	69 955	0.20	5 493	2 660	4 194	6 635	2.5	0.2	43.9	64.4
7.2.4.2 Unstable angina (intermediate coronary syndrome)	205 466	0.59	7 239	3 096	4 985	8 203	3.1	0.4	49.2	65.1
7.2.4.3 Other acute and subacute forms of ischemic heart disease	32 679	0.09	15 224	4 566	8 853	17 772	4.1	0.8	57.3	65.4
7.2.4.4 Coronary atherosclerosis	1 096 640	3.14	21 271	6 353	13 323	28 805	4.7	1.1	62.0	64.7
7.2.4.5 Other forms of chronic heart disease	13 890	0.04	15 497	3 770	5 978	10 431	5.7	3.2	54.2	66.7
7.2.5 Nonspecific chest pain [102.]	514 895	1.48	5 239	2 746	4 292	6 649	2.0	0.1	47.0	57.5
7.2.6 Pulmonary heart disease [103.]	83 931	0.24	15 683	6 819	10 780	17 334	7.5	6.8	42.7	64.2

See footnotes at end of table.

Table 4.14. Reasons Why People Are in the Hospital: 1996—*Continued*

(Principal diagnosis only)

Multilevel Clinical Classifications Software (CCS) category [1]	Number of discharges	Percent of discharges [2]	Mean charges (dollars)	25 percentile charges (dollars)	Median charges (dollars)	75 percentile charges (dollars)	Mean length of stay (days)	Percent died	Percent male	Mean age
7.2.7 Other and ill-defined heart disease [104.]	6 541	0.02	17 526	3 829	6 684	16 491	5.2	2.9	51.4	65.2
7.2.8 Conduction disorders [105.]	62 475	0.18	17 700	8 620	16 064	22 681	4.0	2.1	52.9	71.3
7.2.8.1 Atrioventricular block	44 924	0.13	19 199	10 847	17 560	24 064	4.5	2.7	51.5	75.0
7.2.8.2 Bundle branch block	2 083	0.01	13 038	4 159	9 264	18 625	3.8	0.2	55.5	73.2
7.2.8.3 Anomalous atrioventricular excitation	4 584	0.01	10 062	4 486	8 294	13 719	2.0	0.2	55.7	36.3
7.2.8.4 Other conduction disorders	10 884	0.03	15 336	7 646	12 901	19 454	2.8	0.8	56.9	70.5
7.2.9 Cardiac dysrhythmias [106.]	574 051	1.65	9 941	3 410	5 807	11 289	3.9	1.2	48.1	69.0
7.2.9.1 Paroxysmal supraventricular tachycardia	37 284	0.11	8 071	3 263	5 508	9 304	3.1	0.8	39.0	62.9
7.2.9.2 Paroxysmal ventricular tachycardia	53 677	0.15	22 031	5 293	10 370	30 910	5.6	3.8	70.8	66.4
7.2.9.3 Atrial fibrillation	272 935	0.78	7 520	3 164	5 099	8 580	3.8	1.0	45.8	70.2
7.2.9.4 Atrial flutter	33 478	0.10	7 895	3 186	5 318	9 028	3.6	1.0	64.0	67.7
7.2.9.5 Premature beats	14 423	0.04	5 645	2 883	4 567	6 979	2.7	0.1	48.9	64.5
7.2.9.6 Sinoatrial node dysfunction	66 398	0.19	17 622	9 366	16 564	23 063	4.6	0.7	46.7	76.3
7.2.9.7 Other cardiac dysrhythmias	95 857	0.27	7 167	3 013	4 811	8 254	3.1	1.0	41.0	65.5
7.2.10 Cardiac arrest and ventricular fibrillation [107.]	18 495	0.05	24 152	5 623	11 791	30 272	5.4	50.0	60.8	66.3
7.2.11 Congestive heart failure, nonhypertensive [108.]	990 090	2.84	11 247	4 544	7 353	12 407	6.0	5.2	46.1	73.8
7.2.11.1 Congestive heart failure	970 361	2.78	11 220	4 535	7 337	12 383	6.0	5.2	46.2	73.8
7.2.11.2 Heart failure	19 729	0.06	12 603	5 023	8 161	13 852	6.2	5.5	38.8	74.7
7.3 Cerebrovascular disease	1 044 326	2.99	12 857	5 029	8 131	13 572	6.2	6.8	46.0	72.1
7.3.1 Acute cerebrovascular disease [109.]	654 605	1.88	14 775	5 424	8 740	15 162	7.6	10.6	45.3	72.3
7.3.1.1 Intracranial hemorrhage	113 056	0.32	27 331	6 455	13 212	29 823	9.7	26.9	47.5	67.1
7.3.1.2 Occlusion of cerebral arteries	411 213	1.18	13 016	5 700	8 860	14 554	7.4	7.1	45.8	73.0
7.3.1.3 Acute but ill-defined cerebrovascular accident	130 336	0.37	9 553	4 382	6 716	10 611	6.3	7.4	42.1	74.9
7.3.2 Occlusion or stenosis of precerebral arteries [110.]	167 750	0.48	12 291	6 818	10 140	14 648	3.4	0.5	55.2	71.2
7.3.3 Other and ill-defined cerebrovascular disease [111.]	25 070	0.07	15 144	4 463	7 707	15 962	5.9	1.7	38.2	67.5
7.3.4 Transient cerebral ischemia [112.]	195 864	0.56	6 657	3 558	5 360	8 045	3.8	0.2	41.4	72.7
7.3.5 Late effects of cerebrovascular disease [113.]	1 037	0.00	15 199	2 922	8 133	22 653	15.0	2.9	47.9	70.7
7.4 Diseases of arteries, arterioles, and capillaries	367 957	1.06	21 964	6 540	13 289	25 367	6.9	7.0	53.1	68.7
7.4.1 Peripheral and visceral atherosclerosis [114.]	140 667	0.40	20 493	7 765	13 519	23 062	6.9	6.5	47.4	69.5
7.4.1.1 Atherosclerosis of arteries of extremities	78 169	0.22	19 117	9 163	14 775	22 881	6.1	1.8	54.3	69.5
7.4.1.2 Peripheral vascular disease unspecified	13 211	0.04	16 774	6 139	11 239	20 093	7.6	3.2	54.6	70.0
7.4.1.3 Other peripheral and visceral atherosclerosis	49 287	0.14	23 673	6 321	11 753	24 657	7.9	14.8	34.4	69.4
7.4.2 Aortic, peripheral, and visceral artery aneurysms [115.]	83 317	0.24	36 454	14 083	24 737	40 495	9.0	13.1	72.8	70.8
7.4.2.1 Abdominal aortic aneurysm, without rupture	43 546	0.12	33 666	17 569	25 955	37 997	9.1	4.4	78.2	71.9
7.4.2.2 Other aneurysm	39 771	0.11	39 501	9 959	22 148	45 826	8.9	22.7	66.8	69.5
7.4.3 Aortic and peripheral arterial embolism or thrombosis [116.]	55 300	0.16	22 047	8 846	15 540	26 551	7.4	5.4	49.4	69.1
7.4.3.1 Arterial embolism and thrombosis of lower extremity artery	36 917	0.11	21 546	8 658	15 012	25 779	7.7	5.4	51.8	70.5
7.4.3.2 Other arterial embolism and thrombosis	18 383	0.05	23 056	9 254	16 488	27 891	6.9	5.5	44.4	66.2
7.4.4 Other circulatory disease [117.]	88 673	0.25	10 681	3 578	6 169	10 945	4.7	2.8	46.2	65.3
7.4.4.1 Hypotension	47 249	0.14	6 990	3 141	5 058	8 065	4.0	2.8	47.4	71.1
7.4.4.2 Other and unspecified circulatory disease	41 424	0.12	14 912	4 491	8 234	15 744	5.6	2.9	44.8	58.6
7.5 Diseases of veins and lymphatics	243 041	0.70	8 472	3 779	5 723	9 267	5.9	1.1	44.0	63.1
7.5.1 Phlebitis, thrombophlebitis, and thromboembolism [118.]	188 566	0.54	8 533	3 885	5 816	9 320	6.2	1.1	43.1	63.7
7.5.1.1 Phlebitis and thrombophlebitis	44 664	0.13	7 567	3 525	5 348	8 521	5.9	0.8	40.3	63.3
7.5.1.2 Other venous embolism and thrombosis	143 902	0.41	8 832	4 000	5 973	9 555	6.3	1.2	44.0	63.9
7.5.2 Varicose veins of lower extremity [119.]	15 962	0.05	9 482	4 123	6 454	10 850	6.8	0.3	40.4	65.6
7.5.3 Hemorrhoids [120.]	25 813	0.07	6 108	3 088	4 525	7 007	3.0	0.3	52.0	58.0
7.5.4 Other diseases of veins and lymphatics [121.]	12 700	0.04	11 103	3 685	6 458	11 692	6.0	2.0	44.8	61.6
8 DISEASES OF THE RESPIRATORY SYSTEM	3 235 193	9.28	11 787	3 770	6 537	11 982	5.9	5.8	47.4	54.6
8.1 Respiratory infections	1 574 992	4.52	10 704	3 678	6 334	11 373	5.8	5.0	49.2	51.6
8.1.1 Pneumonia (except that caused by TB or STD) [122.]	1 234 579	3.54	12 176	4 356	7 345	12 945	6.5	6.3	48.8	59.1
8.1.1.1 Pneumococcal pneumonia	57 458	0.16	14 169	4 650	7 612	13 409	7.0	5.1	52.6	59.6
8.1.1.2 Other bacterial pneumonia	258 425	0.74	18 777	6 482	11 034	20 024	8.9	10.1	51.4	69.0
8.1.1.3 Pneumonia, organism unspecified	792 231	2.27	9 810	4 002	6 540	11 020	5.8	5.6	47.2	58.6
8.1.1.4 Other pneumonia	126 466	0.36	12 554	3 815	6 847	12 860	6.2	4.2	51.1	41.6
8.1.2 Influenza [123.]	13 576	0.04	6 927	2 340	3 859	6 588	4.1	1.5	42.9	48.2
8.1.3 Acute and chronic tonsillitis [124.]	37 849	0.11	3 966	2 080	2 925	4 541	2.0	0.0	50.7	18.8
8.1.4 Acute bronchitis [125.]	203 700	0.58	5 781	2 607	4 130	6 649	3.6	0.2	50.5	24.5
8.1.5 Other upper respiratory infections [126.]	85 288	0.24	4 804	1 978	3 255	5 417	2.7	0.1	52.2	23.8
8.1.5.1 Acute upper respiratory infections of multiple or unspecified sites	24 299	0.07	4 535	2 129	3 334	5 173	2.8	0.2	49.3	22.9
8.1.5.2 Chronic sinusitis	10 930	0.03	7 140	3 317	4 936	8 181	3.1	0.1	48.3	38.6
8.1.5.3 Croup	17 499	0.05	2 897	1 313	2 060	3 359	1.7	0.0	69.0	2.1
8.1.5.4 Other and unspecified upper respiratory infections	32 560	0.09	5 241	2 146	3 438	5 739	3.1	0.1	46.7	31.2
8.2 Chronic obstructive pulmonary disease and bronchiectasis [127.]	547 480	1.57	10 552	4 386	6 869	11 219	5.9	2.9	44.1	68.3
8.2.1 Emphysema	21 650	0.06	15 781	4 629	7 565	14 030	7.3	5.8	48.3	69.2
8.2.2 Chronic airway obstruction, not otherwise specified	77 287	0.22	11 468	4 313	6 986	11 981	6.7	5.4	46.7	70.6
8.2.3 Obstructive chronic bronchitis	419 831	1.20	9 895	4 439	6 842	10 917	5.7	2.4	43.4	68.8
8.2.4 Other chronic pulmonary disease	28 713	0.08	13 753	3 577	6 409	12 961	5.9	1.7	44.7	53.2
8.3 Asthma [128.]	418 227	1.20	6 366	2 704	4 350	7 240	3.6	0.4	39.9	33.1
8.3.1 Chronic obstructive asthma	78 207	0.22	9 801	4 190	6 701	10 857	5.5	1.4	31.8	62.7
8.3.1.1 Chronic obstructive asthma without status asthmaticus	45 979	0.13	9 096	4 089	6 436	10 157	5.3	1.3	32.3	64.1
8.3.1.2 Chronic obstructive asthma with status asthmaticus	32 228	0.09	10 815	4 368	7 158	11 994	5.8	1.6	31.2	60.7
8.3.2 Other and unspecified asthma	340 020	0.98	5 576	2 509	3 961	6 425	3.1	0.2	41.7	26.3
8.3.2.1 Other asthma without status asthmaticus	159 639	0.46	5 033	2 453	3 796	5 987	3.1	0.1	39.2	29.4
8.3.2.2 Other asthma with status asthmaticus	180 381	0.52	6 059	2 574	4 131	6 861	3.2	0.2	43.9	23.6
8.4 Aspiration pneumonitis, food/vomitus [129.]	173 114	0.50	19 155	6 823	11 909	21 457	9.4	19.7	54.0	73.8
8.5 Pleurisy, pneumothorax, pulmonary collapse [130.]	101 960	0.29	14 465	4 488	8 271	15 926	7.2	4.4	56.1	58.1
8.5.1 Pleurisy, pleural effusion	54 411	0.16	12 760	4 629	7 955	14 177	6.5	5.0	48.2	66.1
8.5.2 Pulmonary collapse, interstitial and compensatory emphysema	5 264	0.02	11 790	3 620	6 554	11 333	5.2	4.2	53.4	47.9
8.5.3 Empyema and pneumothorax	42 286	0.12	17 001	4 419	9 284	19 421	8.3	3.6	66.7	49.1
8.6 Respiratory failure, insufficiency, arrest (adult) [131.]	202 314	0.58	29 780	7 660	14 906	30 938	10.3	23.3	46.0	66.7
8.6.1 Respiratory failure	187 130	0.54	29 749	7 872	15 132	30 982	10.4	23.4	44.7	67.8
8.6.2 Other respiratory insufficiency	15 184	0.04	30 167	5 026	11 672	30 282	9.1	22.5	49.6	53.8
8.7 Lung disease due to external agents [132.]	7 793	0.02	13 422	4 100	7 484	14 625	6.1	7.7	57.2	58.9
8.8 Other lower respiratory disease [133.]	161 760	0.46	9 407	3 100	5 288	9 441	4.0	3.1	47.7	56.9
8.8.1 Postinflammatory pulmonary fibrosis	16 850	0.05	16 106	6 191	10 445	17 039	6.6	7.7	48.1	65.4

See footnotes at end of table.

Table 4.14. Reasons Why People Are in the Hospital: 1996—*Continued*

(Principal diagnosis only)

Multilevel Clinical Classifications Software (CCS) category [1]	Number of discharges	Percent of discharges [2]	Mean charges (dollars)	25 percentile charges (dollars)	Median charges (dollars)	75 percentile charges (dollars)	Mean length of stay (days)	Percent died	Percent male	Mean age
8.8.2 Painful respiration	71 195	0.20	4 983	2 664	4 077	6 234	2.1	0.0	46.2	58.8
8.8.3 Other and unspecified lower respiratory disease	73 715	0.21	12 128	3 477	6 386	12 368	5.2	5.0	49.1	53.2
8.9 Other upper respiratory disease [134.]	47 553	0.14	8 029	2 704	4 734	8 340	3.5	0.5	55.1	46.3
9 DISEASES OF THE DIGESTIVE SYSTEM	3 001 774	8.61	11 569	4 052	7 091	12 471	5.1	2.2	44.2	55.5
9.1 Intestinal infection [135.]	120 783	0.35	6 013	2 083	3 497	6 123	3.8	0.7	40.5	39.7
9.2 Disorders of teeth and jaw [136.]	30 750	0.09	10 494	4 562	8 375	13 849	2.4	0.1	38.9	34.3
9.3 Diseases of mouth, excluding dental [137.]	16 308	0.05	7 870	3 153	5 312	8 992	3.8	0.7	47.2	46.7
9.4 Upper gastrointestinal disorders	401 430	1.15	9 348	3 526	5 829	9 804	4.4	1.3	44.0	58.0
9.4.1 Esophageal disorders [138.]	158 071	0.45	8 597	3 366	5 621	9 284	3.8	0.6	45.6	56.2
9.4.1.1 Esophagitis	42 227	0.12	7 933	3 502	5 686	9 084	3.7	0.6	45.4	57.9
9.4.1.2 Other esophageal disorders	115 844	0.33	8 840	3 309	5 596	9 376	3.9	0.7	45.7	55.6
9.4.2 Gastroduodenal ulcer (except hemorrhage) [139.]	55 149	0.16	15 047	4 365	7 753	15 228	6.3	3.9	43.9	60.7
9.4.2.1 Gastric ulcer	24 319	0.07	15 824	4 977	8 472	16 021	6.6	3.8	38.5	61.7
9.4.2.2 Duodenal ulcer	20 356	0.06	17 638	4 845	9 286	17 897	7.1	5.2	51.9	60.7
9.4.2.3 Peptic ulcer, site unspecified	9 466	0.03	7 001	2 850	4 613	7 346	3.7	1.6	41.5	58.2
9.4.2.4 Gastrojejunal ulcer	1 007	0.00	19 506	5 557	10 434	22 027	7.9	2.6	35.5	57.5
9.4.3 Gastritis and duodenitis [140.]	144 505	0.41	7 494	3 451	5 506	8 807	4.0	0.9	43.5	58.7
9.4.3.1 Acute gastritis	41 217	0.12	7 012	3 079	5 033	8 485	3.9	1.1	40.6	57.8
9.4.3.2 Other specified gastritis	57 534	0.16	8 165	3 968	6 167	9 617	4.3	0.9	46.0	60.0
9.4.3.3 Unspecified gastritis and gastroduodenitis	37 226	0.11	6 951	3 157	5 035	8 151	3.9	0.9	40.7	58.4
9.4.3.4 Duodenitis	8 529	0.02	7 688	3 658	5 608	8 603	3.9	0.7	53.4	55.7
9.4.4 Other disorders of stomach and duodenum [141.]	43 705	0.13	10 989	3 564	6 081	11 217	5.4	1.8	40.2	59.2
9.5 Abdominal hernia [143.]	161 359	0.46	11 262	4 660	7 444	12 180	4.4	1.2	48.4	60.7
9.5.1 Inguinal hernia	43 588	0.12	8 558	3 949	6 010	9 394	3.3	1.0	84.8	59.8
9.5.1.1 Inguinal hernia with obstruction or gangrene	21 618	0.06	10 339	4 412	6 839	11 101	4.0	1.4	82.7	61.5
9.5.1.2 Inguinal hernia without obstruction or gangrene	21 970	0.06	6 810	3 602	5 402	8 131	2.6	0.5	86.9	58.1
9.5.2 Diaphragmatic hernia	20 133	0.06	13 339	4 455	8 293	14 182	5.1	1.3	35.0	62.9
9.5.3 Other abdominal hernia	97 638	0.28	12 049	5 151	8 082	12 939	4.7	1.3	35.0	60.6
9.5.3.1 Femoral hernia with obstruction/gangrene	5 794	0.02	15 827	5 634	9 626	17 390	6.3	3.8	24.9	73.6
9.5.3.2 Femoral hernia without obstruction/gangrene	595	0.00	6 477	3 751	5 013	8 141	2.7	0.0	36.7	64.9
9.5.3.3 Umbilical hernia with obstruction/gangrene	9 298	0.03	10 504	4 379	6 978	11 408	4.0	2.0	42.1	57.0
9.5.3.4 Umbilical hernia without obstruction/gangrene	4 014	0.01	7 573	3 821	6 172	9 186	2.7	0.3	39.2	53.2
9.5.3.5 Ventral hernia with obstruction/gangrene	9 559	0.03	14 678	5 423	9 021	15 502	5.7	2.9	31.1	62.1
9.5.3.6 Ventral hernia without obstruction/gangrene	10 233	0.03	9 229	4 777	7 089	10 875	3.6	0.4	35.3	58.4
9.5.3.7 Incisional hernia with obstruction/gangrene	17 310	0.05	14 847	6 018	9 740	16 125	6.1	1.8	26.0	61.8
9.5.3.8 Incisional hernia without obstruction/gangrene	36 319	0.10	9 662	4 999	7 546	11 203	3.7	0.3	39.5	59.3
9.5.3.9 Other and unspecified hernia	4 515	0.01	24 410	9 701	16 643	27 997	9.8	3.3	34.5	65.3
9.6 Lower gastrointestinal disorders	848 980	2.43	12 419	4 437	7 473	13 404	5.8	1.9	46.0	54.5
9.6.1 Appendicitis and other appendiceal conditions [142.]	221 465	0.64	9 976	5 035	7 507	11 356	3.7	0.2	58.0	30.7
9.6.1.1 Acute appendicitis with abscess or peritonitis	74 090	0.21	15 178	7 547	11 327	17 126	6.2	0.5	59.8	36.0
9.6.1.2 Acute appendicitis without abscess or peritonitis	133 096	0.38	7 346	4 453	6 329	8 917	2.4	0.0	58.2	27.8
9.6.1.3 Acute appendicitis, not otherwise specified	7 108	0.02	7 352	4 273	6 259	9 058	2.6	0.2	51.6	28.8
9.6.1.4 Other appendiceal conditions	7 171	0.02	7 749	4 272	6 455	9 175	2.8	0.1	41.4	30.1
9.6.2 Regional enteritis and ulcerative colitis [144.]	66 307	0.19	13 577	4 651	8 329	15 495	7.0	0.7	41.8	45.4
9.6.3 Intestinal obstruction without hernia [145.]	271 840	0.78	13 301	3 757	7 000	14 690	6.7	3.6	41.0	65.0
9.6.3.1 Paralytic ileus	47 066	0.13	8 380	3 381	5 488	9 568	5.2	2.9	42.3	66.2
9.6.3.2 Impaction of intestine	31 242	0.09	7 818	2 910	4 943	8 769	5.1	2.8	36.9	70.4
9.6.3.3 Peritoneal or intestinal adhesions	72 306	0.21	22 208	7 076	14 369	26 586	9.8	3.5	37.2	63.1
9.6.3.4 Other intestinal obstruction	121 227	0.35	11 330	3 444	6 036	11 890	6.0	4.1	43.8	64.4
9.6.4 Diverticulosis and diverticulitis [146.]	227 690	0.65	12 859	4 649	7 657	13 914	6.1	1.4	40.2	67.9
9.6.4.1 Diverticulosis	77 278	0.22	11 356	4 238	6 826	11 846	5.4	1.4	42.9	73.5
9.6.4.2 Diverticulitis	150 412	0.43	13 632	4 889	8 153	15 183	6.4	1.4	38.8	65.0
9.6.5 Anal and rectal conditions [147.]	40 737	0.12	9 535	3 660	5 983	10 497	4.5	0.8	51.1	54.2
9.6.6 Peritonitis and intestinal abscess [148.]	20 939	0.06	23 966	6 906	13 117	24 990	9.5	7.6	49.5	54.7
9.7 Biliary tract disease [149.]	477 671	1.37	12 358	5 919	9 426	14 693	4.3	0.7	31.6	55.4
9.7.1 Cholelithiasis with acute cholecystitis	144 364	0.41	14 095	7 502	11 122	16 711	4.7	0.7	36.6	55.8
9.7.2 Cholelithiasis with other cholecystitis	182 250	0.52	10 936	5 700	8 668	13 131	3.4	0.4	24.9	53.0
9.7.3 Cholelithiasis without mention of cholecystitis	29 295	0.08	7 434	3 249	5 654	9 242	3.2	0.4	29.0	56.3
9.7.4 Calculus of bile duct	45 664	0.13	15 244	6 634	11 413	18 265	5.8	1.2	34.2	60.9
9.7.5 Cholecystitis without cholelithiasis	45 336	0.13	12 154	5 375	8 974	14 497	4.6	1.0	37.4	54.5
9.7.6 Other biliary tract disease	30 762	0.09	13 385	4 824	8 388	14 694	5.8	1.8	38.4	59.9
9.8 Liver disease	142 107	0.41	17 777	4 970	8 942	16 657	7.1	11.3	59.4	56.1
9.8.1 Liver disease, alcohol-related [150.]	63 776	0.18	17 180	5 268	9 419	17 223	7.1	11.3	71.2	51.9
9.8.2 Other liver diseases [151.]	78 331	0.22	18 261	4 737	8 562	16 089	7.2	11.3	49.8	59.5
9.8.2.1 Cirrhosis of liver without mention of alcohol	27 948	0.08	22 764	5 511	9 865	18 172	7.7	11.2	45.6	63.2
9.8.2.2 Liver abscess and sequelae of chronic liver disease	29 428	0.08	16 553	4 794	8 539	16 471	7.5	13.1	57.6	59.2
9.8.2.3 Ascites	3 817	0.01	8 806	3 242	5 806	10 204	5.1	4.3	46.9	57.6
9.8.2.4 Other and unspecified liver disorders	17 138	0.05	15 960	4 108	7 328	14 072	6.2	10.0	44.0	54.3
9.9 Pancreatic disorders (not diabetes) [152.]	198 191	0.57	14 779	4 524	7 810	14 525	6.7	1.8	50.0	52.7
9.9.1 Acute pancreatitis	163 287	0.47	14 495	4 442	7 626	13 993	6.6	2.0	50.2	53.1
9.9.2 Chronic pancreatitis	27 035	0.08	13 764	4 613	8 062	15 244	6.7	0.7	47.8	50.4
9.9.3 Other pancreatic disorders	7 869	0.02	24 170	6 591	12 964	25 471	10.2	1.6	53.4	53.1
9.10 Gastrointestinal hemorrhage [153.]	318 119	0.91	10 956	4 189	6 771	11 287	5.1	4.4	52.3	67.7
9.10.1 Hemorrhage from gastrointestinal ulcer	149 879	0.43	13 075	4 792	7 436	12 429	5.6	3.5	55.7	67.8
9.10.2 Melena	28 313	0.08	8 513	3 590	5 864	9 727	4.3	3.6	46.4	68.4
9.10.3 Gastroesophageal laceration syndrome	12 601	0.04	10 040	3 900	6 407	10 749	4.1	1.9	64.0	55.5
9.10.4 Other esophageal bleeding	8 197	0.02	12 771	5 425	8 670	14 738	5.4	4.2	60.1	62.3
9.10.5 Hemorrhage of rectum and anus	10 377	0.03	6 847	2 876	4 719	7 848	4.1	3.5	41.8	68.2
9.10.6 Hematemesis	16 124	0.05	8 174	3 165	5 343	9 104	4.2	7.6	50.2	61.8
9.10.7 Hemorrhage of gastrointestinal tract	92 629	0.27	9 210	3 827	6 337	10 435	4.9	6.1	47.8	70.4
9.11 Noninfectious gastroenteritis [154.]	130 521	0.37	4 306	1 899	3 005	5 027	2.9	0.2	39.1	39.5
9.12 Other gastrointestinal disorders [155.]	155 555	0.45	13 082	3 799	7 571	14 157	6.0	2.4	38.9	57.9
9.12.1 Constipation	18 611	0.05	4 761	2 054	3 262	5 473	3.2	0.8	40.1	60.1
9.12.2 Dysphagia	6 535	0.02	7 979	2 878	5 135	9 034	5.4	1.8	43.1	67.6
9.12.3 Other and unspecified gastrointestinal disorders	130 409	0.37	14 524	4 488	8 662	15 683	6.5	2.7	38.5	57.1

See footnotes at end of table.

Table 4.14. Reasons Why People Are in the Hospital: 1996—*Continued*

(Principal diagnosis only)

Multilevel Clinical Classifications Software (CCS) category [1]	Number of discharges	Percent of discharges [2]	Mean charges (dollars)	25 percentile charges (dollars)	Median charges (dollars)	75 percentile charges (dollars)	Mean length of stay (days)	Percent died	Percent male	Mean age
10 DISEASES OF THE GENITOURINARY SYSTEM	1 592 254	4.57	8 382	3 940	6 257	9 601	3.9	1.4	32.9	53.7
10.1 Diseases of the urinary system	824 432	2.36	8 927	3 330	5 700	9 824	4.8	2.6	44.4	57.2
10.1.1 Nephritis, nephrosis, renal sclerosis [156.]	11 290	0.03	10 550	2 939	5 779	11 623	5.1	0.8	54.9	39.4
10.1.2 Acute and unspecified renal failure [157.]	88 120	0.25	17 029	5 811	10 675	19 634	8.3	13.1	53.0	69.8
10.1.2.1 Acute renal failure	82 552	0.24	17 513	6 076	11 054	20 223	8.5	12.9	53.1	69.6
10.1.2.2 Unspecified renal failure	5 567	0.02	9 879	3 990	6 280	11 260	6.3	16.3	51.3	72.4
10.1.3 Chronic renal failure [158.]	28 832	0.08	18 515	4 130	8 549	19 783	6.9	7.2	52.4	60.1
10.1.4 Urinary tract infections [159.]	404 515	1.16	7 531	3 435	5 345	8 624	5.0	1.7	28.9	58.6
10.1.4.1 Infections of kidney	116 859	0.34	6 405	2 965	4 562	7 243	4.1	0.3	15.9	40.3
10.1.4.2 Cystitis and urethritis	17 762	0.05	9 595	3 684	6 120	10 359	4.9	1.3	43.8	65.9
10.1.4.3 Urinary tract infection, site not specified	269 894	0.77	7 881	3 664	5 687	9 135	5.5	2.3	33.5	66.0
10.1.5 Calculus of urinary tract [160.]	187 450	0.54	6 155	2 300	4 409	7 748	2.4	0.1	62.7	48.1
10.1.5.1 Calculus of kidney	45 415	0.13	7 577	2 365	4 698	9 786	2.9	0.1	53.7	48.9
10.1.5.2 Calculus of ureter	122 845	0.35	5 635	2 328	4 437	7 387	2.2	0.1	64.9	47.0
10.1.5.3 Other and unspecified urinary calculus	19 190	0.06	5 635	2 014	3 766	6 993	2.5	0.2	69.9	52.9
10.1.6 Other diseases of kidney and ureters [161.]	41 985	0.12	11 087	4 976	8 195	13 009	4.7	1.1	43.8	48.4
10.1.6.1 Hydronephrosis	6 969	0.02	10 233	3 965	7 530	12 352	4.5	1.7	47.7	53.6
10.1.6.2 Other and unspecified diseases of kidney and ureters	35 015	0.10	11 259	5 159	8 327	13 187	4.7	1.0	43.1	47.4
10.1.7 Other diseases of bladder and urethra [162.]	31 768	0.09	9 947	3 999	6 418	10 637	4.4	1.0	73.9	64.9
10.1.7.1 Bladder neck obstruction	9 955	0.03	6 963	3 576	5 387	7 917	3.5	0.6	97.4	72.6
10.1.7.2 Other and unspecified diseases of bladder and urethra	21 814	0.06	11 309	4 306	7 084	12 563	4.8	1.1	63.2	61.3
10.1.8 Genitourinary symptoms and ill-defined conditions [163.]	30 471	0.09	7 361	2 898	5 233	8 918	3.7	1.0	70.5	65.3
10.1.8.1 Hematuria	13 116	0.04	6 875	2 645	4 627	8 356	3.7	1.0	75.6	65.8
10.1.8.2 Retention of urine	7 769	0.02	6 126	2 802	4 759	7 375	3.7	1.0	79.8	68.6
10.1.8.3 Other and unspecified genitourinary symptoms	9 586	0.03	9 041	3 672	6 578	11 367	3.8	0.9	56.1	62.0
10.2 Diseases of male genital organs	157 751	0.45	7 268	3 925	5 760	8 565	3.1	0.3	100.0	66.9
10.2.1 Hyperplasia of prostate [164.]	120 640	0.35	7 171	4 151	5 898	8 482	3.1	0.3	100.0	72.1
10.2.2 Inflammatory conditions of male genital organs [165.]	21 370	0.06	6 613	2 934	4 674	7 449	4.1	0.4	100.0	52.8
10.2.3 Other male genital disorders [166.]	15 741	0.05	8 909	3 466	6 093	11 092	2.5	0.4	100.0	46.3
10.3 Diseases of female genital organs	610 071	1.75	7 929	4 835	6 921	9 636	2.9	0.1	0.1	45.6
10.3.1 Nonmalignant breast conditions [167.]	27 974	0.08	7 890	4 419	6 881	9 859	2.2	0.1	2.8	40.3
10.3.2 Inflammatory diseases of female pelvic organs [168.]	80 190	0.23	7 973	3 866	6 343	9 638	3.6	0.0	0.0	34.2
10.3.2.1 Pelvic peritoneal adhesions	17 430	0.05	8 594	5 650	7 673	10 159	3.0	0.0	0.0	37.7
10.3.2.2 Cervicitis and endocervicitis	6 292	0.02	7 904	5 290	7 256	9 781	2.8	0.0	0.0	41.3
10.3.2.3 Pelvic inflammatory disease (PID)	16 179	0.05	5 123	2 624	3 905	6 449	3.0	0.0	0.0	26.6
10.3.2.4 Other inflammatory diseases of female pelvic organs	40 290	0.12	8 872	3 865	6 487	10 540	4.2	0.1	0.0	34.6
10.3.3 Endometriosis [169.]	87 684	0.25	8 430	5 555	7 545	10 138	2.8	0.0	0.0	39.2
10.3.4 Prolapse of female genital organs [170.]	158 995	0.46	7 952	5 113	7 111	9 692	2.8	0.0	0.0	59.0
10.3.5 Menstrual disorders [171.]	71 111	0.20	7 344	4 790	6 640	9 018	2.5	0.0	0.0	39.5
10.3.6 Ovarian cyst [172.]	61 571	0.18	7 431	4 190	6 576	9 454	2.7	0.0	0.0	35.7
10.3.7 Menopausal disorders [173.]	10 281	0.03	7 911	4 780	6 878	9 799	3.0	0.1	0.0	57.9
10.3.8 Female infertility [174.]	1 256	0.00	6 494	4 008	5 993	8 040	2.1	0.0	0.0	32.8
10.3.9 Other female genital disorders [175.]	111 009	0.32	8 149	4 910	6 901	9 570	2.9	0.1	0.0	49.3
10.3.9.1 Female genital pain and other symptoms	65 714	0.19	7 203	4 692	6 509	8 833	2.5	0.0	0.0	50.6
10.3.9.2 Other and unspecified female genital disorders	45 295	0.13	9 524	5 281	7 598	10 702	3.5	0.3	0.0	47.4
11 COMPLICATIONS OF PREGNANCY, CHILDBIRTH, AND THE PUERPERIUM	4 346 935	12.47	4 528	2 554	3 624	5 386	2.2	0.0	0.0	27.1
11.1 Contraceptive and procreative management [176.]	3 513	0.01	6 703	4 184	5 908	8 125	2.0	0.0	1.0	33.3
11.1.1 Sterilization	1 430	0.00	6 349	3 412	5 181	7 687	1.9	0.0	0.9	32.8
11.1.2 Other contraceptive and procreation management	2 083	0.01	6 940	4 622	6 313	8 359	2.1	0.0	1.0	33.7
11.2 Abortion-related disorders	44 510	0.13	4 381	2 120	3 343	5 107	1.4	0.0	0.0	27.2
11.2.1 Spontaneous abortion [177.]	28 420	0.08	4 126	2 117	3 289	4 963	1.2	0.0	0.0	27.4
11.2.2 Induced abortion [178.]	12 469	0.04	4 550	2 075	3 327	5 177	1.6	0.0	0.0	27.1
11.2.3 Postabortion complications [179.]	3 621	0.01	5 824	2 410	3 870	6 344	2.6	0.3	0.0	25.9
11.3 Complications mainly related to pregnancy	1 064 815	3.05	5 083	2 401	3 734	5 940	2.7	0.0	0.0	26.7
11.3.1 Ectopic pregnancy [180.]	41 084	0.12	7 541	4 803	6 872	9 390	2.3	0.1	0.0	29.2
11.3.2 Hemorrhage during pregnancy, abruptio placenta, placenta previa [182.]	58 896	0.17	6 515	2 485	4 503	7 440	3.8	0.0	0.0	28.4
11.3.2.1 Placenta previa	13 493	0.04	10 801	4 686	6 937	10 409	6.7	0.0	0.0	30.5
11.3.2.2 Abruptio placenta	23 490	0.07	6 639	3 304	5 330	7 904	3.3	0.0	0.0	27.5
11.3.2.3 Other hemorrhage during pregnancy, childbirth, and the puerperium	21 913	0.06	3 753	1 590	2 547	4 228	2.6	0.0	0.0	28.2
11.3.3 Hypertension complicating pregnancy, childbirth, and the puerperium [183.]	174 351	0.50	6 271	3 079	4 837	7 588	3.2	0.0	0.0	26.9
11.3.3.1 Preeclampsia and eclampsia	96 997	0.28	7 464	3 642	5 799	9 104	3.7	0.1	0.0	26.3
11.3.3.2 Other hypertension in pregnancy	77 354	0.22	4 774	2 648	3 954	5 862	2.5	0.0	0.0	27.6
11.3.4 Early or threatened labor [184.]	269 765	0.77	5 155	2 030	3 442	5 755	3.0	0.0	0.0	26.0
11.3.4.1 Threatened premature labor	108 075	0.31	4 173	1 529	2 719	4 780	2.8	0.0	0.0	25.8
11.3.4.2 Early onset of delivery	140 984	0.40	6 393	2 892	4 237	6 903	3.5	0.0	0.0	26.3
11.3.4.3 Other early or threatened labor	20 707	0.06	1 829	807	1 228	2 060	0.9	0.0	0.0	25.1
11.3.5 Prolonged pregnancy [185.]	101 055	0.29	4 456	2 816	3 885	5 402	2.1	0.0	0.0	26.6
11.3.6 Diabetes or abnormal glucose tolerance complicating pregnancy, childbirth, or the puerperium [186.]	77 816	0.22	4 385	2 429	3 570	5 312	2.5	0.0	0.0	29.7
11.3.7 Other complications of pregnancy [181.]	341 849	0.98	4 221	2 179	3 209	4 814	2.3	0.0	0.0	25.9
11.3.7.1 Infections of genitourinary tract during pregnancy	63 066	0.18	3 980	2 287	3 230	4 813	2.4	0.0	0.0	24.2
11.3.7.2 Anemia during pregnancy	53 020	0.15	3 708	2 340	3 118	4 260	1.9	0.0	0.0	24.7
11.3.7.3 Mental disorders during pregnancy	16 204	0.05	4 466	2 354	3 352	4 873	3.4	0.0	0.0	27.2
11.3.7.4 Missed abortion	16 317	0.05	4 314	2 340	3 373	5 126	1.4	0.1	0.0	28.6
11.3.7.5 Hyperemesis gravidarum	38 501	0.11	3 266	1 527	2 337	3 746	2.8	0.0	0.0	25.5
11.3.7.6 Infectious and parasitic complications in mother affecting pregnancy	36 870	0.11	5 324	2 656	3 914	5 904	2.5	0.1	0.0	26.1
11.3.7.7 Other and unspecified complications of pregnancy	117 871	0.34	4 505	2 145	3 282	5 009	2.2	0.1	0.0	26.9
11.4 Indications for care in pregnancy, labor, and delivery	1 209 231	3.47	5 520	3 257	4 816	6 909	2.6	0.0	0.0	27.8
11.4.1 Malposition, malpresentation [187.]	156 507	0.45	6 151	4 038	5 617	7 435	3.0	0.0	0.0	28.1
11.4.1.1 Breech presentation	79 649	0.23	6 091	4 230	5 611	7 192	3.0	0.0	0.0	28.1
11.4.1.2 Other malposition, malpresentation	76 859	0.22	6 214	3 807	5 625	7 724	2.9	0.0	0.0	28.2
11.4.2 Fetopelvic disproportion, obstruction [188.]	149 232	0.43	6 073	3 766	5 594	7 774	2.9	0.0	0.0	27.4

See footnotes at end of table.

Table 4.14. Reasons Why People Are in the Hospital: 1996—*Continued*

(Principal diagnosis only)

Multilevel Clinical Classifications Software (CCS) category [1]	Number of discharges	Percent of discharges [2]	Mean charges (dollars)	25 percentile charges (dollars)	Median charges (dollars)	75 percentile charges (dollars)	Mean length of stay (days)	Percent died	Percent male	Mean age
11.4.2.1 Fetopelvic disproportion	36 857	0.11	6 863	4 931	6 365	8 207	3.4	0.0	0.0	27.1
11.4.2.2 Other disproportion or obstruction	112 375	0.32	5 811	3 404	5 216	7 592	2.7	0.0	0.0	27.6
11.4.3 Previous C-section [189.]	268 315	0.77	5 519	3 680	5 122	6 845	2.5	0.0	0.0	29.7
11.4.4 Fetal distress and abnormal forces of labor [190.]	428 172	1.23	5 169	2 868	4 300	6 632	2.4	0.0	0.0	27.1
11.4.4.1 Fetal distress	189 093	0.54	5 345	3 023	4 446	6 715	2.5	0.0	0.0	27.0
11.4.4.2 Uterine inertia	150 119	0.43	5 962	3 523	5 296	7 742	2.8	0.0	0.0	27.0
11.4.4.3 Precipitate labor	56 890	0.16	3 023	2 010	2 709	3 580	1.4	0.0	0.0	27.7
11.4.4.4 Other abnormal forces of labor	32 071	0.09	4 193	2 634	3 559	4 984	2.2	0.0	0.0	27.0
11.4.5 Polyhydramnios and other problems of amniotic cavity [191.]	207 004	0.59	5 365	2 929	4 169	6 123	2.8	0.0	0.0	27.1
11.4.5.1 Premature rupture of membranes	106 374	0.31	4 581	2 736	3 809	5 356	2.3	0.0	0.0	27.6
11.4.5.2 Infection of amniotic cavity	12 734	0.04	6 145	3 510	5 027	7 257	2.8	0.0	0.0	25.6
11.4.5.3 Other problems of amniotic cavity	87 895	0.25	6 209	3 195	4 619	6 978	3.5	0.0	0.0	26.7
11.5 Complications during labor	1 066 508	3.06	3 491	2 397	3 173	4 184	1.7	0.0	0.0	26.9
11.5.1 Umbilical cord complication [192.]	267 207	0.77	3 570	2 419	3 206	4 263	1.7	0.0	0.0	26.9
11.5.1.1 Cord around neck with compression	39 568	0.11	3 599	2 459	3 235	4 303	1.6	0.0	0.0	27.0
11.5.1.2 Other and unspecified cord entanglement with or without compression	213 903	0.61	3 500	2 398	3 173	4 194	1.6	0.0	0.0	26.8
11.5.1.3 Other umbilical cord complications	13 736	0.04	4 574	2 696	3 800	5 594	2.2	0.0	0.0	27.6
11.5.2 Trauma to perineum and vulva [193.]	693 212	1.99	3 413	2 339	3 106	4 098	1.7	0.0	0.0	27.0
11.5.2.1 First-degree perineal laceration	318 116	0.91	3 350	2 311	3 062	4 016	1.6	0.0	0.0	26.8
11.5.2.2 Second-degree perineal laceration	270 327	0.78	3 380	2 292	3 067	4 076	1.6	0.0	0.0	27.5
11.5.2.3 Third-degree perineal laceration	67 307	0.19	3 659	2 547	3 334	4 375	1.8	0.0	0.0	26.8
11.5.2.4 Fourth-degree perineal laceration	29 615	0.08	3 818	2 625	3 434	4 522	1.9	0.0	0.0	25.8
11.5.2.5 Other perineal laceration and trauma	7 847	0.02	3 486	2 419	3 227	4 114	1.7	0.0	0.0	25.8
11.5.3 Forceps delivery [194.]	106 089	0.30	3 784	2 713	3 488	4 517	1.8	0.0	0.0	26.2
11.6 Other complications of birth, puerperium affecting management of mother [195.]	379 466	1.09	4 517	2 550	3 597	5 191	2.1	0.0	0.0	27.6
11.6.1 Postpartum hemorrhage	21 779	0.06	4 769	2 432	3 502	5 108	2.0	0.0	0.0	26.7
11.6.2 Complications of the puerperium	32 817	0.09	5 872	2 589	3 885	6 054	3.2	0.3	0.0	27.2
11.6.3 Cervical incompetence	11 946	0.03	6 657	2 574	3 837	6 345	4.2	0.0	0.0	28.9
11.6.4 Rhesus isoimmunization	18 625	0.05	3 739	2 527	3 396	4 464	1.7	0.0	0.0	26.7
11.6.5 Intrauterine death	14 869	0.04	4 981	2 718	4 000	5 838	2.0	0.0	0.0	27.5
11.6.6 Failed induction	15 027	0.04	4 908	1 774	3 574	7 117	2.4	0.0	0.0	27.5
11.6.7 Other obstetrical trauma	71 793	0.21	3 659	2 389	3 183	4 228	1.7	0.0	0.0	25.3
11.6.8 Other and unspecified complications of birth, puerperium affecting management of mother	192 610	0.55	4 449	2 663	3 771	5 347	2.1	0.0	0.0	28.6
11.7 Normal pregnancy and/or delivery [196.]	578 892	1.66	3 355	2 269	3 008	3 945	1.6	0.0	0.0	26.1
11.7.1 Normal delivery	549 771	1.58	3 222	2 261	2 976	3 855	1.5	0.0	0.0	26.0
11.7.2 Multiple gestation	21 694	0.06	7 192	3 990	5 730	8 109	3.6	0.0	0.0	28.8
11.7.3 Outcome of delivery (V codes)	7 426	0.02	1 945	1 003	1 621	2 514	1.3	0.0	0.0	26.6
12 DISEASES OF THE SKIN AND SUBCUTANEOUS TISSUE	423 323	1.21	9 516	3 450	5 839	10 342	6.3	1.1	49.8	54.7
12.1 Skin and subcutaneous tissue infections [197.]	325 223	0.93	7 912	3 196	5 262	8 988	5.4	0.6	51.5	52.6
12.1.1 Cellulitis and abscess	313 505	0.90	7 958	3 215	5 292	9 055	5.4	0.6	51.5	53.1
12.1.1.1 Cellulitis and abscess of fingers and toes	20 654	0.06	6 933	2 895	4 872	8 214	4.8	0.3	55.8	48.4
12.1.1.2 Cellulitis and abscess of face	21 974	0.06	6 135	2 598	4 310	6 963	3.9	0.3	48.4	37.7
12.1.1.3 Cellulitis and abscess of arm	31 710	0.09	7 102	2 850	4 637	7 989	4.6	0.5	51.7	49.6
12.1.1.4 Cellulitis and abscess of hand	21 620	0.06	6 124	2 440	3 879	7 073	4.0	0.4	61.9	44.6
12.1.1.5 Cellulitis and abscess of leg	145 608	0.42	8 213	3 503	5 639	9 370	6.0	0.7	49.4	59.1
12.1.1.6 Cellulitis and abscess of foot	40 277	0.12	8 514	3 315	5 591	9 738	6.0	0.5	56.2	55.1
12.1.1.7 Other cellulitis and abscess	31 662	0.09	10 122	3 749	6 278	11 041	5.6	0.8	47.2	45.8
12.1.2 Other skin and subcutaneous infections	11 718	0.03	6 673	2 868	4 488	7 368	4.2	0.2	52.1	39.7
12.2 Other inflammatory condition of skin [198.]	9 806	0.03	13 263	3 242	5 820	11 714	6.9	2.6	41.5	46.9
12.3 Chronic ulcer of skin [199.]	76 025	0.22	15 998	5 502	9 494	17 454	10.8	3.2	45.6	66.3
12.3.1 Decubitus ulcer	38 207	0.11	20 048	6 534	11 719	21 923	13.4	5.0	45.5	67.0
12.3.2 Chronic ulcer of leg	35 081	0.10	11 866	4 856	7 885	13 410	8.1	1.4	45.7	66.3
12.3.3 Other chronic skin ulcer	2 738	0.01	12 447	4 627	7 978	14 734	7.4	0.9	45.8	56.8
12.4 Other skin disorders [200.]	12 269	0.04	8 744	3 716	6 275	10 612	3.5	0.2	37.6	43.4
13 DISEASES OF THE MUSCULOSKELETAL SYSTEM AND CONNECTIVE TISSUE	1 391 458	3.99	14 032	5 732	11 165	18 547	4.7	0.4	44.5	59.2
13.1 Infective arthritis and osteomyelitis (except that caused by TB or STD) [201.]	68 133	0.20	17 744	6 443	11 239	20 209	9.6	1.2	59.9	54.2
13.2 Non-traumatic joint disorders	482 011	1.38	18 252	12 819	17 366	22 826	5.1	0.2	38.6	67.5
13.2.1 Rheumatoid arthritis and related disease [202.]	26 068	0.07	14 600	5 856	12 237	19 479	5.5	0.7	25.1	60.6
13.2.2 Osteoarthritis [203.]	415 264	1.19	19 423	14 131	18 209	23 488	5.2	0.2	38.9	69.3
13.2.2.1 Osteoarthritis, localized	239 763	0.69	19 901	14 327	18 778	24 136	5.0	0.2	39.4	69.1
13.2.2.2 Osteoarthritis, generalized and unspecified	175 501	0.50	18 776	13 906	17 512	22 599	5.3	0.2	38.3	69.6
13.2.3 Other non-traumatic joint disorders [204.]	40 680	0.12	8 686	3 508	6 007	10 825	3.9	0.2	44.2	53.7
13.3 Spondylosis, intervertebral disc disorders, other back problems [205.]	519 130	1.49	10 576	4 874	7 966	12 780	3.4	0.2	51.5	53.4
13.3.1 Spondylosis and allied disorders	60 123	0.17	13 576	5 664	10 025	16 174	4.4	0.4	47.3	62.6
13.3.2 Intervertebral disc disorders	329 181	0.94	10 110	5 018	7 849	12 143	2.9	0.1	55.4	48.2
13.3.3 Other back problems	129 826	0.37	10 378	4 125	7 543	13 031	4.2	0.3	43.7	62.1
13.3.3.1 Cervical radiculitis	5 453	0.02	8 298	3 425	6 523	11 326	2.9	0.1	48.9	54.0
13.3.3.2 Spinal stenosis, lumbar region	65 792	0.19	13 056	6 577	10 024	15 812	4.6	0.3	45.3	67.7
13.3.3.3 Lumbago	20 057	0.06	5 548	2 306	3 805	6 426	3.9	0.2	38.7	55.9
13.3.3.4 Sciatica	3 988	0.01	5 570	2 546	4 115	6 657	4.1	0.1	33.9	59.9
13.3.3.5 Thoracic or lumbosacral neuritis or radiculitis, unspecified	9 401	0.03	7 940	3 399	5 907	9 848	4.0	0.0	43.9	55.7
13.3.3.6 Backache, unspecified	7 022	0.02	5 630	2 436	3 953	6 389	3.7	0.9	34.5	59.5
13.3.3.7 Other back pain and disorders	18 114	0.05	10 882	3 754	7 340	13 801	4.1	0.4	47.8	55.8
13.4 Osteoporosis [206.]	1 900	0.01	8 419	3 460	5 450	9 047	6.4	0.8	13.8	76.4
13.5 Pathological fracture [207.]	75 655	0.22	11 092	4 157	7 132	13 536	7.1	2.3	21.3	76.6
13.6 Acquired deformities	35 854	0.10	17 885	6 691	12 145	22 310	4.7	0.2	44.0	47.1
13.6.1 Acquired foot deformities [208.]	7 424	0.02	8 049	4 821	6 741	9 977	2.2	0.0	33.0	47.4
13.6.2 Other acquired deformities [209.]	28 430	0.08	20 457	8 144	15 139	25 397	5.3	0.2	46.9	47.0
13.7 Systemic lupus erythematosus and connective tissue disorders [210.]	18 421	0.05	15 948	4 221	7 833	14 629	7.3	3.5	17.0	43.9
13.8 Other connective tissue disease [211.]	104 078	0.30	9 663	3 514	5 688	9 225	4.1	0.6	49.9	55.0

See footnotes at end of table.

Table 4.14. Reasons Why People Are in the Hospital: 1996—*Continued*

(Principal diagnosis only)

Multilevel Clinical Classifications Software (CCS) category [1]	Number of discharges	Percent of discharges [2]	Mean charges (dollars)	25 percentile charges (dollars)	Median charges (dollars)	75 percentile charges (dollars)	Mean length of stay (days)	Percent died	Percent male	Mean age
13.9 Other bone disease and musculoskeletal deformities [212.]	86 274	0.25	14 218	5 269	10 094	18 950	4.0	0.3	42.5	49.8
14 CONGENITAL ANOMALIES	108 510	0.31	23 193	5 414	10 146	22 932	5.9	1.6	54.3	16.2
14.1 Cardiac and circulatory congenital anomalies [213.]	33 321	0.10	40 911	9 125	21 983	43 281	8.0	3.5	50.5	17.1
14.1.1 Transposition of great vessels	711	0.00	89 740	20 158	53 446	98 177	17.0	6.1	65.5	2.1
14.1.2 Tetralogy of Fallot	2 430	0.01	60 650	10 697	36 533	66 315	11.7	5.5	52.0	3.4
14.1.3 Ventricular septal defect	3 460	0.01	31 914	7 220	22 750	39 035	6.7	2.9	53.3	6.1
14.1.4 Atrial septal defect	4 685	0.01	26 224	14 303	23 409	32 240	4.9	0.3	35.4	24.1
14.1.5 Endocardial cushion defects	1 370	0.00	54 184	14 138	32 179	54 463	10.5	4.7	38.7	5.0
14.1.6 Pulmonary valve atresia and stenosis	922	0.00	36 128	7 307	12 489	40 119	6.9	3.2	55.2	6.1
14.1.7 Aortic valve stenosis	1 044	0.00	43 466	14 178	36 360	53 120	6.5	3.3	66.0	24.5
14.1.8 Patent ductus arteriosus	1 749	0.01	25 015	6 804	11 212	17 610	6.2	0.6	38.1	5.5
14.1.9 Coarctation of aorta	1 588	0.00	40 182	12 778	20 367	35 840	8.9	2.4	67.7	7.7
14.1.10 Pulmonary artery anomalies	1 349	0.00	54 959	8 984	17 216	42 443	8.3	4.0	52.0	8.0
14.1.11 Cerebrovascular anomalies	3 329	0.01	27 981	7 350	15 739	32 519	5.8	1.7	46.2	39.6
14.1.12 Other cardiac and circulatory congenital anomalies	10 683	0.03	45 762	8 054	23 542	50 657	9.1	5.5	55.0	20.9
14.2 Digestive congenital anomalies [214.]	18 071	0.05	15 201	4 400	7 122	13 512	5.8	0.4	67.3	9.6
14.2.1 Esophageal atresia/tracheoesophageal fistula	739	0.00	54 247	7 944	26 684	61 844	18.2	1.8	54.0	11.8
14.2.2 Pyloric stenosis	8 105	0.02	6 294	3 782	5 080	7 251	2.9	0.0	80.7	0.8
14.2.3 Rectal and large intestine atresia/ stenosis	1 158	0.00	20 274	6 259	10 970	20 663	7.0	0.3	52.2	0.7
14.2.4 Hirshsprung's disease	1 535	0.00	21 672	7 202	14 074	23 750	8.2	0.2	74.2	3.4
14.2.5 Other digestive congenital anomalies	6 534	0.02	19 402	5 940	10 410	18 966	7.2	0.9	53.1	23.5
14.3 Genitourinary congenital anomalies [215.]	12 394	0.04	11 846	4 719	7 452	12 387	4.0	0.4	57.4	22.7
14.3.1 Undescended testicle	660	0.00	5 847	3 440	4 719	6 683	1.7	0.0	100.0	10.7
14.3.2 Hypospadias and epispadias	1 744	0.01	7 928	4 583	6 461	10 079	2.7	0.0	100.0	5.0
14.3.3 Obstructive genitourinary defect	2 896	0.01	10 522	6 018	8 498	12 814	3.9	0.0	64.1	16.0
14.3.4 Other genitourinary congenital anomalies	7 094	0.02	13 910	4 449	7 694	13 458	4.6	0.7	40.2	30.9
14.4 Nervous system congenital anomalies [216.]	5 695	0.02	21 272	6 973	13 222	24 067	7.4	2.1	44.9	16.4
14.4.1 Spina bifida	1 526	0.00	26 290	8 846	15 868	32 890	8.8	1.0	44.9	13.9
14.4.2 Congenital hydrocephalus	1 238	0.00	18 971	5 802	9 824	18 663	6.9	2.0	52.8	6.4
14.4.3 Other nervous system congenital anomalies	2 931	0.01	19 647	7 243	13 651	23 429	6.8	2.7	41.5	21.9
14.5 Other congenital anomalies [217.]	39 029	0.11	15 760	5 037	8 207	15 908	4.5	0.8	52.0	16.5
14.5.1 Cleft palate without cleft lip	2 538	0.01	7 506	4 214	5 617	7 498	2.0	0.0	44.8	4.6
14.5.2 Cleft lip with or without cleft palate	4 294	0.01	7 393	4 434	5 958	8 100	1.9	0.0	59.9	4.2
14.5.3 Congenital hip dislocation	2 077	0.01	13 393	7 180	11 490	16 476	4.0	0.0	31.8	11.4
14.5.4 All other congenital anomalies	30 119	0.09	17 817	5 236	9 330	18 277	5.1	1.0	52.9	19.6
15 CERTAIN CONDITIONS ORIGINATING IN THE PERINATAL PERIOD	3 948 024	11.32	3 786	618	899	1 528	3.0	0.4	51.4	0.0
15.1 Liveborn [218.]	3 827 666	10.98	3 279	611	880	1 451	2.8	0.3	51.2	0.0
15.2 Short gestation, low birth weight, and fetal growth retardation [219.]	23 154	0.07	50 254	6 937	18 612	49 695	22.5	4.7	55.1	0.0
15.3 Intrauterine hypoxia and birth asphyxia [220.]	1 018	0.00	31 823	5 413	15 944	41 414	11.1	22.2	49.7	0.0
15.4 Respiratory distress syndrome [221.]	5 961	0.02	56 606	16 924	31 474	59 813	22.0	3.2	62.6	0.0
15.5 Hemolytic jaundice and perinatal jaundice [222.]	37 691	0.11	2 687	1 094	1 706	2 698	2.2	0.0	58.2	0.0
15.6 Birth trauma [223.]	831	0.00	15 881	1 717	5 716	13 981	6.5	3.9	59.4	0.0
15.7 Other perinatal conditions [224.]	51 702	0.15	14 209	2 757	5 593	13 039	6.6	1.1	56.0	0.0
15.7.1 Respiratory conditions of fetus and newborn, other than respiratory distress	22 072	0.06	18 785	3 510	8 639	18 766	8.0	1.1	56.7	0.0
15.7.2 Infections specific to the perinatal period	11 711	0.03	9 671	3 196	5 174	9 980	5.4	0.6	55.7	0.0
15.7.3 Endocrine and metabolic disturbances of fetus and newborn	3 096	0.01	10 202	2 144	4 282	10 738	5.2	0.5	54.5	0.0
15.7.4 Other and unspecified perinatal conditions	14 823	0.04	11 770	2 141	3 625	7 990	5.6	1.5	55.5	0.0
16 INJURY AND POISONING	2 718 444	7.80	14 646	4 283	8 350	15 616	5.4	1.9	49.6	53.1
16.1 Joint disorders and dislocations, trauma-related [225.]	61 531	0.18	9 843	4 858	7 583	11 641	2.6	0.2	59.6	38.3
16.2 Fractures	984 454	2.82	13 873	5 546	10 007	16 277	5.7	1.5	40.1	60.4
16.2.1 Fracture of neck of femur (hip) [226.]	351 036	1.01	16 747	9 927	13 868	19 539	7.5	3.0	25.3	79.2
16.2.2 Skull and face fractures [228.]	53 093	0.15	13 501	4 194	7 791	13 991	3.6	0.5	73.8	33.3
16.2.3 Fracture of upper limb [229.]	142 836	0.41	9 668	4 091	6 770	11 270	3.4	0.4	47.3	47.5
16.2.3.1 Fracture of humerus	59 487	0.17	10 168	4 091	6 968	12 359	4.0	0.8	36.4	52.2
16.2.3.2 Fracture of radius and ulna	59 940	0.17	9 594	4 322	6 930	10 963	3.0	0.2	48.7	45.2
16.2.3.3 Other fracture of upper limb	23 408	0.07	8 581	3 660	5 901	9 684	2.8	0.2	71.4	41.4
16.2.4 Fracture of lower limb [230.]	270 703	0.78	13 362	5 286	8 759	14 792	5.0	0.5	48.0	47.2
16.2.4.1 Fracture of tibia and fibula	68 934	0.20	14 856	5 041	9 559	16 144	5.4	0.4	56.3	44.6
16.2.4.2 Fracture of ankle	105 711	0.30	9 708	5 075	7 438	11 045	3.5	0.2	41.5	47.8
16.2.4.3 Other fracture of lower limb	96 058	0.28	16 309	5 867	10 843	18 802	6.5	0.9	49.1	48.5
16.2.5 Other fractures [231.]	166 787	0.48	12 368	3 519	5 985	11 795	6.0	1.3	41.8	61.8
16.2.5.1 Fracture of vertebral column without mention of spinal cord injury	59 940	0.17	12 313	3 521	6 111	12 437	5.9	1.1	46.1	59.4
16.2.5.2 Fracture of ribs, closed	34 792	0.10	11 134	3 510	5 930	11 059	5.0	1.3	51.3	63.2
16.2.5.3 Fracture of pelvis	58 163	0.17	12 867	3 475	5 879	12 073	6.8	1.5	30.5	65.9
16.2.5.4 Other and unspecified fracture	13 892	0.04	13 594	3 714	6 042	10 469	5.0	1.8	46.6	52.0
16.3 Spinal cord injury [227.]	12 835	0.04	56 786	10 132	27 557	62 705	16.3	4.8	73.0	43.4
16.4 Intracranial injury [233.]	167 335	0.48	22 787	3 776	8 258	19 927	6.9	7.4	64.8	42.1
16.4.1 Concussion	33 687	0.10	7 134	2 474	4 374	7 906	2.6	0.4	60.8	38.3
16.4.2 Other intracranial injury	133 648	0.38	26 763	4 512	10 150	25 101	8.0	9.2	65.8	43.1
16.5 Crushing injury or internal injury [234.]	97 681	0.28	24 832	5 833	11 656	23 655	6.9	4.5	72.4	38.7
16.6 Open wounds	110 202	0.32	8 760	3 274	5 646	9 577	3.0	0.3	74.3	35.0
16.6.1 Open wounds of head, neck, and trunk [235.]	50 740	0.15	8 502	3 200	5 553	9 606	2.5	0.5	73.4	34.2
16.6.2 Open wounds of extremities [236.]	59 462	0.17	8 980	3 324	5 708	9 550	3.4	0.2	75.1	35.6
16.7 Sprains and strains [232.]	86 184	0.25	6 368	3 471	5 436	8 099	2.3	0.1	56.7	50.9
16.8 Superficial injury, contusion [239.]	50 680	0.15	5 602	2 493	4 059	6 748	3.3	0.4	44.3	54.2
16.9 Burns [240.]	40 087	0.11	29 422	3 630	9 061	24 547	9.8	3.1	68.5	32.3
16.10 Complications	804 970	2.31	16 867	5 124	9 939	19 106	6.1	1.8	50.4	58.8
16.10.1 Complication of device, implant, or graft [237.]	469 564	1.35	19 460	6 677	12 534	22 796	6.0	1.9	52.1	60.2
16.10.1.1 Malfunction of device, implant, and graft	222 594	0.64	20 269	7 314	13 863	24 452	5.2	1.4	53.5	63.4
16.10.1.2 Infection and inflammation—internal prosthetic device, implant, and graft	106 178	0.30	19 694	6 415	11 823	22 443	8.5	2.8	51.7	55.9
16.10.1.3 Other complications of internal prosthetic device, implant, and graft	118 590	0.34	16 791	6 261	11 266	20 036	4.9	1.8	48.6	61.4

See footnotes at end of table.

Table 4.14. Reasons Why People Are in the Hospital: 1996—*Continued*

(Principal diagnosis only)

Multilevel Clinical Classifications Software (CCS) category [1]	Number of discharges	Percent of discharges [2]	Mean charges (dollars)	25 percentile charges (dollars)	Median charges (dollars)	75 percentile charges (dollars)	Mean length of stay (days)	Percent died	Percent male	Mean age
16.10.1.4 Complications of transplants and reattached limbs	21 243	0.06	24 934	5 343	10 356	22 365	7.4	2.8	59.6	40.8
16.10.2 Complications of surgical procedures or medical care [238.]	335 406	0.96	13 265	3 876	7 122	13 591	6.2	1.6	47.9	56.8
16.10.2.1 Cardiac complications	16 573	0.05	13 209	4 403	7 656	13 088	4.7	2.5	54.4	66.3
16.10.2.2 Respiratory complications	7 925	0.02	13 752	4 131	7 261	13 483	5.7	3.4	50.8	55.1
16.10.2.3 Gastrointestinal complications	45 590	0.13	13 804	3 651	6 685	13 171	6.4	1.7	36.3	55.4
16.10.2.4 Urinary complications	12 637	0.04	8 419	2 928	5 253	9 229	3.8	1.1	66.5	59.9
16.10.2.5 Hemorrhage or hematoma complicating a procedure	43 603	0.13	8 094	2 772	4 892	8 775	3.5	0.7	53.5	55.8
16.10.2.6 Postoperative infection	114 084	0.33	15 885	4 664	8 686	16 933	8.0	1.5	48.1	56.0
16.10.2.7 Other complications of surgical and medical procedures	94 994	0.27	12 839	3 915	7 160	13 185	5.8	1.9	47.0	57.0
16.11 Poisoning	220 692	0.63	6 204	2 445	3 805	6 368	2.6	0.9	42.5	36.3
16.11.1 Poisoning by psychotropic agents [241.]	69 607	0.20	6 032	2 540	3 803	6 294	2.3	0.6	38.2	37.1
16.11.2 Poisoning by other medications and drugs [242.]	125 152	0.36	6 115	2 464	3 849	6 402	2.6	1.1	41.2	36.5
16.11.3 Poisoning by nonmedicinal substances [243.]	25 933	0.07	7 096	2 112	3 552	6 356	2.8	1.2	60.6	33.3
16.12 Other injuries and conditions due to external causes [244.]	81 793	0.23	8 208	2 483	4 415	8 590	3.2	2.1	58.2	42.3
17 SYMPTOMS, SIGNS, AND ILL-DEFINED CONDITIONS AND FACTORS INFLUENCING HEALTH STATUS	979 806	2.81	11 132	3 442	6 595	13 130	8.2	1.6	41.6	61.1
17.1 Symptoms, signs, and ill-defined conditions	548 714	1.57	7 824	2 796	4 745	8 247	4.1	1.7	42.6	56.0
17.1.1 Syncope [245.]	189 193	0.54	6 244	3 031	4 841	7 577	3.2	0.3	44.3	68.3
17.1.2 Fever of unknown origin [246.]	62 289	0.18	6 729	2 804	4 532	7 808	4.0	0.7	51.6	39.5
17.1.3 Lymphadenitis [247.]	19 694	0.06	6 116	2 661	4 527	7 362	3.1	0.1	50.1	23.2
17.1.4 Gangrene [248.]	55 791	0.16	23 327	8 662	15 205	27 804	11.3	6.4	52.1	72.8
17.1.5 Shock [249.]	7 334	0.02	19 984	4 873	9 809	20 079	6.0	49.8	48.4	67.4
17.1.6 Nausea and vomiting [250.]	30 000	0.09	5 300	2 270	3 695	6 099	3.2	0.7	31.1	53.7
17.1.7 Abdominal pain [251.]	152 157	0.44	5 154	2 294	3 854	6 352	2.7	0.4	34.8	45.6
17.1.8 Malaise and fatigue [252.]	13 398	0.04	6 561	2 698	4 294	7 092	5.9	1.4	39.4	68.5
17.1.9 Allergic reactions [253.]	18 858	0.05	4 865	1 893	3 092	5 174	3.0	0.5	40.5	44.4
17.2 Factors influencing health care	431 092	1.24	15 375	5 705	10 848	19 262	13.4	1.5	40.4	67.5
17.2.1 Rehabilitation care, fitting of prostheses, and adjustment of devices [254.]	335 978	0.96	17 289	7 337	12 627	21 241	15.0	1.0	40.4	69.8
17.2.2 Administrative/social admission [255.]	5 159	0.01	5 009	1 029	2 250	4 837	5.5	6.1	44.8	58.8
17.2.3 Medical examination/evaluation [256.]	14 740	0.04	3 054	617	1 711	3 576	2.7	0.1	51.9	32.1
17.2.4 Other aftercare [257.]	74 484	0.21	9 650	3 146	6 027	11 197	9.0	4.1	37.8	65.1
17.2.5 Other screening for suspected conditions (not mental disorders or infectious disease) [258.]	731	0.00	9 532	5 322	9 867	13 227	5.1	0.0	36.2	30.0
18 RESIDUAL CODES, UNCLASSIFIED, ALL E CODES [259. AND 260.]	43 572	0.12	7 704	2 815	5 024	9 069	4.2	2.3	46.1	54.7

SOURCE: Agency for Health Care Policy and Research (AHCPR) [AHCPR is now known as the Agency for Healthcare Research and Quality (AHRQ)], Center for Organization and Delivery Studies, Healthcare Cost and Utilization Project (HCUP): Table 1.

1. CCS categories are presented in bold lettering with the CCS category number at the end of the word label, in brackets. See the AHRQ Web site for definitions of CCS categories: <http://www.ahrq.gov/data/hcup>.
2. Numbers of discharges are weighted national estimates based on 100% of the data from the HCUP Nationwide Inpatient Sample. Results are not presented for any diagnosis category for which the unweighted number of discharges is less than 70. Estimates presented here have a relative error of less than 30%. Out of the "All Discharges" category, 12,218 discharges had missing or invalid diagnosis codes and are not presented in the table details.

NOTE: Acronyms used in Table 1: CNS—central nervous system; GI—gastrointestinal; HIV—human immunodeficiency virus; OR—operating room; STD—sexually transmitted disease; and TB—tuberculosis.

Table 4.15. Hospital Procedures: 1996

(Principal procedure only)

Multilevel Clinical Classifications Software (CCS) category [1]	Number of discharges	Percent of discharges [2]	Mean charges (dollars)	25 percentile charges (dollars)	Median charges (dollars)	75 percentile charges (dollars)	Mean length of stay	Percent died	Percent male	Mean age
ALL DISCHARGES	34 872 474	100.00	10 647	2 911	5 737	11 414	5.0	2.5	41.3	47.1
1 Operations on the nervous system	828 046	2.37	15 526	5 293	9 074	16 276	5.5	2.4	52.7	43.0
1.1 Incision and excision of CNS [1.]	70 597	0.20	36 364	15 569	25 031	41 603	10.2	8.6	56.6	55.3
1.1.1 Craniotomy and craniectomy	10 807	0.03	35 442	13 236	22 325	41 609	10.5	8.2	59.7	48.7
1.1.2 Incision of cerebral meninges	17 513	0.05	36 861	14 453	23 691	42 156	10.9	14.1	67.7	65.4
1.1.3 Other incision and excision of CNS	42 278	0.12	36 398	16 747	26 217	41 343	9.9	6.4	51.2	52.8
1.2 Insertion, replacement, or removal of extracranial ventricular shunt [2.]	25 133	0.07	26 921	8 417	13 189	25 497	8.9	2.9	53.9	36.6
1.3 Laminectomy, excision intervertebral disc [3.]	340 481	0.98	11 538	5 755	8 692	13 273	3.2	0.2	56.0	51.4
1.3.1 Excision of intervertebral disc	249 609	0.72	10 428	5 374	8 068	12 157	2.7	0.1	57.7	47.6
1.3.2 Laminectomy	90 872	0.26	14 602	7 180	10 721	16 636	4.7	0.4	51.3	61.9
1.4 Diagnostic spinal tap [4.]	251 437	0.72	10 963	3 842	6 659	12 270	6.0	2.3	50.3	25.1
1.5 Insertion of catheter or spinal stimulator and injection into spinal canal [5.]	50 490	0.14	10 096	3 828	6 746	11 992	5.7	1.2	37.1	57.1
1.6 Decompression peripheral nerve [6.]	4 655	0.01	9 396	3 961	6 285	10 362	3.8	0.1	47.6	49.0
1.6.1 Release of carpal tunnel	2 102	0.01	10 327	4 143	6 608	11 204	4.3	0.0	43.8	54.7
1.6.2 Other lysis of adhesion and decompression of peripheral nerves	2 553	0.01	8 630	3 772	6 051	9 811	3.4	0.2	50.8	44.2
1.7 Other diagnostic nervous system procedures [7.]	14 608	0.04	33 173	10 643	19 157	36 316	10.0	12.7	57.5	50.9
1.8 Other non-OR or closed therapeutic nervous system procedures [8.]	12 090	0.03	10 535	3 636	6 589	12 214	6.5	1.4	37.6	49.9
1.9 Other OR therapeutic nervous system procedures [9.]	58 555	0.17	30 582	8 850	16 255	31 536	8.2	6.6	54.3	42.9
2 OPERATIONS ON THE ENDOCRINE SYSTEM	76 315	0.22	10 527	4 938	7 342	11 429	3.0	0.3	25.0	50.5
2.1 Thyroidectomy, partial or complete [10.]	47 752	0.14	7 732	4 529	6 476	9 129	2.0	0.1	17.3	49.2
2.2 Diagnostic endocrine procedures [11.]	2 196	0.01	14 401	6 869	10 766	16 699	6.9	2.3	34.5	62.1
2.3 Other therapeutic endocrine procedures [12.]	26 367	0.08	15 278	6 235	10 252	17 572	4.6	0.6	38.0	51.8
3 OPERATIONS ON THE EYE	71 238	0.20	8 733	3 592	5 515	9 139	3.3	0.5	52.7	55.6
3.1 Corneal transplant [13.]	3 185	0.01	6 927	4 841	5 524	7 585	2.0	0.0	40.0	66.4
3.2 Glaucoma procedures [14.]	5 463	0.02	4 260	2 613	3 297	4 561	1.9	0.0	39.3	67.7
3.3 Lens and cataract procedures [15.]	7 208	0.02	6 497	2 984	4 454	7 074	3.1	0.1	35.5	72.4
3.3.1 Insertion of prosthetic lens	185	0.00	—	—	—	—	—	—	—	—
3.3.2 Phacoemulsification and aspiration of cataract	4 943	0.01	5 843	2 893	4 158	6 364	2.5	0.2	34.5	73.3
3.3.3 Other extracapsular extraction of lens	1 197	0.00	7 250	3 387	5 269	8 597	4.2	0.0	34.2	74.2
3.3.4 Other lens and cataract procedures	882	0.00	8 789	2 756	4 933	9 438	4.7	0.0	43.1	64.7
3.4 Repair of retinal tear, detachment [16.]	9 466	0.03	6 889	3 738	5 463	8 196	1.8	0.1	58.8	55.7
3.5 Destruction of lesion of retina and choroid [17.]	1 279	0.00	41 449	4 721	10 471	16 670	17.1	0.9	50.4	38.3
3.6 Diagnostic procedures on eye [18.]	1 025	0.00	9 385	3 412	6 187	10 562	5.2	0.5	45.9	55.5
3.7 Other therapeutic procedures on eyelids, conjunctiva, cornea [19.]	20 792	0.06	10 117	3 984	6 700	11 349	4.2	1.2	62.5	46.0
3.8 Other intraocular therapeutic procedures [20.]	15 725	0.05	6 911	3 692	5 061	7 848	2.3	0.3	49.2	59.7
3.9 Other extraocular muscle and orbit therapeutic procedures [21.]	7 094	0.02	11 781	4 526	7 868	12 641	3.7	0.6	58.5	46.2
4 OPERATIONS ON THE EAR	23 899	0.07	10 066	3 770	5 993	10 637	3.9	0.4	53.6	34.3
4.1 Tympanoplasty [22.]	1 403	0.00	6 920	3 595	5 080	9 357	1.4	0.0	47.5	32.3
4.2 Myringotomy [23.]	5 690	0.02	10 579	3 293	5 561	10 062	4.4	1.1	54.8	15.5
4.3 Mastoidectomy [24.]	3 997	0.01	11 341	4 730	6 524	11 319	2.9	0.2	53.3	38.6
4.4 Diagnostic procedures on ear [25.]	278	0.00	—	—	—	—	—	—	—	—
4.5 Other therapeutic ear procedures [26.]	12 531	0.04	9 780	3 691	6 036	10 764	4.2	0.2	53.6	41.2
5 OPERATIONS ON THE NOSE, MOUTH, AND PHARYNX	145 124	0.42	9 733	3 429	5 725	9 960	3.9	0.7	55.3	41.7
5.1 Control of epistaxis [27.]	18 365	0.05	7 920	2 845	4 978	8 772	4.3	2.0	52.7	63.9
5.2 Plastic procedures on nose [28.]	10 978	0.03	7 925	3 596	5 699	8 945	2.5	0.3	59.7	44.0
5.3 Dental procedures [29.]	10 928	0.03	11 541	4 313	7 018	12 490	7.0	0.7	51.4	43.9
5.4 Tonsillectomy and/or adenoidectomy [30.]	21 707	0.06	5 020	2 277	3 196	5 154	1.7	0.1	52.8	13.7
5.4.1 Tonsillectomy without adenoidectomy	6 774	0.02	5 562	2 352	3 676	5 913	1.9	0.1	45.9	25.1
5.4.2 Tonsillectomy with adenoidectomy	11 427	0.03	4 794	2 330	3 007	4 675	1.7	0.0	55.8	6.6
5.4.3 Adenoidectomy without tonsillectomy	987	0.00	5 280	2 016	2 322	4 262	1.9	0.0	65.5	6.1
5.4.4 Control of hemorrhage after tonsillectomy or adenoidectomy	2 518	0.01	4 484	2 370	3 622	5 173	1.5	0.0	52.8	18.0
5.5 Diagnostic procedures on nose, mouth, and pharynx [31.]	6 627	0.02	15 263	4 842	8 990	16 928	7.8	2.9	53.7	54.7
5.5.1 Diagnostic procedures on nasal sinuses	896	0.00	15 660	4 777	8 713	16 526	7.0	2.3	47.5	50.0
5.5.2 Other diagnostic procedures on nose, mouth and pharynx	5 730	0.02	15 201	4 842	9 140	17 141	7.9	3.0	54.6	55.4
5.6 Other non-OR therapeutic procedures on nose, mouth, and pharynx [32.]	12 762	0.04	9 473	3 378	5 875	10 580	4.3	0.6	57.0	42.2
5.6.1 Non-OR procedures on nasal sinuses	1 733	0.00	19 430	5 489	8 797	17 968	7.2	0.6	51.6	44.0
5.6.2 Other non-OR procedures on nasal sinuses	11 030	0.03	7 908	3 149	5 533	9 703	3.8	0.6	57.8	41.9
5.7 Other OR therapeutic procedures on nose, mouth, and pharynx [33.]	63 756	0.18	11 334	4 210	6 573	11 111	3.6	0.5	56.6	42.7
5.7.1 OR procedures on nasal sinuses	10 436	0.03	15 222	4 695	8 102	15 085	4.9	1.1	51.9	46.6
5.7.2 Excision salivary gland	12 235	0.04	7 910	4 348	6 428	9 540	2.0	0.2	48.9	56.5
5.7.3 Repair cleft lip	1 998	0.01	6 654	4 105	5 531	7 180	1.8	0.0	60.2	2.6
5.7.4 Correction cleft palate	2 768	0.01	7 594	4 320	5 775	7 683	2.0	0.0	49.8	3.6
5.7.5 Incision and drainage of tonsils	6 185	0.02	6 710	2 505	4 061	7 029	3.1	0.1	54.8	28.8
5.7.6 Other procedures on nose, mouth, and pharynx	30 135	0.09	12 972	4 487	7 126	12 643	4.2	0.6	62.1	44.9
6 OPERATIONS ON THE RESPIRATORY SYSTEM	595 608	1.71	35 655	8 341	15 919	30 862	12.2	8.5	55.4	58.8
6.1 Tracheostomy, temporary and permanent [34.]	69 003	0.20	147 197	55 455	111 301	193 419	36.7	25.1	56.9	60.3
6.2 Tracheoscopy and laryngoscopy with biopsy [35.]	27 963	0.08	8 426	985	3 125	8 813	4.7	1.7	47.9	24.9
6.3 Lobectomy or pneumonectomy [36.]	64 052	0.18	29 800	15 362	21 982	32 601	9.3	3.2	55.5	61.7
6.4 Diagnostic bronchoscopy and biopsy of bronchus [37.]	172 664	0.50	21 879	9 191	15 214	25 201	9.9	6.8	56.6	61.9

See footnotes at end of table.

Table 4.15. Hospital Procedures: 1996—*Continued*

(Principal procedure only)

Multilevel Clinical Classifications Software (CCS) category [1]	Number of discharges	Percent of discharges [2]	Mean charges (dollars)	25 percentile charges (dollars)	Median charges (dollars)	75 percentile charges (dollars)	Mean length of stay	Percent died	Percent male	Mean age
6.4.1 Bronchoscopy without biopsy	28 446	0.08	22 232	7 855	13 878	24 974	9.7	9.5	56.3	53.9
6.4.2 Endoscopic biopsy of bronchus	75 131	0.22	21 599	9 377	15 188	24 681	9.9	6.8	56.9	62.9
6.4.3 Needle biopsy of lung	15 867	0.05	14 670	6 820	11 289	18 197	7.9	3.4	56.3	68.0
6.4.4 Endoscopic biopsy of lung	53 220	0.15	24 225	10 750	17 276	28 101	10.5	6.5	56.6	62.8
6.5 Other diagnostic procedures on lung and bronchus [38.]	14 231	0.04	33 360	12 004	19 919	37 510	10.3	10.1	53.5	58.9
6.6 Incision of pleura, thoracentesis, chest drainage [39.]	172 856	0.50	15 657	5 932	10 608	18 921	8.2	8.2	53.1	61.5
6.6.1 Closed chest drainage	62 712	0.18	14 663	4 829	8 736	16 492	7.5	7.2	61.9	51.6
6.6.2 Open chest drainage	9 663	0.03	19 120	5 778	11 110	21 523	8.7	7.5	61.9	52.1
6.6.3 Thoracentesis	100 480	0.29	15 942	6 828	11 637	19 837	8.7	8.9	46.8	68.6
6.7 Other diagnostic procedures of respiratory tract and mediastinum [40.]	17 673	0.05	20 227	7 784	14 046	24 550	8.4	4.2	56.2	60.2
6.8 Other non-OR therapeutic procedures on respiratory system [41.]	16 410	0.05	18 680	6 607	11 902	21 851	8.7	6.6	51.6	55.2
6.9 Other OR therapeutic procedures on respiratory system [42.]	40 756	0.12	32 178	10 450	19 649	35 666	10.9	3.6	64.0	51.3
7 OPERATIONS ON THE CARDIOVASCULAR SYSTEM	2 887 188	8.28	24 974	9 438	16 672	30 750	6.5	3.7	58.1	63.4
7.1 Heart valve procedures [43.]	75 687	0.22	65 730	38 715	53 672	76 212	12.1	7.1	55.4	65.1
7.2 Coronary artery bypass graft (CABG) [44.]	367 647	1.05	46 990	29 529	39 856	54 893	9.4	3.0	70.5	65.6
7.2.1 Bypass of one coronary artery	37 260	0.11	42 192	27 459	36 763	49 567	8.9	2.7	64.8	63.1
7.2.2 Bypass of two coronary arteries	95 009	0.27	45 039	28 964	38 814	52 188	9.3	2.9	68.3	65.4
7.2.3 Bypass of three coronary arteries	108 640	0.31	47 941	30 282	40 435	55 096	9.7	3.2	70.5	66.5
7.2.4 Bypass of four coronary arteries	74 940	0.21	52 032	32 168	43 812	60 639	10.0	3.7	75.2	66.9
7.2.5 Other bypass of coronary arteries	51 798	0.15	44 724	27 410	37 820	54 724	8.6	2.2	72.1	64.1
7.3 Percutaneous transluminal coronary angioplasty (PTCA) [45.]	479 449	1.37	21 617	12 674	18 455	27 103	3.8	1.0	66.8	63.4
7.3.1 Single vessel PTCA	424 202	1.22	21 319	12 505	18 237	26 688	3.8	1.0	66.6	63.3
7.3.2 Multiple vessel PTCA	55 247	0.16	24 009	14 164	20 389	30 468	3.8	0.8	68.5	64.6
7.4 Coronary thrombolysis [46.]	268	0.00	—	—	—	—	—	—	—	—
7.5 Diagnostic cardiac catheterization, coronary arteriography [47.]	651 303	1.87	12 540	6 800	10 034	14 968	4.1	1.1	56.5	62.9
7.5.1 Coronary arteriography	18 902	0.05	7 354	2 757	4 289	8 921	3.3	0.9	58.8	63.6
7.5.2 Cardiac catheterization	632 401	1.81	12 696	6 960	10 162	15 090	4.1	1.1	56.5	62.9
7.6 Insertion, revision, replacement, removal of cardiac pacemaker or cardioverter/defibrillator [48.]	195 402	0.56	27 020	14 830	20 879	31 602	6.0	2.9	54.5	74.0
7.6.1 Insertion, revision, replacement, or removal of pacemaker leads	72 689	0.21	22 725	13 711	19 815	27 971	5.4	5.7	51.4	74.6
7.6.2 Insertion, revision, replacement, or removal of pacemaker device	98 023	0.28	23 038	14 575	19 452	26 907	5.8	1.3	50.9	75.8
7.6.3 Insertion, revision, replacement, or removal of cardioverter/defibrillator	24 689	0.07	59 890	41 703	54 618	71 546	8.9	0.7	78.3	65.2
7.7 Other OR heart procedures [49.]	62 244	0.18	42 226	15 232	29 138	50 789	8.1	13.1	55.3	51.2
7.8 Extracorporeal circulation auxiliary to open heart procedures [50.]	785	0.00	99 234	22 520	61 205	123 237	15.0	23.2	58.9	27.3
7.9 Endarterectomy, vessel of head and neck [51.]	151 273	0.43	13 706	7 679	11 080	16 177	3.6	0.6	56.6	71.1
7.1 Aortic resection, replacement or anastomosis [52.]	43 740	0.13	40 631	20 652	29 054	43 837	10.1	10.9	78.6	70.5
7.11 Varicose vein stripping, lower limb [53.]	3 768	0.01	7 196	3 540	5 504	8 584	2.6	0.2	33.6	52.3
7.12 Other vascular catheterization, not heart [54.]	211 430	0.61	23 883	7 861	14 409	26 267	10.7	12.8	43.5	49.8
7.12.1 Arterial catheterization	34 841	0.10	32 273	7 917	15 938	32 684	12.5	10.8	54.3	23.1
7.12.2 Umbilical vein catheterization	7 422	0.02	29 814	4 150	12 048	30 369	12.3	3.3	53.3	0.3
7.12.3 Venous catheterization	169 167	0.49	21 909	7 988	14 213	25 160	10.3	13.7	40.8	57.5
7.13 Peripheral vascular bypass [55.]	106 286	0.30	26 439	13 075	19 759	31 250	8.7	2.9	57.4	68.2
7.14 Other vascular bypass and shunt, not heart [56.]	10 675	0.03	46 216	16 306	27 689	51 704	10.4	10.3	52.3	49.6
7.15 Creation, revision and removal of arteriovenous fistula or vessel-to-vessel cannula for dialysis [57.]	64 457	0.18	21 566	9 132	15 305	25 878	8.2	2.7	49.0	61.3
7.16 Hemodialysis [58.]	152 801	0.44	11 473	4 686	7 794	13 251	5.6	4.6	48.5	60.6
7.17 Other OR procedures on vessels of head and neck [59.]	5 558	0.02	30 196	10 609	17 435	33 456	7.2	3.3	50.4	51.4
7.18 Embolectomy and endarterectomy of lower limbs [60.]	19 102	0.05	24 210	10 934	17 533	28 609	8.1	8.6	51.8	70.5
7.19 Other OR procedures on vessels other than head and neck [61.]	193 181	0.55	28 388	9 764	17 254	31 917	8.1	5.1	50.7	62.1
7.19.1 Interrupt vena cava	30 174	0.09	29 008	12 178	19 392	33 177	11.8	8.7	45.6	67.7
7.19.2 Other OR procedures on blood vessels	116 557	0.33	31 743	9 597	18 143	35 290	8.5	5.5	52.0	59.2
7.20 Other diagnostic cardiovascular procedures [62.]	40 537	0.12	14 612	7 346	11 199	17 466	5.4	0.9	55.3	61.5
7.21 Other non-OR therapeutic cardiovascular procedures [63.]	51 597	0.15	22 565	8 871	16 020	26 950	7.9	9.8	54.7	60.3
8 OPERATIONS ON THE HEMIC AND LYMPHATIC SYSTEM	140 103	0.40	28 175	7 825	13 506	25 620	9.4	5.0	51.4	56.1
8.1 Bone marrow transplant [64.]	8 556	0.02	136 524	64 419	98 036	157 701	27.8	8.8	39.8	41.3
8.2 Bone marrow biopsy [65.]	62 603	0.18	20 705	7 336	12 359	22 076	9.6	5.9	50.5	61.1
8.3 Procedures on spleen [66.]	19 583	0.06	32 156	11 659	18 480	32 796	8.9	6.0	55.4	44.4
8.4 Other therapeutic procedures, hemic and lymphatic system [67.]	49 361	0.14	17 091	6 702	11 132	19 037	6.3	2.7	52.8	56.9
8.4.1 Biopsy of lymphatic structure	16 572	0.05	20 386	8 321	14 172	24 172	8.6	5.2	53.0	57.3
8.4.2 Simple excision of lymphatic structure	10 635	0.03	14 861	5 530	9 313	16 419	5.8	3.0	47.5	56.0
8.4.3 Regional lymph node excision	7 001	0.02	11 497	5 279	8 093	12 903	3.9	0.7	46.8	58.2
8.4.4 Radical excision lymph nodes	12 818	0.04	18 488	7 936	12 052	19 138	5.0	0.7	60.8	59.8
8.4.5 Other hemic and lymphatic procedures	2 335	0.01	13 150	5 072	8 271	12 462	5.5	1.1	50.2	38.7
9 OPERATIONS ON THE DIGESTIVE SYSTEM	2 897 334	8.31	16 447	6 074	10 219	17 932	7.0	3.0	44.5	58.2
9.1 Therapeutic procedures on the esophagus	11 968	0.03	11 111	4 612	7 600	12 620	6.6	1.9	46.4	69.0
9.1.1 Injection or ligation of esophageal varices [68.]	101	0.00	—	—	—	—	6.6	1.9	46.3	69.2
9.1.2 Esophageal dilatation [69.]	11 867	0.03	10 969	4 599	7 584	12 502	6.6	1.9	46.3	69.2
9.2 Upper gastrointestinal endoscopy, biopsy [70.]	627 552	1.80	11 408	5 130	8 044	13 126	6.1	2.4	46.1	64.2

See footnotes at end of table.

Table 4.15. Hospital Procedures: 1996—*Continued*

(Principal procedure only)

Multilevel Clinical Classifications Software (CCS) category [1]	Number of discharges	Percent of discharges [2]	Mean charges (dollars)	25 percentile charges (dollars)	Median charges (dollars)	75 percentile charges (dollars)	Mean length of stay	Percent died	Percent male	Mean age
9.2.1 Esophagoscopy	10 409	0.03	12 337	4 771	8 098	14 098	6.2	3.8	54.6	55.3
9.2.2 Gastroscopy	6 910	0.02	13 296	4 905	7 807	13 255	7.2	5.1	45.9	64.0
9.2.3 Esophagogastroduodenoscopy (EGD) without biopsy	238 029	0.68	11 808	5 112	8 135	13 619	6.2	3.3	47.3	64.4
9.2.4 Esophagogastroduodenoscopy (EGD) with biopsy	370 027	1.06	11 072	5 152	7 990	12 797	6.0	1.7	45.1	64.3
9.2.5 Endoscopic biopsy small intestine	2 177	0.01	14 431	5 025	7 834	13 130	6.9	1.9	46.9	58.1
9.3 Gastrostomy, temporary and permanent [71.]	94 510	0.27	22 798	9 415	16 163	27 103	13.7	8.4	43.0	74.7
9.4 Colostomy, temporary and permanent [72.]	10 867	0.03	32 905	13 639	22 062	37 433	13.2	6.9	48.3	62.7
9.5 Ileostomy and other enterostomy [73.]	6 657	0.02	35 256	11 576	21 083	36 944	16.1	10.1	50.2	62.4
9.6 Gastrectomy, partial and total [74.]	21 552	0.06	45 411	19 658	30 861	51 774	15.3	8.5	55.7	65.3
9.7 Small bowel resection [75.]	45 319	0.13	42 051	15 721	25 722	44 260	14.6	9.1	42.7	59.7
9.8 Colonoscopy and biopsy [76.]	242 734	0.70	10 922	4 847	7 733	12 547	6.4	1.5	38.7	66.4
9.8.1 Closed endoscopic biopsy of large intestine	100 620	0.29	11 623	5 086	8 047	13 112	6.6	1.5	36.6	62.4
9.8.2 Other endoscopy of large intestine	142 114	0.41	10 426	4 688	7 510	12 184	6.2	1.5	40.2	69.3
9.9 Proctoscopy and anorectal biopsy [77.]	15 280	0.04	12 783	4 642	7 789	13 791	7.0	2.1	45.2	60.1
9.10 Colorectal resection [78.]	253 439	0.73	27 811	13 350	19 725	30 842	10.8	4.5	46.6	66.0
9.10.1 Right hemicolectomy	76 093	0.22	26 751	12 844	18 932	29 724	10.7	4.6	44.4	69.0
9.10.2 Left hemicolectomy	29 816	0.09	30 738	14 902	22 141	34 457	11.5	5.6	47.7	67.1
9.10.3 Sigmoidectomy	71 629	0.21	26 540	12 939	18 952	29 722	10.5	4.0	46.8	65.3
9.10.4 Resection of rectum	33 695	0.10	24 462	13 465	19 149	27 661	9.8	2.0	50.0	65.7
9.10.5 Other colorectal resections	42 206	0.12	32 466	13 949	21 471	35 635	11.8	6.4	46.7	61.0
9.11 Local excision of large intestine lesion (not endoscopic) [79.]	1 563	0.00	14 689	7 532	11 367	16 822	6.4	1.5	51.7	60.7
9.12 Appendectomy [80.]	229 728	0.66	9 632	4 996	7 370	11 003	3.6	0.2	56.3	29.9
9.13 Hemorrhoid procedures [81.]	15 509	0.04	6 480	3 211	4 652	7 121	3.0	0.4	56.0	52.8
9.14 Endoscopic retrograde cannulation of pancreas (ERCP) [82.]	37 826	0.11	13 924	6 381	10 307	16 387	6.7	2.2	39.1	60.6
9.15 Biopsy of liver [83.]	27 259	0.08	18 344	6 838	11 989	21 056	8.6	8.0	52.3	58.3
9.16 Cholecystectomy and common duct exploration [84.]	408 355	1.17	14 309	7 101	10 718	16 557	4.7	0.9	30.7	54.4
9.16.1 Open cholecystectomy	100 128	0.29	20 123	9 613	14 544	23 115	7.6	2.1	41.1	60.2
9.16.2 Laparoscopic cholecystectomy	303 881	0.87	12 234	6 553	9 720	14 582	3.6	0.4	27.1	52.4
9.16.3 Incision of bile duct	4 346	0.01	26 259	12 055	19 248	30 008	10.1	5.2	39.3	65.6
9.17 Inguinal and femoral hernia repair [85.]	51 849	0.15	13 062	4 151	6 339	10 244	5.3	0.9	80.0	59.5
9.17.1 Unilateral repair inguinal hernia	37 599	0.11	10 012	4 087	6 183	9 640	4.0	0.9	85.4	61.5
9.17.2 Bilateral repair inguinal hernia	9 051	0.03	25 888	4 036	6 231	11 237	10.6	0.2	87.9	44.5
9.17.3 Femoral hernia repair	5 199	0.01	12 945	4 838	8 048	13 754	5.4	2.0	27.0	71.3
9.18 Other hernia repair [86.]	87 133	0.25	12 265	5 262	8 133	12 806	4.7	1.1	37.5	58.6
9.18.1 Umbilical hernia repair	13 567	0.04	11 507	4 383	6 906	11 454	4.4	1.8	43.3	54.4
9.18.2 Incisional hernia repair	47 855	0.14	10 321	5 198	7 791	11 887	4.1	0.5	36.2	59.8
9.18.3 Other abdominal wall hernia repair	18 118	0.05	11 271	5 201	7 975	12 358	4.4	0.9	34.9	58.8
9.18.4 Other hernia repair	7 592	0.02	28 330	9 942	15 672	28 428	9.6	3.3	41.5	57.9
9.19 Laparoscopy [87.]	19 075	0.05	11 169	5 737	8 494	12 620	3.7	0.8	14.0	36.6
9.20 Abdominal paracentesis [88.]	60 664	0.17	14 828	5 826	10 071	17 419	7.8	10.9	52.1	58.5
9.21 Exploratory laparotomy [89.]	25 262	0.07	25 635	8 512	14 262	26 271	8.3	15.8	45.6	50.9
9.22 Excision, lysis peritoneal adhesions [90.]	67 116	0.19	22 343	9 328	14 812	25 287	9.2	3.2	30.1	55.8
9.23 Peritoneal dialysis [91.]	20 971	0.06	10 867	4 537	7 516	12 912	5.7	3.4	48.9	52.6
9.24 Other bowel diagnostic procedures [92.]	6 716	0.02	15 536	5 488	10 026	17 957	6.6	5.3	50.0	50.1
9.25 Other non-OR upper GI therapeutic procedures [93.]	96 497	0.28	11 963	4 217	7 653	13 575	5.5	4.2	51.8	54.6
9.26 Other OR upper GI therapeutic procedures [94.]	83 253	0.24	28 633	9 431	15 587	29 060	9.5	5.5	50.8	47.6
9.27 Other non-OR lower GI therapeutic procedures [95.]	65 164	0.19	10 546	4 832	7 720	12 624	6.0	1.4	47.6	70.8
9.28 Other OR lower GI therapeutic procedures [96.]	101 359	0.29	20 249	6 788	12 289	21 749	8.2	2.7	52.6	53.4
9.28.1 Closure of stoma of large intestine	18 690	0.05	16 622	9 395	13 241	18 859	7.5	0.5	55.4	56.3
9.28.2 Local excision of rectal lesion	3 461	0.01	9 333	4 310	6 327	10 740	4.1	0.4	46.3	70.7
9.28.3 Incision of perirectal tissue	10 435	0.03	8 756	3 841	5 800	9 590	4.0	0.8	63.2	45.2
9.28.4 Incision of perianal abscess	5 850	0.02	8 715	3 617	5 686	9 007	4.0	0.6	65.3	45.9
9.28.5 Incision/excision of anal fistula	2 385	0.01	7 709	3 249	4 843	8 335	3.6	0.0	71.8	46.7
9.28.6 Other lower GI procedures	60 537	0.17	25 608	8 645	15 388	27 977	10.0	4.2	48.3	54.0
9.29 Other gastrointestinal diagnostic procedures [97.]	14 669	0.04	19 701	7 832	12 937	22 761	8.9	6.3	42.4	64.5
9.30 Other non-OR gastrointestinal therapeutic procedures [98.]	52 681	0.15	14 005	5 813	9 746	16 075	6.2	2.3	39.8	62.7
9.31 Other OR gastrointestinal therapeutic procedures [99.]	94 808	0.27	31 798	9 759	17 989	34 584	11.1	5.7	46.7	53.3
9.31.1 Radical pancreaticoduodenectomy	4 925	0.01	58 826	27 638	42 280	67 874	19.0	7.9	51.1	63.4
9.31.2 Incision abdominal wall	10 898	0.03	16 245	5 418	9 425	16 717	7.2	2.1	45.8	51.6
9.31.3 Excision or destruction of peritoneal tissue	9 658	0.03	22 264	8 893	14 830	26 051	8.2	3.3	30.2	53.9
9.31.4 Creation of cutaneoperitoneal fistula	9 292	0.03	27 672	7 982	14 852	28 570	11.0	8.3	51.3	55.1
9.31.5 Other gastrointestinal therapeutic procedures	60 035	0.17	34 560	11 153	19 681	36 714	11.7	6.2	48.4	52.4
10 OPERATIONS ON THE URINARY SYSTEM	452 535	1.30	14 050	5 199	8 474	14 876	5.4	1.5	51.9	57.3
10.1 Cystoscopy and other transurethral procedures	191 400	0.55	10 156	4 711	7 238	11 601	4.8	1.1	61.5	61.2
10.1.1 Endoscopy and endoscopic biopsy of the urinary tract [100.]	65 718	0.19	11 703	5 205	8 331	13 916	7.0	1.5	57.0	63.9
10.1.2 Transurethral excision, drainage, or removal of urinary obstruction [101.]	93 616	0.27	8 980	4 351	6 556	10 084	3.6	0.7	69.0	62.2
10.1.3 Ureteral catheterization [102.]	32 066	0.09	10 391	5 026	7 600	11 969	4.2	1.2	48.8	52.7
10.2 Nephrotomy and nephrostomy [103.]	24 521	0.07	19 347	8 518	13 633	22 940	7.3	3.0	50.9	56.8
10.3 Nephrectomy, partial or complete [104.]	39 927	0.11	21 574	10 421	14 826	23 007	7.4	1.9	53.3	56.9
10.4 Kidney transplant [105.]	13 025	0.04	66 239	41 325	57 545	75 523	10.6	1.1	58.2	44.0
10.5 Genitourinary incontinence procedures [106.]	49 128	0.14	7 352	4 853	6 561	8 916	2.5	0.0	0.7	57.3
10.6 Extracorporeal lithotripsy, urinary [107.]	5 596	0.02	10 578	6 679	9 444	12 821	3.2	0.1	62.1	51.7
10.7 Indwelling catheter [108.]	14 412	0.04	8 969	3 701	6 181	11 007	6.0	8.5	52.3	70.1
10.8 Procedures on the urethra [109.]	20 917	0.06	10 680	4 877*	7 908	13 000	5.0	1.6	76.5	58.0
10.9 Other diagnostic procedures of urinary tract [110.]	18 613	0.05	13 625	3 754	8 428	16 796	6.4	1.0	53.8	47.3
10.10 Other non-OR therapeutic procedures of urinary tract [111.]	21 619	0.06	8 156	2 675	4 669	9 344	4.3	1.8	38.3	45.4
10.11 Other OR therapeutic procedures of urinary tract [112.]	53 377	0.15	19 037	7 060	11 605	21 627	7.0	1.7	56.3	51.9

See footnotes at end of table.

Table 4.15. Hospital Procedures: 1996—*Continued*

(Principal procedure only)

Multilevel Clinical Classifications Software (CCS) category [1]	Number of discharges	Percent of discharges [2]	Mean charges (dollars)	25 percentile charges (dollars)	Median charges (dollars)	75 percentile charges (dollars)	Mean length of stay	Percent died	Percent male	Mean age
11 OPERATIONS ON THE MALE GENITAL ORGANS	1 336 229	3.83	3 407	739	1 125	2 926	2.6	0.1	100.0	13.5
11.1 Transurethral resection of prostate (TURP) [113.]	155 861	0.45	8 246	4 384	6 240	9 249	3.8	0.3	100.0	73.1
11.2 Open prostatectomy [114.]	70 994	0.20	13 496	8 533	11 989	16 003	4.5	0.2	100.0	63.8
11.3 Circumcision [115.]	1 072 116	3.07	1 764	678	940	1 418	2.3	0.0	100.0	0.1
11.4 Diagnostic procedures, male genital [116.]	4 039	0.01	14 131	6 471	10 875	17 807	8.5	1.9	100.0	70.5
11.5 Other non-OR therapeutic procedures, male genital [117.]	4 567	0.01	10 518	3 784	6 414	11 791	5.5	1.2	100.0	47.4
11.6 Other OR therapeutic procedures, male genital [118.]	28 651	0.08	10 522	4 412	7 807	12 835	3.6	0.6	100.0	52.2
11.6.1 Unilateral orchiectomy	4 057	0.01	10 766	4 199	6 463	11 970	4.2	1.0	100.0	42.4
11.6.2 Bilateral orchiectomy	3 392	0.01	13 472	5 481	9 119	16 411	6.8	1.7	100.0	76.4
11.6.3 Orchiopexy	2 573	0.01	6 596	2 864	4 149	5 643	2.2	0.0	100.0	15.5
11.6.4 Insert or replace penile prosthesis	7 556	0.02	12 102	8 842	11 670	15 176	1.8	0.0	100.0	60.3
11.6.5 Other male genital procedures	11 072	0.03	9 385	3 928	6 384	10 386	3.9	0.6	100.0	51.4
12 OPERATIONS ON THE FEMALE GENITAL ORGANS	964 302	2.77	8 771	5 160	7 283	10 183	3.1	0.1	0.0	44.3
12.1 Oophorectomy, unilateral and bilateral [119.]	70 079	0.20	10 526	5 740	8 137	11 769	3.8	0.2	0.0	44.5
12.2 Other operations on ovary [120.]	32 847	0.09	8 603	5 220	7 284	10 028	2.9	0.1	0.0	31.2
12.3 Ligation of fallopian tubes [121.]	71 517	0.21	6 025	4 221	5 601	7 177	1.9	0.0	0.0	29.6
12.4 Other operations on fallopian tubes [123.]	11 632	0.03	7 903	5 020	6 865	9 569	2.6	0.0	0.0	32.9
12.5 Hysterectomy, abdominal and vaginal [124.]	564 328	1.62	9 273	5 799	7 909	10 776	3.2	0.1	0.0	47.0
12.5.1 Total abdominal hysterectomy	354 001	1.02	9 656	6 096	8 157	11 044	3.6	0.1	0.0	46.7
12.5.2 Vaginal hysterectomy	192 185	0.55	8 118	5 252	7 273	9 906	2.4	0.0	0.0	47.6
12.5.3 Other hysterectomy	18 142	0.05	14 120	7 319	10 960	16 881	4.8	0.3	0.0	47.1
12.6 Other excision of cervix and uterus [125.]	32 386	0.09	8 393	5 409	7 600	10 152	2.9	0.0	0.0	37.6
12.7 Abortion (termination of pregnancy) [126.]	3 679	0.01	7 450	2 570	4 477	7 608	2.9	0.5	0.0	27.7
12.8 Dilatation and curettage (D&C), aspiration after delivery or abortion [127.]	44 709	0.13	5 341	2 768	4 017	6 068	1.6	0.1	0.0	28.2
12.9 Diagnostic dilatation and curettage (D&C) [128.]	14 750	0.04	8 434	3 976	6 130	9 402	3.7	0.2	0.0	48.4
12.1 Repair of cystocele and rectocele, obliteration of vaginal vault [129.]	45 825	0.13	6 740	4 337	5 972	8 164	2.5	0.0	0.0	62.5
12.11 Other diagnostic procedures, female organs [130.]	8 871	0.03	11 941	4 940	7 999	13 855	6.2	1.9	0.0	53.6
12.12 Other non-OR therapeutic procedures, female organs [131.]	7 022	0.02	5 862	2 137	3 987	6 979	2.8	0.3	0.0	34.9
12.13 Other OR therapeutic procedures, female organs [132.]	56 656	0.16	9 976	4 358	6 822	10 449	3.7	0.2	0.0	47.6
13 OBSTETRICAL PROCEDURES	3 718 075	10.66	4 561	2 639	3 684	5 408	2.2	0.0	0.0	27.1
13.1 Episiotomy [133.]	708 684	2.03	3 668	2 501	3 265	4 345	1.8	0.0	0.0	26.8
13.2 Cesarean section [134.]	791 779	2.27	7 590	4 995	6 595	8 619	3.7	0.0	0.0	28.5
13.3 Forceps, vacuum, and breech delivery [135.]	375 942	1.08	4 115	2 771	3 660	4 910	1.9	0.0	0.0	27.0
13.3.1 Low forceps delivery with episiotomy	84 388	0.24	4 253	2 897	3 785	5 078	2.1	0.0	0.0	27.0
13.3.2 Vacuum extraction with episiotomy	189 157	0.54	4 017	2 745	3 622	4 823	1.9	0.0	0.0	26.8
13.3.3 Other vacuum extraction	75 406	0.22	4 003	2 657	3 539	4 761	1.8	0.0	0.0	27.2
13.3.4 Other forceps or breech delivery	26 990	0.08	4 689	2 872	3 918	5 348	2.2	0.0	0.0	27.0
13.4 Artificial rupture of membranes to assist delivery [136.]	69 516	0.20	3 383	2 231	3 004	4 053	1.6	0.0	0.0	25.7
13.5 Other procedures to assist delivery [137.]	1 097 378	3.15	3 692	2 368	3 186	4 318	1.8	0.0	0.0	26.6
13.5.1 Induction of labor by artificial rupture of membranes	12 177	0.03	3 187	2 156	2 863	3 776	1.8	0.0	0.0	27.1
13.5.2 Medical induction of labor	72 563	0.21	3 892	2 356	3 336	4 667	1.9	0.0	0.0	27.0
13.5.3 Other manually assisted labor	1 006 992	2.89	3 685	2 374	3 182	4 301	1.8	0.0	0.0	26.6
13.5.4 Other delivery procedures	5 645	0.02	3 574	1 909	2 873	4 482	1.9	0.0	0.0	27.2
13.6 Diagnostic amniocentesis [138.]	8 169	0.02	8 022	3 194	5 322	9 182	5.2	0.0	0.0	25.8
13.7 Fetal monitoring [139.]	59 905	0.17	3 512	1 843	2 691	3 931	2.3	0.0	0.0	26.4
13.8 Repair of current obstetric laceration [140.]	573 118	1.64	3 476	2 365	3 120	4 085	1.7	0.0	0.0	26.9
13.8.1 Repair of obstetric laceration of uterus or cervix	4 232	0.01	4 786	2 842	3 792	5 192	2.3	0.0	0.0	26.4
13.8.2 Repair of obstetric laceration of bladder or urethra	21 179	0.06	3 884	2 559	3 362	4 534	1.7	0.0	0.0	25.5
13.8.3 Repair of obstetric laceration of rectum or sphincter	46 338	0.13	3 807	2 623	3 454	4 501	1.9	0.0	0.0	26.7
13.8.4 Repair of other obstetric laceration	501 368	1.44	3 417	2 330	3 075	4 015	1.7	0.0	0.0	27.0
13.9 Other therapeutic obstetrical procedures [141.]	9 248	0.03	4 119	2 194	3 174	4 747	1.9	0.0	0.0	27.2
13.10 Removal of ectopic pregnancy [122.]	24 337	0.07	7 827	5 153	7 112	9 606	2.4	0.1	0.0	29.7
14 OPERATIONS ON THE MUSCULOSKELETAL SYSTEM	1 864 658	5.35	16 838	7 819	13 403	20 529	5.5	1.1	44.7	59.1
14.1 Partial excision bone [142.]	37 481	0.11	16 089	5 801	9 405	16 760	5.7	0.6	54.6	48.8
14.2 Bunionectomy or repair of toe deformities [143.]	4 319	0.01	6 978	4 163	5 772	8 291	2.7	0.0	19.6	56.9
14.3 Treatment of fracture or dislocation	634 520	1.82	14 136	6 613	10 488	16 095	5.2	1.1	42.7	56.2
14.3.1 Treatment, facial fracture or dislocation [144.]	28 094	0.08	14 496	6 269	10 109	16 077	3.8	0.2	76.4	33.3
14.3.2 Treatment, fracture or dislocation of radius and ulna [145.]	55 979	0.16	9 541	4 441	6 921	10 768	3.0	0.2	49.3	44.4
14.3.3 Treatment, fracture or dislocation of hip and femur [146.]	286 194	0.82	16 850	9 379	13 172	18 802	6.9	2.1	31.6	70.9
14.3.4 Treatment, fracture or dislocation of lower extremity (other than hip or femur) [147.]	183 730	0.53	11 877	5 612	8 457	12 979	4.0	0.2	48.8	45.6
14.3.5 Other fracture and dislocation procedure [148.]	80 523	0.23	12 710	4 943	7 938	13 539	4.1	0.6	52.2	44.0
14.4 Arthroscopy [149.]	4 661	0.01	10 294	5 532	7 916	11 529	3.4	0.2	61.2	42.2
14.4.1 Arthroscopy of knee	2 739	0.01	10 869	5 449	7 897	12 729	4.2	0.4	62.6	40.7
14.4.2 Other arthroscopy	1 922	0.01	9 471	5 613	7 944	10 874	2.2	0.0	59.2	44.2
14.5 Division of joint capsule, ligament or cartilage [150.]	4 796	0.01	8 545	4 736	6 681	10 087	2.7	0.0	43.9	38.8
14.6 Excision of semilunar cartilage of knee [151.]	8 941	0.03	9 730	5 444	8 279	11 822	2.4	0.0	61.2	43.1
14.7 Arthroplasty	668 991	1.92	19 382	13 202	17 748	23 529	5.1	0.7	38.7	67.5
14.7.1 Arthroplasty knee [152.]	315 940	0.91	19 481	13 859	18 077	23 591	4.6	0.2	40.8	65.0
14.7.2 Hip replacement, total and partial [153.]	291 457	0.84	21 350	14 547	18 951	24 736	6.2	1.4	34.2	72.5
14.7.3 Arthroplasty other than hip or knee [154.]	61 594	0.18	9 544	4 892	7 520	12 306	2.3	0.1	49.4	56.2
14.8 Arthrocentesis [155.]	29 466	0.08	9 742	3 750	6 409	11 410	6.5	1.0	53.0	59.7
14.9 Injections and aspirations of muscles, tendons, bursa, joints, and soft tissue [156.]	5 121	0.01	11 125	3 943	7 030	12 843	7.5	1.6	50.0	59.5

See footnotes at end of table.

Table 4.15. Hospital Procedures: 1996—*Continued*

(Principal procedure only)

Multilevel Clinical Classifications Software (CCS) category [1]	Number of discharges	Percent of discharges [2]	Mean charges (dollars)	25 percentile charges (dollars)	Median charges (dollars)	75 percentile charges (dollars)	Mean length of stay	Percent died	Percent male	Mean age
14.10 Amputation of lower extremity [157.]	109 972	0.32	23 339	8 702	14 613	26 767	11.8	4.7	56.9	68.0
14.10.1 Amputation of toe	31 103	0.09	16 283	6 808	11 241	19 513	9.3	1.2	62.2	63.7
14.10.2 Amputation through foot	13 997	0.04	24 137	9 347	16 486	29 856	13.2	2.2	64.6	64.3
14.10.3 Below knee amputation	32 781	0.09	26 309	10 208	16 749	30 656	12.7	4.9	58.5	68.0
14.10.4 Above knee amputation	30 088	0.09	25 913	9 353	15 339	28 989	12.6	9.2	45.7	74.7
14.10.5 Other lower extremity amputation	2 003	0.01	39 955	11 336	20 990	42 157	14.8	8.4	62.5	58.1
14.11 Spinal fusion [158.]	99 149	0.28	24 147	10 905	17 286	28 874	5.0	0.4	49.1	47.7
14.12 Other diagnostic procedures on musculoskeletal system [159.]	22 834	0.07	20 106	7 758	13 379	23 000	9.3	3.5	48.9	57.4
14.13 Other therapeutic procedures on muscles and tendons [160.]	95 143	0.27	9 978	4 506	6 668	10 335	3.4	0.5	61.6	47.1
14.13.1 Rotator cuff repair	26 651	0.08	6 558	4 162	5 834	8 081	1.8	0.0	56.7	61.1
14.13.2 Other suture of muscle, tendon, and fascia	12 000	0.03	7 831	4 051	6 112	8 960	2.4	0.2	73.5	40.4
14.13.3 Other muscle and tendon procedures	56 493	0.16	12 044	4 843	7 391	12 274	4.4	0.8	61.4	41.9
14.14 Other OR therapeutic procedures on bone [161.]	34 881	0.10	14 204	6 395	9 663	15 304	4.3	0.5	53.5	38.1
14.15 Other OR therapeutic procedures on joints [162.]	59 269	0.17	14 169	6 211	9 617	15 903	5.4	0.8	55.3	50.9
14.16 Other non-OR therapeutic procedures on musculoskeletal system [163.]	10 085	0.03	10 283	4 242	7 021	11 611	7.9	0.6	33.2	69.8
14.17 Other OR therapeutic procedures on musculoskeletal system [164.]	35 030	0.10	14 350	6 559	10 715	16 704	4.4	1.0	48.4	40.7
15 OPERATIONS ON THE INTEGUMENTARY SYSTEM	721 061	2.07	15 703	5 255	8 946	16 581	7.5	2.1	41.5	54.0
15.1 Procedures on the breast	123 302	0.35	8 527	4 856	6 903	9 917	2.8	0.3	0.9	61.8
15.1.1 Breast biopsy and other diagnostic procedures on breast [165.]	4 717	0.01	13 090	5 562	8 881	16 377	7.5	3.2	1.7	62.6
15.1.2 Lumpectomy, quadrantectomy of breast [166.]	28 319	0.08	7 517	4 234	6 125	8 736	2.4	0.4	0.6	60.3
15.1.3 Mastectomy [167.]	90 266	0.26	8 605	5 027	7 090	10 144	2.7	0.1	0.9	62.3
15.2 Incision and drainage, skin and subcutaneous tissue [168.]	63 493	0.18	9 875	3 973	6 673	11 501	5.9	0.6	55.8	47.1
15.3 Debridement of wound, infection, or burn [169.]	219 226	0.63	21 061	6 830	12 194	23 306	10.7	3.2	55.2	56.0
15.4 Excision of skin lesion [170.]	24 137	0.07	13 124	4 899	8 137	14 521	6.8	1.5	46.9	58.5
15.5 Suture of skin and subcutaneous tissue [171.]	72 043	0.21	7 899	3 209	5 441	9 359	3.9	1.3	59.4	49.0
15.6 Skin graft [172.]	33 973	0.10	29 033	7 226	13 726	30 062	11.7	1.2	59.1	49.6
15.7 Other diagnostic procedures on skin and subcutaneous tissue [173.]	13 494	0.04	14 654	5 543	9 595	16 639	8.6	3.7	47.4	54.7
15.8 Other non-OR therapeutic procedures on skin and breast [174.]	123 879	0.36	19 624	6 575	12 058	21 941	9.8	4.0	44.0	53.4
15.8.1 Aspiration of skin and subcutaneous tissue	6 885	0.02	9 891	3 904	6 913	12 181	6.6	0.7	51.7	53.0
15.8.2 Insertion of totally implantable vascular access device	63 098	0.18	25 542	9 557	15 823	27 796	10.7	6.4	43.7	55.3
15.8.3 Debridement of nail	16 479	0.05	15 136	6 914	11 258	18 337	14.7	1.8	43.5	73.8
15.8.4 Other skin and breast procedures, non-OR	37 416	0.11	13 385	3 580	7 440	15 226	6.6	1.6	44.3	41.4
15.9 Other OR therapeutic procedures on skin and breast [175.]	47 515	0.14	10 990	5 210	8 336	12 916	2.8	0.5	13.8	43.1
15.9.1 Bilateral reduction mammoplasty	16 721	0.05	7 941	5 020	7 299	9 932	1.4	0.0	1.3	35.8
15.9.2 Excision pilonidal cyst or sinus	1 733	0.00	5 761	3 351	4 520	6 804	2.5	0.0	61.5	28.6
15.9.3 Other skin and breast procedures, OR	29 061	0.08	13 072	5 735	9 717	16 007	3.6	0.8	18.2	48.2
16 MISCELLANEOUS DIAGNOSTIC AND THERAPEUTIC PROCEDURES	4 520 869	12.96	11 630	3 168	6 212	12 140	6.4	5.8	46.8	49.8
16.1 Other organ transplantation [176.]	5 732	0.02	190 833	90 125	142 682	227 885	32.6	9.7	60.2	45.6
16.2 Computerized axial tomography (CT) scan	430 011	1.24	8 915	3 871	6 301	10 511	5.7	3.7	46.0	61.5
16.2.1 Computerized axial tomography (CT) scan head [177.]	295 541	0.85	8 807	3 750	6 143	10 340	5.7	4.2	46.2	63.1
16.2.2 CT scan chest [178.]	28 870	0.08	10 651	4 948	7 868	12 718	6.9	3.3	50.1	64.6
16.2.3 CT scan abdomen [179.]	87 289	0.25	8 908	4 135	6 492	10 488	5.2	2.4	44.1	56.3
16.2.4 Other CT scan [180.]	19 012	0.05	7 983	3 494	5 573	9 476	5.5	1.6	45.5	54.7
16.3 Myelogram [181.]	11 584	0.03	7 548	2 698	5 353	9 232	4.1	0.6	47.8	54.7
16.4 Mammography [182.]	1 130	0.00	10 399	4 055	6 503	10 270	9.8	0.4	1.4	59.8
16.5 Routine chest X-ray [183.]	12 881	0.04	5 951	2 631	4 246	7 219	5.2	2.7	45.2	49.1
16.6 Intraoperative cholangiogram [184.]	778	0.00	18 098	7 067	11 976	19 215	6.9	1.9	43.0	60.7
16.7 Upper gastrointestinal X-ray [185.]	17 022	0.05	10 701	3 791	6 554	12 231	7.7	1.8	45.2	56.0
16.8 Lower gastrointestinal X-ray [186.]	4 519	0.01	7 955	3 153	5 337	8 979	5.7	1.4	43.0	59.6
16.9 Intravenous pyelogram [187.]	30 987	0.09	4 858	2 073	3 250	5 439	3.1	0.2	54.1	48.4
16.10 Cerebral arteriogram [188.]	36 828	0.11	13 772	7 226	10 976	16 558	5.5	2.0	50.1	61.1
16.11 Contrast aortogram [189.]	14 750	0.04	12 733	5 811	9 326	15 609	4.8	2.7	55.1	65.7
16.12 Contrast arteriogram of femoral and lower extremity arteries [190.]	13 993	0.04	13 570	4 877	9 003	17 180	5.6	2.7	54.6	67.0
16.13 Arterio or venogram (not heart and head) [191.]	32 602	0.09	12 605	5 193	9 027	15 347	5.7	1.8	44.9	58.4
16.14 Diagnostic ultrasound	443 216	1.27	9 336	3 982	6 635	11 047	5.2	1.7	41.7	58.5
16.14.1 Diagnostic ultrasound of head and neck [192.]	31 972	0.09	10 884	4 042	6 656	11 578	6.0	0.7	43.8	59.1
16.14.2 Diagnostic ultrasound of heart (echocardiogram) [193.]	234 607	0.67	10 238	4 812	7 597	12 222	5.3	2.0	46.9	65.5
16.14.3 Diagnostic ultrasound of gastrointestinal tract [194.]	13 869	0.04	6 753	3 012	4 904	8 071	4.5	1.4	36.5	54.0
16.14.4 Diagnostic ultrasound of urinary tract [195.]	31 430	0.09	8 546	3 417	5 692	9 951	5.5	1.8	43.2	45.7
16.14.5 Diagnostic ultrasound of abdomen or retroperitoneum [196.]	58 694	0.17	7 839	3 241	5 419	9 251	4.5	1.7	37.8	49.6
16.14.6 Other diagnostic ultrasound [197.]	72 644	0.21	7 799	2 886	5 143	9 183	5.2	1.2	27.4	49.4
16.15 Magnetic resonance imaging [198.]	81 939	0.23	10 393	4 963	7 634	12 231	6.3	1.5	45.6	57.3
16.16 Electroencephalogram (EEG) [199.]	22 458	0.06	11 270	4 217	7 398	12 905	7.1	2.3	48.6	48.1
16.17 Nonoperative urinary system measurements [200.]	542	0.00	11 418	3 438	6 935	11 844	7.0	2.0	42.3	54.8
16.18 Cardiac stress tests [201.]	84 248	0.24	6 586	3 548	5 394	8 141	2.8	0.1	50.5	60.4
16.19 Electrocardiogram [202.]	37 073	0.11	5 668	2 440	4 005	6 664	4.1	2.2	45.1	59.9
16.20 Electrographic cardiac monitoring [203.]	108 238	0.31	6 055	2 769	4 442	7 366	3.3	2.3	46.7	64.7
16.21 Swan-Ganz catheterization for monitoring [204.]	20 287	0.06	27 225	11 707	20 089	33 924	8.8	34.0	53.5	69.1
16.22 Arterial blood gases [205.]	68 626	0.20	8 755	3 393	5 894	10 383	5.2	5.4	46.6	57.5

See footnotes at end of table.

Table 4.15. Hospital Procedures: 1996—*Continued*

(Principal procedure only)

Multilevel Clinical Classifications Software (CCS) category [1]	Number of discharges	Percent of discharges [2]	Mean charges (dollars)	25 percentile charges (dollars)	Median charges (dollars)	75 percentile charges (dollars)	Mean length of stay	Percent died	Percent male	Mean age
16.23 Microscopic examination (bacterial smear, culture, toxicology) [206.]	10 923	0.03	4 653	1 289	2 584	6 062	4.5	1.3	40.3	34.5
16.24 Radioisotope scan	85 610	0.25	9 977	4 742	7 325	11 929	5.9	1.8	41.0	62.3
16.24.1 Radioisotope bone scan [207.]	16 916	0.05	9 713	4 467	6 862	11 475	7.4	2.1	41.0	66.0
16.24.2 Radioisotope pulmonary scan [208.]	35 512	0.10	10 481	5 021	7 822	12 655	5.6	2.4	38.9	62.4
16.24.3 Radioisotope scan and function studies [209.]	30 281	0.09	9 395	4 568	7 015	11 194	5.2	0.8	43.1	60.6
16.24.4 Other radioisotope scan [210.]	2 901	0.01	11 548	4 833	7 734	13 679	8.1	3.1	44.8	58.4
16.25 Therapeutic radiology [211.]	73 945	0.21	11 916	4 784	8 170	14 126	6.8	5.0	42.1	61.5
16.26 Physical therapy	259 939	0.75	13 336	4 829	8 870	16 498	11.6	1.2	40.5	64.9
16.26.1 Diagnostic physical therapy [212.]	11 921	0.03	16 059	5 848	11 048	21 121	14.6	1.5	40.5	68.9
16.26.2 Physical therapy exercises, manipulation, and other procedures [213.]	159 590	0.46	14 246	5 250	9 438	17 535	12.1	1.3	38.1	71.5
16.26.3 Traction, splints, and other wound care [214.]	38 894	0.11	8 497	2 758	5 105	10 109	5.9	1.3	48.5	47.3
16.26.4 Other physical therapy and rehabilitation [215.]	49 535	0.14	13 547	5 685	9 693	16 791	13.7	0.8	42.3	56.5
16.27 Respiratory intubation and mechanical ventilation [216.]	466 077	1.34	32 813	8 620	18 720	38 698	10.9	31.1	51.1	49.7
16.27.1 Endotracheal intubation	140 280	0.40	26 181	4 590	12 813	29 844	9.0	28.8	50.5	41.6
16.27.2 Continuous mechanical ventilation less than 96 hours	203 468	0.58	21 676	8 578	15 353	26 684	7.4	33.0	51.2	55.5
16.27.3 Continuous mechanical ventilation 96 hours or more	95 903	0.28	69 268	30 633	49 152	80 885	21.4	36.5	51.5	54.7
16.27.4 Other respiratory intubation and mechanical ventilation	26 427	0.08	20 862	5 685	12 479	24 649	10.7	9.8	51.6	30.8
16.28 Other respiratory therapy [217.]	171 478	0.49	7 001	2 575	4 743	8 335	4.6	3.3	46.0	41.6
16.28.1 Respiratory medication administered by nebulizer	81 763	0.23	7 532	3 162	5 263	9 114	4.8	2.6	46.5	43.6
16.28.2 Oxygen therapy	74 196	0.21	6 262	1 783	3 961	7 511	4.3	3.5	46.0	36.3
16.28.3 Other respiratory treatments	15 519	0.04	7 673	3 154	5 033	8 144	5.2	5.7	43.6	56.6
16.29 Psychological and psychiatric evaluation and therapy [218.]	137 802	0.40	12 204	4 346	8 291	15 438	13.6	0.2	45.7	43.4
16.29.1 Psychiatric drug therapy	44 447	0.13	11 825	4 720	8 297	14 475	13.6	0.3	51.2	38.4
16.29.2 Electroconvulsive therapy	29 725	0.09	18 734	8 904	14 880	23 840	20.4	0.2	30.8	39.4
16.29.3 Individual psychotherapy	27 971	0.08	8 616	3 274	5 561	10 524	9.4	0.2	46.5	41.1
16.29.4 Other psychological and psychiatric evaluation and therapy	35 659	0.10	10 025	3 440	6 537	12 180	11.4	0.1	50.6	38.4
16.3 Alcohol and drug rehabilitation/ detoxification [219.]	400 264	1.15	4 636	2 140	3 339	5 448	6.1	0.1	68.4	39.4
16.30.1 Alcohol rehabilitation	13 503	0.04	7 548	2 434	5 090	10 668	13.3	0.0	72.6	41.1
16.30.2 Alcohol detoxification	129 474	0.37	4 591	2 004	3 202	5 273	4.2	0.2	74.4	44.6
16.30.3 Alcohol rehabilitation and detoxification	35 751	0.10	5 505	2 818	4 387	6 566	7.8	0.0	71.4	45.2
16.30.4 Drug rehabilitation	7 680	0.02	6 396	2 536	4 330	7 929	10.7	0.0	50.5	31.7
16.30.5 Drug detoxification	71 837	0.21	3 542	1 906	2 918	4 170	4.3	0.0	58.7	35.7
16.30.6 Drug rehabilitation and detoxification	19 979	0.06	5 351	2 632	4 104	6 384	7.4	0.0	56.5	35.9
16.30.7 Alcohol and drug rehabilitation	21 201	0.06	7 271	3 403	6 535	11 119	16.2	0.0	66.0	32.3
16.30.8 Alcohol and drug detoxification	70 293	0.20	3 256	1 732	2 682	3 781	4.3	0.0	70.4	35.9
16.30.9 Alcohol and drug rehabilitation and detoxification	30 546	0.09	5 518	2 943	4 491	6 616	8.3	0.0	69.4	35.3
16.31 Ophthalmologic and otologic diagnosis and treatment [220.]	2 366	0.01	15 370	2 085	7 812	18 059	9.8	0.0	44.1	20.7
16.32 Nasogastric tube [221.]	31 565	0.09	7 853	3 094	5 145	9 134	4.8	6.0	44.9	56.7
16.33 Blood transfusion [222.]	217 819	0.62	10 961	4 216	7 333	12 870	6.3	7.5	43.6	64.1
16.34 Enteral and parenteral nutrition [223.]	46 842	0.13	18 737	6 920	12 356	22 308	11.8	14.6	40.5	58.7
16.35 Cancer chemotherapy [224.]	255 054	0.73	11 699	4 312	6 969	11 542	4.4	1.3	44.4	52.4
16.36 Conversion of cardiac rhythm [225.]	77 581	0.22	9 261	3 295	6 008	11 011	4.3	21.8	59.6	68.2
16.37 Other diagnostic radiology and related techniques [226.]	55 477	0.16	10 300	3 908	6 896	11 918	5.8	1.7	46.8	51.4
16.38 Other diagnostic procedures (interview, evaluation, consultation) [227.]	47 393	0.14	11 910	4 164	7 427	13 536	6.8	4.9	43.1	47.8
16.39 Prophylactic vaccinations and inoculations [228.]	309 025	0.89	1 559	582	828	1 330	2.2	0.0	30.8	0.3
16.40 Nonoperative removal of foreign body [229.]	4 768	0.01	7 397	2 815	4 542	8 183	3.5	1.3	60.2	37.8
16.41 Extracorporeal shock wave lithotripsy, other than urinary [230.]	60	0.00	—	—	—	—	—	—	—	—
16.42 Other therapeutic procedures [231.]	386 736	1.11	9 452	3 013	5 851	11 221	5.5	2.5	46.5	39.3
16.42.1 Inject antibiotic	123 400	0.35	8 673	3 436	5 762	10 070	6.0	2.9	45.2	43.9
16.42.2 Other phototherapy (newborn)	64 436	0.18	10 128	1 792	3 550	10 900	7.1	0.1	48.9	0.1
16.42.3 Other therapies	198 900	0.57	9 721	3 356	6 501	12 037	4.8	2.9	46.4	49.1
NO PROCEDURE LISTED	13 618 888	39.05	5 801	2 017	4 043	7 234	4.2	2.2	41.2	46.8

SOURCE: Agency for Health Care Policy and Research (AHCPR) [AHCPR is now known as the Agency for Healthcare Research and Quality (AHRQ)], Center for Organization and Delivery Studies, Healthcare Cost and Utilization Project (HCUP): Table 2.

1. CCS categories are presented in bold lettering with the CCS category number at the end of the word label, in brackets. See the AHRQ Web site for definitions of CCS categories: <http://www.ahrq.gov/data/hcup>.
2. Numbers of discharges are weighted national estimates based on 100% of the data from the HCUP Nationwide Inpatient Sample. Results are not presented for any diagnosis category for which the unweighted number of discharges is less than 70. Estimates presented here have a relative error of less than 30%. Out of the "All Discharges" category, 12,218 discharges had missing or invalid diagnosis codes and are not presented in the table details.
— Data not available.

NOTE: Acronyms used in Table 1: CNS—central nervous system; GI—gastrointestinal; HIV—human immunodeficiency virus; OR—operating room; STD—sexually transmitted disease; and TB—tuberculosis.

Table 4.16. Treatment for Alcohol and Drug Abuse: 1997

(Percent receiving treatment)

Characteristic	Receive treatment			(Unweighted n)
	Drug abuse treatment [1]	Alcohol abuse treatment [2]	Any substance abuse treatment [3]	
Total	0.9	1.4	1.6	(24 503)
AGE				
12–17 years	1.0	1.0	1.2	(7 844)
18–25 years	1.4	1.8	2.0	(6 238)
26–34 years	1.2	2.1	2.2	(4 387)
35 years and over	0.8	1.3	1.4	(6 034)
SEX				
Male	1.1	2.1	2.2	(10 835)
Female	0.8	0.8	0.9	(13 668)
RACE/ETHNICITY [4]				
White, non-Hispanic	0.9	1.4	1.6	(12 442)
Black, non-Hispanic	1.0	1.4	1.6	(4 638)
Hispanic	0.8	1.0	1.2	(6 259)
POPULATION DENSITY				
Large metro	0.8	1.0	1.1	(12 963)
Small metro	1.1	1.7	1.9	(7 136)
Nonmetro	0.9	1.8	1.9	(4 404)
REGION				
Northeast	1.5	1.5	1.8	(2 905)
North central	0.9	1.2	1.3	(3 255)
South	0.6	1.5	1.6	(7 553)
West	1.0	1.5	1.6	(10 790)

SOURCE: Office of Applied Studies, Substance Abuse and Mental Health Services Administration, National Household Survey on Drug Abuse (NHSDA), 1997: Table 12.2.

1. This category may include some individuals who have also received alcohol abuse treatment.
2. This category may include some individuals who have also received other drug abuse treatment.
3. This category includes individuals who have received alcohol abuse treatment, drug abuse treatment, or both.
4. The category "other" for race/ethnicity is not included.

NOTE: The unweighted n' s for alcohol abuse treatment and drug abuse treatment are slightly smaller than those shown for any substance abuse treatment because of differing patterns of nonresponse across the demographic groups. Because of improved procedures implemented in 1994, these estimates are not comparable with those presented in NHSDA Main Findings prior to 1994. The percentage receiving treatment includes only those respondents who reported having received treatment in the past year and having used alcohol or illicit drugs in their lifetime. Those who reported receiving treatment but never having used the substance were excluded from the analysis.

Table 4.17. Number, Percent Distribution, and Rate[1] of 24-hour Hospital and Residential Treatment Residents, by Type of Mental Health Organization[2]

Type of organization	1969	1975	1979	1986	1990	1992	1994[3]
NUMBER OF HOSPITAL AND RESIDENTIAL TREATMENT RESIDENTS AT END OF YEAR							
Total	471 451	284 158	230 216	237 845	226 953	214 714	236 110
State and county mental hospitals	369 969	193 436	140 355	111 135	90 572	83 180	72 096
Private psychiatric hospitals	10 963	11 576	12 921	24 951	32 268	24 053	26 519
Nonfederal general hospitals with psychiatric services	17 808	18 851	18 753	34 474	38 237	35 611	35 841
VA medical centers[4]	51 696	31 850	28 693	24 322	17 233	18 531	18 019
Federally funded community mental health centers	5 270	10 818	10 112	—	—	—	—
Residential treatment centers for emotionally disturbed children	13 489	16 307	18 276	23 171	27 785	27 751	29 493
All other organizations[5]	2 256	1 320	1 076	20 152	20 768	25 588	54 142
PERCENT DISTRIBUTION OF HOSPITAL AND RESIDENTIAL TREATMENT RESIDENTS							
Total	100.0	100.0	100.0	100.0	100.0	100.0	100.0
State and county mental hospitals	78.5	68.1	61.0	46.7	39.9	38.7	30.6
Private psychiatric hospitals	2.3	4.1	5.6	10.3	14.2	11.2	11.2
Nonfederal general hospitals with psychiatric services	3.8	6.6	8.1	14.5	16.9	16.6	15.2
VA medical centers[4]	11.0	11.2	12.5	10.2	7.6	8.6	7.6
Federally funded community mental health centers	9.0	—	—	—	—	—	—
Residential treatment centers for emotionally disturbed children	2.9	5.7	7.9	9.7	12.2	12.9	12.5
All other organizations[5]	0.5	0.5	0.5	8.5	9.2	11.9	22.9
HOSPITAL AND RESIDENTIAL TREATMENT RESIDENTS PER 100,000 CIVILIAN POPULATION							
State and county mental hospitals	185.8	91.5	63.0	46.5	37.1	33.0	27.8
Private psychiatric hospitals	5.5	5.5	5.8	10.3	13.2	9.5	10.2
Nonfederal general hospitals with psychiatric services	8.9	8.9	8.6	14.4	15.7	14.1	13.8
VA medical centers[4]	26.0	15.1	13.3	10.2	7.1	7.4	7.0
Federally funded community mental health centers	2.7	5.1	4.5	—	—	—	—
Residential treatment centers for emotionally disturbed children	6.8	7.7	8.2	9.7	11.4	11.0	11.4
All other organizations[5]	1.1	0.6	0.5	8.5	8.5	10.2	20.9
All organizations	236.8	134.4	103.9	99.6	93.0	85.2	91.1

SOURCE: Published and unpublished inventory data from the Survey and Analysis Branch, Division of State and Community Systems Development, Center for Mental Health Services, Substance Abuse and Mental Health Services Administration (SAMHSA). M.J. Witkin, J.E. Atay, R.W. Manderscheid, J. DeLozier, A. Male, and R. Gillespe, "Highlights of Organized Mental Health Services in 1994 and Major National and State Trends," pp. 143-175. ed. R.W. Manderscheid and M.J. Henderson, *Mental Health U.S. 1998*, DHHS Pub. No. (SMA) 99-3285. SAMHSA Center for Mental Health Services. (Washington, D.C.: Supt. of Docs., U.S. Govt. Printing Office, 1998.): 143–175.

— Data not available.

1. The population used in the calculation of these rates is the January 1 civilian population of the United States for the respective years.

2. Some organizations were reclassified as a result of changes in reporting procedures and definitions. For 1979–1980, comparable data were not available for certain organization types, and data for either an earlier or a later period were substituted. These factors influence the comparability of 1980, 1986, 1990, 1992, and 1994 data from those earlier years.

3. The number of residents increased in 1994 because all residential treatment and residential supportive patients were combined with 24-hour care hospital residents; in previous years, residential supportive patients were excluded.

4. Includes Department of Veterans Affairs (formerly Veterans Administration, VA) neuropsychiatric hospitals, VA general hospital psychiatric services, and VA psychiatric outpatient clinics.

5. Includes free-standing psychiatric partial care organizations, free-standing psychiatric outpatient clinics, and multiservice mental health organizations. Multiservice mental health organizations were redefined in 1984.

Table 4.18. Hospice Care Agencies: 1993–1996

Characteristic	Agencies		Current patients		Discharges	
	Number	Percent	Number	Percent	Number	Percent
1996						
Total	1 800	100.0	59 400	100.0	393 200	100.0
Ownership						
Proprietary	*	*	6 500	11.0	52 400	13.3
Voluntary nonprofit	1 500	83.5	50 500	84.6	334 900	85.2
Government and other	*100	*4.8	2 600	4.4	*5 900	*1.5
Affiliation						
Operated by hospital	700	40.1	16 300	27.4	123 700	31.5
Part of group or chain	700	36.7	21 000	35.4	132 700	33.8
Geographic region						
Northeast	200	9.7	8 900	15.0	71 700	18.2
Midwest	600	34.5	21 300	33.9	99 000	25.2
South	700	39.5	19 000	32.0	151 200	38.5
West	300	16.3	10 100	17.1	71 400	18.1
Location of agency						
MSA [1]	1 100	63.0	48 100	81.1	331 300	84.2
Not MSA [1]	700	37.0	11 200	18.9	62 000	15.8
Certified	1 700	93.9	58 000	97.7	385 400	98.0
Both Medicare and Medicaid	1 600	89.3	55 100	92.9	360 200	91.6
Medicare only	*	*	*2 300	*3.9	*14 600	*3.7
Not certified	*	*	1 400	2.3	*7 800	*2.0
1993–1994						
Total	1 300	100.0	—	—	328 000	100.0
Ownership						
Proprietary	*100	*9.4	—	—	33 300	10.2
Voluntary nonprofit	1 100	83.8	—	—	285 300	87.0
Government and other	*	*	—	—	*9 300	*2.8
Affiliation						
Operated by hospital	400	35.5	—	—	93 200	28.4
Part of group or chain	500	41.5	—	—	155 700	47.5
Geographic region						
Northeast	300	24.8	—	—	109 800	33.5
Midwest	300	26.4	—	—	73 600	22.4
South	400	34.8	—	—	97 900	29.8
West	200	14.0	—	—	46 800	14.3
Location of agency						
MSA [1]	800	61.0	—	—	272 200	83.0
Not MSA [1]	*500	*39.0	—	—	55 800	17.0
Medicare certification						
As hospice	900	74.2	—	—	287 400	87.6
As home health agency	500	41.9	—	—	180 300	55.0
Medicaid certification						
As hospice	800	67.2	—	—	279 700	85.3
As home health agency	500	43.4	—	—	181 300	55.3

SOURCE: B.J. Haupt, "Characteristics of Hospice Care Users; Data from the 1996 National Home and Hospice Care Survey." NCHS Advance Data, *Vital and Health Statistics*, no. 299, (August 28, 1998): Table 1. B.J. Haupt, Characteristics of Hospice Care Discharges: United States, 1993–94. NCHS Advance Data, *Vital and Health Statistics*, no. 287, (April 25, 1997): Table 1.

* Figure does not meet standard of reliability or precision.
— Data not available.
1. MSA is metropolitan statistical area.

NOTE: Numbers may not add to totals because of rounding. Percents are based on the unrounded figures. Numbers may not add to total since not all agencies are certified or affiliated and an agency may have more than one type of certification or affiliation.

Table 4.19. Hospice Care Patients: 1996

Characteristic	Number			Percent distribution		
	Total	Male	Female	Total	Male	Female
All patients	59 400	26 600	32 700	100.0	100.0	100.0
AGE AT ADMISSION [1]						
Under 65 years	13 100	6 100	7 000	22.1	22.9	21.4
Under 45 years	4 300	2 400	1 900	7.3	8.9	5.9
45–64 years	8 800	3 700	5 100	14.8	14.0	15.5
65 years and over	46 100	20 400	25 700	77.7	76.6	78.6
65–69 years	5 000	2 800	2 200	8.4	10.6	6.6
70–74 years	9 600	5 800	3 800	16.2	21.9	11.5
75–79 years	9 800	4 900	4 900	16.6	18.4	15.0
80–84 years	9 100	3 300	5 800	15.2	12.2	17.7
85 years and over	12 700	3 600	9 100	21.3	13.4	27.8
RACE						
White	49 700	22 000	27 700	83.7	82.5	84.6
Black and other [2]	5 700	3 100	2 500	9.6	11.8	7.8
Black	4 900	2 600	2 300	8.3	9.8	7.1
Unknown	4 000	*1 500	*2 500	6.7	*5.7	*7.6
CURRENT MARITAL STATUS						
Married	25 900	17 600	8 300	43.7	66.1	25.4
Not married [3]	29 700	8 200	21 500	50.0	30.9	65.6
Widowed	19 100	3 000	16 100	32.2	11.4	49.1
Unknown	*3 700	*	*2 900	*6.3	*	*9.0

SOURCE: B.J. Haupt, "Characteristics of Hospice Care Users; Data from the 1996 National Home and Hospice Care Survey." NCHS Advance Data, *Vital and Health Statistics*, no. 299, (August 28, 1998): Table 2.

*Figure does not meet standard of reliability or precision.
1. Excludes unknown.
2. Includes races other than white.
3. Includes separated.

NOTE: Numbers may not add to totals because of rounding. Percents are based on the unrounded figures.

Table 4.20. Hospice Care Discharges by Selected Patient Characteristics by Sex: 1993–1996

Characteristic	Number			Percent distribution		
	Total	Male	Female	Total	Male	Female
1995–1996						
Total	393 200	197 700	195 500	100.0	100.0	100.0
Age at admission [1]						
Under 65 years	121 100	74 000	47 100	30.8	37.4	24.1
Under 45 years	31 700	20 000	*11 700	8.1	10.1	*6.0
45–64 years	89 400	54 000	35 300	22.7	27.3	18.1
65 years and over	265 200	120 900	144 400	67.5	61.1	73.8
65–69 years	34 100	16 200	18 000	8.7	8.2	9.2
70–74 years	61 300	30 100	31 200	15.6	15.2	15.9
75–79 years	57 000	29 200	27 800	14.5	14.8	14.2
80–84 years	48 300	19 100	29 300	12.3	9.6	15.0
85 years and over	64 500	26 300	38 200	16.4	13.3	19.5
Race						
White	310 300	157 500	152 800	78.9	79.7	78.1
Black and other [2]	48 500	21 100	27 400	12.3	*10.7	14.0
Black	43 900	*18 200	25 700	11.2	*9.2	13.1
Unknown	34 500	*19 200	*15 300	8.8	*9.7	*7.8
Marital status at discharge						
Married	190 300	131 600	58 600	48.4	66.6	30.0
Not married [3]	177 700	59 500	118 100	45.2	30.1	60.4
Widowed	115 600	24 800	90 800	29.4	12.5	46.5
Unknown	25 300	*	*18 800	6.4	*	*9.6
Reason for discharge						
Deceased	322 200	160 600	160 600	81.9	81.7	82.1
Services provided by another source	21 300	*16 700	*4 600	5.4	*8.5	*2.4
Other reason for discharge	52 100	*19 600	33 400	13.2	*9.9	17.1
1993–1994						
Total	328 000	171 500	156 500	100.0	100.0	100.0
Age at admission						
Under 65 years	88 400	45 700	42 800	27.0	26.6	27.3
Under 45 years	18 600	12 200	*6 400	5.7	7.1	*4.1
45–64 years	69 900	33 500	36 300	21.3	19.5	23.2
65 years and over	239 100	125 800	113 300	72.9	73.4	72.4
65–69 years	38 000	24 400	13 600	11.6	14.2	8.7
70–74 years	53 200	32 400	20 800	16.2	18.9	13.3
75–79 years	50 700	23 900	26 800	15.5	13.9	17.1
80–84 years	40 700	19 200	21 500	12.4	11.2	13.8
85 years and over	56 500	25 900	30 600	17.2	15.1	19.6
Race						
White	260 400	142 500	117 900	79.4	83.1	75.3
Black and other [2]	25 600	12 700	12 900	7.8	7.4	8.3
Black	24 000	11 800	12 200	7.3	6.9	7.8
Unknown	42 000	16 300	25 700	12.8	9.5	16.4
Married status at discharge						
Married	160 300	108 700	51 600	48.9	63.4	33.0
Not married [3]	145 600	58 100	87 500	44.4	33.9	55.9
Widowed	97 300	32 900	64 400	29.7	19.2	41.1
Unknown	22 200	*	*17 400	*6.8	*	11.1
Reason for discharge						
Deceased	288 000	150 600	137 400	87.8	87.8	87.8
Admitted to inpatient facility	13 000	*	*5 800	4.0	*	*3.7
Admitted to hospital	*10 200	*	*	*3.1	*	*
Other reason for discharge	26 300	*13 700	*12 600	8.0	*8.0	*8.1

SOURCE: B.J. Haupt, "Characteristics of Hospice Care Users; Data from the 1996 National Home and Hospice Care Survey." NCHS Advance Data, *Vital and Health Statistics*, no. 299, (August 28, 1998): Table 5. B.J. Haupt, Characteristics of Hospice Care Discharges: United States, 1993–94. NCHS Advance Data, *Vital and Health Statistics*, no. 287, (April 25, 1997): Table 2.

*Figure does not meet standard of reliability or precision.
1. Excludes unknown.
2. Includes other races than white.
3. Includes separated.

NOTE: Numbers may not add to totals because of rounding. Percents are based on the unrounded figures.

Table 4.21. Nursing Home Residents: 1996

(Percent distribution, except where noted.)

Characteristic	Nursing home residents		Facility ownership			Type of nursing home		
	Number	Percent	For profit	Nonprofit	Government	Hospital based	With independent living for personal care unit [1]	With only nursing home beds [2]
TOTAL								
Number	1 563 900		1 028 700	383 500	151 700	104 900	192 600	1 266 300
Percent		100.0	65.8	24.5	9.7	6.7	12.3	81.0
SEX								
Male	443 500	28.4	27.6	23.3	46.5	37.8	28.8	27.5
Female	1 120 300	71.6	72.4	76.7	53.5	62.2	71.2	72.5
AGE								
Under 65 years	138 400	8.8	9.1	5.7	14.8	14.4	5.5	8.9
65–74 years	186 000	11.9	12.7	7.5	17.7	12.4	10.4	12.1
75–84 years	469 300	29.9	30.3	27.8	33.3	32.3	25.5	30.4
85 years and over	771 200	49.3	48.0	58.9	34.2	40.9	58.7	48.6
RACE								
White	1 387 000	88.7	87.8	91.4	88.0	86.7	94.6	88.0
Black	138 400	8.9	9.5	7.2	8.8	10.4	4.1	9.4
Other	38 500	2.5	2.8	*1.4	*3.1	*2.9	*1.2	2.6
MARITAL STATUS [3]								
Married	258 300	16.6	16.6	14.6	21.8	19.5	19.2	16.0
Widowed	928 200	59.8	60.0	63.9	47.7	50.8	62.6	60.1
Divorced/separated	143 500	9.2	9.9	6.4	12.0	9.1	7.5	9.5
Never married	222 900	14.4	13.5	15.1	18.5	20.7	10.7	14.4
CENSUS REGION								
Northeast	349 000	22.3	18.2	30.5	29.8	23.6	17.8	22.9
Midwest	485 100	31.0	27.6	38.6	35.0	27.2	40.3	29.9
South	490 900	31.4	36.6	20.2	24.1	23.5	33.7	31.7
West	238 900	15.3	17.6	10.7	*11.1	25.7	*8.2	15.5
MSA	1 080 200	69.1	69.3	72.4	59.5	57.8	65.1	70.6
Not MSA	483 700	30.9	30.7	27.6	40.5	42.2	34.9	29.4
INSURANCE [3,4]								
Medicare only	455 600	29.7	27.2	37.5	26.4	34.4	44.9	27.0
Medicaid only	68 200	4.4	5.1	2.8	4.5	6.6	*2.1	4.6
Medicare and Medicaid	974 500	63.5	65.3	58.6	63.3	50.8	50.4	66.5
Neither Medicare nor Medicaid	37 300	2.4	*2.4	*1.2	5.8	*8.2	*2.6	1.9

SOURCE: N.A. Krauss and B.M. Altman, "Characteristics of Nursing Home Residents—1996," (Rockville, Md.: Agency for Health Care Policy and Research 1998. Medical Expenditure Panel Survey, Nursing Home Component, MEPS Research Findings No. 5 AHCPR Pub No. 99-0006): Table 1.

* Relative standard error is equal to or greater than 0.3 and should not be assumed reliable.
1. Nursing homes with independent living or personal care unit include continuing care retirement communities and retirement centers that include independent living and/or personal care units, as well as nursing homes that contain or are affiliated with personal care units.
2. Nursing homes with only nursing home beds include a small number of nursing homes (less than 1%) with an intermediate care facility for the mentally retarded.
3. Marital status and insurance status exclude less than 2% missing data.
4. Medicare only includes less than 1.5% of residents with other public coverage such as veterans' benefits and excludes persons with Medicaid. Medicaid only includes less than 1% of residents with other public overage such as veterans' benefits or some form of private coverage, and excludes persons with Medicare. Medicare and Medicaid includes less than 2% of residents with other public coverage such as veterans' benefits. Neither Medicare nor Medicaid includes less than 1% of residents with other private coverage only and less than 1% with public coverage (such as veterans benefits) with or without private coverage.

NOTE: Categories may not add to totals because of rounding, and in the case of marital status and insurance enrollment, because of nonresponse.

Table 4.22. Health Problems of Nursing Home Residents: 1996

(Percent distribution, except where noted)

Health conditions and characteristics	All nursing home residents		Age in years				Sex	
	Number	Percent	Under 65 years	65–74 years	75–84 years	85 years and over	Males	Females
TOTAL								
Number	1 563 900		138 400	186 000	468 300	771 200	443 500	1 120 300
Percent		100.0	8.8	11.9	29.9	49.3	28.4	71.6
MOST FREQUENT CONDITIONS [1]								
Dementia [2]	746 100	47.7	17.7	39.1	50.2	53.6	44.6	48.9
Heart disease [3]	711 700	45.5	16.6	33.8	42.2	55.6	44.0	46.1
Hypertension	572 400	36.6	25.3	41.1	37.6	37.0	32.0	38.4
Arthritis	379 300	24.3	4.5	16.9	22.5	30.6	17.5	26.9
CVA [4]	332 300	21.2	18.9	28.6	24.3	18.0	26.3	19.2
Depression	315 600	20.2	17.2	23.8	23.1	18.1	17.0	21.4
Diabetes	281 500	18.0	18.8	25.9	21.2	14.0	18.8	17.7
Anemia	271 300	17.4	14.5	12.5	16.0	19.9	15.2	18.2
Allergies	267 200	17.1	15.0	17.4	19.3	16.1	12.6	18.9
COPD [5]	197 900	12.7	6.9	21.2	15.4	10.0	17.9	10.6
HEARING [6]								
Adequate	994 000	64.4	89.0	82.6	71.2	51.6	65.1	64.1
Impaired	354 600	23.0	6.7	12.3	21.4	29.4	21.3	23.6
Highly impaired [7]	194 300	12.6	4.3	5.1	7.4	19.0	13.5	12.2
SIGHT [6]								
Adequate	931 900	60.8	71.1	68.4	65.1	54.4	62.4	60.1
Impaired	396 700	25.9	16.4	22.7	22.9	30.1	24.4	26.4
Highly impaired [7]	205 300	13.4	12.5	8.9	12.0	15.5	13.2	13.5
COMMUNICATIONS [6]								
No problem	618 200	39.9	46.5	45.4	40.8	36.9	41.2	39.5
Problem being understood ...	76 700	5.0	11.2	7.7	4.8	3.3	7.4	4.0
Problem understanding other ...	168 400	10.9	*3.2	6.8	9.7	13.9	10.3	11.1
Both	685 800	44.3	39.1	40.1	44.8	45.9	41.1	45.5

SOURCE: N.A. Krauss and B.M. Altman, "Characteristics of Nursing Home Residents—1996," (Rockville, Md.: Agency for Health Care Policy and Research, Center for Cost and Financing Studies: Medical Expenditure Panel Survey, Nursing Home Component, Round 1,1996): Table 5.

* Relative standard error is equal to or greater than 0.3 and should not be assumed reliable.
1. Persons may have more than one condition. Conditions are calculated separately and do not add to 100%.
2. Includes Alzheimer's disease and related dementia.
3. Includes arteriosclerotic heart disease, cardiac dysrhythmias, cardiovascular disease, and congestive heart failure.
4. Cerebrovascular accident (stroke).
5. Chronic obstructive pulmonary disease.
6. Excludes less than 2 percent missing data.
7. Responses of highly impaired and severely impaired, were combined and classified as highly impaired.

NOTE: Categories may not add to totals because of rounding and, in case of hearing, sight, and communication, nonresponse.

Table 4.23. Unmet Medical Needs: 1993

(Percent)

Characteristic	Any unmet need[1]	Needed, but not able to get care	Delayed medical care because of cost	Needed dental care	Needed prescription	Needed glasses	Needed mental health care
0–17 YEARS OF AGE							
Total[2]	10.8	1.9	4.1	6.2	1.3	1.4	0.4
Sex							
Male	10.4	2.0	4.0	6.1	1.2	1.1	0.5
Female	11.1	1.9	4.3	6.4	1.5	1.7	0.4
Age							
0–4 years	6.2	1.7	2.5	2.4	0.9	*0.1	*—
5–17 years	12.6	2.0	4.8	7.8	1.5	1.9	0.6
Race and/or Ethnicity							
White, non-Hispanic	11.2	1.7	4.4	6.5	1.2	1.3	0.6
Black, non-Hispanic	10.2	2.3	3.1	5.9	1.8	2.0	0.2
Hispanic	10.9	2.7	4.6	5.8	1.8	1.4	*0.3
Mexican-American	11.9	*3.4	5.6	6.3	1.6	1.7	*0.1
Other Hispanic	9.0	*1.6	2.8	5.0	*2.1	*0.9	*0.5
Region							
Northeast	9.3	1.2	3.7	5.2	1.0	*1.0	*0.5
Midwest	9.4	1.7	4.2	4.7	1.2	1.5	*0.2
South	12.6	2.0	4.4	7.6	1.7	1.7	0.4
West	10.8	2.7	4.1	6.6	1.3	1.0	0.7
Place of residence							
MSA[3]	10.0	2.0	3.8	5.6	1.4	1.3	0.5
Central city	10.3	2.2	3.8	6.1	1.5	1.4	0.4
Noncentral city	9.8	1.8	3.7	5.3	1.3	1.2	0.5
Not MSA[3]	13.4	1.8	5.4	8.4	1.2	1.6	0.3
Family structure							
Both parents	10.0	1.6	4.0	5.8	1.1	1.2	0.3
Mother only	14.3	3.3	4.9	8.1	2.5	2.1	1.1
Mother and other adult	10.2	2.1	4.0	6.0	*1.1	*0.8	*0.3
Other	11.3	*2.8	*3.5	5.6	*1.0	2.2	*0.8
Family income							
Less than $10,000	14.0	3.4	4.7	7.5	2.8	1.7	*0.3
$10,000–$19,999	18.0	4.2	6.8	11.2	2.3	2.6	0.8
$20,000–$34,999	13.9	1.5	5.3	8.4	1.7	1.9	0.7
$35,000–$49,000	8.9	1.2	3.3	5.0	*0.3	1.0	*0.4
$50,000 or more	3.2	0.7	1.6	1.2	*0.2	*0.3	*0.2
18–64 YEARS OF AGE							
Total[2]	20.9	3.7	12.5	11.0	3.6	4.9	1.0
Sex							
Male	18.7	3.0	10.8	10.3	2.8	3.9	0.7
Female	22.9	4.3	14.2	11.7	4.3	5.9	1.4
Age							
18–44 years	22.5	3.9	13.2	12.3	3.7	4.5	1.1
45–64 years	17.5	3.2	11.1	8.2	3.3	5.9	0.9
Race and/or ethnicity							
White, non-Hispanic	20.8	3.4	12.8	10.9	3.2	4.7	1.1
Black, non-Hispanic	22.4	4.4	11.2	12.1	5.2	6.8	1.2
Hispanic	21.7	5.1	13.6	12.0	4.7	4.7	0.6
Mexican-American	23.5	5.6	14.9	13.0	4.8	4.5	*0.5
Other Hispanic	19.2	4.5	11.7	10.5	4.7	4.9	*0.7
Region							
Northeast	16.8	3.0	9.9	8.6	2.9	3.8	0.8
Midwest	19.8	3.4	12.1	10.0	3.5	5.0	0.9
South	23.8	3.9	14.7	12.5	4.1	6.1	1.0
West	21.2	4.3	12.0	11.9	3.5	4.1	1.4
Place of residence							
MSA[3]	19.9	3.7	11.9	10.6	3.5	4.6	1.1
Central city	23.0	4.8	13.5	12.4	4.5	5.6	1.3
Noncentral city	18.0	3.1	10.8	9.5	2.9	4.0	0.9
Not MSA[3]	24.4	3.5	15.0	12.3	3.8	6.0	0.9
Employment status							
Currently in labor force	19.7	3.2	12.0	10.3	3.0	4.5	0.9
Currently employed	19.1	3.0	11.6	9.9	2.8	4.2	0.8
Currently unemployed	32.3	6.9	20.2	19.4	6.1	8.8	2.2
Not in labor force	25.0	5.4	14.3	13.4	5.7	6.7	1.6
Family income							
Less than $10,000	39.3	10.3	23.1	23.4	10.2	12.0	2.8
$10,000–$19,999	37.7	7.4	23.9	21.4	8.4	10.7	2.2
$20,000–$34,999	23.6	3.0	13.9	11.8	3.0	4.9	0.9
$35,000–$49,000	14.7	1.9	8.5	6.9	1.5	2.7	0.5
$50,000 or more	7.7	1.1	4.3	3.3	0.4	1.1	0.4

See footnotes at end of table.

Table 4.23. Unmet Medical Needs: 1993—*Continued*

(Percent)

Characteristic	Any unmet need [1]	Needed, but not able to get care	Delayed medical care because of cost	Needed dental care	Needed prescription	Needed glasses	Needed mental health care
65 YEARS OF AGE AND OVER							
Total [2]	10.6	1.6	4.7	4.4	2.0	3.2	*0.2
Sex							
Male	8.7	1.4	3.3	3.7	1.6	2.5	*0.2
Female	12.0	1.8	5.6	4.9	2.3	3.7	*0.2
Age							
65–74 years	11.4	1.6	5.3	5.0	2.1	3.5	*0.2
75 years and over	9.3	1.7	3.8	3.6	1.9	2.6	0.2
Race							
White, non-Hispanic	9.9	*1.6	4.6	4.2	1.7	2.6	*0.2
Black, non-Hispanic	18.4	*1.7	4.8	7.5	4.8	9.0	—
Region							
Northeast	7.5	0.9	3.3	2.9	1.2	2.0	*0.1
Midwest	9.4	1.7	4.8	3.6	1.4	2.4	*0.1
South	14.1	2.3	5.8	5.8	*3.3	4.9	*0.4
West	9.5	1.2	4.1	4.9	*1.4	2.4	*0.2
Place of residence							
MSA [3]	10.3	1.5	4.4	4.4	1.8	2.9	*0.2
Central city	11.0	1.4	4.6	5.1	2.1	3.2	*0.3
Noncentral city	9.8	1.6	4.2	4.0	1.5	2.7	*0.1
Not MSA [3]	11.5	2.0	5.5	4.4	2.7	3.9	*0.4
Family income							
Less than $10,000	24.9	3.7	10.9	10.6	7.9	9.4	*0.7
$10,000–$19,999	13.3	2.1	5.9	5.3	2.1	3.6	*0.1
$20,000–$34,999	6.0	*0.8	*2.7	*2.6	*0.4	1.5	*0.1
$35,000–$49,000	3.0	*0.8	*1.0	*1.0	*0.2	0.9	—
$50,000 or more	3.8	*1.1	*1.2	*1.4	*0.1	0.5	*0.2

SOURCE: G. Simpson, B. Bloom, R.A. Cohen, and P.E. Parsons, "Access to Health Care—Part 1: Children," *Vital and Health Statistics* (National Center for Health Statistics—NCHS) 10, no. 196 (1997): Table 9. B. Bloom, G. Simpson, R.A. Cohen, and P.E. Parsons, "Access to Health Care—Part 2: Working-Age Adults," *Vital and Health Statistics* (NCHS) 10, no. 197 (1997): Table 10. R.A. Cohen, B. Bloom, G. Simpson, and P.E. Parsons, "Access to Health Care—Part 3: Older Adults," *Vital and Health Statistics* (NCHS) 10, no. 198 (1997): Table 3. Based on data from the National Health Interview Survey.

* Figure does not meet standard of reliability or precision.
*— Figure does not meet standard of reliability or precision and quantity zero.
— Data not available.
1. Respondents who answered yes to any of the following questions were classified as having an unmet need: needed medical care or surgery, but did not get it; delayed medical care because of cost; and needed dental care, prescription medicine, eyeglasses, or mental health services, but could not get it.
2. Includes non-Hispanic persons of races other than white or black; persons of unknown insurance coverage; persons with unknown family structure; and persons with unknown income, unknown poverty status, and unknown health status.
3. MSA is metropolitan statistical area.

Table 4.24. Persons Who Did Not See a Physician in the Past Two Years: 1993–1996

(Percent)

	1993	1994	1995	1996
Total	11.8	11.7	11.4	11.7
SEX				
Males	16.1	16.0	15.5	15.1
Under 18 years	6.7	6.6	6.1	5.8
18–44 years	23.5	23.7	23.8	22.6
45–64 years	18.0	17.2	16.1	17.2
65 years and over	8.3	7.8	7.0	6.4
Females	7.6	7.6	7.5	6.7
Under 18 years	6.0	6.3	6.3	5.9
18–44 years	8.2	8.4	13.8	7.1
45–64 years	9.3	9.4	8.9	7.9
65 years and over	6.7	5.5	5.4	5.6
RACE				
White	11.8	11.6	11.4	10.7
Under 18 years	6.4	6.1	6.2	5.9
18–44 years	15.8	15.8	17.6	14.5
45–64 years	13.5	13.2	12.5	12.6
65 years and over	7.4	6.5	5.9	5.9
Black	10.3	10.2	9.9	9.1
Under 18 years	6.2	6.1	5.6	5.1
18–44 years	13.8	14.2	15.5	13.0
45–64 years	11.4	10.6	9.7	9.3
65 years and over	7.7	5.9	6.6	6.0
FAMILY INCOME				
Less than $10,000	11.1	11.1	10.3	9.8
Under 18 years	6.0	6.1	6.7	6.5
18–44 years	15.1	15.3	17.0	14.8
45–64 years	13.8	14.5	11.7	13.7
65 years and over	8.7	7.7	6.9	6.7
$10,000-19,999	14.0	14.0	13.3	13.1
Under 18 years	8.8	8.8	8.9	7.1
18–44 years	19.5	19.9	22.2	18.6
45–64 years	17.0	17.1	15.8	17.1
65 years and over	8.2	7.1	6.2	7.5
$20,000-34,999	12.9	12.6	12.7	12.4
Under 18 years	7.5	7.9	7.4	7.7
18–44 years	17.3	16.7	20.1	16.5
45–64 years	15.0	14.7	14.2	14.5
65 years and over	6.3	5.6	5.4	5.6
Over $35,000	9.9	9.9	9.9	9.0
Under 18 years	4.7	4.8	4.5	4.5
18–44 years	13.0	13.2	14.4	11.7
45–64 years	11.1	10.9	10.5	10.6
65 years and over	5.5	4.6	5.6	4.5

SOURCE: Compiled from National Health Interview Surveys from 1993 to 1996. National Center for Health Statistics.

Table 4.25. Health Insurance Coverage: 1993–1996

(Percent, except where noted.)

Length of Coverage	Total	Male	Female	Non-Hispanic White	Non-Hispanic Black	Hispanic [1]	Asian or Pacific Islander
All persons (number)	246 155 876	119 523 412	126 632 464	18 416 348	31 316 305	23 949 729	8 441 272
COVERED BY PRIVATE OR GOVERNMENT HEALTH INSURANCE							
Less than 36 months	29.0	30.7	27.4	24.8	37.4	49.8	32.3
No months	3.7	4.5	3.0	2.9	3.9	9.9	4.0
I to 35 months	25.3	26.2	24.5	21.9	33.5	39.9	28.3
1 to 6 months	2.4	2.8	2.0	1.8	3.2	5.2	3.9
7 to 12 months	3.1	3.3	3.0	2.5	4.3	6.5	3.2
13 to 18 months	2.4	2.5	2.3	2.1	3.0	3.9	3.5
19 to 24 months	4.2	4.3	4.2	3.4	6.2	7.9	3.9
25 to 30 months	4.6	4.8	4.5	3.9	6.4	7.6	4.9
31 to 35 months	8.6	8.6	8.5	8.2	10.3	8.9	8.8
36 months	71.0	69.3	72.6	75.2	62.6	50.2	67.7
1 to 36 months	96.3	95.5	97.0	97.1	96.1	90.1	96.0
COVERED BY PRIVATE HEALTH INSURANCE							
Less than 36 months	41.0	40.7	41.3	33.9	62.0	66.9	47.6
No months	13.5	13.1	14.0	8.8	26.1	33.0	19.0
I to 35 months	27.5	27.6	27.3	25.0	35.9	34.0	28.6
I to 6 months	4.2	4.1	4.2	3.0	8.1	6.6	5.7
7 to 12 months	4.1	4.0	4.1	3.4	6.2	6.9	3.9
13 to 18 months	2.4	2.5	2.4	2.2	3.0	3.3	2.8
19 to 24 months	4.2	4.2	4.2	3.8	5.9	5.4	3.0
25 to 30 months	4.2	4.4	4.0	3.9	4.9	4.9	5.4
31 to 35 months	8.5	8.5	8.4	8.8	7.8	6.8	7.9
36 months	59.0	59.3	58.7	66.1	38.0	33.1	52.4
1 to 36 months	86.5	86.9	86.0	91.2	73.9	67.0	81.0
COVERED BY MEDICAID							
Less than 36 months	94.2	95.5	93.0	97.1	83.3	87.8	88.5
No months	83.2	86.3	80.2	89.1	62.7	64.7	77.4
I to 35 months	11.1	9.2	12.8	8.0	20.6	23.1	11.2
I to 6 months	3.1	2.6	3.4	2.3	4.9	6.6	2.8
7 to 12 months	2.3	1.9	2.7	1.7	3.3	5.3	2.4
13 to 18 months	1.3	1.0	1.5	0.9	2.7	2.3	1.8
19 to 24 months	1.7	1.4	1.9	1.2	3.6	3.2	1.3
25 to 30 months	1.3	1.0	1.6	0.8	2.5	2.9	1.0
31 to 35 months	1.5	1.2	1.8	1.0	3.6	2.8	1.9
36 months	5.8	4.5	7.0	2.9	16.7	12.2	11.5
1 to 36 months	16.8	13.7	19.8	10.9	37.3	35.3	22.6

SOURCE: U.S. Bureau of the Census, Survey of Income and Program Participation, 1993 Panel, SIPP, Table 4.

1. Persons of Hispanic origin may be of any race.

Table 4.26. People without Health Insurance for the Entire Year

(Number in thousands, except where noted)

Characteristic	1998			1999			Change 1998–1999	
	Total	Uninsured		Total	Uninsured		Uninsured	
		Number	Percent		Number	Percent	Number	Percent
All persons	271 743	44 281	16.3	274 087	42 554	15.5	*-1 727	*-0.8
SEX								
Male	132 764	23 014	17.3	133 933	22 073	16.5	*-941	*-0.8
Female	138 979	21 266	15.3	140 154	20 481	14.6	*-785	*-0.7
RACE AND HISPANIC ORIGIN								
White	223 294	33 588	15.0	224 806	31 863	14.2	*-1 725	*-0.9
Non-Hispanic	193 074	22 890	11.9	193 633	21 363	11.0	*-1 527	*-0.8
Black	35 070	7 797	22.2	35 509	7 536	21.2	*-261	*-1.0
Asian and Pacific Islander	10 897	2 301	21.1	10 925	2 272	20.8	-29	-0.3
Hispanic origin [1]	31 689	11 196	35.3	32 804	10 951	33.4	*-245	*-2.0
AGE								
Under 18 years	72 022	11 073	15.4	72 325	10 023	13.9	*-1 050	*-1.5
18 to 24 years	25 967	7 776	30.0	26 532	7 688	29.0	-88	*-1.0
25 to 34 years	38 474	9 127	23.7	37 786	8 755	23.2	*-372	-0.5
35 to 44 years	44 744	7 708	17.2	44 805	7 377	16.5	*-331	*-0.8
45 to 64 years	58 141	8 239	14.2	60 018	8 288	13.8	49	-0.4
65 years and over	32 394	358	1.1	32 621	422	1.3	*64	*0.2
NATIVITY								
Native	245 295	35 273	14.4	245 708	33 089	13.5	*-2 184	*-0.9
Foreign-born	26 448	9 008	34.1	28 379	9 465	33.4	*457	-0.7
REGION								
Northeast	51 876	7 247	14.0	52 038	6 641	12.8	*-606	*-1.2
Midwest	63 295	7 685	12.1	63 595	7 075	11.1	*-610	*-1.0
South	94 887	17 209	18.1	95 928	16 887	17.6	-322	*-0.5
West	61 684	12 140	19.7	62 526	11 950	19.1	-190	*-0.6
HOUSEHOLD INCOME								
Less than $25,000	68 422	17 229	25.2	64 628	15 577	24.1	*-1 652	*-1.1
$25,000–$49,999	78 973	14 807	18.8	77 119	13 996	18.2	*-811	*-0.6
$50,000–$74,999	57 324	6 703	11.7	56 873	6 706	11.8	3	0.1
$75,000 or more	67 023	5 542	8.3	75 467	6 275	8.3	*733	—
EDUCATION (AGE 18 YEARS AND OLDER)								
No high school diploma	34 811	9 294	26.7	34 087	9 111	26.7	-183	—
High school graduate only	66 054	12 094	18.3	66 141	11 619	17.6	*-475	*-0.7
Some college, no degree	39 087	6 211	15.9	39 940	6 051	15.2	-160	*-0.7
Associate degree	14 114	1 730	12.3	14 715	1 902	12.9	*172	0.7
Bachelor's degree or higher	45 655	3 880	8.5	46 880	3 848	8.2	-32	-0.3
WORK EXPERIENCE (AGE 18 TO 64 YEARS)								
Worked during year	137 003	24 655	18.0	139 218	24 187	17.4	-468	*-0.6
Worked full time	113 638	19 244	16.9	115 973	18 984	16.4	-260	*-0.6
Worked part time	23 365	5 411	23.2	23 245	5 204	22.4	-207	-0.8
Did not work	30 323	8 194	27.0	29 923	7 921	26.5	-273	-0.6

SOURCE: R.J. Mills, "Health Insurance Coverage: 1999," Current Population Reports, P60–211 (September 2000): Table B.

* Statistically significant at the 90% level.
— Represents zero or rounds to zero.
1. Hispanics may be of any race.

Table 4.27. Percent of People without Health Insurance Coverage

(Throughout the year by state: 1996 to 1998)

Area	1998	1997	1996	3-year average 1996–1998	2-year moving average 1997–1998	2-year moving average 1996–1997	Difference in 2-year moving averages (1997/98)–(1996/97)
United States	16.3	16.1	15.6	16.0	16.2	15.9	*0.3
STATE							
Alabama	17.0	15.5	12.9	15.1	16.2	14.2	*2.0
Alaska	17.3	18.1	13.5	16.3	17.7	15.8	*1.9
Arizona	24.2	24.5	24.1	24.3	24.3	24.3	NC
Arkansas	18.7	24.4	21.7	21.6	21.5	23.1	*-1.5
California	22.1	21.5	20.1	21.2	21.8	20.8	*1.0
Colorado	15.1	15.1	16.6	15.6	15.1	15.9	-0.8
Connecticut	12.6	12.0	11.0	11.8	12.3	11.5	0.8
Delaware	14.7	13.1	13.4	13.7	13.9	13.3	0.6
Florida	17.5	19.6	18.9	18.7	18.5	19.3	*-0.7
Georgia	17.5	17.6	17.8	17.6	17.5	17.7	-0.2
Hawaii	10.0	7.5	8.6	8.7	8.8	8.1	0.7
Idaho	17.7	17.7	16.5	17.3	17.7	17.1	0.6
Illinois	15.0	12.4	11.3	12.9	13.7	11.9	*1.8
Indiana	14.4	11.4	10.6	12.1	12.9	11.0	*1.9
Iowa	9.3	12.0	11.6	11.0	10.7	11.8	*-1.1
Kansas	10.3	11.7	11.4	11.1	11.0	11.6	-0.5
Kentucky	14.1	15.0	15.4	14.8	14.6	15.2	-0.6
Louisiana	19.0	19.5	20.9	19.8	19.2	20.2	-1.0
Maine	12.7	14.9	12.1	13.2	13.8	13.5	0.3
Maryland	16.6	13.4	11.4	13.8	15.0	12.4	*2.6
Massachusetts	10.3	12.6	12.4	11.8	11.4	12.5	*-1.1
Michigan	13.2	11.6	8.9	11.2	12.4	10.3	*2.2
Minnesota	9.3	9.2	10.2	9.6	9.2	9.7	-0.5
Mississippi	20.0	20.1	18.5	19.6	20.1	19.3	0.8
Missouri	10.5	12.6	13.2	12.1	11.6	12.9	*-1.3
Montana	19.6	19.5	13.6	17.6	19.5	16.6	*3.0
Nebraska	9.0	10.8	11.4	10.4	9.9	11.1	*-1.2
Nevada	21.2	17.5	15.6	18.1	19.3	16.6	*2.8
New Hampshire	11.3	11.8	9.5	10.9	11.5	10.7	0.9
New Jersey	16.4	16.5	16.7	16.5	16.5	16.6	-0.1
New Mexico	21.1	22.6	22.3	22.0	21.9	22.5	-0.6
New York	17.3	17.5	17.0	17.2	17.4	17.3	0.1
North Carolina	15.0	15.5	16.0	15.5	15.2	15.8	-0.5
North Dakota	14.2	15.2	9.8	13.1	14.7	12.5	*2.2
Ohio	10.4	11.5	11.5	11.1	11.0	11.5	*-0.5
Oklahoma	18.3	17.8	17.0	17.7	18.1	17.4	0.7
Oregon	14.3	13.3	15.3	14.3	13.8	14.3	-0.5
Pennsylvania	10.5	10.1	9.5	10.0	10.3	9.8	*0.5
Rhode Island	10.0	10.2	9.9	10.0	10.1	10.1	NC
South Carolina	15.4	16.8	17.1	16.4	16.1	17.0	-0.8
South Dakota	14.3	11.8	9.5	11.9	13.1	10.7	*2.4
Tennessee	13.0	13.6	15.2	13.9	13.3	14.4	*-1.1
Texas	24.5	24.5	24.3	24.4	24.5	24.4	0.1
Utah	13.9	13.4	12.0	13.1	13.7	12.7	*1.0
Vermont	9.9	9.5	11.1	10.1	9.6	10.3	-0.7
Virginia	14.1	12.6	12.5	13.1	13.4	12.6	0.8
Washington	12.3	11.4	13.5	12.4	11.8	12.4	-0.6
West Virginia	17.2	17.2	14.9	16.5	17.2	16.1	*1.2
Wisconsin	11.8	8.0	8.4	9.4	9.9	8.2	*1.7
Wyoming	16.9	15.5	13.5	15.3	16.2	14.5	*1.7
OTHER							
District of Columbia	17.0	16.2	14.8	16.0	16.6	15.5	1.1
Median	14.6	14.3	13.5	13.9	14.3	13.9	0.4
Low	24.5	24.5	24.3	24.4	24.5	24.4	3.0
Average	9.0	7.5	8.4	8.7	8.8	8.1	-1.5

SOURCE: U.S. Census Bureau, Current Population Surveys, March 1997, 1998, and 1999.

*Statistically significant at the 90% level.
NC is no change

Table 4.28. Insurance Coverage

(Percent of population, except where noted)

Characteristic	Private insurance											
	Under 65 years of age						65 years of age and over [1]					
	1984	1989	1994 [2]	1995	1996	1997 [2,3]	1984	1989	1994 [2]	1995	1996	1997 [2,3]
Total (in millions) [4]	157.5	162.7	160.7	165.0	165.9	165.8	19.4	22.4	24.0	23.5	22.9	22.3
Total, age adjusted [4]	76.6	75.7	69.9	71.2	71.1	70.4	73.5	76.6	77.5	74.9	72.0	69.6
Total, crude [4]	76.8	75.9	70.3	71.6	71.4	70.7	73.3	76.5	77.3	74.8	72.0	69.5
AGE												
Under 18 years	72.6	71.8	63.8	65.7	66.4	66.1						
Under 6 years	68.1	67.9	58.3	60.1	61.1	61.3						
6–17 years	74.9	74.0	66.8	68.7	69.1	68.5						
18–44 years	76.5	75.5	69.8	71.2	70.6	69.4						
18–24 years	67.4	64.5	58.3	61.2	60.4	59.3						
25–34 years	77.4	75.9	69.4	70.3	69.5	68.1						
35–44 years	83.9	82.7	77.1	78.0	77.5	76.4						
45–64 years	83.3	82.5	80.3	80.4	79.5	79.1						
45–54 years	83.3	83.4	81.3	81.1	80.4	80.4						
55–64 years	83.3	81.6	78.8	79.3	78.1	76.9						
65–74 years							76.5	78.2	78.4	75.3	72.4	69.9
75 years and over							68.1	73.9	75.8	74.2	71.3	69.1
75–84 years							70.8	75.9	77.9	76.0	73.3	70.2
85 years and over							56.8	65.5	67.9	67.8	63.9	64.7
SEX [5]												
Male	77.1	76.0	70.4	71.6	71.4	70.7	74.3	77.5	78.9	76.5	73.6	72.0
Female	76.0	75.4	69.5	70.8	70.8	70.1	72.9	76.2	76.5	73.9	71.0	67.8
RACE [5]												
White	79.7	79.0	73.5	74.4	74.2	74.1	76.8	80.3	81.2	78.6	75.3	72.9
Black	58.3	57.8	51.5	54.2	54.9	54.9	42.3	43.0	44.7	41.9	44.0	43.5
Asian or Pacific Islander	69.8	71.1	67.3	68.0	67.8	68.0	—	—	—	—	—	—
HISPANIC ORIGIN AND RACE [5]												
All Hispanic	56.3	52.6	48.6	47.3	47.5	47.3	40.5	44.6	51.2	40.9	38.6	31.9
Mexican	54.3	48.0	45.7	43.9	43.8	43.3	41.4	36.6	44.6	33.0	35.6	32.4
Puerto Rican	48.8	45.9	48.3	47.9	50.7	47.2	—	—	—	—	—	—
Cuban	71.7	69.0	63.9	62.4	65.4	70.5	—	—	—	—	—	—
Other Hispanic	61.6	61.9	52.3	52.2	52.6	50.7	—	—	—	—	—	—
White, non-Hispanic	82.3	82.4	77.3	78.6	78.5	77.9	77.9	81.5	82.6	80.7	77.2	75.0
Black, non-Hispanic	58.5	57.9	51.9	54.6	55.4	55.1	42.0	43.1	45.2	41.7	44.8	43.7
AGE AND PERCENT OF POVERTY LEVEL												
All ages [5]												
Below 100 percent	32.4	26.7	21.3	21.9	20.0	22.7	43.0	45.3	40.1	36.8	32.7	31.0
100–149 percent	62.4	54.9	46.8	47.8	47.1	42.1	67.3	66.7	68.0	67.4	58.8	53.2
150–199 percent	77.7	71.3	65.7	66.5	67.9	64.0	78.6	81.1	81.3	77.4	75.0	69.0
200 percent or more	91.7	91.2	88.9	89.3	89.5	87.7	85.7	86.2	88.9	86.6	84.0	81.4
Under 18 years												
Below 100 percent	28.7	22.3	14.9	16.8	16.1	17.4						
100–149 percent	66.2	59.6	47.8	48.5	49.5	42.5						
150–199 percent	80.9	75.9	69.3	68.5	73.0	66.8						
200 percent or more	92.3	92.7	89.7	90.4	90.7	88.9						
GEOGRAPHIC REGION												
Northeast	80.1	81.8	74.8	75.1	74.9	74.0	76.8	76.7	78.3	76.0	72.9	73.0
Midwest	80.4	81.4	77.2	77.2	78.4	76.9	79.6	82.3	84.6	82.5	80.8	78.5
South	74.0	71.1	65.0	66.7	65.9	66.8	68.0	73.5	71.2	71.6	67.2	66.3
West	71.8	71.3	65.2	67.9	67.1	65.3	70.8	75.1	78.2	69.3	69.0	59.5
LOCATION OF RESIDENCE [5]												
Within MSA [6]	77.2	76.3	70.4	72.1	72.5	71.0	74.5	77.2	78.0	75.1	72.2	68.4
Outside MSA [6]	75.1	73.6	68.1	67.7	65.8	68.0	71.8	75.1	76.0	74.4	71.3	73.6

See footnotes at end of table.

Table 4.28. Insurance Coverage—*Continued*

(Percent of population, except where noted)

Characteristic	Private insurance obtained through workplace [7]											
	Under 65 years of age						65 years of age and over [1]					
	1984	1989	1994 [2]	1995	1996	1997 [2,3]	1984	1989	1994 [2]	1995	1996	1997 [2,3]
Total (in millions) [4]	141.8	146.3	146.7	151.4	151.4	152.5	10.2	11.2	12.5	12.5	12.1	12.0
Total, age adjusted [4]	68.9	68.1	63.8	65.4	64.8	64.7	39.1	38.8	41.0	40.1	38.6	38.2
Total, crude [4]	69.1	68.3	64.2	65.7	65.1	65.0	38.8	38.4	40.4	39.6	38.1	37.5
AGE												
Under 18 years	66.5	65.8	59.0	60.9	61.1	61.3						
Under 6 years	62.1	62.3	53.9	55.6	56.5	57.3						
6–17 years	68.7	67.7	61.8	63.7	63.4	63.4						
18–44 years	69.6	68.4	63.9	65.6	64.7	64.4						
18–24 years	58.7	55.3	50.7	53.9	52.3	53.8						
25–34 years	71.2	69.5	64.1	65.3	64.4	63.6						
35–44 years	77.4	76.2	71.6	72.9	72.0	71.2						
45–64 years	71.8	71.6	71.8	72.4	71.4	70.8						
45–54 years	74.6	74.4	74.6	74.9	74.0	73.6						
55–64 years	69.0	68.3	67.9	68.6	67.5	66.6						
65–74 years							45.1	43.7	45.6	43.3	41.5	42.0
75 years and over							28.6	30.2	33.0	34.3	33.3	31.6
75–84 years							30.8	32.0	35.0	36.1	35.5	33.2
85 years and over							18.9	22.8	25.1	27.5	25.3	25.6
SEX [5]												
Male	69.7	68.6	64.3	65.9	65.2	65.0	44.2	43.4	45.1	44.3	42.7	42.9
Female	68.1	67.6	63.4	64.8	64.4	64.4	35.7	35.6	38.1	37.0	35.5	34.9
RACE [5]												
White	71.9	71.1	67.0	68.4	67.6	67.9	40.9	40.3	42.7	41.6	39.8	39.1
Black	52.4	52.9	48.8	50.4	51.8	52.6	24.0	24.9	26.5	26.4	30.1	32.1
Asian or Pacific Islander	63.6	60.2	57.4	59.8	59.3	60.4	—	—	—	—	—	—
HISPANIC ORIGIN AND RACE [5]												
All Hispanic	52.3	48.0	44.5	44.0	43.8	44.0	25.4	24.3	22.1	20.1	19.4	19.0
Mexican	51.1	45.2	43.7	41.9	40.9	41.2	25.5	22.4	23.1	17.4	18.7	19.0
Puerto Rican	46.4	42.6	45.2	44.7	48.1	44.6	—	—	—	—	—	—
Cuban	57.7	55.8	46.5	53.1	54.4	56.0	—	—	—	—	—	—
Other Hispanic	57.4	55.4	46.2	47.1	47.6	47.1	—	—	—	—	—	—
White, non-Hispanic	74.0	74.1	70.4	72.1	71.5	71.4	41.4	40.9	43.8	42.9	40.8	40.2
Black, non-Hispanic	52.6	53.0	49.2	50.9	52.2	52.8	23.8	24.9	26.8	26.1	30.7	32.1
AGE AND PERCENT OF POVERTY LEVEL												
All ages [5]												
Below 100 percent	23.7	19.4	16.1	17.0	15.5	18.9	13.4	11.5	10.6	11.3	10.2	7.3
100–149 percent	51.9	45.8	40.9	41.9	40.8	37.0	27.8	22.4	25.2	25.3	22.3	17.2
150–199 percent	69.5	62.9	59.0	60.4	60.9	58.7	41.4	39.8	37.3	39.9	37.3	32.9
200 percent or more	85.2	84.2	83.0	83.7	83.2	82.0	52.8	51.5	54.0	51.7	49.9	49.4
Under 18 years												
Below 100 percent	23.2	17.5	12.4	13.4	13.4	15.4						
100–149 percent	58.3	52.5	43.2	43.6	43.7	38.5						
150–199 percent	75.8	70.1	64.0	63.0	67.4	63.1						
200 percent or more	86.9	86.7	84.5	85.5	84.6	83.7						
GEOGRAPHIC REGION												
Northeast	73.8	74.9	69.5	69.5	68.7	69.4	43.9	44.2	45.2	45.3	42.5	43.8
Midwest	71.9	73.3	71.0	71.1	72.3	71.1	40.6	41.4	43.6	46.0	42.3	41.9
South	65.9	63.3	59.1	61.7	60.4	61.0	35.3	33.5	36.8	35.1	34.7	34.2
West	64.5	63.9	58.1	60.7	59.6	58.9	38.2	38.5	40.1	34.9	36.2	34.4
LOCATION OF RESIDENCE [5]												
Within MSA [6]	70.6	69.5	64.8	66.6	66.5	65.6	42.3	41.6	42.6	42.0	40.5	39.8
Outside MSA [6]	65.1	63.4	60.4	60.5	58.6	61.4	33.7	31.3	36.5	33.5	32.2	33.0

See footnotes at end of table.

Table 4.28. Insurance Coverage—*Continued*
(Percent of population, except where noted)

Characteristic	Medicaid or other public assistance [8]											
	Under 65 years of age						65 years of age and over [1]					
	1984	1989	1994 [2]	1995	1996	1997 [2,3]	1984	1989	1994 [2]	1995	1996	1997 [2,3]
Total (in millions) [4]	14.0	15.4	24.1	25.3	25.0	22.9	1.8	2.0	2.5	2.9	2.7	2.5
Total, age adjusted [4]	7.3	7.8	11.5	12.0	11.7	10.7	6.9	7.0	7.8	9.0	8.3	7.8
Total, crude [4]	6.8	7.2	10.6	11.0	10.8	9.7	7.0	7.0	7.9	9.2	8.5	7.9
AGE												
Under 18 years	11.9	12.6	20.0	20.6	20.1	18.4						
Under 6 years	15.5	15.7	27.2	28.3	27.4	24.7						
6–17 years	10.1	10.9	16.2	16.6	16.4	15.2						
18–44 years	5.1	5.2	7.3	7.4	7.3	6.6						
18–24 years	6.4	6.8	9.6	9.7	9.2	8.8						
25–34 years	5.3	5.2	7.7	7.7	7.5	6.8						
35–44 years	3.5	4.0	5.4	5.6	6.0	5.2						
45–64 years	3.4	4.3	4.5	5.3	5.2	4.6						
45–54 years	3.2	3.8	3.8	4.9	4.8	4.0						
55–64 years	3.6	4.9	5.5	6.0	5.7	5.6						
65–74 years							6.0	6.3	6.8	8.3	7.5	7.5
75 years and over							8.5	8.2	9.6	10.4	9.9	8.4
75–84 years							7.7	7.9	8.4	9.5	9.0	7.9
85 years and over							11.7	9.7	14.2	13.7	13.0	10.2
SEX [5]												
Male	6.1	6.5	9.8	10.3	10.1	9.4	4.5	5.0	4.7	5.6	5.5	5.2
Female	8.5	9.1	13.2	13.6	13.3	11.9	8.6	8.4	10.0	11.5	10.4	9.7
RACE [5]												
White	5.0	5.6	8.7	9.4	9.3	8.2	5.0	5.4	6.0	6.9	6.6	6.4
Black	20.5	19.3	27.0	27.0	24.5	22.7	24.9	20.4	21.7	26.8	21.8	19.3
Asian or Pacific Islander	10.1	11.8	10.2	11.4	12.4	10.3	—	—	—	—	—	—
HISPANIC ORIGIN AND RACE [5]												
All Hispanic	13.1	13.5	19.6	21.2	20.1	17.8	24.9	25.6	26.5	31.1	28.9	27.6
Mexican	11.8	12.3	18.3	20.1	19.0	17.1						
Puerto Rican	31.1	28.0	36.2	32.7	33.8	30.9						
Cuban	5.0	8.0	9.8	15.3	13.9	9.2	—	—	—	—	—	—
Other Hispanic	8.0	11.2	16.2	18.4	16.3	15.6	—	—	—	—	—	—
White, non-Hispanic	4.0	4.6	7.1	7.5	7.5	6.8	4.4	4.7	5.1	5.6	5.4	5.4
Black, non-Hispanic	20.8	19.4	27.0	26.7	24.2	22.5	25.2	20.4	21.2	27.0	21.7	19.0
AGE AND PERCENT OF POVERTY LEVEL												
All ages [5]												
Below 100 percent	32.1	37.0	45.0	46.9	46.8	41.6	28.0	29.0	37.4	40.6	39.9	41.0
100–149 percent	7.7	11.2	16.0	18.4	17.2	19.1	6.9	9.2	10.8	13.3	12.5	14.6
150–199 percent	3.3	5.1	5.9	7.7	7.7	8.0	3.3	4.7	3.8	5.2	4.6	5.1
200 percent or more	0.6	1.1	1.4	1.6	1.6	1.9	1.8	2.3	1.8	1.8	1.9	2.5
Under 18 years												
Below 100 percent	43.1	47.8	63.6	65.6	65.9	59.9						
100–149 percent	9.0	12.3	22.9	26.3	24.8	30.2						
150–199 percent	4.4	6.1	8.6	11.7	10.8	12.2						
200 percent or more	0.8	1.6	2.2	2.7	2.6	2.9						
GEOGRAPHIC REGION												
Northeast	9.4	7.4	12.0	12.5	12.3	12.4	5.3	5.4	7.3	8.9	7.3	6.4
Midwest	7.9	8.2	10.4	11.0	9.4	9.2	4.2	3.6	3.7	5.6	5.1	5.0
South	5.5	7.0	11.3	11.6	12.0	9.8	9.5	9.1	10.3	10.8	9.9	9.7
West	7.5	9.1	12.6	13.2	13.4	12.5	7.9	9.3	9.4	10.8	10.8	9.9
LOCATION OF RESIDENCE [5]												
Within MSA [6]	7.8	7.7	11.7	11.8	11.1	10.6	6.2	6.4	7.3	8.4	7.7	7.4
Outside MSA [6]	6.4	8.3	11.1	12.8	13.9	11.0	8.1	8.4	9.2	11.1	10.4	9.2

See footnotes at end of table.

Table 4.28. Insurance Coverage—*Continued*

(Percent of population, except where noted)

Characteristic	Not covered [9]						Medicare only [10]					
	Under 65 years of age						65 years of age and over					
	1984	1989	1994 [2]	1995	1996	1997 [2,3]	1984	1989	1994 [2]	1995	1996	1997 [2,3]
Total (in millions) [4]	29.8	33.4	40.4	37.4	38.9	41.0	4.7	4.5	4.1	4.6	5.7	6.7
Total, age adjusted [4]	14.2	15.2	17.1	15.6	16.1	16.8	17.7	15.3	13.1	14.7	18.1	20.7
Total, crude [4]	14.5	15.6	17.7	16.2	16.7	17.5	17.9	15.4	13.2	14.8	18.1	20.8
AGE												
Under 18 years	13.9	14.7	15.3	13.6	13.4	14.0						
Under 6 years	14.9	15.1	13.7	11.9	11.9	12.5						
6–17 years	13.4	14.5	16.2	14.5	14.1	14.7						
18–44 years	17.1	18.4	21.9	20.5	21.2	22.4						
18–24 years	25.0	27.1	31.1	28.2	29.6	30.1						
25–34 years	16.2	18.3	22.1	21.3	22.5	23.8						
35–44 years	11.2	12.3	16.0	15.2	15.2	16.7						
45–64 years	9.6	10.5	12.0	11.0	12.1	12.4						
45–54 years	10.5	11.0	12.6	11.7	12.5	12.8						
55–64 years	8.7	10.0	11.2	10.0	11.6	11.8						
65–74 years							15.2	13.8	12.3	14.4	18.0	20.3
75 years and over							22.3	17.8	14.5	15.2	18.2	21.5
75–84 years							20.6	16.2	13.3	14.1	16.8	20.5
85 years and over							29.8	24.9	19.1	19.3	23.4	25.2
SEX[5]												
Male	14.8	16.1	18.1	16.7	17.2	17.8	17.4	14.6	12.9	14.4	17.1	19.6
Female	13.6	14.3	16.1	14.6	15.1	15.9	18.1	15.6	13.3	14.9	18.7	21.5
RACE[5]												
White	13.3	14.1	16.4	15.0	15.4	15.8	16.5	13.4	11.6	13.4	16.9	19.2
Black	19.5	21.0	19.5	17.9	19.0	19.3	30.7	34.5	28.7	28.6	30.1	33.9
Asian or Pacific Islander	17.8	18.2	19.9	17.8	18.6	18.8	—	—	—	—	—	—
HISPANIC ORIGIN AND RACE[5]												
All Hispanic	29.0	32.4	31.4	30.8	31.6	33.2	28.5	21.6	18.7	24.5	29.0	34.9
Mexican	33.1	38.6	35.7	35.4	36.7	38.1						
Puerto Rican	17.9	23.3	15.4	17.8	14.4	18.5	—	—	—	—	—	—
Cuban	21.6	21.8	26.1	21.6	17.6	19.8	—	—	—	—	—	—
Other Hispanic	27.1	24.8	30.2	29.0	29.8	31.8	—	—	—	—	—	—
White, non-Hispanic	11.6	11.7	14.2	12.7	12.9	13.3	16.1	13.1	11.3	12.8	16.3	18.3
Black, non-Hispanic	19.2	20.8	19.1	17.8	18.9	19.3	30.8	34.5	28.8	28.7	29.3	34.0
AGE AND PERCENT OF POVERTY LEVEL												
All ages[5]												
Below 100 percent	34.0	35.2	32.7	30.9	32.7	32.8	27.5	26.0	23.0	22.1	25.6	26.9
100–149 percent	26.4	30.6	34.0	31.2	32.8	34.8	22.5	21.1	19.0	18.3	26.6	28.6
150–199 percent	16.7	21.0	24.9	22.8	22.5	25.1	16.2	13.5	12.8	16.2	19.6	23.1
200 percent or more	5.6	6.5	8.4	7.8	7.4	8.5	11.0	10.4	7.8	9.9	12.4	15.0
Under 18 years												
Below 100 percent	28.9	31.6	23.3	20.6	21.3	22.4						
100–149 percent	22.8	26.1	27.7	25.5	25.2	26.1						
150–199 percent	12.7	15.8	19.0	17.7	16.1	19.7						
200 percent or more	4.2	4.4	6.8	6.0	5.3	6.1						
GEOGRAPHIC REGION												
Northeast	9.8	10.5	13.3	12.7	13.2	12.8	17.1	16.8	14.0	15.4	20.3	19.5
Midwest	10.9	10.2	11.9	11.8	11.9	12.6	15.2	13.4	10.7	10.9	12.8	15.2
South	17.4	19.4	20.9	19.1	19.7	20.3	19.8	16.3	16.0	15.8	19.7	21.3
West	17.6	18.1	20.2	17.3	18.1	19.8	18.4	13.8	10.3	17.3	18.6	28.5
LOCATION OF RESIDENCE[5]												
Within MSA [6]	13.2	14.7	16.6	14.9	15.3	16.2	17.6	15.3	12.9	14.9	18.7	22.2
Outside MSA [6]	16.3	16.7	18.8	18.4	19.2	19.4	17.9	15.2	13.9	14.1	15.9	15.6

SOURCE: E. Kramarow, H. Lentzner, R. Rooks, J. Weeks, and S. Saydah, *Health and Aging Chartbook. Health, United States, 1999.* (Hyattsville, Md.: National Center for Health Statistics. 1999): Tables 129 and 130. Data are from the National Health Interview Survey.

* Relative standard error greater than 30 percent
— Data not available.
1. Almost all persons 65 years of age and over are covered by Medicare also. In 1997, 92 percent of older persons with private insurance also had Medicare.
2. The questionnaire changed compared to that used in previous years. See Appendix II of *Health, United States, 1999,* Health Insurance Coverage.
3. Preliminary data.
4. Includes all other races not shown separately and unknown poverty level.
5. Age adjusted. See Appendix II of *Health, United States, 1999.*
6. Metropolitan statistical area.
7. Private insurance originally obtained through a present or former employer or union.
8. Includes public assistance through 1996. In 1997 includes state-sponsored health plans. In 1997 the age-adjusted percent of the population 65 years of age and over covered by Medicaid was 7.4 percent, and 0.4 percent were covered by state-sponsored health plans.
9. Includes persons not covered by private insurance, Medicaid or other public assistance (through 1996), state-sponsored or other government-sponsored health plans (1997), Medicare, or military plans. Estimates of the percentage of persons lacking health care coverage based on the National Health Interview Survey (NHIS) are slightly higher than those based on the March Current Population Survey (CPS) (table 146). See Appendix I of *Health, United States, 1999,* Health Insurance Coverage.
10. Persons coverd by Medicaid but not covered by private health insurance, Medicaid, public assistance (through 1996), state-sponsored or other government-sponsored health plans (1997), or military plans. See Appendix II of *Health, United States, 1999,* Health Insurance Coverage.

NOTE: Data are based on household interviews of a sample of the civilian noninstitutionalized population. Percents do not add to 100 because the percent with other types of health insurance (for example, Medicare, military) is not shown, and because persons with both private insurance and Medicaid appear in both columns. Persons 65 years of age and over without health insurance (1.1 percent in 1997) is not shown.

Table 4.29. Infections Following Surgery: October 1986–July 1996

(Per 100 operative procedures)

Operative procedure	Number of risk factors for wound infections							
	None		One		Two		Three	
	Number	Rate	Number	Rate	Number	Rate	Number	Rate
HEART AND CHEST								
Cardiac surgery	848	0.7	9 829	1.8	2 933	3.6		
CABG- chest and leg [1]	830	0.8	65 595	3.3	14 178	5.6	28	17.9
CABG- chest only [2]	4 343	3.7						
Other cardiovascular	4 890	0.7			1 275	1.4		
Other respiratory system	1 245	3.6						
Thoracic surgery	1 197	0.5	3 028	1.6	1 060	3.5		
DIGESTIVE TRACT								
Appendectomy	4 472	1.3	4 177	3.1	1 664	6.2		
Liver/ pancreas surgery	357	2.8	689	6.1	343	10.2		
Cholecystectomy [3]	16 477	0.5	5 893	0.8	5 554	2.2	2 010	4.0
Colon surgery	5 606	4.3	9 352	6.5	4 171	10.5	518	13.9
Gastric surgery	1 469	2.8	2 461	5.6	1 067	12.4		
Other digestive tract surgery	1 068	2.1	1 555	4.0	489	9.0		
Small bowel surgery	758	5.3	1 519	7.7	1 005	10.6		
Laparotomy	4 030	1.9	4 151	3.3	1 966	6.9	283	9.9
GENITOURINARY								
Nephrectomy	1 785	1.7						
Other genitourinary	12 185	0.5	4 747	1.3	1 025	4.3		
Prostatectomy	1 524	1.0	1 134	2.6	211	5.2		
HEAD AND NECK								
Head and neck surgery	804	2.0	816	4.2	369	12.7		
Other ENT surgery	1 883	0.3	945	0.8	181	5.0		
Herniorrhaphy	7 307	0.9	3 941	2.1	743	3.1		
Mastectomy	9 486	1.7			665	5.0		
NERVOUS SYSTEM								
Craniotomy	2 029	1.0	5 992	1.6				
Other nervous system surgery	2 140	1.5						
Ventricular shunt	1 289	3.6	2 918	4.8				
OBSTETRIC								
Cesarean section	45 441	3.4	16 610	4.4	1 221	7.2		
Abdominal hysterectomy	16 035	1.6	8 445	2.8	1 633	6.1		
Other obstetric surgery	455	0.4						
Vaginal hysterectomy	6 497	1.0	3 235	1.7				
MUSCULOSKELETAL								
Limb amputation	6 260	4.6						
Spinal fusion	5 995	1.3	3 625	3.1	994	7.8		
Open reduction of fracture	8 309	0.8	11 558	1.4	2 615	2.9		
Hip prosthesis	4 504	0.7	10 873	1.7				
Knee prosthesis	5 601	0.9	7 510	1.2	2 314	1.8		
Other joint prosthesis	836	0.7						
Laminectomy	9 702	0.7	6 686	1.4	1 919	2.4		
Other musculoskeletal	18 176	0.7			1 598	2.1		
ENDOCRINE/EYE								
Other hematologic/ lymphatic surgery	583	0.9	526	2.8				
Other endocrine surgery	1 423	0.1	988	1.1				
Other eye surgery	1 417	0.1						
Other integumentary system surgery	5 652	1.4			1 113	2.5		
ORGAN TRANSPLANT/GRAFTS								
Splenectomy	777	2.3			250	5.6		
Organ transplant	1 449	4.9			958	9.9	202	21.3
Vascular surgery	3 819	1.3	24 031	2.0	9 649	5.2	283	8.8
Skin graft	924	1.2	1 521	3.0	785	5.0	164	9.2

SOURCE: National Nosocomial Infections Surveillance (NNIS) System Report, Data Summary for October 1986–April 1998, issued June 1998 Hospital Infections Program, National Center for Infectious Diseases, Centers for Disease Control and Prevention, Public Health Service, U.S. Department of Health and Human Services, Atlanta, Ga.: Table 7.

1. Coronary artery bypass graft with both chest and leg (or other donor site) incisions.
2. Coronary artery bypass graft with chest incision only (example: internal mammary artery graft).
3. Risk categories are defined as
0 if the risk index = 0;
1 if the risk index = 1 and SCOPE (use of laparoscope) = Yes;
2 if the risk index = 1 and SCOPE = No or risk index = 2,3 and SCOPE = Yes;
3 if the risk index = 2,3 and SCOPE = No.
See Appendix C of NNIS report for further discussion of CHOL risk index.

Table 4.30. Hospital Infections Following Surgery for Specific Procedures: October 1986–July 1996

(Infections per 100 operative procedures)

Operative procedure category	Risk index category	Number of hospitals	Pooled mean rate	Percentile				
				10%	25%	50% (median)	75%	90%
HEART AND CHEST								
Cardiac surgery	1	57	1.8	0.0	0.0	1.3	2.4	3.1
Cardiac surgery	2, 3	38	3.6	0.0	1.3	2.9	5.4	8.0
CABG-chest and leg [1]	1	104	3.3	1.2	1.9	3.1	4.2	6.3
CABG-chest and leg [1]	2	84	5.6	0.0	2.9	4.9	8.0	10.7
CABG-chest only [2]	0, 1, 2, 3	42	3.7	0.0	0.0	0.0	3.8	4.9
Other cardiovascular	0, 1	28	0.7	0.0	0.0	0.0	0.9	2.2
DIGESTIVE TRACT								
Thoracic surgery	1	33	1.6	0.0	0.0	0.0	2.2	3.4
Appendectomy	0	34	1.3	0.0	0.0	0.7	2.0	3.6
Appendectomy	1	38	3.1	0.0	0.0	2.5	5.3	5.9
Appendectomy	2, 3	25	6.2	0.0	1.9	5.0	8.0	9.5
Cholecystectomy [3]	0	64	0.5	0.0	0.0	0.0	0.8	1.3
Cholecystectomy [3]	1	47	0.8	0.0	0.0	0.5	1.3	1.9
Cholecystectomy [3]	2	53	2.2	0.0	0.0	2.1	4.3	5.6
Cholecystectomy [3]	3	36	4.0	0.0	1.2	2.9	6.7	9.1
Colon surgery	0	55	4.3	0.0	1.8	3.4	6.0	9.0
Colon surgery	1	66	6.5	0.0	3.4	5.6	8.1	10.1
Colon surgery	2	45	10.5	4.5	6.6	9.3	16.2	17.5
Gastric surgery	0	23	2.8	0.0	0.0	1.8	5.2	7.0
Gastric surgery	1	29	5.6	1.5	2.3	4.9	8.4	10.2
Small bowel surgery	1	23	7.7	3.5	4.8	7.3	13.2	15.9
Laparotomy	0	31	1.9	0.0	0.0	1.5	2.5	4.4
Laparotomy	1	35	3.3	0.0	1.4	3.4	5.1	7.8
Laparotomy	2	23	6.9	0.3	2.3	6.3	9.3	14.5
GENITOURINARY								
Nephrectomy	0, 1, 2, 3	22	1.7	0.0	0.0	1.1	2.2	4.6
Other genitourinary	0	33	0.5	0.0	0.0	0.3	1.1	2.5
Other genitourinary	1	28	1.3	0.0	0.0	0.5	2.0	3.3
Prostatectomy	0	23	1.0	0.0	0.0	0.0	1.7	3.6
HEAD AND NECK								
Herniorrhaphy	0	36	0.9	0.0	0.0	0.5	1.5	2.4
Herniorrhaphy	1	37	2.1	0.0	0.0	1.1	3.1	5.1
Mastectomy	0, 1	45	1.7	0.0	0.0	1.3	2.0	4.3
NERVOUS SYSTEM								
Craniotomy	0	23	1.0	0.0	0.0	1.2	2.4	3.9
Craniotomy	1, 2, 3	41	1.6	0.0	0.0	1.0	2.0	3.4
Ventricular shunt	1, 2, 3	27	4.8	0.0	0.0	3.6	4.9	7.5
OBSTETRIC								
Cesarean section	0	80	3.4	0.4	1.3	2.8	5.0	7.8
Cesarean section	1	75	4.4	0.0	1.3	3.7	6.8	9.5
Abdominal hysterectomy	0	60	1.6	0.0	0.4	1.4	2.6	5.0
Abdominal hysterectomy	1	55	2.8	0.0	0.0	1.8	3.2	4.8
Abdominal hysterectomy	2, 3	28	6.1	0.0	2.8	4.9	8.2	10.8
Vaginal hysterectomy	0	34	1.0	0.0	0.0	0.0	1.6	2.5
Vaginal hysterectomy	1, 2, 3	32	1.7	0.0	0.0	1.3	2.5	4.8
MUSCULOSKELETAL								
Limb amputation	0, 1, 2, 3	36	4.6	0.0	0.9	2.9	4.8	7.8
Spinal fusion	0	35	1.3	0.0	0.0	0.3	1.9	2.3
Spinal fusion	1	35	3.1	0.0	0.0	2.2	4.1	5.6
Open reduction fracture	0	51	0.8	0.0	0.0	0.0	1.2	2.4
Open reduction fracture	1	60	1.4	0.0	0.0	1.0	1.6	2.9
Open reduction fracture	2, 3	35	2.9	0.0	0.0	2.4	4.4	8.7
Hip prosthesis	0	51	0.7	0.0	0.0	0.0	1.2	1.8
Hip prosthesis	1, 2, 3	84	1.7	0.0	0.0	1.0	2.6	3.7
Knee prosthesis	0	59	0.9	0.0	0.0	0.0	1.5	2.7
Knee prosthesis	1	72	1.2	0.0	0.0	1.0	1.7	3.4
Knee prosthesis	2, 3	36	1.8	0.0	0.0	1.4	3.3	5.4
Laminectomy	0	57	0.7	0.0	0.0	0.0	1.0	1.8
Laminectomy	1	53	1.4	0.0	0.0	0.6	2.4	3.1
Laminectomy	2, 3	30	2.4	0.0	0.0	1.7	3.2	5.8
Other musculoskeletal	0, 1	38	0.7	0.0	0.0	0.5	1.1	1.7
Other musculoskeletal	2, 3	20	2.1	0.0	0.0	0.5	2.9	4.1
ENDOCRINE/EYE								
Other integumentary system	0, 1	27	1.4	0.0	0.0	1.1	1.7	2.5
ORGAN TRANSPLANT/GRAFTS								
Vascular surgery	0	40	1.3	0.0	0.0	0.0	1.8	2.9
Vascular surgery	1	76	2.0	0.0	0.0	1.5	2.6	3.5
Vascular surgery	2	65	5.2	0.0	2.3	4.8	7.1	9.2

SOURCE: National Nosocomial Infections Surveillance (NNIS) System Report, Data Summary for October 1986–April 1998, issued June 1998 Hospital Infections Program, National Center for Infectious Diseases, Centers for Disease Control and Prevention, Public Health Service, U.S. Department of Health and Human Services, Atlanta, Ga.: Table 8.

1. CBGB: CABG-Chest and leg = Coronary artery bypass graft with chest and leg (or other donor site) incisions.
2. CBGB: CABG-Chest only = Coronary artery bypass graft with chest incision only (example: internal mammary artery graft.)
3. Risk categories for CHOL are defined as
0 if the risk index = 0;
1 if the risk index = 1 and SCOPE (use of laparoscope) = Yes;
2 if the risk index = 1 and SCOPE = No, or risk index = 2, 3 and SCOPE = Yes;
3 if the risk index = 2,3 and SCOPE = No.

NOTE: Includes only those procedure-risk categories for which at least 20 hospitals have reported at least 30 operations.

Table 4.31. Availability of Physicians for Mental Health Treatment by Urban/Rural Status: 1994

County type and population size	Number of counties	Percent with any mental health physician	Mean number mental health physicians per county	Rate per 100,000 population	Maximum rate of mental health physicains
NON-FEDERAL PSYCHIATRISTS					
Metropolitan Counties					
Metro Central >1,000,000	168	100.0	141.2	17.2	134.4
Metro fringe>1m	132	60.6	3.2	3.0	42.9
Metro 250,000–1,000,000	318	74.8	22.3	8.1	135.4
Metro <250,000	198	83.3	11.0	8.9	84.1
Non-Metropolitan Counties					
Urban adjacent >20,000	133	85.7	3.9	4.8	55.7
Urban nonadjacent >20,000	110	88.2	4.7	7.2	72.6
Urban adjacent 2,500–20,000	611	27.7	0.7	2.2	60.7
Urban nonadjacent 2,500–20,000	642	26.6	0.7	2.6	142.5
Rural adjacent <2,500	247	7.7	0.1	1.0	34.9
Rural nonadjacent <2,500	522	5.2	0.1	0.7	53.9
CHILD PSYCHIATRISTS					
Metropolitan Counties					
Metro Central >1,000,000	168	88.1	20.5	2.6	14.9
Metro fringe>1m	132	26.5	0.5	0.6	12.1
Metro 250,000–1,000,000	318	49.4	3.3	1.2	25.6
Metro <250,000	198	53.5	1.5	1.2	13.9
Non-Metropolitan Counties					
Urban adjacent >20,000	113	21.1	0.3	0.3	3.5
Urban nonadjacent >20,000	110	37.3	0.6	0.9	10.3
Urban adjacent 2,500–20,000	611	4.9	0.1	0.2	9.4
Urban nonadjacent 2,500–20,000	642	4.8	0.1	0.2	10.5
Rural adjacent <2,500	247	2.0	0.0	0.2	10.8
Rural nonadjacent <2,500	522	0.4	0.0	0.0	7.5
FAMILY PRACTICE PHYSICIANS IN NON-FEDERAL FAMILY PRACTICE					
Metropolitan Counties					
Metro Central >1,000,000	168	100.0	126.1	18.9	59.4
Metro fringe>1m	132	97.7	12.1	15.8	54.7
Metro 250,000–1,000,000	318	99.1	41.1	20.5	77.7
Metro <250,000	198	98.0	27.4	23.9	72.0
Non-Metropolitan Counties					
Urban adjacent >20,000	133	100.0	14.4	19.2	62.4
Urban nonadjacent >20,000	110	99.1	14.5	23.6	82.1
Urban adjacent 2,500–20,000	611	95.6	5.3	19.8	98.2
Urban nonadjacent 2,500–20,000	642	94.5	4.8	24.5	107.5
Rural adjacent <2,500	247	68.4	1.6	14.9	100.6
Rural nonadjacent <2,500	522	58.8	1.4	19.9	217.7

SOURCE: C.E. Holzer, H.F. Goldsmith, and J.A. Ciarlo, "Effects of Rural-Urban County Type on the Availability of Health and Mental Health Care Providers," *Mental Health, United States, 1998*, ed. R.W. Manderscheid and M.J. Henderson, DHHS Pub. No. (SMA) 99-3285 Substance Abuse and Mental Health Services Administration, Center for Mental Health Services. (Washington, D.C.: Supt. of Docs., U.S. Govt. Printing Office, 1998) pp. 204–213.

Table 4.32. Estimated Supply of Selected Health Personnel and Practitioner-to-Population Ratios

Health occupation	1970	1975	1980	1985	1990	1995	1996
NUMBER OF PRACTITIONERS							
Physicians	323 800	380 400	453 100	533 600	601 700	681 700	701 200
Allopathic (MD) [1]	311 200	366 400	435 500	511 100	572 700	646 000	663 900
Osteopathic (DO) [2]	12 600	14 000	17 600	22 500	29 000	35 700	37 300
Dentists	96 000	107 100	121 900	133 500	147 500	153 300	154 900
Optometrists	18 400	19 900	21 900	24 000	26 000	28 900	29 500
Pharmacists	112 600	121 800	142 400	153 500	166 700	182 300	185 000
Veterinarians	25 900	31 100	36 500	42 600	48 700	55 400	56 700
Registered nurses	750 000	961 000	1 272 900	1 538 100	1 789 600	2 115 800	2 161 700
Allied	750 000	1 013 000	1 276 000	1 554 500	1 833 000	2 222 040	2 319 300
Total	2 076 700	2 634 300	3 324 700	3 979 800	4 613 200	5 439 440	5 608 300
PRACTITIONERS PER 100,000 POPULATION							
Physicians	155.6	173.5	195.9	220.5	237.6	255.1	260.0
Allopathic (MD) [1]	149.6	167.1	188.3	211.2	226.1	241.8	246.1
Osteopathic (DO) [2]	6.1	6.4	7.6	9.3	11.5	13.4	13.8
Dentists	46.5	49.3	53.2	55.7	58.7	58.0	58.1
Optometrists	8.9	9.2	9.6	10.0	10.3	10.9	11.1
Pharmacists	54.5	56.1	62.2	64.1	66.3	68.9	69.4
Veterinarians	12.5	14.3	15.9	17.8	19.4	21.0	21.3
Registered nurses	366.0	449.0	555.0	640.0	710.0	798.0	808.0

SOURCE: Data estimated by Health Resources and Service Administration, Bureau of Health Professions. unpublished data.

1. The numbers of active MDs include those MDs whose activity status is not classified by the American Medical Association.
2. 1970 data estimated using 1975 proportion of listed DOs to active DOs.

NOTE: MD data for 1990 are as of January 1. Data for all other years are as of December 31.

Table 4.33. Number and Rate of Clinically Trained and Clinically Active Mental Health Personnel

(Rate per 100,000 population)

Health discipline and year of study	Number	Rate
CLINICALLY TRAINED		
Psychology (1997)	73 018	27.5
Social work (1998)	96 273	36.2
Psychiatric nursing (1995) [1]	6 800	2.6
Counseling (1998) [2]	96 263	36.2
CLINICALLY ACTIVE		
Psychiatry (1996)	29 803	11.3
Marriage and family therapy (1998) [3]	44 225	16.7
Psychosocial rehabilitation (1996)	100 000	37.7
School psychology (1995) [4]	22 285	8.4

SOURCE: B.D. Peterson, J. West, T.L. Tanielian, et al., "Mental Health Practitioners and Trainees," *Mental Health, United States, 1998,* ed. R.W. Manderscheid and M.J. Henderson, DHHS Pub. No. (SMA) 99-3285 Substance Abuse and Mental Health Services Administration, Center for Mental Health Services. (Washington, D.C.: Supt. of Docs., U.S. Govt. Printing Office, 1998): pp. 214–246.

1. Twenty-four individuals live in foreign countries. Source: American Nurses Credentialing Center, 1996, page 4; based on certified nurses only.
2. Data from American Counseling Association Educational, Experiential, and Examination requirements of Credentialed Professional Counselors (1995); National Board for Certified Counselors 1998 State Counseling Board Survey; comparison with similar states; and/or number of National Certified Counselors. Counseling count is for clinically trained, because count is more accurate.
3. Total represents clinically active marriage and family therapists.
4. The total and state figures represent the number of employed school psychologists during the 1994–1995 school year reported in Nineteenth Annual Report to Congress on the Individuals with Disabilities Act (U.S. Department of Education 1997).

Table 4.34. Employment, Hours, and Earnings in Private [1] Health Service Establishments, by Selected Type of Establishment

Type of establishment	1995	1996	1997	1998
TOTAL EMPLOYMENT (IN THOUSANDS)				
Nonfarm private sector	97 885	100 189	103 133	106 007
Health services	9 230	9 478	9 703	9 846
Offices and clinics of physicians	1 609	1 678	1 739	1 803
Offices and clinics of dentists	592	611	629	646
Nursing homes	1 691	1 730	1 756	1 762
Private hospitals	3 772	3 812	3 860	3 926
Home health care services	629	675	710	672
NONSUPERVISORY EMPLOYMENT (IN THOUSANDS)				
Nonfarm private sector	80 125	82 092	84 541	86 762
Health services	8 178	8 405	8 599	8 724
Offices and clinics of physicians	1 314	1 377	1 428	1 486
Offices and clinics of dentists	517	535	550	563
Nursing homes	1 526	1 559	1 579	1 585
Private hospitals	3 450	3 489	3 537	3 598
Home health care services	582	624	655	618
AVERAGE WEEKLY HOURS				
Nonfarm private sector	34.5	34.4	34.6	34.6
Health services	32.8	32.7	33.0	33.1
Offices and clinics of physicians	32.5	32.9	33.2	33.0
Offices and clinics of dentists	28.0	28.2	28.4	28.3
Nursing homes	32.5	32.4	32.4	32.6
Private hospitals	34.5	34.4	34.9	35.0
Home health care services	28.6	28.1	28.9	29.0
AVERAGE HOURLY EARNINGS (IN DOLLARS)				
Nonfarm private sector	$11.4	$11.8	$12.3	$12.8
Health services	12.4	12.8	13.3	13.7
Offices and clinics of physicians	12.5	13.2	13.8	14.3
Offices and clinics of dentists	12.4	12.9	13.6	14.2
Nursing homes	8.8	9.0	9.3	9.8
Private hospitals	14.3	14.7	15.0	15.5
Home health care services	10.9	11.2	11.4	11.5
HOSPITAL EMPLOYMENT (IN THOUSANDS)				
Total	5 069	5 067	5 077	5 132
Private	3 772	3 812	3 860	3 926
Federal	233	232	224	223
State	395	376	360	348
Local	669	648	632	635

SOURCE: (1) Health Care Financing Administration.Health Care Indicators: Key Trends in the Health Care Sector–First Quarter 1999. Table 4. (2) U.S. Department of Labor, Bureau of Labor Statistics, Employment and Earnings. (Washington, D.C.: U.S. Govt. Printing Office): Monthly reports for January 1995–March 1999.

1. Excludes hospitals, clinics, and other health-related establishments run by all governments.

NOTE: Data presented here conform to the 1987 Standard Industrial Classification.

Table 4.35. Who Pays for National Health Expenditures

(Millions of dollars)

Type of service provided and year	Total national health expenditures	Private				Public					State and local		
		Total private	Out of pocket	Insurance	Other	Total public	Total federal	Medicare	Medicaid	Other	Total state and local	Medicaid	Other
NATIONAL HEALTH EXPENDITURES													
1965	41 145	30 867	18 539	10 026	2 302	10 278	4 820	0	0	4 820	5 458	0	5 458
1966	45 263	31 600	18 839	10 344	2 418	13 663	7 614	1 846	635	5 133	6 050	676	5 374
1967	50 969	31 964	18 826	10 651	2 487	19 005	12 106	4 939	1 532	5 635	6 899	1 625	5 274
1968	57 684	35 880	20 771	12 169	2 940	21 804	14 190	6 240	1 844	6 106	7 615	1 715	5 900
1969	64 792	40 247	22 715	13 839	3 693	24 545	16 049	7 070	2 309	6 671	8 496	1 886	6 610
1970	73 243	45 536	24 901	16 283	4 353	27 706	17 816	7 701	2 856	7 260	9 890	2 459	7 431
1971	81 018	49 829	26 405	18 555	4 869	31 189	20 403	8 470	3 828	8 105	10 787	2 900	7 887
1972	90 943	55 808	28 989	21 307	5 512	35 135	22 974	9 360	4 568	9 047	12 161	3 783	8 378
1973	100 838	61 550	31 954	23 938	5 658	39 288	25 199	10 777	4 954	9 468	14 089	4 509	9 580
1974	114 265	67 668	34 837	26 818	6 012	46 597	30 575	13 485	6 301	10 789	16 022	4 815	11 207
1975	130 727	75 695	38 094	31 269	6 333	55 032	36 407	16 397	7 437	12 573	18 625	6 060	12 565
1976	149 856	87 434	41 938	37 861	7 634	62 422	42 952	19 764	9 190	13 999	19 470	6 058	13 411
1977	170 375	100 158	46 405	45 857	7 896	70 217	47 693	22 973	9 935	14 784	22 524	7 599	14 926
1978	190 601	111 048	49 733	52 514	8 802	79 553	54 325	26 763	10 961	16 600	25 228	8 580	16 648
1979	215 201	125 054	54 317	60 935	9 802	90 147	61 384	31 037	12 753	17 594	28 763	9 663	19 100
1980	247 273	142 493	60 254	69 758	12 482	104 780	71 958	37 516	14 504	19 938	32 823	11 631	21 192
1981	286 908	165 715	68 492	82 185	15 039	121 193	83 711	44 883	17 223	21 605	37 482	13 155	24 327
1982	322 978	188 397	75 448	95 404	17 545	134 581	93 038	52 470	17 480	23 088	41 543	14 637	26 906
1983	355 291	207 746	82 319	106 161	19 266	147 545	103 126	59 762	19 264	24 100	44 419	16 069	28 350
1984	390 076	229 937	90 857	119 200	19 880	160 139	113 207	66 447	20 626	26 134	46 932	17 623	29 309
1985	428 720	254 518	100 659	132 845	21 014	174 202	123 171	72 084	22 829	28 258	51 032	18 424	32 607
1986	461 229	271 398	108 081	140 555	22 762	189 831	132 634	76 838	25 493	30 304	57 197	20 049	37 147
1987	500 502	293 291	116 053	152 446	24 793	207 211	143 096	82 711	27 844	32 541	64 115	22 576	41 539
1988	560 379	334 251	127 458	178 060	28 733	226 127	156 359	90 100	31 035	35 225	69 769	24 084	45 685
1989	623 536	371 413	133 208	208 466	29 740	252 122	174 766	102 423	35 414	36 930	77 357	26 837	50 520
1990	699 361	416 187	145 032	239 555	31 601	283 174	195 181	111 496	42 669	41 016	87 993	32 703	55 290
1991	766 783	448 859	153 335	261 737	33 787	317 923	222 550	121 139	56 797	44 615	95 374	37 145	58 228
1992	836 537	483 553	161 758	285 490	36 306	352 984	251 759	136 164	67 991	47 604	101 225	38 379	62 846
1993	898 496	513 172	167 051	306 799	39 322	385 323	275 353	148 701	76 842	49 809	109 970	44 906	65 064
1994	947 717	524 908	168 502	315 109	41 298	422 810	301 171	166 883	81 478	52 810	121 638	53 113	68 525
1995	993 725	538 507	170 991	324 282	43 235	455 218	325 989	185 220	86 345	54 423	129 229	59 760	69 469
1996	1 042 522	561 141	178 124	337 108	45 908	481 382	348 009	200 086	92 279	55 644	133 373	61 827	71 546
1997	1 092 385	585 312	187 551	348 020	49 741	507 073	367 050	214 569	95 428	57 053	140 023	64 462	75 561
1998	1 151 700	622 285	197 505	371 610	53 169	529 415	380 076	220 004	101 195	58 877	149 339	69 197	80 142
1999	1 228 540	669 237	208 827	403 694	56 716	559 303	399 758	230 110	108 044	61 604	159 545	74 000	85 546
2000	1 316 179	722 574	222 011	440 075	60 487	593 606	423 909	244 520	114 895	64 493	169 697	78 524	91 173
2001	1 403 603	774 900	236 462	474 157	64 281	628 703	447 726	257 382	122 738	67 605	180 977	83 992	96 985
2002	1 495 545	825 907	250 746	507 114	68 047	669 638	476 171	273 184	132 077	70 911	193 466	90 496	102 970
2003	1 590 359	874 303	265 451	536 832	72 020	716 056	508 847	291 603	142 817	74 427	207 208	97 908	109 301
2004	1 690 417	926 148	280 700	569 226	76 222	764 269	542 068	309 543	154 670	77 854	222 202	106 200	116 001
2005	1 799 543	982 062	297 011	604 346	80 706	817 481	578 653	329 036	168 024	81 594	238 828	115 573	123 255
2006	1 917 273	1040569	314 603	640 467	85 500	876 703	619 812	351 481	182 716	85 615	256 891	125 915	130 976
2007	2 043 132	1102243	334 069	677 529	90 646	940 889	664 513	376 051	198 575	89 887	276 376	137 109	139 266
2008	2 176 620	1166936	355 536	715 321	96 080	1009684	712 506	402 691	215 430	94 385	297 177	149 027	148 150
HEALTH SERVICES AND SUPPLIES													
1965	37 708	29 417	18 539	10 026	852	8 290	3 271	0	0	3 271	5 020	0	5 020
1966	41 706	30 120	18 839	10 344	938	11 586	5 972	1 846	635	3 491	5 614	676	4 939
1967	47 229	30 561	18 826	10 651	1 084	16 668	10 335	4 939	1 532	3 863	6 333	1 625	4 708
1968	53 523	34 262	20 771	12 169	1 322	19 261	12 297	6 240	1 844	4 214	6 963	1 715	5 249
1969	59 894	38 047	22 715	13 839	1 493	21 847	14 120	7 070	2 309	4 741	7 728	1 886	5 842
1970	67 894	42 957	24 901	16 283	1 774	24 937	15 879	7 701	2 856	5 323	9 057	2 459	6 598
1971	75 035	46 915	26 405	18 555	1 954	28 121	18 316	8 470	3 828	6 018	9 804	2 900	6 905
1972	84 322	52 522	28 989	21 307	2 226	31 801	20 688	9 360	4 568	6 761	11 113	3 783	7 330
1973	94 102	58 211	31 954	23 938	2 319	35 891	22 875	10 777	4 954	7 144	13 016	4 509	8 507
1974	106 992	64 288	34 837	26 818	2 632	42 704	28 017	13 485	6 301	8 231	14 687	4 815	9 872
1975	122 344	72 274	38 094	31 269	2 911	50 070	33 155	16 397	7 437	9 322	16 915	6 060	10 855
1976	140 533	83 807	41 938	37 861	4 007	56 726	39 239	19 764	9 190	10 285	17 488	6 058	11 429
1977	161 143	96 621	46 405	45 857	4 359	64 521	43 849	22 973	9 935	10 940	20 673	7 599	13 074
1978	180 750	107 432	49 733	52 514	5 185	73 318	49 875	26 763	10 961	12 150	23 444	8 580	14 863
1979	204 934	121 193	54 317	60 935	5 941	83 740	56 808	31 037	12 753	13 018	26 932	9 663	17 270
1980	235 637	138 041	60 254	69 758	8 029	97 596	66 744	37 516	14 504	14 725	30 851	11 631	19 220
1981	273 680	160 297	68 492	82 185	9 620	113 383	78 274	44 883	17 223	16 168	35 109	13 155	21 954
1982	308 295	181 844	75 448	95 404	10 992	126 451	87 424	52 470	17 480	17 474	39 027	14 637	24 391
1983	339 315	200 372	82 319	106 161	11 892	138 943	97 262	59 762	19 264	18 236	41 681	16 069	25 612
1984	373 654	222 755	90 857	119 200	12 697	150 899	106 663	66 447	20 626	19 590	44 236	17 623	26 614
1985	412 350	248 018	100 659	132 845	14 514	164 332	115 998	72 084	22 829	21 086	48 333	18 424	29 909
1986	444 410	264 844	108 081	140 555	16 209	179 566	124 999	76 838	25 493	22 668	54 567	20 049	34 518
1987	482 179	285 982	116 053	152 446	17 484	196 197	134 949	82 711	27 844	24 394	61 248	22 576	38 672
1988	539 164	325 592	127 458	178 060	20 074	213 572	147 167	90 100	31 035	26 033	66 405	24 084	42 322
1989	601 313	362 361	133 208	208 466	20 688	238 952	165 084	102 423	35 414	27 248	73 868	26 837	47 031
1990	674 837	405 939	145 032	239 555	21 353	268 898	184 814	111 496	42 669	30 649	84 084	32 703	51 381
1991	741 851	438 737	153 335	261 737	23 664	303 115	211 887	121 139	56 797	33 952	91 227	37 145	54 082
1992	808 994	472 546	161 758	285 490	25 299	336 448	239 968	136 164	67 991	35 812	96 480	38 379	58 101
1993	869 488	501 275	167 051	306 799	27 425	368 212	263 276	148 701	76 842	37 732	104 936	44 906	60 030
1994	917 239	513 136	168 502	315 109	29 526	404 103	287 992	166 883	81 478	39 630	116 111	53 113	62 998
1995	963 084	527 555	170 991	324 282	32 282	435 530	312 002	185 220	86 345	40 437	123 527	59 760	63 767
1996	1 010 560	549 454	178 124	337 108	34 222	461 106	333 606	200 086	92 279	41 241	127 499	61 827	65 673
1997	1 057 492	571 946	187 551	348 020	36 376	485 546	351 791	214 569	95 428	41 795	133 755	64 462	69 293
1998	1 114 688	607 809	197 505	371 610	38 694	506 879	364 075	220 004	101 195	42 876	142 803	69 197	73 607
1999	1 189 703	653 898	208 827	403 694	41 377	535 805	383 085	230 110	108 044	44 931	152 720	74 000	78 720
2000	1 275 521	706 439	222 011	440 075	44 353	569 081	406 524	244 520	114 895	47 109	162 557	78 524	84 033
2001	1 360 980	757 964	236 462	474 157	47 345	603 016	429 529	257 382	122 738	49 409	173 488	83 992	89 495
2002	1 451 000	808 287	250 746	507 114	50 427	642 714	457 098	273 184	132 077	51 837	185 616	90 496	95 120
2003	1 543 723	855 923	265 451	536 832	53 641	687 800	488 814	291 603	142 817	54 394	198 986	97 908	101 078
2004	1 641 513	906 946	280 700	569 226	57 020	734 566	520 982	309 543	154 670	56 768	213 584	106 200	107 384
2005	1 748 184	961 978	297 011	604 346	60 622	786 205	556 419	329 036	168 024	59 360	229 786	115 573	114 213
2006	1 863 329	1019568	314 603	640 467	64 499	843 761	596 356	351 481	182 716	62 159	247 405	125 915	121 490
2007	1 986 454	1080282	334 069	677 529	68 685	906 172	639 753	376 051	198 575	65 127	266 419	137 109	129 310
2008	2 117 060	1143970	355 536	715 321	73 113	973 090	686 366	402 691	215 430	68 245	286 724	149 027	137 697

See footnotes at end of table.

Table 4.35. Who Pays for National Health Expenditures—*Continued*

(Millions of dollars)

Type of service provided and year	Total national health expenditures	Private				Public					State and local		
		Total private	Out of pocket	Insurance	Other	Total public	Total federal	Medicare	Medicaid	Other	Total state and local	Medicaid	Other
PERSONAL HEALTH CARE													
1965	35 165	27 910	18 539	8 677	693	7 256	2 970	0	0	2 970	4 286	0	4 286
1966	38 839	28 524	18 839	8 895	791	10 315	5 466	1 725	609	3 132	4 850	650	4 199
1967	44 141	28 993	18 826	9 236	931	15 148	9 628	4 746	1 468	3 415	5 519	1 566	3 954
1968	49 844	32 405	20 771	10 486	1 149	17 438	11 401	5 952	1 762	3 688	6 037	1 640	4 398
1969	56 236	36 508	22 715	12 436	1 357	19 728	13 080	6 758	2 206	4 116	6 649	1 797	4 852
1970	63 825	41 312	24 901	14 776	1 636	22 512	14 704	7 302	2 721	4 681	7 808	2 343	5 465
1971	70 054	44 681	26 405	16 463	1 813	25 373	16 893	8 062	3 661	5 170	8 479	2 781	5 698
1972	78 043	49 313	28 989	18 255	2 069	28 731	19 067	8 884	4 380	5 803	9 664	3 628	6 035
1973	87 066	54 744	31 954	20 618	2 173	32 321	21 164	10 227	4 717	6 220	11 157	4 334	6 823
1974	99 868	61 434	34 837	24 118	2 478	38 434	26 000	12 803	6 017	7 181	12 434	4 614	7 819
1975	114 506	69 211	38 094	28 368	2 750	45 294	30 931	15 668	7 076	8 188	14 363	5 812	8 551
1976	130 532	79 284	41 938	33 507	3 839	51 249	36 653	18 881	8 696	9 075	14 596	5 790	8 806
1977	147 735	89 669	46 405	39 076	4 188	58 067	41 254	22 216	9 355	9 683	16 813	7 232	9 580
1978	164 839	99 333	49 733	44 597	5 002	65 506	46 896	25 758	10 261	10 877	18 611	8 219	10 392
1979	187 496	112 798	54 317	52 738	5 743	74 698	53 750	30 011	11 952	11 787	20 948	9 264	11 684
1980	217 039	130 053	60 254	62 014	7 785	86 986	63 399	36 384	13 668	13 346	23 587	11 125	12 462
1981	252 006	150 737	68 492	72 901	9 344	101 269	74 579	43 564	16 248	14 767	26 691	12 615	14 076
1982	283 277	170 088	75 448	83 979	10 660	113 190	83 744	51 174	16 442	16 128	29 445	14 078	15 368
1983	311 514	186 563	82 319	92 743	11 502	124 950	93 268	58 313	18 196	16 759	31 683	15 352	16 331
1984	341 472	205 208	90 857	102 097	12 253	136 265	102 297	64 833	19 413	18 052	33 967	16 776	17 191
1985	376 442	228 754	100 659	114 065	14 031	147 688	111 051	70 049	21 495	19 507	36 637	17 574	19 063
1986	410 504	248 746	108 081	124 932	15 734	161 757	119 929	74 791	24 072	21 065	41 828	19 099	22 730
1987	449 709	273 234	116 053	140 200	16 982	176 475	129 533	80 636	26 340	22 558	46 942	21 454	25 489
1988	499 257	307 813	127 458	160 788	19 567	191 444	140 846	87 575	29 360	23 910	50 598	22 843	27 756
1989	550 132	336 612	133 208	183 251	20 154	213 520	157 917	99 575	33 478	24 864	55 603	25 466	30 137
1990	614 680	373 536	145 032	207 744	20 761	241 144	176 952	108 601	40 360	27 991	64 191	31 029	33 162
1991	679 563	406 200	153 335	229 814	23 050	273 364	203 167	117 849	54 336	30 981	70 197	35 272	34 925
1992	740 518	437 115	161 758	250 649	24 709	303 564	230 515	132 690	65 379	32 445	73 050	36 169	36 880
1993	790 518	459 128	167 051	265 236	26 841	331 390	252 305	144 708	73 522	34 075	79 085	42 243	36 842
1994	833 969	471 969	168 502	274 548	28 920	362 000	275 727	162 594	77 697	35 436	86 272	49 216	37 056
1995	879 332	489 192	170 941	286 587	31 613	390 140	298 956	180 717	82 014	36 225	91 185	55 229	35 955
1996	923 996	511 405	178 124	299 778	33 503	412 591	319 755	194 860	87 954	36 941	92 837	58 377	34 459
1997	969 005	536 651	187 551	313 451	35 650	432 354	337 257	208 853	91 106	37 298	95 097	61 205	33 892
1998	1 017 973	570 131	197 505	334 723	37 903	447 841	347 656	213 294	96 233	38 129	100 186	65 429	34 756
1999	1 078 330	607 178	208 827	357 921	40 431	471 151	365 113	222 801	102 462	39 850	106 038	69 762	36 277
2000	1 150 860	651 632	222 012	386 349	43 271	499 228	387 064	236 339	109 084	41 642	112 164	74 113	38 051
2001	1 227 320	699 044	236 462	416 394	46 189	528 276	408 821	248 500	116 743	43 578	119 455	79 440	40 015
2002	1 310 035	747 501	250 534	447 533	49 223	562 534	434 940	263 622	125 671	45 647	127 594	85 632	41 962
2003	1 397 891	796 156	265 451	478 277	52 429	601 735	465 140	281 318	135 942	47 880	136 595	92 688	43 907
2004	1 488 599	846 407	280 700	509 933	55 774	642 192	495 831	298 625	147 268	49 938	146 361	100 580	45 780
2005	1 586 429	899 475	297 011	543 142	59 322	686 954	529 719	317 474	160 055	52 191	157 234	109 523	47 712
2006	1 692 119	955 157	314 603	577 410	63 144	736 962	567 900	339 131	174 136	54 632	169 062	119 401	49 661
2007	1 805 177	1013993	334 069	612 651	67 274	791 183	609 427	362 872	189 339	57 217	181 756	130 097	51 659
2008	1 925 159	1075916	355 536	648 735	71 646	849 243	654 054	388 638	205 488	59 928	195 189	141 479	53 709
HOSPITAL CARE													
1965	14 040	8 756	2 751	5 738	267	5 284	2 166	0	0	2 166	3 118	0	3 118
1966	15 802	8 393	2 356	5 715	321	7 409	3 888	1 255	355	2 278	3 521	379	3 142
1967	18 439	8 046	1 864	5 779	404	10 393	6 591	3 229	794	2 568	3 802	846	2 956
1968	21 232	9 268	2 218	6 527	523	11 964	7 809	4 119	890	2 800	4 155	829	3 326
1969	24 140	10 534	2 210	7 668	656	13 606	9 000	4 822	1 130	3 048	4 607	920	3 686
1970	28 003	12 493	2 518	9 070	905	15 510	10 197	5 371	1 436	3 390	5 312	1 235	4 078
1971	30 994	13 701	2 523	10 136	1 041	17 294	11 578	5 932	1 900	3 746	5 716	1 448	4 268
1972	34 887	15 453	3 054	11 191	1 209	19 434	12 997	6 553	2 098	4 346	6 437	1 707	4 730
1973	39 046	17 256	3 697	12 376	1 183	21 791	14 484	7 569	2 122	4 793	7 306	1 976	5 330
1974	45 566	20 093	4 083	14 683	1 327	25 473	17 479	9 434	2 482	5 563	7 994	1 884	6 110
1975	52 571	23 130	4 382	17 304	1 445	29 441	20 445	11 564	2 876	6 005	8 996	2 371	6 625
1976	60 786	27 275	4 571	20 373	2 332	33 511	24 524	13 988	3 776	6 760	8 987	2 340	6 647
1977	68 772	30 931	4 894	23 573	2 464	37 841	27 572	16 296	4 035	7 241	10 269	3 142	7 127
1978	77 255	34 821	5 004	26 878	2 939	42 434	31 247	18 773	4 330	8 144	11 187	3 481	7 706
1979	88 128	40 052	5 169	31 526	3 357	48 076	35 622	21 796	4 930	8 896	12 454	3 876	8 578
1980	102 700	46 814	5 334	36 469	5 011	55 886	42 136	26 441	5 750	9 945	13 750	4 862	8 888
1981	119 872	54 726	6 247	42 451	6 029	65 146	49 460	31 665	6 727	11 068	15 686	5 566	10 121
1982	136 183	63 172	7 180	49 093	6 900	73 011	55 913	36 829	6 855	12 230	17 098	6 119	10 978
1983	147 588	68 033	7 610	53 182	7 241	79 554	61 583	41 257	7 589	12 736	17 972	6 484	11 488
1984	157 620	71 226	8 100	55 822	7 305	86 394	67 508	45 757	8 005	13 745	18 887	7 118	11 769
1985	168 290	76 035	8 811	58 953	8 271	92 255	72 307	48 986	8 552	14 769	19 948	7 174	12 774
1986	179 825	80 559	8 549	62 938	9 073	99 266	76 155	50 959	9 473	15 724	23 111	7 667	15 444
1987	194 099	87 770	8 696	69 324	9 750	106 329	80 500	53 508	10 303	16 689	25 829	8 560	17 269
1988	211 585	97 203	10 390	75 668	11 146	114 382	86 718	57 719	11 596	17 403	27 665	9 205	18 460
1989	231 603	106 532	9 658	86 254	10 619	125 072	95 195	63 500	13 330	18 366	29 876	10 273	19 604
1990	256 447	116 805	11 054	95 569	10 182	139 642	105 416	68 716	16 559	20 141	34 226	12 872	21 354
1991	282 272	126 180	12 962	101 906	11 312	156 092	121 369	73 888	25 239	22 242	34 723	12 532	22 190
1992	305 313	132 512	13 715	107 156	11 640	172 801	138 713	84 019	31 478	23 216	34 088	10 875	23 213
1993	322 995	136 708	14 080	109 922	12 707	186 287	148 789	90 086	34 314	24 390	37 498	14 096	23 401
1994	335 717	134 892	12 662	108 561	13 669	200 825	159 896	99 717	35 274	24 905	40 929	17 568	23 361
1995	347 227	133 692	11 526	107 290	14 877	213 535	170 591	108 945	36 197	25 449	42 944	20 502	22 442
1996	360 777	137 980	11 832	110 020	16 128	222 798	179 569	116 290	37 367	25 912	43 229	21 629	21 600
1997	371 062	142 642	12 418	112 990	17 233	228 420	185 634	123 714	36 200	25 720	42 785	21 377	21 408
1998	382 729	151 495	12 847	120 145	18 502	231 234	187 589	125 004	36 572	26 013	43 644	21 790	21 854
1999	401 271	160 890	13 429	127 580	19 880	240 382	194 773	129 547	38 394	26 832	45 609	22 987	22 621
2000	424 002	172 300	14 118	136 920	21 261	251 702	204 294	136 630	39 912	27 752	47 408	23 844	23 564
2001	447 506	184 615	14 851	147 144	22 619	262 891	213 547	143 494	41 321	28 732	49 344	24 684	24 660
2002	473 917	197 048	15 349	157 651	24 048	276 869	225 464	152 596	43 062	29 805	51 405	25 719	25 687
2003	502 525	209 200	16 024	167 576	25 600	293 324	239 660	163 413	45 278	30 969	53 664	27 022	26 642
2004	530 677	221 407	16 816	177 451	27 141	309 270	253 332	173 733	47 561	32 038	55 937	28 387	27 551
2005	560 276	233 762	17 754	187 242	28 767	326 514	268 232	185 057	49 977	33 199	58 282	29 832	28 450
2006	591 747	246 194	18 810	196 883	30 501	345 553	284 930	198 024	52 463	34 443	60 623	31 321	29 302
2007	624 883	258 931	19 988	206 609	32 334	365 952	302 994	212 291	54 963	35 740	62 958	32 821	30 138
2008	659 470	271 809	21 358	216 195	34 255	387 661	322 388	227 861	57 449	37 077	65 273	34 311	30 962

See footnotes at end of table.

Table 4.35. Who Pays for National Health Expenditures—*Continued*

(Millions of dollars)

Type of service provided and year	Total national health expenditures	Private				Public					State and local		
		Total private	Out of pocket	Insurance	Other	Total public	Total federal	Medicare	Medicaid	Other	Total state and local	Medicaid	Other
PHYSICIAN SERVICES													
1965	8 191	7 633	4 964	2 659	10	558	115	0	0	115	443	0	443
1966	8 807	7 643	4 819	2 813	10	1 165	626	446	68	112	538	73	465
1967	9 867	7 661	4 679	2 972	9	2 206	1 528	1 234	169	125	679	180	499
1968	10 754	8 219	4 840	3 369	10	2 535	1 840	1 466	223	151	695	207	488
1969	12 059	9 325	5 320	3 994	11	2 734	2 052	1 581	286	185	682	233	449
1970	13 579	10 523	5 729	4 781	12	3 056	2 215	1 656	349	210	841	301	540
1971	15 033	11 485	6 221	5 251	13	3 548	2 596	1 867	481	248	953	365	588
1972	16 656	12 586	6 783	5 785	18	4 070	2 926	2 041	594	290	1 144	499	645
1973	18 417	13 723	7 010	6 688	25	4 695	3 280	2 271	706	303	1 415	647	768
1974	20 974	15 340	7 815	7 489	36	5 634	4 060	2 817	873	370	1 574	667	908
1975	23 909	17 277	8 777	8 448	52	6 632	4 758	3 371	976	411	1 875	808	1 067
1976	27 101	19 711	9 985	9 652	74	7 391	5 400	3 936	1 042	422	1 991	781	1 210
1977	31 387	22 892	11 560	11 223	108	8 495	6 292	4 752	1 075	466	2 203	822	1 380
1978	33 810	24 211	11 814	12 225	172	9 600	7 188	5 577	1 104	508	2 412	888	1 524
1979	38 814	27 797	13 107	14 430	260	11 017	8 334	6 560	1 216	558	2 683	937	1 746
1980	45 232	32 156	14 651	17 129	376	13 076	10 010	7 978	1 401	632	3 066	1 108	1 958
1981	52 164	36 991	16 517	19 956	518	15 173	11 773	9 475	1 599	699	3 400	1 237	2 163
1982	57 692	40 386	17 669	22 050	667	17 306	13 591	11 295	1 513	783	3 715	1 304	2 411
1983	64 626	44 817	19 212	24 753	852	19 808	15 800	13 316	1 590	894	4 008	1 387	2 621
1984	72 586	50 736	21 317	28 344	1 074	21 851	17 491	14 744	1 775	972	4 359	1 435	2 924
1985	83 618	59 312	24 431	33 508	1 373	24 305	19 404	16 325	1 983	1 096	4 901	1 539	3 362
1986	93 068	65 293	26 349	37 265	1 679	27 775	22 241	18 669	2 307	1 265	5 534	1 722	3 811
1987	104 138	72 370	28 612	41 710	2 048	31 768	25 546	21 487	2 539	1 521	6 222	1 940	4 283
1988	118 692	83 588	30 704	50 547	2 337	35 104	28 118	23 479	2 854	1 784	6 987	2 060	4 927
1989	131 301	91 505	31 192	57 681	2 633	39 796	31 926	26 779	3 297	1 851	7 870	2 304	5 566
1990	146 346	101 674	32 173	66 845	2 656	44 673	35 576	29 232	4 132	2 212	9 097	2 893	6 203
1991	162 167	113 364	33 296	77 156	2 911	48 804	38 249	30 458	5 304	2 487	10 555	3 806	6 749
1992	175 912	123 648	33 688	86 766	3 194	52 264	40 433	31 267	6 623	2 544	11 831	4 526	7 305
1993	185 929	130 421	32 977	94 114	3 330	55 508	43 444	33 192	7 666	2 587	12 064	5 047	7 017
1994	192 998	133 883	31 370	98 940	3 573	59 115	46 760	36 189	8 052	2 519	12 355	5 541	6 814
1995	201 863	138 617	30 023	104 401	4 194	63 246	50 875	39 869	8 479	2 528	12 370	5 956	6 415
1996	208 509	142 285	31 131	106 886	4 268	66 224	54 398	42 760	9 066	2 572	11 826	6 124	5 702
1997	217 628	147 512	34 072	109 148	4 292	70 116	58 419	46 390	9 345	2 684	11 697	6 386	5 312
1998	227 992	154 447	36 151	113 800	4 496	73 545	61 591	49 138	9 604	2 849	11 954	6 592	5 362
1999	241 508	162 556	38 053	119 741	4 763	78 952	66 276	52 764	10 365	3 147	12 676	7 110	5 566
2000	258 718	173 614	40 635	127 877	5 102	85 104	71 650	57 016	11 199	3 434	13 454	7 621	5 833
2001	275 854	185 691	43 326	136 925	5 440	90 163	75 711	59 745	12 217	3 749	14 452	8 319	6 133
2002	293 332	197 634	46 072	145 778	5 785	95 698	80 143	62 690	13 375	4 078	15 555	9 113	6 442
2003	310 669	208 692	48 670	153 896	6 127	101 977	85 223	66 132	14 663	4 428	16 753	9 994	6 759
2004	328 660	220 202	51 226	162 495	6 481	108 457	90 424	69 593	16 093	4 737	18 034	10 987	7 047
2005	347 896	232 313	54 050	171 402	6 861	115 583	96 114	73 302	17 733	5 079	19 469	12 127	7 342
2006	369 010	245 093	57 330	180 485	7 277	123 918	102 870	77 845	19 570	5 455	21 048	13 406	7 642
2007	391 794	258 673	60 948	189 999	7 726	133 120	110 357	82 906	21 591	5 860	22 763	14 816	7 947
2008	416 119	272 953	64 816	199 931	8 206	143 166	118 561	88 482	23 786	6 293	24 606	16 348	8 257
DENTAL SERVICES													
1965	2 793	2 759	2 704	55	0	35	17	0	0	17	18	0	18
1966	2 961	2 897	2 829	68	0	64	32	0	21	12	32	22	9
1967	3 409	3 255	3 151	104	0	153	77	0	67	10	77	71	6
1968	3 664	3 436	3 323	113	0	228	118	0	104	14	110	98	12
1969	4 174	3 968	3 788	180	0	206	117	0	93	24	89	75	15
1970	4 669	4 452	4 240	212	0	217	127	0	87	41	90	75	15
1971	5 181	4 920	4 672	249	0	261	167	0	101	66	94	77	16
1972	5 516	5 226	4 934	292	0	290	188	0	100	88	102	83	19
1973	6 323	5 987	5 605	378	4	336	205	0	120	86	131	109	22
1974	7 076	6 688	6 131	550	8	389	234	0	166	67	155	128	27
1975	7 956	7 481	6 530	939	11	475	283	0	200	84	192	164	28
1976	8 972	8 467	6 965	1 486	15	506	316	0	233	84	190	158	32
1977	10 055	9 508	7 582	1 908	19	547	321	0	241	81	226	184	42
1978	10 957	10 445	7 918	2 504	22	512	295	0	217	78	217	175	42
1979	11 893	11 336	8 237	3 072	27	557	322	0	247	75	235	192	43
1980	13 323	12 670	8 833	3 811	27	652	367	0	273	94	286	232	53
1981	15 698	14 960	10 082	4 839	39	738	409	0	320	90	329	262	67
1982	16 953	16 328	10 547	5 737	43	626	328	0	258	70	298	228	70
1983	18 271	17 632	11 011	6 578	44	639	335	0	269	66	303	230	73
1984	19 833	19 242	11 578	7 613	51	591	308	0	242	65	283	212	71
1985	21 650	20 997	12 243	8 682	73	653	352	1	280	72	301	231	71
1986	23 108	22 415	12 658	9 677	81	693	379	1	309	70	314	246	68
1987	25 343	24 613	13 118	11 409	86	730	402	1	326	75	328	266	62
1988	27 460	26 697	13 845	12 759	94	763	431	1	348	82	331	269	62
1989	29 496	28 710	14 485	14 115	110	786	441	2	362	77	345	277	69
1990	31 566	30 647	15 379	15 144	124	919	512	2	425	85	407	331	76
1991	33 348	32 221	16 120	15 967	134	1 127	631	2	528	101	496	417	79
1992	37 013	35 611	17 750	17 718	143	1 402	801	5	679	117	601	517	84
1993	39 526	37 626	18 806	18 666	154	1 900	1 081	18	953	110	819	729	91
1994	42 394	40 420	20 011	20 224	185	1 974	1 094	25	957	112	880	779	101
1995	45 000	42 965	21 074	21 677	214	2 036	1 137	37	981	119	898	800	99
1996	47 541	45 448	22 059	23 165	224	2 093	1 203	55	1 032	116	890	802	88
1997	50 648	48 371	23 862	24 268	241	2 277	1 312	74	1 120	117	965	871	94
1998	53 524	51 164	25 324	25 585	255	2 360	1 330	95	1 100	135	1 030	933	97
1999	56 573	54 061	26 766	27 025	270	2 512	1 440	111	1 143	187	1 072	958	114
2000	60 193	57 534	28 401	28 846	287	2 659	1 552	134	1 197	221	1 107	980	128
2001	63 883	61 043	30 052	30 687	304	2 839	1 687	153	1 274	260	1 153	1 009	144
2002	67 653	64 635	31 724	32 589	322	3 017	1 816	170	1 354	292	1 202	1 043	159
2003	71 518	68 321	33 423	34 558	341	3 197	1 946	188	1 439	319	1 252	1 080	172
2004	75 330	71 977	35 076	36 542	359	3 353	2 053	202	1 522	329	1 300	1 120	180
2005	79 328	75 807	36 898	38 532	378	3 521	2 168	217	1 611	339	1 353	1 165	188
2006	83 681	79 978	38 881	40 698	399	3 704	2 292	235	1 707	350	1 411	1 215	196
2007	88 237	84 340	40 998	42 922	420	3 897	2 423	254	1 808	361	1 474	1 269	205
2008	93 093	88 990	43 254	45 293	444	4 103	2 563	274	1 917	371	1 540	1 327	213

See footnotes at end of table.

Table 4.35. Who Pays for National Health Expenditures—*Continued*

(Millions of dollars)

Type of service provided and year	Total national health expenditures	Private				Public					State and local		
		Total private	Out of pocket	Insurance	Other	Total public	Total federal	Medicare	Medicaid	Other	Total state and local	Medicaid	Other
OTHER PROFESSIONAL CARE													
1965	865	774	686	40	48	91	36	0	0	36	54	0	54
1966	955	822	715	50	58	133	70	8	6	57	63	6	57
1967	1 060	873	748	64	61	187	111	22	14	75	76	15	62
1968	1 140	907	761	76	70	233	146	28	16	102	87	15	72
1969	1 252	973	801	93	79	279	187	32	16	139	93	13	80
1970	1 406	1 057	855	112	90	349	238	36	21	181	111	19	92
1971	1 601	1 155	910	143	102	446	325	44	32	249	121	24	97
1972	1 847	1 339	1 032	189	118	508	377	52	37	287	131	31	100
1973	2 103	1 579	1 192	250	137	525	372	74	47	250	153	43	110
1974	2 380	1 759	1 295	306	157	622	454	127	61	265	168	47	121
1975	2 730	1 995	1 436	379	180	735	544	198	75	271	191	61	130
1976	3 216	2 372	1 673	490	209	845	635	269	86	280	210	65	145
1977	3 793	2 865	1 981	637	247	928	703	350	89	264	225	68	157
1978	4 518	3 439	2 352	780	308	1 078	847	439	80	329	231	65	167
1979	5 464	4 192	2 835	970	388	1 272	975	501	95	380	296	75	222
1980	6 352	4 889	3 288	1 142	459	1 463	1 090	575	104	411	374	87	286
1981	8 180	6 478	4 235	1 638	605	1 702	1 264	669	136	458	438	89	349
1982	9 423	7 506	4 796	2 017	693	1 917	1 390	841	114	436	527	100	427
1983	10 709	8 459	5 319	2 368	772	2 250	1 630	1 036	126	468	620	103	517
1984	13 623	11 038	6 829	3 235	974	2 586	1 825	1 199	120	505	761	106	655
1985	16 639	13 633	8 052	4 343	1 238	3 006	2 061	1 385	138	538	945	118	827
1986	19 285	15 701	8 952	5 320	1 429	3 585	2 403	1 671	163	569	1 181	135	1 046
1987	22 606	18 410	10 197	6 582	1 632	4 197	2 732	1 925	188	619	1 465	157	1 308
1988	26 787	22 176	11 668	8 593	1 915	4 612	2 940	2 102	204	635	1 672	163	1 509
1989	29 785	24 420	12 171	10 099	2 150	5 365	3 438	2 554	217	667	1 927	170	1 757
1990	34 675	28 188	13 699	12 036	2 452	6 487	4 270	3 270	266	734	2 217	207	2 011
1991	38 267	30 545	13 962	13 887	2 696	7 722	5 234	4 130	334	770	2 487	270	2 218
1992	42 089	33 085	15 219	14 833	3 033	9 004	6 276	5 019	393	864	2 728	303	2 424
1993	46 145	36 198	17 020	15 779	3 399	9 948	7 136	5 668	577	891	2 812	450	2 362
1994	49 612	38 478	18 300	16 443	3 734	11 134	8 292	6 723	621	948	2 842	477	2 365
1995	53 627	41 238	19 904	17 212	4 123	12 389	9 528	7 781	777	970	2 860	577	2 283
1996	57 472	44 264	21 945	18 036	4 283	13 208	10 370	8 401	925	1 043	2 838	660	2 178
1997	61 916	48 312	24 641	18 901	4 770	13 604	10 822	8 752	986	1 085	2 782	701	2 080
1998	66 765	52 732	27 172	20 394	5 167	14 033	11 189	9 083	990	1 116	2 844	708	2 135
1999	72 103	57 240	29 632	22 003	5 604	14 864	11 863	9 624	1 060	1 179	3 001	756	2 245
2000	77 876	62 117	32 238	23 800	6 079	15 759	12 553	10 176	1 138	1 239	3 206	805	2 401
2001	83 929	67 249	34 996	25 673	6 580	16 680	13 229	10 692	1 233	1 304	3 451	871	2 581
2002	90 075	72 387	37 649	27 646	7 092	17 688	13 970	11 259	1 340	1 371	3 718	945	2 773
2003	96 362	77 530	40 276	29 633	7 620	18 832	14 829	11 928	1 458	1 443	4 004	1 026	2 977
2004	102 818	82 748	42 975	31 608	8 165	20 070	15 769	12 670	1 588	1 512	4 301	1 118	3 183
2005	109 659	88 240	45 834	33 660	8 746	21 419	16 799	13 477	1 737	1 585	4 620	1 222	3 398
2006	116 807	93 960	48 787	35 818	9 355	22 847	17 886	14 319	1 904	1 663	4 961	1 338	3 623
2007	124 355	99 961	51 883	38 076	10 002	24 393	19 069	15 235	2 087	1 746	5 324	1 466	3 858
2008	132 420	106 348	55 182	40 471	10 695	26 071	20 362	16 242	2 287	1 833	5 709	1 606	4 103
HOME HEALTH CARE													
1965	89	89	13	3	74	0	0	0	0	0	0	0	0
1966	108	96	16	3	78	11	10	9	1	0	2	1	1
1967	164	111	18	4	89	53	51	49	2	0	3	2	1
1968	238	163	26	7	131	74	71	68	3	0	4	2	1
1969	272	184	31	9	145	87	81	77	5	0	6	5	1
1970	219	143	26	9	109	76	67	60	7	0	9	7	2
1971	194	120	25	9	85	74	64	53	11	0	10	8	2
1972	220	134	30	12	92	86	74	62	12	0	12	10	2
1973	276	171	37	18	116	105	92	81	12	0	13	11	3
1974	423	251	62	33	156	172	151	130	21	0	21	17	4
1975	622	340	106	65	170	282	240	192	48	0	42	38	4
1976	895	479	160	111	208	416	357	278	79	0	60	56	4
1977	1 147	622	203	161	258	524	450	359	92	0	74	70	4
1978	1 555	917	301	250	366	638	549	443	106	0	89	85	4
1979	1 898	1 103	384	301	418	795	684	550	134	0	112	106	5
1980	2 376	1 424	523	392	509	952	805	651	155	0	147	141	6
1981	2 954	1 687	641	419	627	1 267	1 079	846	233	0	188	181	7
1982	3 551	1 964	758	490	716	1 587	1 357	1 095	262	0	230	221	9
1983	4 295	2 339	918	586	836	1 956	1 672	1 336	336	0	284	273	11
1984	5 080	2 775	1 105	699	972	2 305	1 955	1 572	383	0	350	338	12
1985	5 642	3 162	1 277	800	1 085	2 481	2 053	1 596	457	0	428	415	13
1986	6 382	3 824	1 567	972	1 286	2 558	2 068	1 532	536	0	491	475	16
1987	6 654	3 954	1 787	1 089	1 078	2 700	2 105	1 485	619	0	595	569	27
1988	8 421	5 472	2 501	1 499	1 472	2 949	2 315	1 618	697	0	634	610	25
1989	10 233	6 542	2 895	1 888	1 759	3 691	2 901	2 014	887	0	789	768	22
1990	13 117	8 014	3 613	2 245	2 155	5 103	4 114	3 023	1 091	0	989	962	27
1991	16 050	9 352	4 310	2 527	2 516	6 698	5 497	4 230	1 267	0	1 202	1 153	48
1992	19 624	10 841	5 040	2 885	2 915	8 783	7 392	5 880	1 512	0	1 392	1 317	75
1993	22 966	11 900	5 592	3 111	3 201	11 062	9 516	7 747	1 768	0	1 546	1 467	79
1994	26 194	12 523	5 904	3 251	3 368	13 671	11 920	9 989	1 931	0	1 751	1 662	90
1995	29 084	13 117	6 220	3 369	3 528	15 967	14 046	11 936	2 110	0	1 921	1 818	103
1996	31 162	13 667	6 505	3 486	3 676	17 495	15 474	13 168	2 306	0	2 021	1 891	130
1997	32 318	14 665	7 024	3 698	3 944	17 652	15 387	12 767	2 620	0	2 266	2 135	130
1998	32 314	15 082	7 232	3 802	4 048	17 232	14 672	11 707	2 962	3	2 560	2 419	141
1999	33 795	15 734	7 544	3 966	4 224	18 060	15 309	12 123	3 173	12	2 752	2 589	163
2000	35 957	16 865	8 088	4 251	4 525	19 092	16 105	12 674	3 411	19	2 987	2 798	189
2001	38 262	18 164	8 716	4 578	4 870	20 098	16 833	13 086	3 719	28	3 265	3 048	217
2002	41 017	19 456	9 336	4 904	5 217	21 561	17 983	13 881	4 067	35	3 578	3 330	248
2003	43 927	20 788	9 974	5 240	5 574	23 139	19 215	14 717	4 455	43	3 925	3 642	283
2004	47 382	22 556	10 824	5 685	6 046	24 826	20 510	15 571	4 892	47	4 317	3 996	321
2005	51 135	24 409	11 715	6 152	6 541	26 727	21 960	16 516	5 392	51	4 767	4 402	365
2006	55 389	26 547	12 744	6 691	7 113	28 842	23 570	17 561	5 952	57	5 272	4 855	417
2007	60 216	29 090	13 969	7 331	7 790	31 126	25 297	18 669	6 565	63	5 829	5 351	478
2008	65 368	31 800	15 274	8 014	8 512	33 568	27 130	19 831	7 230	69	6 438	5 889	548

See footnotes at end of table.

Table 4.35. Who Pays for National Health Expenditures—*Continued*

(Millions of dollars)

Type of service provided and year	Total national health expenditures	Private				Public					State and local		
		Total private	Out of pocket	Insurance	Other	Total public	Total federal	Medicare	Medicaid	Other	Total state and local	Medicaid	Other
NONDURABLE MEDICAL PRODUCTS													
1965	3 715	3 571	3 441	130	0	144	59	0	0	59	85	0	85
1966	3 985	3 775	3 594	182	0	210	95	0	50	45	115	53	62
1967	4 227	3 950	3 712	238	0	278	128	0	99	29	150	106	44
1968	4 742	4 436	4 120	317	0	306	141	0	114	27	164	106	59
1969	5 149	4 760	4 361	399	0	389	192	0	165	27	197	135	62
1970	5 497	5 014	4 530	484	0	483	238	0	225	13	245	193	53
1971	5 877	5 309	4 751	558	0	568	297	0	281	16	271	214	57
1972	6 324	5 678	5 034	644	0	646	328	0	308	20	318	255	63
1973	6 817	6 081	5 340	741	0	736	357	0	336	21	379	308	71
1974	7 422	6 575	5 718	857	0	847	445	0	419	26	402	321	81
1975	8 052	7 055	6 070	985	0	997	508	0	478	30	489	392	97
1976	8 722	7 609	6 482	1 127	0	1 113	609	0	576	33	504	394	110
1977	9 196	8 003	6 752	1 252	0	1 193	624	0	587	37	569	449	119
1978	9 891	8 617	7 056	1 562	0	1 274	653	0	614	39	621	494	128
1979	10 744	9 285	7 355	1 930	0	1 459	741	0	701	40	718	536	183
1980	12 049	10 375	7 948	2 427	0	1 674	853	0	810	43	821	599	223
1981	13 398	11 482	8 629	2 853	0	1 916	974	0	927	47	942	684	258
1982	15 029	13 014	9 308	3 706	0	2 015	967	0	917	51	1 047	753	294
1983	16 844	14 572	10 328	4 244	0	2 273	1 109	1	1 052	57	1 164	828	336
1984	18 688	16 103	10 939	5 164	0	2 585	1 251	5	1 188	58	1 334	936	399
1985	21 157	18 058	11 729	6 329	0	3 099	1 512	22	1 427	63	1 587	1 069	517
1986	23 905	20 176	13 145	7 031	0	3 729	1 811	31	1 712	68	1 918	1 261	657
1987	26 533	22 287	14 246	8 041	0	4 246	2 039	39	1 920	81	2 207	1 463	744
1988	29 419	24 662	15 306	9 356	0	4 758	2 303	50	2 157	95	2 455	1 581	874
1989	32 873	27 485	16 898	10 587	0	5 388	2 589	66	2 420	103	2 799	1 746	1 053
1990	37 677	31 162	18 189	12 973	0	6 515	3 131	78	2 928	125	3 384	2 145	1 238
1991	42 148	34 472	19 295	15 178	0	7 676	3 753	91	3 520	142	3 923	2 655	1 268
1992	46 598	38 329	20 400	17 929	0	8 269	4 167	108	3 897	162	4 102	2 811	1 291
1993	50 632	41 284	21 175	20 109	0	9 348	4 915	150	4 571	194	4 433	3 181	1 252
1994	55 189	44 823	21 368	23 455	0	10 366	5 448	255	4 965	229	4 918	3 589	1 329
1995	61 060	49 351	20 702	28 649	0	11 710	6 274	450	5 561	263	5 436	4 084	1 352
1996	69 111	55 696	21 797	33 899	0	13 414	7 533	721	6 501	312	5 881	4 556	1 325
1997	78 888	62 920	23 016	39 905	0	15 968	9 157	961	7 774	423	6 812	5 451	1 361
1998	89 963	71 014	24 764	46 250	0	18 949	10 977	1 274	9 189	514	7 972	6 456	1 515
1999	100 628	79 225	26 641	52 584	0	21 403	12 449	1 518	10 279	652	8 954	7 226	1 728
2000	112 122	87 884	28 804	59 080	0	24 238	14 185	1 846	11 559	780	10 053	8 115	1 939
2001	124 416	96 935	31 284	65 651	0	27 481	16 150	2 110	13 111	930	11 331	9 199	2 132
2002	137 731	106 718	33 905	72 813	0	31 013	18 294	2 353	14 850	1 091	12 719	10 411	2 308
2003	152 363	117 498	36 761	80 737	0	34 865	20 634	2 603	16 760	1 271	14 231	11 737	2 494
2004	167 967	128 946	39 711	89 235	0	39 021	23 125	2 809	18 868	1 449	15 896	13 211	2 685
2005	185 178	141 559	42 878	98 681	0	43 619	25 875	3 010	21 210	1 655	17 744	14 849	2 896
2006	203 584	154 960	46 256	108 704	0	48 624	28 886	3 266	23 730	1 890	19 739	16 612	3 126
2007	223 012	169 133	50 135	118 998	0	53 879	32 045	3 529	26 367	2 149	21 833	18 458	3 376
2008	243 437	184 163	54 508	129 655	0	59 275	35 293	3 805	29 056	2 433	23 981	20 339	3 642
PRESCRIPTION DRUGS [1]													
1965	2 178	2 178	2 178	0	0	0	0	0	0	0	0	0	0
1966	2 329	2 329	2 329	0	0	0	0	0	0	0	0	0	0
1967	2 527	2 527	2 527	0	0	0	0	0	0	0	0	0	0
1968	2 736	2 736	2 736	0	0	0	0	0	0	0	0	0	0
1969	2 942	2 942	2 942	0	0	0	0	0	0	0	0	0	0
1970	3 314	3 314	3 314	0	0	0	0	0	0	0	0	0	0
1971	3 447	3 447	3 447	0	0	0	0	0	0	0	0	0	0
1972	3 671	3 671	3 671	0	0	0	0	0	0	0	0	0	0
1973	4 031	4 031	4 031	0	0	0	0	0	0	0	0	0	0
1974	4 492	4 492	4 492	0	0	0	0	0	0	0	0	0	0
1975	4 970	4 970	4 970	0	0	0	0	0	0	0	0	0	0
1976	5 522	5 522	5 522	0	0	0	0	0	0	0	0	0	0
1977	6 083	6 083	6 083	0	0	0	0	0	0	0	0	0	0
1978	7 062	7 062	7 062	0	0	0	0	0	0	0	0	0	0
1979	8 287	8 287	8 287	0	0	0	0	0	0	0	0	0	0
1980	9 572	9 572	9 572	0	0	0	0	0	0	0	0	0	0
1981	11 153	11 153	11 153	0	0	0	0	0	0	0	0	0	0
1982	12 580	12 580	12 580	0	0	0	0	0	0	0	0	0	0
1983	13 723	13 723	13 723	0	0	0	0	0	0	0	0	0	0
1984	14 924	14 924	14 924	0	0	0	0	0	0	0	0	0	0
1985	15 903	15 903	15 903	0	0	0	0	0	0	0	0	0	0
1986	17 026	17 026	17 026	0	0	0	0	0	0	0	0	0	0
1987	18 269	18 269	18 269	0	0	0	0	0	0	0	0	0	0
1988	19 671	19 671	19 671	0	0	0	0	0	0	0	0	0	0
1989	20 846	20 846	20 846	0	0	0	0	0	0	0	0	0	0
1990	22 241	22 241	22 241	0	0	0	0	0	0	0	0	0	0
1991	23 411	23 411	23 411	0	0	0	0	0	0	0	0	0	0
1992	24 578	24 578	24 578	0	0	0	0	0	0	0	0	0	0
1993	25 602	25 602	25 602	0	0	0	0	0	0	0	0	0	0
1994	26 401	26 401	26 401	0	0	0	0	0	0	0	0	0	0
1995	27 852	27 852	27 852	0	0	0	0	0	0	0	0	0	0
1996	29 208	29 208	29 208	0	0	0	0	0	0	0	0	0	0
1997	29 984	29 984	29 984	0	0	0	0	0	0	0	0	0	0
1998	30 894	30 894	30 894	0	0	0	0	0	0	0	0	0	0
1999	31 988	31 988	31 988	0	0	0	0	0	0	0	0	0	0
2000	33 362	33 362	33 362	0	0	0	0	0	0	0	0	0	0
2001	34 727	34 727	34 727	0	0	0	0	0	0	0	0	0	0
2002	36 127	36 127	36 127	0	0	0	0	0	0	0	0	0	0
2003	37 573	37 573	37 573	0	0	0	0	0	0	0	0	0	0
2004	38 951	38 951	38 951	0	0	0	0	0	0	0	0	0	0
2005	40 395	40 395	40 395	0	0	0	0	0	0	0	0	0	0
2006	41 823	41 823	41 823	0	0	0	0	0	0	0	0	0	0
2007	43 305	43 305	43 305	0	0	0	0	0	0	0	0	0	0
2008	44 861	44 861	44 861	0	0	0	0	0	0	0	0	0	0

See footnotes at end of table.

Table 4.35. Who Pays for National Health Expenditures—*Continued*

(Millions of dollars)

Type of service provided and year	Total national health expenditures	Private				Public					State and local		
		Total private	Out of pocket	Insurance	Other	Total public	Total federal	Medicare	Medicaid	Other	Total state and local	Medicaid	Other
DURABLE MEDICAL EQUIPMENT													
1965	1 000	971	920	51	0	30	13	0	0	13	17	0	17
1966	1 123	1 081	1 020	61	0	42	23	7	0	16	19	0	19
1967	1 057	996	929	67	0	62	42	22	0	20	20	0	20
1968	1 229	1 154	1 085	69	0	75	52	28	0	24	23	0	23
1969	1 420	1 332	1 249	83	0	88	61	32	0	29	27	0	27
1970	1 623	1 523	1 431	92	0	100	70	37	0	33	30	0	30
1971	1 642	1 524	1 427	96	0	118	86	46	0	40	32	0	32
1972	1 875	1 740	1 623	117	0	135	101	55	0	46	34	0	34
1973	2 085	1 931	1 800	131	0	154	115	67	0	48	39	0	39
1974	2 271	2 077	1 928	149	0	194	148	94	0	55	45	0	45
1975	2 550	2 315	2 133	182	0	235	184	123	0	60	51	0	51
1976	2 730	2 459	2 266	193	0	271	213	150	0	63	58	0	58
1977	2 921	2 596	2 368	229	0	325	260	194	0	66	65	0	65
1978	3 184	2 777	2 502	275	0	407	335	260	0	76	72	0	72
1979	3 517	3 034	2 681	353	0	483	405	322	0	82	78	0	78
1980	3 769	3 167	2 733	433	0	602	521	434	0	87	81	0	81
1981	3 967	3 222	2 751	471	0	745	663	572	0	91	82	0	82
1982	4 264	3 337	2 826	512	0	927	842	748	0	94	85	0	85
1983	4 849	3 681	3 141	541	0	1 168	1 082	974	0	108	86	0	86
1984	5 768	4 435	3 843	592	0	1 334	1 246	1 129	0	117	88	0	88
1985	6 749	5 249	4 611	637	0	1 500	1 409	1 284	0	125	91	0	91
1986	7 449	5 743	5 047	696	0	1 706	1 613	1 478	0	135	93	0	93
1987	8 115	6 182	5 422	760	0	1 933	1 847	1 709	0	138	86	0	86
1988	8 894	6 765	5 926	840	0	2 129	2 033	1 888	0	145	95	0	95
1989	9 552	7 100	6 257	843	0	2 452	2 333	2 169	0	164	119	0	119
1990	10 456	7 578	6 748	830	0	2 879	2 744	2 548	0	197	134	0	134
1991	11 184	7 702	6 896	806	0	3 482	3 337	3 116	0	221	146	0	146
1992	11 893	7 991	7 276	715	0	3 903	3 756	3 520	0	236	147	0	147
1993	12 299	7 993	7 270	723	0	4 306	4 165	3 902	0	264	141	0	141
1994	12 483	7 850	7 200	649	0	4 633	4 490	4 184	0	305	144	0	144
1995	13 095	7 662	7 065	596	0	5 433	5 295	4 965	0	330	138	0	138
1996	13 390	7 488	6 934	554	0	5 902	5 773	5 429	0	344	129	0	129
1997	13 878	7 312	6 793	519	0	6 567	6 442	6 047	0	395	125	0	125
1998	13 785	7 333	6 814	519	0	6 453	6 330	5 920	0	410	123	0	123
1999	14 310	7 450	6 920	531	0	6 860	6 737	6 286	0	451	123	0	123
2000	15 031	7 720	7 168	552	0	7 311	7 187	6 694	0	493	124	0	124
2001	15 818	8 079	7 500	579	0	7 739	7 614	7 080	0	534	125	0	125
2002	16 638	8 438	7 832	606	0	8 200	8 073	7 498	0	575	127	0	127
2003	17 575	8 764	8 132	632	0	8 811	8 682	8 067	0	615	129	0	129
2004	18 497	9 037	8 381	656	0	9 460	9 329	8 674	0	656	131	0	131
2005	19 466	9 290	8 610	680	0	10 177	10 044	9 348	0	696	132	0	132
2006	20 522	9 512	8 810	702	0	11 010	10 876	10 139	0	737	134	0	134
2007	21 663	9 721	8 996	725	0	11 942	11 806	11 029	0	777	136	0	136
2008	22 899	9 917	9 169	749	0	12 981	12 843	12 025	0	818	138	0	138
NURSING HOME CARE													
1965	1 471	969	884	2	84	502	221	0	0	221	281	0	281
1966	1 812	1 262	1 160	3	99	550	279	0	98	180	271	105	166
1967	2 338	1 330	1 199	8	123	1 009	613	190	304	120	395	324	71
1968	2 982	1 821	1 663	8	150	1 161	736	243	366	128	425	340	85
1969	3 568	2 198	2 012	12	174	1 370	861	215	425	220	509	346	163
1970	4 217	2 480	2 256	16	207	1 738	1 045	142	505	398	692	436	257
1971	4 762	2 685	2 428	21	236	2 078	1 267	120	779	369	810	588	222
1972	5 516	3 127	2 829	25	273	2 389	1 385	120	1 163	102	1 004	983	21
1973	6 352	3 600	3 242	37	321	2 752	1 570	165	1 281	124	1 182	1 161	21
1974	7 393	3 728	3 314	51	363	3 665	2 203	201	1 858	145	1 462	1 440	22
1975	8 668	4 171	3 691	65	415	4 497	2 647	220	2 248	179	1 850	1 838	12
1976	9 907	4 850	4 315	74	461	5 057	3 182	260	2 708	214	1 875	1 861	14
1977	11 499	5 554	4 983	94	478	5 945	3 573	267	3 053	254	2 371	2 355	16
1978	13 439	6 348	5 724	124	500	7 091	4 187	268	3 629	290	2 904	2 887	17
1979	15 304	6 932	6 263	157	512	8 373	4 996	282	4 394	320	3 377	3 359	17
1980	17 649	8 115	7 370	212	533	9 534	5 608	307	4 931	370	3 926	3 899	27
1981	20 201	9 061	8 237	274	550	11 140	6 770	337	6 010	423	4 370	4 345	25
1982	22 785	10 722	9 784	376	562	12 063	7 025	367	6 157	500	5 038	5 013	25
1983	25 477	12 118	11 058	491	568	13 359	7 716	393	6 763	560	5 644	5 614	30
1984	27 919	13 417	12 222	629	565	14 503	8 301	426	7 202	673	6 202	6 176	26
1985	30 679	14 980	13 601	813	565	15 699	9 181	452	8 003	725	6 518	6 491	28
1986	33 507	16 441	14 790	1 033	618	17 066	10 064	450	8 779	835	7 002	6 971	31
1987	36 329	17 665	15 707	1 285	674	18 664	10 886	482	9 501	902	7 779	7 750	29
1988	39 773	19 712	17 449	1 527	736	20 061	11 988	719	10 314	955	8 073	8 039	35
1989	44 936	21 421	18 806	1 784	831	23 516	14 785	2 492	11 349	944	8 731	8 683	48
1990	50 928	24 979	21 936	2 102	942	25 949	15 774	1 732	13 000	1 043	10 174	10 107	67
1991	57 164	26 528	23 085	2 386	1 056	30 637	18 363	1 935	15 267	1 162	12 274	12 213	61
1992	62 301	27 894	24 091	2 646	1 157	34 407	21 221	2 872	17 098	1 251	13 185	13 117	69
1993	66 447	28 551	24 529	2 814	1 209	37 896	24 040	3 946	18 675	1 419	13 856	13 774	82
1994	71 092	29 644	25 284	3 025	1 335	41 448	26 499	5 513	19 438	1 549	14 948	14 826	123
1995	75 467	31 439	26 624	3 395	1 420	44 028	28 397	6 734	20 053	1 610	15 631	15 522	108
1996	79 385	31 941	26 712	3 731	1 498	47 443	31 288	8 034	21 582	1 671	16 156	16 034	121
1997	82 774	31 325	25 741	4 022	1 562	51 449	34 522	10 150	22 641	1 731	16 927	16 799	128
1998	86 979	32 186	26 308	4 227	1 650	54 793	36 814	11 075	23 957	1 782	17 979	17 844	136
1999	90 124	34 058	27 853	4 491	1 714	56 066	37 480	10 826	24 797	1 857	18 585	18 440	145
2000	94 133	36 012	29 196	5 022	1 793	58 121	38 887	11 169	25 779	1 939	19 234	19 078	156
2001	99 218	38 061	31 009	5 157	1 894	61 158	41 076	12 141	26 902	2 033	20 082	19 916	166
2002	104 910	40 306	32 752	5 547	2 007	64 604	43 533	13 175	28 223	2 134	21 072	20 894	178
2003	111 101	42 751	34 618	6 004	2 129	68 350	46 198	14 270	29 684	2 244	22 152	21 961	191
2004	117 648	45 259	36 741	6 261	2 258	72 388	49 030	15 373	31 294	2 363	23 358	23 154	204
2005	124 946	48 070	38 877	6 793	2 401	76 876	52 154	16 547	33 115	2 492	24 722	24 503	219
2006	132 864	51 146	41 161	7 429	2 556	81 717	55 492	17 742	35 122	2 629	26 225	25 990	235
2007	141 452	54 561	43 846	7 991	2 724	86 890	59 033	18 958	37 302	2 773	27 857	27 605	252
2008	150 680	58 443	47 114	8 427	2 902	92 237	62 654	20 118	39 610	2 926	29 583	29 312	271

See footnotes at end of table.

Table 4.35. Who Pays for National Health Expenditures—*Continued*

(Millions of dollars)

Type of service provided and year	Total national health expenditures	Private				Public					State and local		
		Total private	Out of pocket	Insurance	Other	Total public	Total federal	Medicare	Medicaid	Other	Total state and local	Medicaid	Other
OTHER PERSONAL HEALTH CARE													
1965	823	210	0	0	210	613	343	0	0	343	270		270
1966	957	225	0	0	225	732	443	0	11	432	289	12	278
1967	1 053	246	0	0	246	807	489	0	21	468	319	23	296
1968	1 128	266	0	0	266	862	488	0	47	441	374	43	331
1969	1 261	292	0	0	292	969	530	0	85	444	439	71	369
1970	1 298	313	0	0	313	985	506	0	91	415	478	78	400
1971	1 323	336	0	0	336	987	513	0	76	437	474	57	417
1972	1 532	359	0	0	359	1 173	692	0	68	624	481	60	421
1973	1 615	387	0	0	387	1 228	689	0	93	596	539	81	458
1974	1 870	431	0	0	431	1 439	826	0	137	689	613	110	502
1975	2 477	477	0	0	477	2 000	1 323	0	175	1 148	678	141	537
1976	2 681	541	0	0	541	2 140	1 417	0	198	1 219	723	137	586
1977	2 884	614	0	0	614	2 270	1 459	0	183	1 275	811	141	670
1978	3 168	695	0	0	695	2 473	1 596	0	181	1 415	877	145	733
1979	3 448	782	0	0	782	2 666	1 671	0	236	1 435	995	183	812
1980	4 018	871	0	0	871	3 147	2 010	0	245	1 765	1 137	197	940
1981	4 419	976	0	0	976	3 443	2 187	0	296	1 891	1 256	252	1 004
1982	4 817	1 079	0	0	1 079	3 738	2 331	0	368	1 963	1 407	338	1 069
1983	5 133	1 189	0	0	1 189	3 944	2 342	0	470	1 871	1 602	433	1 169
1984	5 429	1 313	0	0	1 313	4 116	2 413	0	496	1 916	1 704	455	1 249
1985	6 117	1 426	0	0	1 426	4 691	2 774	0	655	2 118	1 918	537	1 381
1986	6 949	1 568	0	0	1 568	5 381	3 195	0	795	2 399	2 186	623	1 563
1987	7 622	1 714	0	0	1 714	5 908	3 476	0	944	2 532	2 432	750	1 682
1988	8 555	1 868	0	0	1 868	6 687	4 001	0	1 191	2 811	2 685	916	1 769
1989	9 507	2 052	0	0	2 052	7 455	4 309	0	1 617	2 692	3 146	1 246	1 900
1990	11 228	2 250	0	0	2 250	8 978	5 415	0	1 960	3 455	3 563	1 512	2 051
1991	13 552	2 426	0	0	2 426	11 126	6 735	0	2 879	3 856	4 392	2 225	2 167
1992	15 360	2 627	0	0	2 627	12 733	7 755	0	3 700	4 056	4 978	2 704	2 273
1993	17 977	2 841	0	0	2 841	15 136	9 220	0	4 999	4 221	5 916	3 499	2 417
1994	21 890	3 056	0	0	3 056	18 834	11 329	0	6 460	4 869	7 505	4 776	2 729
1995	25 057	3 259	0	0	3 259	21 798	12 813	0	7 857	4 956	8 986	5 970	3 015
1996	27 441	3 427	0	0	3 427	24 014	14 148	0	9 174	4 973	9 867	6 681	3 186
1997	29 909	3 606	0	0	3 606	26 303	15 563	0	10 421	5 143	10 739	7 485	3 255
1998	33 027	3 785	0	0	3 785	29 242	17 164	0	11 858	5 306	12 079	8 686	3 393
1999	36 029	3 977	0	0	3 977	32 052	18 785	0	13 251	5 533	13 268	9 696	3 571
2000	39 466	4 224	0	0	4 224	35 242	20 652	0	14 889	5 763	14 590	10 872	3 718
2001	43 709	4 482	0	0	4 482	39 227	22 975	0	16 966	6 009	16 252	12 395	3 857
2002	48 636	4 752	0	0	4 752	43 884	25 665	0	19 400	6 265	18 219	14 178	4 041
2003	54 278	5 037	0	0	5 037	49 240	28 754	0	22 206	6 548	20 487	16 225	4 262
2004	60 670	5 324	0	0	5 324	55 346	32 258	0	25 450	6 808	23 088	18 609	4 480
2005	68 148	5 629	0	0	5 629	62 519	36 374	0	29 279	7 095	26 115	21 423	4 722
2006	76 691	5 944	0	0	5 944	70 747	41 098	0	33 690	7 409	29 649	24 663	4 986
2007	86 260	6 278	0	0	6 278	79 983	46 402	0	38 655	7 747	33 581	28 311	5 270
2008	96 813	6 631	0	0	6 631	90 181	52 260	0	44 152	8 108	37 921	32 347	5 574
PRIVATE HEALTH INSURANCE [2]													
1965	1 928	1 508	0	1 349	159	420	87	0	0	87	333		333
1966	2 142	1 596	0	1 449	147	546	212	120	26	65	334	25	308
1967	2 233	1 568	0	1 415	153	665	306	194	64	48	360	59	301
1968	2 716	1 857	0	1 684	173	860	426	288	82	56	434	75	359
1969	2 492	1 539	0	1 403	136	952	475	311	103	62	477	89	389
1970	2 722	1 645	0	1 507	138	1 078	581	398	135	48	496	116	380
1971	3 317	2 233	0	2 092	141	1 084	632	408	167	57	452	119	333
1972	4 434	3 209	0	3 052	157	1 225	727	475	188	64	498	154	344
1973	4 923	3 466	0	3 320	146	1 456	857	550	237	70	599	175	424
1974	4 544	2 854	0	2 700	154	1 690	1 048	682	284	82	642	201	442
1975	4 910	3 063	0	2 902	161	1 848	1 181	729	361	91	667	248	419
1976	6 680	4 523	0	4 355	168	2 157	1 476	883	494	100	681	268	413
1977	9 313	6 953	0	6 782	171	2 361	1 442	757	581	105	918	366	552
1978	11 027	8 099	0	7 916	183	2 928	1 825	1 005	701	118	1 103	362	741
1979	11 819	8 395	0	8 197	198	3 424	1 952	1 026	801	125	1 472	398	1 074
1980	11 867	7 988	0	7 744	244	3 879	2 100	1 132	836	133	1 778	505	1 273
1981	13 851	9 560	0	9 284	276	4 291	2 437	1 318	976	143	1 854	541	1 313
1982	16 153	11 757	0	11 425	332	4 396	2 489	1 296	1 038	155	1 907	559	1 348
1983	18 317	13 808	0	13 418	390	4 509	2 701	1 449	1 069	183	1 808	716	1 092
1984	22 011	17 547	0	17 103	444	4 464	3 011	1 614	1 213	184	1 453	847	606
1985	24 290	19 264	0	18 781	483	5 026	3 551	2 034	1 334	182	1 475	851	625
1986	21 199	16 098	0	15 623	475	5 101	3 652	2 046	1 421	185	1 449	951	499
1987	18 550	12 748	0	12 246	502	5 802	3 781	2 075	1 504	202	2 021	1 122	899
1988	24 346	17 779	0	17 272	507	6 567	4 428	2 524	1 674	230	2 139	1 241	898
1989	33 121	25 749	0	25 215	534	7 373	5 030	2 848	1 936	246	2 343	1 370	973
1990	40 544	32 403	0	31 811	592	8 141	5 485	2 895	2 309	281	2 656	1 674	982
1991	40 866	32 537	0	31 923	614	8 329	6 016	3 289	2 460	266	2 313	1 874	440
1992	44 901	35 431	0	34 841	590	9 470	6 410	3 473	2 612	325	3 060	2 209	851
1993	53 660	42 148	0	41 564	584	11 513	7 693	3 993	3 321	379	3 820	2 663	1 157
1994	55 108	41 167	0	40 561	606	13 941	8 476	4 289	3 781	407	5 465	3 897	1 568
1995	53 337	38 363	0	37 694	669	14 974	9 244	4 503	4 331	409	5 730	4 531	1 199
1996	52 519	38 049	0	37 330	719	14 469	9 937	5 226	4 326	385	4 532	3 450	1 083
1997	49 998	35 296	0	34 570	726	14 703	10 403	5 716	4 322	366	4 299	3 257	1 042
1998	54 454	37 678	0	36 887	791	16 776	12 039	6 710	4 963	366	4 737	3 768	970
1999	65 138	46 720	0	45 774	946	18 418	13 261	7 309	5 582	370	5 157	4 238	919
2000	74 497	54 808	0	53 726	1 082	19 689	14 374	8 182	5 811	381	5 315	4 412	903
2001	79 640	58 919	0	57 763	1 156	20 721	15 272	8 882	5 996	395	5 449	4 552	897
2002	82 920	60 785	0	59 581	1 204	22 134	16 377	9 561	6 406	410	5 757	4 864	894
2003	83 470	59 768	0	58 556	1 212	23 702	17 587	10 285	6 875	427	6 115	5 220	895
2004	85 828	60 539	0	59 293	1 246	25 289	18 767	10 918	7 402	446	6 522	5 620	902
2005	89 464	62 503	0	61 204	1 299	26 961	19 999	11 562	7 969	468	6 962	6 050	911
2006	93 265	64 411	0	63 057	1 354	28 854	21 420	12 350	8 580	490	7 435	6 514	921
2007	97 163	66 288	0	64 878	1 411	30 875	22 930	13 180	9 236	514	7 945	7 012	933
2008	101 084	68 054	0	66 587	1 468	33 030	24 535	14 052	9 942	541	8 495	7 548	947

See footnotes at end of table.

Table 4.35. Who Pays for National Health Expenditures—*Continued*

(Millions of dollars)

Type of service provided and year	Total national health expenditures	Private				Public					State and local		
		Total private	Out of pocket	Insurance	Other	Total public	Total federal	Medicare	Medicaid	Other	Total state and local	Medicaid	Other
PUBLIC HEALTH ACTIVITY													
1965	615	0	0	0	0	615	214	0	0	214	401	0	401
1966	725	0	0	0	0	725	294	0	0	294	431	0	431
1967	855	0	0	0	0	855	401	0	0	401	454	0	454
1968	963	0	0	0	0	963	471	0	0	471	492	0	492
1969	1 166	0	0	0	0	1 166	564	0	0	564	602	0	602
1970	1 347	0	0	0	0	1 347	594	0	0	594	753	0	753
1971	1 664	0	0	0	0	1 665	791	0	0	791	873	0	873
1972	1 845	0	0	0	0	1 845	893	0	0	893	952	0	952
1973	2 114	0	0	0	0	2 114	854	0	0	854	1 260	0	1 260
1974	2 580	0	0	0	0	2 580	969	0	0	969	1 611	0	1 611
1975	2 928	0	0	0	0	2 928	1 043	0	0	1 043	1 885	0	1 885
1976	3 321	0	0	0	0	3 321	1 110	0	0	1 110	2 211	0	2 211
1977	4 094	0	0	0	0	4 094	1 152	0	0	1 152	2 942	0	2 942
1978	4 884	0	0	0	0	4 884	1 155	0	0	1 155	3 730	0	3 730
1979	5 618	0	0	0	0	5 618	1 106	0	0	1 106	4 512	0	4 512
1980	6 732	0	0	0	0	6 732	1 246	0	0	1 246	5 486	0	5 486
1981	7 823	0	0	0	0	7 823	1 258	0	0	1 258	6 565	0	6 565
1982	8 866	0	0	0	0	8 866	1 191	0	0	1 191	7 675	0	7 675
1983	9 484	0	0	0	0	9 484	1 294	0	0	1 294	8 190	0	8 190
1984	10 171	0	0	0	0	10 171	1 355	0	0	1 355	8 816	0	8 816
1985	11 618	0	0	0	0	11 618	1 397	0	0	1 397	10 221	0	10 221
1986	12 707	0	0	0	0	12 707	1 418	0	0	1 418	11 289	0	11 289
1987	13 919	0	0	0	0	13 919	1 635	0	0	1 635	12 285	0	12 285
1988	15 561	0	0	0	0	15 561	1 893	0	0	1 893	13 668	0	13 668
1989	18 060	0	0	0	0	18 060	2 138	0	0	2 138	15 922	0	15 922
1990	19 613	0	0	0	0	19 613	2 377	0	0	2 377	17 237	0	17 237
1991	21 422	0	0	0	0	21 422	2 705	0	0	2 705	18 717	0	18 717
1992	23 413	0	0	0	0	23 413	3 043	0	0	3 043	20 371	0	20 371
1993	25 310	0	0	0	0	25 310	3 278	0	0	3 278	22 032	0	22 032
1994	28 162	0	0	0	0	28 162	3 788	0	0	3 788	24 374	0	24 374
1995	30 416	0	0	0	0	30 416	3 803	0	0	3 803	26 612	0	26 612
1996	34 045	0	0	0	0	34 045	3 915	0	0	3 915	30 130	0	30 130
1997	38 490	0	0	0	0	38 490	4 131	0	0	4 131	34 359	0	34 359
1998	42 261	0	0	0	0	42 261	4 381	0	0	4 381	37 880	0	37 880
1999	46 236	0	0	0	0	46 236	4 711	0	0	4 711	41 525	0	41 525
2000	50 164	0	0	0	0	50 164	5 086	0	0	5 086	45 078	0	45 078
2001	54 019	0	0	0	0	54 019	5 436	0	0	5 436	48 584	0	48 584
2002	58 045	0	0	0	0	58 045	5 781	0	0	5 781	52 264	0	52 264
2003	62 363	0	0	0	0	62 363	6 087	0	0	6 087	56 276	0	56 276
2004	67 085	0	0	0	0	67 085	6 384	0	0	6 384	60 701	0	60 701
2005	72 291	0	0	0	0	72 291	6 701	0	0	6 701	65 590	0	65 590
2006	77 944	0	0	0	0	77 944	7 036	0	0	7 036	70 908	0	70 908
2007	84 114	0	0	0	0	84 114	7 396	0	0	7 396	76 718	0	76 718
2008	90 817	0	0	0	0	90 817	7 777	0	0	7 777	83 040	0	83 040
RESEARCH													
1965	1 523	176	0	0	176	1 347	1 253	0	0	1 253	95	0	95
1966	1 623	186	0	0	186	1 437	1 333	0	0	1 333	104	0	104
1967	1 771	198	0	0	198	1 573	1 462	0	0	1 462	111	0	111
1968	1 884	208	0	0	208	1 676	1 547	0	0	1 547	129	0	129
1969	1 921	213	0	0	213	1 708	1 551	0	0	1 551	157	0	157
1970	1 956	215	0	0	215	1 741	1 559	0	0	1 559	182	0	182
1971	2 097	233	0	0	233	1 864	1 651	0	0	1 651	214	0	214
1972	2 375	227	0	0	227	2 148	1 910	0	0	1 910	238	0	238
1973	2 506	232	0	0	232	2 274	2 027	0	0	2 027	248	0	248
1974	2 745	252	0	0	252	2 493	2 224	0	0	2 224	269	0	269
1975	3 326	264	0	0	264	3 062	2 762	0	0	2 762	300	0	300
1976	3 728	267	0	0	267	3 461	3 141	0	0	3 141	320	0	320
1977	3 891	220	0	0	220	3 671	3 296	0	0	3 296	375	0	375
1978	4 457	236	0	0	236	4 221	3 774	0	0	3 774	447	0	447
1979	4 776	254	0	0	254	4 522	4 054	0	0	4 054	467	0	467
1980	5 461	292	0	0	292	5 169	4 651	0	0	4 651	519	0	519
1981	5 694	312	0	0	312	5 382	4 778	0	0	4 778	604	0	604
1982	6 040	390	0	0	390	5 650	4 970	0	0	4 970	680	0	680
1983	6 425	456	0	0	456	5 969	5 211	0	0	5 211	758	0	758
1984	7 138	506	0	0	506	6 632	5 801	0	0	5 801	831	0	831
1985	7 840	538	0	0	538	7 302	6 354	0	0	6 354	948	0	948
1986	8 625	782	0	0	782	7 843	6 734	0	0	6 734	1 110	0	1 110
1987	9 129	800	0	0	800	8 329	7 092	0	0	7 092	1 237	0	1 237
1988	10 505	839	0	0	839	9 666	8 289	0	0	8 289	1 377	0	1 377
1989	11 259	882	0	0	882	10 377	8 835	0	0	8 835	1 543	0	1 543
1990	12 214	960	0	0	960	11 254	9 520	0	0	9 520	1 734	0	1 734
1991	12 918	1 090	0	0	1 090	11 828	9 938	0	0	9 938	1 890	0	1 890
1992	14 178	1 183	0	0	1 183	12 995	11 008	0	0	11 008	1 987	0	1 987
1993	14 486	1 215	0	0	1 215	13 271	11 144	0	0	11 144	2 128	0	2 128
1994	15 883	1 276	0	0	1 276	14 607	12 299	0	0	12 299	2 308	0	2 308
1995	16 710	1 325	0	0	1 325	15 385	12 916	0	0	12 916	2 468	0	2 468
1996	17 151	1 432	0	0	1 432	15 718	13 174	0	0	13 174	2 544	0	2 544
1997	17 956	1 488	0	0	1 488	16 467	13 820	0	0	13 820	2 647	0	2 647
1998	18 818	1 555	0	0	1 555	17 263	14 515	0	0	14 515	2 747	0	2 747
1999	19 668	1 631	0	0	1 631	18 037	15 154	0	0	15 154	2 882	0	2 882
2000	20 593	1 721	0	0	1 721	18 873	15 842	0	0	15 842	3 030	0	3 030
2001	21 640	1 822	0	0	1 822	19 818	16 621	0	0	16 621	3 197	0	3 197
2002	22 771	1 933	0	0	1 933	20 838	17 461	0	0	17 461	3 377	0	3 377
2003	24 009	2 055	0	0	2 055	21 954	18 379	0	0	18 379	3 575	0	3 575
2004	25 367	2 191	0	0	2 191	23 176	19 385	0	0	19 385	3 791	0	3 791
2005	26 851	2 340	0	0	2 340	24 510	20 482	0	0	20 482	4 028	0	4 028
2006	28 435	2 502	0	0	2 502	25 932	21 651	0	0	21 651	4 281	0	4 281
2007	30 131	2 679	0	0	2 679	27 452	22 900	0	0	22 900	4 553	0	4 553
2008	31 936	2 870	0	0	2 870	29 066	24 223	0	0	24 223	4 843	0	4 843

See footnotes at end of table.

Table 4.35. Who Pays for National Health Expenditures—*Continued*
(Millions of dollars)

Type of service provided and year	Total national health expenditures	Private				Public					State and local		
		Total private	Out of pocket	Insurance	Other	Total public	Total federal	Medicare	Medicaid	Other	Total state and local	Medicaid	Other
CONSTRUCTION													
1965	1 914	1 273	0	0	1 273	641	297	0	0	297	344	0	344
1966	1 934	1 294	0	0	1 294	640	308	0	0	308	332	0	332
1967	1 969	1 205	0	0	1 205	764	309	0	0	309	455	0	455
1968	2 277	1 410	0	0	1 410	868	346	0	0	346	522	0	522
1969	2 977	1 987	0	0	1 987	990	379	0	0	379	611	0	611
1970	3 393	2 364	0	0	2 364	1 029	378	0	0	378	651	0	651
1971	3 886	2 682	0	0	2 682	1 204	436	0	0	436	769	0	769
1972	4 246	3 060	0	0	3 060	1 186	377	0	0	377	809	0	809
1973	4 230	3 107	0	0	3 107	1 123	297	0	0	297	826	0	826
1974	4 528	3 128	0	0	3 128	1 400	334	0	0	334	1 066	0	1 066
1975	5 057	3 158	0	0	3 158	1 899	490	0	0	490	1 409	0	1 409
1976	5 595	3 360	0	0	3 360	2 235	573	0	0	573	1 662	0	1 662
1977	5 342	3 317	0	0	3 317	2 025	549	0	0	549	1 477	0	1 477
1978	5 394	3 380	0	0	3 380	2 014	676	0	0	676	1 338	0	1 338
1979	5 492	3 607	0	0	3 607	1 885	522	0	0	522	1 363	0	1 363
1980	6 175	4 161	0	0	4 161	2 014	562	0	0	562	1 453	0	1 453
1981	7 534	5 107	0	0	5 107	2 428	659	0	0	659	1 769	0	1 769
1982	8 643	6 163	0	0	6 163	2 481	645	0	0	645	1 836	0	1 836
1983	9 552	6 919	0	0	6 919	2 634	653	0	0	653	1 980	0	1 980
1984	9 285	6 677	0	0	6 677	2 608	743	0	0	743	1 865	0	1 865
1985	8 531	5 962	0	0	5 962	2 569	818	0	0	818	1 751	0	1 751
1986	8 193	5 771	0	0	5 771	2 422	901	0	0	901	1 520	0	1 520
1987	9 194	6 509	0	0	6 509	2 685	1 055	0	0	1 055	1 630	0	1 630
1988	10 710	7 820	0	0	7 820	2 890	903	0	0	903	1 987	0	1 987
1989	10 963	8 170	0	0	8 170	2 793	847	0	0	847	1 946	0	1 946
1990	12 310	9 288	0	0	9 288	3 022	847	0	0	847	2 175	0	2 175
1991	12 014	9 033	0	0	9 033	2 981	725	0	0	725	2 257	0	2 257
1992	13 364	9 824	0	0	9 824	3 541	783	0	0	783	2 758	0	2 758
1993	14 522	10 682	0	0	10 682	3 840	934	0	0	934	2 907	0	2 907
1994	14 596	10 496	0	0	10 496	4 100	881	0	0	881	3 219	0	3 219
1995	13 932	9 628	0	0	9 628	4 304	1 070	0	0	1 070	3 234	0	3 234
1996	14 812	10 254	0	0	10 254	4 558	1 229	0	0	1 229	3 329	0	3 329
1997	16 937	11 877	0	0	11 877	5 060	1 439	0	0	1 439	3 621	0	3 621
1998	18 194	12 920	0	0	12 920	5 274	1 486	0	0	1 486	3 788	0	3 788
1999	19 169	13 708	0	0	13 708	5 461	1 518	0	0	1 518	3 943	0	3 943
2000	20 065	14 413	0	0	14 413	5 652	1 542	0	0	1 542	4 110	0	4 110
2001	20 983	15 114	0	0	15 114	5 869	1 576	0	0	1 576	4 293	0	4 293
2002	21 774	15 687	0	0	15 687	6 086	1 613	0	0	1 613	4 473	0	4 473
2003	22 626	16 324	0	0	16 324	6 302	1 655	0	0	1 655	4 648	0	4 648
2004	23 538	17 011	0	0	17 011	6 527	1 701	0	0	1 701	4 826	0	4 826
2005	24 509	17 743	0	0	17 743	6 765	1 752	0	0	1 752	5 013	0	5 013
2006	25 509	18 499	0	0	18 499	7 010	1 805	0	0	1 805	5 205	0	5 205
2007	26 547	19 282	0	0	19 282	7 265	1 861	0	0	1 861	5 404	0	5 404
2008	27 623	20 096	0	0	20 096	7 527	1 917	0	0	1 917	5 610	0	5 610

SOURCE: Health Care Financing Administration, Office of the Actuary, National Health Care Expenditures Projections. National Health Expenditures 1965–2008.

1. Part of nondurable products.
2. Administration and net cost of private health insurance.

NOTE: Estimates for the years 1998–2008 were projections based on the 1997 release of the National Health Expenditure data.

Table 4.36. Expenditures on Mental Health Care

Type of organization	1969 [2]	1975	1979	1986	1990	1992	1994
EXPENDITURES (THOUSANDS OF DOLLARS)							
Total	3 292 563	6 564 312	8 763 795	18 457 741	28 410 261	29 765 202	33 136 440
State and county mental hospitals	1 814 101	3 185 049	3 756 754	6 325 844	7 774 482	7 970 163	7 824 661
Private psychiatric hospitals	220 026	466 720	743 037	2 629 009	6 101 063	5 301 940	6 468 184
Nonfederal general hospitals with psychiatric services	298 000	621 284	722 868	2 877 739	4 661 574	5 192 984	5 344 188
VA medical centers [3]	450 000	699 027	848 469	1 337 943	1 480 082	1 529 745	1 386 213
Federally funded community mental health centers	143 491	775 580	1 480 890	—	—	—	—
Residential treatment centers for emotionally disturbed children	122 711	278 950	436 246	977 616	1 969 283	2 167 324	2 360 363
All other mental health organizations [4]	244 234	537 702	775 531	4 309 590	6 423 777	9 603 066	9 752 831
PERCENT DISTRIBUTION OF EXPENDITURES							
All organizations	100.0	100.0	100.0	100.0	100.0	100.0	100.0
State and county mental hospitals	55.1	48.5	42.9	34.3	27.4	26.8	23.6
Private psychiatric hospitals	6.7	7.1	8.5	14.2	21.5	17.8	19.5
Nonfederal general hospitals with psychiatric services	9.1	9.5	8.2	15.6	16.4	17.4	16.1
VA medical centers [3]	13.7	10.6	9.7	7.2	5.2	5.1	4.2
Federally funded community mental health centers	4.4	11.8	16.9	—	—	—	—
Residential treatment centers for emotionally disturbed children	3.7	4.2	5.0	5.3	6.9	7.3	7.1
All other mental health organizations [4]	7.4	8.2	8.8	23.3	22.6	32.3	29.5
EXPENDITURES PER CAPITA [1] CIVILIAN POPULATION							
All organizations	16.53	31.05	39.61	77.10	116.39	116.69	127.86
State and county mental hospitals	9.11	15.06	16.86	26.43	31.85	31.25	30.19
Private psychiatric hospitals	1.10	2.21	3.34	10.98	24.99	20.78	24.96
Nonfederal general hospitals with psychiatric services	1.50	2.94	3.37	12.02	19.10	20.36	20.62
VA medical centers [3]	2.26	3.31	3.95	5.59	6.06	6.00	5.35
Federally funded community mental health centers	0.72	3.67	6.65	—	—	—	—
Residential treatment centers for emotionally disturbed children	0.62	1.32	1.96	4.08	8.07	8.50	9.11
All other mental health organizations [4]	1.22	2.54	3.48	18.00	26.32	29.80	37.63

SOURCE: Published and unpublished inventory data from the Survey and Analysis Branch, Division of State and Community Systems Development, Center for Mental Health Services, Substance Abuse Mental Health Services Administration (SAMHSA). M.J. Witkin, J.E. Atay, R.W. Manderscheid, J. DeLozier, A. Male, and R. Gillespe, "Highlights of Organized Mental Health Services in 1994 and Major National and State Trends," *Mental Health, United States, 1998*, DHHS Pub. No. (SMA) 99-3285. SAMHSA Center for Mental Health Services. (Washington, D.C.: Supt. of Docs., U.S. Govt. Printing Office, 1998): Table 8a.

— Data not available.
1. The population used in the calculation of these rates is the January 1 civilian population of the United States for the respective years.
2. Some organizations were reclassified as a result of changes in reporting procedures and definitions. For 1979–1980, comparable data were not available for certain organization types, and data for either an earlier or a later period were substituted. These factors influence the comparability of 1980, 1986, 1990, 1992, and 1994 data from those earlier years.
3. Includes Department of Veterans Affairs (formerly Veterans Administration, VA) neuropsychiatric hospitals, VA general hospital psychiatric services, and VA psychiatric outpatient clinics.
4. Includes free-standing psychiatric partial care organizations, free-standing psychiatric outpatient clinics, and multiservice mental health organizations. Multiservice mental health organizations were redefined in 1984.

NOTES

1. See P. R. Lee, C. L. Estes, and L. Close, *The Nation's Health*, 5th ed. (Boston: Jones and Bartlett Publishers, 1997).

2. See M. Millman, *Access to Health Care in America* (Washington, D.C.: National Academy of Sciences Press, 1993).

3. See G. Simpson, B. Bloom, R. A. Cohen, and P. E. Parsons, "Access to Health Care, Parts I, II, and III," *Vital and Health Statistics* 10 (1977):196–197. Data are based on the Access to Care and Health Insurance components of the 1993 National Health Interview Survey. *Regular source of medical care* was defined as having at least one particular person or place respondents usually went to when sick or when they needed health advice. For a more recent review, see David Barton Smith, *Health Care Divided: Race and Healing a Nation* (Ann Arbor: University of Michigan Press, 1999). Professor Smith shows how current differences in care received can be traced to patterns established before the passage of the civil rights laws.

4. D. A. Woodwell, "National Ambulatory Medical Care Survey: 1997 Summary," *Vital and Health Statistics*, Advance Data No. 305 (May 20, 1999).

5. The data are based on the National Health Interview Survey interviews. Classification of the acute conditions was based on information provided by the respondent and not from medical records.

6. Substance Abuse and Mental Health Services Administration, Office of Applied Studies, *National Household Survey on Drug Abuse, Main Findings 1997*, Department of Health and Human Services Publication No. (SMA) 99-3295 (1999).

7. Substance Abuse and Mental Health Services Administration, Office of Applied Studies, *Uniform Facility Data Set (UFDS):1997*, DHHS Publication No. (SMA) 99-3314 (1999).

8. Substance Abuse and Mental Health Services Administration, Office of Applied Studies, *Mental Health Estimates from the 1994 National Household Survey on Drug Abuse*, Advance Report No. 15 (July 1996).

9. Data were based on the National Home and Hospice Care Survey, first conducted in 1991 and 1992. The information is obtained from the medical records of a sample of patients from a representative sample of hospices and home health care agencies. Current patients were those who were on the agency rolls as of midnight the day before the date of the survey. Discharges were the number of episodes of care that ended during the 12 months prior to the survey. Patients may be included more than once if they had more than one episode of care during the survey period. Discharges can occur because services were provided at another hospice or other source of care, such as an inpatient health care facility, family care, or a home health care agency. The most common reason for discharge (81.9 percent), however, is death of the patient.

10. J. A. Rhoades and N. A. Krauss, "Nursing Home Trends, 1987 and 1996," *Medical Expenditure Panel Survey Chartbook No. 3*, AHCPR Publication No. 99-0032 (1999).

11. M. L. Berk and C. L. Schur, "Measuring Access to Care: Improving Information for Policymakers," *Health Affairs* 17, no. 1 (1998):180–186.

12. R. L. Bennefield, "Dynamics of Economic Well-Being: Health Insurance, 1993 to 1995: Who Loses Coverage and for How Long?" *Current Population Reports*, P70-64 (August 1998). See also R. J. Mills, "Health Insurance Coverage: 1999," *Current Population Reports*, P60-211 (September 2000).

13. From a statement by Michael Hash, deputy administrator, Health Care Financing Administration, before the Senate Special Committee on Aging and Nursing Home Quality, July 28, 1998.

14. Clinton administration sets new initiatives to improve the quality of care in nursing homes. See the *HCFA Medicare/Medicaid Health Watch* IV (September 1998).

15. National Committee for Quality Assurance (NCQA), *The State of Managed Care Quality* (Washington, D.C.: NCQA, July 28, 1999).

16. S. B. Soumerai, T. J. McLaughlin, D. Spiegelman, E. Hertzmark, G. Thibault, and L. Goldman, "Adverse Outcomes of Underuse of Beta-blockers in Elderly Survivors of Acute Myocardial Infarction," *Journal of the American Medical Association* 277, no. 2 (1997):115–121.

17. Centers for Disease Prevention and Control, Hospital Infections Program, National Center for Infectious Diseases, "Public Health Focus: Surveillance, Prevention, and Control of Nosocomial Infections," *Morbidity and Mortality Weekly Report* 41, no. 42 (October 23, 1992):783–787.

18. Centers for Disease Prevention and Control, Hospital Infections Program, National Center for Infectious Diseases, "National Nosocomial Infections Surveillance (NNIS) System Report, Data Summary from January 1990–May 1999, Issued June 1999," *American Journal of Infection Control* 27 (1999):520–532.

19. E. Bergogne-Berezin, "Current Guidelines for the Treatment and Prevention of Nosocomial Infections," *Drugs* 58, no. 1 (July 1999):51–67.

20. J. Stoddard, E. Sekscenski, and J. Weiner, "The Physician Workforce: Broadening the Search for Solutions," *Health Affairs* 17, no. 1 (January/February

1998):252–257. Also see Institute of Medicine, *The Nation's Physician Workforce Options for Balancing Supply and Requirements* (Washington, D.C.: National Academy of Sciences Press, 1996).

21. M. Whitcomb, "A Cross National Comparison of Generalist Physician Workforce Data," *Journal of the American Medical Association (JAMA)* 274 (1995):692–695; R. Cooper, "Seeking a Balanced Physician Workforce for the 21st Century," JAMA 272 (1994):680–687; D. Kindig and D. Libby, "Setting State Health Spending Limits," *Health Affairs* 13, no. 2 (1994):288–289; J. Weiner, "Forecasting the Effects of Health Reform on U.S. Physician Workforce Requirements," *JAMA* 272 (1994):222–230; J. Wennberg, D. Goodman, R. Nease, and R. Keller, "Finding Equilibrium in U.S. Physician Supply," *Health Affairs* 12, no. 2 (1993):89–104; and E. Ginsberg, "Physician Supply Policies and Health Reform," *JAMA* 268 (1992):3,115–3,118.

22. B. J. McClendon, R. M. Politzer, E. Christian, and E. S. Fernandez, "Downsizing the Physician Workforce," *Public Health Reports* 112 (May/June 1997):231–239.

23. L. H. Aiken, J. Sochalski, and G. F. Anderson, "Downsizing the Hospital Nursing Workforce," *Health Affairs* 15, no. 4 (Winter 1996):88–92.

24. K. Grumbach, K. Vranizan, and A. B. Bindman, "Physician Supply and Access to Care in Urban Communities," *Health Affairs* 16, no. 1 (January/February 1997):71–86.

25. M. Komaromy, K. Grumbach, M. Drake, K. Vranizan, N. Lurie, D. Keane, and A. B. Bindman, "The Role of Black and Hispanic Physicians in Providing Health Care for Under-served Populations," *New England Journal of Medicine* 334, no. 20 (1996):1305–1310; E. Moy and B. A. Bartman, "Physician Race and Care of Minority and Medically Indigent Patients," *Journal of the American Medical Association* 273, no. 19 (1995):1515–1520 and J. C. Cantor, E. L. Miles, L. C. Baker, and D. C. Barker, "Physician Service to the Under-served: Implications for Affirmative Action in Medical Education," *Inquiry* 33, no. 2 (Summer 1996):167–180.

26. C. J. Simon, D. Dranove, and W. D. White, "The Impact of Managed Care on the Physician Marketplace," *Public Health Reports* 112 (May/June 1997):222–230.

27. G. F. Anderson, "In Search of Value: An International Comparison of Cost, Access, and Outcomes," *Health Affairs* 16, no. 6 (November/December 1997):163–171.

28. P. R. Lee, C. L. Estes, and L. Close, *The Nation's Health*, 5th ed. (Boston: Jones and Bartlett Publishers, 1997).

29. K. R. Levit, H. C. Lazenby, B. R. Braden, and the National Health Accounts Team, "National Health Spending Trends in 1996," *Health Affairs* 17, no. 1 (January/February 1998):35–51.

30. Health Care Financing Administration, Office of the Actuary, *National Health Statistics Group Annual Health Accounts* (Baltimore: HCFA, 2000), Table 2.

31. G. Wunderlich, *Towards a National Health Care Survey: A Data System for the 21st Century* (Washington, D.C.: National Academy Press, 1992). Also see A. M. Pollock and D. P. Rice, "Monitoring Health Care in the United States: A Challenging Task," *Public Health Reports* 112 (March/April, 1997):108–115.

32. L. Etheredge and S. B. Jones, "What Is Driving Health System Change?" *Health Affairs* 15, no. 4 (Winter 1996):93–104. Also see J. M. Davis, "Predicting Future Health System Change," *Health Affairs* 15, no. 4 (Winter 1996):107–108.

33. J. Gabel, "Ten Ways HMOs Have Changed During the 1990s," *Health Affairs* 16, no. 3 (May/June 1997):134–145.

34. J. Needleman, D. J. Chollet, and J. Lamphere, "Hospital Conversion Trends," *Health Affairs* 16, no. 2 (March/April 1997):187–195.

35. G. Claxton, J. Feder, D. Shactman, and S. Altman, "Public Policy Issues in Nonprofit Conversions: An Overview," *Health Affairs* 16, no. 2 (March/April 1997):9–28.

36. G. J. Young, K. R. Desai, and C. V. Lukas, "Does the Sale of Nonprofit Hospitals Threaten Health Care for the Poor?" *Health Affairs* 16, no. 1 (January/February 1997):137–141.

37. S. Q. Duffy and D. E. Farley, "Patterns of Decline Among Inpatient Procedures," *Public Health Reports* 110 (November/December 1995):674–681.

38. K. R. Levit, H. C. Lazenby, B. R. Braden, and the National Health Accounts Team, "National Health Spending Trends in 1996," *Health Affairs* 17, no. 1 (January/February 1998):35–51.

39. P. A. Lamarche, "Our Health Paradigm in Peril," *Public Health Reports* 110 (September/October 1995):556–560.

Health affects individuals' lives by determining longevity, facilitating or limiting the enjoyment of activity, and shaping individuals' participation in the economy. Health correlates, conditions, and care are major factors affecting our nation's productivity and consume more than 13.0 percent of the gross domestic product. According to one estimate, illness and injury cost Americans more than $2 trillion a year. (See Table 5J.) As health conditions changed during the 20th century, the size and types of effects on the population and community altered as well.

Estimates of the impact of health and illness depend critically on whether analysts focus on the cost of care or on the effects on productivity, livelihood, and enjoyment of people. This chapter presents statistics that show how health affects individuals and society. The consequences of disease, injury, and other measures of health are presented in terms of their effect on longevity, ability to live independently, quality of life, productivity, and the cost of medical care.

MAIN TRENDS

The health of Americans in the last decade has improved greatly because of concerted public health programs, community actions, and healthier individual lifestyles. As discussed in chapter 3, infectious diseases, hazardous occupations, unsafe environmental exposures, and a short life span plagued America in the 19th and early 20th centuries.

Conditions such as typhoid fever, cholera, pellagra, polio, diphtheria, and smallpox are no longer major health problems in the United States. However, chronic diseases, traffic-related fatalities, violence, emerging food-borne pathogens, and other new infectious diseases continue to take their toll on America's health. Controlling environmental hazards and sexually transmitted diseases also continues to be important. This chapter presents statistics on the consequences of these conditions. It begins with examples showing how health practices lead to personal and societal consequences.

CONSEQUENCES OF HEALTH PRACTICES

Lifestyle, nutrition, and environmental exposures affect health. For example, people who have lost their natural teeth are less able to enjoy food and digest it effectively. They must also bear the costs and pain of continuing dental care. Drinking fluoridated water reduces the risk of losing one's natural teeth. As shown in Figure 5A, increased exposure to fluoridated drinking water reduces the number of decayed, missing, and filled teeth, especially among children. Between 1960 and 1991, regular dental hygiene and better diets contributed to a 50 percent decline in the number of people who lost all of their natural teeth. Nevertheless, by the end of the 1980s, more than 40 percent of the population age 75 and older had lost all of their natural teeth. (See Table 5A.)[1]

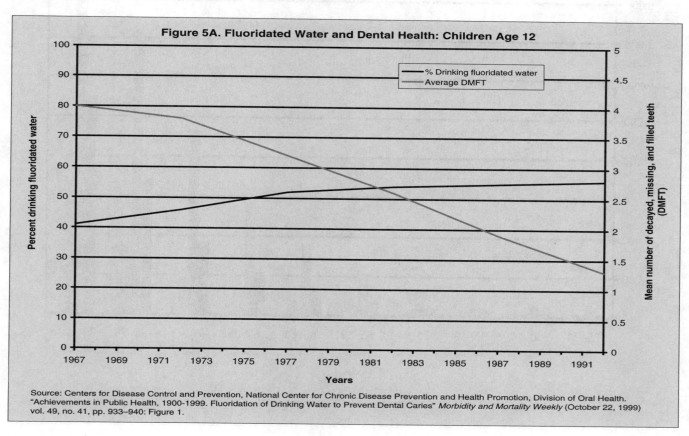

Figure 5A. Fluoridated Water and Dental Health: Children Age 12

Source: Centers for Disease Control and Prevention, National Center for Chronic Disease Prevention and Health Promotion, Division of Oral Health. "Achievements in Public Health, 1900-1999. Fluoridation of Drinking Water to Prevent Dental Caries" *Morbidity and Mortality Weekly* (October 22, 1999) vol. 49, no. 41, pp. 933–940: Figure 1.

Table 5A. Tooth Loss: 1988–1991

(Percent of adults who have lost all of their teeth)

Age	Total	Males	Females	Non-Hispanic white	Non-Hispanic black	Mexican-American
18 years and over	10.5	10.4	10.7	10.9	10.3	6.2
18–24 years	0.0	0.0	0.0	0.0	0.0	0.0
25–29 years	0.6	1.1	0.0	0.8	0.0	0.0
30–34 years	1.3	1.0	1.7	1.7	0.0	0.0
35–39 years	2.5	2.2	2.7	2.7	1.8	0.3
40–44 years	5.8	4.8	6.7	6.8	4.1	0.0
45–49 years	9.2	9.1	9.2	10.5	3.9	2.4
50–54 years	11.8	9.2	14.2	13.2	11.6	4.3
55–59 years	17.6	17.9	17.4	17.8	21.3	3.7
60–64 years	23.8	23.3	24.2	24.1	23.5	11.3
65–69 years	26.0	27.0	25.1	25.8	25.8	13.3
70–74 years	31.1	29.1	32.7	31.4	29.9	28.6
75 years and over	43.9	46.6	42.2	42.8	53.0	44.4

SOURCE: S.E. Marcus, T.F. Drury, L.J. Brown, and G.R. Zion, "Tooth Retention and Tooth Loss in the Permanent Dentition of Adults: United States, 1988–1991," *Journal of Dental Research,* 75 (Special Issue), (February, 1996): 684–695, based on Table 1. Data are from oral health component of Phase 1 of the Third National Health and Nutrition Examination Survey (NHANES III) conducted 1988–1991 and based on dental examinations.

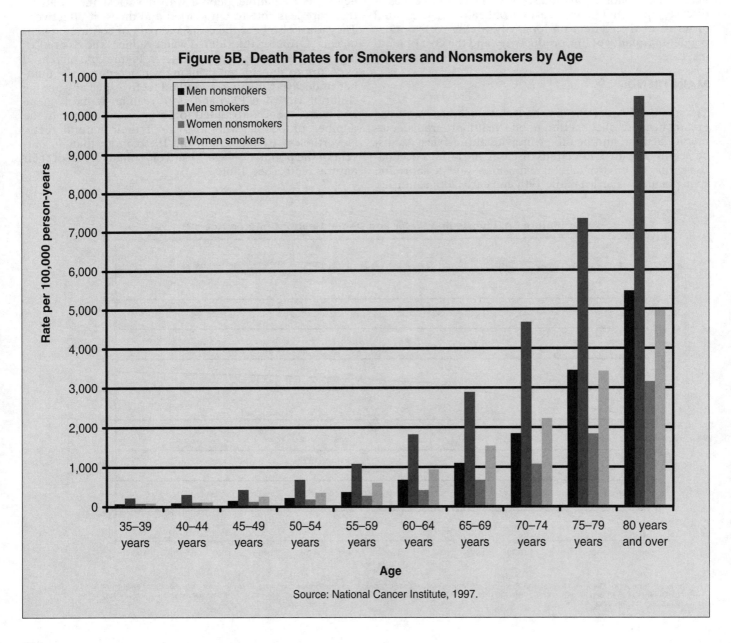

Figure 5B. Death Rates for Smokers and Nonsmokers by Age

Source: National Cancer Institute, 1997.

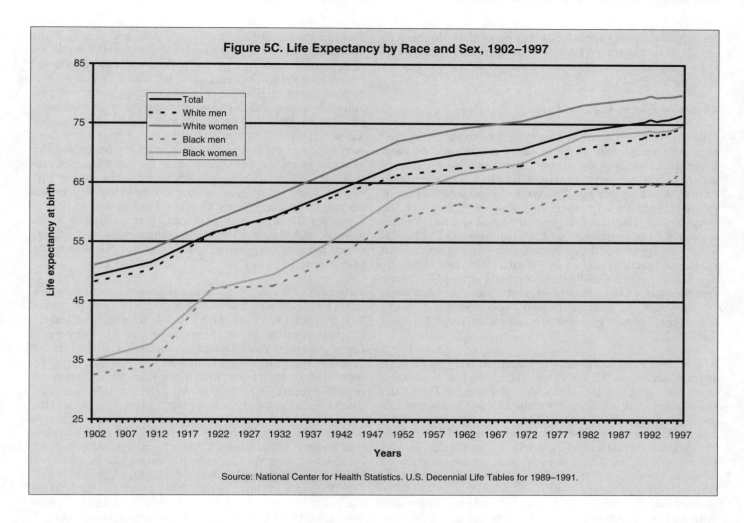

Figure 5C. Life Expectancy by Race and Sex, 1902–1997

Source: National Center for Health Statistics. U.S. Decennial Life Tables for 1989–1991.

Some correlates, like smoking, can greatly increase the risk of developing a disease and dying. Smokers are more likely to die prematurely than nonsmokers from all causes combined. (See Figure 5B.) Smokers are particularly at risk to die from lung cancer and other smoking-related cancers such as those of the throat, pancreas, bladder, and kidney. Other smoking-related conditions include heart disease, stroke, and chronic obstructive pulmonary disease. The risk of these diseases for the smoker increases with the number of years and the number of cigarettes smoked.[2]

Smoking can also pollute the environment and increase the severity of respiratory conditions, especially in children. One of the consequences of passive smoking is that children of smoking parents experience more emergency room visits per year than those of nonsmoking parents.[3]

CONSEQUENCES OF ENVIRONMENTAL EXPOSURE

Environmental exposures such as air pollution, contaminated water, and exposure to toxic chemicals on the skin have been found to correlate with several conditions,

including birth defects and other unhealthy reproductive outcomes such as babies with low birth weight. Unfortunately, birth defects are the leading cause of infant mortality. Some birth defects, including congenital heart defects, Down's syndrome, cerebral palsy, and spina bifida, result in high disability rates. Other birth defects, such as cleft lip or palate, deformed arms or legs, and other physical malformations, often result in high costs of medical care, special education or child care, or structural changes to the home environment to accommodate the child's special needs.

LIFE EXPECTANCY

Shortened life span is the most important effect of illness and injury. A child born in 1902 had a life expectancy of 49.2 years. By 1997, life expectancy at birth had increased to 76.5 years. (See Table 5.1.) This increase in life expectancy in the 20th century was caused in large part by improved health practices, advanced medical technology, and informed health policies. The most dramatic increase in life expectancy has been for Blacks. The average Black child born in 1902 could expect to live to age 33.8. By 1997, the life expectancy for Blacks had more than doubled to age 71.1. In general, Whites have longer life expectancies than Blacks, and women have longer life expectancies than men. (See Figure 5C.)

CAUSES OF POTENTIAL YEARS LOST

One way of understanding longevity is to consider the reasons why people die early in life. Epidemiologists have invented a conventional way of expressing this premature death as the years of potential life lost because death occurred before old age. Studying the leading causes of premature death helps them to find ways to improve the longevity of Americans in general and of specific population groups in particular. At the same time, the potential years lost by cause of death shows the consequences and timing of specific diseases and injuries. Because the average life expectancy at birth is currently around 75 years, one measure of the effect of premature death is the number of years the average person's life expectancy is cut short (that is, their age at death subtracted from 75). (See Table 5.2.)

The leading causes of premature death in the general population under age 75 are cancer, heart disease, and unintentional injuries. (See Table 5B and Figure 5D.) In fact, intentional injuries caused by suicide and homicide are more responsible for cutting life short than HIV/AIDS. Rates of suicide are probably underestimated because of the difficulty of determining suicidal intent. Some deaths (like single-car fatalities in good weather on unoccupied roads or homicides of individuals going into high-risk situations) may be suspicious but are difficult to establish as unintended or suicidal. In addition, the stigma associated with suicide may lead to a bias for classifying the death as unintentional when in doubt.

The life span of Black men could increase greatly if the homicide rate were reduced or if HIV/AIDS could be eliminated. Cancers, especially prostate, colorectal, and respiratory system cancers, also are major causes of premature death in Black men. For example, years lost prematurely among Black men from prostate cancer are three times more than among White men. (See Figure 5E and Table 5.2.) Unintentional injuries are a major cause of death for American Indian and Alaska Native men; twice as many years are lost prematurely for American Indians and Alaska Natives than for White men. The rate of premature death from breast cancer among White women has decreased in recent years. Currently the years lost prematurely for Black women are about 1.5 times that of White women, and almost all of the leading causes of death are major sources of potential years lost for Black women. (See Figure 5F and Table 5.2.)

Between 1980 and 1997, the age-adjusted rate of potential years lost from all causes in the total population improved 24.6 percent. (See Table 5B.) Chronic liver disease and cirrhosis showed the greatest improvement with 45.3 percent fewer potential years lost between 1980 and 1997. Heart diseases and unintentional injuries also showed improvement during this period with more than 30 percent fewer potential years lost. In addition, between 1990 and 1997 the potential years of life lost prematurely because of HIV decreased 43 percent; the improvement was primarily among White men. Among the racial and ethnic groups, the largest improvement for all causes occurred for American Indian or Alaska Native men (29.6 percent) and women (28.1 percent) and for White men (28.2 percent). (See Table 5.2.) For American Indians and Alaska Natives, the years lost prematurely to chronic liver disease, pneumonia, and unintentional injuries decreased more than 30 percent.

Table 5B. Premature Death: 1980–1997

(Age-adjusted rates of years lost; per 100,000 population under age 75)

Condition	Number of years lost per 100,000 persons						Percent change from 1980–1997
	1980	1985	1990	1995	1996	1997	
All causes	9 813.0	8 793.0	8 518.0	8 128.0	7 748.0	7 398.0	-24.6
Diseases of heart	1 877.0	1 664.0	1 363.0	1 259.0	1 222.0	1 190.0	-36.6
Cancer	1 815.0	1 776.0	1 713.0	1 587.0	1 554.0	1 523.0	-16.1
Unintentional injuries	1 688.0	1 365.0	1 263.0	1 155.0	1 136.0	1 115.0	-33.9
Homicide [1]	460.9	357.1	466.4	436.4	394.7	368.9	-20.0
Suicide	402.8	404.5	405.9	405.6	387.8	378.0	-6.2
HIV	—	—	366.2	570.3	401.9	208.7	-43.0
Cerebrovascular disease	302.9	250.8	221.1	211.5	210.2	207.1	-31.6
Chronic liver disease and cirrhosis	259.1	196.0	168.8	149.7	145.7	141.7	-45.3
Pneumonia and influenza	149.1	130.4	128.5	115.3	114.5	112.6	-24.5
Chronic obstructive pulmonary diseases	141.4	156.2	156.9	151.4	161.1	158.9	12.4
Diabetes mellitus	115.1	109.8	133.0	149.9	153.5	149.9	30.2

SOURCE: E. Kramarow, H. Lentzner, R. Rooks, J. Weeks, and S. Saydah, *Health and Aging Chartbook. Health, United States*, 1999. Hyattsville, Md.: National Center for Health Statistics, 1999: Table 31. Data from the National Health Interview Survey.

— Data not available.
1. Includes legal intervention.

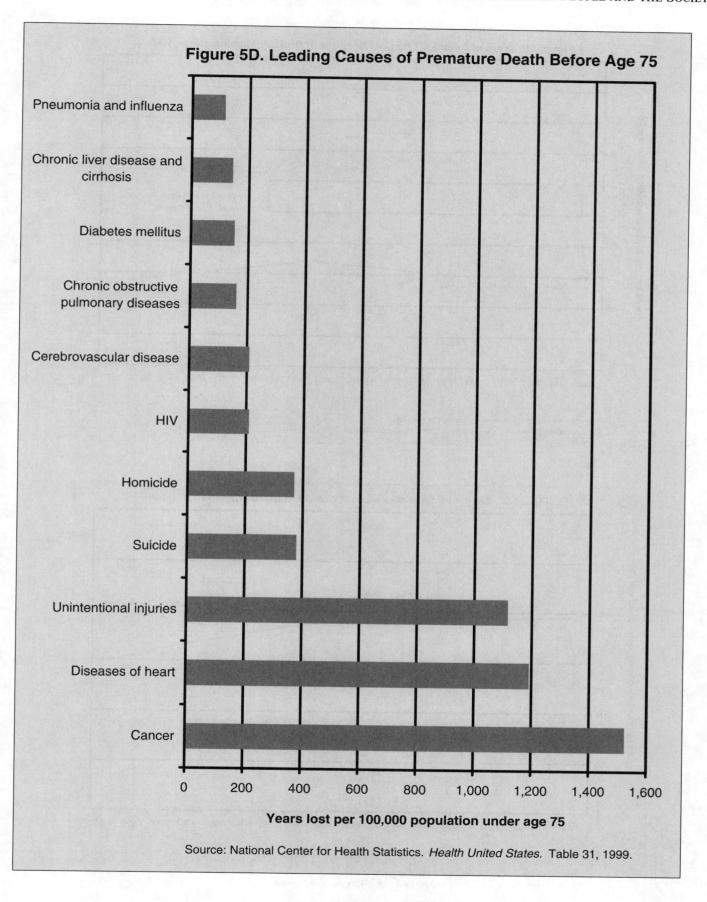

Figure 5D. Leading Causes of Premature Death Before Age 75

Source: National Center for Health Statistics. *Health United States.* Table 31, 1999.

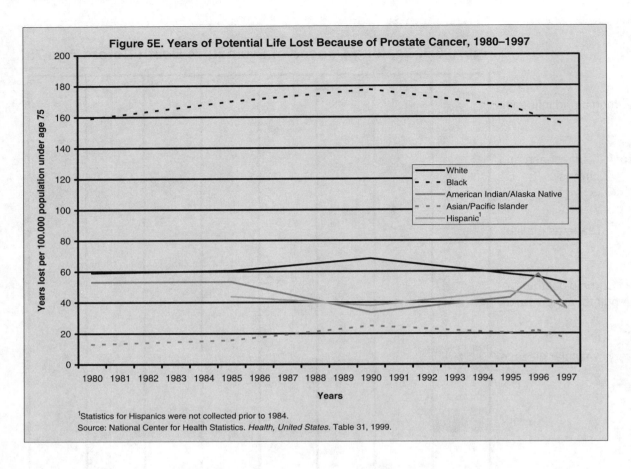

Figure 5E. Years of Potential Life Lost Because of Prostate Cancer, 1980–1997

[1]Statistics for Hispanics were not collected prior to 1984.
Source: National Center for Health Statistics. *Health, United States*. Table 31, 1999.

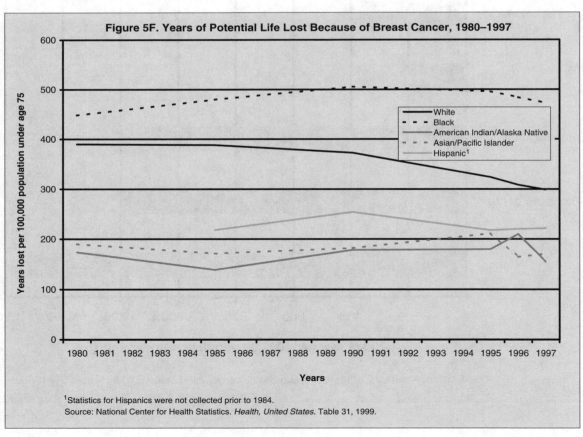

Figure 5F. Years of Potential Life Lost Because of Breast Cancer, 1980–1997

[1]Statistics for Hispanics were not collected prior to 1984.
Source: National Center for Health Statistics. *Health, United States*. Table 31, 1999.

Table 5C. Expected Years of Healthy Life, 1990–1996

Year	Life expectancy at birth			Years of healthy life		Percent fully functional	
	Total	White	Black	Total	Black	Total	Black
1990	75.4	76.1	69.1	64.0	56.0	84.8	81.0
1991	75.5	76.3	69.3	63.9	56.0	84.6	80.8
1992	75.8	76.5	69.6	63.7	55.6	84.0	79.9
1993	75.5	76.3	69.2	63.5	55.2	84.1	79.8
1994	75.7	76.5	69.5	63.8	55.6	84.3	80.0
1995	75.8	76.5	69.6	63.9	56.0	84.3	80.5
1996	76.0	76.8	70.2	64.2	56.5	84.5	80.5

SOURCE: For life expectancy at birth: S.L. Murphy, "Deaths: Final Data for 1998." *National Vital Statistics Reports*, vol. 48, no. 11, July 24, 2000. For years of healthy life, 1990: P. Erickson, R. Wilson, and L. Shannon, *Years of Healthy Life. Healthy People 2000 Statistical Notes*, no. 7, April 1995. 1991–1996: National Center for Health Statistics. *Healthy People 2000 Review. 1998–1999* (Objective 21.1) Hyattsville, MD, 1999.

NOTE: Percent fully functional is calculated as the percent of total life expectancy attributed to years of healthy life. Lack of full function is measured by activity limitations and perceived health status in the National Health Interview Survey.

Although between 1980 and 1997 many conditions leading to premature death in the general population were diminished or delayed, leading to fewer years of potential life lost, some conditions caused increased loss of premature years of life. Between 1980 and 1997, the potential years of life lost from diabetes increased from 115.1 to 149.9 per 100,000 persons or by 30.2 percent. During this period the age-adjusted rate for American Indian and Alaska Native men increased from 255.3 to 358.1. Although chronic obstructive pulmonary disease also resulted in an increase of 12.4 percent in potential years lost for the total population, the American Indian and Alaska Native men had an increase of 88.4 percent and the women had an increase of 72.4 percent. American Indian and Alaska Native men were the only group to have an increase in potential years lost because of cancer (from 912.9 to 1,261 per 100,000 or by 38.1 percent). At the same time, premature deaths from cancer among the total population declined from 1,815 to 1,523 per 100,000 persons or by about 16 percent.

YEARS OF POTENTIAL LIFE LOST: THE MEASURE

Years of potential life lost (YPLL) is a measure of premature death. Dempsey developed this method to take into account the death of younger persons when she was examining the changing consequences of tuberculosis deaths.[4] YPLL is calculated as the sum of the years of life lost annually before a set age, in many cases, age 75. The rate of YPLL is the average number of years of life lost to each person who died. For the calculation of the YPLL for age 75, the persons at risk of premature death are those ages zero to 74. When a measure of working years of life lost is used, then the persons used in the statistic are those between the ages of 15 and 65. Methods of actual calculations of YPLL can differ, especially in the way years lost for older persons are counted. For example, the Centers for Disease Prevention and Control (CDC) calculated only five years of life lost for persons age 55 to 64, even though the life expectancy for this age group is much longer.[5]

QUALITY OF LIFE

Merely extending life is not a totally satisfactory outcome. A primary goal of health care is to improve an individual's quality of life. Although good health facilitates and poor health limits life enjoyment, health alone does not determine the quality of life but interacts with social, economic, and public conditions.[6]

Even though medical technology, early detection, and improved therapies increased survival rates for several diseases, some survivors have experienced severe limitations that caused them to spend their extra years in nursing homes or other long-term care facilities. Others suffered disabilities or other conditions that impaired their ability to independently carry out the usual activities of living. Quality of life goes beyond freedom from injury and disease to include a sense of well-being and the ability to function well psychologically, physically, and socially. Several indicators for monitoring the nation's quality of life have been developed, including Disability Free Life Years, Healthy Life Expectancy, and Disability Adjusted Life Years.[7] The National Center for Health Statistics (NCHS) has constructed the Years of Healthy Life Index, which is used to monitor Healthy People 2000 goals.[8] Using this measure, the NCHS concludes that in recent years, most people can expect 64.2 years of their average life expectancy of 76 years to be healthy and fully functional. That is, the average person born in 1996 can expect that 84.5 percent of his or her life will be fully functional, in excellent perceived health, and without major restricted activities. (See Table 5C.)

However, not all of the nation's population shared equally in this increased quality of life. For example, the average Black person can expect that about 80.5 percent of his or her life will be fully functional, in excellent perceived health, and without major restricted activities. (See Table 5C.) Persons with inadequate economic, nutritional, and social resources or living in areas without access to medical facilities and health care professionals are less likely to share in the increased quality of life.

YEARS OF HEALTHY LIFE INDEX

The Years of Healthy Life Index is based on core questions from the National Health Interview Survey (NHIS) regarding perceived health status and restriction in activity caused by chronic conditions or other impairments or health problems. The perceived health status question is: Would you say your health in general is excellent, very good, good, fair, or poor?

Restricted activities status is based on expectations concerning age-related ability to perform usual activities. Persons are classified as (1) not limited: not limited in any way; (2) limited—other: not limited in major activity, but limited in other activities; (3) limited—major: limited in major activity; (4) unable—major: unable to perform major activity; (5) limited in instrumental activities of daily living (IADL): unable to perform necessary daily tasks without the help of other persons; and (6) limited in activities of daily living (ADL): unable to perform activity of daily living without the help of other persons.

The National Health Interview Survey is limited to persons living in households. Therefore, health status was assigned to institutionalized persons on the basis of assumptions. This method applied to persons living in institutions such as nursing and other health care facilities, as well as in the military and correctional institutions. Years of healthy life for the total population and for groups were calculated by combining the health status information with the life expectancy for each group.

In addition, CDC has developed a state-based index, the Health Related Quality of Life (HR-QOL) Index. This index enables states to monitor their health-related quality of life. It includes measures such as self-perceived excellent health, days of good physical health during the previous 30 days, days without activity limitations during the previous 30 days, and days of good mental health during the previous 30 days. This index is based on data collected from the Behavioral Risk Factor Surveillance System since January 1993.[9] The HR-QOL Index is based on the following four questions:

1. Would you say that in general your health is excellent, very good, good, fair, or poor?

2. Now thinking about your physical health, which includes physical illness and injury, for how many days during the past 30 days was your physical health not good?

3. Now thinking about your mental health, which includes stress, depression, and problems with emotions, for how many days during the past 30 days was your mental health not good?

4. During the past 30 days, for about how many days did poor physical or mental health keep you from doing your usual activities, such as self-care, work, or recreation?

USE OF ASSISTIVE DEVICES

Assistive devices help people overcome their limitations. At the same time, the number of people using such devices is an indicator of the amount of limitation experienced by the population. More Americans are using some kind of device to help them with vision, hearing, mobility, or orthopedic impairments than ever before. Most of the people (about 7.4 million) who need some device to maintain their ability to conduct their own daily activities use it to move about. (See Table 5.3.) Such mobility devices include crutches, wheelchairs, and walkers. About 4.6 million people in the United States used an anatomical device such as an artificial leg, foot, arm, or hand or a body brace. About 4.5 million people used a hearing device and about a half million used Braille, a white cane, or other vision device. (See Table 5.3.)

Some people used more than one device. People were especially more likely to be using a wheelchair, walker, back brace, or other brace in 1994 than in 1980. (See Table 5D.) Fewer people are using crutches. Because the likelihood of an impairment increases with age, unless some other medical technology intervenes, even more people can be expected to use an assistive device in the next

Table 5D. Persons Using Mobility Assistive Technology

(Number in thousands, except where noted)

Assistive device	Number			Percent change			Age-adjusted number		Age-adjusted difference in percent		
	1980	1990	1994	From 1980 to 1990	From 1990 to 1994	From 1980 to 1994	1990	1994	From 1980 to 1990	From 1990 to 1994	From 1980 to 1994
Total population	217 923	246 099	259 626	12.9	5.5	19.1	246 099	259 626	12.9	5.5	19.1
Leg or foot brace	472	1 048	834	122.0	-20.4	76.7	924	718	95.8	-22.3	52.1
Brace other than leg or foot	1 000	2 740	3 651	174.0	33.2	265.1	2 436	3 192	143.6	31.0	219.2
Artificial limb	177	218	199	23.2	-8.7	12.4	189	174	6.8	-7.9	-1.7
Crutch	588	671	575	14.1	-14.3	-2.2	590	501	0.3	-15.1	-14.8
Cane or walking stick [1]	2 878	4 400	4 762	52.9	8.2	65.5	3 626	3 944	26.0	8.8	37.0
Walker	866	1 687	1 799	94.8	6.6	107.7	1 363	1 473	57.4	8.1	70.1
Wheelchair	720	1 411	1 564	96.0	10.8	117.2	1 185	1 315	64.6	11.0	82.6

SOURCE: J. Neil Russell, Gerry E. Hendershot, Felicia LeClere, L. Jean Howie, "Trends and Differential Use of Assistive Technology Devices: United States, 1994," *Vital and Health Statistics*, Centers for Disease Control and Prevention, National Center for Health Statistics, Advance Data no. 292 (November 13, 1997): Table 6. Based on data from the National Health Interview Survey (Disability Component).

1. The 1994 NHIS-D, Phase I, only asked about use of "canes" not walking sticks.

NOTE: Age-adjusted by the direct method using the 1980 population as standard and age groups 44 years and under, 45–64 years, 65–74 years, and 75 years and over.

decade. In the meantime, such devices help people be more independent and help them have a better quality of life.

VISION AND HEARING IMPAIRMENT AMONG OLDER ADULTS

One effect of increased longevity is an increase in the number of people with hearing or vision impairments. However, most people who live to older ages do not lose their ability to see and hear. In fact, 18.1 percent of persons age 70 and older had difficulty seeing, 33.2 percent had a hearing impairment, and 8.6 percent had both impairments. (See Table 5E.) Most of those (91.5 percent) with visual impairments wore glasses. Only 11.6 percent of those with a hearing impairment used a hearing aid during the prior year. Although fewer older persons had difficulty seeing than hearing, those with a vision impairment experienced more limitations in their daily activities, such as walking, getting into and out of bed, preparing meals, and managing their medications. Older persons with difficulty seeing were about twice as likely to be frequently depressed or anxious than those without a vision impairment (13.3 percent versus 7 percent). Those with a hearing difficulty and no other impairment are about as likely as those without such an impairment to be frequently depressed or anxious (9.9 percent versus 7.2 percent). However, those with either a vision or hearing impairment or both were just as likely as those without such an impairment to socialize with friends and relatives. Vision impairment does seem to deter older persons from going out to eat at a restaurant. Part of this may be because older persons with a vision impairment are more likely to have fallen during the prior year and to have suffered a broken hip, heart disease, or stroke. Older persons with both vision and hearing impairments are also more restricted in their activities. (See Tables 5.4 and 5.5.)

ACTIVITY LIMITATIONS[10]

Both acute and chronic health conditions can affect a person's ability to conduct his or her usual activities. Older persons are more restricted by health conditions than younger persons, partially because they have more things to do and partially because they suffer from more debilitating conditions with age. Overall, the average American had 14.5 days of restricted activity caused by an acute or chronic health condition; on 5.9 of these days, the average person was bedridden. Persons with low family income are the most likely to be restricted in their activities. In 1996, persons of working age (18 and older) with annual family incomes less than $10,000 had almost four times more bedridden days than the same age group with annual family incomes of $35,000 or more (15.1 versus 3.8 days). The data cannot show if poor health led to lower incomes or if those with lower incomes were more likely to have more days of limited activity. Some persons may be in poor health because they do not have the income to provide proper nutrition, sanitation, or other health needs whether or not they are working. (See Table 5.6.)

Most people, especially the young, are not restricted in their activities because of a chronic condition. However, about 10 percent of the population suffers from a major restriction. (See Table 5.7.) Limitations in a major activity include the inability for persons to carry on usual daily activities such as working, housekeeping, going to school, or living independently. Limitations in other activities, including civic, church, or recreational tasks, are counted as a limitation but not in a major activity.

The very young and the very old are the most likely to be limited in their daily activities because of an acute condition. Acute conditions are short term, last fewer than three months, and include infective and parasitic conditions, digestive system conditions, and various other short-term conditions such as ear or eye infections and headaches. In 1996, the average person had to limit his or her activities on 6.2 days because of acute conditions. (See Table 5.8.)

In 1996, 20.5 episodes resulted in injuries for every 100 persons in the population. These episodes resulted in 226.4 days of restricted activity and 71.8 days of bed rest. In all, 54.3 million episodes resulted in injuries. (See Table 5.9.)

Table 5E. Visual and Hearing Impairment in Adults Age 70 Years and Over: 1994

Sensory characteristic	Number	Percent
VISION IMPAIRMENTS	3 652 626	18.1
Blind in one eye	879 215	4.4
Blind in both eyes	338 492	1.7
Any other trouble seeing	2 853 053	14.4
Glaucoma	1 601 041	7.9
Cataract	5 125 760	24.5
Lens implant	3 038 524	15.1
Used magnifier	3 376 160	17.0
Wear glasses	18 127 245	91.5
HEARING IMPAIRMENTS	6 697 497	33.2
Deaf in one ear	1 542 163	8.3
Deaf in both ears	1 478 727	7.3
Any other trouble hearing	4 193 478	22.5
Used hearing aid during preceding 12 months	2 343 064	11.6
Cochlear implant	28 018	0.1
Both vision and hearing impairment	1 724 000	8.6

SOURCE: V.A. Campbell, J.E. Crews, D.G. Moriarty, M.M. Zack, and D.K. Blackman, "Surveillance for Sensory Impairment, Activity Limitation, and Health-Related Quality of Life Among Older Adults–United States," 1993–1997. *Morbidity and Mortality Weekly Report* 48, no. SS08 (December 17, 1999): 131-156: Table 2.

Table 5F. Mental Health and Disability: 1994

Characteristic	Number (in thousands)		Percent	
	Household population	Mental/ emotional problem	Household population	Mental/ emotional problem
ACTIVITY LIMITATION				
Not limited	141 999	3 410	84.4	41.4
Unable to do major activity	9 686	2 740	5.8	33.3
Limited in in-kind/amount	9 588	1 297	5.7	15.7
Limited to other activity	6 966	792	4.1	9.6
ACTIVITIES OF DAILY LIVING [1]				
None	165 500	7 206	98.4	87.5
One or more	2 733	1 033	1.6	12.5
INSTRUMENTAL ACTIVITIES OF DAILY LIVING [2]				
None	159 300	5 606	94.7	68.1
One or more	8 971	2 633	5.3	32.0
RESTRICTED ACTIVITY DAYS [3]				
None	150 700	5 419	89.6	65.8
One or more	17 540	2 820	10.4	34.2
BED DAYS				
None	92 650	2 450	55.1	29.7
1–7 days	57 740	2 526	34.3	30.7
8–30 days	11 600	1 647	6.9	20.0
31–365	4 968	1 453	3.0	17.6
RESPONDENT-ASSESSED HEALTH STATUS				
Excellent	58 996	875	35.1	10.6
Very good	50 091	1 444	29.8	17.5
Good	40 659	2 360	24.2	28.6
Fair	12 793	1 951	7.6	23.7
Poor	4 837	1 579	2.9	19.2

SOURCE: 1994 National Health Interview Survey, A.G. Willis, G.B. Willis, A. Male, M.J. Henderson, and R.W. Manderscheid, "Mental Illness and Disability in the U.S. Adult Household Population," *Mental Health U.S., 1998*, ed. R.W. Manderscheid and M.J. Henderson, DHHS Pub. No. (SMA) 99-3285. Substance Abuse and Mental Health Services Administration, Center for Mental Health Services. (Washington, D.C.: Supt. of Docs., U.S. Govt. Printing Office, 1998): 113–123.

1. The Activities of Daily Living (ADL) Scale consists of bathing, dressing, eating, walking, and other activities of personal functioning.
2. The Instrumental Activities of Daily Living (IADL) Scale consists of preparing meals, shopping, doing laundry, using the phone, and other measures of living independently.
3. For two-week period.

NOTE: Some percentages total less than 100 because values for "Don't know" and "Refusal" are not listed.

Persons with mental or emotional problems are more likely to consider themselves in poor health and to be severely restricted in their ability to conduct their daily activities of living. (See Table 5F.) About 33 percent of the 8.2 million persons with a mental or emotional problem in the past year were unable to perform major activities of daily life because of a chronic impairment or mental health problem. In addition, persons with a mental health problem lack the social and economic resources to deal with their poor health and activity limitations because they are more likely not to be currently married or in the labor force. In other words, they are more likely to live alone and to be poor.

DISABILITY

A large number of Americans have a disability of some type.[11] In 1994, 53.9 million persons (20.6 percent of the population) had some functional limitation; of these, 26 million (9.9 percent of the population) had a severe disability. Young boys between the ages of 6 and 14 were more likely than girls their age to have a disability. Almost half of those persons age 65 to 79 reported a disability along with 71.5 percent of those age 80 and over. (See Table 5G.)

LEADING CAUSES OF DISABILITY

Disabilities may result from conditions such as injury, disease, and mental, emotional, or developmental disorders. Arthritis,[12] back or spine problems, heart disease, respira-

tory difficulties, and diabetes are among the leading self-reported causes of disability. (See Table 5H and Figure 5G.) A survey conducted at the start of the 1990s found that about 7.2 million persons reported an activity restriction that they attributed to arthritis, making it the single most prevalent condition resulting in restricted activities or other disabilities.

Diabetes not only is a leading cause of disability but also is among the leading causes of other serious health consequences, such as blindness, kidney failure, end-stage renal disease (kidney failure that requires either a transplant or dialysis for the patient to survive), and amputations. Like most chronic diseases, many of the complications can be prevented, delayed, or made less severe by early detection and treatment as well as by enlightened self-management of the condition.

Black persons are more likely not only to develop diabetes but also to suffer the severe consequences of the disease. For example, the hospital discharge rate for leg or foot amputation not caused by an accident (that is, nontraumatic) is almost two times higher among Black persons with diabetes than among Whites with the disease. (See Figure 5H for the rate expressed in terms of the total population and Table 5.10 for the rates in terms of the number of persons with diabetes.) Between 1983 and 1994, about one-third of White persons with diabetes had some activity restriction. Black persons with diabetes, however, although having higher activity restriction rates than Whites, showed greater improvement.

Table 5G. Prevalence of Disabilities: 1994

Characteristic	Number (in thousands)	Percent of age group
Total	53 907	20.6
0–2 years	313	2.6
3–5 years	652	5.2
Male	442	6.9
Female	210	3.5
6 years and over	52 942	22.3
6–14 years	4 462	12.7
Male	2 824	15.8
Female	1 638	9.6
15 years and over	48 481	24.0
15–21 years	3 047	12.1
22–44 years	14 105	14.9
45–54 years	7 412	24.9
55–64 years	7 497	36.3
65–79 years	11 568	47.3
80 years and over	4 853	71.5

SOURCE: J.M. McNeil, "Americans with Disabilities: 1994–1995," U.S. Census Bureau, Household Economic Studies, Current Population Reports P70-61 (1997). Data from the Survey of Income and Program Participation.

NOTE: Disability in children under age three is defined as a developmental condition for which the child received therapy or diagnostic services. For children age three to six, disability is defined as either a developmental condition or a chronic condition that limited the child's ability to walk, run, or climb the stairs.

Table 5H. Conditions Leading to Disabilities: 1991–1992

(Self-reported causes of disability among persons age 15 years and over)

Condition	Percent distribution of disabilities	Number of persons (thousands)
Total	100.0	41 969
Arthritis or rheumatism	17.1	7 184
Back or spine problems	13.5	5 679
Heart trouble	11.1	4 649
Lung or respiratory trouble	6.8	2 840
High blood pressure	5.1	2 161
Stiffness/deformity of limbs, hands, or feet	4.8	2 024
Diabetes	3.9	1 619
Blindness or other visual impairment	3.5	1 481
Deafness/serious trouble hearing	2.6	1 099
Stroke	2.5	1 047
Cancer	2.1	896
Broken bone/fracture	2.0	830
Mental/emotional problem	1.9	784
Paralysis of any kind	1.7	716
Head or spinal cord injury	1.4	592
Stomach trouble	1.3	537
Mental retardation	1.2	501
Hernia or rupture	1.0	413
Kidney stones/chronic kidney trouble	1.0	400
Senility/dementia/Alzheimer's	0.9	381
Missing limbs, hands, or fingers	0.7	302
Alcohol or drug related	0.7	300
Epilepsy	0.6	259
Learning disability	0.6	235
Cerebral palsy	0.4	182
Tumor, cyst, or growth	0.4	176
Speech disorder	0.4	151
Thyroid trouble or goiter	0.3	139
AIDS or AIDS related	0.3	105
Other	10.2	4 287

SOURCE: J.M. McNeil, "Current Trends Prevalence of Disabilities and Associated Health Conditions—United States, 1991–1992," (from Survey of Income and Program Participation) *Morbidity and Mortality Weekly Report* 43, no. 40 (October 14, 1994): 730–731, 737–739: Table 2.

NOTE: Participants who had difficulty with activities other than seeing, hearing, and having their speech understood by others were asked to select up to three conditions. Back or spine problems include chronic stiffness or deformity of the back or spine. Heart trouble includes coronary arteriosclerosis. Lung or respiratory trouble includes asthma, bronchitis, emphysema, respiratory allergies, TB, or other lung trouble. Stomach trouble includes ulcers, gall bladder, or liver conditions.

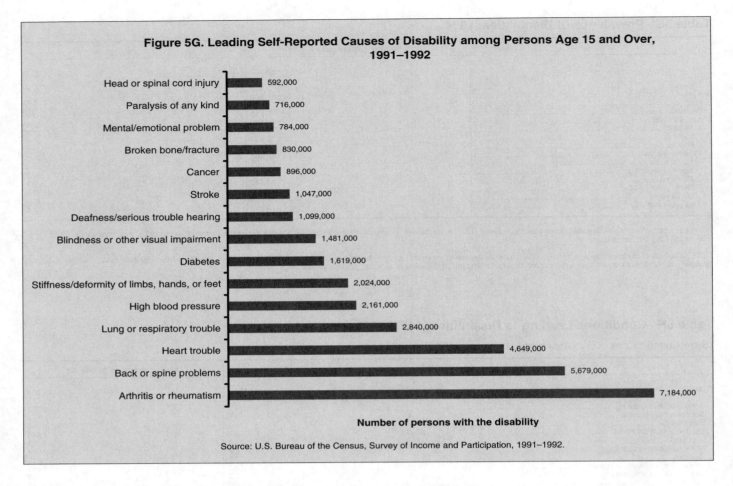

Figure 5G. Leading Self-Reported Causes of Disability among Persons Age 15 and Over, 1991–1992

Cause	Number of persons with the disability
Head or spinal cord injury	592,000
Paralysis of any kind	716,000
Mental/emotional problem	784,000
Broken bone/fracture	830,000
Cancer	896,000
Stroke	1,047,000
Deafness/serious trouble hearing	1,099,000
Blindness or other visual impairment	1,481,000
Diabetes	1,619,000
Stiffness/deformity of limbs, hands, or feet	2,024,000
High blood pressure	2,161,000
Lung or respiratory trouble	2,840,000
Heart trouble	4,649,000
Back or spine problems	5,679,000
Arthritis or rheumatism	7,184,000

Source: U.S. Bureau of the Census, Survey of Income and Participation, 1991–1992.

In 1983, about half of the Blacks had some activity restriction, but by 1994, closer to 40 percent had such limitations. (See Figure 5I and Table 5.11.) Black men especially experienced improvements between 1983 and 1994 regarding work limitations. (See Figure 5J and Table 5.12.) In 1983, 50.4 percent of the Black men had work limitations because of their diabetes compared with 23.1 percent of the White men. By 1994, only 26.3 percent of the Black men compared with 28.2 percent of the White men had work limitations caused by their disease.

CHILDREN WITH DISABILITIES

Children under age six years were considered disabled if they had a learning or other developmental disability, including mental retardation, autism, and cerebral palsy. About 313,000 children under age three years had such a disability, and an additional 652,000 children age three to five years were disabled either because of a developmental or a mobility disability. Among children age 6 to 14, about 2.2 million had difficulty doing regular schoolwork, about 1.6 million had a learning disability, and about half a million had a developmental disability. Young boys age 6 to 14 were almost twice as likely as girls their age to have a disability. (See Table 5.13.)

ADULTS WITH DISABILITIES

The likelihood of a disability increases with age to the extent that 71.5 percent of persons age 80 and over have a disability of some kind, and 53.5 percent have a severe disability. (See Table 5.13.) In this oldest age group, women are more likely than men and Blacks and Hispanics are more likely than Whites to have a severe disability. (See Table 5.13.) Fewer than 15 percent of adults under age 45 have any disability. In 1994, among the 26 million persons of all ages who had a severe disability, 19.3 million were non-Hispanic Whites; 4.2 million were non-Hispanic Blacks; 197,000 were American Indian, Eskimo, or Aleuts; 465,000 were Asian or Pacific Islanders; and 2.1 million were Hispanics.

People without disabilities are more likely to be employed, but employment of persons with disabilities is increasing even for persons with a severe disability. (See Table 5I.) About one-fourth of the people with a severe disability have a job. In 1997, 48.1 percent of the adults age 21 to 64 with a disability were employed. (See Table 5I.) Persons with hearing difficulties (62.4 percent) were more likely to be employed than those with vision difficulties (42.2 percent) or mental disabilities (38.8 percent).

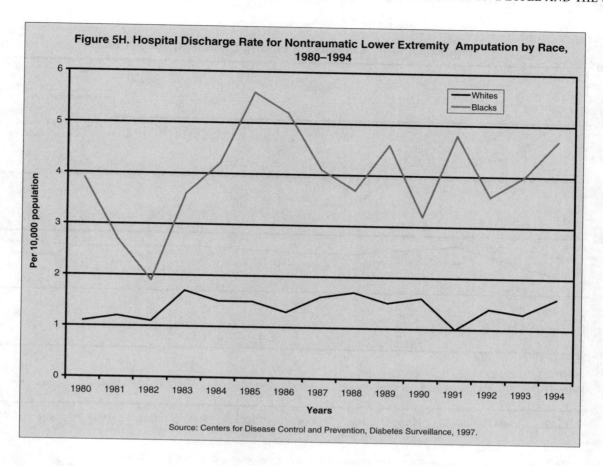

Figure 5H. Hospital Discharge Rate for Nontraumatic Lower Extremity Amputation by Race, 1980–1994

Source: Centers for Disease Control and Prevention, Diabetes Surveillance, 1997.

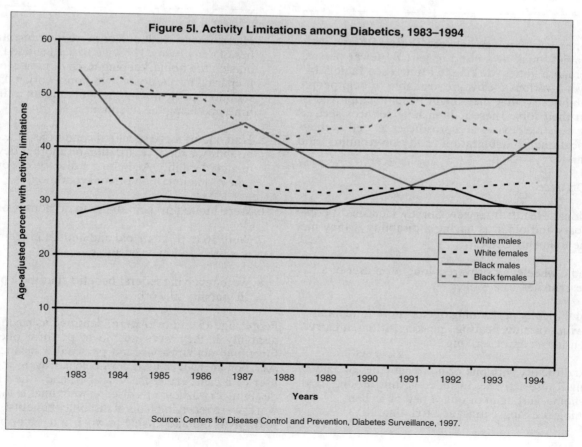

Figure 5I. Activity Limitations among Diabetics, 1983–1994

Source: Centers for Disease Control and Prevention, Diabetes Surveillance, 1997.

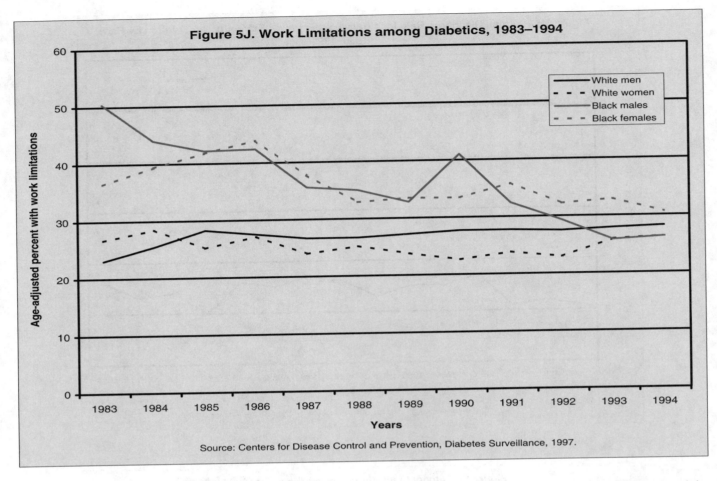

Figure 5J. Work Limitations among Diabetics, 1983–1994

Source: Centers for Disease Control and Prevention, Diabetes Surveillance, 1997.

The difference in earnings between those with and without a disability may be caused in part by fewer persons with severe disabilities working full-time. (See Table 5.14.) In any event, various means are available to help people with disabilities so that they might become employed or remain in their jobs. These aids include services such as providing assistive devices and prostheses as well as treatment, vocational rehabilitation, and job training and placement.

WHO IS DISABLED?

The National Health Interview Survey identified people age 15 years and older as having a disability if they met any of the following criteria:

1. Used a wheelchair or were a long-term user of a cane, crutches, or a walker.

2. Had difficulty performing one or more functional activities (seeing, hearing, speaking, lifting or carrying, using stairs, or walking).

3. Had difficulty with one or more activities of daily living. These activities included getting around inside the home, getting in or out of bed or a chair, bathing, dressing, eating, and toileting.

4. Had difficulty with one or more instrumental activities of daily living. These activities included going outside the home, keeping track of money and bills, preparing meals, doing light housework, taking prescription medicines in the right amount at the right time, and using the telephone.

5. Had one or more specified conditions (a learning disability, mental retardation or another developmental disability, Alzheimer's disease, or some other type of mental or emotional condition).

6. Were limited in their ability to do housework.

7. Were 16 to 67 years old and limited in their ability to work at a job or business.

8. Were receiving federal benefits that were based on an inability to work.

People age 15 and over were identified as having a severe disability if they were unable to perform one or more functional activities; needed personal assistance with an ADL or an IADL; used a wheelchair; were a long-term user of a cane, crutches, or walker; had a developmental disability or Alzheimer's disease; were unable to do housework; were receiving federal disability benefits; or were 16 to 67 years old and unable to work at a job or business.

At present, there is no consensus on the questions that should be asked to determine the disability status of young children. The NHIS asked whether children under six years of age had a "developmental condition for which he/she has received therapy or diagnostic services," and asked whether children three to five years of age had a "long lasting condition that limits his/her ability to walk, run, or use stairs."

DATA SOURCES ON DISABILITY

Four sources provide national data on disability: the National Health Interview Survey, the Survey of Income and Program Participation (SIPP), the Current Population Survey (CPS), and the Decennial Census. The Bureau of the Census does the fieldwork for the National Health Interview Survey, which is designed and analyzed by the National Center for Health Statistics. The bureau also collects disability-related data on the Survey of Income and Program Participation and the Current Population Survey. For the past three decades it has included questions on disability status on the Decennial Census of Population and Housing. The NHIS, SIPP, and CPS are household surveys and therefore do not include persons with disabilities who are in institutions, such as correctional facilities, long-term health care facilities, and the military. All four data sources rely on self-reported conditions and disabilities. Respondents are probably good sources of information on activity limitations. However, unless they receive regular health screening and medical care and are aware of their diagnoses, they may underreport diseases and other health conditions.

The National Health Interview Survey provides a large, cross-sectional sample and is conducted annually.

Periodically the NHIS adds a special module on disability. The NHIS defines *disability* in terms of restricted activities caused by injuries, chronic conditions, or other impairments, and *persons* are described in terms of the number and kind of limitations.

The Survey of Income and Program Participation is relatively smaller and provides data on a panel of households that are interviewed quarterly for several years. The SIPP was first conducted in 1984 and contained some questions about disability. Beginning in 1991, a more consistent and expanded set of questions on disability was included. The SIPP defines disability as a physical or mental impairment that substantially limits one or more of the major life activities. It collects extensive information in order to describe people in terms of types of limitations in functional activities, ADL, IADL, use of wheelchairs and other devices, and the presence of selected conditions related to mental functioning. In addition, the SIPP collects information on work disability and disability among children. Functional activities include seeing, hearing, speaking, lifting, carrying, walking, and using stairs. ADL consist of activities such as getting in and out of bed, bathing, dressing, and moving around in the house. IADL consist of preparing meals, doing light housework, using the telephone, keeping track of money or bills, and going out of the house.

The Current Population Survey has collected information on disability since 1980. It defines *disability* as a health problem that prevents an individual from working or limits the kind or amount of work that a person can do. Estimates of disability based on the CPS, therefore, will be lower than those from the other sources because the CPS deals with limitations influencing work.

Table 5I. Employment of Persons with Disabilities

(Number in thousands, except where noted)

Characteristic	1991–1992		1993–1994		1994–1995		1997	
	Total	Percent employed	Total	Percent employed	Total	Percent employed	Total	Percent employed
Persons 21 to 64 years old	144 075	75.1	148 244	75.1	149 369	76.2	152 886	78.2
With any disability	22 628	50.2	24 363	51.3	23 606	50.4	22 321	48.1
Severe	8 798	30.7	9 857	32.8	9 580	34.1	10 220	29.4
Not severe	13 830	62.7	14 506	63.9	14 026	61.6	12 101	63.9
Uses a wheelchair	495	18.4	582	20.9	685	22.0	874	21.9
Does not use a wheelchair but uses a cane, crutches, or a walker	1 484	25.2	1 840	29.2	1 609	27.5	2 173	24.8
Difficulty seeing	4 567	45.5	5 155	45.5	4 002	43.7	3 484	42.2
Difficulty hearing	5 222	63.7	5 650	65.4	4 489	64.4	3 416	62.4
Difficulty with speech	1 340	35.0	1 351	34.1	1 019	27.4	1 276	36.9
Difficulty lifting	7 548	32.1	8 149	34.5	8 026	34.8	7 232	30.0
Difficulty with stairs	7 803	30.1	8 584	31.6	8 517	33.9	9 420	34.9
Difficulty walking	7 672	31.5	8 600	31.9	8 697	33.5	9 129	33.9
Difficulty with one or more ADLs	3 313	25.3	3 820	26.8	3 640	27.1	4 008	26.2
Difficulty with one or more IADLs	4 811	22.9	5 375	25.4	5 272	26.0	5 620	24.0
Needs personal assistance with one or more ADL and/or IADL	3 704	21.2	4 021	23.1	3 974	24.0	4 379	20.7

SOURCE: J.M. McNeil, Data from the Survey of Income and Program Participation. Presented at the 75th Annual Conference of the Western Economic Association, June 30–July 3, 2000, Vancouver, British Columbia.

ADL - activity of daily living, including getting around inside the home, getting in or out of bed or a chair, bathing, dressing, eating, and toileting.
IADL - instrumental activity of daily living, including going outside the home, keeping track of money and bills, preparing meals, doing light housework, taking prescription medicines in the right amount at the right time, and using the telephone). Disability is defined as having one of the difficulties specified in this table. It does not include being unable to work at a job or receiving federal benefits based on disability as a part of the criteria for disability estimates.

The Decennial Census is conducted every 10 years, and since 1970 has contained questions on disability included on the "long form" asked of a sample of households. All of the last four censuses have included questions on work disability. The 1980 Census also asked about the ability to use public transportation. The 1990 and 2000 Censuses asked about work disability, the ability to go outside the home alone, and the ability to take care of personal needs.

PRODUCTIVITY (WORK AND SCHOOL)

The workforce is currently at its healthiest. The rate of injuries and illnesses among full-time workers in private industry has declined between 1994 and 1998. In 1998, of the 5.9 million injuries and illnesses reported on the job, 5.5 million were injuries.[13] The rate was 6.7 cases per 100 full-time equivalent employees (FTEs), the lowest rate of workplace injury and illness since the early 1970s when the Bureau of Labor Statistics (BLS) first reported such health data. Most of the workplace illnesses were caused by repeated injuries, such as carpal tunnel syndrome and noise-induced hearing loss. Employers report these data to the Department of Labor as part of its Survey of Occupational Injuries and Illnesses. Data on workplace injury, illness, and lost productivity also are available through self-reports, medical records, and workers' compensation claims. Less than half of the workplace injuries or illnesses, however, resulted in lost workdays for recovery or in restricted work activities. The rate of lost workdays (2.0 per 100 FTEs) also is at an all-time low. In addition, all of the major industries have reduced their rate of injuries with lost workdays between 1980 and 1997. (See Table 5.15.)

The consequences for persons with injury, disease, or illness in the workplace include lost productivity, lost wages, and increased risk of further loss of quality of life. Back disorders account for the greatest number of workplace injuries for both men and women. (See Table 5.16.) Most of the known injuries are strains, sprains, fractures, and wounds caused by bodily exertions, falls, or contact with objects. Respiratory conditions are most responsible for illnesses causing absences from work. (See Table 5.17.)

Table 5.15 shows the number and rate of occupational injuries that resulted in lost workdays per 100 FTE workers for the major types of industries (as classified by the Standard Industrial Classification Manual). The private sector includes all industrial categories except public administration and the military. Trends are shown from 1980 to 1997, and the data are based on the Survey of Occupational Injuries and Illnesses conducted by the BLS in the Department of Labor. The survey collects data from a scientifically selected sample of establishments based on type of industry and size of workforce. Employers provide the data using definitions and record-keeping guidelines established by the Department of Labor's Occupational Safety and Health Administration. About 250,000 private industry establishments participate. The survey collects data only on nonfatal work-related injuries and illnesses. A *work-related injury* is any injury that resulted from a

work-related event or exposure in the work environment. Such injuries include sprains, cuts, fractures, and amputations. A *work-related illness* is any condition that may be caused by exposure to factors associated with employment whether inhaled, absorbed, ingested, or contacted directly. Such illnesses include contact dermatitis, dust-related diseases of the lung, toxic-agent poisoning, and cancers. Also included are disorders associated with repeated injuries such as noise-induced hearing loss and carpal tunnel syndrome. Work-related injuries and illnesses not included are those that occurred to the self-employed, farm workers on small farms (10 or fewer employees), private household workers, or government workers (federal, state, or local).

Table 5.18 shows that persons who are unable to control their substance abuse and who engage in heavy drinking or illegal drug use are more likely than nonusers to change jobs often and to skip work.

School children between the ages of 5 and 17 are most likely to miss school if they are White, female, and from a low-income family. (See Table 5.19.) Respiratory conditions account for the greatest loss of school days for all groups of school children.

COSTS TO SOCIETY FROM POOR HEALTH

Society bears an enormous cost from treating disease, injury, and illness as well as from treating their complications and resulting disabilities. In addition, both individuals and society suffer a loss in productivity and quality of life. Chapter 1 includes estimates of national health care expenditures prepared by the Health Care Financing Administration (HCFA). These estimates show that 13.5 percent of the gross domestic product was used to pay for health care in 1998. In its estimates, HCFA included preventive care, public health expenditures, and care for illness and injuries.

According to recent estimates developed by Christopher Conover, the total cost of disease and injury in the United States amounts to $2.015 trillion.[14] (Table 5J provides the breakdown by disease category.) These estimates include the direct cost of providing care as well as productivity losses and are based on a composite approach that summarizes a large number of sector studies. The analysis shows that the injuries caused by violent crime result in greater total cost than any other single category of health event. In terms of direct costs, cardiovascular disease ($172.9 billion), musculoskeletal conditions ($143.2 billion), and mental illness ($138.2 billion) together account for 39.5 percent of the $1,150.9 billion spent in care and prevention.

Estimating the costs of illness and injury serves several purposes. Analysts have produced different estimates to meet these particular needs. In an effort to determine the cost-effectiveness of prevention, researchers have conducted studies to determine the costs associated with preventing certain conditions.

Table 5J. Annual Cost of Illness and Most Costly Illnesses: 2000

(Billions of dollars)

Disease/category	Total costs	Direct costs	Productivity losses			Intangible losses	Rank	Type of estimate	Base year	Source
			Total	Morbidity	Mortality					
GENERAL DISEASE CATEGORIES										
All diseases	2 015.4	1 150.9	864.5	240.5	624.0	NM	NA	Prevalence	1980	[S8, S29]
Violent crime	364.6	21.7	41.8	0.0	0.0	301.1	NA	Incidence	1989	[S18]
Cardiovascular disease	359.2	172.9	186.3	40.6	145.7	NM	NA	Prevalence	1980	[S8]
Injuries	326.5	NA	NA	NA	NA	NM	NA	Prevalence	1985	[S5]
Smoking	281.7	56.7	225.0	90.3	134.7	NM	NA	Prevalence	1993	[S25]
Cancer	257.2	96.4	193.0	25.4	167.5	NM	NA	Prevalence	1985	[S8]
Musculoskeletal conditions	253.0	143.2	109.7	100.7	9.0	NM	NA	Prevalence	1988	[S12]
Mental illness	237.9	138.2	132.6	110.9	21.7	NM	NA	Prevalence	1985	[S3]
Senile dementia	147.3	76.8	70.6	NA	NA	NM	NA	Prevalence	1985	[S14]
Coronary heart disease	94.9	25.1	69.8	0.0	0.0	NM	NA	Incidence	1975	[S17]
SPECIFIC ILLNESSES										
AIDS	168.9	8.5	160.4	4.1	156.2	NM	1	Prevalence	*1991	[S9, S10]
Alcoholism	141.1	20.9	120.2	64.1	56.1	NM	2	Prevalence	1985	[S3]
Alzheimer's	114.4	92.5	21.9	NR	NR	NM	3	Prevalence	1991	[S13]
Arthritis	110.8	29.9	80.8	80.4	0.5	NM	4	Prevalence	1988	[S12]
Falls	94.9	45.1	49.8	49.3	0.6	NM	5	Prevalence	1991	[S5]
Obesity (BMI>30)	92.8	92.8	0.0	NR	NR	NM	6	Prevalence	1995	[S24]
Motor vehicle accidents	80.6	21.1	59.5	31.2	28.3	NM	7	Prevalence	1991	[S5]
Depression	76.2	23.4	52.9	40.2	12.7	NM	8	Prevalence	1990	[S2]
Anxiety disorders	55.9	49.2	6.8	5.4	1.3	NM	9	Prevalence	1990	[S27]
Stroke	51.5	28.6	22.9	2.4	20.5	NM	10	Prevalence	1990	[S11]
Coronary other MI	48.5	15.1	33.4	NR	NR	NM	11	Prevalence	1975	[S17]
Schizophrenia	48.0	32.5	15.4	13.7	1.7	NM	12	Incidence	1975	[S6]
Reproductive cancer	45.6	22.5	23.1	NR	NR	NM	13	Prevalence	1975	[S17]
Diabetes	38.9	25.2	13.7	6.8	6.8	NM	14	Prevalence	1987	[S7]
Firearm injuries	35.5	3.3	32.2	3.4	28.8	NM	15	Incidence	1987	[S16]
Respiratory cancer	31.7	8.3	23.4	NR	NR	NM	16	Prevalence	1975	[S17]
Urinary incontinence (65 years and over)	27.4	27.2	0.2	0.0	0.2	NM	17	Prevalence	1984	[S20]
Parkinson's disease	27.3	18.9	8.4	8.4	0.0	NM	18	Prevalence	1994	[S26]
Drug abuse	26.4	6.4	20.0	14.0	6.0	NM	19	Prevalence	1985	[S3]
Non-Hip fractures	25.4	22.2	3.3	2.7	0.6	NM	20	Prevalence	1988	[S12]
Coronary sudden death	24.3	0.1	24.2	NR	NR	NM	21	Prevalence	1975	[S17]
Hip fractures	19.4	16.6	2.8	2.4	0.4	NM	22	Prevalence	1988	[S12]
Insomnia	18.5	18.5	0.0	0.0	0.0	NM	23	Prevalence	1995	[S28]
Coronary insufficiency	18.2	6.1	12.2	NR	NR	NM	24	Prevalence	1975	[S17]
Migraine headaches	16.8	1.4	15.4	15.4	0.0	NM	25	Incidence	1975	[S15]
Obsessive-compulsive disorder	14.6	4.2	10.4	10.0	0.4	NM	26	Prevalence	**1997	[S23]
Multiple Sclerosis	128.4	6.2	6.9	6.9	0.0	115.3	27	Incidence	1994	[S19, S22]

SOURCE: Unpublished estimates developed by Christopher J. Conover, Center for Health Policy, Law and Management, Duke University, February 2000. An electronic version of this table and updates can be found on the World Wide Web at <http://www.hpolicy.duke.edu/cyberexchange/coirank.htm>. Used with permission.

NOTE: Rankings based on direct and indirect costs only. NR=not reported. NM=not measured. Year 2000 figures obtained by inflating base-year direct costs by the increase in national health expenditures between the base year and 2000 (except for *All diseases*, in which total personal health expenditures for 2000 are directly reported by HCFA), indirect and intangible costs were inflated using the increase in gross domestic product. Note that these estimates are extremely crude as they do not account for shifting age composition, changes in disease prevalence, or changes in medical technology/treatment. Moreover, methods of estimating costs vary widely across studies (e.g., not all medical services are included and not all studies account for informal care-giving). Thus, the rankings shown are extremely approximate and should be used cautiously.

* Figure for direct cost is 1996 (S9). Figures for morbidity and mortality costs are willingness to pay estimates for 1991 (S10).
** Figure for direct costs is for 1994. Figure for morbidity costs is for 1997.

Sources:
[S1] Tom Reynolds, *Journal of the National Cancer Institute*, February 17, 1993, cited in Medical Benefits, March 15, 1993.
[S2] Paul E. Greenberg, Laura E. Stiglin, Stan N. Finkelstein and Ernst R. Berndt. "The Economic Burden of Depression in 1990," *Journal of Clinical Psychology* 54:11 (November 1993): 405–426.
[S3] Dorothy P. Rice, Sander Kelman, Leonard S. Miller, Sarah Dunmeyer. *The Economic Costs of Alcohol and Drug Abuse and Mental Illness: 1985.* Report submitted to Office of Financing and Coverage Policy of the Alcohol, Drug Abuse, and Mental Health Administration, U.S. Department of Health and Human Services. San Francisco: Institute for Health and Aging, University of California, 1990.
[S4] Fred Hellinger. "Forecasts of the Costs of Medical Care for Persons with HIV: 1992-1995," Inquiry (Fall, 1992), cited in Medical Benefits 9(22): 4.
[S5] Dorothy P. Rice, E.J. McKenzie and Associates. Cost of Injury in the United States: A Report to Congress. San Francisco and Baltimore Injury Prevention Center, Johns Hopkins University, 1989, cited in Jeffrey W. Runge. "The Cost of Injury, Emergency Medicine Clinics of North America" 11, No. 1 (February 1993): 241–253.
[S6] Dorothy P. Rice and L.S. Miller, The Economic Burden of Schizophrenia, Paper presented at the Sixth Biennial Research Conference on the Economics of Mental Health, Bethesda, Md, September 21–22, 1992, pp 1-17, cited in Agnes Rupp and Samuel J. Keith, The Costs of Schizophrenia: Assessing the Burden. Psychiatric Clinics of North America 16, no. 2 (June 1993): 413–423.
[S7] Daniel M. Huse, Gerry Oster, Alice R. Killen, Michael J. Lacey, and Graham A. Colditz. The Economic Costs of Non-Insulin-Dependent Diabetes Mellitus, *Journal of the American Medical Association* 262, no. 19 (November 17, 1989): 2708–2713.
[S8] Dorothy P. Rice, Thomas A. Hodgson and Andrea N. Kopstein. "The Economic Costs of Illness: A Replication and Update." *Health Care Financing Review* 7, no. 1 (Fall 1985): 61–80.
[S9] S.A. Bozzette, S.H. Berry, N. Duan, M.R. Frankel, A.A. Leibowitz, D. Lefkowitz, C.A. Emmons, J.W. Senterfitt, M.L. Berk, S.C. Morton, M.F. Shapiro. "The Care of HIV-Infected Adults in the United States." *New England Journal of Medicine* 339, no. 26 (November 26, 1998): 1897–1904.
[S10] Mark S. Thompson and Heidi J. Meyer, "The Cost of AIDS: Alternative Methodological Approaches," in Lee Sechrest, Howard Freeman and Albert Mulley, eds., *Health Services Research Methodology: A Focus on AIDS.* National Center for Health Services Research and Health Care Technology Assessment, September 1989: 95–106.
[S11] Mark S. Adelman, *National Survey of Stroke,* Chapter 6: Economic Impact. Stroke 12, Supplement 1, March-April 1981: 69–87.
[S12] A. Praemer, S. Furner, and D.P. Rice. "Section 5: Costs of Musculoskeletal Conditions. Musculoskeletal Conditions in the United States." American Academy of Orthopedic Surgeons, 1992.
[S13] Richard L. Ernst and Joel W. Hay. The U.S. Economic and Social Costs of Alzheimer's Disease Revisited. *American Journal of Public Health* 84, no. 8 (August 1994): 1261–1264.
[S14] Lien-Fu Huang, William S. Cartwright, and Teh-Wei Hu. "The Economic Cost of Senile Dementia in the United States, 1985" Public Health Reports 103, no. 1 (January-February 1988): 3–7.
[S15] Gregory de Lissovoy and Stephanie S. Lazarus. "The Economic Cost of Migraine: Present State of Knowledge." Neurology 44 (Suppl 4) June 1994: S56–S62.
[S16] Wendy Max and Dorothy P. Rice. Unpublished manuscript cited at, "What is the Cost of Gun Death and Injury?" Pacific Center for Violence Prevention. <http://www.pcvp.org/pcvp/firearms/facts/costs.shtn>.
[S17] Nelson S. Hartunian, Charles N. Smart, and Mark S. Thompson. "The Incidence and Economic Costs of Cancer, Motor Vehicle Injuries, Coronary Heart Disease, and Stroke: A Comparative Analysis," *American Journal of Public Health* 70, no. 12 (December 1980): 1249–1260.
[S18] Ted R. Miller, M.A. Cohen and S. B. Rossman. "Victim Costs of Violent Crime and Resulting Injuries." *Health Affairs* 12(4): 195–197.
[S19] Kathryn Whetten-Goldstein, Frank A. Sloan, Larry B. Goldstein, and Elizabeth D. Kulas. "A Comprehensive Assessment of the Cost of Multiple Sclerosis in the United States." *Multiple Sclerosis* 4 (3) (1998).
[S20] Teh-wei Hu. "The Economic Impact of Urinary Incontinence." *Clinics in Geriatric Medicine* 2, no. 4 (November 1986): 673–687.
[S21] Robert L. DuPont et al. Medical Interface. April 1995, cited in Medical Benefits June 15, 1995, p. 5.
[S22] Frank A. Sloan, W. Kip Viscusi, Harrel W. Chesson, Christopher J. Conover, and Kathryn Whetten-Goldstein. "Alternative Approaches to Valuing Intangible Health Losses: The Evidence for Multiple Sclerosis." *Journal of Health Economics* 17 (1998): 475–497.
[S23] X.H. Hu, L.E. Markson, R.B. Lipton, W. F. Stewart and M.L. Berger. Burden of Migraine in the United States: Disability and Economic Costs. *Archives of Internal Medicine* 159, no. 8 (April 26, 1999): 813–8.
[S24] G.A. Colditz. "Economic Costs of Obesity and Inactivity." *Medical Science and Sports Exercise* 31, 11 Suppl (November 1999): S663–7.
[S25] U.S. Department of Treasury. Deputy Treasury Secretary Lawrence H. Summers Remarks before the George Washington School of Public Health. Press release RR-2321., March 25, 1998. <http://www.treas.gov/press/releases/pr2321.htm>.
[S26] Kathryn Whetten-Goldstein, Frank A. Sloan, and Elizabeth D. Kulas, Toni Cutson, and Margaret Schenkman. "The Burden of Parkinson's Disease on Society, Family, and the Individual." *Journal of the American Geriatric Society* 45, no. 7 (July 1997): 844–849.
[S27] P.E. Greenberg, T. Sisitsky, R.C. Kessler, S.N. Finkelstein, E.R. Berndt, J.R. Davidson, J.C. Ballenger, and A.J. Fryer. "The Economic Burden of Anxiety Disorders." *Journal of Clinical Psychiatry* 60, no. 7 (July 1999): 427–35.
[S28] J.K. Walsh and C.L. Englehardt. "The Direct Economic Costs of Insomnia in the United States for 1995," Sleep 22, Supplement no. 2 (May 1999): S386–93.
[S29] Health Care Financing Administration, National Health Expenditure Projections, 1998–2008. <http://www.hcfa.gov/stats/NHE-Proj/proj1998/proj1998.pdf>.

Martone and others estimated the additional hospital costs associated with hospital-acquired infections on a medical ward to be about $2,100 per infected patient, and bloodstream infections alone to be about $3,517 per infected patient.[15] Magid and others estimated that early diagnosed Lyme disease cases cost about $74 in direct medical treatment costs; when delayed diagnosis and treatment lead to complications, Lyme disease cases cost about $2,228 to $6,724 per infected patient in direct medical costs in the first year.[16] Fahs et al. estimated that the cost of surgery to remove a precancerous cervical lesion ranges from $1,100 to $4,360 compared to the direct medical cost of treating a patient with cervical cancer, which can range from $9,200 to $13,360.[17] Not counting multidrug therapy, the lifetime discounted direct medical cost of treating a person infected with HIV was estimated to be about $96,000.[18] Gorsky estimated the direct medical costs to treat each child with HIV from birth to be about $161,000.[19]

To do an economic assessment of the value of regulations, health practices, and other means of reducing the effects of injury and disease, one must also calculate costs of illness. For example, an attempt has been made to do an economic assessment of various meat, poultry, and other food inspections and regulations instituted to prevent or control food-borne illnesses. Such an economic assessment of the value of these regulations and practices needs to take into account not only the costs of implementing the regulations and practices but also the benefits received from preventing such illnesses.

Table 5K shows the range of costs associated with food-borne illnesses under varying assumptions and methodological approaches.[20] It presents the range of estimated combined costs of medical care and productivity lost because of six major bacterial agents or diseases that are responsible for food-borne illnesses. Medical costs include those for physician and hospital services, supplies, medications, and procedures unique to treating food-borne ill-

nesses. Productivity costs were calculated on the basis of BLS estimates of usual weekly earnings for those who missed work because of food-borne illnesses (forgone earnings caused by death or missed work days). The table presents two approaches to estimating costs of food-borne illnesses. They differ primarily in the method used to calculate the economic value of lost productivity and premature death due to the illness. This cost-of-illness measure is called the *value of a statistical life* (VOSL). Both methods produce a range of estimated costs that depend in part on the range of estimated number of diseases and deaths resulting from these disease-causing agents.

The first cost-of-illness method is the approach taken by Landefeld and Seskin.[21] Estimates of lost productivity because of permanent disability or premature death based on the Landefeld and Seskin approach take into account the after-tax income lost, cost of housekeeping services, and a "risk aversion factor," which includes life insurance premiums as a proxy. The VOSL in this approach depends on age and ranges from about $15,000 to $1,979,000 in 1995 dollars. This method produces lower estimates of the costs of illness to society because it includes a limited number of factors associated with lost productivity and premature death. It does not include the value of factors such as reduced productivity while on the job, time off to see the doctor, reduced quality of life, complications that may develop later, increased burden on family members, and pain and suffering.

The second cost-of-illness method is based on Viscusi's studies of the monetary value that workers themselves place on nonfatal injuries, illness, and death. This approach examines the effect of job characteristics such as health risks, fringe benefits, and other intrinsic factors on pay. The estimates from this approach are based on labor market data that estimate how much more pay an employer must offer to get workers to take risky jobs compared to similar jobs with no risks.[22] Viscusi found a range of $3 million to $7 million in 1995 dollars for extra wages for jobs associ-

Table 5K. Medical Costs and Productivity Losses from Food-Borne and Meat/Poultry Diseases: 1995

(Billions of dollars)

Illness	All food sources		Meat/poultry alone	
	Low	High	Low	High
Landefeld and Seskin estimations [1]				
Salmonella	0.9	3.5	0.5	2.6
Campylobacter jejuni/ coli	0.7	4.3	0.5	3.2
E. coli O157: H7	0.3	0.7	0.2	0.5
Listeria monocytogenes	0.1	0.3	0.1	0.2
Staphylococcus aureus	1.2	1.2	0.6	0.6
Clostridium perfringens	0.1	0.1	0.1	0.1
Total	3.3	10.1	2.0	7.2
Viscusi estimations [2]				
Salmonella	4.8	12.2	2.4	9.2
Campylobacter jejuni/ coli	1.2	6.6	0.9	5.0
E. coli O157: H7	0.9	2.2	0.7	1.7
Listeria monocytogenes	1.3	2.4	0.7	1.2
Staphylococcus aureus	3.3	3.3	1.7	1.7
Clostridium perfringens	0.5	0.5	0.3	0.3
Total	12.0	27.2	6.7	19.1

SOURCE: Stephen R. Crutchfield, Jean C. Buzby, Tanya Roberts, Michael Ollinger, and C.T. Jordan Lin. *An Economic Assessment of Food Safety Regulations: The New Approach to Meat and Poultry Inspection.* Stephen R. Crutchfield, Jean C. Buzby, Tanya Roberts, Michael Ollinger, and C.T. Jordan Lin. Food Safety Branch, Food and Consumer Economics Division, Economic Research Service, U.S. Department of Agriculture, *Agricultural Economic Report* no. 755: Table 3.

1. Cost of illness includes estimates of productivity loss calculated using the value of expected lifetime earnings if illness or premature death had not occurred plus estimated amount or willingness to pay for life insurance premiums. (Reference: J.S. Landefeld and E.P. Seskin, Eugene. The economic value of life: linking theory to practice. *American Journal of Public Health* no. 6 (1982): 555–566.
2. Cost of illnesses estimates that the VOSL (value of statistical life) is about $5 million. (Reference: W.K. Viscusi. The value of risks to life and health. *Journal of Economic Literature* no. 31 (December 1993): 1912–1946.

ated with an increased risk of injury and death. The VOSL value used in Table 5K for the Viscusi approach is $5 million.

Table 5L provides a cost summary for one of the food-borne diseases, salmonellosis. Salmonellosis comes from eating contaminated food. It is the primary documented food-borne illness in most developed countries and in the United States. Infected persons can have fever, nausea, abdominal cramps, diarrhea, and sometimes vomiting. The most severe cases can result in death. Infants, the elderly, and those with immune deficiencies are at highest risk for severe complications associated with this condition. The range of estimates for the number of cases is based on the largest outbreak of salmonellosis in the United States. This outbreak occurred in Chicago in 1985 with an estimated 185,000 cases. Surveys of randomly selected households in the area were used to estimate the number of cases and the percentages of those who visited a physician, were hospitalized, and died. Those estimates were applied to the estimated number of annual cases of salmonellosis in the nation.

The National Safety Council has estimated various direct and indirect costs associated with unintentional injuries on the highway, in the home, and related to work. These data do not include costs associated with quality of life. The council estimated that the direct and indirect costs per motor vehicle crash were as follows: death—$980,000; nonfatal disabling injury—$34,100; and property damage crash—$6,400. The direct and indirect costs per case for other disabling unintentional injuries excluded property damage or nondisabling injury costs and were as follows:

	DEATH	INJURY
Public nonmotor vehicle injuries	$700,000	$7,000
Home injuries	$700,000	$9,900
Work injuries:		
Without employer costs	$870,000	$25,000
With employer costs	$890,000	$28,000

Table 5L. Cost Summary for U.S. Salmonellosis Cases: 1993

Severity of illness	Cost per case		Estimated cases and total costs			
	Cohen et al. (1976 dollars)	This analysis (1993 dollars)	Low		High	
			Cases (number)	Costs (millions of dollars)	Cases (number)	Costs (millions of dollars)
No physician visit [1]	125	371	746 880	276.8	3 734 400	1 384.1
Physician visit [2]	222	794	40 320	32.0	201 600	160.0
Hospitalized [3]	1 750	9 087	12 000	109.0	60 000	545.2
Death [4]	—	385 355	800	308.3	4 000	1 541.4
Total [5]	—	—	800 000	726.1	4 000 000	3 630.8

If 87–96% are food-borne, food-borne costs are $0.6–3.5 billion annually.[6]

SOURCE: J.C. Burby, T. Roberts, C.T. Jordan Lin, J.M. MacDonald, "Bacterial Food-borne Disease: Medical Costs and Productivity Losses," Food and Consumer Economics Division, Economic Research Service, U.S. Department of Agriculture. *Agricultural Economic Report* no. 741: Table 7.

— Data not available.

1. Cases in this category were calculated as a residual. We use the Cohen et al. estimate that the costs per case are $125 (1976 dollars) after we increase this value by 39% to account for fringe benefits and update to 1993 dollars using average weekly earnings for nonagricultural workers from the U.S. Department of Commerce, Bureau of Labor Statistics (BLS).
2. Assuming 5.04% of all cases visit a physician (Ryan, personal communication, 1987). Cost per case is from the Cohen et al. (1978) estimate of $222 (1976 dollars), updated to 1993 dollars using BLS's Consumer Price Index for physician services (U.S. Department of Commerce, Bureau of the Census).
3. This category is for those who were hospitalized and survived. Assuming 1.5% of all cases are hospitalized (Ryan et al. 1987). Cost per case is from Cohen et al. (1978) estimate of $1,750 (1976 dollars), updated to 1993 dollars using BLS's CPI for hospital rooms (U.S. Bureau of the Census).
4. Deaths are calculated using a case fatality rate of 1/1,000. Those who die are assumed to be hospitalized prior to their deaths and incur the same costs as those who are hospitalized and survive. Therefore, the total number of salmonellosis patients hospitalized each year is 12,800 for the low estimate and 64,000 for the high estimate. Costs for those who die are the sum of the cost per hospitalized case ($9,087) and Landefeld and Seskin's (1982) average value of a statistical life for the age distribution ($376,268 after averaging across gender and updating to 1993 values using the average weekly earnings.)
5. The low estimate of 800,000 cases was calculated by multiplying CDC's estimate of 40,000 Salmonella isolates (Tauxe 1991) by Chalker and Blaser's (1988) low estimate of the number (20) of unreported cases to each reported case. The high estimate of 4 million cases was calculated by multiplying CDC's estimate of 40,000 Salmonella isolates (Tauxe 1991) by Chalker and Blaser's (1988) high estimate of the number (100) of unreported cases to each reported case.
6. The 87% food-borne estimate is from Tauxe and Blake (1992) and the 96% food-borne estimate is from Bennett et al. (1987).

NOTE: Some numbers have been rounded. The full sources of the above-listed citations are as follows:
M.L. Cohen, R.E. Fountaine, R.A. Pollard, S.D. VonAllmen, T.M. Vernon, and E.J. Gangarosa, An Assessment of Patient-Related Economic Costs in an Outbreak of Salmonellosis. *New England Journal of Medicine* 299, no 22 (1978): 459–460.
C.A. Ryan, J.K. Nickels, N.T. Hargrett-Bean, M.D. Potter, T. Endo, L. Mayer, D.W. Langkop, C. Gibson, R.C. McDonald, R.T. Kenney, N.D. Purh, P.J. McDonnell, R.J. Martin, M.L. Cohen, and P.A. Blake, Massive Outbreak of Antimicrobial-Resistant Salmonellosis Traced to Pasteurized Milk. *Journal of the American Medical Association* 258, no. 22 (December 1987): 3269–3274.
J.S. Landefeld and E.P. Seskin, The Economic Value of Life: Linking Theory to Practice. *American Journal of Public Health* no. 6 (1982): 555–566.
R.V. Tauxe, *Salmonella*: A Postmodern Pathogen. *Journal of Food Protection* 54, no. 7 (July 1991): 563–568.
R.B. Chalker and M.J. Blaser, A Review of Human Salmonellosis: III. Magnitude of Salmonella Infection in the United States. *Reviews of Infectious Diseases.* 10, no. 10 (1988): 111–124.
R.V. Tauxe and P.A. Blake, Salmonellosis. Chapter 12 in J.M. Last, R.B. Wallace, and E. Barrett-Connoer (eds.) *Public Health and Preventive Medicine* 13th ed. Norwalk, Conn.: Appleton and Lange, 1992, pp. 266–268.
J.V. Bennett, S.D. Homberg, M.F. Rogers, and S.L. Soloman, Infectious and Parasitic Diseases. In R.W. Amler and H.B. Dull (eds.) *Closing the Gap: The Burden of Unnecessary Illness* New York: Oxford University Press, 1987: pp.102–114.

SUMMARY

In this chapter, we reported trends that show the large effect that health conditions and steps taken to respond to them have on people, our society, and our economy. Health conditions determine the length and quality of life. They set limits on the productive capacity of the nation. Disability is a personal as well as a societal impediment. Health has a direct effect on personal and national fulfillment. The level and distribution of health care are also critical factors in social equity. Lacking care, individuals suffer disability that could be prevented. Increased national attempts to meet these challenges have increased the direct cost of medical care. At the same time, access to care is a critical indicator of personal control. The large number of families and individuals who lack adequate medical care because they do not have insurance is a national concern and the focus of continued policy debates.

Table 5.1. Life Expectancy at Birth

Year	All Races			White			Black		
	Total	Men	Women	Total	Men	Women	Total	Men	Women
1902	49.2	47.9	50.7						
1911	51.5	49.9	53.2	49.6	48.2	51.1	33.8	32.5	35.0
1921	56.5	55.7	57.5	51.9	50.2	53.6	35.9	34.1	37.7
1931	59.3	57.8	61.1	57.5	56.3	58.5	47.1	47.1	46.9
1941	63.6	61.6	65.9	60.9	59.1	62.7	48.4	47.6	49.5
1951	68.1	65.5	71.0	64.9	62.8	67.3	53.9	52.3	55.6
1961	69.9	66.8	73.2	69.0	66.3	72.0	60.7	58.9	62.7
1970	70.8	67.1	74.7	70.7	67.6	74.2	63.9	61.5	66.5
1975	72.6	68.8	76.6	71.7	68.0	75.6	64.1	60.0	68.3
1976	72.9	69.1	76.8	73.4	69.5	77.3	66.8	62.4	71.3
1977	73.3	69.5	77.2	73.6	69.9	77.5	67.2	62.9	71.6
1978	73.5	69.6	77.3	74.0	70.2	77.9	67.7	63.4	72.0
1979	73.9	70.0	77.8	74.1	70.4	78.0	68.1	63.7	72.4
1980	73.7	70.0	77.4	74.6	70.8	78.4	68.5	64.0	72.9
1981	74.1	70.4	77.8	74.4	70.7	78.1	68.1	63.8	72.5
1982	74.5	70.8	78.1	74.8	71.1	78.4	68.9	64.5	73.2
1983	74.6	71.0	78.1	75.1	71.5	78.7	69.4	65.1	73.6
1984	74.7	71.1	78.2	75.2	71.6	78.7	69.4	65.2	73.5
1985	74.7	71.1	78.2	75.3	71.8	78.7	69.5	65.3	73.6
1986	74.7	71.2	78.2	75.3	71.8	78.7	69.3	65.0	73.4
1987	74.9	71.4	78.3	75.4	71.9	78.8	69.1	64.8	73.4
1988	74.9	71.4	78.3	75.6	72.1	78.9	69.1	64.7	73.4
1989	75.1	71.7	78.5	75.6	72.2	78.9	68.9	64.4	73.2
1990	75.4	71.8	78.8	75.9	72.5	79.2	68.8	64.3	73.3
1991	75.5	72.0	78.9	76.1	72.7	79.4	69.1	64.5	73.6
1992	75.8	72.3	79.1	76.3	72.9	79.6	69.3	64.6	73.8
1993	75.5	72.2	78.8	76.3	73.2	79.8	69.6	65.0	73.9
1994	75.7	72.4	79.0	76.5	73.1	79.5	69.2	64.6	73.7
1995	75.8	72.5	78.9	76.5	73.3	79.6	69.5	64.9	73.9
1996	76.1	73.1	79.1	76.5	73.4	79.6	69.6	65.2	73.9
1997	76.5	73.6	79.4	76.8	73.9	79.7	70.2	66.1	74.2
				77.1	74.3	79.9	71.1	67.2	74.7

SOURCE: R.N. Anderson, United States Life Tables, 1997. *National and Vital Statistics Reports* vol. 47 no. 28. Hyattsville, Md.: National Center for Health Statistics, 1999: Table 11. D.L. Hoyert, K.D. Kochanek, and S.L. Murphy, Deaths: Final Data for 1997. *National and Vital Statistics Reports* vol. 47 no. 19. Hyattsville, Md.: National Center for Health Statistics. 1999: Table 6.

Table 5.2. Years Lost by Cause of Death

(Years lost before age 75 per 100,000 population under 75 years of age)

Sex, race, Hispanic origin, and cause of death	Crude						Age-adjusted					
	1980	1985	1990	1995	1996	1997	1980	1985	1990	1995	1996	1997
ALL PERSONS												
All causes	10 267.0	9 255.0	8 997.0	8 595.0	8 210.0	7 873.0	9 813.0	8 793.0	8 518.0	8 128.0	7 748.0	7 398.0
Diseases of heart	2 065.0	1 842.0	1 517.0	1 430.0	1 396.0	1 368.0	1 877.0	1 664.0	1 363.0	1 259.0	1 222.0	1 190.0
Ischemic heart disease	1 454.0	1 207.0	942.1	841.8	820.4	786.4	1 307.0	1 078.0	834.8	727.9	704.9	670.2
Cerebrovascular diseases	332.9	277.3	246.2	241.1	240.7	238.5	302.9	250.8	221.1	211.5	210.2	207.1
Malignant neoplasms	1 932.0	1 911.0	1 863.0	1 779.0	1 755.0	1 734.0	1 815.0	1 776.0	1 713.0	1 587.0	1 554.0	1 523.0
Respiratory system	521.1	536.1	538.0	495.9	490.2	479.9	479.5	488.1	486.3	432.7	424.1	410.6
Colorectal	175.8	168.8	153.4	146.8	142.2	143.0	158.5	151.0	137.3	128.3	123.5	123.3
Prostate	78.8	81.5	89.5	77.8	75.5	69.7	67.2	69.2	76.6	66.6	64.6	59.7
Breast	408.5	417.1	416.5	389.0	375.5	368.1	393.0	392.7	381.9	340.0	324.3	314.3
Chronic obstructive pulmonary diseases	164.5	182.6	182.5	188.0	187.9	187.0	141.4	156.2	156.9	161.4	161.1	158.9
Pneumonia and influenza	156.4	139.3	139.9	126.5	125.6	123.8	149.1	130.4	128.5	115.3	114.5	112.6
Chronic liver disease and cirrhosis	254.1	199.4	178.4	166.4	164.1	161.7	259.1	196.0	168.8	149.7	145.7	141.7
Diabetes mellitus	124.6	120.3	147.0	169.6	174.6	172.0	115.1	109.8	133.0	149.9	153.5	149.9
Human immunodeficiency virus infection	—	—	391.2	615.0	435.1	225.3	—	—	366.2	570.3	401.9	208.7
Unintentional injuries	1 688.0	1 344.0	1 221.0	1 098.0	1 079.0	1 060.0	1 688.0	1 365.0	1 263.0	1 155.0	1 136.0	1 115.0
Motor vehicle-related injuries	1 017.0	803.1	752.4	634.1	626.9	608.6	1 010.0	817.0	788.8	687.9	680.8	661.1
Suicide	401.6	407.5	404.8	395.0	380.8	371.5	402.8	404.5	405.9	405.6	387.8	378.0
Homicide and legal intervention	459.5	358.0	452.3	399.1	360.4	335.7	460.9	357.1	466.4	436.4	394.7	368.9
WHITE MALE												
All causes	12 454.0	11 168.0	10 629.0	10 120.0	9 558.0	9 116.0	11 877.0	10 594.0	10 064.0	9 546.0	8 980.0	8 533.0
Diseases of heart	2 907.0	2 551.0	2 058.0	1 918.0	1 866.0	1 826.0	2 681.0	2 329.0	1 856.0	1 678.0	1 623.0	1 576.0
Ischemic heart disease	2 241.0	1 839.0	1 416.0	1 254.0	1 214.0	1 162.0	2 060.0	1 673.0	1 269.0	1 085.0	1 044.0	990.1
Cerebrovascular diseases	309.0	258.0	222.9	224.3	223.6	219.8	280.2	231.6	198.6	195.7	194.4	189.8
Malignant neoplasms	2 087.0	2 042.0	1 970.0	1 868.0	1 842.0	1 806.0	1 939.0	1 875.0	1 793.0	1 653.0	1 620.0	1 576.0
Respiratory system	744.8	725.9	700.1	621.6	611.2	591.9	680.6	655.6	627.7	537.8	525.5	503.6
Colorectal	194.2	191.0	174.7	166.6	160.9	160.3	176.2	170.9	155.7	144.8	138.8	137.5
Prostate	72.6	75.6	85.0	72.3	70.1	64.0	59.1	60.5	68.3	58.1	56.3	51.5
Chronic obstructive pulmonary diseases	219.3	222.4	208.9	200.7	198.3	201.4	187.1	187.6	177.2	169.4	167.5	169.3
Pneumonia and influenza	156.0	146.5	143.3	131.1	128.1	129.5	147.4	135.2	130.5	117.9	115.1	116.1
Chronic liver disease and cirrhosis	306.4	249.1	233.5	235.2	233.7	231.8	307.9	242.6	219.1	208.8	205.1	200.8
Diabetes mellitus	114.7	114.7	141.0	165.6	174.8	166.5	107.4	105.4	127.5	145.7	153.0	143.4
Human immunodeficiency virus infection	—	—	589.3	775.8	492.5	220.1	—	—	544.3	707.8	448.0	200.7
Unintentional injuries	2 553.0	1 990.0	1 766.0	1 556.0	1 513.0	1 486.0	2 523.0	2 004.0	1 821.0	1 638.0	1 591.0	1 561.0
Motor vehicle-related injuries	1 579.0	1 198.0	1 085.0	878.7	857.6	824.6	1 549.0	1 209.0	1 134.0	957.0	933.1	897.1
Suicide	663.0	691.5	694.0	687.4	657.0	636.6	656.4	680.2	692.2	703.8	665.7	644.7
Homicide and legal intervention	455.2	341.8	384.7	344.0	303.6	290.5	452.6	338.0	391.6	372.5	327.7	314.5
BLACK MALE												
All causes	21 081.0	18 896.0	20 744.0	19 543.0	18 140.0	16 621.0	22 338.0	20 016.0	21 250.0	20 272.0	18 994.0	17 373.0
Diseases of heart	3 383.0	3 166.0	2 769.0	2 718.0	2 585.0	2 576.0	4 179.0	3 864.0	3 338.0	3 151.0	2 969.0	2 918.0
Ischemic heart disease	1 805.0	1 538.0	1 249.0	1 180.0	1 125.0	1 128.0	2 283.0	1 929.0	1 561.0	1 411.0	1 326.0	1 308.0
Cerebrovascular diseases	714.1	597.6	546.4	522.4	509.5	515.8	870.2	727.3	655.6	601.0	583.0	578.8
Malignant neoplasms	2 495.0	2 474.0	2 444.0	2 236.0	2 197.0	2 178.0	3 070.0	3 058.0	3 021.0	2 654.0	2 576.0	2 517.0
Respiratory system	911.8	916.1	899.8	766.2	759.6	727.8	1 160.0	1 167.0	1 150.0	941.0	918.1	865.6
Colorectal	176.1	183.8	188.6	187.7	192.1	196.9	215.9	226.0	234.0	223.7	225.6	229.1
Prostate	136.9	141.1	143.7	135.4	130.8	127.4	159.1	170.0	177.6	166.5	160.2	154.6
Chronic obstructive pulmonary diseases	223.3	236.1	241.4	244.6	239.0	226.4	258.7	273.9	278.7	275.3	266.7	250.8
Pneumonia and influenza	467.1	391.5	399.2	305.8	311.3	276.2	492.6	424.3	416.8	321.2	328.4	291.7
Chronic liver disease and cirrhosis	610.1	480.8	390.5	285.3	265.8	239.5	791.8	588.5	461.4	320.5	293.5	265.3
Diabetes mellitus	199.8	204.8	263.0	319.5	310.7	336.0	245.5	249.4	317.8	373.8	357.4	380.2
Human immunodeficiency virus infection	—	—	1 622.0	2 939.0	2 293.0	1 300.0	—	—	1 625.0	2 928.0	2 270.0	1 288.0
Unintentional injuries	2 934.0	2 420.0	2 308.0	2 049.0	1 985.0	1 929.0	2 931.0	2 395.0	2 265.0	2 042.0	1 983.0	1 925.0
Motor vehicle-related injuries	1 289.0	1 127.0	1 163.0	1 008.0	994.4	982.7	1 281.0	1 099.0	1 143.0	1 007.0	997.1	987.6
Suicide	415.7	432.5	482.3	482.0	459.7	436.8	428.1	428.6	478.0	489.3	465.6	443.1
Homicide and legal intervention	2 872.0	2 128.0	3 197.0	2 635.0	2 417.0	2 216.0	2 939.0	2 079.0	3 096.0	2 663.0	2 448.0	2 251.0
AMERICAN INDIAN OR ALASKA NATIVE MALE [1]												
All causes	16 368.0	12 443.0	11 879.0	11 670.0	11 023.0	11 278.0	16 915.0	12 848.0	12 125.0	12 349.0	11 607.0	11 907.0
Diseases of heart	1 667.0	1 391.0	1 287.0	1 285.0	1 285.0	1 328.0	2 299.0	1 887.0	1 660.0	1 592.0	1 564.0	1 616.0
Ischemic heart disease	1 024.0	846.3	712.6	792.0	771.1	809.3	1 511.0	1 207.0	985.1	1 016.0	965.7	1 007.0
Cerebrovascular diseases	190.2	165.1	160.3	225.5	200.3	165.2	256.4	220.3	194.1	270.1	234.2	196.2
Malignant neoplasms	661.4	799.1	725.2	839.5	821.9	1 042.0	912.9	1 056.0	948.4	1 053.0	1 030.0	1 261.0
Respiratory system	174.5	202.9	206.2	243.2	267.5	280.6	256.6	297.1	293.1	325.1	358.1	366.9
Colorectal	44.9	75.3	53.1	77.7	80.0	113.0	64.6	105.5	68.9	97.4	103.6	135.5
Prostate	34.2	35.2	22.5	30.5	42.1	25.5	53.1	53.3	33.5	43.0	58.3	36.4
Chronic obstructive pulmonary diseases	78.2	98.9	100.3	106.5	80.6	166.8	106.2	128.8	128.2	134.3	99.1	200.1
Pneumonia and influenza	343.1	222.4	230.2	225.8	261.7	239.1	370.1	233.4	227.5	240.0	274.9	249.0
Chronic liver disease and cirrhosis	943.9	526.0	445.9	669.3	504.7	539.3	1 259.0	658.7	530.2	735.9	555.6	586.7
Diabetes mellitus	183.1	155.5	191.6	257.9	291.7	284.8	255.3	220.0	256.1	324.7	360.0	358.1
Human immunodeficiency virus infection	—	—	130.2	436.2	271.0	145.1	—	—	130.3	429.3	264.8	139.7
Unintentional injuries	5 731.0	4 092.0	3 600.0	3 321.0	3 175.0	3 125.0	5 509.0	3 897.0	3 508.0	3 289.0	3 130.0	3 107.0
Motor vehicle-related injuries	3 329.0	2 374.0	2 095.0	1 934.0	1 955.0	1 802.0	3 146.0	2 240.0	2 047.0	1 936.0	1 925.0	1 786.0
Suicide	984.6	961.7	968.2	879.2	877.2	917.1	921.0	900.9	945.1	880.4	867.0	913.0
Homicide and legal intervention	1 029.0	821.3	778.2	829.3	682.3	743.7	1 003.0	805.3	754.5	823.3	677.3	731.5

See footnotes at end of table.

Table 5.2. Years Lost by Cause of Death—*Continued*

(Years lost before age 75 per 100,000 population under 75 years of age)

Sex, race, Hispanic origin, and cause of death	Crude						Age-adjusted					
	1980	1985	1990	1995	1996	1997	1980	1985	1990	1995	1996	1997
ASIAN OR PACIFIC ISLANDER MALE [2]												
All causes	6 131.0	5 582.0	5 414.0	5 158.0	4 981.0	4 853.0	6 342.0	5 841.0	5 638.0	5 310.0	5 101.0	4 944.0
Diseases of heart	1 027.0	870.9	740.6	763.5	804.5	795.9	1 237.0	1 059.0	877.9	852.2	873.7	855.5
Ischemic heart disease	697.6	532.9	413.4	429.6	445.4	441.7	863.6	675.0	507.1	487.2	493.2	485.7
Cerebrovascular diseases	201.0	154.2	176.2	212.5	202.5	211.1	238.4	188.3	208.1	234.7	219.3	224.9
Malignant neoplasms	969.1	996.4	965.7	975.0	952.8	997.0	1 160.0	1 193.0	1 132.0	1 072.0	1 031.0	1 062.0
Respiratory system	239.3	211.9	192.8	199.9	199.7	213.5	304.7	275.8	245.4	231.4	227.6	236.6
Colorectal	84.1	89.0	85.6	98.4	80.4	96.7	104.8	112.8	103.7	109.2	89.1	103.0
Prostate	10.3	11.5	18.6	16.1	18.3	14.1	12.9	15.6	25.0	20.1	21.9	16.7
Chronic obstructive pulmonary diseases	67.1	66.8	61.6	65.7	79.4	68.1	76.8	83.5	77.7	75.1	88.3	75.7
Pneumonia and influenza	94.1	76.9	72.2	69.3	72.4	74.2	93.9	81.3	79.4	73.3	75.5	78.9
Chronic liver disease and cirrhosis	94.7	92.6	84.8	62.5	60.1	60.1	112.1	106.7	95.7	64.4	61.8	59.9
Diabetes mellitus	63.6	49.8	60.2	71.3	89.9	77.4	76.6	63.5	74.1	82.2	98.5	85.9
Human immunodeficiency virus infection	—	—	145.8	221.5	146.2	60.5	—	—	134.5	202.4	133.0	54.7
Unintentional injuries	1 196.0	1 058.0	986.7	789.5	776.6	747.9	1 143.0	1 020.0	957.1	797.1	788.6	755.2
Motor vehicle-related injuries	732.6	668.3	657.3	494.3	466.3	418.7	699.8	641.6	634.9	505.4	477.7	425.7
Suicide	320.0	326.0	336.5	355.5	326.4	319.5	308.9	311.9	320.5	361.0	324.6	324.1
Homicide and legal intervention	317.1	257.3	347.5	359.0	317.4	285.4	304.4	244.2	330.7	371.5	323.8	291.9
HISPANIC MALE [3]												
All causes	—	9 338.0	10 217.0	9 583.0	8 477.0	7 677.0	—	9 872.0	10 469.0	9 989.0	8 861.0	8 054.0
Diseases of heart	—	975.8	897.3	846.4	825.4	806.6	—	1 478.0	1 301.0	1 155.0	1 124.0	1 079.0
Ischemic heart disease	—	564.7	483.5	445.2	432.8	412.6	—	917.1	759.4	650.8	631.2	596.6
Cerebrovascular diseases	—	189.8	168.7	183.5	183.6	178.5	—	275.8	228.9	232.4	233.5	228.9
Malignant neoplasms	—	753.2	810.1	838.1	791.9	796.5	—	1 055.0	1 131.0	1 104.0	1 042.0	1 041.0
Respiratory system	—	138.0	169.2	158.4	149.3	141.8	—	226.0	267.8	235.0	224.2	210.5
Colorectal	—	56.1	64.1	68.8	64.7	69.4	—	91.7	98.7	98.5	91.8	98.8
Prostate	—	24.4	22.0	29.3	27.2	22.5	—	43.8	37.8	46.9	44.4	35.9
Chronic obstructive pulmonary diseases	—	50.8	54.6	60.9	53.6	55.4	—	76.5	74.8	79.0	72.2	73.2
Pneumonia and influenza	—	151.5	139.4	118.8	111.6	107.9	—	173.3	152.5	129.1	119.0	118.0
Chronic liver disease and cirrhosis	—	418.8	340.2	309.6	301.7	281.1	—	572.1	454.0	395.8	377.9	350.7
Diabetes mellitus	—	77.4	107.2	144.2	142.5	141.6	—	125.1	160.0	206.8	204.0	200.9
Human immunodeficiency virus infection	—	—	964.3	1 332.0	871.8	434.6	—	—	972.6	1 330.0	869.6	434.1
Unintentional injuries	—	2 092.0	2 120.0	1 794.0	1 679.0	1 600.0	—	1 936.0	1 972.0	1 757.0	1 632.0	1 551.0
Motor vehicle-related injuries	—	1 182.0	1 305.0	1 024.0	951.4	900.2	—	1 076.0	1 202.0	1 002.0	922.9	872.0
Suicide	—	412.7	450.2	462.7	420.5	390.1	—	391.0	434.3	464.3	413.3	383.7
Homicide and legal intervention	—	1 261.0	1 466.0	1 209.0	993.2	877.3	—	1 152.0	1 330.0	1 182.0	949.7	841.0
WHITE, NON-HISPANIC MALE [3]												
All causes	—	10 733.0	10 530.0	9 992.0	9 528.0	9 197.0	—	10 091.0	9 803.0	9 226.0	8 744.0	8 407.0
Diseases of heart	—	2 528.0	2 175.0	2 034.0	1 988.0	1 962.0	—	2 246.0	1 877.0	1 697.0	1 643.0	1 607.0
Ischemic heart disease	—	1 827.0	1 515.0	1 346.0	1 309.0	1 265.0	—	1 614.0	1 294.0	1 107.0	1 065.0	1 018.0
Cerebrovascular diseases	—	244.9	228.8	226.0	224.6	223.2	—	213.1	195.0	188.5	185.9	183.9
Malignant neoplasms	—	2 046.0	2 102.0	1 988.0	1 974.0	1 943.0	—	1 833.0	1 835.0	1 679.0	1 651.0	1 610.0
Respiratory system	—	732.9	760.4	677.3	671.3	655.8	—	642.8	649.2	554.8	544.1	524.7
Colorectal	—	194.4	187.9	178.6	173.5	172.6	—	168.7	159.8	147.5	141.5	139.8
Prostate	—	74.7	92.8	77.8	75.8	69.8	—	57.7	70.4	58.6	56.8	52.4
Chronic obstructive pulmonary diseases	—	234.5	227.2	216.7	216.1	222.0	—	192.6	183.2	173.2	172.0	175.8
Pneumonia and influenza	—	147.7	141.3	130.1	127.6	130.6	—	134.6	125.3	113.6	110.9	113.3
Chronic liver disease and cirrhosis	—	234.4	219.1	219.5	218.4	219.3	—	221.8	198.2	187.3	183.8	181.6
Diabetes mellitus	—	107.7	144.7	166.4	176.7	168.1	—	96.0	125.9	140.0	147.5	137.8
Human immunodeficiency virus infection	—	—	531.4	684.0	425.7	181.6	—	—	485.9	618.2	384.0	164.1
Unintentional injuries	—	1 829.0	1 689.0	1 484.0	1 451.0	1 444.0	—	1 858.0	1 769.0	1 581.0	1 549.0	1 540.0
Motor vehicle-related injuries	—	1 097.0	1 041.0	837.9	821.8	799.8	—	1 122.0	1 111.0	928.0	914.2	889.4
Suicide	—	702.9	719.4	705.2	681.0	665.5	—	689.1	720.9	723.2	692.1	676.5
Homicide and legal intervention	—	254.3	239.2	207.0	189.1	191.4	—	253.0	242.3	219.0	200.3	204.4
WHITE FEMALE												
All causes	6 655.0	6 116.0	5 740.0	5 533.0	5 443.0	5 373.0	6 185.0	5 606.0	5 225.0	5 005.0	4 899.0	4 821.0
Diseases of heart	1 142.0	1 044.0	864.1	811.8	798.8	784.8	915.3	832.2	689.3	648.9	637.1	626.2
Ischemic heart disease	758.1	653.5	521.1	464.1	459.5	434.3	584.8	501.0	399.6	356.1	352.2	332.0
Cerebrovascular diseases	275.0	226.7	200.1	193.4	193.7	189.8	231.4	188.8	165.4	156.8	157.3	153.2
Malignant neoplasms	1 774.0	1 793.0	1 760.0	1 701.0	1 684.0	1 668.0	1 595.0	1 584.0	1 528.0	1 425.0	1 403.0	1 379.0
Respiratory system	305.8	360.5	391.8	393.1	392.3	388.2	267.5	307.0	326.9	316.0	312.3	305.4
Colorectal	165.1	151.3	133.2	125.6	120.8	122.1	137.5	124.5	109.5	101.2	96.8	97.6
Breast	418.8	426.2	420.7	383.8	369.1	361.3	390.0	388.3	373.0	324.1	308.5	298.9
Chronic obstructive pulmonary diseases	117.4	152.8	164.6	183.6	183.7	182.4	94.8	120.9	128.9	143.4	142.0	140.1
Pneumonia and influenza	103.6	91.7	92.3	89.8	90.8	90.5	97.0	83.4	81.8	78.8	79.8	79.0
Chronic liver disease and cirrhosis	145.2	110.8	95.5	89.4	91.4	92.0	138.7	102.0	84.6	75.9	77.1	76.3
Diabetes mellitus	108.0	101.4	121.8	135.8	136.5	136.6	91.4	84.5	101.0	110.3	110.9	111.1
Human immunodeficiency virus infection	—	—	43.4	102.6	76.4	40.2	—	—	41.8	98.1	73.2	38.5
Unintentional injuries	793.0	656.1	610.1	577.6	584.4	576.8	816.8	690.3	654.1	629.2	634.9	627.6
Motor vehicle-related injuries	525.0	440.1	426.7	382.7	387.6	379.9	539.1	465.5	464.8	429.5	434.7	428.0
Suicide	193.0	181.0	166.1	153.4	153.8	156.5	196.1	181.2	165.3	154.0	153.6	155.3
Homicide and legal intervention	132.0	119.0	117.2	114.0	102.5	92.9	136.1	122.7	123.5	124.0	111.1	101.2

See footnotes at end of table.

Table 5.2. Years Lost by Cause of Death—*Continued*

(Years lost before age 75 per 100,000 population under 75 years of age)

Sex, race, Hispanic origin, and cause of death	Crude						Age-adjusted					
	1980	1985	1990	1995	1996	1997	1980	1985	1990	1995	1996	1997
BLACK FEMALE												
All causes	11 795.0	10 576.0	10 966.0	10 373.0	10 054.0	9 560.0	11 863.0	10 630.0	10 662.0	10 179.0	10 012.0	9 475.0
Diseases of heart	2 020.0	1 867.0	1 665.0	1 594.0	1 618.0	1 535.0	2 189.0	1 993.0	1 756.0	1 627.0	1 636.0	1 534.0
Ischemic heart disease	987.7	852.4	711.9	661.6	670.3	634.2	1 078.0	917.5	762.1	680.9	682.3	636.6
Cerebrovascular diseases	600.9	506.3	458.3	415.6	425.1	426.7	656.7	544.5	481.2	417.3	422.9	419.4
Malignant neoplasms	1 855.0	1 833.0	1 893.0	1 856.0	1 822.0	1 839.0	2 085.0	2 019.0	2 041.0	1 911.0	1 845.0	1 837.0
Respiratory system	279.5	306.7	344.9	330.9	328.6	341.4	322.0	344.7	382.4	347.6	337.5	345.2
Colorectal	162.6	171.6	164.4	160.7	157.5	153.3	179.2	187.1	178.3	165.8	160.8	153.2
Breast	382.8	424.0	465.4	484.2	484.4	479.4	448.6	479.8	505.6	495.9	484.0	472.7
Chronic obstructive pulmonary diseases	109.0	132.4	149.0	169.6	185.7	172.7	116.3	139.7	157.4	172.8	187.4	172.2
Pneumonia and influenza	252.3	204.3	214.2	189.1	179.1	180.5	245.2	203.9	206.1	184.0	177.2	177.9
Chronic liver disease and cirrhosis	323.8	227.1	193.2	128.9	121.7	115.8	378.0	250.2	203.4	130.0	119.8	113.2
Diabetes mellitus	248.3	229.2	279.1	307.2	321.9	314.6	271.6	246.7	299.0	318.0	329.5	318.3
Human immunodeficiency virus infection	—	—	427.1	956.6	801.2	517.8	—	—	402.5	913.5	757.5	492.1
Unintentional injuries	898.9	769.7	767.7	740.1	753.1	735.7	876.0	754.6	748.3	730.1	751.9	734.6
Motor vehicle-related injuries	362.9	349.5	381.2	367.2	389.4	394.5	354.7	342.3	376.7	370.2	396.9	400.4
Suicide	88.3	76.4	90.0	77.6	74.1	73.6	91.2	76.8	89.0	77.5	74.7	74.5
Homicide and legal intervention	605.3	491.6	619.7	505.1	467.1	417.7	593.1	474.9	596.5	505.6	470.5	422.2
AMERICAN INDIAN OR ALASKA NATIVE FEMALE [1]												
All causes	9 077.0	6 853.0	6 086.0	6 586.0	6 560.0	6 368.0	9 126.0	6 974.0	6 192.0	6 788.0	6 797.0	6 563.0
Diseases of heart	714.8	664.1	647.0	679.4	651.4	684.4	870.8	811.5	753.2	781.6	738.7	754.3
Ischemic heart disease	323.4	320.0	299.7	342.6	315.7	323.3	442.1	422.4	381.1	408.3	376.3	365.1
Cerebrovascular diseases	158.3	163.8	167.1	178.3	175.5	200.4	204.2	196.0	191.7	199.2	194.6	218.5
Malignant neoplasms	775.0	690.8	860.2	875.1	994.6	942.9	980.9	856.7	1 012.0	978.0	1 105.0	1 035.0
Respiratory system	67.2	97.1	138.6	146.8	152.3	150.3	94.9	125.3	177.3	170.1	178.1	177.4
Colorectal	45.8	40.4	56.2	83.4	73.3	78.2	63.9	50.8	68.3	92.3	85.7	87.0
Breast	125.9	108.9	150.1	158.5	188.8	140.9	173.5	138.8	178.3	179.5	210.0	154.7
Chronic obstructive pulmonary diseases	*	54.7	80.1	107.7	95.6	*	—	69.1	94.2	126.1	110.1	119.1
Pneumonia and influenza	216.4	146.3	152.9	143.5	137.6	118.1	210.9	140.3	154.4	144.7	141.1	128.1
Chronic liver disease and cirrhosis	681.0	461.1	381.8	396.6	411.4	408.2	842.4	537.3	415.9	427.7	428.0	423.1
Diabetes mellitus	190.5	199.5	186.6	270.1	276.6	269.2	260.4	256.1	233.0	318.5	317.8	306.4
Human immunodeficiency virus infection	—	*	—	96.5	*	—	—	*	—	*	*	—
Unintentional injuries	2 170.0	1 521.0	1 185.0	1 354.0	1 360.0	1 327.0	2 056.0	1 461.0	1 155.0	1 337.0	1 350.0	1 302.0
Motor vehicle-related injuries	1 486.0	967.6	778.5	955.7	923.7	846.9	1 412.0	924.3	772.9	955.5	924.6	844.2
Suicide	211.6	202.5	153.9	172.3	238.5	160.1	212.9	192.6	152.8	176.3	243.1	164.0
Homicide and legal intervention	342.9	192.8	226.8	242.9	218.9	227.5	345.9	194.4	219.8	238.7	211.8	223.4
ASIAN OR PACIFIC ISLANDER FEMALE [2]												
All causes	3 893.0	3 520.0	3 264.0	3 178.0	2 990.0	3 060.0	3 918.0	3 580.0	3 308.0	3 159.0	2 949.0	2 992.0
Diseases of heart	378.1	361.4	318.1	353.5	319.1	326.1	420.4	396.9	343.0	358.9	318.8	322.5
Ischemic heart disease	167.1	174.1	148.3	151.7	137.8	145.8	200.5	199.5	164.1	157.6	139.0	143.8
Cerebrovascular diseases	192.2	164.8	175.3	153.3	161.6	173.1	215.6	184.1	190.0	157.3	158.6	168.0
Malignant neoplasms	870.0	881.9	847.0	960.6	910.8	896.4	949.9	946.4	893.7	959.1	886.9	863.2
Respiratory system	98.1	92.9	110.7	126.7	106.7	125.2	113.1	106.1	121.6	129.8	106.4	121.0
Colorectal	79.7	79.6	69.7	71.3	78.6	76.3	89.9	86.6	75.7	70.0	77.5	72.5
Breast	175.7	156.8	173.1	215.9	175.9	181.7	190.0	171.0	182.0	211.1	164.1	170.4
Chronic obstructive pulmonary diseases	22.1	47.6	47.4	42.0	52.6	43.3	23.2	53.4	50.4	41.5	52.8	42.2
Pneumonia and influenza	49.6	42.9	59.6	47.4	46.7	47.3	52.3	43.5	60.7	46.6	45.8	47.4
Chronic liver disease and cirrhosis	34.0	30.8	30.3	24.8	19.0	20.2	39.6	35.0	32.2	25.1	18.8	19.1
Diabetes mellitus	53.1	30.9	44.5	61.8	61.6	60.6	62.6	35.0	50.2	64.7	61.4	60.7
Human immunodeficiency virus infection	—	—	*	25.6	20.4	—	—	—	*	23.3	18.2	—
Unintentional injuries	486.4	472.6	419.6	380.0	340.0	396.9	481.7	467.1	424.0	398.0	349.5	412.5
Motor vehicle-related injuries	338.1	307.2	325.0	281.5	241.5	279.4	333.1	301.2	328.3	297.2	246.4	293.7
Suicide	159.2	145.6	114.7	129.4	119.8	116.5	151.0	144.7	111.3	132.2	116.5	118.6
Homicide and legal intervention	131.0	123.2	117.9	113.3	93.8	93.0	124.8	121.0	113.0	113.0	97.4	94.8
HISPANIC FEMALE [3]												
All causes	—	4 427.0	4 753.0	4 395.0	4 219.0	4 137.0	—	4 567.0	4 662.0	4 378.0	4 211.0	4 114.0
Diseases of heart	—	478.8	442.2	402.6	385.0	391.4	—	641.5	556.9	485.5	458.9	466.2
Ischemic heart disease	—	246.6	219.8	193.8	189.3	190.2	—	356.7	297.0	249.6	241.9	242.3
Cerebrovascular diseases	—	143.8	151.9	140.8	130.0	135.8	—	184.0	182.8	165.6	155.1	155.8
Malignant neoplasms	—	740.9	828.7	793.1	807.4	810.4	—	944.4	1 014.0	937.1	942.3	936.4
Respiratory system	—	49.3	66.3	64.5	68.3	72.6	—	68.7	88.9	82.1	85.3	90.4
Colorectal	—	48.4	54.4	54.8	52.1	52.7	—	65.8	70.9	67.2	64.8	63.7
Breast	—	164.1	201.4	180.0	187.8	189.3	—	218.2	254.2	217.8	220.2	221.7
Chronic obstructive pulmonary diseases	—	41.3	50.6	55.0	49.6	51.1	—	52.4	61.6	64.2	58.0	58.4
Pneumonia and influenza	—	89.4	93.0	73.3	78.2	80.0	—	87.5	87.7	71.2	74.8	79.3
Chronic liver disease and cirrhosis	—	105.4	93.1	75.3	82.1	81.8	—	139.7	115.7	90.2	95.5	95.2
Diabetes mellitus	—	83.4	103.4	132.4	131.1	133.8	—	115.9	137.0	168.8	164.2	167.9
Human immunodeficiency virus infection	—	—	152.9	312.6	225.8	114.6	—	—	146.0	309.8	224.2	114.4
Unintentional injuries	—	549.6	556.5	515.8	536.9	516.0	—	513.7	526.1	501.7	520.7	505.9
Motor vehicle-related injuries	—	347.7	382.4	354.7	361.9	349.4	—	330.7	368.1	349.7	355.6	348.6
Suicide	—	61.8	89.8	73.8	82.3	64.6	—	64.4	88.4	75.9	84.8	66.7
Homicide and legal intervention	—	203.1	227.5	202.4	165.4	146.6	—	188.4	214.0	197.1	158.8	142.5

See footnotes at end of table.

Table 5.2. Years Lost by Cause of Death—*Continued*

(Years lost before age 75 per 100,000 population under 75 years of age)

Sex, race, Hispanic origin, and cause of death	Crude						Age-adjusted					
	1980	1985	1990	1995	1996	1997	1980	1985	1990	1995	1996	1997
WHITE, NON-HISPANIC FEMALE [3]												
All causes	—	6 037.0	5 788.0	5 591.0	5 519.0	5 474.0	—	5 495.0	5 189.0	4 968.0	4 874.0	4 814.0
Diseases of heart	—	1 046.0	902.4	853.4	842.8	832.5	—	816.2	691.9	654.2	643.8	636.7
Ischemic heart disease	—	660.4	549.4	492.7	489.0	464.6	—	493.7	402.7	360.4	356.9	337.8
Cerebrovascular diseases	—	219.7	205.5	197.5	199.2	195.2	—	178.2	163.4	153.7	155.6	151.2
Malignant neoplasms	—	1 807.0	1 861.0	1 804.0	1 787.0	1 772.0	—	1 560.0	1 563.0	1 453.0	1 429.0	1 404.0
Respiratory system	—	377.8	428.1	433.3	433.2	429.9	—	314.4	343.6	333.1	328.9	321.8
Colorectal	—	151.7	142.6	134.1	128.9	130.9	—	122.0	112.6	103.3	98.6	99.9
Breast	—	436.1	444.4	407.0	390.3	381.9	—	387.9	381.3	330.9	313.4	303.0
Chronic obstructive pulmonary diseases	—	164.5	176.9	198.4	199.8	199.4	—	126.9	132.5	147.7	147.0	145.2
Pneumonia and influenza	—	96.2	90.2	90.4	91.0	90.6	—	86.9	78.1	77.7	78.0	76.6
Chronic liver disease and cirrhosis	—	115.8	95.6	90.1	91.9	91.9	—	104.0	82.0	74.0	74.9	73.5
Diabetes mellitus	—	97.7	123.2	134.4	135.2	134.6	—	80.2	98.9	105.1	105.7	104.4
Human immunodeficiency virus infection	—		29.1	72.2	53.4	28.6	—		28.2	69.4	51.2	27.6
Unintentional injuries	—	639.9	607.4	574.7	577.0	577.8	—	682.3	661.1	636.4	637.3	639.6
Motor vehicle-related injuries	—	419.7	425.1	378.8	381.4	379.2	—	450.2	470.9	433.2	436.7	436.0
Suicide	—	195.6	172.6	161.0	161.0	168.2	—	194.5	170.9	160.7	159.8	165.8
Homicide and legal intervention	—	115.0	102.3	96.1	90.9	83.3	—	119.3	108.3	105.9	99.5	92.0

SOURCE: E. Kramarow, H. Lentzner, R. Rooks, J. Weeks, and S. Saydah, *Health and Aging Chartbook. Health, United States,* 1999. Hyattsville, Md.: National Center for Health Statistics. 1999: Table 31.

* Based on fewer than 20 deaths.
— Data not available.
1. Interpretation of trends should take into account that population estimates for American Indians increased by 45 percent between 1980 and 1990, partly because of better enumeration techniques in the 1990 decennial census and to the increased tendency for people to identify themselves as American Indian in 1990.
2. Interpretation of trends should take into account that the Asian population in the United States more than doubled between 1980 and 1990, primarily because of immigration.
3. Excludes data from states lacking a Hispanic-origin item on their death certificates.

NOTE: For data years shown, the code numbers for cause of death are based on the International Classification of Diseases, Ninth Revision. Categories for coding human immunodeficiency virus infection were introduced in the United States in 1987. Years of potential life lost (YPLL) before age 75 provides a measure of the impact of mortality on the population under 75 years of age. These data are presented as YPLL–75 because the average life expectancy in the United States is over 75 years. YPLL–65 was calculated in *Health, United States, 1995* and earlier editions. The race groups, White, Black, Asian or Pacific Islander, and American Indian or Alaska Native, include persons of Hispanic and non-Hispanic origin. Conversely, persons of Hispanic origin may be of any race. Consistency of race identification between the death certificate (source of data for numerator of death rates) and data from the Census Bureau (denominator) is high for individual White and Black persons; however, persons identified as American Indian, Asian, or Hispanic origin in data from the Census Bureau are sometimes misreported as white or non-Hispanic on the death certificate, causing death rates to be underestimated by 22–30 percent for American Indians, about 12 percent for Asians, and about 7 percent for persons of Hispanic origin. (P.D. Sorlie, E. Rogot, and N.J. Johnson, "Validity of Demographic Characteristics on the Death Certificate," *Epidemiology* 3, no. 2 (1992):181–184. YPLL rates for minority groups may also be underestimated.

Table 5.3. Using Assistive Devices: 1994

(Number in thousands)

Assistive device	All ages	44 years and under	45–64 years	65 years and over
ANATOMICAL DEVICES				
Any anatomical devices [1]	4 565	2 491	1 325	748
Back brace	1 688	795	614	279
Neck brace	168	76	78	*13
Hand brace	332	171	119	*42
Arm brace	320	209	86	*25
Leg brace	596	266	138	192
Foot brace	282	191	59	31
Knee brace	989	694	199	96
Other brace	399	239	104	56
Any artificial limb	199	69	59	70
Artificial leg or foot	173	58	50	65
Artificial arm or hand	*21	*9	6	6
MOBILITY DEVICES				
Any mobility device [1]	7 394	1 151	1 699	4 544
Crutch	575	227	188	160
Cane	4 762	434	1 116	3 212
Walker	1 799	109	295	1 395
Medical shoes	677	248	226	203
Wheelchair	1 564	335	365	863
Scooter	140	12	53	75
HEARING DEVICES				
Any hearing device [1]	4 484	439	969	3 076
Hearing aid	4 156	370	849	2 938
Amplified telephone	675	73	175	427
TDD/TTY	104	58	*25	*21
Closed caption television	141	*66	*32	43
Listening device	106	*26	*22	58
Signaling device	95	*37	*23	35
Interpreter	57	*27	*21	9
Other hearing technology	93	*28	*24	41
VISION DEVICES				
Any vision device [1]	527	123	135	268
Telescopic lenses	158	*40	*49	70
Braille	59	*28	*23	*8
Readers	68	*15	*14	39
White cane	130	*35	48	47
Computer equipment	*34	*19	8	7
Other vision technology	277	51	76	151

Source: J. Russell, G. Hendershot, F. LeClere, L. Howie, "Trends and Differential Use of Assistive Technology Devices: United States, 1994." National Center for Health Statistics. *Vital and Health Statistics* no. 292 (November 13, 1997): Table 1. Based on data from the National Health Interview Survey.

* Figure does not meet standard of reliability or precision.
1. Numbers do not add to these totals because categories are not mutually exclusive; a person could have used more than one device within a category.

Table 5.4. Difficulties Experienced by Persons with Vision and Hearing Impairments: 1994 [1]

(Percent of persons age 70 years and over)

Category	Vision		Hearing		Vision and hearing	
	Reported impairment	No impairment	Reported impairment	No impairment	Reported impairment	No impairment
ACTIVITY LIMITATIONS						
Difficulty walking	43.3	20.2	30.7	21.3	48.3	22.2
Difficulty getting outside	28.6	10.4	17.3	12.0	32.8	11.9
Difficulty getting into and out of bed or a chair	22.1	9.3	15.1	9.8	25.0	10.4
Difficulty managing medication	11.8	4.4	7.7	4.8	13.4	5.0
Difficulty preparing meals	18.7	6.7	11.6	7.6	20.7	7.8
COMORBIDITIES AND SECONDARY HEALTH CONDITIONS						
Fallen during preceding 12 months	31.2	19.2	28.4	17.8	37.4	19.8
Broken hip	7.1	4.2	5.4	4.4	7.6	4.5
Hypertension	53.7	43.1	46.7	44.3	53.4	44.3
Heart disease	30.2	19.7	27.6	18.6	32.4	20.6
Stroke	17.4	7.3	11.8	7.8	19.9	8.1
PARTICIPATION RESTRICTIONS						
Frequently depressed or anxious	13.3	7.0	9.9	7.2	15.6	7.4
Get together with friends	65.3	72.5	68.6	72.4	63.3	71.9
Get together with relatives	74.2	76.1	76.9	75.2	75.5	75.8
Go out to eat at restaurant	55.7	65.1	62.7	63.7	55.8	64.1

SOURCE: V.A. Campbell, J.E. Crews, D.G. Moriarty, M.M. Zack, and D.K. Blackman, Surveillance for Sensory Impairment, Activity Limitation, and Health-Related Quality of Life Among Older Adults—United States, 1993–1997. *Morbidity and Mortality Weekly Report* 48, no. SS08 (December 17, 1999): 131-156: Table 2.

1. Total population = 8,767.

Table 5.5. Vision and Hearing Impairments in Adults Age 70 Years and Over: 1994 [1]

Characteristic	Vision impairment		Hearing impairment		Vision and hearing impairment	
	Population	Percent	Population	Percent	Population	Percent
Total	3 652 626	18.1	6 697 497	33.2	1 724 277	8.6
SEX						
Male	1 319 000	16.4	3 214 181	40.0	726 200	9.0
Female	2 333 626	19.2	3 483 316	28.7	998 077	8.2
RACE [2]						
White	3 246 700	17.9	6 243 983	34.5	1 588 000	8.8
Black	307 273	19.6	303 450	19.3	82 604	5.3
Other	98 653	20.6	150 064	31.3	53 673	*
HISPANIC ETHNICITY [3]						
Yes	137 787	18.7	215 513	29.3	69 401	8.2
No	3 469 017	18.1	6 405 472	33.4	1 644 370	8.6
REGION [4]						
Northeast	654 391	14.3	1 396 180	30.6	314 159	6.9
Midwest	959 465	18.7	1 744 938	34.0	457 091	8.9
South	1 304 254	19.9	2 176 528	33.3	604 377	9.2
West	734 516	18.8	1 379 851	35.3	348 650	8.9

SOURCE: V.A. Campbell, J.E. Crews, D.G. Moriarty, M.M. Zack, and D.K. Blackman. Surveillance for Sensory Impairment, Activity Limitation, and Health-Related Quality of Life Among Older Adults—United States, 1993–1997. *Morbidity and Mortality Weekly Report* 48, no. SS08 (December 17, 1999): 131-156: Table 1.

* Analyses were not performed for subgroups when the relative standard error of an estimate was 30% or more.
1. Total population = 8,767.
2. Race data are presented only for whites, blacks, and others because sample sizes for other racial groups were too small for meaningful analysis.
3. Persons of Hispanic origin can be of any race.
4. Northeast = Connecticut, Maine, Massachusetts, New Hampshire, New Jersey, New York, Pennsylvania, Rhode Island, and Vermont; Midwest = Illinois, Indiana, Iowa, Kansas, Michigan, Minnesota, Missouri, Nebraska, North Dakota, Ohio, South Dakota, and Wisconsin; South = Alabama, Arkansas, Delaware, District of Columbia, Florida, Georgia, Kentucky, Louisiana, Maryland, Mississippi, North Carolina, Oklahoma, South Carolina, Tennessee, Texas, Virginia, and West Virginia; and West = Alaska, Arizona, California, Colorado, Hawaii, Idaho, Montana, Nevada, New Mexico, Oregon, Utah, Washington, and Wyoming.

Table 5.6. Activity Restriction Because of Acute and Chronic Conditions: 1996

(Restricted activity days)

Characteristic	Type of restriction					
	Number of days per person			Number of days in the thousands		
	All types	Bed disability	Work or school loss[1]	All types	Bed disability[1]	Work or school loss
All persons[2]	14.5	5.9	4.6	3 824 530	1 566 166	808 570
AGE						
Under 5 years	8.0	3.8	—	160 931	76 273	—
5–17 years	7.5	3.3	4.0	382 431	169 314	205 582
18 years and over	17.0	6.8	4.8	3 281 168	1 320 579	602 988
18–24 years	9.3	3.7	4.1	229 274	89 839	67 318
25–44 years	13.1	5.0	4.7	1 090 104	416 059	319 548
45–64 years	18.7	7.8	5.3	993 935	415 629	201 410
65 years and over	30.5	12.6	3.7	967 855	399 052	14 711
SEX AND AGE						
Male						
All ages	12.3	4.9	4.0	1 587 090	626 154	382 425
Under 5 years	8.8	4.1	—	89 991	41 698	—
5–17 years	7.2	3.0	3.8	188 822	78 859	100 375
18 years and over	14.2	5.5	4.1	1 308 277	505 597	282 050
18–24 years	7.3	2.5	3.8	88 650	29 891	33 438
25–44 years	10.1	3.9	3.8	414 014	159 065	139 378
45–64 years	16.2	6.0	5.0	415 007	159 143	101 275
65 years and over	29.3	12.1	*3.4	390 607	161 498	7 959
Female						
All ages	16.5	6.9	5.1	2 237 441	940 012	426 145
Under 5 years	7.2	3.5	—	70 941	34 575	—
5–17 years	7.7	3.6	4.2	193 609	90 455	105 207
18 years and over	19.6	8.1	5.6	1 972 891	814 982	320 938
18–24 years	11.4	4.8	4.4	140 624	59 947	33 880
25–44 years	16.0	6.1	5.8	676 090	256 994	180 170
45–64 years	21.1	9.5	5.7	578 929	260 486	100 135
65 years and over	31.3	12.9	*4.0	577 248	237 554	6 753
RACE AND AGE						
White						
All ages	14.3	5.6	4.5	3 154 220	1 237 153	661 190
Under 5 years	8.0	3.7	—	128 889	58 889	—
5–17 years	7.8	3.5	4.2	318 271	142 336	168 978
18 years and over	16.6	6.3	4.6	2 707 060	1 035 929	492 213
18–24 years	9.5	3.7	4.1	187 578	72 405	57 124
25–44 years	12.4	4.4	4.4	861 480	307 019	251 062
45–64 years	17.9	7.1	5.2	819 962	326 707	171 741
65 years and over	29.3	11.5	3.4	838 040	329 798	12 286
Black						
All ages	16.4	8.1	5.3	543 067	269 850	115 430
Under 5 years	6.7	*3.6	—	21 685	11 726	—
5–17 years	6.4	2.6	3.6	51 686	21 266	29 234
18 years and over	21.5	10.9	6.3	469 695	236 859	86 196
18–24 years	9.0	3.7	*3.5	31 069	12 611	7 078
25–44 years	18.8	9.3	7.2	194 427	96 266	57 014
45–64 years	25.0	12.7	6.1	135 670	68 738	20 964
65 years and over	41.6	22.7	*3.6	108 530	59 244	1 141
FAMILY INCOME AND AGE						
Less than $10,000						
All ages	27.9	12.2	6.2	554 008	243 175	53 862
Under 5 years	10.2	*6.0	—	20 052	11 839	—
5–17 years	10.8	5.0	6.5	41 328	19 089	24 692
18 years and over	3.5	15.1	5.9	492 629	212 247	29 170
18–24 years	11.8	5.2	*3.9	39 116	17 033	6 627
25–44 years	31.7	15.7	7.1	144 105	71 259	15 138
45–64 years	51.8	24.1	*7.7	140 393	65 229	6 563
65 years and over	4.8	16.7	*3.5	169 015	58 726	842
$10,000–$19,000						
All ages	21.1	9.2	6.2	778 798	338 458	125 634
Under 5 years	8.8	5.0	—	28 489	16 197	—
5–17 years	8.3	3.6	4.5	56 970	24 430	31 115
18 years and over	25.9	11.1	7.1	693 338	297 831	94 519
18–24 years	13.5	4.3	5.5	58 764	18 762	15 801
25–44 years	20.9	8.5	7.6	204 403	83 006	51 800
45–64 years	33.5	18.1	8.7	186 183	100 823	25 024
65 years and over	34.4	13.4	*2.6	243 988	95 241	1 895
$20,000–$34,999						
All ages	1.3	5.2	4.5	701 730	281 969	162 814
Under 5 years	8.7	3.1	—	36 654	13 262	—
5–17 years	7.1	2.6	3.5	71 472	26 468	35 530
18 years and over	14.9	6.1	4.9	593 604	242 239	127 284
18–24 years	9.6	3.9	4.9	47 023	19 075	17 744
25–44 years	1.1	3.8	4.6	198 462	68 614	70 325
45–64 years	18.3	7.9	5.8	171 636	73 506	37 293
65 years and over	23.6	10.8	*1.9	176 483	81 043	1 920

See footnotes at end of table.

Table 5.6. Activity Restriction Because of Acute and Chronic Conditions: 1996—*Continued*

(Restricted activity days)

Characteristic	Type of restriction					
	Number of days per person			Number of days in the thousands		
	All types	Bed disability	Work or school loss [1]	All types	Bed disability [1]	Work or school loss
FAMILY INCOME AND AGE						
$35,000 or more						
All ages	9.9	3.6	3.9	1 083 239	399 448	337 814
Under 5 years	7.9	3.7	—	61 707	29 045	—
5–17 years	7.1	3.2	3.8	165 987	74 922	87 640
18 years and over	10.9	3.8	4.0	855 545	295 481	250 174
18–24 years	7.6	3.4	3.3	59 256	26 198	18 618
25–44 years	9.7	3.1	3.7	371 520	119 059	125 435
45–64 years	11.9	3.9	4.8	313 681	101 129	103 403
65 years and over	18.1	8.0	*2.1	111 088	49 095	2 717
GEOGRAPHIC REGION						
Northeast	13.3	5.1	3.9	716 221	273 540	138 514
Midwest	12.9	5.0	4.3	819 101	317 806	192 138
South	15.8	6.9	4.9	1 432 125	624 840	297 360
West	15.2	6.2	4.8	857 083	349 980	180 559
PLACE OF RESIDENCE						
MSA [3]	1.4	5.7	4.6	2 912 534	1 183 878	643 351
Central city	15.3	6.6	4.9	1 198 046	512 632	251 830
Not central city	13.2	5.2	4.3	1 714 487	671 246	391 521
Not MSA [3]	16.3	6.8	4.5	911 997	382 288	165 220

SOURCE: P.F. Adams, G.E. Hendershot, and M.A. Marano, "Current Estimates from the National Health Interview Survey, 1996." National Center for Health Statistics. *Vital and Health Statistics* 10, no. 200 (1999): Table 69.

— Category not applicable.
* Figure does not meet standard of reliability or precision.
1. Sum of school days lost for children 5–17 years of age and work days lost for currently employed persons 18 years of age and over. School days lost are shown for the age group 5–17 years, work days lost are shown for the age group 18 years and over and each older age group.
2. Includes other races and unknown family income.
3. MSA is metropolitan statistical area.

NOTE: A condition is considered acute if (a) it was first noticed no longer than three months before the reference date of the interview, and (b) it is not one of the conditions considered chronic regardless of the time of onset. (See definition of chronic condition.) However, any acute condition not associated with either at least one doctor visit or at least one day of restricted activity during the reference period is considered to be of minor consequence and is excluded from the final data produced by the survey.

Table 5.7. Restricted Activity Because of Chronic Conditions: 1996

Characteristic	All persons	Degree of activity limitation (percent distribution)					
		With no activity limitations	With activity limitations	With limitations in major activity	Unable to carry on major activity	Limited in amount or kind of major activity	Limited, but not in major activity
All persons [1]	100	85.6	14.4	10.0	4.7	5.3	4.5
AGE							
Under 18 years	100	93.9	6.1	4.4	0.5	3.8	1.7
18–44 years	100	90.3	9.7	7.0	3.4	3.6	2.7
45–64 years	100	78.0	22.0	16.5	9.4	7.2	5.5
65 years and over	100	63.7	36.3	21.5	10.5	11.0	14.8
65–69 years	100	66.6	33.4	26.4	15.1	11.4	7.0
70 years and over	100	62.4	37.6	19.3	8.4	10.9	18.3
SEX							
Male							
Under 18 years	100	86.1	13.9	9.7	4.9	4.9	4.2
18–44 years	100	92.6	7.4	5.5	0.6	4.8	1.9
45–64 years	100	90.4	9.6	7.1	3.7	3.4	2.5
65 years and over	100	78.8	21.2	16.7	10.4	6.4	4.5
65–69 years	100	68.1	31.9	25.9	16.2	9.7	6.0
70 years and over	100	63.3	36.7	15.1	7.4	7.7	21.5
Female							
Under 18 years	100	85.1	14.9	10.2	4.5	5.7	4.7
18–44 years	100	95.3	4.7	3.2	0.4	2.8	1.5
45–64 years	100	90.1	9.9	7.0	3.1	3.9	2.9
65 years and over	100	77.2	22.8	16.4	8.4	7.9	6.4
65–69 years	100	65.3	34.7	26.9	14.1	12.8	7.8
70 years and over	100	61.8	38.2	22.2	9.1	13.0	16.1
RACE							
White							
Under 18 years	100	85.7	14.3	9.7	4.4	5.3	4.6
18–44 years	100	94.3	5.7	4.1	0.4	3.7	1.6
45–64 years	100	90.5	9.5	6.8	3.1	3.7	2.7
65 years and over	100	78.8	21.2	15.7	8.6	7.0	5.5
65–69 years	100	68.0	32.0	25.2	13.9	11.3	6.7
70 years and over	100	62.6	37.4	18.6	8.1	10.4	18.8
Black							
Under 18 years	100	83.7	16.3	12.5	6.4	6.1	3.8
18–44 years	100	91.5	8.5	6.2	1.0	5.2	2.3
45–64 years	100	87.3	12.7	10.0	5.8	4.2	2.7
65 years and over	100	70.7	29.3	23.7	14.7	8.9	5.6
65–69 years	100	53.3	46.7	37.2	24.5	12.7	9.5
70 years and over	100	59.8	40.2	27.1	11.6	15.4	13.1
FAMILY INCOME							
Less than $10,000							
Under 18 years	100	71.1	28.9	22.7	12.9	9.8	6.2
18–44 years	100	90.5	9.5	7.3	1.6	5.7	2.2
45–64 years	100	77.1	22.9	18.3	10.8	7.5	4.6
65 years and over	100	39.9	60.0	54.1	38.9	15.2	5.9
65–69 years	100	42.8	57.2	51.3	37.5	13.9	*
70 years and over	100	51.8	48.2	28.9	10.5	18.5	19.3
$10,000–$19,999							
Under 18 years	100	77.3	22.7	15.8	7.9	7.9	6.9
18–44 years	100	90.2	9.8	7.2	1.0	6.2	2.6
45–64 years	100	84.8	15.2	11.5	6.3	5.2	3.7
65 years and over	100	58.5	41.5	33.7	22.0	11.7	7.7
65–69 years	100	57.3	42.7	34.0	18.9	15.1	8.7
70 years and over	100	59.2	40.8	18.0	6.2	11.8	22.8
$20,000–$34,999							
Under 18 years	100	85.6	14.4	9.8	4.4	5.4	4.6
18–44 years	100	93.6	6.4	4.9	*0.4	4.5	1.5
45–64 years	100	90.3	9.7	6.9	3.0	3.9	2.9
65 years and over	100	76.4	23.6	17.6	9.4	8.3	6.0
65–69 years	100	67.1	32.9	26.5	16.6	9.9	6.5
70 years and over	100	67.8	32.2	14.4	7.3	7.1	17.9
$35,000 or more							
Under 18 years	100	95.7	4.3	2.9	0.3	2.6	1.4
18–44 years	100	93.7	6.3	4.0	1.3	2.7	2.3
45–64 years	100	85.8	14.2	8.8	3.5	5.3	5.4
65 years and over	100	77.1	22.9	15.3	6.1	9.2	7.6
65–69 years	100	69.2	30.8	14.4	7.3	7.1	16.4
GEOGRAPHIC REGION							
Northeast	100	86.0	14.0	9.3	4.1	5.2	4.6
Midwest	100	86.3	13.7	9.7	4.2	5.5	4.1
South	100	84.9	15.1	10.9	5.3	5.6	4.2
West	100	85.4	14.6	9.4	4.8	4.7	5.1
PLACE OF RESIDENCE							
MSA [2]	100	86.3	13.7	9.3	4.3	5.1	4.4
Central city	100	85.1	14.9	10.7	4.9	5.7	4.2
Not central city	100	87.0	13.0	8.5	3.9	4.7	4.4
Not MSA [2]	100	82.9	17.1	12.3	6.2	6.2	4.8

SOURCE: P.F. Adams, G.E. Hendershot, and M.A. Marano, "Current Estimates from the National Health Interview Survey, 1996." National Center for Health Statistics. *Vital and Health Statistics* 10, no. 200 (1999): Table 67.

* Figure does not meet standard of reliability or precision.
1. Includes other races and unknown family income.
2. MSA is metropolitan statistical area.

NOTE: A condition is considered chronic if (a) the respondent indicates it was first noticed more than three months before the reference date of the interview, or (b) it is a type of condition that ordinarily has a duration of more than three months. Examples of conditions that are considered chronic regardless of their time of onset are diabetes, heart conditions, emphysema, and arthritis. A complete list of these conditions may be obtained by contacting the Division of Health Interview Statistics, National Center for Health Statistics.

Table 5.8. Restricted Activity Associated with Acute Conditions: 1996

(Number of restricted activity days per 100 persons)

Characteristic	All acute conditions	Infective and parasitic diseases	Respiratory conditions	Digestive system conditions	Injuries	Other acute conditions
All persons	624.0	64.1	269.6	26.2	133.5	84.9
AGE						
Under 5 years	717.5	166.2	335.1	*18.7	*23.2	146.6
5–17 years	531.2	111.7	272.0	32.7	51.7	45.2
18–24 years	615.1	56.9	263.8	*33.2	128.4	86.8
25–44 years	638.4	38.6	249.3	26.0	182.4	99.8
45 years and over	646.3	38.2	274.2	22.2	162.3	79.0
45–64 years	548.9	43.7	232.9	*18.1	156.8	61.7
65 years and over	809.1	*29.0	343.4	*29.1	171.4	108.0
SEX						
Male						
All ages	546.0	54.2	236.4	26.2	127.5	59.5
Under 5 years	785.1	165.6	349.3	*27.1	*11.4	197.2
5–17 years	487.6	102.4	253.7	*25.3	52.0	*41.2
18–44 years	498.5	32.8	193.6	*22.5	164.0	37.8
45 years and over	587.2	*21.5	253.5	31.6	159.2	65.1
Female						
All ages	698.1	73.4	301.1	26.2	139.1	109.0
Under 5 years	646.6	166.7	320.3	*9.9	*35.6	*93.6
5–17 years	577.0	121.4	291.1	*40.4	51.5	49.3
18–44 years	764.0	52.5	310.0	32.6	176.0	154.2
45 years and over	696.5	52.4	291.9	*14.3	164.9	90.8
RACE						
White						
All ages	630.2	68.0	278.8	26.4	131.8	78.0
Under 18 years	620.3	139.7	311.9	28.4	41.7	77.5
18–44 years	619.1	45.1	256.2	29.5	160.6	85.6
45 years and over	651.0	40.7	280.6	21.1	166.2	69.2
Black						
All ages	604.9	46.5	216.4	*28.6	162.0	111.9
Under 18 years	425.2	*80.2	192.1	*24.6	*51.8	*53.7
18–44 years	776.7	*32.4	238.1	*26.0	262.8	162.4
45 years and over	564.1	*22.9	213.7	*38.7	*144.7	*107.4
FAMILY INCOME						
Less than $10,000						
All ages	1 021.5	96.9	410.1	63.0	193.3	157.2
Under 18 years	817.8	*152.5	408.0	*49.3	*53.2	*126.0
18–44 years	980.3	*66.3	371.6	*74.5	270.8	*147.1
45 years and over	1 262.6	*84.0	460.6	*61.3	225.5	199.1
$10,000–$19,999						
All ages	770.8	64.1	298.9	34.2	205.9	97.1
Under 18 years	572.3	*115.6	221.9	*43.6	*56.9	*70.2
18–44 years	804.9	*37.9	301.4	*37.4	249.1	119.7
45 years and over	891.0	*52.2	357.5	*23.1	276.6	*93.3
$20,000–$34,999						
All ages	582.2	54.2	258.0	29.3	106.4	92.2
Under 18 years	550.9	103.0	259.0	*43.7	*40.4	90.0
18–44 years	600.7	*31.5	249.3	*38.6	146.0	100.3
45 years and over	583.4	*43.9	268.9	*4.3	108.2	83.0
$35,000 or more						
All ages	536.4	70.7	242.4	17.5	108.0	67.6
Under 18 years	614.8	156.4	313.1	*16.1	48.0	71.9
18–44 years	541.6	42.1	232.7	*17.9	130.5	80.1
45 years and over	454.1	*29.4	188.8	*18.4	133.2	45.6

SOURCE: P.F. Adams, G.E. Hendershot, and M.A. Marano, "Current Estimates from the National Health Interview Survey, 1996." National Center for Health Statistics. *Vital and Health Statistics* 10, no. 200 (1999): Tables 16–19.

* Figure does not meet standard of reliability or precision.

NOTE: A condition is considered acute if (a) it was first noticed no longer than three months before the reference date of the interview, and (b) it is not one of the conditions considered chronic regardless of the time of onset. However, any acute condition not associated with either at least one doctor visit or at least one day of restricted activity during the reference period is considered to be of minor consequence and is excluded from the final data produced by the survey.

Table 5.9. Effect of Injuries: 1996

(Rate per 100 persons)

	Episodes of injury	Restricted activity days	Days in bed
All persons	20.5	226.4	71.8
AGE			
Under 5 years	22.4	22.7	6.2
5–17 years	21.1	60.9	15.2
18–24 years	28.0	168.6	25.1
25–44 years	23.2	263.8	82.9
45–64 years	13.9	352.7	117.3
65 years and over	16.7	357.4	135.4
SEX AND AGE			
Male			
All ages	23.1	216.9	57.8
Under 18 years	27.3	50.2	13.0
18–44 years	26.4	231.9	54.6
45 years and over	14.8	352.8	104.1
Female			
All ages	18.1	235.4	85.1
Under 18 years	15.3	50.2	12.2
18–44 years	22.3	252.1	84.5
45 years and over	15.1	355.9	141.0
RACE AND AGE			
White			
All ages	20.8	222.4	68.1
Under 18 years	21.9	49.5	9.8
18–44 years	24.7	229.9	65.1
45 years and over	15.3	345.5	116.3
Black			
All ages	20.3	274.1	105.0
Under 18 years	20.3	53.3	25.4
18–44 years	25.3	349.8	112.8
45 years and over	11.6	456.6	204.3
FAMILY INCOME AND AGE			
Under $10,000			
All ages	26.5	466.0	166.2
Under 18 years	22.6	62.7	25.4
18–44 years	38.5	494.4	182.4
45 years and over	14.8	804.7	276.5
$10,000–$19,999			
All ages	24.6	357.8	133.9
Under 18 years	23.9	57.1	23.5
18–44 years	31.1	431.8	140.0
45 years and over	17.8	515.1	215.1
$20,000–$34,999			
All ages	21.1	177.6	47.6
Under 18 years	23.5	61.1	6.8
18–44 years	21.7	208.2	47.4
45 years and over	18.1	234.5	82.5
$35,000 or more			
All ages	19.5	151.4	39.6
Under 18 years	22.0	49.7	13.0
18–44 years	21.1	159.4	28.5
45 years and over	14.7	237.3	80.8
GEOGRAPHIC REGION			
Northeast	20.8	219.2	61.7
Midwest	23.5	212.9	76.1
South	19.3	227.6	78.3
West	18.9	246.5	66.1
PLACE OF RESIDENCE			
MSA [1]	20.1	220.9	72.1
Central city	19.5	250.6	81.5
Not central city	20.5	203.1	66.4
Not MSA [1]	22.0	246.8	70.7

SOURCE: P.F. Adams, G.E. Hendershot, and M.A. Marano, "Current Estimates from the National Health Interview Survey, 1996." National Center for Health Statistics. *Vital and Health Statistics* 10, no. 200 (1999): Tables 51–56.

1. MSA is metropolitan statistical area.

Table 5.10. Hospital Discharge Rate for Nontraumatic Lower Extremity Amputation among Diabetics

(Per 1,000 diabetic persons)

Year	0–64 years	65–74 years	75 years and over	Total	Age-adjusted rate
1980	3.8	8.1	13.0	6.3	6.3
1981	3.2	6.0	11.5	5.1	5.2
1982	3.3	6.6	11.7	5.3	5.4
1983	5.3	11.2	12.6	7.9	7.9
1984	5.6	8.7	13.7	7.8	7.6
1985	6.6	9.3	11.8	8.3	8.1
1986	4.8	9.9	11.1	7.2	7.0
1987	4.7	12.4	14.9	8.4	8.2
1988	5.9	7.7	17.6	8.3	8.1
1989	5.4	11.0	12.7	8.1	7.9
1990	5.9	8.6	14.1	8.0	7.8
1991	5.0	6.9	9.7	6.4	6.2
1992	5.9	8.9	10.5	7.5	7.4
1993	5.3	8.6	11.6	7.3	7.1
1994	6.5	10.2	11.9	8.4	8.2

Year	Male		Female		White		Black	
	Total	Age-adjusted rate	Total	Age-adjusted rate	Total	Age-adjusted rate	Total	Age-adjusted rate
1980	7.7	8.3	5.2	4.9	4.7	4.6	9.2	10.7
1981	5.8	6.4	4.6	4.5	4.9	4.8	6.2	7.0
1982	6.0	6.4	4.8	4.6	5.0	4.9	4.5	4.7
1983	9.3	9.7	7.0	6.8	7.5	7.4	7.4	8.7
1984	8.6	8.7	7.2	6.9	6.5	6.4	9.1	9.7
1985	8.7	8.8	7.9	7.5	6.2	6.0	12.3	12.4
1986	9.0	9.1	5.8	5.5	5.3	5.1	11.7	12.2
1987	9.1	9.3	7.8	7.1	6.6	6.3	8.7	8.8
1988	11.7	12.1	5.5	5.1	7.2	6.9	8.3	8.2
1989	10.3	10.6	6.3	5.9	6.7	6.4	10.7	10.9
1990	9.7	9.9	6.6	6.2	6.5	6.4	8.0	8.0
1991	7.7	7.7	5.4	5.2	4.0	3.9	11.4	12.0
1992	9.8	9.9	5.8	5.7	5.2	5.0	8.3	8.6
1993	8.4	8.4	6.4	6.1	4.9	4.7	8.7	8.8
1994	10.9	11.0	6.2	5.9	5.8	5.7	9.3	10.2

SOURCE: L.M. Geiss, Diabetes Surveillance, 1997. Centers for Disease Control and Prevention: Atlanta, GA, 1997: Tables 6.4, 6.5, and 6.6.

Table 5.11. Activity Limitations Because of Diabetes

(Numbers in thousands; rate per 100 diabetic population)

Year	Total population								
	All people			Male			Female		
	Number	Rate	Age-adjusted rate	Number	Rate	Age-adjusted rate	Number	Rate	Age-adjusted rate
1983	1,978	34.0	34.0	737	30.9	30.9	1,240	36.3	36.1
1984	2,093	35.4	35.3	794	31.8	31.9	1,299	38.0	37.7
1985	2,203	35.3	35.3	870	32.3	32.3	1,333	37.7	37.4
1986	2,277	35.4	35.5	944	32.0	32.1	1,333	38.3	38.5
1987	2,147	33.3	33.5	941	31.3	31.3	1,206	35.1	35.3
1988	2,051	32.0	32.3	897	30.4	30.2	1,153	33.4	33.8
1989	2,018	32.1	32.2	852	30.4	29.9	1,165	33.5	33.7
1990	2,225	33.6	33.8	940	32.4	32.2	1,285	34.4	34.8
1991	2,401	34.7	34.9	1,009	33.4	33.4	1,392	35.6	36.3
1992	2,602	34.9	35.1	1,108	33.5	33.5	1,494	36.1	36.4
1993	2,591	34.0	34.2	1,075	31.2	31.2	1,516	36.2	36.5
1994	2,611	33.6	33.8	1,083	30.2	30.6	1,529	36.5	36.6

Year	White					
	Male			Female		
	Number	Rate	Age-adjusted rate	Number	Rate	Age-adjusted rate
1983	554	27.4	27.5	867	32.7	32.6
1984	614	29.3	29.5	927	34.4	34.1
1985	700	30.9	30.9	988	34.8	34.7
1986	755	30.3	30.4	991	35.4	36.0
1987	745	29.6	29.7	885	32.7	33.1
1988	703	29.1	29.1	870	32.1	32.5
1989	670	29.5	29.1	874	31.9	32.0
1990	756	31.8	31.5	972	32.8	33.0
1991	853	33.4	33.3	1,003	32.6	33.0
1992	924	33.2	33.1	1,077	33.0	33.0
1993	877	30.5	30.5	1,084	33.6	33.9
1994	847	28.9	29.1	1,106	34.5	34.5

Year	Black					
	Male			Female		
	Number	Rate	Age-adjusted rate	Number	Rate	Age-adjusted rate
1983	183	53.0	53.4	349	50.3	51.5
1984	170	45.3	44.6	347	52.9	53.0
1985	159	39.7	38.2	320	50.2	49.8
1986	172	42.6	42.1	306	49.0	49.2
1987	185	43.4	44.9	291	44.0	44.2
1988	184	40.7	40.8	270	41.1	42.0
1989	170	37.8	36.8	282	43.1	44.0
1990	172	39.6	36.8	281	43.1	44.5
1991	134	33.7	33.6	339	47.5	49.4
1992	166	35.8	36.8	331	45.2	46.6
1993	168	34.5	37.2	345	43.0	44.0
1994	205	37.1	42.7	320	39.6	40.6

SOURCE: L.M. Geiss, Diabetes Surveillance, 1997. Centers for Disease Control and Prevention: Atlanta, GA, 1997: Tables 9.9 and 9.10.

NOTE: Three-year moving averages.

Table 5.12. Work Limitations among Diabetics

(Per 100 diabetic population)

Year	Limited in work among people with diabetes						
	Total			White		Black	
	Total	Male	Female	Male	Female	Male	Female
1983	43.9	40.1	46.7	36.5	45.8	58.8	52.6
1984	44.8	40.5	48.1	38.3	47.1	48.9	54.2
1985	44.2	41.9	46.2	40.3	43.6	49.0	61.0
1986	43.4	41.0	45.6	40.4	42.8	46.9	58.3
1987	41.0	40.0	43.0	39.2	39.9	49.9	56.3
1988	41.0	39.8	42.2	39.1	41.0	50.2	48.2
1989	41.5	40.5	42.4	40.1	41.5	48.7	48.1
1990	41.7	43.6	40.0	43.0	39.7	52.6	43.2
1991	42.6	44.1	41.2	44.1	39.8	48.7	47.0
1992	41.8	43.7	40.2	43.8	38.2	44.4	45.8
1993	43.3	42.7	43.9	43.5	40.5	40.8	51.4
1994	43.5	42.5	44.4	43.7	40.7	37.2	51.4

Year	Limited in work attributed to diabetes						
	Total			White		Black	
	Total	Male	Female	Male	Female	Male	Female
1983	27.9	27.2	28.4	23.1	26.7	50.4	36.5
1984	29.8	28.9	30.5	25.5	28.5	44.0	39.4
1985	29.2	30.8	27.9	28.3	25.2	42.2	41.8
1986	29.9	29.6	30.2	27.5	27.1	42.4	43.9
1987	27.1	27.6	26.6	26.7	24.0	35.6	37.7
1988	26.8	27.3	26.3	26.7	25.2	35.0	32.9
1989	26.5	27.6	25.4	27.2	23.8	32.8	33.5
1990	26.5	29.2	24.1	27.7	22.6	41.0	33.4
1991	27.0	28.0	26.1	27.7	23.8	32.4	35.8
1992	26.2	27.3	25.2	27.5	22.9	29.3	32.2
1993	27.7	27.1	28.3	27.9	25.9	25.8	32.9
1994	27.9	27.4	28.3	28.2	26.3	26.3	30.6

SOURCE: L.M. Geiss, Diabetes Surveillance, 1997. Centers for Disease Control and Prevention: Atlanta, GA, 1997: Tables 9.21 and 9.22.

NOTE: Three-year moving average.

Table 5.13. Disability Status: 1994–1995

(Number in thousands)

Characteristic	Number	Percent distribution
All persons (total population)	261 749	100.0
With any disability	53 907	20.6
With a severe disability	25 968	9.9
Under 6 years		
Age 0 to 2 years (total population)	11 942	100.0
With a developmental condition	313	2.6
Age 3 to 5 years (total population)	12 427	100.0
With any disability	652	5.2
With a developmental condition	510	4.1
Difficulty walking or running	235	1.9
Males 3 to 5 years (total population)	6 419	100.0
With any disability	442	6.9
Females 3 to 5 years (total population)	6 009	100.0
With any disability	210	3.5
Age 6 years and over (total population)	237 379	100.0
With any disability	52 942	22.3
With a severe disability	25 968	10.9
Difficulty seeing words and letters	8 797	3.7
Unable to see words and letters	1 593	0.7
Difficulty hearing normal conversation	10 110	4.3
Unable to hear normal conversation	977	0.4
Difficulty with one or more ADLs	8 575	3.6
Needs personal assistance with one or more ADLs	4 078	1.7
Uses a wheelchair	1 812	0.8
Does not use a wheelchair, has used a cane, crutches, or a walker for 6 months or more	5 210	2.2
Age 6 to 14 years (total population)	35 011	100.0
With any disability	4 462	12.7
With a severe disability	659	1.9
Difficulty doing regular school work	2 170	6.2
With a learning disability	1 559	4.5
With a developmental disability	451	1.3
Difficulty with one or more ADLs	381	1.1
Needs personal assistance with one or more ADLs	272	0.8
Males 6 to 14 years (total population)	17 896	100.0
With any disability	2 824	15.8
Females 6 to 14 years (total population)	17 115	100.0
With any disability	1 638	9.6
Age 15 years and over (total population)	202 368	100.0
With any disability	48 481	24.0
With a severe disability	25 309	12.5
Difficulty with one or more functional activities	33 238	16.4
Severe difficulty with one or more functional activities	15 314	7.6
Difficulty with one or more ADLs	8 194	4.1
Needs personal assistance with one or more ADLs	3 806	1.9
Difficulty with one or more IADLs	12 260	6.1
Needs personal assistance with one or more IADLs	8 986	4.4
Needs personal assistance with one or more ADLs and/or IADLs	9 473	4.7
Age 15 to 21 years (total population)	25 146	100.0
With any disability	3 047	12.1
With a severe disability	813	3.2
Difficulty with one or more ADLs	154	0.6
Needs personal assistance with one or more ADLs	91	0.4
Difficulty with one or more IADLs	385	1.5
Needs personal assistance with one or more IADLs	306	1.2
Needs personal assistance with one or more ADLs and/or IADLs	318	1.3
Age 22 to 44 years (total population)	95 002	100.0
With any disability	14 105	14.9
With a severe disability	6 071	6.4
Difficulty with one or more ADLs	1 425	1.5
Needs personal assistance with one or more ADLs	663	0.7
Difficulty with one or more IADLs	2 364	2.5
Needs personal assistance with one or more IADLs	1 664	1.8
Needs personal assistance with one or more ADLs and/or IADLs	1 777	1.9
Age 45 to 54 years (total population)	30 316	100.0
With any disability	7 412	24.5
With a severe disability	3 472	11.5
Difficulty with one or more ADLs	952	3.1
Needs personal assistance with one or more ADLs	324	1.1
Difficulty with one or more IADLs	1 360	4.5
Needs personal assistance with one or more IADLs	927	3.1
Needs personal assistance with one or more ADLs and/or IADLs	984	3.3
Age 55 to 64 years (total population)	20 647	100.0
With any disability	7 497	36.3
With a severe disability	4 528	21.9
Difficulty with one or more ADLs	1 235	6.0
Needs personal assistance with one or more ADLs	509	2.5
Difficulty with one or more IADLs	1 662	8.1
Needs personal assistance with one or more IADLs	1 160	5.6
Needs personal assistance with one or more ADLs and/or IADLs	1 268	6.1

See footnotes at end of table.

Table 5.13. Disability Status: 1994–1995—*Continued*

(Number in thousands)

Characteristic	Number	Percent distribution
Age 65 to 79 years (total population)	24 471	100.0
With any disability	11 568	47.3
With a severe disability	6 798	27.8
Difficulty with one or more ADLs	2 565	10.5
Needs personal assistance with one or more ADLs	1 181	4.8
Difficulty with one or more IADLs	3 747	15.3
Needs personal assistance with one or more IADLs	2 675	10.9
Needs personal assistance with one or more ADLs and/or IADLs	2 814	11.5
Age 80 years and over (total population)	6 785	100.0
With any disability	4 853	71.5
With a severe disability	3 627	53.5
Difficulty with one or more ADLs	1 864	27.5
Needs personal assistance with one or more ADLs	1 039	15.3
Difficulty with one or more IADLs	2 743	40.4
Needs personal assistance with one or more IADLs	2 254	33.2
Needs personal assistance with one or more ADLs and/or IADLs	2 312	34.1
Age 22 to 44 years, by sex and race		
Males, 22 to 44 years (total population)	47 090	100.0
With a severe disability	2 624	5.6
Females, 22 to 44 years (total population)	47 912	100.0
With a severe disability	3 446	7.2
Whites, not Hispanic origin, 22 to 44 years (total population)	70 242	100.0
With a severe disability	3 903	5.6
Blacks, 22 to 44 years (total population)	12 010	100.0
With a severe disability	1 421	11.8
Of Hispanic origin, 22 to 44 years (total population)	10 176	100.0
With a severe disability	685	6.7
Age 45 to 54 years, by sex and race		
Males, 45 to 54 years (total population)	14 825	100.0
With a severe disability	1 529	10.3
Females, 45 to 54 years (total population)	15 491	100.0
With a severe disability	1 943	12.5
Whites, not Hispanic origin, 45 to 54 years (total population)	24 082	100.0
With a severe disability	2 516	10.5
Blacks, 45 to 54 years (total population)	3 138	100.0
With a severe disability	577	18.4
Of Hispanic origin, 45 to 54 years (total population)	2 263	100.0
With a severe disability	355	15.7
Age 55 to 64 years, by sex and race		
Males, 55 to 64 years (total population)	9 798	100.0
With a severe disability	1 881	19.2
Females, 55 to 64 years (total population)	10 849	100.0
With a severe disability	2 647	24.4
Whites, not Hispanic origin, 55 to 64 years (total population)	16 788	100.0
With a severe disability	3 364	20.0
Blacks, 55 to 64 years (total population)	2 015	100.0
With a severe disability	705	35.0
Of Hispanic origin, 55 to 64 years (total population)	1 390	100.0
With a severe disability	385	27.7
Age 65 to 79 years, by sex and race		
Males, 65 to 79 years (total population)	10 693	100.0
With a severe disability	2 649	24.8
Females, 65 to 79 years (total population)	13 777	100.0
With a severe disability	4 149	30.1
Whites, not Hispanic origin, 65 to 79 years (total population)	20 918	100.0
With a severe disability	5 403	25.8
Blacks, 65 to 79 years (total population)	2 040	100.0
With a severe disability	905	44.3
Of Hispanic origin, 65 to 79 years (total population)	1 197	100.0
With a severe disability	396	33.1
Age 80 years and over, by sex and race		
Males, 80 years or more (total population)	2 371	100.0
With a severe disability	1 065	44.9
Females, 80 years or more (total population)	4 415	100.0
With a severe disability	2 563	58.1
Whites, not Hispanic origin, 80 years or more (total population)	5 962	100.0
With a severe disability	3 127	52.4
Blacks, 80 years or more (total population)	544	100.0
With a severe disability	344	63.2
Of Hispanic origin, 80 years or more (total population)	251	100.0
With a severe disability	156	62.1

SOURCE: J.M. McNeil, "Americans with Disabilities: 1994–1995," U.S. Census Bureau, Household Economic Studies: 1991, 1993, and 1994, Current Population Reports P70-61 (August 1997): Table 1. Data from the Survey of Income and Program Participation.

ADL - activity of daily living, including getting around inside the home, getting in or out of bed or a chair, bathing, dressing, eating, and toileting.
IADL - instrumental activity of daily living, including going outside the home, keeping track of money and bills, preparing meals, doing light housework, taking prescription medicines in the right amount at the right time, and using the telephone.

NOTE: People 15 years old and over were identified as having a disability if they met any of the following criteria: used a wheelchair or were a long-term user of a cane, crutches, or a walker; had a difficulty performing one or more functional activities (seeing, hearing, speaking, lifting/carrying, using stairs, or walking); had difficulty with one or more ADLs; had difficulty with one or more instrumental activities of daily living; had one or more specific conditions (a learning disability, mental retardation or another development disability, Alzheimer's disease, or some other type of mental or emotional condition); were limited in their ability to do housework; were 16 to 67 years old and limited in their ability to work at a job or business; were receiving federal benefits based on an inability to work. People 15 years old and over were identified as having a severe disability if they were unable to perform one or more functional activities; needed personal assistance with an ADL or IADL; used a wheelchair; were a long-term user of a cane, crutches, or a walker; had a developmental disability or Alzheimer's disease; were unable to do housework; were receiving federal disability benefits; or were 16 to 67 years old and unable to work at a job or business. This survey asked whether children under 6 years of age had a "developmental condition for which he/she has received therapy or diagnostic services," and asked whether children 3 to 5 years of age had a "long-lasting condition that limits his/her ability to walk, run, or use stairs." The survey asked a wider set of questions to determine the disability status of children aged 6 to 14 years. The survey asked about the following: the ability to perform the functional activities of seeing, hearing, walking, running, and using stairs; the ability to perform ADL's. the use of wheelcairs, canes, crutches, and walkers; the ability to do regular schoolwork; the presence of a learning disability, mental retardation or some other developmental disability, or any other developmental condition for which the child received therapy or diagnostic services.

Table 5.14. How Disability Affects Economic Status

(Number in thousands)

Characteristic	No disability	Nonsevere disability	Severe disability
MALES 21–64 YEARS OLD	59 478	7 768	6 109
Number of workers	53 382	6 610	1 701
Employment rate	89.8	85.1	27.8
Median monthly earnings	$2 190	$1 857	$1 262
Number of full-time workers	46 999	5 194	1 105
Rate of full-time employment	79.0	66.9	18.1
Median monthly earnings	$2 353	$2 125	$1 880
FEMALES 21–64 YEARS OLD	60 424	7 480	8 110
Number of workers	45 015	5 119	2 006
Employment rate	74.5	68.4	24.7
Median monthly earnings	$1 470	$1 200	$1 000
Number of full-time workers	32 138	3 140	1 070
Rate of full-time employment	53.2	42.0	13.2
Median monthly earnings	$1 750	$1 600	$1 400
PERSONS AGE 0–21 YEARS	76 053	7 001	1 472
With low relative income	22 196	2 221	602
Percent	29.2	31.7	40.9
PERSONS AGE 22–64 YEARS	116 953	14 943	14 071
With low relative income	15 503	2 878	5 944
Percent	13.3	19.3	42.2
PERSONS AGE 65 YEARS AND OVER	14 836	5 994	10 426
With low relative income	2 471	1 501	3 704
Percent	16.7	25.0	35.5
PERSONS AGE 22–64 YEARS	116 953	14 943	14 071
Covered by private health insurance	93 469	10 631	6 144
Percent	79.9	71.1	43.7
Covered by government, not private	3 515	913	5 576
Percent	3.0	6.1	39.6
Not covered by health insurance	19 968	3 399	2 351
Percent	17.1	22.7	16.7
PERSONS AGE 22–64 YEARS	116 953	14 943	14 071
Received cash, food, or rent assistance	6 415	1 337	5 221
Percent	5.5	8.9	37.1
Did not receive assistance	110 538	13 606	8 850
PERSONS AGE 65 YEARS AND OVER	14 836	5 994	10 426
Received cash, food, or rent assistance	711	596	1 872
Percent	4.8	10.0	18.0
Did not receive assistance	14 125	5 398	8 554

SOURCE: J.M. McNeil, "Americans with Disabilities: 1994–1995," U.S. Census Bureau, Household Economic Studies: 1991, 1993, and 1994, Current Population Reports P70-61 (1997): Table 3. Data from the Survey of Income and Program Participation.

Table 5.15. How Injuries Affect Work

Industry	1980	1985	1990	1991	1992	1993	1994	1995	1996	1997
NUMBER OF INJURIES WITH LOST WORKDAYS (IN THOUSANDS)										
Total private sector [1]	2 491.0	2484.7	2987.3	2 794.0	2776.1	2772.5	2848.3	2767.6	2646.3	2682.6
Agriculture, fishing, and forestry [1]	39.3	45.2	57.2	54.3	52.3	51.2	48.5	51.7	49.0	53.8
Mining	66.2	43.9	35.6	31.4	25.6	24.2	24.0	22.8	19.5	22.6
Construction	242.6	272.8	296.3	239.9	226.8	226.5	241.7	217.9	216.8	227.4
Manufacturing	1009.5	825.1	975.0	886.0	833.7	819.5	859.4	838.1	782.9	785.4
Transportation, communication, and public utilities	263.0	243.5	293.3	283.5	266.1	284.1	301.5	289.2	293.0	281.3
Wholesale	191.1	188.4	211.5	204.1	205.3	205.3	214.0	214.7	203.9	200.7
Retail	330.2	399.9	483.9	457.0	476.7	480.4	477.7	459.6	433.9	456.9
Finance, insurance, and real estate	38.1	45.5	63.7	62.2	64.4	61.7	58.8	52.2	49.5	47.6
Services	311.1	420.6	570.8	575.6	625.1	619.6	622.8	621.4	597.8	606.9
INJURIES WITH LOST WORKDAYS PER 100 FULL-TIME EQUIVALENTS [2]										
Total private sector [1]	3.9	3.6	3.9	3.7	3.6	3.5	3.5	3.4	3.1	3.1
Agriculture, fishing, and forestry [1]	5.6	5.6	5.7	5.2	5.2	4.8	4.6	4.2	3.8	4.0
Mining	6.4	4.7	4.9	4.4	4.0	3.8	3.8	3.8	3.2	3.7
Construction	6.5	6.8	6.6	6.0	5.7	5.4	5.4	4.8	4.4	4.4
Manufacturing	5.2	4.4	5.3	5.0	4.7	4.6	4.7	4.6	4.3	4.2
Transportation, communication, and public utilities	5.4	4.9	5.4	5.3	4.9	5.2	5.3	5.0	5.0	4.7
Wholesale	3.8	3.5	3.6	3.6	3.6	3.6	3.6	3.5	3.3	3.1
Retail	2.9	3.1	3.4	3.3	3.3	3.2	3.2	2.9	2.7	2.8
Finance, insurance, and real estate	0.8	0.9	1.1	1.0	1.1	1.0	0.9	0.9	0.8	0.8
Services	2.3	2.5	2.7	2.8	2.9	2.7	2.7	2.7	2.5	2.4

SOURCE: E. Kramarow, H. Lentzner, R. Rooks, J. Weeks, and S. Saydah, *Health and Aging Chartbook. Health, United States, 1999*. Hyattsville, Maryland: National Center for Health Statistics. 1999: Table 74.

1. Excludes farms with fewer than 11 employees.
2. Incidence rate calculated as (N/EH) x 200,000, where N = total number of injuries with lost workdays in a calendar year, EH = total hours worked by all full-time and part-time employees in a calendar year, and 200,000 = base for 100 full-time equivalent employees working 40 hours per week, 50 weeks per year.

NOTE: Industry is coded based on various editions of the Standard Industrial Classification Manuals: data for 1980–1987 are based on the 1972 edition, 1977 supplement; and data for 1988–1996 are based on the 1987 edition (see *Health, United States, 1998*: Appendix II, Industry).

Table 5.16. Job-Related Injuries: 1994

(Number of events involving one day or more away from work)

Characteristic	Sex		
	Men	Women	Unknown
BODY PART AFFECTED [1]	1 257 018	594 347	18 683
Shoulder	70 620	37 741	1 182
Knee	101 999	45 396	1 666
Head [2]	44 048	22 902	688
Eyeball	69 391	13 451	706
Back	396 624	203 771	6 150
Hand, wrist, or finger	254 891	127 802	3 052
Foot, toe, or ankle	150 458	66 188	2 305
Leg	145 840	60 709	2 290
Neck	23 147	16 387	644
NATURE OF INJURY/ ILLNESS	1 169 081	574 591	17 970
Burns	39 695	16 114	351
Surface wounds and bruises	182 548	87 000	3 161
Fractures	102 076	34 992	1 476
Open wounds	171 270	41 334	1 416
Strain or sprain	620 299	332 454	10 742
Nervous system diseases	22 926	30 620	359
Musculoskeletal disorder [3]	21 651	25 435	328
Disorders of the skin	7 630	4 554	98
Infectious and parasitic	986	2 088	39
EVENT OR EXPOSURE	1 457 727	719 138	19 882
Contact with objects	464 398	138 267	4 408
Falls	235 210	155 122	2 976
Bodily exertion, except repetitive	579 943	292 356	9 376
Repetitive motion	31 788	60 076	712
Exposure to harmful substances	72 306	37 745	892
Transportation incidents	58 264	20 070	1 270
Fires and explosions	4 397	630	20
Assaults and violent acts	11 421	14 872	228

SOURCE: D.K. Wagener, J. Walstedt, L. Jenkins, et al. "Women: Work and Health." *Vital and Health Statistics* 3, no. 31 (1997): Table 23.

1. Does not include unspecified or multiple body parts.
2. Head, not including eye.
3. Includes musculoskeletal system and connective tissue diseases and disorders.

NOTE: Data are based on employer records.

Table 5.17. Lost Work Days Associated with Acute Conditions: 1996

(Number of restricted activity days per 100 persons)

Characteristic	All acute conditions	Infective and parasitic	Respiratory conditions	Digestive system conditions	Injuries	Other acute conditions
All persons 18 years and over	284.0	19.2	99.3	11.1	102.6	31.8
AGE						
18–44 years	303.5	20.6	111.4	13.9	103.5	34.4
18–24 years	297.0	*33.0	111.0	*21.8	82.1	*30.6
25–44 years	305.1	17.6	111.5	*12.0	108.7	35.3
45 years and over	244.5	*16.5	74.8	*5.3	100.7	26.6
45–64 years	255.4	*17.7	75.7	*5.8	110.7	25.8
SEX						
Male						
18 years and over	260.9	15.8	77.0	*8.9	119.2	22.4
18–44 years	266.4	*18.0	86.4	*11.7	110.3	21.6
45 years and over	249.5	*11.2	58.0	*3.2	137.2	*24.0
Female						
18 years and over	311.3	23.4	125.6	*13.6	82.9	43.0
18–44 years	347.6	23.7	141.1	*16.6	95.3	49.7
45 years and over	238.7	*22.6	94.5	*7.7	58.1	*29.7
RACE						
White						
18 years and over	265.4	18.4	95.5	11.3	95.5	25.7
18–44 years	281.5	19.3	108.3	14.6	93.2	28.3
45 years and over	234.3	*16.7	70.7	*4.8	99.9	*20.7
Black						
18 years and over	425.0	*22.8	128.0	*12.8	166.6	66.9
18–44 years	457.1	*27.1	133.4	*14.0	180.2	*71.1
45 years and over	339.9	*11.4	*113.6	*9.5	*130.7	*55.8
FAMILY INCOME						
Less than $10,000						
18 years and over	388.8	*31.1	*114.5	*49.7	*80.9	*109.9
18–44 years	440.3	39.9	122.7	56.0	94.4	127.2
45 years and over	*208.3	. . .	*85.5	*27.6	*33.6	*49.3
$10,000-$24,999						
18 years and over	326.7	*29.0	100.6	*6.6	126.9	*32.6
18–44 years	355.0	*24.1	115.5	*6.0	146.4	*34.2
45 years and over	254.2	*41.7	*62.4	*8.3	*76.9	*28.5
$25,000 or more						
18 years and over	256.5	15.8	99.3	*11.0	86.7	24.2
18–44 years	263.3	*16.6	110.9	*14.5	76.5	26.0
45 years and over	243.8	*14.2	77.2	*4.4	106.1	*20.8

SOURCE: P.F. Adams, G.E. Hendershot, and M.A. Marano, Current Estimates from the National Health Interview Survey, 1996. National Center for Health Statistics. *Vital and Health Statistics* 10, no. 200 (1999): Table 38.

* Figure does not meet standard of reliability or precision.

NOTE: A condition is considered acute if (a) it was first noticed no longer than three months before the reference date of the interview, and (b) it is not one of the conditions considered chronic regardless of the time of onset. However, any acute condition not associated with either at least one doctor visit or at least one day of restricted activity during the reference period is considered to be of minor consequence and is excluded from the final data produced by the survey.

Table 5.18. Effect of Illicit Drug Use and Heavy Drinking on Work

(Percent of full-time workers)

Workplace outcome	Current illicit drug use				Heavy alcohol use [1]			
	Yes		No		Yes		No	
	1994	1997	1994	1997	1994	1997	1994	1997
Worked for 3 or more employers in the past year	8.9	9.3	**4.0	**4.3	7.8	8.0	*4.0	*4.4
Missed 2 or more days in the past month due to illness or injury	10.9	12.8	9.1	8.5	9.5	12.4	9.2	8.5
Skipped 1 or more days of work in the past month	12.1	12.9	**6.0	**5.0a	10.9	11.3	*5.1	*5.1
Voluntarily left an employer in the past year	25.8	24.8	**13.6	**15.4	21.7	19.7	**13.9	15.8
Fired by an employer in the past year	4.6	2.3	*1.4	1.2	3.6	0.9	1.4	1.4
Had a workplace accident in the past year	7.7	5.1	5.6	5.5	7.7	8.5	5.6	5.3

SOURCE: Substance Abuse and Mental Health Services Administration (SAMHSA), Office of Applied Studies. Worker Drug Use and Workplace Policies and Programs. Results from the 1994 and 1997 National Household Survey on Drug Abuse. Rockville, Md. DHHS Pub. no. (SMA) 99-3352, 1999: Table 3.1.

* Difference between users and nonusers is statistically significant at the .05 level.
** Difference between users and nonusers is statistically significant at the .01 level.
a. Difference between 1997 estimate and 1994 estimate is statistically significant at the .05 level.
1. Current heavy alcohol use is defined as drinking five or more drinks on the same occasion on each of at least five days in the previous 30 days.

Table 5.19. Lost School Days Associated with Acute Conditions: 1996

(Per 100 schoolchildren per year)

Characteristic	All acute conditions	Infective and parasitic diseases	Respiratory conditions	Digestive system conditions	Injuries	Other acute conditions
All ages 5–17 years	296.9	76.4	152.2	18.1	*16.7	20.5
SEX						
Male	266.8	70.6	141.6	*9.1	*15.8	*19.9
Female	328.6	82.6	163.3	27.5	*17.6	*21.1
RACE						
White	316.0	80.5	166.2	*18.6	*13.2	22.9
Black	226.8	*57.5	*101.5	13.3	37.4	*11.1
FAMILY INCOME						
Less than $10,000	427.6	*106.5	*175.3	*50.1	*37.6	*31.9
$10,000–$19,999	287.9	64.9	118.0	31.8	28.6	19.9
$20,000–$34,999	260.8	*49.9	151.5	25.1	*6.9	*15.9
$35,000 or more	316.2	98.8	160.8	8.4	*16.2	*24.9
GEOGRAPHIC REGION						
Northeast	250.9	*61.7	131.9	*17.8	*6.9	*13.4
Midwest	274.6	*68.6	164.7	12.8	*11.5	12.9
South	270.4	94.3	109.4	*12.3	*15.6	26.0
West	404.5	*71.0	222.3	*33.4	*33.0	*26.9
PLACE OF RESIDENCE						
All MSA [1]	307.0	78.2	155.0	*20.9	*20.3	*18.5
Central city	271.9	*49.8	158.1	*10.6	*28.8	*14.5
Not central city	325.9	93.5	153.4	26.4	15.7	*20.6
Not MSA [1]	259.8	69.9	141.7	7.8	3.5	*27.8

SOURCE: P.F. Adams, G.E. Hendershot, and M.A. Marano, Current Estimates from the National Health Interview Survey, 1996. National Center for Health Statistics. *Vital and Health Statistics* 10, no. 200 (1999): Tables 46 and 47.

* Figure does not meet standard of reliability or precision.
1. MSA is metropolitan statistical area.

NOTE: A condition is considered acute if (a) it was first noticed no longer than three months before the reference date of the interview, and (b) it is not one of the conditions considered chronic regardless of the time of onset. However, any acute condition not associated with either at least one doctor visit or at least one day of restricted activity during the reference period is considered to be of minor consequence and is excluded from the final data produced by the survey.

NOTES

1. Based on the National Health and Nutrition Examination Survey conducted from 1988 to 1991.

2. M. J. Thun, D. G. Myers, C. Day-Lally, M. M. Namboodiri, E. E. Calle, W. D. Flanders, S. L. Adams, and C. W. Heath Jr., "Age and the Exposure-Response Relationships between Cigarette Smoking and Premature Death in Cancer Prevention Study II," in *Smoking and Tobacco Control Monograph No. 8: Changes in Cigarette Related Disease Risks and Their Implications for Prevention and Control* (Bethesda, Md.: National Cancer Institute, February 1997).

3. M. Lipsett, D. Shusterman, and J. Mann, "Respiratory Health Effects," in *Smoking and Tobacco Control Monograph No. 10: Health Effects of Exposure to Environmental Tobacco Smoke* (Bethesda, Md.: National Cancer Institute, 1999).

4. M. Dempsey, "Decline in Tuberculosis: Death Rate Fails to Tell Entire Story," *American Review of Tuberculosis* 56 (1947):157–164.

5. Centers for Disease Prevention and Control, "Premature Mortality in the United States: Public Health Issues in the Use of Years of Potential Life Lost," *Morbidity and Mortality Weekly Report* 35(2S) (December 19, 1986):1s–11s.

6. See Amartya Sen, "Capability and Well-Being," *The Quality of Life* (New York: Oxford University Press, 1993).

7. D. F. Sullivan, "Disability Components for an Index of Health," *Vital and Health Statistics* 2, no. 42 (1971); J. M. Robine, J. P. Michel, and L. G. Branch, "Measurement and Utilization of Healthy Life Expectancy: Conceptual Issues," *Bulletin of the World Health Organization* 70, no. 6 (1992):791–800; J. M. Robine and K. Ritchie, "Health Life Expectancy: Evaluation of Global Indicator of Change in Population of Health," *British Medical Journal* 302, no. 6774 (1991):457–460; World Bank, World Development Report 1993: *Investing in Health* (New York: Oxford University Press, 1993).

8. P. Erickson, R. Wilson, and I. Shannon, "Years of Healthy Life," in *Healthy People 2000: Statistical Notes No. 7* (April 1995).

9. Centers for Disease Prevention and Control, "Current Trends Quality of Life as a New Public Health Measure: Behavioral Risk Factor Surveillance System, 1993," *Morbidity and Mortality Weekly Report* 43, no. 20 (May 27, 1994):375–380.

10. Restricted activity is measured as the number of days people have been unable to do their usual activities because of illness, injury, or other disability. The types of restricted activity included are (1) workdays lost by currently employed adults age 18 and over, (2) school days missed by children age 5 to 17, (3) days spent in bed because of ill health, and (4) days persons have to cut down on their usual daily activity because of ill health.

11. Various terms are used to describe disability and its different aspects. In this document, *impairment* is used to refer to the individual's difficulties in body functions such as seeing, hearing, and speaking. *Activity limitations* or *restricted activities* are used to refer to the individual's inability to conduct the usual activities of daily life. *Participation restriction* is used to refer to the individual's interactions with others and includes activities such as meeting with family and friends. *Disability* is the general term used to include any and all aspects of disability: impairment, activity limitations, and participation restriction. In the first version of the International Classification of Impairments, Disabilities, and Handicaps, the consequences of injury and disease were conceptualized as (1) impairment (loss of psychological, physiological, or anatomical structure or function), (2) disability (limitation in functional performance as a result of impairment), and (3) handicap (limitation in interacting with the physical and social environment). This terminology currently is undergoing review.

12. The category of Arthritis and Other Rheumatic Conditions consists of more than 100 diseases and conditions affecting the joints, surrounding tissues, and other connective tissues. It involves several different types of arthritic conditions such as infectious, degenerative, metabolic, and systemic autoimmune. The most common types of arthritis in the United States include osteoarthritis and rheumatoid arthritis.

13. Department of Labor, Bureau of Labor Statistics, "Workplace Injuries and Illnesses in 1998," Department of Labor news release, December 16, 1999.

14. In these estimates, direct costs represent the total cost of medical care for illness or injury. This category includes formal care costs for all the services that HCFA includes (whether the patient actually paid for these services is irrelevant since the provider incurred a cost to provide them). But in some cost-of-illness studies, direct costs include the monetary value of informal care (that is, care provided by family or friends). Economists have several different ways of measuring these costs, but the basic idea is to measure the opportunity cost of using someone's time to care for a family member rather than, say, work in a factory. Often this measurement is a matter of counting the total hours of such care; determining the average hourly earnings for an individual of similar age, gender, and race, and so forth; and multiplying. HCFA does not include these informal care costs in its estimates.

15. W. J. Martone, W. R. Jarvis, D. H. Culver, and R. W. Haley, "Incidence and Nature of Endemic and Epidemic Nosocomial Infections," in J. V. Bennett and P. S. Brachman, eds., *Hospital Infections* (Boston: Little, Brown (1992):577–596.

16. D. Magid, B. Schwartz, J. Craft, and J. S. Schwartz, "Prevention of Lyme Disease after Tick Bites: A Cost Effectiveness Analysis," *New England Journal of Medicine* 327, no. 8 (1992): 534–541.

17. M. C. Fahs, J. Mandelblatt, C. Schechter, and C. Muller, "Cost Effectiveness of Cervical Cancer Screening for the Elderly," *Annals of Internal Medicine* 177, no. 6 (1992):520–527.

18. S. D. Pinkerton, D. R. Holtgrave, and H. J. Pinkerton, "Cost-effectiveness of Chemoprophylaxis after Occupational Exposure to HIV," *Archives of Internal Medicine* 157, no. 17 (1997):1972–1980. See also M. C. Guinan, P. G. Farnham, and D. R. Holtgrave, "Estimating the Value of Preventing a Human Immunodeficiency Virus Infection," *American Journal of Preventive Medicine* 10, no. 1 (1994):1–4.

19. R. D. Gorsky, P. G. Farnham, W. L. Straus, B. Caldwell, D. R. Holtgrave, R. J. Simonds, M. F. Rogers, and M. C. Guinan, "Preventing Perinatal Transmission of HIV: Costs and Effectivness of a Recommended Intervention," *Public Health Reports* 111, no. 4 (1996):335–341.

20. The number and therefore the costs of food-borne illnesses may be underestimated because many affected people may not seek medical care and because of the delay between exposure and observed illness, and the similarity between the symptoms for food-borne and other gastroenteric illness and reported as such.

21. J. S. Landefeld and E. P. Seskin, "The Economic Value of Life: Linking Theory to Practice," *American Journal of Public Health* 6 (1982):555–566.

22. W. K. Viscusi ("The Value of Risks to Life and Health," *Journal of Economic Literature* 31 [December 1993]:1912–1946). Meat and poultry products are the major food sources for the six disease-causing agents in this table. An update of these estimates may be found in Table 5K and Jean C. Buzby and Tanya Roberts, "ERS Updates U.S. Food-Borne Disease Costs for Seven Pathogens," *Food Review* (September/December 1996):20–25.

Because so much information is available on health correlates, conditions, care, and consequences, keeping track of health statistics can be a daunting and difficult job. Many different federal, state, and local agencies, along with private organizations, issue relevant data, making it challenging to locate the specific information that one might need. This chapter presents a guide to current sources, particularly those found on the Internet. It features the sources used in preparing this book and includes others as well. Additional information can be found in library collections.[1]

FINDING HEALTH STATISTICS IN LIBRARIES

Readers who need to consult trend data may find that their only choice is to work with printed materials. Others may find that the material they are seeking is available only in journal articles or publications that are not yet available on the Internet. Those readers will find that on-line library catalogues and bibliographic databases are the best place to start. For example, the National Library of Medicine's (NLM) LOCATORplus system offers information on the NLM's holdings of books, journals, and audiovisual materials. It also guides users to other medical research tools; see <http://locatorplus.gov>. The Web site of the National Library of Medicine also provides access to the NLM's on-line bibliographic database—Medline; see <http://www.nlm.nih.gov/databases/freemedl.html>. This database provides good coverage of the literature; it reports on a significant portion of the published sources for health statistics.

Although these resources lead users to the published reports, they are not indexed or catalogued in sufficient detail to help users find the specific data series that will answer their questions; however, the published reports provide clues that lead users to the original sources.

THE INDEX TO HEALTH INFORMATION

One resource, the Congressional Information Service (CIS) Index to Health Information, is available in some specialized health libraries, such as the NLM. This resource and its accompanying microfiche collection cover material issued by trade and professional associations, business organizations, commercial publishers, the U.S. Congress, federal administrative agencies, international intergovernmental organizations, state government agencies, and universities since 1988. The CIS updates this resource quarterly.

USING THE INTERNET

The Web sites of federal, state, and local government statistics agencies, as well as of private organizations, expand resources by placing a large body of data on desktops. Issuing statistical reports on the Web is now the norm rather than the exception. Researchers face the task of navigating these sources to answer their questions.[2]

However, information on the Web is created by individual Web masters who do not follow a uniform scheme. There is no catalogue of Web-site information. In its place, librarians and researchers have established special Web sites—called *portals*—that provide a linked table of contents leading users to material. Each of these portals reflects the particular interests of its creators.

Successful searchers realize that this complexity reflects the many perspectives driving the work of people who create health statistics. These points of view not only shape what is collected and how it is compiled, but they also influence where it is reported.

Readers can find many of the series reported in this book in the statistical publications issued by federal government agencies—such as the National Center for Health Statistics (NCHS) at <http://www.cdc.gov/nchs>. Other useful data come from surveillance reports filed by public health agencies—for example, the Centers for Disease Control and Prevention's (CDC) *Morbidity and Mortality Weekly Report* (MMWR) at <http://www2.cdc.gov/mmwr/>.

In addition, many health research reports contain statistical data. For example, the results from the National Health and Nutrition Examination Survey are more frequently accessible in the medical literature. A bibliography of these reports is available on the NCHS Web site at <http://www.cdc.gov/nchs/nhanes.htm>. Other sources are scattered among the work of several agencies and private organizations. To find current results from statistical series, readers should visit the Web sites of the issuing agencies.

GUIDE TO HEALTH STATISTICS SOURCES ON THE INTERNET

The following guide directs readers to some of the most important Web sites that provide health statistics. It also describes the major federal projects that provide health statistics.[3]

GENERAL PURPOSE WEB SITES

The best way to use the Internet is to find the Web sites that are portals where information is organized. These portals provide links to more detailed data. Some portals are merely lists of important sites. Others attempt to organize information by topic or subject. Each one is based on the designer's selection of key places to find information.

PORTALS

In the field of health statistics, several government and private sites provide portals. Because health statistics information is often produced by organizations with a broader mandate, searchers need to consider beginning with a more general portal.

CDC DATA AND SURVEILLANCE LINKS PAGE

The CDC Data and Surveillance Links Page, at <http://www.cdc.gov/scientific.htm>, guides users to statistical sources within the CDC. Many of these sources are collected within the surveillance components of the individual CDC centers. These sites sometimes draw on data from the NCHS but present it in formats that are more directly related to their subject areas. The NCHS Web site is also accessible from this portal.

CDC WONDER

The CDC WONDER site <http://wonder.cdc.gov/> provides a single point of access to CDC reports, guidelines, and public health-related statistical data. This site allows readers to conduct integrated searches of literature and to request information directly from statistical databases on the CDC's mainframe and other computers through "fill-in-the blanks" request screens. It contains data about AIDS, behavioral risk factors, cancer incidence, diabetes, hospital discharges, mortality, and many other topics. To gain premium access, users must first obtain a WONDER identity number and password. The CDC issues these at no cost; however, it can take a few days to get one. Users interested in brief access may sign on as anonymous users, but such access is somewhat limited.

The CDC WONDER page also provides access to a large number of data sets, including special coverage of AIDS; the Combined Health Information Database; the Surveillance, Epidemiology, and End Results (SEER) program; the Fatal Accident Reporting System; the Healthy People 2010 database; a special facility to help users find International Classification of Diseases, 9th revision (ICD-9) codes; an Injury Mortality Database; the MMWR; NCHS data on mortality and natality; data from

the CDC's National Institute for Occupational Safety and Health; data on sexually transmitted diseases; and tuberculosis.

DATA COUNCIL INVENTORY OF DATABASES

The Data Council Inventory of Databases, at <http://aspe.hhs.gov/datacncl/datadir/>, is a compilation of information about major data collection systems sponsored by the U.S. Department of Health and Human Services (DHHS). The site was developed by the Working Group on Racial and Ethnic Data, which is part of DHHS's Data Council. It includes data resources with "current utility, or the potential for use by a wide variety of audiences." It covers recurring surveys and disease registries, one-time studies, and data collections. It does not cover "funded research at a university where the data were applicable only to a specific and narrow issue in the funded study and/or the data are not readily accessible to the public for secondary data analysis." Each record identifies the survey, the sponsoring agency, a description of the data collection, and its race and ethnicity categories, as well as data limitations. Also included are periodicity of collection and reporting, availability of the results and data files, Web site information, and a contact person. The information on this site is periodically updated.

FEDSTATS

The Interagency Council on Statistical Policy sponsors FEDSTATS at <http://www.fedstats.gov/>. The site provides data connections for the more than 100 federal agencies that collect and report statistical information. FEDSTATS presents excellent coverage of health statistics information. It is particularly valuable because large amounts of statistical information related to health are actually collected by agencies outside of the Public Health Service.

GLOBAL HEALTH RESOURCES

The Global Health Resources portal, at <http://www.pitt.edu/HOME/GHNet/GHKR.html>, lists Web sites that provide international health data.

HEALTH, UNITED STATES APPENDIX

Each year the National Center for Health Statistics prepares its summary of health indicators, *Health, United States*. The appendix to this publication contains extensive notes on sources, including URLs indicating where additional information is available. These source notes, located at <http://www.cdc.gov/nchs>, provide an excellent starting point for readers who would like additional information.

Lexis-Nexis Statistical Universe

The Congressional Information Service, a part of Lexis-Nexis, has developed a subscription service that allows users to search for statistical publications and reports from federal, state, and local governments, private publishers, and intergovernmental organizations. For information about this service, see <http://www.lexisnexis.com/business/promotions/su.html>. Because of the depth of this database, users can find material located in publications that are not obviously related to their interests but that do have valuable information. Starting with its paper and microfiche collection (called the American Statistics Index), the CIS compiled an extensive archive of statistical material including practically all of the relevant federal reports relating to health statistics in the United States. It also covers state, local, and intergovernmental sources. This archive has extensive indexing that makes it possible to search for individual tables with information relating to a user's needs. For many reports, the Statistical Universe provides direct links to nearly 25,000 published tables in various formats, including many in spreadsheet formats ready for immediate analysis.

The Web-based interface readers use to access information is well designed and easy to use. It contains many aids, including a very useful on-line link helping searchers find the right category of information. Readers working in libraries with this facility will find it an invaluable resource and the most likely starting point for their search. Although this service is available with a Web-based interface for individual users, its cost is high. Therefore, most researchers will try to find a library that has access. However, readers needing access on their desktop who can afford the service will find it a good investment of their research resources. The one drawback of this service is that there is a brief lag between the time when material is publicly available and the time when it appears on the service. Users of the service should supplement their searches with visits to agency Web sites to be sure they have the latest information. Using the Statistical Universe site together with the source Web sites is likely to produce the most complete set of information available.

NCHS Links

The Web site of the National Center for Health Statistics, at <http://www.cdc.gov/nchs/sites.htm>, provides a list of key health statistics Web sites organized by topic. This list covers government and nongovernment sites. The NCHS's own data can be found by starting with its home page <http://www.cdc.gov/nchs>.

White House Office of National Drug Control Policy

The White House Office of National Drug Control Policy's web site, <http://www.whitehousedrugpolicy.gov/drugfact/index.html>, offers summaries of the prevalence and impacts of the use of various subtances, including club drugs; cocaine; crack; heroin; inhalants; LSD; marijuana; methamphetamines; and steroids. The web site also includes data on drug use among juveniles, minorities, and women as well as references to agency reports.

Social Statistics Briefing Room

The Social Statistics Briefing Room site, <http://www.whitehouse.gov/fsbr/health.html>, located on the White House Web page, provides indicators of major health trends. These data are prepared by government statistical agencies and changed regularly. The site displays links to agency Web sites for more detailed information. This site tends to emphasize current newsworthy results.

Statistical Resources on the Web (University of Michigan)

The University of Michigan's library staff created a specialized portal at <http://www.lib.umich.edu/libhome/Documents.center/sthealth.html>. It includes demographic, economic, environmental, education, and health statistics. The Health Statistics page on this Web site has current links to federal, state, local, and nongovernmental sites. In particular, it includes direct links to major reports. One advantage of this site is that the library staff members who maintain it fill it with current and useful information that is easy to use and well organized. This site also has an excellent explanation showing readers how to use the Lexis-Nexis Statistical Universe service.

Women with Disabilities—Statistical Information

The National Women's Health Information Center Web site, <http://www.4women.gov/wwd/index.htm>, features a list of publications and organizations that provide facts and figures on many of the health issues specifically affecting women with disabilities.

Interactive Web Sites

Interactive Web sites allow users to build their own tables using the templates provided by the statistical agencies. These sites are designed to protect the privacy of individual respondents while allowing users to obtain much more information than is available in published tables. Many of them are easy to use, but some require advanced knowledge about the design and content of data collections. Researchers using these services should always check the literature and Web sites of agencies for their own analyses because interpretation of health statistics data can be difficult.

COMPUTER-ASSISTED SURVEY (UC-BERKELEY)

The Computer-Assisted Survey Web site at <http://csa.Berkeley.edu:7502/> allows users to search data sets from the 1972–1994 General Social Survey, the 1972–1992 National Election Survey, and the 1991 National Health Interview Survey. Users can create spreadsheets with the desired vertical and horizontal variables, and they can choose output as statistics or percentages.

FEDSTATS LIST OF INTERACTIVE SITES

The FEDSTATS list of interactive sites at <http://www.fedstats.gov/toolkit.html> contains links to other government Web sites that provide access similar to FERRET (see below). This list is particularly valuable because it identifies some resources that have health-related material even though they come from agencies outside of the Public Health Service.

FEDERAL ELECTRONIC RESEARCH AND REVIEW EXTRACTION TOOL (FERRET)

The FERRET site, <http://www.cdc.gov/nchs/datawh/ ferret/ferret.htm>, provides access to the information provided by individual respondents. Users can therefore create their own tabulations and go beyond the tables specified by the government agencies. FERRET is a joint effort of the Bureau of the Census, the Bureau of Labor Statistics, and the National Center for Health Statistics. Currently it includes data files from the National Health Interview Survey and the National Health and Nutrition Examination Survey and allows table construction through the World Wide Web. The NCHS has imposed restrictions on FERRET's use to protect the privacy of respondents.

INTERUNIVERSITY CONSORTIUM FOR POLITICAL AND SOCIAL RESEARCH (ICPSR) ARCHIVE

The ICPSR archive, <http://www.icpsr.umich.edu>, housed at the University of Michigan, provides access to microdata files from the NCHS, the Substance Abuse and Mental Health Services Administration (SAMHSA), the Agency for Healthcare Research and Quality (AHRQ), and other government agencies. Researchers can download these files together with extensive documentation,

which is provided in Adobe Acrobat portable document format (PDF). Some studies are available for use with an on-line data analysis system that features the ability to download subsets. The site presents three health-related "topical" archives:

1. Substance Abuse and Mental Health Data Archive (SAMHDA) <http://www.icpsr.umich.edu/ SAMHDA>. This site provides access to microdata from government drug abuse and mental health surveys, including surveys conducted from 1970 to the present. It includes codebooks in compressed and uncompressed format and allows users to generate their own tables. Data from the Drug Abuse Warning Network, Monitoring the Future, the National Household Survey on Drug Abuse, the Treatment Episode Data Set, and the Washington, D.C., Metropolitan Area Drug Study (DC*MADS) are currently available for on-line analysis. Other data sets, including the comorbidity study, can be downloaded for analysis in a statistical package. This site contains links to Web pages that provide additional information on each survey as well as extensive documentation.

2. National Archive of Computerized Data on Aging <http://www.icpsr.umich.edu/NACDA>. This site provides individual- and facility-level data on mental and physical health, health care needs, use, and financing.

3. Health and Medical Care Archive <http://www.icpsr.umich.edu/HMCA>. This page includes use, facility- and individual-level data, and regional studies.

MASSACHUSETTS COMMUNITY HEALTH INFORMATION PROFILE (MASSCHIP)

The MassCHIP site, <http://www.state.ma.us/dph/ose/mchphome.htm>, maintained by the Massachusetts Department of Public Health, provides detailed statistical information for the cities and towns of the state. MassCHIP provides free on-line access to many health and social indicators. To obtain access, users currently must first sign a user agreement and download the MassCHIP software from the Web site. MassCHIP 3.0, which is expected to be available in 2001, will be entirely Web based. MassCHIP provides access to 24 health status, health outcome, program utilization, and demographic data sets, from which users create standard and custom reports and charts and maps.

TRENDS IN HEALTH AND AGING (NCHS DATA ARCHIVE ON AGING)

This specialized Web site, located at <http://www.cdc.gov/nchs/about/otheract/aging/ trenddata.htm>, gives users access to an electronic data warehouse on trends in health and aging. Sponsored by the NCHS and the National Institute on Aging (NIA) of the National Institutes of Health (NIH), the site covers trends in health-related behaviors, health status, health care use, and cost of care and provides data by age, gender, race, and ethnic groups. Users can generate their own tables following the NCHS specified table shells and can download specialized software (Beyond 20/20) or use an embedded query system. Because this site is intended to allow users to see the effects of age on health, it includes data for younger as well as older people—thereby allowing users to make comparisons.

WEB-BASED INJURY STATISTICS QUERY AND REPORTING SYSTEM (WISQARS)

The CDC's National Center for Injury Prevention and Control provides injury-related mortality data in an interactive format at <http://www.cdc.gov/ncipc/osp/wisqars_intro.htm>. This site provides injury deaths and death rates for specific causes of injuries and leading causes of death and includes mortality data from 1981 to 1997. Tables by year, age, race, sex, Hispanic origin, and state are also presented. Death data come from a national mortality database compiled by the CDC's National Center for Health Statistics on the basis of death certificates filed in state vital statistics offices. This site is easy to use. It contains aggregate information for all of the leading causes of death but features more detail for those related to injuries.

HEALTH STATISTICS AGENCIES' WEB SITES

The original source for the most current information about health statistics in the United States is the Web site of the issuing agency. The following entries provide a guide to the major sites. (Additional sites can be found by searching the portals listed in the previous section.) The material in this section describes the sources and provides information about how to find them.

CENTERS FOR DISEASE CONTROL AND PREVENTION, U.S. DEPARTMENT OF HEALTH AND HUMAN SERVICES

NATIONAL CENTER FOR HEALTH STATISTICS

The National Center for Health Statistics Web site, <http://www.cdc.gov/nchs/>, provides an organized set of materials on the programs of the NCHS. Users will find it best to consult the individual pages dedicated to the specific programs of the agency. They can also search the subject index provided. The site notes: "some NCHS data systems and surveys are ongoing annual systems while others are conducted periodically. NCHS has two major

types of data systems: systems based on populations, containing data collected through personal interviews or examinations; and systems based on records, containing data collected from vital and medical records."

Many NCHS programs issue their reports in html or Adobe Acrobat PDF format, making it easy for users to download this material. Data are also available from FERRET (see above) and the NCHS Interactive Database on Health and Aging (see above). Users would do best to start with *Health, United States*, the leading publication of the agency, which has an excellent appendix describing key sources (see above).

National Vital Statistics System

The NCHS draws on state compilations of birth and death certificates to compile statistical information about trends in vital events and their effect on the population. The vital records system serves the social function of recording the entrance and passage of people in the nation. In the 20th century, health statisticians developed a way to use this key social process as a checkpoint where they could record important information associated with these "vital events." In many cases, analysts use these data to make inferences about health conditions—such as inferences about the illnesses that afflict people based on the recorded cause of deaths.

Birth and Death Data

State laws require birth and death certificates to be completed for all births and deaths. The NCHS compiles this information, with the cooperation of state health departments, as a product of the National Vital Statistics System. The NCHS and the state health departments agree on standard forms and procedures to facilitate this effort.

The birth data is located at <http://www.cdc.gov/nchs/births.htm>. The mortality data, located at <http://www.cdc.gov/nchs/about/major/dvs/mortdata.htm>, are the most extensive and detailed source of information on health conditions. They provide demographic, geographic, and cause-of-death information. Of particular interest is that they provide standard health data for small geographic areas over a long time period (at least for the past 50 years).

The data are also used to present the characteristics of those dying in the United States, to determine life expectancy, and to compare mortality trends with other countries. Funeral directors provide the demographic information on death certificates on the basis of information supplied by an informant, such as the next of kin. A physician, medical examiner, or coroner provides the medical certification for the cause of death. Codes for the causes of death are based on the ICD-9.

For a detailed history of this system, see *U.S. Vital Statistics System, Major Activities and Developments: 1950–1995* at <http://www.cdc.gov/nchs/products/pubs/pubd/other/miscpub/miscpub.htm>.

Fetal Death Data

The NCHS collects information on all fetal deaths occurring in the United States and the District of Columbia at <http://www.cdc.gov/nchs/about/major/fetaldth/abfetal.htm>. Beginning in 1994, fetal deaths for Puerto Rico, the Virgin Islands, and Guam were also compiled. The NCHS obtains this data from fetal death reports filed in each state. States set their own reporting requirements; however, most require the reporting of fetal deaths of gestations of 20 weeks or more; some require reporting of all periods of gestation.

National Mortality Followback Survey

The National Mortality Followback Survey site, <http://www.cdc.gov/nchs/about/major/nmfs/ nmfs.htm>, contains detailed data about a sample of deaths collected from the next of kin or another person familiar with the decedent's life history and integrated with information from administrative records to provide more information on health conditions related to deaths. The site also covers socioeconomic variation, health insurance, and health care. Special topics include smoking, comorbid conditions, disabilities, alcohol use, and access to health care services.

National Health Interview Survey

The NCHS conducts the National Health Interview Survey (NHIS) and provides data from the survey at <http://www.cdc.gov/nchs/nhis/htm>. The NHIS is a multipurpose health survey, and the NCHS calls it "the principal source of information on the health of the civilian, household population of the United States." The survey has been conducted from July 1957 to the present and includes all persons in the U.S. civilian population other than those who are patients in long-term care facilities or other institutions (such as prisons or jails). The Bureau of the Census conducts the field work. Topics include "the amount, distribution, and effects of illness and disability in the United States and the services rendered for or because of such conditions." The National Survey of Family Growth, the Medical Expenditure Panel Survey, and the National Health Interview Survey on Disability

use the NHIS respondent sample as a sampling frame, obtain additional information from their sample drawn from the NHIS, and then combine that data with the information collected in the original NHIS interview. NHIS data are collected annually from approximately 43,000 households, which together contain about 106,000 persons. For design details and a description of procedures used, see *National Health Interview Survey: Research for the 1995–2004 Redesign*, NCHS Vital and Health Statistics, series 2, number 126 (Hyattsville, Md.: Centers for Disease Control and Prevention).

National Immunization Survey

The National Immunization Survey, at <http://www.cdc.gov/nis/> and also at <http://www.nisabt.org/>, provides immunization rates of young children since 1994. It includes a household telephone survey of parents of children age 19 months to 35 months and a survey of doctors and other vaccination providers.

National Health Interview Survey on Disability

The National Health Interview Survey on Disability (NHIS-D), at <http://www.cdc.gov/nchs/about/major/nhis_dis/nhis_dis.htm>, shares the sample, staff, and operations of the National Health Interview Survey. The NHIS-D was last conducted in 1994 and 1995 and presents data on persons to ascertain those who suffer from disabilities. It collects data on a wide variety of disabling conditions including those affecting vision, hearing, learning development, and the ability to perform the activities of daily living (ADL) and related functional problems. It also records information about related health and support services. Because the NHIS-D is a part of the NHIS, it is possible to correlate disabilities with their underlying health conditions.

National Health and Nutrition Examination Survey

The NCHS's National Health and Nutrition Examination Survey (NHANES), at <http://www.cdc.gov/nchs/nhanes.htm>, collects data on health conditions by simulating the experience of clinical observation. The NCHS has conducted seven examination surveys since 1960.

The procedure is as follows. Each participant is first interviewed at home. Respondents are then recruited for a physical examination, a dental examination, and a nutritional profile conducted in a mobile examination center. Depending on the age of the respondent and the results of the interviews, various tests and measurements are performed.

In the past, the NCHS has not had the resources to conduct these surveys rapidly. For example, the most recent data available from NHANES III were collected over a three-year period. In April 1999, the NCHS began continuous data collection that could allow for annual reporting of key indicators. Nearly 5,000 persons will be interviewed and examined each year.

Results are typically reported in the medical literature. For more information, see U.S. Department of Health and Human Services, National Center for Health Statistics, *Third National Health and Nutrition Examination Survey, 1988–1994*, series 11, number 1A (ASCII Version) (Hyattsville, Md.: Centers for Disease Control and Prevention, 1997). See also U.S. Department of Health and Human Services, National Center for Health Statistics, *Third National Health and Nutrition Examination Survey, 1988–1994*, series 11, number 2A (ASCII Version) (Hyattsville, Md.: Centers for Disease Control and Prevention, 1998).

NHANES I Epidemiologic Follow-up Study

The NHANES I Epidemiologic Follow-up Study was a longitudinal study of the participants in the NHANES that was conducted in 1971–1975. It collected data that made it possible to examine the relationships between clinical, nutritional, and behavioral factors assessed in the NHANES, on the one hand, and health conditions and subsequent care, on the other. Selected respondents who were age 25 to 74 in 1971–1975 were re-interviewed in 1982, 1986, 1987, and 1992.

National Health Care Survey

The National Health Care Survey (NHCS), at <http://www.cdc.gov/nchs/nhcs.htm>, consists of four health care provider surveys. The NHCS provides data on the use of health care, the effect of medical technology, and the quality of care. It is based on compilations of patient records and covers hospital discharges, ambulatory medical care, nursing homes, ambulatory surgery, hospital ambulatory medical care, hospital outpatient departments, and emergency rooms.

The National Ambulatory Medical Care Survey and the National Hospital Ambulatory Medical Care Survey measure health care use in physician offices and hospital emergency and outpatient departments, respectively. These surveys collect information on patient characteristics, patient symptoms or reasons for visit, provider diagnosis, and whether the patient was hospitalized.

The National Hospital Discharge Survey collects discharge records from approximately 475 nonfederal short-stay hospitals.

CDC SURVEILLANCE REPORTS

To meet the need to take action to protect the public health, government agencies in the states and at the federal government's Centers for Disease Control and Prevention track and record information on more than 50 notifiable diseases and conditions. State laws require physicians and other caregivers to inform state agencies about each case involving a notifiable disease. These reports are forwarded to the CDC. Analysts at the CDC aggregate them and issue periodic reports. The CDC issues a weekly update informing physicians and the public health community about the most recently reported cases. (See the MMWR.)

This surveillance is targeted to produce information that the CDC and the public health community use to intervene and prevent or respond to emerging threats to health. At the same time, the surveys, administrative records, surveillance data, vital statistics, and controlled clinical observations provide important information about the health of our population.

National Nosocomial Infections Surveillance (NNIS) System

The NNIS system, at <http://www.cdc.gov/ncidod/hip/surveill/nnis.htm>, tracks the surveillance of the epidemiology of nosocomial (care-caused) infections in hospitals in the United States. Approximately 245 hospitals voluntarily report their nosocomial infection data. This site covers infections from acute-care general hospital patients only and excludes those from rehabilitation, mental health, nursing home, and other extended-care services. See "National Nosocomial Infections Surveillance (NNIS) Report, Data Summary from October 1986–April 1998, Issued June 1998," *American Journal of Infection Control* 24 (1996):380–388.

Behavioral Risk Factor Surveillance System (BRFSS)

The BRFSS tracks health risks in the United States at <http://www.cdc.gov/nccdph/brfss>. Each state health department conducts a telephone survey in cooperation with the CDC. Analysts at the CDC compile data from the state surveys into national summaries. Topics covered include immunizations, nutrition habits, regular preventive medical exams, and weight control.

Youth Risk Behavior Surveillance (YRBS) System

The Youth Risk Behavior Surveillance site, <http://www.cdc.gov/nccdphp/dash/yrbs/index.htm>, provides national data since 1990 on health risks taken by high school students, including information on nutrition, riding motorcycles without a helmet, school violence, and unprotected sex.

State and local health departments conduct these surveys with support and participation from the CDC. In 1997 participating jurisdictions were Alabama, Arkansas, California, Colorado, Connecticut, Delaware, the District of Columbia, Florida, Georgia, Hawaii, Idaho, Iowa, Kansas, Kentucky, Louisiana, Maine, Massachusetts, Michigan, Mississippi, Missouri, Montana, Nebraska, Nevada, New Hampshire, New Jersey, New York, North Carolina, North Dakota, Ohio, Oregon, Rhode Island, South Carolina, South Dakota, Tennessee, Utah, Vermont, West Virginia, Wisconsin, and Wyoming. The territories of American Samoa, Guam, Northern Mariana Islands, and the U.S. Virgin Islands also participated, as well as the following cities: Baltimore, Boston, Chicago, Dallas, Detroit, Fort Lauderdale, Houston, Jersey City, Los Angeles, Miami, Newark, New Orleans, New York, Philadelphia, San Diego, and San Francisco.

Also see *Assessing Health Risk Behaviors Among Young People: Youth Risk Behavior Surveillance System, At-A-Glance 1999* at <http://www.cdc.gov/nccdphp/dash/yrbs/yrbsaag1999.htm>.

Other CDC Surveillance Sites

Assisted Reproductive Technology Success Rates: <http://www.cdc.gov/nccdphp/drh/art.htm>

Birth Defects Surveillance: <http://www.cdc.gov/nceh/pubcatns/1994/cdc/brosures/neural.htm#neural>

Cancer Registries Program: <http://www.cdc.gov/nccdphp/dcpc/npcr/>

HIV/AIDS Surveillance Reports: <http://www.cdc.gov/nchstp/hiv_aids/stats/hasrlink.htm>

Pregnancy Risk Assessment Monitoring System: <http://www.cdc.gov/nccdphp/drh/srv_prams.htm>

Sexually Transmitted Diseases: <http://www.cdc.gov/nchstp/dstd/Stats_Trends/Stats_and_Trends.htm>

Tuberculosis Surveillance Reports: <http://www.cdc.gov/nchstp/tb/surv/surv.htm>

HEALTH CARE FINANCING ADMINISTRATION

The Health Care Financing Administration site, <http://www.hcfa.gov/stats/stats.htm>, contains data on health care, including reports on national health care expenditures and specific reports on Medicare and Medicaid.

SUBSTANCE ABUSE AND MENTAL HEALTH SERVICES ADMINISTRATION

SAMHSA's Office of Applied Studies (OAS), at <http://www.DrugAbuseStatistics.samhsa.gov>, reports national and state statistics on the prevalence, incidence, and characteristics of persons with substance abuse and mental health problems. This site also reports data on treatment facilities. This site contains some web-only reports that include tables of detailed data not found in published reports. Some of the key sources are listed below.

DRUG AND ALCOHOL SERVICES INFORMATION SYSTEM (DASIS)

The DASIS, at <http://www.samhsa.gov/OAS/DASIS.htm>, is the primary source of national information on substance abuse treatment services and the characteristics of individuals admitted into treatment. The DASIS data sets are maintained with the cooperation and support of the states. This Web site provides data from the following DASIS data sets:

1. *National Survey of Substance Abuse Treatment Services (N-SSATS),* formerly *Uniform Facility Data Set*. The N-SSATS collects information on the location, organization, structure, services, and use of substance abuse treatment facilities in the United States. Information from the survey is also used to compile and update the on-line Substance Abuse Treatment Facility Locator, a widely used resource for referrals to treatment that is located at <http://findtreatment.samhsa.gov>.

2. *Treatment Episode Data Set (TEDS)*. The TEDS collects demographic and drug history information about individuals admitted to treatment, primarily by providers receiving public funding.

NATIONAL HOUSEHOLD SURVEY ON DRUG ABUSE

The National Household Survey on Drug Abuse, at <http://www.samhsa.gov/OAS/NHSDA.htm>, reports on the "prevalence, patterns, and consequences of drug and alcohol use and abuse in the general U.S. civilian noninstitutionalized population aged 12 and over." It also covers the use of illicit drugs, alcohol, and tobacco, as well as the nonmedical use of other drugs. State level estimates are now available on this Web site.

DRUG ABUSE WARNING NETWORK

The Drug Abuse Warning Network site, <http://www.samhsa.gov/OAS/p0000018.htm>, provides semiannual estimates of the number of drug-related visits to hospital emergency departments in the nation and drug-related deaths from selected medical examiner offices. Emergency room estimates are produced for 21 large metropolitan areas and for the nation. Drug-related death data are produced for more than 40 metropolitan areas.

National Substance Abuse Web Index

The National Substance Abuse Web Index site, <http://nsawi.health.org/>, maintained for SAMHSA by the National Clearinghouse for Alcohol and Drug Information, provides an index of 24 state, federal, and private Web sites with substance abuse information. Users can search for statistical data within these sites. The site covers statistical reports, research summaries, and advocacy material.

Agency for Healthcare Research and Quality (Formerly the Agency for Health Care Policy and Research)

The Agency for Healthcare Research and Quality, at <http://www.ahrq.gov>, provides statistics on heath care utilization. Also see the Health Care Utilization Project (HCUP) of the AHRQ at <http://198.179.0.16/HCUPnet.asp> and the Medical Expenditure Panel Survey (MEPS) at <http://www.meps.ahrq.gov/>.

Medical Expenditure Panel Survey

The MEPS is cosponsored by the AHRQ and the NCHS. The survey covers health care use, expenditures, sources of payment, and insurance coverage for the U.S. civilian noninstitutionalized population, as well as including a national survey of nursing homes and their residents. It provides estimates for the level and distribution of health care use and expenditures, monitors the dynamics of the health care delivery and insurance systems, and assesses health care policy implications.

The MEPS is the third in a series of national probability surveys conducted by the AHRQ on the financing and use of medical care in the United States. The National Medical Care Expenditure Survey (NMCES, also known as NMES-1) was conducted in 1977, and the National Medical Expenditure Survey (NMES-2) in 1987.

The MEPS collects data from medical providers, insurance companies, and nursing homes as well as from households. A sample of households provides the core survey from which the other samples are drawn (that is, providers, insurance companies, and nursing homes are selected for the sample because persons living in households included in the sample made use of those services).

Householders are asked about their demographic characteristics, health conditions, health status, use of medical care services, charges and payments, access to care, satisfaction with care, health insurance coverage, income, and employment. Providers are asked to supplement and validate information on medical care events reported by householders. Insurance companies are asked to provide information on the plans covering the householders. The nursing home survey asks about the characteristics, health care use, and expenditures of nursing home residents and the characteristics of nursing home facilities.

Healthcare Cost and Utilization Project

HCUP, at <http://www.ahrq.gov/data/hcup/hcup-pkt.htm>, is a federal-state-industry partnership that is building a standardized, multistate health data system. HCUP includes state-specific hospital-discharge databases and a national sample of discharges from community hospitals. Data users can access the results through Web-based table production software. HCUP has already released two data sets providing information for inpatient hospital stays from 1988 to 1997. The Nationwide Inpatient Sample (NIS) includes inpatient data from a national sample of about 1,000 hospitals. The State Inpatient Database (SID) covers inpatient care in community hospitals in 22 states that represent more than half of all U.S. hospital discharges. The data in HCUP cover the use and cost of hospital care and provide information about diagnoses and procedures. HCUP uses specialized Clinical Classifications Software (CCS), which classifies diagnoses or procedures into clinically meaningful categories. For more information, see *Healthcare Cost and Utilization Project (HCUP), 1988–1997: A Federal-State-Industry Partnership in Health Data* at <http://www.ahrq.gov/data/hcup/hcup-pkt.htm>.

Indian Health Service

The Indian Health Service (IHS) reports statistics on the health of American Indians living on or near reservations—its service population. It issues two reports that are available on the IHS Web site, <http://www.ihs.gov/publicinfo/publications/>:

1. *Trends in Indian Health*, at <http://www.ihs.gov/publicinfo/publications/trends97/trends97.asp>, contains tables and charts that present trends in key health status indicators for the IHS service population, American Indians, and Alaskan Natives, compared to all races in the U.S. population.

2. *Regional Differences in Indian Health* compares key health status indicators among the 12 IHS areas or regions and the United States. It also shows how American Indians and Alaskan Natives compare to the rest of the population.

NATIONAL INSTITUTES OF HEALTH

NATIONAL INSTITUTE ON ALCOHOL ABUSE AND ALCOHOLISM (NIAAA)

The NIAAA, at <http://silk.nih.gov/silk/niaaa1/publication/manual.htm>, conducts epidemiologic research on the causes, incidence, and prevalence of alcohol abuse and alcoholism. This site provides information on the NIAAA's research.

NATIONAL CANCER INSTITUTE (NCI)

CancerNet

CancerNet, at <http://cancernet.nci.nih.gov/statistics.shtm>, leads users to key statistical data sources relating to cancer.

Surveillance, Epidemiology, and End Results Program

Since its inception in 1973, SEER, at <http://www.seer.cancer.gov>, has collected information on cancer incidence and survival in the United States based on registers of persons diagnosed with cancer maintained in Connecticut, Iowa, New Mexico, Utah, and Hawaii and the metropolitan areas of Detroit and San Francisco–Oakland, Atlanta, the 13-county Seattle–Puget Sound area, 10 predominantly Black rural counties in Georgia, and American Indians residing in Arizona. In 1999, coverage of cancer cases among Alaskan Native populations residing in Alaska became part of SEER. The following areas also participated: New Orleans, Louisiana (1974–1977); four counties in New Jersey (1979–1989); and Puerto Rico (1973–1989). In 1992, the SEER program was expanded to increase coverage of minority populations, especially Hispanics, with the addition of Los Angeles County and four counties in the San Jose–Monterey area south of San Francisco. Federally coordinated expansion efforts in 2000 target regions with non-Mexican Hispanics, rural White and Black populations with high poverty levels, American Indians, and states with high cancer rates. According to the NCI, "Geographic areas were selected for inclusion in the SEER Program based on their ability to operate and maintain a high quality population-based cancer reporting system and for their epidemiologically significant population subgroups." The NCI provides national estimates of incidence and survival based on the registry areas it covers, combined with mortality data for the entire United States reported by the NCHS and benchmarked using data from the Bureau of the Census. In collaboration with other federal and private organizations, the NCI provides an annual report to the nation that includes cancer-related data on health behavior, screening, treatment patterns, and other outcomes, as well as cancer incidence rates from other registries that meet established standards for quality. The Web site includes incidence, mortality, and survival data for specific types of cancer sites and detailed population groups.

NATIONAL INSTITUTE FOR CHILD HEALTH AND HUMAN DEVELOPMENT (NICHD)

The Demographic and Behavioral Sciences Branch within the NICHD, at <http://www.nichd.nih.gov/cpr/dbs/dbs.htm>, supports research and data collection on "the processes that determine population size, growth, composition and distribution, and on the determinants and consequences of" population processes. Its research portfolio covers fertility and family planning, HIV and sexually transmitted disease, family and household demography, mortality and health, and population composition, change, and movement.

The NICHD has supported several statistical data collections, including the National Survey of Family Growth, the Current Population Survey—Nativity Supplement, the National Longitudinal Study of Adolescent Health (AddHealth), and the National Survey of Adolescent Males.

NATIONAL INSTITUTE ON DRUG ABUSE (NIDA)

The NIDA site, <http://www.drugabuse.gov/DrugPages/Stats.html>, covers NIDA summaries of drug abuse trends, results from the Monitoring the Future surveys, and reports by the Community Epidemiology Work Group (CEWG).

Monitoring the Future

A school-based survey, located at <http://monitoringthefuture.org/>, has been conducted by the University of Michigan since 1975. It collects information on 8th, 10th, and 12th graders' attitudes and behaviors toward alcohol and drug abuse.

NATIONAL HEART, LUNG, AND BLOOD INSTITUTE

The National Heart, Lung, and Blood Institute sponsors epidemiological studies that can be found at <http://www.nhlbi.nih.gov/index.htm>. It issues an annual *Chartbook* that summarizes current statistics for cardiovascular diseases. The *Chartbook*, at <http://www.nhlbi.nih.gov/resources/docs/cht-book.htm>, features information on the size and trends of morbidity and mortality from the cardiovascular, lung, and blood diseases. It covers prevalence, hospitalizations, and mortality statistics for the nation and some state and county information. It also includes risk factors and the costs of these diseases.

NATIONAL INSTITUTE OF MENTAL HEALTH

The Web site of the National Institute of Mental Health, <http://www.nimh.nih.gov/publicat/stats.cfm>, provides easy access to the *Surgeon General's Report on Mental Health*, which contains a summary of statistical findings on mental health. U.S. Department of Health and Human Services, *Mental Health: A Report of the Surgeon General* (Rockville, Md.: U.S. DHHS, Substance Abuse and Mental Health Services Administration, Center for Mental Health Services, National Institutes of Health, National Institute of Mental Health, 1999).

ADMINISTRATION ON AGING

The Administration on Aging site, <http://www.aoa.dhhs.gov/aoa/stats/statpage.html>, links to statistical data on the aging population and features a special report on aging in the 21st century.

OTHER FEDERAL AGENCIES

BUREAU OF THE CENSUS DISABILITY STATISTICS

A page on the Bureau of the Census Web site, <http://www.census.gov/hhes/www/disable.html>, provides links to Census Bureau data on disability. It covers disability data from the Survey of Income and Program Participation (SIPP), the Decennial Census of Population, and the Current Population Survey (CPS). Since 1984, the SIPP has collected data from panels of households that are interviewed at four-month intervals over a period of at least two years. Detailed questions on disability were asked four times in the SIPP (October 1991 to January 1992, October 1993 to January 1994, October 1994 to January 1995, and August 1997 to November 1997). In 1970, 1980, 1990, and 2000, the decennial censuses asked a sample of respondents questions about disability status. The monthly CPS identifies persons who are out of the labor force because of a disability, and, in each March survey since 1980, has identified persons who have a health problem that "prevents them from working or limits the kind or amount of work they can do."

See also Americans with Disabilities, 1994–1995, at <http://www.census.gov/hhes/www/disable/sipp/disable9495.html> and <http://www.census.gov/hhes/www/disable.html>, and the Presidential Task Force on Employment of Adults with Disabilities at <http://www.dol.gov/dol/_sec/public/programs/ptfead/rechart/index.htm>.

BUREAU OF LABOR STATISTICS

OCCUPATIONAL HEALTH STATISTICS

The Bureau of Labor Statistics (BLS), at <http://www.bls.gov/oshhome.htm>, began collecting safety data in 1912. Each year since 1972, the BLS has reported on the number of workplace injuries, illnesses, and fatalities. This site covers the number of workplace injuries and illnesses in private industry and the frequency of those incidents; it was enhanced in 1992 with more detailed information on characteristics of workers and incidents for the more seriously injured or ill workers. It contains summary data on the number and rate of injuries and illnesses by industry and case and demographic data providing information on injured workers, their disabling condition, and the accident or illness responsible. Fatality data including 28 separate data elements concerning the worker, the fatal incident, and the machinery or equipment involved are also provided. Also see the Occupational Safety and Health Administration's Workplace Injury and Illness Statistics site at <http://www.osha.gov/oshstats/bls/index1.html>.

DEPARTMENT OF TRANSPORTATION

FATALITY ANALYSIS REPORTING SYSTEM (FARS)

The FARS Web site, <http://www-fars.nhtsa.dot.gov/>, contains data on "motor vehicle traffic crashes that result in fatality to a vehicle occupant or non-motorist, from injuries resulting from a traffic crash, that occur within 30 days of the crash." The National Highway Traffic Safety Administration (NHTSA) has compiled this information since 1975. Several resulting databases are maintained by the NHTSA's National Center for Statistics and Analysis (NCSA) at <http://www.nhtsa.dot.gov/people/ncsa/index.html>. It contains data on vehicle crashes and safety-related data and has query capabilities. The site is updated annually.

BUREAU OF TRANSPORTATION STATISTICS

The Bureau of Transportation Statistics site, <http://www.bts.gov>, presents information on accident-related injuries and deaths.

U.S. DEPARTMENT OF AGRICULTURE

The site of the U.S. Department of Agriculture, <http://www.barc.usda.gov/bhnrc/foodsurvey/home.htm>, contains the 1994–1996 Continuing Survey of Food

Intakes by Individuals, one of the two national surveys that collect data on the kinds and amounts of food eaten by Americans. The survey is a national representative sample of about 5,500 participants taken each year. Participants are asked to recall all of the foods eaten by them over a 24-hour period. Information on their food consumption is used to calculate the Healthy Eating Index. Their dietary intake also is compared with the 1989 Recommended Dietary Allowances (RDAs). Also see *Recommended Dietary Allowances*, 10th ed. (Washington, D.C.: National Academy Press, 1989).

FoodNet

Established in 1996, FoodNet, located at <http://www.cdc.gov/ncidod/dbmd/foodnet/>, is a collaborative effort by the Centers for Disease Control and Prevention, the U.S. Department of Agriculture, the U.S. Food and Drug Administration, and the California, Colorado, Connecticut, Georgia, New York, Maryland, Minnesota, Oregon, and Tennessee state health departments. FoodNet actively monitors the occurrence of seven bacterial and two parasitic food-borne diseases within the covered states. It also monitors the frequency of diarrhea in the general population, the proportion of ill persons seeking care for diarrhea, and the frequency of stool culturing by physicians and laboratories for selected food-borne pathogens.

Also see Paul S. Mead, Laurence Slutsker, Vance Dietz, Linda McCaig, Joseph Bresee, Craig Shapiro, Patricia Griffin, and Robert V. Tauxe, "Food-Related Illnesses and Death in the United States," *Emerging Infectious Diseases 5*, no. 5 (September–October 1999). A copy is also available at <http://www.cdc.gov/ncidod/eid/vol5no5/mead.htm>.

STATE DATA

DIRECTORY OF STATE GOVERNMENT OFFICES

An interactive directory of state government offices is provided at <http://www.nasire.org/stateSearch/>. This site has a health and human services category that leads users to state offices responsible for health statistics.

NCHS STATE DATA SITES

The NCHS home page, <http://www.cdc.gov/nchs>, has links to tabulations of health statistics by state.

CDC LIST OF STATE HEALTH DEPARTMENTS

The CDC maintains a list of state departments of public health at <http://www.cdc.gov/other.htm> with links to their Web sites.

INTERNATIONAL SITES

UNITED NATIONS STATISTICS OFFICE

The United Nations Statistics Office, at <http://www.un.org/Depts/unsd/>, provides links to national statistics agency sites around the world.

INFO NATION

The Info Nation site, <http://www.un.org/Pubs/CyberSchoolBus/infonation/e_infonation.htm>, provides statistical information—including basic health statistics indicators for the members of the United Nations—through a convenient lookup tool.

WORLD HEALTH ORGANIZATION'S STATISTICAL INFORMATION SYSTEM

The World Health Organization, at <http://www.who.int/whosis/>, provides worldwide health indicators, including information about the burden of disease, health personnel, international classifications, and HIV/AIDS. The site provides links to health-related Web sites of individual countries.

HEALTH-RELATED WEB SITES OF WORLD HEALTH ORGANIZATION MEMBER NATIONS

The World Health Organization, at <http://www.nt.who.int/whosis/statistics/national_sites/national_sites.cfm?path=statistics,national_sites>, provides links to the public health Web sites of its member states.

ORGANIZATION FOR ECONOMIC COOPERATION AND DEVELOPMENT (OECD)

The Organization for Economic Cooperation and Development, at <http://www.oecd.org/statlist.htm>, provides health statistics relating to the leading industrial countries of the world, including the United States, Canada, Japan, and various European countries.

PAN AMERICAN HEALTH ORGANIZATION

The Pan American Health Organization site, <http://www.paho.org/english/sha/ihomeibs.htm>, contains links to health statistics from Central and South America.

PROGRESS OF NATIONS, 1998

UNICEF's summary of social and health indicators is located at <http://www.unicef.org/pon98/>. The table at this site is produced annually.

NONGOVERNMENTAL ORGANIZATIONS

NATIONAL SAFETY COUNCIL'S STATISTICS DEPARTMENT

The National Safety Council's Statistics Department site, <http://www.nsc.org/lrs/statstop.htm>, reports data on the nation's unintentional-injury experience and trends. It contains current estimates of deaths, nonfatal injuries, and costs caused by unintentional events; *Accident Facts®*; and analyses of injury data and related economic, social, and demographic data for internal use and public dissemination.

NORTH AMERICAN ASSOCIATION OF CENTRAL CANCER REGISTRIES

The North American Association of Central Cancer Registries, at <http://www.naaccr.org>, works to enhance quality and use of cancer registry data. The Web site contains cancer incidence data from a broader set of states than those participating in the SEER program.

THE ALAN GUTTMACHER INSTITUTE (AGI)

The AGI site, <http://www.agi-usa.org/>, reports statistics on pregnancy, family planning, and contraception.

PARTNERSHIP FOR A DRUG-FREE AMERICA

The Partnership for a Drug-Free America site, <http://www.drugfreeamerica.org/>, provides results from surveys conducted by the partnership, including the Partnership Attitude Tracking Survey, which reports on attitudes toward using drugs.

KAISER FAMILY FOUNDATION—STATE HEALTH FACTS

The Kaiser Family Foundation, at <http://www.kff.org/docs/state/>, summarizes indicators for each state including information about conditions and care. The site includes information on health needs, insurance coverage, and Medicaid enrollment and use.

CENTER FOR INTERNATIONAL HEALTH INFORMATION

The Center for International Health Information (CIHI), at <http://www.cihi.com/>, is a health data reference bureau for the Population, Health, and Nutrition Center (PHNC) of the U.S. Agency for International Development's Global Bureau. This site provides access to statistical data including reports, tables, and DOLPHN (Data On-Line for Population, Health, and Nutrition). DOLPHN, an electronic publication, "gives the user access to international data ... drawn from ... demographic and health surveys, the World Health Organization, the United Nations Population Division (UNICEF and other United Nations agencies), the U.S. Bureau of the Census,

and the World Bank." Program information and data are available for free downloading and are updated periodically.

AMERICAN CANCER SOCIETY

The American Cancer Society Web site, <http://www.cancer.org/statistics/index.html>, tracks cancer statistics. The site includes "cancer occurrence, including the number of deaths, cases, and how long people survive after diagnosis."

AMERICAN HEART ASSOCIATION

The American Heart Association and the Stroke Association have jointly issued the *2000 Heart and Stroke Statistical Update* (Dallas, Tex.: American Heart Association, 1999). The publication, which is detailed at <http://www.americanheart.org>, provides prevalence and care statistics for heart disease and stroke. Rates include data benchmarked to the 2000 age-adjusted figures.

PUBLICATIONS

This section covers specialized bibliographic resources and also lists several important publications.

COMBINED HEALTH INFORMATION DATABASE (CHID)

CHID, at <http://chid.aerie.com/>, is a bibliographic database produced by health-related agencies of the federal government. This database provides titles, abstracts, and availability information for health information and health education resources, including health statistics publications. CHID is updated four times a year. The updated database is available at the end of the following months: January, April, July, and October. CHID covers the following topics: AIDS education, Alzheimer's disease, arthritis and musculoskeletal and skin diseases, cancer prevention and control, complementary and alternative medicine, deafness and communication disorders, diabetes, digestive diseases, disease prevention/health promotion, epilepsy education and prevention, health promotion and education, kidney and urologic diseases, maternal and child health, medical genetics and rare disorders, oral health, prenatal smoking cessation, and weight control.

MORBIDITY AND MORTALITY WEEKLY REPORT

The journal *Morbidity and Mortality Weekly Report*, located at <http://www2.cdc.gov/mmwr/mmwr_wk.html>, is edited by the CDC's Epidemiology Program Office. This resource provides articles based on health statistics sources. Some data are issued here rather than being included in regular statistical reports. Surveillance summaries, which summarize long-term trends drawn from surveillance data, are issued occasionally.

VITAL AND HEALTH STATISTICS SERIES (NCHS)

The Vital and Health Statistics Series, at <http://www.cdc.gov/nchs/products/pubs/pubd/series/ser.htm>, presents data on vital and health statistics. See also <http://www.cdc.gov/nchswww/products/pubs/pubd/series/ser.htm>, which contains a linked list of the complete series of NCHS serial reports.

NATIONAL VITAL STATISTICS REPORT

The *Monthly Vital Statistics Report* was renamed the *National Vital Statistics Report* beginning in 1998 with volume 47. It can be found at <http://www.cdc.gov/nchs/products/pubs/pubd/nvsr/nvsr.htm> and <http://www.cdc.gov/nchs/products/pubs/pubd/mvsr/mvsr.htm>. It presents monthly national and state birth, death, marriage, and divorce figures. Mortality statistics are categorized by age, race, sex, or disease on a national level. Monthly data begin with the July 1994 issue.

CHANGING AMERICA: INDICATORS OF SOCIAL AND ECONOMIC WELL-BEING BY RACE AND HISPANIC ORIGIN

A report, located at <http://w3.access.gpo.gov/eop/ca/index.html>, was prepared by the President's Council of Economic Advisors to review the social and economic status of Americans. It compares the situation of Blacks, Hispanics, Asian Americans, and American Indians. A chapter on health provides an overview of key indicators.

SURGEON GENERAL REPORTS

The surgeon general issues reports at <http://www.surgeongeneral.gov/library/reports.htm> about public health issues. These reports frequently contain statistical tables and charts.

WOMEN OF COLOR HEALTH DATA BOOK (NWHIC)

The *Women of Color Health Data Book*, located at <http://www.4women.gov/owh/pub/woc/index.htm>, was prepared by NIH and provides statistical data on the health status of minority women.

MENTAL HEALTH, UNITED STATES (CENTER FOR MENTAL HEALTH SERVICES, SAMHSA)

At <http://www.mentalhealth.org/specials/mentalhealth98/mh98.htm>, the executive summary and some summary statistics from the report, *Mental Health, United States* are available.

ECONOMIC COSTS OF ALCOHOL AND DRUG ABUSE IN THE UNITED STATES, 1992

Written by Henrick Harwood, Douglas Fountain, and Gina Livermore, a report on the economic costs of alcohol and drug abuse is available on-line at <http://www.drugabuse.gov/EconomicCosts/Intro.html>. The report was sponsored by the NIDA.

ATLAS OF UNITED STATES MORTALITY

The Atlas of United States Mortality, at <http://www.cdc.gov/nchswww/products/pubs/pubd/other/atlas/atlas.htm>, presents cause-of-death maps based on death certificate data from the U.S. Vital Statistics program. The site includes 18 leading causes of death by race and sex for health service areas (HSAs) and covers 83 percent of deaths in the United States between 1988 and 1992. It also shows age-adjusted death rates for each HSA and comparisons with the national rate.

ATLAS OF CANCER MORTALITY, 1950–1994

The *Atlas of Cancer Mortality*, at <http://www.nci.nih.gov/atlas/>, presents maps, text, tables, and figures showing cancer death rates by county and state economic areas in 1950–1994 for more than 40 cancers. Maps compare rates for 1950–1969 and 1970–1994.

CHRONIC DISEASE PREVENTION FILE

The Chronic Disease Prevention (CDP) File (CD-ROM version) contains six comprehensive bibliographic data sets:

1. The Health Promotion and Education Data Set, focusing on disease prevention and health promotion
2. The Comprehensive School Health Data Set
3. The Cancer Prevention and Control Data Set
4. The Prenatal Smoking Cessation Data Set
5. The Epilepsy Education and Prevention Activities Data Set
6. The Smoking and Health Data Set

The CDP File is updated every six months and is available on CD-ROM or via the CDC WONDER site. The CDP site is located at <http://www.cdc.gov/nccdphp>.

Alcohol Epidemiologic Data Directory

The Alcohol Epidemiologic Data Directory, at <http://silk.nih.gov/silk/niaaa1/publication/ publication.htm>, is a guide to data sets that have data about alcohol problems. It is presented by the Division of Biometry and Epidemiology, NIAAA.

Mental Health: A Report of the Surgeon General

A report located at <http://www.surgeongeneral.gov/Library/MentalHealth/ summary.html> contains a summary of available statistical information on mental health.

SAMHSA Statistics Source Book

The *SAMHSA Statistics Source Book*, at <http://www.DrugAbuseStatistics.samhsa.gov>, presents a "comprehensive and objective overview of substance abuse, mental illness, and co-occurring disorders" in the United States. It contains statistics and graphics covering "the current extent, costs, impact, and treatment of the addictive and mental illnesses."

Women and Heart Disease (CDC)

At<http://www.cdc.gov/nccdphp/cvd/womensatlas/ index.htm>, the CDC presents *Women and Heart Disease: An Atlas of Racial and Ethnic Disparities in Mortality*, published by the National Center for Chronic Disease Prevention and Health Promotion of the CDC. The site provides extensive information about cardiovascular disease among women. It is illustrated with county maps and graphs and is available on-line or in a printed version.

NOTES

1. These sources are described in Frieda O. Weise et al., *Health Statistics: An Annotated Bibliographic Guide to Information Resources*, 2d ed. (Lanham, Md.: Medical Library Association and Scarecrow Press, 1997), and also Frieda Weise, *Health Statistics: A Guide to Information Sources* (Detroit, Mich.: Gale Research Co., 1980), and Frieda Weise, *A Bibliographic Guide to Statistics and Health Planning Information*, rev. ed. (Springfield, Ill.: Cooperative Health Information System, State Center for Health Statistics, 1976).

2. One of the editors of this book (Daniel Melnick) has prepared a course for the staffs of medical libraries featuring the best strategies for finding health statistics on the Internet. A Web version of this course can be found at the National Library of Medicine (NLM) Web site. See <http://www.NLM.NIH.gov/NICHSR/outreach.html>.

3. The Internet addresses of Web sites frequently change. This chapter shows the Universal Reference Locators (URLs) current as of July 2000. In many cases, when changes are introduced, links will be provided to the new sites. Readers experiencing difficulty are advised to try the first part of the URL. For example, try <http://www.NLM.NICHSR.gov> rather than <http://www.NLM.NIH.gov/NICHSR/outreach.html> if the longer version does not work. Checking for the most recent link on a portal or at the "Finding Health Statistics" course site at the NLM Web site may also provide a more current link. A CD-ROM of this course is available. For more information send an email to course@melnickresearch.net.